THE PICTORIAL FIELD-BOOK
OF THE REVOLUTION

MILITARY COSTUME of the REVOLUTION.

B.J.Lossing inv.

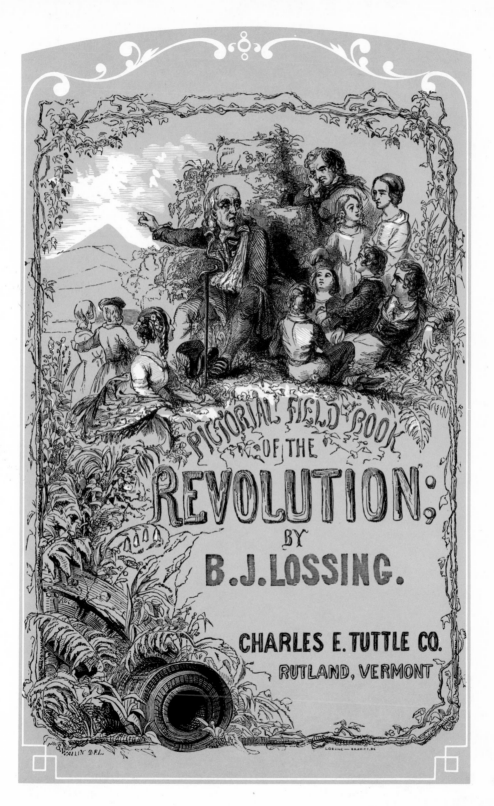

PICTORIAL FIELD BOOK OF THE

REVOLUTION;

BY

B.J. LOSSING.

CHARLES E. TUTTLE CO.
RUTLAND, VERMONT

THE PICTORIAL FIELD-BOOK OF THE REVOLUTION

or illustrations, by pen and pencil, of the history
biography, scenery, relics, and traditions
of the war for independence

by BENSON J. LOSSING

with eleven hundred engravings on wood by
LOSSING AND BARRITT
chiefly from original sketches by the
AUTHOR

and with an introduction to the new edition by
TERENCE BARROW, Ph.D.

IN TWO VOLUMES
VOL. I

CHARLES E. TUTTLE COMPANY
Rutland, Vermont

Representatives

Continental Europe: BOXERBOOKS, INC., *Zurich*
British Isles: PRENTICE-HALL INTERNATIONAL, INC., *London*
Australasia: PAUL FLESCH & CO., PTY. LTD., *Melbourne*
Canada: M. G. HURTIG LTD., *Edmonton*

*Published by the Charles E. Tuttle Company, Inc.
of Rutland, Vermont & Tokyo, Japan
with editorial offices at
Suido 1-chome, 2-6, Bunkyo-ku, Tokyo, Japan*

Copyright in Japan, 1972, by Charles E. Tuttle Co., Inc.

Library of Congress Catalog Card No. 72-77516

International Standard Book No. 0-8048-1046-X

*First edition published 1859 by Harper & Brothers, Publishers, New York
First Tuttle edition published 1972*

PRINTED IN JAPAN

INTRODUCTION TO THE NEW EDITION

IN 1848 Benson John Lossing, author, artist, and woodblock engraver, proposed the original idea of writing a comprehensive narrative sketchbook of the American Revolution of 1776. He succeeded admirably. All who are concerned with American history today can be thankful to this man for giving his plan substantial reality in the form of this mammoth two-volume folio book he called *The Pictorial Field-Book of the Revolution*. As a historian Lossing was indefatigable and timely. If he had set out to gather his facts a decade or two later, he would have been too late; or if he had lacked tenacity, he would have failed.

The idea of an exhaustive survey of the Revolution appears to have been born with Lossing's writing of a brief account of that war, *Seventeen Seventy-six*, published in 1847. His reputation as a writer on American history was established with this book, which received wide popular acclaim. Harper and Brothers of New York readily advanced funds for a five-year plan of research and travel to enable him to gather materials for his magnum opus. So Benson Lossing soon took off on research and travel which was eventually to carry him over 8,000 miles through the thirteen original states and Canada. He tactfully questioned anyone he thought might have information and sketched any place or object that had relevance to the Revolution. When his materials grew heavy, he withdrew to the peace of his farm to write and engrave. Then he would set out again on his quest for fact.

Lossing worked with such untiring industry that the first supplementary parts of *The Field-Book of the Revolution* were issued in 1850. In 1851 the parts were completed and sold in bound form. The great public response to his book was due to the interesting subject, authentic detail, and a national hunger for popular education in a new era of commerce that was transforming American society by replacing the old basis of a rural subsistence economy with industrialism. In addition the book had the charm of the illustrated pictorial presentation that took hold of busy readers of books then, as it does today. Benson Lossing produced about forty illustrated books before his death in 1891.

The Pictorial Field-Book of the Revolution is Lossing's most enduring book. Its compilation is an object lesson in scholarly endurance and practical tact in eliciting information from the thousands of people he interviewed. He was never rebuffed or treated with discourtesy. Everywhere he found hospitality of the style of old America.

The index of some 10,000 or more entries is testimony to his patience in searching out facts, while the 1,100 engravings made from his sketches exhibit a skill which modern photographic processes have rendered superfluous in contemporary publications. It should be noted that the order of the book follows the sequence of Lossing's travels rather than any orderly plan of textual arrangement. The index redeems any shortcoming that arises out of this circumstance or the supplement style.

Benson Lossing's life had a hard beginning. He was born in the town of Beekham, N.Y., in 1813, of good Dutch forefathers who had settled the lower Hudson valley. Unfortunately his mother died when he was an infant in his first year. At the age of twelve he was orphaned when his father died. Thrown on his own resources he first worked as a farm boy, then as apprentice to a watchmaker-silversmith. Later he entered newspaper work as a jack-of-all-trades journalist to become a partner in a Poughkeepsie newspaper at the age of twenty. As someone was needed to engrave illustrations, he learned the art with his usual enthusiasm and dispatch. The illustrations of *The Pictorial Field-Book of the Revolution* he engraved from his drawings, with the assistance of a Mr. Barritt.

The age was ripe for Benson John Lossing's talents; so he did not go unnoticed among his contemporaries. The University of Michigan conferred on him the degree of doctor of laws, while the seventeen learned societies to which he belonged applauded his researches. Lossing preferred the quiet life in which he could think, engrave his blocks, and labor over his manuscripts in peace on his farm on the Connecticut boundary at Dover Plains, N. Y. He loved the simple, unpretentious life.

Many professional historians who are university trained and at times a little arrogant toward the amateur will turn to *The Pictorial Field-Book of the Revolution* with respectful condescension. Benson John Lossing was a self-made historian of patience, industry, insight—and above all a deeply patriotic American. In fact, historians need his book, which is a mine of facts about the Revolution of 1776.

TERENCE BARROW PH.D.

HE story of the American Revolution has been well and often told, and yet the most careless observer of the popular mind may perceive that a large proportion of our people are but little instructed in many of the essential details of that event, so important for every intelligent citizen to learn. Very few are ignorant of the more conspicuous circumstances of that period, and all who claim to be well-informed have a correct general knowledge of the history of our war for independence. But few even of that intelligent class are acquainted with the location of the various scenes depicted by the historian, in their relation to the lakes and rivers, towns and cities, whose names are familiar to the ears of the present generation. For example : the citizen of Saratoga may have a thorough knowledge of the memorable places in his own vicinage, and of the incidents which have hallowed them, yet how puzzled he would be if asked to tell the inquiring stranger, or his more inquisitive children, upon what particular stream, or lofty height, or broad plain, or in what mountain gorge, occurred the battles of Rocky Mount, King's Mountain, Eutaw Springs, or the Cowpens. These are places widely known in their respective districts, and the events connected with them form as important links in the chain of circumstances which were developed in the progress of the colonies toward independence, as the surrender of Burgoyne and his army upon the plain at Saratoga. Among this class, claiming to be generally informed, but ignorant in many particulars, especially in relation to the character and situation of localities, the writer places himself; and to an appreciation of the necessity of a more thorough knowledge of these places, and of the men who are identified with the Revolution, the reader is partially indebted for the pages which follow this confession.

To obtain this accurate chorographical knowledge of our early history as a confederation of states, was not the only incentive to undertake a journey to the battle-fields and other localities hallowed by the events of the Revolution. My limited observation had perceived many remaining physical vestiges of that struggle. Half-hidden mounds of old redoubts; the ruined walls of some stronger fortification; dilap-idated buildings, neglected and decaying, wherein patriots met for shelter or in council; and living men, who had borne the musket and knapsack day after day in that conflict, occasionally passed under the eye of my casual apprehension. For years a strong desire was felt to embalm those precious things of our cherished house-hold, that they might be preserved for the admiration and reverence of remote pos-terity. I knew that the genius of our people was the reverse of antiquarian rever-ence for the things of the past; that the glowing future, all sunlight and eminence, absorbed their thoughts and energies, and few looked back to the twilight and dim valleys of the past through which they had journeyed. I knew that the invisible fingers of decay, the plow of agriculture, and the behests of Mammon, unrestrained in their operations by the prevailing spirit of our people, would soon sweep away every tangible vestige of the Revolution, and that it was time the limner was abroad. I knew that, like stars at dawn which had beamed brightly through a long night, the men of old were fast fading away, and that relics associated with their trials and triumphs would soon be covered up forever. Other men, far more competent than myself to use the pen and pencil, appeared indisposed to go out into the ap-parently shorn and unfruitful field upon which I looked with such covetous delight, except to pick up a grain here and there for special preservation. I knew that the vigorous reapers who had garnered the products of that broad field, must have let fall from their full hands many a precious ear loaded with choice grain, and I re-solved to go out as a gleaner, carefully gather up what they had left behind, and add the winnings to their store. Like the servants of Boaz, when Ruth followed the reapers, they seem to have "let fall also some of the *handfuls* of purpose for me, that I might glean them," for I found a far greater abundance than hope had promised. I have "gleaned in the field until even, and beat out that I have gleaned," and here is my "ephah of barley."

In the arrangement of a plan for presenting the result of these labors to the public in an acceptable form many difficulties were perceptible. Other histories of our Revolution had been written, embellished, and read; what could be produced more attractive than they? The exciting literature of the day, ranging in its in-toxicating character from the gross pictures of sensual life drawn by the French wri-ters of fiction, to the more refined, but not less intoxicating works of popular and esteemed novelists, so cheaply published and so widely diffused, has produced a degree of mental dissipation throughout our land, destructive, in its tendency, to sober and rational desires for imbibing useful knowledge. Among the young, where this dissipation is most rife, and deleterious in its effects, it seemed most desi-rable to have the story of our Revolution known and its salutary teachings pondered and improved, for they will be the custodians of our free institutions when the active men of the present generation shall step aside into the quiet shadows of old age. Next to tales of love and gallantry, the young mind is most charmed by the narra-tives of the traveler. The woof of our history is too sacred to be interwoven with the tinsel filling of fiction, and we should have too high a regard for truth to seek the potential aid of its counterfeit in gaining audience in the ear of the million; but to the latter taste we may consistently pay court, and in behalf of sober history, use its power in disputing for the preference with the tourist. As my journey was among scenes and things hallowed to the feelings of every American, I felt a hope that a record of the pilgrimage, interwoven with that of the facts of past history, would attract the attention, and win to the perusal of the chronicles of our Revolution many who could not be otherwise decoyed into the apparently arid and flowerless domains of mere history. I accordingly determined to make the record of the tour to the important localities of the Revolution a leading feature in the work. Here another difficulty was encountered. So widely scattered are those localities, and so simultaneous were many of the events, that a connected narrative of the journey must necessarily break up the chronological unity of the history, and, at times, produce some confusion. To give incidents of the journey, and sketches and descriptions of the scenery and relics as they appear at present, in fragmentary notes, would deny to the work the charm of a book of travel, and thus almost wholly remove the prime object in view in giving such narrative. The apparently less objectionable course was chosen, and the history was broken into fragments, arranged, in the exhibition, in accordance with the order in which each locality was visited, the fragments individualized as much as possible, yet always maintaining a tie of visible relationship with the whole. The apparent difficulties in the way of the student which this plan suggests, are removed by the aid of a complete Analytical Index at the close of the work, while the narrative of the tour remains unbroken, except by the continually recurring appendices of history. How far this arrangement shall accomplish the desired result the candid judgment of the reader must determine.

To collect the pictorial and other materials for this work, I traveled more than eight thousand miles in the Old Thirteen States and Canada, and visited every important place made memorable by the events of the war; yet, in all that long and devious journey, through cities and villages, amid mountains and vast pine forests, along rivers and over fertile plantations, from New England to Georgia, with no passport to the confidence, no claim to the regard of those from whom information was sought, except such as the object of my errand afforded, and communing with men of every social and intellectual grade, I never experienced an unkind word or cold repulsion of manner. On the contrary, politeness always greeted my first salutation, and, when the object of my visit was announced, hospitality and friendly services were freely bestowed. Every where the memorials of our Revolution are cherished with devotional earnestness, and a feeling of reverence for these things abounds, though kept quiescent by the progressive spirit of the age. To those who thus aided and cheered me in my enterprise, I here proffer my sincere thanks. I can not name them all, for they are too numerous, but they will ever remain cherished "pictures on memory's wall."

It has been said that "diligence and accuracy are the only merits which a historical writer may ascribe to himself." Neither labor nor care has been spared in the collection of materials, and in endeavors to produce a work as free from grave errors as possible. It has imperfections; it would be foolish egotism to assert the contrary. In the various histories of the same events many discrepancies appear; these I have endeavored to reconcile or correct by documentary and other reliable

testimony ; and if the work is not more accurate than its predecessors, it is believed
to be equally so with the most reliable. Free use has been made of the available
labors of others in the same department of literature, always accrediting the source
from whence facts were derived. I have aimed to view men and events with an
impartial eye, censuring friends when they deserved censure, and commending enemies when truth and justice demanded the tribute. The historical events recorded
were those of a family quarrel concerning vital principles in jurisprudence ; and
wisely did a sagacious English statesman console himself, at the close of the war,
with the reflection, " We have been subdued, it is true, but, thank Heaven, the
brain and the muscle which achieved the victory were nurtured by English blood ;
Old England, upon the Island of Great Britain, has been beaten only by Young
England, in America."

In the pictorial department, special care has been observed to make faithful de-
lineations of fact. If a relic of the Revolution was not susceptible of picturesque
effect in a drawing, without a departure from truth, it has been left in its plainness,
for my chief object was to illustrate the *subject*, not merely to embellish the *book*. I
have endeavored to present the features of things as I found them, whether homely
or charming, and have sought to delineate all that fell in my way worthy of preservation. To do this, it was necessary to make the engravings numerous, and no
larger than perspicuity demanded, else the work would be filled with pictures to
the exclusion of essential reading matter.

The plans of military movements have been drawn chiefly from British sources,
for very few were made by the engineers in the Continental service. These appear
to be generally pretty correct, so far as they represent the immediate movements
of the armies in actual conflict ; but the general topographical knowledge possessed
by those engineers, was quite defective. I have endeavored to detect and correct their
inaccuracies, either in the drawings or in the illustrative descriptions.

With these general remarks respecting the origin and construction of the work,
it is submitted to the reading public. If a perusal of its pages shall afford as
much pleasure and profitable knowledge as were derived from the journey and in
the arrangement of the materials for the press, the effort has not been unfruitful
of good results. With an ardent desire that it may prove a useful worker in the
maintenance and growth of true patriotism,

ILLUSTRATIONS—Vol. I.

INTRODUCTION.

Far o'er yon azure main thy view extend,
Where seas and skies in blue confusion blend:
Lo, there a mighty realm, by Heaven design'd,
The last retreat for poor, oppress'd mankind;
Form'd with that pomp which marks the hand divine,
And clothes yon vault, where worlds unnumber'd shine.
Here spacious plains in solemn grandeur spread;
Here cloudy forests cast eternal shade;
Rich valleys wind, the sky-tall mountains brave,
And inland seas for commerce spread the wave
With nobler floods the sea-like rivers roll,
And fairer luster purples round the pole.

TIMOTHY DWIGHT.

VERY nation eminent for its refine ment, displayed in the cultivation of the arts, had its heroic age; a period when its first physical and moral conquests were achieved, and when rude society, with all its impurities, was fused and re-fined in the crucible of progress. When civilization first set up its standard as a permanent ensign in the Western hemisphere, north-ward of the Bahamas and the great Gulf, and the contests for possession began between the wild Aborigines, who thrust no spade into the soil, no sickle into ripe harvests, and those earnest delvers from the Old World, who came with the light of Christianity to plant a new empire and redeem the wilderness by cultivation, then commenced the heroic age of America. It ended when the work of the Revolution, in the eighteenth century, was accomplished; when the bond of vassalage to Great Britain was severed by her colonies, and when the thirteen confed-erated States ratified a federal Constitution, and upon it laid the broad found-ation of our Republic.

Those ancient civilizations, registered by the stylus of history, were mere gleamings of morning compared with the noontide radiance which now lights up the Western World; and even the more modern nations of Europe, brilliant as they appear, have so many dark spots upon the disk of their enlightenment, that their true glory is really less than that of the waxing Star in the West. These ancient and modern civilizations, now past or at their culminating points, were the results of the slow progress of centuries; the heroic age of America, meteor-like, was brilliant and rapid in its course, occupying the space of only a century and a half of time from the permanent implanting of a British colony, weak and dependent, to the founding of our government, which, like Pallas Athena, was, at its birth, full panoplied, strong, eminently individual in its character, and full of recuperative energies. The head of Britannia was cleft by the Vulcan of the Revolution, and from its teeming brain leaped the full-grown daughter, sturdy and defiant.

Long anterior to the advent of Europeans in America, a native empire, but little inferior to Old Rome in civilization, flourished in that region of our continent which now forms the southwestern portion of the Republic. The Aztec empire, which reached the acme of its refinement during the reign of Montezuma, and crumbled into fragments when Cortez dethroned 1521. and murdered that monarch, extended over the whole of Central America ; and when the Spaniards came it was gradually pushing its conquests northward, where all was yet darkness and gloom. To human apprehension, this people, apparently allied by various ties to the wild nations of North America, appeared to be the most efficient instruments in spreading the light of civilization over the whole continent ; yet they were not only denied this glorious privilege, but, by the very race which first attempted to plant the seeds of European refinement in Florida and among the Mobilian tribes, and to shed the illumination of their dim Christianity over the dreary regions of the North, was their own bright light extinguished. The Aztecs and their neighbors were beaten into the dust of debasement by the falchion blows of avarice and bigotry, and they form, apparently, not the most insignificant atom of the chain of events which connects the history of the empires of the Old World with that of our Republic.

It is believed that, two hundred years before the Aztecs subdued the more ancient people of the Mexican valley and founded Tenochtitlan,[1] a handful of rough, half-civilized adventurers from the wintery shores of Iceland and the neighboring main, driven by adverse winds they knew not whither, touched upon the bleak shores of Labrador, and traversed the American continent southward as far as Rhode Island, and, it may be, the capes of Virginia.[2] These supposed first modern discoverers of America were the children of the " mighty sea kings" of the Teutonic romances—the Scandinavian *reguli*, who, scorning to own *Gorm the Old* of Norway, and *Harold Fairhair* of Denmark, their conquerors, as masters, forsook their country and colonized Iceland, Greenland, Shetland, and the Orkney Islands, whence they sent forth piratical expeditions, which became a terror to Western Europe. They traded as well as plundered, and by commerce and conquest became potential. Every coast was visited by their squadrons, either for war or traffic. They swept over Denmark and Germany, and by conquest obtained possession of the best portions of Gaul.[3] They invaded 1014. the British Islands, and placed the renowned Canute upon the throne of Alfred.

Long before Christianity had shed its genial rays over their frozen territory of the North, and banished the barbarous rites of Pagan worship, the lamp of learning had been

---

[1] This city was founded about the year 1210, and was afterward called *Mexico*, which signifies *the place of Mexitli*, the Aztec god of war. The present capital of Mexico is upon the site of that ancient city. The Aztecs, at that time, were settled in Lower California. They were divided into six tribes. The Mexican tribe wandered off southward, subdued the Toltecs, and founded the city around which the whole Aztec nation subsequently gathered. The Toltecs were far more refined than their conquerors, and from members of that dispersed nation the Aztecs were first made acquainted with painting, sculpture, astronomy, and many of the useful arts, such as working in metals, building bridges and aqueducts, agriculture, &c.

[2] See note on page 633.

[3] Charles III., called the Simple, the eighth of the Carlovingian kings of France, ceded to Rolf or Rollo, one of the Northmen chiefs, the large province called by them Normandy. This event occurred in the year 918. Rollo and his subjects embraced Christianity, and became the guardians of France against further invasion from the Northmen.

taken from the cloisters of the South and placed within their temples, and upon dreary and desolate Iceland and Norway civilization erected its humanizing altars. Ardent, imaginative, and devotional, they eagerly accepted Christianity, and it became to them really a "Star in the East," leading to where "the infant Jesus laid." It was not to them so much a personal treasure to be valued for its immortal blessings, as a glorious idea full of temporal advantage. It became an intense passion, not a sober belief, and its warmth generated mighty events. Among them the spirit of chivalry had its birth and early nurture, and in those unholy wars against the possessors of the land of Palestine and of the sepulcher of Christ, called the Crusades, which shook the nations during three consecutive centuries, these Northmen furnished the bravest leaders.

From such a people, possessed of every attribute necessary to the successful founding of new empires, having the ocean pathway to a broad and fertile continent made clear before them, what great results might not be expected? But, with the prize just within their grasp, they, too, were denied the honor of first peopling our land; yet their mixed descendants, the Anglo-Saxons, now possess it. It is supposed that they attempted settlements, but failed, and in the lapse of centuries their voyages were forgotten, or only remembered in the songs of their bards or the sagas of their romancers. For more than five hundred years after the voyages of those navigators, America was an unknown region; it had no place upon maps, unless as an imaginary island without a name, nor in the most acute geographical theories of the learned.[1] It was reserved for the son of an humble wool-carder of Genoa to make it known to the world.

During the first half of the fifteenth century, maritime discoveries were prosecuted with untiring zeal by the people inhabiting the great peninsula of Southwestern Europe. The incentives to make these discoveries grew out of the political condition of Europe and the promises of great commercial advantages. The rich commerce of the East centered in Rome, when that empire overshadowed the known world; when it fell into fragments, the Italian cities continued their monopoly of the trade of the Indies. Provinces which had become independent kingdoms became jealous of these cities, so rapidly outstripping them in power and opulence; and Castile and Portugal, in particular, engaged in efforts to open a direct trade with the East. The ocean was the only highway for such commerce toward which they could look with a hope of success. The errors of geographical science interposed their obstacles; the belief that a belt of impassable heat girdled the earth at the equator intimidated mariners, and none were willing to double Cape Bojador, beyond which was the fancied region of fire.

Prince Henry of Portugal, son of John the First and Philippa of Lancaster (sister of Henry the Fourth of England), having accompanied his father into Africa, in an expedition against the Moors, received much information concerning the mineral riches and fertility of Guinea and other portions of the coast. The idea of making discoveries along the African shores filled his mind, and on his return to Portugal he abandoned the court, retired to a secluded spot near Cape St. Vincent, in full view of the ocean, and drawing around him the most eminent scientific men in the kingdom, pursued geographical and nautical inquiries with untiring zeal. He became convinced that Africa was circumnavigable, and that the

---

[1] "The [Atlantic] Ocean," observes Xerif al Edrisi, an eminent Arabian writer, quoted by Irving, "encircles the ultimate bounds of the inhabited earth, and all beyond is unknown. No one has been able to verify any thing concerning it, on account of its difficult and perilous navigation, its great obscurity, its profound depth, and frequent tempests; through fear of its mighty fishes and its haughty winds; yet there are many islands in it, some of which are peopled and others uninhabited. There is no mariner who dares to enter into its deep waters; or, if any have done so, they have merely kept along its coasts, fearful of departing from them. The waves of this ocean, although they roll as high as mountains, yet maintain themselves without breaking, for if they broke, it would be impossible for a ship to plow through them."

Indies might be reached by doubling its most southerly headlands. Expeditions were fitted out; the Cape de Verd and the Azore Islands were discovered; Cape Bojador was passed; the tropical region was penetrated, and divested of its terrors; and at length the lofty promontory which terminates Africa on the south, was descried. It was hailed as a harbinger of the coveted passage to the Indian Seas, and on that account King John gave it the appellation of the *Cape of Good Hope*

1486.

The Spaniards were also making maritime discoveries at the same time, but Lisbon was the point of great attraction to the learned, the curious, and the adventurous, who were desirous to engage in the expeditions then continually fitting out there. Among them came Christopher Columbus, or Colombo, a native of Genoa, then in the vigor of maturity.[1] Already he had made many a perilous voyage upon the ocean, having engaged in the life of a mariner at the age of fourteen years. The bent of his mind for such pursuits was early discovered by his father, and in the University of Pavia he was allowed, by a short course of study, to obtain sufficient elementary knowledge of geometry, astronomy, geography, and navigation, and of the Latin language, to enable him to make those sciences afterward subservient to his genius. From the commencement of his nautical career to his landing in Portugal, his history is very obscure.

---

[1] There is some obscurity and doubt respecting the precise year in which Columbus was born. Muñoz, in his History of the New World, places it in 1446. Mr. Irving, relying upon the authority of Bernaldez, who says that "he died in 1506, in a good old age, at the age of seventy, a little more or less," places it in 1436, which would make him about forty-eight years old when he landed in Portugal.

[2] This peculiar signature of Columbus is attached to various documents written by him subsequent to his first voyage. It was customary, in his time, to precede a signature with the initials (and sometimes with the words in full) of some pious ejaculation. We accordingly find the signature of Columbus with initial prefixes, thus:

S
S A S
X M Y
χρο FERENS

The interpretation is supposed to be "Sancta! Sancta, Ave, Sancta! Christo, Maria, Yoseph;" *id est. Christ, Mary, Joseph.* The χρο are Greek letters; the word FERENS Roman capitals. X, or a cross. is the sign for Christo or Christ, and χρο is an abbreviation of χριστος, anointed, and expressed the first and chief portion of the Christian name of Columbus. The Latin word *ferens* (bearing, carrying, or enduring) expressed not only the latter portion of his name, but also his character, according to his own lofty conceptions of his mission. He believed himself to be *Christo ferens*, Christ-bearer or Gospel-bearer, to the heathen inhabitants of an unknown world. It may be added, that Colombo (Columbus), a dove or

In person, Columbus was tall and commanding; in manners, exceedingly winning and graceful for one unaccustomed to the polish of courts or the higher orders in society. He was a strict observer of the rituals of his religion. His piety was not a mere form, but an elevated and solemn enthusiasm, born of a deep conviction of the vital truths of Christianity. While in Lisbon, he never omitted religious duties in the sanctuary. At the chapel of the Convent of *All Saints*, where he was accustomed to worship, he became acquainted with a young lady of rank named Donna Felipa, the daughter of Moñis de Palestrello, an Italian cavalier, who had been one of the most distinguished navigators in the service of Prince Henry. They loved, and were married. His wife's sister was married to Pedro Correo, a navigator of note. In the family of his mother-in-law he learned all the incidents of the voyages of her husband; and the charts, journals, and other manuscripts of that navigator she delivered to Columbus. These possessions awakened new aspirations in his mind. He had made himself familiar, by study and large experience, with all the nautical knowledge of the day, and, in common with the most enlightened men of his time, he was disposed to credit the narratives of Plato and other ancient writers respecting the existence of a continent beyond a glorious island called Atlantis,[1] in the waste of waters westward of Europe. Such a continent was necessary to make his own geographical theory perfect. The gorgeous pictures of Zipango or Cipangi and Cathay, on the eastern coast of Asia, drawn by Marco Polo and Mandeville, also excited his warm imagination; and the alleged apparitions of land seen to the westward by the people of the Canary Isles were treasured in his mind as great realities.[2] His comprehensive genius constructed a new and magnificent theory, and his bold spirit stood ready to act in unison with his genius. He based his whole theory upon the fundamental principle that the earth was a terraqueous globe, which might be traveled round from east to west, and that men stood foot to foot at opposite points.

---

pigeon, was doubtless associated, in his imagination, with the carrier-bird, and had its due weight, not only in his conceptions of his destiny, but in forming his sign-manual. The signature to his will is EL ALMIRANTE (the Admiral), with the above letters, instead of χρο FERENS.

[1] Ancient writers speak of an island which existed at a very early period in the Atlantic Ocean, and said to have been eventually sunk beneath its waves. Plato, who gave the first account of it, says he obtained his information from the priests of Egypt. The island was represented to be larger than Asia and Africa, as they were then known, and beyond it was a large continent. Nine thousand years before Plato's time, this island was thickly inhabited and very powerful, its sway extending over all Africa, including Egypt, and also a large portion of Europe. A violent earthquake, which lasted for the space of a day and a night, and was accompanied by inundations of the sea, caused the island to sink, and, for a long period subsequent to this, the sea in this quarter was impassable by reason of slime and shoals. Learned men of modern times have been disposed to believe in the ancient existence of such an island, and suppose the West India Islands to be the higher portions of the sunken land. If this belief is correct, then the continent beyond was America.

According to the account given to Plato, Atlantis was the most productive region upon the earth. It produced wine, grain, and delicious fruits in abundance. It had wide-spread forests, extensive pasture-grounds, mines of gold and silver, hot springs, and every luxury for human enjoyment. It was divided into ten kingdoms, governed by as many kings, all descendants of Neptune, and living in perfect harmony with each other. It had splendid cities, rich and populous villages, vast fortifications, arsenals, and equipments for navies. There was a temple in the island a stadium (six hundred and six feet nine inches) in length, dedicated to Neptune. It was ornamented with gold, silver, orichalcium, and ivory. It contained a golden statue of Neptune, representing the god as standing in his chariot, and holding the reins of his winged steeds. Such was the ancient vision.

[2] So confident were the people of the Canaries that land lay to the westward of them, that they sought and obtained permission from the King of Portugal to fit out various expeditions in search of it. A belief was so prevalent that a Scottish priest named Brandon discovered an island westward of the Canaries, in the sixth century, that maps, in the time of Columbus, had the Island of *St. Brandon* upon them. It was placed under the equator.

a 1543. This was seventy years before Copernicus announced his theory of the form and motion of the planets,[a] and one hundred and sixty years before Galileo was obliged, before the court of the Inquisition at Rome, to renounce his belief in the diurnal revolution of the earth.[b]

b 1633.

Columbus divided the circumference of the earth at the equator, according to Ptolemy's system, into twenty-four hours of fifteen degrees each, making three hundred and sixty degrees. Of these he imagined that fifteen hours had been known to the ancients, extending from the Fortunate or Canary Islands to the city of Thinœ in Asia, the western and eastern boundaries of the known world. By the discovery of the Cape de Verd and the Azore Islands, the Portuguese had advanced the western frontier one hour, leaving about one eighth of the circumference of the globe yet to be explored. The extent of the eastern region of Asia was yet unknown, although the travels of Polo in the fourteenth century had extended far beyond the Oriental boundary of Ptolemy's map. Columbus imagined that the unexplored part of Asia might occupy a large portion of the yet undefined circumference of the earth, and that its eastern headlands might approach quite near to those of Western Europe and Africa. He therefore concluded that a navigator, pursuing a direct course from east to west, must arrive at the extremity of Asia by a far easier and shorter route than following the coast of Africa around the Cape of Good Hope. Fortunately, he adopted the opinions of Aristotle, Pliny, and other writers, who considered the ocean as but of moderate breadth, so that it might be crossed from Europe in the space of a few days. A knowledge or suspicion of its actual extent would have deterred even the bold enterprise of Columbus from attempting an exploration of its waters in the small ships of that day. Reports of strange trees, reeds of immense size, curiously-carved pieces of wood, and the bodies of two men—unlike, in color and visage, any of the known races extant—having drifted ashore upon the Canary and Azore Islands by westerly winds, confirmed him in his belief, and a desire and determination to undertake a demonstration of his theory by an exploring voyage absorbed his whole attention. " He never spoke in doubt or hesitation," says Irving, " but with as much certainty as if his eyes had beheld the Promised Land. A deep religious sentiment mingled with his thoughts, and gave them at times a tinge of superstition, but of a sublime and lofty kind. He looked upon himself as standing in the hand of Heaven, chosen from among men for the accomplishment of its high purpose. He read, as he supposed, his contemplated discovery foretold in Holy Writ, and shadowed forth darkly in the prophecies. The ends of the earth were to be brought together, and all nations, and tongues, and languages united under the banner of the Redeemer."[1] The prophetic passage in Pulci's " Morgante Maggiore" was to him full of promise :

> " Know that this theory is false ; his bark
> The daring mariner shall urge far o'er
> The Western wave, a smooth and level plain,
> Albeit the earth is fashion'd like a wheel.
> Man was in ancient days of grosser mold,
> And Hercules might blush to learn how far
> Beyond the limits he had vainly set[2]
> The dullest sea-boat soon shall wing her way.
> Men shall descry another hemisphere,
> Since to one common center all things tend.
> So earth, by curious mystery divine

---

[1] *Life and Voyages of Columbus.*

[2] Calpe and Abila, or *Gibraltar*, on the Spanish, and *Cape Serra*, on the African shore of the Straits of Gibraltar, were called the Pillars of Hercules ; it being said, in ancient fable, that Hercules placed them there as monuments of his progress westward, and beyond which no mortal could pass.

Well balanced, hangs amid the starry spheres.
At our antipodes are cities, states,
And thronged empires, ne'er divined of yore.
But see, the sun speeds on his western path
To glad the nations with expected light."
PRESCOTT'S TRANSLATION OF STANZA 229, 230, CANTO XXV.

While maturing his plans, Columbus extended the bounds of his observation and study by a voyage to Thule, or Iceland, from which remote point he says he advanced one hundred leagues northward, penetrated the polar circle, and convinced himself of the fallacy of the popular belief that the frozen zone was uninhabitable.[1] Whether he saw, in Iceland, written accounts of the voyages of the Northmen to America, or heard of them as related by tradition or chanted in songs, we have no means of determining. If he did, it is singular, as Prescott remarks, that they were not cited by him in support of his hypothesis, while earnestly pressing his suit for aid before the courts of Portugal and Spain ; and it is equally surprising that he did not, in his first voyage to America, pursue the route traversed by those early navigators. He probably heard little more than vague rumors of their voyages, such as presented insufficient data even for a plausible opinion. His magnificent idea was all his own, sustained by the opinions of a few learned men, and confirmed by his observations while on this northern voyage.

Filled with his noble resolutions and lofty anticipations, Columbus submitted the theory on which rested his belief in a practicable western route to Asia, to King John the Second of Portugal. That monarch's sagacity perceived the promised advantages to be derived from such an enterprise, and he eagerly sought the counsel of his ministers and wise men. But his court and the college of scientific sages could not comprehend the sublime project ; and after a long and fruitless negotiation, during which the Portuguese meanly attempted to avail themselves clandestinely of his information, Columbus quitted Lisbon in disgust, determined to submit his proposals to Ferdinand and Isabella, the Spanish sovereigns, whose wisdom and liberal views were the admiration of men of science and learning. His wife was dead ; his feelings had no hold upon Portugal, and he quitted it forever.

It was toward the close of 1484 when Columbus appeared at the Spanish court.[2] It was an unpropitious hour, for the whole resources of the nation were then employed in prosecuting a war with the Moors. For a long time he awaited the decision of the sovereigns, employing his leisure in the alternate pursuits of science, and engagements in some of the military campaigns. He was treated with great deference, and, after much delay, a council of learned men were convened at Salamanca to consider his plans and propositions. After mature deliberation, they pronounced his scheme "vain, impracticable, and resting on grounds too weak to merit the support of government." A minority of the council were far from acquiescing in this decision, and, with the Cardinal Mendoza and other officers of government, and Fray Juan Perez de Marchena, guardian of the ancient monastery of La Rabida,

[1] In the age of Columbus, Greenland was laid down upon the maps as a continuation or projection westward of Scandinavia. Columbus discovered this error in his northern voyage, which discovery was a new fact in support of his theory of a continent lying westward from Europe, or at least a proximity of the eastern coast of Asia. At that time the climate of Iceland and Greenland was far more genial than at present, and there is reason to believe that those portions of the latter country which for two or three hundred years have been ice-bound and uninhabitable, were then tillable. Philosophers of our day, who have studied the phenomena of terrestrial magnetism with care, have advanced a plausible theory whereby to explain this fact.

[2] It is asserted, but without positive proof, that Columbus, before going to Spain, made application to the authorities of his native city, Genoa, for aid in his enterprise ; but failing in this he went to Venice, and also sent his brother Bartholomew to England, to lay his plans before Henry the Seventh. If these statements are true, they exhibit his perseverance in a still stronger light than truthful history presents it.

they induced the sovereigns to soften the decisions of the council by a promise to give the proposition a fair audience when their pressing state engagements should be ended. Columbus, wearied by procrastination, at length lost all hope of effecting any thing with the Spanish court. He turned from it with disgust, and made application to two wealthy and enlightened Southern dukes, who had ample means at command. He was unsuccessful, and with a heavy heart he left Spain, to carry his proposals to the King of France.

Isabella of Castile and Leon, sister of the profligate Henry the Fourth, was the successor of that monarch to the throne. She married Ferdinand, the son of old John the Second of Aragon, and, associating him with herself in the government, united the two monarchies into one great kingdom, the renowned modern Spain. Isabella was emi-

October 19, 1469.

ISABELLA OF CASTILE.[1]

nently virtuous, and her piety and daily goodness were the fruit of a deep religious feeling. Ferdinand was ambitious, and, in the midst of his perplexity with the Moors, he felt a strong desire to advance the interests and glory of the new kingdom, by maritime discoveries; yet he could not comprehend the vast plans of Columbus, and he looked coldly upon the project. To the pious sentiments of the queen, Father Perez, a former confessor of Isabella and a friend of Columbus, appealed with success; and before the navigator had entered the dominions of France, he was summoned back to the court, then in the camp at Santa Fé. He arrived in time to witness the surrender of Grenada. Joy and exultation pervaded all classes. Columbus took advantage of this state of things, and while he excited

the acquisitiveness of the nobles by reciting wonderful tales of the riches of Cipangi and Cathay, he eloquently portrayed to the queen the glorious prospect of extending the influence of the Gospel over benighted heathens, promising to devote the profits of the enterprise to the recovery of the Holy Sepulcher at Jerusalem from the hands of the Paynim. His eloquence was seconded by that of Louis de St. Angel, a favorite officer of the crown. The religious zeal of Isabella was fired, and, notwithstanding the extravagant demands of Columbus,[2] she resolved, in opposition to the wishes of Ferdinand, to aid him in fitting out an ex-

---

[1] Isabella was of middle size, and well formed, with a fair complexion, auburn hair, and clear, blue eyes. There was a mingled gravity and sweetness in her countenance, and a singular modesty, gracing, as it did, great firmness of purpose and earnestness of spirit. Though strongly attached to her husband, and studious of his fame, yet she always maintained her distinct rights as an allied prince. She exceeded him in beauty, personal dignity, acuteness of genius, and grandeur of soul. Combining the active and resolute qualities of man with the softer charities of woman, she mingled in the warlike councils of her husband, and, being inspired with a truer idea of glory, infused a more lofty and generous temper into his subtile and calculating policy.—*Washington Irving.*

[2] Columbus, in the demands set forth in his proposition, stipulated for himself and heirs the title and authority of admiral and viceroy over all lands discovered by him. This demand was inadmissible, yet the navigator persisted in it, though it appeared an effectual bar to any arrangement with the queen. His stipulations were finally acceded to, and Columbus always regarded the queen with feelings of the liveliest gratitude. "In the midst of the general incredulity," he said in a letter, "the Almighty infused into the queen, my lady, the spirit of intelligence and energy, and while every one else, in his ignorance, was expatiating only on the inconvenience and cost, her highness approved it, on the contrary, and gave it all the support in her power."

pedition   These demands almost frustrated his designs, and Columbus had again turned his back upon the Spanish court, when, through the wise counsels of friends, the queen's objections were overcome, and the warmest impulses of her nature aroused. " I will assume the undertaking," she said, when opposed by her husband and his counselors, " for my own crown of Castile, and am ready to pawn my jewels to defray the expense of it, if the funds in the treasury shall appear inadequate."

A SPANISH CARAVEL.

All preliminaries being arranged, the queen lost no time in fitting out two vessels,[1] and Columbus, aided chiefly by the wealthy and enterprising family of the Pinzons,

VIEW OF PALOS.[2]

equipped a third. With this feeble squadron, manned with timid mariners, Columbus left the little port of Palos, upon the Tinto River, in Andalusia, on Friday, the third of August, 1492, and, spreading his sails to an easterly breeze, turned his prow toward the waste of waters in the direction of the setting sun. He had no reliable chart for his guidance, no director in his course but the sun and stars, and the imperfect mariner's compass, then used only by a few in

---

[1] The vessels furnished by Isabella were only *caravels*, light coasting ships, without decks, and furnished with oars like the ancient galleys.   The picture here given is from a low relief sculpture, on the tomb of Fernando Columbus, a son of the navigator, in the Cathedral of Seville.   Such a vessel would be considered quite inadequate to perform a coasting voyage at the present day.   The larger vessel, with a deck, fitted out by Columbus and his friends, was called the *Santa Maria ;* the caravels were named respectively *Pinta* and *Miña*.   Martin Alonzo Pinzon commanded the *Pinta*, and Vincent Yanez Pinzon the *Miña*. Garcia Fernandez, the physician of Palos, accompanied the expedition as steward.   The whole number of persons that embarked was one hundred and twenty.   The whole expenditure of the queen in fitting out the caravels amounted to only seventeen thousand florins, or between eight and nine thousand dollars.*   These were small preparations for an exploring expedition of such vast extent and importance.

The descendants of the Pinzons are still quite numerous in the vicinity of Palos.   When Mr. Irving visited that town in 1828, he saw the ruins of a family mansion which belonged to one of the two Pinzons who sailed with Columbus on his first voyage.   Mr. Irving was accompanied in his visit to Palos, the monastery of Ribida, and other localities in the vicinity, by *Juan Fernandez Pinzon, a descendant of one of the companions of Columbus.*

THE PINZON MANSION.

[2] The pile of buildings in this view, standing upon the bluff, is the ancient Church of St. George.   For some misdemeanor, the people of Palos were obliged to serve the crown for one year with two armed car

---

* This is the amount given by Muñoz, one of the most reliable of Spanish authors. Others have named a much higher sum Dr. Robertson rates the amount at £4000 sterling, or about $20,000, but does not give his authority.

navigating the pleasant seas of the Old World. After various delays at the Canary Islands, they passed and lost sight of Ferro, the most westerly one of the group, on Sunday, the ninth of September. Now Europe was left behind, and the broad Atlantic, mysterious and unknown, was before them. As the space widened between them and their homes, the hearts September, of the mariners failed; and when, on the thirteenth, the commander and his 1492. pilots discovered the variations of the magnetic needle, misgivings arose in the stout hearts of the explorer and his friends, the Pinzons. They were now six hundred miles westward of the Canaries, in an unknown sea. It was a phenomenon unknown to the world of science, and Columbus tried in vain to satisfy himself respecting the cause. He could not long conceal the fact from his seamen. It filled them with consternation and awe; for they believed they were entering another world, subject to the influence of laws unknown and dreadful. Columbus quieted their apprehensions by telling them that the needle did not point to the north star, but to an invisible point around which that star revolved daily. Thus he explained a phenomenon now well known; and his companions, relying upon his astronomical knowledge, received his theory as truth, and their alarm subsided.

For several days after this event they were wafted pleasantly by the trade winds, which blow continually from east to west. The air was balmy, and soon vast fields of sea-weeds, and an occasional petrel upon the wing, heralded an approach to land; but head winds and days of profound calm deferred the joyful consummation of their hopes; and the seamen, wearied and home-sick, resolved to retrace their path, and seek the shores of Spain. Even the little land birds that came upon the spars, and sung merrily their welcome to the New World, and then left at evening for their distant perches in the orange groves, failed to inspire the mariners with confidence in the truth of their commander's reasonings, and open mutiny manifested itself. With gentle words, promises of rewards, and threats of punishment against the most refractory, Columbus kept them from actual violence for sev- September 25. eral days. One evening, just at sunset, Martin Alonzo Pinzon, mounted on the stern of the Pinta, shouted, "Land! land! Señor, I claim the reward!"[1] Along the southwestern horizon was stretched an apparent island. Columbus, throwing himself upon his knees, with all the crews, chanted *Gloria in Excelsis!* In the morning the island had vanished, for it was nothing but a cloud. For a fortnight longer they floated upon an almost unruffled sea, when land birds came singing again, and green herbage floated by; but days passed on, and the sun, each evening, set in the waves. Again the seamen mutinied, and Columbus was in open defiance with his crew; for he told them that the expedition had been sent by their sovereigns, and, come what might, he was determined to accomplish his purpose. They were on the point of casting him into the sea, when, just at sunset, a coast-fish glided by; a branch of thorn, with berries upon it, floated near; and a staff, artificially carved, came upon the waters to tell them of human habitations not far off. The vesper hymn to the Virgin was now sung, and Columbus, after recounting the blessings of God thus far manifested on the voyage, assured the crews that he confidently expected to see land in the morning. On the high poop of his vessel he sat watching until

---

avels. They were under this penalty when Columbus made his arrangement with Isabella, and they were ordered to fit out the two caravels for the expedition. In the porch of the old Church of St. George, Columbus first proclaimed this order to the inhabitants of Palos. Mr. Irving, who visited Palos in 1828, says of this edifice, "It has lately been thoroughly repaired, and, being of solid mason-work, promises to stand for ages, a monument of the discoverers. It stands outside of the village, on the brow of a hill, looking along a little valley to the river. The remains of a Moorish arch prove it to have been a mosque in former times. Just above it, on the crest of the hill, is the ruin of a Moorish castle."

[1] Columbus agreed to give a silk waistcoat, besides the royal pension of thirty dollars, to the person who first discovered land.—*Muñoz*

near midnight, when he saw the glimmer of moving lights upon the verge of the horizon Fearing his hopes might have deceived his vision, he called Pedro Gutierrez, gentleman of the king's bed-chamber, and also Rodrigo Sanchez, of Segovia, to confirm his discovery. They also saw the gleams of a torch. All night the overjoyed Columbus watched. At dawn, beautiful wooded shores were in full view ; the perfumes of flowers came upon the light land breeze ; and birds in gorgeous plumage hovered around the vessels, caroling morning hymns, which seemed like the voices of angels to the late despairing seamen. In small boats

October 12, 1492.

they landed, the naked natives, who stood upon the beach in wonder, fleeing to the deep shadows of the forest in alarm. Columbus, dressed in gold-embroidered scarlet, bearing the royal standard, first stepped upon the shore. He was followed by the Pinzons, each bearing the banner of the enterprise.[1] On reaching the land, they all fell upon their knees, kissed the earth, and, with tears of joy in their eyes, chanted the *Te Deum Lauda-*

LANDING OF COLUMBUS.[3]

mus. Rising from the ground, Columbus displayed the royal standard, drew his sword, and took possession of the land in the name of the Spanish sovereigns, giving the island the title of San Salvador [2] With the most extravagant demonstrations of joy, his followers crowded around him. The most insolent in the mutinous displays were the most abject in making vows of service and faithfulness. All present took an oath of obedience to him as admiral and viceroy, and representative of Ferdinand and Isabella. The triumph of Columbus was complete.

BANNER OF THE EXPEDI-
TION.

The natives had beheld the approaching ships at dawn with fear

---

[1] This was a white banner, emblazoned with a green cross, having on each side the letters F. and Y., the Spanish initials of Ferdinand and Ysabel, surmounted by golden crowns.

[2] The island on which Columbus first set his foot in the New World is one of the Lucayas or Bahama group, and was called by the natives *Guanahana.* The Spaniards and others still call it *San Salvador ;* the English have given it the vulgar name of *Cat Island.* It lies between the twenty-fourth and twenty-fifth degrees of north latitude, and the second and third degrees of longitude east of the meridian of Washington city, eighty or ninety miles northeast of Havana, Cuba. *Muñoz,* a learned Spanish writer, thinks Watling's Island, and not the one called San Salvador on our maps, was the first landing-place.

[3] This is copied, by permission of the author, from Irving's *Life of Columbus.* It is a fac-simile of a sketch supposed to have been made by Columbus, in a letter written by him to Don Raphael Xansis, treasurer of the King of Spain.

and awe, regarding them as monsters of the deep. By degrees their alarm subsided, and they approached the Europeans. Each party was a wonder to the other. The glittering armor, shining lace, and many-colored dresses of the Spaniards filled the natives with admiration and delight; while they, entirely naked, with skins of a dark copper hue, painted with a variety of colors and devices, without beards and with straight hair, were objects of great curiosity to the Spaniards. They were unlike any people of whom they had knowledge. Not doubting that he was upon an island near the coast of Farther India, Columbus called these wild inhabitants *Indians*, a name which all the native tribes of America still retain.

It is not within the scope of my design to relate, in detail, the subsequent career of Columbus in the path of discovery, nor of those navigators who succeeded him, and share with him the honor of making known our continent to the Old World. He was the bold pioneer who led the way to the New World, and as such, deserves the first and highest reward; yet he was not truly the first discoverer of the *continent* of North America. Eager in his search for Cathay, he coasted almost every island composing the groups now known as the West Indies, during his several voyages, but he never saw the shores of the Northern August, Continent. He did, indeed, touch the soil of South America, near the mouth of 1498. the Oronoco, but he supposed it to be an island, and died in the belief that the lands he had discovered were portions of Farther India.[1]

Intelligence of the great discovery of Columbus, though kept concealed as much as possible by the Spanish court, for reasons of state policy, nevertheless went abroad, and aroused the ambition of other maritime powers. The story that Columbus had found vast and populous gold-producing regions in the Western Ocean excited the cupidity of individuals, and

---

[1] Columbus returned to Europe in March, 1493. Ferdinand and Isabella bestowed upon him every mark of honor and distinction; and the nobles were obsequious in their attentions to the favorite of royalty. On the 25th of September, 1493, he left Cadiz, on a second voyage of discovery. He had three large ships and fourteen caravels under his command. His discoveries were principally among the West India Islands, where he founded settlements. He returned to Spain in June, 1496. Misfortunes had attended him, yet the sovereigns treated him with distinguished favor. On the 30th of May, 1498, Columbus sailed from San Lucar de Barrameda, with a squadron of six vessels, on a third voyage of discovery. He found the settlements which had been planted in great confusion, and civil war among the Spaniards and natives was rife in Hispaniola. In the mean while, intrigues against him were having due weight in the Spanish court. It was alleged that Columbus designed to found an empire in the New World, cast off all allegiance to Spain, and assume the title and pomp of king. He had already offended the conscientious Isabella by persisting in making slaves of the natives, and she readily gave her consent to send out a commissioner to investigate the conduct of the navigator. Bobadilla, a tool of Columbus's enemies, was intrusted with that momentous duty; and, as might have been expected, he found Columbus guilty of every charge made against him. Bobadilla seized Columbus, and sent him in chains to Spain. His appearance excited the indignation of the sovereigns, and they declared to the world that Bobadilla had exceeded his instructions; yet justice was withheld, through the influence of Ferdinand, and Columbus was not reinstated as viceroy of Hispaniola.

While these events were occurring, Vasco de Gama, a Portuguese navigator, had reached Calicut, in the East Indies, by doubling the Cape of Good Hope, and traversing the Indian Ocean. But Columbus still persevered in his determination to reach Asia by a western route. He induced Isabella to fit out a fourth expedition for him, and on the 9th of May, 1502, he sailed for Hispaniola. After many troubles and hardships, he returned to Spain in 1504. His patron and best friend, the queen, died that same year. Old age had made its deep furrows, and, in the midst of disappointment and neglect, the great discoverer died on the 20th of May, 1506, at the age of seventy. He never realized his grand idea of reaching India by a western route. The honor of that achievement was reserved for the expedition of Magellan, fourteen years after the death of Columbus. That navigator passed through the straits which bear his name, at the southern extremity of our continent, and launched boldly out upon the broad Pacific. He died on the ocean, but his vessels reached the Philippine Islands, near the coast of India, in safety. Magellan gave the name of PACIFIC to the pleasant ocean over which he was sailing.

many adventurers offered their services to sovereigns and men of wealth. Almost simultaneously, Sebastian Cabot, of Bristol, and Amerigo Vespucci, a Florentine, sailed for the lands discovered by Columbus ; the former under the auspices of Henry the Seventh of England, and the latter in the employment of Spanish merchants, with the sanction of Ferdinand. Cabot's father was an Italian, and had been long a resident of Bristol, then the chief commercial mart of England. The Northwestern seas were often traversed as far as Iceland by the Bristol mariners, and they had probably extended their voyages westward to Greenland in their fishing enterprises. Cabot seems to have been familiar with those seas, and the English merchants had great confidence in his abilities. He obtained a commission from Henry the Seventh, similar, in its general outline, to that given to Columbus by Ferdinand and Isabella. It empowered him and his three sons, their heirs or deputies, to discover and settle unknown lands in the Eastern, Northern, or Western seas, such lands to be taken possession of in the name of the King of England. He fitted out two vessels at his own expense, which were freighted by merchants of London and Bristol ; and it was stipulated that, in lieu of all customs and imposts, Cabot was to pay to the King one fifth part of all the gains.

Cabot's son, Sebastian, a talented young man of only twenty years, with about three hundred red men, sailed from harbor of Bristol in May, 1497. He directed his course to the northwest, until he reached the fifty-eighth degree of north latitude, when floating ice and intense cold induced him to steer to the southwest. Fair winds produced a rapid voyage, and he discovered land on the twenty-fourth of June, which he called PRIMA VISTA, because it was his *first view* of a new region. The exact point of this first discovery is not certainly known ; some supposing it to have been on the coast of Labrador, and others the Island of Newfoundland or the peninsula of Nova Scotia. He touched at other points, but did not attempt a settlement ; the climate seemed too rigorous, the people too fierce, and he returned to Bristol.

Cabot made arrangements for a second voyage. He did not go in person, but fitted out

February, 1498.

SEBASTIAN CABOT.

vessels for the purpose. His son, Sebastian, was placed at the head of the expedition, and in May, 1498, the month in which De Gama reached Calicut, in the East Indies, by way of the Cape of Good Hope, he sailed for the New World with several ships. He visited the region first discovered by his father and himself, and called it NEWFOUNDLAND. It was not rich in gold and spices, but its shoals abounded with vast schools of codfish ; and within a few years after his return to England a permanent fishery was established there. Cabot sailed along the whole coast of the present United States, beginning at latitude fifty-six degrees, and terminating at about thirty-six degrees, or Albemarle Sound. His provisions ailing, he returned to England. He made another voyage in 1517, as far south as the

Brazils ; but failing to discover a western passage to the East Indies, he again returned to England.[1]

In the same month when young Cabot sailed from Bristol, Amerigo Vespucci departed

AMERIGO VESPUCCI.[2]

from Cadiz on his first voyage to the New World. In that voyage he appears to have held a subordinate station. May, 1497 The expedition under Ojeda, which Amerigo calls his *second* voyage, was not undertaken until 1499. Whether any vessel in that expedition was under his command is questionable. Spanish writers assert to the contrary, and say that he was first a captain when in the service of Emanuel of Portugal ; but it is not my province to inquire into this disputed matter. Spanish historians, jealous of the fame of Columbus, charge Vespucci with falsehood and fraud ; but early Spanish authors were not always scrupulous in regard to truth when national pride demanded prevarication, or even absolute falsehood. It was

---

[1] After his second voyage, Sebastian Cabot was invited to Spain, and sailed on a voyage of discovery, in the service of the Spanish monarch, in 1525. He visited Brazil, and, coasting southward to the thirty-fifth degree, he entered a large river, which he called *Rio de la Plata*. Up this river he sailed one hundred and twenty leagues. After an absence of six years, he returned to Spain, but seems not to have been well received by the sovereign. He made other, but less conspicuous voyages, and in his old age retired to Bristol, where he died about the year 1557, at the age of eighty years. He received a pension from Edward the Sixth, and was appointed governor of a company of merchants associated for the purpose of making discoveries.

[2] The name of the Florentine is variously spelled, Amerigo Vespucci, Americus Vespucius, Amerigo Vespuche. The latter orthography is according to the entry in an account-book containing the expenditure of the treasurer of the royal mercantile house of Seville, quoted by Muñoz, tome i., page xix of the Introduction. It appears by that account, that on the 24th of February, 1512, was paid to Manuel Catano, executor of the will of Amerigo, "10937 and a half maravedis," which was due to him for services as chief steersman to his majesty. Amerigo was appointed to that office in March, 1508, with a salary of 50,000 maravedis a year.

Whether he ever commanded an expedition in the Spanish service is a disputed question. He made several voyages to the New World between 1497 and 1512, the year of his death. With an expedition under the command of Ojeda, in 1499, he visited the Antilles and the coast of Guiana and Venezuela. On his return, Emanuel, king of Portugal, invited him to his capital, and gave him the command of three ships for a voyage of discovery. He left Lisbon May 10th, 1501, visited Brazil, and traversed the coast of South America as far as Patagonia, but failed to discover the straits through which Magellan passed at a later day. He returned to Lisbon in 1502. He made a fourth voyage, and returned to Portugal in 1504. Soon after this he wrote an account of his voyage. The book was dedicated to Rene II., duke of Lorraine. He again entered the service of the King of Spain, who appointed him to draw sea-charts, and gave him the title and salary of chief steersman or pilot, which commission he held until his death. According to some accounts, he died in the Island of Terceria, one of the Azores, in 1514 ; others affirm that his death occurred at Seville.

The portrait of the navigator, here given, was copied, by permission, from the original picture by Bronzino, now in possession of C. Edwards Lester, Esq., late United States consul at Genoa. It was committed to his care by the Vespucci family, to be placed in the possession of our government. No arrangement for its purchase has yet been made, I believe.

An Italian woman named Elena Vespucci, bearing proofs of her lineal descent from the famous navigator, came to America a few years ago, and made application to our Congress for a grant of land, on account of her relationship to the Florentine from whom our continent derived its name. Subsequently, her

natural that they should be tender of the reputation of Columbus, although he was not a Spaniard, for his discoveries reflected great luster upon the Spanish crown. For this reason they have ever disputed the claims of Vespucci, and denounced him as a liar and a charlatan. These denunciations, however, prove nothing, and the fame of Columbus loses none of its brightness by admitting the claims of the Florentine; claims, it must be acknowledged, that have sound logic and fair inferences as a basis. Amerigo seems to have been the first who published an account of the discoveries in the New World, and for this priority the narrow and selfish policy of the Spanish government is responsible. His first announcement was made in a letter to Lorenzo de Medici,[a] and soon afterward he published a volume giving an account of his four voyages, which he dedicated to the Duke of Lorraine.[b] In these he claims the merit of discovering the continent, having landed upon the coast of Paria,[c] in Colombia, South America, and traversed the shores, according to his own account, as far northward as the Gulf of Mexico. If this statement is true, he visited the continent nearly a year previous to the landing of Columbus at the mouth of the Oronoco, in the same district of Paria. From the circumstance of Amerigo making the first publication on the subject, and claiming to be the discoverer of the continent, the New World was called AMERICA, and the Florentine bears the honor of the name; but to neither Columbus nor Vespucci does the honor of first discoverer of America properly belong, but to young Cabot, for he and his crew first saw its soil and inhabitants. He alone, of all those voyagers in the fifteenth century, beheld North America. Whether to Columbus, Vespucci, or Cabot, truth should award the palm, Italy bears the imperishable and undisputed honor of giving birth to all three.

[a] 1504.
[b] 1507.
[c] 1497

The expeditions of the Cabots turned attention to the regions north of the West India Islands. Emanuel of Portugal dispatched some vessels, under the command of Gaspar Cortereal, in 1501, to follow in the track of the English. Cortereal sailed between two and three hundred leagues along the North American coast, but his voyage was fruitless of good results, either to science or humanity. He made few discoveries of land, carried on no traffic, planted no settlements, but kidnapped and carried to Portugal several friendly natives, to be sold as slaves! Perfidy and cruelty marked the first intercourse of the whites with the tribes of our continent; is it to be wondered that the bitter fruits of suspicion and hostility should have flourished among them?

Ponce de Leon, one of the companions of Columbus, and first governor of Porto Rico, a small island sixty miles east of Haiti, sailed on a voyage of discovery among the Bahamas, in search of the fabled Fountain of Youth. It was generally believed in Porto Rico, and the story had great credence in Old Spain, that the waters of a clear spring, bubbling up in the midst of a vast forest, upon an island among the Bahamas, possessed the singular property of restoring age and ugliness to youth and beauty, and perpetuating the lives of those who should bathe in its stream. De Leon was an old man, and, impressed with the truth of this legend, he sought that wonderful fountain. After cruising for a while among the Bahamas, he landed upon the peninsula of Florida, in the harbor of St. Augustine. It was on Palm Sunday when he debarked. That day is called by the Spaniards *Pasqua de Flores* and, partly from that circumstance, and partly on account of the great profusion of flowers which, at that early season of the year, were blooming on every side,

1512.

brother and two sisters, Amerigo, Eliza, and Teresa Vespucci, made a similar petition to Congress. They mention the fact that Elena, " possessing a disposition somewhat indocile and unmanageable, absented herself from her father's house, and proceeded to London. Hence she crossed the ocean, and landed upon the shores of Brazil, at Rio Janeiro. From that city she proceeded to Washington, the capital of the United States." Elena Vespucci was treated with respect. Possessed of youth and beauty, she attracted much attention at the metropolis, but the prayer in the petition of both herself and family was denied. She was living at Ogdensburgh, New York, when I visited that place in 1848.

Ponce de Leon gave the country (which he supposed to be a large island like Cuba) the name of FLORIDA. He took formal possession in the name of the Spanish monarch ; but, feeling unauthorized to proceed to making conquests without a royal commission, he sailed for Spain to obtain one, after failing in his search after the Fountain of Youth.

He had plunged into every stream, however turbid, with the vain expectation of rising from it young and blooming ; but, according to Oviedo, instead of returning to vigorous youth, he arrived at a second childhood within a few years. He was afterward appointed Governer of Florida, and was killed while on an expedition against the natives.

While Ponce de Leon was in Europe, where he remained several years, some wealthy gentlemen of Haiti fitted out two vessels to explore the Bahamas. The squadron was commanded by Lucas Vasquez d'Aillon or Allyon, a Spanish navigator. Their vessels were driven northward by a hurricane, and came near being stranded upon the low coasts. They finally made land in St. Helen's Sound, near the mouth of the Combahee River, in South Carolina, about half way between Charleston and Savannah. D'Aillon called the river Jordan, and the country Chicora. He carried off several natives, whom he enticed on board his ships, with the intention of selling them as slaves in Haiti. A storm destroyed one of the vessels, and the captured Indians in the other voluntarily starved themselves to death, so the avaricious whites were disappointed in their expectations of gain. D'Aillon afterward returned, with three ships, to conquer the whole of Chicora. The natives feigned friendship, decoyed the whites on shore, and then, with poisoned arrows, massacred nearly the whole of them, in revenge for their former perfidy. But few returned with D'Aillon to Haiti. This was the first discovery of the Carolina coast.

While these events were in progress, Cortez, at the head of an expedition fitted out by Velasquez, the governor of Cuba, was destroying the empire of Montezuma, in Mexico, then recently discovered. The success of Cortez excited the jealousy of Velasquez, for he feared a renunciation of his authority by that bold leader. He sent Pamphilo de Narvaez, with a strong force, to arrest and supersede Cortez ; but he was defeated. and most of his troops joined his enemy. Narvaez afterward obtained from the Spanish court a commission as *adelantado* or Governor of Florida, a territory quite indefinite in extent, reaching from the southern capes of the peninsula to the Panuco River in Mexico. With a force of three hundred men, eighty of whom were well mounted, Narvaez landed in Florida, where he raised the royal standard, and took possession of the country for the crown of Spain. With the hope of finding some wealthy region like Mexico and Peru, he penetrated the vast swamps and everglades in the interior of the flat country along the northern shore of the Gulf of Mexico. His men suffered terribly from the almost daily attacks of the natives and the nightly assaults of the deadly malaria of the fens. They reached the fertile regions of the Appalachians ; but the capital of the tribe, instead of being a gorgeous city like Mexico or Cuzco, was a mean village of two hundred huts and wigwams. Disappointed, and one third of his number dead, Narvaez turned southward, reached the Gulf near the present site of St. Mark's, on the Appalachie Bay, constructed five frail barks, and launched upon the waters. Nearly all his men, with himself, perished during a storm. Four of the crew, who were saved, wandered for years through the wild regions of Louisiana and Texas, and finally reached a Spanish settlement in Northern Mexico. These men gave the first intelligence of the fate of the expedition.

Two years after the return of these members of the expedition of Narvaez, Fernando de Soto planned an expedition to explore the interior of Florida, as all North America was then called, in search of a populous and wealthy region supposed to exist there. By permission of the Spanish monarch, he undertook the exploration and conquest of Florida

April 22, 1528.

June, 1528.

1536.

1538.

1520.

at his own risk and expense. He was commissioned governor-general of that country and of Cuba for life. Leaving his wife to govern Cuba during his absence, he sailed in

FERNANDO DE SOTO.

June, 1539, and landed at Tampa Bay with a force of six hundred men in complete armor. There he established a small garrison, and then sent most of the vessels of his fleet back to Cuba. He found a Spaniard, one of Narvaez's men, who had learned the native language. Taking him with him as interpreter, De Soto marched with his force into the interior. For five months they wandered among the swamps and everglades, fighting their way against the natives, when they reached the fertile region of the Flint River, in the western part of Georgia. There they passed the winter, within a few leagues of the Gulf, making, through exploring parties, some new discoveries, among which was the harbor of Pensacola. Early in May they broke up their encampment,

June 25, 1539.

1540

and, marching northeasterly, reached the head-waters of the Savannah River. After a brief tarry there, they turned their faces westward, and, on the twenty-eighth of October, came upon a fortified town, near the junction of the Alabama and Tombeckbee Rivers. A severe battle of nine hours' duration ensued. Several thousands of the half-naked Indians were slain, and their village reduced to ashes. Several of the mailed Spaniards were killed, and the victory availed De Soto nothing. All his baggage was consumed, and much provision was destroyed.

The wild tribes, for many leagues around, were aroused by this event. De Soto went into winter quarters in a deserted Indian village on the Yazoo. There he was attacked by the swarming natives, bent on revenge. The town was burned, all the clothing of the Spaniards, together with many horses and nearly all the swine which they brought from Cuba, were destroyed or carried away, and several of the whites were killed. Early in the spring the shorn invaders pushed westward, and discovered the Mississippi. They crossed it at the Chickasaw Bluffs, and traversed the country on its western shore up to the thirty-seventh degree, nearly opposite the mouth of the Ohio. They penetrated the wilderness almost three hundred miles west of the Mississippi during the summer, and wintered upon the Washita, in Arkansas. They passed down the Red River to the Mississippi in the spring, where De Soto sickened and died.[a] He had appointed a successor, who now attempted to lead the remnant of the expedition to Spanish settlements in Mexico.

a May 31, 1542.

For several months they wandered in the wilderness, but returned in December,[b] to winter upon the Mississippi, a short distance above the mouth of the Red River. There they constructed seven large boats, and in July following embarked in them. On reaching the Gulf of Mexico, they crawled cautiously along its sinuous coast, until the twentieth of September, when, half naked and almost famished, they reached a white settlement near the mouth of the Panuco River, about thirty miles north of Tampico.

b 1543

While the Spaniards were making these useless discoveries of the southern regions of our Republic along the Gulf of Mexico, the French fitted out several expeditions to explore the coast between the peninsula of Florida and the banks of Newfoundland. John Verrazzani, a celebrated Florentine navigator, proceeded to America with a squadron of four ships, under

the auspices of Francis the First of France, in 1523. Three of his vessels were so dam
aged by a storm that they were sent back; in the fourth, he proceeded on his voyage.

VERRAZZANI.

Weathering a terrible tempest, he reached our
coast near the mouth of Cape Fear River, in
North Carolina. He explored the whole coast
from the Carolinas to Nova Scotia, and taking
formal possession of the country in the name
of the French king, he called it NEW FRANCE,
the title held by Canada while it remained in
possession of the French. Verrazzani was followed, the next year, by Cartier (also in the
service of the French king), who discovered
the Gulf and River St. Lawrence;[1] and soon
afterward by the Lord of Roberval, a wealthy
nobleman, who proposed to plant a colony in
the New World. Roberval failed in his undertaking, and returned to France. He sailed
on another voyage, and was never heard of afterward. Other efforts at settlement along the
southern coasts were made by the French, but

were unsuccessful. A Protestant French colony, planted in Florida, was destroyed by the
Spaniards in 1564, and over the dead bodies of the Huguenots the murderers placed the
inscription, "We do this not as unto Frenchmen, but as unto Heretics." In 1567, De
Gourgues, a Gascon soldier, fitted out an expedition at his own expense, to avenge this out
rage. He surprised the Spanish forts erected near St. Augustine, and hung the soldiers of
the garrison upon the trees. Over them he placed the inscription, "I do this not as unto
Spaniards or mariners, but as unto traitors, robbers, and murderers." Thus white people
were exterminated by white people, and Indians again posessed the land.

The history of the early discoveries in North America forms a wonderful chapter in the
great chronicle of human progress and achievements, and in its details there are narratives
of adventure, prowess, love, and all the elements of romance, more startling and attractive
than the most brilliant conceptions of the imagination ever evolved. The story of the progress of settlements which followed is equally marvelous and attractive. These tempt the
pen on every side, but as they are connected only incidentally with my subject, I pass them
by with brevity of notice. In the preceding pages I have taken a very brief survey of
events in the *progress of discovery* which opened the way to settlements in the New World;
a brief survey of the *progress of settlements* will be found interwoven with the records upon
the pages which follow. They are all united by the often invisible threads of God's providence; and each apparently insignificant event in the wondrous history of our continent is a
link as important in the great chain of human deeds, directed by divine intelligence, as those
which arrest the attention and command the admiration of the world. Never was this
truth oftener and more strikingly illustrated than in our history of the war for independ
ence; and the student of that history, desirous of understanding its true philosophy, should
make himself familiar with the antecedents which have a visible relation thereto.

[2] See page 178, vol. i.

PICTORIAL FIELD-BOOK

OF

THE REVOLUTION.

CHAPTER I.

" Our young wild land, the free, the proud !
    Uncrush'd by power, unawed by fear,
Her knee to none but God is bow'd,
    For Nature teaches freedom here :
From gloom and snow to light and flowers
Expands this heritage of ours :
Life with its myriad hopes, pursuits,
Spreads sails, rears roofs, and gathers fruits.
But pass two fleeting centuries back ;
    This land, a torpid giant, slept,
Wrapp'd in a mantle thick and black
    That o'er its mighty frame had crept,
Since stars and angels sang, as earth
Shot, from its Maker, into birth."
                                        STREET.

HE love of country, springing up from
the rich soil of the domestic affections, is a
feeling coexistent and coextensive with social
union itself. Although a dreary climate, barren
lands, and unrighteous laws, wickedly administered, may
repress the luxuriant growth of this sentiment, it will still
maintain firm root in the heart, and bear with patience the
most cruel wrongs. Man loves the soil that gave him birth as
the child loves the mother, and from the same inherent impulses. When exiled from his father-land, he yearns for it as a
child yearns for home ; and though he may, by legal oath, dis-
claim allegiance to his own and swear fealty to another government,
the invisible links of patriotism which bind him to his country can
not be severed ; his lips and hand bear false witness against his truthful heart.

Stronger far is this sentiment in the bosom of him whose country
is a pleasant land, where nature in smiling beauty and rich beneficence
woos him on every side ; where education quickens into refining activity
the intellect of society ; and where just laws, righteously administered,
impress all possession, whether of property or of character, with the broad
seal of security. An honest, justified pride elevates the spirit of the citizen of a land so favored ; makes him a vigilant guardian of its rights and
honor, and inspires him with a profound reverence for the men and deeds
consecrated by the opinions of the just as the basis upon which its glory rests.

It was under the influence of this sentiment, so natural to every American, and a strong desire to make a personal visit to the classic grounds of my country, and portray their features before every ancient lineament should be effaced, that, during the sultriness of midsummer, I left behind me the cares of business life within the confines of our commercial metropolis, and commenced a pilgrimage to the most important localities connected with the events of the war for our national independence. For many years, as I occasionally saw some field consecrated by revolutionary blood, or building hallowed as a shelter of the heroes of that war, I have felt emotions of shame, such as every American ought to feel, on seeing the plow leveling the breast-works and batteries where our fathers bled, and those edifices, containing the council-chambers of men who planned the attack, the ambuscade, or the retreat, crumbling into utter ruin. While England erects a monument in honor of the amputated leg of a hero who fought for personal renown, we allow these relics, sanctified by the deeds of soldiers who were more than heroes as the world regards heroism, to pass away and be forgotten. Acquisitiveness is pulling down walled fortresses ; the careless agriculturist, unmindful of the sacredness of the ditch and mound that scar his fields, is sowing and reaping where marble monuments should stand ; and improvement, a very Cambyses among achievements of labor of former times, under the fair mask of refined taste, is leveling nearly all that remains of the architecture of the Revolution. To delineate with pen and pencil what is left of the physical features of that period, and thus to rescue from oblivion, before it should be too late, the mementoes which another generation will appreciate, was my employment for several months ; and a desire to place the result of those journeyings, with a record of past events inseparably connected with what I have delineated, in an enduring form before my countrymen, has given birth to these pages.

I resolved to visit the scenes of the northern campaigns during the summer and early autumn. With the exception of the historic grounds lying around New York and among the Hudson Highlands, the fields of Saratoga, in point of importance and distance, invited the initial visit.

I left New York on the evening of the 24th of July for Poughkeepsie, on the banks of the Hudson, there to be joined by a young lady, my traveling companion for the   1848. summer. For many days the hot sun had been unclouded, and neither shower nor dew imparted grateful moisture to town or country.

> " The whispering waves were half asleep,
> The clouds were gone to play,
> And on the woods and on the deep
> The smiles of Heaven lay."
>
> SHELLEY.

During the afternoon the barometer indicated a change, and portents of a gathering storm arose in the west. At twilight we entered the great amphitheater of the Highlands, and darkness came down suddenly upon us as a tempest of wind, thunder, and rain burst over the Dunderberg and the neighboring heights. A thunder-storm at night in the Hudson Highlands ! It is a scene of grandeur and sublimity vouchsafed to few, and never to be forgotten. The darkness became intense, and echo confused the thunder-peals into one continuous roar. The outlines of the hills disappeared in the gloom, and our vessel seemed the only object wrapped in the bosom of the tempest, except when, at every flash of lightning, high wooded cones, or lofty ranges, or rocky cliffs burst into view like a sudden creation of the Omnipotent fiat, and then melted into chaos again. The storm continued until we passed West Point. The clouds then broke, and as we emerged from the upper gate of the Highlands into the beautiful expanse of Newburgh Bay, the moon came forth, like a queen from her pavilion, in beauty and majesty, the winds were quiet, the waters placid, and the starry sky serene, for

> " The thunder, tramping deep and loud
> Had left no foot-marks there."

The next morning the air was clear and cool as in September. At noon we took passage in one of those floating palaces which are the pride of the Hudson River. What a contrast to the awkward contrivance—the mere germ of the steam-boat of the present day—that gave such glory to Fulton, and astonished the world.[1] Her saloon, like a ducal drawing-room; her table, spread as with a royal banquet; her speed, like that of the swift bird, are all the creations of one generation, and seem like works of magic. Among the passengers there were a few—plain and few indeed—who attracted general attention. They were a remnant of a regiment of Volunteers returning home, weary and spirit-broken, from the battle-fields of Mexico. Of the scores who went with them, these alone returned to tell of havoc in battle and slaughter by the deadly *vomito*. They were young, but the lesson of sad experience might be read on each brow, and the natural joy of the homeward-bound beamed not in their eyes. To them military glory was a bubble burst; and the recollections of the recent past brought not to them that joy which the soldier feels who has battled in defense of country and home. At Albany preparations had been made to receive them, and for half a mile the wharves, bridges, vessels, and houses were thickly covered with people anxious to see the returning heroes. We landed with difficulty in the midst of the excitement and noise, for cannon-peals, and drum and fife, and the rattle of military accouterments, and wild huzzas of the crowd, and the coaxing and swearing of porters and coachmen, were enough to confound confusion itself. How changed was the scene when we returned, a few weeks later. Wharves, bridges, and houses had been swept by conflagration, and acres of the dense city were strewn with smoking ruins.

Early on the morning of the 26th we left Albany for Bemis's Heights, near the village of Stillwater. An omnibus ride of an hour, over a fine McAdam road, placed us in Troy, where we took stage for the Waterford ferry at Lansingburgh, four miles above. The day was excessively warm, and eleven passengers occupied "seats for nine." Not a zephyr stirred the waters or the leaves. A funny little water-man, full of wine and wit, or something stronger and coarser, offered to row us across in his rickety skiff. I demanded the price for ferriage.

---

[1] For the gratification of the curious, I here present a drawing of the "CLERMONT," Fulton's *experiment* boat, with some notices of her earlier voyages.

It was constructed under the personal supervision of Fulton, in 1807. It was one hundred feet long, twelve feet wide, and seven feet deep. In 1808 it was lengthened to one hundred and fifty feet, widened to eighteen, and its name changed to NORTH RIVER. The engine was constructed by Watt & Bolton, England, and the hull by David Brown, of New York. In August, 1807, the boat was propelled from the East River to the Jersey shore; and about the first of September it was started on its first trip to Albany.

The following advertisement appeared in the Albany Gazette, September 1st, 1807:

THE CLERMONT.

"The *North River steam-boat* will leave Paulus's Hook [Jersey City] on Friday, the 4th of September, at 9 in the morning, and arrive at Albany on Saturday, at 9 in the afternoon. Provisions, good berths, and accommodations are provided. The charge to each passenger is as follows:

To Newburgh,	dolls. 3,	time 14 hours.
" Poughkeepsie,	" 4,	" 17 "
" Esopus,	" 5,	" 20 "
" Hudson,	" 5½,	" 30 "
" Albany,	" 7,	" 36 " "

It is noticed in the same paper, of October 5th, 1807, that "Mr. Fulton's new steam-boat left New York on the 2d, at 10 o'clock A.M., against a strong tide, very rough water, and a violent gale from the north. She made a headway against the most sanguine expectations, and without being rocked by the waves." What a change in about forty years! Forty years ago a steam-boat voyage from Albany to New York, one hundred and sixty miles, was accomplished in thirty-six hours, at an expense of seven dollars, exclusive of cost of meals. Now the passage is easily and often made in nine and a half hours, at a cost of one dollar, and frequently for less. Now our first class steam-boats are nearly four hundred feet long, and of proportionate depth and breadth of beam.

" Five thousand dollars," hiccoughed the Charon. I did not object to the price, but. valuing safety at a higher figure, sought the owner of a pretty craft near by, while the little votary of Bacchus was tugging manfully, but unsuccessfully, at a huge trunk, to lift it into his boat. Before he was fairly conscious that he was not yet toiling at our luggage, we were out upon the stream in the " Lady of the Lake." I compensated the tipsy boatman for his labor of love by a brief temperance lecture ; but the seed doubtless fell upon " stony ground," for he had the hard-heartedness to consign me to the safe keeping of him whom

> " The old painters limned with a hoof and a horn,
>   A beak and a scorpion tail."

We pushed across the Hudson to the upper mouth or " sprout" of the Mohawk, and, gliding under the rail-road bridge and along a sluice of the Champlain Canal, clambered up a high bank, and reached the packet office at Waterford[1] toward noon. The suppressed roar of Cohoes' Falls, two miles distant, wooed us to the pleasures of that fashionable resort, to while away the three hours before the arrival of the canal packet.

These falls, though not so grand as many others either in volume or altitude of cataract, or in the natural scenery around, nevertheless present many points of beauty and sublimity exceedingly attractive to the tourist. The Mohawk is here more than one hundred yards wide, and perfectly rock-ribbed on both sides. The fall is nearly seventy feet perpendicular, in addition to the turbulent rapids above and below. A bridge, eight hundred feet long, spans the river half a mile below the falls, from which a fine view may be obtained of the whole scene.

Before entering the Hudson, the river is divided into four mouths or *sprouts*, as they are called, by three rocky islands, Haver's, Van Schaick's or Cohoes', and Green's or Tibbetts's Islands, which form a scene that is singularly picturesque. It is generally supposed that Henry Hudson, the discoverer of the river bearing his name, ascended as far as this point in 1609, and that he and his boat's crew were the first white men who beheld the cataract of Cohoes.

The mouth of the Mohawk was a point of much interest toward the close of the summer of 1777, when Van Schaick's Island was fortified by General Schuyler, then in command of the northern division of the Continental army. Properly to understand the position of affairs at that period, it is necessary to take a brief view of events immediately antecedent to, and intimately connected with, the military operations at this point, and at Stillwater a few weeks later.

Incensed at the audacity of the American Congress in declaring the colonies free and independent states ; piqued at the consummate statesmanship displayed by the members of that Congress, and foiled in every attempt to cajole the Americans by delusive promises, or to crush the spirit of resistance by force of arms, the British ministry, backed by the stubborn king and a strong majority in both Houses of Parliament, determined to open the campaign of 1777 with such vigor, and to give to the service in America such material, as should not fail to put down the rebellion by midsummer, and thus vindicate British valor, which seemed to be losing its invincibility. So long as the Americans were tolerably united ; so long as there remained a free communication between Massachusetts and Virginia, or, in other words, between the Eastern and the Middle and Southern States, permanent success of the British arms in America was very questionable. The rebellion was hydra-headed, springing into new life and vigor suddenly and powerfully, from the inherent energies of union, in places where it seemed to be subdued and destroyed. To sever that union, and to paralyze the vitality dependent thereon, was a matter of great importance, and to effect this was a paramount object of the British government.

General Howe was then in the quiet possession of the city of New York and its vicinity ;

---

[1] Waterford is on the west bank of the Hudson, at the head of sloop navigation.

OF THE REVOLUTION.   37

English Preparations for the Campaign of 1777.   Instructions of Lord George Germain.   Biographical Sketch of Burgoyne

a strong British force occupied Rhode Island and overawed the eastern coast; the patriot insurgents had been driven out of Canada by General Carleton, and nothing remained to complete the separation of the two sections of the American States but to march an invad-

ing army from the north, which, forming a junction with Howe, should secure the country and the strong-holds upon Lakes Champlain and George and the Hudson River.[1] Such an expedition was planned jointly by the king, Lord George Germain, and General Burgoyne, and agreed upon in council.[2] The general command was intrusted to Burgoyne, who was a natural son of Lord Bingley, and at that time high in the confidence of the king and his advisers.[3] He was brave, skillful, and humane, proud of distinction, sanguine of success, and eager for military renown. If the tactics of European warfare had been appropriate for the expedition, success might have attended his efforts. But in his appointment, as well as in the minute and positive instructions given him, without reference to any contingency that might demand a wide departure from their letter and spirit, the British ministry, always at fault in the management of

LIEUTENANT GENERAL BURGOYNE
From an English print, 1783.

---

[1] Lord George Germain, then colonial secretary, in a letter to Governor Carleton, of Canada, dated March 26th, 1777, observes, "With a view of quelling the rebellion as soon as possible, it is become highly necessary that the most speedy junction of the two armies should be effected [the forces from Canada and those of General Howe at New York]; and, therefore, as the security and good government of Canada absolutely require your presence there, it is the king's determination to leave about 3000 men under your command for the defense and duties of that province, and to employ the remainder of your army upon two expeditions, the one under the command of Lieutenant General Burgoyne, who is to force his way to Albany, and the other under Lieutenant Colonel St. Leger, who is to make a diversion on the Mohawk River."—*Burgoyne's Statement of the Expedition from Canada*, &c. (Appendix), p. xiii., London, 1780.

[2] Pictorial History of George III., vol. i., p. 306.

[3] Lieutenant General Burgoyne was an illegitimate son of Lord Bingley. He entered the army at an early age, and his education and the influence of his father soon placed him in the line of promotion. In 1762 he was sent into Portugal with an English force to assist in the defense of that kingdom against the Spaniards. He then held the commission of a brigadier, and distinguished himself in the capture of the garrison of Almeida. After his return to England, he became a privy councillor, and was elected to a seat in Parliament as representative for Preston, in Lancashire. He came over to America in 1775, and was at Boston at the time of the battle of Bunker Hill. He was sent to Canada the same year, but early in 1776 returned to England. Through the influence of the king and Lord George Germain, he was appointed to the command of the northern British army in America in the spring of 1777. After some successes, he was captured, with all his army, at Saratoga, in October of that year. After some delay, he was allowed to return to England on parole, and he was actually engaged in debates upon the floor of the British House of Commons at the very time he was a prisoner to the Americans. His misfortunes lost him the friendship of the king, and he was denied access to his presence. In 1780 he published a narrative of his Expedition, together with the proceedings of his trial before a committee of Parliament, in which he well vindicated his character. He soon afterward resigned his emoluments from government, amounting to $15,000 a year. In 1781 he joined the opposition in Parliament, and opposed the further prosecution of the war against the Americans as impolitic and cruel. From the conclusion of peace until his death, he devoted his time to pleasure and literary pursuits. He died of an attack of gout, on the 4th of August, 1792. Among his literary productions are *The Maid of the Oaks*, *Bon Ton*, and *The Heiress*, dramas which at one time were highly popular. Benevolence and humanity were strong features in Burgoyne's character, and I think the fierce anathema of Philip Freneau, a poet of the Revolution, was altogether too severe. After giving Burgoyne several hard rubs in the course of his epic, he describes an ice-bound, fog-covered, dreary island north of Scotland, and there consigns the Tories, with Burgoyne at their head, as follows:

> "There, Loyals, there, with loyal hearts retire,
> There pitch your tents, and kindle there your fire,
> There desert Nature will her stings display,
> And fiercest hunger on your vitals prey;
> And with yourselves let John Burgoyne retire,
> To reign your monarch, whom your hearts desire."
> FRENEAU's *Poems*, p. 246

38   PICTORIAL FIELD-BOOK

Burgoyne's Arrival in Canada.   His Preparations for the Campaign.   Appointment of General Schuyler to the Command.

American affairs, made a most egregious blunder. Sir Guy Carleton, then Governor of Canada, and perfectly acquainted with the people and country, should have been placed in command. Burgoyne was almost totally ignorant of the Canadians and Indians, who formed a large part of his force, and he knew absolutely nothing of the true character and temper of the people he was sent to oppose and oppress.

Burgoyne arrived at Quebec in March, 1777, bearing the commission of a lieutenant general. Carleton, though greatly aggrieved, nobly aided Burgoyne in preparing the expedition. By extraordinary activity, vessels were constructed, stores were collected, and a force of more than seven thousand men was mustered at St. John's, at the foot of Lake Champlain, on the first of June. Lieutenant Colonel St. Leger, with a detachment of seven hundred Rangers, was sent up the St. Lawrence and Lake Ontario to Oswego, to penetrate the country from that point, arouse and conciliate the Indians, capture Fort Schuyler,[1] sweep the valley of the Mohawk with the aid of Johnson and his Tories, and join Burgoyne at Albany when Lake Champlain and the valley of the Upper Hudson should lie prostrate at his feet.

As soon as Congress perceived the storm that was gathering on the northern frontier, they felt the necessity of prompt action and the services of an influential commander. Fear, loyalty, British gold, would undoubtedly lead the van of the invading army, and none but a wise and tried man could quiet the alarm of the people and command the fidelity of the militia.

Philip Schuyler,[2] a gentleman of fortune, and possessed of military skill, experience, sound judgment, prudent forethought, and lofty patriotism, was reappointed to the command of the forces of the north, in which position he had been superseded, in effect, a few weeks before, by Horatio Gates, the Adjutant General of the Continental army. No appointment could have been more popular with the people of Northern New York, who were in a state of great excitement and alarm. In the late campaigns against the French and Indians upon Lakes George and Champlain, he had rendered essential service to the colony and to the people of the northern frontier, and his many virtues endeared him to all who knew him. His large estate was lying directly in the path of the invader; and if a mercenary feeling could have existed in a soul so noble as his, the defense of his own broad acres and costly mansion would have made him vigilant and brave.

General Schuyler arrived in Albany on the third day of June, where he 1777 met General Gates, and, with all the frankness of a generous and unsuspecting

[1] Fort Schuyler stood at the head of boat navigation, on the Mohawk, where the village of Rome now is. It was erected in 1758, and was then called Fort Stanwix. It was repaired in 1776, and named Fort Schuyler, in honor of General Schuyler, in whose military department it was located.

[2] General Philip Schuyler was born at Albany, on the 22d of November, 1733. His grandfather, Peter Schuyler, was Mayor of Albany, and commander of the northern militia in 1690. His father, John Schuyler, married Cornelia Van Courtlandt, a woman of strong mind, and Philip was their eldest son. By virtue of primogeniture law, he inherited the real estate of his father at his death, but he generously shared it with his brothers and sisters. His father died when Philip was young, and to the thorough training of

nature, sought the aid of his counsel and his sword. But he encountered a smaller mind than his own, and both counsel and sword were refused. He was coldly received by the adjutant general, who was deeply offended because Congress had not allowed him to retain his command. A brave soldier always seeks the post of greatest danger; and General Schuyler, not doubting the courage or devotion of Gates, offered him the command of Ticonderoga, the point where the first conflict with Burgoyne would inevitably take place, and where the first laurels were to be won. But the pride of Gates stifled his patriotism. He refused to serve under Schuyler, and, at his own request, had leave to withdraw from the department, where, indeed, he had done literally nothing.

All was terror and alarm among the inhabitants of the north, as Burgoyne victoriously swept Champlain from St. John's to Crown Point, and with his formidable force, daily augmented by loyalists and savage allies, prepared to beleaguer the strong fortress of Ticonderoga. Mount Hope, commanding the road to Lake George, was occupied; the American outposts were driven in; the lake was studded with armed vessels, and the formidable height of Mount Defiance was scaled, and artillery planted upon its very summit, seven hundred feet above the fort below.

General St. Clair, who commanded the garrison, when he saw the battery above him, and the girdle of strong battalions that was closing around him, knew that resistance would be madness. Under cover of night, he retreated across to Mount Independence, and, with the small garrison there, fled toward Fort Edward by the way of Castleton and Skenesborough, leaving the stores and ammunition behind. The British eagerly pursued the flying Americans. The battle of Hubbardton, so disastrous to the patriots, was fought. The boom across the lake at Ticonderoga was broken, and a free passage made for the vessels of the enemy. They swept the lake to Skenesborough (now Whitehall), when the American works and the stores that were left became an easy prey to the invaders.

The army under General Schuyler was in a wretched condition, and daily diminishing. Food, clothing, ammunition, and artillery were all wanting. The pecuniary resources and credit of Congress were daily failing, and all the future seemed dark, and foreboding of evil. The Eastern militia, sick and disheartened by late reverses, became restless and insubordi-

---

his gifted mother he was greatly indebted for his success in life. He entered the army against the French and Indians in 1755, and commanded a company which attended Sir William Johnson to Fort Edward and Lake George. He soon attracted the attention of Lord Howe, who commanded the first division of the British army against the forts on Lake George and Lake Champlain, and was placed in the commissariat department. When Lord Howe fell at Ticonderoga, to Colonel Schuyler was intrusted the duty of conveying the body of that greatly-beloved young nobleman to Albany for sepulture. After the peace of 1763, he was much in active service in the civil government of his state. In the Colonial Assembly of New York, he was one of the warmest opponents of the British government in its attempts to tax the colonies without their consent. He was elected a delegate to the Continental Congress which assembled in May, 1775, and in June following he was appointed by that body one of the major generals (the third) of the American army. He was charged by Washington with the command of the army in the province of New York, and directed to secure the lakes and prepare for invading Canada. He was taken sick, and the command devolved on Montgomery. During 1776, he was active in Indian affairs, and in perfecting the order and discipline of the northern army. For causes quite inexplicable, he was superseded, in effect, by Gates in March, 1777, but was reinstated in May. Again, when Burgoyne drove St. Clair from Ticonderoga, and prudence caused General Schuyler to retreat with his army from Fort Edward down the Hudson River, calumny, that had successfully poisoned the minds of the Eastern people and the militia, became so clamorous for his removal, that Congress placed Gates again in charge of the army in August. Injured and insulted, the patriot still continued to devote his services and his fortune in aid of his country. He demanded a court of inquiry, and its verdict, acquitting him of all blame, conferred as much honor upon him as his successes won at Saratoga. He was urged by Washington to accept military command, but he preferred to lend his aid to his country in another way. He was a member of the old Congress under the Confederation; and after the adoption of the Constitution of the United States, he was a senator from New York, with Rufus King. He was again a senator, in place of Aaron Burr, in 1797. He died at Albany, November 18th, 1804, aged 71 years. He has two daughters still living—Elizabeth, the venerable widow of General Alexander Hamilton, and now (1849) ninety-two years of age; and Catharine, his youngest daughter, widow of the late Major Cochrane, of Oswego, son of Dr. Cochrane, the distinguished Surgeon General of the Revolutionary Army. See page 199 Vol. II.

nate, and nearly all of them left the army and returned home. These things were exceedingly discouraging to the commander, yet his stout heart never failed. " Should it be ask
July 24, ed," he said, in a letter to the Albany Committee, from Moses's Creek, four miles be-
1777. low Fort Edward, " what line of conduct I mean to hold amid this variety of difficulties and distress, I would answer, *to dispute every inch of ground with General Burgoyne, and retard his descent into the country as long as possible.*"

Burgoyne's force, in the mean while, was constantly augmented by accessions from the families of the loyal and the timid. Slowly and surely he advanced from Skenesborough to Fort Anne, and was pressing onward, in the midst of fearful obstacles, toward the Hudson.

Under all these circumstances, General Schuyler thought it prudent to retreat until new recruits, or a re-enforcement from Washington, should give more strength to his army. He accordingly fell back from Fort Edward, the general rendezvous of his forces after the evacuation of Ticonderoga, Mount Independence, and Fort George. As Burgoyne approached, the people fled, in terror and dismay, toward Albany, leaving their ripe harvest fields and pleasant homes to be trodden down or burned by the enemy. Burgoyne at length reached Fort Edward ; and as he marched slowly down the valley of the Hudson, Schuyler retreated in good order to Saratoga, then to Stillwater, and finally to Cohoes' Falls.

In the mean while the people in the Mohawk Valley were in the greatest consternation. St. Leger had arrived from Oswego, and was besieging Fort Schuyler, while the Tories and Indians were spreading death and desolation on every hand. Colonel Gansevoort, with a handful of men, was closely shut up in the fort ; General Herkimer, with the brave militia
August 6. of Tryon county, had been defeated at Oriskany, and the people below hourly expected the flood of destroyers to pour down upon them. It was a fearful emergency. Without aid all must be lost. Brave hearts were ready for bold deeds, and during a night of fearful tempest of thunder and rain, Colonel Willett and Lieutenant Stockwell crept stealthily from the fort, through groups of sleeping besiegers, beyond their lines, and at dawn on the second day, mounted upon fleet horses, sped down the valley to the headquarters of General Schuyler, at Stillwater, and, in the name of the beleaguered garrison and the people of Tryon county, implored assistance.

Not a moment was to be lost. The subjugation of the whole valley would inevitably follow the surrender of Fort Schuyler, and the victors, gathering strength, would fall like an avalanche upon Albany, or, by junction, swell the approaching army of Burgoyne. The prudent foresight and far-reaching humanity of General Schuyler at once dictated his course. He called a council,[1] and proposed sending a detachment immediately to the relief of Fort Schuyler. His officers opposed him, with the plea that his whole force was not then sufficient to stay the oncoming of Burgoyne. The clearer judgment of Schuyler made him persist in his opinion, and he earnestly besought them to agree with him. While pacing the floor in anxious solicitude, he overheard the half-whispered remark, " He means to weaken the army."[2] Treason in the heart of Philip Schuyler ! Never was a thought more foul

---

[1] General Schuyler was then quartered in the house of Derrick Swart, Esq., at Stillwater. The house is still standing, just at the foot of the hill.—*Charles Neilson, Esq.*

[2] At this time jealousy had created secret enemies for General Schuyler, and he was even charged with being associated with St. Clair in preliminary acts of treason, about the time the latter evacuated Ticonderoga. The ridiculous story got abroad that they had been paid for their treason by the enemy in *silver balls*, shot from Burgoyne's guns into the American camp !—*See Thatcher's Military Journal,* p. 86.

NOTE.—It will be observed that, in this rapid view of events connected with the American encampment at the mouth of the Mohawk, I have avoided all details, where, perhaps, the reader may have wished more minute information. The necessity for this course arises from the nature of the plan of my work, which is to notice in detail the various important localities, *in the order in which I visited them, and not in chronological succession,* as the mere historian would do. For example, I visited Cohoes' and Bemis's Heights before Fort Edward and Ticonderoga. I therefore describe the scenery and events of the former places minutely, and reserve similar minute details concerning the latter until, in the order of the narrative of my tour, I reach them. This explanation is necessary, as some might suppose that important places are to be slightly noticed, while others of less moment have an undue share of attention. I have visited all the

or charge more wicked.   Wheeling suddenly toward the slanderer and those around him, and unconsciously biting into several pieces a pipe he was smoking, he indignantly exclaimed, " Gentlemen, I shall take the responsibility upon myself; where is the brigadier that will take command of the relief?   I shall beat up for volunteers to-morrow."   The brave and impulsive Arnold, ever ready for deeds of daring, at once stepped forward and offered his services.   The next morning the drum beat, and eight hundred stalwart men   August 15 were enrolled for the service before meridian.   Fort Schuyler was saved, and the   1777. forces of St. Leger scattered to the winds.   In after years the recollection of those burning words of calumny always stirred the breast of the veteran patriot with violent emotions If ever a bosom glowed with true devotion to country, it was that of Philip Schuyler.

Such, in brief, were the events which placed the remnant of the main army of the north at the mouth of the Mohawk in August, 1777, and caused Van Schaick's and Haver's Islands to be fortified.   That seemed to be the most eligible point at which to make a stand in defense of Albany against the approaches of the enemy from the north and from the west. Nowhere else could the comparatively feeble force of the Americans so effectually oppose the overwhelming number of the invaders.   At that time there were no bridges across the Hudson or the Mohawk, and both streams were too deep to be fordable except in seasons of extreme drought.   There was a ferry across the Mohawk, five miles above the falls,[1] and one across the Hudson at Half Moon Point,[2] or Waterford.   The " sprouts" of the Mohawk, between the islands, were usually fordable ; and as Burgoyne would not, of course, cross the Hudson, or attempt the ferry upon the Mohawk, where a few resolute men could successfully oppose him, his path was of necessity directly across the mouth of the river.   Fortifications were accordingly thrown up on the islands and upon the main land, faint traces of which are still visible.

In this position, with his headquarters at Stillwater, in advance of his army, General Schuyler brought all his energies and resources into requisition for the augmentation and discipline of his troops, preparatory to a first determined conflict with Burgoyne.   His private purse was freely opened,[3] and by unwearied exertions day and night the army rapidly improved in numbers, discipline, and spirits.   His correspondence at that time with men of every degree, from the President of Congress and the commander-in-chief to subordinate officers and private gentlemen, was very extensive, all having relation to the one great wish of his heart, the checking of the progress of the British army.   He addressed the civil and military authorities in every direction, urging them to assist him with men and arms.   The Council of Safety, at Albany, was appealed to.   " Every militia-man," he said, " ought to turn out without delay in a crisis the most alarming since the contest began."   He appealed to the Eastern States.   " If," he said, in a letter to Governor Trumbull, of Connecticut, " the Eastern militia do not turn out with spirit and behave better, we shall be ruined." To Washington he repeated, in substance, what he had said on the 12th of July previous. " If my countrymen will support me with vigor and dexterity, and do not meanly despond,

---

most important localities of the Revolution, and each in its turn, in the course of the work, will receive its full share of notice.

It is my intention to give in notes, in the course of the work, brief biographical sketches of all the most important actors in our Revolutionary war, both domestic and foreign.   These sketches will be introduced at points where the record exhibits the most prominent events in the life of the subject.   Prominent men will, therefore, be mentioned often before a biography will be given; but the reader may rely upon finding it in the work, if a memoir can be found.

[1] Loudon's ferry.   At this place the left wing of the army rested, under the command of General Arnold.

[2] So called from the name of Henry Hudson's ship, the Half Moon.

[3] General Schuyler never allowed his private interest to interfere in the least degree with the public good.   When the Continental army was retreating from Fort Edward, Mrs. Schuyler rode up from Albany to their beautiful country seat at Saratoga, and superintended the removal of their furniture.   While there she received direction from her husband to set fire with her own hands to his extensive fields of wheat, and to request his tenants to do the same, rather than suffer them to be reaped by the enemy.— *Women of the Revolution*, vol. i., p. 60.

we shall be able to prevent the enemy from penetrating much further into the country."
At the same time all was life and activity in his camp.   From his own state recruits were
constantly filling his thinned regiments, and the heart of the patriot was cheered with the
prospect of soon winning back those laurels which, by the late reverses and the events of
the last campaign, had been, in a measure, stripped from his brow.

But secret enemies had been for some time plotting his disgrace by poisoning the minds
of the Eastern people, and raising a clamor in favor of the reinstatement of Gates, who as
yet, for obvious reasons, had met with no reverses.   The friends of that officer were an active
faction in Congress at that time, *sub rosâ*, but the next year were far more undisguised in
favoring the scheme for giving Gates the chief command in place of Washington.   We are
so accustomed to look upon all the men of the Revolution who took sides with the friends
of America as pure and holy in all their thoughts and actions, that we reluctantly yield to
the conviction that they were ever actuated by motives less worthy and exalted than those
of the loftiest patriotism.   This is claiming too much for human nature.   While we may
award to them all that is noble and disinterested in feeling, when the good of the common
cause demanded personal sacrifice and pliancy of opinion, it is folly to deny that the spirit
of faction was rife among the members of the Old Continental Congress, and that selfish
motives often controlled their actions.   Congress, listening to the clamors from the East,
the importunities of Gates's friends, and the suggestions of a false military philosophy, deprived General Schuyler of his command just as he was about to lead his troops to victory.

General Gates, with his new commission, arrived at Van Schaick's on the 19th of August, three days after the battle of Bennington, a battle which, in its effect upon the British
army, gave full assurance of future victory to the Americans.   How nobly did the conduct
of Schuyler on this occasion contrast with that of Gates a few weeks previous.   On Gates's
arrival, without the slightest indication of ill humor, the patriot resigned his command, communicated all the intelligence he possessed, and put every interesting paper into his hands
simply adding, " I have done all that could be done, as far as the means were in my power,
to injure the enemy, and to inspire confidence in the soldiers of our own army, and, I flatter
myself, with some success ; but the palm of victory is denied me, and it is left to you, general, to reap the fruit of my labors.   I will not fail, however, to second your views ; and
my devotion to my country will cause me with alacrity to obey all your orders."[1]   " I am
sensible," he said, in a letter to Congress, " of the indignity of being ordered from the command of the army at the time when an engagement must soon take place ;" yet he preferred
to suffer reproach in silence rather than allow his bleeding country to be injured by the withdrawal of a single arm from its support.   Although disgraced by the act of Congress, he
persevered assiduously in strengthening the army and preparing for the coming conflict.
" I shall go on," he said to Washington, " in doing my duty and endeavoring to deserve
your esteem."   And when General Gates arrived, he cordially proffered his co-operation,
was very active in promoting the success of the battles which soon after took place, was
present at Saratoga when Burgoyne surrendered his sword, and rejoiced, because his country
was the gainer, when the laurels which should have graced his brow were placed upon that
of another.   Warmed by such impulses, who can doubt that the bosom of the generous
patriot on that day heaved with nobler pride and purer joy than that of the lauded victor?

---

[1] Garden, p. 359.

CHAPTER II.

" Led on by lust of lucre and renown,
Burgoyne came marching with his thousands down ;
High were his thoughts and furious his career,
Puff'd with self-confidence and pride severe ;
Swoll'n with the idea of his future deeds,
Onward to ruin each advantage leads."

PHILIP FRENEAU, 1778.

E left Waterford at two o'clock P.M. for Bemis's Heights, the famous battle-ground where Burgoyne was checked and defeated in the autumn of 1777, a few weeks after General Gates succeeded to the command of the northern army. Our conveyance was a neat canal packet, its cabin crowded with passengers and a well-supplied dinner-table, and its deck piled with as much luggage and as many loungers as low bridges and a hot sun would allow. For a loiterer who takes no note of passing hours but to mark and mourn their excessive length, and who loves to glide along listlessly among green fields and shady woods without the disturbance of even a carriage ride, a day voyage upon a canal is really delightful, especially if the face of nature is attractive, and a pleasant companion or agreeable book assists in smoothing the passage of time. Such seemed to be the character of nearly all our fellow-passengers, pleasure from personal enjoyment being their chief object. When dinner was over, some slept some read, and every body talked to every body as freely as old acquaintances would chat.

The country through which we passed is very fertile, and beautifully diversified in aspect. The plain over which the Hudson here flows is a narrow alluvial bottom, of garden richness, along the western edge of which passes the canal. Green woods and cultivated fields skirted the river on either side, and those conical hills and knolls, like western tumuli, which are prominent features from Stillwater to Sandy Hill, here begin to appear. Some of them were still covered with the primeval forest, and others were cultivated from base to summit, giving a pleasing variety to the ever-changing landscape. The dark green corn, just flowering ; the wheat ears, fading from emerald to russet ; the blackberries, thick in the hedges ; the flowers innumerable, dotting the pasture fields, and the fragrance of the new-mown hay, scattered in wind-rows along the canal, were pleasant sights to one just escaped from the dust and din of the city, and imparted a gratification which only those can feel and appreciate who seldom enjoy it. There was one thing wanting, which leafy June would have supplied——the melody of birds.

" Silence girt the woods ; no warbling tongue
Talks now unto the echo of the groves ;
Only the curled stream soft chidings kept ;
And little gales that from the green leaves swept
Dry summer's dust, in fearful whisperings stirr'd,
As loth to waken any singing bird,"

for it was just the season when the warblers of the forest are still, except at early morning, when they carol a brief matin hymn, and then are quiet. Yet

" The poetry of earth is never dead.
When all the birds are faint with the hot sun,
And hide in cooling trees, a voice will run

> From hedge to hedge about the new-mown mead ;
> That is the grasshopper's."
>
> KEATS.

At the Borough, or Mechanicsville, nine miles above Waterford, the rail-road from Saratoga Springs reaches the canal. Here our boat was filled to repletion with a bevy of young people, who, tired of medicinals and midnight merriment at that Mecca of fashion in summer, had determined to take a " slow coach" to Whitehall, and meet the stronger tide of gay tourists flowing to Ticonderoga from Lake George. They were full of life, and not one of them had ever passed a night upon a canal-boat. Poor souls ! how we pitied them, while we rejoiced at our own better fortune, intending, as we did, to debark toward cooling sunset. If " affliction is necessary to temper the over-joyous," our young travelers were doubtless well annealed before morning in the vapor bath of a packet cabin.

One of the passengers was a roving journeyman printer, full of the general intelligence of the craft, an inveterate tobacco chewer, and evidently a boon companion of John Barleycorn and his cousins. His hat was a-slouch and his coat seedy. His wit kept the deck vocal with laughter ; yet, when at times he talked gravely, the dignity of intelligence made us all respectful listeners. He was perfectly familiar with the history of the classic grounds through which we were then passing. His father was one of the special adjutants appointed by General Gates on the morning of the action of the 19th of September, and from him he had often received minute details of the events of that contest. He mentioned a circumstance connected with the commander on that occasion, which, in some degree, explains the singular fact that he was not upon the field of action—a fact which some have adduced as evidence of cowardice. It is admitted that General Gates did not leave his camp during the contest ; and the special adjutant referred to asserted boldly that *intoxication* was the chief cause. That, in the opinion of the world at that time, was a weakness far more excusable, and a crime less heinous, than cowardice ; for a night's debauch and a morning of dullness and stupidity were things too common among *gentlemen* to affect reputation seriously, unless bad consequences ensued. He was not alone in devotion to the wine-cup at that very time, for it is said that Burgoyne and Earl Balcarras did not leave their flagon and their cards until dawn that morning. Burgoyne and the earl, however, had either stouter heads or stouter hearts than Gates, for they were on duty in the field when the contest was raging. It may be that neither wine nor cowardice controlled the American commander. Let us charitably hope that it did not, and charge the fault upon a weak judgment ; for we should be ever ready to act toward erring brother-man according to the glorious injunction of Prior :

> " Be to his faults a little blind ;
> Be to his virtues very kind."

We reached Bemis's Heights between five and six o'clock in the evening. The hotel is situated a few rods south of the site of the old residence of Bemis. The obliging landlord anticipated our impatience to view the battle-ground, and when supper was over we found a horse and light wagon in readiness to carry us to the residence of Charles Neilson, Esq., on the summit of the heights, whence a fine view of the whole scene of conflict and of the surrounding country might be obtained.[1] It was too late for much observation, for twilight soon spread its veil over every object. After spending an hour pleasantly and profitably with Mr. Neilson and his family, I made an engagement to meet him early next morning, to ride and ramble over the historic grounds in the neighborhood.

---

[1] Mr. Neilson occupies the mansion owned by his father, an active Whig, at the time of the battles there. He has written and published a volume entitled " An original, compiled, and corrected Account of Burgoyne's Campaign and the memorable Battles of Bemis's Heights." It contains many details not found in other books, which he gathered from those who were present, and saw and heard what they related It is valuable on that account.

The morning broke with an unclouded sky, and before the dew was off the grass I was upon Bemis's Heights, eager to see what yet remained of the military works of a former time.   Alas ! hardly a vestige is to be seen ; but a more beautiful view than the one from Mr. Neilson's mansion I have seldom beheld.   The ground there is higher than any in the vicinity, except the range of hills on the east side of the Hudson, and the eye takes in a varied landscape of a score of miles in almost every direction.   Bounding the horizon on the north and west are the heights of Saratoga and the high mountains on the eastern shore of Lake George.   On the south stretch away into the blue distance toward Albany the gentle hills and the pleasant valley of the Hudson.   On the east, not far distant, rises Willard's Mountain, and over and beyond its southern neighbors of less altitude may be seen the heights of Bennington on the Walloomscoik,[1] the Green Mountains, and the lofty summit of far-famed Mount Tom.

Bemis's Heights are situated on the right bank of the Hudson, about four miles north of the pleasant village of Stillwater (which is on the same side of the river), and about twenty-five miles from Albany.   The ground here rises abruptly from an extensive alluvial flat about half a mile in width a little above, but here tapering until it forms quite a narrow defile of not more than thirty or forty rods on each side of the river.   At the time of the Revolution, the whole country in this vicinity was covered with a dense forest, having only an occasional clearing of a few acres ; and deep ravines furrowed the land in various directions.   Fronting the river, a high bluff of rocks and soil, covered with stately oaks and maples, presented an excellent place on which to plant a fortification to command the passage of the river and the narrow valley below.   The bluff is still there, but the forest is gone, and many of the smaller ravines have been filled up by the busy hand of cultivation.

The only road then much traveled passed along the margin of the river.   Upon the road, at the southern extremity of the bluff, was a tavern kept by a man named Bemis, the only one of note between Albany and Fort Edward.   Good wines and long pipes, a spacious ball-room and a capital larder, made Bemis's house a famous place of resort for sleighing parties in winter, throughout the whole of the Saratoga valley of the Hudson.   He owned a portion of the heavy-timbered heights near him, and from that circumstance the hill derived its name.

On the summit of the height, three fourths of a mile northwest of Bemis's, the father of Mr. Neilson owned a clearing of a few acres when the war broke out, and he had erected a small dwelling and a log barn thereon.   The dwelling, with large additions, is still there, but the log barn, which was picketed and used for a fort, has long since given place to another.   Around that old mansion cluster many interesting historic associations, and if its walls could articulate, they might tell of heroism in action and patient endurance which the pen of history has never yet recorded.

Upon the next page are given a group of localities about Bemis's Heights and a miniature map of the engagements there.   The picture at the top of the page represents the mansion of Mr. Neilson, as seen from the opposite side of the road, looking eastward.   It stands upon the east side of the highway leading to Quaker Springs, about one hundred rods north of the road from Bemis's Heights to the watering places of Ballston and Saratoga.   It is a frame house, and the part next to the road is modern compared with the other and smaller portion, which is the original dwelling.   The room in the old part (a sketch of which is given in the third picture from the top) is quite large, and was occupied by Brigadier-general Poor and Colonel Morgan as quarters at the time of the encampments there.   It was in this room that Major Ackland, the brave commander of the British Grenadiers, who was severely wounded in the battle of the 7th of October, was kindly received by the American officers, and visited and nursed by his heroic wife, Lady Harriet Ackland, of whom, and the event in question, I shall hereafter speak.   The bed of the wounded officer was beneath

---

[1] It is said that the smoke of the battle of Bennington, thirty miles distant, was distinctly seen from Bemis's Heights.

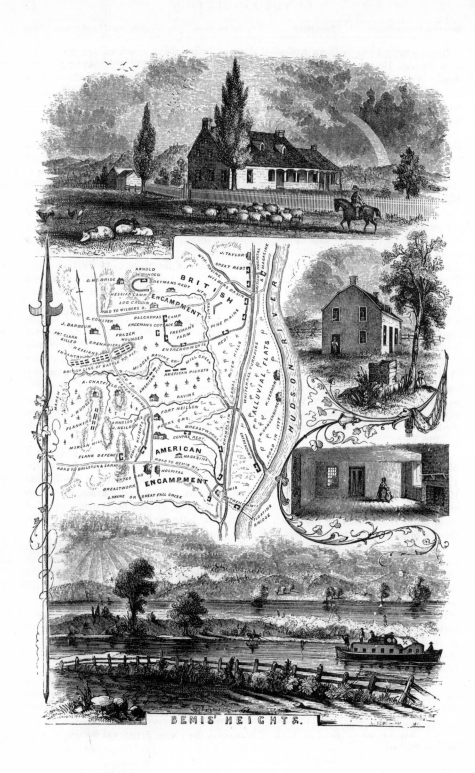

BEMIS' HEIGHTS.

the window on the left. The door in the center opens into a small bed-room ; and this as well as every thing else about the room, is carefully preserved in its original condition. Where the smaller poplar tree stands was a building which General Arnold occupied ; and further to the left the small buildings are upon the spot where the fortified log barn stood, which was at the northwest angle of the American works. In compliment to the owner, the rude fortification was called Fort Neilson.

Between the smaller poplar tree and the house is seen Willard's Mountain, five miles distant, on the east side of the Hudson. This eminence commands a fine view of the valley for many miles. From its summit a Mr. Willard and a few others, with a good spy-glass, watched all the movements of Burgoyne, and made regular reports to General Gates. This service was exceedingly valuable, for a fair estimate of the number of troops, their baggage, stores, artillery, &c., was made from his observations. His name is immortalized by a gigantic monument, which has borne it ever since.

The second vignette from the top is a view of Gates's headquarters at the time of the battle of the 7th of October. He first made his headquarters at Bemis's house, but afterward removed them hither. This house was demolished about four years ago, but, from a sketch furnished by Mr. Neilson, I am enabled to give a correct view. The old well curb is still there, and seems as though it might survive a generation yet. This house stood about one hundred and fifty rods south of Fort Neilson, and the traces of the cellar may now be seen a few yards to the left of the Ballston road, ascending from the river.

The third vignette represents the room mentioned above. The picture at the bottom of the page is a view from the Bemis's Heights Hotel, representing the Champlain Canal, the Hudson River, and the hills on the eastern side. Near the large trees on the left may be seen traces of a redoubt which defended a floating bridge that was thrown across the river here, and so constructed that one end could be detached at pleasure, allowing the bridge to swing around with the current, and thus prevent the enemy from entering upon it. The lumber for this bridge was furnished by General Schuyler, at his own private expense, and floated down the river from Saratoga or Schuylerville.

The map I shall have occasion to refer to when noticing the fortifications and the battles. The halbert, represented on the left of the picture, was plowed up in the neighborhood, and is in the possession of Mr. Neilson. When found, it had a small British flag or cloven pennon attached to it, which soon occupied the utilitarian and more peaceful position of patches in the bed-quilt of a prudent housewife.

When General Gates took the command of the Northern army,[a] events were occurring favorable to his success. Burgoyne was at Fort Edward, paralyzed with alarm and perplexity on account of the failure of an expedition to Bennington—a failure, in its immediate as well as prospective effects, extremely disastrous. The obstructions which General Schuyler had thrown in the way on his retreat from Fort Anne, made the march of the enemy slow and toilsome in the extreme.[1] The plethora of the commissariat department was rapidly subsiding by the delay ; the supplies of the surrounding country, already heavily levied on, were totally inadequate to the demand, and the capture of American stores was an object called for by stern necessity. Burgoyne, therefore, halted at Fort Edward, and sent an expedition to Bennington to seize a large quantity of clothing and pro-

[a] August 19, 1777.

---

[1] General Schuyler felled large trees across the roads and bridle-paths through the woods, sunk deep ditches, and destroyed all the bridges. These evils Burgoyne was obliged to overcome and repair. With immense toil, the obstructions were removed, and no less than forty bridges over streams and morasses were constructed, so as to allow the passage of artillery. It must be remembered, too, that a soldier in actual service is not so lightly accoutered as a soldier on parade. Besides the actual fatigue of traveling and labors, he has a heavy back-burden to bear. Respecting this, we quote Burgoyne's own words : " It consists of a knapsack, containing his bodily necessaries, a blanket, a haversack with provisions, a canteen, a hatchet, and a fifth share of the general camp equipage belonging to his tent." These articles (reckoning the provisions to be for four days), added to his accouterments, arms, and sixty rounds of ammunition, make a bulk totally incompatible with combat, and a weight of about sixty pounds.

visions which the Americans had collected there. The detachment sent thither so weakened his forces that he dared not proceed until it should return, bringing back, as he confidently expected, ample provisions for his army until he should enter Albany triumphant. But the New England militia were on the alert, and they not only saved their stores and live cattle at Bennington, but defeated and dispersed the enemy, capturing a large number, August 16. together with arms and ammunition, then much needed by the growing ranks of the volunteers.

Burgoyne had hardly recovered from this shock, before a courier, guided by a friendly Indian, came in breathless haste by the way of Saratoga Lake and Glenn's Falls, bearing the direful news of the desertion of the Indians, the defection of the loyalists of the Mohawk August 22. Valley, and the complete defeat of St. Leger at Fort Schuyler. These reverses fell like an incubus upon the spirits of his army. The Indians in his camp, already vexed because Burgoyne's humanity had restrained their purposes of rapine and murder, began to waver in their fidelity, and the Canadians and timid loyalists became luke warm through very cowardice, and deserted by hundreds.

Burgoyne was greatly perplexed. To proceed at that time would be madness ; to retreat would not only lose him a promised *order*, perhaps a peerage, but would operate powerfully in giving friends to the republicans. The idea of British invincibility would be dissipated, and thousands who favored the cause of the king on account of that supposed invincibility and the hopelessness of resistance, would join the patriots, or would, at least, become mere *passive* loyalists. In view of all these difficulties, the British commander wisely resolved to remain at Fort Edward until the panic should subside and stores should be brought forward from his posts on Lake George and Lake Champlain. He was also in daily expectation of advices from General Howe or Sir Henry Clinton, at New York, announcing a movement upon the Hudson for the purpose of producing a diversion in favor of Burgoyne, by drawing away a portion of the American army from the North.

These disasters of the enemy greatly inspirited the Americans, and the Eastern militia, among whom Gates was very popular, flocked to his standard with great alacrity. The murder of Jane M Crea at Fort Edward (of which I shall hereafter speak) was another powerful agency in swelling the ranks of the patriots. Fierce indignation was aroused in every honest heart by the highly-colored recital of that event, and loyalists by hundreds withdrew their support from a cause which employed such instrumentalities as savage warriors to execute its purposes.

Perceiving the disposition of Burgoyne to halt at Fort Edward, and the difficulties that were gathering around him, General Gates advanced up the Hudson to Stillwater, and prepared to act offensively or defensively, as circumstances should dictate. It was at first resolved to throw up fortifications at the place where the village of Stillwater now is ; but the narrowness of the valley and the abruptness of the bank on the western margin of the flat at Bemis's offered a more advantageous position, and there, by the advice of Kosciusko, who was an engineer in the army, General Gates made his encampment and fortified it.[1]

---

[1] Thaddeus Kosciusko was born in Lithuania in 1736, of an ancient and noble family. He was educated at the military school of Warsaw, and afterward became a student in France. There he became acquainted with Dr. Franklin, and was by him recommended to General Washington. Before leaving Poland, he had eloped with a beautiful lady of high rank. They were overtaken in their flight by her father, who made a violent attempt to rescue his daughter. The young Pole had either to slay the father or abandon the young lady. Abhorring the former act, he sheathed his sword, and soon after obtained permission of his sovereign to leave his country. He came to America, and presented himself to the commander-in-chief He answered the inquiry of his excellency, "What do you seek here ?" by saying, "I come to fight as a volunteer for American independence." "What can you do ?" asked Washington. "Try me," was Kosciusko's laconic reply. Greatly pleased with him, Washington made him his aid. In October, 1776, he was appointed engineer by Congress, with the rank of colonel. In the autumn of 1777 he fortified the camp of Gates at Bemis's Heights, and afterward superintended the construction of the works at West Point, among the Hudson Highlands. He was greatly esteemed by the American officers, and admitted a member of the Cincinnati Society At the close of our Revolution he returned to Poland, and was made

THADDEUS KOSCIUSKO.

Along the brow of the hill toward the river a line of breast-works was thrown up, about three fourths of a mile in extent, with a strong battery at each extremity, and one near the center in such position as to completely sweep the valley, and command even the hills upon the eastern side of the river. Faint traces of these redoubts and the connecting breast-works are still visible. At the northern extremity, where the largest and strongest battery was erected, the mound is leveled, but the ditch is quite deep, and may be traced many rods westward from the brow of the hill, along the line of breast-works that were thrown up after the first battle. But every year the plow casts in the soil of its furrows, and ere long no vestige will remain of these intrenchments. Within the area of the northeast redoubt, at the time of my visit, potatoes in desecrating luxuriance were flourishing, except upon a very small spot occupied as a burial-place for a few of the Vanderburgh family. It really seemed sacrilegious for the vulgar vines of the nutritious tuber to intertwine with the long grass and beautiful wild flowers that covered the graves. The elder one of those buried there was an active republican, and had his house burned by the enemy. A few plain slabs with inscriptions tell who lie beneath the several mounds, but no stone marks the grave where sleeps that venerable patriot.

From the foot of the hill, across the flats to the river, an intrenchment was opened, and at the extremity, on the water's edge, a strong battery was erected, which guarded the floating bridge constructed there, and also commanded the plain on the east side of the river in such a manner that the enemy might have been terribly enfiladed in case they had attempted to pass down the river or the valley.

Near where the road crossed Mill Creek, a small stream nearly half a mile above Bemis's tavern, were a short line of breast-works and a strong battery, which, with those mentioned above, composed all the fortifications previous to the first battle. These being completed about the 15th of September, and the enemy approaching, General Gates made preparations for resistance. Brave officers and determined soldiers, in high spirits, were gathered around him, and the latter were hourly increasing in numbers. The counsels of General Schuyler and the known bravery of General Arnold were at his command ; and he felt confident of victory, aided by such men as Poor, Learned, Stark, Whipple, Paterson, Warner, Fellows,

---

a major general under Poniatowski. He commanded judiciously and fought bravely ; and when, in 1794, a new revolution broke out in Poland, he was made generalissimo, and vested with the power of a military dictator. In October of that year he was overpowered, wounded, and taken prisoner. In reference to this event, Campbell, in his Pleasures of Hope, says,

"Hope for a season bade the world farewell,
And freedom shrieked when Kosciusko fell."

He was kept in prison in St. Petersburg until the death of the Empress Catharine, when he was liberated by Paul, loaded with honors, and offered a command in the Russian service, which he declined. The emperor besought him to accept the proffered honor, and presented him with his own sword. But bitterly reflecting that his country had been annihilated, he refused to receive his sword, saying, " I no longer need a sword, since I have no longer a country to defend." He visited the United States in 1797, and received from Congress a grant of land for his services. He returned to Switzerland toward the close of his life, and died there October the 16th, 1817. His remains were taken to Cracow, and at Warsaw a public funeral was made for him. At West Point, on the Hudson, the cadets erected a monument to his memory. We have given a drawing of the monument, and a more particular notice, on page 705, of this volume

Bailey, Glover, Wolcott, Bricketts, and Tenbroeck, with their full brigades, and the brave Virginian, Colonel Morgan, with his unerring marksmen, supported by the regiments of Dearborn, Brooks, Cilley, Scammel, and Hull.

Small successes about this time, important in the aggregate result, tended materially to keep up the spirits of the American troops, and made them eager to encounter the main body of the enemy. General Lincoln, with about two thousand militia, got in the rear of Burgoyne, and, by dividing his force into detachments, operated with much effect. One detachment, under Colonel Brown, surprised the British posts on Lake George, captured a vessel containing provisions for the enemy, took possession of Mount Hope and Mount Defiance, and, appearing before Ticonderoga, demanded its surrender. But the walls and garrison were too strong, and, after a cannonade of four days, the siege was abandoned, and all the troops prepared to unite and attack the enemy in the rear. The threatening aspect of this movement of Lincoln at the beginning, and the probability of having his supplies from the lakes cut off, induced Burgoyne, in self-defense, to move forward and execute promptly what he intended to do. Having, by great diligence, brought forward provisions for about thirty days, he advanced along the left bank of the Hudson to the mouth of the Batten Kill, where he encamped preparatory to crossing the river.[1] His officers were somewhat divided in opinion in regard to the expediency of further attempts to reach Albany; and it had been plainly intimated to Burgoyne that it might be greater wisdom to fall back from Fort Edward, rather than advance, for it was evident that perils of no ordinary kind were gathering around the invading army.

Unwilling to act in opposition to the *expressed* opinions of his officers, Burgoyne avoided any intimations of judgment on their part by omitting to consult them at all; and he assumed the responsibility of crossing the Hudson, resting for his defense, if adversity should ensue, upon the peremptory nature of his instructions.[2] He constructed a bridge of boats, and on the 13th and 14th of September passed his whole army over, and encamped on the heights and plains of Saratoga, at the mouth of the Fish Creek, where Schuylerville now is, and within about five miles of the American works below. On the 15th, having succeeded in getting his artillery, baggage, and stores across the river, Burgoyne moved down as far as Do-ve-gat (now Coveville), where he halted until the morning of the 17th, for the purpose of repairing the roads and bridges before him, when he advanced as far as Swords's house and encamped for the night. On the morning of the 18th he moved down as far as the place now called Wilbur's Basin, within two miles of the American camp, and here he made preparations for battle. His chief officers were Major-general Phillips, of the artillery, who had performed signal service in Germany; Brigadier-general Fraser, commander of the grenadiers and light infantry; Brigadiers Hamilton and Powell; and the Brunswick major general, Baron de Riedesel, with his brigadiers, Specht and Gall. Earl Balcarras, Colonel Breyman, Major Ackland, Lieutenant Kingston, and others of minor grade, were men of tried courage, and ardently attached to their general and the service.

When the defeat of Burgoyne, a few days later, became known in England, the crossing of the Hudson River and his persistence in pressing toward Albany, with the American army in front and a wilderness filling with armed republicans in his rear, formed the chief theme for the vituperative assaults of his enemies; and to these steps all his subsequent misfortunes were attributed. But, as we have seen, he retreated behind the peremptory instructions of ministers; and Botta very justly observes, " that at that time he had not

---

[1] His place of encampment was about one hundred rods north of Lansing's saw-mill. The farm, till within a few years, was occupied by Mr. Thomas Rogers. Burgoyne had quite an extensive slaughter-yard there, which so enriched the soil, that its effects are still visible on the corn crops and other produc tions.—*C. Neilson.*

[2] In his dispatch to Lord George Germain, dated at Albany, October 20th, 1777, Burgoyne alludes to this fact, and says, " I did not think myself authorized to call any men into council, where the peremptory tenor of my orders and the season of the year admitted no alternative."—*State of the Expedition, &c.*, Appendix, p. lxxxiv.

yet received any intelligence either of the strength of the army left at New York, or the movements which Sir Henry Clinton intended to make, or had made, up the North River toward Albany. He calculated on a powerful co-operation on the part of that general. Such was the plan of the ministers, and such the tenor of their peremptory instructions."[1]

Whether the movement was judicious or injudicious we will not stop to inquire, but, having arranged the two armies within cannon-shot of each other, will pass on to the consideration of an event which solved the question by arguments far more potential than logic can command—

THE FIRST BATTLE OF STILLWATER.[2]

1777. The morning of the 19th of September was clear and calm, and every thing without was white with hoar-frost. The hostile armies, within ear-shot of each other's *reveille*, were disposed in similar order, each extending from the river westward over the hills. The main body of the American army composing the right wing, which consisted chiefly of Glover's, Nixon's, and Patterson's brigades, was under the immediate command of General Gates, and occupied the hills near the river and the narrow flats below them. The left wing, composed of the brigade of General Poor, consisting of Cilley's, Scammel's, and Hale's regiments, of New Hampshire; Van Courtlandt's and Henry Livingston's, of New York: Latimer and Cook's Connecticut militia; the corps of riflemen under Morgan, and infantry under Dearborn, was posted on the heights about three fourths of a mile from the river, and commanded by General Arnold.[3] The center, on the elevated plain near the residence of Mr. Neilson, was composed of Learned's brigade, with Bailey's, Wesson's, and Jackson's regiments, of Massachusetts, and James Livingston's, of New York.

The left wing of the British army, which included the immense train of artillery under Generals Phillips and Riedesel, rested upon the flats upon the bank of the river. The center and the right wing, composed principally of Hessians,[4] extended westward upon the hills, and were commanded by Burgoyne in person, covered by General Fraser and Colonel Breyman, with the grenadiers and light infantry. The front and flanks were covered by the Indians, Canadians, and loyalists, who still remained in the camp.

General Gates resolved to maintain a defensive position, and await the approach of Burgoyne, who, on the contrary, had made every preparation for advancing. Phillips and Reidesel were to march with the artillery along the road on the margin of the river. The Canadians and Indians in front were to attack the central outposts of the Americans, while Burgoyne and Fraser, with the grenadiers and infantry, in separate bodies, and strongly flanked by Indians, were to make a circuitous route through the woods back of the river hills, form a junction, and fall upon the rear of the American camp. It was arranged that three minute-guns should be fired when Burgoyne and Fraser should join their forces, as a signal for the artillery to make an attack upon the American front and right, force their way through the lines, and scatter them in confusion.

At an early hour the American pickets observed great activity in the British camp; the glitter of bayonets and sabers and the flashing of scarlet uniforms were distinctly seen through

---

[1] Otis's Botta, vol. ii., p. 9.

[2] The conflicts at this point are known by the several titles *Bemis's Heights*, *Stillwater*, and *Saratoga*, from the fact that the battles occurred upon Bemis's Heights, in the town of Stillwater, and county of Saratoga.

[3] These were the same troops which formed the left wing of the army when encamped at the mouth of the Mohawk. They were stationed at Loudon's ferry, five miles from the mouth of the river, and there Arnold took the command after his return from Fort Schuyler.

[4] The *Hessians* were some of the German soldiers, hired by Great Britain of their masters, petty German princes, at a stipulated sum per head, to come to America and butcher her children. The Landgrave of Hesse-Cassel furnished the larger number, and from that circumstance all of the Germans received the general appellation of *Hessians*. I have given a minute account of them, and of the debates in Parliament which the infamous bill providing for the hiring of these mercenaries produced, on page 589, of this volume.

the vistas of the forest as the troops of the enemy marched and countermarched to form the various lines for battle. These movements were constantly reported to General Gates, yet he issued no orders and evinced no disposition to fight. About ten o'clock it was clearly perceived that the whole of the enemy's force was in motion, and separated into three divisions. Phillips and Reidesel, with the artillery, commenced marching slowly down the road along the river; Burgoyne, with the center division, followed the course of the stream, now forming Wilbur's Basin, westward; and Fraser and Breyman commenced a circuitous route along a new road partially opened from the basin, and intersecting the road from Bemis's about two and a half miles north of the American lines.

Arnold was fully apprised of all this, and became as impatient as a hound in the leash His opinion, earnestly and repeatedly expressed to the commander during the morning, that a detachment should be sent out to make an attack, was at length heeded. About noon, Colonel Morgan with his light-horse, and Major Dearborn with his infantry, were detached from Arnold's division, and, marching out, made a vigorous attack upon the Canadians and Indians who swarmed upon the hills. They met at the middle ravine, south of Freeman's cottage.[1] The enemy was repulsed; but so furious was Morgan's charge, that his men became scattered in the woods, and a re-enforcement of loyalists under Major Forbes soon drove the Americans back. Captain Vàn Swearingen and Lieutenant Morris, with twenty privates, fell into the hands of the British. For a moment, on finding himself almost alone, Morgan felt that his corps was ruined; but his loud signal-whistle soon gathered his brave followers around him, and the charge was renewed. Dearborn seconded him, and Cilley and Scammel hastened to their support. The contest was quite equal, and both parties at length retired within their respective lines.

About the same time a party of Canadians, savages, and loyalists were detached through the skirt of the woods along the margin of the flats near the river. They were met by the American pickets on a flat piece of ground near Mill Creek, and a smart skirmish ensued. The enemy was much cut up and broken, and finally fled, leaving thirteen dead on the field and thirty-five taken prisoners. In the mean while, Burgoyne and Fraser were making rapid movements for the purpose of falling upon the Americans in front and on the left flank. The center division marched through some partial clearings to Freeman's farm,[2] while Fraser, having reached a high point about one hundred and fifty rods north of the "cottage," moved rapidly southward for the purpose of turning the left flank of the Americans. Arnold, at the same time, made a similar attempt upon Fraser. He called upon Gates for a re-enforcement from the right wing, but the commander deemed it prudent not to weaken it, for the left of Burgoyne's army was then within half a mile of his lines, and spreading out upon the heights.

Arnold resolved to do what he could with those under his command, which consisted of General Learned's brigade and the New York troops. With these he attempted to turn the enemy's right, and, if possible, cut off the detachment of Fraser from the main army. So dense was the forest and so uneven was the ground, that neither party fairly comprehended the movements of the other, or knew that each was attempting the same maneuver. They met suddenly and unexpectedly upon the level ground near Mill Creek, or Middle Ravine, about sixty yards west of Freeman's cottage, and at once an action, warm and destructive, began. Arnold led the van of his men, and fell upon the foe with the fury and impetuosity of a tiger. By voice and action he encouraged his troops; but the overwhelming numbers of the enemy for a time repulsed them. By a quick movement, Fraser attacked the left flank of the right wing of the American army; but fearing that Arnold (who had

---

[1] The attention of the reader is called to the small map or plan of the engagement, upon page 46, while perusing the notices of the battle.

[2] Freeman's farm, as it was called, was a small cultivated clearing, about half a mile east of the present road leading to Quaker Springs. The farm was an oblong clearing in front of the cottage, about sixty rods in length from east to west, skirted by thick woods, and sloping south.—*Neilson*, p. 141.

rallied his troops, and was re-enforced by four regiments under Lieutenant-colonels Brooks, Cilley, and Scammel, and Majors Dearborn and Hull) might cut the British lines and separate the two wings, he brought up the twenty-fourth regiment, some light infantry, and Breyman's riflemen, to strengthen the point of attack. The Americans made such a vigorous resistance, that the British began to give way and fall into confusion; but General Phillips, who, from his position below the heights, heard the din of conflict on the right wing of his army, hurried over the hills, through the thick woods, with fresh troops and part of the artillery under Captain Jones, and appeared upon the ground at the very moment when victory seemed within the grasp of the Americans. For an hour the republicans had disputed the ground inch by inch, but the crushing force of superior numbers pressed them back to their lines.

THE BATTLE-GROUND.[1]

It was now about three o'clock. The contest suddenly ceased, but it was only the lull which precedes a more furious burst of the tempest. Each army took breath, and gathered up new energies for a more desperate conflict. They were beyond musket-shot of each other, and separated by a thick wood and a narrow clearing. Each was upon a gentle hill, one sloping toward the south, the other toward the north. The Americans were sheltered by the intervening wood; the British were within an open pine forest. The Americans stood

---

[1] This view is taken from near the house of Mr. Neilson, looking northwest. In the foreground, on the right, are seen the remains of the intrenchments which here crossed the road from Fort Neilson, the fortified log barn. The light field in the distance, toward the right of the picture, with a small house within it, is the old clearing called "Freeman's farm." On the rising ground over the tree upon the slope, near the center of the foreground, is the place where Fraser wheeled southward to turn the right flank of the Americans. On the level ground, near the small trees on the right of the large tree upon the slope, is the place where Arnold and Fraser met and fought. On the high middle ground beyond the woods, toward the left, where several small houses are seen, the British formed their line for the second battle on the 7th of October. The detachments under Poor, Learned, and Morgan, which marched to the attack on that day, diverged from near the point seen in the foreground on the right, and marched down the slope by the sheep, across the flat. The brigade of Learned passed on where are seen the dark trees on the left. Morgan kept further to the extreme left, and Poor made a direct line across the level ground and up the hill in the direction marked by the four slender trees by the fence in the center of the picture. The range of mountains in the extreme distance borders the eastern shore of Lake George. The highest peak in the center is Buck Mountain, and that upon the extreme left is French Mountain, at the foot of which are the remains of Forts George and William Henry, at the head of Lake George.

in determined silence, and heard distinctly the voices of the officers upon the opposite hill as they gave their orders along the lines.

Again the enemy made the first hostile movement, and from a powerful battery opened a terrible fire, but without effect. To this the Americans made no reply. Burgoyne then ordered the woods to be cleared by the bayonet, and soon, across the open field, column after column of infantry steadily advanced toward the patriot lines. The Americans kept close within their intrenchments until the enemy fired a volley and pressed onward to the charge, when they sprang upon their assailants with a force that drove them far back across the clearing. Like the ebbing and flowing of the tide, the contending armies alternately advanced and retreated, and for more than three hours the conflict was severe and the result doubtful. And it was not until the sun went down and darkness came upon them, that the warriors ceased their horrid strife. Even amid the gloom of evening there were furious contentions. Just at dusk, Lieutenant-colonel Marshall, with the tenth Massachusetts regiment, encountered some British grenadiers and infantry on a rise of ground a little west of Freeman's cottage, and a brisk but short action ensued.[1] The commander of the enemy was killed, and the troops fled in confusion. Lieutenant-colonel Brooks, of the eighth Massachusetts regiment, remained upon the field until eleven o'clock at night, and in the course of the evening he had a skirmish on the extreme left with some of Breyman's riflemen, whom he knew as such only by the brass match-cases upon their breasts. He was the last to leave the field of action. The conflict at length ended. The Americans retired within their lines, and the British rested on their arms all night upon the field of battle.[2]

The loss of the Americans was, officers included, sixty-four killed, two hundred and seventeen wounded, and thirty-eight missing; in all, three hundred and nineteen.[3] The British lost, in killed, wounded, and prisoners, "rather more than less than five hundred."[4] Both parties claimed the honor of victory. The British, it is true, remained masters, or, at least, possessors, of the field, but this was not their ultimate object. It was to *advance*, and that they failed to do; while the Americans were intent only upon maintaining their ground, and this they accomplished. The advantage, therefore, was certainly on the side of the republicans.

Very few battles have been marked by more determined bravery and patient endurance on both sides than this. Phillips and Riedesel, who had served in the wars in Flanders and other parts of Europe, said they never knew so long and hot a fire; and Burgoyne, in his defense before Parliament, remarked, "few actions have been characterized by more obstinacy in attack or defense." The number of Americans engaged in the action was about two thousand five hundred, and of the British about three thousand. The whole British army in camp and on the field numbered about five thousand, and that of the American about seven thousand.

Although the aggregate number of killed on both sides did not exceed one hundred and fifty, the slaughter and maiming were dreadful in particular instances. Major Jones, of the British army, commanded a battery, and fell, while at his post, during the swaying to and fro of the armies across the clearing, toward evening, when several of the cannons were taken and retaken a number of times. Thirty-six out of forty-eight of his artillery-men were killed or wounded. Lieutenant Hadden was the only officer unhurt, and he had his cap shot from his head by a musket-ball while spiking the cannon. The sixty-second regiment[5]

---

[1] At the urgent solicitation of Arnold, Gates sent out this feeble re-enforcement, which was all that was detached from the right wing during the action. Had fresh troops been supplied to support the left wing, no doubt the Americans would have gained a decided victory.

[2] See Gordon, Ramsay, Botta, Marshall, Sparks, Pictorial History of the Reign of George III., Stedman, Burgoyne's State of the Expedition, Thatcher, Neilson, &c.

[3] Report to the Board of War.

[4] Lieutenant-colonel Kingston, the adjutant general, before a committee of Parliament.

[5] The particular troops engaged in this action were, of the British, the ninth, twenty-first, sixty-second, and twentieth of Hamilton's brigade; the twenty-fourth, belonging to Fraser's brigade; Breyman's rifle-

OF THE REVOLUTION. 5 5

Baroness Reidesel's Notice of the Battle.   Major Hull.   Narrow Escape of Burgoyne.   Arnold, and the Testimony of History

of Hamilton's brigade, which consisted of six hundred when it left Canada, was so cut in pieces, that only sixty men and five officers were left capable of duty. The commander, Colonel Anstruther, and Major Harnage, were both wounded.

The Baroness Riedesel, wife of General Riedesel, who accompanied her husband through this whole campaign, wrote an admirable narrative of the various events connected there-with. In relation to the battle of the 19th of September, she says, " An affair happened, which, though it turned out to our advantage, yet obliged us to halt at a place called Free-man's farm. I was an eye-witness to the whole affair, and, as my husband was engaged in it, I was full of anxiety, and trembled at every shot I heard. I saw a great number of the wounded, and, what added to the distress of the scene, three of them were brought into the house in which I took shelter. One was a Major Harnage, of the sixty-second regi-ment, the husband of a lady of my acquaintance ; another was a lieutenant, married to a lady with whom I had the honor to be on terms of intimacy ; and the third was an officer by the name of Young."

More than one half of an American detachment under Major Hull,[1] consisting of two hundred men, was killed or wounded. Some of the Americans ascended high trees, and from their concealed perches picked off the British officers in detail. Several were killed by the bullets of these sure marksmen. Burgoyne himself came very near being made a victim to this mode of warfare. A bullet, intended for him, shattered the arm of Captain Green, aid-de-camp to General Phillips, who at that moment was handing a letter to Bur-goyne. The captain fell from his horse. In the confusion of the smoke and noise, it was supposed to be Burgoyne, and such was the belief, for some hours, in the American camp. Among the Americans who were killed in the battle were Colonels Adams and Colburn, valuable officers. But it is unpleasant and unprofitable to ponder upon the painful details of a battle, and we will pass on to the consideration of subsequent events.

Let us pause a moment, however, and render justice to as brave a soldier as ever drew blade for freedom. Although in after years he was recreant to the high and sacred responsi-bilities that rested upon him, and committed an act deserving the execrations of all good men, strict justice demands a fair acknowledgment of his brave deeds. I mean Benedict Arnold

The testimony of historians is in conflict respecting the part which Arnold performed in the battle just noticed ; and prejudice and evident falsehood have denied him the honor of being personally engaged in it. Gordon says, " Arnold's division was out in the action, but he himself did not head them ; he remained in the camp the whole time." General Wil-kinson, the adjutant general of Gates at that time, says in his *Memoirs* that " no general officer was on the field of battle during the day," and intimates that he himself chiefly con ducted affairs. He further says, that when, toward evening, Gates and Arnold were to-gether in front of the camp, Major Lewis[2] came in from the scene of action, and announced that its progress was undecisive. Arnold immediately exclaimed, " I will soon put an end to it," and set off in a full gallop from the camp. Gates dispatched an officer after him, and ordered him back. Botta, who was acquainted with many of the foreign officers who served in this war, and whose sources of correct information were very ample, observes,

---

men ; a corps of grenadiers ; a part of the artillery, and a motley swarm of Indians and loyalists. The American troops in action were those under Morgan and Dearborn ; the first, second, and third New Hamp-shire regiments ; the eighth, ninth, and tenth Massachusetts regiments ; the second and third of New York, and a Connecticut regiment of militia.

[1] He was a major general in our war with Great Britain in 1812. He surrendered his whole army, with all the forts and garrisons in the neighborhood of Detroit, to General Brock on the 16th of August of that year. His wife, Sarah Hull, to whom he had been married but a few weeks when the battle of Stillwater occurred, determined to share the fortunes and perils of her husband, was in the camp, and was active among those Amer-ican women who extended comfort and kind attentions to the ladies of the British army after the surrender of Burgoyne. Because of his surrender at Detroit, General Hull was tried for cowardice, treason, &c., and condemned to be shot ; but, in consideration of his Revolutionary services and his age, he was pardoned He lived to see his character vindicated, and died in 1825. His wife died the following year.

[2] Morgan Lewis, afterward governor of the state of New York.

" Arnold exhibited upon this occasion all the impetuosity of his courage ; he encouraged his men by voice and example." Stedman, a British officer who served under Cornwallis here, says, in his " History of the American War," " The enemy were led to the battle by General Arnold, who distinguished himself in an extraordinary manner." Allen, in his Biographical Dictionary, says, " In the battle near Stillwater, September the 19th, he conducted himself with his usual intrepidity, being engaged incessantly for four hours." M‘Farlane, in the Pictorial History of England, says, " Gates's detachment, being re-enforced and led on by Arnold, fell upon Burgoyne and the right wing." Again : " Arnold behaved with extraordinary gallantry, but he could make an impression nowhere." Again : " Every time that Arnold was beaten back, Gates sent him more men from the star redoubt." The well-founded traditions of the vicinity support the position that Arnold was actively engaged in the conflict, and a knowledge of the locality is sufficient to cause a doubt of the correctness of Wilkinson's statement.

Finally, Colonel Varick, writing from camp to General Schuyler, three days after the action, said, " He [Gates] seems to be piqued that Arnold's division had the honor of beating the enemy on the 19th. This I am certain of, that Arnold has all the credit of the action. And this I further know, that Gates asked where the troops were going when Scammel's battalion marched out, and, upon being told, he declared no more troops should go ; he would not suffer the camp to be exposed. Had Gates complied with Arnold's repeated desires, he would have obtained a general and complete victory over the enemy. But it is evident to me he never intended to fight Burgoyne, till Arnold urged, begged, and entreated him to do it." In another letter which he wrote to Schuyler, about a month afterward, from Albany, Colonel Varick observed, " During Burgoyne's stay here, he gave Arnold great credit for his bravery and military abilities, especially in the action of the 19th, whenever he spoke of him, and once in the presence of Gates."

Under ordinary circumstances, the statements of General Wilkinson, he being adjutant general at that time, and presumed to be cognizant of all the events of the battle, ought to be received as semi-official ; but in this case they must be taken with great allowance. Gates was evidently jealous of Arnold's well-earned reputation and growing popularity with the army ; and Wilkinson, who was his favorite, and seemed ever ready to pander to his commander's vanity, caused, by his officious interference at that very time, a serious misunderstanding between the two generals, which resulted in an open rupture. In the first place, he caused a part of Arnold's division to be withdrawn without his knowledge, and he was put in the ridiculous light of presuming to give orders which were contravened by the general orders of the commander-in-chief. Wilkinson also insisted on the return of a part of Arnold's division (Morgan's corps) being made directly to him, and Gates sustained the unjust demand in general orders. And then, to crown his injustice toward a brave officer, Gates, in his communication to Congress respecting the battle, said nothing of Arnold or his division, but merely observed that " the action was fought by detachments from the army." This was ungenerous, not only to Arnold, but to the troops under his command, and he justly complained of the neglect when it became known. Harsh words passed between the two officers, and Gates even told Arnold that he thought him of little consequence in the army, that when Lincoln arrived he should take away his command, and that he would give him a pass to leave the camp as soon as he pleased.[1]

Under the excitement of his feelings, Arnold demanded a pass for himself and suite to join General Washington. The pass was granted, but in his cooler moments he saw how injurious it might be to the cause, and how hazardous to his reputation, if he should voluntarily leave the army when another battle was hourly expected. He remained, but without any employment in the camp, for Gates put his threat into execution, took command of Arnold's division himself, and, on the arrival of General Lincoln, on the 29th, placed him over the right wing.

---

[1] Sparks's Life of Arnold.

The morning of the 20th of September was cloudy, dull, and cheerless, and with the gloomy aspect of nature the spirits of the British army sympathized. The combatants had slumbered upon the field during the night, and at dawn, seeing no disposition on the part of the Americans to renew the conflict, they retired to their camp on the river hills, and upon the flats at the mouth of the creek, now Wilbur's Basin.

BURGOYNE'S ENCAMPMENT ON THE WEST BANK OF THE HUDSON, SEPTEMBER 20, 1777.
From a print published in London, 1779.

Burgoyne was surprised and mortified at the bold and successful resistance of the Americans, and saw clearly that it would be useless to attempt to carry the works by storm, or in any other way to push forward toward Albany. He resolved to strengthen his position, endeavor to communicate with Howe and Clinton at New York, and effect by their co-operation what his own unaided troops could not accomplish. Had he been aware of the true condition of the Americans on the morning after the battle, he might easily have won a victory, for the soldiers composing the left wing, which sustained the conflict, had only a single round of cartridges left. Nor was the magazine in a condition to supply them, for such was the difficulty of procuring ammunition at that time, that the army had a very meager quantity when the conflict began the day previous, and now there were not in the magazine forty rounds to each man in the service. At no time was there more than three days' provisions in the camp, and on the day of action there was no flour. A supply arrived on the 20th, and the disheartening contingency of short allowance to the weary soldiers was thus prevented. General Gates alone was privy to this deplorable deficiency, and it was not until after a supply of powder and window-leads for bullets was received from Albany that he made the fact known, and thus gave a plausible reason for not complying with Arnold's urgent request to commence the battle early again the next morning.

Both parties now wrought diligently in strengthening their respective positions. The Americans extended and completed their line of breast-works from the northeastern angle on the river hills,[1] westward about three fourths of a mile, to the heights, a few rods north

---

[1] See the small map on page 46.

of the dwelling of Mr. Neilson. From this point they were extended south and southwest to a large ravine, now on the south side of the road leading to Saratoga Springs. At the northwest angle, near Mr. Neilson's, stood the log barn before alluded to. This was strengthened by a double tier of logs on three sides. Strong batteries, in circular form, extended about one hundred and fifty feet south. The whole was encircled by a deep trench and a row of strong palisades. The area within was about half an acre. When completed. it formed quite a strong bulwark, and was named Fort Neilson.

About fifty rods south of the fort was a strong battery; and in the rear, near the center of the encampment, stood the magazine, made bomb-proof. The front of the camp was covered by a deep ravine skirted by a dense forest, running nearly parallel with the lines. from the river hills westward. For some distance west of the fort, large trees were felled, and presented a strong *abatis* toward the enemy.[1]

Burgoyne was equally busy in strengthening his position. His camp was pitched within cannon-shot of the American lines. Across the plain to the river hills a line of intrenchments, with batteries, was thrown up, crossing the north ravine not far from its junction with the Middle Ravine or Mill Creek. The intrenchments extended northward on the west side of Freeman's farm. The Hessian camp was pitched upon an eminence about half a mile northwest of Freeman's farm, where a strong redoubt was reared, and a line of intrenchments of a horse-shoe form was thrown up. Intrenchments were also made along the hills fronting the river; and four redoubts, upon four hills or huge knolls, were erected. two above and two below Wilbur's Basin. A short line of intrenchments, with a battery, extended across the flats to the river, and covered their magazine and hospital in the rear. These composed the principal defenses of the enemy. In many places these works may still be traced, especially by mounds and shallow ditches in the woods.

As soon as the works were completed, General Gates moved his quarters from Bemis's house to the one delineated in the second picture from the top, among the group of localities on page 46. The house belonged to Captain Ephraim Woodworth. A barn, which stood about fifteen rods east of the house, was used for a hospital.

September, 1777. General Lincoln, with two thousand New England troops, joined the main army on the 29th. Gates at once gave up the right wing to him, and assumed the command of the left, which was composed of two brigades under Generals Poor and Learned. Colonel Morgan's rifle corps, and a part of the fresh New England militia. Morgan occupied the heights immediately south of the fort; Learned's brigade the plain on the east, and General Poor's brigade the heights south of Morgan, between him and Gates's headquarters.[2] In fact, the position of the American army was about the same as at the time of the battle of the 19th. Burgoyne disposed his troops to the best advantage. The Hessians, under Colonel Breyman, occupied a height on the extreme right, and formed a flank defense rather than a wing of the main army. The light infantry, under Earl Balcarras. with the choicest portion of Fraser's corps, flanked on the left by the grenadiers and Hamilton's brigade, occupied the vicinity of Freeman's farm; the remainder of the army, including the artillery under Phillips and Reidesel, occupied the plain and the high ground north of Wilbur's Basin; and the Hessians of Hanau, the forty-seventh regiment, and some loyalists, were situated upon the flats near the river, for the protection of the bateaux, hospital, and magazine. Thus in parallel lines to each other, and within cannon-shot, the two armies lay in menacing attitude from the 20th of September until the 7th of October. Each exercised the utmost vigilance, expecting the other to fall upon them in full power, or entangle them by strategy. There were constant skirmishes between small detachments, sometimes foraging parties, and at others a few pickets; and not a night passed without the per-

---

[1] *Abatis* is a French word signifying trees cut down. It is a phrase used in fortifications; and an *abatis* which is composed of trees felled, so as to present their branches to the enemy, is frequently found in woody country one of the most avail ble and efficient kir ds of defense.

[2] Neilson, p. 15, 35

formance of some daring exploit, either for the sake of adventure, or to annoy each other. The Americans were constantly gaining strength, and their superiority of numbers enabled them to form expeditions to harass the British, without weakening their lines by fatigue or endangering the safety of the camp.

The success of the Americans in the late battle, and the rapid increment of the army, almost annihilated loyalty in the neighborhood, and made every republican, whether soldier or citizen, bold and adventurous.   At one time about twenty young Americans, farmers residing in the vicinity, not belonging to the camp, and intent on having a frolic, resolved to capture an advance picket-guard of the enemy, stationed on the north bank of the middle ravine.   They selected their officers, and each being armed with a fowling-piece and plenty of powder and shot, they marched silently through the woods in the evening, until they got within a few yards of the picket.   The captain of the party then gave a tremendous blast upon an old horse-trumpet which he carried, and, with yells and the noise of a whole regiment, they rushed through the bushes upon the frightened enemy.   No time was given for the sentinel's hail, for, simultaneously with their furious onset, the captain of the frolickers cried out lustily, " Ground your arms, or you are all dead men !"   Supposing half the American army was upon them, the astonished pickets obeyed, and thirty British soldiers were taken by the jolly young farmers into the republican camp with all the parade of regular prisoners of war.   This was one of many similar instances, and thus the British camp was kept in a state of constant alarm.[1]

Burgoyne saw, with deep anxiety, the rapid increase of the American forces, while his own were daily diminishing by desertion.   Nearly one hundred and fifty Indian warriors, from the tribes of the Oneidas, Tuscaroras, Onondagas, and Mohawks, accepted the war-belt, partook of the feast, and joined the republican army within three days after the battle of the 19th.   The Indians with Burgoyne were so dissatisfied with the results of that battle, and so disappointed in their hopes of blood and plunder, that they deserted him in large numbers in that hour of his greatest peril.   It was their hunting season, too, and this was another strong inducement to return to their wives and children, to keep starvation from their wigwams.   The Canadians and loyalists were not much more faithful.[2]

Burgoyne used every means in his power to transmit intelligence of his situation to Howe, and to implore his assistance either by co-operation or a diversion in his favor.   But the American pickets, vigilant and wary, were planted in all directions ; and it was by the merest chance that the British commander received a letter from Sir Henry Clinton, at New York,[3] written in cipher on the 10th, informing him that he should make a diversion in his favor by attacking Forts Clinton and Montgomery, in the Hudson Highlands, on the 20th.   This information raised the hopes of Burgoyne, for he supposed that the attack at those points would draw off large detachments from Gates for their defense, and render the belligerent forces at Stillwater nearly equal in numbers.   He immediately dispatched two officers in disguise, and several other persons in different directions, to Sir Henry Clinton, with a letter, urging him to make the diversion without fail, and saying that he had provisions enough to hold out until the 12th of October.

Time rolled on, and Burgoyne heard nothing further from Clinton.   His provisions began to fail, and on the 1st of October he was obliged to put his troops on short allowance.   Not a man or a biscuit was allowed to reach him from any quarter.   The militia were flocking into Gates's camp from all directions, and perils of every kind were weaving their web around the proud Briton.   At last he was reduced to the alternative to fight or fly.

---

[1] " I do not believe either officer or soldier ever slept during that interval without his clothes, or that any general officer or commander of a regiment passed a single night without being upon his legs occasionally at different hours, and constantly an hour before daylight."—*Burgoyne's " Review of the Evidence,"* p. 166.

[2] Marshall's Life of Washington.

[3] General Howe had left Clinton in command at New York, and was then engaged against Washington on the Delaware, for the purpose of making a conquest of Philadelphia.

The latter was both impracticable and inglorious, and at a council of officers it was resolved to fight.

On the morning of the 7th of October, Burgoyne, at the head of fifteen hundred regular troops, with two twelve pounders, two howitzers, and six six pounders, moved toward the American left, to the northern part of a low ridge of land about three fourths of a mile northwest from the American camp, where they formed a line in double ranks. He was seconded by Phillips, Riedesel, and Fraser. The guard of the camp upon the high grounds was committed to Brigadiers Hamilton and Specht, and that of the redoubts and plain near the river to Brigadier-general Gall. This movement was for a two-fold purpose, to cover a foraging party sent out to supply the pressing wants of the camp, and, if the prospect was favorable, to turn the left of the American army, and fall upon its flank and rear. Small parties of loyalists and Indians were sent around through by-paths, to hang upon the American rear and keep them in check.

Before this movement was known to General Gates, he had ordered out a detachment of three hundred men under Colonel Brooks, to gain the rear of the enemy and fall upon his outposts. While Brooks was at headquarters, receiving his instructions, a sergeant arrived with intelligence of the movement of the British army. The order to Colonel Brooks was revoked, the officers in camp were summoned to their posts, and an aid was sent out by the commander-in-chief to ascertain the exact position and probable intentions of the enemy. He proceeded to a rise of ground covered with woods, half a mile from Fort Neilson (near the house of Asa Chatfield), where he discovered the British in a wheat field cutting straw, and several officers on the top of a cabin (Joseph Munger's) with a spy-glass, endeavoring to ascertain the condition of the American left. The aid returned, and had just reached headquarters with his intelligence, when a party of Canadians, Indians, and loyalists, who had been sent forward to scour the woods, attacked the American pickets near the middle ravine. They were soon joined by a detachment of grenadiers, drove the Americans before them, and pressed forward until within musket-shot of the republican lines. For half an hour a hot engagement ensued at the breast-work, a little south of the fort. Morgan, with his riflemen, supported by a corps of infantry, at length charged the assailants with such deadly effect, that they retreated in confusion to the British line, which was forming upon a newly-cleared field, preparatory to marching into action.

It was now two o'clock, about the same hour at which the two armies summoned their strength for combat on the 19th of September. The grenadiers, under Major Ackland, and the artillery, under Major Williams, were stationed on the left, upon a gentle eminence on the borders of a wood, and covered in front by Mill Creek or Middle Ravine. The light infantry, under Earl Balcarras, were placed on the extreme right, and the center was composed of British and German troops, under Generals Phillips and Reidesel. Near the cabin of Mr. Munger, and in advance of the right wing, General Fraser had command of a detachment of five hundred picked men, destined to fall upon the American flank as soon as the action in front should commence.

This design was at once perceived, and, at the suggestion of Morgan, Gates dispatched that sagacious officer, with his rifle corps and other troops amounting to fifteen hundred men, in a circuitous route to some high ground on the extreme right of the enemy, thence to fall upon the flanking party under Fraser at the same moment when an attack should be made upon the British left. For the latter service the brigade of General Poor, composed of New York and New Hampshire troops, and a part of Learned's brigade, were detached.

About half past two the conflict began. The troops of Poor and Learned marched steadily up the gentle slope of the eminence on which the British grenadiers, and part of the artillery under Ackland and Williams, were stationed, and, true to their orders not to fire until after the first discharge of the enemy, pressed on in awful silence toward the battalions and batteries above them. Suddenly a terrible discharge of musket-balls and grape-shot made great havoc among the branches of the trees over their heads, but scarcely a shot took effect among the men. This was the signal to break the silence of our troops, and, with a loud shout, they sprang forward, delivered their fire in rapid volleys, and opened right and left to avail themselves of the covering of the trees on the margin of the ridge on which the artillery was posted.

The contest now became fierce and destructive.   The Americans rushed up to the very mouths of the cannon, and amid the carriages of the heavy field-pieces they struggled for victory.   Valor of the highest order on both sides marked the conflict, and for a time the scale seemed equipoised.   Five times one of the cannon was taken and retaken, but at last it remained in possession of the republicans as the British fell back.   Colonel Cilley, who, during the whole contest, had fought at the head of his troops, leaped upon the captured piece, waved his sword high in air, dedicated the brazen engine of death to " the American cause," wheeled its muzzle toward the enemy, and with their own ammunition opened its thunder upon them.   It was all the work of a moment of exultation when the enemy fell back from their vantage ground.   The effect was electrical, and seemed to give the republicans stronger sinews and fiercer courage.   The contest was long and obstinate, for the enemy were brave and skillful.   Major Ackland, who was foremost in the conflict, was at last severely wounded, and Major Williams was taken prisoner.   Suddenly deprived of their superior officers, the grenadiers and artillery-men fled in confusion, and left the field in possession of the Americans.

Almost simultaneously with the attack on the British left, Morgan with his corps rushed down the hills that skirted the flanking party of Fraser in advance of the enemy's right, and opened upon them such a destructive storm of well-aimed bullets, that they were driven hastily back to their lines.   Then, with the speed of the wind, Morgan wheeled and fell upon the British right flank with such appalling force and impetuosity, that their ranks were at once thrown into confusion.   The mode and power of attack were both unexpected to the enemy, and they were greatly alarmed.   While thus in confusion, Major Dearborn, with some fresh troops, came up and attacked them in front.   Thus assailed, they broke and fled in terror, but were rallied by Earl Balcarras, and again led into action.   The shock on right and left shook the British center, which was composed chiefly of Germans and Hessians, yet it stood firm.

General Arnold had watched with eager eye and excited spirit the course of the battle thus far.   Deprived of all command, he had no authority even to *fight*, much less to *order* Smarting under the indignity heaped upon him by his commander ; thirsting for that glory which beckoned him to the field ; burning with a patriotic desire to serve his country, now bleeding at every pore ; and stirred by the din of battle around him, the brave soldier became fairly maddened by his emotions, and, leaping upon his large brown horse, he started off on a full gallop for the field of conflict.   Gates immediately sent Major Armstrong[1] after him to order him back.   Arnold saw him approaching, and, anticipating his errand, spurred his horse and left his pursuer far behind, while he placed himself at the head of three regiments of Learned's brigade, who received their former commander with loud huzzas.   He immediately led them against the British center, and, with the desperation of a madman, rushed into the thickest of the fight, or rode along the lines in rapid and erratic movements, brandishing his broadsword above his head, and delivering his orders every where in person. Armstrong kept up the chase for half an hour, but Arnold's course was so varied and perilous that he gave it up.

The Hessians received the first assault of Arnold's troops upon the British center with a brave resistance ; but when, upon a second charge, he dashed furiously among them at the head of his men, they broke and fled in dismay.   And now the battle became general along the whole lines.   Arnold and Morgan were the ruling spirits that controlled the storm on the part of the Americans, and the gallant General Fraser was the directing soul of the British troops in action.   His skill and courage were every where conspicuous.   When the

---

[1] The author of the celebrated " Newburgh letters," written in the spring of 1783. See pages 672 to 678, inclusive, of this volume.

lines gave way, he brought order out of confusion ; when regiments began to waver, he in-fused courage into them by voice and example.   He was mounted upon a splendid iron-gray gelding ; and, dressed in the full uniform of a field officer, he was a conspicuous object for the Americans.   It was evident that the fate of the battle rested upon him, and this the keen eye and sure judgment of Morgan perceived.[1]   In an instant his purpose was con-ceived, and, calling a file of his best men around him, he said, as he pointed toward the British right, " That gallant officer is General Fraser.   I admire and honor him, but it is necessary he should die ; victory for the enemy depends upon him.   Take your stations in that clump of bushes, and do your duty."   Within five minutes Fraser fell mortally wound-ed, and was carried to the camp by two grenadiers.   Just previous to being hit by the fatal bullet, the crupper of his horse was cut by a rifle-ball, and immediately afterward another passed through the horse's mane, a little back of his ears.   The aid of Fraser noticed this, and said, " It is evident that you are marked out for particular aim ; would it not be pru-dent for you to retire from this place ?"   Fraser replied, " My duty forbids me to fly from danger," and the next moment he fell.[2]

Morgan has been censured for this order, by those who profess to understand the rules of war, as guilty of a highly dishonorable act ; and others, who gloat over the horrid details of the slaying of thousands of humble rank-and-file men as deeds worthy of a shout for glory, and drop no tear for the slaughtered ones, affect to shudder at such a cold-blooded murder of an officer upon the battle-field.   War is a monstrous wrong and cruel injustice at all times ; but if it is right to kill at all upon the field of battle, I can perceive no greater wrong in slaying a *general* than a *private*.   True, he wears the badge of distinction, and the trumpet of Renown speaks his name to the world, but his life is no dearer to himself, and wife, and children, and friends, than that of the humblest private who obeys his com-mands.   If Daniel Morgan was guilty of no sin, no dishonor, in ordering his men to fall upon and slay those under the command of Fraser, he was also guiltless of sin and dishonor in ordering the sacrifice of their chief.   Indeed, it is probable that the sacrifice of *his* life saved that of hundreds, for the slaughter was stayed.

As soon as Fraser fell, a panic spread along the British line.   It was increased by the appearance, at that moment, of three thousand New York troops, under General Tenbroeck. Burgoyne, who now took command in person, could not keep up the sinking courage of his men.   The whole line gave way, and fled precipitately within the intrenchments of the

---

[1] Samuel Woodruff, Esq., of Connecticut, a volunteer in the army at the time, visited Bemis's Heights some years since, and wrote an interesting account of some of the transactions of the day.   He says the importance of the death of Fraser was suggested to Morgan by Arnold.

[2] The name of the rifleman who killed General Fraser was Timothy Murphy.   He took sure aim from a small tree in which he was posted, and saw Fraser fall on the discharge of his rifle.   Fraser told his friends before he died that he saw the man who shot him, and that he was in a tree.   Murphy afterward accompanied General Sullivan in his expedition against the Indians in Central and Western New York, where he had a narrow escape from death.   In the fall of 1778 he was stationed in Schoharie county, where he became enamored of a young girl of sixteen, named Margaret Feeck.   He was twelve years her senior, yet his love was reciprocated.   Her parents " denied the bans," and attempted to break off the engagement by a forcible confinement.   But " love laughs at locksmiths," and, under pretense of going after a cow some distance from home to milk her, she stole away one evening barefooted, to meet her lover, according to an appointment through a trusty young friend, upon the bank of the Schoharie Creek.   He was not there, and she forded the stream, determined to go to the fort where Murphy was stationed.   She found him, however, upon the opposite side of the stream, and, mounting his horse behind him, they en-tered the fort amid the cheering of the inmates.   The young females there fitted her up with comfortable attire, and the next day they set out for Schenectady.   There the soldier purchased for his intended bride silk for a gown, and several dress-makers soon completed it.   They repaired to the house of Rev. Mr. Johnson, where they were married, and then returned to Schoharie.   The parents became reconciled, and they lived happily together many years.   Murphy was an uneducated man, but was possessed of a strong intellect, and had a good deal of influence over a certain class.   He was an early friend of the Hon. William C. Bouck, late governor of New York, and was among the most active in bringing him forward in public life.   He lost his Margaret in 1807, and in 1812 married Mary Robertson.   He died of a cancer in his throat in 1818.—*See* Simm's " *History of Schoharie County.*"

camp. The tumultuous retreat was covered by Phillips and Reidesel. The Americans pursued them up to their very intrenchments in the face of a furious storm of grape-shot and musket-balls, and assaulted their works vigorously without the aid of field pieces or other artillery.

The conflict was now terrible indeed, and in the midst of the flame, and smoke, and metal hail, Arnold was conspicuous. His voice, clear as a trumpet, animated the soldiers, and, as if ubiquitous, he seemed to be every where amid the perils at the same moment. With a part of the brigades of Patterson and Glover, he assaulted the works occupied by the light infantry under Earl Balcarras, and at the point of the bayonet drove the enemy from a strong *abatis*, through which he attempted to force his way into the camp. He was obliged to abandon the effort, and, dashing forward toward the right flank of the enemy, exposed to the cross-fire of the contending armies, he met Learned's brigade advancing to make an assault upon the British works at an opening in the *abatis*, between Balcarras's light infantry and the German right flank defense under Colonel Breyman. Canadians and loyalists defended this part of the line, and were flanked by a stockade redoubt on each side.

Arnold placed himself at the head of the brigade, and moved rapidly on to the attack. He directed Colonel Brooks to assault the redoubt, while the remainder of the brigade fell upon the front. The contest was furious, and the enemy at length gave way, leaving Breyman and his Germans completely exposed. At this moment Arnold galloped to the left, and ordered the regiments of Wesson and Livingston, and Morgan's corps of riflemen, to advance and make a general assault. At the head of Brooks's regiment, he attacked the German works. Having found the sally-port, he rushed within the enemy's intrenchments. The Germans, who had seen him upon his steed in the thickest of the fight for more than two hours, terrified at his approach, fled in dismay, delivering a volley in their retreat, which killed Arnold's horse under him, and wounded the general himself very severely, in the same leg which had been badly lacerated by a musket-ball at the storming of Quebec, two years before. Here, wounded and disabled, at the head of conquering troops led on by his valor to the threshold of victory, Arnold was overtaken by Major Armstrong, who delivered to him Gates's order to return to camp, fearing he "might do some rash thing!" He indeed did a rash thing in the eye of military discipline. He led troops to victory without an order from his commander. His conduct was rash indeed, compared with the stately method of General Gates, who directed by orders from his camp what his presence should have sanctioned. While Arnold was wielding the fierce sickle of war without, and reaping golden sheaves for Gates's garner, the latter (according to Wilkinson) was within his camp, more intent upon discussing the merits of the Revolution with Sir Francis Clarke, Burgoyne's aid-de-camp, who had been wounded and taken prisoner, and was lying upon the commander's bed at his quarters, than upon winning a battle, all-important to the ultimate triumph of those principles for which he professed so warm an attachment. When one of Gates's aids came up from the field of battle for orders, he found the general very angry because Sir Francis would not allow the force of his arguments. He left the room, and, calling his aid after him, asked, as they went out, " Did you ever hear so impudent a son of a b——h ?" Poor Sir Francis died that night upon Gates's bed.

" It is a curious fact," says Sparks, " that an officer who really had not command in the army was the leader of one of the most spirited and important battles of the Revolution. His madness, or rashness, or whatever it may be called, resulted most fortunately for himself. The wound he received at the moment of rushing into the arms of danger and of death added fresh luster to his military glory, and was a new claim to public favor and applause. In the heat of the action, he struck an officer on the head with his sword, an indignity and offense which might justly have been retaliated upon the spot in the most fatal manner. The officer forbore ; and the next day, when he demanded redress, Arnold declared his entire ignorance of the act, and expressed his regret."[1]

---

[1] Life of Arnold, p. 118.

It was twilight when Arnold was wounded and conveyed by Major Armstrong and a sergeant (Samuel Woodruff) from the field. The Germans who fled at his approach. finding the assault general, threw down their arms and retreated to the interior of the camp, leaving their commander, Colonel Breyman, mortally wounded. The camp of Burgoyne was thus left exposed at a strong point. He endeavored to rally the panic-stricken Germans in the midst of the increasing darkness, but they could not be again brought into action.[1] In truth, both armies were thoroughly fatigued, and the Americans were as loth to follow up the advantage thus presented as were the British to repair their discomfiture. As night drew its curtain over the scene, the conflict ended, the clangor of battle was hushed, and all was silent except the groans of the wounded, an occasional word of command, and the heavy tread of retiring columns, seeking for a place of repose.

About midnight, General Lincoln, with his division, which had remained in camp during the action, marched out to relieve those upon the field, and to maintain the ground acquired. Perceiving this, and knowing the advantage the Americans would possess with fresh troops and such an easy access to his camp, Burgoyne felt the necessity of guarding against the peril at once by changing his position. Before dawn he removed the whole of his army, camp, and artillery about a mile north of his first position, above Wilbur's Basin, whence he contemplated a speedy retreat toward Fort Edward.

October, 1777.   Early on the morning of the 8th the Americans took possession of the evacuated British camp, and skirmishes took place between detachments from the two armies during the day, in one of which General Lincoln was badly wounded in the leg. As the news that the British had retreated spread over the surrounding country, a great number of men, women, and children came flocking into camp to join in the general joy, or to perform the more sorrowful duty of seeking for relatives or friends among the wounded and slain.

The loss of the Americans in killed and wounded did not exceed one hundred and fifty. Arnold was the only commissioned officer who received a wound. The British army suffered severely, and their loss in killed, wounded, and prisoners was about seven hundred.[2] Among the officers killed were the gallant Fraser, Sir Francis Clarke (Burgoyne's aid-de-camp,) Colonel Breyman, and Lieutenant Reynell. The latter two died on the field; Sir Francis Clarke was taken prisoner and carried to Gates's quarters, where he died that night. Major Ackland, who was severely wounded, was also taken prisoner, and, with Major Will-

iams, was carried into the American camp; and Fraser, who was conveyed to the house of John Taylor, near Wilbur's Basin, expired the next morning at about eight o'clock October 8.   Burgoyne had several narrow escapes. One ball passed through his hat and another his coat.

The house in which General Fraser died stood until 1846, upon the right bank of the Hudson, about three miles above Bemis's Heights, near Ensign's store, and exhibited the marks of the conflict there in numerous bullet-holes. It was used by Burgoyne

HOUSE IN WHICH GENERAL
FRASER DIED.

---

[1] Evidence of Captain Money before a committee of Parliament in the case of Burgoyne.

[2] " The British and Hessian troops killed in the foregoing actions were slightly covered with earth and brush on the battle-field. It was not uncommon, after the land was cleared and cultivated, to see many, sometimes twenty, human skulls piled upon stumps in the fields. I have myself, when a boy, seen human bones thickly strewn about the ground, which had been turned up by the plow."—C. Neilson. Burgoyne's Campaign, p. 182.

I saw, in the possession of Mr. Neilson, many relics plowed up from the battle-field, such as cannon-balls,

No. 1.   No. 2.

grape-shot, tomahawks, arrow-heads. buttons, knives, &c., and among them were some teeth, evidently front ones, but double. It is supposed that they belonged to the Hessians, for it is said that many of them had double teeth all around, in both jaws. The annexed are drawings of two tomahawks in my possession. No. 1 is made of iron, No 2 of stone. It is graywacke, and is creased for the purpose of securing the handle by a string or by green withes

for quarters when he first pitched his camp there, and it was a shelter to several ladies attached to the British army, among whom were the Baroness Riedesel and Lady Harriet Ackland. General Fraser was laid upon a camp-bed near the first window on the right of the door, where he expired. I can not narrate this event and its attendant circumstances better than by quoting the simple language of the Baroness Riedesel.

" But," she says, " severer trials awaited us, and on the 7th of October our misfortunes began. I was at breakfast with my husband, and heard that something was intended. On the same day I expected Generals Burgoyne, Phillips, and Fraser to dine with us. I saw a great movement among the troops; my husband told me it was merely a reconnoissance, which gave me no concern, as it often happened. I walked out of the house, and met several Indians in their war dresses, with guns in their hands. When I asked them where they were going, they cried out, ' War! war!' meaning that they were going to battle. This filled me with apprehension, and I had scarcely got home before I heard reports of cannon and musketry, which grew louder by degrees, till at last the noise became excessive.

" About four o'clock in the afternoon, instead of the guests whom I expected, General Fraser was brought on a litter, mortally wounded. The table, which was already set, was instantly removed, and a bed placed in its stead for the wounded general. I sat trembling in a corner; the noise grew louder, and the alarm increased; the thought that my husband might, perhaps, be brought in, wounded in the same manner, was terrible to me, and distressed me exceedingly. General Fraser said to the surgeon, ' *Tell me if my wound is mortal; do not flatter me.*' The ball had passed through his body, and, unhappily for the general, he had eaten a very hearty breakfast, by which the stomach was distended, and the ball, as the surgeon said, had passed through it. I heard him often exclaim, with a sigh, ' *O fatal ambition! Poor General Burgoyne! Oh! my poor wife!*' He was asked if he had any request to make, to which he replied that, *if General Burgoyne would permit it, he should like to be buried at six o'clock in the evening, on the top of a mountain, in a redoubt which had been built there.* I did not know which way to turn; all the other rooms were full of sick. Toward evening I saw my husband coming; then I forgot all my sorrows, and thanked God that he was spared to me. He ate in great haste, with me and his aid-de-camp, behind the house. We had been told that we had the advantage over the enemy, but the sorrowful faces I beheld told a different tale; and before my husband went away, he took me aside, and said every thing was going very badly, and that I must keep myself in readiness to leave the place, but not to mention it to any one I made the pretense that I would move the next morning into my new house, and had every thing packed up ready.

" I could not go to sleep, as I had General Fraser and all the other wounded gentlemen in my room, and I was sadly afraid my children would wake, and, by their crying, disturb the dying man in his last moments, who often addressed me and apologized ' *for the trouble he gave me.*' About three o'clock in the morning I was told that he could not hold out much longer; I had desired to be informed of the near approach of this sad crisis, and I then wrapped up my children in their clothes, and went with them into the room below About eight o'clock in the morning *he died.*

" After he was laid out, and his corpse wrapped up in a sheet, we came again into the room, and had this sorrowful sight before us the whole day; and, to add to the melancholy scene, almost every moment some officer of my acquaintance was brought in wounded. The cannonade commenced again; a retreat was spoken of, but not the smallest motion was made toward it. About four o'clock in the afternoon I saw the house which had just been built for me in flames, and the enemy was now not far off. We knew that General Burgoyne would not refuse the last request of General Fraser, though, by his acceding to it, an unnecessary delay was occasioned, by which the inconvenience of the army was much increased. At six o'clock the corpse was brought out, and we saw all the generals attend it to the mountain. The chaplain, Mr. Brudenell, performed the funeral service, rendered unusually solemn and awful from its being accompanied by constant peals from the enemy's artillery.   Many cannon-balls flew close by me, but I had my eyes directed toward the mountain[1] where my husband was standing amid the fire of the enemy, and of course I could not think of my own danger."

It was just at sunset, on that calm October evening, that the corpse of General Fraser was carried up the hill to the place of burial within the "great redoubt."   It was attended only by the members of his military family and Mr. Brudenell, the chaplain ; yet the eyes

of hundreds of both armies followed the solemn procession, while the Americans, ignorant of its true character, kept up a constant cannonade upon the redoubt.   The chaplain, unawed by the danger to which he was exposed, as the cannon-balls that struck the hill threw the loose soil over him, pronounced the impressive funeral service of the Church of England with an unfaltering voice.[3]   The growing darkness added solemnity to the scene.

FRASER'S BURIAL-PLACE.[2]

Suddenly the irregular firing ceased, and the solemn voice of a single cannon, at measured intervals, boomed along the valley, and awakened the responses of the hills.   It was a minute-gun fired by the Americans in honor of the gallant dead.   The moment information was given that the gathering at the redoubt was a funeral company, fulfilling, amid imminent perils, the last-breathed wishes of the noble Fraser, orders were issued to withhold the cannonade with balls, and to render military homage to the fallen brave.

How such incidents smooth the rough features of war !   In contrast with fiercer ages gone by, when human sympathy never formed a holy communion between enemies on the battle-field, they seem to reflect the radiance of the future, and exhibit a glimpse of the time to which a hopeful faith directs our vision, when " nation shall not war against nation," when " one law shall bind all people, kindreds. and tongues, and that law shall be the law of UNIVERSAL BROTHERHOOD."

The case of Major Ackland and his heroic wife presents kindred features.   He belonged to the corps of grenadiers, and was an accomplished soldier.   His wife accompanied him to Canada in 1776, and during the whole campaign of that year, and until his return to England after the surrender of Burgoyne, in the autumn of 1777, endured all the hardships, dangers, and privations of an active campaign in an enemy's country.   At Chambly, on the Sorel, she attended him in illness, in a miserable hut ; and when he was wounded in the battle of Hubbardton, Vermont, she hastened to him at Skenesborough from Montreal, where she had been persuaded to remain, and resolved to follow the army thereafter.   Just before crossing the Hudson, she and her husband came near losing their lives in consequence of their tent taking fire from a candle overturned by a pet dog.   During the terrible engagement of the 7th of October she heard all the tumult and dreadful thunder of the battle in which her husband was engaged ; and when, on the morning of the 8th, the British fell

---

[1] The height occupied by Burgoyne on the 18th, which ran parallel with the river till it approached General Gates's camp.

[2] The hill on which the "great redouht" was erected, and where General Fraser was buried, is about one hundred feet high, and almost directly west from the house wherein he died.   The relative situation of this eminence to the Hudson will be best understood by looking at the view of Burgoyne's encampment, page 57.   The center hill in that drawing is the one here represented.   The grave is within the inclosure on the summit of the hill.

[3] Burgoyne's " State of the Expedition," p. 169.   Lieutenant Kingston's Evidence, p. 107.

back in confusion to Wilbur's Basin, she, with the other women, was obliged to take refuge among the dead and dying, for the tents were all struck, and hardly a shed was left standing. Her husband was wounded, and a prisoner in the American camp. That gallant officer was shot through both legs when Poor and Learned's troops assaulted the grenadiers and artillery on the British left, on the afternoon of the 7th. Wilkinson, Gates's adjutant general, while pursuing the flying enemy when they abandoned their battery, heard a feeble voice exclaim, "Protect me, sir, against that boy." He turned and saw a lad with a musket, taking deliberate aim at a wounded British officer, lying in a corner of a worm fence. Wilkinson ordered the boy to desist, and discovered the wounded man to be Major Ackland. He had him conveyed to the quarters of General Poor (now the residence of Mr. Neilson), on the heights, where every attention was paid to his wants.

When the intelligence that he was wounded and a prisoner reached his wife, she was greatly distressed, and, by the advice of her friend, the Baroness Riedesel, resolved to visit the American camp, and implore the favor of a personal attendance upon her husband. On the 9th she sent a message to Burgoyne by Lord Petersham, his aid, asking permission to depart. "Though I was ready to believe," says Burgoyne, "that patience and fortitude, in a supreme degree, were to be found, as well as every other virtue. under the most tender forms, I was astonished at this proposal. After so long an agitation of spirits, exhausted not only for want of rest, but absolutely want of food, drenched in rains for twelve hours together, that a woman should be capable of such an undertaking as delivering herself to an enemy, probably in the night, and uncertain of what hands she might fall into, appeared an effort above human nature. The assistance I was enabled to give was small indeed ; I had not even a cup of wine to offer her ; but I was told she had found, from some kind and fortunate hand, a little rum and dirty water. All I could furnish to her was an open boat and a few lines, written upon dirty wet paper, to General Gates. recommending her to his protection."[1]

October.
1777.

She set out in an open boat upon the Hudson, accompanied by Mr. Brudenell the chaplain, Sarah Pollard her waiting-maid, and her husband's valet, who had been severely wounded while searching for his master upon the battle-field. It was about sunset when they started, and a violent storm of rain and wind, which had been increasing since morning, rendered the voyage tedious and perilous in the extreme. It was long after dark when they reached the American outposts. The sentinel heard their oars and hailed them. Lady Harriet returned the answer herself. The clear, silvery tones of a woman's voice amid the darkness filled the soldier on duty with superstitious fear, and he called a comrade to accompany him to the river bank. The errand of the voyagers was made known, but the faithful guard, apprehensive of treachery, would not allow them to land until they sent for Major Dearborn. This delay was only for a few minutes, not "seven or eight dark and cold hours," as asserted by Burgoyne. They were invited by that officer to his quarters, where a cup of tea and other comforts were provided ; and Lady Harriet was also comforted by the joyful tidings that her husband was safe. In the morning she experienced parental tenderness from General Gates, who sent her to her husband at Poor's quarters, under a suitable escort. There she remained until he was removed to Albany.[2]

---

[1] The following is a copy of the note from Burgoyne to General Gates : " Sir—Lady Harriet Ackland. a lady of the first distinction of family, rank, and personal virtues, is under such concern on account of Major Ackland, her husband, wounded and a prisoner in your hands, that I can not refuse her request to commit her to your protection. Whatever general impropriety there may be in persons in my situation and yours to solicit favors, I can not see the uncommon perseverance in every female grace and exaltation of character of this lady, and her very hard fortune, without testifying that your attentions to her will lay me under obligations.　　　　　　　　　　　　" I am, sir, your obedient servant,
" J. BURGOYNE."*

[2] Major Ackland reciprocated the generous treatment here extended, by doing all in his power, while on parole in New York, to alleviate the condition of distinguished American prisoners there. After his

* The original is among Gates's papers (vol. x.), in the possession of the New York Historical Society, from which this was copied.

When we consider the delicate form, the gentleness and refinement in which she had been nurtured in the lap of rank and fortune, the shining virtues of connubial constancy, heroic devotion, and unbending fortitude stand out in bold relief in the character of Lady Harriet Ackland; and these, in their practical development in her case, furnish romance with a stranger page than imagination can command, and lend to poetry half its inspiration. They gave impulse to the lyre of the accomplished lady of Perez Morton, Esq.; and I will close this chapter with an extract from her poem, suggested by the events above noticed.

> " To gallant Gates, in war serenely brave,
> The tide of fortune turns its refluent wave;
> Forced by his arms, the bold invaders yield
> The prize and glory of the well-fought field:
> Bleeding and lost, the captured *Ackland* lies,
> While leaden slumber seals his Fraser's eyes;
> *Fraser!* whose deeds unfading glories claim,
> Endeared by virtues and adorned by fame.
>   *   *   *   *   *   *   *
> 'Twas now the time, when twilight's misty ray
> Drops the brown curtain of retiring day,
> The clouds of heaven, like midnight mountains, lower,
> Waft the wild blast and dash the drizzly shower,
> Through the wet path her restless footsteps roam,
> To where *the leader* spread his spacious dome.
> Low at his feet she pours the desperate prayer—
> Give my lost husband to my soothing care,
> Give me in yonder solitary cave,
> With duteous love, his burning wounds to lave;
> On the warm pillow which his breast supplies,
> Catch his faint breath and close his languid eyes,
> Or in his cause my proffered life resign—
> Mine were his blessings, and his pains were mine."

return to England, he warmly defended American courage, at a dinner party, against the aspersions of a Lieutenant Lloyd. High words passed, and a duel ensued. The major was shot dead; Lady Harriet became a maniac, and remained so two years. After her recovery, she married Mr Brudenell, the chaplain already mentioned.

CHAPTER III.

URGOYNE and his army are at Wilbur's Basin, prepared to retreat toward Lake Champlain, but lingering to pay a last sad tribute of affectionate regard to the remains of the accomplished Fraser. Night has drawn its veil over the scene, and we will turn away for a moment from the sorrowful contemplation of war and its horrid retinue, to glance at a picture lovely to the eye, ennobling to the spirit, and fruitful of pleasant impressions upon the heart and memory.

Like a " dissolving view," the smoking ruins, the sodden field, the trailing banner, the tent and breast-work and abatis, and slaughtered hundreds, and wailing families, painted in gore by the hand of human discord ; and the roar of cannon, the rattle of musketry, the roll of drums, the hiss and detonation of bombs, the savage yell, the loud huzza, the shriek and groan, the prayer and curse made audible by the boastful voice of physical strength, have all passed away with the darkness, and a bright summer's sunlight is upon the landscape. Turning the eye northward from the American camp, there are the same gentle slopes, and deep ravines, and clustering hills, and flowing river ; and the heights of Saratoga in the far distance loom up as of yore. But herds are grazing upon the lowlands, and flocks are dotting the hills ; the ring of the mower's scythe is heard in the meadow, and the merry laugh goes up from the russet harvest-field. Art, with its strong arm of industry, has dug another river along the plain for the use of commerce ; the forest has been reaped by agriculture, habitations of prosperity are on every hand, and the white wing of peace is spread out over all. It is a pleasant sight ; therefore let us enjoy it, and, for a while, forget the dark picture of the past which we have been contemplating.

I spent nearly the whole of the day rambling and sketching upon the camp and battle grounds of Stillwater. It was excessively warm, although a strong breeze $\quad$ July 27 1848. from the south constantly prevailed. As early as ten o'clock dark clouds began to rise in the west, and the rumbling of distant thunder was audible. All day long, shower after shower arose threateningly, sometimes approaching so near that sharp claps of thunder would startle us ; but they all swept along the horizon west and north, and disappeared behind the eastern hills. Not a drop of rain fell at Bemis's. I remarked the phenomenon, and was told that showers never reached there from the west. Their birth-place seems to be Saratoga Lake, about six miles westward from the Hudson, and the summer rain-clouds which rise there generally pass up the lake to its outlet, the Fish Creek, and, traversing that stream until it falls into the Hudson, cross the valley and pass on to the Green Mountains, or spend their treasures upon the intervening country.

About half past three in the afternoon a canal packet arrived from the south, and we embarked for Schuylerville, nine miles above Bemis's. As usual, the boat was crowded to excess, and, the sun being veiled by the clouds in the west, the passengers covered the deck. As we passed quietly along the base of the hills whereon was Gates's camp, crossed Mill Creek or Middle Ravine, and approached Wilbur's Basin, it required but small exercise of the imagination, while listening to the constant roll of thunder beyond the heights, to realize the appalling sounds of that strife of armies which shook those hills seventy years before, as it fell upon the eager ears of wives, and sisters, and children whose cherished ones were in the midst of the storm.

Proceeding northward, we approached the track of the showers, and, just before we reached Wilbur's Basin, a cloud, black as Erebus, and so low that it seemed to rest upon the hill-tops, spread out above us like the wings of a monster bird ; and in its wake huge masses of vapor, wheeling like the eddies of a whirlpool, came hastening on.   The experienced boatmen understood these portents, and covering the baggage with strong canvas, lashed it tightly to the vessel.   The breeze was still, and a hot, suffocating calm ensued. The passengers, warned by the helmsman, retreated into the cabin, and the windows were closed.   The cattle in the fields huddled in groups, and every bird and fowl, conscious of impending danger, sought shelter.   A flash of lightning, followed instantly by a crashing thunder-peal, broke over the valley, and seemed to sever the fetters of the wind.   A sullen roar was heard in the distance, like the rush of great waters ; the trees of the forest began to rock, and from the roads behind us clouds of dust arose and filled the air.   In a few moments a tornado was upon us in its strength.   It lasted only two minutes, but in its track the results of the labor of the farmer for many days were destroyed.   Hay-cocks and wheat sheaves were scattered like thistle-down, and the standing grain was laid upon the earth as by the tread of a giant footstep.   As the wind passed by, the rain came down gently, and continued to fall until we reached Schuylerville.

There came on the boat at Bemis's " a poor exile from Erin," with a patched coat and pair of thin pantaloons hanging over one arm.   He was immediately introduced to the captain by the attentive steward, when he pleaded poverty, and declared that he hadn't a "cint in the world."   He was ordered ashore, and the boat was guided accommodatingly near the bank.   The poor fellow urged fatigue, and the weight of his brogans testified to the truth of the appeal, if he had walked a mile.   It was cruel to doubt the honesty of that hard-favored face, and fifty cents were soon collected for him as a peace-offering to the captain.   When the gust came on, he refused to go into the cabin.   He had been in a three days' gale upon the Atlantic, and was not to be frightened by a squall on land.   The first blast of the hurricane wheeled him several times around upon deck, and came very near putting him ashore, willing or not willing.   While he was endeavoring to seize a support, the wind grasped his extra pantaloons, and, in utter dismay, he saw them gyrating, like a spread eagle, high in air, and becoming " small by degrees and beautifully less" in the distance.   The loss distressed him greatly—far more than the helmsman thought necessary, and he ordered him to be quiet.   " Indade," said the poor fellow, " do ye think a man can be quiet when the wind is rolling him like a bag o' feathers tied fast at one end, and all he has in the world snatched from him by the blackguard gale ?" and he looked agonizingly toward the point where his pantaloons had vanished.

" Precious small estate," answered the amused helmsman, " if a pair of old pantaloons is all you have in the world.   I'll give you a better pair than that if you'll stop your noise."

" An' wid three Vickeys sowed up in the waistbands ?" eagerly inquired the exile.

His cautiousness was here at fault.   He hadn't a " cint in the world," but he had three sovereigns sewed up in the waistbands of the pantaloons which had gone a-ballooning.   As soon as the gale passed by, a child of the Green Isle was a foot-passenger upon the towpath, bearing sorrowful testimony to the truth of the ethical maxim, that retributive justice is always swift to punish offenders against truth and honesty.   No doubt his thoughts were all with his absconded sub-treasurer, and the prose of Holmes's poem evidently engrossed his mind :

> "I saw them straddling through the air,
>   Alas ! too late to win them;
> I saw them chase the clouds as if
>   The devil had been in them.
> They were my darlings and my pride,
>   *They carried all my riches :*
> 'Farewell, farewell !' I faintly cried,
>   ' My breeches ! O my breeches !' "

It was about four o clock when we passed the burial-place of General Fraser.   It had been my intention to stop there for an hour, and visit the last earth-home of the illustrious dead.   But the rain fell fast, and the day was so far consumed that I was obliged to forego the melancholy pleasure.   The canal is so near the base of the hill, that I easily made the sketch of it (printed on page 67) from the cabin-window.   Many years ago a distant rela-tive of the general proposed to remove his remains to Scotland, and lay them beside those of his mother ; but they are still undisturbed where his sorrowing comrades laid them.

We reached the little settlement of Coveville at half past four, the rain still falling gently. This was formerly Do-ve-gat, or Van Vechten's Cove, as it was sometimes called, the place where the British tarried from the 15th till the 17th of September, while a working party repaired the roads and bridges in advance to Wilbur's Basin.   Here was the residence of Colonel Van Vechten, of the Saratoga militia, one of General Gates's staff.   He was a zealous Whig, and the active Tories, whose plans his vigilance often frustrated, were greatly imbittered against him politically, while they honored him as a brave man and good neighbor.[1]   Burgoyne, on his retreat to Saratoga after the battle of the 7th of October, ordered the dwellings of several Whigs to be destroyed ; and at Do-ve-gat the buildings of Colonel Van Vechten were the first to which the torch of the invader was laid.   His family fled to Albany on the approach of Burgoyne from Fort Edward ; and when they returned, late in October, their fine estate was a perfect wreck, and they had no shelter for their heads.

Colonel Van Vechten was at Albany, on public business, at the time of the first battle on Bemis's Heights.   He had received an order from the Committee of Safety at that city, when Burgoyne marched from Fort Edward, to remove every Tory or disaffected person from his vicinage into Connecticut.   This order touched his excellent heart with grief, for many of those included in the proscription were his neighbors, and some were his personal friends, who honestly differed from him in relation to the momentous political questions at issue.   Within six hours after receiving the order he was in Albany, and procured its re-call.   The humanity, policy, and sound wisdom of that step were soon illustrated by the firm support which some of these disaffected ones gave to the American cause.

We landed at Schuylerville in the midst of " sun and shower," for the sky was clear in the west, yet the rain-drops came glittering down profusely.   The Fish Creek, which here has a succession of falls and rapids for nearly a mile, affording fine water-power for several mills, was brimful with the showers of the day, and poured its flood, roaring and foaming, under the canal viaduct with such force as to shake the solid masonry.   It empties its waters into the Hudson about one hundred rods east of the canal, at the southeast angle of Old Fort Hardy, now among the buried things of the past.   Upon the plain north of the creek, near the old fort, the forces of Burgoyne laid down their arms ; and on every side of that pleas-ant village scenes of historic interest lie scattered.   The earth was too wet to invite a sun-set ramble, and we contented ourselves with viewing the beauty of the scene that spread out before us eastward while loitering upon the upper piazza of the Schuylerville House.

1777.

1777.

---

[1] I have already had occasion to use the terms *Whig* and *Tory*, and shall do so often in the course of this work.   They were copied by us from the political vocabulary of Great Britain, and were first used here, to distinguish the opposing parties in the Revolution, about 1770.   The term originated during the reign of Charles II., or about that time.   Bishop Burnet, in his *History of his own Times*, gives the following explanation : " The southwest counties of Scotland have seldom corn enough to serve them round the year : and the northern parts producing more than they need, those in the west come in the summer to buy at Leith the stores that come from the north ; and, from a word, *whiggam*, used in driving their horses, all that drove were called *whiggamores*, and shorter, *whiggs*.   Now in that year, after the news came down of Duke Hamilton's defeat, the ministers animated their people to rise and march to Edinburgh, and then came up marching at the head of their parishes, with unheard-of fury, praying and preaching all the way as they came.   The Marquis of Argyle and his party came and headed them, they being about six thou-sand.   This was called the Whiggamore's inroad, and ever after that *all that opposed the courts* came, in contempt, to be called Whigg ; and from Scotland the word was brought into England, where it is now one of our unhappy terms of distinction."   Subsequently all whose party bias was *democratic* were called Whigs.   The origin of the word *Tory* is not so well attested.   The Irish malcontents, half robbers and half insurgents, who harassed the English in Ireland at the time of the massacre in 1640, were the first to whom this epithet was applied.   It was also applied to the court party as a term of reproach.—*See, also,* *Macaulay's History of England*, i., 240.

It was, indeed, a charming scene, enhanced by the associations of the vicinity. The face of nature was washed clean by the drenching showers; the trees and shrubs were brilliant green; and from the clustering knolls or loftier hills beyond the Hudson, once bristling with bayonets or wreathed by the smoke of cannon, the evening sunlight was reflected back by the myriad rain-drops lying upon trees, and grass, and blooming corn. Nor was this all. Upon the dark background of the hills was Iris,

> "That beautiful one,
> Whose arch is refraction, whose keystone the sun;
> In the hues of its grandeur sublimely it stood
> O'er the river, the village, the field, and the wood."
>
> CHARLES SWAIN.

Springing from the plain, its double arch spanned the whole ground where British pride was humbled and American valor acknowledged. I never gazed upon the "bow of promise" with so much interest, for thought unconsciously bridged over the chasm of seventy buried years, and it seemed for a moment as if the dark hours of our rebellious conflict had returned, and that in the covenant seal before me the eye of hope read prophetically the history of the happy present. As the sun went down and the bow faded, the Spirit of Beauty left traces of its pencil on my thoughts, and I felt, with "AMELIA," that

> "There are moments, bright moments, when the spirit receives
> Whole volumes of thought on its unwritten leaves,
> When the folds of the heart in a moment unclose,
> Like the innermost leaves from the heart of the rose;
> And thus, when the rainbow had passed from the sky,
> The thoughts it awoke were too deep to pass by;
> It left my full soul like the wings of a dove,
> All flutt'ring with pleasure, and flutt'ring with love."

In the evening I visited the son of Colonel Van Vechten just named, a man of three score and ten years. His memory is unclouded, and extends back to the closing scenes of the Revolution. His father stored that memory with the verbal history of his times, and every noteworthy locality of Saratoga is as familiar to him as the flower-beds of his beautiful garden. He kindly offered to be my guide in the morning to all the places here made memorable by the events connected with the surrender of Burgoyne.

While awaiting the dawn, let us turn to the past, and view occurrences from the burial of Fraser to the closing scenes of the drama.

October, 1777. As soon as the funeral ceremonies at Fraser's burial were ended on the evening of the 8th, Burgoyne, fearing that the Americans (whose forces constantly increased, and whose activity denoted preparations for some bold movement) might succeed in turning his right and surrounding him, commenced a night march toward Saratoga. A retreat was anticipated by General Gates, and, previous to the action on the 7th, he sent General Fellows with a detachment of fourteen hundred men to occupy the high grounds east of the Hudson, opposite the Saratoga ford, intending, in case the enemy retreated, to follow so closely in pursuit as to be able to re-enforce that officer from the ranks of the main army. He also sent another detachment, after the action, to occupy ground higher up near Fort Miller, and ordered a selected corps of two thousand men to push forward and occupy the heights beyond Saratoga, in the direction of Lake George. But the retreat of Burgoyne was at a time when Gates least expected it. The troops of the former had been in motion all the night before, and under arms all day on the 8th, and he supposed that they would tarry for rest until the morning of the 9th.

At sunset on the 8th a lurid haziness in the west indicated an approaching storm, and before midnight the rain began to fall. The enemy felt that his situation was too perilous to be maintained, and the whole British army commenced its march at nine o'clock in the evening. The loss of Fraser was now severely felt, for he had always showed as consummate skill in managing a retreat as bravery in leading to an attack. General Riedesel commanded the van-guard and General Phillips the rear-guard.   The night was so dark, the rain so incessant in the morning, and the roads were so bad, that the royal army did not reach Saratoga until the evening of the 9th.   They made a halt about six o'clock in the morning, and General Riedesel, exhausted by fatigue, went into the caleche in which his wife and children were, and slept soundly for about three hours.   Wet and weary, and harassed by the Americans all the way, the poor soldiers were too much exhausted even to cut wood for fires, and they lay down upon the cold, wet ground and slept.   The generals reposed in the open air, upon mattresses, with no other covering than oil-cloth.   The Baroness Reidesel and other women of the British camp were obliged to submit to these privations.   " My dress," the former says, " was wet through and through with rain, and in this state I had to remain the whole night, having no place to change it ; I, however, got close to a large fire, and at last lay down on some straw.   At this moment General Phillips came up to me, and I asked him why he had not continued our retreat, as my husband had promised to cover it and bring the army through.   ' Poor dear woman,' he said, ' I wonder how, drenched as you are, you have the courage still to persevere, and venture further in this kind of weather.   I wish,' he continued, ' you were our commanding general ; General Burgoyne is tired, and means to halt here to-night and give us our supper.' "[1]   No doubt there was more sincerity than compliment in General Phillips's wish, for the frequent halts and great delays of Burgoyne had dissatisfied his officers, and were, doubtless, chief causes of his misfortunes.   His ambition and his love of ease were often wrestling, and the latter too frequently gained the mastery.

The retreat of Burgoyne was so sudden, that he left all his sick and wounded in the hospital behind him, together with a great number of wheel carriages and other things collected at Wilbur's Basin.   The invalids, amounting to about three hundred, were treated by General Gates with the utmost humanity, which Burgoyne afterward gratefully acknowledged. On retiring, the English burned the houses they had occupied, and many other things which they could not carry away with them.   They also wantonly set fire to several buildings on the way, by order of Burgoyne himself ; and among others, when they crossed the Fish Creek, the mansion of General Schuyler, his mills and other property, amounting in value to twenty thousand dollars, were destroyed by them.

The house of General Schuyler was elegant for the times, and was very pleasantly situated upon the south bank of the Fish Kill or Fish Creek.   It was rebuilt after the war but in a style much inferior in beauty and expense.   It is still standing, and in the present possession of George Strover, Esq.   The broad lawn in front is beautifully shaded with venerable trees ; and the falls of the Fish Creek close by contribute, by their music and wild beauty, much to the interest of the scene.   The mill was also rebuilt in the same style.   In the engraving is given a correct representation of it.   Many of the logs in the dam are the same that curbed the stream in the time of the Revolution ; and I was told that little was wanted to make the whole appear as at that period, but that the surrounding hills should be covered with dense woods.

SCHUYLER'S MILLS, SARATOGA.

The rain was so heavy on the 9th, that General Gates did not commence his pursuit until nearly noon on the tenth.   The

[1] Letters of the Baroness Riedesel.

detachment under Fellows was unconsciously in a perilous situation for want of re-enforce-

GENERAL SCHUYLER'S MANSION.

ments. Resting in supposed security on the night of the 9th, his camp was left so entirely unguarded that an officer, who had been sent forward by Burgoyne to reconnoiter, marched all around it without meeting a sentinel! This neglect would have been fatal if Burgoyne had known the exact position of his enemies around him. The officer urged him to allow him to surprise Fellows, but misfortune had made the British general wary and suspicious, and, fortunately for the Americans, the request was denied.

The main army of Gates reached the high ridge between Saratoga Church and the Fish Creek at about four in the afternoon of the 10th. The British had crossed over the creek, and were encamped upon the high grounds on the slope of which Schuylerville is now built.[1] The two armies were within the sound of each other's music. The boats of Burgoyne, with his baggage and provisions, were at the mouth of the creek. A fatigue party began to carry the stores from the boats to the heights, but Fellows constantly played upon them with two field pieces stationed on the flats beyond the river, and they were obliged to retreat to the camp. Several of the bateaux of the enemy, with their provisions, were captured, and immediately became objects of plunder for the raw militia and motley followers of the army. Even the Continental troops were implicated in taking "pay and rations" for services, directly from the enemy, instead of receiving them through the paymaster. These irregularities became so extensive that General Gates issued an order on the 12th, in which he declared that he "saw so many scandalous and mean transactions committed by persons who sought more after plunder than the honor of doing their duty, that it was his unalterable resolution to have the first person who should thereafter be detected in pillaging the baggage and stores taken from the enemy, tried and punished with the utmost severity of the military law."[2]

Finding the ford across the Hudson strongly guarded by the Americans, Burgoyne resolved to continue his retreat up the right bank of the river to the front of Fort Edward, force his way across, and take possession of that fortress. He sent forward a working party, consisting chiefly of loyalists, guarded by Fraser's marksmen, to repair the bridges and open the roads, and also a detachment of troops to take possession of the fort. The Americans, who were spreading out in small detachments upon every height, on all sides, soon drove the workmen back into the camp; and the British troops found the fort in the possession of two hundred Americans, under Colonel Cochrane. The militia were flocking to the fort to strengthen the garrison, and the enemy, believing the Americans to be as numerous in front as in rear, hastily retreated back to their lines.

---

[1] The village of Schuylerville is on the north bank of the Fish Creek. Old Saratoga, with its church, was on the south side. The church was about eight hundred yards south of the creek, on the road to Albany.

[2] It is said that when Burgoyne proposed in council, on the 13th, to retreat precipitately, he mildly reproached Major Skene, a stanch loyalist, with having brought him into this difficulty by injudicious advice, particularly with regard to the expedition to Bennington. "You have brought me into this difficulty," he said; "now advise me how to get out of it." "Scatter your baggage, stores, and every thing else that can be spared, at proper distances," replied the major, "and the militia will be so engaged in collecting and securing the same, that the troops will have an opportunity of getting clear off."

[3] The two victories on Bemis's Heights greatly inspirited the Americans, and when, after the last battle, General Gates, in order to make victory secure, applied to the Legislature of New Hampshire for more troops, the militia turned out with alacrity. The speaker of the Assembly, John Langdon, Esq., upon receiving the application, immediately proposed an adjournment, and that as many members as could should set off directly as volunteers for the cause, taking with them all the men they could collect. It was agreed to, and done by himself and others.—*Gordon,* ii., 262.

Thus the cloud of perils thickened around Burgoyne. He now abandoned all idea of saving his artillery and baggage, and saw no other mode of escape than a precipitate retreat. The provisions and other stores in his bateaux were captured or destroyed by the republicans, and from every direction he was galled by a desultory fire from cannon and small arms. So overwhelming was the number of the Americans, that to fight would be madness, and Burgoyne lost all hope of saving his doomed army.

But in the midst of all these perils and despondencies, a stratagem of the British commander, suggested by an erring apprehension on the part of General Gates, aided by the occurrence of a natural phenomenon, came very near being successful, and for a time greatly cheered the drooping spirits of the enemy. Rumor reached General Gates that the whole British army had moved toward Fort Edward, leaving only a small detachment, as a rear-guard, in defense of the camp. This rumor originated from the march of the detachment already mentioned, which was sent forward to Fort Edward. General Gates, therefore, determined to cross the Fish Creek on the morning of the 11th, fall in full force upon and crush the British rear-guard, and make a vigorous pursuit after the main body.

By some means this determination of Gates's became known to Burgoyne, and he resolved to profit by the false rumor. He left a strong guard at the battery on the creek, and concealed his troops in the thicket, a few rods in the rear. In the morning the sky was cloudless, but a thick fog rested upon the whole country and obscured every object. This was hailed as a favorable event by both generals, Gates supposing that it would veil his movements from the British rear-guard, and Burgoyne confidently believing that it would conceal his ambush, and that victory was now certain.

The brigades of Generals Nixon and Glover, and Morgan's corps, were ordered to cross the creek and fall upon the enemy's camp. Morgan advanced at about daylight, the fog being so thick that he could see but a few rods around him. He at once fell in with the British pickets, who poured in a volley upon him and killed a lieutenant and several privates. Morgan instantly conceived that the rumor was false, and that the enemy was in force near. At that moment Deputy Adjutant-general Wilkinson, who had been sent by Gates to reconnoiter, rode up, and, coinciding in opinion with Morgan, hastened to report to his commander the supposed peril of his corps. The brigades of Patterson and Learned were immediately dispatched to its support. Nixon and Glover were at the same time pressing forward to attack the camp, while the whole army advanced to the heights immediately south of the creek. Nixon crossed the creek to the plain, and surprised a picket guard at Fort Hardy; and Glover was about to follow him, when a British soldier was seen hastily fording the stream. He was captured, and professed to be a deserter. Glover questioned him, and was informed that the entire British army were in their camp, drawn up in order of battle. The general suspected him of untruth, and threatened him with instant death if he should deceive him. The soldier declared that he was an honest deserter, and solemnly affirmed the truth of his tale, which was soon confirmed by a German deserter, and by

the capture of a reconnoitering party, consisting of a subaltern and thirty-five men, by the advance guard, under Captain Goodale, of Putnam's regiment. The deserter was immediately sent with one of Glover's aids to General Gates, and information was forwarded to General Nixon, with urgent advice to halt. Satisfied of the deserter's truth, Gates revoked all the orders of the evening previous, and directed the troops to return to their respective positions. His headquarters were nearly a mile in the rear of his army, and his order came almost too late to save the troops, who had

GENERAL GATES'S HEADQUARTERS AT SARATOGA.[1]

---

[1] This house is still standing. The view is taken from the road, a few rods southwest of the building.

already crossed the creek, from destruction, for the fog soon passed away and discovered them to the enemy, then in full view, and under arms upon the heights. Nixon, however, had retreated, and the cannonade opened upon him by the British took effect only upon the rear of his brigade.[1]

General Learned, in the mean while, with his own and Patterson's brigades, had reached Morgan's corps, and was pressing on rapidly to the attack when Wilkinson came up, not with a counter order from Gates, but with the intelligence that the right wing of the Americans had given way. The brave veteran disliked the idea of retreating, preferring to carry out the standing order of the previous day to the very letter;[2] but, on counseling with Colonels Brooks and Tupper, and some other officers, a retreat was deemed advisable. As they turned, the British, who were awaiting an attack, opened a fire upon them; but the Americans were soon masked by the woods, and Morgan took post upon the flank and rear of the enemy.

Thus, by the providential circumstance of a deserter flying to our camp, our army was saved from a terrible, perhaps fatal, loss; for, had the several brigades of Nixon, Glover, Learned, and Patterson been cut off, Burgoyne might have so much weakened the American army, and strengthened his own by the adherence of the now wavering loyalists and Indians, as to scatter the remainder of the Continental forces and reach Albany, the darling object of all his efforts. But the breath of the deserter blasted all his hopes, and the incident was, to use his own words, "one of the most adverse strokes of fortune during the campaign."[3]

Burgoyne now saw no way of escape. He sent out scouts toward the north, who reported the roads impassable and the woods swarming with republicans. The few Indians who had remained now left him, utterly disheartened; and the loyalists, feeling that their personal security would be jeoparded in case of a surrender, left the army every hour. It was proposed to make a scattered retreat, each soldier carrying in his knapsack provisions enough for two or three days, Fort George being the place of rendezvous; but such a step would be perilous in the extreme, for the Americans, apparently as numerous as the leaves upon the trees, and ever on the alert, would cut them off in detail. In battle, a fortunate circumstance might occur in their favor; but General Gates, assured that he had his enemy in his power, could not be induced to jeopard the lives of his troops by an engagement. Burgoyne's only hope rested upon aid from Clinton below. Not a word, however, could he get from that general; yet, clinging with desperation to every hope, however feeble, he resolved to await that succor quietly in his strong camp as long as his exhausted stores and a powerful enemy would allow.

Burgoyne's camp, upon the heights near the Fish Creek, was fortified, and, extending more than half a mile in the rear, was strengthened by artillery. On an elevated plain, northwest of the village of Schuylerville, his heavy guns were chiefly posted. Directly in his rear Morgan and his corps were stationed. In front, on the east side of the Hudson,

---

It is of wood, and has been somewhat enlarged since the Revolution. It was used by General Gates for his quarters from the 10th of October until after the surrender of Burgoyne on the 17th. It belonged to a Widow Kershaw, and General Gates amply compensated her for all he had. on leaving it. It is now well preserved. It stands on the east side of the Albany and Whitehall turnpike, about a mile and a half south of the Fish Creek. The Champlain Canal passes immediately in the rear of it; and nearly half a mile eastward is the Hudson River.

[1] John Nixon was born at Framingham, Massachusetts, March 4th, 1725. He was at the siege of Louisburg in 1745, was captain in the provincial troops under Abercrombie at Ticonderoga, and was esteemed a valiant soldier during the whole of the French and Indian war. He took the patriot side when our Revolution broke out. He was one of the minute men at the Lexington battle, was at the head of a regiment in the battle of Bunker Hill, and was made a brigadier in the Continental army in August, 1776. He was then placed in command at Governor's Island, near New York. In the battle of Bemis's Heights a cannon-ball passed so near his head it impaired the sight of one eye and the hearing of one ear. On account of ill health, he resigned his commission in 1780. He died March 24th, 1815, aged 90 years.

[2] The standing order was, "In case of an attack against any point, whether front, flank, or rear, the troops are to fall on the enemy at all quarters."

[3] Letter to Lord George Germain, dated Albany 20th, 1777.

Fellows, with three thousand troops, was strongly intrenched. The main body of the Amer ican army, under Gates, was on the south side of the Fish Creek; and in every direction small detachments of Continentals or republican militia were vigorously watching the enemy at bay.[1] Fort Edward was in possession of the Americans, and upon high ground in the vicinity of Glenn's Falls they had a fortified camp.

Burgoyne was completely environed, and every part of the royal camp was exposed to

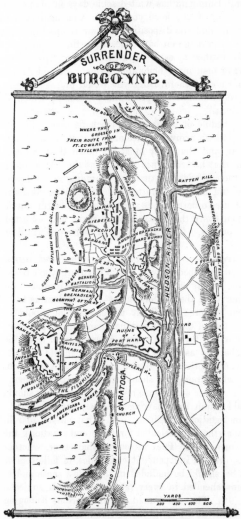

the fire of cannon and musketry. The soldiers slept under arms continually. There was not a place of safety for the sick, wounded, and dying, or for the wom en and children of the officers and soldiers. There was no secure place for a council. None dared go to the river for water, and thirst began to distress the camp.[2] The desertions of the Indians and Canadians, the cowardice and disaffection of the loy alists, and the losses in killed and wound ed, had so thinned Burgoyne's ranks, that his army was reduced one half, and a large proportion of those who remained were not Englishmen. There was not bread for three days in store, and of course none could be obtained. Not a word came from General Clinton, and Burgoyne was totally ignorant of his having made any movement up the Hudson. The last ray of hope faded away, and toward the even ing of the 12th the British commander held a council with Generals Reidesel, Phillips, and Hamilton. It was decided to retreat before morning, if possible; but returning scouts brought only hopeless in telligence respecting the roads and the strength of the enemy.

On the morning of the 13th Burgoyne called a general council of all officers, in cluding captains of companies. Their de liberations were held in a large tent, which was several times perforated by musket balls from the Americans. Several grape shot struck near the tent, and an eighteen pound cannon-ball swept across the table at which sat Burgoyne and the other gen erals. Their deliberations were short, as might be expected, and it was unanimous ly resolved to open a treaty with General Gates for an honorable surrender. It was a bitter pill for the proud lieutenant general, but there was no alternative.

---

[1] By reference to the above map, the position of the two armies at this juncture will be more clearly un derstood. They held the same relative position until the surrender on the 17th.

[2] The consideration of Americans for women was conspicuously displayed at this time. While every man who went to the river for water became a target for the sure marksmen of the Americans, a soldier's wife went back and forth as often as she pleased, and not a gun was pointed at her.

Proposition of Burgoyne to surrender his Troops.	Terms proposed by Gates.	Terms finally agreed upon.

Toward evening a flag was sent to General Gates, with a note, intimating that General Burgoyne was desirous of sending a field officer to him upon a matter of great moment to both armies, and wishing to know at what hour the next morning it would suit General Gates to receive him. The reply was, " At ten o'clock, at the advanced post of the army of the United States." Accordingly, Lieutenant Kingston, Burgoyne's adjutant general, appeared at the appointed hour and delivered the following note from his commander : " After having fought you twice, Lieutenant-general Burgoyne has waited some days in his present position, determined to try a third conflict against any force you could bring against him. He is apprized of your superiority of numbers, and the disposition of your troops to impede his supplies, and render his retreat a scene of carnage on both sides. In this situation, he is impelled by humanity, and thinks himself justified by established principles and precedents of state and war, to spare the lives of brave men upon honorable terms. Should Major general Gates be inclined to treat upon that idea, General Burgoyne would propose a cessa tion of arms during the time necessary to communicate the preliminary terms by which, in any extremity, he and his army mean to abide."

General Gates had already prepared a schedule of terms upon which he was willing to treat. It enumerated the distresses of the British army, and declared that they could only be allowed to surrender as prisoners of war, and that they must lay down their arms in their camp. Burgoyne replied, with spirit, that he would not admit that the retreat of his army was cut off while they had arms in their hands, and that the degrading act of laying down their arms within their own camp would not be submitted to. The latter condition was waived, and in the afternoon General Gates ordered a cessation of hostilities till sunset. Negotiations continued until the 16th, when every thing was agreed upon and adjusted, ready for the signatures of the contracting parties. This last act was to be performed on the morning of the 17th.

The substance of the " *Convention between Lieutenant-general Burgoyne and Major-general Gates*," as the British commander superscribed it, was, 1st. That Burgoyne's troops were to march out of their camp with all the honors of war, the artillery to be moved to the verge of the Hudson, and there left, together with the soldiers' arms—the said arms to be piled by word of command from their own officers ; 2d. That a free passage should be granted the troops to Great Britain, on condition of their not serving again during the war ; 3d. That if any cartel should take place by which Burgoyne's army, or any part of it, should be exchanged, the foregoing article should be void as far as such exchange should extend ; 4th. That the army should march to the neighborhood of Boston by the most expeditious and convenient route, and not be delayed when transports should arrive to receive them ; 5th. That every care should be taken for the proper subsistence of the troops till they should be embarked ; 6th. That all officers should retain their carriages, horses, bat-horses, &c., and their baggage, and be exempt from molestation or search ; 7th. That on the march, and while the army should remain at Boston (the port selected for their embarkation), the officers should not be separated from their men ; 8th. That all corps whatsoever, whether composed of sailors, bateaux-men, artificers, drivers, independent companies, or followers of the army, of whatever country they might be, should be included in the fullest sense and to the utmost extent of the articles, and comprehended in every respect as British subjects, whose general had capitulated for them ;[1] 9th. That all Canadians and persons belonging to the Canadian establishment should be permitted a free return to Canada, should be conducted by the shortest route to the British posts on Lake George, should be treated in all respects like the rest of the army, and should be bound by the same conditions not to serve during the war, unless exchanged ; 10th. That passports should be immediately granted for three officers, to carry Burgoyne's dispatches to General Howe at Philadelphia, to Sir Guy Carleton in Canada, and to the government of Great Britain by way of New York ; 11th. That all officers, during their stay in Boston, should be admitted to parole, and from

---

[1] This was to afford protection to the loyalists or Tories.

first to last be permitted to wear their side-arms ; 12th. That if the army found it necessary to send for their clothing and other baggage from Canada, they should be permitted to do so, and have the necessary passports granted them ; 13th. That these articles should be signed and exchanged on the following morning at nine o'clock, the troops to march out of their intrenchments at three o'clock in the afternoon.   Appended October 17. to these articles was an addendum or postscript, signed by General Gates, declaring that General Burgoyne, whose name was not mentioned in the above treaty, was fully comprehended in it.[1]

FAC-SIMILE OF THE SIGNATURES OF BURGOYNE AND GATES TO THE "CONVENTION."

During the night of the 16th Captain Campbell succeeded in eluding the American sentinels, and reached the British camp with dispatches from Sir Henry Clinton announcing his capture of the forts among the Hudson Highlands, and the expedition of Vaughan and Wallace as far up the river as Esopus.   Here was a ray of hope, and Burgoyne felt disposed to withhold his signature from the "convention."   General Gates was apprized of this, and of the cause which had excited new hopes in the British commander.   He was better acquainted, too, with the threatening aspect below than Burgoyne, and he knew that "delays are dangerous."   He drew up his army on the morning of the 17th in order of battle, and then sent a peremptory message to Burgoyne, that if the articles were not signed by him immediately, he should open a fire upon him.   Under the circumstances, the terms were exceedingly humane and honorable ; far more so than might be expected if the negotiation should be here broken off and again commenced. With reluctance Burgoyne subscribed his name, and preparations were immediately made for the ceremonies of surrender.

The British army left their camp upon the hills, and marched sorrowfully down upon the "green" or level plain in front of old Fort Hardy,[2] where the different companies were drawn up in parallel lines, and, by order of their several commanders, grounded their arms and emptied their cartridge-boxes.   They were not subject to the mortification of thus submitting under the gaze of an exulting foe, for General Gates, with a delicacy and magna-

---

[1] A copy of these articles, said to be in the handwriting of General Gates, and signed by the two commanders, is in the possession of the New York Historical Society, from which the above fac-similes were copied.

[2] Fort Hardy was situated at the junction of the Fish Creek with the Hudson River, on the north side of the former.   It was built of earth and logs, and was thrown up by the French, under Baron Dieskau, in 1755, when Sir William Johnson was making preparations at Albany to march against the French on Lakes Champlain and George.   It was abandoned by the French, and named by the English Fort Hardy, in honor of Sir Charles Hardy, who was that year appointed Governor of New York.   The lines of the intrenchments of the fort inclosed about fifteen acres, bounded south by the Fish Creek and east by the Hudson River.   This fort was a ruin at the time of the Revolution ; yet, when I visited it (July, 1848), many traces of its outworks were still visible.   Its form may be seen by reference to the map, page 77.   Many military relics have been found near the fort, and I was told that, in excavating for the Champlain Canal, a great number of human skeletons were found.   The workmen had, doubtless, struck upon the burial-place of the garrison.

nimity of feeling which drew forth the expressed admiration of Burgoyne and his officers, had ordered all his army within his camp, out of sight of the vanquished Britons.[1] Colonel Wilkinson, who had been sent to the British camp, and, in company with Burgoyne, selected the place where the troops were to lay down their arms, was the only American officer present at the scene.[2]

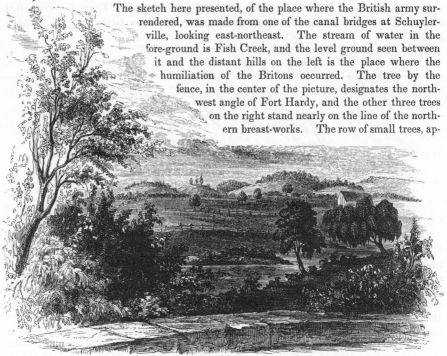

The sketch here presented, of the place where the British army surrendered, was made from one of the canal bridges at Schuylerville, looking east-northeast. The stream of water in the fore-ground is Fish Creek, and the level ground seen between it and the distant hills on the left is the place where the humiliation of the Britons occurred. The tree by the fence, in the center of the picture, designates the northwest angle of Fort Hardy, and the other three trees on the right stand nearly on the line of the northern breast-works. The row of small trees, ap-

VIEW OF THE PLACE WHERE THE BRITISH LAID DOWN THEIR ARMS.

parently at the foot of the distant hills, marks the course of the Hudson ; and the hills that bound the view are those on which the Americans were posted. This plain is directly in front of Schuylerville, between that village and the Hudson. General Fellows was stationed upon the high ground seen over the barn on the right, and the eminence on the extreme left is the place whence the American cannon played upon the house wherein the Baroness Reidesel and other ladies sought refuge.

As soon as the troops had laid down their arms, General Burgoyne proposed to be introduced to General Gates. They crossed Fish Creek, and proceeded toward headquarters, Burgoyne in front with his adjutant general, Kingston, and his aids-de-camp, Captain Lord Petersham and Lieutenant Wilford, behind him. Then followed Generals Phillips, Riedesel, and Hamilton, and other officers and suites, according to rank. General Gates was informed of the approach of Burgoyne, and with his staff met him at the head of his camp, about a mile south of the Fish Creek, Burgoyne in a rich uniform of scarlet and gold, and Gates in a plain blue frock-coat. When within about a sword's length, they reined up and halted. Colonel Wilkinson then named the gentlemen, and General Burgoyne, raising his hat gracefully, said, "The fortune of war, General Gates, has made me your prisoner." The victor promptly replied, "I shall always be ready to bear testimony that it has not

---

[1] Letter of Burgoyne to the Earl of Derby. Stedman, i., 352. Botta, ii., 21.   [2] See Wilkinson.

OF THE REVOLUTION. 81

Humiliating Review of the British Prisoners.   Burgoyne's Surrender of his Sword.   The Spoils of Victory.   Yankee Doodle.

been through any fault of your excellency." The other officers were introduced in turn, and the whole party repaired to Gates's headquarters, where a sumptuous dinner was served.[1]

SITE OF THE FIRST INTERVIEW BETWEEN GATES AND BURGOYNE.[2]

After dinner the American army was drawn up in parallel lines on each side of the road, extending nearly a mile. Between these victorious troops the British army, with light infantry in front, and escorted by a company of light dragoons, preceded by two mounted officers bearing the American flag, marched to the lively tune of Yankee Doodle.[3] Just as they passed, the two commanding generals, who were in Gates's marquee, came out together, and, fronting the procession, gazed upon it in silence a few moments. What a contrast, in every particular, did the two present! Burgoyne, though possessed of coarse features, had a large and commanding person ; Gates was smaller and far less dignified in appearance. Burgoyne was arrayed in the splendid military trappings of his rank ; Gates was clad in a plain and unassuming dress. Burgoyne was the victim of disappointed hopes and foiled ambition, and looked upon the scene with exceeding sorrow ; Gates was buoyant with the first flush of a great victory. Without exchanging a word, Burgoyne, according to previous understanding, stepped back, drew his sword, and, in the presence of the two armies, presented it to General Gates. He received it with a courteous inclination of the head, and instantly returned it to the vanquished general. They then retired to the marquee together, the British army filed off and took up their line of march for Boston, and thus ended the drama upon the heights of Saratoga.

The whole number of prisoners surrendered was five thousand seven hundred and ninety-one, of whom two thousand four hundred and twelve were Germans and Hessians. The force of the Americans, at the time of the surrender, was, according to a statement which General Gates furnished to Burgoyne, thirteen thousand two hundred and twenty-two, of which number nine thousand and ninety-three were Continentals, or regular soldiers, and four thousand one hundred and twenty-nine were militia. The arms and ammunition which came into the possession of the Americans were, a fine train of brass artillery, consisting of 2 twenty-four pounders, 4 twelve pounders, 20 sixes, 6 threes, 2 eight inch howitzers, 5 five and a half inch royal howitzers, and 3 five and a half inch royal mortars ;[4] in all forty-two

---

[1] See Wilkinson.

[2] This view is taken from the turnpike, looking south. The old road was where the canal now is, and the place of meeting was about at the point where the bridge is seen.

[3] Thatcher, in his Military Journal (p. 19), gives the following account of the origin of the word *Yankee* and of *Yankee Doodle :* "A farmer of Cambridge, Massachusetts, named Jonathan Hastings, who lived about the year 1713, used it as a favorite cant word to express excellence, as a *yankee* good horse or *yankee* good cider. The students of the college, hearing him use it a great deal, adopted it, and called him *Yankee Jonathan ;* and as he was a rather weak man, the students, when they wished to denote a character of that kind, would call him *Yankee Jonathan.* Like other cant words, it spread, and came finally to be applied to the New Englanders as a term of reproach. Some suppose the term to be the Indian corruption of the word English—*Yenglees, Yangles, Yankles,* and finally *Yankee.*

"A song, called *Yankee Doodle,* was written by a British sergeant at Boston, in 1775, to ridicule the people there, when the American army, under Washington, was encamped at Cambridge and Roxbury." See "Origin of Yankee Doodle," page 480, of this volume.

[4] Two of these, drawings of which will be found on page 700, are now in the court of the laboratory of the West Point Military Academy, on the Hudson.

pieces of ordnance.   There were four thousand six hundred and forty-seven muskets, and six thousand dozens of cartridges, besides shot, carcasses, cases, shells, &c.   Among the English prisoners were six members of Parliament.[1]

Cotemporary writers represent the appearance of the poor German and Hessian troops as extremely miserable and ludicrous.   They deserved commiseration, but they received none. They came not here voluntarily to fight our people ; they were sent as slaves by their masters, who received the price of their hire.   They were caught, it is said, while congregated in their churches and elsewhere, and forced into the service.   Most of them were torn reluctantly from their families and friends ; hundreds of them deserted here before the close of the war ; and many of their descendants are now living among us.   Many had their wives with them, and these helped to make up the pitiable procession through the country. Their advent into Cambridge, near Boston, is thus noticed by the lady of Dr. Winthrop of that town, in a letter to Mrs. Mercy Warren, an early historian of our Revolution : " On Friday we heard the Hessians were to make a procession on the same route.   We thought we should have nothing to do but view them as they passed.   To be sure, the sight was truly astonishing.   I never had the least idea that the creation produced such a sordid set of creatures in human figure—poor, dirty, emaciated men.   Great numbers of women, who seemed to be the beasts of burden, having bushel baskets on their backs, by which they were bent double.   The contents seemed to be pots and kettles, various sorts of furniture, children peeping through gridirons ánd other utensils.   Some very young infants, who were born on the road ; the women barefooted, clothed in dirty rags.   Such effluvia filled the air while they were passing, that, had they not been smoking all the time, I should have been apprehensive of being contaminated."[2]

The whole view of the vanquished army, as it marched through the country from Saratoga to Boston, a distance of three hundred miles, escorted by two or three American officers and a handful of soldiers, was a spectacle of extraordinary interest.   Generals of the first order of talent ; young gentlemen of noble and wealthy families, aspiring to military renown ; legislators of the British realm, and a vast concourse of other men, lately confident of victory and of freedom to plunder and destroy, were led captive through the pleasant land they had coveted, to be gazed at with mingled joy and scorn by those whose homes they came to make desolate.   " Their march was solemn, sullen, and silent ; but they were every where treated with such humanity, and even delicacy, that they were overwhelmed with astonishment and gratitude.   Not one insult was offered, not an opprobrious reflection cast ;"[3] and in all their long captivity[4] they experienced the generous kindness of a people warring only to be free.

---

[1] Gordon, ii., 267.

[2] Women of the Revolution, i., 97.

[3] Mercy Warren, ii., 40.

[4] Although Congress ratified the generous terms entered into by Gates with Burgoyne in the *convention* at Saratoga, circumstances made them suspicious that the terms would not be strictly complied with. They feared that the Britons would break their parole, and Burgoyne was required to furnish a complete roll of his army, the name and rank of every officer, and the name, former place of abode, occupation, age, and size of every non-commissioned officer and private soldier.   Burgoyne murmured and hesitated.   General Howe, at the same time, was very illiberal in the exchange of prisoners, and exhibited considerable duplicity.   Congress became alarmed, and resolved not to allow the army of Burgoyne to leave our shores until a formal ratification of the convention should be made by the British government.   Burgoyne alone was allowed to go home on parole, and the other officers, with the army, were marched into the interior of Virginia, to await the future action of the two governments.   The British ministry charged Congress with positive perfidy, and Congress justified their acts by charging the ministers with *meditated* perfidy. That this suspicion was well founded is proved by subsequent events.   In the autumn of 1778, Isaac Ogden, a prominent loyalist of New Jersey, and then a refugee in New York, thus wrote to Joseph Galloway, an American Tory in London, respecting an expedition of four thousand British troops which Sir Henry Clinton sent up the Hudson a week previous : " Another object of this expedition was to open the country for many of Burgoyne's troops that had escaped the vigilance of their guard, to come in.   About forty of these have got safe in.   If this expedition had been a week sooner, greater part of Burgoyne's troops probably would have arrived here, as a disposition of rising on their guard strongly prevailed, and all they wanted to effect it was some support near at hand."

The surrender of Burgoyne was an event of infinite importance to the struggling republicans. Hitherto the preponderance of success had been on the side of the English, and only a few partial victories had been won by the Americans. The defeat on Long Island had eclipsed the glory of the siege of Boston ; the capture of Fort Washington and its garrison had overmatched the brilliant defense of Charleston ; the defeat at Brandywine had balanced the victory at Trenton ; White Plains and Princeton were in fair juxtaposition in the account current ; and at the very time when the hostile armies at the north were fighting for the mastery, Washington was suffering defeats in Pennsylvania, and Forts Clinton, Montgomery, and Constitution were passing into the hands of the royal forces. Congress had fled from Philadelphia to York, and its sittings were in the midst of loyalists, ready to attack or betray. Its treasury was nearly exhausted ; its credit utterly so. Its bills to the amount of forty millions of dollars were scattered over the country. Its frequent issues were inadequate to the demands of the commissariat, and distrust was rapidly depreciating their value in the public mind. Loyalists rejoiced ; the middlemen were in a dilemma ; the patriots trembled. Thick clouds of doubt and dismay were gathering in every part of the political horizon, and the acclamations which had followed the Declaration of Independence, the year before, died away like mere whispers upon the wind.

All eyes were turned anxiously to the army of the north, and upon that strong arm of Congress, wielded, for the time, by Gates, the hopes of the patriots leaned. How eagerly they listened to every breath of rumor from Saratoga ! How enraptured were they when the cry of victory fell upon their ears ! All over the land a shout of triumph went up, and from the furrows, and workshops, and marts of commerce ; from the pulpit, from provincial halls of legislation, from partisan camps, and from the shattered ranks of the chief at White Marsh, it was echoed and re-echoed. Toryism, which had begun to lift high its head, retreated behind the defense of inaction ; the bills of Congress rose twenty per cent. in value ; capital came forth from its hiding-places ; the militia readily obeyed the summons to the camp, and the great patriot heart of America beat strongly with pulsations of hope. Amid the joy of the moment, Gates was apotheosized in the hearts of his countrymen, and they

MEDAL STRUCK IN HONOR OF GENERAL GATES AND HIS ARMY.

The engraving exhibits a view of both sides of the medal, drawn the size of the original. On one side is a bust of General Gates, with the Latin inscription, "HORATIO GATES DUCI STRENUO COMITIA AMERICANA ;" The American Congress, to *Horatio Gates, the valiant leader.* On the other side, or reverse, Burgoyne is represented in the attitude of delivering up his sword ; and in the background, on either side of them, are seen the two armies of England and America, the former laying down their arms. At the top is the Latin inscription, "SALUS REGIONUM SEPTENTRIONAL :" literal English, *Safety of the northern region or department.* Below is the inscription, "HOSTE AD SARATOGAM IN DEDITION, ACCEPTO DIE XVII. OCT. MDCCLXXVII. ;" English, *Enemy at Saratoga surrendered October 17th, 1777.*

generously overlooked the indignity offered by him to the commander-in-chief when he refused, in the haughty pride of his heart in that hour of victory, to report, as in duty bound, his success to the national council through him.   Congress, too, overjoyed at the result, forgot its own dignity, and allowed Colonel Wilkinson,[1] the messenger of the glad tidings, to stand upon their floor and proclaim, " The whole British army have laid down their arms at Saratoga ; our own, full of vigor and courage, expect your orders ; it is for your wisdom to decide where the country may still have need of their services."   Congress voted thanks to General Gates and his army, and decreed that he should be presented with a medal of gold, to be struck expressly in commemoration of so glorious a victory.

This victory was also of infinite importance to the republicans on account of its effects beyond the Atlantic.   The highest hopes of the British nation, and the most sanguine expectations of the king and his ministers, rested on the success of this campaign.   It had been a favorite object with the administration, and the people were confidently assured that, with the undoubted success of Burgoyne, the turbulent spirit of rebellion would be quelled, and the insurgents would be forced to return to their allegiance.

Parliament was in session when the intelligence of Burgoyne's defeat reached England ; December 3, and when the mournful tidings were communicated to that body, it instantly 1777. aroused all the fire of opposing parties.[2]   The opposition opened anew their eloquent batteries upon the ministers.   For several days misfortune had been suspected.   The last arrival from America brought tidings of gloom.   The Earl of Chatham, with far-reaching comprehension, and thorough knowledge of American affairs, had denounced the mode of warfare and the material used against the Americans.   He refused to vote for the laudatory address to the king.   Leaning upon his crutch, he poured forth his vigorous denunciations against the course of the ministers like a mountain torrent.   " This, my lords," he said, " is a perilous and tremendous moment !   It is no time for adulation.   The smoothness of flattery can not now avail—can not save us in this rugged and awful crisis.   It is now necessary to instruct the throne in the language of truth. . . . . You can not. I venture to say it, you can not conquer America.   What is your present situation there ? We do not know the worst, but we know that in three campaigns we have suffered much and gained nothing, and perhaps at this moment the northern army (Burgoyne's) may be a total loss. . . . . You may swell every expense, and every effort, still more extravagantly ; pile and accumulate every assistance you can buy or borrow ; traffic and barter with every little pitiful German prince that sells and sends his subjects to the shambles of a foreign power ; your efforts are forever vain and impotent ; doubly so from this mercenary aid on which you rely, for it irritates to an incurable resentment the minds of your enemies. To overrun with the mercenary sons of rapine and plunder, devoting them and their possessions to the rapacity of hireling cruelty !   If I were an American, as I am an Englishman, while a foreign troop was landed in my country, I never would lay down my arms—never, never, never !"[3]

The Earl of Coventry, Earl Temple Chatham's brother-in-law, and the Duke of Richmond, all spoke in coincidence with Chatham.   Lord Suffolk, one of the Secretaries of State, undertook the defense of ministers for the employment of Indians, and concluded by saying, " It is perfectly justifiable to use all the means that God and nature have put into our hands."   This sentiment brought Chatham upon the floor.   " That God and nature put

---

[1] James Wilkinson was born in Maryland about 1757, and, by education, was prepared for the practice of medicine.   He repaired to Cambridge as a volunteer in 1775.   He was captain of a company in a regiment that went to Canada in 1776.   He was appointed deputy adjutant general by Gates, and, after the surrender of Burgoyne, Congress made him a brigadier general by brevet.   At the conclusion of the war he settled in Kentucky, but entered the army in 1806, and had the command on the Mississippi.   He commanded on the northern frontier during our last war with Great Britain.   At the age of 56 he married a young lady of 26.   He died of diarrhea, in Mexico, December 28th, 1825, aged 68 years.

[2] Pitkin, i., 399.

[3] Parliamentary Debates.

into our hands!" he reiterated, with bitter scorn. "I know not what idea that lord may entertain of God and nature, but I know that such abominable principles are equally abhorrent to religion and humanity. What! attribute the sacred sanction of God and nature to the massacres of the Indian scalping-knife, to the cannibal and savage, torturing, murdering, roasting, and eating—literally, my lords, *eating*—the mangled victims of his barbarous battles. . . . . These abominable principles, and this most abominable avowal of them, demand most decisive indignation. I call upon that right reverend bench (pointing to the bishops), those holy ministers of the Gospel and pious pastors of the Church—I conjure them to join in the holy work, and to vindicate the religion of their God."

In the Lower House, Burke, Fox, and Barré were equally severe upon the ministers; and on the 3d of December, when the news of Burgoyne's defeat reached London, the latter arose in his place in the Commons, and, with a severe and solemn countenance, asked Lord George Germain, the Secretary of War, what news he had received by his last expresses from Quebec, and to say, upon his word of honor, what had become of Burgoyne and his brave army. The haughty secretary was irritated by the cool irony of the question, but he was obliged to unbend and to confess that the unhappy intelligence had reached him, but added it was not yet authenticated.[1]

Lord North, the premier, with his usual adroitness, admitted that misfortune had befallen the British arms, but denied that any blame could be imputed to ministers themselves, and proposed an adjournment of December, 1777. Parliament on the 11th (which was carried) until the 20th of January.[2] It was a 1778. clever trick of the premier to escape the castigations which he knew the opposition would inflict while the nation was smarting under the goadings of mortified pride.

The victory over Burgoyne, unassisted as our troops were by foreign aid, placed the prowess of the United States in the most favorable light upon the Continent. Our urgent solicitations for aid, hitherto but little noticed except by France, were now listened to with respect, and the American commissioners at Paris. Dr. Franklin, Silas Deane,[3] and Arthur Lee.[4] occupied a commanding position among the diplomatists of Europe. France, Spain, the States General of Holland, the Prince of Orange, and even Catharine of Russia and Pope Clement XIV. (Ganganelli), all

Silas Deane

---

[1] History of the Reign of George III., i., 326.

[2] Pitkin, i., 397. Annual Register, 1778, p. 74.

[3] Silas Deane was a native of Groton, Connecticut. He graduated at Yale College, 1758, and was a member of the first Congress, 1774. He was sent to France Early in 1776, as political and commercial agent for the United Colonies, and in the autumn of that year was associated with Franklin and Lee as commissioner. He seems to have been unfit, in a great degree, for the station he held, and his defective judgment and extravagant promises greatly embarrassed Congress. He was recalled at the close of 1777, and John Adams appointed in his place. He published a defense of his character in 1778, and charged Thomas Paine and others connected with public affairs with using their official influence for purposes of private gain. This was the charge made against himself, and he never fully wiped out all suspicion. He went to England toward the close of 1784, and died in extreme poverty at Deal, 1789.

[4] Dr. Lee was born in Virginia in 1740—a brother to the celebrated Richard Henry Lee. He was educated at Edinburgh, and, on returning to America, practiced medicine at Williamsburgh about five years. He went to London in 1766, and studied law in the Temple. He kept his brother and other patriots of the Revolution fully informed of all political matters of importance abroad, and particularly the movements of the British ministry. He wrote a great deal, and stood high as an essayist and political pamphleteer. He was colonial agent for Virginia in 1775. In 1776 he was associated with Franklin and Deane, as minister at the court of Versailles. He and John Adams were recalled in 1779. On returning to the United States, he was appointed to offices of trust. He died of pleurisy, December 14th, 1782, aged nearly 42.

of whom feared and hated England because of her increasing potency in arms, commerce, diplomacy, and the Protestant faith, thought kindly of us and spoke kindly to us. We were loved because England was hated ; we were respected because we could injure England by dividing her realm and impairing her growing strength beyond the seas. There was a perfect reciprocity of service ; and when peace was ordained by treaty, and our independence was established, the balance-sheet showed nothing against us, so far as the governments of continental Europe were concerned.

November.   In the autumn of 1776, Franklin and Lee were appointed, jointly with Deane, resident commissioners at the court of Versailles, to negotiate a treaty of amity and commerce with the French king. They opened negotiations early in December with the Count De Vergennes, the premier of Louis XVI. He was distinguished for sound wisdom, extensive political knowledge, remarkable sagacity, and true greatness of mind. He foresaw that generous dealings with the insurgent colonists at the outset would be the surest means of perpetuating the rebellion until a total separation from the parent state would be accomplished—an event eagerly coveted by the French government. France hated England cordially, and feared her power. She had no special love for the Anglo-American colonies, but she was ready to aid them in reducing, by disunion, the puissance of the British empire. To widen the breach was the chief aim of Vergennes. A haughty reserve, he knew, would discourage the Americans, while an open reception, or even countenance, of their deputies might alarm the rulers of Great Britain, and dispose them to a compromise with the colonies, or bring on an immediate rupture between France and England. A middle line was, therefore, pursued by him.[1]

While the French government was thus vacillating during the first three quarters of 1777, secret aid was given to the republicans, and great quantities of arms and ammunition were sent to this country, by an agent of the French government, toward the close of the year, ostensibly through the channel of commercial operations.[2] But when the capture of

---

[1] Ramsay, ii., 62, 63.

[2] In the summer of 1776, Arthur Lee, agent of the Secret Committee of Congress, made an arrangement by which the French king provided money and arms secretly for the Americans. An agent named Beaumarchais was sent to London to confer with Lee, and it was arranged that two hundred thousand Louis d'ors, in arms, ammunition, and specie, should be sent to the Americans, but in a manner to make it appear as a commercial transaction. Mr. Lee assumed the name of Mary Johnson, and Beaumarchais that of Roderique, Hortales, & Co. Lee, fearing discovery if he should send a written notice to Congress of the arrangement, communicated the fact verbally through Captain Thomas Story, who had been upon the continent in the service of the Secret Committee. Yet, after all the arrangements were made, there was hesitation, and it was not until the autumn of 1777 that the articles were sent to the Americans. They were shipped on board *Le Henreux*, in the fictitious name of Hortales, by the way of Cape François, and arrived at Portsmouth, New Hampshire, on the 1st of November of that year. The brave and efficient Baron Steuben was a passenger in that ship.

This arrangement, under the disguise of a mercantile operation, subsequently produced a great deal of trouble, a more minute account of which is given in the Supplement to this work.

Beaumarchais was one of the most active business men of his time, and became quite distinguished in the literary and political world by his "*Marriage of Figaro*," and his connection with the French Revolution in 1793. Börne, in one of his charming *Letters from Paris*, after describing his visit to the house where Beaumarchais had lived, where "they now sell kitchen salt," thus speaks of him : " By his bold and fortunate commercial undertakings, he had become one of the richest men in France. In the war of American liberty, he furnished, through an understanding with the French government, supplies of arms to the insurgents. As in all such undertakings, there were captures, shipwrecks, payments deferred or refused, yet Beaumarchais, by his dexterity, succeeded in extricating himself with personal advantage from all these difficulties.

" Yet this same Beaumarchais showed himself, in the (French) revolution, as inexperienced as a child and as timid as a German closet-scholar. He contracted to furnish weapons to the revolutionary government, and not only lost his money, but was near losing his head into the bargain. Formerly he had to deal with the ministers of an absolute monarchy. The doors of great men's cabinets open and close softly and easily to him who knows how to oil the locks and hinges. Afterward Beaumarchais had to do with honest, in other words with dangerous people ; he had not learned to make the distinction, and accordingly he was ruined." He died in 1799, in his 70th year, and his death, his friends suppose, was voluntary.

OF THE REVOLUTION. 87

Unmasking of the French King.   Independence of the United States acknowledged by France.   Letter of Louis XVI.

Burgoyne and his army (intelligence of which arrived at Paris by express on the 4th of December) reached Versailles, and the ultimate success of the Americans was hardly problematical, Louis cast off all disguise, and informed the American commissioners, through M. Gerard, one of his Secretaries of State, that the treaty of alliance and commerce, already negotiated, would be ratified, and "that it was decided to acknowledge the independence of the United States." He wrote to his uncle, Charles IV. of Spain, urging his co-operation; for, according to the family compact of the Bourbons, made in 1761, the King of Spain was to be consulted before such a treaty could be ratified.[1] Charles refused to co-operate, but Louis persevered, and in February, 1778, he acknowledged the independence of the United States, and entered into treaties of alliance and commerce with them on a footing of perfect equality and reciprocity. War against England was to be made a common cause, and it was agreed that neither contracting party should conclude truce or peace with Great Britain without the formal consent of the other first obtained; and it was mutually covenanted not to lay down their arms until the independence of the United States should be formally or tacitly assured by the treaty or treaties that should terminate the war.[2] Thus allied, by treaty, with the ancient and powerful French nation, the Americans felt certain of success.

February 6.

---

[1] This letter of Louis was brought to light during the Revolution of 1793. It is a curious document, and illustrates the consummate duplicity practiced by that monarch and his ministers. Disclosing, as it does, the policy which governed the action of the French court, and the reasons which induced the king to accede to the wishes of the Americans, its insertion here will doubtless be acceptable to the reader. It was dated January 8th, 1778.

"The sincere desire," said Louis, "which I feel of maintaining the true harmony and unity of our system of alliance, which must always have an imposing character for our enemies, induces me to state to your majesty my way of thinking on the present condition of affairs. England, our common and inveterate enemy, has been engaged for three years in a war with her American colonies. We had agreed not to intermeddle with it, and, viewing both sides as English, we made our trade free to the one that found most advantage in commercial intercourse. In this manner America provided herself with arms and ammunition, of which she was destitute; *I do not speak of the succors of money and other kinds which we have given her, the whole ostensibly on the score of trade.* England has taken umbrage at these succors, and has not concealed from us that she will be revenged sooner or later. She has already, indeed, seized several of our merchant vessels, and refused restitution. We have lost no time on our part. We have fortified our most exposed colonies, and placed our fleets upon a respectable footing, which has continued to aggravate the ill humor of England.

"Such was the posture of affairs in November last. The destruction of the army of Burgoyne and the straitened condition of Howe have lately changed the face of things. America is triumphant and England cast down; but the latter has still a great, unbroken maritime force, *and the hope of forming a beneficial alliance with the colonies,* the impossibility of their being subdued by arms being now demonstrated. All the English parties agree on this point. Lord North has himself announced in full Parliament a plan of pacification for the first session, and all sides are assiduously employed upon it. Thus it is the same to us whether this minister or any other be in power. From different motives they join against us, and do not forget our bad offices. They will fall upon us in as great strength as if the war had not existed. This being understood, and our grievances against England notorious, I have thought, after taking the advice of my council, and particularly that of M. D'Ossune, and having consulted upon the propositions which the insurgents make, to treat with them, *to prevent their reunion with the mother country.* I lay before your majesty my views of the subject. I have ordered a memorial to be submitted to you, in which they are presented in more detail. I desire eagerly that they should meet your approbation. Knowing the weight of your probity, your majesty will not doubt the lively and sincere friendship with which I am yours," &c.— *Quoted by Pitkin* (i., 399) *from* Histoire, &c., de la Diplomatique Française, vol. vii.

[2] Sparks's Life of Franklin, 430, 433.

CHAPTER IV.

" The sun has drunk
The dew that lay upon the morning grass ;
There is no rustling in the lofty elm
That canopies my dwelling, and its shade
Scarce cools me. All is silent save the faint
And interrupted murmur of the bee,
Sitting on the sick flowers, and then again
Instantly on the wing. The plants around
Feel the too potent fervors ; the tall maize
Rolls up its long green leaves ; the clover droops
Its tender foliage, and declines its blooms.
But far in the fierce sunshine tower the hills,
With all their growth of woods, silent and stern,
As if the scorching heat and dazzling light
Were but an element they loved."

BRYANT.

T was early in the morning of such a day as the poet refers to that we commenced a ride and a ramble over the historic grounds of Saratoga near Schuylerville, accompanied by the friendly guide whose proffered services I have already mentioned. We first rode to the residence of Mrs. J—n, one of the almost centenarian representatives of the generation cotemporary with our Revolution, now so few and hoary. She was in her ninety-second year of life, yet her mental faculties were quite vigorous, and she related her sad experience of the trials of that war with a memory remarkably tenacious and correct. Her sight and hearing were defective, and her skin wrinkled ; but in her soft blue eye, regular features, and delicate form were lingering many traces of the beauty of her early womanhood. She was a young lady of twenty years when Independence was declared, and was living with her parents at Do-ve-gat (Coveville) when Burgoyne came down the valley. She was then betrothed, but her lover had shouldered his musket, and was in Schuyler's camp.

While Burgoyne was pressing onward toward Fort Edward from Skenesborough, the people of the valley below, who were attached to the patriot cause, fled hastily to Albany. Mrs. J—n and her parents were among the fugitives. So fearful were they of the Indian scouts sent forward, and of the resident Tories, not a whit less savage, who were emboldened by the proximity of the invader, that for several nights previous to their flight they slept in a swamp, apprehending that their dwelling would be burned over their heads or that murder would break in upon their repose. And when they returned home, after the surrender of Burgoyne, all was desolation. Tears filled her eyes when she spoke of that sad return. " We had but little to come home to," she said. " Our crops and our cattle, our sheep, hogs, and horses, were all gone, yet we knelt down in our desolate room and thanked God sincerely that our house and barns were not destroyed." She wedded her soldier soon afterward, and during the long widowhood of her evening of life his pension has been secured to her, and a few years ago it was increased in amount. She referred to it, and with quivering lip—quivering with the emotions of her full heart—said, " The government has been very kind to me in my poverty and old age." She was personally acquainted with General Schuyler, and spoke feelingly of the noble-heartedness of himself and lady in all the relations of life. While pressing her hand in bidding her farewell, the thought occurred that we

OF THE REVOLUTION   89

Remains of the Fortifications of Burgoyne's Camp.   The Riedesel House.   Narrative of the Baroness Riedesel.

represented the linking of the living, vigorous, active present, and the half-buried, decaying past ; and that between her early womanhood and now all the grandeur and glory of our Republic had dawned and brightened into perfect day.

From Mrs. J——n's we rode to the residence of her brother, the house wherein the Baroness Riedesel, with her children and female companions, was sheltered just before the surrender of Burgoyne.   It is about a mile above Schuylerville, and nearly opposite the mouth of the Batten Kill.   On our way we paused to view the remains of the fortifications of Burgoyne's camp, upon the heights a little west of the village.   Prominent traces of the mounds and ditches are there visible in the woods.   A little northwest of the village the lines of the defenses thrown up by the Germans, and Hessians of Hanau may be distinctly seen.   (See map, page 77.)

The house made memorable by the presence and the pen of the wife of the Brunswick

THE RIEDESEL HOUSE, SARATOGA.

general is well preserved.   At the time of the Revolution it was owned by Peter Lansing, a relative of the chancellor of that name, and now belongs to Mr. Samuel Marshall, who has the good taste to keep 1848. up its original character.   It is upon the high bank west of the road from Schuylerville to Fort Miller, pleasantly shaded in front by locusts, and fairly embowered in shrubbery and fruit trees.

We will listen to the story of the sufferings of some of the women of Burgoyne's camp in that house, as told by the baroness herself : " About two o'clock in the afternoon we again heard a firing of cannon and small arms ; instantly all was alarm, and every thing in motion.   My husband told me to go to a house not far off.   I immediately seated myself in my caleche, with my children, and drove off ; but scarcely had we reached it before I discovered five or six armed men on the other side of the Hudson.   Instinctively I threw my children down in the caleche, and then concealed myself with them.   At this moment the fellows fired, and wounded an already wounded English soldier, who was behind me.   Poor fellow ! I pitied him exceedingly, but at this moment had no power to relieve him.

" A terrible cannonade was commenced by the enemy against the house in which I sought to obtain shelter for myself and children, under the mistaken idea that all the generals were in it.   Alas ! it contained none but wounded and women.   We were at last obliged to re-sort to the cellar for refuge, and in one corner of this I remained the whole day, my children sleeping on the earth with their heads in my lap ; and in the same situation I passed a sleepless night.[1]   Eleven cannon-balls passed through the house, and we could distinctly hear them roll away.   One poor soldier, who was lying on a table for the purpose of having his leg amputated, was struck by a shot, which carried away his other ; his comrades had

CELLAR OF THE RIEDESEL HOUSE.

left him, and when we went to his assistance we found him in a corner of the room, into which he had crept, more dead than alive, scarcely breathing.[2]   My reflections on the danger to which my husband was exposed now agonized me exceedingly, and the thoughts of my children, and the necessity of struggling for their preservation, alone sustained me.

---

[1] The cellar is about fifteen by thirty feet in size, and lighted and ventilated by two small windows only.
[2] The place where this ball entered is seen under the window near the corner, and designated in the picture by a small black spot.

" The ladies of the army who were with me were Mrs. Harnage, a Mrs. Kennels the widow of a lieutenant who was killed, and the lady of the commissary.   Major Harnage, his wife, and Mrs. Kennels made a little room in a corner with curtains to it, and wished to do the same for me, but I preferred being near the door, in case of fire.   Not far off my women slept, and opposite to us three English officers, who, though wounded, were determined not to be left behind ; one of them was Captain Green, an aid-de-camp to Major-general Phillips, a very valuable officer and most agreeable man.   They each made me a most sacred promise not to leave me behind, and, in case of sudden retreat, that they would each of them take one of my children on his horse ; and for myself one of my husband's was in constant readiness. . . . . The want of water distressed us much ; at length we found a soldier's wife who had courage enough to fetch us some from the river, an office nobody else would undertake, as the Americans shot at every person who approached it ; but, out of respect for her sex, they never molested her.

" I now occupied myself through the day in attending the wounded ; I made them tea and coffee, and often shared my dinner with them, for which they offered me a thousand expressions of gratitude.   One day a Canadian officer came to our cellar, who had scarcely the power of holding himself upright, and we concluded he was dying for want of nourishment ; I was happy in offering him my dinner, which strengthened him, and procured me his friendship.   I now undertook the care of Major Bloomfield, another aid-de-camp of General Phillips ; he had received a musket-ball through both cheeks, which in its course had knocked out several of his teeth and cut his tongue ; he could hold nothing in his mouth, the matter which ran from his wound almost choked him, and he was not able to take any nourishment except a little soup or something liquid.   We had some Rhenish wine, and, in the hope that the acidity of it would cleanse his wound, I gave him a bottle of it.   He took a little now and then, and with such effect that his cure soon followed ; thus I added another to my stock of friends, and derived a satisfaction which, in the midst of sufferings. served to tranquilize me and diminish their acuteness.

" One day General Phillips accompanied my husband, at the risk of their lives, on a visit to us.   The general, after having beheld our situation, said to him, ' I would not for ten thousand guineas come again to this place ; my heart is almost broken.'

" In this horrid situation we remained six days ; a cessation of hostilities was now spoken of, and eventually took place."

The baroness, in the simple language of her narrative, thus bears testimony to the generous courtesy of the American officers, and to the true nobility of character of General Schuyler in particular : " My husband sent a message to me to come over to him with my children.   I seated myself once more in my dear caleche, and then rode through the American camp.   As I passed on I observed, and this was a great consolation to me, that no one eyed me with looks of resentment, but they all greeted us, and even showed compassion in their countenances at the sight of a woman with small children   I was, I confess, afraid to go over to the enemy, as it was quite a new situation to me.   When I drew near the tents a handsome man approached and met me, *took my children from the calèche, and hugged and kissed them, which affected me almost to tears.*   ' You tremble,' said he, addressing himself to me ; ' be not afraid.'   ' No,' I answered, ' you seem so kind and tender to my children, it inspires me with courage.'   He now led me to the tent of General Gates, where I found Generals Burgoyne and Phillips, who were on a friendly footing with the former.   Burgoyne said to me, ' Never mind ; your sorrows have now an end.'   I answered him that I should be reprehensible to have any cares, as he had none ; and I was pleased to see him on such friendly footing with General Gates.   All the generals remained to dine with General Gates.

" The same gentleman who received me so kindly now came and said to me, ' You will be very much embarrassed to eat with all these gentlemen ; *come with your children to my tent, where I will prepare for you a frugal dinner, and give it with a free will.'*   I said, ' *You are certainly a husband and a father, you have shown me so much kindness.*'

I now found that he was GENERAL SCHUYLER.   He treated me with excellent smoked

GENERAL SCHUYLER AND BARONESS RIEDESEL.

tongue, beef-steaks, potatoes, and good bread and butter !   Never could I have wished to eat a better dinner ; I was content ; I saw all around me were so likewise ; and, what was better than all, my husband was out of danger.

"When we had dined he told me his residence was at Albany, and that General Burgoyne intended to honor him as his guest, and invited myself and children to do so likewise.   I asked my husband how I should act ; he told me to accept the invitation.   As it was two days' journey there, he advised me to go to a place which was about three hours' ride distant.

"Some days after this we arrived at Albany, where we so often wished ourselves ; but we did not enter it as we expected we should—victors !¹   We were received by the good General Schuyler, his wife, and daughters, not as enemies, but kind friends ; and they treated us with the most marked attention and politeness, as they did General Burgoyne, who had caused General Schuyler's beautifully-finished house to be burned.   In fact, they behaved like persons of exalted minds, who determined to bury all recollections of their own injuries in the contemplation of our misfortunes.   General Burgoyne was struck with General Schuyler's generosity, and said to him, ' You show me great kindness, though I have done you much injury.'   ' That was the fate of war,' replied the brave man ; ' let us say no more about it.' "

General Schuyler was detained at Saratoga when Burgoyne and suite started for Albany.

¹ General Burgoyne boasted at Fort Edward that he should eat a Christmas dinner in Albany, surrounded by his victorious army.

92   PICTORIAL FIELD-BOOK

British Officers at Schuyler's House.   Execution-place of Lovelace.   Active and Passive Tories.   Rendezvous of Lovelace.

He wrote to his wife to give the English general the very best reception in her power. "The British commander was well received," says the Marquis de Chastellux,[1] in his Travels in America, "by Mrs. Schuyler, and lodged in the best apartment in the house. An excellent supper was served him in the evening, the honors of which were done with so much grace that he was affected even to tears, and said, with a deep sigh, 'Indeed, this is doing too much for the man who has ravaged their lands and burned their dwellings.' The next morning he was reminded of his misfortunes by an incident that would have amused any one else. His bed was prepared in a large room ; but as he had a numerous suite, or family, several mattresses were spread on the floor for some officers to sleep near him. Schuyler's second son, a little fellow about seven years old, very arch and forward, but very amiable, was running all the morning about the house. Opening the door of the saloon, he burst out a laughing on seeing all the English collected, and shut it after him, exclaiming, 'You are all my prisoners !' This innocent cruelty rendered them more melancholy than before."

We next visited the headquarters of General Gates, south of the Fish Creek, delineated on page 75. On our way we passed the spot, a few rods south of the creek, where Lovelace, a prominent Tory, was hung. It is upon the high bluff seen on the right of the road in the annexed sketch, which was taken from the lawn in front of the rebuilt mansion of General Schuyler.

Lovelace was a fair type of his class, the bitterest and most implacable foes of the republicans. There were many Tories who were so from principle, and refused to take sides against the parent country from honest convictions of the wrongfulness of such a course. They looked upon the Whigs as rebels against their sovereign ; condemned the war as unnatural, and regarded the final result as surely disastrous to those who had lifted up the arm of oppo-

PLACE WHERE LOVELACE WAS EXECUTED.

sition. Their opinions were courteously but firmly expressed ; they took every opportunity to dissuade their friends and neighbors from participation in the rebellion ; and by all their words and acts discouraged the insurgent movement. But they shouldered no musket, girded on no sword, piloted no secret expedition against the republicans. They were passive, noble-minded men, and deserve our respect for their consistency and our commiseration for their sufferings at the hands of those who made no distinction between the man of honest opinions and the marauder with no opinions at all.

There was another class of Tories, governed by the footpad's axiom, that "might makes right." They were Whigs when royal power was weak, and Tories when royal power was strong. Their god was mammon, and they offered up human sacrifices in abundance upon its altars. Cupidity and its concomitant vices governed all their acts, and the bonds of consanguinity and affection were too weak to restrain their fostered barbarism. Those born in the same neighborhood ; educated (if at all) in the same school ; admonished, it may be, by the same pastor, seemed to have their hearts suddenly closed to every feeling of friendship or of love, and became as relentless robbers and murderers of neighbors and friends as the savages of the wilderness. Of this class was Thomas Lovelace, who, for a time, became a terror to his old neighbors and friends in Saratoga, his native district.

At the commencement of the war Lovelace went to Canada, and there confederated with five other persons from his own county to come down into Saratoga and abduct, plunder, or betray their former neighbors. He was brave, expert, and cautious. His quarters were in a large swamp about five miles from the residence of Colonel Van Vechten at Do-ve-gat, but his place of rendezvous was cunningly concealed. Robberies were frequent, and several inhabitants were carried off. General Schuyler's house was robbed, and an attempt was

---

[1] A French officer, who served in the army in this country during a part of the Revolution.

made by Lovelace and his companions to carry off Colonel Van Vechten; but the active vigilance of General Stark, then in command of the barracks north of the Fish Creek,[1] in furnishing the colonel with a guard, frustrated the marauder's plans.   Intimations of his intentions and of his place of concealment were given to Captain Dunham, who commanded a company of militia in the neighborhood, and he at once summoned his lieutenant, ensign, orderly, and one private to his house.[2]   At dark they proceeded to the "Big Swamp," three miles distant, where two Tory families resided.   They separated to reconnoiter, but two of them, Green and Guiles, were lost.   The other three kept together, and at dawn discovered Lovelace and his party in a hut covered over with boughs, just drawing on their stockings. The three Americans crawled cautiously forward till near the hut, when they sprang upon a log with a shout, leveled their muskets, and Dunham exclaimed, "Surrender, or you are all dead men!"   There was no time for parley, and, believing that the Americans were upon them in force, they came out one by one without arms, and were marched by their captors to General Stark at the barracks.   They were tried by a court-martial as spies, traitors, and robbers, and Lovelace, who was considered too dangerous to be allowed to escape, was sentenced to be hung.   He complained of injustice, and claimed the leniency due to a prisoner of war; but his plea was disallowed, and three days afterward he was hung upon the brow of the hill at the place delineated, during a tremendous storm of rain and wind, accompanied by vivid lightning and clashing thunder-peals.   These facts were communicated to me by the son of Colonel Van Vechten, who accompanied me to the spot, and who was well acquainted with all the captors of Lovelace and his accomplices.

The place where Gates and Burgoyne had their first interview (delineated on page 81) is about half way between the Fish Creek and Gates's headquarters.   After visiting these localities, we returned to the village, and spent an hour upon the ground where the British army laid down their arms.   This locality I have already noted, and will not detain the reader longer than to mention the fact that the plain whereon this event took place formed a part of the extensive meadows of General Schuyler, and to relate a characteristic adventure which occurred there.

While the British camp was on the north side of the Fish Creek, a number of the officers' horses were let loose in the meadows to feed.   An expert swimmer among the Americans who swarmed upon the hills east of the Hudson, obtained permission to go across and capture one of the horses.   He swam the river, seized and mounted a fine bay gelding, and in a few moments was recrossing the stream unharmed, amid a volley of bullets from a party of British soldiers.   Shouts greeted him as he returned; and, when rested, he asked permission to go for another, telling the captain that *he* ought to have a horse to ride as well as a private.   Again the adventurous soldier was among the herd, and, unscathed, returned with an exceedingly good match for the first, and presented it to his commander.[3]

Bidding our kind friend and guide adieu, we left Schuylerville toward evening, in a private carriage, for Fort Miller, six miles further up the Hudson.   The same beautiful and diversified scenery, the same prevailing quiet that charmed us all the way from Waterford, still surrounded us; and the river and the narrow alluvial plain through which it flows, bounded on either side by high undulations or abrupt pyramidal hills, which cast lengthened shadows in the evening sun across the meadows, presented a beautiful picture of luxurious repose.   We crossed the Hudson upon a long bridge built on strong abutments, two miles and a half above Schuylerville, at the place where Burgoyne and his army crossed on the 12th of September, 1777.   The river is here quite broad and shallow, and broken by frequent rifts and rapids.

We arrived at Fort Miller village, on the east bank of the river, between five and six o'clock; and while awaiting supper, preparatory to an evening canal voyage to Fort Edward, nine miles above, I engaged a water-man to row me across to the western bank, to

---

[1] The place where these barracks were located is just within the northern suburbs of Schuylerville.
[2] Davis, Green, Guiles, and Burden.   [3] Neilson, 223

94   PICTORIAL FIELD-BOOK

Visit to the Site of old Fort Edward.   Tragedy of "Bloody Run."   Daring Feat by Putnam.   Fort Miller Fording-place.

view the site of the old fort. He was a very obliging man, and well acquainted with the localities in the neighborhood, but was rather deficient in historical knowledge. His attempts to relate the events connected with the old fort and its vicinity were amusing; for Putnam's ambush on Lake Champlain, and the defeat of Pyles by Lee, in North Carolina, with a slight tincture of correct narrative, were blended together as parts of an event which occurred at Fort Miller.

We crossed the Hudson just above the rapids. A dam for milling purposes spans the stream, causing a sluggish current and deeper water for more than two miles above. Here was the scene of one of Putnam's daring exploits. While a major in the English provincial army, nearly twenty years before the Revolution, he was lying in a bateau on the east side of the river, and was suddenly surprised by a party of Indians. He could not cross the river swiftly enough to escape the balls of their rifles, and there was no alternative but to go down the foaming rapids. In an instant his purpose was fixed, and, to the astonishment of the savages, he steered directly down the current, amid whirling eddies and over shelving rocks. In a few moments his vessel cleared the rush of waters, and was gliding upon the smooth current below, far out of reach of the weapons of the Indians. It was a feat they never dared attempt, and superstition convinced them that he was so favored by the Great Spirit that it would be an affront to Manitou to attempt to kill him with powder and ball. Other Indians of the tribe, however, soon afterward gave practical evidence of their unbelief in such interposition.

There is not a vestige of Fort Miller left, and maize, and potatoes, and pumpkin vines were flourishing where the rival forces of Sir William Johnson and the Baron Dieskau alternately paraded. At the foot of the hill, a few rods below where the fort stood, is a part of the trench and bank of a redoubt, and this is all that remains even of the outworks of the fortification.

An eighth of a mile westward is Bloody Run, a stream which comes leaping in sparkling cascades from the hills, and affords fine trout fishing. It derives its name from the fact that, while the English had possession of

BLOODY RUN.

the fort in 1759, a party of soldiers from the garrison went out to fish at the place represented in the picture. The hills, now cultivated, were then covered with dense forests, and afforded the Indians excellent ambush. A troop of savages, lying near, sprang silently from their covert upon the fishers, and bore off nine reeking scalps before those who escaped could reach the fort and give the alarm.

This clear mountain stream enters the Hudson a little above Fort Miller, where the river makes a sudden curve, and where, before the erection of the dam at the rapids, it was quite shallow, and usually fordable. This was the crossing-place

FORT MILLER FORDING-PLACE.[1]

for the armies; and there are still to be seen some of the logs and stones upon the shore which formed a part of the old "King's Road" leading to the fording-place. They are now sub-

---

[1] This view is taken from the site of the fort, looking northward. The fort was in the town of Northumberland. It was built of logs and earth, and was never a post of great importance.

merged, the river having been made deeper by the dam ; but when the water is limpid they can be plainly seen.   It was twilight before we reached the village on the eastern shore We supped and repaired to the packet office, where we waited until nine o'clock in the evening before the shrill notes of a tin horn brayed out the annunciation of a packet near. Its deck was covered with passengers, for the interesting ceremony of converting the dining-room into a dormitory, or swinging the hammocks or berths and selecting their occupants, had commenced, and all were driven out, much to their own comfort, but, strange to say, to the dissatisfaction of many who lazily preferred a sweltering lounge in the cabin to the delights of fresh air and the bright starlight.   Having no interest in the scramble for beds, we enjoyed the evening breeze and the excitement of the tiny tumult.   My companion, fearing the exhalations upon the night air, did indeed finally seek shelter in one end of the cabin, but was driven, with two other young ladies, into the captain's state-room, to allow the "hands" to have full play in making the beds.   Imprisoned against their will, the ladies made prompt restitution to themselves by drawing the cork of a bottle of sarsaparilla and sipping its contents, greatly to the consternation of a meek old dame, the mother of one of

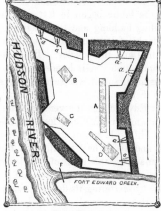

FORT EDWARD.[2]

the girls, who was sure it was "bed-bug pizen, or something a pesky sight worse."   We landed at Fort Edward at midnight, and took lodgings at a small but tidily-kept tavern close by the canal.

Fort Edward was a military post of considerable importance during the French and Indian wars and the Revolution.[1]   The locality, previous to the erection of the fortress, was called the *first carrying-place*, being the first and nearest point on the Hudson where the troops, stores, &c., were landed while passing to or from the south end of Lake Champlain, a distance of about twenty-five miles.   The fort was built in 1755, when six thousand troops were collected there, under General Lyman, waiting the arrival of General Johnson, the commander-in-chief of an expedition against Ticonderoga and Crown Point.   It was at first called Fort Lyman, in honor of the general who superintended its erection.   It

---

[1] I refer particularly to the war between England and France, commonly called, in Europe, the *Seven Years' War*.   It was declared on the 9th of June, 1756, and ended with the treaty at Paris, concluded and signed February 10th, 1763.   It extended to the colonies of the two nations in America, and was carried on with much vigor here until the victory of Wolfe at Quebec, in 1759, and the entire subjugation of Canada by the English.   The French managed to enlist a large proportion of the Indian tribes in their favor, who were allied with them against the Britons.   It is for that reason that the section of the *Seven Years' War* in America was called by the colonists the "French and Indian War."   I would here mention incidentally that that war cost Great Britain five hundred and sixty millions of dollars, and laid one of the largest foundation stones of that national debt under which she now groans.   It was twenty millions in the reign of William and Mary, in 1697, and was then thought to be enormous ; in 1840 it was about four thousand millions of dollars !

[2] EXPLANATION : *a a a a a a*, six cannons; A, the barracks; B, the store-house; C, the hospital; D, the magazine; E, a flanker; F, a bridge across Fort Edward Creek; and G, a balm of Gilead tree which then overshadowed the massive water-gate.   That tree is still standing, a majestic relic of the past, amid the surrounding changes in nature and art.   It is directly upon the high bank of the Hudson, and its branches, heavily foliated when I was there, spread very high and wide. At the union below its three trunks it measures more than twenty feet in circumference.

BALM OF GILEAD AT FORT EDWARD

was built of logs and earth, sixteen feet high and twenty-two feet thick, and stood at the junction of Fort Edward Creek and the Hudson River. From the creek, around the fort to the river, was a deep fosse or ditch, designated in the engraving by the dark dotted part outside of the black lines.

There are still very prominent traces of the banks and fosse of the fort, but the growing village will soon spread over and obliterate them forever. Already a garden was within the lines; and the old parade-ground, wherein Sir William Johnson strutted in the haughty pride of a victor by accident,[1] was desecrated by beds of beets, parsley, radishes, and onions

Fort Edward was the theater of another daring achievement by Putnam. In the winter of 1756 the barracks, then near the northwestern bastion, took fire. The magazine was only twelve feet distant, and contained three hundred barrels of gunpowder. Attempts were made to batter the barracks to the ground with heavy cannons, but without success. Putnam, who was stationed upon Rogers's Island, in the Hudson, opposite the fort, hurried hither, and, taking his station on the roof of the barracks, ordered a line of soldiers to hand him water. But, despite his efforts, the flames raged and approached nearer and nearer to the magazine. The commandant, Colonel Haviland, seeing his danger, ordered him down; but the brave major did not leave his perilous post until the fabric began to totter. He then leaped to the ground, placed himself between the falling building and the magazine, and poured on water with all his might. The external planks of the magazine were consumed, and there was only a thin partition between the flames and the powder. But Putnam succeeded in subduing the flames and saving the ammunition. His hands and face were dreadfully burned, his whole body was more or less blistered, and it was several weeks before he recovered from the effects of his daring conflict with the fire.

The first place of historic interest that we visited at Fort Edward was the venerable and blasted pine tree near which, tradition asserts, the unfortunate Jane M'Crea lost her life while General Burgoyne had his encampment near Sandy Hill. It stands upon the west side of the road leading from Fort Edward to Sandy Hill, and about half a mile from the canal-lock in the former village. The tree had exhibited unaccountable signs of decadence for several years, and when we visited it, it was sapless and bare. Its top was torn off by a November gale, and almost every breeze diminishes its size by scattering its decayed twigs. The trunk is about five feet in diameter, and upon the bark is engraved, in bold letters, JANE M'CREA, 1777. The names of many ambitious visitors are intaglioed upon it, and reminded me of the line " Run, run, Orlando, carve on every tree." I carefully sketched all its branches, and the engraving is a faithful portraiture of the interesting relic, as viewed from the opposite side of the road. In a few years this tree, around which history and romance have clustered so many associations, will crumble and pass away forever.[2]

The sad story of the unfortunate girl is so interwoven in our history that it has become a component part; but it is told with so many variations, in essential and non-essential par-

---

[1] Sir William Johnson had command of the English forces in 1755, destined to act against Crown Point He was not remarkable for courage or activity. He was attacked at the south end of Lake George by the French general, Deiskau, and was wounded at the outset. The command then devolved on Major-general Lyman, of the Connecticut troops, who, by his skill and bravery, secured a victory over the French and Indians. General Johnson, however, had the honor and reward thereof. In his mean jealousy he gave General Lyman no praise; and the British king (George II.) made him a baronet, and a present of twenty thousand dollars to give the title becoming dignity.

NOTE.—As I shall have frequent occasion to employ technical terms used in fortifications, I here give a diagram, which, with the explanation, will make those terms clear to the reader. The figure is a vertical section of a fortification. The mass of earth, $a\ b\ c\ d\ e\ f\ g\ h$, forms the *rampart* with its *parapet*; $a\ b$ is the interior slope of the rampart; $b\ c$ is the *terre-plein* of the rampart, on which the troops and cannon are placed; $d\ e$ is the *banquette*, or step, on which the soldiers mount to fire over the parapet; $e\ f\ g$ is the parapet; $g\ h$ is the exterior slope of the parapet; $h\ i$ is the *revêtment*, or wall of masonry, supporting the rampart; $h\ k$, the exterior front covered with the revetment, is called the *escarp*; $i\ k\ l\ m$ is the *ditch*; $l\ m$ is the *counterscarp*; $m\ n$ is the *covered way*, having a banquette $n\ o\ p$; $s\ r$ is the *glacis*. When there are two ditches, the works between the inner and the outer ditch are called *ravelins*, and all outside of the ditches, *outworks.*—See Brande's Cyc., art. *Fortification*.

[2] It was cut down in 1853, and converted into canes, boxes, &c.

ticulars, that much of the narratives we have is evidently pure fiction ; a simple tale of Indian abduction, resulting in death, having its counterpart in a hundred like occurrences, has been garnished with all the high coloring of a romantic love story. It seems a pity to spoil the *romance* of the matter, but truth always makes sad havoc with the frost-work of the imagination, and sternly demands the homage of the historian's pen.

All accounts agree that Miss M'Crea was staying at the house of a Mrs. M'Neil, near the fort, at the time of the tragedy. A granddaughter of Mrs. M'Neil (Mrs. F—n) is now living at Fort Edward, and from her I received a minute account of the whole transaction, as she had heard it a "thousand times" from her grandmother. She is a woman of remarkable intelligence, about sixty years old. When I was at Fort Edward she was on a visit with her sister at Glenn's Falls. It had been my intention to go direct to Whitehall, on Lake Champlain, by way of Fort Ann, but the traditionary accounts in the neigh-

1848.

JANE M'CREA TREE, FORT EDWARD.

borhood of the event in question were so contradictory of the books, and I received such assurances that perfect reliance might be placed upon the statements of Mrs. F—n, that, anxious to ascertain the truth of the matter, if possible, we went to Lake Champlain by way of Glenn's Falls and Lake George. After considerable search at the falls, I found Mrs. F—n, and the following is her relation of the tragedy at Fort Edward :

Jane M'Crea was the daughter of a Scotch Presbyterian clergyman of Jersey City, opposite New York ; and while Mrs. M'Neil (then the wife of a former husband named Campbell) was a resident of New York City, an acquaintance and intimacy had grown up between Jenny and her daughter. After the death of Campbell (which occurred at sea) Mrs. Campbell married M'Neil. He, too, was lost at sea, and she removed with her family to an estate owned by him at Fort Edward.   Mr. M·Crea, who was a widower, died, and Jane went to live with her brother near Fort Edward, where the intimacy of former years with Mrs. M·Neil and her daughter was renewed, and Jane spent much of her time at Mrs. M·Neil's house.   Near her brother's lived a family named Jones, consisting of a widow and six sons, and between Jenny and David Jones, a gay young man, a feeling of friendship budded and ripened into reciprocal love.   When the war broke out the Joneses took the royal side of the question, and David and his brother Jonathan went to Canada in the autumn of 1776. They raised a company of about sixty men, under pretext of re-enforcing the American garrison at Ticonderoga, but they went further down the lake and joined the British garrison at June 1, 1777. Crown Point.   When Burgoyne collected his forces at St. John's, at the foot of Lake Champlain, David and Jonathan Jones were among them.   Jonathan was made captain and David a lieutenant in the division under General Fraser, and at the time in question they were with the British army near Sandy Hill.   Thus far all accounts nearly agree.

The brother of Jenny was a Whig, and prepared to move to Albany ; but Mrs. M·Neil, who was a cousin of General Fraser (killed at Stillwater), was a stanch loyalist, and intended to remain at Fort Edward.   When the British were near, Jenny was at Mrs. M·Neil's, and lingered there even after repeated solicitations from her brother to return to his house, five miles further down the river, to be ready to flee when necessity should compel.   A faint hope that she might meet her lover doubtless was the secret of her tarrying.   At last her brother sent a peremptory order for her to join him, and she promised to go down in a large bateau[1] which was expected to leave with several families on the following day.

Early the next morning a black July 27, 1777. servant boy belonging to Mrs. M·Neil espied some Indians stealthily approaching the house, and, giving the alarm to the inmates, he fled to the fort, about eighty rods distant.

A RIVER BATEAU.

Mrs. M·Neil's daughter, the young friend of Jenny, and mother of my informant, was with some friends in Argyle, and the family consisted of only the widow and Jenny, two small children, and a black female servant.   As usual at that time, the kitchen stood a few feet from the house ; and when the alarm was given the black woman snatched up the children, fled to the kitchen, and retreated through a trap-door to the cellar.[2]   Mrs. M·Neil and Jenny followed, but the former being aged and very corpulent, and the latter young and agile, Jenny reached the trap-door first.   Before Mrs. M·Neil could fully descend, the Indians were in the house, and a powerful savage seized her by the hair and dragged her up.   Another went into the cellar and brought out Jenny, but the black face of the negro woman was not seen in the dark, and she and the children remained unharmed.

With the two women the savages started off, on the road toward Sandy Hill, for Burgoyne's camp ; and when they came to the foot of the ascent on which the *pine tree* stands, where the road forked, they caught two horses that were grazing, and attempted to place their prisoners upon them.   Mrs. M·Neil was too heavy to be lifted on the horse easily, and as she signified by signs that she could not ride, two stout Indians took her by the arms and hurried her up the road over the hill, while the others, with Jenny on the horse, went along the road running west of the tree.

The negro boy who ran to the fort gave the alarm, and a small detachment was imme-

---

[1] Bateaux were rudely constructed of logs and planks, broad and without a keel.   They had small draught, and would carry large loads in quite shallow water.   In still water and against currents they were propelled by long driving-poles.   The ferry-scows or flats on the southern and western rivers are very much like the old bateaux.   They were sometimes furnished with a mast for lakes and other deep water, and had cabins erected on them.

[2] Traces of this cellar and of th foundation of the house are still visible in the garden of Dr. Norton, in Fort Edward village, who is a relative of the family by marriage.

diately sent out to effect a rescue.   They fired several volleys at the Indians, but the savages escaped unharmed.   Mrs. M‹Neil said that the Indians, who were hurrying her up the hill, seemed to watch the flash of the guns, and several times they threw her upon her face at the same time falling down themselves, and she distinctly heard the balls whistle above them.   When they got above the second hill from the village the firing ceased ; they then stopped, stripped her of all her garments except her chemise, and in that plight led her into the British camp.   There she met her kinsman, General Fraser, and reproached him bitterly for sending his " scoundrel Indians" after her.   He denied all knowledge of her being away from the city of New York, and took every pains to make her comfortable.   She was so large that not a woman in camp had a gown big enough for her, so Fraser lent her his camp-coat for a garment, and a pocket-handkerchief as a substitute for her stolen cap.

Very soon after Mrs. M‹Neil was taken into the British camp, two parties of Indians arrived with scalps.   She at once recognised the long glossy hair of Jenny,[1] and, though shuddering with horror, boldly charged the savages with her murder, which they stoutly denied.

THE SPRING.[3]

They averred that, while hurrying her along the road on horseback, near the spring west of the *pine tree*, a bullet from one of the American guns, intended for them, mortally wounded the poor girl, and she fell from the horse.   Sure of losing a prisoner by death, they took her scalp as the next best thing for them to do, and that they bore in triumph to the camp, to obtain the promised reward for such trophies.   Mrs. M‹Neil always believed the story of the Indians to be true, for she knew that they were fired upon by the detachment from the fort, and it was far more to their interest to carry a prisoner than a scalp to the British commander, the price for the former being much greater.   In fact, the Indians were so restricted by Burgoyne's humane instructions respecting the taking of scalps, that their chief solicitude was to bring a prisoner alive and unharmed into the camp.[2]   And the probability that Miss M‹Crea was killed as they alleged is strengthened by the fact that they took the corpulent Mrs. M‹Neil, with much fatigue and difficulty, uninjured to the British lines, while Miss M‹Crea, quite light and already on horseback, might have been carried off with far greater ease.

It was known in camp that Lieutenant Jones was betrothed to Jenny, and the story got abroad that he had sent the Indians for her, that they quarreled on the way respecting the reward he had offered, and murdered her to settle the dispute.   Receiving high touches of coloring as it went from one narrator to another, the sad story became a tale of darkest horror, and produced a deep and wide-spread indignation.   This was heightened by a published letter from Gates to Burgoyne, charging him with allowing the In-   September 2, 1777.

---

[1] It was of extraordinary length and beauty, measuring a yard and a quarter.   She was then about twenty years old, and a very lovely girl ; not lovely in beauty of face, according to the common standard of beauty, but so lovely in disposition, so graceful in manners, and so intelligent in features, that she was a favorite of all who knew her.

[2] " I positively forbid bloodshed when you are not opposed in arms.   Aged men, women, children, and prisoners must be held sacred from the knife and hatchet, even in the time of actual conflict.   You shall receive compensation for the prisoners you take, but you shall be called to account for scalps.   In conformity and indulgence of your customs, which have affixed an idea of honor to such badges of victory, you shall be allowed to take the scalps of the dead when killed by your fire and in fair opposition ; but on no account, or pretense, or subtilty, or prevarication are they to be taken from the wounded, or even the dying ; and still less pardonable, if possible, will it be held to kill men in that condition on purpose, and upon a supposition that this protection to the wounded would be thereby evaded."—*Extract from the Speech of Burgoyne to the Indians assembled upon the Bouquet River, June 21, 1777.*

[3] This is a view of a living spring, a few feet below the noted *pine tree*, the lower portion of which is seen near the top of the engraving.   The spring is beside the old road, traces of which may be seen.

dians to butcher with impunity defenseless women and children.   " Upward of one hundred men, women, and children," said Gates, " have perished by the hands of the ruffians, to
whom, it is asserted, you have paid the price of blood."   Burgoyne flatly denied this assertion, and declared that the case of Jane M'Crea was the only act of Indian cruelty of which
he was informed.   His information must have been exceedingly limited, for on the same
day when Jenny lost her life a party of savages murdered the whole family of John Allen,
of Argyle, consisting of himself, his wife, three children, a sister-in-law, and three negroes.
The daughter of Mrs. M'Neil, already mentioned, was then at the house of Mr. Allen's
father-in-law, Mr. Gilmer, who, as well as Mr. Allen, was a Tory.   Both were afraid of
the savages, nevertheless, and were preparing to flee to Albany.   On the morning of the
massacre a younger daughter of Mr. Gilmer went to assist Mrs. Allen in preparing to move.
Not returning when expected, her father sent a negro boy down for her.   He soon returned,
screaming, " They are all dead—father, mother, young missus, and all !"   It was too true.
That morning, while the family were at breakfast, the Indians burst in upon them and
slaughtered every one.   Mr. Gilmer and his family left in great haste for Fort Edward,
but proceeded very cautiously for fear of the savages.   When near the fort, and creeping
warily along a ravine, they discovered a portion of the very party who had plundered Mrs.
M'Neil's house in the morning.   They had emptied the straw from the beds and filled the
ticks with stolen articles.   Mrs. M'Neil's daughter, who accompanied the fugitive family,
saw her mother's looking-glass tied upon the back of one of the savages.   They succeeded
in reaching the fort in safety.

Burgoyne must soon have forgotten this event and the alarm among the loyalists because
of the murder of a Tory and his family ; forgotten how they flocked to his camp for protection, and Fraser's remark to the frightened loyalists, " It is a conquered country, and we
must wink at these things ;" and how his own positive orders to the Indians, not to molest
those having protection, caused many of them to leave him and return to their hunting-
grounds on the St. Lawrence.   It was all dark and dreadful, and Burgoyne was willing to
retreat behind a false assertion, to escape the perils which were sure to grow out of an admission of half the truth of Gates's letter.   That letter, as Sparks justly remarks, was more
ornate than forcible, and abounded more in bad taste than simplicity and pathos ; yet it was
suited to the feelings of the moment, and produced a lively impression in every part of America.   Burke, in the exercise of all his glowing eloquence, used the story with powerful effect
in the British House of Commons, and made the dreadful tale familiar throughout Europe.

Burgoyne, who was at Fort Ann, instituted an inquiry into the matter.   He summoned
the Indians to council, and demanded the surrender of the man who bore off the scalp, to
be punished as a murderer.   Lieutenant Jones denied all knowledge of the matter, and utterly disclaimed any such participation as the sending of a letter to Jenny, or of an Indian
escort to bring her to camp.   He had no motive for so doing, for the American army was
then retreating ; a small guard only was at Fort Edward, and in a day or two the British
would have full possession of that fort, when he could have a personal interview with her.
Burgoyne, instigated by motives of policy rather than by judgment and inclination, pardoned
the savage who scalped poor Jenny, fearing that a total defection of the Indians would be
the result of his punishment.[1]

Lieutenant Jones, chilled with horror and broken in spirit by the event, tendered a resignation of his commission, but it was refused.   He purchased the scalp of his Jenny, and
with this cherished memento deserted, with his brother, before the army reached Saratoga,
and retired to Canada.   Various accounts have been given respecting the subsequent fate
of Lieutenant Jones.   Some assert that, perfectly desperate and careless of life, he rushed
into the thickest of the battle on Bemis's Heights, and was slain ; while others allege that
he died within three years afterward, heart-broken and insane.   But neither assertion is
true.   While searching for Mrs. F—n among her friends at Glenn's Falls, I called at the

----

[1] Earl of Harrington's Evidence in Burgoyne's "*State of the Expedition*," p. 66.

house of Judge R——s, whose lady is related by marriage to the family of Jones. Her aunt married a brother of Lieutenant Jones, and she often heard this lady speak of him. He lived in Canada to be an old man, and died but a few years ago. The death of Jenny was a heavy blow, and he never recovered from it. In youth he was gay and exceedingly garrulous, but after that terrible event he was melancholy and taciturn. He never married, and avoided society as much as business would permit. Toward the close of July in every year, when the anniversary of the tragedy approached, he would shut himself in his room and refuse the sight of any one; and at all times his friends avoided any reference to the Revolution in his presence.

At the time of this tragical event the American army under General Schuyler was encamped at Moses's Creek, five miles below Fort Edward. One of its two divisions was placed under the command of Arnold, who had just reached the army. His division included the rear-guard left at the fort. A picket-guard of one hundred men, July 23, 1777. under Lieutenant Van Vechten, was stationed on the hill a little north of the pine tree; and at the moment when the house of Mrs. M'Neil was attacked and plundered, and herself and Jenny were carried off, other parties of Indians, belonging to the same expedition, came rushing through the woods from different points, and fell upon the Americans. Lieutenant Van Vechten and several others were killed and their scalps borne off. Their bodies, with that of Jenny, were found by the party that went out from the fort in pursuit. She and the officer were lying near together, close by the spring already mentioned, and only a few feet from the pine tree. They were stripped of clothing, for plunder was the chief incentive of the savages to war. They were borne immediately to the fort, which the Americans at once evacuated, and Jane did indeed go down the river in the bateau in which she had intended to embark, but not glowing with life and beauty, as was expected by her fond brother. With the deepest grief, he took charge of her mutilated corse, which was buried at the same time and place with that of the lieutenant, on the west bank of the Hudson, near the mouth of a small creek about three miles below Fort Edward.

Mrs. M'Neil lived many years, and was buried in the small village cemetery, very near the ruins of the fort. In the summer of 1826 the remains of Jenny were taken up and deposited in the same grave with her. They were followed by a long train of young men and maidens, and the funeral ceremonies were conducted by the eloquent but unfortunate Hooper Cummings, of Albany, at that time a brilliant light in the American pulpit, but destined, like a glowing meteor, to go suddenly down into darkness and gloom. Many who were then young have a vivid recollection of the pathetic discourse of that gifted man, who on that occasion "made all Fort Edward weep," as he delineated anew the sorrowful picture of the immolation of youth and innocence upon the horrid altar of war.

GRAVE OF JANE M'CREA.

A plain white marble slab, about three feet high, with the simple inscription *Jane M'Crea*, marks the spot of her interment. Near by, as seen in the picture, is an antique brown stone slab, erected to the memory of Duncan Campbell, a relative of Mrs. M'Neil's first husband, who was mortally wounded at Ticonderoga in 1758.[1] Several others of the same name lie near, members of the family of Donald Campbell, a brave Scotchman who was with Montgomery at the storming of Quebec in 1775.

We lingered long in the cool shade at the spring before departing for the village burial-ground where the remains of Jenny rest. As we emerged from the woods we saw two or

---

[1] The following is the inscription:

HERE LYES THE BODY OF DUNCAN CAMPBELL, OF INVERSAW. ESQR., MAJOR TO THE OLD HIGHLAND REGT., AGED 55 YEARS, WHO DIED THE 17TH JULY, 1758, OF THE WOUNDS HE RECEIVED IN THE ATTACK OF THE RETRENCHMENTS OF TICONDEROGA OR CARILLON THE 8TH JULY, 1758.

102   PICTORIAL FIELD-BOOK

Young Girl struck by Lightning.   Village Burial-ground.   Colonel Cochran and his Adventures.   Rogers's Island.

three persons with a horse and wagon, slowly ascending the hill from the village.   In the wagon, upon a mattress, was a young girl who had been struck by lightning, two days before, while drawing water from a well.[1]   Although alive, her senses were all paralyzed by the shock, and her sorrowing father was carrying her home, perhaps to die.   With brief words of consoling hope, we stepped up and looked upon the stricken one.   Her breathing was soft and slow—a hectic glow was upon each cheek ; but all else of her fair young face was pale as alabaster except her lips.   It was grievous, even to a stranger, to look upon a young life so suddenly prostrated, and we turned sadly away to go to the grave of another, who in the bloom of young womanhood was also smitten to the earth, not by the lightning from Heaven, but by the arm of warring man.

The village burial-ground is near the site of the fort, and was thickly strewn with wild flowers.   We gathered a bouquet from the grave of Jenny, and preserved it for the eye of the curious in an impromptu herbarium made of a city newspaper.   A few feet from her "narrow house" is the grave of Colonel Robert Cochran, whom I have already mentioned as commanding a detachment of militia at Fort Edward at the time of Burgoyne's surrender.   He was a brave officer, and was warmly attached to the American cause.   In 1778 he was sent to Canada as a spy.   His errand being suspected, a large bounty was offered for his head.   He was obliged to conceal himself, and while doing so at one time in a brush-heap, he was taken dangerously ill.   Hunger and disease made him venture to a log cabin in sight.   As he approached he heard three men and a woman conversing on the subject of the reward for his head, and discovered that they were actually forming plans for his capture.   The men soon left the cabin in pursuit of him, and he immediately 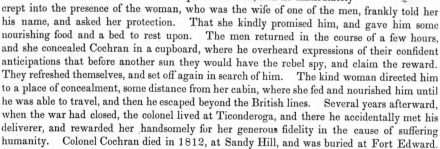 crept into the presence of the woman, who was the wife of one of the men, frankly told her his name, and asked her protection.   That she kindly promised him, and gave him some nourishing food and a bed to rest upon.   The men returned in the course of a few hours, and she concealed Cochran in a cupboard, where he overheard expressions of their confident anticipations that before another sun they would have the rebel spy, and claim the reward.   They refreshed themselves, and set off again in search of him.   The kind woman directed him to a place of concealment, some distance from her cabin, where she fed and nourished him until he was able to travel, and then he escaped beyond the British lines.   Several years afterward, when the war had closed, the colonel lived at Ticonderoga, and there he accidentally met his deliverer, and rewarded her handsomely for her generous fidelity in the cause of suffering humanity.   Colonel Cochran died in 1812, at Sandy Hill, and was buried at Fort Edward.

It was hot noon when I left the village cemetery, and took shelter under the shadow of the venerable balm of Gilead tree at the place of the water-gate of the fort.   A few rods be-

MOUTH OF FORT EDWARD CREEK.[2]

low is the mouth of Fort Edward Creek, on the south of which the British army were encamped when Burgoyne tarried there to send an expedition to Bennington, and, after that disastrous affair, to recruit and discipline his forces.   Dividing the waters of the Hudson in front of the fort is Rogers's Island, a beautiful and romantic spot, which was used as a camp-ground by the English and French alternately during the French and Indian war.   Almost every year the

[1] This mournful event occurred in the village, very near the same spot where, a year before, five men in a store were instantly killed by one thunder-bolt.

[2] This sketch is taken from within the intrenchments of Fort Edward, near the magazine, looking southwest.   On the left, just beyond the balm of Gilead tree, is seen the creek, and on the right, across the water, Rogers's Island.

plow turns up some curious relics of the past upon the island, such as bayonets, tomahawks, buttons, bullets, cannon-balls, coin, arrow-heads, &c.   Dr. Norton, of Fort Edward, gave me a skull that had been exhumed there, which is remarkable for its excessive thickness; not so thick, however, as to resist the force of a musket-ball which penetrated it, and doubtless deprived its owner of life.   It is three eighths of an inch thick where the bullet entered in front, and, notwithstanding its long inhumation, the sutures are perfect.   Its form is that of the negro, and it probably belonged to the servant of some officer stationed there.

The silver coin found in the vicinity of Fort Edward is called by the people "cob money." The derivation of this name I could not learn.   I obtained two pieces of it, both of which are Spanish coin.   The larger one is a cross-pistareen, of the value of sixteen cents; the other is a quarter fraction of the same coin.   They are very irregular in form, and the devices and dates are quite imperfect.   The two in my possession are dated respectively 1741, 1743 These Spanish small coins composed the bulk of specie circulation among the French in Canada at that time

TWO SIDES OF A CROSS-PISTAREEN.

CHAPTER V.

" Though of the past from no carved shrines,
　　Canvass, or deathless lyres, we learn,
　Yet arbor'd streams and shadowy pines
　　Are hung with legends wild and stern :
　In deep dark glen—on mountain side,
　　Are graves whence stately pines have sprung,
　Naught telling how the victims died,
　　Save faint tradition's faltering tongue."
　　　　　　　　　　　　　　　STREET.

E dined at three, and immediately left the pleasant little village of Fort Edward in a barouche for Glenn's Falls, by the way of Sandy Hill, a distance of six miles.   The latter village is beautifully situated upon the high left bank of the Hudson, where the river makes a sudden sweep from an easterly to a southerly course. Here is the termination of the Hudson Valley, and above it the river courses its way in a narrow channel, among rugged rocks and high, wooden bluffs, through as wild and romantic a region as the most enthusiastic traveler could desire.

It was early in the afternoon when we reached the Mansion House at Glenn's Falls, near the cataract.   All was bustle and confusion, for here is the brief tarrying-place of fashionable tourists on their way from Saratoga Springs to Lake George. There was a constant arrival and departure of visitors.   Few remained longer than to dine or sup, view the falls at a glance, and then hasten away to the grand summer lounge at Caldwell, to hunt, fish, eat, drink, dance, and sleep to their heart's content.   We were thoroughly wearied by the day's ramble and ride, but time was too precious to allow a moment of pleasant weather to pass by unimproved.   Comforted by the anticipation of a Sabbath rest the next day, we brushed the dust from our clothes, made a hasty toilet, and started out to view the falls, and search for the tarrying-place of Mrs. F—n, of Fort Edward.

Here the whole aspect of things is changed.   Hitherto our journey had been among the quiet and beautiful ; now every thing in nature was turbulent and grand.   The placid river was here a foaming cataract, and gentle slopes, yellow with the ripe harvest, were exchanged for high, broken hills, some rocky and bare, others green with the oak and pine or dark with the cedar and spruce.   Here nature, history, and romance combine to interest and please, and geology spreads out one of its most wonderful pages for the scrutiny of the student and philosopher.   All over those rugged hills Indian warriors and hunters scouted for ages before the *pale face* made his advent among them ; and the slumbering echoes were often awakened in the last century by the crack of musketry and the roar of cannon, mingled with the loud war-hoop of the Huron, the Iroquois, the Algonquin, the Mohegan, the Delaware, the Adirondack, and the Mohawk, when the French and English battled for mastery in the vast forests that skirted the lakes and the St. Lawrence.   Here, amid the roar of this very cataract, if romance may be believed, the voice of Uncas, the last of the Mohegans, was heard and heeded ; here Hawk Eye kept his vigils ; here David breathed his nasal melody ; and here Duncan Heyward, with his lovely and precious wards, Alice and Cora Monroe, fell into the hands of the dark and bitter Mingo chief.[1]

---

[1] See Cooper's " Last of the Mohicans."

The natural scenery about the falls is very picturesque, but the accompaniments of puny art are exceedingly incongruous, sinking the grand and beautiful into mere burlesque. How expertly the genius of man, quickened by acquisitiveness, fuses the beautiful and useful in the crucible of gain, and, by the subtle alchemy of profit, transmutes the glorious cascade and its fringes of rock and shrub into broad arable acres, or lofty houses, or speeding ships, simply by catching the bright stream in the toils of a mill-wheel. Such meshes are here spread out on every side to ensnare the leaping Hudson, and the rickety buildings, the clatter of machinery, and the harsh grating of saws, slabbing the huge black marble rocks of the shores into city mantels, make horrid dissonance of that harmony which the eye and ear expect and covet where nature is thus beautiful and musical.

A bridge, nearly six hundred feet long, and resting in the center upon a marble island, spans the river at the foot of the falls, and from its center there is a fine view of the cataract. The entire descent of the river is about sixty feet. The undivided stream first pours over a precipice nine hundred feet long, and is then separated into three channels by rocks piled in confusion, and carved, and furrowed, and welled, and polished by the rushing waters.

Below, the channels unite, and in one deep stream the waters flow on gently between the quarried cliffs of fine black marble, which rise in some places from thirty to seventy feet in height, and are beautifully stratified. Many fossils are imbedded in the rocks, among which the *trilobite* is quite plentiful. Here the heads (so exceedingly rare) are frequently found.

By the contribution of a York shilling to an intelligent lad who kept "watch and ward" at a flight of steps below the bridge, we procured his permission to descend to the rocks below, and his services as guide to the "Big Snake" and the "Indian Cave." The

VIEW BELOW THE FALLS.[1]

former is a petrifaction on the surface of a flat rock, having the appearance of a huge serpent ; the latter extends through the small island from one channel to the other, and is pointed out as the place where Cooper's sweet young heroines, Cora and Alice, with Major Heyward and the singing-master, were concealed. The melody of a female voice, chanting an air in a minor key, came up from the cavern, and we expected every moment to hear the pitch-pipe of David and the "Isle of Wight." The spell was soon broken by a merry laugh, and three young girls, one with a torn barege, came clambering up from the narrow entrance over which Uncas and Hawk Eye cast the green branches to conceal the fugitives. In time of floods this cave is filled, and all the dividing rocks below the main fall are covered with water, presenting one vast foaming sheet. A long drought had greatly diminished the volume of the stream when we were there, and materially lessened the usual grandeur of the picture.

We passed the Sabbath at the falls. On Monday morning I arose at four, and went down to the bridge to sketch the cascade. The whole heavens were overcast, and a fresh breeze from the southeast was driving portentous scuds before it, and piling them in dark masses along the western horizon. Rain soon began to fall, and I was obliged to retreat under the bridge, and content myself with sketching the more quiet scene of the river and shore below the cataract.

We left Glenn's Falls in a "Rockaway" for Caldwell, on Lake George, nine miles northward, at nine in the morning, the rain falling copiously. The road passes over a wild,

---

[1] This view was taken from under the bridge, looking down the river. The noted cave opens upon the river just below where the figures stand.

broken, and romantic region.   Our driver was a perfect Jehu.   The plank road (since finished) was laid a small part of the way, and the speed he accomplished thereon he tried to
keep up over the stony ground of the old track, to "*prevent jolting!*"

On the right side of the road, within four miles of Lake George, is a huge boulder called
"Williams's Rock."   It was so
named from the fact that near it
Colonel Ephraim Williams was
killed on the 8th of September,
1755, in an engagement with
the French and Indians under
Baron Dieskau.   Major-general
(afterward Sir William) Johnson was at that time at the head
of Lake George, with a body of
provincial troops, and a large

WILLIAMS'S ROCK.[1]

party of Indians under Hendrick,
the famous Mohawk sachem.
Dieskau, who was at Skenesborough, marched along the course
of Wood Creek to attack Fort
Edward, but the Canadians and
Indians were so afraid of cannon
that, when within two miles of
the fort, they urged him to change
his course, and attack Johnson in
his camp on Lake George.   To

this request he acceded, for he ascertained by his scouts that Johnson was rather carelessly
encamped, and was probably unsuspicious of danger.
Information of his march was communicated to the
English commander at midnight, September 7th,
and early in the morning a council of war was   1755.
held.   It was determined to send out a small party to
meet the French, and the opinion of Hendrick was asked.   He shrewdly said, "If they are to fight, they are
too few; if they are to be killed, they are too many."
His objection to the proposition to separate them into
three divisions was quite as sensibly and laconically expressed.   Taking three sticks and putting them together, he remarked, "Put them together, and you can't
break them.   Take them one by one, and you can break
them easily."   Johnson was guided by the opinion of
Hendrick, and a detachment of twelve hundred men in
one body, under Colonel Williams, was sent out to meet
the approaching enemy.

Before commencing their march, Hendrick mounted
a gun-carriage and harangued his warriors in a strain
of eloquence which had a powerful effect upon them.   He was then about sixty-five years
old.   His head was covered with long white locks, and every warrior loved him with the
deepest veneration.[3]   President Dwight, referring to this speech, says, "Lieutenant-colonel

HENDRICK.[2]

---

[1] This view is taken from the road, looking northward.   In the distance is seen the highest point of the
French Mountain, on the left of which is Lake George.   From this commanding height the French scouts
had a fine view of all the English movements at the head of the lake.

[2] The portrait here given of the chief is from a colored print published in London during the lifetime of
the sachem.   It was taken while he was in England, and habited in the full court dress presented to him
by the king.   Beneath the picture is engraved, "The brave old Hendrick, the great sachem or chief of the
Mohawk Indians, one of the six nations now in alliance with, and subject to, the King of Great Britain."

[3] Hendrick (sometimes called King Hendrick) was born about 1680, and generally lived at the *Upper
Castle*, upon the Mohawk.   He stood high in the estimation of Sir William Johnson, and was one of the
most active and sagacious sachems of his time.   When the tidings of his death were communicated to his
son, the young chief gave the usual groan upon such occasions, and, placing his hand over his heart, exclaimed, "My father still alive here.   The son is now the father, and stands here ready to fight."—*Gentlemen's Magazine.*

Sir William Johnson obtained from Hendrick nearly one hundred thousand acres of choice land, now
lying chiefly in Herkimer county, north of the Mohawk, in the following manner: The sachem, being at
the baronet's house, saw a richly-embroidered coat and coveted it.   The next morning he said to Sir William, "Brother, me dream last night."   "Indeed," answered Sir William; "what did my red brother

Pomeroy, who was present and heard this effusion of Indian eloquence, told me that, although he did not understand a word of the language, such were the animation of Hendrick, the fire of his eye, the force of his gestures, the strength of his emphasis, the apparent propriety of the inflections of his voice, and the natural appearance of his whole manner, that himself was more deeply affected with this speech than with any other he had ever heard."

The French, advised by scouts of the march of the English, approached with their line in the form of a half moon, the road cutting the center. The country was so thickly wooded that all correct observation was precluded, and at Rocky Brook, four miles from Lake George, Colonel Williams and his detachment found themselves directly in the hollow of the half moon. A heavy fire was opened upon them in front and on both flanks at the same moment, and the slaughter was dreadful. Colonel Williams was shot dead near the rock before mentioned, and Hendrick fell, mortally wounded by a musket-ball in the back. This circumstance gave him great uneasiness, for it seemed to imply that he had turned his back upon his enemy. The fatal bullet came from one of the extreme flanks. On the fall of Williams, Lieutenant-colonel Whiting succeeded to the command, and effected a retreat so judiciously that he saved nearly all of the detachment who were not killed or wounded by the first onslaught.[1]

So careless and apathetic was General Johnson, that he did not commence throwing up breast-works at his camp until after Colonel Williams had marched, and Dieskau was on the road to meet him. The firing was heard at Lake George, and then the alarmed commander began in earnest to raise defenses, by forming a breast-work of trees, and mounting two cannon which he had fortunately received from Fort Edward the day before, when his men thus employed should have been sent out to reenforce the retreating regiment. Three hundred were, indeed, sent out, but were totally inadequate. They met the flying English, and, joining in the retreat, hastened back to the camp, closely pursued by the French.

A short distance from Williams's Rock is a small, slimy, bowl-shaped pond, about three hundred feet in diameter, and thickly covered with the leaves of the water-lily. It is near the battle-ground where Williams and his men were slain, and the French made it the sepulcher for the slaughtered Englishmen. Tradition avers that for many years its waters bore a bloody hue,

BLOODY POND.

dream?" "Me dream that coat be mine." "It is yours," said the shrewd baronet. Not long afterward Sir William visited the sachem, and he too had a dream. "Brother," he said, "I dreamed last night." "What did my pale-faced brother dream?" asked Hendrick. "I dreamed that this tract of land was mine," describing a square bounded on the south by the Mohawk, on the east by Canada Creek, and north and west by objects equally well known. Hendrick was astonished. He saw the enormity of the request, but was not to be outdone in generosity. He sat thoughtfully for a moment, and then said, "Brother, the land is yours, but you must not dream again." The title was confirmed by the British government, and the tract was called the Royal Grant.—*Simms's Schoharie County*, p. 124.

[1] Colonel Ephraim Williams was born in 1715, at Newton, Massachusetts. He made several voyages to Europe in early life. Being settled at Stockbridge when the war with France, in 1740, commenced, and possessed of great military talent, he was intrusted with the command of the line of Massachusetts forts on the west side of the Connecticut River. He joined General Johnson, at the head of a regiment, in 1755, and, as we have seen, fell while gallantly leading his men against the enemy. By his will, made before joining Johnson, he bequeathed his property to a township west of Fort Massachusetts, on the condition that it should be called Williamstown, and the money used for the establishment and maintenance of a free school. The terms were complied with, and the school was afterward incorporated (1793) as a college. Such was the origin of Williams's College. Colonel Williams was forty years old at the time of his death.

108 PICTORIAL FIELD-BOOK

Arrival at Caldwell.   Indian and French Names of Lake George.   Fort William Henry.   Attack upon Johnson's Camp, 1755

and it has ever since been called *Bloody Pond*.   I alighted in the rain, and made my way through tall wet grass and tangled vines, over a newly-cleared field, until I got a favorable view for the sketch here presented, which I hope the reader will highly prize, for it cost a pair of boots, a linen "sack" ruined by the dark droppings from a cotton umbrella, and a box of cough lozenges.

It was almost noon when we reined up at the Lake House at Caldwell.   We had anticipated much pleasure from the first sight of Horicon, but a mist covered its waters, and its mountain frame-work was enveloped in fog ; so we reserved our sentiment for use the next fair day, donned dry clothing, and sat quietly down in the parlor to await the sovereign pleasure of the storm.

Lake George is indeed a beautiful sheet of water, and along its whole length of thirty-six miles almost every island, bay, and bluff is clustered with historic associations.   On account of the purity of its waters, the Indians gave it the name of *Horicon*, or *Silver Water*.   They also called it *Canideri-oit*, or *The Tail of the Lake*, on account of its connection with Lake Champlain.[1]   It was visited by Samuel Champlain in 1609, and some suppose that he gave his name to this lake instead of the one which now bears it.   It is fair to infer, from his own account, that he penetrated southward as far as Glenn's Falls ; and it is not a little remarkable that in the same year, and possibly at the same season, Hendrick Hudson was exploring below the very stream near the head-waters of which the French navigator was resting.   Strange that two adventurers, in the service of different sovereigns ruling three thousand miles away, and approaching from different points of the compass, so nearly met in the vast forests of wild America.   The French, who afterward settled at Chimney Point, on Lake Champlain, frequently visited this lake, and gave it the name of *Sacrament*, its pure waters suggesting the idea.[2]

The little village of Caldwell contains about two hundred inhabitants, and is situated

FORT WILLIAM HENRY.[3]

near the site of Fort William Henry, at the head of the lake, a fortress erected by General Johnson toward the close of 1755, after his battle there with the French under Dieskau.   That battle occurred on the same day when Colonel Williams and his detachment were routed at Rocky Brook.   The French pursued the retreating English vigorously, and about noon they were seen approaching in considerable force and regular order, aiming directly toward the center of the British encampment.   When within one hundred rods of the breast-works, in the open valley in front of the elevation on which Fort George (now a picturesque ruin) was afterward built, Dieskau halted and disposed his Indians and Canadians upon the right and left flanks.   The regular troops, under the immediate command of the baron, attacked the English center, but, having only small arms, the effect was trifling.   The English reserved their fire until the Indians and Canadians were close upon them, when with sure aim they poured upon them a volley of musket-balls which mowed them down like grass before the

---

[1] Spafford's Gazetteer of New York.

[2] The bed of the lake is a yellowish sand, and the water is so transparent that a white object, such as an earthen plate, may be seen upon the bottom at a depth of nearly forty feet.   The delicious salmon trout, that weigh from five to twenty pounds, silver trout, pike, pickerel, and perch are found here in great abundance, and afford fine sport and dainty food for the swarms of visitors at the Lake House during the summer season.

[3] The extent of the embankments and fosse of this fort was fourteen hundred feet, and the barracks were built of wood upon a strong foundation of lime-stone, which abounds in the neighborhood.   This plan is copied from a curious old picture by Blodget, called a " Prospective Plan of the Battles near Lake George 1755."

scythe.   At the same moment a bomb-shell was thrown among them by a howitzer, while two field pieces showered upon them a quantity of grape-shot.   The savage allies, and almost as savage colonists, greatly terrified, broke and fled to the swamps in the neighborhood. The regulars maintained their ground for some time, but, abandoned by their companions, and terribly galled by the steady fire from the breast-works, at length gave way, and Dieskau attempted a retreat.   Observing this, the English leaped over their breast-works and pursued them.   The French were dispersed in all directions, and Dieskau, wounded and helpless, was found leaning upon the stump of a tree.   As the provincial soldier[1] who discovered him approached, he put his hand in his pocket to draw out his watch as a bribe to allow him to escape.   Supposing that he was feeling for a pocket pistol, the soldier gave him a severe wound in the hip with a musket-ball.   He was carried into the English camp in a blanket and tenderly treated, and was soon afterward taken to Albany, then to New York, and finally to England, where he died from the effects of his wounds.   Johnson was wounded at the commencement of the conflict in the fleshy part of his thigh, in which a musket-ball lodged, and the whole battle was directed for five consecutive hours by General Lyman, the second in command.[2]

Johnson's Indians, burning with a fierce desire to avenge the death of Hendrick, were eager to follow the retreating enemy ; and General Lyman proposed a vigorous continuation of efforts by attacking the French posts at Ticonderoga and Crown Point, on Lake Champlain.   But Johnson, either through fear, a love of ease, or some other inexplicable cause, withheld his consent, and the residue of the autumn was spent in erecting Fort William Henry.

In the colonial wars, as well as in the war of our Revolution, the British government was often unfortunate in its choice of commanders.   Total inaction, or, at best, great tardiness, frequently marked their administration of military affairs.   They could not comprehend the elastic activity of the provincials, and were too proud to listen to their counsels.   This tardiness and pride cost them many misfortunes, either by absolute defeat in battle, or the theft of glorious opportunities for victory through procrastination.   Their shrewd savage allies saw and lamented this, and before the commissioners of the several colonies, who met at Albany in 1754 to consult upon a plan of colonial alliance, in which the SIX NATIONS[3] were invited to join, Hendrick administered a pointed rebuke to the governor and military commanders.   The sachems were first addressed by James Delancy, then lieutenant-governor of New York ; and Hendrick, who was a principal speaker, in the course of a reply remarked, " Brethren, we have not as yet confirmed the peace with them (meaning the French-Indian allies).   'Tis your fault, brethren ; we are not strengthened by conquest, for we should have gone and taken Crown Point, but you hindered us.   We had concluded to go and take it, but were told it was too late, that the ice would not bear us.   Instead of this, you burned your own fort at *Sar-ragh-to-gee* [near old Fort Hardy], and ran away from it, which was a shame and a scandal to you.   Look about your country, and see ; you have no fortifications about you—no, not even to this city.   'Tis but one step from Canada hither, and the French may easily come and turn you out of doors.

" Brethren, you were desirous we should open our minds and our hearts to you : look at

---

[1] This soldier is believed to have been General Seth Pomeroy, of Northampton, Massachusetts.—*Everett's Life of Stark.*

[2] At this battle General Stark, the hero of Bennington, then a lieutenant in the corps of Rogers's Rangers, was first initiated in the perils and excitements of regular warfare.

[3] The SIX NATIONS consisted of the tribes of the *Mohawks, Onondagas, Oneidas, Senecas, Cayugas,* and *Tuscaroras.*   The first five were a long time allied, and known as the *Five Nations.*   They were joined by the *Tuscaroras* of North Carolina in 1714, and from that time the confederation was known by the title of the *Six Nations.*   Their great council fire was in the special keeping of the Onondagas, by whom it was always kept burning.   This confederacy was a terror to the other Indian tribes, and extended its conquests even as far as South Carolina, where it waged war against, and nearly exterminated, the once powerful Catawbas.   When, in 1744, the Six Nations ceded a portion of their lands to Virginia, they insisted on the continuance of a free war-path through the ceded territory.

the French, they are men—they are fortifying every where; but, we are ashamed to say it, you are like women, bare and open, without any fortifications."[1]

The head of Lake George was the theater of a terrible massacre in 1757. Lord Loudon, a man of no energy of character, and totally deficient in the requisites for a military leader, was appointed that year governor of Virginia, and commander-in-chief of all the British forces in North America. A habit of procrastination, and his utter indecision, thwarted all his active intentions, if he ever had any, and, after wasting the whole season in getting here and preparing to do something, he was recalled by Pitt, then prime minister, who gave as a reason for appointing Lord Amherst in his place, that *the minister never heard from him, and could not tell what he was doing.*[2]

Opposed to him was the skillful and active French commander, the Marquis Montcalm, who succeeded Dieskau. Early in the spring he made an attempt to capture Fort William
March 16, Henry. He passed up Lake George on St. Patrick's eve, landed stealthily behind
1757. Long Point, and the next afternoon appeared suddenly before the fort. A part of the garrison made a vigorous defense, and Montcalm succeeded only in burning some buildings and vessels which were out of reach of the guns at the fort.[3] He returned to Ticonderoga, at which post and at Crown Point he mustered all his forces, amounting to nine thousand men, including Canadians and Indians, and in July prepared for another attempt to capture Fort William Henry.

General Webb, who was commander of the forces in that quarter, was at Fort Edward with four thousand men. He visited Fort William Henry under an escort of two hundred men commanded by Major Putnam, and while there he sent that officer with eighteen Rangers down the lake, to ascertain the position of the enemy on Champlain. They were discovered to be more numerous than was supposed, for the islands at the entrance of Northwest Bay were swarming with French and Indians. Putnam returned, and begged General Webb to let him go down with his Rangers in full force and attack them, but he was allowed only to make another reconnoissance, and bring off two boats and their crews which he left fishing. The enemy gave chase in canoes, and at times nearly surrounded them, but they reached the fort in safety.

Webb caused Putnam to administer an oath of secrecy to his Rangers respecting the proximity of the enemy, and then ordered him to escort him back immediately to Fort Edward. This order was so repugnant to Putnam, both as to its perfidy and unsoldierly character, that he ventured to remonstrate by saying, " I hope your excellency does not intend to neglect so fair an opportunity of giving battle should the enemy presume to land." Webb coolly and cowardly replied, " What do you think we should do here ?" The near approach of the enemy was cruelly concealed from the garrison, and under his escort the general returned to Fort Edward. The next day he sent Colonel Monroe with a regiment to re-enforce and to take command of the garrison at Lake George.

Montcalm, with more than nine thousand men, and a powerful train of artillery, landed

[1] Reported for the *Gentlemen's Magazine*, London, 1755.

[2] This is asserted by Dr. Franklin in his Autobiography (Sparks's Life, 219), where he gives an anecdote illustrative of the character of Loudon. Franklin had occasion to go to his office in New York, where he met a Mr. Innis, who had brought dispatches from Philadelphia from Governor Denny, and was awaiting his lordship's answer, promised the following day. A fortnight afterward he met Innis, and expressed his surprise at his speedy return. But he had not yet gone, and averred that he had called at Loudon's office every morning during the fortnight, but the letters were not yet ready. " Is it possible," said Franklin, " when he is so great a writer ? I see him constantly at his escritoire." " Yes," said Innis, " but he is like St. George on the signs, *always on horseback, but never rides forward.*"

[3] The garrison and fort were saved by the vigilance of Lieutenant Stark, who, in the absence of Rogers, had command of the Rangers, a large portion of which were Irishmen. On the evening of the 16th he overheard some of these planning a celebration of St. Patrick's (the following day). He ordered the sutler not to issue spirituous liquors the next day without a written order. When applied to he pleaded a lame wrist as an excuse for not writing, and his Rangers were kept sober. The Irish in the regular regiments got drunk, as usual on such an occasion. Montcalm anticipated this, and planned his attack on the night of St. Patrick's day. Stark, with his sober Rangers, gallantly defended and saved the fort.

at the head of the lake, and beleaguered the garrison, consisting of less than three thousand men.[1] He sent in proposals to Monroe for a surrender of the fort, urging his humane desire to prevent the bloodshed which a stubborn resistance would assuredly cause. Monroe, confidently expecting re-enforcements from Webb, refused to listen to any such proposals. The French then commenced the siege, which lasted six consecutive days, without much slaughter on either side. Expresses were frequently sent to General Webb in the mean while, imploring aid, but he remained inactive and indifferent in his camp at Fort Edward. General Johnson was at last allowed to march, with Putnam and his Rangers, to the relief of the beleaguered garrison ; but when about three miles from Fort Edward, Webb recalled them, and sent a letter to Monroe, saying he could render him no assistance, and advising him to surrender. This letter was intercepted by Montcalm, and gave him great joy, for he had been informed by some Indians of the movements of the provincials under Johnson and Putnam, who represented them to be as numerous as the leaves on the trees. Alarmed at this, Montcalm was beginning to suspend the operations of the siege preparatory to a retreat, when the letter from the pusillanimous Webb fell into his hands. He at once sent it in to Monroe, with proposals for an immediate surrender.

Monroe saw that his case was hopeless, for two of his cannon had bursted, and his ammunition and stores were nearly exhausted. Articles of capitulation were agreed upon, and, under promise of protection, the garrison marched out of the fort preparatory to being escorted to Fort Edward.[2]

The savages, two thousand warriors in number, were enraged at the terms of capitulation, for they were induced to serve in this expedition by a promise of plunder.[3] This was denied them, and they felt at liberty to throw off all restraint. As soon as the last man left the gate of the fort, they raised the hideous war-whoop, and fell upon the English with the fury of demons. The massacre was indiscriminate and terrible, and the French were idle spectators of the perfidy of their allies. They refused interference, withheld the promised escort, and the savages pursued the poor Britons with great slaughter, half way to Fort Edward.[4] Fifteen hundred of them were butchered or carried into hopeless captivity. Montcalm utterly disclaimed all connivance, and declared his inability to prevent the massacre without ordering his men to fire upon the Indians. But it left a deep stain upon his otherwise humane character, and the indignation excited by the event aroused the English colonists to more united and vigorous action.

Montcalm burned and otherwise destroyed every thing connected with the fortification. Major Putnam, who had been sent with his Rangers from Fort Edward to watch the movements of Montcalm, reached Lake George just as the rear of the enemy left the shore, and truly awful was the scene there presented, as described by himself : " The fort was entirely demolished ; the barracks, out-houses, and buildings were a heap of ruins ; the cannon, stores, boats, and vessels were all carried away. The fires were still burning, the smoke and stench offensive and suffocating. Innumerable fragments, human skulls and bones, and carcasses half consumed, were still frying and broiling in the decaying fires.

August 9, 1757.

---

[1] The place where Montcalm landed is a little north of the Lake House, at Caldwell, and about a mile from the site of the fort.

[2] It was stipulated, 1st. That the garrison should march out with their arms and baggage ; 2d. Should be escorted to Fort Edward by a detachment of French troops, and should not serve against the French for a term of eighteen months ; 3d. The works and all the warlike stores should be delivered to the French ; 4th. That the sick and wounded of the garrison should remain under the protection of Montcalm, and should be permitted to return as soon as they were recovered.

[3] Dr. Belknap.

[4] The defile through which the English retreated, and in which so many were slaughtered, is called the Bloody Defile. It is a deep gorge between the road from Glenn's Falls to Lake George and the high range of hills northward, called the French Mountain. In excavations for the plank road near the defile a large number of skeletons were exhumed. I saw the skull of one, which was of an enormous size, at least one third larger than any other human head I ever saw. The occipital portion exhibited a long fracture, evidently made by a tomahawk.

Dead bodies, mangled with scalping-knives and tomahawks in all the wantonness of Indian fierceness and barbarity, were every where to be seen.   More than one hundred women, butchered and shockingly mangled, lay upon the ground, still weltering in their gore.   Devastation, barbarity, and horror every where appeared, and the spectacle presented was too diabolical and awful either to be endured or described."

Fort William Henry was never rebuilt.   Upon an eminence about a mile southeast of it, and half a mile from the lake, Fort George was erected, but it was never a scene of very stirring events.   A little south of Fort George was a small fortification called Fort Gage, so named in honor of General Gage, who served under Lord Amherst, and succeeded him in the command of the forces in America in 1760, and was Governor of Massachusetts when the Revolution broke out.   Hardly a vestige of this fort can now be seen.

The English, under General Abercrombie and the young Lord Howe, quartered at Fort George in 1758, preparatory to an attack upon the French posts upon Lake Champlain. Seven thousand regulars and nine thousand provincial troops were there assembled, with a one train of artillery and all necessary military stores, the largest and best-appointed army yet seen in America.   On the 5th of July they embarked on Lake George, on board nine hundred bateaux and one hundred and thirty-five whale-boats, and the next day landed at the foot of the lake and pushed on toward Ticonderoga.   Of the events which befell them there I shall hereafter write.   Let us glance a moment at the present.

Toward evening the rain abated, and, accompanied by an old resident shoemaker as guide, I made a visit to the remains of the two English forts.   The elder one (Fort William Henry) stood directly upon the lake shore, on the west side of a clear mountain stream called West Creek, the main inlet of Lake George.   Nothing of it now remains but a few mounds and shallow ditches, so leveled and filled that the form of the works can not be distinctly traced. The road along the lake shore passes across the northeast and northwest angles, but the features of the past are hardly tangible enough to attract the attention of a passer-by.   A little southwest of the fort, at the base of Rattlesnake or Prospect Hill, is a level clearing called the French Field.   It is the place where Dieskau halted and disposed his troops for action. Many of the slain were buried there; and I saw a rough-hewn stone at the head of a grave, upon which was inscribed, in rude characters, "Jacques Cortois, 1755."

Fort George, the remains of which are scattered over several acres, was situated about a mile southeast from William Henry, upon an eminence gently sloping back from the lake. The dark limestone or black marble, such as is found at Glenn's Falls, here every where approaching near the surface or protruding above, formed a solid foundation, and supplied ample materials for a fortress.   A quadrangular citadel, or sort of castle, was built within the lines of breast-works, and the ruins of this constitute all that is left of the old fort.   I observed vestiges of the foundations of the barracks and other buildings; and the quarries whence materials were taken for the buildings and ramparts seem almost as fresh as if just opened.   The wall of the citadel, on the eastern side (the left of the picture), is now about twenty feet high.   Within the ancient area of the fort there is just sufficient earth to nourish a thick growth of dark juniper bushes, which, with the black rocks and crumbling masonry, presented a somber aspect.   Both forts commanded a fine view of the lake for ten miles north.

The indications of fair weather which lured me out suddenly disappeared, and before I reached the Lake House the heavy clouds that came rolling up from the south poured down their contents copiously.   Dark masses

RUINS OF THE CITADEL OF FORT GEORGE.

of vapor hovered upon the mountains that begirt the lake, and about sunset the tops of all were buried in the driving mists. We seemed to be completely shut up within mighty prison walls, and early in the evening vivid lightning and heavy thunder-peals contributed to produce a scene of singular grandeur and awe. In the midst of the elemental strife the steam-boat arrived with passengers from Ticonderoga, and those pleasure seekers who came in her, bedraggled and weary, were capital studies for an artistic Jeremiah in search of lamentations personified. But an excellent supper, in dry quarters, soon brought the sunshine of gladness to every face, and before ten o'clock more than half the new-comers were among the liveliest in quadrille, cotillion, waltz, or gallopade.

I arose the next morning at four. The scene from my chamber window was one of quiet beauty. The sky was cloudless, and the lake, without a ripple, was spread out before me,

> "A glorious mirror of the Almighty's form."

The east was all glowing with the soft radiance of approaching sunlight, giving a deeper gray to the lofty hills that intervened, and every tree was musical with the morning song of the birds.

> "The south wind was like a gentle friend,
> Parting the hair so softly on my brow.
> It had come o'er the gardens, and the flowers
> That kissed it were betrayed; for as it parted
> With its invisible fingers my loose hair,
> I knew it had been trifling with the rose
> And stooping to the violet. There is joy
> For all God's creatures in it."
>   WILLIS.

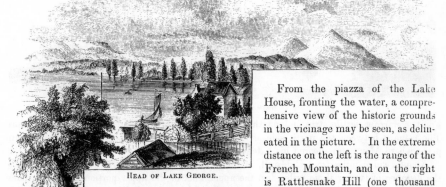

HEAD OF LAKE GEORGE.

From the piazza of the Lake House, fronting the water, a comprehensive view of the historic grounds in the vicinage may be seen, as delineated in the picture. In the extreme distance on the left is the range of the French Mountain, and on the right is Rattlesnake Hill (one thousand five hundred feet high), with other lofty elevations, heavily wooded to their very summits. By the trees on the shore, in the center of the picture, is the site of Fort William Henry ; and further on the left, and directly over the flag-staff, is the site of Fort George.

We left this fine summer resort in the steam-boat William Caldwell, at eight in the morning. The air was clear and cool, the company agreeable, and the voyage down the lake delightful. The mountain shores, the deep bays, and the numerous islands (said to be three hundred and sixty-five, the number of days in the year) present a constant variety, and all that the eye takes in on every side is one vision of beauty. I procured a seat in the pilot's room aloft, whence I had a broad view of the whole ever-changing panorama of the lake in the course of the voyage.

The first island which we passed, of any considerable size, was Diamond Island,[1] lying

---

[1] This name was given it on account of the number and beauty of the quartz crystals which are found upon it. In shape and brilliancy they resemble pure diamonds.

directly in front of Dunham's Bay.   Here was a depôt of military stores for Burgoyne's
army in 1777, and the scene of a sharp conflict between the small garrison that defended
it and a detachment of Americans under Colonel Brown.   Between the actions of the 19th
of September and 7th of October at Bemis's Heights, General Lincoln, with a body of New
England militia, got in the rear of Burgoyne near Lake Champlain.   He sent Colonel Brown
with a strong division to attempt the recapture of Ticonderoga and the posts in the vicinity,
and thus to cut off the retreat of the British as well as their supplies.   It was a service
September 25,   exactly suited to Brown's active and energetic character, and, by a rapid and
1777.   stealthy movement on a stormy night, he surprised and captured all the British outposts between the landing-place at the north end of Lake George and the main fortress at Ticonderoga.   Mount Hope, Mount Defiance, the French lines, and a block-house,
with an armed sloop, two hundred bateaux, and several gun-boats, fell into his hands.   He
also captured two hundred and ninety-three prisoners, and released one hundred Americans ;
and, among other things, he retook the old Continental standard which St. Clair left at Ticonderoga when he evacuated that post.   He then attacked the fortress, but its walls were
impregnable, and he withdrew.

Flushed with success, Colonel Brown determined to sweep Lake George, and in the vessels they had captured the Americans proceeded to Diamond Island.   The little garrison
there made a vigorous resistance, and the republicans were repulsed with some loss.   They
then pushed for the shore on the south side of Dunham's Bay, where they burned all the
vessels they had captured, and returned to Lincoln's camp.

A little north of Diamond Island is Long Island, which lies directly in front of Long

LONG POINT AND VICINITY.[1]

Point, a narrow, fertile strip of land that projects far into the lake from the eastern shore.
The estuary between the north side of the point and the mountains is Harris's Bay, the
place where Montcalm moored his bateaux and landed on the 16th of March, 1757.

About twelve miles from Caldwell, in the center of the lake, is Dome Island, which, at
the distance of two or three miles, has the appearance of the upper portion of a large dome,
with an arch as regular as if made by art.   This island was the shelter for Putnam's men
whom he left in the two boats while he informed General Webb of the presence of the French
and Indians upon the two islands near the entrance of Northwest Bay, and nearly in front
of the landing-place at Bolton, on the western shore.

Shelving Rock, a lofty cliff on the eastern shore, and Tongue Mountain, a bold, rocky
promontory on the west, flank the entrance to the Narrows, where the islands are so numerous, varying in size from a few rods to an acre, that there is only a very narrow channel for
a steam-boat to pass through.   A little north of Shelving Rock is the Black Mountain, its
summit twenty-two hundred feet high, thickly covered with the dark spruce, and its sides
robed with the cedar, fir, pine, and tamarac.   There the wild deer, the bear, and the cata-
mount have free range, for the hunter seldom toils up its weary ascent.

---

[1] This little sketch was taken from the steam-boat, near the south end of Long Island, which appears in
the foreground.   Long Point is seen in the center, and on the right are Dunham's Bay and the northern
extremity of the French Mountain.   The highest peak on the left is Deer Pasture, or Buck Mountain

OF THE REVOLUTION. 115

Sabbath Day Point.   Skirmish in 1756.   Halt of Abercrombie's Army.   Splendid Appearance of the Armament.

A few miles beyond the entrance to the Narrows, on the western shore, is another fertile strip of land projecting into the lake, called Sabbath Day Point. It is between three and four miles from the little village of Hague, in the midst of the most picturesque scenery imaginable. Here, in 1756, a small provincial force, pressed by a party of French and Indians, and unable to escape across the lake, made a desperate resistance, and defeated the enemy with

SABBATH DAY POINT.

considerable slaughter. Here, in the summer of 1758, General Abercrombie, with his fine army, already noticed as having embarked in bateaux and whale-boats at the head of the lake, landed for refreshments. It was just at dark, on a sultry Saturday evening, when the troops debarked and spread over the beautiful cape for a few hours' repose. The young Lord Howe, the well-beloved of both officers and soldiers, was there, and called around him, in serious consultation, some of the bravest of the youthful partisans who accompanied the expedition. Captain Stark (the Revolutionary general) was invited to sup with him; and long and anxious were the inquiries the young nobleman made respecting the fortress of Ticonderoga and its outposts, which they were about to assail, as if a presentiment of personal disaster possessed his mind.

July 5, 1758.

It was after midnight when the whole armament moved slow-

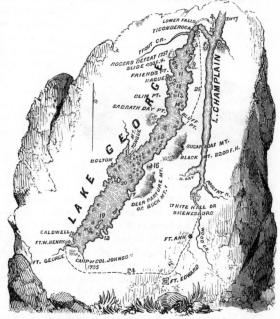

LAKE GEORGE AND PART OF LAKE CHAMPLAIN.[1]

ly down the lake, and it was late on the Sabbath morning before they reached the landing-place at the foot of it.[2] The scene exhibited by this strong and well-armed force of sixteen thousand men was very imposing. "The order of march," says Major Rogers, "exhibited a splendid military show." Howe, in a large boat, led the van of the flotilla. He was accompanied by a guard of Rangers and boatmen. The regular troops occupied the center and the provincials the wings. The sky was clear and starry, and not a breeze ruffled the dark waters as they slept quietly in the shadows of the mountains. Their oars were muf-

---

[1] Explanation of the references: 1. Fort Ticonderoga. 2. Fort Howe. 3. Mount Defiance. 4. Mount Independence. 5. Village of Alexandria. 7. Black Point. 8. Juniper Island. 9. Anthony's Nose. 10. M'Donald's Bay. 11. Rogers's retreat on the ice to Fort William Henry. 12. Cook's Islands. 13. Scotch Bonnet. 14. Odell Island. 15. Buck Mountain and Rattlesnake Dens. 16. Shelving Rock. 17. Phelps's Point. 18. Long Point. 19. Long Island. 20. Dome Island. 21. Diamond Island. 22. Dunham's Bay. 23. Harris's Bay. 24. The route of Dieskau from Skenesborough to Fort William Henry.

[2] It being early on Sunday morning when the army left the point, General Abercrombie named the place Sabbath Day Point. The little sketch here given was taken from the steam-boat, half a mile above, looking northeast.

116   PICTORIAL FIELD-BOOK

Skirmish at Sabbath Day Point, 1776.   Rogers's Slide.   Narrow Escape of Major Rogers.   Prisoners' Island.

fled ; and so silently did they move on in the darkness, that not a scout upon the hills observed them. Day dawned just as they were abreast of the Blue Mountain, four miles from the landing-place ; and the first intimation which the outposts of the enemy, stationed there, had of the approach of the English was the full blaze of red uniforms which burst upon their sight as the British army swept around a point and prepared to land.

At Sabbath Day Point a party of American militia of Saratoga county had a severe battle with Tories and Indians in 1776. Both were scouting parties, and came upon each other unexpectedly. The Americans repulsed the enemy, and killed and wounded about forty. There are now a few buildings upon the point, and the more peaceful heroism of the culturist, in conflict with the unkindness of nature, is beautifying and enriching it.

On the western shore of the lake, three miles northward of the little village of Hague, is

ROGERS'S ROCK.[1]

Rogers's Rock, or Rogers's Slide. The lake is here quite narrow, and huge masses of rocks, some a hundred feet high, are piled in wild confusion on every side. The whole height of Rogers's Rock is about four hundred feet, and the "slide," almost a smooth surface, with a descent on an angle of about twenty-five degrees from meridian, is two hundred feet. This hill derives its name from the fact, that from its summit Major Rogers, commander of a corps of Rangers, escaped from Indian pursuers. With a small party who were reconnoitering at the outlet of the lake, in the winter of 1758, he was surprised and put to flight by a band of Indians. He was equipped with snow-shoes, and eluded pursuit until he came to the summit of the mountain. Aware that they would follow his track, he descended to the top of the smooth rock, and, casting his knapsack and his haversack of provisions down upon the ice, slipped off his snow-shoes, and, without moving them, turned himself about and put them on his feet again. He then retreated along the southern brow of the rock several rods, and down a ravine he made his way safely to the lake below, snatched up his pack, and fled on the ice to Fort George. The Indians, in the mean while, coming to the spot, saw the two tracks, both apparently approaching the precipice, and concluded that two persons had cast themselves down the rock rather than fall into their hands. Just then they saw the bold leader of the Rangers making his way across the ice, and believing that he had slid down the steep face of the rock, considered him (as did the Indians Major Putnam at Fort Miller) under the special protection of the Great Spirit, and made no attempt at pursuit.[2]

In consequence of a detention at Bolton, we did not reach the landing-place at the outlet of the lake until noon. Within a mile of the landing is a small island covered with shrubbery, called Prisoners' Island, where the French, in the Seven Years' War, kept their English captives who were taken in that vicinity. The first party confined there easily es-

---

[1] This sketch is from the lake, a little south of Cook's Point, seen just over the boat on the left. Immediately beyond is seen the smooth rock. Nearly opposite the "slide" is Anthony's Nose, a high, rocky promontory, having the appearance of a human nose in shape when viewed from a particular point.

[2] Major Rogers was the son of an Irishman, who was an early settler of Dumbarton, in New Hampshire. He was appointed to the command of a party of Rangers in 1755, and with them did signal service to the British cause. In 1759 he was sent by General Amherst from Crown Point to destroy the Indian village of St. Francis. He afterward served in the Cherokee war. In 1766 he was appointed governor of Michillimackinac. He was accused of constructive treason, and was sent in irons to Montreal for trial. In 1769 he went to England, was presented to the king, but soon afterward was imprisoned for debt. He returned to America, and in the Revolution took up arms for the king. In 1777 he returned to England, where he died. His name was on the proscription list of Tories included in the act of New Hampshire against them, in 1778. His journal of the French War, first published at London in 1765, was republished at Concord in 1831.

caped, in consequence of the carelessness of the victors in not ascertaining the depth of the water, which on one side is fordable. A small guard was left in charge of them, and, as soon as the main body of the French had retreated, the English prisoners *waded* from the island and escaped.

Directly west of this island is Howe's Landing, the place where Lord Howe with the van-guard of Abercrombie's army first landed, the outlet, a mile below, being in possession of the enemy. The whole British force debarked here on the morning after leaving Sabbath Day Point, and before noon the Rangers under Rogers and Stark were pushing July 6, forward toward Ticonderoga, as a flank or advance-guard to clear the woods, while 1758. the main army pressed onward.

The distance from the steam-boat landing to Fort Ticonderoga is four miles. We found vehicles in abundance awaiting our arrival, and prepared to carry passengers with all their baggage, from a clean dickey only to a four-feet trunk, for twenty-five cents each. I succeeded in securing my favorite seat on a pleasant day, the coachman's perch. At the Lake House we became acquainted with a young lady from the vicinity of the lofty Catskills. whose love of travel and appreciation of nature made her an enthusiast, and one of the most agreeable companions imaginable. She fairly reveled in the beauties of Lake George, not exhibited in the simpering lip-sentimentality, borrowed from the novelist, which so often annoys the sensible man when in the midst of mere fashionable tourists, but in hearty, intelligent, and soul-stirring emotions of pleasure, which lie far deeper in the heart than mortal influence can fathom, and which gleam out in every lineament of the face. While others were afraid of spoiling their complexions in the sun, or of crumpling their smooth dresses or fine bonnets, she bade defiance to dust and crowds, for her brown linen " sack," with its capacious pockets for a guide-book and other accessories, and her plain sun-bonnet gave her no uneasiness ; and her merry laughter, which awoke ringing echoes along the hills as she. too, mounted the coachman's seat to enjoy the fresh air and pleasant landscape, was the very soul of pleasure. We rambled with herself and brother that afternoon over the ruins of Ticonderoga, and at evening parted company. We hope her voyage of life may be as pleasant and joyous as those few hours which she spent that day, where,

> " In the deepest core
> Of the free wilderness, a crystal sheet
> Expands its mirror to the trees that crowd
> Its mountain borders."

The road from the foot of Lake George to Fort " Ty" is hilly, but the varied scenery makes the ride a pleasant one. We crossed the outlet of the lake twice ; first at the Upper Falls, where stands the dilapidated village of Alexandria, its industrial energies weighed down, I was told, by the narrow policy of a " lord of the manor" residing in London, who owns the fee of all the land and of the water privileges, and will not sell, or give long leases The good people of the place pray for his life to be a short and a happy one—a very generous supplication. From the high ground near the village a fine prospect opened on the eastward ; and suddenly, as if a curtain had been removed, the cultivated farms and pleasant villages of Vermont along the lake shore, and the blue line of the Green Mountains in the far distance, were spread out before us.

The second or Lower Falls is half way between the two lakes, and here the thriving village of Ticonderoga is situated. A bridge and a saw-mill were there many years before the Revolution ; and this is the spot where Lord Howe, at the head of his column, crossed the stream and pushed forward through the woods toward the French lines, a mile and a quarter beyond. We arrived at the Pavilion near the fort at one o'clock, dined, and with a small party set off immediately to view the interesting ruins of one of the most noted fortresses in America. Before noticing its present condition and appearance, let us glance at its past history.

Ticonderoga is a corruption of Cheonderoga, an Iroquois word, signifying *Sounding wa ters,* and was applied by the Indians to the rushing waters of the outlet of Lake George at the falls.   The French, who first built a fort at Crown Point (Fort St. Frederic), estab-lished themselves upon this peninsula in 1755, and the next year they began the erection of a strong fortress, which they called *Fort Carillon.*[1]   The Indian name was generally applied to it, and by that only was it known from the close of the French and Indian war in 1763.[2]

The peninsula is elevated more than one hund-red feet above the lake, and contains about five hundred acres.   Nature and art made it a strong place.   Water was upon three sides, and a deep swamp extended nearly across the fourth.   Within a mile north of the fortress intrenchments were thrown up, the remains of which may still be seen at each side of the road, and are known as the French lines.   The whole defenses were completed by the erection of a breast-work nine feet high, upon the narrowest part of the neck between the swamp and the outlet of Lake George ; and before the breast-work was a strong *abatis.*

Here, as I have already mentioned, was the general rendezvous of the French under Montcalm,

GROUND PLAN.

August 3, 1757.   preparatory to the attack on Fort William Henry.   It continued to be the head-quarters of that general until Quebec was threatened by an expedition under Wolfe, 1759.   up the St. Lawrence, when he abandoned the posts on Lake Champlain, and mustered all his forces at the capital of Lower Canada.

Montcalm commanded a force of four thousand men at Ticonderoga when Abercrombie July 6, 1758.   approached, and was in daily expectation of receiving a re-enforcement of three thou-sand troops under M. de Levi.   The English commander was advised of this ex-pected re-enforcement of the garrison, and felt the necessity of making an immediate attack upon the works.   His army moved forward in three columns ; but so dense was the forest that covered the whole country, that their progress was slow.   They were also deficient in suitable guides, and in a short time were thrown into a great deal of confusion.   They pressed steadily forward, and the advanced post of the French (a breast-work of logs) was set fire to by the enemy themselves and abandoned.   Lord Howe, who was Abercrombie's lieutenant, or second in command, led the advanced column ; and as they pressed onward after crossing the bridge, Major Putnam, with about one hundred men, advanced as a scouting party to reconnoiter.   Lord Howe, eager to make the first attack, proposed to accompany Putnam, but the major tried to dissuade him, by saying, " My lord, if I am killed the loss of my life will be of little consequence, but the preservation of yours is of infinite importance to this army."   The answer was, " Putnam, your life is as dear to you as mine is to me.   I am determined to go."[3]   They dashed on through the woods, and in a few minutes fell in with the advanced guard of the French, who had retreated from the first breast-works, and, with-out a guide and bewildered, were endeavoring to find their way back to the lines.   A sharp skirmish ensued, and at the first fire Lord Howe, another officer, and several privates were

---

[1] This is a French word, signifying chime, jingling, noise, bawling, scolding, racket, clatter, riot.— *Boyer.*   Its application to this spot had the same reference to the rush of waters as the Indian name *Che- onderoga.*

[2] This fortress was strongly built.   Its walls and barracks were of limestone, and every thing about it was done in the most substantial manner.

Explanation of the ground plan : a, entrance and wicket gate ; b, counterscarp twenty feet wide ; c c, bastions ; d, under-ground room and ovens ; e e e e, barracks and officers' quarters ; f, court or parade-ground ; g g, trench or covert-way, sixteen feet wide and ten feet deep ; h, the place where Ethan Allen and his men entered by a covert-way from the outside.

[3] Humphrey's Life of Putnam.

killed.[1] The French were repulsed with a loss of three hundred killed and one hundred and forty-eight taken prisoners. The English columns were so much broken, confused, and fatigued, that Abercrombie marched them back to the landing-place on Lake George, to bivouac for the night. Early the next morning Colonel Bradstreet advanced and took possession of the saw-mills, near the present village of Ticonderoga, which the enemy had abandoned.

Abercrombie sent an engineer to reconnoiter, and on his reporting that the works were unfinished and might easily be taken, the British troops were again put in motion toward the fortress. As they approached the lines, the French, who were completely shel- July 8, 1758. tered behind their breast-works, opened a heavy discharge of artillery upon them, but they pressed steadily forward in the face of the storm, determined to assault the works, and endeavor to carry them by sword and bayonet. They found them so well defended by a deep *abatis*, that it was almost impossible to reach them ; yet, amid the galling fire of the enemy, the English continued for four hours striving to cut their way through the limbs and bushes to the breast-works with their swords. Some did, indeed, mount the parapet, but in a moment they were slain. Scores of Britons were mowed down at every discharge of cannon. Perceiving the rapid reduction of his army, Abercrombie at last sounded a retreat , and, without being pursued by the French, the English fell back to their encampment at the foot of Lake George, from which the wounded were sent to Fort Edward and to Albany The English loss was nearly two thousand men and · twenty-five hundred stand of arms. Never did troops show bolder courage or more obstinate persistence against fearful obstacles. The whole army seemed emulous to excel, but the Scotch Highland regiment of Lord John Murray was foremost in the conflict, and suffered the severest loss. One half of the privates and twenty-five officers were slain on the spot or badly wounded. Failing in this attempt, Abercrombie changed his plans. He dispatched General Stanwix to build a fort near the head-waters of the Mohawk, at the site of the present village of Rome, Oneida county. Colonel Bradstreet, at his own urgent solicitation, was ordered, with three thousand troops, mostly provincials, to proceed by the way of Oswego and Lake Ontario, to attack Fort Frontenac, where Kingston, in Upper Canada, now stands ; and himself, with the rest of the army, returned to Albany.[2]

While misfortunes were attending the English under the immediate command of Abercrombie, and the power and influence of the French were gaining strength on the lake, a British force was closely beleaguering Louisburg, on the Island of Cape Breton, at the mouth of the St. Lawrence, then the strongest fortification in America, and the rallying point May 28. of French power on this Continent. Early in 1758 Admiral Boscawen sailed from

---

[1] George, Lord-viscount Howe, was the eldest son of Sir E. Scrope, second Viscount Howe in Ireland. He commanded five thousand British troops which landed at Halifax in 1757, and, as we have seen, the next year accompanied General Abercrombie against Ticonderoga. Alluding to his death, Mante observes, "With him the soul of the army seemed to expire." He was the idol of his soldiers, and, in order to accommodate himself and his regiment to the nature of the service, he cut his hair short, and fashioned his clothes for activity. His troops followed his example, and they were, indeed, the soul of Abercrombie's army. He was in the thirty-fourth year of his age when he fell. The General Court of Massachusetts Bay, as a testimony of respect for his character, appropriated two hundred and fifty pounds sterling for the erection of a monument in Westminster Abbey.

Captain (afterward general) Philip Schuyler, who was highly esteemed by Lord Howe, and who at that time was employed in the commissary department, was commissioned to carry the young nobleman's remains to Albany and bury them with appropriate honors. They were placed in a vault, and I was informed by a daughter of General Schuyler (Mrs. Cochran, of Oswego) that when, many years afterward, the coffin was opened, his hair had grown to long, flowing locks, and was very beautiful.

[2] General James Abercrombie was descended from a wealthy Scotch family, and, in consequence of signal services on the Continent, was promoted to the rank of major general. In 1758 fifty thousand troops were placed under his command by Mr. Pitt, and sent with him to America to attempt a recovery of all that the French had taken from the English. He was the successor of Lord Loudon, but was not much superior to the earl in activity or military skill. He was superseded by Amherst after his defeat at Ticonderoga, and in the spring of 1759 he returned to England.

Halifax, Acadia,[1] with forty armed vessels, bearing a land force of twelve thousand men under General Amherst.   General Wolfe was second in command ; and in appointing that young soldier to a post so important, Pitt showed that sagacity in correctly appreciating character for which he was so remarkable.

On the 2d of June the fleet anchored in Gabarus Bay, and the whole armament reached the shore on the 8th.   The French, alarmed at such a formidable force, called in their outposts, dismantled the royal battery, and prepared for a retreat.   But the vigilance and activity of Wolfe prevented their escape.   He passed around the Northeast Harbor, and erected a battery at the North Cape, from which well-directed shots soon silenced the guns of the smaller batteries upon the island.   Hot shots were also poured into the small fleet of French vessels lying in the harbor of Louisburg, and three of them were burned.   The town was greatly shattered by the active artillery ; the vessels which were not consumed were dismantled or sunken ; and several breaches were made in the massive walls.   Certain destruction awaited the garrison and citizens, and at last the fortress, together with the town and St. John's (now Prince Edward's) Island, was surrendered into the hands of the English by capitulation.

June 12.

June 25.

July 21.

July 26.

The skill, bravery, and activity of General Amherst, exhibited in the capture of Louisburg, gained him a vote of thanks from Parliament, and commended him to Pitt, who, the next year, appointed him to the chief command in America, in place of the less active Abercrombie.   So much did Pitt rely upon his judgment and ability, that he clothed him with discretionary powers to take measures to make the complete conquest of all Canada in a single campaign.   His plans were arranged upon a magnificent scale.   Appreciating the services of Wolfe, one expedition was placed under his command, to ascend the St. Lawrence and attack Quebec.   General Prideaux was sent with another expedition to capture the strong-hold of Niagara, while Amherst himself took personal command of a third expedition against the fortress on Lake Champlain.   It was arranged for the three armies to form a junction as conquerors at Quebec.   Prideaux, after capturing the fort at Niagara, was to proceed down the lake and St. Lawrence to attack Montreal and the posts below, and Amherst was to push forward after the capture of Ticonderoga and Crown Point, down the Richelieu or Sorel River to the St. Lawrence, and join with Wolfe at Quebec.

Amherst collected about eleven thousand men at Fort Edward and its vicinity, and, moving cautiously along Lake Champlain, crossed the outlet of Lake George, and appeared before Ticonderoga on the 26th of July.   He met with no impediments by the way, and at once made preparations for reducing the fortress by a regular siege.   The garrison were strong, and evinced a disposition to make a vigorous resistance.   They soon discovered, however, that they had not Abercrombie to deal with, and, despairing of being able to hold out against the advancing English, they dismantled and abandoned the fort, and fled to Crown Point.   Not a gun was fired or a sword crossed ; and the next day Amherst marched in and took possession of the fort.   He at once set about repairing and enlarging it, and also arranging an expedition against the enemy at Crown Point, when, to his astonishment, he learned from his scouts that they had abandoned that post also, and fled down the lake to Isle Aux Noix in the Richelieu or Sorel.   Of his operations in that direction I shall hereafter write.

1759.

---

[1] Acadia was the ancient name of the whole country now comprehended within the boundaries of Nova Scotia, or New Scotland.

CHAPTER VI.

"I'm not romantic, but, upon my word,
  There are some moments when one can't help feeling
As if his heart's chords were so strongly stirred
  By things around him, that 'tis vain concealing
A little music in his soul still lingers,
Whene'er the keys are touched by Nature's fingers."

C. F. HOFFMAN.

ATURE always finds a chord of sympathy in the human heart harmoniously respondent to her own sweet music ; and when her mute but eloquent language weaves in with its teachings associations of the past, or when, in the midst of her beauties, some crumbling monument of history stands hoary and oracular, stoicism loses its potency, and the bosom of the veriest churl is opened to the genial warmth of the sun of sentiment. Broken arches and ruined ramparts are always eloquent and suggestive of valiant deeds, even where their special teachings are not comprehended ; but manifold greater are the impressions which they make when the patriotism we adore has hallowed them. To impressions like these the American heart is plastic while tarrying among the ruins of Ticonderoga, for there the first trophy of our war for independence was won, and there a soldier of the British realm first stooped a prisoner to the aroused colonists, driven to rebellion by unnatural oppression.

A glimpse from the coach, of the gray old ruins of the fortress of " Ty," as we neared the Pavilion, made us impatient as children to be among them. Our own curiosity was shared by a few others, and a small party of us left early and ascended the breast-works, over scattered fragments of the walls, and eagerly sought out the most interesting localities, by the aid of a small plan of the fort which I had copied for the occasion. Without a competent guide, our identifications were not very reliable, and our opinions were as numerous and diverse as the members of our party. We were about to send to the Pavilion for a guide and umpire, when a venerable, white-haired man, supported by a rude staff, and bearing the insignia of the " Order of Poverty," came out from the ruins of the northern line of barracks, and offered his services in elucidating the confused subject before us. He was kind and intelligent, and I lingered with him among the ruins long after the rest of the party had left, and listened with pleasure and profit to the relation of his personal experience, and of his familiar knowledge of the scene around us.

Isaac Rice was the name of our octogenarian guide, whose form and features, presented upon the next page, I sketched for preservation.[1] Like scores of those who fought our battles for freedom, and lived the allotted term of human life, he is left in his evening twilight to depend upon the cold friendship of the world for sustenance, and to feel the practical ingratitude of a people reveling in the enjoyment which his privations in early manhood contributed to secure He performed garrison duty at Ticonderoga under St. Clair, was in the field at Saratoga in 1777, and served a regular term in the army ; but, in consequence of some lack of doc-

---

[1] Mr. Rice sat down in the cool shadow of the gable of the western line of barracks while I sketched his person and the scenery in the distance. He is leaning against the wall, within a few feet of the entrance of the covert-way to the parade-ground, through which Allen and his men penetrated. In the middle ground is seen the wall of the ramparts, and beyond is the lake sweeping around the western extremity of Mount Independence, on the left beyond the steam-boat. For a correct apprehension of the relative position of Mount Independence to Ticonderoga, the reader is referred to the map, ante page 115.

uments or some technical error, he lost his legal title to a pension, and at eighty-five years of age that feeble old soldier was obtaining a precarious support for himself from the free-will offerings of visitors to the ruins of the fortress where he was garrisoned when it stood in the pride of its strength, before Burgoyne scaled the heights of Mount Defiance. He is now alone, his family and kindred having all gone down into the grave. His elder brother, and the last of his race, who died in 1838, was one of the little band who, under Colonel Ethan Allen, surprised and captured Fort Ticonderoga in the spring of 1775. We will consider that event and its consequences before further examining the old ruins around us.

The contempt with which the loyal and respectful addresses of the first Continental Congress of 1774 were treated by the British ministry and a majority in Parliament; the harsh measures adopted by the government early in 1775, to coerce the colonists into submission, and the methodical tyranny of General Gage at Boston, and of other colonial governors, convinced the Americans that an appeal to arms was inevitable. They were convinced, also, that the province of Quebec, or Canada, would remain loyal,[1] and that there would be a place of rendezvous for British troops when the colonies should unite in open and avowed rebellion. The strong fortresses of Ticonderoga and Crown Point formed the key of all communication between New York and Canada, and the vigilant patriots of Massachusetts, then the very hot-bed of rebellion, early perceived the necessity of securing these posts the moment hostilities should commence. Early in March, Samuel Adams and Joseph Warren, members of the Committee of Correspondence of Boston, sent a secret agent into Canada to ascertain the opinions and temper of the people of that province concerning the great questions at issue and the momentous

---

[1] On the 26th of October, 1774, the Congress adopted an address to the people of Canada, recounting the grievances the American colonies suffered at the hands of the parent country, and including that province in the category of the oppressed, urging them to affiliate in a common resistance. But its Legislative Assembly made no response, and Congress construed their silence into a negative.—*Journals of Congress*, i., 55

OF THE REVOLUTION. 123

Report of the secret Agent.   Plan formed in Connecticut to Capture Ticonderoga.   Expedition under Ethan Allen.

events then pending.   After a diligent but cautious performance of his delicate task, the agent sent word to them from Montreal that the people were, at best, lukewarm, and advised that, the moment hostilities commenced, Ticonderoga and its garrison should be seized. This advice was coupled with the positive assertion that the people of the New Hampshire Grants were ready to undertake the bold enterprise.[1]

Within three weeks after this information was received by Adams and Warren, the battle of Lexington occurred.   The event aroused the whole country, and the patriots April 19, flocked to the neighborhood of Boston from all quarters.   The provincial Assembly 1775. of Connecticut was then in session, and several of its members[2] concerted and agreed upon a plan to seize the munitions of war at Ticonderoga, for the use of the army gathering at Cambridge and Roxbury.   They appointed Edward Mott and Noah Phelps a committee to proceed to the frontier towns, ascertain the condition of the fort and the strength of the garrison, and, if they thought it expedient, to raise men and attempt the surprise and capture of the post.   One thousand dollars were advanced from the provincial treasury to pay the expenses of the expedition.

The whole plan and proceedings were of a private character, without the public sanction of the Assembly, but with its full knowledge and tacit approbation.   Mott and Phelps collected sixteen men as they passed through Connecticut; and at Pittsfield, Massachusetts, they laid their plans before Colonel Easton and John Brown (the latter was afterward the Colonel Brown whose exploits on Lake George have been noticed), who agreed to join them. Colonel Easton enlisted volunteers from his regiment of militia as he passed through the country, and about forty had been engaged when he reached Bennington.   There Colonel Ethan Allen, a man of strong mind, vigorous frame, upright in all his ways, fearless in the discharge of his duty, and a zealous patriot, joined the expedition with his *Green Mountain Boys*, and the whole party, two hundred and seventy men, reached Castleton, fourteen miles east of Skenesborough, or Whitehall, at dusk on the 7th of May.   A council of war was immediately held, and Allen was appointed commander of the expedition, Colonel James Easton, second in command, and Seth Warner, third.   It was arranged that Allen and the principal officers, with the main body, should march to Shoreham, opposite Ticonderoga; that Captain Herrick, with thirty men, should push on to Skenesborough, and capture the young Major Skene (son of the governor, who was then in England), confine his people, and, seizing all the boats they might find there, hasten to join Allen at Shoreham;

---

[1] By the grant of Charles II. to his brother James, duke of York, the tract in America called New York was bounded on the east by the Connecticut River, while the charters of Massachusetts and Connecticut gave those provinces a westward extent to the "South Sea" or the Pacific Ocean.   When, toward the middle of the last century, settlements began to be made westward of the Connecticut River, disputes arose, and the line between Connecticut and New York was finally drawn, by mutual agreement, twenty miles east of the Hudson.   Massachusetts claimed a continuation of the Connecticut line as its western boundary, but New York contested the claim as interfering with prior grants to that colony.   New Hampshire, lying north of Massachusetts, was not as yet disturbed by these disputes, for the country west of the Green Mountains was a wilderness, and had never been surveyed.   When Benning Wentworth was made Governor of New Hampshire, he was authorized to issue patents for unimproved lands within his province, and in 1749 applications were made to him for grants beyond the mountains.   He gave a patent that year for a township six miles square, having its western line twenty miles east of the Hudson, and in his honor it was named Bennington.   The Governor and Council of New York remonstrated against this grant, yet Wentworth continued to issue patents; and in 1754 fourteen townships of this kind were laid out and settlements commenced.   During the French and Indian war settlements increased tardily, but after the victory of Wolfe at Quebec numerous applications for grants were made; and at the time of the peace, in 1763, one hundred and thirty-eight townships were surveyed west of the Connecticut River, and these were termed the New Hampshire Grants.   The controversy between New York and the *Grants* became so violent that military organizations took place in the latter section to resist the civil power of New York, and about 1772 the military thus enrolled were first called *Green Mountain Boys*; among the most active and daring of whom were Ethan and Ira Allen and Remember Baker, men of whom I shall have occasion to speak hereafter.—See *Sparks's Life of Ethan Allen, and Thompson's Vermont*, part ii.

[2] Among these were Silas Deane, David Wooster, Samuel H. Parsons, and Edward Stevens, all distinguished men during the Revolution.

and that Captain Douglas should proceed to Panton, beyond Crown Point, and secure every boat or bateau that should fall in his way.

Benedict Arnold, who joined the army about this time, doubtless received a hint of this expedition before he left New Haven, for the moment he arrived at Cambridge with the company of which he was captain, he presented himself before the Committee of Safety, and proposed a similar expedition in the same direction. He made the thing appear so feasible, May 3, that the committee eagerly accepted his proposal, granted him a colonel's commission, 1775. and gave him the chief command of troops, not exceeding four hundred in number, which he might raise to accompany him on an expedition against the lake fortresses. Not doubting his success, Arnold was instructed to leave a sufficient garrison at Ticonderoga, and with the rest of the troops return to Cambridge with the arms and military stores that should fall into his possession. He was also supplied with one hundred pounds in cash, two hundred pounds weight each of gunpowder and leaden balls, one thousand flints, and ten horses, by the provincial Congress of Massachusetts. His instructions were to raise men in Western Massachusetts, but, on reaching Stockbridge, he was disappointed in finding that another expedition had anticipated him, and was on its way to the lake. He remained only long enough to engage a few officers and men to follow him, and then hastened onward and May 9, joined the other expedition at Castleton. He introduced himself to the officers, pulled 1775. a bit of parchment from his pocket, and, by virtue of what he averred was a superior commission, as it was from the Massachusetts Committee of Safety, claimed the supreme command. This was objected to, for he came single-handed, without officers or troops ; and the soldiers, a large proportion of whom were Green Mountain Boys, and who were much attached to Allen, declared that they would shoulder their muskets and march home rather than serve under any other leader. Arnold made a virtue of necessity, and united himself to the expedition as a volunteer, maintaining his rank, but having no command.

The momentary interruption of Arnold produced no change in the plans, and Allen marched to the shore of the lake, opposite Ticonderoga, during the night. He applied to a farmer in Shoreham, named Beman, for a guide, who offered his son Nathan, a lad who passed a good deal of time within the fort, with the boys of the garrison, and was well acquainted with every secret way that led to or within the fortress.[1] But a serious difficulty now occurred. They had but a few boats, and none had been sent from Skenesborough or May 10, Panton. The day began to dawn, and only the officers and eighty-three men had 1775. crossed the lake. Delay was hazardous, for the garrison, if aroused, would make stout resistance. Allen, therefore, resolved not to wait for the rear division to cross, but to attack the fort at once. He drew up his men in three ranks upon the shore, directly in front of where the Pavilion now stands, and in a low but distinct tone briefly harangued them ; and then, placing himself at their head, with Arnold by his side, they marched quickly but stealthily up the height to the sally port. The sentinel snapped his fusee at the commander, but it missed fire, and he retreated within the fort under a covered way. The Americans followed close upon his heels, and were thus guided by the alarmed fugitive directly to the parade within the barracks. There another sentinel made a thrust at Easton, but a blow upon the head from Allen's sword made him beg for quarter, and the patriots met with no further resistance.

As the troops rushed into the parade under the covered way, they gave a tremendous shout, and, filing off into two divisions, formed a line of forty men each along the southwestern and northeastern range of barracks. The aroused garrison leaped from their pallets, seized their arms, and rushed for the parade, but only to be made prisoners by the intrepid New Englanders. At the same moment Allen, with young Beman at his elbow as guide, ascended the steps to the door of the quarters of Captain Delaplace, the commandant

---

[1] He died in December, 1846, in Franklin county, New York, when nearly ninety years old. He had lived to see our confederacy increase from *thirteen* to *thirty* states, and from *three millions* of people to *twenty millions*.

of the garrison, and, giving three loud raps with the hilt of his sword, with a voice of peculiar power, ordered him to appear, or the whole garrison should be sacrificed. It was about four o'clock in the morning. The loud shout of the invaders had awakened the captain and his wife, both of whom sprang to the door just as Allen made his strange demand. Delaplace appeared in shirt and drawers, with the frightened face of his pretty wife peering over his shoulder. He and Allen had been old friends, and, upon recognition, the captain assumed boldness, and authoritatively demanded his disturber's errand. Allen pointed to his men and sternly exclaimed, " I order you instantly to surrender." " By what authority do *you* demand it ?" said Delaplace. " In the name of the Great Jehovah and the Continental Congress !"[1] thundered Allen, and, raising his sword over the head of the captain, who was about to speak, ordered him to be silent and surrender immediately. There was no alternative. Delaplace had about as much respect for the " Continental Congress" as Allen had for " Jehovah," and they respectively relied upon and feared powder and ball more than either. In fact, the Continental Congress was but a shadow, for it did not meet for organization until six hours afterward,[2] and its " authority" was yet scarcely acknowledged even by the patriots in the field. But Delaplace ordered his troops to parade without arms, the garrison of forty-eight men were surrendered prisoners of war, and, with the women and children, were sent to Hartford, in Connecticut. The spoils were one hundred and twenty pieces of iron cannon, fifty swivels, two ten-inch mortars, one howitzer, one cohorn, ten tons of musket-balls, three cart-loads of flints, thirty new carriages, a considerable quantity of shells, a ware-house full of material for boat building, one hundred stand of small arms, ten casks of poor powder, two brass cannon, thirty barrels of flour, eighteen barrels of pork, and some beans and peas.

Warner crossed the lake with the rear division, and marched up to the fort just after the surrender was made. As soon as the prisoners were secured, and all had breakfasted, he was sent off with a detachment of men in boats to take Crown Point ; but a strong head wind drove them back, and they slept that night at Ticonderoga. Another and successful attempt was made on the 12th, and both fortresses fell into the hands of the patriots without bloodshed.

Arnold, who yielded his claims to supreme command at Castleton, assumed control the moment the fort was surrendered. But his orders were not heeded, and the Connecticut Committee,[3] of semi-official origin, which accompanied the expedition, interposed, formally installed Colonel Allen in the command of Ticonderoga and its dependencies, and authorized him to remain as such until the Connecticut Assembly or the Continental Congress should send him instructions. They affirmed that the government of Massachusetts had no part in the transaction ; that the men from Pittsfield were paid by Connecticut ; and that Arnold could be considered only as a volunteer. Finding his commands unheeded, and unwilling to allow personal considerations to affect, inimically, the public good, Arnold again yielded He sent a written protest, with a statement of his grievances, to the Massachusetts Legislature. The Connecticut Committee also sent a statement to the same body. The appointment of Allen was confirmed, and the Assembly of Massachusetts directed Arnold not to interfere. He soon afterward went down the lake to seize a British sloop of war at St. John's, and to seek other occasions where glory might be won in the service of his country.

The capture of Ticonderoga and Crown Point was an event wholly unlooked for by the

---

[1] According to Mr. Rice, history has omitted the suffix to this demand, which in those days was considered a necessary clincher to all solemn averments. It is characteristic of the man and the times. Rice's brother was within a few feet of Allen, and said he exclaimed, " In the name of the Great Jehovah and the Continental Congress, *by God.*"

[2] The second Continental Congress assembled at Philadelphia at ten o'clock that day (May 10th), and chose Peyton Randolph *President,* and Charles Thompson *Secretary.*

[3] One of the committee, Mr. Phelps, visited the fort, in disguise, the day before Allen and his men arrived. He pretended to be a countryman wishing to be shaved, and, while looking about for the garrison barber, observed every thing carefully, and saw the dilapidation of the walls and the laxity of duty and discipline, particularly as to sentinels.

Continental Congress, then in session at Philadelphia, and many members were alarmed at the serious aspect of affairs at the east and north, for as yet the Americans had harbored no distinct thought or wish derogatory to the truest loyalty.   They were aggrieved by the rulers and legislators of the parent country, and were earnestly seeking redress.   Ten years they had been petitioning the king and Parliament to exercise righteousness and equity toward them, but their prayers were unheeded and their warnings were scoffed at and answered by new oppressions.   Yet the colonists remained loyal, and never breathed an aspiration for political independence.   The colonial Assemblies, as well as the mass of the people, looked forward with anxiety for a reconciliation, for they felt proud of their connection with the British realm, whose government was then among the most powerful upon earth.[1]

When the news of the capture of the forts on Champlain reached Congress, they recommended to the committees of New York and Albany to remove the cannon and stores to the south end of Lake George, and to erect a strong post at that place.   They also directed an exact inventory of the cannon and military stores to be taken, " in order," as the dispatch said, " that they may be safely returned when the restoration of harmony between Great Britain and the colonies, *so ardently desired by the latter*, shall render it prudent and consistent with the over-ruling law of self-preservation."[2]

1774.   The delegates to the first Continental Congress, who met in September of the previous year, while they exhibited rare firmness of purpose in tone and manner, again and again avowed their loyalty, and made most humble petitions to the king and the Legislature for a redress of grievances.   And those of the Congress in session when the first hostile movements on Lake Champlain occurred, while they saw clearly that nothing but a general resort to arms was now left for the colonists, resolved to make fresh appeals to the king and Parliament before taking decidedly offensive steps in acts of open hostility.   They felt quite certain, however, that the haughtiness of power would not bend so long as its pride was wounded, and that it would never yield to an agreement for a reconciliation upon terms other than the absolute submission of the insurgents.   Congress, therefore, correctly representing the public sentiment, resolved to be, at the same time, *free men* and *loyal subjects* as long as a link of consistency should bind those conditions in unity.   They adopted an address to the inhabitants of Canada ;[a] a declaration, setting forth the causes and the necessity for the colonies to take up arms ;[b] an humble petition to the king ;[c] an address to the Assembly of Jamaica ;[d][3] and an address to the people of Ireland.[e][4]   To the king they expressed their continued devotion to his person, and their deep regret that circumstances had in the least weakened their attachment to the crown.   To the people of Great Britain they truthfully declared that their acts were wholly defensive ; that the charge which had been made against them, of seeking absolute independence, was a malicious slander ; and that they had never, directly or indirectly, applied to a foreign power for countenance or aid in prosecuting a rebellion.   They truly set forth that the rejection of their petitions and the accumulation of oppressive acts of Parliament were the causes that placed them in the attitude of resistance which they then assumed—an atti-

[a] May 29, 1775.
[b] July 6.
[c] July 8.
[d] July 25.
[e] July 28.

---

[1] The affections of the people of the colonies were very much alienated by the grievances of the *Stamp Act* in 1765, and kindred measures, yet they still had a strong attachment to the mother country, even when the Revolution finally broke out.   Dr. Franklin's testimony in 1766 may be quoted as illustrative of the temper of the people nearly ten years later.   In answer to the question concerning the feelings of the people of America toward Great Britain before the passage of the Stamp Act, he said, " They had not only a respect but an affection for Great Britain, for its laws, its customs, and its manners, and even a fondness for its fashions, that greatly increased the commerce.   Natives of Britain were always treated with particular regard ; and to be an *Old Englandman* was of itself a character of some respect, and gave a kind of rank among us."—*Examination of Dr. Franklin before the British House of Commons relative to the Repeal of the American Stamp Act.*

[2] Pitkin, i., 355.

[3] Jamaica, one of the West India Islands, was then a British colony, with a provincial Legislature like those on the American Continent.

[4] See Journals of Congress, i., p. 100–168.

tude at once necessary and justifiable, and worthy of the free character of subjects of the British realm. "While we revere," they said, "the memory of our gallant and virtuous ancestors, we never can surrender these glorious privileges for which they fought, bled, and conquered : your fleets and armies can destroy our towns and ravage our coasts ; these are inconsiderable objects—things of no moment to men whose bosoms glow with the ardor of liberty. We can retire beyond the reach of your navy, and, without any sensible diminution of the necessaries of life, enjoy a luxury which, from that period, you will want—the luxury of being free."

TICONDEROGA AT SUNSET

While petitions and addresses were in course of preparation and adoption, Congress proceeded to make extensive military arrangements. The militia of the various colonies, and such volunteers as could be obtained, were mustered into service under the title of the CONTINENTAL ARMY ; and the troops which had flocked to the vicinity of Boston from all parts of New England after the skirmishes at Lexington and Concord,[a] and were then investing that city, were adopted and enrolled under the same title.[b] Congress voted to issue bills of credit, or paper money, to the amount of three millions of dollars, for the pay of the army, and also took measures for the establishment of provisional Assemblies in the several colonies instead of the royal governments ; for acts of Parliament, declaring the colonies in a state of rebellion, and providing for the destruction of the commerce of several sea-port towns, and for the sending of fleets and armies to enforce submission, were regarded by the Americans as virtual acknowledgments of the abdication of all power here.[1] Thus, while the colonists kept the door of reconciliation wide open, they prepared to maintain the righteous position which they had assumed at all hazards.

a April 19, 1775
b June, 1775.

Let us for a moment close the chronicles of the past, and consider one of the most interesting relics of the Revolution yet remaining—the ruins of Ticonderoga. I lingered with the old soldier among the fragments of the fortress until sunset ; and just as the luminary

[1] See Parliamentary Register (1775) p 6–69.

went down behind Mount Defiance I made the preceding sketch, which may be relied upon as a faithful portraiture of the present features of Fort Ticonderoga. The view is from the remains of the counterscarp, near the southern range of barracks, looking northward. The barracks or quarters for the officers and soldiers were very substantially built of limestone, two stories high, and formed a quadrangle. The space within was the parade. Upon the good authority of his brother, our venerable guide pointed out the various localities of interest, and, having no doubt as to the correctness of his information, I shall accord it as truth The most distinct and best-preserved building seen in the sketch is the one in which the commandant of the garrison was asleep when Allen and his men entered the fort. On the left of the group of figures in the fore-ground is the passage leading from the covered way into the parade, through which the provincials passed. The two lines of forty men each were drawn up along the range of buildings, the remains of which are seen on the right and left of the picture. The most distant building was the officers' quarters. A wooden piazza, or sort of balcony, extended along the second story, and was reached from the ground by a flight of stairs at the left end. The first door in the second story, on the left, was the entrance to Delaplace's apartment. It was up those rickety steps, with young Beman at his side, that Colonel Allen ascended; and at that door he thundered with his sword-hilt, confronted the astonished captain, and demanded his surrender. Between the ruined walls on the extreme left is seen Mount Defiance, and on the right is Mount Hope. The distant wall in the direction of Mount Hope is a part of the ramparts or out-works, and the woods beyond it mark the location of the remains of the "French lines," the mounds and ditches of which are still very conspicuous.

Near the southeastern angle of the range of barracks is the bakery; it is an under-ground arched room, and was beneath the *glacis*, perfectly bomb-proof, and protected from all danger from without. This room is very well preserved, as the annexed sketch of it testifies; but the entrance steps are much broken, and the passage is so filled with rubbish that a descent into it is difficult. It is about twelve feet wide and thirty long. On the right is a window, and at the end were a fire-place and chimney, now in ruins. On either side of the fire-place are the ovens, ten feet deep. We had no light to explore them, but they seemed to be in good condition This bakery and the ovens are the best-preserved portions of the fortress. For more

THE BAKERY.

than half a century the walls of the fort have been common spoil for all who chose to avail themselves of such a convenient quarry; and the proximity of the lake affords rare facility for builders to carry off the plunder. The guide informed me that sixty-four years ago he assisted in the labor of loading a vessel with bricks and stones taken from the fort, to build an earthen-ware factory on Missisqui Bay, the eastern fork of the lower end of Lake Champlain. Year after year the ruins thus dwindle, and, unless government shall prohibit the robbery, this venerable landmark of history will soon have no abiding-place among us. The foundation is almost a bare rock, earthed sufficient to give sustenance to mullens, rag-weed, and stinted grass only, so that the plowshare can have no effect; but desecrating avarice, with its wicked broom, may sweep the bare rock still barer, for the site is a glorious one for a summer hotel for invalids. I shall, doubtless, receive posthumous laudation for this suggestion from the money-getter who here shall erect the colonnade, sell cooked fish and flavored ices, and coin wealth by the magic of the fiddle-string.

On the point of the promontory, just above the steam-boat landing, are the remains of the "Grenadiers' Battery," a strong redoubt built of earth and stone. It was constructed by the French, and enlarged by the English. It commanded the narrow part of the lake, between that point and Mount Independence, and covered the bridge, which was made by the Americans, extending across to the latter eminence. The bridge was supported by twenty-two sunken piers of large timber, at nearly equal distances ; the space between was made of separate floats, each about fifty feet long and twelve feet wide, strongly fastened together by chains and rivets, and also fastened to the sunken piers.   Before this bridge was a boom, made of very large pieces of timber, fastened together by riveted bolts and chains of iron, an inch and a half square.[1]   There was a battery at the foot of Mount Independence, which covered that end of the bridge ; another half way up the hill ; and upon the table-land summit was a star fort well picketed.   Here, strongly stationed, the Americans held undisputed possession from the 10th of May, 1775, until the 5th of July, 1777, when they were dislodged by Burgoyne, who began to plant a battery upon Sugar Hill, or Mount Defiance.   This event we shall consider presently.

I went up in the evening to view the solitary ruins by moonlight, and sat upon the green sward of the old esplanade near the magazine.   All was hushed, and association, with its busy pencil, wrought many a startling picture.   The broken ruins around me, the lofty hills adjacent, the quiet lake at my feet, all fading into chaos as the evening shadows came on, were in consonance with the gravity of thought induced by the place and its traditions.

> " The darkening woods, the fading trees,
>   The grasshopper's last feeble sound,
> The flowers just waken'd by the breeze,
>   All leave the stillness more profound.
> The twilight takes a deeper shade,
>   The dusky pathways blacker grow,
> And silence reigns in glen and glade—
>   All, all is mute below."
>   MILLER'S EVENING HYMN.

So smoothly ran the current of thought, that I was almost dreaming, when a footstep startled me.   It was that of the old patriot, who came and sat beside me.   He always spends the pleasant moonlight evenings here, for he has no companions of the present, and the sight of the old walls kept sluggish memory awake to the recollections of the light and love of other days.   " I am alone in the world," he said, " poor and friendless ; none for me to care for, and none to care for me.   Father, mother, brothers, sisters, wife, and children have all passed away, and the busy world has forgotten *me*.   I have been for almost eighty years a toiler for bread for myself and loved ones, yet I have never lacked for comforts.   I can say with David, 'Once I was young, but now I am old, yet I have never seen the righteous forsaken or his seed begging bread.'   I began to feel my strength giving way last spring, and looked fearfully toward the poor-house, when I heard that the old man who lived here, to show visitors about, was dead, and so I came down to take his place and die also."   He brushed away a tear with his hard and shriveled hand, and, with a more cheerful tone, talked of his future prospects.   How true it is that blessed

> " Hope springs immortal in the human breast,"

for this poor, friendless, aged man had bright visions of a better earthly condition even in the midst of his poverty and loneliness.   He took me to an opening in the broken wall, which fronted a small room near the spot where the provincials entered, and with a low voice, as if afraid some rival might hear his business plans, explained how he intended, another year, to clear away the rubbish, cover the room over with boards and brush, arrange a sleeping-place in the rear, erect a rude counter in front, and there, during the summer, sell cakes, beer, and fruit to visitors.   Here I saw my fancied hotel in embryo.   He estimated the cash capital necessary for the enterprise at eight dollars, which sum he hoped to save from his season's earnings, for the French woman who gave him food and shelter charged him but a trifling weekly sum for his comforts.   He calculated upon large profits and extensive sales, and hoped, if no opposition marred his plans, to make enough to keep him comfortable through

---

[1] Burgoyne's Narrative, Appendix, p. xxx.

life. He entertained me more than an hour with a relation of his own and his father's adventures,[1] and it was late in the evening when I bade him a final adieu. "God bless you, my son," he said, as he grasped my hand at parting. "We may never meet here again, but I hope we may in heaven!"

August 2, 1848. Early the next morning I started for Mount Defiance in company with an English gentleman, a resident of Boston. We rode to the "lower village," or Ticonderoga, where we left our ladies to return by the same stage, while we climbed the rugged heights. We hired a horse and vehicle, and a lad to drive, who professed to know all about the route to the foot of the mountain. We soon found that he was bewildered ; and, unwilling to waste time by losing the way, we employed an aged resident near the western slope to pilot us to the top of the eminence. He was exceedingly garrulous, and boasted, with much self-gratulation, of having assisted in dragging a heavy six pounder up to the top of the mountain, five years ago, for the purpose of celebrating the "glorious Fourth" on the very spot where Burgoyne planted his cannon sixty-six years before. We followed him along a devious cattle-path that skirted a deep ravine, until we came to a spring that bubbled up from beneath a huge shelving rock whose face was smooth and mossy. The trickling of the water through the crevices within, by which the fountain below was supplied, could be distinctly heard. From a cup of maple-leaves we took a cool draught, rested a moment, and then pursued our toilsome journey.

Our guide, professing to know every rock and tree in the mountain, now left the cattle-path for a "shorter cut," but we soon wished ourselves back again in the beaten track The old man was evidently "out of his reckoning," but had too much "grit" to acknowledge it. For nearly an hour we followed him through thickets tangled with vines, over the trunks of huge trees leveled by the wind, and across a dry morass covered with brakes and wire-grass shoulder high, where every trill of the grasshopper sounded to our suspicious and vigilant ears like the warning of a rattle-snake, until at length we were confronted by a wall of huge broken rocks, almost perpendicular, and at least fifty feet high. It seemed to extend north and south indefinitely, and we almost despaired of scaling it. The guide insisted upon the profundity of his knowledge of the route, and we, being unable to contradict his positive assertions that he was in the right way, followed him up the precipice. It was a toilsome and dangerous ascent, but fortunately the sun was yet eastward of meridian, and we were in shadow. We at last reached a broad ledge near the summit, where, exhausted, we sat down and regaled ourselves with some mulberries which we had gathered by the way. A large wolf-dog, belonging to our guide, had managed to follow his master, and seemed quite as weary as ourselves when he reached us. Another scramble of about twenty minutes, over broken rocks and ledges like a giant's stair-case, brought us upon the bold, rocky summit of the mountain. The view from this lofty hill is one of great interest and beauty, including almost every variety of natural scenery, and a region abounding with historical

---

[1] His father was a lieutenant in the English service, and belonged to the Connecticut troops that were with Amherst when he took Ticonderoga. While the English had possession of that post, before seizing Crown Point, he was much annoyed by a swaggering English major, who boasted that no American in the country could lay him upon his back. Lieutenant Rice accepted the general challenge. For twenty minutes it was doubtful who the successful wrestler would be. Rice was the more agile of the two, and, by a dexterous movement, tripped his adversary and brought him upon his back. The burly major was greatly nettled, and declared the act unfair and unmanly. Rice made a rejoinder, and hard words passed, which ended in a challenge from the major for a duel. It was accepted, and the place and time of meeting were appointed. But the fact having reached the ears of Amherst, he interposed his persuasion. The Englishman was resolved on fighting, and would listen to no remonstrance until Amherst touched his national and military pride. "Consider," he said, "how glorious is our conquest. We have taken this strong fortress without shedding one drop of blood. Shall Britons be such savages, that, when they can not spill the blood of enemies, they will shed that of each other?" The appeal had the desired effect, and the parties sealed their reconciliation and pledged new friendship over a glass of grog. They then tried their strength again. The major was prostrated in an instant by a fair exertion of superior strength, and from that hour he was Rice's warmest friend. The major's name was Church. He was a lieutenant colonel under Prevost, and was killed at Savannah on the 16th of September, 1779.

associations.   The fore-ground of the picture represents the spot whereon Burgoyne began the erection of a battery ; and a shallow hole, drilled for the purpose of making fastenings

VIEW FROM THE TOP OF MOUNT DEFIANCE.

for the cannon, may still be seen.   The sheet of water toward the left is the outlet of Lake George, where it joins Lake Champlain, which sweeps around the promontory in the middle ground, whereon Fort Ticonderoga is situated.   Gray, like the almost bald rock on which they stand, the ruins were scarcely discernible from that height, and the Pavilion appeared like a small white spot among the green foliage that embowers it.   On the point which the steam-boat is approaching is the *Grenadiers' Battery* already mentioned, and on the extreme right is seen a portion of Mount Independence at the mouth of East Creek.   This eminence is in Vermont—Mount Defiance and Fort Ticonderoga are in New York.   The point beyond the small vessel with a white sail is the spot whence the Americans under Allen and Arnold crossed the lake to attack the fort ; and between Mount Independence and the *Grenadiers' Battery* is the place where the bridge was erected.   The lake here is quite narrow, and, sweeping in serpentine curves around the two points, it flows northward on the left, and expands gradually into a sheet of water several miles wide.   The hills seen in the far distance are the Green Mountains of Vermont, between which lofty range and the lake is a beautifully diversified and fertile agricultural country twelve miles wide, a portion of the famous New Hampshire Grants.   From this height the eye takes in a range along the lake of more than thirty miles, and a more beautiful rural panorama can not often be found.   Let us retreat to the cool shadow of the shrubbery on the left, for the summer sun is at meridian ; and, while gathering new strength to make our toilsome descent, let us open again the volume of history, and read the page on which are recorded the stirring events that were enacted within the range of our vision.

Lieutenant-general Burgoyne, with a strong and well-appointed army of more than seven thousand men,[1] including Indians, came up Lake Champlain and appeared before Crown Point on the 27th of June.   The few Americans in garrison there abandoned the fort and retreated to Ticonderoga.   The British quietly took possession, and, after establishing a magazine, hospital, and stores there, proceeded to invest Ticonderoga on the 30th. Some light infantry, grenadiers, Canadians, and Indians, with ten pieces of light artillery, under Brigadier-general Fraser, were encamped on the west side of the lake, at the mouth of Putnam's Creek.   These moved up the shore to Four Mile Point, so called from being that distance from Ticonderoga.   The German reserve,

1777.

consisting of the chasseurs, light infantry, and grenadiers, under Lieutenant-colonel Breyman, were moved at the same time along the eastern shore, while the remainder of the army, under the immediate command of Burgoyne himself, were on board the Royal George and Inflexible frigates and several gun-boats, which moved up the lake between the two strong wings on land.   The land force halted, and the naval force was anchored just beyond cannon-shot from the American works.

Major-general Arthur St. Clair[2] was in command of the American garrison at Ticonderoga, a post of honor which Schuyler had offered to Gates.   He found the garrison only about two thousand strong; and so much were the stores reduced, that he was afraid to make any considerable addition to his force from the militia who were coming in from the east, until a replenishment of provisions could be effected.   Had the garrison been well supplied with stores, six or eight thousand men might have been collected there before the arrival of the enemy.

[1] The day when the British army encamped before Ticonderoga (July 1st), the troops consisted of British, rank and file, three thousand seven hundred and twenty-four; Germans, rank and file, three thousand and sixteen; Canadians and provincials about two hundred and fifty, and Indians about four hundred, making a total of seven thousand four hundred and ninety.

[2] Arthur St. Clair was a native of Edinburgh, in Scotland.   He was born in 1734, and came to America with Admiral Boscawen in 1759.   He served in Canada in 1759 and 1760, as a lieutenant under General Wolfe, and, after the peace of 1763, was appointed to the command of Fort Ligonier, in Pennsylvania.   In January, 1776, he was appointed a colonel in the Continental army, and was ordered to raise a regiment destined for service in Canada.   Within six weeks from his appointment his regiment was on its march. He was appointed a brigadier in August of that year, and was an active participant in the engagements at Trenton and Princeton.   In February, 1777, he received the appointment of major general, and on the 5th of June was ordered by General Schuyler to the command of Ticonderoga.   He reached that post on the 12th, and found a garrison of two thousand men, badly equipped and very short of ammunition and stores. He was obliged to evacuate the post on the 5th of July following.   In 1780 he was ordered to Rhode Island, but circumstances prevented him from going thither.   When the allied armies marched toward Virginia, in 1781, to attack Cornwallis, St. Clair was directed to remain at Philadelphia with the recruits of the Pennsylvania line, for the protection of Congress.   He was, however, soon afterward allowed to join the army, and reached Yorktown during the siege.   From Yorktown he was sent with a considerable force to join Greene, which he did at Jacksonville, near Savannah.   He resided in Pennsylvania after the peace; was elected to Congress in 1786, and was president of that body in 1787.   Upon the erection of the Northwestern Territory into a government in 1788, he was appointed governor, which office he held until 1802. when Ohio was admitted as a state into the Union, and he declined an election to the post he had held. His military operations within his territory against the Indians were disastrous, and when he retired from office he was almost ruined in fortune.   He made unsuccessful applications to Congress for the payment of certain claims, and finally died almost penniless, at Laurel Hill in Western Pennsylvania, Aug. 31, 1818, aged 84 years.

St. Clair was an officer of acknowledged bravery and prudence, yet he was far from being an expert and skillful military leader. His self-reliance and his confidence in the valor and strength of those under him often caused him to be less vigilant than necessity demanded ; and it was this fault, in connection with the weakness of the garrison, which gave Burgoyne his only advantage at Ticonderoga. He soon perceived, through the vigilance of his scouts, that St. Clair had neglected to secure those two important eminences, Mount Hope and Sugar Loaf Hill (Mount Defiance), and, instead of making a direct assault upon the fortress, the British general essayed to possess himself of these valuable points.

When Burgoyne approached, a small detachment of Americans occupied the old French lines north of the fort, which were well repaired and guarded by a block-house. They also had an outpost at the saw-mills (now the village of Ticonderoga), another just above the mills, and a block-house and hospital at the entrance of the lake. Between the lines and the old fort were two block-houses, and the Grenadiers' Battery on the point was manned.

The garrison in the star fort, on Mount Independence, was rather stronger than that at Ticonderoga, and better provisioned. The fort was supplied with artillery, strongly picketed, and its approaches were well guarded by batteries. The foot of the hill on the northwestern side was intrenched, and had a strong *abatis* next to the water. Artillery was placed in the intrenchments, pointing down the lake, and at the point, near the mouth of East Creek, was a strong circular battery. The general defenses of the Americans were formidable to an enemy, but the tardiness of Congress in supplying the garrison with food, clothing, ammunition, and re-enforcements, made them quite weak.[1] Their lines and works were extensive, and instead of a full complement of men to man and defend them, and to occupy Sugar Loaf Hill and Mount Hope, the whole force consisted of only two thousand five hundred and forty-six Continentals and nine hundred militia. Of the latter not one tenth had bayonets.

While at Crown Point, Burgoyne sent forth a pompous and threatening proclamation, intended to awe the republicans into passiveness, and confirm the loyalists June 29. in their position by a sense of the presence of overshadowing power.[2] In his proclamation the British commander set forth the terrible character of the Indians that accompanied him, greatly exaggerated their numbers, and magnified their eagerness to be let loose upon the republicans, whether found in battle array or in the bosom of their families. " I have," he said, " but to give stretch to the Indian forces under my direction, and they amount to thousands, to overtake the hardened enemies of Great Britain and America. I consider them the same wherever they may lurk." Protection and security, clogged with conditions, were held out to the peaceable who remained in their habitations. All the outrages of war, arrayed in their most terrific forms, were denounced against those who persisted in their

---

[1] It was generally believed, until Burgoyne appeared at St. John's, that the military preparations in progress at Quebec were intended for an expedition by sea against the coast towns still in possession of the Americans; and influenced by this belief, as well as by the pressing demands for men to keep General Howe and his army from Philadelphia, Congress made but little exertion to strengthen the posts on Lake Champlain. This was a fatal mistake, and it was perceived too late for remedy.

[2] This swaggering proclamation commenced as follows : " By John Burgoyne, Esquire, lieutenant general of his majesty's forces in America, colonel of the Queen's regiment of Light Dragoons, governor of Fort William, in North Britain, one of the Commons of Great Britain in Parliament, and commanding an army and fleet employed on an expedition from Canada," &c. " From the pompous manner in which he has arrayed his titles," says Dr. Thatcher, " we are led to suppose that he considers them as more than a match for all the military force which we can bring against them."—*Military Journal*, p. 82.

General Washington, from his camp at Middlebrook, in New Jersey, issued a manifesto or counter proclamation, which, in sincerity and dignity, was infinitely superior to that issued by Burgoyne. He alluded to the purity of motives and devotion of the patriots, the righteousness of their cause, and the evident guardianship of an overruling Providence in the direction of affairs, and closed by saying, " Harassed as we are by unrelenting persecution, obliged by every tie to repel violence by force, urged by self-preservation to exert the strength which Providence has given us to defend our natural rights against the aggressor, we appeal to the hearts of all mankind for the justice of our cause; its event we leave to Him who speaks the fate of nations, in humble confidence that as his omniscient eye taketh note even of the sparrow that falleth to the ground, so he will not withdraw his countenance from a people who humbly array themselves under his banner in defense of the noblest principles with which he has adorned humanity."

hostility.　But the people at large, and particularly the firm republicans, were so far from being frightened, that they treated the proclamation with contempt, as a complete model of pomposity.[1]

1777.　On the 2d of July the right wing of the British army moved forward, and General St. Clair believed and hoped that they intended to make a direct assault upon the fort.　The small American detachments that occupied the outposts toward Lake George made but a feeble resistance, and then set fire to and abandoned their works.　Generals Phillips and Fraser, with an advanced corps of infantry and some light artillery, immediately took possession of Mount Hope, which completely commanded the road to Lake George, and thus cut off all supplies to the patriot garrison from that quarter.　This accomplished, extraordinary energy and activity were manifested by the enemy in bringing up their artillery, ammunition, and stores to fortify the post gained, and on the 4th Fraser's whole corps occupied Mount Hope.[2]　In the mean while Sugar Loaf Hill had been reconnoitered by Lieutenant Twiss, the chief engineer, who reported that its summit had complete command of the whole American works at Ticonderoga and Mount Independence, and that a road to the top, suitable for the conveyance of cannons, though difficult, might be made in twenty-four hours.　It was resolved to erect a battery on the height, and, by arduous and prolonged labor, a road was cleared on the night of the 4th.　The Thunderer, carrying the battery train and stores, arrived in the afternoon, and light twelve pounders, medium twelves, and eight-inch howitzers were landed.

July.

So completely did the enemy occupy the ground between the lake, Mount Hope, and Sugar Loaf Hill, that this important movement was concealed from the garrison ; and when, at dawn on the morning of the 5th, the summit of Mount Defiance[3] glowed with the scarlet uniforms of the British troops, and heavy artillery stood threateningly in their midst, the Americans were paralyzed with astonishment, for that array seemed more like the lingering apparitions of a night vision than the terrible reality they were forced to acknowledge. From that height the enemy could look down into the fortress, count every man, inspect all their movements, and with eye and cannon command all the extensive works of Ticonderoga and Mount Independence.　St. Clair immediately called a council of war, and presented to them the alarming facts, that the whole effective strength of the garrison was not sufficient to man one half of the works ; that, as the whole must be constantly on duty, they could not long endure the fatigue ; that General Schuyler, then at Fort Edward, had not sufficient troops to re-enforce or relieve them ; that the enemy's batteries were nearly ready to open upon them, and that a complete investment of the place would be accomplished within twenty-four hours.　It seemed plain that nothing could save the troops but evacuation, and the step was proposed by the commander and agreed to by his officers.　It was a critical and trying moment for St. Clair.　To remain would be to lose his army, to evacuate would be to lose his character.　He chose to make a self-sacrifice, and at about two o'clock on the following morning the troops were put in motion.

July 6, 1777.

As every movement of the Americans could be seen through the day from Mount Defiance, no visible preparations for leaving the fort were made until after dark, and the purpose of the council was concealed from the troops until the evening order was given.　It was arranged to place the baggage, and such ammunition and stores as might be expedient, on board two hundred bateaux, to be dispatched, under a convoy of five armed galleys, up the lake to Skenesborough (Whitehall), and the main body of the army to proceed by land to

---

[1] Gordon, ii., 205.

[2] This title was given to it by General Fraser, in allusion to the hope they entertained of dislodging the Americans.

[3] I was informed by an old man, ninety years of age, residing at Pittsford, not far from the battle-ground at Hubbardton, that the British gave the name of Mount Defiance to Sugar Loaf Hill on the day when they erected their battery upon it, for from that height they defied the Americans either to resist or dislodge them.　The old man was one of the British regulars under Burgoyne, but soon afterward deserted to the Continentals.

the same destination, by way of Castleton.   The cannons that could not be moved were to be spiked ; previous to striking the tents, every light was to be extinguished ; each soldier was to provide himself with several days' provisions ; and, to allay any suspicions on the part of the enemy of such a movement, a continued cannonade was to be kept up from one of the batteries in the direction of Mount Hope until the moment of departure.

These arrangements were all completed, yet so short was the notice that a good deal of confusion ensued.   The garrison of Ticonderoga crossed the bridge to Mount Independence at about three o'clock in the morning, the enemy all the while unconscious of the escape of their prey.   The moon was shining brightly, yet her pale light was insufficient to betray the toiling Americans in their preparations and flight, and they felt certain that, before day light should discover their withdrawal, they would be too far advanced to invite pursuit. But General De Fermoy, who commanded on Mount Independence, regardless of express orders, set fire to the house he had occupied as the troops left.   The light of the conflagration revealed the whole scene and every movement to the enemy, and the consciousness of discovery added to the confusion and disorder of the retreating republicans.   The rear-guard, under Colonel Francis, left the mount at about four o'clock in the morning, and the whole body pressed onward in irregular order toward Hubbardton, where, through the energy and skill of the officers, they were pretty well organized after a halt of two hours.   The main army then proceeded to Castleton, six miles further, and the rear-guard, with stragglers picked up by the way, were placed under the command of Colonel Seth Warner, and remained at Hubbardton until some, who were left behind, should come up.   Here a desperate, and, to the Americans, a disastrous battle was fought the next morning, the details of which will be given hereafter.

As soon as the movement of the Americans was perceived by the British, General Fraser commenced an eager pursuit with his pickets, leaving orders for his brigade to follow.   At daylight he unfurled the British flag over Ticonderoga, and before sunrise he had passed the bridge and Mount Independence, and was in close pursuit of the flying patriots.[1]   Major-general Riedesel and Colonel Breyman, with their Germans and Hessians, soon followed to sustain Fraser, while Burgoyne, who was on board the Royal George, prepared for an immediate pursuit of the bateaux and convoy by water.   The Americans placed great reliance upon their strong boom at Ticonderoga, and regarded pursuit by water as almost impossible ; but the boom and bridge were speedily cleft by the enemy.   Long before noon a free passage was made for the gun-boats and frigates, and the whole flotilla were crowding all sail to overtake the American bateaux.   These, with the baggage and stores, were all destroyed at Skenesborough before sunset.

The evacuation of Ticonderoga, without efforts at defense, was loudly condemned throughout the country, and brought down a storm of indignant abuse upon the heads of Generals St. Clair and Schuyler, for much of the responsibility was laid upon the latter because he was the commander-in-chief of the northern department.   The weakness of the garrison, the commanding position of the enemy upon Mount Defiance, where they could not be reached by the guns of the fort, and the scarcity of stores and ammunition, were not taken into the account, and, consequently, the verdict of an excited public was very unjust toward those unfortunate officers.   Washington had placed great reliance upon them both ; nor did the event destroy his confidence in their ability and bravery, yet he was perplexed,[2] and

---

[1] This was the third time in consecutive order that the fortress was captured by an enemy to the garrison without bloodshed, namely, in 1759, by the English under General Amherst ; in 1775, by the New England provincials under Colonel Ethan Allen, and now (1777) by the British under Lieutenant-general Burgoyne.

[2] The chief thus wrote to General Schuyler on hearing of the disaster : " The evacuation of Ticonderoga and Mount Independence is an event of chagrin and surprise not apprehended nor within the compass of my reasoning.   I know not upon what principle it was founded, and I should suppose it would be still more difficult to be accounted for if the garrison amounted to five thousand men in high spirits, healthy, well supplied with provisions and ammunition, and the Eastern militia were marching to their succor, as you mentioned in your letter of the 9th [June] to the Council of Safety of New York."

clearly foresaw that some other leader would be necessary to inspire sufficient confidence in the minds of the Eastern militia to cause them to turn out in force to oppose the progress of Burgoyne. Accordingly, he recommended Congress to send an " active, spirited officer to conduct and lead them (the militia) on."[1] But Congress went further. Unwisely listening to and heeding the popular clamor, they suspended St. Clair from command, and appointed Adjutant-general Gates to supersede General Schuyler. St. Clair did not leave the army, but was with Washington at the battle of Brandywine. By a general court-martial, held in the autumn of 1778, he was acquitted of all blame, with the highest honor, and this decision was fully confirmed by Congress in December following. The noble conduct of General Schuyler toward Gates, and his continued patriotic efforts in behalf of his country after suffering the injustice inflicted by Congress, have been mentioned in another chapter. After the lapse of several months the public mind was brought to bear with calmness upon the subject, and, before the close of the war, both generals were fully reinstated in the confidence of the people.

Our historic picnic upon the mountain-top is ended, and, being well rested, let us " gather up the fragments, that nothing be lost," and descend to the village of " Ty," by the way of the military road which was made impromptu by General Phillips for his cannon, up the northern slope of Defiance. Very slight traces of it are now visible, and these consist chiefly of a second growth of timber, standing where the road was cut.

We parted with our guide at the foot of the mountain. Our boy-driver and the vehicle had disappeared, and we were obliged to walk in the hot sun to the village. Our good tempers were not at all improved when we learned the fact that the stage from Lake George had passed nearly an hour before, and that no conveyance could be procured until toward evening to take us to the fort, unless the boy, who had not returned, should make his appearance ; and where he had gone was a mystery. Dinner at the Pavilion was an event only a half hour in the future, and two miles in distance stretched between us and the viands. So we stopped grumbling, trudged on, and, whiling away the moments by pleasant conversation, we reached the Pavilion in time to take our places at table, too much heated and fatigued, however, to enjoy the luxuries set before us. Our Boston friends left that afternoon, but we tarried until two o'clock the next morning, when we departed on the Burlington for Whitehall.

The air was cool and the sky unclouded when we left Ticonderoga. The moon had gone down, and it was too dark to see more than the outlines of the romantic shores by which we were gliding, so we took seats upon the upper deck and surveyed the clear heavens, jeweled with stars. The Pleiades were glowing in the southern sky, and beautiful Orion was upon the verge of the eastern horizon. Who can look upward on a clear night and not feel the spirit of worship stirring within ! Who can contemplate those silent watchers in the firmament and not feel the impulses of adoration !

> " I know they must be holy things
> That from a roof so sacred shine,
> Where sounds the beat of angels' wings,
> And footsteps echo all divine.
> Their mysteries I never sought,
> Nor hearken to what science tells ;
> For oh, in childhood I was taught
> That God amid them dwells."
> MILLER.

---

[1] In his letter to Congress (from which this sentence is quoted), dated at Morristown, July 10th, 1777, Washington continues, " If General Arnold has settled his affairs, and can be spared from Philadelphia, I would recommend him for this business, and that he should immediately set out for the northern department. He is active, judicious, and brave, and an officer in whom the militia will repose great confidence. Besides this, he is well acquainted with that country, and with the routes and most important passes and defiles in it. I do not think he can render more signal services, or be more usefully employed at this time, than in this way. I am persuaded his presence and activity will animate the militia greatly, and spur them on to a becoming conduct." Arnold was sent accordingly, and his signal services at Bemis's Heights we have already considered.

Just as the day dawned tiny spiral columns of vapor began to rise from the lake, and before sunrise we were completely wrapped in a dense fog. After passing the bay south of Mount Independence, the lake becomes very narrow, and the channel is so sinuous that our vessel proceeded very cautiously in the dense mist. At the *Elbow,* half a mile from White-hall Landing, a rocky point containing " Putnam's Ledge" projects from the west, and occasions such a short and narrow turn in the lake, that it is with much difficulty large class steam-boats make their way through. It can only be done by the use of hawsers attached to the bow and stern, and this process requires an annoying delay. We reached Whitehall, at the mouth of Wood Creek,[1] at the head of the lake, about seven in the evening, and found comfortable quarters at a well-conducted temperance hotel near the landing.[2]

This is ancient Skenesborough, and was a point of considerable importance during the wars on our northern frontier, from 1745 till the close of the Revolution. Here armies halted, and provisions, ammunition, and stores were collected and distributed. A picketed fort was erected here during the French and Indian war, upon the brow of the hill east of Church-street. Soon after the peace of Paris, in 1763, Philip K. Skene, an English major under half pay, purchased several soldiers' grants located here, and, to make his title secure, procured a royal patent. He effected a small settlement at this point, and named it Skenesborough, which title it bore until after the Revolution. He had procured a second patent, and became possessor of the whole of the land comprised within the present township of Whitehall, except four thousand acres on its eastern border. He was a magistrate of the crown, the owner of black slaves, and was sometimes honored with the title of governor, on account of having held the office of Lieutenant-governor of Crown Point and Ticonderoga. In addition to a stone residence, he erected another stone edifice, one hundred and thirty feet long, for a military garrison and depôt, upon the spot used as a garden by the family of the late Judge Wheeler. Near the east end was an arched gateway, the key-stone of which is now in the north basement wall of the Baptist Church, and bears the initials "P. K. S.," and date "1770."

Skenesborough was a point included in the programme of operations against Ticonderoga, in the expedition under Colonel Allen in 1775. The council held at Castleton, where Allen was appointed commander-in-chief, resolved to send thirty men, under Captain Herrick, to surprise Skenesborough, capture the son of the proprietor (the latter was then in Europe), his negroes and tenantry, seize all the boats and other vessels that might be found there, and hasten down the lake with them to Shoreham. The surprise was so complete, that the plan was all accomplished without bloodshed. Major Skene the younger was captured while out shooting ; the twelve negroes and fifty tenants were secured, and the governor's strong stone buildings were taken possession of by the captors. In the cellar of his house was found the body of the wife of the elder Skene, where it had been preserved many years to secure to the husband an annuity devised to her " while she remained above ground !" The Amer-

---

[1] In the older histories and in the geographies of the state of New York the whole narrow part of Lake Champlain south of Ticonderoga was called respectively *Wood Creek* and *South River.* For fifty years these names for that portion of the lake have become obsolete, and as historians write for the future, they should be careful to note these changes, so as not to mislead the student. Mr. Headly carelessly observes, when speaking of the retreat from Ticonderoga, that " their long procession of boats began by moonlight to wind up Wood Creek," &c. Again, speaking of Putnam's position when he attacked the French and Indians in their canoes, he represents the place as upon " Wood Creek where it falls into the lake." The fact is, the spot is upon the lake, about a mile below where Wood Creek proper " falls into the lake." He says again, " A whole fleet of canoes, filled with soldiers, was entering the mouth of the creek." The mouth of the creek being a cascade, it would have been difficult for the canoes to enter it. Wood Creek proper rises in French Pond, in Warren county, and, flowing by Fort Anne in a deep and sluggish stream, receives the waters of the Pawlet, and falls into Lake Champlain at Whitehall.

[2] Whitehall is a growing and flourishing village. It is within a rocky ravine at the foot of a high eminence called Skene's Mountain, at the mouth of Wood Creek and the northern terminus of the Champlain Canal and Rail-road. It has a beautiful agricultural country behind it, and the natural scenery in the vicinity is very picturesque. The Indian name of the locality, when the whites first explored the neighborhood, was *Kah-cho-qua-na,* which, literally interpreted, is, " place where dip fish."

icans buried the body in the rear of the house, and, embarking on board a schooner in the harbor, belonging to Skene, they sailed down the lake to join Allen at Shoreham.[1]

A garrison was stationed at Skenesborough in 1776, and there the vessels of the little fleet which Arnold commanded in an action on the lake, below Crown Point, were constructed and partially armed. The Americans strengthened the military works there, and made it quite a strong post. This was the stipulated point for rendezvous of the army under St. Clair, on its retreat from Ticonderoga in 1777. I have already observed that those who escaped by water were unsuspicious of pursuit, and that the flotilla was scarcely moored at Skenesborough before the frigates appeared and attacked the galleys. Two of them were captured, and the other three were blown up. Unsupported by the feeble garrison at Skenesborough or by detachments from the army retreating by land,[2] and conscious of the futility of contention with such a force as Burgoyne presented, the Americans abandoned their bateaux, set fire to them, together with the fort, mills, block-houses, &c., and fled toward the camp of General Schuyler at Fort Edward.[3] At Fort Anne they were joined by a few other troops sent forward with provisions and ammunition by General Schuyler, but it was a feeble re-enforcement, for he had with him at Fort Edward only about seven hundred Continentals and fifteen hundred militia. The supplies which he sent so reduced the ammunition and stores of his garrison, that they were several days without lead, except a small quantity which they received from Albany, and which was obtained by stripping the windows.

The troops borne by the flotilla under Burgoyne, and those that marched from Ticonderoga in pursuit of the Americans, conjoined at Skenesborough, where the British commander resolved to make thorough preparations for pushing forward to the Hudson River. He was informed by the people at Skenesborough that the Americans were retreating toward Fort Edward. Lieutenant-colonel Hill, of the ninth regiment, was sent forward on the 7th to take post at Fort Anne and watch the movements of the republicans. The rest of the British army were encamped at Skenesborough and vicinity, where they remained nearly three weeks, while detachments were repairing the roads and bridges, and constructing new ones on the way to Fort Anne. Burgoyne and his staff were entertained at the mansion of Major Skene, whose familiarity with the country and the people caused him to be introduced into the military family of the commander. He was considered a valuable acquisition, but the result proved otherwise. He advised the disastrous expedition to Bennington, and accompanied the enemy there. He was personally known to many of the Americans engaged in that affair, who made great efforts to capture him alive. Four horses were shot under him, but, mounting a fifth, he made his escape, although the poor animal fell and expired from the effects of a shot, after carrying his rider beyond the reach of his foes. Skene was with Burgoyne when his army surrendered at Saratoga. He dared not return home under his parole, but went to England. He ordered his house to be burned, to prevent its falling into the hands of the Americans. His lands were confiscated and sold by the state,[4] and soon after the Revolution the name of Skenesborough was repudiated by the people, and that of Whitehall substituted. Hardly a vestige of the Revolution

July, 1777.

1788.

---

[1] See Reverend Lewis Kellogg's *Historical Discourse*, Whitehall, 1847.

[2] At Castleton St. Clair was informed of the approach of Burgoyne by water, and, instead of marching to Skenesborough, he struck off into the woods on the left, fearing that he might be intercepted by the enemy at Fort Anne.

[3] General Mattoon, late of Amherst, Massachusetts, was a subaltern in the American convoy. According to his account, there were then only four houses at Skenesborough, besides those belonging to Skene. While he was in one of them, occupied by a French family, and just in the act of partaking of some refreshments, a cannon-ball from the enemy's fleet entered, crushed the table, and scattered the victuals in all directions over the room.—*Kellogg's Discourse*, p. 6.

[4] The place was very unhealthy at that time. The mortality from sickness among the troops stationed there during the Revolution was fearful ; and so bad was the reputation of Whitehall in this particular at the close of the war, that, when the lands of Skene were offered for sale, no competitor appeared, and 29,000 acres were struck off at the first offer of £14 10s. to an agent of the purchasers, John Williams, Joseph Stringham, and John Murray.—*Kellogg's Discourse*, p. 14.

A remarkable case of longevity occurred near Whitehall. Henry Francisco, a native of England, died

is now left there.   When another war was waged against us by the same enemy, in 1812, this was again the theater of hostile preparations.   The block-house within the old fort was repaired, furnished with artillery, and garrisoned for the defense of the place.   Intrench-ments and a magazine were constructed on an island a few hundred yards north of the vil-lage, and barracks were erected on the brow of the hill west of Church Street, the remains of which have but recently been demolished.   The American fleet engaged in ⎫ September 11, the battle of Plattsburgh, with the vessels captured from the enemy in that en- ⎬ 1814. gagement, were anchored in the harbor at Whitehall soon after that event ; and the remains of some of the vessels of both nations may now be seen decaying together in the lake, a short distance from the harbor.

After breakfast, on the morning of our arrival at Whitehall, I rode to Fort Anne ⎫ August 3, Village, eleven miles south, accompanied by the editor of the " *Democrat*,"[1] whose ⎬ 1848. kind attentions and free communications of valuable knowledge concerning historical locali-ties in the vicinity contributed much to the pleasure and instruction of the journey thither. It is a pleasant little village, situated upon a gently undulating plain near the junction of Wood Creek and East Creek, and exhibited a charming picture of quiet and prosperity There I found a venerable kinsman, nearly eighty years of age, who, in the vigor of manhood, fifty years ago, purchased an extensive tract of land in this then almost unbroken wilderness.[2] His dwelling, store-house, and barns occupy the site of Fort Anne, the only traces of which

SITE OF FORT ANNE.[3]

are the stumps of the strong pine pickets with which it was stockaded.   It was built by the English, under General Nicholson, in 1757, two years after the construction of Fort Ed-ward.   It was a small fortress, and was never the scene of any fierce hostility.   Although ninety years had elapsed since its pickets were set in the ground, what remained of them

near there in November, 1820, aged one hundred and thirty-four years.   He was present at the corona-tion of Queen Anne, March 8th, 1702.   He served in the French wars and in the Revolution, and lived in this country nearly ninety years; since deceased.

[1] D. S. Murray, Esq.

[2] William A. Moore, Esq., president of the Whitehall Bank.

[3] This view is from the bridge which crosses Wood Creek, looking south.   The distant building on the right is the dwelling of Mr. Moore.   Nearer is his store-house, and on the left are his out-houses.   The stumps of the pickets may be traced in a circular line from his dwelling along the road to the crook in the fence, and so on to the barns and in their yards.

exhibited but slight tokens of decay, and the odor of turpentine was almost as strong and fresh when one was split as if it had been planted but a year ago.

August, About a mile northwest of Fort Anne is the place where a severe battle was
1758.   fought between a corps of five hundred Rangers, English and provincials, under Putnam and Rogers, and about the same number of French and Indians, under the famous partisan Molang. Putnam and Rogers were sent by Abercrombie to watch the enemy in the neighborhood of Ticonderoga. When they arrived at South Bay, an expansion of Lake Champlain near Whitehall, the two leaders separated, taking with them their respective divisions, but, being discovered by the watchful Molang, they deemed it expedient to reunite and return immediately to Fort Edward. Their troops were marched in three divisions, the right commanded by Rogers, the left by Putnam, and the center by Captain Dalyell (sometimes written D'Ell). They halted at evening on the border of Clear River, a fork of Wood Creek before its junction with East Creek, and within a mile of Fort Anne. Early in the morning, while the lines were forming, Major Rogers, regardless of the teachings of the Ranger's great virtue, precaution, amused himself by firing at a target with a British officer. The sound reached the vigilant ears of Molang and his Indian allies, who, unknown to the Americans, were then encamped within a mile of them. He had been searching for the Rangers to intercept them, and the firing was a sure guide. His men were posted in ambush along the paths which he knew they must take, and as the Americans, just at sunrise, emerged from a dense thicket into the open woods, Molang and his followers fell upon them with great fury. Rogers seemed to be appalled by the fierce onslaught and fell back, but Put-

nam and Dalyell sustained their position and returned the fire. The conflict became desperate. At length Putnam's fusee missed fire when the muzzle was within a few inches of the breast of a giant savage, who thrust it aside and fell upon the major with the fierceness of a panther, made him prisoner, bound him firmly to a tree, and then returned to the battle. Captain Dalyell now assumed the command. The provincials fell back a little, but, rallying, the fight continued with great vigor. The tree to which Putnam was bound was about midway between the combatants, and he stood in the center of the hottest fire of both, utterly unable to move body or limb, so firmly had the savage secured him. His garments were riddled by bullets, but not one touched his person. For an hour he remained in this horrible position, until the enemy were obliged to retreat, when he was unbound and carried off by his savage captors.[1]

MAJOR ISRAEL PUTNAM IN BRITISH UNIFORM.

From an old picture in the possession of a gentleman in New London, Connecticut.

Wounded, exhausted, and dispirited, Putnam was forced to make a weary march over a rough country, led on by

[1] At one time, when the provincials fell back, and the Indians were near him, a young warrior amused himself by trying his skill in throwing his tomahawk as near Putnam's head as possible without hitting him. When he was tired of his amusement, a French subaltern, more savage than the Indian, leveled his musket at Putnam's breast, but it missed fire. The major claimed the consideration due to a prisoner of war, but the barbarous Frenchman was unmoved, and, after striking him a violent blow upon his cheek with the butt end of his musket, left him to die, as he thought.

the savages, who had tied cords so tightly around his wrists that his hands were swollen and dreadfully tortured.   He begged for release either from the pain or from life.   A French officer interposed and unbound the cords ; and just then his captor came up, and, with a sort of savage humanity, supplied him with moccasins, and expressed great indignation because of the harsh treatment his prisoner had endured.   I say *savage humanity*, for it was present kindness, exercised while a dark and atrocious intention for the future made the Indian complaisant—the prisoner was reserved for the stake, and all those exquisite tortures with which savage cruelty imbitters the death of its victims.   Deep in the forest he was stripped naked, and with green withes was bound fast to a sapling.   The wood was piled high around him, and the wild death-songs of the savages, mingled with fierce yells, were chanted.   The torch was applied, and the crackling flame began to curl around the fagots, when a black cloud, that for an hour had been rising in the west, poured down such a volume of water that the flames were nearly extinguished.   But they burst forth again in fiercer intensity, and Putnam lost all hope of escape, when a French officer dashed through the crowd of savages, scattered the burning wood, and cut the cords of the victim.   It was Molang himself.   Some relenting savage had told him of the horrid orgies in the forest, and he flew to the rescue of Putnam, just in time to save him.   After enduring much suffering, he was delivered to Montcalm at Ticonderoga, and by him sent to Montreal, where he experienced great kindness from Colonel Peter Schuyler, a fellow-prisoner, through whose influence he was exchanged for a prisoner taken by Colonel Bradstreet at Fort Frontenac.[1]

About three fourths of a mile north of Fort Anne is a narrow, rocky defile, through which Wood Creek and the Champlain Canal flow and the rail-road is laid.   Art has widened the defile by excavation, and cultivation has swept away much of the primitive forest.   Here in this rocky gorge, then just wide enough for the stream and a narrow pathway, a severe

BATTLE-GROUND NEAR FORT ANNE.[2]

engagement occurred between the ninth British regiment, under Lieutenant-colonel Hill, and a detachment of Americans, under Colonel Long.   This officer, with about five hundred republicans, principally of the invalids and convalescents of the army, was   July 8, 1777.   posted at Fort Anne by General Schuyler, with directions to defend it.   Warned of the approach of the enemy, Colonel Long prepared not only for defense, but to go out and meet him.   The Americans fit for duty were mustered, and early in the morning they marched up to the southern edge of the defile.   " At half past ten in the morning," said Major

---

[1] See Humphrey's and Peabody's Biographies of Putnam.
[2] This sketch was taken from the rail-road, looking north.   The forest upon the left is the " thick wood" of the Revolution, but on the right cultivated fields have taken the place of the forest to a considerable extent.   On the right is seen the Champlain Canal, here occupying the bed of Wood Creek.   The fence on the left indicates the place of the public road between Fort Anne and Whitehall   When this sketch was made (1848) the rail-road was unfinished.

Forbes in his testimony on the trial of Burgoyne, " they attacked us in front with a heavy and well-directed fire ; a large body of them passed the creek on the left, and fired from a thick wood across the creek on the left flank of the regiment ; they then began to recross the creek and attack us in the rear ; we then found it necessary to change our ground, to prevent the regiment being surrounded ; we took post on a high hill to our right. As soon as we had taken post, the enemy made a very vigorous attack, which continued upward of two hours ; and they certainly would have forced us, had it not been for some Indians that arrived and gave the Indian hoop, which we answered with three cheers ; the rebels soon after that gave way."[1] The major's *facts* are correct, but his *inferences* are wide of the mark. The Americans were not frightened by the Indian war-hoop, for it was a sound very familiar to their ears, but they " gave way" because their ammunition gave out Had Colonel Long been well supplied with powder and ball, the British troops would have been destroyed or made prisoners. Captain Montgomery, of Hill's regiment, was severely wounded and captured by the Americans, who, when they gave way, set fire to Fort Anne and retreated to the headquarters of General Schuyler at Fort Edward.

We returned to Whitehall toward evening. The ride was delightful through a country ever-changing and picturesque, particularly when approaching the lake. On the left rise the lofty summits of the hills on Lake George ; on the east those of Vermont and Massachusetts ; and down the lake, northward, Mount Defiance may be plainly seen. After an early evening meal, I procured a water-man and his boat, and, accompanied by my traveling companion and Mr. M., proceeded to "Put's Rock," near "the Elbow," a mile from the landing, and near the entrance of South Bay.[2] The lake is here very narrow, and the shores on either side are abrupt, rocky, and wooded. It was about sunset when we arrived at the scene of Putnam's exploit, and the deep shadows that gathered upon the western shore, where the famous ledge is situated, heightened the picturesque character of the scenery and the force of the historical associations which lionize the spot. Upon the rough ledge of rocks seen on the right of the picture Major Putnam and fifty men boldly opened a musket battery upon about five hundred French and Indian warriors under the famous Molang, who were in canoes upon the water.[3] This event occurred a few days previous to the unfortunate battle

VIEW AT PUTNAM'S ROCK.

---

[1] *Burgoyne's State of the Expedition*, &c., p. 81.

[2] Here I will correct a serious geographical error which I find in Peabody's *Life of Putnam*. He says. " Abercrombie ordered Major Putnam to proceed with fifty men to South Bay, in Lake George." Again. " The detachment marched to Wood Creek, near the point where it flows into South Bay." South Bay is in Lake Champlain, and Wood Creek does not flow into it at all. See note respecting Wood Creek, ante, page 137.

[3] The view is taken from the Vermont shore, where rafts of timber and piles of lumber (as seen on the left) betoken the chief article of commerce here. The ledge of rocks, which rises about fourteen feet in height, is on the New York side. From the perpendicular point, rugged and broken, there is a gentle slope thickly covered with timber and shrubbery, and affording an excellent place for an ambuscade. The small trees in the distance mark the point at the *Elbow*, and the hill beyond is a portion of Skene's Mountain which overlooks the harbor at Whitehall.

near Fort Anne, where Putnam was taken prisoner.   Major Rogers, who was also sent by Abercrombie to watch the movements of the enemy, had taken a station twelve miles distant, and Putnam and his fifty rangers composed the whole force at this point.   Near the front of the ledge he constructed a parapet of stone, and placed young pine trees before it in such a natural manner that they seemed to have grown there, and completely hid the defense from observers on the water below.   Fifteen of his men, disabled by sickness, were sent back to the camp at Fort Edward, and with his thirty-five he resolved to attack whatever force might appear upon the lake.   Four days he anxiously awaited the appearance of the enemy, when early one evening he was gratified by the intelligence that a large fleet of canoes, filled with warriors, was leisurely approaching from South Bay.   It was the time of full moon, the sky was unclouded, and from his hiding-place every movement of the Indians could be distinctly seen.   Putnam called in all his sentinels, and in silence every man was stationed where his fire might be most effective.   Not a musket was to be moved until orders were given by the commander.   The advanced canoes had passed the parapet, when one of the soldiers hit his firelock against a stone.   The sound was caught by the watchful ears of Molang and his followers.   The canoes in the van halted, and the whole fleet was crowded in confusion and alarm directly beneath the ledge.   A brief consultation ensued, and then they turned their prows back toward South Bay.   As they wheeled the voice of Putnam shouted " Fire," and with sure aim each bullet reached a victim.   The enemy returned the fire, but without effect, and for a time the carnage produced by the Rangers was dreadful in that dense mass upon the waters.   Molang soon perceived by the firing that his assailants were few, and detached a portion of his men to land below and attack the provincials in the rear.   Putnam had perceived this movement, and sent a party of twelve men, under Lieutenant Durkee, who easily repulsed them when they attempted to land.   About daybreak he learned that the enemy had actually debarked at a point below, and was marching to surround him.   This fact, and the failure of his ammunition, warned him to retreat. Nearly half the number of the enemy perished on that fatal night, while Putnam lost but two men, who were wounded.[1]   While retreating through the thick forest, an unexpected enemy fired upon them, but wounded only one man.   Putnam instantly ordered his men to charge, when his voice was recognized by the other leader, who cried out, " Hold, we are friends !"   " Friends or foes," shouted Putnam, " you deserve to perish for doing so little execution with so fair a shot."   The party proved to be a detachment sent to cover their retreat.

It was late in the evening twilight before I finished my sketch, but our obliging waterman would not consent to row us back until we should go to his house near by and see his " pullet and chickens"—his wife and children.   His dwelling was at the foot of the steep Vermont shore, completely hemmed in by rocks and water, but embowered in shrubbery. His children brought us fruit, and we were refreshed by draughts of water from a mountain spring close by, of icy coldness.   The moon was shining brightly when we passed the Elbow on our return, and by its pale light we could see the ribs and other decaying timber of the British ship of war *Confiance* and the American ship *Saratoga*.   The former was sunk there in 1814, and the latter, which was afterward used as a store-ship, was scuttled by some miscreants while her officers and crew were at the village participating in a Fourth of July celebration.   It was about nine in the evening when we reached the hotel.   There I met that distinguished and venerable divine, Rev. Mr. Pierce, of Brookline, Massachusetts, and was charmed and edified by his conversation for more than an hour.[2]   His memory was

---

[1] These men, one a provincial, the other an Indian, were placed under an escort of two others, and sent toward the camp.   They were pursued and overtaken by the Indians.   The wounded men told the escort to leave them to their fate, which they did.   When the savages came up, the provincial, knowing that he would be put to death, fired and killed three.   He was instantly tomahawked.   The Indian was kept a prisoner, and from him Putnam learned the above facts when they met some time afterward in Canada.

[2] Mr. Pierce was seventy-five years old.   He distinctly remembered Washington's visit to Boston in 1789. The cavalcade halted near the entrance to the city, and Washington was obliged to sit on horseback two hours, while the state authorities and the selectmen decided a point of etiquette—whose province it was to

richly stored with historic learning, and our intercourse was to me a pleasant and profitable appendix to the events and studies of the day.

Early the next morning we left Whitehall on the steamer *Saranac*, and landed at Chipman's Point, or Sholes's Landing, the port of Orwell, and the most eligible point whence to reach the battle-ground of Hubbardton. The morning was delightful, and the ride in a light wagon, accompanied by the intelligent son of Mr. Sholes, proved to be one of peculiar pleasure. Our route was through the pleasant little village of Orwell, five miles southeast of the landing. There we turned southward, and followed the margin of the broad ravine or valley through which the retreating Americans and pursuing British passed when St. Clair evacuated Ticonderoga. The road was made very tortuous to avoid the high ridges and deep valleys which intersect in all directions, while at the same time it gradually ascends for several miles. I never passed through a more picturesque country. The slopes and valleys were smiling with cultivation, and in every direction small lakes were sparkling in the noonday sun. Within about six miles of the battle-ground we descended into a romantic valley imbosomed in a spur of the Green Mountains. We passed several small lakes, lying one below another, over which arose rough and lofty precipices, their summits crowned with cedar, hemlock, pine, and spruce. The tall trunks of the pines, black and branchless, scathed by lightning and the tempest, arose above the surrounding forests like mighty sentinels, and added much to the wild grandeur of the scene. From the rough and narrow valley we ascended to a high, rolling table-land, well cultivated ; and upon the highest part of July 7, this tract, surrounded on the south and east by loftier hills, the battle of Hubbardton 1777. occurred.

General Fraser, whom I have already mentioned as having started after the Americans July 6. from Ticonderoga, continued his pursuit of St. Clair and his army through the day, and, learning from some Tory scouts that they were not far in advance, he ordered his men to lie that night upon their arms, to be ready to push forward at daybreak. About three in the morning his troops were put in motion, and about five o'clock his advanced scouts discovered the American sentries, who discharged their pieces and retreated to the main body of the detachment, which was left behind by St. Clair, under the command of Colonels Warner and Francis. Their place of encampment was in the southeast part of Hubbardton, Rutland county, near the Pittsford line, upon the farm of John Selleck,[1] not far from the place where the Baptist meeting-house now stands. The land is now owned by a son of Captain Barber, who was in the engagement. He kindly accompanied me to the spot, and pointed out the localities, according to the instructions of his patriotic father. The engraving on the opposite page represents the general view of the place of encampment and the battle-ground. When the British advanced guard discovered the Americans, they were breakfasting near a dwelling which stood close by the Baptist meeting-house, the two-story building seen in the center of the picture. The dark spot near the fence, seen between the larger trees in the foreground (I in the map of the battle), marks the remains of the cellar of the old house. The road on the right is that leading toward Ticonderoga ; and the roofs of the houses, seen over the orchard on the right, mark the direction of the road lead-

receive him. The selectmen carried the day. He explained to me the nature of the apparent error in the registration of the birth and christening of Dr. Franklin. The entries of both events are upon the same day, Sunday, 17th of January, 1706. An old man, who remembered the circumstance well, for it caused some gossip at the time, told him that Dr. Franklin's mother went to church and received the communion in the morning, gave birth to her son at noon, and in the afternoon the child was christened.

[1] The first settlement in this town was in the spring of 1774, and consisted of only two families. In 1775 seven other families joined them, among whom was Mr. Selleck, and these nine constituted the whole population of the town when the battle occurred. On the day previous a party of Indians and Tories, under Captain Sherwood, came upon the inhabitants and made prisoners of two farmers named Hickock, and their families, and two young men named Keeler and Kellogg. They captured two or three others, and carried them all off to Ticonderoga, leaving their families to shift for themselves. The sorrowing wives and children made a toilsome journey over the mountains to Connecticut, whence they had emigrated. The men remained prisoners at Ticonderoga (except two who escaped) until after the surrender of Burgoyne in October, when that fortress was retaken by the Americans.—See *Thompson's Gazetteer of Vermont.*

ing down to the valley toward Castleton. The large boulder in front is famed by local tra-

THE BATTLE-GROUND OF HUBBARDTON.

dition as the observatory of the first man of the British van who discovered the Americans; and it is related that he was shot by a sentinel before he could leap down. The range of hills in the distance are the Pittsford Mountains, over which a portion of the Americans fled toward Rutland. A small branch of a tributary of Castleton Creek runs through the intervale between the meeting-house and the hills beyond. The hottest of the fight occurred upon the slope between the large tree and the meeting-house. It was covered with ripe grain when I visited it, and August, 1848. the achievements of the tiller gathering his sheaves seemed more truly great than all the honors and renown which wholesale slaughter ever procured for a warrior chieftain.

It was an excessively hot morning in July when the battle of Hubbardton com- July 7, 1777. menced. The American force consisted of the three regiments of Warner, Francis, and Hale, and such stragglers from the main army then at Castleton (six miles in advance) as had been picked up on the way. The Americans were about thirteen hundred strong, and the British, under Fraser, about eight hundred. Reidesel and his Germans were still in the rear, but, expecting his arrival every moment, Fraser began the attack at seven in the morning, fearing that the Americans might escape if he delayed. The charge of the enemy was well received, and the battle raged furiously. Had Warner been well sustained by the militia regiment under Colonel Hale, he might have secured a victory; but that officer, with his troops, fled toward Castleton, hoping to join the main army there under St. Clair, leaving the commander with only seven hundred men to oppose the enemy. On the way, Hale and his men fell in with an inconsiderable party of British soldiers, to whom they surrendered, without offering any resistance, although the numbers were about equal.[1] They

---

[1] Colonel Hale has been severely censured for this act of apparent cowardice, but when every circumstance is taken into account, there is much to induce a mitigation of blame. Himself and a large portion of his men were in feeble health, and quite unfit for active service, and his movement was one of precaution rather than of cowardly alarm. Rivals, soon after he surrendered, circulated reports unfavorable to his reputation. On hearing of them, he wrote to General Washington, asking him to obtain his exchange, that he might vindicate his character by a court-martial; but before this could be accomplished he died, while a prisoner on Long Island, in September, 1780.

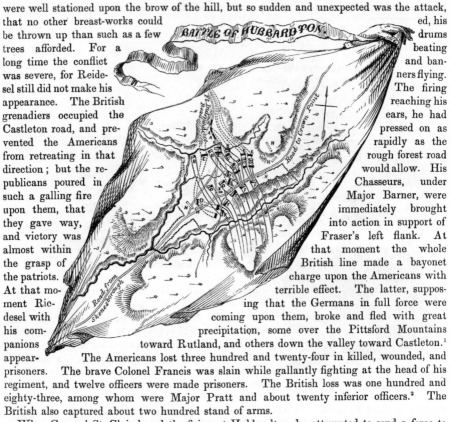

were well stationed upon the brow of the hill, but so sudden and unexpected was the attack, that no other breast-works could be thrown up than such as a few trees afforded. For a long time the conflict was severe, for Reidesel still did not make his appearance. The British grenadiers occupied the Castleton road, and prevented the Americans from retreating in that direction; but the republicans poured in such a galling fire upon them, that they gave way, and victory was almost within the grasp of the patriots. At that moment Riedesel with his companions appeared, his drums beating and banners flying. The firing reaching his ears, he had pressed on as rapidly as the rough forest road would allow. His Chasseurs, under Major Barner, were immediately brought into action in support of Fraser's left flank. At that moment the whole British line made a bayonet charge upon the Americans with terrible effect. The latter, supposing that the Germans in full force were coming upon them, broke and fled with great precipitation, some over the Pittsford Mountains toward Rutland, and others down the valley toward Castleton.[1] prisoners. The brave Colonel Francis was slain while gallantly fighting at the head of his regiment, and twelve officers were made prisoners. The British loss was one hundred and eighty-three, among whom were Major Pratt and about twenty inferior officers.[2] The British also captured about two hundred stand of arms.

When General St. Clair heard the firing at Hubbardton, he attempted to send a force to the relief of Warner, but the militia absolutely refused to go, and the regulars and others were too far on their way to Fort Edward to be recalled. St. Clair had just learned, too, that Burgoyne was at Skenesborough, and he hastened forward to join General Schuyler, which he did on the 12th, with his troops worn down by fatigue and lack of provisions. The loss to the Americans by the evacuation of these posts on the lake was one hundred and twenty-eight pieces of cannon and a considerable quantity of ammu-

July, 1777.

EXPLANATION OF THE MAP.—A, advanced corps of General Fraser, attacked at B; C, position of the corps while it was forming; D, Earl of Balcarras detached to cover the right wing; E, the van-guard and Brunswick company of Chasseurs coming up with General Reidesel; F, position of the Americans after Riedesel arrived. The lines extending downward show the course of the retreat of the Americans over the Pittsford Mountains. H, position of the British after the action; I, house where the wounded were carried, mentioned in the description of the picture on page 144; O, position of the Americans previous to the action. This map is a reduced copy of one drawn by P. Gerlach, Burgoyne's deputy quartermaster general.

[1] Many of the Americans, in their precipitate retreat, threw away their muskets to rid themselves of the encumbrance. Some have been found, within a few years, in the woods on the line of the retreat. One of them, of American manufacture, is in my possession, and dated 1774. The bayonet is fixed, the flint is in the lock, and the powder and ball are still in the barrel.

[2] The statements concerning the loss in this battle are various and contradictory. Some accounts say that nearly six hundred, who were wounded, crawled off into the woods and died; and others, again, put the American loss down at less than three hundred. There is a preponderance of testimony in favor of the number I have given, and it is, doubtless, near the truth.

nition and stores. In every respect the event was disastrous, and, as we have seen, produced much discontent in the army and disappointment throughout the country.

General Schuyler summoned the fragments of the broken armies to his camp at Fort Edward. All united, numbered only four thousand four hundred men, and this was the whole effective force opposed to the southward progress of Burgoyne. Nearly one half of these deserted, not to the enemy, but to their homes, before the end of the month. Yet the general neither despaired nor remained idle. He kept his men busily engaged in destroying bridges, felling trees, digging deep trenches, and making other obstructions in the forest paths from Fort Anne to Fort Edward, to delay the progress of the enemy ; and this labor resulted in greatly impeding Burgoyne's march, and in delaying his arrival upon the Hudson. The subsequent events connected with these two armies, excepting the battle of Bennington and the expedition of St. Leger, have already been noticed in detail. The latter will be considered in their proper order.

I lingered upon the battle-ground in Hubbardton as long as time would allow, for the view from that lofty table-land is both beautiful and grand, particularly in the direction of Castleton, on the southwest. A broad valley, bounded on either side by ranges of high hills, cultivated to their summits, and diversified by rich intervales covered with ripe harvests and dark green corn, spread out below us, a lovely picture of peace and prosperity. The view at its further extremity is bounded by the high hills near the Hudson, and on the left some of the higher summits were dark with spruce and cedar trees. We returned to Sholes's by the way of Hyde's, in Sudbury, where we dined. As usual, every delicacy of the season was upon his table. Indeed, "a table equal to Hyde's" has become a proverbial expression of praise among tourists, for it is his justifiable boast that he spreads the choicest repasts that are given between Montreal and New Orleans. His beautifully embowered mansion is near the base of the Green Mountains, by the margin of a charming lake, on the borders of a rich valley, about twelve miles east of Lake Champlain, and a more delightful summer retreat can not well be imagined. Our route thither was over a rough mountain road. Among the rugged hills we met a venerable, white-haired man leaning upon two canes, and greatly bowed by the weight of years. I accosted him with reverence, and, in answer to my inquiry whether he was a soldier of the Revolution, he informed me that he was with General Sullivan on Rhode Island, and was on duty in the fort on Butt's Hill at the time of the engagement there on the 29th of August, 1778, known as the battle of Quaker Hill.

We arrived at Sholes's between five and six o'clock in the evening. Our excellent host and his neighbor and friend, living at the foot of Mount Independence, anticipating my wishes, had a skiff in readiness to convey us across the bay to visit that memorable spot. Although I had ridden forty miles during the day, and storm-clouds had been gathering thick and fast for two hours, and now threatened a speedy down-pouring, I was too anxious for the visit to allow fatigue or rain to thwart my purpose. Accompanied by my companion and another young lady, the daughter of Mr. S., we pushed across the bay—five of us in a light skiff, and the wind rising—to the foot of Mount Independence, on its steep southern side.

We ascended by the old road constructed in 1776. The top of the summit is flat table-land, and afforded a very eligible site for strong military works. It was first occupied by the Americans early in 1776, when they commenced the erection of batteries, barracks, and houses, with the view of making it a place of general rendezvous, and a recruiting station for the army of the north.[1] It was heavily timbered when they took possession of it, but almost all the trees were felled for building purposes and for fuel. A second growth of tim-

---

[1] Mount Independence is situated in the southwest corner of Orwell, in Vermont, one mile north of Sholes's Landing, and contains about two hundred and fifty acres of land, some of which is arable. The troops stationed there in 1776 received the news of the adoption of the *Declaration of Independence*, by the Continental Congress, with the most extravagant demonstrations of joy. It was just after the reveille, on the morning of the 18th of July, that a courier arrived with the glad tidings ; and, by a general order, a gala day for the soldiers ensued. At sunset they fired a salute of thirteen guns, in honor of the confederation, and named the place on which they were encamped Mount Independence, in commemoration of the event.

ber now covers it, except where the parades were.   The trees are chiefly maple, some of them twenty inches in diameter.   There are about two hundred of them on the mount, large enough for the extraction of sap for sugar.   The young shoots never sprang up where the old parades were, and they present bald spots, bearing only stinted vegetation.

During the summer and autumn of 1776 the Americans were diligent in fortifying this spot.   They erected a picketed fort and several batteries, dug many wells, and constructed nearly three hundred houses for the use of the soldiers.   The remains of these are scattered in all directions upon the mount ; and the foundation walls of the hospital, just commenced when the evacuation in 1777 took place, are now nearly as perfect as when first laid.   Narrow ditches, indicating the line of pickets on the north part of the mount, and running in various directions and at every angle, are distinctly seen ; and the remains of the " horseshoe battery," on the extreme north end, are very prominent.   Near this battery is a flint quarry, which seems to have been well known and used by the Indians, for arrow-heads in every stage of manufacture, from the almost unshapen flint to the perfect weapon, are found there, I was told, in abundance.   Toward the close of 1776 a fatal epidemic prevailed in the garrison there, called the " camp distemper," and the graves of the victims are thickly strewn among the trees.   At one time the deaths were so numerous that it was found impossible to dig a grave for each, and the spot was shown to me where fourteen bodies were deposited in a single broad grave, about daylight one morning.   Among the hundreds of these mounds of the dead, scattered over the mount, there was only one individualized by an

inscribed stone.   The rude monument is a rough limestone, and the inscription, " M. Richardson Stoddard," appeared as if carved with the point of a bayonet.   The tenant was probably an officer of militia from a town formerly named Stoddard, in Vermont.   Already some Vandal visitor had broken off a " relic" from its diminutive bulk, and ere this some patriotic antiquary has doubtless slipped the whole stone into his pocket, and secured a legacy of rare value for his wondering children !   A propensity to appropriate to private use a fragment of public monuments, and a pitiful ambition, allied in kind to that of the Ephesian incendiary, to associate one's name by pencil or penknife inscription with places of public resort, have already greatly marred and disfigured a large proportion of our few monuments, and can not be too severely condemned.   Charity, that " covereth the multitude of sins," has not a mantle broad enough to hide this iniquity, for none but heartless knaves or brainless fools would thus deface even the meanest grave-stone in a church-yard.   Wolfe's monument on the Plains of Abraham, and the monuments at Red Bank and Paoli, bear mournful testimony of this barbarism which is abroad.

At various times Mount Independence, as well as Crown Point and other localities in the neighborhood of Lake Champlain, has been scarred by money-diggers.   In 1815 a company came hither from Northern Vermont, to search for military treasures which wise seers and the divining rod declared were buried there.   The chief of the party, entertaining misgivings on his arrival as to the success of money-digging, purchased land in the neighborhood, and while his more credulous companions were digging deep into the mount, he was plowing deep into his land.   He raised grain and esculent roots—they raised gravel and worthless clay.   When their patience and money were exhausted, they shouldered their picks and departed for Western New York.   He remained, became a thrifty farmer, and, by the unerring divining rod of industry, found the treasure.   Credulous people still dig at these localities, and several pits were pointed out to me which had been recently excavated.[1]

---

[1] Three or four years ago the white wife of a negro dreamed three times—the cabalistic number—that at a certain place on Mount Independence immense treasures were buried when the Americans evacuated that post.   They were, doubtless, the identical silver balls which calumny asserted Burgoyne fired into St. Clair's camp as the price of treason.   The negro procured aid, and a pure white dog to watch them while digging.   A moonlight night was the chosen time.   The secret leaked into the ears of some boys, and set their mischievous wits at work.   A large pumpkin was emptied of its seeds, and staring eyes, wide nos

OF THE REVOLUTION.   149

Return to Sholes's.   Darkness on the Lake.   View from Sholes's Landing.

Darkness came on, and the rain pattered upon the leaves before we descended to the shore ; and by the time we were fairly out upon the lake our destined haven was invisible. The wind was fresh and the waters rough.   One of the ladies guided the helm, but her bright eyes could not discern the distant shore, and her nautical skill was unavailing.   The son of Mr. S., anticipating such a dilemma, discharged a small swivel at the landing, and by its beacon flash we were safely guided until we came within the rays of the candles at the house.   Wet and weary, we supped and retired early, to resume our journey in the morning.

VIEW FROM SHOLES'S LANDING [1]

trils, and grinning teeth were cut out of the rind, and a lighted candle was placed within the sphere.   This hideous head, with its fiery eyes and nostrils, was placed on the caput of a bold boy, who marched up to the pit where the money-diggers were at work.   The dog first discovered the grinning specter, and, with a loud yell, leaped from the cavity and ran for life.   The men followed, leaving pick, spade, hat, and coat behind, quite sure that the " gentleman in black" was close upon their heels ; and they have ever since believed that he guards the treasures, and sometimes takes an evening stroll on Mount Independence.

[1] This is a view from Chipman's Point, or Sholes's Landing, looking north.   The high ridge on the right, in the distance, is Mount Independence.   The higher and more distant hill on the left, over the cedar, is Mount Defiance, and the elevation beyond is Mount Hope.   Fort Ticonderoga is on the other side of Mount Independence, in a line with the highest part.

150   PICTORIAL FIELD-BOOK

Chimney Point.   First Settlement by the French.   Fort St. Frederic.   Distant View of Crown Point.

CHAPTER VII.

"The green earth sends its incense up from every mountain shrine,
From every flower and dewy cup that greeted the sunshine.
The mists are lifted from the rills like the white wing of prayer;
They lean above the ancient hills, as doing homage there.
The forest-tops are lowly cast o'er breezy hill and glen,
As if a prayerful spirit pass'd on nature as on men."

WHITTIER.

LIGHT mist was upon the water when we departed from Sholes's, but a gentle breeze swept it off to the hills as we turned the point of Mount Independence and entered the broader expanse near Ticonderoga. We caught a last glimpse of the gray ruins as our boat sped by, and before nine o'clock we landed at Chimney Point, opposite Crown Point, where the lake is only half a mile wide.[1] Here the French established their first settlement on Lake Champlain, in 1731, and commenced the cultivation of the grains of the country. They erected a stone wind-mill in the neighborhood, which was garrisoned and used as a fort during the wars with the English colonies. When Professor Kalm, the Swedish naturalist and traveler, during his botanical tour through New York and Canada in 1749, visited this settlement, five or six cannons were mounted in the mill. The place was then called Wind-mill Point.[2]

The same year in which the French settled at Chimney Point, they built a strong fort upon the shore opposite, and called it *Fort St. Frederic*, in honor of Frederic Maurepas, the then Secretary of State. It was a starwork, in the form of a pentagon, with bastions at the angles, and surrounded by a ditch walled in with stone. Kalm says there was a considerable settlement around the fort, and pleasant, cultivated gardens adorned the rude dwellings. There was a neat little church within the ramparts, and every thing betokened a smiling future for a happy and prosperous colony. But the rude clangor of war disturbed their repose a few years afterward; the thunder of British artillery frightened them away, and they retired to the north end of the lake. For many years the chimneys of their deserted dwellings on the eastern shore were standing, and gave the name of Chimney Point to the bold promontory.

CHIMNEY POINT LANDING.[3]

---

[1] Chimney Point is in the southwestern corner of Addison town, Vermont, and is the proper landing-place for those who desire to visit the ruins of Crown Point fortress, on the opposite side of the lake.

[2] From Kalm's account it appears probable that the wind-mill was upon the shore opposite, at the point where now may be seen the ruins of what is called the *Grenadiers' Battery*. He says it was "within one or two musket-shots of Fort St. Frederic," a fortification immediately on the shore opposite Chimney Point.

[3] This view is taken from the green in front of the inn at Chimney Point, looking west-southwest. The first land seen across the lake is Crown Point, with the remaining barracks and other works of the fortress, and the dwellings and outhouses of Mr. Baker, a resident farmer. Beyond the point is Bulwaggy Bay, a broad, deep estuary much wider than the lake at Chimney Point. Beyond the bay, and rising from its western shore, is Bulwaggy Mountain, varying in perpendicular height from four to nine hundred feet, and distant from the fort between one and two miles. A little to the right of the larger tree on the shore is the

OF THE REVOLUTION. 151

Visit to Crown Point.   Description of the Fortress.   Its present Appearance.

Anxious to leave in the evening boat for Burlington, we sent our light baggage to the inn, and immediately crossed over to Crown Point on a horse-boat, the only ferry vessel there. Mr. Baker, an aged resident and farmer upon the point, kindly guided us over the remains of the military works in the vicinity, where we passed between three and four hours. We first visited old Fort St. Frederic, the senior fortress in chronological order. It is upon the steep bank of the lake, and the remains of its bomb-proof covered way, oven, and magazine can still be traced; the form of its ramparts is indicated by a broken line of mounds.

The average width of the peninsula of Crown Point is one mile, and the principal works are upon its highest part, near the northern end. The peninsula is made up of dark limestone, covered quite slightly with earth. This physical characteristic lent strength to the post, for an enemy could not approach it by parallels or regular advances, but must make an open assault. *St. Frederic*, standing close by the water, lacked this advantage; and the French, feeling their comparative weakness, exercised the valor of prudence, and abandoned it on the approach of the English and provincials under General Amherst, in 1759, and retired to the Isle Aux Noix,[1] in the Sorel. The British commander took immediate possession, but the works were so dilapidated that, instead of repairing them, he at once began the erection of a new and extensive fortress about two hundred yards southwest of it, and upon more commanding ground. The ramparts were about twenty-five feet thick, and nearly the same in height, of solid masonry.

July 26.

WESTERN LINE OF BARRACKS.[2]

PLAN OF THE FORT.

The curtains varied in length from fifty-two to one hundred yards, and the whole circuit, measuring along the ramparts, and including the bastions, was eight hundred and fifty-three yards, a trifle less than half a mile. A broad ditch cut out of solid limestone surrounded it. The fragments taken from the excavation were used to construct the reveting, and the four rows of barracks erected within. On the north was a gate, and from the northeastern bastion was a covered way leading to the lake. Within this bastion a well, nearly eight feet in diameter and ninety feet deep, was sunk, from which the garrison was supplied with water. This fortress was never entirely finished, although the British government spent nearly ten millions of dollars upon it and its outworks. Its construction was a part of the grand plan devised by Pitt to crush French power in America, and hence, for

site of Fort St. Frederic, and at the edge of the circle on the left, along the same shore, is the locality of the *Grenadiers' Battery*. The wharf and bridge in the foreground form the steam-boat and ferry landing at Chimney Point.   [1] This is pronounced *O Noo-ah.*

[2] There were four large buildings used for barracks within the fort, the walls or chimneys of which were built of limestone. One of them has been entirely removed, and another, two hundred and eighty-seven feet long, is almost demolished. Portions of it are seen on the left, in the foreground of the picture. The walls of the other two—one, one hundred and ninety-two, and the other two hundred and sixteen feet long, and two stories high—are quite perfect, and one of them was roofed and inhabited until within two or three years. At each end, and between these barracks, are seen the remains of the ramparts. The view is from the northwestern angle of the fort, a little south of the remains of the western range of barracks, and looking southeast. The hills in the distance are the Green Mountains on the left, and the nearer range called Snake Mountain, on the right.

Explanation of the Plan.—A, B, C, the *barracks;* D, the *well;* the black line denotes the *ramparts,* with its *parapet;* the white space next to it the *ditch,* and the shaded part outside, the *covered way, banquette,* and *glacis.*

this as well as for every other part of the service here, the most extraordinary efforts were made, and pecuniary means were freely lavished.[1]

Amherst constructed several small vessels at Crown Point, and, leaving a garrison to defend the partly finished fort, embarked with the rest of his troops, and sailed down the lake, to attack the French in their new position in the Sorel. Storm after storm arose upon the lake, and greatly endangered the safety of his men and munitions in the frail vessels. The season being considerably advanced, he abandoned the design, and resolved not to risk the snow-storms that would soon ensue, and the general barrenness of food and forage that now
October 2, 1759. prevailed in an enemy's country. So he returned to Crown Point, and went into winter-quarters.

The works at Crown Point are much better preserved than those at Ticonderoga, and the

CROWN POINT.

present owner of the ground, with a resolution which bespeaks his taste and patriotism, will not allow a stone to be removed. The view here given is from the parapet near the end of the southeastern range of barracks, where the flag-staff was, looking down the lake northwest. At the foot of the hills on the lake shore, toward the left, is Cedar Point, at the entrance of Bulwaggy Bay, and a little north of it is the village of Port Henry, the location of the works of a large iron company, composed chiefly of Bostonians. There is a ferry between this place and Chimney Point, the boats touching at Crown Point.

In the gable wall of the nearest barracks in the view are two inscribed stones, faced smooth where the inscription is carved. One bears the initials "G. R.," George Rex or King; the rude form of an anchor, a mark peculiar to Great Britain, and placed upon her cannon-balls and other military articles; and the date of the construction of the fortress, "1759." The other stone has the initial "G." without the R., the monogram of Amherst, the anchor, and a number of rectangular and diagonal lines of inexplicable meaning. The deep well, already alluded to, is close by the covered way that leads to the lake, and a few rods northeast from the eastern range of barracks. It was nearly filled with rubbish,

and almost hidden from view by the weeds and shrubbery upon its margin. I was informed that a general impression prevailed in the vicinity, about twenty-five years ago, that this deep well was the depository of vast treasures, which were cast into it by the French for conceal-

[1] For the campaign of 1759 the Legislature of New York authorized the levy of two thousand six hundred and eighty men, and issued the sum of five hundred thousand dollars in bills of credit, bearing interest, and redeemable in 1768 by the proceeds of an annual tax.

OF THE REVOLUTION. 153

Search for Treasure in the Well.   A venerable Money-digger.   Capture of Crown Point by the Patriots.   Seth Warner.

ment when they abandoned the fort in 1759. Accordingly, a stock company of fifty men, whose capital was labor, and whose dividends were to be the treasure found, cleared the well of all its rubbish, in search of the gold and silver. One of the company furnished the whisky which was drunk on the occasion, and agreed to wait for his pay until the treasure was secured. The men " kept their spirits up by pouring spirits down," and before the work was completed nearly three hogsheads of alcohol were swallowed by them. They cleared and drained the well to its rocky bottom, and all the metal which they found was iron in the form of nails, spikes, bolts, axes, shovels, &c. The whisky and the labor were lost to the owners, but they found the saying correct, that " truth lies at the bottom of a well," for they discovered, when at the bottom, the important truth, which doubtless taught them wisdom, that credulity is a faithless though smiling friend, and a capricious and hard master to serve. Money-digging still continues in the

THE WELL.

neighborhood, and several excavations within the fort were pointed out as the scene of quite recent labor in that line.

In 1844 a venerable, white-haired man, apparently between eighty and ninety years of age, leaning upon a staff, and accompanied by two athletic men, came to the fort and began to dig. They were observed by Mr. B., and ordered away. The old man was urgent for leave to dig, for he had come from the northern part of Vermont, was very poor, knew exactly where the treasure was, as he had assisted in concealing it, and asked but thirty minutes to finish his work. Mr. B. left them, and, returning an hour afterward, saw quite a deep hole, but no man was near. The diggers were gone, and the impression is that they really " found something !" There has been a great deal of money-digging upon Snake Mountain, on the eastern side of the lake, induced, to some extent, by the wonderful discovery of a crucible there. Among those rugged hills was doubtless the residence of " May Martin," the lovely heroine of the " Money-diggers."[1]

Crown Point remained in the quiet possession of the British from 1759 until 1775, when it was surprised and taken by a small body of provincials called " Green Mountain Boys," under Colonel Seth Warner.[2] I have already mentioned the fact that he attempted its capture on the same day that Delaplace surrendered Ticonderoga to Ethan Allen, but was thwarted and driven back by a storm. That was on the 10th of May. The attempt was renewed on the 12th, with success, and the garrison, consisting of only a sergeant and eleven men, were made prisoners without firing a shot.[3] Among the spoils were a hundred and fourteen cannons, of which only sixty-one were fit for service.

1775.

---

[1] See Thompson's pretty fiction, " *May Martin, or the Money-diggers.*"

[2] Seth Warner was born in Woodbury, Connecticut, about 1744. He moved to Bennington, Vermont, in 1773, and was noted for his skill in hunting. He and Ethan Allen were the leaders of the people of the New Hampshire Grants in their controversy with New York, and on the 9th of March, 1774, the Legislature of the latter province passed an act of outlawry against them. After the capture of Ticonderoga and Crown Point, he received a colonel's commission from the Continental Congress, and joined Montgomery in Canada. His regiment was discharged at St. John's, and, after the death of his general, he raised another body of troops and marched to Quebec. He covered the retreat of the Americans from Canada to Ticonderoga, was with the troops when they evacuated that post in 1777, and commanded the rear-guard that fought a severe battle at Hubbardton. He was one of General Starks's aids at the battle of Bennington, and then joined the army under Gates at Stillwater. His health soon afterward gave way, and he died at Woodbury in 1785, aged forty-one years. The state of Vermont gave his widow and children a valuable tract of land.—*Allen's American Biography.*

[3] On the day when Allen captured Ticonderoga, he sent a message to Captain Remember Baker, one of his colleagues in the violent boundary disputes between the New Yorkers and the people of the New Hampshire Grants, to join him at that post. Baker obeyed the summons, and when he was coming up

Arnold arrived at Ticonderoga the same evening, and on the 14th about fifty men, who had enlisted in compliance with his orders given by the way while hurrying on to Castleton to overtake Allen, arrived from Skenesborough, and brought with them the schooner which belonged to Major Skene. He manned this vessel instantly, armed it with some of the guns taken at the fort, and sailed down the lake to St. John's, on the Sorel. There he surprised and made prisoners the garrison, consisting of a sergeant and twelve men ; captured a king's sloop with seven men ; destroyed five bateaux ; seized four others ; put on board some of the valuable stores from the fort, and with his prisoners, and favored by a fair wind which had chopped around from south to north just as he had secured his prizes, he returned to Ticonderoga. Colonel Allen, with one hundred and fifty men in bateaux, started upon the same expedition, but Arnold's schooner outsailed the flat-boats, and Allen met him within fifteen miles of St. John's, returning with his prizes. Arnold was on board the king's sloop, where Allen visited him, and, after ascertaining the actual state of affairs, the latter determined to go on to St. John's and garrison the fort with about one hundred men. He landed just before night, marched about a mile toward Laprairie, and formed his men in ambush to attack an expected re-enforcement for the enemy. He soon learned that the approaching force was much larger than his own, and retired across the river, where he was attacked early in the morning by two hundred men. He fled to his boats and escaped to Ticonderoga, with a loss of three men taken prisoners. Thus within one week the strong fortresses of Ticonderoga and Crown Point, with all their dependencies upon the lake, were snatched from the British by the bold provincials, without their firing a gun or losing a man ; and their little fleet upon the lake, their only strength left, was captured and destroyed in a day.

These events aroused General Carleton, the governor of Canada, and a re-enforcement of more than four hundred British and Canadians was speedily sent to St. John's. It was determined to send small water craft from Chambly and Montreal, to be armed and manned at St. John's ; and other measures were planned for dispatching a sufficient force up the lake to recapture Ticonderoga and Crown Point. Tidings of these preparations soon reached the cars of Arnold, and afforded him an opportunity to sever his connection with Allen, so ill suited to his restless and ambitious spirit. A fleet to oppose the enemy was now necessary, and, having had some experience at sea in earlier life, Arnold assumed to be the commander of whatever navy should be fitted out. His assumption was not complained of, and he proceeded vigorously in arming and manning Skene's schooner, the king's corvette, and a small flotilla of bateaux. With these and about one hundred and fifty men, he took post at Crown Point to await the approach of the enemy. There he organized his little navy by the appointment of a captain and subordinate officers for each vessel. He mounted six carriage guns and twelve swivels in the sloop, and four carriage guns and eight swivels in the schooner. He was also active in sending off the ordnance from Crown Point to the army at Cambridge, and at the same time he sent emissaries to Montreal and the Caughnawagas to sound the intentions of the Canadians and Indians, and ascertain what was the actual force under Carleton and the nature of his preparations. He also wrote to the Continental Congress in June, 1775. proposing a plan of operations whereby, he confidently believed, the whole of Canada might be conquered by two thousand men. He asserted that persons in Montreal had agreed to open the gates when a strong Continental force should appear before the city ; assured Congress that Carleton had only five hundred and fifty effective men under him ; and offered to lead the expedition and to be responsible for consequences. His representations were doubtless true, but Congress was not prepared to sanction such an expedition. Allen, in a letter dated Crown Point, June 2d, 1775, made a similar proposition to the Provincial Congress of New York. In the mean while letters had been sent from Ticonderoga to the Provincial Congress of Massachusetts, complaining of Arnold's arrogant assumptions, and otherwise dis-

---

the lake with his party, he met two small boats with British soldiers, going to St. John's with the intelligence of the reduction of Ticonderoga, and to solicit a re-enforcement of the garrison at Crown Point. Baker seized the boats, and with his prisoners arrived at the fort just in time to join Warner in taking possesrion of it.—*Sparks's Life of Ethan Allen.*

paraging his deeds. A committee of inquiry was appointed, who proceeded to Lake Champlain. Arnold was at Crown Point, acting as commandant of the fort and commodore of the navy, and, not suspecting the nature of their visit, he was enthusiastic in his discourse to them of his expected victories. The first intimation of their errand aroused Arnold's indignation ; and when he fully understood the purport of their commission, he wrote them a formal letter of resignation, discharged his men, and returned to Cambridge, uttering loud complaints of ill usage by the Provincial Congress of Massachusetts. Thus ended the naval operations upon the lake in 1775.

When Ticonderoga and Crown Point were securely in the power of the provincials, Colonel Easton went to Massachusetts and Connecticut, and explained to the respective governments all the transactions connected with the reduction of these important posts. The Massachusetts Assembly wrote to Governor Trumbull, of Connecticut, expressing their willingness to allow that colony all the honor, and to withhold all interference in future operations in that quarter. Trumbull immediately prepared to send a re-enforcement for the garrisons, of four hundred men. Meanwhile messages were sent to the Continental Congress, and, through courtesy, to the Provincial Congress of New York, within whose jurisdiction the fortresses were situated, to ascertain their views. The Continental Congress approved the measures of Governor Trumbull, and requested the Convention of New York to supply the troops with provisions. The four hundred men were immediately sent, under Colonel Hinman, who superseded Colonel Allen in the command at Ticonderoga. The latter, with Warner, set off for the Continental Congress at Philadelphia, to procure pay for their soldiers, whose terms had expired, and to solicit authority to raise a new regiment in Vermont. The appearance of these men occasioned a great sensation in Philadelphia, and they were introduced upon the floor of Congress, to make their communications to that body orally. Congress at once acquiesced in their wishes, granted the soldiers the same pay as was received by those of the Continental army, and recommended to the New York Convention that, after consulting General Schuyler, they should " employ in the army to be raised in defense of America those called Green Mountain Boys, under such officers as the said Green Mountain Boys should choose." This resolution was dispatched to the New York Convention, and thither Allen and Warner repaired, and obtained an audience.[1] The Assembly resolved that a regiment of Green Mountain Boys, consisting of seven companies, and not exceeding five hundred men in number, should be raised. The matter was referred to General Schuyler, who immediately notified the people of the New Hampshire Grants, and ordered them to raise the regiment. Allen and Warner were not members of the regiment, but soon afterward they both joined General Schuyler at Ticonderoga, where he was stationed with about three thousand troops from New York and New England, preparatory to an invasion of Canada. Early in September Generals Schuyler and Montgomery sailed from Ticonderoga and Crown Point with their whole force, and appeared before St. John's, on the Sorel. Let us for a moment take a general view of affairs having a relation to the northern section of operations at this juncture and immediately antecedent thereto.

August,
1775.

---

[1] The Assembly of New York was embarrassed when Allen and Warner appeared at the door of its hall and asked for admission, and a warm debate ensued. During the then recent controversy of the Legislature of New York with the people of the New Hampshire Grants, these men had been proclaimed outlaws, and that attainder had never been wiped off by a repeal. There were members of that body who had taken a very active part, personally, in the controversy, and they were unwilling to give their old enemies a friendly greeting. Their prejudices, and the scruples of others who could not recognize the propriety of holding public conference with men whom the law of the land had declared to be rioters and felons, produced a strong opposition to their admission to the hall. The debates were becoming very warm, when Captain Sears (the noted " King Sears") moved that " Ethan Allen be admitted to the floor of the House." It was carried by a very large majority, as was also a similar resolution in regard to Warner. Allen afterward wrote a letter of thanks to the New York Assembly, in which, after referring to the formation of the battalion of Green Mountain Boys, he concluded by saying, " I will be responsible that they will reciprocate this favor by boldly hazarding their lives, if need be, in the common cause of America."

. The British ministry, alarmed at the rapid progress of the rebellion in America, and particularly at the disaffection to the royal government which was manifest in Canada, and observing that all their coercive measures in relation to Massachusetts had thus far augmented rather than diminished the number and zeal of the insurgents in that colony, determined, in 1774, to try a different policy with Canada, to secure the loyalty of the people. A large proportion of the inhabitants were of French descent, and members of the Romish communion. Those who composed the most influential class were of the old French aristocracy, and any concessions made in favor of their caste weighed more heavily with them than any that might be made to the whole people, involving the extension of the area of political freedom, an idea which was a mere abstraction to them. Religious concessions to the other and more ignorant class were a boon of great value, and by these means the king and his advisers determined to quiet the insurrectionary spirit in Canada. A bill was accordingly introduced into Parliament, " For making more effectual provision for the government of the province of Quebec, in North America." It provided for the establishment of a Legislative Council, invested with all powers except that of levying taxes. It was provided that its members should be appointed by the crown, and continue in authority during its pleasure ; that Canadian subjects professing the Catholic faith might be called to sit in the Council ; that the Catholic clergy, with the exception of the regular orders, should be secured in the enjoyment of their professions, and of their tithes from all those who professed their religion ; that the French laws without jury should be re-established, preserving, however, the English laws, with trial by jury, in criminal cases. The bill also provided that the limits of Canada should be extended so as to inclose the whole region between the lakes and the Ohio and Mississippi Rivers, regardless of the just claims of other colonies under old and unrepealed charters.[1] These liberal concessions to the Canadians would have been highly commendable, had not other motives than a spirit of liberality manifestly actuated ministers. The most obtuse observer could plainly perceive their object to be to secure a strong footing north and west of the refractory colonies, where troops might be concentrated and munitions of war collected, to be used at a moment's warning, if necessary, in crushing rebellion near. Such a design was at once charged upon ministers by the ever-vigilant Colonel Barré, on the floor of the British House of Commons. " A very extraordinary indulgence," he said, " is given to the inhabitants of this province, and one calculated to gain the hearts and affections of these people. To this I can not object, if it is to be applied to good purposes ; but if you are about to raise a popish army to serve in the colonies, from this time all hope of peace in America will be destroyed. The Americans will look on the Canadians as their task-masters, and, in the end, their executioners." It was urged by ministers that common justice demanded the adoption of such a measure, for a very large proportion of the people of Canada were Roman Catholics.[2] Edmund Burke, Thomas Townshend, Charles Fox, Sergeant Glynn, and others joined Colonel Barré in his denunciations of the bill, particularly in relation to the clauses concerning the Roman Catholic religion, and that providing for the establishment of a Legislative Council to be appointed by the crown. The former were considered a dangerous precedent for a Protestant government, and the latter was regarded as shadowing forth the ultimate design of the king and his ministers to subvert the popular form of government in America, and to make the legislators mere creatures of the crown. By its provisions the Governor of Canada was vested with almost absolute and illimitable power, and permitted to be nearly as much a despot, if he chose, as any of the old Spanish viceroys of

[1] Thomas and John Penn, son and grandson of William Penn, then the proprietaries of Pennsylvania and Delaware, entered a protest against the boundary section of this bill, because it contemplated an encroachment upon their territory. Burke, who was then the agent of the colony of New York, also opposed this section of the bill for the same reason, in behalf of his principal. The letter of that statesman to the Assembly of New York on the subject is published among the Collections of the New York Historical Society, and is said to be the only one known to be extant of all those which he wrote to that body

[2] Governor Carleton asserted, on oath, before a committee of Parliament, that there were then only about three hundred and sixty Protestants in Canada, while the Roman Catholics numbered one hundred and fifty thousand.

South America.   On this point Lord Chatham (William Pitt) was particularly eloquent, and he also took ground against the religious features of the bill, as an innovation dangerous to the Protestant faith and to the stability of the throne.   The bill, however, with all its exceptionable clauses, was adopted by quite a large majority in both Houses, and received the royal assent on the 22d of June.   It was introduced into the House of Lords by the Earl of Dartmouth, and passed that House without opposition.   This bill is refer- 1774. red to in our Declaration of Independence as one of the " acts of pretended legislation" that justified the separation from the parent country.

While this act, with the Boston Port Bill, that for the subversion of the charter of Massachusetts, and the law authorizing the transportation of criminals to Great Britain for trial, were in transit through Parliament and receiving the royal signature, the colonists were preparing to make a successful resistance against further legislative encroachments.   Throughout the whole summer and autumn of 1774 the greatest excitement prevailed.   The committees of correspondence were every where active and firm, and were constantly supplied with minute knowledge of all the movements of the home government by secret agents in the British metropolis.   The people by thousands signed non-importation agreements, and otherwise attested their willingness to make personal sacrifices in the cause of freedom.   The press spoke out boldly, and orators no longer harangued in parables, but fearlessly called upon the people to UNITE.   The events of the French and Indian war had demonstrated the prowess and strength of the Anglo-Americans against the foes of Britain, and they felt confident in that strength against Britain herself, now that she had become the oppressor of her children, if a bond of union could be made that should cause all the colonies to act in concert.   A general Congress, similar to that which convened in New York in 1765, was therefore suggested.   Throughout the colonies the thought was hailed as a happy one, and soon was developed the most energetic action.   The Congress met in September, adopt- 1774 ed loyal addresses to the king and Parliament, to the people of the colonies, of Canada, of Ireland, and of Great Britain, and took precautionary measures respecting future aggressions upon their rights.   The people, highly indignant, every where evinced the strength of that feeling by open contempt for all royal authority exercised by officers of the crown.   The acts alluded to were denounced as " barbarous and bloody," the British ministry were published in the gazettes, and placarded upon the walls as *papists* and as *traitors to the Constitution*, and the patriots even had the boldness to lampoon the king and Parliament.   (For an illustration, see next page.)

Such was the temper of the Americans at the opening of the year 1775.   The events at Lexington and Concord added fuel to the flame of indignation and rebellion.   As we have seen, Ticonderoga and other posts on Lake Champlain were assailed, and fell into the hands of the Americans.   In June the battle of Bunker Hill was fought.   A Continental June 17, army was speedily organized.   Hope of reconciliation departed.   The sword was 1775. fairly drawn, and at the close of summer an expedition was arranged to invade Canada, for which an armament was collected at Ticonderoga.   Such a step seemed essential for two reasons : first, to confirm the Canada patriots (who were chiefly in the neighborhood of Montreal) in their opposition to Great Britain by the pressure of armed supporters ; and, secondly, to secure the strong-hold of Quebec while its garrison was yet weak, and before General Carleton could organize a sufficient force to defend it.   That officer, it was well known, was vested with almost unlimited power as governor of the province, under the act which we have just considered ; and it was also well known that he was using every means at his command to induce the Canadians to take up arms against the rebellious colonists.   Neither bribes nor promises were spared.   The imperial government resolved to send out fifteen thousand muskets to arm the French Catholics, and agents of the crown were busy among the Indian tribes upon the St. Lawrence and the Ottawa, inciting them to an alliance with the army of the king.

Congress had already sent an affectionate address " To the oppressed inhabitants May 29. of Canada," and its effects were so palpable to Governor Carleton, that he feared 1775.

158   PICTORIAL FIELD-BOOK

| The British Government caricatured. | Carleton's attempt to seduce the Bishop of Quebec. | Consistency of the Prelate |

entire disaffection to the royal government would ensue. The people were disappointed in the operations of the act of 1774, and all but the nobles regarded it as tyrannical. Unable

VIRTUAL REPRESENTATION, 1775.[1]

April 1, 1775.   Price, 6d.

1. One String Jack, Deliver your property.
2. Begar, just so in France. } Accomplices.
3. Te Deum.
4. I give you that man's money for my use.
5. I will not be robbed.
6. I shall be wounded with you.
7. I am blinded.
8. The French Roman Catholic town of Quebec.
9. The English Protestant town of Boston.

to make an impression favorable to the king upon the Canadians by an appeal to their loyalty, Carleton had recourse to the authority of religion. He endeavored to seduce Brand, the Roman Catholic bishop of Quebec, from his exalted duties as a Christian pastor, to engage in the low political schemes of a party placeman, and publish a *mandement*, to be read from the pulpit by the curates in time of divine service. He also urged the prelate to exhort the people to take up arms against the colonists. But the consistent bishop refused to exert his influence in such a cause, and plainly told Carleton that such conduct would be unworthy of a faithful pastor, and derogatory to the canons of the Romish Church. A few priests, however, with the nobility, seconded Carleton's views, but their influence was feeble with the mass of the people, who were determined to remain neutral. The governor now tried another scheme, and with better effect. He could make no impression upon the masses by appeals to their loyalty or their religious prejudices, and he determined to arouse them by

---

[1] The above engraving is an exact copy, reduced, of a caricature which I found in the possession of the Massachusetts Historical Society at Boston, entitled "*Virtual Representation.*" On the back of it, apparently in the hand-writing of the time, is the following :

"A full explanation of the within print.—No. 1 intends the K—g of G. B., to whom the House of Commons (4) gives the Americans' money for the use of that very H. of C., and which he is endeavoring to take away with the power of cannon. No. 2, by a Frenchman, signifies the tyranny that is intended for America. No. 3, the figure of a Roman Catholic priest with his crucifix and gibbet, assisting George in enforcing his tyrannical system of civil and religious government. Nos. 5 and 6 are honest American yeomen, who oppose an oaken staff to G—'s cannon, and determine they will not be robbed. No. 7 is poor Britannia blindfolded, falling into the bottomless pit which her infamous rulers have prepared for the Americans. Nos. 8, 9 represent Boston in flames and Quebec triumphant, to show the probable consequence of submission to the present wicked ministerial system, that popery and tyranny will triumph over true religion, virtue, and liberty.

"N.B. Perhaps this may remind the Bostonians of the invincible attachment of the Numantines* to their liberty," &c.

* The Numantines inhabited a city on the banks of the Douro, in Spain. Twenty years they were besieged by the Romans, until at length the younger Scipio Africanus entered their city (one hundred and thirty-three years B.C., and twelve years after the destruction of Carthage). The Numantines, seeing all hope gone, set fire to their city and perished in the flames rather than become slaves to their oppressors.

OF THE REVOLUTION. 159

Royal Highland Regiment, how raised.   Our Departure from Crown Point.   Split Rock.   War-feast on the Bouquet River.

appealing to their cupidity. Accordingly, he caused the drums to beat up for volunteers in Quebec, and by offers of good pay, privileges, and bounties, he succeeded in enrolling a few, under the title of the *Royal Highland Regiment*.[1] About the same time Colonel July, 1775. Guy Johnson arrived at Montreal with a large number of Indian chiefs and warriors of the Six Nations, who, despite their solemn promises of neutrality, were induced to join the soldiers of the king. They made oath of allegiance to the crown in the presence of Carleton, and were held in readiness to serve him when he should call.

A small number of regular British troops, with the volunteers and Indians, composed the bulk of Carleton's army at the close of the summer of 1775, the time when General Schuyler was preparing, at Ticonderoga and Crown Point, for a campaign against Canada. We thus come back from our historic ramble to our starting-place at Crown Point. The ruins are sufficiently explored; let us pass over to Chimney Point and dine, for the steamer will soon come down the lake to convey us to our Sabbath resting-place at Burlington.

We left Chimney Point in the evening, a cool, gentle breeze blowing from the northwest. The western shore is bold, and in many places precipitous, and in the distance the blue peaks and lofty ridges of the Adirondack Mountains skirt the horizon. The eastern margin is the termination of the pleasant slopes and beautiful intervales between the Green Mountains and the lake, cultivated and wooded alternately to the water's verge. At dusk we reached the

SPLIT ROCK.

famous *Split Rock*. The moon was shining brightly in the west, where faint tints of daylight still lingered, and we passed so near that we had a fine view of that geological wonder. It is on the west side of the lake, about thirty miles below Crown Point. Here is a sharp promontory jutting into the lake, the point of which, containing about half an acre, and covered with bushes, is separated from the main land by a cleft fifteen feet wide. It was observed as a curiosity by the old French explorers. Soundings to the depth of five hundred feet have been made between the fragment and the main rock, without finding a bottom. Geologists differ in opinion respecting the cause which formed the chasm, some ascribing it to an earthquake, and others to the slow attrition of the current upon a portion of the rock of softer texture than the rest. A light-house stands near as a guide to the navigator, for the lake is only a mile wide at this point. Here it suddenly expands, and at the mouth of the Bouquet River, eight miles above, it is about five miles wide.

At the falls in the Bouquet, two miles from the lake, is the village of Willsborough, the place where Burgoyne encamped and gave a war-feast to about four hundred Indians of the tribes of the Algonquins, Iroquois, and Ottawas, who, accompanied by a Roman Catholic priest, joined him there. Both he and Carleton were averse to the measure of em- June 21, 1777. ploying the savages in the British army, but the express instructions of ministers demanded it, and he dared not disobey.[2] He made a speech to them, in which he humanely endeavored to soften their savage ferocity and restrain their thirst for rapine and blood. His exordium was words of flattery in praise of their sagacity, faithfulness, forbearance, and loyalty. He then spoke of the abused clemency of the king toward the colonies, and declared to the warriors their relief from restraint. " Go forth," he said, " in the might of your valor

---

[1] Their time of service was limited to the continuance of the disturbances; each soldier was to receive two hundred acres of land in any province in North America he might choose; the king paid himself the accustomed duties upon the acquisition of lands; for twenty years new proprietors were to be exempted from all contribution for the benefit of the crown; every married soldier obtained other fifty acres, in consideration of his wife, and fifty more for account of each of his children, with the same privilege and exemptions, besides the bounty of a guinea at the time of enlistment.—Botta, vol. i., p. 220.

[2] The employment of Indians by the British ministry, in this campaign, has been excused upon the lame plea, which has not the shadow of truth, that, unless they were thus employed, the Americans would have mustered them into their service.—See Knight's *Pictorial England*, vol. v., p. 306.

and your cause.   Strike at the common enemies of Great Britain and of America ; disturb-
ers of public order, peace, and happi-
ness ; destroyers of commerce ; parricides of the state."   He told them
that his officers and men would endeavor to imitate their example in
perseverance, enterprise, and constancy, and in resistance of hunger,
weariness, and pain.   At the same
time he exhorted them to listen to
his words, and allow him to regulate
their passions, and to conform their
warfare to his, by the rules of European discipline and the dictates of
his religion and humanity.   He reminded them that the king had many
faithful subjects in the provinces,
and, therefore, indiscriminate butch-
ery of the people might cause the
sacrifice of many friends.   He then
charged them, in the words quoted
from his speech in the note on ante,
page 99, not to kill for scalps, or destroy life except in open warfare, and
claimed for himself the office of um-
pire on all occasions.   When he had finished, an old Iroquois chief arose and said :

BURGOYNE ADDRESSING THE INDIANS.

" I stand up in the name of all the nations present, to assure our father that we have at-
tentively listened to his discourse.   We receive you as our father, because when you speak
we hear the voice of our great father beyond the great lake.   We rejoice in the approbation
you have expressed of our behavior.   We have been tried and tempted by the Bostonians,[1]
but we loved our father, and our hatchets have been sharpened upon our affections.   In
proof of the sincerity of our professions, our whole villages able to go to war are come forth.
The old and infirm, our infants and wives, alone remain at home.   With one common assent we promise a constant obedience to all you have ordered and all you shall order ; and
may the Father of Days give you many and success."[2]

These promises were all very fine, and Burgoyne, to his sorrow, had the credulity to rely
upon them.   At first the Indians were docile, but as soon as the scent of blood touched their
nostrils their ferocious natures were aroused, and the restraints imposed by the British commander were too irksome to be borne.   Their faithfulness disappeared ; and in the hour of
his greatest need they deserted him, as we have seen, by hundreds, and returned home.

As the lake widened and the evening advanced, the breeze freshened almost to a gale,
and, blowing upon our larboard quarter, it rolled up such swells on our track that the vessel
rocked half the passengers into silent contemplation of the probability of casting their supper
to the fishes.   The beacon upon Juniper Island was hailed with delight, for the Burlington
break-water was just ahead.   We entered the harbor between nine and ten in the evening,

---

[1] The old chief spoke truly.   They had been " tempted by the Bostonians," but not by the Boston patriots.   General Gage, then governor of Massachusetts, and other loyalists in Boston, sent emissaries among
the Indians in various ways, and these were the tempters which the old chief confounded with the enemies
of the crown.   I shall have occasion hereafter to speak of Connelly, one of Gage's emissaries, who went
to Virginia, and, under the auspices of Lord Dunmore, carried promises and money to the Indians on the
frontier, to instigate them to fall upon the defenseless republicans of that stanch Whig state.
[2] So interpreted by Burgoyne in his " State of the Expedition," &c.

and were soon in comfortable quarters at the American, fronting the pleasant square in the center of the village.

The next morning dawned calm and beautiful. The wind was hushed, and the loveliness of repose was upon the village, lake, and country. It was our second Sabbath from home, and never was its rest more welcome and suggestive of gratitude, for the preceding week had been to me one of unceasing toil, yet a toil commingled with the most exalted pleasure. I had been among scenes associated with the noblest sentiments of an American's heart ; and when, mingling with the worshipers in St. Paul's Church, the clear voice of Bishop Hopkins repeated the divine annunciation, " From the rising of the sun unto the going down of the same, my name shall be great among the heathen, saith the Lord," I felt that our own country, so late a wilderness and abiding-place for pagans, but now blooming under the beneficent culture of free institutions that were born amid the labor-throes of the Revolution, was a special illustration of that glorious declaration.

Early on Monday morning we procured saddle horses and rode out to the resting-place of General Ethan Allen, a burial-ground embowered in shrubbery, lying upon the brow of the hill overlooking the Winooski, and within sound of its cascades. It is on the south side of the road leading east from Burlington, nearly half a mile from the University of Vermont, that stands upon the summit of the hill, upon the western slope of which is the village. Allen's monument is a plain marble slab, resting upon a granite foundation, and bears the following inscription :

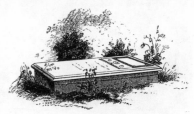

TOMB OF ETHAN ALLEN.

THE

CORPOREAL PART

OF

GENERAL ETHAN ALLEN

RESTS BENEATH THIS STONE,

THE 12TH DAY OF FEB., 1789,

AGED 50 YEARS.

HIS SPIRIT TRIED THE MERCIES OF HIS GOD,

IN WHOM ALONE HE BELIEVED AND STRONGLY TRUSTED.

Near his are the graves of his brother Ira[1] and several other relatives. The whole are inclosed within a square defined by a chain supported by small granite obelisks. A willow drooped over the tombs of the patriot dead, and rose-bushes clustered around the storm-worn monuments. The dew was yet upon the grass, and its fragrant exhalations filled the air with such grateful incense, that we were loth to leave the spot. We galloped our horses back to the village in time for breakfast, delighted and profited by our morning's ride. Halt-

---

[1] Ira Allen was born in Salisbury, Connecticut, in 1752. He went to Vermont in early life, and became one of the most active citizens of that state, particularly in the controversy between Vermont and New York respecting the territory called the New Hampshire Grants. It is said that when the Revolution broke out he sided with the crown and went to Canada. His stanch Whig brother, Ethan, indignant at his choice, recommended the Vermont Assembly to confiscate his brother's property. Ira heard of it, and challenged Ethan to fight a duel. Ethan refused, on the ground that it would be " disgraceful to fight a Tory," and so the matter ended. Ira finally became a warm republican, and was active during the remainder of the war. He was a member of the Convention which formed the Constitution of Vermont, and became the first secretary of the state. He was afterward treasurer, member of the council, and surveyor general. He rose to the rank of major general of militia, and in 1795 he went to Europe to purchase arms for the supply of his state. Returning with several thousand muskets and some cannon, he was captured by an English vessel and carried to England, where he was accused of supplying the Irish rebels with arms. A litigation for eight years, in the Court of Admiralty, was the consequence, but a final decision was in his favor He died at Philadelphia, January 7th, 1814, aged 62 years.

ing near the university a few minutes, we enjoyed the beautiful view which the height commands. The Green Mountains stretched along the east; the broken ranges of the Adirondack, empurpled by the morning sun, bounded the western horizon; and below us, skirting the lake, the pleasant village lay upon the slope, and stretched its lengthening form out toward the rich fields that surrounded it. To the eye of a wearied dweller in a dense city all villages appear beautiful in summer, but Burlington is eminently so when compared with others.

We left the metropolis of the lake for Plattsburgh about noon. On our left, as we emerged from the harbor, were the Four Brothers, small islands swarming with water-fowl, and the bald point of Rock Dunder, a solitary spike rising, shrubless and bare, about twenty feet above the water. Before us spread out the two Heros (North and South), green islands, which belonged to the Allen family during the Revolution. The first landing-place below Burlington is Port Kent, on the west side of the lake, ten miles distant. A little below is Port Jackson, nearly west of the south end of Valcour's Island. This is an interesting por-

SCENE OF ARNOLD'S NAVAL BATTLE.[1]

tion of the lake to the American tourist, for it is the place where our first naval battle with Great Britain was fought. This event took place October the 11th, 1776. The American flotilla was commanded by Benedict Arnold, and the English vessels by Captain Pringle, accompanied by Governor Carleton. In order to a lucid understanding of the position of affairs at that time, we must consider for a moment the connecting chain of events from the autumn of 1775, when General Schuyler was at Ticonderoga and Crown Point preparing to invade Canada, to the meeting of the belligerents in question.

The forces under Generals Schuyler and Montgomery proceeded to execute the will of September 10, Congress, and in September appeared before St. John's, at the Sorel. Finding 1775. the fort, as they supposed, too strong for assault, they returned to and fortified *Isle Aux Noix.* Schuyler went back to Ticonderoga and hastened forward re-enforcements, but was unable to return on account of sickness. Montgomery succeeded him in command. He captured Fort St. John's and Fort Chambly, and entered Montreal in triumph. He then pushed on to Quebec, when he was joined by a force under Arnold, and early in December laid siege to that city. After besieging it unsuccessfully for three weeks, the Amer-December 31, icans commenced an assault. Montgomery was killed, the Americans were re-1775. pulsed, and many of them made prisoners. Arnold was wounded. He became the chief in command, and kept the remnant of the republican army together in the vicinity 1776. of Quebec, until the arrival of General Wooster early in the spring and General Thomas in May. General Carleton soon afterward received re-enforcements from England, and by the middle of June the Americans, after retreating from post to post, were driven out of Canada.

Not doubting that Carleton would follow up his successes by providing water craft upon the lake, to attempt the capture of Ticonderoga and Crown Point, a council of officers, under General Gates, who in June was appointed to the command of the Northern army, resolved to abandon the latter post and concentrate all their forces at the former. Accord-

---

[1] This sketch was made from the pilot's room of the steam-boat just after leaving Port Jackson. On the left is a point of the main land, and on the right is seen a portion of Valcour's Island. The high ground in the extreme distance, on the left, is Cumberland Head, and that dimly seen in the center of the picture is the Vermont shore.

ingly, General Sullivan, who was at Crown Point, withdrew with his forces to Ticonderoga, and active measures for offensive and defensive operations were there adopted.   Materials for constructing vessels, as well as skillful artisans, were scarce.   The latter had to be obtained from the sea-ports ; yet such was the zeal of the Americans, that by the middle of August a small squadron, consisting of one sloop, three schooners, and five gondolas, was in readiness and rendezvoused at Crown Point under Arnold, who received the command of it from General Gates.   The sloop carried twelve guns, one schooner the same number, the others eight, and the gondolas three each.   Toward the close of the month Arnold sailed down the lake, under positive instructions from Gates not to pass beyond *Isle Aux Têtes*, near what is now called Rouse's Point, and to act only on the defensive.   He halted at Wind-mill Point, four miles above *Isle Aux Têtes*, to reconnoiter, and anchored his vessels across the lake, to prevent any boats of the enemy from passing up.

As soon as Carleton was advised of the movements of the Americans at Ticonderoga, he sent seven hundred men from Quebec to St. John's, to construct a fleet, and in the course of a few weeks several strong vessels were finished and armed for duty.   A radeau called the *Thunderer* (a kind of flat-bottomed vessel carrying heavy guns), and twenty-four gunboats, armed each with a field piece or carriage gun, were added to the fleet.   Forty boats with provisions accompanied the expedition.

Convinced that his position was dangerous, for the British and Indians were collecting on the shores, Arnold fell back about ten miles to *Isle La Motte*, where he need not fear an attack from the main land.   Here his fleet was considerably increased, and consisted of three schooners, two sloops, three galleys, eight gondolas, and twenty-one gun-boats.   Ignorant of the real strength of the armament which he knew Carleton was preparing at St. John's, and unwilling to engage a superior force on the broad lake, Arnold withdrew his fleet still further back, and anchored it across the narrow channel between Valcour's Island and the western shore.

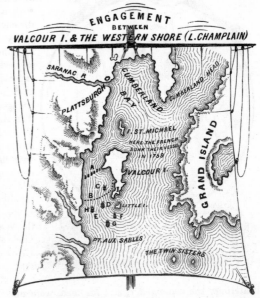

1776.   Early on the morning of the 11th of October the British fleet appeared off Cumberland Head, moving up the lake, and in a short time it swept around the southern point of Valcour's Island.   The enemy's force was formidable, for the vessels were manned by seven hundred chosen seamen.   Captain Pringle was commodore, and made the *Inflexible* his flagship.   Among the young officers in the fleet was Edward Pellew, afterward Admiral Viscount Exmouth, one of the most distinguished of England's naval commanders.   The action began about twelve o'clock, by the attack of the Carleton upon the American schooner *Royal Savage* and three galleys.   The latter, in attempting to return to the line, grounded,

EXPLANATION OF THE MAP.—A, American fleet under Arnold ; B, 21 gun-boats; C, schooner Carleton, 12 six pounders ; D, ship Inflexible, 18 twelve pounders ; E, anchorage of the British fleet during the night, to cut off the Americans' retreat; F, radeau Thunderer, 6 twenty-four pounders and 12 six pounders; G, gondola *Loyal Convert*, 7 nine pounders ; H, schooner *Maria*, 14 six pounders, with General Carleton on board ; I, the place where the American schooner *Royal Savage*, of 8 six pounders and 4 four pounders, was burned.   This plan is copied from *Brasrier's Survey of Lake Champlain*, edition of 1779.

164　　　　　　　PICTORIAL FIELD-BOOK

Severe Battle on the Lake.　　Escape of the Americans through the British Line.　　Chase by the Enemy.　　Another Battle

and was burned, but her men were saved. Arnold was on board the *Congress* galley, and conducted matters with a great deal of bravery and skill. About one o'clock the engagement became general, and the American vessels, particularly the *Congress*, suffered severely. It was hulled twelve times, received seven shots between wind and water, the main-mast was shattered in two places, the rigging cut to pieces, and many of the crew were killed or wounded. Arnold pointed almost every gun on his vessel with his own hands,[1] and with voice and gesture cheered on his men. In the mean while the enemy landed a large body of Indians upon the island, who kept up an incessant fire of musketry, but with little effect. The battle continued between four and five hours, and the Americans lost, in killed and wounded, about sixty men.

Night closed upon the scene, and neither party were victors. The two fleets anchored within a few hundred yards of each other. Arnold held a council with his officers, and it was determined to retire during the night to Crown Point, for the superiority of the vessels, and the number and discipline of the men composing the British force, rendered another engagement extremely hazardous. Anticipating such a movement on the part of the Americans, the British commander anchored his vessels in a line extending across from the island

ACTION of the 13TH of OCT.
A. *Place of action.*
B. *Congress Galley and 5 Gondolas.*
C. *Bulwaggy Bay.*

to the main land. A chilly north wind had been blowing all the afternoon, and about sunset dark clouds overcast the sky. It was at the time of new moon, and, therefore, the night was very dark, and favored the design of Arnold. About ten o'clock he weighed anchor, and with the stiff north wind sailed with his whole flotilla, unobserved, through the enemy's lines. Arnold, with his crippled galley, brought up the rear. It was a bold movement. At daybreak the English watch on deck looked with straining eyes for their expected prey, but the Americans were then at Schuyler's Island, ten miles south, busily engaged in stopping leaks and repairing sails. The British weighed anchor and gave chase. Toward evening the wind changed to the south, and greatly retarded the progress of both fleets during the night. Early on the morning of the 13th the enemy's vessels were observed under full sail, and rapidly gaining upon the Americans. The *Congress* galley (Arnold's "flag-ship") and the Washington, with four gondolas, were behind, and in a short time the British vessels *Carleton*, *Inflexible*, and *Maria* were alongside, pouring a destructive fire upon them. The Washington soon struck, and General Waterbury the commander, and his men, were made prisoners.[2] The whole force of the

October, 1776.

---

[1] Sparks's Life of Arnold.

[2] Among the prisoners was Joseph Bettys, afterward the notorious outlaw and bitter Tory, better known as "Joe Bettys." He was a native of Saratoga county, and joined the Whigs on the breaking out of the Revolution. While a captive in Canada, after the battle on Lake Champlain, he was induced to join the royal standard, and was made an ensign. He became notorious as a spy, and, having been caught by the Americans, he was at one time conducted to the gallows. At the instance of his aged parents, Washington granted him a reprieve on condition of his thoroughly reforming. But he immediately joined the enemy again, and for a long time his cold-blooded murders, his plunder and incendiarism made him the terror of

attack now fell upon the *Congress*, but Arnold maintained his ground with unflinching resolution for four hours.   The galley was at length reduced almost to a wreck, and surrounded by seven sail of the enemy.   Longer resistance was vain, and the intrepid Arnold ran the galley and four gondolas into a small creek on the east side of the lake, about ten miles below Crown Point, and not far from Panton.   He ordered the marines to set fire to them as soon as they were grounded, leap into the water and wade ashore with their muskets, and form in such a manner upon the beach as to guard the burning vessels from the approach of the enemy.   Arnold remained in his galley till driven off by the fire, and was the last man that reached the shore.   He kept the flags flying, and remained upon the spot until his little flotilla was consumed, and then, with the small remnant of his brave soldiers, marched off through the woods toward Chimney Point, and reached Crown Point in safety. The rapidity of his march saved him from an Indian ambush that waylaid his path an hour after he passed by.   Two schooners, two galleys, one sloop, and one gondola, the remnant of his fleet, were at Crown Point, and General Waterbury and most of his men arrived there on parole the next day, when all embarked and sailed to Ticonderoga.   General October 14, Carleton took possession of Crown Point, and for a few days threatened Ticon-   1776. deroga, but the season was so far advanced that he prudently withdrew. and sailed down the lake to go into winter-quarters in Canada.[1]   The whole American loss in the two actions was between eighty and ninety, and that of the enemy about forty.

Although the republicans were defeated, and the expedition was disastrous in every particular, yet such were the skill, bravery, and obstinate resistance of Arnold and his men against a vastly superior force, the event was hailed as ominous of great achievements on the part of the patriots when such fearful odds should not exist.   Arnold's popularity, so justly gained at Quebec, was greatly increased, and the country rang with his praises. Sparks justly observes, respecting Arnold's conduct in the engagement on the 13th, that " there are few instances on record of more deliberate courage and gallantry than were displayed by him from the beginning to the end of this action."

We arrived at Plattsburgh at about two o'clock in the afternoon.   The day was excessively warm, and I felt more like lounging than rambling.   In fact, the spot has no Revolutionary history worth mentioning, for its existence as a lonely settlement in the wilderness is only coeval with that of our independence.   Count Vredenburgh, a German nobleman, who married a lady of the household of the queen of George II. of England, obtained a grant for thirty thousand acres of land on Cumberland Bay, and just before the Revolution he settled there.   When the war broke out he sent his family to Montreal, and soon afterward his splendid mansion, which stood where the Plattsburgh Hotel now is, and his mills, three miles distant, were burned.   He had remained to look after his property, and it is supposed that he was murdered for his riches, and his house plundered and destroyed.   In 1783 some Canadian and Nova Scotia refugees, under Lieutenant (afterward Major-general) Mooers,[2] who were stationed on the Hudson near Newburgh, left Fishkill Landing in a boat, and, proceeding by the way of Lakes George and Champlain, landed and commenced the first permanent settlement in that neighborhood, within seven or eight miles of the present village of Plattsburgh.   Judge Zephaniah Platt and others formed a company, after the war, to purchase military land-warrants, and they located their lands on Cumberland Bay, and organized the town of Plattsburgh in 1785.   Such is its only connection with the history

the whole region in the neighborhood of Albany.   At last he was captured (1782), and was executed as a spy and traitor, at Albany.

[1] It is related that while Carleton was at Ticonderoga, Arnold ventured in the neighborhood in a small boat.   He was seen and chased by young Pellew (afterward Lord Exmouth), and so rapidly did his pursuers gain upon him, that he ran his boat ashore and leaped on land, leaving his stock and buckle behind him. It is said that the stock and buckle are still in possession of the Pellew family.—See *Ostler's Life of Admiral Viscount Exmouth.*

[2] Benjamin Mooers served as a lieutenant and adjutant in the Revolution.   He commanded the militia in the battle of Plattsburgh in 1814.   For thirty years he was county treasurer, and often represented his county in the Assembly and Senate of New York.   He died in February, 1838

of our Revolution.   It is a conspicuous point, however, in the history of our war with Great Britain commenced in 1812, for it is memorable as the place where one of the severest engagements of that contest took place, on the 11th of September, 1814, between the combined naval and military forces of the Americans and British.   General Macomb commanded the land, and Commodore M'Donough the naval forces of the former, and General Prevost and Commodore Downie[1] those of the latter.   The engagements on the land and water were simultaneous, and for some time the issue was doubtful.   The Americans, however, were successful.   When the flag of the British commodore's ship was struck, the enemy on land, disheartened and confused, retreated across the Saranac, and the carnage ceased.   The loss of the Americans was about one hundred and fifty; that of the enemy, in killed, wounded, prisoners, and deserters, more than one thousand.

I passed a considerable portion of the afternoon with General St. John B. L. Skinner, who was a volunteer under Macomb in the battle.   He was a member of a company of young men and boys of the village, who, after the military had gone out on the Chazy road, organized and offered their services to the commander-in-chief.   They were accepted, and the brave youths were immediately armed with rifles and ordered to the headquarters of General Mooers.   Only three of the company were over eighteen years old, and not one of them was killed, though for a long time they were exposed to a hot fire while occupying a mill upon the Saranac and keeping the enemy at bay.   General Skinner's beautiful man sion and gardens are upon the lake shore, and from an upper piazza we had a fine view of the whole scene of the naval engagement, from Cumberland Head on the north to Valcour's Island on the south, including in the far distance eastward the blue lines of the northern range of the Green Mountains.   The bay in which the battle occurred is magnificent, fringed with deep forests and waving grain-fields.   A substantial stone break-water defends the harbor from the rude waves which an easterly wind rolls in, and the village is very pleasantly situated upon a gravelly plain on each side of the Saranac River.

A short distance from the village of Plattsburgh are the remains of the cantonments and breast-works occupied by Macomb and his forces; and to the kind courtesy of General Skinner, who accompanied me to these relics of the war, I am indebted for many interesting details in relation to that memorable battle.[2]   But as these have no necessary connection with our subject, on account of their remoteness from the time of the Revolution, I will bid adieu to Plattsburgh, for the evening is far gone, the lights of the "Burlington" are sparkling upon the waters near Valcour's Island, and the coachman at the hotel front is hurrying us with his loud "All aboard!"

It was nearly midnight when we passed the light on Cumberland Head,[3] and we reached

---

[1] Commodore Downie was slain in the battle and buried at Plattsburgh.   His sister-in-law, Mary Downie, erected a plain monument to his memory over his remains.

[2] General S. mentioned one or two circumstances connected with the naval engagement worth recording. He says that, when the fleet of the enemy rounded Cumberland Head, M'Donough assembled his men on board his ship (Saratoga) on the quarter-deck.   He then knelt, and, in humble, fervent supplication, commended himself, his men, and his cause to the Lord of Hosts.   When he arose, the serenity of faith was upon his countenance, and seemed to shed its influence over his men.   A curious incident occurred on his ship during the engagement.   The hen-coop was shot away, and a cock, released from prison, flew into the rigging, and, flapping his wings, crowed out a lusty defiance to the enemy's guns. There he remained, flapping his wings and crowing, until the engagement ceased.   The seamen regarded the event as encouraging, and fought like tigers while the cock cheered them on.   A notice of a relic of Washington, in the possession of General S., may not be inappropriate here. It is a pouch and puff-ball, for hair-powder, which belonged to the chief several years.   It is made of buckskin, and is about twelve inches long.   The puff is made of cotton yarn.   Mr. Gray, who was a number of years sheriff of Clinton county, readily recognized it as the one used by himself in powdering Washington's hair, when he was a boy and attached to the general in the capacity of body servant.   When La Fayette was at Burlington, in 1824, Mr. Gray went up to see him, and the veteran remembered him as the "boy Gray" in Washington's military family.

[3] On this point is situated the farm presented to Commodore M'Donough by the Legislature of Vermont. The point is connected with Grand Island, or North Hero (the largest island in the lake), by a ferry.

OF THE REVOLUTION. 167

Rouse's Point and Military Works. | The Territorial Line. | Isle Aux Noix. | Historical Associations.

Rouse's Point, the last landing-place on the lake within " the States," between one and two in the morning, where we remained until daylight, for the channel here, down the outlet of the lake, is so narrow and sinuous that the navigation is difficult in the night. On a low point a little northward of the landing the United States government commenced building a fort in 1815, and, after expending about two hundred thousand dollars, it was discovered that the ground was British soil. The work was abandoned, and so remained until the conclusion of the treaty formed by Daniel Webster and Lord Ashburton in 1842, when the territorial line was run a little north of the fort. It is now in course of completion.

The morning on which we left Rouse's Point was clear and calm. A slight mist lay upon the water, and over the flat shores of the Richelieu or Sorel River, which we had entered, a thin vapor, like a gauze veil, was spread out. We watched with interest for the line of separation between the territories. It was about four o'clock in the morning when we crossed it, twenty-three miles south of St. John's, and so became "foreigners." A broad stripe like a meadow-swathe, running east and west, cut in the dwarf forest upon either side, denotes the landmark of dominion, and by a single revolution of the paddle-wheel we passed from the waters of our republic to those of the British realm. In less than an hour we were at the landing-place on *Isle Aux Noix*, a small low island in the Sorel, strongly fortified by the British as one of their most important outposts in the direction of the United States. This island is all clustered with historic associations. While the fussy custom-house officer and his attendants are boarding our boat, let us look into the mirror of retrospection.

When the French settlement at Chimney Point was broken up on the approach of Gen-

ISLE AUX NOIX, IN THE SOREL.[1]

eral Amherst, in 1759, the people fled down the lake, and, landing upon this island, fortified it. The walnut and hazel abounded there, and they gave it a name significant of this fact. Commanding, as it does, completely the outlet of Lake Champlain, the importance of its position, in a military view, was at once appreciated. But the French held possession only a few months, for in the spring of 1760 they were driven from it by Amherst in his march toward Montreal. After the treaty of Paris in 1763, the necessity for a garrison upon *Isle Aux Noix* no longer existed, and the fortifications were allowed to crumble into ruins.

In the autumn of 1775 the island was occupied by the Americans, under General Schuyler. With a considerable force, destined to invade Canada, he sailed down the lake and appeared before St. John's. Informed that the garrison there was too strong for him, he returned to *Isle Aux Noix* and fortified it. From this post he sent out a declaration among the Canadians, by Colonel Allen and Major Brown, assuring them that the Americans intended to act only against the British forts, and not to interfere with the people or their religion.

August 8, 1848.

September 6, 1775.

---

[1] The sketch was made from the pilot's room of the steam-boat, about half a mile above the island, looking east-northeast. The landing is a little beyond the trees on the right, where sentinels are stationed. The island is small, and wholly occupied by the military works. A broad fen extends some distance from the northern side, and the wild ducks that gather there afford fine amusement for sportsmen during the hunting season.

Early in October the Americans, under General Montgomery (Schuyler being ill), left the island and proceeded to St. John's, whence they marched victoriously to Quebec. From that time until the close of the Revolution no permanent garrison was established there, but the island was the halting-place for the troops of both parties when passing up and down the lake. It was the principal scene of the negotiations between some of the leading men of Vermont and British officers, which were so adroitly managed by the former as to keep an English army of ten thousand men quite inactive on our northern frontier for about three years.[1] The British strongly fortified it in 1813, and it has been constantly garrisoned since.

We arrived at St. John's, on the Richelieu or Sorel River, between six and seven o'clock in the morning, where our luggage was overhauled by the custom-house officer, who was received on board at *Isle Aux Noix*. The operation was neither long nor vexatious, and seemed to be rather a matter of legal form than induced by a desire or expectation of detecting contraband articles. In fact, the polite government functionary seemed to have great faith in mere assertions, and to rely more upon physiognomy than personal inspection of the luggage for assurance that her majesty's revenue laws were inviolate. He looked every trunk-owner full in the face when he queried about the nature of his baggage, and only two persons were obliged to produce their keys for his satisfaction. Our trunk was of prodigious size and weight, and made him very properly suspicious of the truth of my allegations that its contents were only articles for personal use. A descendant of Abraham at my elbow, with nothing but a rotund bandana handkerchief, appeared to be my scape-goat on the occasion, for while the officer was making him untie its hard knots, he ordered my luggage to pass. I was told that the word of a poor Jew is never believed by the uncircumcised Gentile who "sits at the receipt of customs;" but in this instance his incredulity was rebuked, for the Israelite's bundle contained nothing but a tolerably clean shirt, a cravat, and a small Hebrew Bible. At eight

---

[1] In 1779–80 the partial dismemberment of Vermont and its connection with New York and New Hampshire produced great bitterness of feeling, and the Legislature of the former demanded of Congress the entire separation of that state from the other states, and its admission into the confederacy upon a basis of perfect equality. The disputes ran high, and the British entertained hopes that Vermont would be so far alienated from the rebel cause, by the injustice of Congress, as to be induced to return to its allegiance to the British crown. Accordingly, in the spring of 1780, Colonel Beverly Robinson wrote to Ethan Allen from New York, making overtures to that effect. The letter was not answered, and in February, 1781, he wrote another, inclosing a copy of the first. These letters were shown to Governor Chittenden and a few others, and they concluded to make use of the circumstances for the benefit of Vermont. Allen sent both letters to Congress, and at the same time wrote to that body, urging the justice of the demand of his state. He closed his letter by saying, "I am as resolutely determined to defend the independence of Vermont as Congress is that of the United States; and, rather than fail, I will retire with the hardy Green Mountain Boys into the desolate caverns of the mountains and wage war with human nature at large."* In the mean while, some British scouting parties had captured some Vermonters, and Governor Chittenden sent Ira Allen and others to negotiate with Colonel Dundas for an exchange of prisoners. They met upon *Isle Aux Noix*, and there Dundas, under the direction of General Haldimand, made verbal overtures similar to the written ones of Robinson to Ethan Allen. The proposals of the British officers were received by Allen with apparent favor. Haldimand and Dundas were delighted with their skill in diplomacy, and readily acceded to the proposition of Allen not to allow hostilities on the Vermont frontier until after the next session of its Legislature. The British force, consisting of about ten thousand men, was thus kept inactive. These negotiations with the enemy excited the suspicion of the Whigs and the fears of Congress; yet with such consummate skill did Allen manage the affair, that when he reported the result of his mission to the Legislature of Vermont, where British emissaries as well as ardent Whigs were in waiting, he satisfied both parties. Soon afterward a letter from Lord George Germain to Sir Henry Clinton was intercepted and sent to Congress. It contained so much evidence of the treasonable designs of the leading men in Vermont, that Congress felt more disposed to accede to the demands of that state, and thus retain her in the Union. Peace soon afterward ensued, and Vermont was one of the United States included in the treaty. How far the designs of the Allens, of Chittenden, the Fays, and others, were really treasonable, or were measures of policy to bring Congress to terms, and prevent hostilities upon their weak frontier, can not be certainly determined. The probabilities are in favor of the *ruse* rather than the *treason*. At any rate, they should have the benefit of a doubt, and a verdict of acquittal of all wrong intentions.

* A convention, held at Westminster on the 15th of January, 1777, declared "That the district and territory comprehending and usually known by the name and description of the New Hampshire Grants of right ought to be and is declared forever hereafter to be a free and independent jurisdiction or state, to be forever hereafter called, known, and distinguished by the name of New Connecticut, alias VERMONT."—See *Slade's State Papers*, p. 70.

o'clock my companion and our luggage proceeded by rail-road by way of La Prairie to Mont-real, while I prepared to journey to the same city in a light wagon by way of Chambly and Longueuil.

St. John's is pleasantly situated upon the western side of the Sorel, at the termination of steam-boat navigation on Lake Champlain, and near the head of Chambly Rapids. It has always been a place of considerable importance as a frontier town since the Revolution, al-though its growth has been slow, the population now amounting to not quite four thou-sand. The country on both sides of the river here is perfectly flat, and there is no place whence the town may be seen to advantage. A little south of the village, and directly upon the shore, is a strong military establishment, garrisoned, when we visited it, by three

MILITARY ESTABLISHMENT AT ST. JOHN'S.

companies of Highland infantry. Accompanied by an intelligent young gentleman of the village as guide, I visited all the points of historic interest in the vicinity. We crossed the deep, sluggish river in a light zinc shallop, and from the middle of the stream we obtained a fine view of the long bridge[2] which connects St. John's with St. Athenaise on the opposite shore, where the steep roof and lofty glittering spire of the French church towered above the trees.[3] After visiting the remains of Montgomery's block-house, we recrossed the river and rambled among the high mounds which compose the ruins of old Fort St. John's. They occupy a broad area in the open fields behind the present military works. The embank-ments, covered with a rich green sward, averaged about twelve feet in height, and the whole were surrounded by a ditch with considerable water in it. We lingered half an hour to view a drill of the garrison, and then returned to the village to prepare for a pleasant ride to Chambly, twelve miles distant.

Military works were thrown up at St. John's by the French, under Montcalm, in 1758, and these were enlarged and strengthened by Governor Carleton at the beginning of our Revolution. Here, as we have seen, the first organized American flotilla, under Arnold, made a regular assault upon British vessels and fortifications, and aroused Sir Guy Carleton to a sense of the imminent danger of Montreal and Quebec. Here too was the scene of the first regular siege of a British fort by the rebellious colonists. In September, 1775, the Americans, as we have already noticed, sailed down the Richelieu and appeared before St. John's. They were fired upon by the English garrison when about two miles distant, but without effect. They landed within about a mile and a half of the fort, and, while marching slowly toward the outworks, a small party of Indians attacked them and produced some confusion. In the evening General Schuyler was informed, by a man who appeared to be friendly and intelligent, that, with the exception of only fifty men retained in Montreal by General Carleton, the whole regular British force in Canada was in the garrison at St. John's; that this and the fort at Chambly were strongly fortified and well supplied; that one hundred Indians were in the fort at St. John's, and that another large body, under Colonel John Johnson, was hovering near; that a sixteen gun vessel was

---

[1] This view is taken from the eastern side of the river, near the remains of a block-house erected by Mont-gomery when he besieged the fort in 1775. On the right is seen the fort, which incloses the magazine; in the center is the building occupied by the officers, on either side of which are the barracks of the soldiers. The large building on the left is the hospital, and the smaller one still further left is the dead-house. The river here is about a quarter of a mile wide. The present military works are upon the site of those of the Revolution.

[2] It was built by the Honorable Robert Jones, the proprietor, and is called Jones's Bridge.

[3] This spacious church was not finished. The old one, a small wooden structure, was undisturbed within the new one, and was used for worship until the completion of the exterior of the present edifice.

about ready to weigh anchor at St. John's; and that not a single Canadian could be induced to join the insurgent standard. The informer was doubtless an enemy to the Americans, for his assertions were afterward proved to be untrue. General Schuyler, however, gave credence to them, and returned with his troops to *Isle Aux Noix*, where illness obliged him to leave the army in charge of Montgomery, and retire to the healthier post of Ticonderoga. Thence he soon went to Albany, and, his health being partially restored, he was active in forwarding re-enforcements to *Isle Aux Noix*.

Montgomery, with more impetuosity and less caution than Schuyler, determined to push forward at once, for the season was near when military operations there would be difficult. About this time a small train of artillery and a re-enforcement arrived, and he made vigorous preparations to invade Canada. Before leaving the island, a chevaux-de-frise was thrown across the channel to intercept the progress of Carleton's vessels up the lake. On the seventeenth his whole force was landed on the west side of the Richelieu. On the eighteenth he led a corps of five hundred men, in person, to the north side of the fort, where the village now is. There he met a detachment from the garrison, which had just repulsed and pursued a small party of Americans under Major Brown, and a short skirmish ensued. Two field pieces and the whole detachment would doubtless have been trophies for the Americans had they been true to themselves; but here that insubordination which gave Montgomery so much trouble was strongly manifested, and caution, secrecy, and concert of action were out of the question.[1] Montgomery pushed on a little further northwest, and, at the junction of the roads running respectively to Montreal and Chambly, formed an entrenched camp of three hundred men to cut off supplies for the enemy from the interior, and then hastened back to his camp to bring up his artillery to bear upon the walls of the fort. The supplies for a siege were very meager. The artillery was too light, the mortars were defective, the ammunition scarce, and the artillerists unpracticed in their duties. The ground was wet and swampy, and in many places closely studded with trees. In a day or two disease began to appear among the troops, and, in consequence of their privations, disaffection was working mischief in the army. To escape these unfavorable circumstances, Montgomery proposed to move to the northwest side of the fort, where the ground was firm and water wholesome, and commence preparations for an assault. But the troops, unused to military restraint, and judging for themselves that an attack would be unsuccessful, refused to second the plan of their leader. Unable to punish them or convince them of their error, Montgomery yielded to the pressure of circumstances, and so far gratified the mutinous regiments as to call a council of war. It resulted, as was expected, in a decision against his plan. Disorder continually reigned in the American camp. Irregular firing occurred almost daily, and the enemy threw some bombs, but it was a waste of ammunition by both parties. At length the proposed plan of Montgomery was adopted, and the camp was moved to the higher ground northwest of the fort, where breast-works were thrown up. While the main army was thus circumvallating St. John's, but, for want of ammunition and heavy guns, unable to breach the walls, small detachments of Americans, who were joined by many friendly Canadians, were active in the vicinity. One, under Ethan Allen, attempted the capture of Montreal. Of this foolish expedition I shall hereafter write.

But another, and a successful one, was undertaken, which hastened the termination of the siege of St. John's. Carleton, supposing that the fort at Chambly, twelve miles northward, could not be reached by the Americans unless the one at St. John's was captured, had neglected to arm it, and kept but a feeble garrison there. Montgomery was informed of this by Canadian scouts, and immediately sent Colonel Bedell of New Hampshire, Major Brown of Massachusetts, and Major Livingston of New York, with detachments, to capture the fort. The method of attack was planned by Canadians familiar with the place. Artillery was placed upon bateaux, and during a dark night was conveyed past the fort at St. John's to the head of Chambly Rapids, where it was mounted on carriages and taken to the

Margin notes: September, 1775. / October 7, 1775.

---

[1] Montgomery's dispatch to General Schuyler.

OF THE REVOLUTION. 171

Attack upon and Surrender of Fort Chambly.   Repulse of Carleton at Longueuil.   Surrender of St. John's.   The Spoils

point of attack. The garrison made but a feeble resistance, and soon surrendered. This

FORT AT CHAMBLY.[1]

was a most important event, for it furnished Montgomery with means to carry on the siege
of St. John's vigorously.[2] The large quantity of ammunition that was captured was sent
immediately to the besiegers, who, by vigorous exertions, erected a strong battery within
two hundred and fifty yards of the fort. A strong block-house was also erected before it,
on the opposite side of the river. The former was mounted with four guns and
six mortars, and the latter had one gun and two mortars.   October 30.

While these preparations were in progress, Carleton, informed of the capture of Fort
Chambly, left Montreal with a re-enforcement for the garrison at St. John's. He embarked
upon the St. Lawrence in bateaux and flat-boats, and attempted to land at Longueuil, a mile
and a half below the city. Colonel Seth Warner, with three hundred Green Mountain Boys,
was on the alert in the neighborhood, and lay in covert near the spot where Carleton was
about to land. He allowed the boats to get very near the shore, when he opened a terrible
storm of grape-shot upon them from a four pound cannon, which drove them across the river
precipitately and in great confusion. The tidings of this event reached Mont-   November 1,
gomery toward evening, and Colonel Warner soon afterward came in with several   1775.
prisoners captured from one of Carleton's boats that reached the shore. The commander-
in-chief immediately sent a flag and letter to Major Preston, the commandant of the garrison, by one of Warner's prisoners, informing him of the defeat of Carleton, and demanding
a surrender of the fortress to prevent further effusion of blood. Hostilities ceased for the
night, and in the morning Preston asked for a delay of four days before he should make proposals to surrender. The request was denied and the demand renewed. There was no alternative, and the garrison surrendered prisoners of war. The siege had continued six weeks,
and the bravery and perseverance of the British troops were such, that Montgomery granted
them honorable terms. They marched out of the fort with the honors of war, and the troops

---

[1] This is a view of the south and west sides of the fort, looking toward the river. It stands directly upon
the Richelieu, at the foot of the Chambly Rapids, and at the head of the navigation of the river up from
the St. Lawrence. It is strongly built of stone, and, as seen in the picture, is in a state of excellent preservation.

[2] The spoils taken at Chambly were 6 tons of powder; 80 barrels of flour; a large quantity of rice,
butter, and peas; 134 barrels of pork; 300 swivel shot; 1 box of musket shot; 6364 musket cartridges;
150 stand of French arms; 3 royal mortars; 61 shells; 500 hand grenades; 83 royal fusileer's muskets
with accouterments; and rigging for 3 vessels. The prisoners consisted of 1 major, 2 captains, 3 lieutenants, captain of a schooner, a commissary and surgeon, and 83 privates. The colors of the seventh regiment of British regulars were there, and were captured. These were sent to the Continental Congress,
and were the first trophies of the kind which that body received. There were a great number of women
and children in the fort, and these were allowed to accompany the prisoners, who were sent with their
baggage to Connecticut.

172   PICTORIAL FIELD-BOOK

Surrender of St. John's.   Insubordination.   Retreat of the Americans out of Canada.

November 3.   grounded their arms on the plain near by.   The officers were allowed to keep their side-arms, and their fire-arms were reserved for them.   Canadian gentlemen and others at St. John's were considered a part of the garrison.   The whole number of troops amounted to about five hundred regulars and one hundred Canadian volunteers.[1] The Continental troops took possession of the fort, and Montgomery proposed to push on to Montreal.

Insubordination again raised its hydra-head in the American camp.   The cold season was near at hand, and the raw troops, unused to privations of the field, yearned for home, and refused, at first, to be led further away.   But the kind temper, patriotic zeal, and winning eloquence of Montgomery, and a promise on his part that, Montreal in his possession, no further service would be exacted from them, won them to obedience, and all but a small garrison for the fort pressed onward toward the city.[2]

The fort at St. John's remained in possession of the Americans until the latter part of May, 1776, when they were completely driven out of Canada.   Arnold and Sullivan, with their detachments, were the last to leave that province.   The former remained in Montreal until the last moment of safety, and then pressed on to St. John's, with the enemy close at his heels.   Two days before, he had ordered the encampment closed there, and a vessel upon

ST. JOHN'S, ON THE RICHELIEU OR SOREL.
From a drawing by Captain Aubrey, who assisted at its capture in 1776.

the stocks to be taken apart and sent to Ticonderoga.   Sullivan, who was stationed at the mouth of the Sorel, also retreated to St. John's.   The commanders wished to defend the fort against the pursuing enemy, but the troops absolutely refused to serve longer, and they all embarked, and sailed up the lake to *Isle Aux Noix*.   When every loaded boat had left the shore, Arnold and Wilkinson, his aid, rode back two miles and discovered the enemy in rapid march under Burgoyne.   They reconnoitered them a few moments, and then galloped back,

---

[1] The spoils of victory were 17 brass ordnance, from two to twenty-four pounders; 2 eight-inch howitzers; 7 mortars; 22 iron ordnance, from three to nine pounders; a considerable quantity of shot and small shells; 800 stand of arms, and a small quantity of naval stores.   The ammunition and provisions were in considerable, for the stock of each was nearly exhausted.

[2] Armstrong's Life of Montgomery.

stripped and shot their horses, set fire to the works at St. John's, pushed off from shore in a small boat, and overtook the flotilla before they reached *Isle Aux Noix*. Having no vessels with which to pursue the Americans, Burgoyne rested at St. John's. In the course of the autumn he returned to England.

Early in the summer of 1777 St. John's was the theater of active preparations, on the part of the British, for the memorable campaign which terminated in the capture of Burgoyne and his whole army at Saratoga. This campaign was planned chiefly by Lord George

LORD GEORGE GERMAIN.

Germain, the Secretary of War, and Burgoyne, with the approval of the king and the full sanction of the Council. Burgoyne was made commander of the expedition, and arrived at Quebec on the 6th of May. Carleton gave him his cordial co-operation, and St. John's was the place of general rendezvous for all the regulars, provincials, and volunteers. On the 1st of June an army of six thousand men was collected there, and, embarking in boats, sailed up the lake to Cumberland Head, where it halted to await the arrival of ammunition and stores. These collected, the whole armament moved up the lake to the north of the Bouquet, where, as already narrated, a council was held with the Indian tribes. As the rest of the story of that campaign, so disastrous to British power in America, has been told in preceding chapters, we will return to St. John's, and pass on to Chambly.

1777.

I left St. John's about eleven o'clock in a light wagon, accompanied by the young man who acted as guide among the old military remains. There is but little in the appearance of St. John's to distinguish it from a large village in the States, but the moment we emerged into the country I felt that I was in a strange land. The road traverses the line of the Chambly Canal, which runs parallel with the Richelieu or Sorel River. The farm-houses are thickly planted by the roadside; so thickly that all the way from St. John's to Chambly and Longueuil we seemed to be in a village suburb. The farms are diminutive compared with ours, averaging from fifteen to forty acres each, and hence the great number of dwellings and out-houses. They are generally small, and built of hewn logs or stone. Most of the dwellings and out-houses are whitewashed with lime, even the roofs, which gives them a very neat appearance, and forms a beautiful contrast in the landscape to the green foliage which embowers them. I was told that each house contains a *consecrated broom*. When a new dwelling is erected, a broom is *tabooed* by the priest and hung up in the dwelling by the owner, where it remains untouched, a sort of Lares or household god. Many of them have a cross erected near, as a talisman to guard the dwelling from evil. They are generally dedicated to St. Peter, the chief patron saint of the rural French Canadians. A box, with a glass door, inclosing an image of the saint, a crucifix, or some other significant object, is placed upon or within the body of the cross, and the whole is usually surmounted by a cock. A

singular choice for a crest, for it is a fowl identified with St. Peter's weakness and shame.

It was in the time of hay harvest, and men, women, and children were abroad gathering the crops. As among the peasantry of Europe and the blacks of our Southern States, the women labor regularly in the fields. They are tidily habited in thin stuff of cotton or worsted, generally dyed blue, and all of domestic manufacture. Their costume is graceful, and, sitting loosely, gives full play to the muscles, and contributes to the high health which every where abounds in the rural districts of this region. Their broad-rimmed straw hats, like the Mexican sombrero, afford ample protection against the hot sun. These also are home-made, and the manufacture of them for our markets, during the long Canadian winters, affords quite a cash revenue to most of the families. These simple people are generally

174   PICTORIAL FIELD-BOOK

The Richelieu and its Rapids.   Chambly.   The Fort.   Beloeil Mountain.   Large Cross.

CANADIAN PEASANT GIRL.

uneducated, and superstition is a strong feature in their religious character. They are honest, kind-hearted, and industrious, have few wants, live frugally, and, in their way, seem to enjoy a large share of earthly happiness.

The Richelieu has either a swift current or noisy rapids nearly the whole distance between St. John's and Chambly. The stream is broad, and in many places deep, for it is the outlet for the whole volume of the waters of Lake Champlain into the St. Lawrence. In some places the foaming rapids produce a picturesque effect to the eye and ear, and vary the pleasure of the otherwise rather monotonous journey between the two villages.

Chambly is an old town, at the foot of the rapids, and bears evidence of thrift. A Frenchman bearing that name built a small wood fort there, which was afterward replaced by the solid stone structure pictured on page 171. The latter retained the name of the original fort, as also does the village. It is a military station at present, and, being at the head of the navigation of the Richelieu or Sorel from the St. Lawrence, has a commanding position. The river here, at the foot of the falls, expands into a circular basin about a mile and a half in diameter. The old fort is dismantled and ungarrisoned, and is now used only for a store-house. Near it are seen the remains of the battery erected by Bedell, while preparing to storm the fort in 1775. I tarried at Chambly long enough only to reconnoiter and sketch the old fortress and the features of the Beloeil, the only mountain range in view, and

1848.

BELOEIL MOUNTAIN.[1]

then went to an inn to dine, a mile on the road toward Longueuil. There I learned that a French Canadian, nearly one hundred years old, was living near. Although the sun was declining, and we had seventeen miles' travel before us, I determined to visit the old man

---

[1] This sketch is taken from the southeast angle of old Fort Chambly, showing the rapids in the foreground. The mountain is twenty miles distant, near the Sorel. On the highest point of the range the Bishop of Nancy, a French prelate, erected a huge cross in 1843, the pedestal of which was sufficiently large to form a chapel capable of containing fifty persons. In November, 1847, during a severe thunder-gust, the lightning and wind completely demolished the cross, but spared the pedestal, and that, being white, may be seen at a great distance

and sound his memory.   We met him upon the road, coming toward the inn   He had just left his rake in the field, and had on a leather apron and broad-rimmed hat.   He was a small, firmly-built man, apparently sixty-five years old.   Conversation with him was difficult, for his dialect, professedly French, was far worse than Gascon.   Still we managed to understand each other, and I gleaned from him, during our brief interview, the facts that he was born in Quebec in 1752 ; remembered the storming of the city by the English under Wolfe ; removed to Chambly in 1770 ; was a spectator of the capture of the fort by a detachment from Montgomery's army in 1775 ; assisted in furnishing stores for Burgoyne's army at St John's in 1777 ; and has lived upon and cultivated the same small farm of thirty acres from that time until the present.   He was ninety-six years old, and appeared to have stamina sufficient for twenty years more of active life.   He seemed to be a simple-hearted creature, ignorant of the world beyond the Richelieu and the adjacent village, and could not comprehend my movements while sketching his honest countenance.   He was delighted, however, when he saw the outlines of an old man's face, and knew them to be his own ; and when I presented him with a silver coin, he laughed like a pleased child.   But when the young man who accompanied me, with intended generosity, offered him a glass of brandy, his eyes sparkled with indignation, and in his bad French he uttered an emphatic refusal. *He had signed the temperance pledge a year be-*

FRANCOIS YEST.

fore, and he felt insulted by the seeming attempt to win him from his allegiance.   Glorious old convert, and firm old preacher of principle in the very den of the fierce lion, for decanters were at his elbow, and a friendly hand proffered the contents to his lips !   A vow of total abstinence from intoxicating drinks at the age of ninety-five !   For that I pressed the hard hand of FRANCOIS YEST with a firmer grasp when I bade him adieu.

We had a pleasant ride from Chambly to Longueuil (seventeen miles) over a plank road. Unlike similar roads in New York, the planks were laid diagonally.   They had been in use twelve years, and were but little decayed.   The country all the way to the St. Lawrence is flat.   The soil, though rather wet, is productive, and almost every rood of it was under cultivation.   Here and there were a few groves, but no forests ; and a solitary huge bowlder by the road-side, shivered by lightning, was the only rock that I saw between the Richelieu and the St. Lawrence.   When within three miles of Longueuil, the glittering domes and spires of Montreal appeared in the distance like gems set in the dark mountain that formed a background beyond.

A THUNDER-STRUCK ROCK.

It was five o'clock when we reached Longueuil, a mile and a half below Montreal, on the opposite side of the river.   There I parted from the young gentleman whose light wagon had conveyed me from St. John's, and proceeded to Montreal on the steam ferry-boat that connects it with Longueuil.   Neither cab nor omnibus was in waiting, and I was obliged to ride a mile in a rickety calèche,[1] drawn

---

[1] The calèche is a two-wheeled vehicle, much used in Lower Canada.   It is similar in form to our gig, but, instead of having but one seat, there is one for the driver upon the dash-board.   Four can ride comfortably in one of them.   Some are made elegantly, with a folding cover to ward off the sun or rain, and they are a pleasant vehicle to ride in.   I found them in universal use in the narrow streets of Quebec.   Such was the vehicle in use in Canada at the time of our Revolution, and mentioned by the Baroness Reidesel as the kind in which she and her children traveled with the British army.

176   PICTORIAL FIELD-BOOK

Ride in a Caleche.   Safe Arrival of my Companion.   An Evening Stroll.   Aurora Borealis

by a representative of Rosinante.   The vehicle, horse, driver, and ride altogether made a
funny affair.   The driver was a little Frenchman, with a
jocky-coat and breeches, and a red tasseled skull-cap.   All
the way he belabored his beast with blows and curses, but
the animal's hide and ears seemed impervious.   I could think
of nothing but a parody on a couplet of the old song, "If I
had a donkey," &c.   As we wheeled up a narrow court from
St. Paul's Street to the Exchange Hotel, a merry laugh of
half a furlong's audibility rang out from a group of young
ladies upon an upper piazza, and that was my first evidence
that my traveling companion, Miss B——, had arrived safely,

A CALECHE.

as per consignment in the morning to the care of the urbane proprietors of that excellent
establishment.   She had rambled through the city with pleasant company until thoroughly
wearied, so I took an evening stroll alone.   The day had been very warm, but the evening
was cool.   The stars were brilliant, yet it was too dark to see much beyond the dim forms
of massy buildings, wrapped in deep shadows.   But above, in the far north, a phenomenon
seldom exhibited in summer was gorgeously displayed; more so than we often see it in
lower latitudes in winter, and I stood an hour in the Place d'Arms, watching the ever-
changing beauties of the brilliant Aurora Borealis.   It is a strange sight, and well might
the ignorant and superstitious of other times regard it with fearful wonder.   Lomonosov, a
native Russian poet, thus refers to the sublime spectacle :

> "What fills with dazzling beams the illumined air?
>   What wakes the flames that light the firmament?
> The lightning's flash; there is no thunder there,
>   And earth and heaven with fiery sheets are blent;
> The winter's night now gleams with brighter, lovelier ray
> Than ever yet adorned the golden summer's day.
>
> "Is there some vast, some hidden magazine,
>   Where the gross darkness flames of fire supplies—
> Some phosphorous fabric, which the mountains screen,
>   Whose clouds of light above those mountains rise,
> When the winds rattle loud around the foaming sea,
> And lift the waves to heaven in thundering revelry?"

OF THE REVOLUTION. 177

Montreal.   A Ride to the Mountain.   Interesting View.   Visit to the City Churches.   Parliament House.   Grey Nunnery

CHAPTER VIII.

HE pleasure-seeker will find much about Montreal to amuse him ; and the staid traveler, searching for the gold of general knowledge, might fill a large chapter in his journal, in recording what is noteworthy among present things there.   Mine is a tour too specific in its aim to allow much latitude of departure from historic research, and, therefore, things irrelevant, yet incidentally connected with the objects of the journey, must be passed by with brief notice.

Early on the morning after our arrival we joined purses and company with a young married couple from Burlington, who were on a wedding jaunt, and, procuring a barouche, went out to visit the " lions" of the city and suburbs.   We first rode to the " Mountain," a lofty hill on the west, in the rear of the city, composed chiefly of a sort of compound trap-rock slightly covered with soil upon its summit, and crowned with a forest of small trees.   The road, as it winds up its southern slope, passes the Priests' Farm,[1] the Governor's Palace, and many beautiful villas, and opens to the view a lovely, cultivated country on the western part of the island and the Isle of Jesus beyond.   Near the summit of the mountain is a cottage completely enveloped in trees and shrubbery, where ices, wines, and fruit tempt the appetite. We loitered in its sweet flower-gardens for half an hour, and then ascended to the hill-top. Beautiful panorama !   The city, with its numerous polished tin roofs, lay glittering at our feet in the morning sun.   The broad St. Lawrence, cleft by St. Helen's and one or two smaller islands, was teeming with water craft, and in every direction the landscape was dotted with little villages, each having its church, " pointing its taper spire to Heaven."

We descended the northern slope of the mountain to the city, and visited St. James's or the Bishop's Church, one of the largest and most richly decorated church edifices in the province.   It is the cathedral of the titular Bishop of Montreal, and contains many fine European paintings over the several altars.   There were worshipers at all the altars, and some of the confessionals were occupied by penitents and priests.   An attendant, a devout old Frenchman, showed us a number of relics, and assured us, by a printed placard in French, that certain prayers and money-offerings at the different shrines would blot out a host of transgressions.   Our Protestant education taught us that prayers without faith avail nothing ; and our faith in this particular being like a " grain of mustard seed," we saved our money and time, and hastened to the Parliament House and the Grey Nunnery near.   We stepped into the capacious parish Church or Cathedral of Notre Dame on our way.   It has a marble font said to be twelve hundred years old, having belonged to a church in Rome in the seventh century.   We visited the Legislative chambers and the valuable library in the Parliament House,[2] and then rang for entrance at the gate of the GREY NUNNERY, or *General Hospital of the Charitable Sisters*.   This, as an almoner of comforts to the aged and lonely, is a noble institution, the income of the establishment, and the whole time of the Sis-

margin note: August 9, 1848.

---

[1] The " Priests' Farm" (*La Maison des Prêtres*) is an ecclesiastical establishment situated on the south side of the " Mountain."   The buildings, inclosed within high walls, with massive round towers, are large, and have an antique appearance.   They are surrounded by several fine gardens and orchards, and, in summer, are a weekly resort for the professors and pupils of the seminary and college.

[2] The Parliament House and the valuable library within it, containing the Legislative records of the province, were burned by a political mob in April, 1849.   The loss is irreparable, for many of the books were too rare to be replaced.

ters of Charity connected with it, being devoted to the relief of poor and infirm old persons, and the nurture and education of orphans.[1] The building is spacious, and a large number of both classes are there made comfortable. Our visit was at mid-day. When the clock struck twelve, a long procession of the nuns, veiled, marched slowly into the chapel, singing a Gregorian chant, and knelt within the nave in prayer. We followed in respectful silence. Each nun had a small crucifix and string of beads attached ; and whatever may have been the case with their thoughts, their eyes never wandered, notwithstanding strangers were gazing upon them. They were habited in dark drab dresses, bound with black velvet and looped up behind ; aprons with stripes, and over the head (on which they wore a cap with a deep border), covering the face and neck, a thin black veil was thrown, through which the features were discernible. Some were young and pretty, others old and plain, but the sacred character of their labor of love invested them all with beauty. We visited a few other places of note, and, after "lunch," I left my company and went down to Longueuil, where Carleton was defeated by Warner in 1775. We are upon historic ground ; let us open the old volume a few moments.

GREY NUN PRAYING.

Montreal is built upon an island thirty miles long and twelve wide, and is upon the site of ancient *Hochelaga*, a noted Indian village which gave its name to the river in this vicinity. The first white man who visited the spot was Jaques Quartier or Cartier, a French navigator, who discovered the Gulf and River St. Lawrence, and gave them the name they bear.[2] The vicinity, even up the slopes of the mountain, was tilled and covered with corn-fields. Cartier was enchanted with the view from the mountain—a view of "thirty leagues radius"—and, in honor of his king (Francis I.), he called it Mount Royal. In time the name was modified to Montreal, and in this form was borne by the white settlement that gathered there in 1640. The spot was consecrated by the superior of the Jesuits, and a chapel built in 1642.

October 3, 1535.

The Indians, at first friendly, became jealous, and at length hostile. The town was stockaded and slight bastions were built, but finally a strong wall of masonry was constructed, fifteen feet high, with battlements and six gates. The town gradually increased in size and commercial importance, and at the time of our Revolution was nearly as populous as Quebec. When, toward the middle of the last century, hostilities commenced between the English and French colonies, Montreal was an important place as a frontier town. There Duquesne de Menneville[3] and Vaudreuil de Cavagnal, French governors of Canada, fitted out their expeditions against the English on the Ohio and the unfriendly Indians of New York. Montreal was threatened by the English under Amherst in 1759, but it was not until the autumn of 1760 that it passed out of the possession of the French. Quebec surrendered a year before, and Vaudreuil retreated to Montreal, with a determination to make

September 8, 1760.

---

[1] This hospital was founded by M. Charron and others, in 1692. In 1748 it passed into the hands of a society of ladies, at the head of whom was Madame Youville, who, being left a widow at the age of twenty-eight, determined to devote her life and fortune to the relief of the infirm poor. In 1755 the plan of the establishment was enlarged, so as to embrace orphans, the cause of which was singular, as given in Bosworth's " Picture of Montreal." One winter day, as Madame Y. was passing the " Little River," she saw an infant hard frozen in the ice, with a poniard sticking in its throat, and one of its little hands raised through the ice as if in the attitude of demanding justice against the perpetrator of the crime. Madame Y. was dreadfully shocked at the sight, and, on consultation with her associates, it was resolved to extend their charity and protection to orphans and foundlings.

[2] He arrived in the gulf on the festival of St. Lawrence (10th of August), and, on account of that circumstance, named the waters in honor of the saint.

[3] He built a fort on the Ohio, which was called Fort Duquesne. It is memorable as the place near which Braddock was defeated in 1755, when Washington's military talents were first conspicuously developed. The name of the fort was changed to Pitt, and the present city of Pittsburgh stands upon its site.

there a bold stand in defense of French dominion in Canada. The English invested Mont-

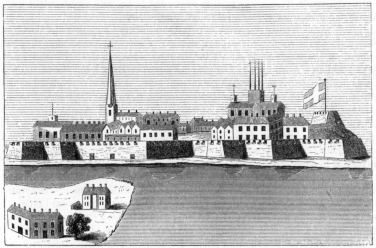

VIEW OF MONTREAL AND ITS WALLS IN 1760.[1]

From an old French print.

real in September, 1760. Amherst approached down the St. Lawrence from Oswego, General Murray advanced up the river from Quebec, and Colonel Haviland took post on the south side of the St. Lawrence, opposite the city. Vaudreuil perceived that re- *September 6,* sistance would be vain, and two days afterward the city was surrendered to the *1760.* English. With this event French dominion ceased in Canada. The terms of capitulation were honorable to both parties. Private property was respected ; the revenues of the priesthood were held sacred to their use ; the Roman Catholic religion was undisturbed ; the privileges of all classes were preserved and guarantied ; and every thing was done to reconcile the people to their new masters. General Gage, afterward Governor of Massachusetts, was appointed Governor of Montreal.

Montreal remained in quiet possession of the English until 1775, when the invading army of the insurgent colonies disturbed its repose, after the capture of Forts St. John's and Chambly. A month previous to these events the town was alarmed by the appearance of an American detachment under Ethan Allen, but the result quieted their fears. When the command of the Northern army devolved upon Montgomery, he sent Allen, who had been traversing Canada in the neighborhood of the St. Lawrence, to retrace his steps and further arouse the people in favor of the rebellion. Active and brave, Allen gathered a large number to his standard. A week after he left the American camp at *Isle Aux Noix* he was at St. Ours, twelve miles south of the·Sorel, with two hundred and fifty Canadians under arms. He wrote to Montgomery that within three days he would join him in laying siege to St. John's, with at least five hundred armed Canadians. On his way to join the main army, he marched up the east side of the St. Lawrence to Longueuil. When between that place and La Prairie, he fell in with Major Brown, at the head of an advanced party of Americans and Canadians, who informed him that Montreal was weak and defenseless, and proposed to make a joint attack upon the city. Allen had confidence in the courage and judgment of Brown, and, as the scheme opened an adventurous field, he agreed to the proposition

---

[1] The island with buildings, seen on the left, is St. Helen's or Helena, now strongly fortified. It is in front of the city, a mile distant, and is a beautiful summer resort. It formerly belonged to the Barons of Longueuil, and is now the property of the crown. The picture is a fac-simile of the print, with all its defects in drawing.

Allen was to return to Longueuil, procure canoes, and cross the St. Lawrence with his troops below the city, while Brown was to cross above the town, with two hundred men, and the attack was to be made at opposite points simultaneously.

September 24, 1775.　　Allen crossed the river at night with eighty Canadians and thirty Americans. It was a rough, windy night, and so few were the canoes that they had to cross three times, yet the whole party passed the foaming waters in the light vessels safely before daylight. At dawn Allen expected to hear the signal of Brown, but the morning advanced, and it was evident that the latter had not crossed over. Guards were placed upon the roads to prevent persons from carrying intelligence into the town, and Allen would have retreated if his boats could have carried all over at once.

The Americans being discovered, armed men were soon seen issuing from the gates. A force of forty British regulars, more than two hundred Canadians, and a few Indians came down upon them from the town ; but, notwithstanding the disparity in numbers, such was the bravery of some of the Americans, that the engagement lasted an hour and three quarters. At length, his men having all deserted but twenty-eight, seven of whom were wounded, Allen agreed to a surrender upon being promised honorable terms. They were marched to Montreal, and the officers who were on the field acted very civilly toward them ; but when they were delivered into the custody of General Prescott, they experienced the most brutal treatment at his hands. On learning, by conversation with Allen, that he was the same man who had captured Ticonderoga, Prescott was greatly enraged, threatened him with a halter, and ordered him to be bound hand and foot in irons and placed on board the Gaspee war schooner. A bar of iron eight feet long was attached to his shackles, and, with his fellow-prisoners, who were fastened together in pairs with handcuffs, he was thrust into the lowest part of the ship, where neither seat nor bed was allowed them.[1] We shall have con-

---

[1] Ethan Allen was born in Roxbury, Litchfield county, in Connecticut. He went to Vermont at an early age, and about 1770 took an active part in the disturbances that occurred between the Hampshire Grants and the state of New York. The Legislature of the latter province proclaimed him an outlaw, and offered fifty pounds sterling for his apprehension. A party, determining to capture him while on a visit to his friends in Salisbury and lodge him in the jail at Poughkeepsie, came near effecting their object. He afterward led the expedition against Ticonderoga, and his former sins were forgotten by his enemies. In the autumn of 1775 he was twice sent into Canada to observe the disposition of the people, and, if possible, win them over to the American cause. On returning from his last tour to camp, he was induced by Major Brown to cross the St. Lawrence and attack Montreal. The former failed to co-operate with him, and he was captured and put in irons. He remained five weeks in irons on board the Gaspee, at Montreal, and when Carleton was repulsed by Warner at Longueuil, the vessel was sent down to Quebec. There he was transferred to another vessel, where he was treated humanely, and sent to England to be tried for treason. He was placed in charge of Brook Watson, a resident of Montreal, and afterward Lord Mayor of London. Allen, in his grotesque garb, attracted great attention in the streets of Falmouth, where he was landed. He was confined for a time in Pendennis Castle, near Falmouth, and was sent to Halifax in the spring of 1776. He was confined in jail there until autumn, and was then sent to New York, then in possession of the British. There he was kept about a year and a half. In May, 1778, he was exchanged for Colonel Campbell, and returned to his fireside in Vermont. He never afterward actively engaged in military service. He died at Colchester, Vermont, February 13th, 1789, and his remains repose in a beautiful cemetery near the Wincoski, at Burlington. Ethan Allen was a blunt, honest man, of purest virtue and sternest integrity. In religion he was a free-thinker, and passed for an infidel. An anecdote is related of him, which illustrates the purity of his principles. He owed a citizen of Boston sixty pounds, for which he gave his promissory note. It was sent to Vermont for collection. It was inconvenient for Allen to pay, and the note was put in suit. Allen employed a lawyer to attend the court, and have the judgment postponed until he could raise the money. The lawyer determined to deny the genuineness of the signature, as the readiest method of postponing the matter, for in that case a witness at Boston would have to be sent for. When the case was called, it happened that Allen was in a remote part of the court-house, and, to his utter astonishment, heard his lawyer gravely deny the signature of the note. With long and fierce strides he rushed through the crowd, and, confronting the amazed "limb of the law," rebuked him in a voice of thunder. "Mr. ——, I did not hire you to come here and lie. That is a true note—I signed it—I'll swear to it—and I'll pay it. I want no shuffling, I want time. What I employed you for was to get this business put over to the next court, not

SIGNATURE OF ETHAN ALLEN.

OF THE REVOLUTION. 181

Montgomery's March upon Montreal.   Flight and Capture of Prescott.   Escape of Carleton.   Mutiny in Montgomery's Camp.

siderable to say of the character and career of the brutal Prescott, while commanding afterward on Rhode Island.

The cause of Major Brown's failure to cross, and, with Allen, attack Montreal, has never been explained. The plan was good, and would doubtless have been successful. Half carried out, it proved disastrous, and both Brown and Allen were blamed, the one for proposing, the other for attempting, such a hazardous enterprise.

After the fall of St. John's, General Montgomery pressed on toward Montreal. Carleton knew its weakness, and at once retreated on board one of the vessels of a small fleet lying in the river. Montgomery entered the town in triumph the day after Carleton and the garrison left it. He treated the people humanely, and secured their confi- November 13, 1775. dence and good will. Finding there a large supply of woolen goods, he set about clothing his army, so that those who accompanied him further in the campaign might be prepared for the rigors of a Canadian winter.

As soon as Montgomery saw the disposition of the garrison to flee, he dispatched Colonel Easton with Continental troops, cannon, and armed gondolas to the mouth of the Sorel. This force was so advantageously posted that the British fleet could not pass, and General Prescott, several officers, members of the Canadian Council, and one hundred and twenty private soldiers, with all the vessels, surrendered by capitulation.[1] At the midnight preceding Governor Carleton was conveyed in a boat, with muffled oars, past the American post to Three Rivers, and arrived safely at Quebec. The Americans were very anxious to secure Governor Carleton, for his talents, judgment, and influence formed the basis of strength against the invaders. They were watchful in their guardboats, but a dark night and a secret way favored his escape, and they secured a far inferior captive in Prescott, whose conduct, on many occasions, made him a disgrace to the British army.

Notwithstanding all

SIR GUY CARLETON.[2]
From a London print dated 1782.

the important posts in Canada except Quebec were now in possession of the Americans, Montgomery justly asserted, in a letter to Congress, that, "till Quebec is taken, Canada is unconquered." Impressed with this idea, he determined to push forward to the capital despite the inclemency of the season and the desertion of his troops. The term of service of many had expired, and others absolutely refused to proceed further. Insubordination manifested itself among the

officers, and it required all the address the general was master of to induce a respectable force to march to Quebec, after garrisoning Montreal. But amid all these discouragements

---

to come here and lie and juggle about it." The result was, that the postponement of the claim was amicably arranged between the two lawyers.

[1] There were eleven sail of vessels. Their contents were 760 barrels of flour, 675 barrels of beef, 376 firkins of butter, 3 barrels of powder, 4 nine and six pounders, cartridges and ball, 2380 musket cartridges, 8 chests of arms, 200 pairs of shoes, and a quantity of intrenching tools.

[2] Guy Carleton, afterward Lord Dorchester, was Wolfe's quartermaster at the storming of Quebec, and was appointed a major in the British army in 1772. In 1774 he was constituted Captain-general and Governor of Quebec or Canada. He successfully commanded the British at Quebec when attacked by Montgomery in 1775, compelled the Americans to raise the siege in 1776, and drove them out of the province. In October he recaptured Crown Point. He was unjustly superseded in military command by Burgoyne in 1777. He was appointed to succeed Sir Henry Clinton in 1782, and was in command of the British troops when they evacuated New York on the 25th of November, 1783. He died in England at the close of 1808, aged 83 years.

the hopeful general did not despair.   He knew that Arnold was traversing the wilderness along the Kennebeck and the Chaudière to join him, and was then, perhaps, menacing Quebec ; and he knew also that the troops under Carleton and M'Lean were hardly adequate to defend the city, even against a smaller force than his own.   He winnowed his army of the recusant and mutinous, and then pushed onward down the St. Lawrence.[1]

I remarked that I left my pleasant company at Montreal, and went down to Longueuil. My object was to ascertain, if possible, the place where Warner planted his battery and repulsed the boats of Carleton.   Longueuil is an old town, chiefly composed of small stone houses with steep roofs.   It has a spacious French church, of antique appearance, though not more than thirty years old.   The people all speak bad French, and for more than an hour I sought the "oldest inhabitant."   That mysterious creature was an old woman of unknown age, and so deaf that she could not hear half I said, or understand a word.   I reciprocated the latter infirmity, and now confess profound ignorance of all she attempted to say.   An intelligent lad came to the rescue, and silenced our jargon batteries by referring me to his uncle, who lived near the beach, and " knew every thing."   He was a man about fifty, and spoke English pretty well.   I made my business known, and he at once assumed the patronizing air of Sir Oracle, said he knew it all, and pointed to the shore a little above as the very spot where " the cavalry horses were stabled," and where " the English dragoons drank a health to King George and vowed death to the Yankees."   He knew Sir George Prevost, and praised the veterans of Wellington who accompanied him.   As British dragoons and Wellington's veterans were not with Carleton, and as my mentor's first birth-day doubtless occurred twenty years after the time in question, I properly doubted his knowledge of the facts I was in search of.   I told him that it was the American Revolution I was inquiring about.   He did not seem to understand me, and I called it *rebellion*.   " Oh oui ! yes, yes, I know," he exclaimed.   " Two hundred crossed here for St. John's.   Captain Glasgow was a fine fellow.   Pity Lord Elgin wasn't as great a man as Sir John Colborne." With exhausted patience, I explained to him the time and nature of the revolution of the last century, but he had never heard of it !   He knew nothing behind his own " life and times."   As he represented the " collective wisdom" of the village, I despaired of better success, and returned to Montreal with the fruit of a three hours' expedition under a hot sun—a Yankee's postulate—a shrewd *guess*.   I was as little successful in my search at Montreal for the battle-ground where Ethan Allen and his men were made prisoners.   An intelligent gentleman, who was one of the leaders in the rebellion there in 1837, assured me that the spot was unknown to the inhabitants, for tradition has but little interest in keeping its finger upon the locality, and not a man was living who had personal knowledge of the event.   It is probable that the northern suburbs of the city now cover the locality, and that the place is not far from the present Longueuil ferry-landing.

Having accomplished my errand at Montreal, we departed for Quebec toward evening, in the fine steamer *John Munn*, accompanied by our Burlington friends of the morning. The magnificent stone quays were crowded with people, and our boat had a full complement of passengers.   At the lower end of St. Helen's we entered the St. Mary's Rapids, and, darting past Longueuil, were soon out of sight of the spires of Montreal.   The banks of the river are low, and on either side villages and cultivated fields exhibited an ever-changing and pleasing panorama.   Belœil Mountain loomed up eastward of us, and the white chapel, the pedestal of the bishop's huge cross upon the loftiest summit, sparkled like a star in the beams of the setting sun.   It was twilight when we arrived at William Henry, or Sorel, an old town, forty-five miles below Montreal, at the mouth of the Richelieu or Sorel River.   A

---

[1] Several hundred of the militia, regardless of order, took the nearest route to their respective homes in New England and New York.   About three hundred arrived in a body at Ticonderoga, and, flinging their heavy packs over their shoulders, crossed the lake on the ice, and traversed the wilderness through the deep snow to their homes in New Hampshire, Massachusetts, and Connecticut.   It was an undertaking quite as perilous as the siege of Quebec.   The endearments of home were the goal of the one, military glory was that of the other.   The choice, though not creditable to them as patriots, deserves our respectful homage.

French engineer named Sorel built a fort there as early as 1665, and the present town occupies its site. Our boat tarried there an hour for passengers and freight, but it grew too dark to see much of the town. A motley group crowded the narrow wharf, and when we left, the forward deck was covered with cabbages, leeks, and onions for the Quebec market, which afforded perfume gratuitously for the whole boat.

Sorel was a place of considerable importance at the time of our Revolution. Standing at the mouth of a navigable river, and at the narrowest part of the St. Lawrence between Montreal and Quebec, its possession was important to both belligerents. When the Americans approached Canada in 1775, Colonel M·Lean, with a Scotch regiment of Royal Highlanders, went up from Quebec and took station there. When Carleton left Montreal to reenforce the garrison at St. John's, M·Lean was to join him near Longueuil; but the unexpected repulse of the former by the Green Mountain Boys, and the spreading of American detachments over the country east of the St. Lawrence, between it and the Richelieu, so alarmed M·Lean, that he not only fell back precipitately to Sorel, but abandoned that post to Colonel Easton, and retired to Quebec. At Sorel, Colonel Easton did good service a few weeks later, when, with floating batteries and cannon on shore, he disputed the passage of the British fleet retreating from Montreal, and captured the whole flotilla, with General Prescott.

Leaving Sorel, we passed several islands, and then entered Lake St. Peter's, an expansion of the St. Lawrence about twenty-five miles long, and having an average width of nine miles. A half moon dimly lighted the sluggish waters, and defined an outline of the huge serpent of smoke which our vessel left trailing behind. The shores disappeared in the night shadows, and one after another of the passengers retired to bed, until the promenade deck was deserted, except by two young ladies, whose sweet voices charmed us for an hour with " Dearest May" and kindred melodies. It was near midnight when the nightingales ceased their warbling, and I sought the repose of my state-room.

Three Rivers, St. Anne's, the Richelieu Rapids, Cape Rouge, Chaudière, Sillery Cove, and New Liverpool were all passed during our slumbers, but we were upon the deck in the morning in time to catch the first glimpse of Quebec in the distance. A forest of masts, above which loomed Cape Diamond crowned with the gray citadel and its threatening ordnance, were the first objects in view. But as our vessel made a graceful sweep toward Point Levi, and " rounded to" at the Queen's Wharf, I think I never saw a more picturesque scene.

It was just at sunrise, and the morning was cloudless. As the orb of day came up from the eastern hills, the city, spread out upon the steep acclivities and along the St. Charles, reflected back its bright ·rays from a thousand windows, and roofs of polished tin. All was a-glow with luster, except the dark walls and the shipping, and for the moment the creations of Aladdin's Lamp seemed before us. The enchantment was soon over, and was succeeded by the sober prose of travel, as we passed slowly to the upper town along the narrow and·crooked Mountain Street, through Prescott Gate, closely jammed in a pigmy coach. We found comfortable quarters at the Albion, on Palace Street, one of the most respectable English hotels in the upper city. After breakfast we ordered a barouche, to visit the Falls of Montmorenci, the Plains of Abraham, and other places of note, and obtained a permit from the commandant to enter the citadel. Before making the interesting tour, let us turn to a map of the city, trace out its walls and gates and general topography, and consult the chronicle of its history; then we shall view its celebrities understandingly.

EXPLANATION OF THE DIAGRAM.—A is the St. Charles River; B, the St. Lawrence; a is Palace Gate; b, Gate St. John's; c, Gate St. Louis; d, Governor's Garden, wherein is a stone monument in memory of Wolfe and Montcalm; e, the portion of Cape Diamond at the foot of which Montgomery was killed; f, the grand battery; g, Prescott Gate; h, Hope Gate; o is a bold point of rock in the Sault-au-Matelot, where Arnold was wounded. The walls here given, with the citadel, inclose the upper town.

Quebec is situated upon and around a lofty promontory at the confluence of the St. Lawrence and the St. Charles Rivers, and is so strongly guarded against intruders, by steep acclivities on nearly three sides, that it has been aptly named the " Gibraltar of America." Art has added strength to these natural defenses, and, except on the rear, it is absolutely impregnable to any known implements of war. Before it spreads out a magnificent basin, where a hundred ships of the line might ride at anchor ; and around it, as far as the eye can reach, industry has planted a beautiful garden. The plains of the St. Charles, the towering Cap Tourment, the Falls of Montmorenci and of the Chaudière, the lovely Island of Orleans, and the pleasant slopes of Point Levi, unite, with the city itself, to make up a cluster of attractions with which those of few places on earth can vie.

July, 1608. The foundation of the city was laid two hundred and forty years ago, by Samuel Champlain, and yet it is just upon the margin of the primeval forest, which extends from a narrow selvage of civilization along the St. Lawrence to the Arctic regions. When Champlain, with great parade, laid the foundation stone of the future city, Old *Hochelaga* (now Montreal), discovered by Cartier more than a hundred years before, was blotted from existence, and but a few whites were planting corn and sowing wheat where the Indian gardens had flourished. Religion and commerce joined hands, and the new city soon became the capital of French dominion in America. From it missionaries and traders went westward to obtain peltry and furs, make geographical discoveries, and convert the heathen, and in a few years the French language was heard in the deep forests that skirted the vast lakes, from the Thousand Islands at the foot of Ontario to the broad waters of the Huron. Immigration steadily augmented the population, churches and convents were erected,[1] and the bastioned walls of old Fort St. Louis, mounted with cannon, were piled around the temples of the Prince of Peace at Quebec ; for the treacherous Algonquin, the wily Iroquois, and the bloody Huron, though mutual enemies, coalesced in jealousy of the French and a desire to crush their rising strength. As the colony increased in power, and, through its missionaries, in influence over the Indian tribes, the more southern English colonies became jealous, and a deep-seated animosity between them prevailed for a generation. At length the two governments quarreled, and their respective colonies gladly espoused each the cause of the parent state. To guard the St. Lawrence, the French built a strong fortress upon the Island of Cape Breton, and also began a cordon of forts along the lakes and the Ohio and Mississippi. Frontenac, Oswego, Niagara, Duquesne, and Detroit arose along the frontier. Fleets and armies came from the Old World ; the colonists armed and formed strong battalions ; the savage tribes were feasted, and bribed, and affiliated with European warriors, and wilderness America became a battle arena. In a little while the different fortresses changed masters ; Louisburgh, the strong-hold of French military power in America, fell before the skill and bravery of Amherst and Wolfe ; and at the beginning of 1759 Quebec was the only place of considerable importance in possession of the French.

We have considered, in a preceding chapter, the success of Amherst and Wolfe in the capture of Louisburgh, and the high reputation which that event gave them. Pitt, relying upon the skill and bravery of these two commanders, resolved, if possible, to conquer all Canada in a single campaign, intrusting the chief command to Amherst. That general, with a large force, attempted to join Wolfe at Quebec, by sweeping Lake Champlain and capturing Montreal ; he was unsuccessful, and Wolfe alone had the glory of the siege of Quebec.

Wolfe embarked eight thousand troops at Louisburgh, under convoy of a fleet of twenty-two ships of the line, and an equal number of frigates and smaller armed vessels, commanded by Admirals Saunders and Holmes. He landed his army safely near the Church of St. Laurent, upon the Island of Orleans, a few miles below Quebec, where, under the direction of Sir Guy Carleton (afterward governor of Canada), batteries were erected.

June 27, 1759.

---

[1] These were placed upon the most accessible portions of the promontory, and near them the rude buildings of the people were erected. To these circumstances Mr. Hawkins, author of a capital " Guide to Quebec," ascribes the present irregular course of the streets.

The brave and accomplished Montcalm, with an army of thirteen thousand men, six battalions of which were regulars, and the others Canadians and Indians, occupied the city with a garrison, and a strongly intrenched camp upon the heights of Beauport, extending from the St. Charles to the River Montmorenci.   The center of the camp and Montcalm's

headquarters were at Beauport. The whole front was intrenched and well defended from the English cannon.   Beyond the right wing a bridge was thrown across the St. Charles, and strongly protected, to keep up a communication with the city.   There were

VIEW OF POINT LEVI, FROM DURHAM TERRACE, QUEBEC.

also two batteries for its defense, placed upon hulks sunk in the channel.

Wolfe sent General Monkton to take possession of Point Levi, opposite Quebec. He landed at Beaumont, and marched up to the point with little opposition, where he erected batteries, from which the shots dealt destruction upon the lower town lying upon the St. Charles, but had no effect upon the walls of the city.   Finding efforts from that point unavailing, Wolfe, with his division on Orleans, crossed the north channel of the St. Lawrence, and encamped near the left bank of the Montmorenci, within cannon-shot of the left wing of the enemy on the other side of the river.   He met with fierce opposition, but succeeded in maintaining his ground and erecting two batteries there. Still, Quebec was too distant to be affected by any of his works, and he resolved upon the bold measure of storming the strong camp of the enemy.   On the last day of July the troops at Point Levi, and a large number of grenadiers under General Monkton, crossed the St. Lawrence in the boats of the fleet, and landed a little above the Montmorenci.   At the same time those below Montmorenci, under Generals Townshend and Murray, crossed that stream by fording it near its mouth, at low water, and joined the other division upon the beach. The enemy at once made arrangements to receive them.   The right of the French was

June 29.

July 10

---

[1] This sketch is taken from Durham Terrace, near the north wall of the Castle Garden.   In the foreground are the tops of the houses below in Champlain, Notre Dame, and St. Peter's Streets, and in the distance, across the St. Lawrence, is seen Point Levi, with its pretty little village, its church and wharves. On the extreme left, in the distance, is the upper end of the Island of Orleans, which divides the channel. The point seen is the place where Wolfe erected batteries.

under Baron de St. Ours, the center under De Senezergues, and the left under M. Herbin
The garrison in the city was commanded by M. de Ramezay.

It was nearly night when the English divisions joined, and heavy thunder-clouds were
rolling up from the west.   The grenadiers, impatient of restraint, rushed madly upon the
enemy's works, before the other troops that were to sustain them had time to form.   Consequently they were driven back to the beach with a severe loss, and sought shelter behind a
redoubt which had been abandoned by the enemy.   The French kept up a galling fire, till
the gathering tempest burst with great fury upon the belligerents.   Night closed in while the
storm was yet raging.   The tide came roaring up against the current of the St. Lawrence with
uncommon strength, and the British were obliged to retreat to their camp across the Montmorenci, to avoid submersion on the beach by the foaming waters.   The loss of the English in that
unfortunate attempt was one hundred and eighty killed and six hundred and fifty wounded.

Wolfe was greatly dispirited by this event, for he was very sensitive to censure, and that
he expected for this miscarriage.   The emotions of his mind, co-operating with fatigue of
body upon his delicate constitution, brought on a fever and dysentery, that nearly proved
fatal.   It was nearly a month before he was able to resume the command.   When sufficiently recovered to write, he drew up a letter to Pitt, in which, after detailing
the events, referring to his illness, and frankly confessing that he had called a
council of war, he said, "I found myself so ill, and am still so weak, that I begged the general officers to consult together for the general safety. . . . . . .   We have almost the whole
force of Canada to oppose us.   In this situation there is such a choice of difficulties, that I
own myself at a loss how to determine.   The affairs of Great Britain require the most vigorous measures ; but then the courage of a handful of brave men should be exerted only
where there is some hope of a favorable event."   When this letter reached England, it excited consternation and anger.[1]   Pitt feared that he had mistaken his favorite general, and
that the next news would be that he had either been destroyed or had capitulated.   But in
the conclusion of his melancholy epistle Wolfe had said he would do his best ; and that best
turned out a miracle of war.   He declared that he would rather die than be brought to a
court-martial for miscarrying, and, in conjunction with Admiral Saunders, he concerted a
plan for scaling the Heights of Abraham, and gaining possession of the elevated plateau at
the back of Quebec, on the side where the fortifications were the weakest, as the French engineers had trusted to the precipices and the river beneath.[2]

The camp at Montmorenci was broken up, and the artillery and troops were conveyed
across to Point Levi, whence they were taken some distance up the river by a
portion of the fleet under Holmes, while Saunders, with the rest of the fleet, remained behind to make a feigned attack upon the intrenchments at Beauport.   Montcalm,
unable to comprehend these movements, remained in his camp, while Bougainville was stationed a little above the Plains of Abraham, to watch the operations of the division of the
English fleet that sailed up the river.

At night the troops were all embarked in flat-boats, and proceeded up the river with the
tide.   Bourgainville saw them, and marched up the shore to prevent their landing.   It was
starlight, yet so cautiously did the boats, with muffled oars, move down the river toward
daylight, with ebb tide, that they were unperceived by the French detachment, and landed
safely in a cove below Sillery, now called *Wolfe's Cove*.   The first division was commanded
by Lieutenant-colonel (afterward General) Sir William Howe, and were all on shore at dawn
The light infantry scrambled up the woody precipice, and dispersed a French guard under
Captain de Verjer,[3] while the rest of the army clambered up a winding and steep ravine.

September 2.

September 12.

---

[1] The news of the failure of Wolfe at Montmorenci reached England on the morning of the 16th of October, and was published in an extra Gazette of that date.   The same evening Captain Hale arrived and
brought the news of the triumph upon the Plains of Abraham.   The general grief was suddenly changed
into great joy, and a day for public thanksgiving was set apart by the old king.

[2] Pictorial History of England, iv., 609.

[3] The French guard, who could not comprehend the noise below them, fired down the precipice at ran-

OF THE REVOLUTION.   187

Ascent of the English to the Plains of Abraham.   The Battle-ground.   Preparations for Battle.   Wolfe's Ravine.

The second division, under General Townshend, landed in good order, and before sunrise five thousand British troops were drawn up in battle array upon the Plains of Abraham, three hundred feet above the St. Lawrence.   September 13, 1759.

The appearance of the English troops upon the heights was the first intimation Montcalm had of the real intentions of his enemy.   He at once saw the imminent danger to which the city and garrison were exposed, and immediately marched his whole army across the St. Charles to attack the English.   He brought his troops into battle line about ten o'clock in the morning.   He had two field pieces; the English but one, a light six pounder, which some sailors succeeded in dragging up the ravine at about eight o'clock in the morning.

WOLFE'S RAVINE.[1]

I am indebted to Alfred Hawkins, Esq., of Quebec, for the following account of the position of the two armies, and the present localities identified therewith : "The battle-ground presents almost a level surface from the brink of the St. Lawrence to the St. Foy Road. The *Grand Allée*, or road to Cape Rouge, running parallel to that of St. Foy, passes through its center.   That road was commanded by a field redoubt, a four-gun battery on the English left, which was captured by the light infantry.   The remains of this battery are distinctly seen near the present race-stand.   There were also two other redoubts, one upon the rising ground in the rear of Mr. C. Campbell's house—the scene of Wolfe's death —and the other toward the St. Foy Road, which it was intended to command.   On the site of the country seat called Marchmont, at present the residence of Major-general Sir James Hope, K.C.B., there was also a small redoubt commanding the intrenched path leading to the cove.   This was taken possession of by the advanced guard of the light infantry immediately on ascending the height.   At the time of the battle the plains were without fences or inclosures, and extended to the walls on the St Louis side.   The surface was dotted over with bushes, and the roads on either side were more dense than at present, affording shelter to the French and Indian marksmen.

" In order to understand the relative position of the two armies, if a line be drawn to the St. Lawrence from the General Hospital, it will give nearly the front of the French army at ten o'clock, after Montcalm had deployed into line.   His right reached beyond the St. Foy Road, where he made dispositions to turn the left of the English.   Another parallel line, somewhat in advance of Mr. C. G. Stewart's house on the St. Foy Road, will give the front of the British army before Wolfe charged at the head of the grenadiers of the twenty-second, fortieth, and forty-fifth regiments, who had acquired the honorable title of the Louisburgh Grenadiers, from having been distinguished at the capture of that place, under his own command, in 1758.   To meet the attempt of Montcalm to turn the British left, General Townshend formed the fifteenth regiment *en potence*, or representing a double front.   The light infantry were in the rear of the left, and the reserve was placed near the right, formed in eight subdivisions, a good distance apart."

Wolfe placed himself on the right, at the head of the twenty-eighth regiment of *Louisburgh Grenadiers*, who were burning with a desire to avenge their defeat at the Montmorenci.   The English had waited four hours for the approach of the French, and were fully

---

dom, and so the British fired up.   They all fled but the captain, who was wounded and taken prisoner. It is said the poor fellow begged the British officer to sign a certificate of his courage and fidelity, lest he should be punished for accepting a bribe, in the belief that Wolfe's bold enterprise would be deemed impossible without corruption.

[1] This scene is about half way up the ravine from Wolfe's Cove, looking down the road, which is a steep and winding way from the river to the summit of the Plains of Abraham.   It is a cool, shaded nook—a delightful retreat from the din and dust of the city in summer.

prepared for action. Montcalm was on the left of the French, at the head of the regiments of *Languedoc, Bearne,* and *Guienne.* Wolfe ordered his men to load with two bullets each, and reserve their fire until the French should be within forty yards. These orders were strictly obeyed, and their double-shotted guns did terrible execution. "The hottest of the fight occurred," says Hawkins, "between the right of the race-stand and the martello towers."[1] After delivering several rounds in rapid succession, which threw the French into confusion, the English charged furiously with their bayonets. While urging on his battalions in this charge, Wolfe was singled out by some Canadians on the left, and was slightly wounded in the wrist. He wrapped a handkerchief around

GENERAL WOLFE.[2]

to stanch the blood, and, while still cheering on his men, received a second wound in the groin ; a few minutes afterward another struck him in the breast and brought him to the ground, mortally wounded. At that moment, regardless of self, he thought only of the victory for his troops. "Support me," he said to an officer near him ; "let not my brave soldiers see me drop. They day is ours—keep it." He was taken to the rear, while his troops continued to charge. The officer on whose shoulder he was leaning exclaimed, "They run, they run !" The light returned to the dim eyes of the dying hero, and he asked, with emotion, "Who runs ?" "The enemy, sir ; they give way every where." "What," feebly exclaimed Wolfe, "do they run already ? Go to Colonel Preston and

tell him to march Webb's regiment immediately to the bridge over the St. Charles, and cut off the fugitives' retreat. Now, God be praised, I die happy !" These were his last words, and in the midst of sorrowing companions, just at the moment of victory, he died. Montcalm, who was gallantly fighting in the front rank of the French left, received a mortal

September 14. wound, and died the next morning about five o'clock, and was buried in an excavation made by the bursting of a shell within the precincts of the Ursuline Convent, where his remains still rest.[3] When Lord Aylmar was Governor of Canada, he

---

[1] The *Martello Towers* are four strong circular structures erected at different distances in rear of the city, between the St. Lawrence and the St. Charles. Cannons are mounted upon their tops. They are very thick on the side toward the open country, but thin toward the city. The object of this manner of construction is, that, if taken by an enemy, they can easily be laid in ruins by the shot of the garrison.

[2] James Wolfe was born in Westerham, in Kent, January 2d, 1727. He entered the army very young, and soon distinguished himself by skill, judgment, and bravery. After his return from the expedition against Louisburgh, in 1758, he was appointed to the command of that section of the expedition against Canada that went up the St. Lawrence. His assault on Quebec was one of the boldest military achievements ever attempted, but, just at the moment of victory, he lost his life, at the early age of 32 years. His body was conveyed to England on board the Royal William, and buried at Greenwich on the 20th of November, 1759, where, in the family vault, the hero rests by the side of his father and mother. His father, Edward Wolfe, was a lieutenant general, and died in March of the same year, aged 74. The British government erected a monument to the memory of the young hero, in Westminster Abbey.

[3] Lewis Joseph de St. Veran, Marquis de Montcalm, descended from a noble family of Candiac, in France. He was educated for a soldier, and distinguished himself at the battle of Placenza in 1746. He rose by degrees to the rank of field marshal, and in 1756 was appointed Governor of Canada. He ably opposed the English under Abercrombie, but fell while gallantly fighting Wolfe at Quebec, on the 13th of September, 1759. His remains are within the grounds of the Ursuline Convent at Quebec. A few years ago a plain marble slab was placed to his memory, in the chapel of that nunnery, by Lord Aylmar, on which is the following inscription :

Honneur
à
MONTCALM
Le destin, en lui derobant
La victoire,
L' a recompensé par
Une mort glorieuse.

caused a small granite pillar. about ten feet high, to be erected upon the spot where Wolfe

WOLFE'S MONUMENT.[1]

fell upon the Plains of Abraham, now just within the southern suburb of Quebec. It bears the brief inscription, HERE DIED WOLFE, VICTORIOUS. That Vandalism under the specious guise of reverence for the great, of which I have already had occasion to speak, has sadly mutilated this monument, as may be seen in the engraving. The pedestal has lost many a pound of *relic*, and the iron railing around the monument has been broken down.

Wolfe and Montcalm were both able commanders, and were idolized by their respective troops. The former, though so young, was almost reverenced by his officers, for to bravery and great military skill he united all the virtues and graces of the perfect gentleman.

The expressions of attachment made by General (afterward Marquis) Townshend illustrate the sentiment of his officers and men. In a letter written just after the battle, he says, " I am not ashamed to own to you that my heart does not exult in the midst of this success. I have lost but a friend in General Wolfe. Our country has lost a sure support and a perpetual honor. If the world were sensible at how dear a price we have purchased Quebec in his death, it would damp the public joy. Our best consolation is, that Providence seemed not to promise that he should remain long among us. He was himself sensible of the weakness of his constitution, and determined to crowd into a few years actions that would have adorned length of life."

Five days after the battle the city of Quebec capitulated and passed into the possession of the English, and the remnant of the grand army of the French, under M. Levi, who succeeded Montcalm, retired to Montreal. General Murray was left to defend battered and half-ruined Quebec, and the British fleet, fearful of frost, retreated down the St. Lawrence to the ocean. Levi determined on attempting to regain all that the French had lost, and in the spring of 1760 he marched upon Quebec with a motley army of ten thousand men, composed of French, Canadians, and Indians. Murray, with seven thousand men, went out and attacked him, but was sorely defeated, lost all his guns, and was nearly cut off in his retreat back to the city. Levi followed up his success vigorously, and as soon as the ice left the St. Lawrence he brought up six French frigates and prepared to beleaguer the city by land and by water. He encamped upon the heights above Point Levi, and felt sure of his prey. Fortunately for the English, Lord Colville arrived at this juncture with two good frigates, and destroyed the French vessels under the eyes of Levi. Thoroughly frightened by the suddenness of the event, and learning that these two fast sailers were only the van of a powerful fleet, the French commander retreated precipitately to Montreal, leaving his artillery and stores behind him. Vaudreuil, the governor general of the province, was at Montreal, and Amherst, Murray, and Haviland proceeded to invest that city. Despairing of succor from abroad, Vaudreuil capitulated on the 8th of September, and on that memorable day French power in Canada expired and hostilities in America ceased. Peace ensued between the two governments by the conclusion and signing of a treaty at Paris, on the 10th of February, 1763. and thus ended the famous " Seven Years' War." From that time the two races have not been arrayed in battle against each other in the Western world, except while the French were here as allies in 1780–81, and assisted in the battle at Yorktown and the capture of Cornwallis.

September 18, 1759.

April 28, 1760.

May 16.

1760.

---

[1] Since my visit to Quebec (August, 1848) the *remains* of this monument have been removed, and a column forty feet high, surmounted by a bronze helmet and sword, has been erected. The monument is from the design of Sir James Alexander.

Quebec enjoyed tranquillity until the Americans, under Montgomery and Arnold, invaded Canada in the autumn and winter of 1775. We left the former pressing forward toward the city, with the rigors of a Canadian winter gathering around him. Let us return and watch the progress of that little army of patriots, and also consider the wonderful expedition of the brave Arnold through the wilderness of the east.

We mentioned incidentally, in a previous chapter, that when the tidings of the capture of the forts on Lake Champlain reached the Continental Congress, that body promptly took action to defend the liberties of the people, and secure their rights by force of arms, if necessary. The skirmishes at Lexington and Concord, the menaces against Massachusetts, and Boston in particular, fulminated by the home government, and the arrival of several regiments of British troops, for the avowed purpose of crushing the anticipated rebellion, aroused a spirit of resistance in the colonies hitherto unknown, even when the Stamp Act, ten years before, had awakened a terrible storm of indignation throughout the land. From all directions men flew to arms, and in a few weeks a large patriot army invested Boston, and threatened Governor Gage and his mercenary troops with destruction. The incongruous material which composed the army was partially organized by appointing Artemas Ward[1] commander-in-chief until the general Congress should act in the premises. That action 1775. was not long delayed, and on the 15th of June Congress adopted a resolution to appoint a general "to command all the Continental forces raised for the defense of American liberty." George Washington was unanimously chosen to fill the important office,[2] July 12, and he repaired to Cambridge, near Boston, and took command of the army. He 1775. set about organizing and disciplining the troops, and making preparations for an active campaign.

About the middle of August, a committee of Congress visited Washington in his camp, and a plan was then devised to send a force to Canada, by way of the Kennebec River, to co-operate with Schuyler, already preparing to invade that province by way of the North ern lakes. Arnold was then at Cambridge, uttering loud complaints of ill usage upon Lake Champlain. His bravery was well known, and the proposed expedition was exactly suited to his adventurous disposition. To silence his complaints and to secure his services, Washington appointed him to the command of that perilous expedition, and at the same time gave him a commission of colonel in the Continental army. Eleven hundred hardy men were detached for the service from the army, consisting of ten companies of musketeers from New England and three companies of riflemen from Virginia and Pennsylvania. Arnold's field officers were Lieutenant-colonel Christopher Greene (the hero of Red Bank, on the Delaware), Lieutenant-colonel Roger Enos, and Majors Meigs and Bigelow. The riflemen were commanded by Captain Daniel Morgan, the renowned partisan leader in subsequent years of the war.

Arnold and his troops marched from Cambridge to Newburyport, where they embarked September 18. on board eleven transports for the mouth of the Kennebec. They reached Gardiner in safety, and found two hundred bateaux ready for them at Pittston, on the opposite side of the river. Carpenters had been previously sent to construct

---

[1] Artemas Ward was a native of Massachusetts, and graduated at Harvard in 1748. He was successively a representative in the Legislature and member of the Council of his state. He was also a justice of the Court of Common Pleas for Worcester county. Having considerable military knowledge, he was chosen to command the army that gathered around Boston in the spring of 1775. Congress appointed him the first of the four major generals under Washington, and to him was assigned the division of the army at Roxbury, when the siege of Boston, in 1776, took place. He resigned his commission a month after that event, yet, at the request of Washington, he continued in command till toward the last of May. He was a member of Congress under the Confederation, and also after the adoption of the present Constitution. He died at Shrewsbury in 1800, aged 73 years.

[2] Four major generals and eight brigadiers were appointed at the same time. To the former rank were chosen Artemas Ward, Charles Lee, Philip Schuyler, and Israel Putnam (the Major Putnam in the French and Indian war) ; to the latter, Seth Pomeroy (supposed to be the soldier who shot Dieskau), Richard Montgomery, David Wooster, William Heath, Joseph Spencer, John Thomas, John Sullivan, and Nathaniel Greene. Horatio Gates was appointed adjutant general, with the rank of brigadier.

these vessels.   The troops then rendezvoused at Fort Western, opposite the present town of Augusta.   This was on the verge of an uninhabited and almost unexplored wilderness,[1] and toward its fearful shadows these brave men turned their faces.

A small reconnoitering party was sent in advance to Lake Megantic, or Chaudière Pond, and another to survey the course and distances of the Dead River, a tributary of the Kennebec. The main body moved forward in four divisions, a day apart in time.   Morgan, with the riflemen, was in the van ; next were Greene and Bigelow, with their companies of musketeers ; Meigs, with four other companies, followed, and the rear was brought up by Enos, with three remaining companies.   Arnold was the last to leave Fort Western.   He proceeded in a birch canoe, passed the several parties, and overtook Morgan on the third day at Norridgewock Falls.   Here, upon a beautiful plain on the eastern bank of the river, the ancient Norridgewock Indians, a tribe of the ABENAKES, had a village, and in the midst of the grandeur, beauty, and fertility of nature, and the barbarous heathenism of man in this picturesque region, Father Ralle, a French Jesuit, had erected a Christian altar, and taught the sublime truths of the Gospel.[2]

Here the first severe toils of the little army began, for they were obliged to carry all their bateaux, provisions, and stores around the falls, a mile and a quarter, into the navigable waters above.   The banks were rocky and precipitous.   They found, too, that their boats were leaky, and much of their provisions was spoiled or greatly damaged. Seven days were consumed in passing the falls and repairing the

NORRIDGEWOCK FALLS, 1775.

vessels.   The same labor, though not so fatiguing, was demanded at the Carratunc Falls.

[1] Colonel Montressor, a British officer, had traversed the wilderness fifteen years before.   He ascended the Chaudière from Quebec, crossed the Highlands near the head waters of the Penobscot, passed through Moose-head Lake, and entered the eastern branch of the Kennebec.   Arnold possessed an imperfect copy of the printed journal of Montressor, and this, with information received from some St. Francis Indians who visited Washington's camp, gave him an idea of the country and the privations his men must suffer.

The same region was traversed by a French missionary named *Dreuillettes*, more than two hundred years before.   He crossed the St. Lawrence to the sources of the Kennebec, down which river he descended to its mouth, and thence coasted eastward to the missionary station on the Penobscot.—*Hildreth*, ii., 84.

[2] Father Ralle resided among the Norridgewocks twenty-six years, and possessed great influence over them.   He was considered an enemy to the British settlers in Massachusetts, and an expedition was planned against him and the settlement.   A party fell upon them suddenly, and killed and scalped the priest and thirty of the Indians.   This event occurred in 1724, and when Colonel Arnold was there, in 1775, the

Desertions and sickness reduced their number to about nine hundred and fifty effective men when they arrived at the great carrying-place, twelve miles below the junction of Dead River with the Kennebec.   So rapid was the stream, that the men waded more than half way, pushing the bateaux against the current ; yet they were in good spirits, and seemed to partake of the enthusiasm of their leader.

Arnold now examined his muster-roll and commissariat.   The troops, though somewhat reduced in number, were strong and enthusiastic, and he ascertained that he had twenty-five days' provisions in store.   The Chaudière, on which were French settlements, he estimated to be at a distance of ten days' travel.   The weather was fine, and the prospect so encouraging that they pushed forward with alacrity.   The great carrying-place was a portage of fifteen miles, broken by three ponds.   Oxen dragged the bateaux part of the way on sleds, and the baggage and stores were carried on the shoulders of the men.   Over craggy knolls and tangled ravines, through deep morasses, creeks, and ponds, they pursued their journey, sometimes carrying their vessels and the vessels sometimes bearing them, until they reached the Dead River.   The ponds afforded an abundance of delicious salmon-trout, and want of food had not yet been among their privations.   The surface of the Dead River was smooth, and the waters flowed on in a gentle current in the midst of the magnificent forest, now rendered gorgeous by the brilliant hues imparted to the foliage by early frost.   Occasional falls interrupted their progress, but the labors of the men were far less severe than hitherto.   Suddenly the monotony of the vast forest was broken by the appearance of a lofty mountain covered with snow, at the foot of which Arnold encamped three days, raising the Continental flag over his tent.[1]   A small hamlet called Flag-staff, in commemoration of the event, is upon the camp-ground, and the lofty eminence bears the name of Mount Bigelow.[2]

When the expedition moved forward, a heavy rain set in, which sent down such torrents from the hills that the river arose eight feet in one night, overflowing its banks and filling its channels with rafts of drift wood.   So suddenly did this freshet occur, that the water came roaring down the valley where the soldiers were encamped, so unexpectedly and powerfully that they had barely time to retreat to their bateaux before the whole plain was overflowed.   Seven boats were overturned and the provisions lost, and others were in imminent peril in the midst of the flood.   They were yet thirty miles from the head of the Chaudière, and but about twelve days' provisions remained.   The storm and exposure made many sick, and despondency supplanted cheerfulness, for the future seemed pregnant with misery.   A council of war was held, and it was decided to send the sick and feeble back, and to press forward with the healthy.   Arnold wrote to Greene and Enos, who were in the rear, to select as many of their best men as they could supply with fifteen days' provisions, and come on with them, leaving the others to return to Norridgewock.   Enos, either through a false construction of the order or willful disobedience, returned to Cambridge with his whole division.   His appearance excited the greatest indignation in the Continental camp, and Enos was looked upon as a traitor for thus deserting his companions and endangering the whole expedition.   He was tried by a court-martial, and it being proved that he was short of provisions, and that none could be procured in the wilderness, he was acquitted.   He never was restored in public estimation, however, and soon afterward left the army.

In the mean while Arnold, with the rest of the troops, pressed onward.   The rain changed to snow, and ice formed upon the water in which the men waded to push the bateaux as

foundations of the church and altar were still visible, but the red men had forever departed.   Father Ralle left a manuscript dictionary of the Abenake language (the dialect of the Norridgewocks), which is preserved in the library of Harvard University.

[1] What the device on this flag, or what its color was, we have no means of ascertaining.   The stripes and stars were not used until 1777.   On the 14th of June that year, Congress " resolved that the flag of the thirteen United States be thirteen stripes, alternate red and white ; that the Union be thirteen stars, white in a blue field, representing a new constellation."   Since then we have added a star for every new state.

[2] Tradition asserts that, while the Americans encamped there, Major Bigelow ascended to the summit of the mountain, with the expectation of seeing the spires of Quebec !   From this supposed adventure the mountain derives its name.

OF THE REVOLUTION.　　193

Lake Megantic and the Chaudière.　　Perilous Voyage.　　Narrow Escape.　　Sertigan.　　Timely Relief for the Troops.

they passed the numerous ponds and marshes near the sources of the Dead River.　Seventeen falls were passed, and on a bleak day, marching through snow two inches deep, they reached the Highlands which separated the waters of New England from Canada.　A portage of four miles brought them to a small stream, down which they pushed their vessels and reached Lake Megantic, the great source of the Chaudière.　There they found Lieutenants Steele and Church, who had been sent forward from the great carrying-place to explore and clear the portages.　Here also was Jakins, who had been sent to the French settlers on the Chaudière to ascertain their political sentiments, which he reported to be favorable.[1]

The little army encamped on the eastern shore of the lake, and the next morning Arnold, with a party of fifty-five men on shore, under Captain Hanchet, and ^October 29.

thirteen men with himself, in five bateaux and a birch canoe, pushed onward down the Chaudière to the French settlements, there to obtain provisions and send them back to meet the main forces.　It was a fearful voyage.　As soon as they left the lake and ^October 27, entered the river, the current ran with great rapidity, boil-^1775. ing and foaming over a rocky bottom.　They had no guide.　They lashed their baggage and provisions to the bateaux and committed themselves to the mercy of the stream.　At length the fearful roar of rushing waters met their ears, and in a few minutes they were plunging amid rapids.　Three of the boats were dashed in pieces upon the rocks and their contents ingulfed, but, fortunately, no lives were lost.　Six men struggled long in the waters, but were saved.　The other bateaux were moored in shallow estuaries, while aid was rendered to those in the stream, and this proved the salvation of the whole party.　The apparent calamity was a mercy in disguise, for had they not been thus checked, they must all have plunged into destruction over a fall just beyond, which was discovered by one of the rescued men.　For seventy miles falls and rapids succeeded each other, but the voyagers reached Sertigan (four miles below the mouth of Des Louis), the first French settlement, in safety.　The people ^October 30 were friendly, and sold provisions freely.　As soon as the wants of his own party were supplied, Arnold sent back some Canadians and Indians with flour and cattle for the approaching troops, who were in great distress, all their boats having been destroyed, with their provisions.　They had slaughtered their last ox several days before.　In a few days the whole army emerged in detachments from the forests, and united at Sertigan.[2]

ROUTE THROUGH THE WILDERNESS.

[1] Two Indians were sent forward with Jakins to carry letters, one to General Schuyler on Lake Champlain, the other to some persons in Quebec.　They betrayed their trusts, for the latter, named Eneas, was known to have reached Quebec, but the letters went into the hands of Lieutenant-governor Carmahé instead of those for whom they were intended.　The letters to General Schuyler never reached him.

[2] Judge Henry, who at the close of the last century was president of the second judicial district in Pennsylvania, was one of the soldiers in this expedition, and has left behind him a lucid and exceedingly interesting narrative of the "hardships and sufferings of that band of heroes."　In reference to the destitute condition of the troops before food was sent back from Sertigan, he says, "Coming to a low, sandy beach of the Chaudière, for we sometimes had such, some of our companies were observed to dart from the file, and with their nails tear out of the sands roots which they esteemed eatable, and ate them raw, even without washing.　The knowing one sprang; half a dozen followed; he who obtained it ate the root instantly. . . . . . They washed their moose-skin moccasins in the river, scraping away the dirt and sand with great care.　These were brought to the kettle and boiled a considerable time, under the vague but consolatory hope that a mucilage would take place.　The poor fellows chewed the leather, but it was leather still.　They had not received food for the last forty-eight hours.　Disconsolate and weary we passed the night."　A dog was killed and furnished material for broth, but starvation would have destroyed them all in a few days.*

* "My dog was very large and a great favorite.　I gave him up to several men of Captain Goodrich's company.　They carried him to their company, and killed and divided him among those who were suffering most severely from hunger.　They ate t every part of him, not excepting his entrails."—Letter of General Dearborn to the Rev. William Allen.

The beautiful valley of the Chaudière was now before them, enlivened with a friendly population and blessed with abundance of provisions. Arnold had been furnished with printed copies, in French, of a manifesto by Washington, to be distributed among the people. It explained the causes of the contest, and asked them, as neighbors and friends, to join the standard of liberty. Arnold, with great discretion, circulated these freely, at the same time acquiescing in the wishes of Washington by treating the inhabitants with the greatest respect. Every thing received from them was paid for, and they rendered aid in return with a hearty good will.[1]

About forty Indians of the Norridgewocks, under the famous *Natanis* and his brother *Sabatis*, here joined the Americans, and on the 9th of November the whole army that remained arrived at Point Levi, opposite Quebec, after one of the most wonderful marches on record, during the space of two months. Thirty-two days they traversed the gloomy wilderness without meeting a human being. Frost and snow were upon the ground, and ice was upon the surface of the marshes and streams, which they were obliged to traverse and ford, sometimes armpit deep in water and mud; yet they murmured not, and even women followed in the train of the suffering patriots.[2] It was an effort in the cause of freedom worthy of its divine character; and the men who thus periled life and endured pain, whatever may have been their course in after life, deserve the highest praise from the hearts and lips of posterity.[3]

---

[1] I met a gentleman at Quebec (August, 1848) who had just made a journey across the country from the Kennebec to the St. Lawrence by the way of the Chaudière. He said that many of the old *habitans* were still living in that beautiful valley, and spoke very highly of the "good Bostonians," whose passage through their country was one of the greatest events in the quiet lives of those isolated and simple people. He showed me an order for flour and cattle, signed by Arnold at Sertigan, which he procured from an old man 93 years of age. Many documents of the kind are, he said, preserved in the families of the old settlers.

[2] Judge Henry speaks of two women, the wives of soldiers attached to the division of the army to which he belonged. Their names deserve preservation for the admiration of posterity. "One was the wife of Sergeant Grier, a large, virtuous, and respectable woman." The other was the wife of a private soldier named Warner. Judge H. says, in reference to their march through the wet country near Megantic Lake, "Entering the ponds, and breaking the ice here and there with the butts of our guns and feet, we were soon waist deep in mud and water. As is generally the case with youths, it came to my mind that a better path might be found than that of the more elderly guide. Attempting this, the water in a trice cooling my armpits, made me gladly return in the file. Now Mrs. Grier had got before me. My mind was humbled, yet astonished, at the exertions of this good woman. Her clothes more than waist high, she waded on before me to firm ground. Not one, so long as she was known to us, dared to intimate a disrespectful idea of her."

[3] Those most prominent afterward in the history of our country, who accompanied Arnold on that expedition, were Morgan, Greene, Dearborn, Febiger, Meigs, and Burr. "Here it was" (near Sertigan), says Judge Henry, "that, for the first time. Aaron Burr. a most amiable youth of twenty, came to my view. He was then a cadet."

OF THE REVOLUTION.   195

American Army at Point Levi.   Alarm of the Canadians.   Storm on the St. Lawrence.   Passage of the Army.

CHAPTER IX.

" Oh, few and weak their numbers were,
     A handful of brave men;
But to their God they gave their prayer,
     And rush'd to battle then.
They left the plowshare in the mold,
Their flocks and herds without a fold,
The sickle in the unshorn grain,
The corn half garner'd on the plain,
And muster'd in their simple dress
For wrongs to seek a stern redress—
To right those wrongs, come weal, come wo,
To perish or o'ercome their foe."
                                        M'LELLAN.

UCH were the men who followed the bold Arnold, through terrible difficulties and privations, from their quiet homes in New England, and, in the midst of light falling snow, appeared like a specter army on the heights of Point Levi, to the wondering people of Quebec.   Through the treachery of the Indian Eneas (who pretended to have been taken prisoner), Cramahé and his council knew that a small American force was in the wilderness, but they would not believe that it would ever reach Quebec; therefore the fact was not made known to the military or the people.   They had taken the precaution, however, to keep all boats on the Quebec side of the river.   It was about eight o'clock in the morning when Arnold and his followers emerged from the forest and displayed upon the banks of the St. Lawrence.   Quebec was at once in a tumult.   The drums beat to arms, and the Canadians were terribly alarmed Some near Point Levi had fled across to the city, and their fears caused them to greatly magnify the number and character of the Americans.   By a mistake of a single word the fears of the people were greatly increased, for the news spread that the mysterious army that descended from the wilderness was clad in *sheet iron*.[1]

Arnold resolved to cross the river immediately, and found means to communicate his intentions to his friends in Quebec.[2]   But for several days and nights a tempest of wind and sleet raged upon the St. Lawrence, and he was obliged to wait its pleasure at Point Levi. In the mean while the garrison of the city was strengthened by troops from Sorel, under M'Lean, and the prospect of success for the patriots was proportionably lessened.   At length the wind ceased.   Between thirty and forty birch canoes were procured, and about nine o'clock in the evening of the 13th the first division crossed; before daylight five hundred Americans landed safely, and rendezvoused at Wolfe's Cove.   The enemy had placed a frigate (the Lizzard) and a sloop in the river, to intercept them, but the vigilance of these they eluded until just as the last party passed a guard-boat.   One hundred and fifty men were at Point Levi, but it was too late to return for them.   No time was

November, 1775

---

[1] Morgan's riflemen wore linen frocks, their common uniform.   The Canadians, who first saw these emerge from the woods, said they were *vêtu en toile*—clothed in linen cloth.   The word *toile* was changed to *tole*, iron plate.

[2] In earlier life Arnold was engaged in trafficking in horses, and shipped many for the West Indies.   He visited Quebec several times to procure stock, and thus became well acquainted with the place and many people there.   His knowledge of the city and vicinity was doubtless one cause that led to his appointment to the command of the expedition.

to be lost, for the garrison would soon be alarmed.   Arnold, placing himself at the head of his little band of heroes, scaled the heights where Wolfe had ascended sixteen years before, and at dawn they stood upon the lofty Plains of Abraham.   That goal where glory was to be won and freedom vindicated, which had lured them from the camp at Cambridge, and haunted them in their disturbed dreams amid the perils of the wilderness, was now befo.ε the zealous patriots; but their hearts sank, and the whisperings of hope were like the breathings of despair, when they saw the dark castle and the massy walls that inclosed the garrison of the enemy.   They numbered only seven hundred and fifty men.   They had no artillery, and nearly half their muskets were rendered useless during their march through the wilderness.   They learned, too, that troops from Sorel and Newfoundland had been added to the garrison, making an attack upon the town a hopeless waste of effort.[1]   But Arnold relied upon the friendly disposition of the Canadian militia and the people of the city, and, to ascertain their feelings, he drew up his men within eight hundred yards of the walls and gave three cheers, hoping that the regulars would sally out to attack them, and that then, the gates being unclosed, he might rush in, and, by the aid of friends within, secure the city. The parapets of the walls were lined by hundreds of the people, and many of them huzzaed in return.   Several guns were fired by the Americans, but without effect.   The British at length brought a thirty-two pounder to bear upon the patriots, but not a shot injured them. Lieutenant-governor Cramahé and M'Lean were too wary to be lured into such a snare as making a sortie, for they knew well the disloyalty of the French citizens and most of the leading men of Quebec.   The English citizens were much dissatisfied with the French laws that had governed them since the passage of the "Quebec Bill," the previous year.

1774.   The French, on the other hand, though petted, so as to be won, could not forget their ancient national animosities, and were willing to see the English discomfited.   The unruly conduct of the soldiery had also disgusted the people, and some were loud in their complaints against Carleton and his deputy, for exposing Quebec, by withdrawing its garrison when Montreal was threatened.   The Royal Scotch, under M'Lean, were all that could be certainly relied upon.   These elements of disaffection combined, made the force in the city, securely sheltered, quite inactive, for M'Lean well knew that Arnold's little army was too weak to attempt an assault, and he felt sure that the fierce winter winds and driving snow would soon force them from their bleak encampment.

Finding his attempts vain, by frequent hostile displays upon the heights, to draw out the garrison, Arnold, in accordance with military usage, sent a flag to M'Lean, with a formal summons to surrender, threatening him with terrible disasters if he refused.   The movement was exceedingly ridiculous, and was not only treated with utter contempt by the British commander, but the bearer was fired upon.[2]   About this time Arnold learned that Carleton, who had fled from Montreal, was approaching Quebec.   He also inspected his ammunition and stores, and to his surprise found that nearly all the cartridges were spoiled, hardly five rounds to a man being left fit for use.   Learning, also, from his friends in the city, that a sortie was about to be made, he broke up his camp and retreated to *Point aux Trembles*, twenty miles above Quebec, to await the approaching troops of Montgomery.   On his arrival at *Aux Trembles*, Arnold was informed that Carleton had gone from that place but a few hours before, and shortly afterward was heard the cannonading at Quebec that welcomed his

---

[1] The garrison, including the regulars and militia within the town, and the marines in the ships, was about eighteen hundred strong.   Surprise has been expressed that these did not march out and destroy the feeble force of the Americans.   The obvious reason was, that the majority of the garrison troops were militia, and supposed to be ready to join the Americans in the event of a battle.

[2] "It must be confessed," says Judge Henry, "that this ridiculous affair gave me a contemptible opinion of Arnold.   Morgan, Febiger, and other officers did not hesitate to speak of it in that point of view.   However, Arnold had a vain desire to gratify.   He was well known at Quebec.   Formerly, he had traded from this port to the West Indies, most particularly in the article of horses; hence he was despised by the principal people.   The epithet of *horse-jockey* was freely and universally bestowed upon him by the British. Having now obtained power, he became anxious to display it in the faces of those who had formerly despised and contemned him."

return to the city.　Montgomery landed at *Point aux Trembles* on the 1st of December, his troops, by sickness and desertion, reduced to a mere handful.　There he took command of the combined troops, amounting to only about nine hundred effective men.　He brought clothing from Montreal for Arnold's half-naked troops.　The next day, in the face of a driving snow-storm, they started for Quebec, and arrived in sight of the city on the 5th.　Their march was slow and excessively fatiguing, for the snow was deep, and drifted high in the roads.　Montgomery established his headquarters at Holland House, and Arnold occupied a house near Scott's Bridge.　The Americans were chiefly encamped near the Intendant's Palace, by the St. Charles, in the suburb St. Roche.

The American forces were considerably inferior in numbers to those of the garrison, but this was unknown within the city.　Montgomery endeavored to send a summons to surrender, but Carleton would not allow a flag to approach the walls.　At length a letter was conveyed by a citizen to Governor Carleton, in which Montgomery demanded an immediate surrender, at the same time magnifying the number of his followers, and threatening all the calamities of an assault.　Although Carleton thought Montgomery's army larger than it really was, he was not easily frightened.　Montgomery, like Arnold, counted upon friends within the city, but they were paralyzed by the presence of troops, and dared do nothing favorable to the besiegers.　With no other ordnance than some light cannon and a few mortars, a feeble, ill-clad, and ill-fed army, exposed to the severest frost in the open fields, and snow falling almost constantly, the American commander nearly despaired of success ; yet the love of his adopted country, and thoughts of the depression of spirit throughout the colonies which a failure would produce, moved him to extraordinary efforts.　He resolved to annoy the people into submission by harassing attacks upon the city, and accordingly attempted to throw bombs over the walls.　These efforts were unavailing, and he then erected a six-gun battery upon some heaps of snow and ice within seven hundred yards of the walls, but his guns were too light for any efficiency.　Nearly three weeks were thus consumed in unavailing attempts to make an entrance.　Mutinous murmurs were audible in the camp, the term of service of many of the troops had nearly expired, the small-pox appeared among the soldiers, and the general looked for a speedy dissolution of his whole army.

Perils were gathering a fearful web around the brave Montgomery.　He called a council of war, and it was resolved, as a last resort, to make a regular assault upon the town at different points.　The troops were accordingly ordered to parade in three divisions at two o'clock on the morning of the 31st of December.　All obeyed with alacrity, except three companies of Arnold's detachment, whose term of service was about expiring.　They threatened to leave the army at once unless transferred to another command, but the firmness and wisdom of Montgomery restored order, and they took their places in the ranks.[1]　The New York regiments and a part of Easton's militia paraded at Holland House, under the immediate command of Montgomery ; the Cambridge detachment and Colonel Lamb's company of artillerists, with one field piece, at Morgan's quarters ; and the two small corps of Livingston and Brown at their respective parade-grounds.　The plan was, for the first and second divisions to assault the lower town on opposite sides, and the third, under Livingston and Brown, to make feigned attacks, from the Plains of Abraham, upon the upper town, in the neighborhood of St. John's and St. Louis Gates and Cape Diamond Bastion.

Montgomery, at the head of the first division, descended from the Plains of Abraham to Wolfe's Cove, south of the city, and commenced his march toward the lower town by a road (now Champlain Street) that ran along the margin of the river, under Cape Diamond.　Ar-

1775

December 2

1775.

---

[1] The cause of this outbreak is not known.　Montgomery, in a letter to Schuyler (the last he ever wrote), spoke of the occurrence, and intimated that Major Brown was at the bottom of it.　He promised a full explanation in his next, but, alas ! " the next" was never written.　It appears that Arnold had quarreled with Hanchet, one of his captains, before reaching Point Levi, and two others took sides with the captain.　Brown and Arnold had quarreled at Ticonderoga, and it is supposed that the former took this opportunity to gall Arnold, by widening the breach between him and his captains, and endeavoring to get them detached from Arnold's command and joined to his own.

nold, at the head of the second division, advanced from the general hospital, around the

ST. JOHN'S GATE, OUTSIDE.

north side of the town, on the St. Charles.   Both parties were to meet at Mountain Street, and force Prescott Gate. The snow was falling fast, and furious winds were piling it in frightful drifts.   Cautiously Montgomery led his men in the dark toward the narrowest point under Cape Diamond, called *Pres de Ville*, where the enemy had planted a battery of three pounders.[1]   This post was in charge of a captain of Canadian militia, with thirty-eight men, and nine British seamen, under Captain Barnsfare, master of a transport, to work the guns.   On the river side was a precipice, and on the left the rough crags of dark slate towered far above him.   When within fifty yards of the battery, the Americans halted to reconnoiter.   The guard at the battery and the artillerymen with lighted matches were perfectly silent, and Montgomery concluded that they were not on the alert. But Barnsfare, through the dim light of early dawn and the drifting snow, saw faintly their movements.   Montgomery, in the van of his troops, cried out, "Men of New York, you will not fear to follow where your general leads.   March on!" and rushed boldly over heaps of ice and snow to charge the battery.   At that moment, when the Americans were within forty paces, Captain Barnsfare gave the word, the match was applied, and a discharge of grape-shot swept the American column with terrible effect.   Montgomery, Major McPhunn his aid, and Captain Cheeseman were killed, together with several privates near.   The rest, appalled at the dreadful havoc and the death of their general, fled in confusion back to Wolfe's Cove, where Colonel Campbell took the command, but made no further attempts to force a junction with Arnold.   Ten minutes the battery belched its iron storm in the dim space, but, after the first discharge, there was no enemy there to slaughter.

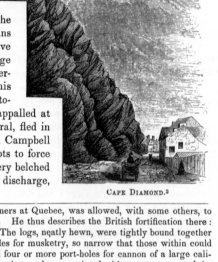

CAPE DIAMOND.[2]

---

[1] Judge Henry, who was one of the American prisoners at Quebec, was allowed, with some others, to go out and see the place where Montgomery was slain.   He thus describes the British fortification there: It was a sort of block-house forty or fifty feet square.   The logs, neatly hewn, were tightly bound together by dove-tail work.   The lower story contained loop-holes for musketry, so narrow that those within could not be harmed by those without.   The upper story had four or more port-holes for cannon of a large caliber.   These guns were charged with grape and canister shot, and were pointed with exactness toward the avenue at Cape Diamond.   The block-house seemed to take up the space between the foot of the hill and the river, leaving only a cart-way on each side.   The bulwarks of the city came only to the edge of the hill, above that place; hence down the side of the precipice, slantingly to the brink of the river, there was a stockade of strong posts fifteen or twenty feet high, knit together by a stout railing at bottom and top with pins.   It was asserted that Montgomery sawed four of these posts himself, so as to admit four men abreast to attack the block-house.

[2] This is a view of the spot where Montgomery was killed.   The cliff is Cape Diamond, crowned with the citadel.   The street at the foot of it is called Champlain, and is inhabited chiefly by a mixed population of French, Canadians, and Irish.   It extends from Mountain Street south almost to Wolfe's Cove.   This view is from Champlain Street, a few rods south of *Près de Ville*, looking north.   High upon the rocks Alfred Hawkins, Esq., of Quebec, has placed a board with this inscription: "HERE MAJOR-GENERAL MONTGOMERY FELL, DECEMBER 31ST, 1775."

While this dreadful scene was in progress at Cape Diamond, Arnold, at the head of the second division, was pressing onward along the St. Charles, where the snow was worse drifted than on the St. Lawrence. He led his men in files until he reached the narrow street called

Sault au Matelot, where, under a high, jutting rock, the enemy had a two-gun picketed battery, well manned. Like Montgomery, he headed his men, and, while leading Lamb's artillery to the attack upon the barrier, was completely disabled by a musket-wound in the knee, and was carried back to the general hospital, where he heard of the death of Montgomery. The command of his division now devolved upon Morgan, and for more than an hour the Americans withstood the storm of grape-shot and musket-balls at the first barrier, and finally carried it, for the deadly aim of the riflemen caused great consternation in the ranks of the enemy. Passing the first barrier, the patriots rushed on to the second, which commanded both *Sault au Matelot* and St. Peter's Streets. The defenses here extended from the cliff to the river ; and the present custom-house, then a private dwelling, had cannons projecting from the windows of the gable. Here a fierce contest of three hours ensued, and many were killed on both sides. At length the Americans took shelter from the fire of the battery, in the houses on both sides of the street, and in the narrow pass that leads up to Hope Gate. The English and Canadians

PLACE WHERE ARNOLD WAS WOUNDED.[1]

already occupied houses near, and the patriots were terribly galled on all sides, and from the walls of the city above them. Captain Lamb was severely wounded by a grape-shot, which carried away a part of his cheek-bone, and other officers were more or less injured. The Americans finally captured the barrier, and were preparing to rush into the town, when Carleton sent a large detachment from the garrison, through Palace Gate, to attack them in the rear. The news of the death of Montgomery and the retreat of his detachment gave the people and the troops within the walls fresh courage. Captain Dearborn, with some provincials, was stationed near Palace Gate, and was completely surprised when its leaves were thrown open and the troops rushed out. It was a movement entirely unlooked for ; and so suddenly and in such overwhelming force did the enemy pour upon them, that they were obliged to surrender.

PALACE GATE, OUTSIDE.[2]

While Morgan was pressing on vigorously into the town, he heard of the death of Montgomery, the capture of Dearborn and his company, and the advance of the enemy in his rear. Surrounded by foes on all sides, and every support cut off,

---

[1] This view is in a narrow alley near the north end of *Sault au Matelot* Street, in the rear of St. Paul's Street. At the time in question St. Paul's Street did not exist, and the water, at high tide, came nearly up to the precipice. The first barrier and battery extended from the jutting rock seen in the picture, to the water. The present alley was then the beach. The circular wall on the top of the rock is a part of the grand battery, one of the most formidable and commanding defenses in the world.

[2] This is one of the most beautiful gates of the city, and opens toward the St. Charles, on the northern side of the town. A strong guard-house is seen at the left, pierced for muskets to defend the entrance. Immediately adjoining this gate are the artillery barracks. The gate is at the northern extremity of Palace Street, one of the broadest in the city, and "so named," says Hawkins, "from the circumstance that it led out to the Intendant's house, or palace, which stood on the beach of the St. Charles, where the queen's wood-yard now is."

the patriots yielded, and surrendered themselves prisoners of war.[1] The remainder of the division in the rear retreated to their camp, leaving behind them one field piece and some mortars in a battery at St. Roche.   The whole loss of the Americans at Cape Diamond and *Sault au Matelot*, in killed and wounded, was about one hundred and sixty.   The British loss was only about twenty killed and wounded.

As soon as hostilities ceased, search was made for the bodies of those who fell with Montgomery. Thirteen were found nearly buried in the snow, and with them was Montgomery's orderly sergeant, dreadfully wounded, but alive.   The sergeant would not acknowledge that his general was killed, and persisted in his silence until he died, an hour afterward.   For several hours Carleton was uncertain whether the general was slain ; but a field officer among the captured troops of Arnold's division recognized the body of the young hero among those in the guard-house, and, it is said, he there pronounced a most touching eulogium on the bravery and worth of the deceased, while tears of grief coursed down his cheeks.[2]   Cramahé, the lieutenant governor, who had known Montgomery years before, took charge of the body, and it was buried within a wall that surrounded a powder magazine, near the ramparts bounding on St. Louis Street, where it remained forty-two years.[3]   It has been well observed that it would be difficult to select, from so small a body of men as that engaged in besieging Quebec, so large a number who afterward distinguished themselves for patriotism and courage, as that little band presented.   Morgan and his rifle corps became world renowned.   Dearborn was distinguished

---

[1] The force that surrendered consisted of 1 lieutenant colonel, 2 majors, 8 captains, 15 lieutenants, 1 adjutant, 1 quartermaster, 4 volunteers, 350 rank and file, and 44 officers and soldiers, who were wounded, making a total of 426.   The prisoners were treated humanely.   The officers were confined in the seminary, the oldest literary institution in Quebec.   Major Meigs was sent out for the clothing and baggage of the prisoners, and all testified to the humanity of Carleton.

[2] Montgomery had a watch in his pocket which Mrs. M. was very desirous of obtaining.   She made her wishes known to Arnold, who sent word to Carleton that any sum would be paid for it.   Carleton immediately sent the watch to Arnold, and refused to receive any thing in return.

[3] Richard Montgomery was born in the north of Ireland in 1737.   He entered the army at the age of twenty, and was with Wolfe at the storming of Quebec in 1759.   He was in the campaign against the Spanish West Indies, and afterward resided some time in this country.   He quitted his regiment and returned to England.   While here he imbibed an attachment for the country, and in 1772, returned to make it his home.   He purchased an estate upon the Hudson, in Rhinebeck, Dutchess county, and married the daughter of Robert R. Livingston.   When the Revolution broke out, he espoused the cause of the colonists, and in the autumn of 1775 was second in command, under Schuyler, in the expedition against Canada, with the rank of brigadier.   The illness of Schuyler caused the chief command to devolve upon Montgomery, and in the capture of St. John's, Chambly, and Montreal, and his attack on Quebec, he exhibited great judgment and military skill.   He was commissioned a major general before he reached Quebec.   In that campaign he had every difficulty to contend with—undisciplined and mutinous troops, scarcity of provisions and ammunition, want of heavy artillery, lack of clothing, the rigor of winter, and desertions of whole companies.   Yet he pressed onward, and, in all probability, had his life been spared, would have entered Quebec in triumph.   His death was a great public calamity, and throughout the land public honors were paid to his memory.   The eloquence of Chatham, Burke, and Barrè sounded his praises upon the floor of the British Parliament, and the prime minister (Lord North), while acknowledging his worth, and reprobating the cause in which he fell, concluded by saying, "Curse on his virtues, they have undone his country."   As soon as the news of his death reached Congress, resolutions of condolence with his family for their bereavement, and expressive of their "grateful remembrance, profound respect, and high veneration," were adopted. It was voted to erect a monument to his memory, which was accordingly done, in the front of St. Paul's Church in New York city, on which is the following inscription :

as a skillful officer at Saratoga and other fields of the Revolution, and commanded the troops that captured York, in Upper Canada, in the spring of 1813. Meigs boldly attacked and destroyed shipping and stores at Sag Harbor, and of his regiment, and that of Febi- *April 27.* ger, were the forlorn hope at Stony Point. Greene's prowess and skill were well attested at Red Bank, on the Delaware. Thayer behaved nobly in defense of Fort Mifflin, opposite Red Bank. Lamb was distinguished at Compo, Fort Montgomery, and Yorktown. Oswald was at Compo, and fought bravely at Monmouth; and Poterfield was killed at Camden, in South Carolina, when Gates was so terribly defeated there. M'Pherson and Cheeseman,[1] Montgomery's aids, were brave and accomplished, and gave assurance of future renown; but they fell with their leader, and share with him the grateful reverence of posterity.

Colonel Arnold took command of the remnant of the patriot army after the death of Montgomery, and was promoted to the rank of brigadier general. He could muster only about eight hundred men; and, feeling unsafe in his camp under the walls of the city, he retired about three miles from the town, intrenched himself as well as circumstances would allow, and assumed the attitude of a blockade, hoping, by cutting off supplies for the city from the country, to bring the enemy to terms. Carleton, feeling secure within the walls, and expecting re-enforcements from England as soon as the ice should move out of the St. Law-

---

MONTGOMERY'S MONUMENT.

THIS
monument is erected by order of Congress,
25th of January, 1776,
to transmit to posterity a grateful remembrance of the patriotic conduct, enterprise, and perseverance
of *Major-general* RICHARD MONTGOMERY,
who, after a series of success amid the most discouraging difficulties, *Fell* in the attack on
QUEBEC, 31st December, 1775, aged 37 years.

In 1818 a request in behalf of the widow of General Montgomery was made to the Governor-in-chief of Canada, Sir John Sherbrooke, to allow his remains to be disinterred and conveyed to New York. The request was readily acceded to, and Mr. James Thompson, of Quebec, who was one of the engineers at the time of the storming of the city, and assisted in burying the general, also assisted in the disinterment, making an affidavit to the identity of the body. He said, in his affidavit, that the body was taken to the house of Mr. Gobert, and placed in a coffin lined with flannel and covered with black cloth; that Rev. Mr. de Montmolin, chaplain to the garrison, performed the funeral service; that Montgomery's aids (M'Pherson and Cheeseman) were buried in their clothes, without coffins; and that he (Thompson) afterward wore Montgomery's sword, but the American prisoners were so affected by the sight of it, that he laid it aside. He identified the coffin taken up on the 16th of June, 1818, as the one. The remains were placed in another coffin and deposited beneath the monument. The following is the inscription upon a silver plate on the coffin: "The state of New York, in honor of General Richard Montgomery, who fell gloriously fighting for the independence and liberty of the United States before the walls of Quebec, the 31st of December, 1775, caused these remains of the distinguished hero to be conveyed from Quebec, and deposited, on the 8th day of July (1818), in St. Paul's Church, in the city of New York, near the monument erected to his memory by the United States."

General Montgomery left no children whom "the state, in gratitude toward their father, distinguished with every mark of kindness and protection," as Botta asserts. His widow survived him more than half a century. When at the house of his brother-in-law, the late Peter R. Livingston, at Rhinebeck, a few years ago, I saw an interesting memento of the lamented general. A day or two before he left home to join the army under Schuyler, he was walking on the lawn in the rear of his brother-in-law's mansion with the owner, and as they came near the house, Montgomery stuck a willow twig in the ground, and said, "Peter, let that grow to remember me by." It did grow, and is now a willow with a trunk at least ten feet in circumference.

[1] This officer had a presentiment that he should not survive the battle. When preparing to go forth on that stormy December morning, he dressed himself with more care than usual, and putting a considerable sum of money, in gold, in his pocket, remarked, with a smile, "This will insure me a decent burial." He was of the New York line. A sergeant and eleven men fell with him. He was not instantly killed, but arose to press forward to charge the battery. It was a feeble effort, and he fell back a corpse, in a winding-sheet of snow.

rence, remained quiet; and in this relative position the belligerents continued until the 1st of April, when General Wooster, who had remained inactive all winter in Montreal, came down, and, being superior in rank to Arnold, took the chief command. The force which he brought with him, and the small addition made by troops that reached the encampment from New England during the winter, and Canadian recruits, swelled the army to nearly three thousand, eight hundred of whom were sick with the small-pox, which raged terribly in the American camp.

Preparations were made to beleaguer the city at once. A battery was erected upon the Plains of Abraham, and another at Point Levi, and a cannonade was opened upon the town, but without effect. At that moment the falling of Arnold's horse upon his wounded leg so disabled him, that he was unfit for active service, and he asked and obtained leave from General Wooster (with whom he was upon unfriendly terms) to retire to Montreal. General Thomas, who was appointed to succeed Montgomery, arrived early in May, but Carleton having received re-enforcements under Burgoyne, the Americans were obliged to make a hasty retreat, leaving their stores and sick behind. The latter were kindly treated, and finally sent home. At the mouth of the Sorel the Americans were re-enforced, but they could not brave the power of the enemy. General Thomas died there of small-pox, and Sullivan succeeded to the command.[1] But Burgoyne, with a considerable force, was pressing forward, and ultimately, as we have noted in a preceding chapter, the patriots were driven out of Canada.

1776.

We have taken a long historic ramble; let us vary our pleasure by a ride to Montmorenci, and a visit to other celebrities about Quebec.

The morning was excessively hot when we left the city for the falls of the Montmorenci Our egress was from the Palace Gate, and with us was quite a train of vehicles destined for the same point. We passed through the suburb of St. Roche, in the lower town, and crossed over Dorchester Bridge, a noble structure which spans the St. Charles, a short distance below the site of the old bridge fortified by Montcalm. The distance from Quebec to the Montmorenci is between seven and eight miles. The road (McAdamized) is very good, and passes through a rich and thoroughly cultivated region. Like the road from St. John's to Chambly and Longueuil, it is so thickly strewn with farmhouses that we seemed to be in a suburban street the whole distance. The village of Beauport, an old town, where Montcalm's headquarters were, is about midway between the St. Charles and the Montmorenci, and, like other Lower Canadian

PALACE GATE, INSIDE.[2]

villages, has an antiquated appearance. Between Quebec and Beauport we passed a large gilt cross reared upon the top of a beautiful Corinthian column, painted white, green, and vermilion. It was erected, as we were told, by some priests in Quebec, and consecrated to the cause of temperance. A strong iron railing incloses it, except in front, where two or three steps lead to a platform at the foot of the column, whereon devout passers-by may kneel in prayer.

---

[1] John Thomas was descended from a respectable family of Plymouth, Massachusetts. He served, with reputation, in the French and Indian war. At the head of a regiment raised by himself in Kingston, Massachusetts, he marched to Roxbury in 1775, and joined the Continental army. Congress appointed him one of the first eight brigadier generals, and he commanded a division at the siege of Boston. In March, 1776, he was appointed a major general, and on the 1st of May following joined the army before Quebec. He died of small-pox, at Chambly, on the second of June. General Thomas was greatly beloved by his soldiers, and his judgment, prudence, and firmness commended him to Washington as one promising to do much for the cause of the colonists.

[2] This sketch is a view from within Palace Street, looking out upon the open country beyond the St Charles. The river, with a few masts, is seen just over the top of the gate. Adjoining the gate, on the right, is seen a portion of the guard-house.

After passing Beauport, we were beset by troops of urchins, who stood in groups making polite bows to win attention and coin, or ran beside the carriage with the speed of trotting horses, lustily crying out, with extended hand, " *un sou ! un sou !* " They were miniature Falstaffs in figure, some not more than four or five years old, with dark skins and lustrous black eyes. It was amusing to see their vigorous but good-natured scrambles for a *sou* when cast among them, and the persevering race of the unsuccessful for the next expected piece of copper. Many a dollar is thus scattered and picked up by the road side to Montmorenci, during " the season," for the amusement of the passengers and the comfort of the *habitans.*

We left our barouche on the south side of the Montmorenci, and crossing, upon a bridge, the turbulent stream that rushes, leaping and foaming among broken rocks, toward the cascade ust below, we paid a *sou* each to a pretty French girl who guarded a gate opening to a winding pathway through the fields to the margin of the bank a little below the falls. The path is down a gentle slope for several rods, and at almost every step the picturesque scenery of the cascade assumes a new aspect.

TEMPERANCE CROSS.

These falls, though much higher than those of Niagara, have none of the grandeur of that great wonder. Our first thought here is, How beautiful ' but when the eye and the ear are first impressed with the avalanche of waters at Niagara, the solemn thought is, How sublime and wonderful ! When we visited the Montmorenci, a long drought had greatly diminished the volume of its waters, yet it exhibited a scene strikingly picturesque and pleasing. For two or three hundred yards the river is confined in a narrow limestone bed,[1] whence it rushes with great velocity to the brink of the precipice, and leaps into a crescent-shaped bay of the St. Lawrence, more than two hundred feet below. There, at low tide, the bare rocks receive the flood, and send up clouds of spray a hundred feet or more, on which the rays of the evening sun often depict the beautiful bow. In front, cleaving the broad bosom of the St. Lawrence, is the Island of Orleans, a paradise of beauty in summer, and a place of much resort by the citizens of Quebec, particularly the English residents, who see in it much that resembles their " sweet Devonshire coast." Its length is nineteen miles, and its average breadth about five. A population of five thousand inhabit it, and its rich soil is thoroughly cultivated for the production of vegetables for the Quebec market. Beyond, on the right, is Point Levi, and up the St. Lawrence, glittering in the sun, lies Quebec. Grouping the beauties of the natural scenery, the historical associations, and the delights of a summer ride, a trip to Montmorenci is an event to be long remembered with pleasure. The sun was at meridian, and the mercury indicated ninety-

MONTMORENCI FALLS.

[1] The river, in this channel, is not more than twelve feet wide, and here the Natural Steps occur. They rise on one side of the stream like irregular stairs. They have been formed by the action of the water on the softer layers of limestone, and present a curiosity for the visitor.

three degrees in the shade. The points of view were sparsely shadowed by trees, and we tarried only long enough to glance at the beauties of the fall and steal its features with a pencil, and then returned to Quebec, where, before dinner, we visited several churches, the chapel of the *Ursuline Convent*,[1] the *Seminary of Quebec*,[2] the chapel of the *Hotel Dieu*,[3] and the citadel.

The citadel crowning Cape Diamond is a combination of powerful works. It is three hundred and fifty feet above the river, and is terminated on the east by a round tower, over which floats the national standard of England, the flag

> " That's braved, a thousand years,
> The battle and the breeze."

The approach to the citadel is by a winding road through the acclivity of the *glacis* from St. Louis Gate. It is foreign to my plan to notice in detail modern fortifications upon Revolutionary ground, and we will stop to consider only a few points of interest in this most perfect military work. The main entrance is through Dalhousie Gate, where we presented our *permit*, and were joined by a young Highland soldier to guide and guard us. On the top of *Dalhousie Bastion* is a covered way with a broad gravel walk, from which is obtained the finest view of the city, harbor, and surrounding country. The St. Charles is seen winding through a beautiful undulating plain, and the spires of Beauport, Charlesbourg, and Lorette with the white cottages around them, form a pleasing feature in the landscape. The citadel and its ravelins cover about forty acres; and the fortifications, consisting of bastions, curtains of solid masonry, and ramparts twenty-five to thirty feet in height, mounted with cannon, are continued entirely around the upper town. Upon the cliff called *Sault au Matelot* is the grand battery, of eighteen thirty-two pounders, commanding the basin and harbor below. At the different gates of the city sentinels are posted day and night, and in front of the jail and other public buildings the solemn march of military guards is seen The garrison at Quebec numbered about three thousand soldiers. Among them was the 79th regiment of Scotch Highlanders, lately from Gibraltar. They were six hundred strong, and, dressed in their picturesque costume, made a fine appearance. To a stranger the military forms a principal feature of Quebec, and the mind is constantly carried back to the era of Froissart, when " Everie fayre towne had strong high walls, and bowmen and spearmen were more numerous than all others."

We left the citadel, emerged from St. Louis Gate, and, after visiting the monument where " Wolfe died victorious," rode over the battle-ground upon the Plains of Abraham, and, crossing to the *St. Foix* Road, went into the country as far as Holland House (the headquarters of Montgomery), and then returned, pleased and wearied, to the Albion. We strolled at evening through the governor's garden, rested upon Durham Terrace (see view on page 185), which was crowded with promenaders, and, losing our way in trying to ferret out the Albion, found ourselves at Hope Gate, where a kind priest, in long black cassock and broad beaver, conducted us back to Palace Street.

I devoted the following day to business. Before breakfast I went to Durham Terrace,

---

[1] The Ursuline Convent is situated on Parloir Street, near the English Cathedral. Influenced by an appeal from the French Jesuits of Canada, a young widow of Alençon, named Madame *de la Peltrie*, resolved to devote her life and fortune to the work of establishing a convent in Quebec. She founded the Ursuline Convent in 1641. An excellent school for the education of females is attached to it. In the chapel, as already noticed, is an inscribed marble slab, in memory of Montcalm, whose body lies within the grounds of the institution.

[2] This literary institution was founded in 1633, by *De Laval de Montmorency*, the first bishop of Canada. The professors, and all attached to it, receive no money compensation; they are simply guarantied "food and raiment, in sickness and in health." The chapel contains several fine paintings. The library has nearly 10,000 volumes.

[3] The Hotel Dieu, a nunnery, stands between Palace and Hope Gates. It was founded in 1636, by the Duchess d'Aquillon, a niece of the famous Cardinal Richelieu. The cardinal was a libera benefactor of the establishment during his life. The chapel is plain, and has but a few paintings.

OF THE REVOLUTION. 205

Historical Localities at Quebec.   An alarmed Englishman.   Wolfe and Montcalm's Monument.   Departure for Montreal.

and sketched Point Levi and the adjacent scenery beyond the St. Lawrence ; and after receiving explicit directions respecting the various historical localities about the city from an old and intelligent resident, I procured a caleche and started in search of them, the result of which is given in the several sketches and the descriptions on preceding pages.   As the day advanced, the heat became almost intolerable, until we reached the cool retreats of Wolfe's Cove, where, in the shade of a maple that overhangs a bubbling spring, I loitered an hour, dreading my intended ramble over the Plains of Abraham above.   We slowly ascended the steep and winding road up Wolfe's Ravine (in pity for the poor horse, walking half the way), and at the top I dismissed the vehicle and went over the plains on foot.   Hardly a shrub breaks the smooth surface.   The ground slopes from the city, and only a few chimney-tops and a roof or two indicated the presence of a populous town.

While sketching the broken monument on the spot where Wolfe fell, a young Englishman, full of zeal for the perpetuity of British colonial rule, was a spectator, and was very inquisitive respecting my intentions.   With a pointer's keen perception, he determined my whereabout when at home, and of course looked upon me as a meddling foreigner.   He saw me using the pencil on Durham Terrace in the morning, and also happened to pass while I was delineating Palace Gate.   The idea of "horrible rebellion" and "Yankee sympathy" seemed to haunt his mind, and I fed his suspicions so bountifully with sinless fibs, that before I finished my sketch he started off for the city, fully impressed with the notion that he had discovered an emissary from the War Department at Washington, collecting military data preparatory to an invasion of her majesty's dominions !   I soon followed him, glad to escape from the burning heat upon the plains, and took shelter under the lofty trees in the governor's garden, near the citadel, a delightful public promenade on the west side of *Des Carrieres* Street.   In the garden, near the street, is a fine monument, consisting of an obelisk and pedestal of granite, erected to the memory of Wolfe and Montcalm.   At the suggestion of Earl Dalhousie, who was Governor of Canada in 1827, a subscription was opened for the purpose, and when it reached seven hundred pounds, the earl made up the deficiency and superintended the erection of the monument.   It bears the names of WOLFE and MONTCALM, and a Latin explanatory inscription.[1]

WOLFE AND MONTCALM'S MONUMENT.

We left Quebec toward evening for Montreal, on our way up the St. Lawrence to Ontario.   A   August 11, 1848.
gentle shower crossed our track two miles distant, leaving a cool breeze upon the waters, and dispelling the haziness of the atmosphere.   Like a thin veil, it hung athwart the eastern sky, not thick enough to cover the face of the moon that gleamed dimly through it, yet sufficiently dense to refract and reflect the solar rays, and exhibit the radiant bow.   While admiring the beautiful phenomenon, I had occasion to administer a quiet rebuke to a young fop, whose attempts at wit, loud tone, and swaggering manner had attracted our attention at the dinner-table at Quebec.   He was accompanied by an elderly lady and two young maidens, and on the boat I observed him contributing largely to the amusement of the latter by asking silly questions of unsuspecting passengers, and receiving grave and polite answers, over which they made merry.   At length it was my turn to be his "subject."   "Can you tell me," he said, "what causes that rainbow ?"   "Do you ask for information ?"   I inquired, in return.   "Well, yes," he said, a little confused.   "Do you understand the Newtonian

---

[1] The following is the inscription : Mortem virtus, communem famam historia, monumentum posteritas dedit.   Hanc columnam in virorum illustrium memoriam WOLFE et MONTCALM P. C. Georgius Comes De Dalhousie in Septentrionalis Americæ partibus ad Britannos pertimentibus summam rerum administrans ; opus per multos annos prætermissum, quid duci egregio convenientius ?   Auctoritate promorens, exemplo stimulans, munificentia fovens A.S., MDCCCXXVII., Georgio IV., Britanniarum Rege.

theory of light? the laws of refraction and reflection? and are you familiar with the science of optics?" I asked, with a serious manner. "No, not much," he mumbled, with an effort to assume a careless air. "I perceive, sir, that you are not far enough advanced in knowledge to understand an explanation if I should give it," I mildly replied, and left him to his own reflections. Perhaps I was rude in the presence of that matron and those young girls, but the injunction of high authority, to "answer a fool according to his folly," did not parley with politeness. The maidens, half smiling, bit their lips, while the young man gazed steadfastly from the window of the saloon upon the beautiful shores we were passing by. They were indeed beautiful, dotted with villages, neat white farm-houses, fields of grain, and wide-spreading woods bathed in the light of the evening sun; and I hope the calm beauty of the scene, above and below, soothed the disquieted spirit of the young gazer, and awakened in his bosom aspirations for that wisdom which leads her willing pupils to perceive

> "Tongues in trees, books in the running brooks,
> Sermons in stones, and good in every thing."

We arrived at Montreal at six in the morning, left it by rail-road at ten for La Chine, nine miles distant, and at the head of La Chine Rapids embarked in the steamer British Queen for Ogdensburgh. We were soon at the foot of the Cascades, or St. Ann's Rapids, near the southwestern extremity of the Island of Montreal.

THE CASCADES, OR ST. ANN'S RAPIDS.[1]

The St. Lawrence here falls eighty-seven feet in the distance of seven miles. Steamboats and other vessels go *down* the rapids, but are obliged to ascend through the Beauharnois Canal, which we entered at about noon. This canal is fifteen miles long, fifty feet wide, and nine feet deep. The navigation of the rapids is very dangerous, and vessels are sometimes wrecked upon the submerged rocks. A sloop, loaded with staves and lumber, was lying in the midst of the foaming rapids, where it had struck the day before while guided by an unskillful pilot. The canal voyage was slow, for we passed nine locks before we reached the waters above Lake St. Louis, an expansion of the river, where the Ottawa or Utawas comes sweeping around each side of Isle Pero, at its mouth, and swells the volume of

---

[1] These rapids are so called from the circumstance that a village of the same name is near. This was considered by the Canadian *voyageurs* the place of departure when going from Montreal on fur-trading excursions, as here was the last church upon the island. This fact suggested to Moore the thoughts expressed in the first verse of his *Canadian Boat Song*:

> "Faintly as tolls the evening chime,
> Our voices keep tune and our oars keep time,
> Soon as the woods on shore look dim,
> We'll sing at St. Ann's our evening hymn.
> Row, brothers, row, the stream runs fast,
> The rapids are near, and the daylight's past."

Moore says, in reference to this song, "I wrote these words to an air which our boatmen sung to us frequently while descending the St. Lawrence from Kingston to Montreal. Our *voyageurs* had good voices, and sung perfectly in tune together. I remember when we had entered, at sunset, upon one of those beautiful lakes into which the St. Lawrence so grandly and unexpectedly opens, I have heard this simple air with a pleasure which the finest compositions of the first masters have never given me."

OF THE REVOLUTION.   2 0 7

Junction of the Ottawa and St. Lawrence.   Cedars Rapids.   Garrison there in 1776.   Conduct of Bedell and Butterfield.

the St. Lawrence with its turbid flood.[1]   We were most of the time in full view of the river, and had a fine opportunity to observe the people, dwellings, and agricultural operations along the line of the canal.

We passed the Cedars Rapids, twenty-four miles from La Chine, at about three o'clock. These rapids vary in intricacy, depth, and rapidity of current, and are nine miles long, running at the rate of nine to twelve miles an hour.   In some places the rocks are covered with only a few feet of water, and the descent is at all times rather perilous.   Small islands, covered with trees and shrubbery, accelerate the speed of the waters.   These rapids derive their

CEDARS RAPIDS, AT ST. TIMOTHY.

name from the village of Cedars, on the north side of the St. Lawrence, in Vaudreuil district.   The sketch was made from the steam-boat, in the canal, while stopping for wood and water at St. Timothy.

The Cedars occupy quite a conspicuous place in the annals of the Northern campaign of 1775–76.   Three hundred and ninety Americans, under Colonel Bedell, of the New Hampshire line, occupied a small fortress there in the spring of 1776.   Early in May, Captain Foster, of the British army, with a detachment of forty regulars, one hundred Canadians, and five hundred Indians, under the celebrated Brant, or Thayendanegea, descended from the British station at the mouth of the Oswegatchie (now Ogdensburgh), and approached the fort.   Bedell, under pretense of going to Montreal for re-enforcements, left the garrison in command of Major Butterfield, an officer quite as void of courage as his superior.   Both have been branded by cotemporary writers as cowards, and their conduct on this occasion confirms the opinion.[2]   Butterfield did not even make a fair show of resistance, but quietly

---

[1] For several miles below the confluence of the two rivers the muddy water of the Ottawa and the clear stream of the St. Lawrence are seen contending for the mastery.   The line of demarkation may be traced by the color even below the St. Ann's Rapids.

[2] Washington, writing to General Schuyler under date of June 10th, 1776, said, "If the accounts of Colonel Bedell and Major Butterfield's conduct be true, they have certainly acted a part deserving the most exemplary notice.   I hope you will take proper measures, and have good courts appointed to bring them, and every other officer that has been or shall be guilty of misconduct, to trial, that they may be punished according to their offenses.   Our misfortunes at the Cedars were occasioned, as it is said, entirely by their base and cowardly behavior, and can not be ascribed to any other cause."   A late writer for one of our weekly papers, in giving a "true account of the Northern campaign," is particularly laudatory of the bravery of Colonel Bedell at St. John's and Chambly.   He seems to regard all the official and other records of the events there as quite erroneous, and "sets the matter right" by quoting a letter written by Bedell to the Committee of Safety of New Hampshire.   He calls the style of the letter "Cæsarean," and in the free use of the pronoun *I* there is certainly a similarity to Cæsar's *Veni, Vidi, Vici*.   Taking the colonel's letter as verity, we must suppose that, in the capture of Forts Chambly and St. John's, Montgomery and all other officers were mere puppets in his hands.   In a postscript he says, "This moment I have got possession of St. John's; and, the post being obliged to set off, have not time to copy the articles of capitulation; and to-morrow shall march for Montreal, leaving a detachment to keep the fort."   Other portions of his letter plainly indicate that he wished to impress those who sent him to the field with the idea that he was the master-spirit there.   I should not have noticed this matter so minutely but for the disposition of a class of writers at present to make prominent the exploits of subalterns, upon ex-parte evidence, by hiding the brilliant deeds of those to whom compatriots and cotemporary historians have awarded the highest meed of praise.   It is an easy, and the only, way to make a sapling conspicuous, to fell the noble trees that surround and overshadow it.

May 15, surrendered the fort and garrison as soon as Foster arrived. Meanwhile, Major
1775. Henry Sherburne was sent by Arnold from Montreal, with one hundred and forty
men, to re-enforce the garrison, but Bedell, "valuing safety more than fidelity and honor,"[1]
refused to accompany him. Sherburne arrived upon the shore of Lake St. Louis on the day
of the surrender, and, having crossed the day after, left forty men as guards, and, with one
hundred, proceeded toward the fort, unconscious of the disgraceful conduct of Butterfield.
About five in the evening the whole force of Foster's Canadians and Indians burst from an
ambuscade and fell upon the republicans. They made a brave defense for nearly an hour
and a half, when the Indians, in number greatly superior, formed a girdle around them, and
at a given signal rushed upon the devoted little band and disarmed them. Infuriated by the
obstinate resistance of the Americans, the Indians butchered about twenty of them with knives
and tomahawks, and, stripping the remainder almost naked, drove them in triumph to the
fort.[2] The loss of the Americans, in the action and by massacre, was fifty-eight; the enemy lost twenty-two, among whom was a brave of the Senecas.

As soon as Arnold heard of the disasters at the Cedars, he marched with about eight
hundred men against the enemy, then at Vaudreuil, for the two-fold purpose of chastising
May, them and releasing the American prisoners. He arrived at St. Ann's on the after-
1776. noon of the 20th, at which time the bateaux of the enemy were distinctly seen taking
the American prisoners from an island three miles distant, toward the main land on the
south side of the St. Lawrence. About the same time a party of Caughnawaga Indians,[3]
whom Arnold had sent to the hostile savages in the morning, demanding a surrender of the
prisoners, and threatening them with extermination if any more murders of Americans should
be perpetrated, returned with an answer of defiance. The Indians sent back word to Ar
nold that they were too numerous to fear him, and that if he should attempt to cross the
river and land, for the purpose of rescuing the Americans, every prisoner should be immediately put to death. Unmindful of this threat, Arnold filled his boats with men, and proceeded to the island which the enemy had just left. Five Americans, naked and almost
famished, were there, and informed him that all the other prisoners, except two (who, being
sick, were butchered), had been taken to *Quinze Chiens*, four miles below. Arnold, with
his flotilla, proceeded thither. The enemy opened an ineffectual fire upon them, but as night
May 26, was closing in, and his men were fatigued, the general returned to St. Ann's and called
1776. a council of war. He there received a flag from the British commander, accompanied by a letter from Major Sherburne, giving him the assurances that if he persisted in his
design of attacking him, it would be entirely out of his power to restrain his savages from
disencumbering themselves of the prisoners, by putting them to death. Major Sherburne
confirmed the information that a massacre had already been agreed upon. Foster also demanded of Arnold an agreement, on his part, to a proposed cartel which Sherburne and the
other officers had been compelled to sign. This agreement covenanted for the delivery of

---

[1] Gordon, ii., 65.

[2] Stone, in his Life of Brant, asserts that that chief used his best endeavors to restrain the fury of the In
dians after the surrender of Sherburne.   Captain M'Kinstry (late Colonel M'Kinstry, of Livingston's Manor,
Columbia county) commanded the company, on that occasion, which fought most obstinately with the In
dians.   On that account the savages had determined to put him to death by the torture, and had made prep
arations for the horrid rite.   Brant interposed, and, in connection with some humane English officers, made
up a purse and purchased an ox, which the Indians roasted for their carousal instead of the prisoner.   Brant
and M'Kinstry became personal friends, and the chief often visited the latter at the manor after the war.—
Life of Brant, i., 155.

[3] The Caughnawagas called themselves the Seven Nations of Canada.   Many of them were with the
Mohawks and others of the Six Nations of New York in the battle of the Cedars, but those upon the Island
of Montreal were friendly to the republicans.   A remnant of the tribe now inhabit a village called Caughnawaga, about twelve miles from Montreal, and profess Christianity.   They have a handsome church, are
industrious, temperate, and orderly, and, unlike others of the Indian tribes, increase rather than diminish in
population.   I saw several of them in Montreal selling their ingenious birch bark and bead work.   They
are quite light, having doubtless a liberal tincture of French blood.   Their language is a mixture of Iroquois and French.

an equal number of British soldiers in exchange for the Americans, with the condition that the latter should immediately return to their homes, and not again take up arms.   Four American captains were to go to Quebec as hostages till the exchange should be effected. Arnold was strongly averse to making such an agreement, but the dictates of humanity and the peculiar circumstances of the case caused him to yield to the terms, except the conditions that the Americans should not again take up arms, and that they should be pledged not to give any information, by words, writings, or signs, prejudicial to his majesty's service.   Foster waived these points, and the convention was signed.[1]

The part performed by Foster in coercing the American officers into compliance with his demands, by suspending the bloody hatchet of the Indians over their heads, was thought disgraceful, and Congress refused to ratify the agreement, except upon such terms as the British government would never assent to.   Although Washington abhorred the act, he considered the convention binding ; and General Howe complained of the bad faith of Congress. The British government, however, indicated its appreciation of the matter by letting the waters of oblivion flow quietly over the whole transaction.   The prisoners were finally released by General Carleton, and the hostages at Quebec were sent home on parole.

Arnold, with his detachment, returned to Montreal, where, a few days afterward, a Committee of Congress, consisting of Franklin, Chase, and Carroll, arrived, to inquire into the state of affairs.   Their mission was fruitless, for all hope of maintaining a foothold in Canada was abandoned by the military leaders, and, as previously noted, the Americans soon afterward withdrew entirely from the province.

We entered the lake near Grand Island, above Cedars Rapids, and, passing the Rapids of *Coteau du Lac*, six miles above the latter, landed at a pretty little village of the same name.   Here the St. Lawrence expands into one of those broad lakes which mark its course from Ontario to the gulf.   It is called Lake St. Francis, and is forty miles long, and in some places twelve or thirteen broad.   Beautiful islands, covered with timber and luxuriant shrubbery, are scattered over its bosom.   We passed many of those floating islands—extensive rafts of lumber—which indicate a chief feature in the commerce of that noble river.   On one of the small islands

LUMBER RAFT ON THE ST. LAWRENCE.

on the northern shore, opposite the district of Glengary, is a huge " cairn," sixty feet high, the pinnacle of which is an iron cannon, from whose muzzle a flag-staff is projected.   A spiral path-way leads from base to summit, sufficiently wide for a person to pass up and down by it in safety. It is built of loose stones, without mortar or cement. The people of the neighboring parish of Glengary (who are chiefly Scotch), under the direction of Colonel Carmichael, reared it, in general testimony of their loyalty during the Canadian rebellion so called, of 1837–8, and in especial honor of Sir John Colborne (now Lord Seaton), who was the commander-in-chief of the British forces in Canada at that time.   In imitation of the manner in which tradition asserts that the ancient *cairns* were built, each person in the district, man, woman, and child, capable of lifting a stone, went to the island and added one to the pile.   We passed St.

CAIRN.[2]

[1] Marshall, Gordon, Allen, Sparks.
[2] This is probably the only structure of the kind on the American continent.   Cairn is a word of Celtic origin, used to denote the conical piles of stones frequently found upon the hills of Britain.   These piles are supposed by some to have been erected as memorials of some local event, while others assign to them a sepulchral character.   Some are supposed to be sacrificial, like the *carnedd* of the Welsh.   They all have a similar appearance wherever found, being composed of loose stones piled in a conical form.

210   PICTORIAL FIELD-BOOK

St. Regis and its ancient Church.   Passage of Rapids.   Wind-mill Point and Ogdensburgh.   Loyalty of a British Veteran.

Regis,[1] the first village upon the St. Lawrence within the territory of the United States, about sunset, and before the twilight had entirely faded we were again out of the river and in the Cornwall Canal, on the north side of the St. Lawrence, to avoid the swift rapids, called the *Long Sault,* nearly two miles in extent. We passed the *Du Platte* Rapids in the night, and at dawn entered the *Gallopes* or *Galoose* Rapids, nine miles below Ogdensburgh. These are a mile and a half long, and present a formidable obstacle to the upward passage of vessels. The channel is exceedingly narrow, and very near the southern shore. With three men at the tiller-wheel, and a full head of steam, our goodly "Queen" came up to the most rapid and intricate part, where, for nearly ten minutes, it was difficult to determine whether an inch of progress was made, and we were more than half an hour in making the mile and a half. The usual time occupied in going down from Ogdensburgh to Montreal by steam-boat is nine hours. On account of rapids and currents, and the canal navigation, the voyage up occupies about seventeen hours.

We caught the first rays of the morning sun reflected from the spires at Prescott and Ogdensburgh, flourishing villages, which flank the St. Lawrence at the head of all its numerous rapids. Wind-mill Point, on the Canada side, is close by, and as we passed the famous cape we were edified with a running commentary on the beneficence of monarchy and the horrors of republicanism, from an old officer of a British corps of marine engineers, who, with his daughter, was a passenger from Montreal. He had amused me for an hour the evening previous, after passing St. Regis, by a relation of his personal adventures in that vicinity during our last war with Great Britain. He then commanded a gun-boat with eighty men ; and he boasted, with much warmth and satisfaction, of the terrible manner in which he galled the Yankees with "grape and cannister" at the time of the engagements at Chrysler's Farm, Williamsburgh, and near St. Regis. He was bubbling over with loyalty, and became rabid at the mere mention of *annexation.* His head was white with the bleaching of threescore and ten years. Great experience and extensive practical knowledge, with frankness and volubility in conversation, made him a most agreeable companion, and we much regretted parting with him and his amiable daughter at Kingston.

I called Wind-mill Point a "famous cape." Its notoriety is very youthful, yet its history is one of those epitomes of progress worth noticing, which make up the movements of the nations. It was here that the Canada patriots (so called) in 1837 took post with a view of attacking Fort Wellington, a small fortification between the point and Prescott. There

---

[1] St. Regis is an old Indian village, and contains a small Roman Catholic Church, built about the year 1700. It is said that the priest informed the Indians that a bell was highly important to their worship, and they were ordered to collect furs sufficient to purchase one. They obeyed, and the money was sent to France for the purpose. The French and English were then at war. The bell was shipped, but the vessel that conveyed it fell into the hands of the English, and was taken into Salem, in the fall of 1703. The bell was purchased for a small church at Deerfield, on the Connecticut River, the pastor of which was the Rev. Mr. Williams. The priest of St. Regis heard of the destination of his bell, and, as the Governor of Canada was about to send an expedition, under Major Rouville, against the colonies of New England, he exhorted the Indians to accompany him and get possession of it. Rouville, with 200 French and 142 Indians, arrived near Deerfield in the evening of the 29th of February, 1704. During the night they attacked the unsuspecting villagers, killed 47, and made 112 prisoners. The latter, among whom were the pastor and a part of his family, were taken to Canada. The only house left standing was that of Mr. Williams, which the assailants themselves occupied in securing their prisoners. It is still standing, near the center of the village, and is represented in the annexed cut. The bell was conveyed in triumph through the forest to Lake Champlain, to the spot where Burlington now stands, and there they buried it with the benedictions of Father Nicolas, the priest of St. Regis, who accompanied them. Thus far they had carried it, by means of timber, upon their shoulders. They hastened home, and returned in early spring with oxen and sled to convey the sacred bell, now doubly hallowed in their minds, to its destination. The Indians of the village had never heard the sound of a bell, and powerful was the impression upon their minds when its deep tones, louder and louder, broke the silence of the forest as it approached their village at evening, suspended upon a cross piece of timber, and rung continually by the delighted carriers. It was hung in the steeple, and there it remains. The material incidents of this narrative doubtless occurred, but later investigations show that the bell was taken to a church at Caughnawaga, near Montreal, instead of St. Regis.—See HOUGH's *Hist. of St. Lawrence and Franklin Counties,* p. 114.

SHELDON HOUSE.

were several stone buildings and a strong stone wind-mill on the point. These were taken possession of by the insurgents toward noon on the 12th of November, 1838. They numbered about two hundred, many of them being from our frontier towns. They came in two schooners, which were towed down the St. Lawrence by the steamer United States, the captain (Van Cleve) supposing them to be, as represented by a passenger, laden with merchandise. As soon as he discovered the character of the vessels, he resolved to go no further, and stopped at Morristown, ten miles above Ogdensburgh. The schooners' lines were cast, and the next morning, filled with armed men, they were at anchor between Ogdensburgh and Prescott. The insurgents landed at Wind-mill Point, and commenced fortifying their position. Recruits from our shores swelled their ranks for the first twelve hours after their landing. Ogdensburgh and Prescott were in great commotion, and before night not a living being was to be seen in the latter place, for there would evidently be the battle-field.

Preparations were immediately made at Fort Wellington to dislodge the patriots, and a British armed steam-boat, lying at Prescott, prepared to co-operate with the garrison. During the evening the steam-boat Telegraph arrived, having on board Colonel Worth, of the United States army, and two companies of troops, with a marshal, to maintain neutrality. Early next morning two armed British steamers arrived with troops, and an assault was

commenced upon the patriots by throwing bombs upon the houses and the mill. The field pieces of their battery on shore returned the fire, and, after a fight of an hour, the British were driven back into the fort, with the loss of about one hundred men killed, and many wounded. Many of the patriots had fled in the morning, and when the action commenced there were only a hundred and twenty-eight left on the point, while the government troops amounted to more than six hundred. The insurgents lost five men killed and thirteen

WIND-MILL POINT.[1]

wounded. The next day they sent out a flag, but the bearer was shot. On the 15th the British received a re-enforcement of four hundred regulars, with cannon and gun-boats. The patriots were also re-enforced, and numbered more than two hundred. The government troops, with volunteers from Kingston, in all about two thousand men, surrounded the patriots by land and water, and kept up a continual cannonading until the evening of the 16th, when the latter surrendered. A white flag was displayed from the mill, and three or four others were sent out by the patriots, but the bearers were shot down.[2] Indeed, there seemed to be but little disposition on the part of the conquerors to give quarter. The dwellings in the vicinity of the wind-mill were burned, and it is asserted that a number of the patriots were consumed in one of them, which stood upon the beach. Other buildings have been burned since, and their blackened ruins, with the wind-mill, battered by cannon-balls, stand there now, gloomy mementoes of an abortive attempt to sever the chains of colonial vassalage.

According to Theller, thirty-six patriots were killed, two escaped, and ninety were made prisoners. The British lost a hundred and fifty men and twenty officers killed, among whom was Captain Drummond. The commander of the insurgents was a young Pole, only thirty-one years of age, named Von Schoultz, who, with ten others, was hung, and a large portion of the remainder of the prisoners was banished to Van Diemen's Land.

At Ogdensburgh we left the British Queen, and went on board the Lady of the Lake, bound for Oswego. Having an hour to pass before her departure, we employed it in a pleas-

---

[1] This view was sketched from the steam-boat, when a little below the wind-mill, looking west-north-west. The mill is a strong stone structure, and answered a very good purpose for a fort or block-house. Its narrow windows were used by the patriots as loop-holes for their muskets during the action.

[2] See "Theller's Canada in 1837-8."

ant ramble through the town and along the banks of the dark Oswegatchie. It was Sabbath morning, and all was quiet in that pleasant village. We traversed the high banks of the stream, along its majestic course from the bridge to the dam, about half a mile. The declivity of the bank is studded with oaks, sycamores, and pines, and lofty trees shade the pleasant pathway the whole distance, making it a delightful promenade either at hot noon or in the evening twilight. The water is of an amber color when not turbid, and from this one of its chief tributaries, the Black Lake, derives its name.

Ogdensburgh is near the site of the old French fort generally known as *Fort Oswegatchie*, but on their maps, as early as 1740, it is called *Fort Presentation*, and sometimes *La Gallette*. This fort was garrisoned by the French during a part of the Seven Years' War, but was taken by the English in 1760, while they were descending the St. Lawrence to attack Montreal. It is related that Putnam, then a lieutenant colonel, performed one of his daring and original feats here, in the attack upon the fort and upon the two armed vessels that lay at the mouth of the Oswegatchie River. Humphreys says that he undertook, with one thousand men in fifty bateaux, to capture the vessels by boarding. With beetle and wedges, he proceeded to secure the rudders, to disable the vessels and prevent them from bringing their broadsides to bear, and then to make a furious attack upon and board them. As they approached, the crew of one of the vessels, panic-struck, forced the commander to surrender, and the other vessel was run ashore. The fort was the next object of solicitude. With the permission of Amherst, Putnam caused a number of boats to be prepared with musket-proof fascines[1] along the sides, so as to form a shelter from the fire of the enemy. The fort was defended by an *abatis* overhanging the water ; and, to overcome such a formidable obstacle, he caused a broad plank, twenty feet in length, to be attached to the bow of each boat, so that it might be raised and lowered at pleasure. This was to form a bridge over the projecting *abatis*, on which the besiegers might pass to the attack on the fort. As soon as the boats, thus strangely equipped, began to move toward the fort, the alarmed garrison, unused to such martial enginery, surrendered without firing a shot.

These tales, like many others of which Putnam is the reputed hero, partake somewhat of the marvelous, and in this instance rather conflict with cotemporary history as well as probability. Colonel Mante, who was intimate with Rogers and Putnam, says that one of the vessels was grounded before the attack, and that an action of *four hours* occurred with the other. He also says that " the general ordered the vessels [of the English] to fall down the stream, post themselves as close to the fort as possible, and man their tops well, in order to fire upon the enemy, and prevent their making use of their guns, while the grenadiers rowed in with their broadswords and tomahawks, fascines and scaling-ladders, under cover of the light infantry, who were to fire into the embrasures."[2] He says nothing about Putnam's project or the " planks." Dr. Trumbull says, " The general, receiving intelligence that one of the enemy's vessels was aground and disabled, and that another lay off La Gallette, determined, with the utmost dispatch, to go down the river and attack Oswegatchie and Isle Royal. On the 17th of August the row-galleys fell in with the French sloop commanded by M. de la Broquirie, who, after a smart engagement, surrendered to the English galleys. . . . . . By the 23d two batteries were opened against the fort, and it was cannonaded by them in concert with the row-galleys in the river. M. Ponchaut, the commander, beat a parley, and surrendered the fort on terms of capitulation."[3] From personal observation of the ground, I am inclined to think that a plank twenty feet long could hardly have *reached the abatis* from the water, even in a perpendicular position, unless the altitude of the shores was less then than now. Very possibly the ingenious idea of wedging up the rudders of the vessels and of scaling the outworks of the fort was conceived by the fertile

[1] Fascines, from the Latin fascina, *fagot*, is a term used in fortifications to denote bundles of fagots, twigs, or branches of trees, which, being mixed with earth, are used for filling up ditches, forming parapets, &c

[2] History of the Late War in North America, &c., by Thomas Mante, major of a brigade in the campaign of 1764 ; London, 1772.

[3] History of Connecticut from 1630 to 1764, by Benjamin Trumbull, D.D.

mind of Putnam, but it is not one of the strong points upon which the reputation of the general for skill and bravery rests, for it must have been a failure if attempted.   One thing is certain—Fort Oswegatchie fell into the hands of the English at that time, after a pretty warm engagement.   Lieutenant-colonel Massey, with the grenadiers, took possession of the fort, the garrison were sent to New York, and the post was named by Amherst Fort William Augustus.

Ogdensburgh was a place of considerable importance, in a military point of view, during our war with England, begun in 1812.   Lying directly opposite a Canadian village (Prescott) and a military post, it was among the earliest of the points of attack from Canada. As early as the 2d of October, 1812, it was assaulted by the enemy.   General Jacob Brown, with four hundred Americans, commanded there in person.   On Sunday, the 4th, the British, one thousand in number, in forty boats, approached to storm the town, but, after a sharp engagement, they were repulsed.   Another attack was planned, and in February following it was carried into effect.   On the 21st of that month, the British, twelve hundred strong, attacked it in two columns, and, after an hour of hard fighting, drove Captain Forsyth and his troops out of the place as far as Black Lake, and took possession of the village.   The Americans lost twenty men in killed and wounded, the British about sixty.

1813.

We can not stay longer upon the beautiful banks of the Oswegatchie, for the signal-bell for departure is ringing merrily upon the Lady of the Lake.

214   PICTORIAL FIELD-BOOK

Departure from Ogdensburgh.   The St. Lawrence and the Thousand Islands.   Kingston.

CHAPTER X.

"Billows! there's not a wave! the waters spread
    One broad, unbroken mirror; all around
    Is hush'd to silence—silence so profound
That a bird's carol, or an arrow sped
    Into the distance, would, like 'larum-bell,
    Jar the deep stillness and dissolve the spell."
                                        PARK BENJAMIN.

CALM, sweetly consonant with ideas of Sabbath rest, was upon the main, the islands, and the river, and all the day long not a breath of air rippled the silent-flowing but mighty St. Lawrence. We passed the morning in alternately viewing the ever-changing scene as our vessel sped toward Ontario, and in perusing Burke's " Essay on the Sublime and Beautiful." I never read that charming production with so much pleasure as then, for illustrative examples were on every side. And when, toward noon, our course was among the Thousand Islands, the propriety of his citation of the stars as an example, by their number and confusion, of the cause of the idea of sublimity was forcibly illustrated. " The apparent disorder," he says, " augments the grandeur, for the appearance of care is highly contrary to our idea of magnificence." So with these islands. They fill the St. Lawrence through nearly sixty miles of its course, commencing fifteen miles below Kingston, and vary in size from a few yards to eighteen miles in length. Some are mere syenite rocks, bearing sufficient alluvium to produce cedar, spruce, and pine shrubs, which seldom grow to the dignity of a tree; while others were beautifully fringed with luxuriant grass and shaded by lofty trees. A few of the larger are inhabited and cultivated. They are twelve hundred and twenty-seven in number. Viewed separately, they present nothing remarkable; but scattered, as they are, so profusely and in such disorder over the bosom of the river, their features constantly changing as we made our rapid way among them, an idea of magnificence and sublimity involuntarily possessed the mind, and wooed our attention from the tuition of books to that of nature.

August 13, 1848.

We reached Kingston, Upper Canada, at about four o'clock, where we remained until nearly sunset. This is a large and flourishing town, at the lower end of Lake Ontario, and its commercial position is valuable and important. It stands near the site of old Fort Frontenac, and is now a British military post. It seems strongly fortified, and completely commands, by its military works, the entrance of the St. Lawrence from Ontario. A strong bomb-proof round tower stands upon Cedar Island, just below the city. Similar structures guard the portals of Fort Henry, the open space between the city and the fort, and one is a huge sentinel in the harbor, directly in front of the magnificent market-house that fronts upon the quay. They are mounted with cannon, and the hollow buttresses are pierced for musketry. A flourishing Indian settlement, called *Candaragui*, was upon the site of Kingston when first discovered by the French, and traces of the builder's art, evidently older than the fortifications of the whites, have been discovered. I was informed by a resident at Kingston, whom I met at Quebec, that while excavating to form a terrace near his residence, a few months previous, his workmen struck the stump of a tree three feet in diameter, and, upon removing it, a stone wall, regularly laid, was found beneath it.

This spot, known as Fort Frontenac, was a place of much importance during the inter-colonial wars of the last century. It was first a fur trading and missionary station of the Quebec colony. In 1673, Count Louis Frontenac, governor of Canada, erected a fort there and gave it his own name, and for eighty years it was one of the strongest military posts in America. It was from this point that Father Marquette (under the patronage of Fronte-nac) and other missionaries took their final departure for explorations in the Far West, and here provisions and stores were kept to supply other military and religious establishments upon the great lakes. Fort Frontenac remained in possession of the French until 1758. when Colonel Bradstreet,[1] with a detachment of men, chiefly provincials of New York and New England, captured it. After the disastrous defeat of Abercrombie at Ticonderoga, Colonel Bradstreet solicited and obtained permission to undertake that expedition. He trav-ersed the wilderness to Oswego, where he embarked in three vessels already prepared for him, descended the lake, and suddenly appeared before Frontenac. The weak garrison, over-whelmed by numbers, surrendered without resistance. The commander of the fort was ex-changed for Colonel Peter Schuyler, then a prisoner in Canada.

Leaving a small garrison to keep the post, Bradstreet and his troops returned and aided in building Fort Stanwix, upon the Mohawk, at the portage between that river and Wood Creek, a tributary of Oneida Lake. Among his officers were, Colonel Charles Clinton, of Ulster county, New York ; Major Nathaniel Woodhull, who fell on Long Island in 1776 , and Goosen Van Schaick, of Albany, and Lieutenant Marinus Willett, of New York, who were afterward colonels in the New York Revolutionary line.[2]

We did not land at Kingston, for the tarrying time of the boat was uncertain. It was nearly sunset when we left, and we passed the southern extremity of Gage Island just in time to see its last rays sparkling upon the tree-tops on Amherst Island, in the far distance. Ontario, like the St. Lawrence, was unruffled, and the evening voyage between Kingston and Sackett's Harbor was exceedingly pleasant, rendered so chiefly by a cool breeze, cush-ioned seats, agreeable company, and the anticipations of meeting dear friends at Oswego the next morning. We landed there a little after daybreak, and tarried three days before start-ing for the " Niagara frontier."

Oswego is beautifully situated upon Lake Ontario, on each side of the Chouegesen or Os-wego River, a large and rapid stream, through which flow the waters of eight considerable lakes in the interior of New York—the Canandagua, Crooked, Seneca, Cayuga, Owasco, Skaneateles, Onondaga, and Oneida, with their numerous little tributaries—and drains a surface of four thousand five hundred square miles. Beautifully significant are the Indian names of Oswego and Ontario—*rapid water* and *pretty lake*—for the river comes foaming

[1] John Bradstreet was a native of England. He was Lieutenant-governor of St. John's, Newfoundland, in 1746, and ten years afterward accompanied the expeditions against the French on the frontier of New York. In 1756 he was commissary general, and engaged in keeping up a communication between Albany and Oswego. He had charge of boats that carried provisions, and so much were they annoyed by the In dians in the French service, while passing down the Onondaga or Oswego River, that it required a great deal of skill and bravery to defend them. A small stockade fort near the site of the present village of Rome was cut off by the enemy, and they were obliged to depend upon their own power, in the open forest, for protection. He had a severe engagement near the margin of Oneida Lake, with a large war party of sav-ages, but gained a victory, leaving nearly two hundred of the enemy dead upon the field. His own loss was about thirty. His capture of Fort Frontenac, in 1758, put into the possession of the English the fort, nine armed vessels, forty pieces of cannon, a vast quantity of provisions and stores, and one hundred and ten prisoners. In the summer of 1764 he was employed against the Indians on the borders of Ontario, and at Presque Isle he compelled the Delawares, Shawnees, and other tribes to agree to terms of peace. He was appointed major general in 1772, and died at New York, October 21st, 1774.

[2] The captains of the New York troops engaged in this expedition were, Jonathan Ogden, of West Ches-ter ; Peter Dubois, of New York ; Samuel Bladgely and William Humphrey, of Dutchess ; Daniel Wright and Richard Howlet, of Queens ; Thomas Arrowsmith, of Richmond ; Ebenezer Seely, of Ulster ; and Peter Yates and Goosen Van Schaick, of Albany.

down broad rapids several miles before it expands into the harbor and mingles its flood with the blue waters of Ontario.   Its hydraulic power, its commercial position relative to Canada and the great West of our own dominion, and the healthfulness of its climate, mark out Oswego for a busy and populous city.   These advantages of locality were early perceived by the English, and were probably not entirely overlooked by the French.   But military occupation, for the purpose of spreading wide the overshadowing wings of empire, through the two-fold influences of religion and traffic, seemed to be the chief design of the French in planting small colonies at commanding points.

As early as July, 1696, Frontenac, governor of Canada, fitted out an expedition to attack the Five Nations in New York,[1] and Oswego was made his place of rendezvous.   There he built a small stockade fort on the west side of the river, and then proceeded with fifty men into the interior as far as the Onondaga Valley.   The Indians fled before him, but upon the shore of Onondaga Lake, near the present Salina, they left their emblem of defiance—two bundles of rushes suspended from a branch.   The governor returned to Oswego, and sailed for Fort Frontenac, without accomplishing any good for himself or harm to the Indians, except burning their dwellings when they fled from them.   Three years previously, Frontenac, by another route, fell upon the Indians on the Mohawk, near Schenectady, slew many, and took about three hundred prisoners.

These expeditions seemed to be a part of the grand scheme of the French to confine the English, now pushing into the wilderness in all directions, to the Atlantic sea-board ; but their forts on the lakes and upon the Ohio, and their extensive alliances with Indian tribes, could not repress the spirit of adventure and love of gain which marked their southern neighbors.   The great confederacy of the FIVE NATIONS of New York remained for a long time the fast friends and allies of the English, none but the Caughnawagas, as the French Jesuits termed their converts of the confederacy, lifting the hatchet against them.   Protected by these friendly savages, trading posts were founded, and these in turn became military establishments.   In 1722, Governor Burnet, of New York (son of the celebrated English bishop of that name), established a trading house at Oswego.   His object seemed to be political rather than commercial, for he desired to gain a foothold there, and thus, in a measure, command Lake Ontario.   He had been advised by the Board of Trade, after the treaty of Utrecht in 1713, "to extend with caution the English settlements as far as possible, as there was no probability of obtaining an arrangement of general boundaries."   Acting under this advice and the promptings of his own clear judgment, he planted the English standard, for the first time, upon the great lakes, and, in spite of the remonstrances of the French and the murmurings of the Oneidas and Senecas (who disliked to see fortresses rising in their neighborhood), he built and armed, at his own expense, a small fort at Oswego in 1727.   The French, in the mean while, had strongly fortified their trading post at the mouth of the Niagara River, and thus outflanked the English so far as the lake was concerned.   Beauharnois, the governor of Canada, ordered Burnet to desist.   Burnet defied, the Frenchman threatened, but, after blustering for a while, the latter, as a countervailing measure, took possession of Crown Point and built Fort St. Frederic there.   From that time until 1755, the English had undisturbed possession of Burnet's fort, and kept it garrisoned by a lieutenant and twenty-five men.

I am indebted to E. W. Clarke, Esq., of Oswego, for much local information concerning that city and neighborhood.   He kindly permitted me to use the manuscript of a lecture delivered by him before a literary society there, and from it I gleaned a description of the trading-house and fort erected by Governor Burnet.   It was situated on the west side of the river, directly on the bank of the lake, and forty feet above the water.   The bank, composed of rock and hard-pan, was almost perpendicular.   The building was of stone, and about ninety feet square.   The eastern end was circular.   It was provided with port-holes and a

---

[1] The name of the Confederation of the Five Nations was changed to that of Six Nations when it was joined by the Tuscaroras of Carolina in 1714.

OSWEGO IN 1755.[1]

deep well. The ascent to it from the south was a flight of stone steps (see engraving), the remains of which have been visible within a few years. The earth embankments of the fort, with its ditch and palisades, were about two hundred feet west of the building, upon higher ground, and traces of these might be seen until the late growth of the city obliterated them. The bluff on which the trading-house and fort rested has been leveled in filling in the basin, for the construction of wharves.

While Braddock was making his fatal march against Fort Duquesne, at the junction of the Ohio and Monongahela, in 1755, Governor Shirley, of Massachusetts, with a force of about one thousand five hundred men, composed of provincials and Indians, was on the march from Albany to Oswego, for the purpose of making attacks simultaneously upon Niagara and Frontenac. His march through the wilderness was perilous and fatiguing, and when he arrived at Oswego in August, his troops were reduced by sickness, and dispirited by the intelligence of Braddock's defeat. But Shirley, who succeeded Braddock in the chief command, was not disheartened. He strengthened Oswego by erecting two other forts ; one   1755.

westward of old Fort Oswego, called New Fort, one hundred and seventy feet square, with bastions and a rampart of earth and stones ; and another on the opposite side of the basin, four hundred and seventy yards distant from the old fort. The east fortification, called Fort Ontario, was built of logs from twenty to thirty inches in diameter. It was eight hundred feet in circumference, and its outer walls were fourteen feet high. Around it was a ditch fourteen feet wide and ten deep, and within were barracks for three hundred men. It was intended to mount sixteen pieces of cannon. This fort was on a commanding site, the perpendicular bank being higher than that upon the west side.[2]

Shirley built vessels and made other great preparations

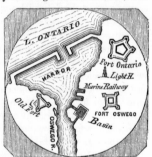

FORTS AT OSWEGO.[3]

at Oswego to proceed against Niagara. He constructed and equipped a sloop and schooner of sixty tons each, two row-galleys of twenty tons each, and eight whale-boats, each capable of carrying sixteen men. His views were promptly seconded by the New York Assembly. That body had already voted eight thousand pounds toward the enlistment of two thousand men in Connecticut, and raised four hundred men of their own in addition to their eight hundred then in the field. Shirley was also directed to complete the forts, and prepare for building one or more vessels of a large class, to mount ten six pounders besides swivels, two more row-galleys, and one hundred whale-boats. But heavy rains delayed his embarkation so long, that winter approached, and he abandoned the expedition against Niagara. He left seven hundred men in garrison at Oswego, and returned to Albany, where the remainder of his troops were disbanded. Additional fortifications, to complete the works, were made to the fort on the west side of the river, and stronger outworks were added to Fort Ontario.

---

[1] This view is looking north toward the lake. It is a reduced copy of the frontispiece to Smith's History of New York, first edition, London, 1757, and represents the encampment of Shirley there at that time.

[2] Smith's *History of New York ;* Clarke's MS.

[3] There are but few traces left of old Fort Oswego. The light-house that stood upon the bluff between the old fort and the present Fort Ontario, is removed, and another substantial one is erected upon the left pier, in front of the harbor. The city, on the east, is now fast crowding upon the ravelins of the old Fort.

218   PICTORIAL FIELD-BOOK

Remains of the "New Fort."   Shirley's Preparations at Albany.   Montcalm's Approach to Oswego.   Attack on the Works.

The remains of the ramparts and ditches of the New Fort are now quite prominent at the junction of Montcalm and Van Buren Streets.   The annexed engraving is a view of the appearance of these remains when I visited them.   The view is from _{August, 1848.}

REMAINS OF "NEW FORT," AT OSWEGO.

appearance of these remains when I visited them.   The view is from Montcalm Street, looking north, toward the lake.   The mounds and ditch were covered with a green sward; and decayed stumps of trees, three feet in diameter, were upon the former.   The fort had been abandoned about ninety years (for Fort Ontario became the main fortification after 1758), and, therefore, those large trees must have been produced within that time.

Shirley made vigorous preparations at Albany to re-enforce Oswego, the following spring, for the Marquis de Montcalm, an _{1756.} enterprising and experienced commander, was governor of Canada, and offensive operations on the part of the French were certainly expected.   Colonel Bradstreet was appointed commissary general, and, aided by Captain (afterward General) Philip Schuyler, forwarded large quantities of provisions to Oswego.   William Alexander, afterward Lord Sterling, of the Revolutionary army, was Shirley's secretary.   Early in the spring an army of seven thousand men, under General Winslow, was at Albany, waiting the arrival of the commander-in-chief, Lord Loudon.   His procrastination, which defeated all the plans for the season's campaign, was fatal in this instance.   He did not arrive until late in the summer. In the mean while the French, about five thousand in number, under the Marquis de Montcalm, came up the lake from Fort Frontenac, and landed stealthily behind a heavily-wooded cape (now called Four-mile Point), a few miles below Oswego.   Montcalm was there nearly two days before the fact was known to the garrison.   He had thirty pieces of heavy artillery, and was about commencing a march through the forest, to take Fort Ontario by surprise, when he was discovered by the English.   Colonel Mercer, the commandant of the garrison, ordered a brigantine to cruise eastward, and prevent any attempt of the enemy to approach the fort by water.   The next day a heavy gale drove the brigantine ashore, and while she was thus disabled, the French transported their cannon, unmolested, to within two _{August 11.} miles of the fort.   One or two other small vessels were sent out to annoy them, but the heavy guns of the French drove them back to the harbor.   The enemy pressed steadily forward through the woods, and toward noon of the same day invested the fort with thirty-two pieces of cannon, ranging from twelve to eighteen pounders, several large brass pounders and hoyets, and about five thousand men, one half of whom were Canadians and _{July 9, 1755.} Indians.   Some of this artillery was taken from the English when Braddock was defeated.   The garrison, under Colonel Mercer, numbered only one thousand four hundred, and a large portion of these were withdrawn to the fort on the west side of the river, to strengthen it, and to place the river between Mercer's main body and the enemy.   The French began the assault with small arms, which were answered by the guns of Fort Ontario, and bombs from the small fort on the other side of the basin.   Finding an open assault danger- _{August 12.} ous, Montcalm commenced approaching by parallels during the night, and the next day he began another brisk fire with small arms.   On the day following he opened a battery of cannons within sixty yards of the fort.   As soon as Colonel Mercer perceived this, he sent word to the garrison, consisting of three hundred and seventy men, to destroy their cannon, ammunition, and provisions, and retreat to the west side.   This they effected without the loss of a man.   During the night of the 13th the enemy were employed, in the face of a destructive cannonade, in erecting a heavy battery to play upon the fort.   On the morning of the 14th they had finished their battery of twelve heavy guns, and under its cover two thousand five hundred Canadians and Indians crossed the river in three divisions. Colonel Mercer was killed during this movement, and the command devolved upon Colonel

Littlehales.   The enemy had a mortar battery in readiness by ten o'clock, and their forces were so disposed that all the works of defense were completely enfiladed.   At the same time, the regulars, under the immediate command of Montcalm, were preparing to cross to the attack.   Colonel Littlehales called a council of war, and, it being agreed that a defense was no longer practicable, a *chamade*, or parley, was beaten by the drums of the fort, and the firing ceased on both sides.   Two officers were sent to the French general to inquire upon what terms he would accept a surrender.   He sent back a polite and generous answer, remarking, at the same, time that the English were an enemy to be esteemed, and that none but a brave nation would have thought of defending so weak a place so long.[1]   The fort, the whole garrison, one hundred and twenty cannons, fourteen mortars, a large quantity of ammunition and stores, and quite a respectable fleet in the harbor, were the spoils of victory The forts were dismantled, the prisoners were placed on transports for Frontenac, and, without leaving a garrison behind, the whole military armament went down the lake, and left Oswego solitary and desolate.

The destruction of the forts was a stroke of policy on the part of Montcalm.   They had been a continual eyesore to the Six Nations, for they had reason to suspect that, if the English became strong enough, their fortifications would be used as instruments to enslave the tribes.   This act of Montcalm was highly approved by the Indians, and caused them to assume a position of neutrality toward the belligerent Europeans.   This was what Montcalm desired, and he gained far more power by destroying the forts than he would by garrisoning them.   French emissaries were sent among the Indians, and by their blandishments, and in consequence of their successes, they seduced four of the tribes wholly from the British interest.   These were the Oneidas, Onondagas, Cayugas, and Senecas.

The following year English troops again took possession of Fort Ontario, and partially restored it to its former strength, and in 1759 it was rebuilt on a larger scale. 1757. They also erected a small stockade fort near the Oswego Falls, and built Fort Stanwix, on the Mohawk.   Thus, in a military point of view, Oswego remained until our 1758. war for independence broke out.[2]

This post was rather too remote for active operations, during the first years of the war, to attract the serious attention of either party, and the fort was garrisoned by only a few men until the summer of 1777, when St. Leger, with seven hundred Rangers, detached from the army of Burgoyne at St. John's, on the Sorel, made this his place of rendezvous preparatory to his incursion into the Valley of the Mohawk.   Here he was joined by Sir John Johnson and Colonel Daniel Claus, with nearly seven hundred Indians, under Brant, and four hundred regular troops.   Here a war feast was given, and, certain of success, the party, in high spirits, departed to invest Fort Stanwix.   A different scene was exhibited a few weeks later at Oswego.   St. Leger, foiled, and his troops utterly routed, came hastening back in all the terror and confusion of a retreat, the victors in hot pursuit.   His Indian allies, greatly alarmed, were scattered over the vast forests, and a mere remnant of his army,

---

[1] His note to Colonel Littlehales was as follows : " The Marquis of Montcalm, army and field marshal, commander-in-chief of his most Christian majesty's troops, is ready to receive a capitulation upon the most honorable conditions, surrendering to him all the forts.   They shall be shown all the regard the politest nation can show.   I send an aid-de-camp on my part, viz., Mons. de Bougainville, captain of dragoons ; they need only send the capitulation to be signed.   I require an answer by noon.   I have kept Mr. Drake for a hostage.   " MONTCALM.
" *August* 14, 1756."

[2] Mrs. Grant, of Edinburgh, Scotland, in her " Memoirs of an American Lady," gives a charming picture of the scenery about Oswego in 1761–2.   She was then a child, and resided there with her father ; and her book presents all the vividness of a child's impressions.   She noted, in particular, a feature in the forest scenery which now delights the sojourner upon the southern shores of Lake Ontario—the sudden bursting forth of leaves and flowers in the spring.   Major Duncan, who was in command of the fort at that time, was a gentleman of taste, and, in addition to a large and well-cultivated garden, he had a bowling green and other pleasure grounds.   These were the delight of the author of the " Memoirs," whose pleasing pictures may be found in chapters xliv. to xlvii. inclusive.

without arms, half naked, and nearly starved, followed him to Fort Ontario, whence he fled
to Montreal. The details of the siege of Fort Stanwix will be given hereafter.

There was no engagement at Oswego during the Revolution. Just at the close of the
war, Washington conceived the design of securing Fort Ontario, and sent an expedition
thither under the command of Colonel Marinus Willett, who had been an efficient officer in
the Mohawk Valley from the time of the siege of Fort Stanwix. Preliminary articles of
peace had been signed in November previous, but as the terms were not definitely agreed
upon, it was the policy of the commander-in-chief to be prepared for the reopening of hostilities, and, therefore, until the settlement was finally made, in September, 1783, by the signing of the definitive treaty, his vigilance was unrelaxed. This enterprise was undertaken in
mid-winter. Willett assembled his troops at Fort Herkimer, on the German Flats, and on
1783. the 9th of February crossed the Oneida Lake on the ice, and reached Oswego Falls
the next morning. Not being strong enough in numbers to attempt a siege or an open
assault, he there prepared scaling-ladders, and determined to surprise the garrison that night.
A deep snow lay upon the ground, and the weather was so intensely cold that one of the soldiers was frozen to death. A young Oneida Indian acted as guide, but the snow and the

darkness caused him to lose his way.
At daylight they found themselves in
sight of the fort, and soon afterward
they discovered three wood-choppers
near. Two of them were captured, but
the third escaped to the fort and gave
the alarm. Willett and his party immediately retreated, and thus ended the
expedition.[1] In 1796 this post, with
all others upon the frontier, was given
up by the English to the United States.

VIEW OF OSWEGO AND THE FORT IN 1798.[2]
From a drawing by Dewitt, surveyor general.

A prize, in the shape of public stores
deposited at the Oswego Falls, attracted
the attention of the British in 1814, and a fleet, bearing three thousand men, appeared before the town on the fifth of May. Fort Oswego, (called Ontario when repaired subsequent to the War,) on the East side of the harbor, was quite dilapidated, and the little
garrison had small means of defense. They had only six cannons, and three of these had
lost their trunnions. As soon as the sail of the enemy appeared, information was sent to
Captain Woolsey, of the navy, then at the village on the west side of the river, and to the
neighboring militia. Four large ships, three brigs, and a number of gun and other boats
1814. appeared, about seven miles distant, at dawn on the morning of the fifth of May.
The Americans prepared a battery on the shore, and gave the enemy such a warm reception, while approaching in boats to land, that they returned to their ships. Early on the
morning of the 6th the fleet came within cannon-shot of the works, and for three hours kept
up a discharge of grape and heavy balls against the fort and batteries.[3] The troops finally
effected a landing, and the little band of Americans, not exceeding three hundred in number, after maintaining their ground as long as possible, withdrew into the rear of the fort,
and halted within four hundred yards of it. After fighting about half an hour, they march-

---

[1] Clarke's MS.

[2] This view is from the west side of the river, near the site of the present United States Hotel.

[3] I visited Fort Ontario, which is now a strong and admirably appointed fortification. A small garrison
is usually stationed there, but at the time of my visit the fort was vacated by troops and left in charge of a
sergeant (Mr. Brown), whose courtesy made our little party feel as much at home amid the equipments of
war as if we were veritable soldiers and our ladies *attachés* of the camp. He gave me a four-pound cannon-ball, which was fired into the fort from the British ship Wolfe, the only ship engaged in the action, on
the morning of the Sixth of May, 1814. It bears the rude anchor mark of British ordnance shot, and
was labeled by the sergeant, "A present from John Bull to Uncle Sam."

ed toward the falls, to defend the stores, destroying the bridges in their rear. The British burned the barracks, and, after spiking some of the guns, evacuated the fort, and retired to their ships at three o'clock on the morning of the 7th. The loss of the Americans was six killed, thirty-eight wounded, and twenty-five missing. The enemy lost, in killed, wounded, drowned, and missing, two hundred and thirty-five.[1] They returned on the 9th, and sent a flag into the village, to inform the people of their intention to land a large force and capture the stores ; but, being informed that the bridges were destroyed and the stores removed, the fleet weighed anchor and returned to Kingston.

Scarcely a feature of old Oswego is left. The little hamlet of the Revolution and the tiny village of 1814 have grown into a flourishing city. Heavy stone piers, built by the United States government, guard the harbor from storms, and a strong fortification protects it from enemies. Lake commerce enlivens the mart, and a canal and rail-road daily pour their freights of goods and travel into its lap.

VIEW OF OSWEGO HARBOR, 1848.[3]

While in Oswego I visited the venerable Major Cochran and his excellent lady, the daughter of General Philip Schuyler. Major Cochran was then nearly eighty years old, and feeble in bodily health, but his mind was active and vigorous. His father was Dr. John Cochran,[2] the surgeon general of the Middle Department of the Revolutionary army ; and himself was a member of Congress during the administration of the elder Adams.[4] His family relationship and position made him acquainted with all the general officers of the Revolution, and his reminiscences afforded me much pleasure and instruction during my brief visit. He has since gone down into the grave, and thus the men of that generation, like the sands of an hour-glass, fall into their resting-

[1] Letter of Commodore Chauncy to the Secretary of the Navy.

[2] Dr. Cochran was born in Chester, Pennsylvania, in 1730. His father came from the north of Ireland. He studied medicine at Lancaster, and served as surgeon's mate in the hospital department during the French and Indian war. At the close of that contest he settled in Albany, and married Gertrude, the only sister of General Schuyler. He entered the Revolutionary army, and in the spring of 1777 Washington appointed him surgeon general of the Middle Department, and in October, 1781, director general of the hospitals of the United States. He removed to New York after the peace, and his eminent services were not forgotten by Washington, who nominated him commissioner of loans for that state. He died at Palatine, Montgomery county, April 6th, 1807, aged 76.

[3] This view is from the top of the United States Hotel, looking east-northeast. It was hastily sketched during the approach of a thunder-storm, and the "huge herald drops" came down just as I traced the distant water-line of the lake. The objects by the figure in the foreground are the balustrade and chimney of the hotel, now (1848) a summer boarding-house for strangers. The first height beyond the water on the right is the point on which stands Fort Oswego. The land in the far distance, on the same side, is Four-mile Point, behind which Montcalm landed his forces. On the left is seen the light-house upon one of the stone piers, and beyond it spread out the waters of Lake Ontario.

[4] Circumstances connected with his election are rather amusing. A vessel was to be lanched upon (I think) Seneca Lake, at Geneva, and, it being an unusual event, people came from afar to see it. The young folks gathered there, determined to have a dance at night. A fiddle was procured, but a fiddler was wanting. Young Cochran was an amateur performer, and his services were demanded on the occasion. He gratified the joyous company, and at the supper-table one of the gentlemen remarked, in commendation of his talents, that he was "fit for Congress." The hint was favorably received by the company, the matter was "talked up," and he was nominated and elected a representative in Congress for the district then comprising the whole state of New York west of Schenectady. He always claimed to have fiddled himself into Congress.

place. His lady, many years his junior, was the youngest and favorite daughter of General Schuyler. She was his traveling companion during his old age, and constantly enjoyed the advantages of the refined society by which he was surrounded. When her mother departed from earth, she was his companion and solace, and was at his bedside, to minister to his wants, in the hour of death.[1] Although the stirring scenes of the Revolution were passed before the years of her infancy were numbered, her intercourse with the great and honorable of that generation, during her youth and early womanhood, brought facts and circumstances to her vigorous mind so forcibly, that their impressions are as vivid and truthful as if made by actual observation. She related many interesting circumstances in the life of her father, and among them that of an attempted abduction of his person in 1781.

At the time in question, General Schuyler was residing in the suburbs of Albany, having left the army and engaged in the civil service of his country. Notwithstanding his comparatively obscure position, his aid and counsel were constantly sought, in both military and civil transactions, and he was considered by the enemy one of the prominent obstacles in the way of their success. He was then charged by Washington with the duty of intercepting all communications between General Haldimand in Canada and Clinton in New York. For some time the Tories in the neighborhood of Albany had been employed in capturing prominent citizens and carrying them off to Canada, for the purpose of exchange. Such an attempt was made upon Colonel Gansevoort, and now a bold project was conceived to carry off General Schuyler. John Waltermeyer, a bold partisan and colleague of the notorious Joe Bettys, was employed for the purpose. Accompanied by a gang of Tories, Canadians, and Indians, he repaired to the neighborhood of Albany, but, uncertain how well General Schuyler might be guarded, he lurked among the pine shrubbery in the vicinity eight or ten days. He seized a Dutch laborer, and learned from him the exact position of affairs at Schuyler's house, after which he extorted an oath of secrecy from the man and let him go. The Dutchman seems to have made a mental reservation, for he immediately gave information of the fact to General Schuyler. A Loyalist, who was the general's personal friend, and cognizant of Waltermeyer's design, also warned him. In consequence of the recent abductions, the general kept a guard of six men constantly on duty, three by day and three by night, and after these warnings they and his family were on the alert.

_{August, 1781.} At the close of a sultry day, the general and his family were sitting in the front hall. The servants were dispersed about the premises. The three guards relieved for the night were asleep in the basement room, and the three on duty, oppressed by the heat, were lying upon the cool grass in the garden. A servant announced to the general that a stranger desired to speak to him at the back gate. The stranger's errand was at once comprehended. The doors of the house were immediately shut and close barred. The family were hastily collected in an upper room, and the general ran to his bed-chamber for his arms. From the window he saw the house surrounded by armed men. For the purpose of arousing the sentinels upon the grass, and perchance to alarm the town, he fired a pistol from the window. The assailants burst open the doors, and at that moment Mrs. Schuyler perceived that, in the confusion and alarm of the retreat from the hall, her infant child, a few months old, had been left in the cradle in the nursery below. Parental love subdued all fear, and she was flying to the rescue of her child, when the general interposed and prevented her. But her third daughter[2] instantly rushed down the two flights of stairs, snatched the still sleeping infant from the cradle, and bore it off safely. One of the miscreants hurled a sharp tomahawk at her as she left the room, but it effected no other harm than a slight injury to her dress, within a few inches of the infant's head. As she ascended a private stair-case she met Waltermeyer, who, supposing her to be a servant, exclaimed, "Wench, wench, where

---

[1] Grief for the loss of his wife, and the melancholy circumstances connected with the death of his son-in-law, General Alexander Hamilton, weighed heavily upon his spirits. His death was hastened by exposure and fatigue while accompanying two French dukes over the battle-ground of Saratoga. He was taken ill there, and never recovered.

[2] Margaret, afterward the first wife of the late venerated General Van Rensselaer (the patroon) of Albany.

is your master ?" With great presence of mind, she replied, " Gone to alarm the town." The Tory's followers were then in the dining-room, plundering it of the plate and other valuables, and he called them together for consultation. At that moment the general threw up a window, and, as if speaking to numbers, called out, in a loud voice, " Come on, my brave fellows, surround the house and secure the villains, who are plundering." The assailants made a precipitate retreat, carrying with them the three guards that were in the house, and a large quantity of silver plate. They made their way to Ballstown by daybreak, where they took General Gordon a prisoner from his bed, and with their booty returned to Canada.[1] The bursting open of the doors of General Schuyler's house aroused the sleeping guards in the cellar, who rushed up to the back hall, where they had left their arms, but they were gone. Mrs. Church,[2] another daughter of General Schuyler, who was there at the time, without the slightest suspicion that they might be wanted, caused the arms to be removed a short time before the attack, on account of apprehended injury to her little son, whom she found playing with them. The guards had no other weapon but their brawny fists, and these they used manfully until overpowered. They were taken to Canada, and when they were exchanged, the general gave them each a farm, in Saratoga county. Their names were John Tubbs, John Corlies, and John Ward.

Mrs. Cochran was the infant rescued by her intrepid sister. The incident is one of deep interest, and shows the state of constant alarm and danger in which the people lived at that day, particularly those whose position made them conspicuous. Mrs. Cochran kindly complied with my solicitation for a likeness of herself to accompany the narrative here given.

---

[1] Major Cochran related to me an incident connected with the booty in question. Among the plundered articles was a silver soup tureen. He was at Washington city at the time of the inauguration of Harrison, in 1841, and while in the rotunda of the Capitol, viewing Trumbull's picture of the surrender of Burgoyne, a stranger at his elbow inquired, " Who is that fine-looking man in the group, in citizen's dress?" " General Schuyler," replied Major Cochran. " General Schuyler !" repeated the stranger. " Why, I ate soup not long since, at Belleville, in Canada, from a tureen that was carried off from his house by some Tories in the Revolution." This was the first and only trace the family ever had of the plundered articles.

[2] She was the wife of John B. Church, Esq., an English gentleman, who was a contractor for the French army in America under Rochambeau. He returned to England, and was afterward a member of Parliament.

It was my intention to go directly from Oswego to Rome, by the plank road that traverses the old war-paths of the last century between those points, for the region westward is quite barren of incident connected with the Revolution.   Old Fort Niagara, at the mouth of the Niagara River, was a place of rendezvous for Tories and Indians while preparing for marauding excursions on the borders of civilization in New York, or when they returned with prisoners and scalps.   Beyond this it offered no attractions, for hardly a remnant of its former material is left.   But having been joined at Oswego by another member of my family, who, with my traveling companion, was anxious to see the great cataract, and desirous myself to look again upon that wonder of the New World, I changed my course, and on a August 17, stormy morning, with a strong north wind awakening the billows of Ontario, we left 1848.   Oswego for Lewiston in the steamer Cataract, commanded by the same excellent Van Cleve whose vessel got a little entangled, ten years before, in the affair at Wind-mill Point, near Ogdensburgh.   The lake was very rough, and nearly all on board turned their thoughts inwardly, conversing but little until we entered the Genesee River in the afternoon. Many lost the breakfast they had paid for, and others, by commendable abstinence and economy, saved the price of dinner by shunning it altogether.

The scenery upon the tortuous course of the Genesee is very picturesque.   The stream is deep and narrow, and its precipitous shores are heavily wooded.   The voyage terminated three fourths of a mile below the Lower Falls of the Genesee, and five miles from Ontario. Here is the port of Rochester.   The city lies upon the plains at the Upper Falls, two miles distant.   Our boat remained there until toward evening, and, the rain having abated, I strolled up the winding carriage-way as far as the Lower Falls.   This road is cut in the precipitous bank of the river, presenting overhanging cliffs, high and rugged, on one side, and on the other steep precipices going down more than a hundred feet below to the sluggish bed of the stream.   Every thing about the falls is broken and confused.   The stream, the rocks, the hills, and trees are all commingled in chaotic grandeur, varying in lineament at each step, and defying every attempt to detect a feature of regularity.   There sandstone may be seen in every stage of formation, from the loose soil to shale, and slate-like lamina, and the solid stratified rock.   The painter and the geologist are well rewarded for a visit to the Lower Falls of the Genesee.

We descended the river toward evening.   Heavy clouds were rolling over the lake ; and the white caps that sparkled upon its bosom, and the spray that dashed furiously over the unfinished stone pier at the mouth of the river, betokened a night of tempest and gloom. The wind had increased almost to a gale upon the lake while we had been quietly lying in the sheltering arms of the Genesee.   Premonitions of sea-sickness alarmed my prudence, and by its wise direction I slipped into my berth before eight o'clock, and slept soundly until aroused by the porter's bell, a little before daybreak, at Lewiston Landing.   The rain continued, though falling gently.   We groped our way up the slippery road to the cars, and, shivering in the damp air, took seats for Niagara, fully resolved to give the bland invitation of the "lake route" a contemptuous refusal on our return eastward.   It may be very pleasant on a calm day or a moonlight night, but *our* experience made us all averse to the aquatic journey.

We passed from Ontario into the Niagara River, seven miles below Lewiston, while slumbering, and, consequently, I have nothing to say of Fort Niagara from personal observation. We will turn to veritable history for the record, and borrow the outlines of an illustration from another pencil.

In 1679, during the administration of Frontenac, a French officer named De Salle inclosed a small spot in palisades at the mouth of the Niagara River, and in 1725, two years before Governor Burnet built his fort at Oswego, a strong fortification was erected there.   It was captured by the British, under Sir William Johnson, in 1759.   The forces, chiefly provincials, that were sent against the fort were commanded by General Prideaux, who sailed 'uly 7, from Oswego, and landed near the mouth of the river in July.   He at once opened 1757.   his batteries upon the fortress, but was soon killed by the bursting of a gun.   The

OF THE REVOLUTION. 225

Attack on Fort Niagara.   Stratagem of the French.   Traditions respecting the Fort.   A Refuge for Tories and Indians.

command then devolved upon Johnson.   An army of French regulars, twelve hundred strong, drawn chiefly from western posts, and accompanied by an equal number of Indians, marching to the relief of the garrison, were totally routed by Johnson, and a large part of them made prisoners.   The siege had then continued more than a fortnight, and the beleaguered garrison, despairing of succor, surrendered the next day.   In addition to the ammunition and stores that fell into their hands, July 23, 1759. the strong fort itself was an important acquisition for the English. Within its dungeons were found instruments for executions or murders and the ears of the English received many horrid tales from the captive

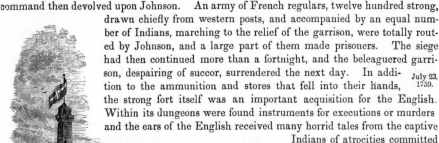

Indians of atrocities committed there during French rule.

It is said that the mess-house, a strong building still standing within the fort, was built by the French by stratagem.   The Indians were opposed to the erection of any thing that appeared like a for-

DISTANT VIEW OF FORT NIAGARA.[1]

tress.   The French troops were kindly received by the savages, and obtained their consent to build a wigwam.   They then induced the Indians to engage in an extensive hunt with some French officers, and when they returned the walls were so far advanced that they might defy the savages if they should attack them.   It grew into a large fort, with bastions and ravelins, ditches and pickets, curtains and counter-scarp, covered way, draw-bridge, raking batteries, stone towers, bakery, blacksmith shop, mess-house, barracks, laboratory, magazine, and a chapel with a dial over its door to mark the progress of the hours.   It covered about eight acres.   A few rods from the barrier-gate was a burial-ground, over the portal of which was painted, in large letters, REST.   The dungeon of the mess-house, called the black-hole, was a strong, dark, and dismal place, and in one corner of the room was fixed an apparatus for strangling those whom the despotic officers chose to kill.   The walls were profusely inscribed with French names and mementos in that language, and the letters and emblems were many of them so well executed as to prove that some of the victims were not of common stamp.   When, in June, 1812, an attack upon the fort by the English was momentarily expected, a merchant, residing near the fort, deposited some valuable articles in the dungeon.   He went there one night with a light, and discovered his own family name upon the walls.   Like other ruins, it has its local legends.   The headless trunk of a French officer has been seen sitting on the margin of the well in the dungeon ; and large sums of money have been buried there, and their localities pointed out by fingers visible only to money-diggers.[2]

During the American Revolution " it was the headquarters," says De Veaux, " of all that was barbarous, unrelenting, and cruel.   There were congregated the leaders and chiefs of those bands of murderers and miscreants who carried death and destruction into the remote American settlements.   There civilized Europe reveled with savage America, and ladies of education and refinement mingled in the society of those whose only distinction was to wield the bloody tomahawk and the scalping-knife.   There the squaws of the forests were raised to eminence, and the most unholy unions between them and officers of the highest rank smiled upon and countenanced.   There, in their strong-hold, like a nest of vultures, securely, for seven years, they ´sallied forth and preyed upon the distant settlements of the Mohawk and

[1] This is copied from one published in Barber and Howe's " Historical Collections of New York."   They copied it from an engraving published during the war of 1812.   It gives the appearance of the locality at that time.   The view is from the west side of the Niagara River, near the light-house.   The fort is on the east side (the right of the picture), at the mouth of the river.   The steam-boat seen in the distance is out on Lake Ontario.   [2] See De Veaux's Niagara Falls.

Susquehanna Valleys.   It was the depôt of their plunder : there they planned their forays, and there they returned to feast, until the time of action came again."

The shores of Niagara River, from Erie to Ontario, abound in historic associations connected with the military operations on that frontier during the war of 1812.   The battles of Chippewa, Lundy's Lane, Queenston, and Fort Erie occurred in this vicinity ; but these events are so irrelevant to our subject, that we must give them but brief incidental notice as we happen to pass by their localities.

Fort Niagara was feebly garrisoned by the Americans, and on the 19th of December, 1813, a British force of twelve hundred men crossed the river and took it by surprise.   The garrison consisted of three hundred and seventy men.   The commanding officer was absent, the gates were open and unguarded, and the fortress, strong as it was, became an easy prey to the enemy.   Sixty-five of the garrison were killed, and twenty-seven pieces of ordnance and a large quantity of military stores were the spoils of victory for the British.

It was broad daylight when our train moved from Lewiston, and across the Niagara, on the Canada shore, the heights of Queenston, surmounted by Brock's monument, were in full view. The battle that renders this towering slope so famous occurred on the 13th of October, 1812. The Americans were commanded by the late General Stephen Van Rensselaer, the British by General Sir Isaac Brock.   The former were about twenty-five hundred strong ; the latter numbered about the same, besides a horde of Chippewa Indians.   The British were 1812. strongly posted upon the heights.   At four o'clock on the morning of the 13th about six hundred Americans, under Colonel Solomon Van Rensselaer and Lieutenant-colonel Christie, crossed over in boats to dislodge the enemy.   The passage was made in the face of a destructive fire, and the brave Americans rushed impetuously up the acclivity and attacked the first battery, captured it, and soon stood victorious upon the height from which they had driven the enemy.   General Brock endeavored, in person, to rally his scattered troops, and was fatally wounded while leading them to the charge.[1]   Dismayed when they saw their leader fall, they fled in great confusion.   At this time Colonel Scott,[2] with a reenforcement of six hundred men, regulars and volunteers, crossed over ; and the enemy was also re-enforced by troops from Fort George, and five hundred Chippewa Indians.   The strife was fierce for a long time.   The British, re-enforced, far outnumbered the Americans, and the militia remaining at Lewiston could not be induced to cross over to support their friends in the combat.   Overwhelming numbers closed in upon the Americans, and, after fighting eleven hours, they were obliged to surrender.   The American loss was about ninety killed and nine hundred wounded, missing, and prisoners.   The behavior of many of our militia on this occasion was extremely disgraceful.   Taking advantage of the darkness when they crossed in the morning, they hid themselves in the clefts of the rocks and clumps of bushes near the shore, where they remained while the fighting ones were periling life upon the heights above.   The cowards were dragged out from their hiding-places by the legs, by the British soldiers, after the surrender.

The rail-road cars from Lewiston to the Falls ascend in their course an inclined plane that winds up what is evidently the ancient southern shore of Lake Ontario.   Deposits of pebbles at the foot of the ridge, and many other facts connected with this physical feature of the country from Niagara to Oswego, prove conclusively, to the mind of the close observer, that this was the shore of Ontario before the great convulsion took place which formed the

---

[1] General Brock was lieutenant governor of Upper Canada.   The Legislature of that province caused a monument to be erected to his memory, on the heights near the spot where he fell.   It is in a position so elevated, that it may be seen at different points nearly fifty miles distant.   The monument is constructed of freestone.   The base, which covers the vault wherein lie the remains of General Brock and his aid, Lieutenant-colonel John M'Donald (who was killed in the same action), is twenty feet square.   The shaft rises one hundred and twenty-six feet from the ground.   A miscreant named Lett attempted to destroy it by gunpowder on the night of the 17th of April, 1840.   The keystone over the door was thrown out, and the shaft was cracked nearly two thirds of its height.

[2] Now Major-general Scott, of the United States army.   The present General Wool was a captain, and commanded a company in the action.

Falls of Niagara.   We leave what questions upon this point remain open, to be settled by wiser minds, and hasten on to the Falls.   We caught a few glimpses of the green waters from the windows of the car, and in a few minutes were in the midst of the tumult of porters at the village, more clamorous for our ears than the dull roar of the cataract near by.   The fasting upon the lake and the early morning ride had given us a glorious appetite for breakfast, and as soon as it was appeased we sallied out, guide-book in hand, to see the celebrities.   These have been described a thousand times.   Poets, painters, travelers, historians, philosophers, and penny-a-liners have vied with each other in magnifying this wonder, and as I can not (if I would) "add one cubit to its stature" for the credulous, a thought concerning its sublimity and beauty for the romantic, a hue to the high coloring of others for the sentimental, or a new fact or theory for the philosophical, I shall pass among the lions in almost perfect silence, and speedily leave the excitements of this fashionable resort for the more quiet grandeur and beauty of the Mohawk Valley, once the " dark and bloody ground," but now a paradise of fertility, repose, and peace.

We crossed the whirling rapids and made the circuit of Goat Island.   In this route all the remarkable points of the great cataract are brought to view.   From the Hog's Back, at the lower end of the island, there is a fine prospect of the river below, and the distant Canada shore beyond.   The almost invisible Suspension Bridge, like a thread in air, was seen two miles distant ; and beneath us, through the mist of the American Fall, glorious with rainbow hues, the little steam-boat, the " Maid of the Mist," came breasting the powerful current.   We looked down from our lofty eyrie (literally, in the clouds), through the mist veil, upon her deck, and her passengers appeared like Lilliputians in a tiny skiff.   From the southern side of the island we had a noble view of the Horse-shoe Fall, over which pours the greater portion of the Niagara River.   The water is estimated to be twenty feet deep upon the crown of the cataract.   Biddle's Tower is a fine observatory, overlooking, on one side, the boiling abyss below the fall, and standing apparently in the midst of the rushing waters as they hurry down the rapids above.   We spent two hours upon the verge of the floods, in the shadows of the lofty trees that cover the island, but these scenes were tame compared with what we beheld from the " Maid of the Mist" toward noon.   We rode nearly to the Suspension Bridge, and, walking down a winding road cleft in the rocks, reached the brink of the river at the head of the great rapids above the whirlpool.   There we embarked on the little steam-boat, and moved up the river to the cataract.   As we approached the American Fall, all retreated into the cabins, and, the windows being closed, we were soon enveloped in spray.   It was a sight indescribably grand.   As we looked up, the waters seemed to be pouring from the clouds.   A feeling of awe, allied to that of worship, pervaded us, and all were silent until the avalanche of waters was passed.   The beautiful lines of Brainerd came vividly up from the shrine of memory, and aided my thoughts in seeking appropriate language :

> " It would seem
> As if God poured thee from his ' hollow hand,'
> And hung his bow upon thine awful front,
> And spoke in that loud voice which seemed to him
> Who dwelt in Patmos for his Savior's sake,
> ' The sound of many waters,' and had bade
> The flood to chronicle the ages back,
> And notch his cent'ries in the eternal rocks.
>
> Deep calleth unto deep.   And what are we
> That hear the question of that voice sublime ?
> Or what are all the notes that ever rung
> From war's vain trumpet, by thy thundering side ?
> Yea, what is all the riot man can make
> In his short life to thy unceasing roar ?
> And yet, bold babbler, what art thou to Him
> Who drowned the world, and heaped the waters far
> Above its loftiest mountains ? a light wave
> That breaks and whispers of its Maker's might."

228   PICTORIAL FIELD-BOOK

Buckingham's Lines.   Voyage of the Maid of the Mist.   Romantic Marriage.   The Whirlpool.   The Suspension Bridge.

Beautifully has Buckingham expressed the reverential thoughts which fill the mind and part the lips for utterance in that majestic presence :

> " Hail ! sovereign of the world of floods ! whose majesty and might
> First dazzles—then enraptures—then o'erawes the aching sight;
> The pomp of kings and emperors in every clime and zone
> Grow dim beneath the splendors of thy glorious watery throne.
>
> " No fleets can stop thy progress, no armies bid thee stay,
> But onward, onward, onward thy march still holds its way;
> The rising mist that veils thee, as thine herald, goes before,
> And the music that proclaims thee is the thundering cataract's roar.
>
> " Thy reign is of the ancient days, thy scepter from on high—
> Thy birth was when the distant stars first lit the gloomy sky;
> The sun, the moon, and all the orbs that shine upon thee now,
> Beheld the wreath of glory which first bound thy infant brow !"

Our little boat, after sweeping around as near the great Horse-shoe Fall as prudence would allow, touched a moment at the landing on the Canada side, and then returned to her moorings.   We felt relieved when we stood again on land, for there is some peril in the voyage ; yet the wonderful scene yields a full compensation for the risk.   It affords an opportunity to exhibit courage more sensibly than the foolish periling of life in clambering over the slippery rocks under the Falls, and sentiment has here some chance for respectable display.   The week previous to our visit a young couple, with a parson, took passage in the " Maid of the Mist,"· and, when enveloped in the spray of the cataract, were united in wedlock.   What an altar before which to make nuptial vows !   Can they ever forget the solemn promises there made, or be unfaithful to the pledge there sealed ?

We visited the whirlpool, and that wonder of art, the Suspension Bridge, before returning to the village.   The former is at the elbow of the Niagara River, two and a half miles below the cataract, and should never be left unseen by the visitor at the Falls.   The Suspension Bridge spans the river near the head of the rapids above the whirlpool.   The present structure is only the *scaffolding* for constructing the one intended for the passage of a train of rail-road cars.   Numerous foot-passengers were upon it, and a coach and horses, with driver and two passengers, crossed it while we were there.   The light structure bent beneath the weight like thin ice under the skater, yet the passage is considered perfectly safe.   I visited it again toward evening, and made the accompanying sketch to illustrate the method of its

construction and its relative position to the Falls.[1] To attempt to sketch the Falls *truthfully* is vain.   They have never yet been portrayed

PART OF NIAGARA SUSPENSION BRIDGE.[2]

---

[1] The bridge from pier to pier is eight hundred feet long.   Its breadth is eight feet.   The whole bridge is suspended upon eight cables, four on each side, which pass over towers fifty-four feet high, built of heavy timbers.   The towers for the large bridge will be of solid masonry eighty feet high.   Each cable is eleven hundred and sixty feet long, and composed of seventy-two number ten iron wires, around which is wrapped small wire three times boiled in linseed oil, which anneals it, and gives it a coat that can not be injured by exposure to the weather, and preserves the wire from rust.   The cables, after passing over the piers on the banks, are fast anchored in masonry fifty feet back of them.   The suspenders are composed of ¸ight wires each, and are placed four and a half feet apart.   The bridge is two hundred feet above the water.

[2] This view, looking up the river, comprises about one half the bridge, a portion of the bank on the Canada side on the right, the American shore on the left, and a part of the Falls, seen under the bridge, in the extreme distance.

in their grandeur, and never can be.   A picture can not convey an idea of their magnificence to the eye.   They must be seen to be known.   Art utterly fails in attempts to transfer their features to canvas, and degrades nature by its puny efforts.   In their *motion* consists their great sublimity, and the painter might as well attempt to delineate the whirlwind as to depict Niagara in its glory.

We left Niagara early on Saturday morning, stopped in Buffalo just long enough to go from one rail-way station to another, and reached Syracuse at about eight in the evening, a distance of two hundred miles.   That day's journey seems more like a dream than reality, for hills and valleys, woods and meadows, hamlets and villages, lakes and rivers, the puff of the engine, the rattle of the train, men, women, and children in serried ranks, are all mingled in confusion in the kaleidescope of memory, and nothing but a map or a Traveler's Guide-book can unravel the tangled skein of localities that was spun out in that rapid journey of fourteen hours.   We remember the broad Niagara, the dark Erie with white sails upon its bosom, the stately houses and busy streets of Buffalo, the long *reaches* of flat, new country, dotted with stumps, from Buffalo to Attica and beyond, the stirring mart of Rochester, the fields, and orchards, and groves of lofty trees that seemed waltzing by us, the beautiful villages of Canandaigua and Geneva, the falls of the Seneca, the long bridge ot Cayuga, the strong prison and beautiful dwellings of Auburn, and the golden sunset and cool breeze that charmed us as we approached Syracuse.   In that flourishing city of the recent wilderness we passed a quiet Sabbath with some friends, and the next morning I journeyed to Rome.

August 19, 1848.

Although a quarter of a century has scarcely passed since Syracuse was a village of mean huts,[1] it has a history connected with European civilization more than two hundred years old.   At Salina, now a portion of the city of Syracuse, where the principal salt-wells are, the French, under the Sieur Dupuys, an officer of the garrison at Quebec, made a settlement as early as 1655.   The Onondaga tribe then had their villages in the valley, a few miles from Syracuse, and a good understanding prevailed between them and the new-comers.   The jealousy of the Mohawks was aroused, and they attempted to cut off the colonists while on their way up the St. Lawrence.   They, however, reached their destination in safety, and upon the borders of the Onondaga Lake they reared dwellings and prepared for a permanent colony.   But the uneasiness of the Indian tribes soon manifested itself in hostile preparations, and in the winter of 1658 Dupuys was informed that large parties of Mohawks, Oneidas, and even Onondagas, were arming.   Unable to procure assistance in time from Quebec, he succeeded, by stratagem, in constructing some bateaux and escaping with the whole colony secretly down the river to Oswego, and thence to Montreal.

Relying implicitly upon the good faith and promised friendship of the Indians, Dupuys had neglected to preserve his canoes.   To construct new ones in view of the Indians would advertise them of his intentions, and bring their hatchets upon the settlement at once.   He therefore had small bateaux made in the garret of the Jesuit's house, and kept them concealed when finished.   A young Frenchman had been adopted into the family of a chief, and had

---

[1] In 1820 the late William L. Stone visited Syracuse in company with Mr. Forman, one of the earliest and most industrious friends of the Erie Canal.   "I lodged for the night," says Mr. Stone, "at a miserable tavern, thronged by a company of salt-boilers from Salina, forming a group of about as rough-looking specimens of humanity as I had ever seen.   Their wild visages, beards thick and long, and matted hair even now rise up in dark, distant, and picturesque effect before me.   I passed a restless night, disturbed by strange fancies, as I yet well remember.   It was in October, and a flurry of snow during the night had rendered the morning aspect of the country more dreary than the evening before.   The few houses I have already described, standing upon low and almost marshy ground, and surrounded by trees and entangled thickets, presented a very uninviting scene.   ' Mr. Forman,' said I, ' do you call this a village ?   It would make an owl weep to fly over it.'   ' Never mind,' said he, in reply, ' you will live to see it a city yet.' "   Mr. Stone did, indeed, live to see it a city in size, when he wrote the above in 1840, and it is now a city in fact, with mayor and aldermen, noble stores and dwellings, and a population of some 14,000.

Judge Forman was one of the projectors of the Erie Canal, and the founder of Syracuse.   He died at Rutherfordton, North Carolina, on the 4th of August, 1849, aged 72 years.

acquired great influence over the tribe.   By their customs an adopted son had all the priv-ileges of a son by birth.   When Dupuys had a sufficient number of bateaux finished, this young man went to his foster-father, and in a solemn manner related that he had dreamed, the previous night, that he was at a feast, where the guests ate and drank every thing that was set before them.   He then asked the old chief to permit him to make such a feast for the tribe.   The request was granted, and the feast was spread.   Many Frenchmen were present, and with horns, drums, and trumpets, they kept a continual uproar.   The French, in the mean while, were diligently embarking and loading their bateaux, unobserved by the feasting savages.   At length the guests, who had been eating and drinking for hours, ceased gormandizing, to take some repose.   The young Frenchman commenced playing upon a guitar, and in a few minutes every red man was in a profound slumber.   He then joined his companions, and before morning the whole colony were far on their way toward Oswego. Late the next day the Indians stood wondering at the silence that prevailed in the dwellings of the whites, and when, at evening, having seen no signs of human life through the day, they ventured to break open the fastened dwellings, they were greatly astonished at finding every Frenchman gone ; and greater was their perplexity in divining the means by which they escaped, being entirely ignorant of their having any vessels.[1]

Ten years afterward another French colony settled in what now is called Pompey, about fourteen miles from Syracuse, and for three years it prospered, and many converts were made to the Catholic faith from the Onondaga tribe.   A company of Spaniards, having been in-formed of a lake whose bottom was covered with brilliant scales like silver, arrived there, and in a short time the animosities of the respective adventurers caused them to accuse each other to the Indians of foul designs upon the tribes.   The Onondagas believed both parties, and determined to rid themselves of such troublesome neighbors.   Assisted by the Oneidas and Cayugas, they fell upon the colony on All-Saints' day, 1669, and every Frenchman and Spaniard was massacred.[2]

Evidences of much earlier visits by Europeans have been found in the vicinity, among which was a sepulchral stone that was exhumed near Pompey Hill.   It was of an oblong

figure, being fourteen inches long by twelve wide, and about eight inch-es in thickness.   In the center of the surface was a figure of a tree, and a serpent climbing it ; and upon each side of the tree was an in-scription, as seen in the cut : " *Leo X., De Vix*, 1520.   *L. S. † Ω*." This inscription may be thus translated : " Leo X., by the grace of God ; sixth year of his pontificate, 1520."   The letters L. S. were doubtless the initials of the one to whose memory the stone was set up. The cross denoted that he was a Roman Catholic, but the meaning of the inverted U is not so clear.   It has been supposed that the stone

SEPULCHRAL STONE.

was carved on the spot by a friend of the deceased, who may have been one of several French or Spanish adventurers that found their way hither from Florida, which was discovered by the Spaniards in 1502.   They were amused and excited by stories of a lake far in the north, whose bottom was lined with silver, and this was sufficient to cause them to peril every thing in searching it out.   De Soto's historian speaks, in the course of his narrative of the adven-tures of that commander in the interior of America, of extreme cold at a place called by the natives *Saquechama*.   It is supposed that this name and *Susquehanna* are synonymous ap-pellations for the country in Central New York, and that the silver-bottomed lake was the Onondaga, the flakes and crystals of salt which cover its bottom giving it the appearance of silver.[3]

---

[1] See extracts from a MS. history of Onondaga county, by Rev. J. W. Adams, of Syracuse, quoted in the Historical Collections of New York, p. 398.

[2] Dewitt Clinton's *Memoir on the Antiquities of Western New York.*

[3] See Clinton's *Memoir*, &c. ; also, Sandford's *Aborigines*, note on page 114.   The crystals of salt on the bottom of the lake, into which the salt springs flow, were, like the scales of mica discovered on the eastern coast by Gosnold and his party, mistaken for laminæ of silver.   There are not many salt springs near the

We have already noticed the expedition of the French, under Frontenac, as far as the Onondaga Valley. From that time nothing but Indian feuds disturbed the repose that rested upon Onondaga Lake and the beautiful country around, until business enterprise within the present century began its warfare upon the forests and the rich soil.

I arrived at Rome, upon the Mohawk, toward noon. It is a pleasant village, and stands upon the site of old Fort Stanwix, on the western verge of the historical ground of the Mohawk Valley. Here was the outpost of active operations in this direction, and here was enacted one of the most desperate defenses of a fortress that occurred during our struggle for

independence. The village, in its rapid growth, has overspread the site of the fortification, and now not a vestige of antiquity remains, except a large elm-tree by the house of Alvah Mudge, Esq., which stood within the southwest angle of the fort. Mr. Mudge kindly pointed out to me the area comprehended within the fort, and the portion of the village seen in the picture covers that area. The mason-work in the foreground is a part of the first lock of the Black River Canal, at present an unproductive work. The large building in the center of the picture is the mansion of John Striker, Esq., president of the Rome Bank, and stands near the site of the northeast angle of the fort. The whole view is only a few rods northwest of the Mohawk River, and a mile eastward of Wood Creek, the main inlet of Oneida Lake. Here was a portage of a

SITE OF FORT STANWIX.

mile, and the only interruption of water communication between Schenectady and Oswego. This inconvenience was obviated by the construction of a canal between the Mohawk and Wood Creek, in 1797.

Fort Stanwix was built in 1758, under the direction of General Stanwix, after the defeat of Abercrombie at Ticonderoga. It was a strong square fortification, having bomb-proof bastions, a glacis, covered way, and a well-picketed ditch around the ramparts. Its position was important in a military point of view, for it commanded the portage between the Mohawk and Wood Creek, and was a key to communication between the Mohawk Valley and Lake Ontario. Other, but smaller, fortifications were erected in the vicinity. Fort Newport, on Wood Creek, and Fort Ball, about half way across the portage, formed a part of the military works there, and afforded not only a strong post of resistance to French aggression in that direction, but also a powerful protection to the Indian trade. The works cost the British and Colonial government two hundred and sixty-six thousand four hundred dollars, yet when the Revolution broke out the fort and its outposts were in ruins.

From the commencement of hostilities the Mohawk Valley was a theater of great activity, and all through the eventful years of the contest it suffered dreadfully from the effects of partisan warfare. Every rood of ground was trodden by hostile parties, and for seven years the fierce Indian, and the ofttimes more ferocious Tory, kept the people in continual alarm, spreading death and desolation over that fair portion of our land. So frequent and sanguinary were the stealthy midnight attacks or open daylight struggles, that Tryon coun-

surface, but under the marshes that surround Onondaga Lake, and beneath the lake itself, there seems to lie a vast salt lake, and shafts are sunken from the surface above into it. The water or brine is pumped up from these shafts or wells, and vast quantities of salt are manufactured annually in the neighborhood of Syracuse. A great number of men find employment there, and the state derives a handsome revenue from the works.

ty[1] obtained the appropriate appellation of "the dark and bloody ground," and, long after peace blessed the land, its forests were traversed with fear and distrust.   Here was the seat

of Sir William Johnson,[2] agent for the British government in its transactions with the SIX NATIONS.   He was shrewd, cunning, and licentious, having little respect for the laws of God or man, and observed them only so far as compliance was conducive to his personal interest.   By presents, conformity in dress and manners, and other appliances, he obtained almost unbounded influence over the tribes of the valley, and at his beck a thousand armed warriors would rush to the field.   He died before the events of our Revolution brought his vast influence over the Indians into play, in active measures against the patriots.   Yet his mantle of power and moral sway fell, in a great degree, upon his son, Sir John Johnson, who succeeded to his title, office, and estates.   The latter, his cousin Guy Johnson, *Thayendanegea* (Brant) the Mohawk sachem, Daniel Claus, and the Butlers were the leading spirits of loyalty in Tryon county, and the actors and abettors of scenes that darken the blackest page in the history of our race.   These will be noticed hereafter.   For the present we will confine our thoughts to the most prominent local events immediately antecedent to the siege of Fort Stanwix, or Schuyler, upon the site of which, at Rome, we are standing.

1765.   The excitement of the Stamp Act reached even the quiet valley of the Mohawk, and implanted there the seeds of rebellion, and the people were eager listeners while the conflict of power and principle was going on upon the sea-board, during the ten years a 1775.   preceding the organization of the Continental army.[a]   The meeting of the general Continental Congress caused opinions to take a definite shape and expression, and in the autumn of that year the demarkation line between patriots and Loyalists was distinctly drawn among the people of this inland district.

In the spring of 1775, just before the second Congress assembled at Philadelphia, at a court holden at Johnstown, the Loyalists made a demonstration against the proceedings of

---

[1] Tryon county then included all the colonial settlements in New York west and southwest of Schenectady.   It was taken from Albany county in 1772, and named in honor of William Tryon, then governor of the province.   The name was changed to Montgomery in 1784.   The county buildings were at Johnstown, where was the residence of Sir William Johnson (still standing).

[2] Sir William Johnson was born in Ireland, about the year 1714.   He was a nephew of Sir Peter Warren, the commodore who was distinguished in the attack on Louisburgh, Cape Breton, 1745.   Sir Peter married a lady (Miss Watts) in New York, purchased large tracts of land upon the Mohawk, and about 1734 young Johnson was induced to come to America and take charge of his uncle's affairs in that quarter.   He learned the Indian language, adopted their manners, and, by fair trade and conciliatory conduct, won their friendship and esteem.   He built a large stone mansion on the Mohawk, about three miles west of Amsterdam, where he resided twenty years previous to the erection of Johnson Hall at Johnstown.   It was fortified, and was called *Fort Johnson*.   It is still standing, a substantial specimen of the domestic architecture of that period.   In 1755 he commanded a force intended to invest Crown Point.   He was attacked by Dieskau at the head of Lake George, where he came off victorious.   For this he was made major general and a knight.   He commanded the assault upon Niagara, after the death of Prideaux, and was successful there.   He was never given credit

FORT JOHNSON.

for great military skill or personal bravery, and was more expert in intriguing with Indian warriors, and sending them to the field, than in leading disciplined troops boldly into action.   He died at Johnson Hall (Johnstown) on the 11th of July, 1774, aged 60 years.

the National Council, by drawing up and obtaining signatures to a declaration disapproving of the acts of that body in the preceding autumn. This proceeding of the Tories aroused the indignation of the Whigs, who composed a considerable majority of the whites in Tryon county. Committees were appointed and public meetings were called in every district in the county. The first was held at the house of John Veeder, in Caughnawaga,[1] where patriotic speeches were made, and a liberty pole, a most offensive object to the eyes of the Loyalists, was erected. Before this was accomplished, Sir John Johnson, accompanied by Colonel Claus, Guy Johnson, and Colonel John Butler, with a large number of their retainers, armed with swords and pistols, arrived upon the ground and interrupted the proceedings.

Guy Johnson mounted a high stoop near the old church and harangued the people. He expatiated upon the strength of the king and government, and the folly of opposing the authority of the crown. He had not a conciliatory word for the people, but denounced their proceedings in virulent and abusive language, so irritating, that Jacob Sammons, a leader among the Whigs, could no longer restrain himself, but boldly pronounced the speaker a liar and a villain. Johnson leaped from his tribune and seized Sammons by the throat; one of his party felled the patriot to the ground by a blow from a loaded whip-handle, and then bestrode his body. When Sammons recovered from the momentary stupor, he hurled the fellow from him, and, springing upon his feet, stripped off his coat and prepared to fight, when he was again knocked down. Most of his Whig friends had fled in alarm, and he was carried to his father's house, " bearing upon his body the first scars

CAUGHNAWAGA CHURCH.[2]

of the Revolutionary contest in the county of Tryon."[3]

A spirited Whig meeting was held soon afterward, in Cherry Valley, where the conduct of the Tories at Johnstown was strongly condemned; but in the Palatine district and other places the threats and the known strength of the Johnsons and their friends intimidated the Whigs for a while.

In the mean time, Colonel Johnson fortified the baronial hall by planting swivels around it. He paraded the militia, armed the Scotch Highlanders (who lived in the vicinity of Johnstown, and were Roman Catholics), and by similar acts, hostile to the popular movement, the suspicions of the Whigs were confirmed that he was preparing for the suppression of all patriot demonstrations in the county, and was inciting the Indians to join the enemies

---

[1] Caughnawaga is the ancient name of the Indian village that stood a little eastward of the present village of Fonda. Its name signifies *coffin*, and was given to the place in consequence of there being in the Mohawk, opposite the village, a black stone (still to be seen) resembling a coffin, and projecting above the surface at low water.—*Historical Collections of New York*, p. 281.

[2] This old church, now (1848) known as the *Fonda Academy*, under the management of Rev. Douw Van Olinda, is about half a mile east of the court-house, in the village of Fonda. It is a stone edifice, and was erected in 1763 by voluntary contributions. Sir William Johnson contributed liberally. Its first pastor was Thomas Romayne, who was succeeded in 1795 by Abraham Van Horn, one of the earliest graduates of King's (now Columbia) College, in the city of New York. He was from Kingston, Ulster county, and remained its pastor until 1840. During his ministry he united in marriage 1500 couples. The church was without a bell until the confiscated property of Sir John Johnson was sold in the Revolution, when the *dinner-bell* of his father was purchased and hung in the steeple. The bell weighs a little more than one hundred pounds, and bears the following inscription : " S. R. William Johnson, baronet, 1774. Made by Miller and Ross, in Eliz. Town."—*Simms's Schoharie County*, &c.

Over the door of the church is a stone tablet, with this inscription in Dutch : " Komt laett ons op gaen tot den Bergh des Heeren, to den huyse des godes Jacobs, op dat hy ons leere van syne wegen, en dat wy wandel in syne paden." *English*, " Come ye, and let us go up to the mountain of the Lord; to the house of the God of Jacob, and he will teach us his ways, and we will walk in his paths."

[3] Stone's Life of Brant, i., 53.

of liberty as soon as actual hostilities should commence.[1]   Another circumstance confirmed these suspicions.   Brant was the secretary of Colonel Guy Johnson, the superintendent of Indian affairs after the death of Sir William, and his activity in visiting the tribes and holding secret conferences with the sachems was unceasing.   Suddenly his former friendly intercourse with Mr. Kirkland, the faithful Christian missionary, was broken off in 1774, and, at Brant's instigation, an Oneida chief preferred charges against the pious minister to Guy Johnson, and asked for his removal.   It was well known that Mr. Kirkland was a Whig,[2] and this movement of the wily sachem could not be misinterpreted.   But the Oneida nation rallied in support of the minister, and his removal was for a time delayed.

During the summer of 1775 the Johnsons were very active in winning the *Six Nations* from their promises of neutrality in the coming contest.[3]   A council of the Mohawks was held at Guy Park in May, 1775. which was attended by delegates from the Albany and the Tryon county Committees. *Little Abraham*, brother of the famous Hendrick who was killed near Lake George, was the principal chief of the Mohawks, and their best speaker on the occasion.   Guy Johnson, the Indian agent, was in attendance

GUY PARK.[4]

at the council, but the result was unsatisfactory to both parties.   The delegates, cognizant of the disaffection and bad faith of the Indians, could not rely upon their present promises ; and Guy Johnson, alarmed by the events at Lexington and Concord, and by intimations which he had received that his person was in danger of seizure by order of the General Congress, broke up the council abruptly, and immediately directed the assembling of another at the Upper Castle, on the German Flats, whither himself and family, attended by a large retinue of Mohawks, at once repaired.   But this council was not held, and Johnson, with his family and the Indians, pushed on to Fort Stanwix.   His sojourn there was brief, and he moved on to Ontario, far beyond the verge of civilization. Brant and the Butlers attended him, and there a large council was held, composed chiefly of Cayugas and Senecas.

Thus far no positive acts of hostility had been committed by Guy Johnson and his friends, yet his design to alienate the Indians and prepare them for war upon the patriots was undoubted.   His hasty departure with his family to the wilderness, accompanied by a large train of Mohawk warriors, and the holding a grand council in the midst of the fierce Cayu-

---

[1] See letter of the Palatine Committee to the Committee of Safety at Albany, dated May 18th, 1775.

[2] Samuel Kirkland was son of the pious minister, Daniel Kirkland, of Norwich, Connecticut.   He learned the language of the Mohawks, was ordained a missionary to the Indians at Lebanon in 1766, and removed his wife to the Oneida Castle in 1769.   The next spring he removed to the house of his friend, General Herkimer, near Little Falls, where his twin children were born, one of whom was the late Dr. Kirkland, president of Harvard College.   The very air of Norwich seemed to give the vitality of freedom to its sons, and Mr. Kirkland early imbibed those patriotic principles which distinguished him through life.   His attachment to the republican cause was well known, and, after the battles of Lexington and Concord, the provincial Congress of Massachusetts, desirous of securing either the friendship or neutrality of the Six Nations, sent a letter to him inclosing an address to the Indians, and requesting him to use his influence in obtaining the ends in view.   Mr. Kirkland succeeded in securing the attachment of the Oneidas to the patriot cause, and continued his religious labors among them during the war, when the other tribes, through the influence of Brant and the Johnsons, had taken up arms for the king.   He officiated as chaplain to the American forces in the vicinity of his labors, and accompanied Sullivan in his expedition in 1779.   The state of New York, in consideration of his patriotic services, gave him the lands of the "Kirkland patent," in the town of Kirkland.   After 40 years' service for his God and country, he fell asleep at Paris, Oneida county, on the 28th of March, 1808, in the 67th year of his age.

[3] General Schuyler had held a conference with the chiefs of the Six Nations during the previous winter, and, setting before them the nature of the quarrel that had led to hostile movements, received from them solemn promises that they would remain neutral.

[4] This was the residence of Guy Johnson, and is still standing, on the north side of the Mohawk, about a mile from the village of Amsterdam, in Montgomery county.   It is substantially built of stone, and may stand a century yet.   Embowered in trees, it is a beautiful summer residence.

gas and Senecas, greatly alarmed the people of the lower valley,[1] inasmuch as his reply to a letter from the Provincial Congress of New York, which he wrote from the council-room in the wilderness, glowed with sentiments of loyalty. It was, moreover, posi- July 8, 1775. tively asserted that he was collecting a large body of savages on that remote frontier, to fall upon the inhabitants of the valley, and this belief was strengthened by the fact that Sir John Johnson, who held a commission of brigadier general of militia, remained at Johnson Hall, then fortified and surrounded by a large body of Loyalists. The alarmed patriots appealed to the Committee of Safety at Albany for protection, and every preparation was made to avert the threatened disaster. Guy Johnson, however, did not return to the valley, but went to Oswego, where he called another council, and then, accompanied by a large number of chiefs and warriors of the Six Nations, among whom was Brant, departed for Canada. He descended the St. Lawrence to Montreal, where he met Sir Guy Carleton and Sir Frederic Haldimand, then governor of Canada, with whom the Indians entered into a formal agreement to take up arms for the king.[2] These were the Indians who appeared against the Americans at St. John's, on the Sorel, and who, in connection with some Caughnawagas, made the terrible massacre of Major Sherburne's corps at the Cedars in the following spring, noticed in a previous chapter.

These movements of the Johnsons and their friends, the strengthening of Johnson Hall, the military organization of the Scotch Highlanders in the vicinity, the increasing alienation of the Indians, the boldness of the Tories, and the continual alarm of the people of Tryon county, caused the General Congress, in December, 1775, to take active measures in that direction. The Dutch and Germans in the Mohawk Valley, Schoharie, Cherry Valley, and, indeed, in all parts of that extensive country, were ardent Whigs; and the Highlanders, with the retainers of the Johnsons and their friends, composed the bulk of the Tory population, except a few desperate men who looked for plunder and reward. Had these alone been inimical to the patriots, there would have been little alarm; but the country swarmed with Indians, who were hourly becoming more and more hostile to the Whigs, through the influence of the Johnsons and their powerful ally, Joseph Brant. It was also reported that military stores were collected at Johnson Hall, and that three hundred Indians were ready to fall upon the whites when Sir John Johnson should give the signal. Congress, therefore, ordered General Schuyler (who had returned to Albany from Lake Champlain, on account of ill health) to take such measures as he should think proper to seize the military stores, to apprehend the Tory leaders, and to disarm the loyal inhabitants. He had no troops at command, but, aided by the Albany Committee of Safety, he soon mustered seven hundred men and marched to Schenectady. The Mohawks of the "Lower Castle" (near Amsterdam), with Little Abraham at their head, had not been seduced by Brant and Johnson, but kept to their promise to remain neutral. To preserve their good-will, Schuyler sent to them a messenger (Mr. Bleecker, the Indian interpreter, then residing at Albany) with a January 15, 1776. belt, informing them of the object of his expedition. They were not pleased with the idea of invasion, and a deputation was sent to the general to persuade him to desist. He conferred with them at Schenectady, satisfied them of his good intentions and the necessity of the movement, and then marched on as far as Guy Park. He dispatched a January 16. letter at the same time to Sir John Johnson, requesting a personal interview with him. They met at Guy Park in a friendly way, and General Schuyler proposed terms by

---

[1] On the 11th of July, Colonel Herkimer wrote from Canajoharie to the Palatine Committee, that he had received credible intelligence that morning that Johnson was ready to march back upon the settlement with a body of 800 or 900 Indians, and that his point of attack would be just below the Little Falls. This intelligence proved to be untrue.

[2] British historians assert that General Carleton was averse to the employment of the savages against the Americans. Mr. Stone, in his Life of Brant, quotes from a speech of that chief, wherein the reverse is asserted. The British commanders never failed to employ Indians in warfare, when their services could be obtained. Their feelings of humanity doubtless revolted when coalescing with the savages of the forest to butcher their brethren, but with them *principle* too often yielded to *expediency* in that unrighteous war.

which the matter might be settled without bloodshed.   He demanded the immediate surrender of all arms, ammunition, and stores in the possession of Johnson, the delivery to him
of all the arms and military accouterments held by the Tories and Indians, and Sir John's
parole of honor not to act inimically to the patriot cause.   Sir John asked twenty-four hours
for consideration.   His reply was unsatisfactory, and Schuyler marched on to
January 18.
Caughnawaga, within four miles of Johnstown.   The militia had turned out with
alacrity, and his force of seven hundred men had increased to three thousand.   Sir John,
alarmed, acceded to all the terms proposed by General Schuyler, and the next day that officer proceeded to Johnson Hall, where arms and other munitions of war were surrendered by
the baronet.   About three hundred Scotchmen also delivered up their arms.   Colonel (afterward General) Herkimer was empowered to complete the disarming of the Tories, and
General Schuyler and his forces marched back to Albany.

It soon afterward became evident that what Sir John had promised when constrained by
fear would not be performed when the cause of that fear was removed.   He violated his
parole of honor, and the Highlanders began to be as bold as ever in their opposition to the
Whigs.   Congress thought it dangerous to allow Johnson his liberty, and directed Schuyler
to seize his person, and to proceed vigorously against the Highlanders in his interest.   Colonel Dayton was intrusted with the command of an expedition for the purpose, and in
1776.
May he proceeded to Johnstown.   The baronet had friends among the Loyalists in
Albany, by whom he was timely informed of the intentions of Congress.   His most valuable
articles were put in an iron chest and buried in his garden[1] when he heard of Dayton's approach, and, hastily collecting a large number of his Scotch tenants and other Tories, he fled to
the woods by the way of the Sacandaga, where it is supposed they were met by Indians sent
from Canada to escort them thither.[2]   Amid perils and hardships of every kind, they traversed the wilderness between the head waters of the Hudson and the St. Lawrence, and,
after nineteen days' wanderings, arrived at Montreal.   Sir John was immediately commissioned a colonel in the British service, raised two battalions of Loyalists called the *Johnson
Greens*, and became one of the bitterest and most implacable enemies of the Americans that
appeared during the war.   He afterward, as we shall observe, scourged the Mohawk Valley
with fire and sword, and spread death and desolation among the frontier settlements even so
far south as the Valley of Wyoming.

After the flight of Johnson and the Tories, Tryon county enjoyed a short season of repose,
and nothing of importance occurred during the remainder of 1776 and the winter of 1777.
Yet the people did not relax their vigilance.   The Declaration of Independence was received
by them with great joy, but they clearly perceived that much was yet to be done to *support*
that declaration.   Congress, too, saw the importance of defending the Northern and Western frontiers of New York from the incursions of the enemy and their savage allies.   The
fortresses on Lake Champlain were already in their possession, and General Schuyler was
ordered to repair and strengthen old Fort Stanwix, then in ruins, and to erect other fortifications, if necessary, along the Mohawk River.   Colonel Dayton was charged with the duty

---

[1] Sir John had a faithful black slave, to whom he intrusted the duty of burying his iron chest.   Colonel
Volkert Veeder bought the slave when Johnson Hall was sold, but he would never tell where the treasure
was concealed.   Sir John visited the Mohawk Valley in 1780, recovered his slave, and by his directions
found the iron chest.—*Simms.*

[2] This is inferred from a sentence in one of Brant's speeches, quoted by Mr. Stone, as follows: "We
then went in a body to a town then in possession of the enemy, and rescued Sir John Johnson, bringing him
fearlessly through the streets."   Brant and Guy Johnson were both in England at that time.

Lady Johnson was conveyed to Albany, and there kept for some time, as a sort of hostage for the good
conduct of her husband.   Among the articles left in Johnson Hall was the family Bible of Sir William.
When the confiscated property was sold, the Bible was bought by John Taylor, who was afterward Lieutenant-governor of New York.   Perceiving that it contained the family record of the Johnsons, Mr. Taylor
wrote to Sir John, offering its restoration.   A rude messenger was sent for the Bible.   "I have come for
Sir William's Bible," he said, "and there are the four guineas which it cost."   The man was asked what
message Sir John had sent.   He replied, "Pay four guineas and take the book."—*Stone's Life of Brant,*
ii., 145

of repairing Fort Stanwix, with the assistance of the Tryon county militia, but he seems to have made little progress, for it was not complete when, in the summer of the next year, it was invested by St. Leger.   He named the new fortress Fort Schuyler, in 1777 honor of the commanding general of the Northern Department, and by that appellation it was known through the remainder of the war.[1]

In the course of the spring of 1777, Brant came from Canada, and appeared among the Mohawks at Oghkwaga,[2] or Oquaca, with a large body of warriors.   He had not yet committed any act of hostility within the borders of New York, nor was his presence at the Cedars known in the Mohawk Valley.   Yet none doubted his hostile intentions, and his presence gave much uneasiness to the patriots, while the Tories became bolder and more insolent. In June his intentions became more manifest, when he ascended the Susquehanna, from Oghkwaga to Unadilla, with about eighty of his warriors, and requested an interview with the Rev. Mr. Johnstone, of the " Johnstone Settlement."   He declared that his object was to procure food for his famished people, and gave the whites to understand that, if provisions were not furnished, the Indians would take them by force.   Mr. Johnstone sounded Brant concerning his future intentions, and the chief, without reserve, told him that he had made a covenant with the king, and was not inclined to break it.   The people supplied him with food, but the marauders, not satisfied, drove off a large number of cattle, sheep, and swine. As soon as the Indians had departed, not feeling safe in their remote settlement, the whites abandoned it, and took refuge in Cherry Valley.   Some families in the neighborhood of Unadilla fled to the German Flats, and others to Esopus and Newburgh, on the Hudson River.

As the Indian forces were constantly augmenting at Oghkwaga, it was determined by General Schuyler and his officers, in council, that Herkimer (now a brigadier) should repair thither and obtain an interview with Brant.   Herkimer took with him three hundred Tryon county militia, and invited Brant to meet him at Unadilla.   This the chief agreed to.   In the mean while, Colonel Van Schaick marched with one hundred and fifty men as far as Cherry Valley, and General Schuyler held himself in readiness to repair to Unadilla if his presence should be needed.   These precautions seemed necessary, for they knew not what might be the disposition of Brant.

It was a week after Herkimer arrived at Unadilla before Brant made his appearance. He came accompanied by five hundred warriors.   He dispatched a runner to Herkimer to inquire the object of his visit.[3]   Herkimer replied that he came to see and converse with

---

[1] This change in the name of the fort, from Stanwix to Schuyler, produced some confusion, for there was already an old fort at Utica called Fort Schuyler, so named in honor of Colonel Peter Schuyler, a commander of provincial troops in the war with the French and Indians.

[2] Toward the close of the winter of 1777 a large gathering of Indians was held at Oghkwaga.   The Provincial Congress of New York dispatched thither Colonel John Harper, of Harpersfield, to ascertain their intentions.   He arrived on the 27th of February, and was well received by the Indians.   They expressed their sorrow for the troubles that afflicted Tryon county, and gave every assurance of their pacific dispositions.   Colonel Harper believed them, and gave them a feast by roasting an ox.   It was afterward discovered that all their friendship was feigned; their professions of peaceful intentions were gross hypocrisy.   A few weeks subsequently, while taking a circuit alone through the woods near the head waters of the Susquehanna, Harper met some Indians, who exchanged salutations with him.   He recognized one of them as Peter, an Indian whom he had seen at Oghkwaga, but they did not know him.   His great-coat covered his uniform, and he feigning to be a Tory, they told him they were on their way to cut off the Johnstone settlement on the east bank of the Susquehanna, near Unadilla.   Colonel Harper hastened back to Harpersfield, collected fifteen stout and brave men, and with them gave chase to the marauders.   In the course of the following night they came upon the Indians in the valley of Charlotte River.   It was almost daylight when their waning fires were discovered.   The savages were in a profound slumber.   Their arms were silently removed, and then each man of Harper's party, selecting his victim, sprang upon him, and before he was fairly awake the savage found himself fast bound with cords which the whites had brought with them.   It was a bolder achievement than if the red men had been killed, and nobler because bloodless. When the day dawned, and the Indians saw their captors, Peter exclaimed, "Ugh! Colonel Harper! Why didn't I know you yesterday?"   They were taken to Albany and surrendered into the hands of the Committee of Safety.

[3] The real object of the conference is not known.   It is supposed that, as Herkimer and Brant had been near neighbors and intimate friends, the former hoped, in a personal interview, to persuade the chief to join

his brother, Captain Brant. "And all these men wish to converse with the chief too?" asked the quick-witted messenger. He returned to Brant and communicated the reply. The parties were encamped within two miles of each other, and the whole assemblage made an imposing display. By mutual agreement, their arms were to be left in their respective encampments. The preliminaries being arranged, Brant and about forty warriors appeared upon the skirt of a distant wood, and the parties met in an open field. A circle was formed, and the two commanders, with attendants, entered it for conference. After exchanging a few words, Brant asked Herkimer the object of his visit. He made the same reply as to the messenger. "And all these have come on a friendly visit too?" said the chief. "All want to see the poor Indians. It is very kind," he added, while his lip curled with a sarcastic smile. After a while the conversation became animated, and finally the chief, being pressed by direct questions concerning his intentions, firmly replied, "That the Indians were in concert with the king, as their fathers had been; that the king's belts were yet lodged with them, and they could not violate their pledge; that General Herkimer and his followers had joined the Boston people against their sovereign; that, although the Boston people were resolute, the king would humble them; that General Schuyler was very smart on the Indians at the treaty of German Flats, but, at the same time, was not able to afford the smallest article of clothing; and, finally, that the Indians had formerly made war on the white people when they were all united, and, as they were now divided, the Indians were not frightened." He also told General Herkimer that a war-path had been opened across the country to Esopus, for the Tories of Ulster and Orange to join them. The conference ended then, with an agreement to meet the next morning at nine o'clock, the respective forces to remain encamped as they were.[1]

During the conference, some remarks made by Colonel Cox greatly irritated the sachem, and on his signal to his warriors, who were near, they ran to their encampment, raised the shrill war-hoop, and returned with their rifles. In the mean while the chief became pacified, and the warriors were kept at a proper distance. Herkimer, however, fearful that Brant's pacific appearance might be feigned, prepared to act with decision on the following morning. He charged an active young soldier, named Wagner, with the duty of shooting Brant, if any hostile movement should appear on the part of the chief. Wagner was to select two assistants, who were to shoot the two attendants of Brant at the same time. He chose Abraham and George Herkimer, nephews of the general, and the three stood by the side of Herkimer the next morning. There was no necessity for their services, and, haply, no blood was shed on the occasion. Mr. Stone seems to have mistaken Herkimer's precaution, in this instance, for premeditated perfidy, and says that, had the intent been perpetrated, the stain upon the character of the provincials would have been such that "all the waters of the Mohawk could not have washed it away." Mr. Wagner was yet living at Fort Plain when I visited that place in 1848, and I have his own authority for saying that the arrangement was only a precautionary one, for which Herkimer deserved praise. Mr. Stone gives his version upon "the written authority of Joseph Wagner himself." Simms has declared, in his "History of Schoharie County," and repeated in conversation with myself, that Wagner told him he never furnished a MS. account of the affair to any one. Here is some mistake in the matter, but the honorable character of General Herkimer forbids the idea of his having meditated the least perfidy.

Again they met, and the haughty chief—haughty because conscious of strength—as he entered the circle, addressed General Herkimer, and said, "I have five hundred warriors with me, armed and ready for battle. You are in my power, but, as we have been friends and neighbors, I will not take advantage of you." He then gave the signal, and all his warriors, painted in the hideous colors that distinguished them when going into battle, burst

the patriots, or, at least, to remain neutral. It is also supposed that he went to demand restitution for the cattle, sheep, and swine of which the savages had plundered the Johnstone and Unadilla settlements.

[1] Campbell's *Annals of Tryon County*.

from the surrounding forest, gave the war-hoop, and discharged their rifles in the air. Brant coolly advised the general to go back to his house, thanked him for his courtesy on the occasion, expressed a hope that he might one day return the compliment, and then turned proudly upon his heel and disappeared in the shadowy forest. " It was early in July, and the morning was remarkably clear and beautiful. But the echo of the war-hoop had scarcely died away before the heavens became black, and a violent storm obliged each party to seek the nearest shelter. Men less superstitious than many of the unlettered yeomen, who, leaning upon their arms, were witnesses of the events of this day, could not fail, in aftertimes, to look back upon the tempest, if not as an omen, at least as an emblem, of those bloody massacres with which these Indians and their associates subsequently visited the inhabitants of this unfortunate frontier."[1]

A few days after this conference, Brant withdrew his warriors from the Susquehanna and joined Sir John Johnson and Colonel John Butler, who were collecting a large body of Tories and refugees at Oswego, preparatory to a descent upon the Mohawk and Schoharie settlements. There Guy Johnson and other officers of the British Indian Department summoned a grand council of the Six Nations. They were invited to assemble " to eat the flesh and drink the blood of a Bostonian"—in other words, to feast on the occasion of a proposed treaty of alliance against the patriots, whom the savages denominated Bostonians, for the reason that Boston was the focus of the rebellion. There was a pretty full attendance at the council, but a large portion of the sachems adhered faithfully to their covenant of neutrality made with General Schuyler, until the appeals of the British commissioners to their avarice overcame their sense of honor. The commissioners represented the people of the king to be numerous as the forest leaves, and rich in every possession, while those of the colonies were exhibited as few and poor; that the armies of the king would soon subdue the rebels, and make them still weaker and poorer; that the *rum* of the king was as abundant as Lake Ontario; and that if the Indians would become his allies during the war, they should never want for goods or money. Tawdry articles, such as scarlet clothes, beads, and trinkets, were then displayed and presented to the Indians, which pleased them greatly, and they concluded an alliance by binding themselves to take up the hatchet against the patriots, and to continue their warfare until the latter were subdued. To each Indian were then presented a brass kettle, a suit of clothes, a gun, a tomahawk and scalping-knife, a piece of gold, a quantity of ammunition, and a promise of a bounty upon every scalp he should bring in.[2] *Thayendanegea* (Brant) was thenceforth the acknowledged grand sachem of the Six Nations, and soon afterward commenced his terrible career in the midst of our border settlements.[3]

We have thus glanced at the most important events that took place in the Mohawk Valley and adjacent districts prior to the attack of St. Leger upon Fort Stanwix, or Schuyler (as it will hereafter be called), which mark the progress of the Revolution there, before Brant and his more savage white associates brightened the tomahawk and musket, and bared the knife, in avowed alliance with the enemies of liberty. Volumes might be, and, indeed, have been, written in giving details of the stirring events in Tryon county during our Revolutionary struggle.[4] To these the reader is referred for local particulars, while we consider transactions there of more prominent and general interest.

---

[1] Campbell's *Annals of Tryon County.*

[2] See *Life of Mary Jemison.* This pamphlet was written in 1823, and published by James D. Bemis of Canandaigua, New York. She was taken a captive near Fort Duquesne (now Pittsburgh) when a child and was reared among the Indians. She married a chief, and became an Indian in every particular, except birth. At the council here spoken of she was present with her husband. Her death occurred at the age of 89. She says that the brass kettles mentioned in the text were in use among the Seneca Indians as late as 1823, when her narrative was printed.

[3] Soon after Brant joined the Indians at Oghkwaga, he made a hostile movement against the settlement of Cherry Valley. He hovered around that hamlet for some days, but did not attack it. Of this a detailed account will be given hereafter.

[4] The most voluminous are Campbell's *Annals of Tryon County*, Stone's *Life of Brant* and Simms's *Schoharie County and Border Wars of New York.*

CHAPTER XI.

"A scream! 'tis but the panther's—naught
 Breaks the calm sunshine there;
A thicket stirs! a deer has sought
 From sight a closer lair;
Again upon the grass they droop,
Then bursts the well-known whoop on whoop,
 Shrill, deafening on the air,
And onward from their ambush deep,
Like wolves, the savage warriors leap."

STREET.

E are now upon an Indian battle-ground, in the bosom of the deep forest, where the cunning and ferocity of the savage had free exercise in the panther-like maneuvers of the ambuscade, and the unrestrained use of the hatchet and knife. Hitherto we have seen the red warriors subordinate, and comparatively ineffective in the conflicts we have considered, except in the battle at Lake George and in the massacre at the Cedars. We have seen their method of warfare wholly subverted by European tactics, and their fiery courage controlled by a policy unknown in their sanguinary battles, unsuited to their martial training, and unsatisfactory to their fierce natures when aroused by the flow of blood. But in the siege of Fort Schuyler, which we are about to chronicle, and particularly in the battle of Oriskany, which formed a part of the operations of that siege, the Indians, commanded by Brant, the most subtle and accomplished war chief of his time, formed the strong right arm of St. Leger, and were left free to fight according to the customs of their race.

In the spring of 1777, Colonel Peter Gansevoort[1] was appointed to the command of Fort Schuyler, and held that post in the summer of that year, when Burgoyne was making his victorious march toward Albany by way of Lake Champlain. The successful progress of the British commander greatly alarmed the people of the north, and those of Tryon county were particularly disturbed by intelligence that a de-

---

[1] Peter Gansevoort was born in Albany, July 17th, 1749. He accompanied Montgomery into Canada in 1775, with the rank of major, and the next year he was appointed a colonel in the New York line, which commission he held when he defended Fort Schuyler against St. Leger. For his gallant defense of that post he received the thanks of Congress, and in 1781 was promoted to the rank of brigadier general by the state of New York. After the war he was for many years a military agent. He held several offices of trust, and was always esteemed for his bravery and judgment as a soldier, and for his fidelity, intelligence, and probity as a citizen. He died July 2d, 1812, aged 62 years.

scent upon them from Oswego might be expected. As early as June, a man from Canada, arrested as a spy, had disclosed the fact that a detachment of British troops, Canadians and Indians, was to penetrate the country by way of Oswego and the Mohawk, to join Burgoyne when he should reach Albany. This intelligence was soon after confirmed by Thomas Spencer, a friendly Oneida half-breed sachem, who was sent to Canada a secret emissary for information. He was present at a council where Colonel Claus,[1] a brother-in-law of Sir John Johnson, presided, and there he became acquainted with the general plans of Burgoyne. The Oneida further informed the inhabitants that Sir John Johnson and Colonel Claus, with their families, were then at Oswego in command of seven hundred Indians and four hundred regular troops; that there were six hundred Tories at Oswegatchie (Ogdensburgh) ready to join them; and that Colonel John Butler was to arrive at Oswego on the 14th of July, from Niagara, with Tories and Indians.

This information, instead of arousing the Whigs of the Mohawk Valley to prompt and efficient action, seemed to paralyze them with alarm. The timid were backward in preparing for the field, and the wavering, considering the patriot cause almost hopeless, became Loyalists, or, at best, passive Whigs. Fort Schuyler was still unfinished, and feebly garrisoned, and certain discomfiture seemed to await the patriots in that region. Colonel Gansevoort, however, was vigilant, active, and hopeful. He wrote spirited letters to General Schuyler, imploring aid, and that officer as urgently laid the condition of Tryon county before the Provincial Congress of New York, and also the General Congress. But it was then too late to expect succor from a distance, and the people of the Mohawk Valley were thrown upon their own feeble resources for defense. St. Leger and his Rangers, with the forces of Johnson, Claus, Butler, and Brant, mentioned by the Oneida chief, were already in motion, and on the 1st of August the enemy, one thousand seven hundred strong, came up Oneida Lake, and near the ruins of old Fort Newport prepared to invest Fort Schuyler. The Indians were led by Brant, and the whole beleaguering force, at the beginning of the march at Oswego Falls, was disposed in admirable order for the journey through the forest. The main body was led by the Indians, under Brant, in five columns, four hundred and sixty paces in front of the advanced guard. The Indians marched in single file, at large distances apart. Between the five columns and the rear-guard a file of Indians, ten paces apart, formed a line of communication. The advanced guard was one hundred paces in front of the main column, which was disposed in Indian file, the right and left flanks covered by a file of savages. The rear-guard was formed of regular troops. The advanced guard was composed of sixty marksmen, selected from the corps of Johnson's Royal Greens, and led by Captain Watts, a brother-

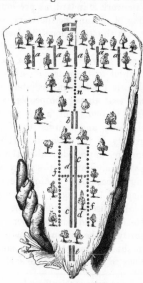

ORDER OF MARCH.[2]

---

[1] Daniel Claus married the daughter of Sir William Johnson, and was a man of considerable influence. Brant entertained for him sentiments of the strongest personal hostility, although both were engaged in the same cause. His wife died in Canada in 1801, and Brant, in the name of the Five Nations, made a speech of condolence on her death. William Claus, deputy superintendent of Indian affairs, was his son.—*Sabine's Lives of the Loyalists.*

[2] This diagram, representing the order of march of the besieging force, is a reduced copy of an engraving in *Stone's Life of Brant.* The original drawing, beautifully colored, was found in the writing-desk of St. Leger, which he left behind when he fled from his camp before Fort Schuyler. The following is an explanation of the diagram: *a a a a a,* five columns of Indians in front, flanking the British flag; *b,* advanced guard; *n,* line of communication between the advanced guard and Indian columns; *c c, d d,* the left and right wings of the eighth and thirty-fourth regiments (the thirty-fourth on the left side); *e,* rear-guard, *f f,* Indians on the right and left flanks; *i i,* line of communication.

in-law of Sir John Johnson.   Each corps was likewise furnished with practiced marksmen at short intervals, who were ordered to concentrate their strength upon any point that might be attacked.   St. Leger, as appears from his private diary, was much annoyed on the way by the disposition of his Indian allies to proceed according to their own notions of expediency. They were averse to approaching the fort in a body, but the commander finally persuaded them to be governed by his directions, which, at Oswego, they had promised to obey, and on the 2d of August Lieutenant Bird and Brant commenced the investment of the fort.

1777.

The garrison, under Colonel Gansevoort, consisted of seven hundred and fifty men.   In July, Colonel Marinus Willett, an active and judicious officer, had joined the garrison with his regiment, and, on the very day when Bird commenced the investiture of the fort, Lieutenant-colonel Mellon, of Colonel Wesson's[1] regiment, arrived with two hundred men, and two bateaux laden with provisions and military stores.   With this timely addition, the garrison had sufficient provision for six weeks, and a plentiful supply of ammunition for small arms.   But for their cannon, their most important means of defense, they had only about four hundred rounds, or nine cartridges for each piece a day for that length of time.   The garrison was also *without a flag* when the enemy appeared, but their pride and ingenuity soon supplied one in conformity to the pattern adopted by the Continental Congress.   Shirts were cut up to form the white stripes, bits of scarlet cloth were joined for the red, and the blue ground for the stars was composed of a cloth cloak belonging to Captain Abraham Swartwout, of Dutchess county, who was then in the fort.[2]   Before sunset the curious mosaic-work standard, as precious to the beleaguered garrison as the most beautifully-wrought flag of silk and needle-work, was floating over one of the bastions.

On the 3d, Colonel St. Leger arrived before the fort with his whole force.   It was a motley collection of British regulars, a few Hessians and Canadians, well-armed Tories, and troops of warriors from the various tribes of the Six Nations, except the Oneidas, who were faithful to their agreement to remain neutral.   St. Leger dispatched an officer, bearing a flag, to the fort, immediately after his arrival, with a copy of a pompous manifesto which he had sent among the people, conceived very much in the vein of the one issued by Burgoyne from Crown Point, a few weeks before.   He magnified the power, clemency, and justice of the king, and charged the General Congress, and other assemblies, committees, &c., with cruelty in the form of " arbitrary imprisonment, confiscation of property, persecution and torture, unprecedented in the inquisitions of the Romish Church."   He also denounced the patriot civil authorities every where as guilty of " the profanation of religion," and of " shocking proceedings" of almost every shade of darkness.   He then exhorted the people who were disposed to do right, to remember that he was " at the head of troops in the full power of health, discipline, and valor, determined to strike when necessary and anxious to spare when possible," and tempted them with offers of employment if they would join his standard, security to the infirm and industrious, and payment in coin for all supplies for his army that might be brought into his camp.   " If, notwithstanding these endeavors and sincere intentions to effect them," he said, in conclusion, " the phrensy of hostility should remain, I trust

---

[1] The name of this officer is variously spelled in the books—Weston, Wesson, and Wessen.   At the close of an autograph letter of his among Gates's Papers (vol. x.), in the New York Historical Society, it is written Wesson, and, presuming that he spelled his own name correctly, I give that orthography.   It will be remembered that Colonel Wesson and his regiment were active participators in the battles of Bemis's Heights, a few weeks later than the time in question.

[2] It was in Captain Swartwout's company, while at Poughkeepsie, that Samuel Geake, an emissary of Sir Henry Clinton, enlisted, in the character of a recruit, insinuated himself into the good graces of the officers at Fort Schuyler, and acquired much valuable information respecting the means, designs, and expectations of the Americans.   He was suspected, arrested, tried by court-martial as a spy, and was condemned to death.   He was spared, however, as a witness against Major Hammell, another recreant American, who had accompanied him to Poughkeepsie, and who was under arrest at that time.   Geake confessed that he was employed for the purpose of which he was accused.   He said that Major Hammell (who had been taken prisoner by the British) had espoused the cause of the enemy, and was promised a colonelcy in the British army, and that he (Geake) was to receive the commission of lieutenant as soon as he should return to New York from Fort Schuyler.

I shall stand acquitted in the eyes of God and man in denouncing and executing the vengeance of the state against the willful outcasts.   The messengers of justice and of wrath await them in the field ; and devastation, famine, and every concomitant horror that a reluctant, but indispensable, prosecution of military duty must occasion, will bar the way to their return."   The patriot people who received the manifesto treated it with derision, and the little garrison, which had already counted the cost of a siege, and determined upon a defense of the fort, laughed at its threats, and regarded its offer of bribes with scorn.

The siege commenced on the 4th.   A few bombs were thrown into the fort, and the Indians, concealed behind trees and bushes, wounded several men who were employed in raising the parapets.   Similar annoyances occurred on the 5th, and toward evening the Indians spread out through the woods, encircled the fort, and, by hideous yells through the night, attempted to intimidate the garrison.   St. Leger, confident of success, sent a dispatch to Burgoyne at this juncture, expressing his assurance that Fort Schuyler would be in his possession directly, and the hope that they would speedily meet as victors at Albany. Let us leave the besiegers and besieged a moment, and ride down to Oriskany, eight miles eastward of Fort Schuyler, where a terrible episode in the siege occurred. _{August, 1777.}

I left Rome (site of Fort Schuyler) at about two o'clock, in an open light wagon, for Oriskany.[1]   The day was very warm ; the road, although nearly level, was excessively stony, and when I arrived at the village I was almost overcome by the heat and fatigue.   Desirous of reaching Utica that evening, I stayed at the village only long enough to procure a competent guide to the battle-ground.   Mr. George Graham, a resident of the village (who was one of the committee of arrangements for the celebration held upon the battle-ground, on the anniversary of the event, in 1844), kindly accompanied me to the spot, and pointed out the various localities which were identified on the occasion referred to by many old men who were present, some of whom were in the battle.   The locality is about two miles west of the canal landing in the village, and in the midst of a beautiful agricultural country.   Let us consult the history while on our way thither, and then we shall better understand our " topographical survey."

As soon as St. Leger's approach up Oneida Lake was known to General Herkimer, he summoned the militia of Tryon county to the succor of the garrison at Fort Schuyler.   The timidity which seemed to have abated the fire of the Whigs, when the first intimations of the invasion were given by the Canada spy and the Oneida sachem, now disappeared, when the threatened danger was at their doors, and the call of Herkimer was responded to with alacrity, not only by the militia, but most of the members of the Tryon county committee entered the field as officers or volunteers.   They rendezvoused at Fort Dayton, on the German Flats, and, on the day when the Indians encircled the fort, Herkimer was near Oriskany with more than eight hundred men, eager to face the enemy.   He sent a messenger to Gansevoort, informing him of his approach, and requesting him to apprise him of the arrival of his courier by discharging three guns in rapid succession, which he knew would be heard at Oriskany.   But the messenger did not arrive until near noon the next day.   Herkimer was brave, but cautious, and determined to halt there until he should receive re-enforcements or hear the signal guns from the fort.   His officers, influenced by the impatience of their men to press on toward the fort, were opposed to delay.   Herkimer, self-relying, was firm.   Harsh words ensued, and two of his colonels, Cox and Paris, more impertinent than generous, denounced the old man as a coward and a Tory.   This bitter taunt sank deep into his heart, but his duty governed his feelings, and he calmly replied, " I am placed over you as a father and guardian, and shall not lead you into difficulties from which I may not be able to extricate you."   But they persisted in their demands for an immediate advance, and continued their ungenerous taunts.   Stung by imputations

---

[1] Oriskany is a little village about eight miles west of Utica, at the junction of the Oriskany Creek with the Mohawk.   The Erie Canal and the rail-road both pass through it, and the establishment of woolen factories there promises growth and prosperity to the pleasant town.

244   PICTORIAL FIELD-BOOK

Herkimer's Advancce to Oriskany.   Sortie from Fort Schuyler, under Colonel Willett.   Biographical Sketch of Willett

of cowardice, Herkimer at length yielded, and gave the word to " March on !" at the same time telling those who boasted loudest of their courage that they would be the first to run on seeing the enemy.

St. Leger had intelligence of the advance of Herkimer, and detached a division of Johnson's Greens, under Major Watts, Colonel Butler with his Rangers, and Brant with a strong body of Indians, to intercept him, and prevent an attack upon his intrenchments. Before the arrival of Herkimer's messenger, Gansevoort had observed the silence of the enemy's camp, and also the movement of a portion of his troops along the margin of a wood down the river. The arrival of the courier dispelled all doubts as to the destination of the detachment, and the signal guns were immediately fired. Herkimer had informed Gansevoort, by the messenger, that he intended, on hearing the signals, to cut his way to the fort through the circumvallating camp of the enemy, and requested him to make a sortie at the same time. This was done as soon as the arrangement could be made, and a detachment of two hundred men, consisting of portions of Gansevoort's and Wesson's regiments, was detailed for the purpose, who took with them an iron three pounder. Fifty men were also added, to protect the cannon, and to act otherwise as circumstances might require. The enterprise was intrusted to Colonel Marinus Willett,[1] who, by quick and judicious movements and daring courage, with his small force, accomplished wonders in a few hours. Rain was falling copiously while preparations for the sortie were in progress, but the moment it ceased Willett sallied out and fell furiously upon that portion of the camp occupied by Sir John Johnson and his Royal Greens, a detachment of whom, as we have seen,

---

[1] Marinus Willett was born at Jamaica, Long Island, July 31st (O.S.), 1740. He was the youngest of six sons of Edward Willett, a Queen's county farmer. He was early imbued with a military spirit, and joined the army, under Abercrombie, as a lieutenant in Colonel Delancy's regiment, in 1758. He was in the disastrous battle at Ticonderoga, and accompanied Bradstreet in his expedition against Fort Frontenac. Exposure in the wilderness injured his health, and he was confined by sickness in the newly-erected Fort Stanwix until the end of the campaign. Willett early espoused the republican cause when British aggression aroused resistance here. When the British troops in the New York garrison were ordered to Boston, after the skirmish at Lexington, they attempted, in addition to their own, to carry off a large quantity of spare arms. Willett resolved to prevent it, and, though opposed by the mayor and other Whigs, he captured the baggage-wagons containing them, and took them back to the city. These arms were afterward used by the first regiment raised by the state of New York. He was appointed second captain of a company in Colonel M'Dougal's regiment, and accompanied Montgomery in his northern expedition. He was placed in command of St. John's, and held that post until January, 1776. He was that year appointed lieutenant colonel, and, at the opening of the campaign of 1777, placed in command of Fort Constitution, on the Hudson. In May he was ordered to Fort Stanwix, or Schuyler, where he performed signal services, as noticed in the text. He was left in command of the fort, and remained there until the summer of 1778 when he joined the army under Washington, and was at the battle of Monmouth. He accompanied Sullivan in his campaign against the Indians in 1779, and was actively engaged in the Mohawk Valley in 1780, 1781, and 1782. In 1792 he was sent by Washington to treat with the Creek Indians at the south; and the same year he was appointed a brigadier general in the army intended to act against the Northwestern Indians. He declined the appointment, for he was opposed to the expedition. He was for some time sheriff of New York, and was elected mayor of the city in 1807. He was chosen elector of President and Vice-president in 1824, and was made president of the Electoral College. He died in New York, August 23d, 1830, in the 91st year of his age.

had been sent to oppose the approach of Herkimer.   The advanced guard, unable to withstand the impetuosity of the attack, were driven in ; and so suddenly was Sir John's camp assailed, that he was not allowed time to put on his coat.   He endeavored to bring his troops into order, but they fled in dismay.   The Indian encampment was then assaulted, and in a few moments the savages, too, were scattered.   Sir John and his troops fled across the river, to the temporary camp of St. Leger, and the Indians buried themselves in the deep forest near.   No less than twenty-one wagon-loads of spoil, consisting of clothing, blankets, stores, camp equipage, five British standards, the baggage of Sir John, with all his papers, and those of other officers, containing every kind of information necessary to the garrison, were captured.   Having secured their prize, Willett and his party returned to the fort without the loss of a man.   The five British colors were raised in full view of the enemy, upon the flag-staff, beneath the uncouth American standard, and the whole garrison, mounting the parapets, made the forest ring with three loud cheers.   This chivalrous exploit was duly noticed by Congress, and an elegant sword was presented to Colonel Willett in the name of the United States.

General Herkimer, in the mean while, had moved from the mills, at the mouth of Oriskany Creek, toward the fort, entirely unconscious of the ambuscade that, in a deep ravine two miles distant, awaited his approach.   The morning was dark, sultry, and lowering. His troops, composed chiefly of the militia regiments of Colonels Cox, Paris, Visscher, and Klock, were quite undisciplined, and their order of march was irregular and without precaution.   The contentions of the morning had delayed their advance until about nine o'clock, and the hard feelings that existed between the commander and some of his officers caused a degree of insubordination which proved fatal in its consequences.   Brant and his Tory asso-

THE BATTLE-GROUND OF ORISKANY.[1]

[1] This sketch was made from the eastern side of the ravine, looking west.   The marsh in the bottom of the ravine, mentioned in the text, is partially drained by a rivulet.   When I visited the spot (August, 1848), many logs of the old causeway were still visible, and afforded a crossing-place for cattle.   These logs are seen in the picture.   The road on the left is the present highway between Oriskany and Rome. The barn stands upon the western side of the ravine, and along the high ground upon which it is situated, and crossing the road southeasterly, the ambush was placed.   The hottest of the battle occurred upon the high plain between the ravine in the foreground and another beyond the most distant trees in the picture The hills seen in the extreme distance, on the right, are those upon the north side of the Mohawk.   The frame-work in the ravine is the remains of the scaffolding erected for the speakers at the celebration alluded to, in 1844.   The chief speakers on the occasion were John A. Dix and Senator Dickinson, and the audi-

ciates had learned from their scouts the exact route the patriots had taken, and arranged an
ambuscade accordingly. A deep ravine crossed the path of Herkimer in a north and south
direction, extending from the high grounds on the south to the river, and curved toward the
east in a semicircular form. The bottom of this ravine was marshy, and the road crossed it
by means of a causeway of earth and logs. On each side of the ravine the ground was nearly
level, and heavily timbered. A thick growth of underwood, particularly along the margin
of the ravine, favored concealment. It was upon the high ground on the western side of
this ravine that the ambush of the Tories and Indians was laid, in such a manner that the
causeway was surrounded by them, as by a circle, leaving only a small segment open where
the road entered. Unsuspicious of the proximity of the enemy, the whole body of provincials, except the rear-guard, composed of Visscher's regiment, descended into the ravine, followed by the baggage-wagons. Brant gave a signal, and in an instant the circle closed, the
war-hoop was sounded, and spear, and hatchet, and deadly rifle-ball fell upon the patriots
like hail from the clouds that hovered over them. The rear-guard, in fulfillment of Herkimer's prediction, instantly fled, and left their companions in the ravine to their fate. They
were pursued by the Indians, and probably suffered more, in their cowardly flight, than if
they had boldly aided their environed companions in arms.

This sudden onslaught produced great confusion in the patriot ranks, but they soon recovered, and fought with the courage and skill of veteran troops. The slaughter, however,
was dreadful. Herkimer was severely wounded at the commencement of the action, and
Colonel Cox and Captain Van Slyk were killed at the first fire. A musket-ball passed
through and killed the horse of the general, and shattered his own leg just below the knee.
With perfect composure and cool courage, he ordered the saddle to be taken from his slaughtered horse and placed against a large beech-tree near. Seated there, with his men falling
like autumn foliage, and the bullets of the enemy, like driving sleet, whistling around him,
the intrepid general calmly gave his orders, and thus nobly rebuked the slanderers who called
him a coward.[1]

For nearly an hour the fierce action continued, and by slow degrees the enemy was closing in upon the republicans. The latter then made an admirable change in their method
of repulsion. They formed themselves into circles, and thus met the enemy at all points.
Their fire became so destructive in this way, that the Johnson Greens and a portion of Butler's Tories attempted a bayonet charge. This was promptly met by the patriots, and the
battle assumed the terrible form of a death-struggle in close personal contact. They

> " Fought eye to eye, and hand to hand,
>   Alas ! 'twas but to die;
> In vain the rifle's deadly flash
> Scorch'd eagle plume and wampum sash;
>   The hatchet hiss'd on high,
> And down they fell in crimson heaps,
> Like the ripe corn the sickle reaps."

At this moment a heavy thunder-peal broke over the forest, and the rain came down in such

---

ence was estimated at 15,000 people. The scaffold was erected upon the spot, as nearly as it could be
defined, where General Herkimer fell. In the middle of the field beyond the scaffold, in the
lightest part near the tree, toward the barn, is seen a dark spot. It marks the site, now indicated by a cavity, where the beech-tree stood under which Herkimer sat and delivered his orders. Avarice cut the tree down about eight years ago, and then uprooted the stump to make
room for a more precious hill of potatoes. This view is about two miles west of Oriskany, on
the north side of the main road. Arrow-heads, bullets, bayonets, tomahawks, pipes, &c., are
still found there by the cultivator. The bowl of an earthen pipe was shown to me by a resident upon the ground (whose house is seen in the distance, beyond the barn), which he had
plowed up the day before. He had several other relics of the battle, but would not part with
any. The above is a drawing of the pipe-bowl.
    [1] It is related that, during the hottest of the action, the general, seated upon his saddle, quietly took his
tinder-box from his pocket, lighted his pipe, and smoked as composedly as if seated at his own fire-side.

torrents that the combatants ceased their strife, and sought shelter beneath the trees. It was during this heavy shower that Willett made his preparations at the fort for the successful sortie just noticed; and, as soon as the rain subsided, he fell upon Johnson's camp, and the battle was renewed at Oriskany.

During the lull in the conflict, both parties viewed the ground, and made new arrangements for attack and defense. It had been observed by the patriots that the Indians, as soon as they saw a gun fired by a provincial behind a tree, would rush forward and tomahawk him before he could reload. To meet such an exigency in the renewed conflict, two men stood together behind a tree, and, while one fired, the other awaited the approach of the savage with his tomahawk, and felled him with his bullet. The provincials had also made choice of more advantageous ground, and, soon after the renewal of the fight, so destructive was their fire that the Indians began to give way. Major Watts came up with a detachment of Johnson's Greens to support them, but the presence of these men, mostly refugees from the Mohawk, made the patriots more furious, and mutual resentments, as the parties faced and recognized each other, seemed to give new strength to their arms. They leaped upon each other with the fierceness of tigers, and fought hand to hand and foot to foot with bayonets and knives. It was a terrible struggle, and exhibited the peculiar cruelty and brutality which distinguishes civil war.

A firing was now heard in the direction of the fort. It was the attack of Willett upon the enemy's camp. Colonel Butler instantly conceived a stratagem, and was nearly successful in its execution. He so changed the dress of a detachment of Johnson's Greens, that they appeared like American troops. These were made to approach from the direction of the fort, and were at first (as intended by Butler) mistaken by the patriots for a re-enforcement from the garrison. But the quick eye of Captain Gardinier, an officer who performed deeds of great valor on that memorable day, discovered their real character, and, ordering his men to fall upon these pretended friends, they were soon scattered in confusion. The Indians, finding their ranks greatly thinned, and the provincials still undismayed, raised the loud retreating cry, *Oonah! Oonah!* and fled in all directions. The panic was communicated to the Tories and Canadians, and the whole force of the enemy retreated in confusion, pursued by the provincials with shouts of victory. Thus, after a conflict of six hours, ended the battle of Oriskany, the bloodiest encounter, in proportion to the numbers engaged, that occurred during the war. Neither party could claim a decided victory. Both had suffered dreadfully. The patriots remained masters of the field, but they did not accomplish the design of the expedition, the relief of the garrison at Fort Schuyler. Their wounded, nearly fifty in number, were carried from the field on litters, and among them was General Herkimer, who was taken to his residence below the Little Falls, on the Mohawk, where he died ten days afterward. The manner and circumstances of his death will be noticed in the relation of my visit to his mansion, which is still standing.

The loss in this battle seems not to have been officially given on either side. St. Leger, in a letter to Burgoyne, dated August 11th, five days after the battle, says, "Above four hundred [patriots] lay dead on the field, among the number of whom were almost all of the principal movers of the rebellion in that county." The enemy also claimed to have taken two hundred prisoners. Dr. Thatcher, in his Military Journal (page 89), records the loss of the Americans at "one hundred and sixty killed, and a great number wounded." This is the number stated by Gordon and other cotemporary writers. The Indians lost about seventy, among whom were several chiefs.[1] Major Watts was badly wounded, and left for dead upon the field. He revived from the faintness produced by loss of blood, crawled to a brook and quenched his thirst, and there remained until he was found, nearly three days afterward, by an Indian scout, and taken into St. Leger's camp. There were many deeds

1777

---

[1] Gordon and others relate that, in the course of the battle, a portion of the Indians became impressed with the belief that there was a coalition between Johnson's and Herkimer's men to destroy them, and that, toward the close of the conflict, the savages killed many of the Tories. "It is thought," says Gordon (i.., 237), "that near as many of Sir John's Tory party were killed by the Indians as by the militia."

of personal courage exhibited in that battle, which, according to the military ethics of a less benevolent age, would entitle the actors to the crown of laurel, the applause of multitudes, and the panegyric of the historian.　But the picture is so revolting to the eye of Christian benevolence, and so repugnant to the nobler feelings of brotherhood, which are now happily impressing their benignant features upon society, that it is far better to draw the curtain of silence before it, and plead for the warriors, in extenuation, the dreadful necessity that impelled them to deeds so shocking to humanity.　It is high time that the practice of pampering a depraved public taste by giving the horrid details of slaughter in battle, and of investing with glory, as models for imitation, those who fight most furiously and slay most profusely, should fall into desuetude.　These details are not essential elements of history.　They contain no useful lesson, no seed of philosophy worthy of germination, no real benefit for the understanding or the heart.[1]　Thus far I have avoided such recitals, and I shall do so through the whole work before me.　Neither pen nor pencil shall intentionally contribute one thought for a panegyric on war or its abettors.　The student of our Revolution, while he may justly rejoice at the vast and invaluable blessings which followed that event, should be taught to *lament* rather than *admire* the dreadful instrumentalities that were necessarily employed. He may thus be taught without lessening the veneration which he ought to feel for those who periled life and fortune in defense of the liberty we now enjoy.　Let us turn from these better contemplations to the more unpleasant task of tracing out the succeeding events of the siege of Fort Schuyler.

So completely was the garrison still environed by the besieging force, after the battle at Oriskany, that no correct intelligence of that event could reach them.　St. Leger took advantage of this circumstance, and, by false representations of victory for himself, the total discomfiture of the provincials, and the victorious advance of Burgoyne, endeavored to bring the garrison to surrender.　Colonel Billenger and Major Frey were made prisoners, and on the evening of the battle they were forced to write a letter to Colonel Gansevoort, which contained many misrepresentations, and a recommendation to cease resistance.　St. Leger's adjutant general, Colonel John Butler, delivered the letter to Gansevoort, and at the same time communicated a verbal demand of surrender from his commander.　Gansevoort refused an answer to a verbal summons, unless made by St. Leger himself.　On the next morning, Colonel Butler and two other officers approached the fort with a white flag, and asked permission to enter as bearers of a message to the commander.　The request was granted ; they were conducted, blind-folded, within the fortress, and received by Gansevoort in his dining-room, which was lighted with candles, the windows being closed.　Colonels Willett and Mellen were present, and the messengers of St. Leger were politely received.　Major Ancram, one of them, more fluent in speech than the others, made known the wishes of St. Leger.　He spoke of the humanity of his feelings, and his desire to prevent further bloodshed.　He assured Gansevoort that it was with much difficulty the Indians were restrained from massacre, and that the only salvation of the garrison was an immediate surrender of the fort and all the public stores.　The officers and soldiers would be allowed to retain their baggage and other private property, and their personal safety should be guarantied.　He expressed a hope that these honorable terms would be immediately complied with, for, if they were not, it would be out of St. Leger's power to renew the proposition.　The Indians, he remarked, were ready and eager to march down the country and destroy the inhabitants, and they were reminded that the total destruction of Herkimer's relief corps, and the fact that *Burgoyne had possession of Albany*, extinguished all hope of succor for the garrison.

[1] An example in an account of the battle in question, given in Stone's *Life of Brant*, may be cited as an illustration.　A Captain Dillenback was assailed by three of Johnson's Greens.　" This officer," says the biographer, " had declared he would not be taken alive, and he was not.　One of his three assailants seized his gun, but he suddenly wrenched it from him and felled him with the butt.　He shot the second dead, and thrust the third through with his bayonet.　But in the moment of his triumph *at an exploit of which even the mighty Hector, or either of the sons of Zeruiah, might have been proud*, a ball laid this brave man low in the dust."　It is the last clause which is chiefly objectionable, for therein the historian, not content with recording the bloody act (justified by the law of self-preservation), lauds it as a deed worthy of the highest praise

This speech, made up of falsehood, persuasion, and threats, excited the indignation of the patriot officers, and Colonel Willett, with the approbation of Colonel Gansevoort, promptly and properly replied. I give his words, as contained in his narrative. They were delivered with emphasis, while he looked the officer, he says, full in the face : " Do I understand you, sir ? I think you say that you came from a British colonel, who is commander of the army that invests this fort ; and, by your uniform, you appear to be an officer in the British service. You have made a long speech on the occasion of your visit, which, stripped of all its superfluities, amounts to this—that you come from a British colonel to the commandant of this garrison, to tell him that, if he does not deliver up the garrison into the hands of your colonel, he will send his Indians to murder our women and children. You will please to reflect, sir, that their blood will be upon your heads, not upon ours. We are doing our duty ; this garrison is committed to our charge, and we will take care of it. After you get out of it, you may turn round and look at its outside, but never expect to come in again, unless you come a prisoner. I consider the message you have brought a degrading one for a British officer to send, and by no means reputable for a British officer to carry. For my own part, I declare, before I would consents to deliver this garrison to such a murdering set as your army, by your own account, consists of, I would suffer my body to be filled with splinters and set on fire, as you know has at times been practiced by such hordes of women and children killers as belong to your army."

These words expressed the sentiments of the garrison, and the officers very justly concluded that Burgoyne could not be at Albany, and the Tryon county militia all slain or dispersed, else such a solicitude on the part of the enemy for an immediate surrender, on such favorable conditions, would not be exhibited. The manner of the messengers and the tenor of their discourse made the besieged feel stronger, and more resolved to defend their post.

On the 9th, St. Leger sent a written demand for a surrender, which contained the substance of Major Ancram's speech Gansevoort immediately replied, in writing, " Sir, your letter of this date I have received, in answer to which I say, that it is my determined resolution, with the force under my command, to defend this fort to the last extremity, in behalf of the United States, who have placed me here to defend it against all their enemies." This prompt and bold stand was unexpected to the British commander. His " cannon had not the least effect upon the sod-work of the fort," and his " royals had only the power of teazing."[1] He therefore commenced approaching the fort by

August, 1777.

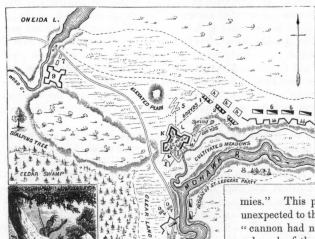

FORT SCHUYLER AND VICINITY.[2]

---

[1] Letter of St. Leger to Burgoyne, dated Oswego, August 27th, 1777.

[2] DESCRIPTION OF THE ENGRAVING.—A, Fort Schuyler ; b, southwest bastion, three guns ; c, northwest bastion, four guns ; d, northeast bastion, three guns ; e, southeast bastion, four guns ; g, laboratory ; h h h, barracks ; I, horn-works begun ; K, covered way ; L L, glacis ; M, sally-port ; N, officers' quarters ; O O, Willett's attack. The figures refer to the redoubts, batteries, &c., of the enemy. 1, a battery of three guns ; 2, bomb battery, four mortars ; 3, bomb battery of three guns ; 4 4 4, redoubts to cover the batteries ; 5, line of approaches, 6 6, British encampment ; 7, Loyalists ; 8, Indians ; 9, ruins of Fort Newport.

" sapping to such a distance that the rampart might be brought within their portices, at the same time all materials were preparing to run a mine under the most formidable bastion."[1]

In the mean while an address to the people of Tryon county, signed by Johnson, Claus, and Butler, was issued, strongly protesting their desire for peace, promising pardon and protection to all that should submit, and threatening all the horrors of Indian cruelty if they resisted.   They called upon the principal men of the valley to come up and oblige the garrison at Fort Schuyler to do at once what they would be forced to do finally—surrender. This document was sent by messengers through Tryon county, but it effected little else than get the messengers themselves into trouble.[2]   The siege, in the mean while, was steadily, but feebly, continued.   The garrison, fearing that re-enforcements for the enemy might arrive, or that the siege might continue until their own provisions and ammunition should fail, resolved to communicate with General Schuyler, then at Stillwater, and implore succor. Colonel Willett volunteered to be the messenger, and on a very stormy night, when shower after shower came down furiously, he and Lieutenant Stockwell left the fort by the sally-port at ten o'clock, each armed with a spear, and crept upon their hands and knees along a morass to the river.   They crossed it upon a log, and were soon beyond the line of drowsy sentinels.   It was very dark, their path-way was in a thick and tangled wood, and they soon lost their way.   The barking of a dog apprised them of their proximity to an Indian camp, and for hours they stood still, fearing to advance or retreat.   The clouds broke away toward dawn, and the morning star in the east, like the light of hope, revealed to them their desired course.   They then pushed on in a zigzag way, and, like the Indians, sometimes traversed the bed of a stream, to foil pursuers that might be upon their trail.   They reached the German Flats in safety, and, mounting fleet horses, hurried down the valley to the headquarters of General Schuyler, who had already heard of the defeat of Herkimer, and was devising means for the succor of the garrison at Fort Schuyler.

August 10, 1777.

August 13.

St. Leger continued the siege.   He advanced, by parallels, within one hundred and fifty yards of the fort, and the garrison, ignorant of the fate of Willett and Stockwell, or the relief that was preparing for them below, began to feel uneasy.   Their ammunition and provisions being much reduced in quantity, some hinted an opinion to their commander that a surrender would be humane policy.   Gansevoort's stout and hopeful heart would not yield admission to such an idea, and he informed the garrison that he had resolved, in case succor should not appear before their supplies were exhausted, to sally out at night and cut his way through the enemy's camp.   Suddenly, and mysteriously to the garrison, the besiegers broke up their camp, and fled so precipitately from before the fort that they left their tents, artillery, and camp equipage behind them.

August 22.

The mystery was soon solved.   We have already noticed the appeal of General Schuyler to his troops at the mouth of the Mohawk, and the readiness with which Arnold and several hundred men volunteered to march to the relief of Gansevoort.   These troops consisted chiefly of the Massachusetts brigade of General Learned.   They marched immediately, under the general command of Arnold, and were joined by the first New York regiment, under Colonel Livingston.   On the 20th, Arnold and a portion of the troops arrived at Fort Dayton, where he intended to wait for the remainder, under Learned, to arrive ; but, hearing of the near approaches of St. Leger to Fort Schuyler, he resolved to push forward, and hazard a battle before it should be too late.   He knew that his small force was too inconsiderable to warrant a regular engagement, and he conceived several stratagems to supply his deficiency of strength.   One, which proved successful, was adopted.   Among the Tory prisoners who were taken with Walter Butler was a coarse, unlettered, half idiot named Hon-

---

[1] Letter of St. Leger to Burgoyne, dated Oswego, August 27th, 1777.
[2] Walter N. Butler, a son of Colonel John Butler, and afterward one of the most brutal of the Tory leaders, with fourteen white soldiers and the same number of Indians, appeared at the German Flats, at the house of a Tory named Shoemaker.   Colonel Wesson was then in command of a small fortification there, called Fort Dayton, and he sent a party to arrest Butler and his associates.   They succeeded, and Butler was tried and condemned as a spy, but was afterward sent a prisoner to Albany, under a reprieve.

Yost Schuyler, a nephew of General Herkimer, who, with his mother and brother, lived near Little Falls. He was tried and condemned to death. His mother hastened to Fort Dayton and pleaded for his life. For a time Arnold was inexorable, but finally consented to spare him, on condition that he should go to Fort Schuyler and endeavor so to alarm St. Leger, by representations of the great number of Americans that were approaching, as to induce him to raise the siege. Hon-Yost readily agreed to perform the duty, for, in reality, his political creed was so chameleon-like, that it would assume any required hue, according to circumstances. His mother offered herself as a hostage for his faithfulness, but Arnold chose his brother Nicholas as security. The latter was placed in confinement, and Hon-Yost, with a friendly Oneida, who promised to aid him, departed for Fort Schuyler.

Arnold, having issued a proclamation[1] from Fort Dayton to counteract the address of Johnson, Claus, and Butler, marched ten miles onward toward Fort Stanwix. There he received a communication from Colonel Gansevoort, announcing that the siege _{August 23, 1777.} had suddenly been raised, and that the enemy had fled, in great haste, toward Wood Creek; why, he could not imagine. Arnold perceived that Hon-Yost had been faithful. He and the Indian had managed the affair adroitly, and the charge of idiotcy against Hon-Yost was wiped out forever. Before leaving Fort Dayton, he had several bullets shot through his coat, and, with these evidences of a "terrible engagement with the enemy," he appeared among the Indians of St. Leger's camp, many of whom knew him personally. He ran into their midst almost out of breath, and apparently much frightened. He told them that the Americans were approaching in great numbers, and that he had barely escaped with his life. His bullet-riddled coat confirmed the story. When they inquired the number of the Americans, he pointed to the leaves on the trees, and shook his head mysteriously. The Indians were greatly agitated. They had been decoyed into their present situation, and had been moody and uneasy since the battle of Oriskany. At the moment of Hon-Yost's arrival they were engaged in a religious observance—a consultation, through their prophet, of Manitou, or the Great Spirit, to supplicate his guidance and protection. The council of chiefs at the *pow-wow* at once resolved upon flight, and told St. Leger so. He sent for and questioned Hon-Yost, who told him that Arnold, with two thousand men, would be upon him in twenty-four hours. At that moment, according to arrangement, the friendly Oneida, who had taken a circuitous route, approached the camp from another direction, with a belt. On his way he met two or three straggling Indians of his tribe, who joined him, and they all confirmed the story of Hon-Yost. They pretended that a bird had brought them the news that the valley below was swarming with warriors. One said that the army of Burgoyne was cut to pieces, and another told St. Leger that Arnold had three thousand men near. They shook their heads mysteriously when questioned about numbers by the Indians, and pointed, like Hon-Yost, upward to the leaves. The savages, now thoroughly alarmed, prepared to flee. St. Leger tried every means, by offers of bribes and promises, to induce them to remain, but the panic, and suspicion of foul play, had determined them to go. He tried to make them drunk, but they refused to drink. He then besought them to take the rear of his army in retreating; this they refused, and indignantly said, "You mean to sacrifice us. When you marched down, you said there would be no fighting for us Indians; we might go down and smoke our pipes; whereas numbers of our warriors have been killed, and you mean

---

[1] The address of Arnold was well calculated to awe the timid and give courage to the wavering Whigs. The prestige of his name gave great weight to it. He prefaced it with a flourish of his title and position, as follows: "By the Honorable Benedict Arnold, Esq., general and commander-in-chief of the army of the United States of America on the Mohawk River." He denominated a certain Barry St. Leger "a leader of a banditti of robbers, murderers, and traitors, composed of savages of America and more savage Britons," and denounced him as a seducer of the ignorant and unthinking from the cause of freedom, and as threatening ruin and destruction to the people. He then offered a free pardon to all who had joined him or upheld him, "whether savages, Germans, Americans, or Britons," provided they laid down their arms and made oath of allegiance to the United States within three days. But if they persisted in their "wicked courses," and "were determined to draw on themselves the just vengeance of Heaven and their exasperated country, they must expect no mercy from either."

August 23, 1777. to sacrifice us also."[1] The council broke up, and the Indians fled. The panic was communicated to the rest of the camp, and in a few hours the beleaguering army were flying in terror toward their boats on Oneida Lake. Hon-Yost accompanied them in their flight as far as Wood Creek, where he managed to desert. He found his way back to the fort that night, and was the first to communicate to Colonel Gansevoort the intelligence of Arnold's approach.[2] The Indians, it is said, made themselves merry at the precipitate flight of the whites,[3] who threw away their arms and knapsacks, so that nothing should impede their progress. The savages also gratified their passion for murder and plunder by killing many of their retreating allies on the borders of the lake, and stripping them of every article of value. They also plundered them of their boats, and, according to St. Leger, "became more formidable than the enemy they had to expect."[4] Half starved and naked, the whites of the scattered army made their way to Oswego, and, with St. Leger, went down Ontario to Canada.

Colonel Gansevoort, on the retreat of St. Leger, sent a dispatch to Arnold, acquainting August 25. him with the fact. That general sent forward nine hundred men, with directions to attempt to overtake the fugitives, and the next day reached the fort himself. Gansevoort had already sent out a detachment to harass the flying enemy, and several prisoners were brought in, with a large quantity of spoil, among which was the *escritoire*, or writing-desk, of St. Leger, containing his private papers. Colonel Willett was left in command of the garrison at the fort, and Arnold and his men marched back to the main army (then at Stillwater, under Gates, who had superseded Schuyler), to perform valiant service in the battle that soon afterward occurred on Bemis's Heights. Thus ended the siege of Fort Schuyler,[5] in the progress of which the courage, endurance, and skill of the Americans, every where so remarkable in the Revolution, were fully displayed.[6]

---

[1] Mary Jemison, whose narrative we have referred to, says that the Indians (at least the Senecas) were greatly deceived. They were sent for to "see the British whip the rebels." They were told that they were not wanted to fight, but might sit down and smoke their pipes, and look quietly on. With this impression, the Seneca warriors accompanied the expedition, and, as we have seen, suffered great loss.

[2] Hon-Yost made his way back to Fort Dayton, to the great joy of his friends. He afterward fled from the valley with his family and fourteen Tory associates, and joined Sir John Johnson. After the war he returned to the valley, where he remained until his death in 1818.

[3] Gordon (ii., 240), on the verbal authority of the Rev. Mr. Kirkland, who was at Fort Schuyler, relates that St. Leger, while standing on the border of a morass alone with Sir John Johnson, reproached the latter with being the cause of the disaffection of the Indians. High words and mutual criminations followed. Two chiefs, standing near, overheard the quarrel, and put an end to it by shouting, "They are coming! they are coming!" Both officers, terribly alarmed, plunged into the morass. This was the signal for the general retreat of the whole army. Such was their haste, that they left their tents, baggage, and artillery behind, and the bombardier was left asleep in the bomb battery! When he awoke he found himself alone, the sole representative in camp of the besieging army. The Indians continued their cry, at intervals, "They are coming! they are coming!" behind the fleeing Tories, and thus amused themselves all the way to Oneida Lake.

[4] Letter of St. Leger to Burgoyne, August 27th, 1777.

[5] Fort Schuyler was destroyed by fire and flood in 1781, and was never rebuilt.

[6] Before the fort was invested by St. Leger, the Indians, in small parties, annoyed the garrison, and frequently attacked individuals when away from their dwellings. On one occasion they fired upon three little girls who were out gathering blackberries. Two were killed and scalped, but the third escaped. The remarkable adventure of Captain Gregg is worthy of notice. He was a soldier of the garrison of Fort Schuyler, and went out one day to shoot pigeons, with two of his soldiers, and a boy named Wilson (who became an ensign in the army at the age of eighteen, and conducted the surrender of the British standards at Yorktown). Fearing the Indians, the boy was sent back. They had not proceeded far before some savages in ambush shot all three down, scalped them, and made off. The captain, though badly wounded, was not killed. His two soldiers, however, were lifeless, and, laying his bleeding head upon the body of one of them, he expected soon to die. His dog had accompanied him, and, in great agitation, whined, licked his wounds, and otherwise manifested his grief and attachment. He told the dog to go for help, and the animal, as if endowed with reason, at once obeyed. He ran about a mile, and found two men fishing. By piteous moans he induced them to follow him to his wounded master. The captain was carried to the fort, and, after suffering much, was restored to health. "He was a most frightful spectacle," says Dr. Thacher, from whose journal (page 144) this account is taken. "The whole of his scalp was removed; in two places on the forepart of his head the tomahawk had penetrated the skull; there was a wound on

On my return to Oriskany village, after visiting the battle-ground, I learned that Mr. Nellis, who was engaged in that conflict, was still living at Whitesborough, three miles eastward. I had dismissed the vehicle that conveyed me from Rome to Oriskany, intending to proceed to Utica from the latter place upon a canal packet. I felt a desire to visit the old veteran, and yet was anxious to reach Utica that evening. While deliberating concerning the matter, a constable from Whitesborough rode up to the hotel in a light wagon, executed his business in haste, and kindly offered me a seat on his return. I gladly placed myself in his custody. He said his errand to Oriskany was in search of a thief, and I have no doubt the people of Whitesborough gave him credit for success, for my " fatigue dress" and soiled " Panama" made me appear more like a prowler than a tourist. Mr. Nellis was not at home, so my visit was fruitless, except in the pleasure derived from a view of the beautiful village, as we rode in from the westward. It lies upon a plain, encircled by the arms of the Erie Canal and the Mohawk River.

At sunset, after partially satisfying a long-suffering appetite from a table at *a restorer*, on the verge of the canal, where dainty guests should eat with closed eyes and unwavering faith in the purity of the viands and the proper proportions of flies and butter, I embarked for Utica, six miles eastward. It was the close of a calm, sultry day, and peculiarly grateful August 20, 1848. was the evening breeze that fanned us as we glided along upon that tiny river, through cultivated fields and pleasant woodlands.

> " Sweet to the pensive is departing day,
> When only one small cloud, so still and thin,
> So thoroughly imbued with amber light,
> And so transparent that it seems a spot
> Of brighter sky, beyond the furthest mount,
> Hangs o'er the hidden orb; or where a few
> Long, narrow stripes of denser, darker grain,
> At each end sharpened to a needle's point,
> With golden borders, sometimes straight and smooth,
> And sometimes crinkling like the lightning's stream,
> A half hour's space above the mountain lie."
>
> CARLOS WILCOX.

This quiet scene was soon exchanged for the bustle and noise of the busy town, and, before the twilight had fairly faded I was jolted over the paved streets of Utica. There I spent some thirty hours with some friends. The city has no noteworthy reminiscences of the Revolution, except the single fact that the army, under Herkimer, crossed the Mohawk at old Fort Schuyler (then a fortress in ruins), while on his way to Oriskany, and the general interest which belongs to it as that portion of Tryon county which was consecrated by the presence and the prowess of the patriots. It is a pleasant and thriving city, upon the southern slope of the Mohawk Valley. Like all other towns in Western New York, it is young and vigorous, and every feature glows with the beauty of youth and health.

I left Utica at noon by rail-road, arrived at Little Falls, twenty miles eastward, at one o'clock, and at two started in a light wagon for Fort Herkimer, or Mohawk, on the German Flats. The driver and guide was a courteous young man, but totally deaf. I never practiced pantomime with better success, for my companion, intelligent, and apparently well versed in all the local history of the region, easily comprehended my awkward manipulations, and answered my mute inquiries promptly and clearly.

The upper valley of the Mohawk, which narrows to a deep, rocky ravine at Little Falls, has, within a few miles of its lower extremity, a rich and fertile alluvial plain on each side of the river, known as the German Flats, so called in consequence of being first settled and cultivated by German families. The settlement was originally called Burnet's Field, from the circumstance that the patent had been granted by Governor Burnet. The patent comprehended the plain and slopes westward of the junction of West Canada Creek 1720

---

his back with the same instrument, besides a wound in his side, and another through his arm with a mus-ket-ball."

and the Mohawk River, and included about ten miles of the valley east and west. Toward the eastern extremity of the Flats, and about four miles west of Little Falls, on the south side of the river, is one of the churches which were erected under the auspices and by the lib-

OLD STONE CHURCH, GERMAN FLATS.

eral contributions of Sir William Johnson.[1] The church is of stone, but is somewhat altered in its external appearance. The walls are very thick, and it has square buttresses at the corners. It was altered and repaired in 1811, at an expense of nearly four thousand dollars. The roof (formerly steep) was raised, an upper row of windows was formed, and a gallery was constructed within. The height of the old windows is indicated by the arches seen over the present square ones, and the eaves were just above the key-stones. The original tower, with its steeple, was similar to the one at Caughnawaga. The tower, or belfry, was open, and in it was placed a swivel for the protection of the inhabitants against the Indians, or to sound an alarm to the people on the neighboring hills. The pulpit, although newly constructed when the church was repaired, is precisely the same, in style, as the original. The sounding-

board and panels in front are handsomely painted in imitation of inlaid work, and the whole has an elegant appearance. This church has never been without a pastor since its construction in 1767, yet only two ministers have presided over the flock during eighty years of its existence. The first was the Rev. Abraham Rosenkrans. Before the church was built, he preached to the people in that region in their dwellings, school-houses, and barns. He was installed pastor of the church in 1767, and remained there until his death in 1796, when his remains were deposited beneath the pulpit. He was succeeded by the Rev. John P. Spinner, from Germany, who preached in the German language exclusively until within twenty years, and afterward in English and German alternately. He died in May, 1848.

A few rods west of the church was the large stone mansion of the

THE PULPIT.

Herkimer family, which was stockaded and called Fort Herkimer. Around this, and the church, the humbler dwellings of the farmers were clustered, for so frequently did the Indian marauder (and as frequently the unprincipled Tory, in the Revolution) disturb them, that they dared not live in isolation. Fort Herkimer became a prey to public vandalism when the Erie Canal was built. The waters flow in part over the site of the fort, and its stones, so easily quarried, were used in the construction of a lock near by.

Two miles further westward, on a gravelly plain upon the north side of the river, is the pretty little village of Herkimer. It occupies the site of old Fort Herkimer, erected in the early part of the Seven Years' War, and known as Fort Dayton during the Revolution, occurrences at which we have already mentioned. This beautiful region, like the "sweet Vale

[1] It was built upon the north side of the old German burying-ground. Near the southern wall of this church is a large brown sandstone slab, placed there by the provincial government, on which is the following inscription: "HERE REPOSES THE BODY OF JOHN RING, ESQ., OF THE KINGDOM OF IRELAND, A CAPTAIN OF HIS MAJESTY'S INDEPENDENT COMPANY OF THE PROVINCE, WHO DEPARTED THIS LIFE THE 20TH DAY OF SEPTEMBER, 1755, IN THE 30TH YEAR OF HIS AGE." Near this church, it is said, was raised the first liberty-pole in 1775. White, the sheriff of Tryon county at that time, came up with a large body of militia from Johnstown and cut it down.

OF THE REVOLUTION.   255

Plan of Fort Herkimer.   Destruction of Andrustown.   Expedition against the German Flats.   Destruction of the Settlement.

of Wyoming," was disturbed and menaced in the earlier periods of the war, and in 1778 it was made a desolation.

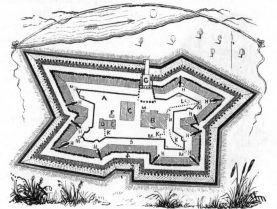

FORT HERKIMER.[1]

Owing to the distant situation of Fort Schuyler, its garrison afforded very slight protection to this portion of the valley, and Fort Dayton had become little better than a dilapidated block-house. The Tories and Indians were, consequently, bold in their marauding expeditions, and the murderer and the incendiary kept the patriots in continual alarm. All the spring and summer succeeding the flight of St. Leger from Fort Schuyler, the various settlements in Tryon county were menaced. In July, a secluded hamlet called Andrustown, situated about six miles southeast of the German Flats, and composed of seven families, was destroyed by a party of savages, under Brant. They owned a thousand fertile acres among the hills and pleasant valleys toward the Otsego Lake, and plunder seemed to be the sachem's chief object. This secured, some of the people murdered, and others made captive, the torch was applied, and the whole settlement utterly laid waste.

Success made the Indians more greedy, and toward the close of August they hung like a gathering storm upon the hills around the German Flats. Aroused and alarmed by the tragedy at Andrustown, the people had kept scouts on the alert, and the approach of Brant from Unadilla toward the settlement was heralded by them in time for the residents to prepare for the coming invasion. These scouts came in hot haste, and informed the inhabitants that the savages would be upon them in a few hours. There was no time to look after and secure their sheep and cattle, but, gathering up the most valuable things which they could carry from their houses, the whole settlement took refuge in Forts Dayton and Herkimer, and in the old church.

Brant, with three hundred Tories and one hundred and fifty Indians, reached the borders of the settlement early in the evening.[2] It was a dark and rainy night, and he lay concealed in a ravine near Shoemakers (where Walter Butler was captured the year before) until near daylight, when his warriors were called to duty, and soon swept, like a fierce wind, over the plain. The houses were assailed, but neither scalps nor prisoners were to be found in them. At dawn the fires were kindled. Barns, filled with the product of an abundant harvest just gathered, the dwellings of the people, and every thing combustible, were set on fire, within view of the sorrowing fugitives in the fort. Having nothing but small arms, the savages did not attack the fort, but, having laid the whole plain in ashes, collected the horses, sheep,

---

[1] I copied this sketch from a manuscript drawing in possession of the New York Historical Society. It was drawn by a private of Captain Ogelvie's company, and presented by him to " Charles Clinton, Esq.,* lieutenant colonel commanding," in July, 1758. Herkimer is there spelled Herekheimer.

EXPLANATION OF THE SKETCH.—A, the parade; B, dwelling-house; C, barracks; D, guard-room; E, officers' kitchen; F, the well; G, draw-bridge; H H, &c., ten swivel guns; K K, stockades; L, the oven; M M, &c., sentry boxes; N, smith's shop; O, the Mohawk River; 1, terrace; 2, trench; 3, palisades; 4, parapet; 5, banqueting.

[2] At the time in question there were thirty-four houses and as many barns in the settlement on the south side of the river, and about an equal number on the north side, at Fort Dayton, now Herkimer village.

---

* Charles Clinton emigrated to America from Ireland (whither his family fled from England for refuge in the time of Cromwell) in 1729, and in 1731 he founded a settlement in Ulster county, New York. He was appointed lieutenant colonel by Governor Delancy, after serving with distinction under Bradstreet. He was the father of General James Clinton (the father of the late Dewitt Clinton) and of Governor George Clinton, of the Revolution. He died November 19, 1773, aged 82 years.

and cattle, and drove them off over the southern hills.   Four hundred militia-men were hastily collected, and pursued them as far as Edmundston's plantation, on the Unadilla River, where they found three scouts dead ; but they effected nothing in the way of retaliation or the recovery of property. A party of friendly Oneidas, however, were more successful. They penetrated the Unadilla settlement, where Brant[1] had his headquarters, burned some of the Tory houses, took several prisoners, and brought away some of the cattle taken from the people at the German Flats. A

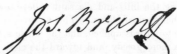

deputation of about one hundred Indian warriors of the Oneidas communicated the result of this expedition to Major Cochran, then in command of the garrison at Fort Schuyler. They were a part of those who proffered their services to General Gates, after the first battle on Bemis's Heights, in the autumn previous.

I returned to Little Falls toward evening, and the lengthened shadows of the hills and trees heightened the picturesque beauty of the scene. The view, on approaching

[1] Joseph Brant (Thayendanegea) was a Mohawk of pure blood. His father was a chief of the Onondaga nation, and had three sons in the army with Sir William Johnson, under King Hendrick, in the battle at Lake George in 1755. Joseph, his youngest son, whose Indian name was Thayendanegea, which signifies *a bundle of sticks*, or, in other words, *strength*, was born on the banks of the Ohio in 1742, whither his parents immigrated from the Mohawk Valley. His mother returned to Canajoharie with two children, Mary, or Molly, who became the concubine of Sir William Johnson, and Thayendanegea. His father, Te howaghwengaraghkwin, a chief of the Wolf tribe* of the Mohawks, seems to have died in the Ohio country.

* According to Colden, each of the original Five Nations was divided into *three* tribes, the Tortoise or Turtle, the Bear, and the Wolf. Others affirm that there were *eight* divisions in each, the other tribes being the Crane, the Snipe, the Hawk, the Beaver, and the Deer. The first three seem to have been pre-eminent; and among the Mohawks, with whom the whites had more direct and extensive business and social intercourse than with any others, these only were known. Title deeds to lands, and other papers, now in the office of the Secretary of State at Albany, have the signatures or marks of the chiefs of these three tribes attached. The annexed cuts are fac-similes, which I copied from the originals. No. 1 is the mark

No. 1.

No. 2.

of *Teyendagages*, or Little Hendrick, of the Turtle tribe ; No. 2, that of *Kanadagea*, or Hans, chief of the Bear tribe, and is intended to represent a bear lying on his back ; No. 3 is the signature and hieroglyphic of Great Hendrick, the celebrated chief of the Wolf tribe, who was killed near Lake George in 1755. *Kanadagea* sometimes

No. 3.

made a simple cross, thus :   Little Abraham, or

Tinyahasara, whom we have noted as friendly to the Americans, made a mark thus :   I found upon several papers the

name of Daniel, a chief of the Tortoise tribe, often associated with that of Little Abraham and of Hans. The signatures of the chiefs of all the three tribes appear to have been essential in making those deeds or conveyances legal. Besides the eight *totums* here named, there appears to have been, at an earlier date, three other tribes, the Serpent, the Porcupine, and the Fox. Giles F. Yates, Esq., of Schenectady, one of our most indefatigable antiquaries, discovered a document having the marks of twenty-one chiefs and that of a woman (Eusena) attached. Among them are those of *Togwayenant*, of the Serpent ; *Sander*, of the Porcupine ; and *Symon*, of the Fox tribe. The date of the document is 1714. It is not my province, neither have I the space, to pursue this interesting subject further, in this connection.

DANIEL'S SIGNATURE.

from the west, changes from the quiet beauty of a rolling plain, enriched by the cultivator's art, and enlivened by a gently gliding river, to the rugged grandeur of lofty hills, craggy steeps, and turbulent cascades. It reminded me of two of Cole's beautiful pictures in his " Voyage of Life," wherein is depicted the course of an ambitious youth. He is out upon a placid stream, so full of self-confidence that his guardian angel is left behind. All around is beauty and repose. The stream meanders on without a riff, but in the distance it sweeps with a majestic curve around a woodland into a mysterious region. Onward speeds the bark of the youthful voyager upon the gentle current, until the valley becomes narrower, the waters run swiftly, the tall trees and beautiful flowers upon its banks disappear, high and barren rocks wall in his view, and just before him is the wild leap of a cataract into a fearful gulf below.

The village of Little Falls is upon the rocky bank of the cascades, and only westward can the eye see any thing from it but rocks, and trees, and running water mingled in wild confusion. Here the high ridge of the Alleghany range, which divides the head waters of the Mohawk and the Ontario streams from the Susquehanna and other Atlantic rivers, crosses the Mohawk Valley, and in ages long past, ere the great Falls of Niagara existed, doubtless formed the crown of a cataract almost as magnificent, when the waters of Ontario covered the upper valley, and a portion of its flood here found its way into the great lake that filled the Hudson basin, whose outlet, in turn, was among the rugged hills of the Highlands at West Point and vicinity. Such is the theory of the geologist; and never had opinion stronger presumptive proofs of its correctness than are found at Little Falls.[1] An obstruction here, seventy feet in height, would cause the waters to overflow the Rome summit, and mingle with those of Ontario by the way of Wood Creek, Oneida Lake, and the Oswego River. The rugged shores present many incontestible evidences of abrasion by the violent action of water, thirty to sixty feet above the present bed of the river. Many of them are circular perpendicular cavities in the hard rocks, which are composed chiefly of gneiss, granite, and hornblende. In some instances masses of stratified rocks present the appearance of Cyclopean architecture, as seen in the above cut,[2] and hundreds of small cavities, far above the present bed of the

His mother, after her return, married an Indian called Carribogo (news-carrier), whom the whites named Barnet; but, by way of contraction, he was called Barnt, and, finally, Brant. Thayendanegea was called Joseph, and was known as Brant's Joseph, or Joseph Brant. Sir William Johnson sent young Brant to the school of Dr. Wheelock, of Lebanon Crank (now Columbia), Connecticut, and, after he was well educated employed him as secretary, and as agent in public affairs. He was employed as missionary interpreter from 1762 to 1765, and exerted himself for the religious instruction of his tribe. When the Revolution broke out, he attached himself to the British cause, and in 1775 left the Mohawk Valley, went to Canada, and finally to England, where his education, and his business and social connection with Sir William Johnson, gave him free access to the nobility. The Earl of Warwick caused Romney, the eminent painter, to make a portrait of him for his collection, and from a print after that picture the engraving on the preceding page was made. Throughout the Revolution he was engaged in warfare chiefly upon the border settlements of New York and Pennsylvania, in connection with the Johnsons and Butlers. He held a colonel's commission from the king, but he is generally called Captain Brant. After the peace in 1783, Brant again visited England, and, on returning to America, devoted himself to the social and religious improvement of the Mohawks. who were settled upon the Ouise or Grand River, in Upper Canada, upon lands procured for them by Brant from Sir Frederic Haldimand, governor of the province. The territory embraced six miles on both sides of the river, from its mouth to its source. He translated the Gospel of St. Mark into the Mohawk language ; and in many ways his exertions for the spiritual and temporal welfare of his people were eminently successful, and endeared him to his nation. He died at his residence at the head of Lake Ontario, November 24th, 1807, aged 65 years. One of his sons (John) was an officer in the British service, on the Niagara frontier, in the war of 1812. His daughter married William J. Kerr, Esq., of Niagara, in 1824, and, I believe, is still living.

[1] This name was given in contradistinction to the Great Falls, now called Cohoes, at the mouth of the Mohawk.

[2] This is a view of a large circular cavity on the western shore of the river a few yards from the railroad, and about thirty feet above its bed. On the side of the cavity toward the river is an opening about

stream, indicate the action of pebbles in eddies of water.   The hills on either side rise to an altitude of nearly four hundred feet, and from that height the ancient cataract may have poured its flood.   Immediately below the present cascades at the foot of Moss Island, or Moss Rock, the river expands into a broader basin, more than one hundred feet deep, from whose depths rocky spikes, like church spires, shoot upward, some of them to the surface of the water.   Into this gulf the great cataract doubtless poured its flood, while the rocky cones, too hard to be abraded, resisted the unceasing attrition of the water for ages.

I strolled along the rail-road at twilight, by the margin of the rapids and of the gulf below ; and before sunrise I went down upon the tow-path to view the scene in the shadows of early morning.   Art and nature here vie with each other in claims upon our admiration. Here the former exhibits its wonderful triumphs, and the latter displays its beauty and grandeur.   On the south side of the river is the Erie Canal, the passage for which was excavated through solid rock a distance of two miles.   This narrow defile presented the most formidable obstruction on the whole line of that great work, and it was supposed that at least two years would be required to complete the excavation.   Skill and persevering industry accomplished the most difficult portion in ninety days.   The waters of the canal here

---

ten feet square, and over the entrance is a massive lintel, which appears as if hewn and placed there by the hands of man.   Within the large cavity, which is open at the top, are smaller ones upon its concave sides.   Two of these concavities are seen in the engraving.   The rocks are covered with a luxuriant growth of shrubbery, springing from the rich alluvial deposits in the fissures.   An exploration of them is dangerous, for some of the fissures are broad and deep.   Indian legends invest these caverns with romantic interest.   One of them I will repeat, in brief, as it was told to me, for it is identified with the spot represented in the picture.

Long ago, when the river was broader and the falls were more lofty, a feud arose between two young chiefs of the respective tribes of the Mohawk nation, the Wolf and the Tortoise.   A maiden of the Bear tribe was the cause of the feud, as maidens often are.   She was loved by both the young chiefs, and for a time she so coquetted that each thought himself beloved by her in return.   Her father was a stern old warrior, and loved his child tenderly.   Both chiefs had fought the Mingoes and Mohegans by his side, and the bravery of each entitled him to the hand of the maiden.   Her affections were at length stirred by the more earnest importunities of the Wolf, and she promised to become his bride.   This decision reached the ears of the Tortoise, and the embers of jealousy, which disturbed both while unaccepted suitors, burst into a flame of ungenerous revenge in the bosom of the disappointed lover.   He determined to possess the coveted treasure before the Wolf should take her to his wigwam.   With well-dissembled acquiescence in her choice, and expressions of warm friendship for herself and her affianced, he allayed all suspicions, and the maiden rambled with him in the moonlight upon the banks of the river when her affianced was away, unconscious of danger.   The day approached for the maiden to go to the wigwam of her lord.   The Tortoise was with her alone in a secluded nook upon the brink of the river.   His light canoe was near, and he proposed a voyage to a beautiful little island in the stream, where the fire-flies sparkled and the whippoorwill whispered its evening serenade.   They lanched, but, instead of paddling for the island, the Tortoise turned his prow toward the cataract.   Like an arrow they sped down the swift current, while the young chief, with vigorous arm, paddled for the western shore.   Skillful as with the bow and hatchet, he steered his canoe to the mouth of the cavern here pictured, then upon the water's brink, seized the affrighted maiden, and leaped ashore, at the same moment securing his canoe by a strong green withe.   The cave was dry, a soft bed of the skins of beasts was spread, and abundance of provision was there stored.   At the top of the cave, far above the maiden's reach, an opening revealed a passage through the fissures to the rocks above. It was known only to the Tortoise ; and there he kept the maiden many months, until her affianced gave her up as lost to him forever.   At length, while hunting on the southern hills in flowery May, the Wolf saw the canoe at the mouth of the cave.   It solved the question in his mind.   The evening was clear, and the full moon shone brightly.   He waited until midnight, when, with an arm as strong and skill as accurate as his rival's, he steered his canoe to the mouth of the cavern, which was lighted up by the moon. By its light he saw the perfidious Tortoise sleeping in the arms of an unwilling bride.   The Wolf smote the Tortoise, but the wound was slight.   The awakened warrior, unable to grasp his hatchet, bounded through the opening at the top of the cavern, and closed it with a heavy stone.   The lovers embraced in momentary joy.   It was brief, for a fearful doom seemed to await them.   The Tortoise would return with power, and they had to make choice of death, by the hatchet of the rival chief, or the waters of the cataract.   The latter was their choice, and, in affectionate embrace, they sat in their canoe and made the fearful leap.   The frail vessel struck propitiously upon the boiling waters, and, unharmed, passed over the gulf below.   Down the broad stream they glided, and far away, upon the margin of the lower lake, they lived and loved for two generations, and saw their children's children go out to the battle and the chase. In the long line of their descent, tradition avers, came Brant, the Mohawk sachem, the strong WOLF of his nation.

OF THE REVOLUTION.   259

View of Little Falls.   First Settlement.   Night Attack upon the Settlement.   Escape of Cox and Skinner.   Ride to Danube.

descend forty feet within a mile, by five locks ; and the traveler has ample time to view the
wild scenery while passing them. On the north side of the river the hard rocks have also been excavated, for the railroad which traverses the high bank in its winding course. Altogether, art and nature have here presented a scene worth a long journey to behold.

VIEW AT LITTLE FALLS.[1]

There was a small settlement at Little Falls at the time of the Revolution.   A Scotchman named Ellis had obtained, through Sir William Johnson, a patent for the mountain gorge, and erected flouring mills there These were important for supplying the people at the German Flats and the small garrisons that were kept at Forts Dayton and Herkimer.   A party of Tories and Indians in 1780 joined in an expedition to destroy the mills, and thus cut off the supply of flour for the Whig garrisons.   They made a stealthy descent, under cover of night.   The mill was garrisoned by about a dozen men, but so sudden and unexpected was the attack, that only a few shots were exchanged, and one man killed, before its defenders fled for safety.   Some leaped from the windows when the Indians entered, and others concealed themselves below.   Two men, Cox and Skinner, hid in the race-way, under the water-wheel, while two others, Edick and Getman, leaped into the race-way above the mill, and attempted to conceal themselves by keeping under the water as much as possible.   In this they would have succeeded, had not the assailants set the mill on fire, the light of which revealed the hiding-place of the latter two, and they were made prisoners.   Cox and Skinner were more fortunate.   The water-wheel protected them from the burning timbers that fell around them, and they remained safe in their hiding-place until the enemy had departed.   The object of the assailants was accomplished, and they returned to their rendezvous among the hills, carrying with them five or six prisoners.

After breakfast I rode down to Danube, to visit the residence of General Herkimer while living, and the old Castle Church near the dwelling-place of Brant in the Revolution.   It was a pleasant ride along the tow-path, between the canal and the river.   Herkimer's residence is about two and a half miles below Little Falls, near the canal, and in full view

[1] This view was taken from the rail-road near the village, looking down the river.   On the right is seen the Erie Canal, and on the left, and more in the foreground, the Mohawk, at the foot of the falls, with the rail-road and the magnetic highway.   The rugged bluff in the center is Moss Rock, at the lower extremity of which is the gulf, seen in the annexed engraving.   This view is from the tow-path, below Moss Rock. On the left is the canal, and on the right are the gulf and a portion of the village in the distance.   Moss Rock is an island, formed by the canal and the river.   The summit of this amorphous pile has been suggested as an appropriate site for the proposed monument to the memory of Dewitt Clinton.   It seems to me that the spot is singularly appropriate for that purpose.   The Erie Canal, with its busy commerce, is his perpetual memorial; and here is the point where the most wonderful triumphs were achieved in the construction of that stupendous work.   Here, too, pass all travelers to and from Niagara and the great West from the eastward, and the monument would be seen, if erected there, by more persons than at any other locality that may be named, out of the city of New York.

of the traveler upon the rail-road, half a mile distant. It is a substantial brick edifice,

was erected in 1764, and was a splendid mansion for the time and place. It is now owned by Daniel Conner, a farmer, who was *modernizing* it when I was there, by building a long, fashionable piazza in front, in place of the small old porch, or stoop, seen in the picture. He was also *improving* some of the rooms within. The one in which General Herkimer died (on the right of the front entrance), and also the one on the opposite side of the passage, are left precisely as they were when the general occupied the house; and Mr. Conner has the good taste and patriotism to preserve them so. These rooms are handsomely wainscoted with white pine, wrought into neat moldings and panels, and the casements of the deep windows are of the same material and in the same style.

GENERAL HERKIMER'S RESIDENCE.

Mr. Conner has carefully preserved the great lock of the front door of the *castle*—for castle it really was, in strength and appointments against Indian assaults. It is sixteen inches long and ten wide. Close by the house is a subterranean room, built of heavy masonry and arched, which the general used as a magazine for stores belonging to the Tryon county militia. It is still used as a store-room, but with more pacific intentions.

The family burial-ground is upon a knoll a few rods southeast of the mansion, and there rest the remains of the gallant soldier, as secluded and forgotten as if they were of "common mold." Seventy years ago the Continental Congress, grateful for his services, resolved to erect a monument to his memory, of the value of five hundred dollars; but the stone that may yet be reared is still in the quarry, and the patriot inscription to declare its intent and the soldier's worth is not yet conceived. Until 1847, no stone identified his grave. Then a plain marble slab was set up, with the name of the hero upon it; and when I visited it (1848), it was overgrown with weeds and brambles. It was erected by his grandnephew, W. Herkimer. The consecrated spot is in the possession

HERKIMER'S GRAVE

of strangers, and, but for this timely effort to preserve the identity of the grave, the visitor might soon have queried, with the poet in search of General Wooster's resting-place

> "O say, can none tell where the chieftain was laid?
> Where our hero in glory is sleeping?
> Alas! shall we never more seek out his grave,
> While fame o'er his memory is weeping?"

Although General Herkimer was severely wounded at the battle of Oriskany, his death was the result of unskillful treatment, and, if tradition speaks truth, of criminal indulgence of appetite on the part of his surgeon. He was conveyed from the field on a litter to his residence. The weather was sultry, and the wound, which was a few inches below the August 16, knee, became gangrenous. Nine days after the battle, a young French surgeon, 1777. who accompanied Arnold in his march up the valley, recommended amputation. Dr. Petrie, the general's medical adviser, was opposed to amputation, but it was done. The performance of the surgeon was so unskillful that the flow of blood was with great difficulty stanched. Indeed, the bleeding was not entirely checked, and it was thought advisable for the surgeon and his assistant to remain with the general, as his situation was very critical. Colonel Willett called to see him soon after the operation, and found him sitting up in his bed, as cheerful as usual, and smoking his pipe.   The blood continued to flow, and what little skill the surgeon possessed was rendered useless by indulgence in wine.   No other physician was at hand, and toward evening, the blood still flowing, the general became convinced that his end was near.   He called for the Bible, and read composedly, in the presence of his family and others, the thirty-eighth psalm, applying the deep, penitential confessions of the poem to his own case.   He closed the book, sank back upon his pillow, and expired Stone justly observes, " If Socrates died like a philosopher, and Rousseau like an unbelieving sentimentalist, General Herkimer died like a CHRISTIAN HERO."[1]

The Castle Church, as it is called—the middle one of the three constructed under the auspices of Sir William Johnson—is still standing (1848), two and a half miles below the Herkimer mansion.   It is a wooden building, and was originally so painted as to resemble stone.   Its present steeple is not ancient, but its form is not unlike that of the original.   Here the pious Kirkland often preached the Gospel to the heathen, and here Brant and his companions received lessons of heavenly wisdom.   The church stood upon land that belonged to the sachem, and the house of Brant, where Christian missionaries

CASTLE CHURCH.

were often entertained before he took up the war-hatchet, stood about seventy-five rods northward of the church.   Bricks and stones of the foundation were still to be seen in an apple orchard north of the road, and the locality was well defined, when I visited it, by rank weeds, nowhere else in the field so luxuriant.   I returned to Little Falls in time to dine and to take the western train at one o'clock for Fort Plain, seventeen miles down the Mohawk.

Fort Plain (near the junction of Osquaga Creek and the Mohawk), one of the numerous comely children brought forth and fostered by the prolific commerce of the Erie Canal, is near the site of the fortification of that name, erected in the Revolution.   This fort was eligibly situated upon a high plain in the rear of the village, and commanded an extensive sweep of the valley on the right and left.   A sort of defense was thrown up there by the people in the early part of the war, but the fort proper was erected by the government after the alarming demonstrations of the Indians in the Mohawk and Schoharie Valleys in 1778.   For a while it was an important fortress, affording protection to the people in the neighborhood, and forming a key to the communication with the Schoharie, Cherry Valley, and Unadilla settlements.   Its form was an irregular quadrangle, with earth and log bastions, embrasures at each corner, and barracks and a strong block-house within.   The plain on which it stood is of peninsular form,

FORT PLAIN.

---

[1] I was unsuccessful in my search for information respecting the career of General Herkimer in youth and early manhood.   He left no children.   Those of the family name are descendants of his only brother, George Herkimer.   His family was among the early settlers of the German Flats, and, though opulent according to the standard of his times, he seems to have been quite uneducated.   An old man whom I saw near the Flats remembered him as " a large, square-built Dutchman," and supposed him to have been about 65 years old when he died.   Should this meet the eye of any of his descendants, they will confer a favor upon the author by communicating to him any information they may possess concerning the general and his immediate family.

[2] An aged resident of Fort Plain, Mr. David Lipe, whose house is near the canal, below the old fortification, went over the ground with me, and I made a survey of the outlines of the fort according to his directions.   He aided in pulling down the block-house when it was demolished after the war, and his memory seemed to be very accurate.   I am indebted to him for much of the information here recorded concerning Fort Plain.

EXPLANATION OF THE PLAN.—The black line represents the parapet; a, the large block-house; b b b b, small block-houses at each bastion; c c, barracks.   There were two large apple-trees within the fort, and on the northern side of the hill is the living spring that supplied the garrison with water.

and across the neck, or isthmus, a breast-work was thrown up.   The fort extended along
the brow of the hill northwest of the village, and the block-
house was a few rods from the northern declivity.   This block-
house was erected in 1780, after the fort and barracks were
found to be but a feeble defense, under the supervision of a
French engineer employed by Colonel Gansevoort.   The latter, by order of General Clinton, then in command of the
Northern Department, had repaired thither with his regiment,
to take charge of a large quantity of stores destined for Fort
Schuyler.   Ramparts of logs and earth were thrown up, and
a strong block-house was erected, a view of which is here
given.   It was octagonal in form, three stories in height, and
composed of hewn timbers about fifteen inches square.   There
were numerous port-holes for musketry, and in the lower story
three or four cannons were placed.   The first story was thirty
feet in diameter, the second forty, and the third fifty.   Each

FORT PLAIN BLOCK-HOUSE.[1]

of the upper stories projected about five feet, and in the floor of each projection there were
also port-holes, through which to fire perpendicularly upon an enemy below.   The powder
magazine of the fort was placed directly under the block-house for protection.

Some time after the completion of the work, doubts were expressed of its being cannon-
ball proof.   A trial was made with a six pounder placed at a proper distance.   Its ball
passed entirely *through* the block-house, crossed a broad ravine, and lodged in the hill on
which the old parsonage stands, an eighth of a mile distant.   This proved the inefficiency
of the building, and its strength was increased by lining it with heavy planks.   In order to
form a protection for the magazine against hot shot, the little garrison that was stationed
there in 1782 commenced throwing up a bank of earth around the block-house.   Rumors
of peace, and the quiet that then prevailed in that valley, caused the work to cease, and,
August, happily, its resumption was never demanded.   The mounds which were raised on
1848.   the south side of the block-house were yet quite prominent when I visited the locality.

This place was included in the Canajoharie settlement, and in 1780 felt severely the
vengeance of the Tories and Indians, inflicted in return for terrible desolations wrought by
an army under Sullivan, the previous year, in the Indian country west of the white settlements.   The whole region on the south of the Mohawk, for several miles in this vicinity,
was laid waste.   The approach of the dreaded Thayendanegea along the Canajoharie Creek,
with about five hundred Indians and Tories, to attack the settlement at Fort Plain, was an-
August 2, nounced to the people, then engaged in their harvest fields, by a woman who fired
1780.   a cannon at the fort.   The larger portion of militia had gone with Gansevoort to
guard provisions on their way to Fort Schuyler, and those who remained, with the boys and
old men, unable to defend their lives or property, fled into the fort for protection.   In their
approach the enemy burned every dwelling and barn, destroyed the crops, and carried off
every thing of value.   Regardless of the strength of the fort, they marched boldly up within
cannon-shot of the intrenchments, burned the church, the parsonage, and many other build-

---

[1] There is considerable confusion in the accounts concerning Fort Plain, for which there is no necessity.
There was a stockade about two miles southwest of Fort Plain, called Fort Clyde, in honor of Colonel Clyde,
an officer in the Tryon county militia; and another about the same distance northwest, called Fort Plank,
or Blank, from the circumstance that it stood upon land owned by Frederic Blank.   The latter and Fort
Plain have been confounded.   Mr. Stone erroneously considered them as one, and says, in his *Life of Brant*
(ii., 95), "The principal work of defense, then called Fort Plank, and subsequently Fort Plain, was situated
upon an elevated plain overlooking the valley, near the site of the village still retaining the name of the
fortress."   Other writers have regarded the block-house as the fort, when, in fact, it was only a part of the
fortifications.   The drawing here given is from one published in Stone's Life of Brant, with a description
from the Fort Plain Journal of December 26th, 1837.   Mr. Lipe considered it a correct view, except the
lower story, which, it was his impression, was square instead of octagonal, and had four port-holes for
heavy ordnance.

ings, and carried off several women and children prisoners. The house of Johannes Lipe, the father of David, my informant, which is still standing, was saved from plunder and fire by the courage and presence of mind of his wife. She had been busy all the evening carrying her most valuable articles from her house LIPE'S HOUSE. to a place of concealment in a hollow at the rear, and had made several deposites there. The last time she returned she met two prowling Indians at the gate. She was familiar with their language, and, without any apparent alarm, inquired of them if they knew any thing of her two brothers, who were among the Tories that fled to Canada. Fortunately, the savages had seen them at Oswegatchie, and, supposing her to be a Tory likewise, they walked off, and the house was spared.

The church spire had a bright brass ball upon it, which the Indians believed was gold.

OLD PARSONAGE AND CHURCH.[1]

While the edifice was burning, they waited anxiously for the steeple to fall, that they might secure the prize. When it fell, the savages rushed forward, scattered the burning timbers, and several of them in succession seized the glittering ball. It was speedily dropped, as each paid the penalty of blistered fingers, and discovered that "all is not gold that glistens."

With the destruction of Fort Plain the devastation was, for the time, stayed. In a day the fairest portion of the valley had been made desolate. Fifty-three dwellings and as many barns were burned, sixteen of the inhabitants were slain, and between fifty and sixty persons, chiefly women and children, were made captives. More than three hundred cattle and horses were driven away, the implements of husbandry were destroyed, and the ripe grain-fields, just ready for the sickle, were laid in ashes.[2] The smoke was seen as far as Johnstown, and the people immediately left the fields and joined the Albany and Schenectady militia, then marching up the valley, under Colonel Wemple. The colonel seemed to be one of those men who deem prudence the better part of valor, and was opposed to forced marches, particularly in pursuit of such fierce enemies as were just then attracting his attention. He managed to reach Fort Plain in time to see the smouldering embers of the conflagration, and to rest securely within its ramparts that night. The work of destruction was over, and the Indians and Tories were away upon another war-path.

At Fort Plain I was joined by my traveling companions, whom I had left at Syracuse, and made it my headquarters for three days, while visiting places of interest in the vicinity. It being a central point in the hostile movements in Tryon county, from the time of the flight of St. Leger from before Fort Stanwix until the close of the war, we will plant our telescope of observation here for a time, and view the most important occurrences within this particular sweep of its speculum. The battle of Minisink, and the more terrible tragedy in the Valley of Wyoming, radii in the hostile operations of the Indians and Tories from our point of view, will be noticed in other chapters. It is difficult to untie the complicated knot of events here, and make all parts perspicuous, without departing somewhat from the plan of the work, and taking up the events in chronological order. Every thing being subordinate to the history, I shall, therefore, make such departure for the present, and reserve my notes of travel until the story of the past is told.

---

[1] This view is from the high plain on the right of the block-house, looking north. The building upon the hill across the ravine is the old parsonage, which was immediately built upon the ruins of the one that was burned. On the left I have placed a church in its proper relative position to the parsonage, as indicated by Mr. Lipe. It was about half a mile northwest of the fort. On the right are seen the Mohawk River and Plain, a train of cars in the distance, and the hills that bound the view on the north side of the Mohawk Valley, in the direction of Stone Arabia and Klock's Field, where two battles were fought in 1780. These will be hereafter noticed.   [2] Letter of Colonel Clyde to Governor Clinton.

264   PICTORIAL FIELD-BOOK

Aspect of Affairs in Tryon County.   The Western Indians.   Girty and his Associates.   Fidelity of White Eyes.

CHAPTER XII.

ARK and threatening was the aspect of affairs for the people of the Mohawk Valley, in the spring of 1778, the year succeeding the dispersion of St. Leger's motley force at Fort Schuyler. Brant, with his warriors, retired to Fort Niagara after that event, and during the autumn and winter he and the British and Tory leaders made extensive preparations for war the ensuing spring. Colonel Hamilton was in command at Detroit, engaged actively in endeavors to induce the tribes along the southern shores of the western lakes and the head waters of the Mississippi to join the four divisions of the Six Nations of New York[1] who were in alliance with the crown against the patriots. He was aided by three malignant Tories, M‘Kee, Elliot, and Simon Girty.[2] They had been confined at Pittsburgh, but, escaping, they traversed the country thence to Detroit, and by proclaiming that the Americans had resolved on the destruction of the Indians, and that their only safety consisted in the immediate alliance of the Delawares and Shawnees with the soldiers of the king, aroused these tribes to a desire for war. Already they had been excited against the whites in general by the irruption into their county of Daniel Boon and others (of which I shall hereafter write), and they listened favorably to the appeal of the refugees. The expedition of M‘Intosh into the Ohio Valley gave apparent confirmation to the assertions of the Tories, and Captain *Pipe* (the rival chief of White Eyes of the Delawares, a fast friend of the Americans) at once assembled his warriors, and urged them to follow him immediately upon the war-path. He proclaimed every one an enemy who should speak against his proposition. But *White Eyes*, the beloved of all, persuaded his people to desist, and sent a message[3] to the Shawnees, which had the effect to keep them in check for a time. We shall consider the Indian wars in the Ohio country in detail in a future chapter.

The Johnsons and Colonel John Butler were also active at this juncture upon the St. Lawrence, recruiting Tory refugees, and inducing the Caughnawagas and other tribes to take up the hatchet; and at the dawn of the year a powerful combination was in progress, which threatened the destruction of all the settlements in the Mohawk and Schoharie Valleys.

Two of the Six Nations, the Oneidas and the Tuscaroras, were still faithful to their pledge of neutrality, nor were the tribes of the other four yet generally in arms. Congress, therefore, resolved to make another effort to secure their neutrality, if not a defensive alliance.[4]

---

[1] The Mohawks, Senecas, Onondagas, and Cayugas.

[2] Girty was an unmitigated scoundrel, and was far more savage in his feelings than the Indians. He was present when Colonel Crawford was tortured by the Indians in 1782, and looked upon his agonies with demoniac pleasure. The same year he caused the expulsion of the peaceful Moravians, who were laboring usefully among the Wyandots; and he personally ill treated them when driven away. He instigated an Indian warrior, at the defeat of St. Clair in 1791, to tomahawk the American General Butler, who lay wounded on the field, and to scalp him, and take out his heart for distribution among the tribes. There were some Tories, even active ones, whom we can respect; but miscreants like Girty and Walter Butler, of the Mohawk Valley, present no redeeming quality to plead for excuse.

[3] The message was as follows: "GRANDCHILDREN, YE SHAWNEES: Some days ago a flock of birds [M‘Kee, Elliot, and Girty], that had come on from the east, lit at Gaschochking, imposing a song of theirs upon us, which song had nigh proved our ruin. Should these birds, which, on leaving us, took their flight toward Scioto, endeavor to impose a song on you likewise, do not listen to them, for they lie."

[4] A resolution to this effect was adopted by Congress on the 2d of February, 1778. They instructed the commissioners to "Speak to the Indians in language becoming the representatives of free, sovereign, and independent states, and in such a tone as to convince them that they felt themselves so."—*Journals of Congress*, iv., 63.

A council was called, and the chiefs of all the Six Nations were invited to attend. General Schuyler and Volkert P. Douw were appointed commissioners to attend the meeting and act in behalf of Congress. They requested Governor Clinton to send a special commissioner to be present at the council, and James Duane was accordingly appointed. The council met at Johnstown on the 9th of March. More than seven hundred Indians were present, consisting of Tuscaroras, Oneidas, and Onondagas, a small number of Mohawks, 1778. three Cayugas, but not one of the Senecas, the most powerful and warlike tribe of the confederacy. The latter not only refused to attend, but sent a message affecting great surprise that they were invited to such a council.[1] It is not certainly known that General Schuyler was present at the meeting. La Fayette accompanied Duane, and the latter seems to have conducted the proceedings on the part of Congress. They were opened by an address from that body, charging the Indians with perfidy, cruelty, and treachery, while the conduct of the United States had been true and magnanimous toward them. An old Onondaga hypocritically acknowledged and bewailed the sins of his tribe, but charged them upon the young and headstrong warriors who had been seduced by the Tory leaders. The Mohawks and Cayugas were sullen and silent, while an Oneida chief, conscious of the faithfulness of his own tribe and of the Tuscaroras, spoke eloquently in behalf of both, concluding with a solemn assurance that the United States might rely upon their abiding friendship. Those two tribes were applauded by the commissioners, while the others were dismissed with an admonition to look well to their ways, as the arm of the United States was powerful, and vengeance might penetrate the remotest settlements of the Senecas. The council, on the whole, was unsatisfactory, for it was evident that the most warlike and important tribes, with Brant at their head, still brooded over their loss at Oriskany, and were determined on revenge.

While La Fayette was at Johnstown, Colonel Samuel Campbell, of Cherry Valley, waited upon him and directed his attention to the exposed condition of that settlement and of those upon the Schoharie Creek. The people had built three slight fortifications the preceding year, but they were quite insufficient for sure protection. They were merely embankments of earth thrown up around strong stone houses, and stockaded, into which the women and children might flee for safety in the event of an invasion. They were respectively known as the Upper, Middle, and Lower Forts.[2] By direction of La Fayette, these were each manned by a company of soldiers, with a small brass field piece. He also directed a fort to be erected in the Oneida country, and Forts Schuyler and Dayton to be strengthened; and, as we have already noticed, Fort Plain was afterward enlarged and more strongly fortified. These and far more efficient preparations for defense were necessary; for the recovery of the Mohawk Valley, where their property was situated, was an object too important to the Johnsons, Butlers, and the large number of refugees who accompanied them to Canada, not to induce extraordinary efforts for its attainment. Their spies and scouts were out in every direction, and, at the very time of the council at Johnstown, Colonel Guy Carleton, a nephew of the Governor of Canada of the same name, was lurking in the neighborhood, to watch the actions and to report upon the dispositions of the chiefs in conclave. His employers at the same time were upon the frontiers, preparing for invasion.

---

[1] "It is strange," said the messenger, "that while your tomahawks are sticking in our heads [referring to the battle of Oriskany], our wounds bleeding, and our eyes streaming with tears for the loss of our friends at German Flats [Oriskany], the commissioners should think of inviting us to a treaty."—*From a MS. Letter of James Duane, cited by Stone.*

[2] These were situated in the Schoharie Valley. The Upper Fort was near the margin of Schoharie Creek, about five miles southeast of Middleburgh village, and within the limits of the present town of Fulton. The remains of the Middle Fort are still visible, near Middleburgh, on the plain east of the road leading to Schoharie. The Lower Fort was five miles north of Middleburgh, at the village of Schoharie. An old stone church (yet standing, but much altered from the original), one mile northward of the court-house, was within the intrenchments, and formed the citadel of the fort. The ramparts inclosed the two story stone house of John Becker, the kitchen part of which was, until recently, well preserved. Temporary dwellings were erected within the inclosure, and in these the inhabitants kept their most valuable things.—See Simms's *Schoharie*, &c., p. 269.

266   PICTORIAL FIELD-BOOK

Settlers of Tryon County.   Destruction of Springfield.   M‘Kean and Brant

1778.　　Early in the spring, Brant and his warriors, with a large number of Tories, appeared at Oghkwaga, his headquarters the previous year.　There he organized scalping
parties and sent them out upon the borderers.　The settlers were cut off in detail.　Marauding parties fell upon isolated families like bolts from the clouds, and the blaze of dwellings upon the hills and in the valleys nightly warned the yet secure inhabitant to be on the

ARMED SETTLERS.

alert.　Their dwellings were transformed into block-houses.　The women were taught the
use of weapons, and stood sentinels when the men were at work.　Half-grown children were
educated for scouts, and taught to discern the Indian trail, and every man worked armed in
his field.　Such was the condition of the dwellers of Tryon county during almost the whole
time of the war.

Brant's first hostile movement of consequence, after his return to Oghkwaga, was the destruction of a small settlement at Springfield, at the head of Otsego lake, ten miles west of
Cherry Valley.　It was in the month of May.　Every house was burned but one, into which
the women and children were collected and kept unharmed.　The absence of Tories in that
expedition, and the freedom to act as he pleased on the part of Brant, may account for this
humanity.　Several men were made captive, and, with considerable property, were carried
off to Oghkwaga.

In June, Captain M‘Kean, at the head of some volunteers, was sent to reconnoiter Brant's
encampment at Oghkwaga.　M‘Kean's headquarters were at Cherry Valley.　On his way
down the valley of the Charlotte River, he learned that large war-parties were out, and,
fearing a surprise, thought it prudent to return.　He halted an hour to refresh, and wrote a
letter to Brant, censuring him for his predatory warfare; he intimating that he was too cowardly to show himself in open and honorable conflict, M‘Kean challenged him to meet him
in single combat, or with an equal number of men, to try their skill, courage, and strength;
and concluded by telling him that if he would come to Cherry Valley, they would change
him from a *Brant* to a *goose*.[1]　This was an injudicious movement, and, doubtless, incited

---

[1] This letter was fastened to a stick and placed in an Indian path.　It soon reached Brant, and irritated

the sachem, in some degree, to join Butler, a few months later, in desolating that settlement.

There was an engagement on the 2d of July, on the upper branch of the Cobelskill, between a party of regular troops and Schoharie militia, fifty-two in number, and an Indian force four hundred and fifty strong. The Americans, commanded by Captain Christian Brown, were overpowered. Fourteen were killed, eight wounded, two were missing, and the remainder escaped. The dwellings were burned, and the horses and cattle, which the victors could not take with them, were slaughtered in the fields. At the same time, Colonel John Butler, who had penetrated the country from Niagara with a body of Indians and Tories, eleven hundred strong, broke into the Valley of Wyoming and laid it waste. July 3-4, Of this I shall write in detail hereafter. We have already considered the destruc- 1778. tion of the settlement at German Flats, toward the close of this summer. Scalping parties continued to infest the Schoharie and neighboring settlements until quite late in September, when troops from the main army checked their depredations for a while. A few days after the battle of Monmouth,[a] Colonel William Butler, with a Pennsylvania regiment [a] June 28, and a detachment of Morgan's rifle corps,[1] was ordered to Tryon county, and took 1778. post at Schoharie, whence parties were sent out to chastise the white and red savages, and to protect threatened settlements. They accomplished but little, however, except in intercepting bands of Tories that were making their way from the Hudson River settlements to join Johnson at Niagara. One of these parties, collected in the vicinity of Catskill, under a Captain Smith, was dispersed, the commander killed, and several of the men made prisoners. This, and a few other exploits of a similar character, inspired the people with confidence, and they anticipated a season of repose. But it was of short duration, for already a cloud was gathering in the west, full charged with desolation.

We have noticed the fact that Walter Butler, a son of Colonel John Butler, was arrested near Fort Dayton in August, 1777, tried, and condemned to death as a spy, but reprieved and sent a prisoner to Albany. He was closely confined in the jail there until the spring of 1778, when, through the interposition of his father's friends, some of them of the highest respectability, he was liberated from prison, and allowed to reside with a private family, having a single sentinel to guard him. This family proved to be Tories in disguise. The sentinel was made drunk, and young Butler, mounting a fleet horse, escaped, and joined his father at Niagara, just after the massacre of Wyoming. On his way through the Seneca country he excited the Indians, by tales of the extensive preparations which the Americans were making to penetrate and lay waste their country, and they were soon ripe for invading the white settlements.

About this time a Seneca chief, called *Great Tree*, who was with Washington during the summer, left for his own country and nation, with the strongest professions of friendship for the Americans. He promised to use his influence in keeping the Senecas neutral, and, if unsuccessful, he was to return with his personal adherents and join the friendly Oneidas. According to his own account, he found his people in arms, and uttering loud defiance against the whites. The chiefs and principal warriors were collected at Kanadaseago and Genesee ; and *Great Tree*, believing the stories of Butler, and finding his people very united, resolved to join his nation in chastising any whites that might penetrate their county. He was a popular orator and warrior, and his adherence gave the Senecas much joy. The Indians west of the Oneidas were thus prepared to follow a leader upon the war-path.

Walter Butler obtained from his father the command of a detachment of his Rangers, and permission to employ them, with the forces of Captain Brant, in an expedition against the

---

him exceedingly. In a letter written soon afterward to a Tory named Cass, he said, " The people of Cherry Valley, though bold in words, will find themselves mistaken in calling me a goose."

[1] Timothy Murphy, the man who shot General Fraser at Bemis's Heights, was in this detachment, and became the terror of the Indians and Tories in the Schoharie country. He used a double-barreled rifle, and the Indians, seeing him fire twice without stopping to load, supposed that he could fire as often as he pleased in the same manner.

settlements in Tryon county.   It was late in the season, but he thirsted for revenge because of his imprisonment, and departed eastward early in October.   While on his way, and near
1778. Genesee, he met Brant, with his warriors, going from his camp upon the Susquehanna to his winter-quarters at Niagara.   Brant felt a deep personal hatred toward young Butler, and this feeling was greatly increased on finding himself made subordinate to the latter.   But the difficulty, which threatened, at first, to be serious, was soon adjusted.   Thayendanegea had thought much of the insulting letter of Captain McKean, and more willingly turned his face back toward the settlements.   The united forces amounted to about seven hundred men.

This movement was known to Mr. Dean, an Indian interpreter in the Oneida country, early in October, and he communicated the information to Major Cochran, then in command at Fort Schuyler.   That officer sent a messenger with the intelligence to Colonel Alden, at Cherry Valley, and also to the garrisons of the Schoharie forts ; but the presence of the Pennsylvania troops and riflemen had lulled the people into fancied security, and the report of the oncoming invasion was treated as an idle Indian tale.

Cherry Valley, the wealthiest and most important settlement near the head waters of the eastern branch of the Susquehanna, was the enemy's chosen point of attack.   Colonel Ichabod Alden, of Massachusetts, was in command of the fort there, with about two hundred and fifty Continental troops.[1]   On the 8th of November the commandant received a dispatch from Fort Schuyler, informing him that his post was about to be attacked by a large force of Indians and Tories, then assembled upon the Tioga River.   Colonel Alden treated the information with unconcern, but the inhabitants were greatly alarmed.   They asked permission to move into the fort or to deposite their most valuable articles there, but the colonel, regarding the alarm as really groundless, refused his consent.   He assured them, at the same time, that he would be vigilant in keeping scouts upon the look-out and the garrison in preparation, and, accordingly, on the 9th parties were sent out in various directions.   One of these, which went down toward the Susquehanna, built a fire at their encampment, fell asleep, and awoke prisoners in the hands of Butler and Brant.   All necessary information concerning the settlement was extorted from them, and the next day the enemy moved forward and encamped upon a lofty hill covered with evergreens, about a mile southwest of the village, and overlooking the whole settlement.   From that observatory they could see almost every house in the village ; and from the prisoners they learned that the officers were quartered out of the fort, and that Colonel Alden and Lieutenant-colonel Stacia were at the house of Robert Wells, recently judge of the county, and formerly an intimate friend of Sir William Johnson and Colonel John Butler.

November 10, Early in the morning the enemy marched slowly toward the village.   Snow
1778. had fallen during the night, and the morning was dark and misty.   When near the village, the Tories halted to examine their muskets, for the dampness had injured their powder.   The Indians, and particularly the ferocious Senecas, eager for blood and plunder, pushed forward in the van during the halt.   A settler, on horseback, going toward the village, was shot, but, being slightly wounded, escaped and gave the alarm.   Colonel Alden could not yet believe that the enemy was near in force, but he was soon convinced by the sound of the war-whoop that broke upon the settlement, and the girdle of fierce savages, with gleaming hatchets, that surrounded the house of Mr. Wells.   They rushed in and murdered the whole family.[2]   Colonel Alden escaped from a window, but was pursued, tomahawked, and scalped.

---

[1] While Brant was collecting his troops at Oghkwaga the previous year, the strong stone mansion of Colonel Samuel Campbell, at Cherry Valley, was fortified, to be used as a place of retreat for the women and children in the event of an attack.   An embankment of earth and logs was thrown up around it, and included two barns.   Small block-houses were erected within the inclosure.   This was the only fort at Cherry Valley at the time in question.

[2] The family of Mr. Wells consisted of himself and wife, mother, brother and sister (John and Jane), and a daughter.   His son John (the late eminent counselor of New York) was then at school in Schenectady, and was the only survivor of the family.   They had all been living at Schenectady for some months, for security, but the alarm in the region of Cherry Valley having subsided, they had just returned.   The de-

The house of the venerable minister, Mr. Dunlap (whose wife was the mother of Mrs. Wells), and that of a Mr. Mitchell, were next attacked, and most of the inmates murdered.[1] Mr. Dunlap and his daughter at home were protected by Little Aaron, a Mohawk chief, who led him to his door and there stood by his side, and preserved his life and property. But the good old man sank under the terrible calamity of that day, and joined his lost ones in the spirit land within a year thereafter. Many other families of less note were cut off. Thirty-two of the inhabitants, mostly women and children, and sixteen soldiers of the garrison, were killed. The whole settlement was plundered after the massacre had ceased, and every building in the village was fired when the enemy left with their prisoners and booty. Among the prisoners were the wife and children of Colonel Campbell, who was absent at the time. He returned to find his property laid waste and his family carried into captivity.

The prisoners, numbering nearly forty, were marched down the valley that night in a storm of sleet, and were huddled together promiscuously, some of them half naked, with no shelter but the leafless trees, or resting-place but the wet ground. The marauders, finding the women and children cumbersome, sent them all back the next day, except Mrs. Campbell, her aged mother,[2] and her children, and a Mrs. Moore, who were kept as hostages for the kind treatment and ultimate exchange of the family of Colonel John Butler. The returning prisoners carried back with them a letter from Walter Butler to General Schuyler, in which he pretended that feelings of mercy for the almost naked and helpless captives were the incentive that caused him to release them ; disclaimed all desire to injure the weak and defenseless ; and closed by assuring him that, if Colonel John Butler's family were longer detained, he would not restrain the Indians from indulgence in murder and rapine. The " tender mercy" of Butler was that of " the wicked." He was the head and front of all the cruelty at Cherry Valley on that day. He commanded the expedition, and while he saw, unmoved, the murder of his father's friend and family, and of others whose age and sex should have secured his regard, his *savage* ally, the " monster Brant," hastened to save that very family, but was too late.[3] Butler would not allow his Rangers even to warn their friends

struction of the Wells family was marked by circumstances of peculiar ferocity, and I mention them to exhibit the infernal character which the passions of men assume when influenced by the horrid teachings in the school of war. One of the Tories boasted that he cleft open the head of Mr. Wells while on his knees in prayer. His sister Jane was distinguished for her beauty, virtues, and accomplishments. When the enemy burst into the house, she fled to a pile of wood and endeavored to conceal herself. An Indian pursued and caught her. He then wiped his knife, dripping with the blood of her relatives, sheathed it, and deliberately took his tomahawk from his girdle. At that moment a Tory, who had been a domestic in the family of Mr. Wells, relented, and, springing forward, claimed her as his sister. The savage thrust him aside and buried his hatchet in her temple. It is said that Colonel John Butler, professedly grieved at the conduct of his son at Cherry Valley, remarked, on one occasion, " I would have gone miles on my knees to save that family, and why my son did not do it, God only knows."

[1] Mr. Mitchell was in the field when the invasion took place, and found safety in the woods. After the enemy had retired, he hastened to the village, when he found his house on fire and the dead bodies of his wife and three children lying within. He extinguished the flames, and discovered his little daughter terribly mangled, but yet alive. He took her to the door, hoping fresh air might revive her, when he discovered a straggling party of the enemy near. He had just time to conceal himself, when a Tory sergeant named Newberry, whose acts in Schoharie entitle him to a seat in the councils of Pandemonium, approached, and, seeing the poor child lying upon the door-stone, dispatched her with a blow of a hatchet. This miscreant was afterward caught and hung by order of General Clinton.

[2] Mrs. Cannon, the mother of Mrs. Campbell, was quite old. She was an encumbrance, and a savage slew her with his tomahawk, by the side of her daughter, who, with a babe eighteen months old in her arms, was driven with inhuman haste before her captors, while, with uplifted hatchets, they menaced her life. Arriving among the Senecas, she was kindly treated, and installed a member of one of the families. They allowed her to do as she pleased, and her deportment was such that she seemed to engage the real affections of the people. Perceiving that she wore caps, one was presented to her, considerably spotted with blood. On examination, she recognized it as one that had belonged to her friend, Jane Wells. She and her children (from whom she was separated in the Indian country) were afterward exchanged for the wife and family of Colonel John Butler, then in the custody of the Committee of Safety at Albany.

[3] There are many well-authenticated instances on record of the humanity of Brant, exercised particularly toward women and children. He was a magnanimous victor, and never took the life of a former friend or acquaintance. He loved a hero because of his heroism, although he might be his enemy ; and he was

in the settlement of the approaching danger, but friend and foe were left exposed to the terrible storm; he had sworn vengeance, and his bad heart would not be content until its cravings were satisfied. Tender charity may seek to cloak his crimes with the plea that partisan warfare justified his deeds; and lapse of time, which mellows such crimson tints in the picture of a man's character, may temper the asperity with which shocked humanity views his conduct; yet a just judgment, founded upon observation of his brief career, must pronounce it a stain upon the generation in which he lived. After the destruction of Cherry Valley his course was short, but bold, cruel, and bloody. British officers of respectability viewed him with horror and disgust; and when, in 1781, he was slain by the Oneidas on the banks of the West Canada Creek, his body was left to decay, while his fallen companions were buried with respect.

SIGNATURE OF WALTER BUTLER.

With the destruction of Cherry Valley all hostile movements ceased in Tryon county, and were not resumed until the following spring, when an expedition was sent against the Onondagas by General Clinton. Frequent messages had been sent by the Oneidas during the winter, all reporting that Brant and his Tory colleagues were preparing for some decisive blow. The Onondagas, in the mean while, were making peaceful professions, expressing a desire to remain neutral, while they were in league and in secret correspondence with the leaders in the hostile camp at Niagara. Policy, and even the necessity born of the law of self-preservation, seemed to demand the infliction of summary and severe chastisement upon the savages who menaced and desolated the Tryon county settlements. Early in the winter General Schuyler had assured Congress that, unless something of the kind was speedily done, Schenectady must soon become the boundary of settlement in that direction.

The arrangement of an expedition against the Indians was intrusted to General Clinton. April 18, 1779. In April he dispatched a portion of the regiments of Colonels Gansevoort and Van Schaick, under the latter officer, against the Onondagas. The party consisted of five hundred and fifty-eight strong men. Van Schaick was instructed to burn their castle and villages in the Onondaga Valley, destroy all their cattle and other effects, and make as many prisoners as possible. He was further instructed to treat the women that might fall into his hands with all the respect due to chastity. The expedition went down Wood Creek and Oneida Lake, and thence up the Oswego River to the point on Onondaga Lake where Salina now is. A thick fog concealed their movements, and they had approached to within four or five miles of the valley before they were discovered. As soon as the first village was attacked, the alarm spread to the others. The people fled to the forests, leaving every thing, even their arms, behind them. Three villages, consisting of about fifty houses, were destroyed; twelve Indians were killed, and thirty-three were made prisoners. A large quantity of

---

never known to take advantage of a conquered soldier. I have mentioned the challenge which Captain M'Kean sent to Brant. After the affair at Cherry Valley, he inquired of one of the prisoners for Captain M'Kean, who, with his family, had left the settlement. "He sent me a challenge," said Brant. "I came to accept it. He is a fine soldier thus to retreat." It was replied, "Captain M'Kean would not turn his back upon an enemy when there was any probability of success." "I know it," replied Brant. "He is a brave man, and I would have given more to take him than any other man in Cherry Valley; but I would not have hurt a hair of his head."

Dr. Timothy Dwight relates that Walter Butler ordered a woman and child to be slain, in bed, at Cherry Valley, when Brant interposed, saying, "What! kill a woman and child! That child is not an enemy to the king nor a friend to Congress. Long before he will be big enough to do any mischief, the dispute will be settled." When, in 1780, Sir John Johnson and Brant led a desolating army through the Schoharie and Mohawk Valleys, Brant's humanity was again displayed. On their way to Fort Hunter an infant was carried off. The frantic mother followed them as far as the fort, but could get no tidings of her child. On the morning after the departure of the invaders, and while General Van Rensselaer's officers were at breakfast, a young Indian came bounding into the room, bearing the infant in his arms and a letter from Captain Brant, addressed to "the commander of the rebel army." The letter was as follows: "Sir—I send you, by one of my runners, the child which he will deliver, that you may know that, whatever others may do, I do not make war upon women and children. I am sorry to say that I have those engaged with me who are more savage than the savages themselves." He named the Butlers and others of the Tory leaders. This incident was related to Mr. Stone by the late General Morgan Lewis.

provisions, consisting chiefly of beans and corn, was consumed. The council-house, or castle, was not burned, but the swivel in it was spiked. All the horses and cattle in the vicinity were slaughtered ; and, when the work of destruction was ended, the expedition returned to Fort Schuyler, after an absence of only six days, and without the loss of a man.

This expedition, cruel and of doubtful policy, alarmed the neutral Oneidas.[1] They were faithful to the Americans, yet, having intermarried freely with the Onondagas, their relations had been slain or impoverished, and this distressed them. They sent a deputation to Fort Schuyler to inquire into the matter. Colonel Van Schaick pacified, if he did not satisfy, them. and they returned to their people. But the ire of the Onondagas was fiercely kindled, not only on account of the destruction of their property, but because of the extinguishment of their council fire. Three hundred braves were immediately sent upon the war-path, charged with the vengeance of the nation. Guided by a Tory, they came down fiercely upon the settlement at Cobelskill,[2] murdering, plundering, and burning. The militia turned out to repulse them, but, being led into an ambuscade, a number of them were killed. They fought desperately, and while the militia was thus contending, and beating back the savages, the people fled in safety to Schoharie. Seven of the militia took post in a strong house, which the savages set fire to, and these brave young men all perished in the flames. The whole settlement was then plundered and burned. The patriots lost twenty-two killed, and forty-two who were made prisoners.

While this expedition was in progress, scalping parties appeared at the different points in the lower section of the Mohawk, and the settlements were menaced with the fate of Cherry Valley. On the south side of the Mohawk a party fell upon the Canajoharie settlement, took three prisoners, captured some horses, and drove the people to Fort Plain. On the same day another party attacked a small settlement at Stone Arabia,[3] burned some houses, and killed several people. A party of Senecas appeared at Schoharie on the same day, drove the people to the fort, plundered the houses, and carried away two men prisoners. These simultaneous attacks were part of a plan for cutting off the settlement in detail. The Indians on the south of the Mohawk were from the Seneca country, and those on the north from Canada, both, doubtless, the advanced parties of larger forces. The settlements were thoroughly alarmed. The Palatine[4] Committee wrote immediately to General Clinton, at Albany, for succor. That efficient officer afforded immediate aid, and, by the timely check thus given to the invaders, the settlers of the valley were prevented from being driven into Schenectady.[5] Other settlements near the Delaware and on the frontiers of Ulster county were visited by the Indians in May and the early part of June ; and in July the battle of Minisink occurred, the particulars of which will be hereafter related. April 18, 1779. July 20, 1779.

In the spring of this year it was determined to send a formidable force into the Indian country of Western New York, for the purpose of chastising the savages and their Tory allies so thoroughly that the settlements upon the Mohawk and the upper branches of the Susquehanna might enjoy a season of repose. The tribes of the Six Nations were then populous. They had many villages, vast corn-fields, and fruitful orchards and gardens in the

---

[1] At the time of this expedition there were about forty Oneida warriors at Fort Schuyler. These were sent, with a party of regulars, under Lieutenants M'Lellan and Hardenburgh, northward to attack the fort at Oswegatchie. This expedition was unsuccessful in its ostensible object, the garrison having been apprised of their approach. It is supposed that the employment of the Oneidas so far away that they could not notify their kinsmen, the Onondagas, of the invasion, was the principal object of this northern movement, and in that it was successful. The Oneidas were really friendly to the patriots, but to their credit it was said by General Clinton (who knew them well), in a letter to General Sullivan, "Their attachment to one another is too strong to admit of their being of any service when employed against their fellows."

[2] Cobelskill was taken from Schoharie. The little village is about ten miles west of the former.

[3] Stone Arabia is about three miles north of the Mohawk, in the rear of Palatine, and thirteen west of Johnstown.

[4] Palatine is on the north side of the Mohawk, opposite Canajoharie, with which it is connected by a bridge.

[5] Campbell's *Annals ;* Stone's *Brant.*

fertile country westward of Otsego Lake.

Jn?. Sullivan

It was supposed that the most effectual method to subdue or weaken them would be to destroy their homes and lay waste their fields, and thus drive them further back into the wilderness toward Lake Erie. Already the Mohawks had been thrust out of the valley of their name, and their families were upon the domains of the Cayugas and Senecas. It was, therefore, determined to make a combined movement upon them of two strong divisions of military, one from Pennsylvania and the other from the north, at a season when their fields and orchards were fully laden with grain and fruits. It was a part of the plan of the expedition to penetrate the country to Niagara, and break up the nest of vipers there.

General Sullivan[1] was placed in the chief command, and led in person the division that ascended the Susquehanna from Wyoming, while General Clinton[2] commanded the forces that penetrated the country from the mouth of the Canajoharie. It was arranged to unite the two divisions at Tioga.

Clinton's troops, fifteen hundred strong, were mustered at Canajoharie on the 15th of June, and on the 17th he commenced the transportation of his bateaux and provisions across the hilly country to Springfield, at the head of Otsego Lake, a distance of more than twenty

[1] John Sullivan was born in Berwick, Maine, on the 17th of February, 1740. His family emigrated to America from Ireland in 1723. He was a farmer in his youth, and, after arriving at maturity, he studied law, and established himself in practice in Durham, New Hampshire. He was chosen a delegate to the first Continental Congress. After retiring from that body, he and John Langdon, the speaker of the Provincial Congress of New Hampshire, commanded a small force which seized Fort William and Mary, at Portsmouth, and carried off all the cannon. He was appointed one of the eight brigadiers when the Continental army was organized in 1775, and early in the following year he was made a major general. He superseded Arnold in the command of the American army in Canada in 1776. When General Greene became ill on Long Island, he took command of his division, and was made prisoner at the battle fought there in August, 1776. He was exchanged, and took command of General Charles Lee's division in New Jersey after the capture of that officer. In the autumn of 1777 he was engaged in the battles at the Brandywine and Germantown, and in the winter following he took command of the troops on Rhode Island. He besieged Newport in August, 1778, was unsuccessful, and retreated from the island after a severe battle near the north end. He commanded the expedition against the Indians in 1779, and this was the last of his military career. Having offended some of the members of the Board of War, and believing himself ill treated, he resigned his commission in 1779. He was afterward a member of Congress, and, for three years from 1786, was President of New Hampshire. In 1789 he was appointed district judge, which office he held until his death, which occurred January 23d, 1795.

[2] James Clinton was born in Ulster county, New York, August 9th, 1736. At the age of twenty (1756) he was captain, under Bradstreet, in the attack on Fort Frontenac. In 1763 he was intrusted with the command of four companies in Ulster and Orange, raised for defense against the inroads of the savages. He, with his brother George (the Governor of New York during the Revolution), early espoused the patriot cause. He was appointed a colonel in 1775, and accompanied Montgomery to Canada. In August, 1776, he was made a brigadier; and he was in command, under Governor Clinton, at Forts Montgomery and Clinton when they fell into the hands of the enemy in 1777. He escaped, and made his way to his residence in safety. Conjointly with Sullivan, he led the expedition against the Indians in 1779. During the remainder of the war he was connected with the Northern Department, having his quarters at Albany. He retired to his estate, near Newburgh, Orange county, New York, after the Revolution, where he died

miles.   It was an arduous duty, for his boats numbered two hundred and twenty, and he had provisions sufficient for three months.   He reached Springfield, with all his luggage, on the 30th.   On his way he captured Hare and Newberry, two notorious spies, the former a lieutenant in the British service, and the latter the miscreant whom we have already noticed as the murderer of Mr. Mitchell's wounded child at Cherry Valley.   They were tried, and hanged "pursuant to the sentence of the court, and to the entire satisfaction of the inhabit-ants of the county."[1]

Clinton, with his division, proceeded to the foot of Otsego Lake, and there awaited orders from Sullivan.   A day or two after his arrival, General Schuyler communica-   July 1, 1779. ted to him the important information that the purpose of the expedition was known to the enemy, and that four hundred and fifty regular troops, one hundred Tories, and thirty In-dians had been sent from Montreal to re-enforce the tribes against whom it was destined. This information General Schuyler received from a spy whom he had sent into Canada. The spy had also informed him that they were to be joined by one half of Sir John John-son's regiment and a portion of the garrison at Niagara.   On the 5th, Mr. Deane,[2] the In-dian interpreter, arrived with thirty-five Oneida warriors, who came to explain the absence of their tribe, whom Clinton, by direction of Sullivan, had solicited to join him.[3]   They con-firmed the intelligence sent by Schuyler, and added that a party of Cayugas and Tories, three hundred in number, were then upon the war-path, and intended to hang upon the outskirts of Clinton's army on its march to Tioga.

Clinton remained at the south end of Otsego Lake, awaiting the tardy movements of Sul-livan, until the first week in August.   His troops became impatient, yet he was not idle. He performed a feat which exhibited much ingenuity and forecast.   He discovered that, in consequence of a long drought, the outlet of the lake was too inconsiderable to allow his boats to pass down upon its waters.   He therefore raised a dam across it at the foot of the lake, by which the waters would be so accumulated that, when it should be removed, the bed of the outlet would be filled to the brim, and bear his boats upon the flood.   The work was soon accomplished, and, in addition to the advantages which it promised to the expedition, the damming of the lake caused great destruction of grain upon its borders, for its banks were overflowed, and vast corn-fields belonging to the Indians were deluged and destroyed. The event also greatly alarmed the savages.   It was a very dry season, and they regarded the sudden rising of the lake, without any apparent cause, as an evidence that the Great Spirit was displeased with them.   And when Clinton moved down the stream with his large flotilla upon its swollen flood, the Indians along its banks were amazed, and retreated into the depths of the forest.

Sullivan and Clinton formed a junction at Tioga on the 22d of August, the entire force amounting to five thousand men, consisting of the brigades of Generals Clinton,   1779.

December 22d, 1812, aged 75 years.   He was the father of De Witt Clinton, the eminent Governor of New York in 1826–7.

[1] So said General Clinton in a letter to General Schuyler.   The latter remarked, in reply, "In executing Hare you have rid the state of the greatest villain in it.   I hope his abettors in the country will meet with a similar exaltation."

[2] James Deane was the first settler in the town of Westmoreland, Oneida county.   He was the son of pious New England parents, and at the age of eleven years was sent among the Indians upon the Susque-hanna to learn their language, for the purpose of becoming a missionary among them.   He was afterward a student in Dartmouth College.   On the breaking out of the war, he was appointed Indian agent, with the rank of major in the army, and during the contest he was most of the time among the Oneidas.   At the close of hostilities the Oneidas granted him a tract of land two miles square, near Rome, in Oneida county, which he afterward exchanged for a tract in Westmoreland, where he removed in 1786, and resided until his death in 1832.

[3] General Clinton was averse to the employment of the Oneidas or any other Indians; but such being the orders of his superior, he engaged Mr. Deane to negotiate with them.   The Oneidas, to a man, volun-teered to accompany the expedition, and the few Onondagas who still adhered to the Americans were also ready to join Clinton.   But on the 23d the Oneidas received an address at Fort Schuyler, from General Haldimand, written in the Iroquois language; and so alarming were the menaces it contained, that they suddenly changed their minds, and determined to stay at home and defend their own castles and dwellings.

Hand, Maxwell, and Poor, together with Proctor's artillery and a corps of riflemen. The movement of the expedition had been so slow that the enemy was prepared to receive them. Near Conewawah[1] (Newtown in the histories of the battle), a considerable Indian village at the junction of the Newtown Creek with the Chemung River, they had thrown up breastworks half a mile in length, where they had determined to make a bold stand against the invaders.

The Americans moved cautiously up the Tioga and Chemung, having large flanking parties on either side, and a strong advanced and rear guard, for they were told that detachments of the enemy were hovering around, ready to strike when an opportunity should offer. On their march they destroyed a small Indian settlement, and the next day Major Parr, of the advanced guard, discovered the enemy's works. These were about a mile in advance of Conewawah, and were so covered by a bend in the river, that only the front and one flank were exposed to the fire of the assailants. That flank rested upon a steep hill or ridge running nearly parallel with the river. Further to the left was another ridge, running in the same direction, and passing in the rear of the American army. Detachments of the enemy were stationed on both hills, having a line of communication ; and they were so disposed that they

August 29, 1779.

ORDER OF MARCH.[2]

might fall upon the assailants, flank and rear, as soon as the action should commence. The Tories and Indians were further protected by the pine-trees and shrub oaks that covered the ground. Hoping that the Americans might not discover their concealed fortification, they had arranged it in such a relative position to the road along which the invaders must pass, that the whole flank of the army would be exposed to an enfilading fire. Happily for the Americans, their preparations were discovered in time.

General Hand[3] formed the light infantry about four hundred yards from the breast-works, and, while thus waiting for the main body to come up, was several times attacked by small parties of Indians, who sallied out, raised the war-whoop, and then retreated within the works. The hill upon the right swarmed with savages, and Sullivan ordered Poor to sweep it with his brigade. He immediately commenced the ascent, and the action became warm. His progress was bravely disputed for two hours, when the enemy slowly gave way. They darted from tree to tree as they yielded inch by inch ; and from behind rocks, and bushes, and trees they galled the Americans terribly with a scattering fire. Brant was at the head of the savages, and Sir John Johnson, aided by the Butlers and Captain M'Donald, one of

---

[1] Conewawah was upon the site of the present village of Elmira. The name is an Iroquois word, signifying *a head on a pole.* It was beautifully situated in the midst of a fertile valley, and, at the time of the invasion, was surrounded by fruitful orchards and broad fields of flowering corn. The place became a white settlement, and was incorporated by the name of Newtown in 1815, which was changed to Elmira in 1825. There are no vestiges to be seen here of the *battle of Chemung,* as the engagement that took place there is sometimes called. The spot where Sullivan landed is a few rods below the "Sullivan Mill," which stands upon the Conewawah or Newtown Creek, near its junction with the Chemung. The works thrown up by Sullivan, and destroyed when he returned from the Genesee country, were a little south of the mill.

[2] EXPLANATION OF THE PLAN.—The advanced guard, composed of light infantry, one mile in advance. *a a*, flanking corps. *b b*, the main body. Clinton's and Hand's brigades were on the right, and Poor's and Maxwell's were on the left. *c,* Proctor's artillery and the pack horses. The rifle corps composed a portion of the strong rear-guard.

[3] General Edward Hand was a native of Leinster province, Ireland, and was born at the close of 1744. His amiable disposition and urbanity of manner endeared him to his men, and he maintained, throughout the war, the unlimited confidence and respect of his superior officers. After the war he was much engaged in civil offices of trust, and his name is attached to the Pennsylvania Constitution of 1790. So highly did Washington esteem him, that when, during Adams's administration, he consented to take the chief command of the American army to be raised to resist the threatened and actual aggressions of France, he desired the appointment of General Hand as adjutant general. He died in 1803.

the Scotch refugees from Johnstown, commanded the Tories. It is believed that Guy Johnson was also in the battle, but this is not certainly known. They fought skillfully and courageously, and, but for the artillery that was brought into play as speedily as possible, the victory would doubtless have been on their side. The cannonade produced a great panic among the Indians, yet their leader, who was seen at all points, and in the hottest of the fight, kept them long from retreating. Poor at length gained the summit of the ridge, out-flanked the enemy, and decided the fortunes of the day. Brant, perceiving that all was lost, raised the loud, retreating cry, *Oonah! Oonah!* and savages and Tories, in great confusion, abandoned their works and fled across the river, pursued by the victors. Thus ended the battle of Chemung. The force of the enemy was estimated by Sullivan at fifteen hundred, including five companies of British troops and Rangers. The Americans numbered between four and five thousand, a considerable portion of whom were not brought into action at all. Considering the length of time occupied in the battle, and the numbers engaged, the loss was very inconsiderable. Only five or six of the Americans were killed, and about fifty wounded. The loss of the enemy was much greater. In their flight eight Indians were slain and *scalped* by their pursuers. Ay, *scalped!* for the Americans had been apt scholars in learning the Indian art of war that had been so terribly taught them in Tryon county for three years.

Sullivan's army rested upon the battle-ground that night, and the next morning pushed onward toward Catharinestown, an Indian settlement northwest from Conewawah, and about three miles from the head of Seneca Lake. The march was difficult and dangerous. The route lay through narrow defiles and a deep valley traversed by a stream so sinuous that they had to ford it several times, the water often waist high. At night they bivouacked in a dark and tangled cedar swamp, without blankets or food, and in continual fear of an enemy in ambush.[1] The whole army reached Catharinestown in safe-ty, and encamped before it on the 2d of September. The people fled, and the next day the village and surrounding corn-fields and orchards were destroyed. August 31.

The flying campaign, charged with destruction, had now fairly begun. "The Indians shall see," said Sullivan, "that there is malice enough in our hearts to destroy every thing that contributes to their support," and cruelly was that menace executed. The Indians fled before him like frightened deer to cover, and the wail of desolation was heard through-out their pleasant land, from the Susquehanna to the Genesee. Village after village was laid waste, and fields and orchards were desolated. Kendaia was swept from existence ;[a] other and smaller villages were annihilated ; and on the 7th of Sep-tember the conquerors sat down before Kanadaseagea, the capital of the Senecas, near the head of the beautiful lake of that name. Sixty indifferent cabins, surrounded by fine or-chards of apple, peach, and pear trees, became a prey to the army. Not a roof was left to shelter the sorrowing inhabitants on their return—not a fruit-tree to shade them or to give them sustenance—not an ear of corn of all the abundance that lay before the invaders when they approached, was saved from the devouring flames. a September 6,
1779.

While the chief portion of the army was engaged in this work, detachments went out and wrought equal devastation elsewhere. Four hundred men went down the west side of the lake and destroyed Gotheseunquean, or Gaghsiungua, and the plantations around it, and an-other party, under Colonel Harper, marched to Schoyere, near Cayuga Lake, and utterly de-stroyed it and its fields of grain.

Taking breath at Kanadaseagea, the invaders marched on to Kanandaigua, at the head of the little lake of that name, and in a few hours after their arrival the "twenty-three very elegant houses, mostly framed, and, in general, large,"[2] with the ex-tensive fields of corn and beans, and orchards of heavily-laden fruit-trees, were destroyed. September 10

---

[1] The enemy might have rallied upon the hills along this perilous route, and greatly thinned, if not quite destroyed or captured, the invading army. But, as Brant afterward said, they did not believe that Sullivan would commence a march so soon over so bad a route ; and the Indians were so terrified by the cannons, and disheartened by the result of the battle, that they could not be readily induced to attempt another.

[2] See General Sullivan's official account of this expedition.

Honeoye, or Anyeaya, a village lying in the path of the invading army in its march toward the Valley of the Genesee, was next swept away, and Sullivan prepared to desolate the broad valley in whose bosom nestled the great capital of the Western tribes, and the most important of all the Indian settlements.

Thus far the enemy had fled in terror before the invading army, and the villages of the Indians were destroyed without an effort being made to defend them. The beautiful Valley of the Genesee, the earthly paradise of the Six Nations, was now menaced. A council of the villages of the plain was held, and they resolved to turn and strike another blow in defense of their homes. Their women and children were removed to the deep shelter of the forest, and the warriors prepared for battle upon a plain between Honeyoe and the head of Connissius Lake, now known as Henderson's Flats. There they waited in ambush the approach of Sullivan's army, and rose upon the advanced guard with the desperation of wounded panthers. The battle was short, the savages were routed, and all that they had gained was the capture of two Oneida chiefs.[1]

On the 12th, Kanaghsaws and its plantations were laid in ashes. Here the progress of the army was temporarily checked by a deep stream, which it was necessary to bridge in order to pass over with the baggage and stores. Before them lay the village of Little Beard's Town, and, while the army was delayed in constructing a bridge, Lieutenant Boyd, of the rifle corps, with a detachment of twenty-six men, went to reconnoiter the town. He found it deserted, except by two Indians, whom he killed and scalped. Returning, his route lay near the party who had captured the two Oneidas. One of them, as we have seen, was killed, the other was spared for torture. He broke loose from his captors, and fled in the direction of Sullivan's camp. Many Indians started in pursuit, and these were joined by Brant and a large body of warriors, who had lain in ambush to cut off Boyd on his return.

September 13, 1779. The pursuing Indians came upon Boyd and his party. Surrounded by overwhelming numbers, he saw no way to escape but by cutting his way through the fierce circle. Three times he made the attempt; almost all his men were killed, and himself and a soldier named Parker were made prisoners and carried in triumph to Little Beard's Town.[2] Brant treated them humanely, but, having business elsewhere, the chief left them in the custody of Colonel John Butler, who, with his Rangers, was there. The unfeeling Tory handed them over to the tender mercies of the Indians. By them Boyd was tortured in the most cruel manner, and then beheaded. Parker was beheaded without being tortured. Among the few who escaped was Timothy Murphy, the slayer of Fraser at Bemis's Heights. The Americans found the bodies of the two victims at Little Beard's Town, and buried them upon the bank of Little Beard's Creek, under a clump of wild plum-trees on the road now running from Moscow to Genesee.

The Tories and Indians now held another council, and it was concluded that further attempts to oppose such an army as Sullivan's was futile. They therefore resolved to leave their beautiful country ; and their women and children were hurried off toward Niagara,

---

[1] One of these was General Sullivan's guide, and had rendered the Americans very important services. He had an elder brother engaged with the enemy, and here they met for the first time since their separation at the Oneida Castle. Fierce was the anger of the elder chief when he recognized his brother in the prisoner. Approaching him with violent gestures, he said, "*Brother!* you have merited death! The hatchet or the war-club shall finish your career!" He then reproached him for aiding the rebellion, for driving the Indians from their fields, and for butchering their children. "No crime can be greater," he said. "But though you have merited death, and shall die on this spot, my hands shall not be stained with the blood of a brother ! *Who will strike?*" Instantly a hatchet gleamed in the hand of Little Beard, the sachem of a village near by,* and the next moment the young Oneida was dead at the feet of his brother. —See Campbell's *Annals.*

[2] Han Yerry, an Oneida sachem, was with Lieutenant Boyd, serving him as guide. He fought with signal courage. The Indians knew him, and, several springing upon him, he was literally hacked in pieces by their hatchets. Han Yerry lived at Oriskany at the time of the battle there, and joined the Americans. He was a powerful man, and did great execution. For this the Indians defeated in that battle entertained toward him feelings of the most implacable hatred.

---

* Little Beard's Town, now Leicester, in Livingston county.

while the warriors hovered around the conquering army, to watch its movements and strike a blow if opportunity should occur.

Sullivan proceeded to the Genesee Valley. Gathtsegwarohare and Little Beard's Town were destroyed, and on the 14th he crossed the river, and the army encamped around Genesee, the Indian capital. Here every thing indicated the presence of civilization. There was not a wilderness feature in the scene. The rich intervales present-ed the appearance of cultivation for many generations,[1] and the farms, and orchards, and gardens bespoke a degree of comfort and refinement that would be creditable to any civilized community. But a terrible doom hung over the smiling country. The Genesee Castle was destroyed, and the capital was laid in ashes. "The town" [Genesee], said Sullivan, in his dispatch to Washington, "contained one hundred and twenty-eight houses, mostly large and very elegant. It was beautifully situated, almost encircled with a clear flat, extending a number of miles, over which extensive fields of corn were waving, together with every kind of vegetable that could be conceived." Yet the contemplation of this scene could not stay the destroyer's hand; and over the whole valley and the surrounding country the troops swept with the besom of desolation. Forty Indian towns were burned; one hundred and sixty thousand bushels of corn in the fields and in granaries were destroyed; a vast number of the finest fruit-trees,[2] the product of years of tardy growth, were cut down; hundreds of gardens covered with edible vegetables were desolated; the inhabitants were driven into the forests to starve, and were hunted like wild beasts; their altars were overturned, and their graves trampled upon by strangers; and a beautiful, well-watered country, teeming with a prosperous people, and just rising from a wilderness state, by the aid of cultivation, to a level with the productive regions of civilization, was desolated and cast back a century within the space of a fortnight.[3] To us, looking upon the scene from a point so remote, it is difficult to perceive the necessity that called for a chastisement so cruel and terrible. But that such necessity seemed to exist we should not doubt, for it was the judicious and benevolent mind of Washington that conceived and planned the campaign, and ordered its rigid execution in the manner in which it was accomplished. It awed the Indians for the moment, but did not crush them. In the reaction they had greater strength. It kindled the fires of deep hatred, which spread far among the tribes upon the lakes and in the valley of the Ohio. Washington, like Demetrius, the son of Antigonus, received from the savages the name of An-na-ta-kau-les, which signifies *a taker of towns*, or TOWN DESTROYER.[4]

September, 1779.

---

[1] The race of Indians that then inhabited the Valley of the Genesee had no knowledge of the earlier cul-tivators of the soil. They asserted, according to Mary Jemison, that another race, of which they had no knowledge, had cultivated the land long before their ancestors came into the valley; and she saw the dis-entombment of skeletons much larger than those of the race she was among.

[2] Many of the orchards were uncommonly large. One that was destroyed by the axe contained fifteen hundred trees.

[3] Stone says (Life of Brant, ii., 25), "It is apprehended that few of the present generation are thoroughly aware of the advances which the Indians, in the wide and beautiful country of the Cayugas and Senecas, had made in the march of civilization. They had several towns and many large villages, laid out with a considerable degree of regularity. They had framed houses, some of them well finished, having chimneys, and painted. They had broad and productive fields; and, in addition to an abundance of apples, were then enjoyment of the pear and the more luscious peach."

[4] At a council held in Philadelphia in 1792, Corn Planter, the distinguished Seneca chief, thus addressed the President: "FATHER—The voice of the Seneca nation speaks to you, the great counselor, in whose heart the wise men of all the thirteen fires have placed their wisdom. It may be very small in your ears, and, therefore, we entreat you to hearken with attention, for we are about to speak to you of things which to us are very great. When your army entered the country of the Six Nations, we called you *The Town Destroyer*; and to this day, when that name is heard, our women look behind them and turn pale, and our children cling close to the necks of their mothers. Our counselors and warriors are men, and can not be afraid; but their hearts are grieved with the fears of our women and children, and desire that it may be buried so deep that it may be heard no more."

Corn Planter was one of the earliest lecturers upon temperance in this country. While speaking upon this subject in 1822, he said, "The Great Spirit first made the world, next the flying animals, and formed all things good and prosperous. He is immortal and everlasting. After finishing the flying animals, he came down to earth and there stood. Then he made different kinds of trees, and woods of all sorts, and

From causes not clearly understood, Sullivan did not extend his victorious march to Niagara, the head-quarters of the Tories and Indians, the breaking up of which would have been far more efficient in bringing repose to the white settlements than the achievements just accomplished ; but, having desolated the Genesee Valley, he crossed the river and retraced his steps. When the army recrossed the outlet of Seneca Lake, Colonel

September 20, 1779.

Zebulon Butler, of Wyoming, was sent with a detachment of five hundred men, to pass round the foot of Cayuga Lake and destroy the Indian towns on its eastern shore. Lieutenant Dearborn was dispatched upon similar service along its western shore ; and both corps, having accomplished their mission, joined the main body on the Chemung.[1]

September 28.

Butler had burned three towns and the capital of the Cayugas, and Dearborn had destroyed six towns and a great quantity of grain and fruit-trees. The army reached Tioga, its starting-place, on the 3d of October, where it was joined by the garrison left in charge of Fort Sullivan. Destroying that stockade, they took up their line of march on the 4th for Wyoming, where they arrived on the 7th, and pitched their tents on the former camp-ground near Wilkesbarre. The next day a large portion of the troops left for Easton, on the Delaware, at which place they were dismissed. Thus ended a campaign before which we would gladly draw the vail of forgetfulness.

Although beaten back into the wilderness, and their beautiful country laid waste, the Indians were not conquered, and in the spring of the following year Brant and some of

1780.

his followers were again upon the war-path. During the winter the threat of Sir Frederic Haldimand against the Oneidas was executed. Their castle, church, and villages were destroyed, and the inhabitants were driven down upon the white settlements for protection. They collected together near Schenectady, where they remained until after the war.[2] These, too, were particular objects for the vengeance of the hostile savages. They regarded the Oneidas as double traitors, and determined to punish them accordingly, should an opportunity offer to do so.

In April, in connection with a band of Tories, the savages destroyed Harpersfield, and then marched to the attack of the Upper Schoharie Fort. On their way they captured Captain Alexander Harper and a small company who were with him, engaged in making maple sugar. Three of the yeomanry were killed, and ten made prisoners and taken to Niagara. With difficulty Brant kept his Indians from murdering them by the way. At Niagara Harper met with his niece, the daughter of Mr. Moore, of Cherry Valley, whose family, with that of Colonel Campbell, was carried into captivity in 1778. She had married a British officer named Powell, and through his exertions Captain Harper and his associates were kindly treated at Niagara. But they were doomed to a long absence from home, for they were not released until the peace in 1783 opened all the prison doors.[3]

The borders of Wyoming, and the Dutch settlements along the western frontiers of the

people of every kind. He made the spring and other seasons, and the weather suitable for planting. These he *did* make. *But stills to make whisky to give to the Indians he* DID NOT *make.* . . . . . . The Great Spirit has ordered me to stop drinking, and he wishes me to inform the people that they should quit drinking intoxicating drinks."

[1] Lieutenant-colonel Hubley, an officer of the Pennsylvania line, has left an interesting account of this expedition in his Journal. He says that, on the 25th of September, the army held a celebration in testimony of their pleasure "in consequence of the accession of the King of Spain to the American alliance, and the generous proceedings of Congress in augmenting the subsistence of the officers and men." General Sullivan ordered five of his fattest bullocks to be slaughtered, one for the officers of each brigade. In the evening, after the discharge of thirteen cannons, the whole army performed a *feu de joie.* Thirteen appropriate toasts were drunk. The last was as follows : " May the enemies of America be metamorphosed into pack horses, and sent on a western expedition against the Indians."

[2] A remnant of this tribe now occupies land in the vicinity of Rome, Oneida county, New York.

[3] Among the Tory captors of Harper and his associates was a brute named Becraft, who boasted of having assisted in the murder of the Vrooman family in Schoharie. He had the audacity to return to Schoharie after the war. The returned prisoners, who had heard his boast, and others, informed of his presence, caught him, stripped him naked, and, tying him to a tree, gave him a severe castigation with hickory whips. They enumerated his several crimes, and then gave him a goodly number of stripes for each. On releasing him, they charged him never to come to the county again. Of course he did not.

present Ulster and Orange counties, suffered from scalping parties during the spring and summer of 1780. We have already noticed the destruction of the settlement and mills at Little Falls, on the Mohawk ; also the devastation of the Canajoharie settlements and the hamlet at Fort Plain, which occurred in August of that year. The irruption of Sir John Johnson into the valley in the neighborhood of Johnstown will be considered when writing of my visit to Johnson Hall.

1780. During the autumn an extensive expedition was planned against the Mohawk and Schoharie settlements. The Indians were thirsting for revenge for the wrongs and misery inflicted by Sullivan. The leaders were Sir John Johnson, Brant, and the famous half-breed Seneca warrior, Corn Planter.[1] The Indians rendezvoused at Tioga Point, and, ascending the Susquehanna, formed a junction at Unadilla with Sir John Johnson and his forces, which consisted of three companies of his Greens, one company of German Yagers, two hundred of Butler's Rangers, one company of British regulars, under Captain Duncan, and a number of Mohawks. They came from Montreal by way of Oswego, bringing with them two small mortars, a brass three pounder, and a piece called a *grasshopper*.

The plan agreed upon by the invaders was, to proceed along the Charlotte River, the east branch of the Susquehanna, to its source, thence across to the head of the Schoharie, sweep all the settlements along its course to its junction with the Mohawk, and then devastate that beautiful valley down to Schenectady. They began their march at nightfall, and before morning they had passed the Upper Fort unobserved, and were applying the torch to dwellings near the Middle Fort (Middleburgh). At daylight signal guns at the Upper Fort announced the discovery of the enemy there, but it was too late to save the property, already in flames. The proceeds of a bountiful harvest were in the barns, and stacks of hay and grain were abundant.

October 15.

Major Woolsey, who seems to have been a poltroon,[2] was the commander of the garrison at the Middle Fort, and sent out a detachment against the foe, under Lieutenant Spencer, who was repulsed, but returned to the fort without losing a man. That post was now formally invested by the enemy, and Sir John Johnson sent a flag, with a summons to surrender. The bearer was fired upon by Murphy, the rifleman already mentioned, but was unhurt ; and, on his return to the camp, Johnson commenced a siege. The feeble garrison had but little ammunition, while the enemy, though well supplied, did very little execution with his own. The siege was a singular, and even ridiculous, military display. While a party of the besiegers were awkwardly trying to cast bomb-shells into the apology for a fort, the rest were valiantly attacking deserted houses and stacks of grain. Failing to make any impression, Sir John sent another flag toward noon. Murphy again fired upon the bearer, and again missed his mark. Woolsey had ordered him to desist, but Murphy plainly told his commanding officer that he was a coward, and meant to surrender the fort ; and excused his breach of the rules of war in firing upon a flag by the plea that the enemy, in all his conduct, paid no regard whatever to military courtesy.

The siege continued, and again a flag was sent, and was fired upon a third time by Murphy. The officers and regulars in the fort had menaced him with death if he should again thus violate the rules of war. But the militia, among whom he was a great favorite, rallied around him, and Woolsey and his men were set at defiance. At length Johnson, suspecting the garrison to be much stronger than it really was, or fearing re-enforcements might arrive from Albany, abandoned the siege, and marched rapidly down the valley, destroying

---

[1] Corn Planter now first became conspicuous. According to Stone, this chief, and the afterward more famous Red Jacket, were among the Indians at the battle of Chemung. They became rivals, and Red Jacket finally supplanted Corn Planter. Brant always despised Red Jacket, for he declared him to have acted the part of a coward during Sullivan's expedition, in trying to get the chiefs to sue for peace upon the most ignominious terms.

[2] Campbell, in his *Annals*, says, " Woolsey's presence of mind forsook him in the hour of danger. He concealed himself at first with the women and children in the house, and, when driven out by the ridicule of his new associates, he crawled around the intrenchments on his hands and knees, amid the jeers and bravos of the militia, who felt their courage revive as their laughter was excited by the cowardice of the major."

with fire every thing combustible in his way.   He attacked the Lower Fort, but, being repulsed by a shower of grape-shot and musket-balls from the garrison in the church, he continued his march down the river to Fort Hunter,[1] at its junction with the Mohawk.   Not
a house, barn, or grain-stack, known to belong to a Whig, was left standing, and it was es
timated that one hundred thousand bushels of grain were destroyed by the invaders in that
one day's march.   The houses and other property of the Tories were spared, but the exasperated Whigs set them on fire as soon as the enemy had gone, and all shared a common
fate.   Only two persons in the besieged fort were killed, but about one hundred of the inhabitants were murdered during the day.   The Vroomans, a numerous family in Schoharie,
suffered much, many of them being among the slain.

October,   Sir John remained at Fort Hunter on the 17th, and destroyed every thing be-
1780.   longing to the Whigs in the neighborhood.   On the 18th he began a devastating
march up the Mohawk Valley.   Caughnawaga was laid in ashes, and every dwelling on
both sides of the river, as far up as Fort Plain, was destroyed.[2]   On the night of the 18th Sir
John encamped with his forces near "The Nose," and the following morning he crossed the
Mohawk at Keder's Rifts,[3] sending a detachment of fifty men to attack a small stockade called
Fort Paris, in Stone Arabia, about three miles north of the river.   The main body kept in motion at the same time, and continued the work of destruction along the wide line of its march.

As soon as the irruption of Johnson into the Schoharie settlement was made known at
Albany, Governor George Clinton, accompanied by General Robert Van Rensselaer, of
Claverack, at the head of a strong body of militia, marched to the succor of the people in
Tryon county.   They arrived at Caughnawaga on the 18th, while it was yet in flames ;
and, ascertaining that Fort Paris was to be attacked the next day, Van Rensselaer dispatched orders to Colonel Brown, then stationed there, to march out and meet the enemy.   Brown
promptly obeyed, and near a ruined military work, called Fort Keyser, confronted the invaders.   A sharp action ensued, and the overwhelming numbers of the enemy bore down
the gallant little band of Brown, who, with forty of his soldiers, was slain.[4]   The remainder of his troops found safety in flight.

---

[1] Fort Hunter was built at the mouth of the Schoharie Creek during the French and Indian war.   It
inclosed an edifice called Queen Anne's Chapel, to which a parsonage, built of stone, was attached.   The
old fort was torn down at the commencement of the Revolution, but it was afterward partially restored and
often garrisoned.   The chapel was demolished in 1820, to make room for the Erie Canal.   The parsonage
is still standing in the town of Florida, half a mile below the Schoharie, and a few rods south of the canal.
[2] Among the many sufferers at this time was Major Jelles Fonda, from whom the present village of
Fonda, near old Caughnawaga, derives its name.   He was absent from home at the time, attending a meeting of the state Legislature, of which he was a member, then in session at Poughkeepsie, Dutchess county.
His mansion was at a place called " The Nose," in the town of Palatine.   His wife escaped under cover
of a thick fog, and on foot made her way to Schenectady.   The house was burned, together with property
valued at $60,000.—Antiquarian Researches, by Giles F. Yates, Esq.
[3] Rifts are short, shallow rapids, the frequent occurrence of which in the Mohawk River makes navigation of that stream, even with bateaux, quite difficult.
[4] Colonel Brown was a distinguished soldier in former campaigns of the Revolution in the Northern Department, as the reader has already noticed.   He was born in Sandersfield, Berkshire county, Massachusetts, October 19th, 1744.   He graduated at Yale College in 1771, and studied law with Oliver Arnold (a
cousin of the traitor), at Providence, Rhode Island.   He commenced practice at Caughnawaga, New York,
and was appointed king's attorney.   He soon went to Pittsfield, Massachusetts, where he became active in
the patriot cause.   He was chosen by the State Committee of Correspondence, in 1774, to go to Canada
to excite rebellion, in which perilous duty he had many adventures.   He was elected to Congress in 1775,
but before the meeting of that body he had joined the expedition under Allen and Arnold against Ticonderoga.   He assisted in the capture of Fort Chambly in the autumn of that year, and planned the attack
on Montreal, which resulted so disastrously to Colonel Ethan Allen.   He was at the storming of Quebec
at the close of the year.   The following year Congress gave him the commission of lieutenant colonel.   In
1777 he conducted the expedition that attacked Ticonderoga and other posts in its vicinity, released one
hundred American prisoners at Lake George, and captured quite a large quantity of provisions and stores
belonging to the enemy.   Soon after this he retired from the service on account of his detestation of Arnold.
Three years before the latter became a traitor, Brown published a hand-bill, in which he denounced him as
an avaricious and unprincipled man, charged him with " selling many a life for gain," and predicted that
he would prove r traitor, in the remarkable words with which the hand-bill closed : " Money is this man's

Sir John now dispersed his forces in small bands to the distance of five or six miles in each direction, to pillage the county. He desolated Stone Arabia, and, proceeding to a place called Klock's Field, halted to rest. General Van Rensselaer, with a considerable force, was in close pursuit. He had been joined by Captain M'Kean, with a corps of volunteers, and a strong body of Oneida warriors, led by their principal chief, Louis Atyataronghta, whom Congress had commissioned a colonel.[1] His whole force was now fifteen hundred strong. Van Rensselaer's pursuit was on the south side of the Mohawk, while Johnson was ravaging the country on the north side. Johnson took care to guard the ford while his halting army was resting, and the pursuers were there kept at bay. The tardy movements of Van Rensselaer, who, instead of pushing across to attack the wearied troops of the invader, *rode off to Fort Plain to dine with Governor Clinton*, were justly censured; and the Oneida chief even denounced him as a Tory. This accusation, and the remonstrances of some of his officers, quickened his movements, and toward evening his forces crossed the river and were arrayed for battle. The whites of the enemy were upon a small plain partially guarded by a bend in the river, while Brant, with his Indians, occupied, in secret, a thicket of shrub oaks in the vicinity. The van of the attack was led by the late General Morgan Lewis, then a colonel. Colonel Dubois commanded the extreme right, and the left was led by Colonel Cuyler, of Albany. Captain M'Kean and the Oneidas were near the right. Johnson's right was composed of regular troops; the center, of his Greens; and his left was the Indian ambuscade. When the patriots approached, Brant raised the war-whoop, and in a few moments a general battle ensued. The charge of the Americans was so impetuous that the enemy soon gave way and fled. Brant was wounded in the heel, but escaped. Van Rensselaer's troops wished to pursue the enemy, but it was then twilight, and he would not allow it. They were ordered to fall back and encamp for the night, a movement which caused much dissatisfaction.[2]

God, and to get enough of it he would sacrifice his country!" This was published at Albany in the winter of 1776–7, while Arnold was quartered there. Arnold was greatly excited when told of it, called Brown a scoundrel, and declared that he would kick him whensoever and wheresoever they might meet. This declaration was communicated to Brown. The next day, Brown, by invitation, went to a dinner where he would meet Arnold. The latter was standing with his back to the fire when the former entered the door, and he and Brown thus met each other face to face. Brown walked boldly up to Arnold, and, looking him sternly in the face, said, "I understand, sir, that you have said you would kick me. I now present myself to give you an opportunity to put your threat into execution." Arnold made no reply. Brown then said, "Sir, you are a dirty scoundrel." Arnold was still silent, and Brown left the room, after apologizing to the gentlemen present for his intrusion.*

Colonel Brown, after he left the army, was occasionally employed in the Massachusetts service. In the fall of 1780, with many of the Berkshire militia, he marched up the Mohawk Valley, to act as circumstances might require. He was slain at Stone Arabia on his birth-day (October 19th, 1780), aged 35 years. On his way to the Mohawk country, he called upon Ann Lee, the founder of the sect of Shaking Quakers in this country, then established near Albany. He assured her, by way of pleasantry, that on his return he should join her society. A fortnight after his death two members of the society waited upon his widow, told her that her husband, in spirit, had joined "Mother Ann," and that he had given express orders for her to become a member. She was not to be duped, and bade them begone. On the anniversary of Colonel Brown's death (as well as of his birth), in 1836, a monument was reared to his memory by his son, the late Henry Brown, Esq., of Berkshire, Massachusetts, near the place where he fell, in the town of Palatine. Upon the monument is the following inscription:

In memory of Colonel JOHN BROWN,
who was killed in battle on the 19th day of October, 1780,
at Palatine, in the county of Montgomery.
Æ. 36.

[1] He was a representative of three nations, for in his veins ran the blood of the French, Indian, and negro.
[2] While some of M'Kean's volunteers were strolling about, waiting for the main army to cross, they came upon a small block-house, where nine of the enemy were in custody, having surrendered during the night. On one of them being asked how he came there, his answer was a sharp commentary upon the criminal inaction of General Van Rensselaer. "Last night, after the battle," he said, "we crossed the river; it was dark; we heard the word 'lay down your arms;' some of us did so. We were taken, nine

---

* Stone's Life of Brant, ii., 117.

Louis and M‘Kean did not strictly obey orders, and early in the morning they started off with their forces in pursuit. Johnson, with the Indians and Yagers, fled toward Onondaga Lake, where they had left their boats concealed. His Greens and the Rangers followed. Van Rensselaer and his whole force pursued them as far as Fort Herkimer, at the German Flats, and there M‘Kean and Louis were ordered to press on in advance after the fugitives. They struck the trail of Johnson the next morning, and soon afterward came upon his deserted camp while the fires were yet burning. Van Rensselaer had promised to push forward to their support; but, having little confidence in the celerity of his movements, and fearing an ambuscade, Louis refused to advance any further until assured that the main body of the Americans was near. The advanced party halted, and were soon informed by a messenger that Van Rensselaer had actually abandoned the pursuit, and was then on his return march! It was a shameful neglect of advantage, for, with proper skill and action, Johnson might have been captured at the Nose,[1] before Stone Arabia was desolated, or else overtaken and secured in his flight.

When Van Rensselaer heard of the concealment of Johnson's boats on the Onondaga, he dispatched a messenger to Captain Vrooman, then in command at Fort Schuyler, ordering him to go with a strong detachment and destroy them. Vrooman instantly obeyed. One of his men feigned sickness at Oneida, and was left behind. He was there when Johnson arrived, and informed him of Vrooman's expedition. Brant and a body of Indians hastened forward, came upon Vrooman and his party while at dinner, and captured the whole of them without firing a gun. Johnson had no further impediments in his way, and easily escaped to Canada by way of Oswego, taking with him Captain Vrooman and his party prisoners, but leaving behind him a great number of his own men.[2] Tryon county enjoyed comparative repose through the remainder of the autumn and part of the winter.

In January, 1781, Brant was again upon the war-path in the neighborhood of Fort Schuyler. The slender barrier of the Oneida nation had been broken the previous year by driving that people upon the white settlements, and the warriors from Niagara had an unimpeded way to the Mohawk Valley. They were separated into small parties, and cut off load after load of supplies on their way to Forts Plain, Dayton, and Schuyler. During the month of March two detachments of soldiers near Fort Schuyler were made prisoners, and the provisions they were guarding were captured. All the information that could be got respecting the movements of the enemy strengthened the belief that it was his determination to make another invasion of the valley, and penetrate, if possible, as far as the settlement at Schenectady, to destroy the Oneidas who had found shelter there.

Already the scarcity of provisions at Forts Schuyler and Dayton warned the people that, if supplies were not speedily obtained, those posts must be abandoned, and the whole county would thus be left open to the savages. The distress at Fort Schuyler was greatly increased by a flood early in May, which overflowed the works and destroyed considerable provisions. The damage was so great, that it was decided, at a council of officers, that the strength of the garrison was totally inadequate to make proper repairs. A few days afterward the destruction of the fort was completed by fire, the work, it was supposed, of an incendiary. The post was then necessarily abandoned, and the garrison was marched down to Forts Dayton and Plain.

May 12, 1781.

---

of us, and marched into this little fort by seven militia men. We formed the rear of three hundred of Johnson's Greens, who were running promiscuously through and over one another. I thought General Van Rensselaer's whole army was upon us. Why did you not take us prisoners yesterday, after Sir John ran off with the Indians and left us? We wanted to surrender." The man was a Tory of the valley.—See *Life of Brant*, ii., 123.

[1] The *Nose*, or Anthony's *Nose*, as it is sometimes called, is a bluff at a narrow part of the Mohawk, in the town of Palatine, and derives its name from the circumstance that its form is something like that of the human nose. Here a ridge evidently once crossed the valley and kept the waters in check above, for the effects of the action of running streams and eddies are very prominent in the rocks. At the upper end of the plain below are bowlders and large gravel stones, which diminish to sand at the lower end.

[2] Campbell's *Annals*.

At this period every thing combined to cast gloom over the Mohawk country.   Vermont, as we have noticed in a former chapter, had assumed an equivocal position, amounting almost, in appearance, to a treasonable rebellion against Congress.   General Haldimand, with a large regular force, was menacing the northern country from his post upon Lake Champlain ; the Johnsons, Butlers, and Brant were laying plans for an extensive invasion of Tryon county and the settlements near the Delaware ; the forts that served for a defense for the people were weak from lack of provisions, ammunition, and men ; the principal one, the key to the Mohawk Valley from the west, was destroyed ; and, worse than all, a spirit of discontent and despondency was rife in that quarter, induced by the inefficiency of Congress in furnishing supplies, and the seeming hopelessness of the patriot cause.   General Schuyler and others expressed their conviction that, if another invading army should come upon the settlements during the existing state of things, large numbers of the people would join the royal standard.   The undisciplined militia, necessarily engaged in farm labor, and often insubordinate, were a weak reliance, and nothing but an efficient military force, either of paid levies or soldiers of the regular army, could give confidence and real protection.

The expectation of such aid was but a feeble ray of hope at the beginning of the summer, for Washington and the French commander (De Rochambeau) were concocting plans far more important than the defense of a single frontier section of the vast extent of the colonies. Governor Clinton was greatly pained and embarrassed by the gloomy prospect in his department.   In this dilemma, his thoughts turned to Colonel Willett, who had just been appointed to the command of one of the two regiments formed by the consolidation of five New York regiments.   His name was a " tower of strength" among the people of the Mohawk Valley, and Clinton implored him to take command of all the militia levies and state troops that might be raised for the summer campaigns.   He consented, left the main army, and established his head-quarters at Fort Rensselaer[1] (Canajoharie), toward the close of June.   1781. The spirits of the people were revived, although the forces of Willett consisted of mere fragments of companies hastily collected from the ruins of the last campaign.   " I confess myself," he said, in a letter to Governor Clinton, " not a little disappointed in having such a trifling force for such extensive business as I have now on my hands ; and, also, that nothing is done to enable me to avail myself of the militia.   The prospect of a suffering country hurts me.   Upon my own account I am not uneasy.   Every thing I can do shall be done ; and more can not be looked for.   If it is, the reflection that I have done my duty must fix my tranquillity."[2]

While the enemy is threatening invasion and Willett is preparing to repel him, let us turn from the exciting chronicle, and resume our quiet journey, in the course of which some of the stirring incidents of the subsequent strife between the patriots and the enemy, in Tryon county, will come up in review.

---

[1] This was upon the Canajoharie Creek, near the junction of its two branches, in the town of Root.
[2] Willett's Narrative.

CHAPTER XIII.

The earth all light and loveliness, in summer's golden hours,
Smiles, in her bridal vesture clad, and crown'd with festal flowers;
So radiantly beautiful, so like to heaven above,
We scarce can deem more fair that world of perfect bliss and love.

ANONYMOUS.

Look now abroad—another race has fill'd
   These populous borders—wide the wood recedes,
And towns shoot up, and fertile plains are till'd;
   The land is full of harvests and green meads;
Streams numberless, that many a fountain feeds,
   Shine, disembower'd, and give to sun and breeze
Their virgin waters; the full region leads
   New colonies forth, that toward the western seas
Spread, like a rapid flame among the autumnal leaves.

BRYANT.

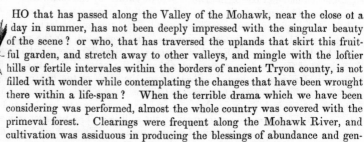

HO that has passed along the Valley of the Mohawk, near the close of a day in summer, has not been deeply impressed with the singular beauty of the scene? or who, that has traversed the uplands that skirt this fruitful garden, and stretch away to other valleys, and mingle with the loftier hills or fertile intervales within the borders of ancient Tryon county, is not filled with wonder while contemplating the changes that have been wrought there within a life-span? When the terrible drama which we have been considering was performed, almost the whole country was covered with the primeval forest. Clearings were frequent along the Mohawk River, and cultivation was assiduous in producing the blessings of abundance and general prosperity; but the southern portions of Herkimer and Montgomery, and all of Schoharie and Otsego, down to the remote settlement of Unadilla, were a wilderness, except where a few thriving settlements were growing upon the water courses. The traveler, as he views the "field joined to field" in the Mohawk Valley, all covered with waving grain, green pastures, or bending fruit-trees, inclosing, in their arms of plenty, elegant mansions; or watches the vast stream of inland commerce that rolls by upon the Erie Canal; or the villages of people that almost hourly sweep along its margin after the vapor steed; or rides over the adjacent hill-country north and south, enlivened by villages and rich in cultivation, can hardly realize the fact that here, seventy years ago, the wild Indian was joint possessor of the soil with the hardy settlers, and that the light of civilization was as scattered and feeble, and for a while as evanescent and fleeting in these broad solitudes, as is the sparkle of the fire-fly on a summer evening. Yet such is the wonderful truth; and as I passed down the canal at the close of the day, from Fort Plain to Fultonville, surrounded with the activity, opulence, and beauty of the Mohawk Valley, I could not, while contrasting this peacefulness and progress with the discord and social inertia of other lands, repress the feelings of the Pharisee.

Fultonville is sixteen miles below Fort Plain, and it was long after dark when I arrived there. Early on the following morning I procured a conveyance to visit old Caughnawaga and Johnstown, north of the Mohawk. A gentleman of leisure and intelligence, residing at Fultonville, kindly offered to accompany me, and his familiarity with the history and localities of the neighborhood, and freedom of communication, made my morning's ride pleasant and profitable. Fultonville is upon the canal, and may be called the *port* of the village of Fonda, which lies upon the rail-road, on the northern verge of the valley.

August 24, 1848.

OF THE REVOLUTION. 285

Caughnawaga.   John Butler's Residence.   Johnstown.   An Octogenarian.   Biography of Butler

The Mohawk cleaves the center of the plain between the two villages, and is spanned by a fine covered bridge. Fonda and Caughnawaga (now Mohawk) lie in close embrace. The former has all the freshness of infancy, while the latter, with its gray old church,[1] has a matronly gravity in its appearance. It is only about half a mile eastward from its blooming daughter, at the foot of the hills over which winds the eastern fork of the road from Johnstown. On a commanding eminence, about a mile north of Fonda, we came to the house

THE BUTLER HOUSE.

where Colonel John Butler resided,[2] which is believed to be the oldest dwelling in that section, and coeval with Caughnawaga Church. It overlooks the Mohawk Valley on the south, and commands an extensive prospect of a fine agricultural country in every direction. It is now owned by a Mr. Wilson, and is often visited by the curious, who are as frequently attracted by the eminently infamous as by the eminently good. It is a fair specimen of the middling class of houses of that period. The posts stand directly upon the stone foundation, without sleepers, and there are no plaster walls or ceilings in the house, the sides of the rooms being lined with pine boards. The bricks of the chimney are the small, imported kind which distinguished many of the edifices in the old states, that were constructed about a century ago.

The village of Johnstown, which was included in the town of Caughnawaga, organized in 1798, lies pleasantly in the bosom and along the slope of an intervale, about four miles north of Fonda.[3] I met there a venerable citizen, John Yost, eighty years of age, who had been a resident of the vicinity from his birth. He was often dandled on the knee of Sir William Johnson, and has a clear recollection of the appearance of the baronet and the circumstances of his death. His father was an adherent of the Whig cause, and instructed him early in the principles of the Revolution. He was several times employed by Colonel Willett as an express to carry dispatches from Fort Plain to Tripe's Hill and other points in the valley, his extreme youth guarding him from suspicion. He was still an active man when I saw him, and his bodily health promised him the honors of a centenarian. _{August, 1848.}

Johnson Hall, the residence of Sir William and Sir John Johnson,[4] is situated upon a

---

[1] See page 263.

[2] John Butler was one of the leading Tories of Tryon county during the whole war of the Revolution. Before the war he was in close official connection with Sir William Johnson, and, after his death, with his son and nephew, Sir John and Guy Johnson. When he fled with the Johnsons to Canada, his family were left behind, and were subsequently held as hostages by the Americans, and finally exchanged for the wife and children of Colonel Samuel Campbell, of Cherry Valley. He was active in the predatory warfare that so long distressed Tryon county, and commanded the eleven hundred men who desolated Wyoming in 1778. He was among those who opposed the progress of Sullivan in the Indian country in 1779, and accompanied Sir John Johnson in his destructive march through the Schoharie and Mohawk settlements in 1780. After the war he went to Canada, where he resided until his death, which occurred about the year 1800. His property upon the Mohawk, by an act of the Legislature of New York, was confiscated; but he was amply rewarded by the British government for his infamous services in its behalf. He succeeded Guy Johnson as Indian agent, with a salary of $2000 per annum, and was granted a pension, as a military officer, of $1000 more. Like his son Walter, he was detested for his cruelties by the more honorable British officers; and, after the massacre at Wyoming, Sir Frederic Haldimand, then Governor of Canada, sent word to him that he did not wish to see him. It is but justice to Colonel Butler to say, that he was far more humane than his son Walter, and that his personal deeds at Wyoming were not so heinous as the common accounts have made them. These will be considered when the attack upon that settlement shall receive a more particular notice.

John Butler

SIGNATURE OF COLONEL JOHN BUTLER.

[3] The old jail in the village was standing when I was there, in August, 1848. It was built in 1762, and was consumed by fire on the 8th of September, 1849.

[4] John Johnson was the son of Sir William Johnson by his first wife. He was born in 1742, and succeeded his father in his title and estates in 1774. He was not as popular as his father, being less social

gentle eminence, about three fourths of a mile northward of the court-house in the village, and near the state road to Black River. This was probably the finest mansion in the province, out of the city of New York, at the time of its erection, about the year 1760. The nall, or main building, is of wood, and double clap-boarded in a manner to represent blocks

NORTH FRONT OF JOHNSON HALL.

of stone. Its exterior dimensions are forty feet wide, sixty feet long, and two stories high. The detached wings, built for flanking block-houses, are of stone. The walls of these are very thick, and near the eaves they are pierced for musketry. The entrance passage, which extends entirely through the house, is fifteen feet wide, from which rises a broad stair-case, with heavy mahogany balustrades, to the second story. The rail of this balustrade is scarred by hatchet blows at regular intervals of about a foot, from the top to the bottom, and tradition avers that it was done by the hands of Brant when he fled from the hall with Sir John Johnson, in 1776, to protect the house from the torch of marauding savages, for he asserted that such a token would be understood and respected by them.

The rooms in both stories are large and lofty, and the sides are handsomely wainscoted with pine panels and carved work, all of which is carefully preserved in its original form by Mr. Eleazer Wells, the present proprietor. He has been acquainted with the house for fifty years, and within that time one of the rooms has been neither painted nor papered.[1] The

and less acquainted with human nature. His official relations to the parent government, and his known opposition to the rebellious movements of the colonies, caused him to be strictly watched, and, as we have noted in the text, not without just cause. Expelled from his estate, his property confiscated, his family in exile, he became an uncompromising enemy of the republicans, and until the close of the war his influence was exerted against the patriots.

John Johnson

SIGNATURE OF SIR JOHN JOHNSON.

Soon after the close of the war Sir John went to England, and, on returning in 1785, settled in Canada. He was appointed superintendent and inspector general of Indian affairs in North America, and for several years he was a member of the legislative council of Canada. To compensate him for his losses, the British government made him several grants of lands. He died at the house of his daughter, Mrs. Bowes, at Montreal, in 1830, aged 88 years. His son, Sir Adam Gordon Johnson, succeeded him in his title.

[1] In that room Mr. Wells was married in 1807, the house then belonging to his mother-in-law. Mr. Wells related to me a fact which illustrates the wonderful progress of Western New York in population

paper hangings upon it have been there that length of time, and are doubtless the same that were first put upon the wall by the baronet.   Every thing of the kind is well preserved, and the visitor is gratified by a view, in its original aspect, of the *only baronial hall in the United States.*

Here Sir William lived in all the elegance and comparative power of an English baron of the Middle Ages.   He had many servants and retainers, " wives and concubines, sons and daughters of different colors."[1]   His hall was his castle, and around it, beyond the wings, a heavy stone breast-work, about twelve feet high, was thrown up.   Invested with the power and influence of an Indian agent of his government in its transactions with the confederated Six Nations, possessed of a fine person and dignity of manners, and of a certain style of oratory that pleased the Indians, he acquired an ascendency over the tribes never before held by a white man.   When, in 1760, General Amherst embarked at Oswego on his expedition to Canada, Sir William brought to him, at that place, one thousand Indian warriors of the Six Nations, which was the largest number that had ever been seen in arms at one time in the cause of England.   He made confidants of many of the chiefs, and to them he

---

and wealth within half a century.   About the time of his marriage he went west, with the intention of purchasing a farm in the Genesee country, always so celebrated for its fertility.   Among other places, he visited the site of the present large city of Rochester.   Then a solitary cabin was there.   The land was offered to him for two dollars an acre, but it seemed too wet for his purpose, and he refused to buy.   " Had I purchased then," said Mr. Wells, " it *might* have made me a *millionaire*, although such a result is by no means certain, for the original owner of all the land where Utica now stands was a tenant, and his descendants still are tenants, of other proprietors of the soil there."   The prize within the reach of the person to whom he alluded was allowed, through lack of prudence and forecast, to slip through his fingers, and not a rood of all the acres of Utica is now his own.

[1] Sir William is said to have been the father of a hundred children, chiefly by native mothers, who were young squaws, or the wives of Indians who thought it an honor to have them intimate with the distinguished king's agent.   He availed himself of a custom which Colden says was then prevalent among the Six Nations.   "They carried their hospitality so far as to allow distinguished strangers," he says, " the choice of a young squaw from among the prettiest in the neighborhood, washed clean and dressed in her best apparel, as a companion during his sojourn with them."   Sir William had two *wives*, although they were not made so until they had lived long with the baronet.   Simms says, on the authority of well-authenticated tradition, that his first wife was a young German girl, who, according to the custom of the times, had been sold to a man named Phillips, living in the Mohawk Valley, to pay her passage money to the captain of the emigrant ship in which she came to this country.   She was a handsome girl, and attracted considerable attention.   A neighbor of Sir William, who had heard him express a determination never to marry, asked him why he did not get the pretty German girl for a housekeeper.   He replied, " I will."   Not long afterward the neighbor called at Phillips's, and inquired where the High Dutch girl was.   Phillips replied, " Johnson, that tarned Irishman, came tother day and offered me five pounds for her, threatening to horsewhip me and steal her if I would not sell her.   I thought five pounds petter than a flogging, and took it, and he's got the gal."   She was the mother of Sir John Johnson, and of two daughters, who became the wives respectively of Guy Johnson and Daniel Claus.*   When she was upon her death-bed, Sir William was married to her in order to legitimate her children.   After her death her place was supplied by Molly Brant, sister of the Mohawk sachem, by whom he had several children.   Toward the close of his life, Sir William married her in order to legitimate her children also, and her descendants are now some of the most respectable people in Upper Canada.   Sir William's first interview and acquaintance with her, as related by Mr. Stone (Note, Life of Brant, i., 387), have considerable romance.   She was a very sprightly and beautiful girl, about sixteen, when he first saw her at a militia muster.   One of the field officers, riding upon a fine horse, came near her, and, " by way of banter, she asked permission to mount behind.   Not supposing she could perform the exploit, he said she might.   At the word, she leaped upon the crupper with the agility of a gazelle.   The horse sprang off at full speed, and, clinging to the officer, her blanket flying and her dark hair streaming in the wind, she flew about the parade-ground as swift as an arrow.   The baronet, who was a witness of the spectacle, admiring the spirit of the young squaw, and becoming enamored of her person, took her home as his wife."   According to Indian customs, this act made her really his wife, and in all her relations of wife and mother she was very exemplary.

---

* These two daughters, who were left by their dying mother to the care of a friend, were educated almost in solitude.   That friend was the widow of an officer who was killed in battle, and, retiring from the world, devoted her whole time to the care of these children.   They were carefully instructed in religious duties, and in various kinds of needle-work, but were themselves kept entirely from society.   At the age of sixteen they had never seen a lady, except their mother and her friend, or a gentleman, except Sir William, who visited their room daily.   Their dress was not conformed to the fashions, but always consisted of wrappers of finest chintz over green silk petticoats.   Their hair, which was long and beautiful, was tied behind with a simple band of ribbon.   After their marriage they soon acquired the habits of society, and made excellent wives.

was in the habit of giving a diploma, testifying to their good conduct.   One of these is in the possession of the New York Historical Society, a copy of which, with the vignette, is given in the note.[1]   His house was the resort of the sachems of the Six Nations for counsel and for trade, and there the presents sent out by his government were annually distributed to the Indians.   On these occasions he amused himself and gratified his guests by fêtes and games, many of which were highly ludicrous.[2]   Young Indians and squaws were often seen running foot-races or wrestling for trinkets, and feats of astonishing agility were frequently performed by the Indians of both sexes.

1774.   Sir William's death was sudden, and was by some ascribed to poison, voluntarily taken by him, and by others to apoplexy, induced by over-excitement.   His possessions, which, with his offices and titles, passed into the hands of his son, did not long remain undisturbed, but were abandoned, as we have seen, in 1776, and were afterward sold to strangers under an act of attainder and confiscation passed by the Legislature of New York.

Sir John, as we have already noted, fled to Canada, where he received a colonel's commission.   The sequestration of his immense landed property inspired him with feelings of implacable revenge, which were manifested by his terrible visitations to the settlements in Tryon county.   One of these was chiefly for the purpose of recovering the plate and other valuables belonging to the baronet, which had been buried near Johnson Hall.   The events of this incursion were as follows:

About midnight on Sunday, the 21st of May, 1780, Sir John, with a force of five hundred Tories and Indians, who had penetrated the country from Crown Point to the Sacondaga River, appeared at Johnson Hall without being seen by any but his friends.   His forces were divided into two detachments, and between midnight and dawn he began to devastate the settlement by burning every building, except those which belonged to Tories.   One division was sent around in an easterly course, so as to strike the Mohawk at Tripes Hill,[3] below Caughnawaga, whence it was ordered to proceed up the valley, destroy Caughnawaga, and form a junction with the other division at the mouth of Cayudutta Creek.   This march was performed; many dwellings were burned and several lives were sacrificed.   Sir John, in the mean while, at the head of one division, proceeded through the village of Johnstown unobserved by the sentinels at the small picketed fort there, and before daylight was at the Hall, once his own, where he secured two prisoners.   On his way to join the other division upon the Cayudutta, he came to the residence of Sampson Sammons, who was, with his

---

[1] "By the Honorable Sir William Johnson, Bart., His Majesty's sole Agent and Superintendant of Indian Affairs for the Northern Department of North America, Colonel of the Six United Nations, their Allies and Dependants, &c., &c.

"To . . . .   WHEREAS, I have received repeated proofs of your attachment to his Britannic Majesty's Interests and Zeal for his service, upon sundry occasions, more particularly . . . . I do therefor give you this public Testimonial thereof, as a proof of his Majesty's Esteem and Approbation, Declaring you, the said . . . . ., to be a . . . . . . of your . . . . ., and recommending it to all his Majesty's Subjects and faithful Indian Allies to Treat and Consider you upon all occasions agreeable to your character, station, and services . . . . . . GIVEN under my hand and seal at Arms, at Johnson Hall, the . . . . . . day of . . . . . ., 17 . .

"By command of Sir W. Johnson."

[2] Among the amusements invented by Sir William were foot-races, in which the competitors had mealbags drawn up over their legs and tied under their arms; a hog, with its tail greased, would be offered as a prize to the one that should catch it by that extremity; a half pound of tea was a prize offered to the one who could make the wryest face; a bladder of Scotch snuff to the greatest scold of two old women; and children might be seen exploring pools of muddy water, into which the baronet had cast several pennies.—*Simms*, 121.

[3] At this place lived Garret Putnam, a very active Whig, and his house was the first one assailed.   Unknown to the invaders, Putnam had rented his house to two Englishmen named Gort and Platto, stanch Tories.   The assailants broke into the house, scalped the two men, who had not time to reveal their characters, and it was not until daylight that they discovered their victims to be their own friends instead of Putnam and his son, as they had supposed.

whole family, among the most active and intrepid patriots in Tryon county. Sir John had always respected Mr. Sammons, and still held him in high estimation, but he was determined to carry him and his family away prisoners, if possible, and thus lessen the number of his more influential enemies in the Mohawk Valley. It was not yet light when a Tory, named Sunderland, with a resolute band, surrounded the house of Sammons, and the first intimation the family had of danger was the arrest of Thomas, the younger of three sons, as he stepped out of the door to observe the weather.[1] The father and three sons were made prisoners, but the females of the family were left undisturbed, after the house was plundered of every thing valuable. The marauders then marched with their prisoners to the mouth of the Cayudutta, and both divisions went up the valley, burning, plundering, and murdering. A venerable old man, named David Fonda, was killed and scalped by an Indian party attached to the expedition, and in its march of a few miles nine aged men, four of them upward of eighty years old, were murdered. Returning to Caughnawaga, the torch was applied, and every building, except the church, was laid in ashes. From Caughnawaga they proceeded to Johnstown[2] by way of the Sammonses, on whose premises every building was burned, and the females, bereft of their protectors and helpers, were left houseless and almost naked. Seven horses that were in the stables were taken away, and that happy family of the morning were utterly destitute at evening.

Toward sunset Johnson perceived that the militia of the neighborhood were gathering, under the direction of Colonel John Harper, and resolved to decamp. Several Loyalists had joined him, and he succeeded in obtaining possession of twenty negro slaves whom he had left behind at the time of his flight, in the spring of 1776. Among these was the faithful negro who buried his chests of plate. With his prisoners, slaves, and much booty, he directed his course toward the Sacondaga. The inhabitants seemed so completely May 22, taken by surprise, and were so panic-stricken by the suddenness and fierceness of the 1780. invasion, that he was unmolested in his retreating march, and reached St. John's, on the Sorel, in safety. The captives were sent to Chambly, twelve miles distant, and confined in the fortress there.[3]

[1] Thomas Sammons, who was then a lad, lived until within a few years, and furnished much of the interesting matter concerning this irruption of Sir John, to the author of the *Life of Brant*, from whose pages I have gleaned much of the narrative here given. Mr. Sammons was a representative in Congress from 1803 to 1807, and again from 1809 to 1813.

[2] I have before mentioned that the silver plate and other valuable articles belonging to Johnson were buried by a faithful slave. When the Hall and other property were taken possession of by the Tryon county Committee, under the act of sequestration, the elder of Mr. Sammon's sons became the lessee, and the purchaser of the slave William, who had buried the plate. This slave Sir John found at the Hall, and while he tarried there for several hours on the day in question, the negro, assisted by four soldiers, disinterred the plate, which filled two barrels. It was then distributed among forty soldiers, who placed it in their knapsacks, the quarter-master making a memorandum of the name of each with the article of plate intrusted to him, and in this way it was carried safely to Montreal.

Johnson Hall, with seven hundred acres of land, had been sold by the commissioners to James Caldwell, of Albany, for $30,000, the payment to be made in *public securities*. To show the real value of such securities—in other words, the state of public credit of the colonies about 1779, it may be mentioned that Mr. Caldwell immediately resold the property for $7000, $23,000 less *on paper* than he gave for it, and then made money by the operation. He had bought the securities for a trifle, and received hard cash from the man who purchased from him.

[3] While halting on the day after leaving Johnstown, the elder Mr. Sammons requested a personal interview with Sir John, which was granted. He asked to be released, but the baronet hesitated. The old man then recurred to former times, when he and Sir John were friends and neighbors. " See what you have done, Sir John," he said. " You have taken myself and my sons prisoners, burned my dwelling to ashes, and left the helpless members of my family with no covering but the heavens above, and no prospect but desolation around them. Did we treat you in this manner when you were in the power of the Tryon county Committee ? Do you remember when we were consulted by General Schuyler, and you agreed to surrender your arms ? Do you not remember that you then agreed to remain neutral, and that upon that condition General Schuyler left you at liberty on your parole ? Those conditions you violated. You went off to Canada ; enrolled yourself in the service of the king ; raised a regiment of the disaffected, who abandoned their country with you ; and you have now returned to wage a cruel war against us, by burning our dwellings and robbing us of our property. I was your friend in the Committee of Safety, and exerted my-

Governor Clinton was at Kingston, Ulster county, when intelligence of this invasion reached him. He repaired immediately to Albany, and sent such forces, composed of militia and volunteers, as he could raise, to overtake and intercept the invaders. One division, commanded by the governor in person, pushed forward to Lakes George and Champlain, and at Ticonderoga was joined by a body of militia from the New Hampshire Grants. At the same time Colonel Van Schaick, with eight hundred militia, pursued the enemy by way of Johnstown. But Sir John was far beyond the reach of pursuers, and too cautious to take a route so well known as that of the lakes. He kept upon the Indian paths through the wilderness west of the Adirondack Mountains, and escaped. This was the last visit made by Johnson to the Mohawk Valley during the war, but his friends invaded the settlement the following year, and near Johnson Hall a pretty severe battle took place.

On the 24th of October, 1781, Major Ross and Walter Butler, at the head of about one thousand troops, consisting of regulars, Indians, and Tories, approached the settlement so stealthily that they reached Warren Bush (not far from the place where Sir Peter Warren made his first settlement, and the place of residence of Sir William Johnson on his arrival in America) without their approach being suspected. The settlement was broken into so suddenly that the people had no chance for escape. Many were killed, and their houses plundered and destroyed. As soon as Colonel Willett, then stationed at Fort Rensselaer, was informed of this incursion, he marched with about four hundred men for Fort Hunter, on the Mohawk. Colonel Rowley, of Massachusetts, with a part of his force, consisting of Tryon county militia, was sent round to fall upon the enemy in the rear, while Willett should attack them in front. The belligerents met a short distance above Johnson Hall, and a battle immediately ensued. The militia under Willett soon gave way, and fled in great confusion to the stone church in the village; and the enemy would have had an easy victory,

---

self to save your person from injury. And how am I requited? Your Indians have murdered and scalped old Mr. Fonda, at the age of eighty years, a man who, I have heard your father say, was like a father to him when he settled in Johnstown and Kingsborough. You can not succeed, Sir John, in such a warfare, and you will never enjoy your property more!" The appeal had its effect. The baronet made no reply, but the old gentleman was set at liberty, and a span of his horses was restored to him. A Tory, named Doxstader (whom we shall soon meet again at Currytown), was seen upon one of the old man's horses, and refused to give him up. After the war he returned to the neighborhood, when Mr. Sammons had him arrested, and he was obliged to pay the full value of the animal.

The two elder sons of Mr. Sammons, Frederic and Jacob, were taken to Canada. At Chambly they concerted a plan for escape by the prisoners rising upon the garrison, but the majority of them were too weak-hearted to attempt it. The brothers, however, succeeded in making their escape a few days afterward, and the narrative of their separate adventures, before they reached their homes, forms a wonderful page in the volume of romance. It may be found in detail in the second volume of Stone's *Life of Brant*. Jacob, after a toilsome journey from St. John's to Pittstown, in Vermont, through the trackless wilderness, reached Schenectady in safety, a few weeks after his capture, where he found his wife and children. But Frederic was recaptured, and it was nearly two years before he returned. His adventures in making his escape from an island among the St. Lawrence rapids, above Montreal, and his subsequent travel through the wilderness from the St. Lawrence to the Mohawk, with a fellow-prisoner, partake of all the stirring character of the most exciting legendary fiction. Almost naked, and with matted hair, they entered the streets of Schenectady, a wonder and a terror to the inhabitants at first, but, when known, they were the objects of profound regard. A strange but well-attested fact is related in connection with the return of Frederic. After the destruction of his property upon the Mohawk, the elder Sammons and his family returned to Marbletown, in Ulster county, whence they had emigrated. On the morning after his arrival at Schenectady, Frederic dispatched a letter to his father, by the hand of an officer on his way to Philadelphia. He left it at the house of Mr. Levi De Witt, five miles distant from Mr. Sammons's. On the night when the letter was left there, Jacob dreamed that his brother Frederic was living, and that a letter, announcing the fact, was at Mr. De Witt's. The dream was twice repeated, and the next morning he related it to the family. They had long given Frederic up as lost, and laughed at Jacob for his belief in the teachings of dreams. Jacob firmly believed that such a letter was at De Witt's, and thither he repaired and inquired for it. He was told that no such letter was there, but urged a more thorough search, when it was found behind a barrel, where it had accidentally fallen. Jacob requested Mr. De Witt to open the letter and examine it, while he should recite its contents. It was done, and the dreamer repeated it word for word! Frederic lived to a good old age, enjoying the esteem and confidence of his fellow-citizens. He was chosen an elector of President and Vice-president in 1837.

had not Rowley emerged from the woods at that moment, and fallen upon their rear.   It was then nearly four o'clock in the afternoon, and the fight was kept up with bravery on both sides until dark, when the enemy retreated, or rather fled, in great disorder, to the woods.   During the engagement, and while Rowley was keeping the enemy at bay, Willett succeeded in rallying the militia, who returned to the fight.   The Americans lost about forty killed and wounded.   The enemy had about the same number killed, and fifty made prisoners.

The enemy continued their retreat westward nearly all the night after the battle, and early in the morning Willett started in pursuit.   He halted at Stone Arabia, and sent forward a detachment of troops to make forced marches to Oneida Lake, where, he was informed, the enemy had left their boats, for the purpose of destroying them.   In the mean while he pressed onward with the main force to the German Flats, where he learned that the advanced party had returned without accomplishing their errand.   From a scouting party he also learned that the enemy had taken a northerly course, along the West Canada Creek. With about four hundred of his choicest men, he started in pursuit, in the face of a driving snow-storm.   He encamped that night in a thick wood upon the Royal Grant,[1] and sent out a scouting party, under Jacob Sammons, to search for the enemy.   Sammons discovered their forces a few miles in advance of the Americans, and, after reconnoitering their camp, communicated the fact to Willett that they were well armed with bayonets.   That officer deferred his meditated night attack upon them, and continued his pursuit early in the morning, but the enemy were as quick on foot as he.   In the afternoon he came up with a lagging party of Indians, and a brisk but short skirmish ensued.   Some of the Indians were killed, some taken prisoners, and others escaped.   Willett kept upon the enemy's trail along the creek, and toward evening came up with the main body at a place called Jerseyfield, on the northeastern side of Canada Creek.   A running fight ensued ; the Indians became terrified, and retreated across the stream at a ford, where Walter Butler, who was their leader, attempted to rally them.   A brisk fire was kept up across the creek by both parties for some time, and Butler, who was watching the fight from behind a tree, was shot in the head by an Oneida, who knew him and took deliberate aim.   His troops thereupon fled in confusion.   The Oneida bounded across the creek, and found his victim not dead, but writhing in great agony.   The Tory cried out, " *Save me!   Save me!   Give me quarters!*" while the tomahawk of the warrior glittered over his head.   " *Me give you Sherry Falley quarters!*" shouted the Indian, and buried his hatchet in the head of his enemy.   He took his scalp, and, with the rest of the Oneidas, continued the pursuit of the flying host.   The body of Butler was left to the beasts and birds, without burial, for charity toward one so blood-stained had no dwelling-place in the bosoms of his foes.   The place where he fell is still called *Butler's Ford.*   The pursuit was kept up until evening, when Willett, completely successful by entirely routing and dispersing the enemy, wheeled his victorious little army, and returned to Fort Dayton in triumph.[2]   This was the closing scene of the bloody drama performed in the Valley of the Mohawk during the Revolution, a tragedy terrible in every aspect ; and we, who are dwelling in the midst of peace and abundance, and so far removed, in point of time, from the events, that hardly an actor is living to tell us of scenes that seem almost fabulous, can not properly estimate the degree of moral and physical courage, long suffering, patient endurance, and hopeful vigilance which the people of that day exhibited.   It was a terrible ordeal for the patriots.   Like the three holy men of Babylon, they passed through a " fiery furnace heated one seven times more than it was wont to

October 29.

---

[1] The Royal Grant, it will be remembered, was the tract of land which Sir William Johnson shrewdly procured from Hendrick, the Mohawk sachem, by outwitting him in a game of dreaming.—See page 106.

[2] The sufferings of the retreating army must have been many and acute.   The weather was cold, and in their hasty flight many of them had cast away their blankets, to make their progress more speedy.   The loss of the Americans in this pursuit was only one man ; that of the enemy is not known.   It must have been very great.   Colonel Willett, in his dispatch to Governor Clinton, observed, " The fields of Johnstown the brooks and rivers, the hills and mountains, the deep and gloomy marshes through which they had to pass they only could tell ; and perhaps the officers who detached them on the expedition."

be," yet they came out unscathed——"neither were their coats changed nor the smell of fire had passed on them." We are yet to visit Currytown, Sharon Springs, and Cherry Valley, and note some incidents of the civil war, reserved for record here, and then we shall leave old Tryon county, with the pleasant anticipations of the "homeward-bound."

We returned to Fultonville, from our excursion to Johnstown, by the western road, and passed the premises formerly owned by Sampson Sammons, near the winding Cayadutta. The house, which was built upon the foundation of the one destroyed by the miscreants under Johnson, has a venerable appearance; but the trailing vines that cover its porch, and the air of comfort that surrounds it, hide all indications of the desolation of former times. We arrived at Fultonville in time to dine, and there I spent an hour pleasantly and profitably with Jeptha R. Simms, Esq., the author of a "History of Schoharie County and the Border Wars of New York," a work of much local and general interest, and a valuable companion to Campbell's "Annals of Tryon County." It is greatly to be lamented that men like Campbell and Simms, and Miner, of Wyoming, who gathered a large proportion of the facts concerning the Revolution from the lips of those who participated in its trials, have not been found in every section of our old thirteen states equally industrious and patriotic. It is now too late, for the men of the Revolution are mostly in the grave. I have found but few, very few, still alive and sufficiently vigorous to tell the tales of their experience with perspicuity; and a hundred times, in the course of my pilgrimage to the grounds where

> Discord raised its trumpet notes
> And carnage beat its horrid drum,

have my inquiries for living patriots of that war been answered with "Five years ago Captain A. was living;" or "three years ago Major B. died;" or "last autumn Mother C. was buried;" all of whom were full of the unwritten history of the Revolution. But they are gone, and much of the story of our struggle for independence is buried with them. They are gone, but not forgotten:

> . . . . "They need
> No statue or inscription to reveal
> Their greatness. It is round them; and the joy
> With which their children tread the hallow'd ground
> That holds their venerated bones, the peace
> That smiles on all they fought for, and the wealth
> That clothes the land they rescued—these, though mute,
> As feeling ever is when deepest—these
> Are monuments more lasting than the fanes
> Rear'd to the kings and demi-gods of old."
> PERCIVAL.

I returned to Fort Plain, by rail-road, toward evening, and the next morning, accompanied by the friend with whom we were sojourning, I started for Currytown.[1] We went by the way of Canajoharie, a pleasant little village on the canal, opposite Palatine, and thence over the rugged hills southward. A little below Canajoharie we sketched an old stone house which was erected before the Revolution, and was used soon afterward by the brothers Kane, then the most extensive traders west of Albany. An anecdote is related in connection with the Kanes, which illustrates the proverbial shrewdness of Yankees, and the confiding nature of the old stock of Mohawk Valley Dutchmen. A peddler (who was, of course, a Yankee) was arrested for the offense of traveling on the Sabbath, contrary to law, and taken before a Dutch justice near Caughnawaga. The peddler pleaded the urgency of his business. At first the Dutchman was inexorable, but

THE KANE HOUSE.

at length, on the payment to him of a small sum, agreed to furnish the Yankee with a written permit to travel on. The justice, not being expert with the pen, requested the peddler to write the "pass." He wrote a draft upon the Kanes for fifty dollars, which the unsus-

[1] The name is derived from William Curry, the patentee of the lands in that settlement.

pecting Dutchman signed. The draft was presented and duly honored, and the Yankee went on his way rejoicing. A few days afterward the justice was called upon to pay the amount of the draft. The thing was a mystery, and it was a long time before he could comprehend it. All at once light broke in upon the matter, and the victim exclaimed, vehemently, in broken English, "Eh, yah! I understhands it now. Tish mine writin', and dat ish de tam Yankee pass!" He paid the money and resigned his office, feeling that it was safer to deal in corn and butter with honest neighbors, than in law with Yankee interlopers.

We reached Currytown, a small village nearly four miles south of Canajoharie, at about noon. The principal object of my visit there was to see the venerable Jacob Dievendorff, who, with his family, was among the sufferers when that settlement was destroyed by Indians and Tories in July, 1781. Accompanied by his son-in-law (Dr. Snow, of Currytown), we found the old patriot busily engaged in his barn, threshing grain; and, although nearly eighty years of age, he seemed almost as vigorous and active as most men are at sixty. His sight and hearing are somewhat defective, but his intellect, as exhibited by his clear remembrance of the circumstances of his early life, had lost but little of its strength. He is one of the largest land-holders in Montgomery county, owning one thousand fertile acres, lying in a single tract where the scenes of his sufferings in early life occurred. In an orchard, a short distance from his dwelling, the house was still standing which was stockaded and used as a fort. It is fast decaying, but the venerable owner allows time alone to work its destruction, and will not suffer a board to be taken from it. The occurrences here have already been recorded, by Campbell and Simms, as related to them long ago by Mr. Dievendorff and others, and from these details I gather the following facts, adding such matters of interest as were communicated to me by Mr. Dievendorff himself and his near neighbor, the venerable John Keller.

On the 9th of July, 1781, nearly five hundred Indians, and a few Loyalists, commanded by a Tory named Doxstader, attacked and destroyed the settlement of Currytown, murdered several of the inhabitants, and carried others away prisoners. The house of Henry Lewis (represented in the engraving) was picketed and used for a fort.[2] The

August, 1848.

Jacob Dievendorff aged 79

[1] I here present a portrait of Mr. Dievendorff, which he kindly allowed me to make while he sat upon a half bushel in his barn. Also, a sketch of the back of his head, showing its appearance where the scalp was taken off. The building is a view of the one referred to in the text as the Currytown fort, now standing in Mr. Dievendorff's orchard. The method used by the Indians in scalping is probably not generally known. I was told by Mr. Dievendorff and others familiar with the horrid practice that the scalping-knife was a weapon not unlike, in appearance, the bowie-knife of the present day. The victim was usually stunned or killed by a blow from the tomahawk. Sometimes only a portion of the scalp (as was the case with Mr. Dievendorff) was taken from the crown and back part of the head, but more frequently the whole scalp was removed. With the dexterity of a surgeon, the Indian placed the point of his knife at the roots of the hair on the forehead, and made a circular incision around the head. If the hair was short, he would raise a lappet of the skin, take hold with his teeth, and tear it instantly from the skull. If long, such as the hair of females, he would twist it around his hand, and, by a sudden jerk, bare the skull. The scalps were then tanned with the hair on, and often marked in such a manner that the owners could tell when and where they were severally obtained, and whether they belonged to men or women. When Major Rogers, in 1759, destroyed the chief village of the St. Francis Indians, he found there a vast quantity of scalps, many of them comically painted in hieroglyphics. They were all stretched on small hoops.

[2] Mr. Dievendorff told me that on one occasion the fort was attacked by a party of Indians. There were

settlers, unsuspicious of danger, were generally at work in their fields when the enemy fell upon them.   It was toward noon when they emerged stealthily from the forest, and with torch and tomahawk commenced the work of destruction.   Among the sufferers were the Dievendorffs, Kellers, Myerses, Bellingers, Tanners, and Lewises.   On the first alarm, those nearest the fort fled thitherward, and those more remote sought shelter in the woods.   Jacob Dievendorff, the father of the subject of our sketch, escaped.   His son Frederic was overtaken, tomahawked, and scalped, on his way to the fort,[1] and Frederic's brother Jacob, then a lad eleven years old, was made prisoner.   A negro named Jacob, two lads named Bellinger, Mary Miller, a little girl ten or twelve years old, Jacob Myers and his son, and two others, were captured.   The Indians then plundered and burned all the dwellings but the fort and one belonging to a Tory, in all about twelve, and either killed or drove away most of the cattle and horses in the neighborhood.   When the work of destruction was finished, the enemy started off in the direction of New Dorlach, or Turlock (now Sharon) with their prisoners and booty.

Colonel Willett was at Fort Plain when Currytown was attacked.   On the previous day he had sent out a scout of thirty or forty men, under Captain Gross, to patrol the country for the two-fold purpose of procuring forage and watching the movements of the enemy. They went in the direction of New Dorlach, and, when near the present Sharon Springs, discovered a portion of the camp of the enemy in a cedar swamp.[2]   Intelligence of this fact reached Willett at the moment when a dense smoke, indicating the firing of a village, was seen from Fort Plain, in the direction of Currytown.   Captain Robert M'Kean, with sixteen levies, was ordered to that place, with instructions to assemble as many of the militia on the way as possible.   With his usual celerity, that officer arrived at the settlement in time to assist in extinguishing the flames of some of the buildings yet unconsumed.   Colonel Willett, in the mean time, was active in collecting the militia.   Presuming that the enemy would occupy the same encampment that night, and being joined during the day by the forces under M'Kean and Gross, he determined to make an attack upon them at midnight, while they were asleep.   His whole strength did not exceed one hundred and fifty effective men, while the enemy's force, as he afterward learned, consisted of more than double that number.   The night was dark and lowering, and the dense forest that surrounded the swamp encampment of the enemy was penetrated only by a bridle path.   His guide became bewildered, and it was six o'clock in the morning before he came in sight of the enemy, who, warned of his approach, had taken a more advantageous position.   From this position it was desirable to draw them, and for that purpose Willett sent forward a detachment from the main body, which he had stationed in crescent form on a ridge now seen on the south side of the turnpike, opposite the swamp, who fired upon the Indians and then retreated. The stratagem succeeded, for the Indians pursued them, and were met by Willett, advancing with one hundred men.   M'Kean was left with a reserve in the rear, and fell furiously upon the flank of the enemy.   A desperate fight for a short time ensued, when the Indians broke and fled, but kept up a fire from behind trees and rocks.   Willett and his men, understanding their desultory warfare, pursued them with bullet and bayonet, until they relinquished the fight, and fled precipitately down their war-path toward the Susquehanna, leaving their camp and all their plunder behind.   They left forty dead upon the field.   The American loss was five killed, and nine wounded and missing.   The brave M'Kean was

several women, but only one man, in the fort.   The savages approached stealthily along a ravine, a little north of the fort, and were about to make an assault upon the frail fortification, when they were saluted with a warm fire from it.   There were several muskets in it, which the women loaded as fast as the man could fire; and so rapid were the discharges, that the Indians, supposing quite a large garrison to be present, fled to the woods.   The remains of the building are still scarred by many bullet marks.

[1] He was not killed, but lay several hours insensible, when he was picked up by his uncle, Mr. Keller, who carried him into the fort.   He recovered, and lived several years, when he was killed by the falling of a tree.

[2] A part of this swamp may still be seen on the north side of the western turnpike, about two miles east of the springs.

mortally wounded, and died at Fort Plain a few days after the return of the expedition to that post. I was informed by Mr. Lipe, at Fort Plain, that the body of the captain was buried near the block-house, and that the fort was afterward called Fort M'Kean, in honor of the deceased soldier.

At the time of the attack, the Indians had placed most of their prisoners on the horses which they had stolen from Currytown, and each was well guarded. When they were about to retreat before Willett, fearing the recapture of the prisoners, and the consequent loss of scalps, the savages began to murder and scalp them. Young Dievendorff (my informant) leaped from his horse, and, running toward the swamp, was pursued, knocked down by a blow of a tomahawk upon his shoulder, scalped, and left for dead. Willett did not bury his slain, but a detachment of militia, under Colonel Veeder, who repaired to the field after the battle, entombed them, and fortunately discovered and proceeded to bury the bodies of the prisoners who were murdered and scalped near the camp. Young Dievendorff, who was stunned and insensible, was seen struggling among the leaves ; and his bloody face being mistaken for that of an Indian, one of the soldiers leveled his musket to shoot him. A fellow-soldier, perceiving his mistake, knocked up his piece and saved the lad's life. He was taken to Fort Plain, and, being placed under the care of Dr. Faught, a German physician, of Stone Arabia, was restored to health. It was five years, however, before his head was perfectly healed ; and when I saw him (August, 1848), it had the tender appearance and feeling of a wound recently healed. He is still living (1849), in the midst of the settlement of Currytown, which soon arose from its ashes, and is a living monument of savage cruelty and the sufferings of the martyrs for American liberty.[1]

Toward evening we left Currytown for Cherry Valley, by the way of Sharon Springs. The road lay through a beautiful, though very hilly, country. From the summits of some of the eminences over which we passed the views were truly magnificent. Looking down into the Canajoharie Valley from the top of its eastern slope, it appeared like a vast enameled basin, having its concavity garnished with pictures of rolling intervales, broad cultivated fields, green groves, bright streams, villages, and neat farm-houses in abundance ; and its distant rim on its northern verge seemed beautifully embossed with wooded hills, rising one above another in profuse outlines far away beyond the Mohawk. We reached the Springs toward sunset, passing the Pavilion on the way.[2] They are in a broad ravine, and along the margin of a hill ; and near them the little village of Sharon has grown up.[3] Our stay was brief—just long enough to have a lost shoe replaced by another upon our horse, and to visit the famous fountains—for, having none of the " ills which flesh is heir to" of sufficient malignity to require the infliction of sulphureted or chalybeate draughts, we were glad to escape to the hills and vales less suggestive of Tophet and the Valley of Hinnom. How any *but invalids*, who find the waters less nauseous than the allopathic doses of the shops,

[1] The little girl (Mary Miller) was found scalped, but alive, and was taken, with the lad Dievendorff, toward Fort Plain. She was very weak when found, and on taking a draught of cold water, just before reaching the fort, instantly expired.

[2] The Pavilion is a very large hotel, situated upon one of the loftiest summits in the neighborhood, and commanding a magnificent view of the country. It was erected in 1836 by a New York company, and is filled with invalids and other visitors during the summer.

[3] The *Sharon Sulphur Springs* have been celebrated for their medical properties many years, and are said to be equal in efficacy to those in Virginia. An analysis of the waters, made by Dr. Chilton, of New York, gives the following result :

Sulphate of magnesia . .	42.40 grains.
Sulphate of lime	111.62 "
Chlorid of sodium	2.24 "
Chlorid of magnesium . .	2.40 "
Hydro-sulphate of sodium } Hydro-sulphate of calcium }	2.28 "
Sulphureted hydrogen gas .	16 cubic inches.

There is a chalybeate spring in the neighborhood. The whole region abounds in fossils, and is an interesting place for the geologist.

296   PICTORIAL FIELD-BOOK

Arrival at Cherry Valley.   Judge Campbell and his Residence.   His Captivity.   Movements of Brant

and, consequently, are happier than at home, can spend a "season" there, within smelling distance of the gaseous fountains, and call the sojourn *pleasure*, is a question that can only be solved by Fashion, the shrewd alchemist in whose alembic common miseries are transmuted into conventional happiness.   The sulphureted hydrogen does not infect the Pavilion, I believe, and a summer residence there secures the enjoyment of pure air and delightful drives and walks in the midst of a lovely hill country.

It was quite dark when we reached Cherry Valley, eight miles west of Sharon Springs.[1] This village lies imbosomed within lofty hills, open only on the southwest, in the direction of the Susquehanna, and as we approached it along the margin of the mountain on its eastern border, the lights sparkling below us, like stars reflected from a lake, gave us the first indication of its presence.   In the course of the evening we called upon the Honorable James S. Campbell, who, at the time of the destruction of the settlement in 1778, was a child six years of age.   He is the son of Colonel Samuel Campbell, already mentioned, and father of the Honorable William W. Campbell, of New York city, the author of the *Annals of Tryon County*, so frequently cited.   With his mother and family, he was carried into captivity. He has a clear recollection of events in the Indian country while he was a captive, his arrival and stay at Niagara, his subsequent sojourn in Canada, and the final reunion of the family after an absence and separation of two years.[2]   His residence, a handsome modern

MANSION OF JUDGE CAMPBELL.[3]

structure, is upon the site of the old family mansion, which was stockaded and used as a fort at the time of the invasion.   The doors and window-shutters were made bullet-proof, and the two barns that were included within the ramparts were strengthened.

In a former chapter we have noticed that Brant's first hostile movement, after his return from Canada and establishment of his head-quarters at Oghkwaga, was an attempt to cut off the settlement of Cherry Valley, or, at least, to make captive the members of the active Committee of Correspondence.   It was a sunny morning, toward the close of May, when Brant and his warriors cautiously moved up to the brow of the lofty hill   1777. on the east side of the town, to reconnoiter the settlement at their feet.   He was astonished and chagrined on seeing a fortification where he supposed all was weak and defenseless, and greater was his disappointment when quite a large and well-armed garrison appeared upon the esplanade in front of Colonel Campbell's house.   These soldiers were not as formidable as the sachem supposed, for they were only half-grown boys, who, full of the martial spirit of the times, had formed themselves into companies, and, armed with wooden guns and swords, had regular drills each day.   It was such a display, on the morning in question, that attracted Brant's attention.   His vision being somewhat obstructed by the trees and

---

[1] Cherry Valley derived its name, according to Campbell, from the following circumstance : " Mr. Dunlop [the venerable pastor whose family suffered at the time of the massacre in 1778], engaged in writing some letters, inquired of Mr. Lindesay [the original proprietor of the soil] where he should date them, who proposed the name of a town in Scotland.   Mr. Dunlop, pointing to the fine wild cherry-trees and to the valley, replied, ' Let us give our place an appropriate name, and call it Cherry Valley,' which was readily agreed to."—*Annals of Tryon County*.

[2] The children of Mrs. Campbell were all restored to her at Niagara, except this one.   In June, 1780, she was sent to Montreal, and there she was joined by her missing boy.   He had been with a tribe of the Mohawks, and had forgotten his own language ; but he remembered his mother, and expressed his joy at seeing her, in the Indian language.   Honorable William Campbell, late surveyor general of New York, was her son   She lived until 1836, being then 93 years of age.   She was the last survivor of the Revolutionary women in the region of the head waters of the Susquehanna.

[3] This pleasant dwelling is upon the northern verge of the town, on the road leading from Cherry Valley to the Mohawk.   The sketch was taken from the road.

shrubs in which he was concealed, he mistook the boys for full-grown soldiers, and, considering an attack dangerous, moved his party to a hiding-place at the foot of the Tekaharawa Falls, in a deep ravine north of the village, near the road leading to the Mohawk.[1] In that deep, rocky glen, "where the whole scene was shadowy and almost dark even at mid-day," his warriors were concealed, while Brant and two or three followers hid themselves in ambush behind a large rock by the road side, for the purpose of obtaining such information as might fall in his way.

On the morning of that day, Lieutenant Wormwood, a promising young officer of Palatine, had been sent from Fort Plain to Cherry Valley with the information, for the committee at the latter place, that a military force might be expected there the next day. His noble bearing and rich velvet dress attracted a good deal of attention at the village ; and when, toward evening, he started to return, accompanied by Peter Sitz, the bearer of some dispatches, the people, in admiration, looked after him until he disappeared beyond the hill. On leaving, he had cast down his portmanteau, saying, "I shall be back for it in the morning." But he never returned. As the two patriots galloped along the margin of the Tekaharawa Glen, they were hailed, but, instead of answering, they put spurs to their horses. The warriors in ambush arose and fired a volley upon them. The lieutenant fell, and Brant, rushing out from his concealment, scalped him with his own hands. Sitz was captured, and his dispatches fell into the hands of Brant. Fortunately they were double, and Sitz had the presence of mind to destroy the genuine and deliver the fictitious to the sachem. Deceived by these dispatches concerning the strength of Cherry Valley, Brant withdrew to Cobelskill, and thence to Oghkawaga, and the settlement was saved from destruction at that time.[2] Its subsequent fate is recorded in a previous chapter.

DISTANT VIEW OF CHERRY VALLEY.

Judge Campbell kindly offered to accompany us in the morning to "Brant's Rock."[3] Having engaged to be back at Fort Plain in time the next day to take the cars for Albany at two o'clock, and the distance from the "rock" being twelve miles, over a rough and hilly road, an early start was necessary, for I wished to make a sketch of the village and valley, as also

---

[1] The *Tekaharawa* is the western branch of the *Canajoharie* or *Bowman's Creek*, which falls into the Mohawk at Canajoharie, opposite Palatine.

[2] Campbell's Annals.

[3] This rock, which is about four feet high, lies in a field on the left of the road leading from Cherry Valley to the Mohawk, about a mile and a half north of the residence of Judge Campbell. It is a fossiliferous mass, composed chiefly of shells. Behind this rock the body of Lieutenant Wormwood, lifeless and the head scalped, was found by the villagers, who had heard the firing on the previous evening. Judge Campbell, who accompanied us to the spot, pointed out the stump of a large tree by the road side, as the place where Lieutenant Wormwood fell. The tree was pierced by many bullets, and Judge Campbell had extracted several of them when a boy

BRANT'S ROCK.

of the rock.   At early dawn, the light not being sufficient to perceive the outline of distant objects, I stood upon the high ridge north of the village which divides the head waters of the eastern branch of the Susquehanna from the tributaries of the Mohawk.   As the pale light in the east grew ruddy, a magnificent panorama was revealed on every side ; and as the stars faded away, and trees, and fields, and hills, and the quiet village arose from the gloom ; and the sun's first rays burst over the eastern hills into the valley, lighting it up with sudden splendor, while the swelling chorus of birds and the hum of insects broke the stillness ; and the perfumes of flowers arose from the dewy grass like sweet incense, the delighted spirit seemed to hear a voice in the quivering light, saying,

> " From the quicken'd womb of the primal gloom
>   The sun roll'd black and bare,
> Till I wove him a vest, for his Ethiop breast,
>   Of the threads of my golden hair ;
> And when the broad tent of the firmament
>   Arose on its airy spars,
> I pencil'd the hue of its matchless blue,
>   And spangled it round with the stars.
>
> .   .   .   .
>
> I waken the flowers in their dew-spangled bowers,
>   The birds in their chambers of green,
> And mountains and plain glow with beauty again
>   As they bask in my matinal sheen.
> Oh, if such the glad worth of my presence to earth,
>   Though fitful and fleeting the while,
> What glories must rest on the home of the blest,
>   Ever bright with the Deity's smile."
>   WILLIAM PITT PALMER.

On the north the Valley of the Canajoharie stretches away to the Mohawk, twelve miles distant, whose course was marked by a white line of mist that skirted the more remote hills ; and on the south Cherry Valley extends down among the mountains toward the Susquehanna proper, and formed the easy war-path to the settlement at its head, from Oghkwaga and Unadilla.   From the bosom of the ridge whereon I stood spring the head waters of the eastern branch of the Susquehanna and those of Canajoharie.   I had finished the sketch here given before the sun was fairly above the tree-tops, and, while the mist yet hovered over the Tehakawara, we were at Brant's Rock, within the sound of the tiny cascades.   There we parted from Judge Campbell, and hastened on toward Fort Plain, where we arrived in time to breakfast, and to take the morning train for Albany.   Before leaving, let us take a parting glance at the Revolutionary history of the Mohawk Valley, for we may not have another opportunity.

Soon after the irruption of Dockstader, or Doxstader, into the Currytown and New Dorlach settlements, a party of Tories and Indians made a descent upon Palatine, under the conduct of a son of Colonel Jacob Klock.   They were betrayed by one of their number, and fled to the woods for safety, without accomplishing any mischief.   At the German Flats and in that vicinity several spirited rencounters took place between the enemy and the patriot militia.   One of them was marked by great bravery on the part of Captain Solomon Woodworth, and a small company of rangers which he had organized.   He marched from Fort Dayton to the Royal Grant for the purpose of observation.   On the way he fell in with an Indian ambush.   Without warning, his little band was surrounded by savages, who made the forest ring with the war-whoop.   One of the most desperate and bloody engagements of the war ensued.   Woodworth and a large number of his rangers were slain, and the victorious Indians took several of them prisoners.   Only fifteen escaped.

Another affair occurred at a settlement called Shell's Bush, about five miles north of Herkimer village, which deserves a passing notice.   A wealthy German named John Christian Shell, or Schell, had built a block-house of his own, two stories high, the upper one projecting so as to allow the inmates to fire perpendicularly upon the assailants.[1]   One sultry

---

[1] At that time there were no less than twenty forts, so called, between Schenectady and Fort Schuyler.

OF THE REVOLUTION. 299

Descent of Tories upon "Shell's Bush." Shell's Block-house. Furious Battle. Capture of M'Donald. Luther's Hymn.

afternoon in August, while the people were generally in their fields, Donald M'Donald, one of the Scotch refugees from Johnstown, with a party of sixty Indians and Tories, made a descent upon Shell's Bush. The inhabitants mostly fled to Fort Dayton, but Shell and his family took refuge in his block-house. He and two of his sons (he had eight in all) were at work in the field. The two sons were captured, but the father and his other boys, who were near, reached the block-house in safety. It was finally besieged, but the assailants were kept at a respectful distance by the *garrison*. Shell's wife loaded the muskets, while her husband and sons discharged them with sure aim. M'Donald tried to burn the block-house, but was unsuccessful. He at length procured a crow-bar, ran up to the door, and attempted to force it. Shell fired upon him, and so wounded him in the leg that he fell. Instantly the beleaguered patriot opened the door and pulled the Scotchman within, a prisoner. He was well supplied with cartridges, and these he was obliged to surrender to his captors. The battle ceased for a time. Shell knew the enemy would not attempt to burn his castle while their leader was a prisoner within it, and, taking advantage of the lull in the battle, he went into the second story, and composedly sang the favorite hymn of Luther amid the perils that surrounded him in his controversies with the pope.[1] But the respite was short. The enemy, maddened at the loss of several of their number killed, and their commander a prisoner, rushed up to the block-house, and five of them thrust the muzzles of their pieces through the loop-holes. Mrs. Shell seized an ax, and, with well-directed blows, ruined every musket by bending the barrels. At the same time Shell and his sons kept up a brisk fire, which drove the enemy off. At twilight he went to the upper story and called out to his wife, in a loud voice, informing her that Captain Small was approaching from Fort Dayton with succor. In a few minutes, with louder voice, he exclaimed, " Captain Small, march your company round upon this side of the house. Captain Getman, you had better wheel your men off to the left, and come upon that side." This was a successful stratagem. There were no troops approaching, but the enemy, deceived by the trick, fled to the woods. M'Donald was taken to Fort Dayton the next day, where his leg was amputated, but the blood flowed so freely that he died in a few hours.[2] The two sons of Shell

They were generally strong dwellings stockaded, and so arranged that fifteen or twenty families might find protection in each.

[1] The following is a literal translation of the hymn, made for the author of the *Life of Brant* by Professor Bokum, of Harvard University. It is from a German hymn book published in 1741.

1.

A FIRM fortress is our God, a good defense and weapon;
He helps us free from all our troubles which have now befallen us.
The old evil enemy, he is now seriously going to work;
Great power and much cunning are his cruel equipments,
There is none like him on the earth.

2.

With our own strength nothing can be done, we are very soon lost:
For us the right man is fighting, whom God himself has chosen.
Do you ask, Who is he? His name is Jesus Christ,
The Lord Jehovah, and there is no other God;
He must hold the field.

3.

And if the world were full of devils, ready to devour us,
We are by no means much afraid, for finally we must overcome
The prince of this world, however badly he may behave,
He can not injure us, and the reason is, because he is the judge,
A little word can lay him low.

4.

That word they shall suffer to remain, and not to be thanked for either;
He is with us in the field, with his spirit and his gifts.
If they take from us body, property, honor, child, and wife,
Let them all be taken away, they have yet no gain from it,
The kingdom of heaven must remain to us.

[2] M'Donald wore a silver-mounted tomahawk, which Shell took from him. Its handle exhibited thirty-two scalp notches, the tally of horrid deeds in imitation of his Indian associates.

were carried into Canada, and they asserted that nine of the wounded enemy died on the way. Their loss on the ground was eleven killed and six wounded, while not one of the defenders of the block-house was injured. Soon after this event Shell was fired upon by some Indians, while at work in his field with his boys. He was severely wounded, and one of his boys was killed. The old man was taken to the fort, where he died of his wound.[1]

1781.   During this summer the Tories and Indians went down upon Warwasing and other portions of the frontier settlements of Ulster and Orange counties. These expeditions will be elsewhere considered. The irruption of Ross and Butler into the Johnstown settlement in October, and their repulse by Colonel Willett, have been related. With that transaction closed the hostilities in Tryon county for the year, and the surrender of Cornwallis October 19, and his whole army at Yorktown, in Virginia, so dispirited the Loyalists that 1781.   they made no further demonstrations, by armed parties, against the settlements. Attempts, some of them successful, were made to carry off prominent citizens.[2] The Indians still hung around the borders of the settlements in small parties during 1782, but they accomplished little beyond producing alarms and causing general uneasiness. Peace ensued, the hostile savages retired to the wilderness, a few of the refugee Tories, tame and submissive, returned, and the Mohawk Valley soon smiled with the abundance produced by peaceful industry.

We left Fort Plain toward noon, and reached Albany in time to depart for New York the same evening. Columns of smoke were yet rising from the smouldering ruins of a large portion of the business part of the city lying near the river, south of State Street ; and the piers along the basin, black and bare, exhibited a mournful contrast to the air of busy activity that enlivened them when we passed through the place a few weeks before. I have been in Albany many times ; let us take a seat upon the promenade deck of the Isaac Newton, for the evening is pleasant, and, as we glide down the Hudson, chat a while about the Dutch city and its associations, and its sister settlement Schenectady, and thus close our FIRST TOUR AMONG THE SCENES OF THE REVOLUTION.

The site of Albany was an Indian settlement, chiefly of the Mohawk tribes, long before Hendrick Hudson sailed up the North River. It was called *Scagh-negh-ta-da*, a word signifying *the end of the pine woods*, or *beyond the pine woods*. Such, and equally appropriate, was also the name of a settlement on the Mohawk, at the lower end of the valley, which still retains the appellation, though a little Anglicised in orthography, being spelled Schenectady. From the account given in Juet's Journal, published in the third volume of Purchas's Pilgrimages, of Hudson's voyage up the river, it is supposed that he proceeded in his vessel (the *Half Moon*) as far as the present site of Albany, and perhaps as high as Troy.[3] But he left no colony there, and the principal fruit of his voyage, which he carried back to the Old World, was intelligence of the discovery of a noble river, navigable one hundred and sixty miles, and passing through the most fertile and romantic region imaginable. This

---

[1] Stone's *Life of Brant*.
[2] The most prominent Tories engaged in this business were Bettys and Waltermeyer. We have noticed in another chapter the attempt of the latter to abduct General Schuyler. Among the prisoners thus made by these two miscreants, from Ballston, were Samuel Nash, Joseph Chaird, Uri Tracy, Samuel Patchin, Epenetus White, John Fulmer, and two brothers named Bontas. They were all taken to Canada, and, after being roughly treated, were either exchanged, or became free at the conclusion of the war.
[3] Henry or Hendrick Hudson was a native of England. While seeking a northwest passage to Japan and China, he explored the coasts of Greenland and Labrador in 1607–8. After returning to England from a second voyage, he went to Holland and entered the service of the Dutch East India Company, who fitted out the *Half Moon* for him to pursue his discoveries. It was during this voyage that he sailed up the river which bears his name. The next year (1610) he was sent out by an association of gentlemen, and in that voyage discovered the great bay at the north called Hudson's Bay, where he wintered. In the spring of 1611 he endeavored to complete his discoveries, but, his provisions failing, he was obliged to relinquish the attempt and make his way homeward. Going out of the straits from the bay, he threatened to set one or two of his mutinous crew on shore. These, joined by others, entered his cabin at night, pinioned his arms behind him, and with his sons, and seven of the sick and most infirm on board, he was put into a shallop and set adrift. He was never heard of afterward.

OF THE REVOLUTION. 301

~arly History of Albany.   Fort Orange.   First Stone House.   The Church.   The Portrait of Hudson.

discovery was made early in the autumn of 1609.   As soon as the intelligence reached the
Dutch East India Company, they sent out men to establish trading posts in the country.
1610. These traders ed in 1614, and the
ascended the river place was named, by
and built a block- the Dutch, Beaver-
house on the north wyck, or Beaver
point of Boyd's Isl- town, from the cir-
and, a little below cumstance that great
Albany ; and it may numbers of beavers
be said that in 1612 were found there.
Albany was founded, A fortification, call-
for in that year the ed Fort Orange, was
first permanent trad- built in 1623.[1] The
ing post was estab- town retained its
lished there.   Next original name until
to Jamestown, in 1664, when the
Virginia, it was the New Netherlands
earliest European (as the country upon
settlement within the Hudson was call-
the thirteen original ed) passed into the
colonies.   A tempo- hands of the En-
rary fort was erect- glish.   It then re-

HENDRICK HUDSON.[2]

ceived the name of Albany, one of the titles of James, duke of York, the brother of Charles
II., afterward King James II. of England.

The first permanent settlement that was made at Albany (the traders resorting thither
only in the autumn and winter) was in 1626, and from that time until 1736 many respectable Dutch families came over and established themselves there and in the vicinity.   Among
them occur the names of Quackenboss, Lansing, Bleecker, Van Ness, Pruyn, Van Wart,
Wendell, Van Eps, and Van Rensselaer, names familiar to the readers of our history, and
their descendants are numerous among us.   The first *stone* building, except the fort, was
erected at Albany in 1647, on which occasion " eight ankers" (one hundred and twenty-
eight gallons) of brandy were consumed.[3]   About this time the little village of Beaverwyck
was stockaded with strong wooden pickets or palisades, the remains of which were visible
until 1812.   The government was a military despotism, and so rigorous were the laws that
quite a number of settlers left it and established themselves upon the present site of Schenectady, about one hundred years since.   A small church was erected in 1655, and the Dutch
East India Company sent a bell and a pulpit for it, about the time when its first pastor,
Rev. Gideon Schaats, sailed for Beaverwyck.   It became too small for the congrega- 1657.
tion, and in 1715 a new and larger edifice was erected on its site.   This stood about ninety-
two years, in the open area formed by the angle of State, Market, and Court Streets.

Albany had become a considerable town when Kalm visited it in 1749.   He says the
people all spoke Dutch.   The houses stood with the gable ends toward the streets, and the
water gutters at the eaves, projecting far over the streets, were a great annoyance to the
people.   The cattle, having free range, kept the streets dirty.   The people were very social,

[1] Eight curious pieces of ordnance were mounted upon the ramparts of Fort Orange, called by the Dutch,
according to Vander Kempt, *stien-gestucken*, or stone pieces, because they were loaded with *stone* instead
of iron balls.   These cannon were formed of long stout iron bars laid longitudinally, and bound with iron
hoops   Their caliber was immense.   The fort does not seem to have been a very strong work, for in 1639
a complaint was made to the Dutch governor that the fort was in a state of miserable decay, and that the
" hogs had destroyed a part of it."

[2] This picture is copied from a painting said to be from life, now in the possession of the Corporation of
the city of New York, and hanging in the " Governor's Room," in the City Hall.   It was in the old Stadt
House, and was in existence in Governor Stuyvesant's time.

[3] Letter of the commissary, De la Montagnie, to the Dutch governor of New Amsterdam (New York).

and the spacious stoops, or porches, were always filled at evening, in summer, with neighbors mingling in chit-chat.   They knew nothing of stoves ; their chimneys were almost as
broad as their houses ; and the people made wampum, a kind of shell on strings, used as
money, to sell to Indians and traders.[1]   They were very cleanly in their houses ; were frugal in their diet, and integrity was a prevailing virtue.   Their servants were chiefly negroes.
In 1777, according to Dr. Thatcher (Military Journal, p. 91), Albany contained "three hundred houses, chiefly in the Gothic style, the gable ends to the streets."   He mentions the "ancient stone church," and also " a decent edifice called City Hall, which accommodates gen
erally their assembly and courts of justice."   It also had " a spacious hospital," erected during the French war.   It was incorporated a city in 1686, and was made the capital of the
state soon after the Revolution.

Albany was an important place, in a military point of view, from the close of the seventeenth century until the hostilities, then begun between the English and French colonies,
ceased in 1763.   It was the place where councils with the Indians were held, and whence
expeditions took their departure for the wilderness beyond.   It never became a prey to French
conquest, though often threatened.   In the depth of the winter of 1690 a party of two hundred Frenchmen and Canadians, and fifty Indians, chiefly Caughnawaga Mohawks, sent out
February 8,   by Frontenac, menaced Albany.   They fell upon Schenectady at midnight, mas-
1691.   sacred and made captive the inhabitants, and laid the town in ashes.   Sixty-
three persons were murdered and twenty-seven carried into captivity.   The church and
sixty-three houses were burned.   A few persons escaped to Albany, traveling almost twenty
miles in the snow, with no other covering than their night-clothes.   Twenty-five of them
lost their limbs in consequence of their being frozen on the way.   Schenectady, like Albany,
was stockaded, having two entrance gates.   These were forced open by the enemy, and the
first intimation the inhabitants had of danger was the bursting in of their doors.[2]   Informed
that Albany was strongly garrisoned, the marauders, thinking it not prudent to attack it,
turned their faces toward Canada with their prisoners and booty.   The settlement suffered
some during the French and Indian war, but it was rather too near the strong post of Albany to invite frequent visits from the enemy.   It is said that Schenectady was the principal seat of the Mohawks before the confederacy of the five Iroquois nations was formed.

One of the most prominent events that occurred at Albany, which has a remote connection with our Revolution, was the convention of colonial delegates held there in 1754.   For
a long time the necessity for a closer political union on the part of the English colonies had
been felt.   They had a common enemy in the French, who were making encroachments
upon every interior frontier, but the sectional feelings of the several colonies often prevented
that harmony of action in the raising of money and troops for the general service which
proper efficiency required.   It was also evident that the Indians, particularly the Six Nations of New York, were becoming alienated from the English, by the influence of French
emissaries among them, and a grand council, in which the several English colonies might
be represented, was thought not only expedient, but highly necessary.   Lord Holderness,

---

[1] Wampum is made of the thick and blue part of sea clam-shells.   The thin covering of this part being
split off, a hole is drilled in it, and the form is produced and the pieces made smooth by a grindstone.   The
form is that of the cylindrical glass beads called *bugles*.   When finished, they are strung upon small hempen
cords about a foot long.   In the manufacture of wampum, from six to ten strings are considered a day's
work.   A considerable quantity is manufactured at the present day in Bergen county, New Jersey.

[2] Walter Wilie, who was one of a party sent from Albany to Schenectady as soon as the intelligence
reached that place of the destruction of the town, wrote a ballad, in the style of Chevy Chase, in which the
circumstances are related in detail.   He says of his ballad, " The which I did compose last night in the
space of one hour, and am now writing, the morning of Friday, June 12th. 1690."   He closes it with,

" And here I end the long ballad,
The which you just have redde ;
I wish that it may stay on earth
Long after I am dead."

the English Secretary of State, accordingly addressed a circular letter to all the colonies, proposing a convention, at Albany, of committees from the several colonial assemblies, the chief design of which was proclaimed to be the renewal of treaties with the Six Nations. Seven of the colonies, namely, New York, Massachusetts, New Hampshire, Connecticut, Rhode Island, Pennsylvania, and Maryland, responded to the call, and the convention assembled at Albany, in the old City Hall, on the 19th of June, 1754.[1] James Delancy was chosen president of the convention. The chiefs of the Six Nations were in full attendance, their principal speaker being Hendrick, the sachem afterward killed near Lake George while in the service of the English. The proceedings were opened by a speech to the Indians from Delancy ; and while the treaty was in progress, the convention was invited, by the Massachusetts delegates, to consider whether the union of the colonies, for mutual defense, was not, under existing circumstances, desirable. The General Court of Massachusetts had empowered its representatives to enter into articles of union and confederation. The suggestion was favorably received, and a committee, consisting of one member from each colony, was appointed.[2] Several plans were proposed. Dr. Franklin, whose fertile mind had conceived the necessity of union, and matured a plan before he went to Albany, now offered an outline in writing, which was adopted in committee, and reported to the convention. The subject was debated " hand in hand," as Franklin observes, " with the Indian business daily," for twelve consecutive days, and finally the report, substantially as drawn by him, was adopted, the Connecticut delegates alone dissenting.[3] It was submitted to the Board of Trade, but that body did not approve of it or recommend it to the king, while the colonial assemblies were dissatisfied with it. " The assemblies did not adopt it," says Franklin, " as they all thought there was too much *prerogative* in it, and in England it was judged to have too much of the *democratic*." The Board of Trade had already proposed a plan of their own —a grand assembly of colonial governors and certain select members of their several councils, with power to draw on the British treasury, the sums thus drawn to be reimbursed by taxes imposed on the colonies by the British Parliament. This did not suit the colonists at all, and Massachusetts specially instructed her agent in England " to oppose every thing that shall have the remotest tendency to raise a revenue in America for any public uses or serv-

---

[1] The following are the names of the commissioners from the several states :
New York.—James Delancy, Joseph Murray, William Johnson, John Chambers, William Smith.
Massachusetts.—Samuel Welles, John Chandler, Thomas Hutchinson, Oliver Partridge, John Worthington.
New Hampshire.—Theodore Atkinson, Richard Wibird, Mesheck Weare, Henry Sherburne.
Connecticut.—William Pitkin, Roger Wolcott, Elisha Williams.
Rhode Island.—Stephen Hopkins, Martin Howard.
Pennsylvania.—John Penn, Benjamin Franklin, Richard Peters, Isaac Norris.
Maryland.—Benjamin Tasker,* Benjamin Barnes.†

[2] The committee consisted of Hutchinson of *Massachusetts*, Atkinson of *New Hampshire*, Pitkin of *Connecticut*, Hopkins of *Rhode Island*, Smith of *New York*, Franklin of *Pennsylvania*, and Tasker of *Maryland*.

[3] The plan proposed a grand council of forty-eight members—seven from Virginia, seven from Massachusetts, six from Pennsylvania, five from Connecticut, four each from New York, Maryland, and the two Carolinas, three from New Jersey, and two each from New Hampshire and Rhode Island. The number of forty-eight was to remain fixed, no colony to have more than seven nor less than two members ; but the apportionment to vary within those limits, with the rates of contribution. This council was to have the general management of civil and military affairs. It was to have control of the armies, the apportionment of men and money, and to enact general laws, in conformity with the British Constitution, and not in contravention of statutes passed by the imperial Parliament. It was to have for its head a president general, appointed by the crown, to possess a negative or veto power on all acts of the council, and to have, with the advice of the council, the appointment of all military officers and the entire management of Indian affairs. Civil officers were to be appointed by the council, with the consent of the president.—*Pitkin,* i., 143. It is remarkable how near this plan, submitted by Franklin, is the basis of our Federal Constitution. Coxe, of New Jersey, who was Speaker of the Assembly of that province, proposed a similar plan in his " Carolana" in 1722, and William Penn, seeing the advantage of union, made a similar proposition as early as 1700.— *Hildreth,* ii., 444.

---

* This name is differently spelled by different writers. Pitkin, in his text (vol. i., p. 142), writes it Trasker, and in the list of delegates in his appendix (429) it is Trasher.
† Williams, in his *Statesman's Manual,* has it Abraham instead of Benjamin. I have followed Pitkin.

ices of government." This was the first proposition to tax the colonies without their consent, and thus early we find Massachusetts raising her voice as fearlessly against it as she did twenty years afterward, when her boldness drew down upon her the vengeance of the British government.

During the Revolution, and particularly after the British took possession of New York city, Albany was the focus of revolutionary power in the state. There the Committee of Safety had its sittings ; and, after the destruction of the forts in the Highlands, and the burning of Esopus (Kingston), it was generally the head-quarters of the military and civil officers in the Northern Department. There the captive officers of Burgoyne's invading army were hospitably entertained by General Schuyler and his family at their spacious mansion, then "half a mile below the town." The house is still standing, at the head of Schuyler Street, a little west of South Pearl Street, upon an eminence some thirty feet high in front, and completely imbosomed in trees and shrubbery. Within it the Baroness Reidesel was entertained, and there occurred those events mentioned by her and Chastellux, which I have noticed in a preceding chapter (pages 91 and 92). It was the scene, also, of the attempted abduction of the general by the Tory, Waltemeyer, when he robbed the patriot of his plate in 1781, mentioned on page 223. There La Fayette, Steuben, Rochambeau, and other foreign officers of eminence were entertained, and there the noblest of the land, as well as distinguished travelers from abroad, were frequent guests during the life of the owner ; and its doors were opened as freely when the voice of poverty pleaded for assistance as when the great claimed hospitality and courtesy.

We arrived in New York on the morning of the 1st of September. The air was cool and bracing, the day was fine, and the lately-deserted streets and shops were thronged with mingled citizens and strangers plunged as deeply in the maze of business as if no forgetfulness of the leger and till had occurred while babbling brooks and shady groves wooed them to Nature's worship. There I rested a few days, preparatory to a visit to the beautiful valley

1777.

SCHUYLER'S MANSION.[1]

"On Susquehanna's side, fair Wyoming !"

---

[1] This view is from Schuyler Street. The edifice is of brick, having a closed octagonal porch or vestibule in front. It was built by Mrs. Schuyler while her husband was in England in 1760-1. The old family mansion, large and highly ornamented, in the Dutch style, stood nearly upon the site of the present City Hall, between State and Washington Streets. It was taken down in 1800.

CHAPTER XIV.

" The sultry summer past, September comes,
Soft twilight of the slow, declining year ;
All mildness, soothing loneliness, and peace ;
The fading season ere the falling come,
More sober than the buxom, blooming May,
And therefore less the favorite of the world,
But dearest month of all to pensive minds."

CARLOS WILCOX.

 N the morning of the 12th of September I left New York on my SECOND TOUR. My chief destination was Wyoming, after a visit to a few noteworthy places in New Jersey, of which Morristown was the first. I was in Newark just in time to be too late for the morning train for Morristown. Newark is beautiful and eligible in location, and a thriving city ; but it has only a few scraps of Revolutionary history, exclusively its own, for the entertainment of an inquirer. The village contained about one thousand inhabitants at that time. British, republicans, and Hessians were alternately billeted upon the people ; and, being on the line of travel from New York to Brunswick and Trenton, its monotony was often broken by the passage of troops. Political parties were nearly balanced at the commencement of the war, and, when the Declaration of Independence was put forth, many of the Loyalists left the place and went to New York, among whom was the pastor of the Protestant Episcopal Church of Newark. It suffered much during the war from the visitations of regular troops of both armies, and of marauders. When Washington fled toward the Delaware, in November, 1776, his army (three thousand in number) encamped there from the 22d to the 28th. On that day Cornwallis entered the town with a pursuing force. Both armies were quartered upon the inhabitants. Cornwallis left a strong guard there, which remained until after the battle of Princeton. Foraging parties and plunderers kept the inhabitants in a state of continual alarm. On the night of the 25th of January, 1780, a party of five hundred of the enemy went from New York to Newark on the ice, burned the academy,[1] carried off an active Whig named Hedden, and would doubtless have laid the town in ashes had not the light of a conflagration at Elizabethtown (the burning of the Presbyterian Church by another party, unknown to the first) alarmed them, and caused them to hasten back to New York. No other events of much general importance occurred there during the war. It seems to have been as famous in early times as now for its *cider*. Governor Carteret wrote, in a letter to the proprietors in 1682, " At Newark are made great quantities of cider, exceeding any we can have from New England, Rhode Island, or Long Island."

I left Newark for Morristown at two o'clock, by rail-road, through a beautifully-diversified region. The road passes above the upper verge of the sandy plains, through a very hilly country, and makes some broad curves in its way from Newark to Morristown, a distance, by the track, of about twenty-two miles. Springfield on the left and the Short Hills

---

[1] In that building the collegiate school, now the College of New Jersey, seated at Princeton, was held. while under the charge of the Rev. Aaron Burr, the father of the Vice-president of the United States of that name. This school was instituted at Elizabethtown by Jonathan Dickinson, in 1746. He died the following year, and the students were sent to Newark, and placed under the charge of Mr. Burr, who thus became the second president of the institution. It continued at Newark eight years, and was then removed to Princeton.

on the right, places of note in our revolutionary history, were pointed out as we sped rapidly by, and, before memory could fairly summon the events which made them famous, we were at the station at Morristown, a quarter of a mile eastward of the village green.   The town is pleasantly situated upon a table land, with steep slopes on two sides.   On the west is a high ridge called Kimble's Mountain, two hundred and fifty feet above the town, its summit commanding a magnificent prospect of the adjacent country, and considerably resorted to during the summer.   It was upon the southern slope of this mountain that the American army, under the immediate command of Washington, was encamped during the winter of 1779–80 ; and upon the same ridge (which terminates abruptly at the village), half a mile from the green, are the remains of Fort Nonsense.   It was nearly sunset when I ascended the hill, accompanied by Mr. Vogt, the editor of one of the village papers.   The embankments and ditches, and the remains of the block-houses of Fort Nonsense, are very prominent, and the form of the embryo fortification may be distinctly traced among the trees.   Its name was derived from the fact that all the labor bestowed upon it was intended merely to counteract the demoralizing effects of idleness.   The American army was comfortably *hutted*, and too remote and secure from the enemy to make camp duty at all active.   Washington foresaw the evil tendency of idleness, and discreetly ordered the construction of a fort upon a hill overlooking the town.   There was no intention to complete it, and when the winter encampment broke up in the spring the work was, of course, abandoned.

From the mountain we saw one of those gorgeous September sunsets so often seen in the Northern States, and so beautifully described by Wilcox :

> " The sky, without the shadow of a cloud,
> Throughout the west is kindled to a glow
> So bright and broad, it glares upon the eye,
> Not dazzling, but dilating, with calm force,
> Its power of vision to admit the whole.
> Below, 'tis all of richest orange dye ;
> Midway, the blushing of the mellow peach
> Paints not, but tinges the ethereal deep;
> And here, in this most lovely region, shines,
> With added loveliness, the evening star.
> Above, the fainter purple slowly fades,
> Till changed into the azure of mid-heaven."

As the warm glow in the west faded, the eastern sky was radiant with the light of the full moon that came up over the hills, and under it we made our way along the sinuous mountain path down to the village.   I spent the evening with the Honorable Gabriel Ford, who owns the fine mansion which was occupied by Washington as his head-quarters during the winter encampment there in 1779–80.   It belonged to Judge Ford's mother, then a widow, himself being a boy about fourteen years old.   His well-stored mind is still active, notwithstanding he is eighty-four years old, and he clearly remembers even the most trifling incidents of that encampment which came under his observation.   He entertained me until a late hour with anecdotes and facts of interest, and then kindly invited me to pass the night under his hospitable roof, remarking, " You shall sleep in the room which General Washington and his lady occupied."   That certainly was the proffer of a rare privilege, and I tarried till morning.   Before making further notes of a personal character, let us look at the history.

Morristown was twice the place of a winter encampment of the division of the American army under the personal command of Washington.   The first time was in 1777, after his brilliant achievements at Trenton, and the battle of Princeton.   When the fortieth and fifty-fifth British regiments, which Washington encountered in that battle, fled, he pursued them as far as Kingston, where he had the bridge taken up, and, turning short to the left, crossed the Millstone River twice, and arrived at Pluckemin the same evening.   It had been his intention to march to New Brunswick, to capture British stores deposited there ; but his troops were so exhausted, not having slept for thirty-six hours, and Cornwallis was so near, that he abandoned the design and advanced to Morristown, where he went into winter quarters.   He had achieved much, far more than the most sanguine patriot hoped for. At the very moment when his army appeared upon the verge of dissolution, and retreating from town to town, he struck a blow so full of strength that it paralyzed the enemy, broke up the British line of cantonments upon the Delaware, and màde Cornwallis turn his eyes back wistfully to more secure quarters at New York, under the wing of General Howe, the British commander-in-chief.   Nor did Washington sit down quietly at Morristown.   He had established cantonments at various points from Princeton on the right, under the control of General Putnam, to the Hudson Highlands on the left, at which post General Heath was still in command, having been left there when the American army fled from Fort Lee, on the Hudson, to the Delaware, the previous autumn.   He was in the midst of hills and a fertile country teeming with abundance, but he did not trust to the strong barriers of nature for his protection.   Weak and poorly clad as was his army, he sent out detachments to harass the British, and with such spirit were those expeditions conducted, that, on or before the 1st of March, not a British or Hessian soldier remained in the Jerseys, except at New Brunswick and Amboy.   Under the circumstances, it was a splendid triumph, and greatly inspirited the friends of the republican cause.   The martial spirit of the people seemed to revive, and it was thought that the thinned battalions of the army would be speedily replenished.   New courage was infused into the Continental Congress, the members of which, alarmed at the rapid approach of the British to Philadelphia, then the national metropolis, had fled to Baltimore, and held their sittings there.

The American army was encamped in log huts at Morristown, and Washington's headquarters were at the old Freeman Tavern, which stood on the north side of the village green.   In the Morris Hotel, a building then used as a commissary's store-house, the chief often participated in the rites of Free-masonry, in a room over the bar, which was reserved for a ball-room and for the meetings of the Masonic Lodge.   There he conferred the degrees of the Order upon his companions-in-arms, and his warm attachment to the institution lasted until his death.

Some writers assert that, toward the close of January, the small-pox broke out violently in the American camp, and that Washington resorted to a general inoculation of the army to stay its fatal progress.   As Dr. Thacher, who performed this service in the camp in the Highlands, opposite West Point, at a later period, does not mention the circumstance in his Journal, and as cotemporary writers are silent on the subject, it was reasonable to conclude that such an event did not occur at Morristown.   But Dr. Eneas Munson, one of Dr. Thacher's assistants, and still living in New Haven, has settled the question.   I wrote to him upon the subject, inquiring also whether *vaccination* was ever substituted for *inoculation* during the Revolution.   It was during the preceding year that Jenner, a young English surgeon, had made his famous discovery of the efficacy of *vaccination*.[1]   It had attracted the attention of Washington, for the soldiers of the Northern army had suffered terribly from the disease in Canada during the spring of 1776, and one of the most promising officers of the Continental army (General Thomas) had fallen a victim to the loathsome malady.   Dr. Munson kindly answered my letter, as follows, under date of November 1st, 1849: " In reply to your inquiries of the 30th ult., I can say that *vaccination* was not practiced

1777.

---

[1] Edward Jenner, who was born in 1749, had his attention turned to the subject of vaccination at about the beginning of 1776, by the circumstance of finding that those who had been affected by the cow-pox, or *kine-pox*, as it is popularly called, had become incapable of receiving the variolous infection.   Inoculation, or the insertion of the virus of the common small-pox, had long been practiced.   It was introduced into general notice by Lady Mary Wortley Montague in 1721, whose son was inoculated at Constantinople, and whose daughter was the first to undergo the operation in England.   It was reserved for Jenner to discover the efficacy and introduce the practice of vaccination, or the introduction of the virus of the cow-pox, more than fifty years afterward.   It was first introduced into the British capital in 1796, but met with great hostility on the part of the medical faculty.   The triumph of Jenner was finally complete, and his fame is world wide.   Oxford presented him with a diploma, the Royal Society admitted him as a member, and the Brit-ish Parliament voted him $100,000.

generally, nor at all, to my knowledge, in the American army of the Revolution. At Morristown there was a partial *inoculation*, but it was not general there. At the Highlands, opposite West Point, it (inoculation) was general, and I assisted in it professionally.[1] Vaccination was practiced by my father one year after the close of the war of the Revolution."[2] This is unquestionable authority.

When the British entered New Jersey, the proclamation of the brothers Howe, offering a free pardon to all rebels who should lay down their arms, and full and ample protection of person and property to those who should take an oath of allegiance to the British crown, was freely circulated.[3] This proclamation was received by the people while the American army was flying before the Britons, and general despondency was crushing every hope for the success of the patriot cause. Its effect was, therefore, powerful and instantaneous, and hundreds, whose sympathies were with the Americans, timid and hopeless, accepted the protection upon the prescribed terms. They generally remained in their houses while the belligerent armies were in motion. But they soon found their hopes cruelly disappointed, and those who should have been their protectors became their worst oppressors. The Hessians, in particular, being entirely mercenary, and influenced by no feelings of sympathy, plundered, burned, and destroyed every thing that came in their way, without discriminating between friend and foe. The people of all parties were insulted and abused in their own houses, their dwellings were rifled, their women were oftentimes ravished by the brutal soldiers, and neither smiling infancy nor decrepit age possessed immunity from their outrages. The British soldiery sometimes participated in these crimes, and upon the British government properly rested the guilt, for the Hessians were its hired fighting machines, hired contrary to the solemn protests and earnest negative pleadings of the best friends of England in its national legislature. But these enormities proved favorable to the republican cause. Those who had received *paper* protections regarded Sir William Howe as a perjured tool of oppression, and the loyalty of vast numbers of the disaffected and lukewarm, that burned so brightly when recording their oaths of allegiance, was suddenly extinguished, and their sad hearts, touched by the persuasions of self-interest, felt a glow of interested patriotism. Washington January 25, took advantage of this state of feeling, and issued a counter proclamation, com- 1777. manding all persons who had received protections from the British commissioners to repair to head-quarters, or to some general officer of the army, to deliver up such protections, and take an oath of allegiance to the United States. It nevertheless granted full liberty to all such as preferred " the interests and protection of Great Britain to the freedom and happiness of their country, forthwith to withdraw themselves and their families within the enemy's lines." The reasonable time of thirty days was allowed the inhabitants to comply with these requisitions, after which those who remained, and refused to give up their protections, were to be regarded and treated as adherents to the king and enemies of the United States.

---

[1] In his *Military Journal*, p. 250, Dr. Thacher, alluding to the inoculation in the Highlands, says, " All the soldiers, with the women and children, who have not had the small-pox, are now under inoculation. . . . . . . Of five hundred who have been inoculated here, four only have died." He mentions a fact of interest connected with the medical treatment of the patients. It was then customary to prepare the system for inoculation, by doses of calomel and jalap. An *extract of butternut*, made by boiling down the inner bark of the tree, was substituted, and found to be more efficacious and less dangerous than the mineral drug. Dr. Thacher considered it " a valuable acquisition to the materia medica."

[2] Dr. Munson's father was an eminent physician, and was for many years the President of the Medical Society of Connecticut. He was a native of New Haven, graduated at Yale College in 1753, and, having been a tutor, he was a chaplain in the army on Long Island in 1775. He died at New Haven in 1826, aged nearly ninety-two years. He was a practicing physician seventy years. Being a man of piety, he often administered medicine to the mind, by kneeling at the bed-side of his patients and commending them to God in prayer.

[3] General Sir William Howe, the commander-in-chief of the British forces in America, and his brother Richard, Earl Howe, the admiral of the fleet on our coast, were appointed by Parliament commissioners to negotiate for peace with the American Congress, or to prosecute the war, as events might determine. They issued a circular letter to all the royal governors, and a proclamation to the people, offering pardon and protection. This commission will be considered hereafter.

Notwithstanding Washington had been vested by Congress with the power of a military dictator, and the wisdom and equity of the proclamation were not questioned, the Legislature of New Jersey regarded it as an infringement upon state rights, that political stumbling-block in the progress of the Revolution ; and even members of the Continental Congress censured the commander-in-chief. The former claimed that each state possessed the exclusive power of requiring such an oath, and the latter deemed the oath absurd when the states were not legally confederated, and such a thing as "United States" did not exist. But Washington, conscious of the necessity and wisdom of his course, did not heed these foolish murmurs. His plan worked admirably, and hundreds flocked to the proper officers to give up their British protections. The state was purged of the most inimical Tories, and the ranks of the army were so rapidly filled by volunteers and new recruits, that, when the campaign opened in June, his force, which numbered about eight thousand men when he left his head-quarters at Morristown, toward the close of May, for Middlebrook (a strong position, twelve miles from the British camp at New Brunswick), had swelled to fourteen thousand. He had previously written to the republican governors of the several states, urging them to adopt prompt and efficient co-operative measures, by raising recruits and filling up the broken regiments. He also wrote stirring appeals to Congress, but that body, acting under powers undefined, and swayed by the jealousies of the several states represented therein, was tardy and inefficient in its action. He was obliged, in his public declarations, to magnify the strength of his army, in order to encourage the desponding people and awe the enemy ; and this justifiable deception made his appeals less effective, for the necessity did not seem so great as represented. These were trying circumstances for the commander-in-chief, but his stout heart did not despond, and his hopeful spirit saw brighter prospects in the future.

December 27, 1776.

WASHINGTON'S HEAD-QUARTERS AT MORRISTOWN.[1]

Morristown was again the head-quarters of Washington during the winter of 1779–80 The campaigns for the season had been fruitless of very favorable results to either party. The war had been carried on chiefly at the extreme south, and in the vicinity of New York city, at the north. Toward the close of the year, Sir Henry Clinton, who had succeeded Sir William Howe in the chief command, sailed from New York for Charleston, and the main body of the American army went into winter quarters near Morristown. They re-

---

[1] This view is from the forks of the road, directly in front of the mansion. The house is of brick, covered with planks, and painted white. The rooms are large and well finished, and it was a fine mansion for the times.

mained in tents until the 14th of February, when log huts were completed for their use. Strong detachments were stationed at West Point and other posts near the Hudson, and the American cavalry were cantoned in the western part of Connecticut. Washington, as we have noted, made his head-quarters at the residence of the widow of Colonel Jacob Ford, who had commanded a regiment of Morris county militia during Washington's retreat through New Jersey. It is situated nearly three fourths of a mile east of the village green, on the Newark and Morristown turnpike. The general and his suite occupied the whole of the large building, except two rooms on the eastern side of the main passage, which were reserved for Mrs. Ford and her family. The lower front room, on the left of the door, was his dining-room, and the apartment immediately over it was his sleeping-room while Mrs. Washington was at head-quarters. He had two log additions made to the house, one for a kitchen, on the east end, and the other, on the west end, was used as the offices of Washington, Hamilton, and Tilghman. In the meadow, a few rods southeast of the dwelling, about fifty log huts were erected for the accommodation of the life-guard, which consisted of two hundred and fifty men, under General William Colfax. In that meadow Count Pulaski exercised his legion of cavalry, and his dexterous movements were the wonder and emulation of the officers, many of whom were considerably injured in attempts to imitate his feats.[1]

The main body of the army, as we have noticed, was encamped upon the southern slope of Kimble's Mountain, beginning about two miles from head-quarters, and extending several miles westward. They were sufficiently near to be called into service instantly, if necessary. During the winter many false alarms occurred, which set the whole camp in motion. Sentinels were placed at intervals between the camp and head-quarters, and pickets were planted at distant points toward the Raritan and the Hudson, with intervening sentinels. Sometimes an alarm would begin by the firing of a gun at a remote point. This would be answered by discharges along the whole line of sentinels to the head-quarters and to the camp. The life-guard would immediately rush to the house of the general, barricade the doors, and throw up the windows. Five soldiers, with their muskets cocked and brought to a charge, were generally placed at each window, and there they would remain until the troops from the camp marched to head-quarters, and the cause of the alarm was ascertained. It was frequently the case that the attempts of some young suitor, who had been *sparking* until a late hour, and attempted to pass a sentinel without giving the countersign, caused the discharge of a musket, and the commotion in the camp. These occasions were very annoying to the ladies of the household, for both Mrs. Washington and Mrs. Ford were obliged to lie in bed, sometimes for hours, with their rooms full of soldiers, and the keen winter air from the open windows piercing through their drawn curtains.

The winter of 1780 was one of uncommon severity, and the troops suffered dreadfully from a lack of provisions, clothing, and shelter.[2] The snow fell in great quantities, and the

---

[1] It is related that, among other feats, that daring horseman would sometimes, while his steed was under full gallop, discharge his pistol, throw it in the air, catch it by the barrel, and then hurl it in front as if at an enemy. Without checking the speed of his horse, he would take one foot from the stirrup, and, bending over toward the ground, recover his pistol, and wheel into line with as much precision as if he had been engaged in nothing but the management of the animal.

[2] Dr. Thacher, in his "*Military Journal*," p. 181, says, "The sufferings of the poor soldiers can scarcely be described; while on duty they are unavoidably exposed to all the inclemency of storms and severe cold, at night they now have a bed of straw upon the ground, and a single blanket to each man; they are badly clad, and some are destitute of shoes. We have contrived a kind of stone chimney outside, and an opening at one end of our tents gives us the benefit of the fire within. The snow is now [January 6th, 1780] from four to six feet deep, which so obstructs the roads as to prevent our receiving a supply of provisions. For the last ten days we have received but two pounds of meat a man, and we are frequently for six or eight days entirely destitute of meat, and then as long without bread. The consequence is, the soldiers are so enfeebled from hunger and cold as to be almost unable to perform their military duty, or labor in constructing their huts. It is well known that General Washington experiences the greatest solicitude for the suffering of his army, and is sensible that they, in general, conduct with heroic patience and fortitude." In a private letter to a friend, Washington said, "We have had the virtue and patience of the army put to the severest trial. Sometimes it has been five or six days together without bread, at other times as many with-

OF THE REVOLUTION. 311

Sufferings and Fortitude of the Army.   Sterling's Secret Expedition.   Extreme Cold.   Chevalier Luzerne.   Death of Miralles.

channels of transportation for provisions being closed, Washington found it necessary to levy contributions upon the inhabitants in neighboring towns.   He applied to the magistrates for aid, apprehending some difficulty in the exercise of his power, but the people cheerfully complied with his requisitions, and the pressing wants of the army were supplied.   The chief was greatly annoyed by complaints of frequent thefts committed by his soldiers ; but such was the force of the first law of nature—self-preservation—when the commissariat was empty, that the severest punishments did not deter them from stealing sheep, hogs, and poultry. Repeated warnings were given to the army, in general orders and otherwise, against the marauding practice, yet many suffered the inflictions of the lash, and in some cases of robbery the death penalty was incurred.[1]

In January, Major-general Lord Sterling, with about fifteen hundred men in sleighs, set off at night on a secret expedition, ostensibly to procure provisions, but really to attack the enemy in their quarters on Staten Island.   They passed over on the ice from Elizabethtown about midnight.   It was a starry night, and the weather was extremely cold. The enemy had notice of their approach, and the object of the expedition was defeated. They captured some blankets and stores, and then returned to camp about daylight.   The snow was three feet deep on the ground, and so excessive was the cold, that five hundred of the party were more or less frozen.[2]   A retaliating movement was made soon afterward by the enemy.   A party attacked the American picket guard, and carried off a major and forty men.   Two or three enterprises of a like nature were all that varied the monotonous round of duties until the arrival at head-quarters of the Chevalier de Luzerne, the minister from the French government.   He succeeded M. Gerard, the first minister sent to the insurgent colonies from France, and had arrived in Philadelphia the September previous.   He was an accomplished and highly honorable gentleman, and was received with much regard by the commander-in-chief.   Don Juan de Miralles, a distinguished Spaniard, accompanied him ; and during their visits the military education which Baron Steuben, the celebrated tactician, had imparted to the army was several times displayed in reviews and difficult evolutions.   Luzerne remained some time at head-quarters, and a ball, which was attended by Washington and his lady, all his officers, Governor Livingston and his lady, and many other distinguished persons, was given in his honor, at the Morris Hotel.   Miralles, in the mean while, was seized, at head-quarters, with a pulmonic fever, and died on the 28th.   The religious ceremonies of the funeral were conducted by a Spanish Catholic priest, and the body was interred with great pomp in the common burying-ground near the church in Morristown.[3]   A guard of soldiers was placed near the grave, to

1780.

January 27, 1780.

April 19.

---

out meat, and once or twice two or three days at a time without either......... At one time the soldiers eat every kind of horse food but hay.   Buckwheat, common wheat, rye, and Indian corn composed the meal which made their bread.   As an army, they bore it with the most heroic patience ; but sufferings like these, accompanied by the want of clothes, blankets, &c., will produce frequent desertions in all armies ; and so it happened with us, though it did not excite a single mutiny."

[1] Dr. Thacher says (Military Journal, p. 182) that whipping with knotted cords, which often cut through the flesh at every blow, applied to the bare back, was the most common punishment.   The drummers and fifers were made the executioners, and it was the duty of the drum major to see that the chastisement was well performed.   The soldiers adopted a method which they said somewhat mitigated the anguish of the lash.   They put a leaden bullet between their teeth, and bit on it while the punishment was in progress. They would thus often receive fifty lashes without uttering a groan or hardly wincing.

[2] So intense was the cold that winter that New York Bay was thickly frozen over, and large bodies of troops, with heavy cannons, were transported on the ice, from New York city to Staten Island, a distance of nine miles.

[3] Dr. Thacher has left a record of the burial.   "The deceased," he says (page 188), "had been about one year a resident with our Congress, from the Spanish court.   The corpse was dressed in rich state, and exposed to public view, as is customary in Europe.   The coffin was most splendid and stately, lined throughout with fine cambric, and covered on the outside with rich black velvet, ornamented in a superb manner. The top of the coffin was removed, to display the pomp and grandeur with which the body was decorated. It was in a splendid full dress, consisting of a scarlet suit embroidered with rich gold lace, a three-cornered gold-laced hat, and a genteel cued wig, white silk stockings, large diamond shoe and knee buckles ; a profusion of diamond rings decorated the fingers, and from a superb gold watch, set with diamonds, several

prevent its desecration in search of hidden treasure, until the body could be removed to Phil
adelphia.

Morristown was the scene of the only serious and decided mutiny in the American army
during the Revolution. It occurred on the 1st of January, 1781. The whole movement,
when all the circumstances are taken into account, should not be execrated as a military rebellion, for, if ever there was just cause for men to lift up their strength against authority,
those mutineers possessed it. They had suffered every privation during a long, and, in many
respects, disastrous campaign, and not a ray of hope appeared in the gloomy future. Their
small stipend of money was paid irregularly, sometimes not at all, and generally in Continental bills, which were every day becoming more valueless. The frequent promises of
Congress had as frequently been unfulfilled, and the illiberal interpretations which the officers gave to the expressed terms of the enlistment of the soldiers produced great dissatisfaction. It was stipulated in those terms that they (the soldiers of the Pennsylvania line, who
revolted) should serve for three years, or during the war. The soldiers interpreted these
words to mean that they should be entitled to a discharge at the end of three years, or sooner,
if the war should terminate. This was doubtless the spirit of the agreement, but the officers read it otherwise, and claimed their service until the conclusion of the war, however
long that time might be. This was the principal cause of dissatisfaction, and a quarrel with
the officers led to open rebellion.

The Pennsylvania line at that time consisted of about two thousand men, and was stationed at the old camp-ground near Morristown. The three years' enlistment had expired
with most of them. A bounty of three half joes (about twenty-five dollars) had been offered
to new recruits, while the pay of these veterans of three years' service was not increased.
There was still due them their pay for twelve months, and nakedness and famine were their
daily companions. The officers had murmured somewhat, and the soldiers, hearing the
whisperings of complaint, took courage and spoke out boldly. They appointed a sergeant
major their commander, styling him major general; and in the evening of the 1st of
January, on a preconcerted signal, the whole line, except a part of three regiments,
paraded under arms without officers, marched to the magazines, supplied themselves with
provisions and ammunition, and, seizing six field pieces, took horses from General Wayne's
stables to transport them. The officers of the line collected those who had not joined the
insurgents, and endeavored to restore order, but some of the revolters fired, killing a Captain
Billings and wounding several others. The mutineers then ordered the minority to come over
to their side immediately, or suffer destruction by the bayonet, and the command was obeyed.

1781.

General Wayne was in command of the Pennsylvania troops, and was much beloved by
them. He exerted all his influence, by threats and persuasions, to bring them back to duty
until their grievances should be redressed. They would not listen to his remonstrances, and,
on his cocking his pistol, they presented their bayonets to his breast, saying, "We respect
and love you; often have you led us into the field of battle, but we are no longer under your
command; we warn you to be on your guard; if you fire your pistol, or attempt to enforce
your commands, we shall put you instantly to death." Wayne appealed to their patriotism; they pointed to the impositions of Congress. He reminded them of the strength their
conduct would give to the enemy; they exhibited their tattered garments and emaciated
forms. They avowed their willingness to support the cause of freedom, for it was dear to

rich seals were suspended. His excellency, General Washington, with several other general officers and members of Congress, attended the funeral solemnities, and walked as chief mourners. The other officers of the
army, and numerous respectable citizens, formed a splendid procession, extending about a mile. The pall-
bearers were six field officers, and the coffin was borne on the shoulders of four officers of artillery, in full
uniform. Minute guns were fired during the procession, which greatly increased the solemnity of the occasion." Dr. Thacher adds, "This gentleman is said to have been in possession of an immense fortune, and
has left to his three daughters, in Spain, one hundred thousand pounds sterling (half a million of dollars)
each. Here we behold the end of all earthly riches, pomp, and dignity. The ashes of Don Miralles mingle
with the remains of those who are clothed in humble shrouds, and whose career in life was marked by sordid poverty and wretchedness."

their hearts, if adequate provision could be made for their comfort, and declared their intention to march directly to Philadelphia, and demand from Congress a redress of their grievances. Finding threats and persuasion useless, Wayne resolved upon a line of policy that proved effective. He supplied them with provisions, and, with Colonels Stewart and Butler, officers whom they greatly respected, marched with them to prevent their depredating upon the inhabitants, and to draw from their leaders a statement of their claims and wishes. They reached Princeton on the 3d, and there a committee of sergeants submitted to Wayne, in writing, the following demands : First, a discharge for all those, without exception, who had served three years under their original engagements, and not received the increased bounty and re-enlisted for the war. Second, an immediate payment of all arrears of pay and clothing, both to those who should be discharged and those who should be retained. Third, the residue of their bounty, to put them on an equal footing with the recently enlisted, and future substantial pay to those who should remain in the service. General Wayne was not authorized to promise a full acquiescence in their demands, and further negotiations were referred to the civil authority of the state of Pennsylvania.

Intelligence of this revolt reached Washington and Sir Henry Clinton on the same day. The head-quarters of the former were at New Windsor, on the Hudson, just above the Highlands; of the latter, in the city of New York. Washington called January 3, 1781. a council of war, and, as the extent of the disaffection was unknown, it was determined to have one thousand men, drafts from the several regiments in the Highlands, held in readiness to march at a moment's notice, to quell the rebellion, if called upon. The council heartily approved of the course pursued by General Wayne; and Washington, whose patience had often been severely tried by the tardy movements of Congress, was willing to have that body aroused to activity by circumstances which should demand immediate and undivided attention. Sir Henry Clinton, mistaking the spirit of the mutineers, thought to gain great advantage by the event. He dispatched two emissaries, a British sergeant, and a New Jersey Tory named Ogden, to the insurgents, with the written offer that, on laying down their arms and marching to New York, they should receive their arrearages, and the amount of the depreciation of the Continental currency, in hard cash; that they should be well clothed, have a free pardon for all past offenses, and be taken under the protection of the British government; and that no military service should be required of them, unless voluntarily offered. Sir Henry requested them to appoint agents to treat with his and adjust the terms of a treaty; and, not doubting the success of his plans, he went to Staten Island himself, with a large body of troops, to act as circumstances might require. Like his masters at home, he entirely misapprehended the spirit and the incentives to action of the American soldiers. They were not mercenary—not soldiers by profession, fighting merely for hire. The protection of their homes, their wives and little ones, and the defense of holy principles, which their general intelligence understood and appreciated, formed the motive power and the bond of union of the American army, and the soldier's money stipend was the least attractive of all the inducements which urged him to take up arms. Yet, as it was necessary to his comfort, and even his existence, the want of it afforded a just pretext for the assumption of powers delegated to a few. The mutiny was a democratic movement; and, while the patriot felt justified in using his weapons to redress grievances, he still looked with horror upon the armed oppressors of his country, and regarded the act and stain of treason, *under any circumstances*, as worse than the infliction of death. Clinton's proposals were, therefore, rejected with disdain. " See, comrades," said one of the leaders, " he takes us for traitors. Let us show him that the American army can furnish but one Arnold, and that America has no truer friends than we." They immediately s..zed the emissaries, who, being delivered, with Clinton's papers, into the hands of Wayne,[1] were tried and executed as spies, and the reward which had been offered for their apprehension was

---

[1] When they were delivered up, the insurgents stipulated that they should not be executed until their own affairs were compromised, and, in case of failure, that the prisoners should be delivered when demanded.

tendered to the mutineers who seized them.　They sealed the pledge of their patriotism by nobly refusing it, saying, " Necessity wrung from us the act of demanding justice from Congress, but we desire no reward for doing our duty to our bleeding country !"

Congress appointed a commissioner to confer with the insurgent troops at Princeton.　The result was, a compliance with their just demands, and the disbanding of a large part of the Pennsylvania line for the winter, which was filled by new recruits in the spring.　Thus " terminated," as Thacher remarks, " a most unfortunate transaction, which might have been prevented had the just complaints of the army received proper attention in due season."

The wisdom of Washington's precaution in having a thousand men ready for sudden marching orders was soon demonstrated.　About the middle of January a portion of the New Jersey line, cantoned at Pompton,[1] followed the example of the Pennsylvania mutineers, and revolted.　The chief resolved not to temporize with them, and ordered a detachment of five hundred men, under Major-general Robert Howe, to reduce them to subordina-

1781.　tion.　Howe reached their encampment, after a fatiguing march of four days through deep snow, on the 27th of January.　His troops were well armed, and, parading them in line, he ordered the insurgents to appear in front of their huts, unarmed, within five minutes.　They hesitated, but a second order, as promptly given, made them obedient.　Three of the ringleaders were tried and condemned to be executed on the spot.　Two of them were shot, and their executioners were twelve of the most prominent of their guilty associates. The other one, less guilty, was pardoned.　Their punishment was quick and terrible, and never were men more humble and submissive than were the remainder of the insurgents. General Howe then addressed them effectively, by platoons, and ordered their officers, whom the mutineers had discarded, to resume their respective commands.　The hopes of Sir Henry Clinton had been again excited, but the emissary whom he sent to the revolted troops, hearing of the fate of the others, played false to his master, by going directly to Howe and delivering the papers into his hands.　Revolt, that followed so closely upon Arnold's treason a few months before, was thus effectually nipped in the bud.

I have said that I spent an evening at Morristown with Judge Ford, the proprietor of the head-quarters of Washington.　I look back upon the conversation of that evening with much pleasure, for the venerable octogenarian entertained me until a late hour with many pleasing anecdotes illustrative of the social condition of the army, and of the private character of the commander-in-chief.　As an example of Washington's careful attention to small matters, and his sense of justice, he mentioned the fact that, when he took up his residence with his (Ford's) mother, he made an inventory of all articles which were appropriated to his use during the winter.　When he withdrew in the spring, he inquired of Mrs. Ford whether every thing had been returned to her.　" All but one silver table-spoon," she answered.　He took note of it, and not long afterward she received from him a spoon bearing his initials, G. W.　That spoon is preserved as a precious relic in the family.　His tender care for the comfort of Mrs. Ford was often evinced.　On the occasions when the alarms, which we have noticed, were given, he always went to her room, drew the curtains close, and soothed her by assurances of safety.　And when her son, a lad of seventeen, was brought home from the Springfield battle, seriously wounded, his first care in the morning was to inquire after the sufferer.[2]　Washington's moral and religious feelings were never blunted by

---

[1] Pompton is a small town upon a fertile plain on the Pompton River, in Pequannock county.

[2] The wounded lad recovered, and afterward became a distinguished lawyer in a southern city.　A remarkable instance of Washington's remembrance of persons was related to me, as having occurred in connection with the wounded boy.　Many years afterward, when success had crowned his professional industry with wealth, and two daughters had nearly reached womanhood, he was returning south with them in his carriage, after a visit to his friends at Morristown, and stopped at Mount Vernon to see the retired chief. Reasonably concluding that Washington had forgotten the boy of 1780, he had procured a letter of introduction.　When he drove up to Mount Vernon, Washington was walking upon the piazza.　He went to the carriage, and as the servant of Mr. Ford threw open the door, and he stepped out, the general extended his hand, and said, with all the confidence of a recent acquaintance, " How do you do, Mr. Ford ?"　Eighteen years had elapsed since Washington had seen his face, and the boy had grown to mature manhood.

the influences of the camp. While at Morristown, he observed that gambling was frequent among the officers and soldiers. This growing vice he arrested by prohibition and threats of punishment, put forth in general orders. It is related that he called upon the Rev. Dr. Jones, the pastor of the Presbyterian Church of Morristown, on learning that the communion service was to be observed in his church on the following Sabbath, and inquired whether communicants of another denomination were permitted to join with them. The doctor replied, " Most certainly ; ours is not the Presbyterian's table, general, but the Lord's ; and hence we give the Lord's invitation to all his followers, of whatever name." " I am glad of it," said the general ; " that is as it ought to be ; but, as I was not quite sure of the fact, I thought I would ascertain it from yourself, as I propose to join with you on that occasion Though a member of the Church of England, I have no exclusive partialities." Washing ton was at the communion table on the following Sabbath.

General Schuyler was with Washington during the winter of 1780. His head-quarters

SCHUYLER'S HEAD-QUARTERS.

were at a house (still standing) a few rods eastward of the rail-way station. A portion of his family was with him, among whom was his daughter Elizabeth, a charming girl, about twenty-two years of age. Colonel Alexander Hamilton, who was Washington's aid and military secretary, was smitten with her charms and accomplishments, and his evenings were usually spent with her at her father's quarters. Mr. Ford, then a lad, was a favorite with Hamilton, and, by permission of the chief, the colonel would give him the countersign, so as to allow him to play at the village after the sentinels were posted for the night. On one occasion he was returning home, about nine o'clock in the evening, and had passed the sentinel, when he recognized the voice of Hamilton in a reply to

the soldier's demand of " Who comes there ?" He stepped aside, and waited for the colonel to accompany him to the house. Hamilton came up to the point of the presented bayonet of the sentinel to give the countersign, but he had quite forgotten it. " He had spent the evening," said Judge Ford, who related the anecdote to me, " with Miss Schuyler, and thoughts of her undoubtedly expelled the countersign from his head." The soldier lover was embarrassed, and the sentinel, who knew him well, was stern in the performance of his duty. Hamilton pressed his hand upon his forehead, and tried hard to summon the cabalistic words from their hiding-place, but, like the faithful sentinel, they were immovable. Just then he recognized young Ford in the gloom. " Ay, Master Ford, is that you ?" he said, in an undertone ; and, stepping aside, he called the lad to him, drew his ear to his mouth, and whispered, " Give me the countersign." He did so, and Hamilton, stepping in front of the soldier, delivered it. The sentinel, seeing the movement, and believing that his superior was testing his fidelity, kept his bayonet unmoved. " I have given you the countersign ; why do you not shoulder your musket ?" asked Hamilton. " Will that do, colonel ?" asked the soldier, in reply. " It will for this time," said Hamilton ; " let me pass." The soldier reluctantly obeyed the illegal command, and Hamilton and his young companion reached head-quarters without further difficulty. Colonel Hamilton afterward married Miss Schuyler. She still survives him (1849), and at the age of ninety-two years is the attractive center of a circle of devoted friends at Washington city, her present place of residence.

I passed the night under the hospitable roof of Judge Ford, and in the room which Washington and his lady had occupied. The carpet upon the floor, dark and of a rich pattern, is the same that was pressed by the feet of the venerated chief nearly seventy years ago ; and in an apartment below were a looking-glass, secretary, and book-case that formed a portion of the furniture of the house at that time.[1] The room fronts south, and, the sky being

[1] Since my interesting visit, Judge Ford has been taken from among the living, and these relics will

September 12, perfectly clear, I had a fine view, from the window, of an almost total eclipse
1848.   of the moon, which occurred at about midnight. As from that interesting observatory I watched the progress of the obscuration, and then the gradual enlightenment
of the satellite, it appeared to me a most significant emblem of the political condition of
America, and the cause of the patriots, at the time when, from the same window, Washington, with anxious eye, had doubtless gazed upon the same moon in its silent path-way among
the stars. It was the gloomiest period of the war. For many months the bright prospects
of the patriots were passing deeper and deeper within the penumbra of British power and oppression, and, at the beginning of 1780. only a faint curve of light was seen upon the disk
of hope ; the eclipse was almost total. *Financial embarrassment* was the chief bane of the
patriots, and the expected antidote of rebellion for the Loyalists and the king. Let us here
take a brief view of the financial affairs of the Revolutionary government.

When the Continental army was organized, in June, 1775, and other methods of defense
were adopted by the General Congress, the necessity for providing pecuniary means for de-
fraying the expenses, demanded and received the most serious attention of the delegates. The
colonies, deprived, in a great measure, of all commercial intercourse with other parts of the
world, by the unwise and oppressive policy of the mother country, a paper medium seemed
to be their only resource. It was a blessing at the beginning, but proved a curse in the end.
To place it upon a footing that should command the public confidence, and to secure it from
depreciation, was important and difficult. The New York Convention, foreseeing the necessity of such a measure, had already considered the subject, and a committee of that body had
reported suggestions a few weeks previously. They proposed three distinct modes of issuing
paper money. First, that each colony should issue, for itself, the sum which might be appropriated to it by Congress. Second, that the united colonies should issue the whole sum
necessary, and each colony become bound to sink its proportionable part ; and, third, that
Congress should issue the whole sum, every colony be bound to discharge its proportion, and
the united colonies be obliged to pay that part which any colony should fail to discharge.
The convention preferred the last mode, as affording higher security to those who should receive the paper, and, of consequence, as likely to obtain more ready, general, and confidential
circulation. It was also believed that it would be an additional bond of union to the associated colonies.[1]

The Continental Congress adopted, substantially, the last proposition, and, in the course
of the session of 1775, three millions of dollars were issued in bills of credit, and the faith
of the confederated colonies was pledged for their redemption.[2] This sum was appropriated

doubtless lose their value, by being separated and distributed among the family. I have preserved drawings of the articles here named. Judge Ford expressed his surprise that the mirror was not demolished, for
the room in which it hung was occupied, at one time, by some of the subalterns of the Pennsylvania line,
who were sons of some of the leading men of that state—gentlemen by birth, but rowdies in practice.
They injured the room very much by their nightly carousals, but the mirror escaped their rough treatment.

[1] Pitkin, i., 347. Records of the New York Convention.

[2] The resolution providing for the first emission of bills was adopted on the 22d of June, 1775, and was
as follows : "*Resolved*, That a sum not exceeding two millions of Spanish milled dollars be emitted by the
Congress in bills of credit, for the defense of America." On the next day the committee appointed for the
occasion reported and offered resolutions (which were adopted) as follows : "*Resolved*, That the number and
denomination of the bills to be emitted be as follows :

49,000	bills of	8	dollars each,	$392,000
49,000	"	7	"	343,000
49,000	"	6	"	294,000
49,000	"	5	"	245,000
49,000	"	4	"	196,000
49,000	"	3	"	147,000
49,000	"	2	"	98,000
49,000	"	1	"	49,000
11,800	"	20	"	236,000
Total, 403,800				$2,000,000

OF THE REVOLUTION. 317

Continental Paper Money.　　Form of the Bills.　　Devices and Mottoes.　　Paul Revere and cotemporary Engravers.

among the colonies according to the supposed number of the inhabitants, including negroes and mulattoes, and each colony was to pay its proportion, in four equal annual payments, the

FAC-SIMILE OF THE CONTINENTAL BILLS.[1]

first by the last of November, 1779, and the fourth by the last of November, 1782. The several Colonial Conventions were to provide, by taxes, for sinking their proportion of the bills, and the bills themselves were to be received in payment for such taxes. Two general treasurers were appointed, and it was recommended to each colony to appoint a treasurer. The amount of the first emission was two millions of dollars.

"*Resolved*, That the form of the bills be as follows :

CONTINENTAL CURRENCY.

No. ——　　　　　　　　　　　　　　　　　　　　—— *Dollars.*

This bill entitles the bearer to receive —— Spanish milled dollars, or the value thereof in gold and silver, according to the resolutions of the Congress, held at Philadelphia on the tenth day of May, A.D. 1775.

"*Resolved*, That Mr. J. Adams, Mr. J. Rutledge, Mr. Duane, ·Dr. Franklin, and Mr. Wilson be a committee to get proper plates engraved, to provide paper, and to agree with printers to print the above bills."*

[1] The paper on which these bills were printed was quite thick, and the enemy called it " the *pasteboard* money of the rebels." The vignettes were generally, both in device and motto, significant. The one most prominent in the engraving represents a beaver in the slow but sure process of cutting down a tree with its teeth. The motto, " PERSEVERANDO—*by Perseverance*," said to the colonists, " Persist, and you will be successful." I will notice a few other devices and mottoes of bills which I have seen. A globe, with the motto, in Latin, " THE LORD REIGNS; LET THE EARTH REJOICE." A candlestick with thirteen branches and burners, denoting the number of states; motto, " ONE FIRE, AND TO THE SAME PURPOSE." A thorn-bush with a hand grasping it; motto, " SUSTAIN OR ABSTAIN." A circular chain bearing on each link the name of a state, an emblem of union; motto, " WE ARE ONE." I have in my possession a coin, made of some composition resembling German silver of the present day (of which the following is a fac-simile the proper

* The plates were engraved on copper by Paul Revere, of Boston. Himself, Nathaniel Hurd, of the same city, Amos Doolittle, of New Haven, and an Englishman named Smithers, in Philadelphia, were the only engravers in America at that time. Hurd engraved as early as 1760. Revere began a little later. In 1766 he engraved a picture emblematic of the repeal of the Stamp Act. This, and a caricature called The Seventeen Rescinders, were very popular, and had an extensive sale. He engraved and published a print in 1770, representing the "Boston Massacre," and in 1774 he engraved another of a similar size, representing the landing of the British troops in Boston. In 1775 he engraved the plates, made the press, and printed the bills of the paper money ordered by the Provincial Congress of Massachusetts. Doolittle was at Lexington and Concord, and made drawings and engravings of the skirmishes at those places. The sketches were made on the morning after the engagements, and were engraved during the summer of 1775. Mr. Doolittle assisted in re-engraving the battle of Lexington on a smaller scale, in 1832, forty-three years afterward, for Barber's "History and Antiquities of New Haven." A copy of it, by permission, is inserted in this work.

1775.   On the 25th of July the Continental Congress ordered the issuing of one million of dollars more,[1] and from time to time new emissions were authorized, to meet the demands upon the treasury, until, at the beginning of 1780, the enormous sum of two hundred millions of dollars had been issued, no part of which had been redeemed.   While the amount of the issues was small, the credit of the bills was good ; but when new emissions took place, and no adequate measures for redemption were exhibited, the people became suspicious of those frail representatives of money, and their value began to depreciate.   This effect did not occur until eighteen months from the time of the first emission had elapsed. Twenty millions of the Continental bills were then in circulation, besides a large amount of local issues by the several states.   It was now perceived that depreciation was inevitable, and Congress proposed, as a substitute for further issues, a loan of five millions, at an interest of four per cent.   A lottery was also authorized, designed to raise a like sum on loan, the prizes being payable in loan office certificates.   These offices were opened in all the states ; the rate of interest was raised from four to six per cent., but the loans came in very slowly.   The treasury ran low, the loan offices were overdrawn by the commissaries' drafts, the issue of bills was reluctantly recommenced, and ten additional millions were speedily authorized.   During the year 1778 sixty millions and a half were added to the issues already made.   The commissioners in France (see page 86) had been instructed to borrow money there, but as yet they had been unsuccessful.

Various plans were proposed at different times to sink those issues of bills of credit, but none could be put into efficient practical operation.   The several states issued paper money independently of the Continental Congress ; and the Loyalists, aided by Sir Henry Clinton, in the autumn of 1778 sent out large quantities of counterfeits of the Continental emissions of May 20th, 1777, and April 11th, 1778, and scattered them as widely among the people as their means would allow.[2]   Under these circumstances, Congress felt the necessity of making an extraordinary effort to sustain the declining credit of the bills, by making some provision for their actual redemption.   On the 2d of January, 1779, it was "*Resolved*, That the United States be called on to pay in their respective quotas of fifteen millions of dollars for the year 1779, and of six millions of dollars annually for eighteen years from and after the year 1779, as a fund for sinking the emissions and loans of the United States to the 31st of December, 1778, inclusive."   It was provided that any bills emitted by order of Congress prior to 1780, and no others, should be received in payment of those quotas.   A period of five months was given for taking out of circulation the emissions which had been counterfeited, during which time they were to be received into the public treasury in pay-

---

size), bearing the same device on one side.   On a three dollar note is a device representing a stork struggling with an eagle—the feeble colonies warring with strong Great Britain; motto, "THE RESULT IS UNCERTAIN." This bill is dated eighteen days after the adoption of the Declaration of Independence. A majestic oak-tree; motto, "I SHALL FLOURISH THROUGH AGES OF AGES." A hand planting a young tree; motto, "FOR POSTERITY." A boar encountering a spear; motto, "DEATH, OR LIFE WITH DECENCY." A harp, denoting harmony; motto, "LARGE THINGS ARE CONSONANT WITH SMALL ONES." A figure of Justice; motto, "THE WILL OF JUSTICE."

FAC-SIMILE OF THE FIRST MONEY COINED BY THE UNITED STATES.

[1] As the signing of so many bills would require more time than the members could spare from public duties, Congress appointed twenty-eight gentlemen to perform the duty, allowing each one dollar and thirty-three cents for every thousand bills signed and numbered by him.   It was necessary for each bill to have the signature of two of them.   [2] See page 662, Vol. II.

ment of debts and taxes, and also into the Continental loan offices, either on loan or to be exchanged for other bills of a new tenor, bearing interest at five per cent., and redeemable in specie within six years. The old bills thus called in were to be destroyed.[1]

This effort, like its predecessors, was unsuccessful. Prices rose as the money sank in value, and every branch of trade was deranged. In several states laws limiting prices were still in force, and the rapid depreciation of the bills threw all contracts into confusion. The amount in circulation on the 1st of September, 1779, was a hundred and sixty millions. Congress resolved that the issues should not exceed two hundred millions in the whole. The loans prior to the 1st of August, 1778, the interest of which was payable in bills on France, were seven millions and a half. The loans contracted since were more than twenty-six millions. The debt abroad was estimated at four millions. Only three millions out of the sixty millions of paper dollars already called for from the states had been paid into the public treasury.

Congress was powerless to stay the downward tendency of the paper currency. It continued to depreciate and prices to rise. Early in 1780, forty paper dollars were worth only one in specie.[2] The commissaries found it extremely difficult to purchase supplies for the army, for the people refused to exchange their articles for the almost worthless paper. Direct taxes had been unsuccessfully tried to replenish the treasury, and, as supplies could not be obtained, a speedy dissolution of the army and abandonment of the rebellion seemed inevitable.

Congress was obliged to open new resources for the supply of the army, and required each state to furnish a certain quantity of beef, pork, flour, corn, forage, and other articles, which were to be deposited in such places as the commander-in-chief should determine. The states were to be credited for the amount at a fixed valuation in specie. This scheme was utterly

---

[1] Journals of Congress, vol. i., p. 5.

[2] The following bill of items is preserved, and illustrates the value of the Continental bills in 1781 :

CAPTAIN A. M'LANE,*

Bo't of W. NICHOLLS,

January 5th, 1781.

1 pair boots	$600
6¾ yds. calico, at 85 ds.	752
6 yds. chintz, at 150 ds.	900
4½ yds. moreen, at 100 ds.	450
4 hdkfs., at 100 ds.	400
8 yds. quality binding, 4 ds.	32
1 skein of silk	10
	$3,144

If paid in specie.......... £18 10s.

Received payment in full,

For WM. NICHOLLS.

JONA. JONES.

The following scale of depreciation is also preserved :

Value of $100 in Specie in Continental Money.

	1777.	1778.	1779.	1780.	1781.
January	$105	$325	$742	$2934	$7400
February	107	350	868	3322	7500
March	109	370	1000	3736	0000
April	112	400	1104	4000	——
May	115	400	1215	4600	——
June	120	400	1342	6400	——
July	125	425	1477	8900	——
August	150	450	1630	7000	——
September	175	475	1800	7100	——
October	275	500	2030	7200	——
November	300	545	2308	7300	——
December	310	634	2593	7400	Nothing.

---

* Captain M'Lane was the father of the late Secretary of the Treasury.

impracticable, from the want of authority to enforce the demands, and the distance of several states from the army, and Congress speedily abandoned it.   The several states were then recommended by Congress to pass laws making paper money a legal tender, at its nominal value, for the discharge of debts which had been contracted to be paid in hard cash.   Such laws were enacted, and many dishonest debtors took advantage of them.   Although the bills were passing at the rate of twenty for one, they were made a lawful tender, and debts were discharged at a cheap rate.   It was one of the most unwise and unjust acts committed by Congress during the war.   The honest and simple were defrauded, and the rogues were immense gainers.[1]   The people justly raised a great clamor, while the friends of the king greatly rejoiced in seeing the growth of what they deemed the canker-worm in the seed of rebellion.[2]

Among the most prominent evils arising from the rapid depreciation of the paper was a spirit of speculation and fraud, which excited unfounded jealousies and suspicions.   The

---

[1] Washington opposed the measure from the beginning as iniquitous, unjust, and fraught with the direst evils.   He was a considerable loser by it.   While at Morristown, a respectable man in the army was very assiduous in his attentions to the chief, and they were generally reciprocated.   This man paid his debts in the depreciated currency, under the law, and the fact became known to Washington.   Some time afterward the man called at head-quarters, but the general hardly noticed him.   This coldness was observed by the officers, and La Fayette remarked, " General, this man seems much devoted to you, and yet you have scarcely noticed him."   Washington replied, smiling, "I know I have not been cordial; I tried hard to be civil, and attempted to speak to him two or three times, but that Continental money stopped my mouth."

[2] Rev. Charles Inglis, who was rector of Trinity Church, in New York, from 1777 until 1782, and, after the peace, was made Lord Bishop of Nova Scotia, in a letter to Joseph Galloway, the great Pennsylvania Loyalist, then in London, thus writes, under date of December 12th, 1778, in reference to the immense issues and the depreciation of the bills of credit: " The fee simple of the thirteen *United States* is not equal to this sum, which is still increasing.   I therefore think it utterly impossible to support the credit of this money; and were there nothing else, *this would be sufficient to destroy the rebellion,* if Britain would hold the places she now possesses, and keep a moderate number of cruisers on the coast.   The mode of securing French debts, by which the colonies became mortgaged for the fripperies of every French peddler, is another embarrassing article on this head, which must prove ruinous to America."   Daniel Coxe, a member of the king's council of New Jersey, and a refugee in New York, writing to Galloway, under date of February 14th, 1779, says, " The *current* depreciation of their money now at Philadelphia is fifteen for one; and tho' there are *clubs* and *private* associations endeavoring to support its credit, nothing will do, nor can any thing, in my opinion, now save 'em on this point but a foreign loan,·and which, though they affect otherwise, I think they can not negotiate any where in Europe, unless all the moneyed nations are turned fools; and if they can not command a loan, and are prevented from all remittances and trade southward, they must sink, never again, I hope, to rise....... In short, they never were so wretched and near destruction as at this moment, and, unless some unforeseen event takes place in their favor soon, I firmly expect the next summer must end their independence and greatness...... For God's sake, then, encourage every degree of spirit and exertion all you can, and quickly; a good push, and they go to the wall infallibly."   Such was the tenor of the letters sent to England by the Loyalists from 1778 until 1781.   The financial embarrassments of Congress gave Loyalists and friends of government strong hopes that it would accomplish what British arms had failed to do.   It may be here remarked that many of the letters which passed between the Loyalists here and their friends abroad were written in cipher, so that, should they fall into the hands of the patriots, they might not be read, to the disadvantage of the writers and

CIPHER ALPHABET.

CLINTON   HAS   SENT   A   SECRET   EXPEDITION   UP

THE   HUDSON   TO   INTERCEPT   WASHINGTON.

FAC-SIMILE OF CIPHER WRITING.

their cause.   I here give, for the gratification of the curious, an alphabetical key, and a fac-simile or two lines of the cipher writing, copied from one of the letters of a distinguished Tory, together with the interpretation.

rapid rise in prices was unjustly attributed to extortion on the part of public officers, and even General Greene, who acted as quarter-master general, was accused of enriching himself at the public expense, because he received for his salary a per centage on all moneys disbursed, and the depreciation made the nominal amount vast. Individual speculators and monopolizers were the extortioners and the oppressors of the people, and of them Washington said, in a letter to President Reed, " I would to God that some of the more atrocious in each state were hung in gibbets upon a gallows four times as high as the one prepared for Haman." It was remarked, " that while the honest and patriotic were impoverished, rogues and Tories were fast growing rich."

Toward the close of the summer of 1779, the country was greatly agitated by the existing financial embarrassments. Meetings were held in the chief cities on the subject. In Philadelphia, party feelings, growing out of the currency question, became so strong and decided that a riot took place under the very eyes of Congress. A committee had undertaken to regulate the prices of flour, rum, sugar, molasses, coffee, salt, and other articles of general use. Robert Morris and other leading merchants refused to conform to the regulation. Wilson, Clymer, and Mifflin, with their friends, were threatened with banishment to New York, as abettors and defenders of the Tories. They armed themselves, and repaired to _{October 4,} Wilson's house. A mob, with fire-arms and two cannons, approached. Some ^{1779.} shots were fired, and one of the defenders of the house was killed. A man and a boy of the mob were also killed. The mob were about to force the door, when Reed, the president of Congress, appeared with some cavalry, and partially restored order, but it was necessary for the citizens to turn out and patrol the streets. It was several days before quiet was restored. In the midst of this general excitement a convention of the five Eastern States _{October 20,} was held at Hartford, and Congress, unable longer to disguise the fact that its ^{1779.} bills of credit were permanently depreciating, approved of, and recommended, a plan elaborated by that convention, to regulate prices on the basis of twenty paper dollars for one of specie. This measure partially quieted the public mind. Before the end of the year the two hundred millions were emitted, and the press was stopped.[1] At that time the depreciation stood thirty for one, and was constantly increasing. The diversion of labor from agricultural and other industrial pursuits, the destruction of grain by the belligerent forces in various parts of the country, combined with the embarrassed state of the finances of government, which we have briefly considered, threatened famine and general bankruptcy; and during the winter and spring of 1780, when Washington had his quarters at Morristown, the hope of the patriot was suffering an almost total eclipse; it was the gloomiest period of the Revolution. The financial operations which subsequently occurred will be noticed hereafter, such as long drafts on the United States commissioners abroad, and foreign loans.

We have made a wide but necessary digression in turning aside to view the financial affairs of the patriots at the period under consideration. Let us resume our journey and historic annotations.

I left Morristown for Springfield in the early morning train. The air was _{September 13,} cool and bracing, and I had a pleasant walk of about a mile from the station, ^{1848.} at the foot of the Short Hills, to the pretty village lying in the bosom of a fertile plain near the banks of the Rahway River. The trees upon the surrounding hills were beginning to assume the variegated livery of autumn, not from the effects of frosts, but of a long drought, yet on the plain every thing was as green as in June, except the ripening maize. I sought for the " oldest inhabitant," and found him in the person of the venerable Gilbert Edwards, who was a half-grown boy at the time of the battle of Springfield, and sold apples to the American soldiers when they came down from the Short Hills to oppose the invasion of the enemy under Knyphausen, the German general.[2] He kindly accompanied me to the place

---

[1] Pitkin, Marshall, Ramsay, Gordon, Sparks, Hildreth.

[2] General, the Baron Knyphausen, was a native of Alsace, then one of the Rhenish provinces. His father was a colonel in the German regiment of Dittforth, in the service of John, Duke of Marlborough. The general was bred a soldier, and served under Frederic the First, father of Frederic the Great of Prussia. The

322   PICTORIAL FIELD-BOOK

| Battle-ground at Springfield. | Invasion by General Knyphausen. | Clinton's Designs. | Plan of the Springfield Battle. |

where the principal engagement occurred, which is on the right of the present turnpike leading from Springfield to Elizabethtown, and a few rods westward of the Rahway.   Nothing
now remains upon the spot to indicate military operations, for no works were thrown up on
the occasion.   The battle was the result of an unexpected invasion.   The knoll on which

the Americans were posted, then covered with apple-trees, is
now bare, only a few stumps remaining ; but on the eastern
slope a few of the trees are left, venerable in form and feature,
and venerated for their associations.   One of them is pictured
in the engraving.   It bears several scars of wounds inflicted
by the cannon-balls of the approaching enemy.   They are "honorable scars," and I bespeak for the veteran a perpetual pension
of respect.

On the 6th of June, 1780, General Knyphausen, then in temporary command of the British troops in New York during the
absence of Sir Henry Clin-
ton at the south, dispatch-
ed Brigadier-general Mathews from Staten Island with
about five thousand troops, who landed at Elizabethtown Point.   He had been informed that the American army at Morristown was much dissatisfied, and
ripe for mutiny and treason, and that the people of New
Jersey were ready to join the royal standard as soon as
ample protection should be guarantied them.   Influenced by these opinions, Knyphausen ordered Mathews
to march toward Morristown, but the annoyances which
he met with on the way soon undeceived him.   He
burned the village of Connecticut Farms, and advanced
on Springfield, but, being informed that Washington
had sent a force to oppose him, he wheeled and returned to Elizabethtown.   Many of his soldiers were cut
off during the recession, by small parties of Jerseymen
concealed behind fences, rocks, and bushes.   On reaching Elizabethtown Point, he intrenched his forces within the old works thrown up there by the Americans,
where they remained about a fortnight.

In the mean while, General Clinton arrived from the

PLAN OF THE BATTLE AT SPRINGFIELD.[1]

south, and determined to carry out the plan arranged by Knyphausen, to capture the stores
at Morristown, and, if possible, draw Washington out from his strong position among the
Short Hills, into a general engagement.   He also took pains to mislead Washington, by em-

twelve thousand German troops hired by the English government, for service in America, were placed under his command, and the Hessians were led by the Baron de Reidesel.   He arrived with his troops, under
convoy of Admiral Lord Howe, in June, 1776, and was engaged in the battle of Long Island in August following.   He was also in the battle of Brandywine, and commanded an expedition to Springfield, New Jersey.   For some months during the absence of Sir Henry Clinton at the south, Knyphausen was in command
of the city of New York.   He was about sixty years of age, possessed of a fine figure, and was remarkably amiable and simple-minded.   La Fayette used to tell an anecdote concerning him, on the authority of
British officers.   The passage to America was very long, and one night, while playing whist in the cabin,
Knyphausen suddenly turned to the captain and said, with an air of much sincerity, "Captain, ain't we hab
sailed past America?"   He died on the frontiers of Germany toward the close of the last century.

[1] EXPLANATION OF THE MAP.—The stream with branches, and running in a southerly direction, is the
Rahway River ; *a* is the house (still standing) of Mrs. Mathews, near which the enemy formed for battle ;
b, the site of *Byram's Tavern*, at the foot of the first range of hills ; *c*, the Springfield and Elizabethtown
turnpike ; *d*, the Vauxhall Road ; *e*, the first position of the brigades of Stark and Maxwell, near the mill,
and north of the rail-road ; *f*, Shrieve's regiment at the second bridge ; *g*, the mill ; *h*, post of the Americans, on the hills in the rear of *Byram's Tavern*.   The other localities are printed on the map.

OF THE REVOLUTION. 323

Washington deceived by Clinton.   Second Invasion under Knyphausen.   Disposition of opposing Troops.   The Battle.

barking troops in transports on the Hudson, as if an expedition was intended against West Point. Washington *was* deceived by this movement, and, with a considerable force, marched toward the Highlands, leaving Major-general Greene in command at Springfield. Clinton, perceiving the success of his stratagem, crossed over to Elizabethtown, with Knyphausen and additional troops, and at break of day on the 23d the whole army, consisting of about five thousand infantry, a considerable body of cavalry, and from fifteen to twenty pieces of artillery, advanced toward Springfield. They moved in two columns, one on the main road (the present turnpike) leading to Springfield, the other on the Vauxhall Road, leading to the principal pass among the Short Hills, a series of high ridges at the head of the Springfield plains. The Americans were under the immediate command of Greene. The right column of the enemy, on the Vauxhall Road, was opposed by Major Henry Lee with his cavalry, and some pickets under Captain Walker, and the left was confronted by Colonel Dayton, of the New Jersey line.[1] The remainder of the American troops had been posted upon the roads leading to the different passes over the mountains, and it was with considerable difficulty that they were collected in force at Springfield to oppose the enemy concentrating there. The latter, after maneuvering to gain the flanks of the Americans, formed upon a gentle eminence on the eastern side of the Rahway, near the

June, 1780.

house of Mrs. Mathews, which is still standing. Colonel Angell, with his regiment, was posted in the orchard upon the knoll west of the stream, with a single field piece under the charge of Captain Littell, to defend the bridge ; and Colonel Shrieve's regiment was drawn up at the second bridge, in the rear of the town, to cover the retreat of the Americans, if such a movement should become necessary. Lee's dragoons, and the pickets under Captain Walker, were stationed at the Vauxhall Bridge, and the militia were drawn up on the flanks, principally under the command of General Dickinson, of New Jersey.

The first attack was made by the enemy upon Lee's force at the Vauxhall Bridge, and the Americans were repulsed. At that instant the British troops near the first Springfield Bridge moved to attack Colonel Angell in the orchard. Captain Littell played his artillery so briskly and well, that he kept the enemy east of the bridge for some time ; but bringing their artillery to bear, they pressed forward, forded the stream (which is there only about two rods wide), and drove the Americans from their position and across the second bridge. The artillery of the British, being leveled too high, did but little execution, except among the branches of the apple-trees, and the Americans retreated with very little loss. The enemy were warmly received at the second bridge by Shrieve's regiment, but overwhelming numbers obliged the gallant little band of Americans to fall back and join the brigades of Maxwell and Stark upon the hill. The situation of the patriot army was now critical. The enemy was pushing vigorously forward on the Vauxhall Road, leading in

MRS. MATHEWS'S HOUSE.[2]

[1] Elias Dayton was born in Elizabethtown, New Jersey, in 1735. He joined the army during the French and Indian war. He was a member of the corps called "Jersey Blues," raised in 1759 by Edward Hart, the father of John, one of the signers of the Declaration of Independence. With that corps he fought under Wolfe at Quebec. He was one of the Committee of Safety at Elizabethtown at the beginning of the Revolution; in February, 1778, Congress appointed him colonel of a New Jersey regiment; and in 1782 he was promoted to the rank of brigadier general. He was in several of the principal battles of the Revolution, and had three horses shot under him—one at Germantown, one at Springfield, and one at Crosswick Bridge. He was the first president of the Cincinnati of New Jersey, and, during the life of Washington, enjoyed the warm personal friendship of that distinguished man. He died at Elizabethtown in 1807.

[2] This sketch was made from the left bank of the Rahway, at the site of the old bridge. This is now the rear of the house, but, at the time of the battle, the road was upon this side of it, which formed the front. The deviation of the road is indicated in the map by a dotted line. Remains of the abutments of the old bridge, where the British crossed, may still be seen.

their rear, and their numbers were too small to guard the several passes through the mountains, and have a respectable force engaged in battle.   Greene accordingly ordered the main body of the army, except the two brigades already mentioned, to take post on the hills in the rear of Byram's Tavern, and detached the regiments of Colonels Webb and Jackson, with one piece of artillery, to check the advance of the enemy on the Vauxhall Road.   The movement was successful, and that important pass was secured.

The Americans were now advantageously posted, and General Greene was anxious for an engagement ; but Knyphausen saw his own disadvantage, and, after setting fire to the village, began a retreat toward Elizabethtown.   Greene ordered out detachments to extinguish the flames of such houses as were not within the reach of the enemy's cannon, but their efforts were of little avail.   The church, and every house and barn in the village but three, were burned.   One of the latter now stands close by the tavern of Mr. Reynolds.   It is a very well built house, and exhibits an orifice in the northwestern gable, made by the passage of a cannon-ball.   The parsonage was saved, and in it the congregation worshiped until a more convenient place was supplied.

As soon as the village was fired, the enemy began their retreat.   Captain Davis, with one hundred and twenty men and large parties of militia, fell upon their flanks and rear, and kept up a continual fire upon them all the way to Elizabethtown.   The retreat was so precipitate that Stark's brigade, which was put in motion, could not overtake them.   At June 23. midnight the enemy began crossing over to Staten Island on a bridge of boats, and by six o'clock in the morning they had evacuated Elizabethtown and removed their bridge.[1]   The loss in killed and wounded has not been fully given on either side.   Lieutenant-colonel Barber, in his return to General Greene, reported thirteen Americans killed, and fifty-eight wounded and missing.   In this report was not included the return of Davis's detachment and of the militia that pursued the enemy to Elizabethtown.   The militia had twelve wounded and none killed.   The loss of the enemy is unknown.   The newspapers of the day put down their loss in the skirmish at Connecticut Farms and vicinity, two weeks previous, at one hundred and fifty killed, and as many wounded.   Colonel Barber, who acted as deputy adjutant general on the occasion, was particularly recommended for his activity, by General Greene, in his report of the engagement.[2]   General Washington, on hearing of the movement of the enemy toward Springfield, sent a re-enforcement, but it was too late to save the town.   Greene, in his report, says, " I lament that our force was too small to save the town from ruin.   I wish every American could have been a spectator ; they would have felt for the sufferers, and joined to revenge the injury."

After much difficulty, I procured a conveyance to Elizabethtown.   Mr. Meeker, a resident of Springfield, seventy-four years old, kindly left his plow, and in a light wagon took me thither, by the way of Connecticut Farms, a small village now called Union, lying four miles northwest of Elizabethtown.   Almost every building in that village was destroyed by the British invaders while on their way to Springfield, on the 6th of June, 1780.   An event occurred there at that time, which excited the greatest indignation throughout the country.   The family of the Rev. James Caldwell, the pastor of the First Presbyterian Church at Elizabethtown, and an ardent Whig, had removed to Connecticut Farms as a place of greater security, and occupied the parsonage.   Mrs. Caldwell was the daughter of John Ogden, of Newark, and was greatly beloved for her piety and benevolence.   When she heard of the

---

[1] Report of General Greene to the commander-in-chief.

[2] Francis Barber was born at Princeton in 1751, and was educated at the College of New Jersey.   He was installed rector of an academic institution connected with the First Presbyterian Church at Elizabethtown, in which situation he remained until the commencement of the Revolution.   He joined the patriot army, and in 1776 was commissioned by Congress a major of the third battalion of New Jersey troops ; at the close of the year was appointed lieutenant colonel, and subsequently became assistant inspector general under Baron Steuben.   He was in constant service during the whole war, was in the principal battles, and was present at the surrender of Cornwallis at Yorktown.   He was with the Continental army at Newburgh in 1783 ; and on the very day when Washington announced the signing of the treaty of peace to the army, he was killed by a tree falling upon him while riding by the edge of a wood.—*Rev. Nicholas Murray.*

approach of the enemy, and the people fled from the town, she resolved to remain, trusting in Providence for protection. When they entered the village, she withdrew, with her infant in her arms, into a private apartment, and engaged in religious devotions. A maid, who had charge of the other children, and accompanied her to the private apartment, saw a " redcoat soldier" jump over the fence into the yard, and told Mrs. Caldwell that he was approaching the window. Mrs. Caldwell arose from a bed on which she had been sitting, and at that moment the soldier discharged his musket at her through the window. It was loaded with two balls, both of which passed through her body, and she fell lifeless upon the floor, in the midst of her children.[1] It was with much difficulty that her body was saved from the conflagration that ensued. It was dragged into the street, and lay exposed for several hours in the hot sun, when some of her friends procured liberty to take it to the house of Captain Wade, on the opposite side of the road. Her husband was at the Short Hills that night, suffering dreadfully from anxiety respecting his family. The next day he procured a flag and went to Connecticut Farms, when he found the village in ruins and his wife no more. That cold-blooded murder, as well as the wanton destruction of the peaceful village, changed many Tories to Whigs, and helped to confirm the settled hatred of the well-affected and the patriots against the British government, whose military officers winked at such atrocities.

On our way, Mr. Meeker related some interesting facts concerning his family. His grandfather was a stanch republican, and had eight sons and four sons-in-law in the Continental army, who were remarkable for their physical strength and moral courage. The father of Mr. Edwards, the old gentleman who went over the Springfield battle-ground with me, was one of the sons-in-law. One of his sons (Mr. Meeker's father) lived up among the Short Hills, and was a substantial farmer. A conversation which he had one day with General Dayton, at Elizabethtown, well illustrates the political character of many of the yeomanry of that period. While a portion of the standing army, under the administration of the elder Adams, was at Elizabethtown, Mr. Meeker went to General Dayton to pay his direct tax, in hard cash, for the support of the army. " Of what use is your standing army?" asked Meeker. " To support Congress," replied Dayton. " Ay, to support Congress indeed," said the old man, bitterly. " To support Congress in taking away our liberties, and in altering the Constitution so as to place men in public offices for life. I fought for freedom through the war for nothing (his Continental money was worthless), and now I want to pay for my land and be *independent* indeed, but tax upon tax keeps me poor. I could at any time raise one hundred men among my neighbors upon the Short Hills, say privately to your standing army, ' Come and help us'—and they would come, and we'd march to Philadelphia and take your Congressmen from their seats. We will not have a standing army. Disband it." " Our standing army," said Dayton, " will intimidate the British." " Look ahere, General Dayton," said Meeker, while his eyes sparkled with emotion, " you are well acquainted in London. Write to your acquaintances there, and tell them that Timothy Meeker is dead, and that he has left seven sons, every one of whom is a stronger man than he. Tell them we are seven times stronger than before, and that will intimidate them more than all your standing armies, that suck the life-blood from the people." Such was the logic of New Jersey farmers in 1798, and our government soon acted in accordance with it.

We reached Elizabethtown at about noon, and having ample time before the departure

---

[1] Such is the current history, and the diabolical act was fixed upon " a British soldier." Some believed that the occurrence was a mere accident, resulting from the cross firing of the combatants, but there is ample evidence that it was a deliberate murder. A correspondent of the Newark Advertiser says that " there is evidence of a very direct character, which affixes the guilt of murder of the poor lady to a particular individual." " A very respectable citizen," he adds, " lately deceased, who was a witness of the scenes of that day, says that a man named M'Donald, from the north of Ireland, who had been in the employment of Mr. Caldwell, or of his family, was the person who committed the atrocious deed. This man, from some unknown cause, had conceived a violent enmity against his employer, and it was in this manner he satiated his revenge. The witness to whom reference is now made, further declared that he saw M'Donald after the murder, and heard him avow it, saying, at the same time, that ' now he was satisfied,' upon which he joined and went off with the enemy."

of the evening train for Middlebrook, my next tarrying-place, I visited the several Revolutionary localities in the vicinity.   The burial-ground of the First Presbyterian Church, on Broad Street, was the chief attraction within the village, for therein repose the remains of many distinguished men of the Revolution.   The church that occupied the site of the present one was burned on the night of the 25th of January, 1780, together with the academy (which stood upon the ground of the present lecture room) and the court-house.   A notorious Tory named Cornelius Hetfield fired the church with his own hands, and was heard to lament that the "black-coated rebel," as he called Dr. Caldwell, the pastor, was not burned

in his pulpit.   Near the Broad Street front of the burying ground stands the monument erected to the memory of the Rev. James Caldwell and his wife, by citizens of Elizabethtown.   It is a handsome marble obelisk, which, with an inscribed pedestal, rests upon a granite base.   On the left in the picture are seen a recumbent slab, and also an upright one.   The former is of brown stone, and covers the grave of Jonathan Dickinson,[1] the founder of the College of New Jersey, now located at Princeton ; the latter is of white marble, and is sacred to the memory of Margaret Van Pelt, a grand-daughter of Mr. Caldwell.   On the west side of the cemetery, in the rear of the church, are several vaults shaded by a venerable oak, among which is that of the celebrated Elias Boudinot, who was president of Congress

CALDWELL'S MONUMENT.[2]

in 1782, and an active patriot during the Revolution.   Of him I shall have occasion to write hereafter.   A little south of Boudinot's vault is that of General Dayton, just mentioned, and in the vicinity are the graves of General Crane, an active patriot of the Revolution ; Colonel Barber, already mentioned ; Moses Ogden, a young American officer, who was killed at Connecticut Farms when that settlement was burned , and of several others of colonial and Revolutionary eminence, among whom is Governor Belcher.

BOUDINOT'S VAULT.

---

[1] Jonathan Dickinson was born in Hatfield, Massachusetts, April 22d, 1688.   He graduated at Yale College in 1706, and two years afterward became the pastor of the First Presbyterian Church at Elizabethtown, New Jersey, where he continued nearly forty years.   He was the cotemporary of Whitfield, Brainard, Edwards, and the Tennants.   He was chiefly instrumental in organizing the academy at Elizabethtown, which was chartered as the College of New Jersey in 1746.   He was made its first president, but the institution did not long enjoy the advantages of his care, as he died on the 7th of October, 1747, aged fifty-nine.   The first commencement of the college was in 1748, when six young men graduated, five of whom became ministers of the Gospel.

[2] The following are the inscriptions upon the Caldwell monument :

EAST SIDE.   "This monument is erected to the memory of the REV. JAMES CALDWELL, the pious and fervent Christian, the zealous and faithful minister, the eloquent preacher, and a prominent leader among the worthies who secured the independence of his country.   His name will be cherished in the church and in the state so long as Virtue is esteemed and Patriotism honored."

WEST SIDE.   "Hannah, wife of the Rev. James Caldwell, and daughter of Jonathan Ogden, of Newark, was killed at Connecticut Farms by a shot from a British soldier, June 25th,* 1780, cruelly sacrificed by the enemies of her husband and of her country."

NORTH SIDE.   " 'The memory of the just is blessed.'   'Be of good courage—and let us behave ourselves valiant for our people, and for the cities of our God, and let the Lord do that which is good in his sight.'   'The glory of children are their fathers.' "

SOUTH SIDE.   "James Caldwell.   Born in Charlotte county, in Virginia, April, 1734.   Graduated at Princeton College, 1759.   Ordained pastor of the First Presbyterian Church of Elizabethtown, 1762.   After serving as chaplain in the army of the Revolution, and acting as commissary to the troops in New Jersey, he was killed by a shot from a sentinel at Elizabethtown Point, November 24th, 1781."

---

* This is an error, as will be perceived by reference to the text.

OF THE REVOLUTION. 327

Death of Mr. Caldwell.　　Execution of his Murderer.　　Mr. Caldwell's Funeral.　　His Orphan Family.

The death of Mr. Caldwell, which occurred a little more than a year subsequent to that of his wife, was regarded as a foul murder. He was shot upon the causeway at old Elizabethtown Point, by an American sentinel named Morgan, who was hung for the deed. The circumstances are substantially as follows. At the time of the occurrence the Americans had possession of Elizabethtown, and there was established there a commissariat of prisoners, under the superintendence of Major Adams. To facilitate the business for which the commissariat was established, a sloop made weekly trips between the Point and New York, then the head-quarters of the British army. Passengers with a flag, and also parcels, were frequently carried by this vessel, and a strong guard was placed at a tavern on the shore, having one or more sentinels upon the causeway that extended across the marsh to the wharf. On the 24th of November, 1781, this vessel arrived at the wharf, having on board a Miss Berlah Murray (afterward Mrs. Martin Hoffman), who had permission to visit her sister (Mrs. Barnett), at Elizabethtown. Mr. Caldwell went down to the sloop in his chaise to receive her, but she was not there. He went on board the vessel, when a small bundle belonging to her was placed in his charge, with which he started for his vehicle. James Morgan, a sentinel on duty upon the causeway, ordered Mr. Caldwell to deliver his bundle to him for examination, as his orders were not to let any thing of the kind pass without strict scrutiny. Mr. Caldwell told him it was the property of a lady, which had been placed in his charge, and refused to give it up. The sentinel reiterated his demand, when Mr. Caldwell turned from him, and, it is said, went toward the vessel to leave the bundle, rather than subject it to the inspection of the soldier. The latter, probably irritated by disobedience of his orders, and, it may be, by words, leveled his musket and shot Mr. Caldwell dead upon the spot. Opinions were, and still are, various as to the motive of the sentinel. Some justify him as acting in strict obedience to his orders ; others believe him to have been bribed to murder the active patriot when the first opportunity should offer ; and others, again, simply condemn him for exceeding the spirit of his instructions. Morgan was arrested, the coroner's inquest brought in a verdict of willful murder against him, and he was tried, found guilty, and executed at Westfield on the 29th of January, 1782. He was taken to the church, where a sermon was preached by the Rev. Jonathan Elmer, from the words of Jeremiah, " O, do not this abominable thing which I hate ;" and immediately after the close of the services the prisoner was hung. The place of his execution is about half a mile north of the church, in Westfield, and still bears the name of Morgan's Hill. A local controversy has arisen upon the subject, which seems to turn more upon the *inferences* of the several writers than upon the material facts here given. " Who shall decide when doctors disagree ?" Cotemporary records form the best umpire in such cases, and correct history, the *patient* in question, is not likely to suffer from such a disagreement.

The death of Mr. Caldwell, a pious and eloquent minister, and such an active patriot, made a powerful impression on the public mind, and there was " a voice of mourning" wherever his eminent virtues were known. It was Saturday afternoon when he was shot. His body was conveyed to the house of his friend, Mrs. Noel, whence it was buried the following Tuesday. " Many," says Dr. Murray, " were ignorant of the tragical deed until they came to church on the Sabbath ; and, instead of sitting with delight under his instructions, there was a loud cry of wailing over his melancholy end. There was a vast concourse assembled to convey him to his tomb. The corpse was placed on a large stone before the door of the house of Mrs. Noel (now the residence of Miss Spalding), where all could take a last view of the remains of their murdered pastor. After all had taken their last look, and before the coffin was closed, Dr. Elias Boudinot came forward, leading nine orphan children, and, placing them around the bier of their parent, made an address of surpassing pathos to the multitude in their behalf."[1]

I rode down to Elizabethtown Point, a place famous in the annals of the Revolution.

---

[1] *Notes on Elizabethtown*, page 77. The funeral sermon was preached by Dr. M'Whorter, of Newark, from Ecclesiastes, viii., 8.

The distance is about two miles, and so nearly adjacent are the houses along the road, that it may be said the village extends all the way to the Point. The old wharf or landing is about three quarters of a mile northeast of the present bustling port, and only a solitary dwelling, the traces of the causeway, and the apparition, at low water, of some of the logs of the ancient wharf, constitute the remains of the Revolution there, except slight indications of the works thrown up by the Americans in the rear. Making a journey in a direct line

through some shrub oaks and a field of tangled buck-wheat, I visited and sketched the old tavern, now the property of Mr. Isham, of New York, where many of the stirring scenes of the Revolution occurred. There American and British officers were alternately quartered, from 1776 until the close of the war, and in that house the corpse of Mr. Caldwell was laid while a wagon was procured to convey it to the town. In front of it is a flat shore, overflowed at high tide, across which was a substantial causeway about seventy-five rods in length, with a wharf at the end. Here was the landing-place of troops passing and repassing to and from Staten Island, closely contiguous; and from

OLD TAVERN AT ELIZABETHPORT.[1]

this wharf extended the bridge of boats over which the British retreated after the battle of Springfield. There Washington embarked in the barge prepared to convey him to New April 24, York, to be inaugurated the first President of the United States, and in the old tav-1789. ern he breakfasted that morning.

When the British fleet appeared off Sandy Hook with the troops of General Howe, in June, 1776, great alarm spread through New Jersey; for, as the Americans then had military occupation of New York city, it was supposed the enemy would land on the Jersey coast. Governor Livingston, at the head of the New Jersey militia, established his camp at Elizabethtown Point, and caused a fortification to be constructed by digging ditches and throwing up breast-works, which extended from the old to the new Point, and on which a few cannons were mounted. These works were never of any material use, and hardly a vestige of them remains.

From the Point several water expeditions were fitted out, for the narrow and tortuous channel, and low, marshy shore protected the place from the visits of large vessels of war. One of these expeditions was under the command of Elias Dayton and William Alexander. The latter is better known in our history as Lord Stirling, and was Governor Shirley's military secretary at Albany twenty years before. Informed that a British transport and provision ship was on the coast, the Committee of Safety at Elizabethtown ordered four armed boats to attempt its capture. They came in sight of the vessel about forty miles from Sandy Hook. The men in the boats were all concealed under hatches, except two in each, unarm-

---

[1] This view is looking eastward. In the distance, on the right, is seen a vessel, at the entrance of Newark Bay, and the land beyond is the high ground intervening between it and Jersey City. In one of the rooms of the old tavern is a Franklin stove, which has probably been a tenant there ever since it came from the foundery. I gave a sketch of it, not only because it is a relic of the time, but because it doubtless shows the form of the stove as invented by Dr. Franklin in 1742,* before an "improvement" was made. On its front, in raised letters, are the words "Ross and Bird's Hibernia Foundry, 1782." Ross had a foundery at Elizabethtown in 1774, as appears by the inscription upon the dinner-bell of Sir William Johnson, now in the belfry of the old Caughnawaga Church at Fonda. See note, page 233.

---

* Franklin says, in reference to this invention, "Governor Thomas was so pleased with the construction of this stove, that he offered to give me a patent for the sole vending of them for a term of years; but I declined it, from a principle which has ever weighed with me on such occasions, viz., that, as we enjoy great advantages from the inventions of others, we should be glad of an opportunity to serve others by an invention of ours; and this we should do freely and generally." A London iron-monger made some alterations, which Franklin says "hurt its operation," got a patent for it there, and made a small fortune by it.

OF THE REVOLUTION.　　　329

Capture of a Provision Ship.　　Privateering.　　"London Trading."　　"Liberty Hall."　　Designs against Governor Livingston.

ed, who managed the oars. The enemy mistook them for fishing vessels, and allowed them to come along side. At a preconcerted signal, the hatches were raised, the armed Americans poured upon the deck of the ship, and in a few minutes she was their prize, hardly a show of resistance having been made. She was taken in triumph to Elizabethtown Point, where her cargo was landed. This exploit was performed in the summer of 1775, soon after the battle on Bunker Hill. Some privateering expeditions were fitted out here and at Amboy during the war; but, with the exception of the invasion already detailed, there were few military operations there. There are a few blemishes in the general good character for Whiggery, claimed by Elizabethtown. During the war there was a great deal of "London trading," or supplying the enemy with provisions and other things, carried on there. The high price paid by the British on Staten Island tempted even the most ardent Whigs to put money in their purses by the traffic. Many took their pay in British goods, and actually opened stores in the village with articles thus obtained. Governor Livingston, alluding to the practice, said, "The village now consists of unknown, unrecommended strangers, guilty-looking Tories, and very knavish Whigs."

Having an hour to spare on my return to the village, I walked out to old "Liberty Hall,"

"LIBERTY HALL."[1]

the former residence of Governor Livingston, now the property of Mr. John Kean. It is a fine old mansion, imbowered in shrubs and overshadowed by venerable trees. It is situated upon the left of the Springfield Turnpike, beyond the Elizabeth River, and about three fourths of a mile north of the rail-way station in the village. Governor Livingston was an active partisan, and during the whole war was continually employed in public duties or in wielding his pen in favor of the Republican cause. For this reason he was extremely obnoxious to the enemy, and particularly to the Tories, whom he cordially hated and despised. Several attempts were made to abduct him, but they were all unsuccessful. It was also said that Sir Henry Clinton offered a bounty for his life, if he could not be taken alive, and that a prominent Tory of New Jersey had been solicited to assassinate him for a price. Of this Governor Livingston accused Clinton, in a letter. The latter did not deny the charge, but, in a very discourteous reply, said, "Had I a soul capable of harboring so infamous an idea as assassination, you, sir, at least, would have nothing to fear; for, be assured, I should not blacken myself with so foul a crime to obtain so trifling an end." Sir Henry, however, thought the "end not too trifling" to fit out an expedition for the express purpose of capturing the "rebel governor." It was midnight, on the 28th of February, 1779, that a party of British troops, sent by Clinton from New York, landed at Elizabethtown Point, and,

---

[1] Some time after the death of Governor Livingston this property was purchased by Lord Bolingbroke, who, under the assumed name of John Belesis, ran away from England with a daughter of Baron Hompasch, a German general. She was at a boarding school there, and Bolingbroke had a wife living. He married the girl here. She died in England in 1848. The grandmother of the present proprietor, Susan, the daughter of Peter Van Burgh Livingston, bought the farm of Lord Bolingbroke, and it has been in possession of the family ever since. Her first husband was John Kean, a member of Congress from South Carolina from 1785 to 1787, and was first cashier of the first United States Bank, chartered by an act of Congress passed February 8th, 1791. Her second husband was Count Niemcewicz, a Polish nobleman.

marching directly to "Liberty Hall," burst open the doors, and shouted vociferously for "the damned rebel governor." Fortunately, the governor had left home some hours before, to pass the night with a friend, a few miles distant. After becoming convinced that he was not there, they demanded his papers. Those of the greatest importance (his recent correspondence with Washington, and with Congress and the state officers) were in the box of his sulky, in his parlor. This box the officer in command was about to seize, when Livingston's daughter Catharine, a girl of great spirit and presence of mind, represented to him that the box contained her private property, and appealed to his courtesy as a gentleman and a soldier to protect it for her. A guard was placed over it, and she then led the men to the library, where they filled their foraging bags with worthless law papers. After threatening to burn the house, they returned to Elizabethtown, burned one or two dwellings in the village, and then departed for New York.[1]

Mr. Sedgwick relates a tradition connected with the family of Governor Livingston. At the time of the invasion, when the village of Connecticut Farms was burned, Governor Livingston was absent from home on official duty. The family had spent the day in great alarm, for immediately in front of their dwelling the smoke and flames of that conflagration of that village were distinctly seen. Late in the evening several British officers came to the house, told them that their troops were retreating, and proposed to pass the night there. The family felt secure from marauders while such protectors were present, and retired to bed. About midnight they were aroused. The officers were called away, and soon afterward some exclaiming, "God! it's Mrs. Caldwell, that we killed to-day!"

drunken soldiers rushed into the hall, swearing that they would burn the "rebel house." There were none but women in the house. The maid servant fastened herself in the kitchen, and the ladies of the family locked themselves in another room. The ruffians discovered their hiding-place, and, fearing to exasperate them by refusing to come out, one of the governor's daughters boldly opened the door. A drunken soldier seized her by the arm, and at the same moment she seized him by the collar with a force that alarmed him At that instant a gleam of light illumined the hall and fell upon the white dress of the lady. The soldier staggered back, They soon left the house.

Wil^s Livingston[2]

---

[1] Sedgwick's *Life of William Livingston*, p. 322.

[2] William Livingston was descended from the old Scotch family of that name, whose first representative in this country was Robert, the "first lord of the manor" upon the Hudson. He was born in November, 1723, and graduated in Yale College in 1741. He was well educated, and possessed many solid as well as brilliant attainments in law and literature. He early espoused the cause of the colonists, and, having removed from New York to New Jersey, was elected a delegate to the first Continental Congress from that state. In 1776, after the people of New Jersey had sent Governor Franklin, under a strong guard, to Connecticut, Mr. Livingston was elected chief magistrate of the state; and such were his acknowledged talents, and republican virtue, and the love of the people for him, that he was annually elected to that office until his death. In 1787 he was a delegate to the convention that formed the Federal Constitution; and, after being actively employed in public life for almost twenty years, he died at "Liberty Hall," near Elizabethtown, July 25th, 1790, aged sixty-seven years. The silhouette here given is copied from one in Sedgwick's *Life of Livingston*, which he says was probably taken from life, about 1773. The Livingstons are descended from a noble Scotch family. Lord Livingston, afterward Earl of Linlithgow, was one of the custodians of Mary, Queen of Scots, while in Dumbarton Castle in 1547. The great-grandson of the Earl was John Livingston, a pious Scotch minister who fled from persecution, and went to Holland. He was the

I left Elizabethtown in the cars, at about three o'clock, and arrived at Middlebrook, a pleasant little village on the Raritan, toward sunset, passing on the way Scotch Plains and the thriving town of Plainfield.   The road passes over an almost level country, and, though the soil is light and sandy, thrift appeared on every side.   Middlebrook and Boundbrook lie close together, and are included in one village.   Here, toward the last of May, 1777, Washington encamped his army, after breaking up his cantonments at Morristown.   His troops rapidly augmented; and when, in June, General Howe began to show some disposition to open the summer campaign, the American army mustered about fourteen thousand effective men.   They were strongly posted upon the Heights of Middlebrook, in the rear of the village, near the place of the winter encampment in 1778–9, which will be presently noticed.   Washington suspected Howe's design to be to make an attempt to capture Philadelphia.   He concentrated the Northern forces on the Hudson; a strong division under Arnold was posted on the Delaware, and a considerable force was under his immediate command at Middlebrook. General Howe had encamped at New Brunswick, ten miles distant, and endeavored to draw Washington out from his strong position, into a general engagement upon the plains.   But the chief would not hazard a battle while his forces were so divided.   Howe remained two days at New Brunswick; but, concluding that Washington was too strongly posted among the hills to be attacked with impunity, the British commander sought to accomplish by stratagem what he had failed to do by open and obvious movements.   For this purpose   June 14, he advanced rapidly toward Somerset Court-house, feigning a design to cross the   1777. Delaware.   Failing to draw Washington from his post by this maneuver, he made another feint, a few days afterward, which succeeded better.   He suddenly retreated, first   a June 19. toward New Brunswick,[a] and then to Amboy,[b] and even sent some detachments   b June 22. over to Staten Island.   Partly deceived by these movements, and hoping to reap some advantage by harassing the British rear, Washington sent strong detachments after the retreating enemy, and also advanced with his whole force to Quibbletown (now New Market), five or six miles from Middlebrook.   This was exactly what Howe desired to accomplish,   June. and, accordingly, on the night of the 25th, he suddenly recalled his troops from Staten Island and Amboy, and early the next morning marched rapidly toward the American lines, hoping to cut off their retreat to Middlebrook, and thus bring on a general action.   Washington was too quick and vigilant for Howe, and reached his strong position again.   The advanced guard of the British fell in with Lord Stirling's division, and a warm skirmish ensued.   On the approach of Cornwallis with a considerable force, Stirling retreated to his camp with inconsiderable loss.   Other skirmishes ensued, but neither party suffered much. At Westfield the British forces wheeled, and, marching back to Amboy, passed over to Staten Island, leaving the Americans in the quiet possession of New Jersey.

It was on the gentle slope from the plain to the steep acclivities of the mountain in the rear of Middlebrook, that seven brigades of the American army were *hutted* during the winter of 1779–80.   After the battle of Monmouth,[c] the American army crossed the   c June 28, Hudson River, and took post chiefly in Westchester county.   The head-quarters   1778. of Washington were at White Plains.   In the mean while the Count d'Estaing had arrived at Sandy Hook with a French fleet; but, being unable to pass the bar with his heavy ships, to attack Lord Howe in the bay, he sailed eastward to co-operate with General Sullivan in a proposed attack upon Newport, on Rhode Island.   Of this expedition, which proved unsuccessful, I shall hereafter write.

Washington continued at White Plains until late in autumn, suspecting the design of Sir Henry Clinton to be to make a movement eastward.   Sir Henry gave currency to the reports that such were his intentions, until Washington moved his head-quarters to Freder-

common ancestor of all the Livingstons in America.   His son Robert, the first " lord of the manor" of Livingston, in Columbia County, New York. came to America about 1675, and from him all the family in this country have descended.   They were all remarkable for their patriotism during the Revolution; and for sixty years afterward the Livingstons were among our prominent public men

332   PICTORIAL FIELD-BOOK

Clinton's Operations in New Jersey.   Disposition of the American Forces.   Encampment at Middlebrook.   Pluckemin.

icsburg, near the Connecticut line, and turned his attention decidedly to the protection of the eastern coast. Clinton then sent foraging parties into New Jersey, and ravaged the whole country, from the Hudson to the Raritan, and beyond. The abandonment of the siege of Newport, the return of Howe's fleet to New York, and the entire withdrawal of forces from the east by Clinton, except those stationed upon Rhode Island, convinced Washington that the British commander had no further designs in that direction, and he prepared to put his army into the most advantageous winter-quarters. Nine brigades were stationed on the west side of the Hudson, exclusive of the garrison at West Point. One of these was at Smith's Cove, in the rear of Haverstraw, one at Elizabethtown, and the other seven were at Middlebrook. Six brigades were cantoned on the east side of the Hudson and at West Point. One was at West Point, two were at Continental Village, a hamlet near Peekskill, and three in the vicinity of Danbury, in Connecticut. The artillery was at Pluckemin, in Bedminster county, New Jersey.[1] The head-quarters of the chief were in the vicinity of Middlebrook. Knox, Greene, and Steuben were among the general officers that accompanied him; and the ladies of several of the officers, among whom was Mrs. Washington, enlivened the camp by their presence during the winter.

The place of encampment was about three fourths of a mile northwest from the village. Log huts were completed, for the use of the soldiers, in February, after they had suffered exposure under canvas tents for several weeks. The huts, according to the description of Dr. Thacher, who was there, were made very comfortable by filling the interstices between the logs with mud, as log houses in our Western and Southwestern states are now·made. The huts were arranged in straight lines, forming a regular and compact village. The officers' huts were arranged in front of the line, according to their rank, with kitchens in the rear; and the whole was similar in form to a tent encampment. Remains of these are still found in the fields where the encampment was. I could not ascertain where Washington was quartered; and, as far as I could learn by inquiries, there is only one house remaining in the neighborhood which was occupied by any of the general officers at that time, and that is the dwelling of Mr. Staats, where Major-general Baron Steuben had his quarters. From a remark by Dr. Thacher, in his Military Journal (page 156), I infer that Washington's quarters were at or near Pluckemin, a few miles from the camp. The doctor speaks of an event that occurred "near head-quarters, at Pluckemin."

In the evening of my arrival at Middlebrook, I called on Mrs. Polly Van Norden, a small, but vigorous old lady, eighty-four years of age. She lived near the Monmouth battle-ground at the time of the conflict there, and was well acquainted with the sufferings of the Whigs in that region from the depredations of the desperate band of Tories called the Pine Robbers. She was a woman of strong but uncultivated mind, and became excited with feelings of the

---

[1] Pluckemin lies at the base of a high mountain, about six miles northwest of Somerville. There the American army halted on the 4th of January, 1777 (the day after the battle of Princeton), on its way to Morristown. In the village burial-ground is the grave of Captain Leslie, of the British army, who was mortally wounded at Princeton. Mr. Custis, in his Recollections of the Life of Washington, says, "It was while the commander-in-chief reined up his horse, upon approaching the spot, in a plowed field, where lay the gallant Colonel Harslet, mortally wounded, that he perceived some British soldiers supporting a wounded officer, and, upon inquiring his name and rank, was answered, 'Captain Leslie.' Dr. Benjamin Rush, who formed a part of the general's suite, earnestly asked, 'A son of the Earl of Levin?' to which the soldiers replied in the affirmative. The doctor then addressed the general-in-chief: 'I beg your excellency to permit this wounded officer to be placed under my care, that I may return, in however small a degree, a part of the obligation I owe to his worthy father for the many kindnesses received at his hands while a student at Edinburgh.' The request was immediately granted; but, alas! poor Leslie was soon *past all surgery*." He died the same evening, after receiving every possible kindness and attention, and was buried the next day at Pluckemin, with the honors of war. His troops, as they lowered the body to the soldier's last rest, shed tears of sorrow over the remains of their much-loved commander. On a plain monument erected to his memory is the following inscription: "In memory of Captain WILLIAM LESLIE, of the seventh British regiment, son of the Earl of Levin, in Scotland. He fell, January 3d, 1777, aged 26 years, at the battle of PRINCETON. His friend, Benjamin Rush, M.D., of Philadelphia, hath caused this stone to be erected, as a mark of his esteem for his worth, and respect for his family."

bitterest hatred against the Tories while telling me of their deeds—a hatred, the keenness of which the lapse of seventy years has scarcely blunted.

Early the following morning, in company with a gentleman of the village, I rode to the residence of the venerable Bergen Bragaw, a hale old man of eighty-seven.   From him I learned the exact locality of the American encampment.   His half-brother was one of the Pennsylvania line, and my informant often visited him in the camp. He said the slope where the huts were erected was heavily timbered at that time, but it was completely cleared in cutting down trees for the log houses, and has been a cultivated tract ever since. September 14, 1848.

From Mr. Bragaw's we rode to the house formerly owned by Abraham Staats, and now in possession of his son. Three sisters survive, one of whom (Mrs. Jane Doty), nearly eighty years of age, who resided there during the Revolution, has a clear recollection of many events connected with Baron Steuben's occupancy of the house.   Although she was then a child eight or ten years old, she remembers the dignity of his appearance, the urbanity of his manners, for which he was noted, and the elegance and richness of the ornaments with which he was adorned.   She spoke of a brilliant medal that hung by a ribbon upon his breast.[1] Mrs. Doty recollected two visits made to the baron by Washington and his lady, one to dine and the other to take tea with him.   On the latter occasion several ladies were present.   She also remembers an entertainment given by the baron to the American officers and their ladies, on which occasion the table was spread in a grove near by.   This occurred a short time before the encampment broke up, which event took place early in June. 1779.

STEUBEN'S HEAD-QUARTERS.[2]

Returning to the village, we proceeded to visit the camp-ground, which is upon the left of the main road over the mountains to Pluckemin ; also "Washington's Rock."   The former exhibits nothing worthy of particular attention ; but the latter, situated upon the highest point of the mountain in the rear of Middlebrook, is a locality, independent of the associations which hallow it, that must ever impress the visitor with pleasant recollections of the view obtained from that lofty observatory.   We left our wagon at a point half way up the mountain, and made our way up the steep declivities along the remains of the old road. How loaded wagons were managed in ascending or descending this mountain road is quite inconceivable, for it is a difficult journey for a foot-passenger to make.   In many places not even the advantage of a zigzag course along the hill sides was employed, but a line as straight as possible was made up the mountain.   Along this difficult way the artillery troops that were stationed at Pluckemin crossed the mountain, and over that steep and rugged road heavy cannons were dragged.   Having reached the summit, we made our way through a narrow and tangled path to the bold rock seen in the picture on the next page.   It is at an elevation of nearly four hundred feet above the plain below, and commands a magnificent view of the surrounding country included in the segment of a circle of sixty miles, having its rundle southward. At our feet spread out the beautiful rolling plains like a map, through which course the wind-

[1] Baron Steuben had received from the King of Prussia a splendid medal of gold and diamonds, designating the Order of *Fidelity*, which he always wore when in full military dress.

[2] This view is from the field in front of the house, looking north.   The dwelling is at the end of a lane several rods from the main road leading to Middlebrook from New Brunswick.   It is on the western side of the Raritan, and about a mile from the bridge near Middlebrook.   Only the center building was in existence at the time in question, and that seems to have been enlarged.   Each wing has since been added. The interior of the old part is kept in the same condition as it was when Steuben occupied it, being, like most of the better dwellings of that time, neatly wainscoted with pine, wrought into moldings and panels.

334 PICTORIAL FIELD-BOOK

View from Washington's Rock.　　　Another similar Rock at Plainfield.　　　Celebration at Pluckemin in 1779.

ing Raritan and the Delaware and Hudson Canal. Little villages and neat farm-houses dotted the picture in every direction. Southward, the spires of New Brunswick shot up above the intervening for-ests, and on the left, as seen in the picture, was spread the expanse of Raritan and Amboy Bays, with many white sails upon their bosoms. Beyond were seen the swelling hills of Staten Island, and the more abrupt heights of Neversink or Navesink Mountains, at Sandy Hook. Upon this lofty rock Washington often stood, with his telescope, and reconnoitered the vicinity. He overlooked his camp at his feet, and could have descried the marchings of the enemy at a great distance upon the plain, or the evolutions of a fleet in the waters beyond. In the rear of Plainfield, at an equal elevation, and upon the same range of hills, is another rock bearing a similar appellation, and from the same cause. It is near the brow of the mountain, but, unlike the one under consideration, it stands quite alone, and rises from a slope of the hill, about twenty-five feet from base to summit. From this latter lofty position, it is said, Washington watched the movements of the enemy in the summer of 1777, recorded on page 331.

While upon the mountains, a haze that dimmed the sky in the morning, gathering into thick clouds, assumed the nimbus form, and menaced us with rain. This fact, and the expectation of the speedy arrival of the train for Somerville, where I was to take stage for Easton, on the Delaware, hurried us back to the village. There I met an old gentleman (whose name I have forgotten), who, though a small boy at the time, remembered the grand display at Pluckemin during the encampment, on February 6, 1778, the anniversary of the alliance of America with France.[1] He remembered an incident which I have not seen mentioned in the published accounts of that

[1] The following account of this celebration, published at the time, will doubtless interest the reader. It must be remembered that on the 6th of February, 1778, Dr. Franklin and other American commissioners, and commissioners appointed by the French government, signed a treaty of friendship and alliance between the two countries. The event alluded to occurred on the first anniversary (1779) of the alliance, or a few days afterward. It was postponed until the 18th, on account of Washington's absence from camp. The general-in-chief, and all the principal officers of the army there, Mrs. Washington, Mrs. Knox, Mrs. Greene, and the ladies and gentlemen for a large circuit around the camp, were of the company; and there was a vast concourse of spectators from every part of New Jersey.

The artillery were posted upon a piece of rising ground, and the entertainment was given by General Knox and the officers of the artillery corps. The entertainment and ball were held at the academy of the Park. The celebration was commenced at about four o'clock in the afternoon, by a discharge of thirteen cannons. The company invited then sat down to dinner in the academy. In the evening a display of fireworks was made, under the direction of Colonel Stevens, "from the point of a temple one hundred feet in length, and proportionately high." The temple showed thirteen arches, each displaying an illuminated painting. The center arch was ornamented with a pediment larger than any of the others; and the whole edifice was supported by a colonnade of the Corinthian order. The illuminated paintings were disposed in the following order: The 1st arch on the right represented the commencement of hostilities at Lexington, with this inscription: "The scene opened." 2d. British clemency, represented in the burning of Charlestown, Falmouth, Norfolk, and Kingston. 3d. The separation of America from Britain. A magnificent arch broken in the center, with this motto: "By your tyranny to the people of America, you have separated the wide arch of an extended empire." 4th. Britain represented as a decaying empire, by a barren country, broken arches, fallen spires, ships deserting its shores, birds of prey hovering over its moldering cities, and a gloomy setting sun. Motto,

"The Babylonian spires are sunk,
Achaia, Rome, and Egypt moldered down;
Time shakes the stable tyranny of thrones,
And tottering empires crush by their own weight."

affair. He said that several boys had possession of a small swivel, and, in firing it, one of them, while loading, had his hand blown off by a premature discharge of the piece. The boy was the son of a widow, and Washington, hearing of the circumstance, sent his mother two guineas.

I left Middlebrook at noon, and within half an hour was at dinner in Somerville, five or six miles distant, whence, at one o'clock, I departed in a stage-coach for Easton. Within the coach were seven grown persons, three children about ten years old, and two babies of a respectable size and sound lungs; while on the outside were four passengers and the driver, and an indefinite quantity of baggage. The roads were excessively dusty. The rain that commenced falling gently soon after leaving Somerville relieved us of that annoyance, but produced a greater—the necessity of having the windows of the coach closed, to keep out the drippings of the increasing storm. A wheezing old gentleman in green goggles insisted upon keeping the window open near him, to save him from suffocation; while a shadowy, middle-aged lady, upon the next seat, wrapped in a cloak, as earnestly declared that it should be closed to save her from an ague that had threatened her for a week. The matter appeared to be very properly a *casus belli*, as prime ministers say; but, unlike the action of prime ministers in general, the controversy was compromised by mutual concessions, the crooked roads over the rough hills presenting a basis for an amicable treaty of peace. It was agreed that, when the course of the road brought the lady to the windward, the window was to be closed, and at other times the gentleman was to be accommodated with fresh air.

The country through which we passed is beautifully diversified with lofty hills and deep ravines, forming numerous water courses, whose irrigating streams fertilize the broad valleys which are found occasionally imbosomed among the less fertile, but cultivated mountains. Of these, the Musconetcong,[1] through which flows a small river of the same euphonious name, dividing the counties of Hunterdon and Warren, is said to be one of the most charming. We crossed the Musconetcong at the pretty little village of Bloomsbury, at twilight, but the *gloaming* and the rain deprived us of the pleasure of a view of the valley and its thriving town. We were now within six miles of the Delaware, and as the darkness deepened the storm increased; and when, at seven o'clock, we crossed the river, and reined up at the hotel in Easton, we seemed to alight in the very court of Jupiter Pluvius.

Easton is upon the right bank of the Delaware, at its confluence with the Lehigh River, thirty-seven miles northwest from Somerville. Arriving there after dark, and departing the next morning before daylight, I had no opportunity to view it. It is said to be a place of much business, and inhabited by a well-educated, social, and highly moral population, and is in the midst of natural scenery singularly picturesque. It has but little Revolutionary history, and that relates chiefly to contests with the Indians. Here the division of the army

5th. America represented as a rising empire. Prospect of a fertile country, harbors and rivers covered with ships, new canals opening, cities arising amid woods, splendid sun emerging from a bright horizon. Motto,

> " New worlds are still emerging from the deep,
> The old descending, in their turns to rise."

6th. A grand illuminated representation of LOUIS THE SIXTEENTH, the encourager of letters, the supporter of the rights of humanity, the ally and friend of the American people. 7th. The center arch, THE FATHERS IN CONGRESS. Motto, " *Nil desperandum reipublicæ.*" 8th. The American philosopher and embassador extracting lightning from the clouds. 9th. The battle near Saratoga, 7th of October, 1777. 10th. The Convention of Saratoga. 11th. A representation of the sea fight, off Ushant, between Count d'Orvilliers and Admiral Keppel. 12th. Warren, Montgomery, Mercer, Wooster, Nash, and a crowd of heroes who have fallen in the American contest, in Elysium, receiving the thanks and praises of Brutus, Cato, and those spirits who in all ages have gloriously struggled against tyrants and tyranny. Motto, " Those who shed their blood in such a cause shall live and reign forever." 13th represented Peace, with all her train of blessings. Her right hand displaying an olive branch; at her feet lay the honors of harvest; the background was filled with flourishing cities; ports crowded with ships; and other emblems of an extensive empire and unrestrained commerce.

When the fire-works were finished, the company concluded the celebration by a splendid ball, which was opened by Washington, whose partner was the lady of General Knox.

[1] This is an Indian word, signifying " *a rapid-running stream.*"

PICTORIAL FIELD-BOOK

of Sullivan, under his immediate command, rendezvoused previous to its flying and desolating campaign against the Six Nations in central New York in 1779, and hither came the poor fugitives from the blackened Valley of Wyoming, after the terrible massacre and burning there in 1778. It has history antecedent to this, but in a measure irrelevant to our subject. Here, in 1758, the chiefs of the Indian tribes, the Delawares, Shawnees, Miamis, Nanticokes, Mohicans, Conoys, Monseys, and all of the Six Nations, assembled in grand council with the Governors of Pennsylvania and New Jersey, Sir William Johnson, and other distinguished men ; and the eloquence and good sense of the great Indian diplomatist, Teedyuscung, were here displayed on several occasions. Here, too, before the cabin of the white man was built upon the Delaware above Trenton, the surrounding hills echoed the voices of the eminent Whitefield and Brainerd,[1] as they proclaimed the Gospel of Peace to the heathen ; and here the good Moravians sang their hymns and held their love-feasts in the wigwams of the Indians.

---

[1] GEORGE WHITEFIELD was born in Gloucester, England, December 16th, 1714. After making some progress in learning, he was obliged to assist his mother, who kept an inn. At the age of eighteen he entered Oxford, where he became acquainted with the Wesleys (John and Charles), the founders of the Methodists. He joined these eminent Christians, took orders, and was ordained by the bishop in June, 1736. Mr. John Wesley was then in Georgia, and by his persuasion Whitefield embarked for America. He arrived at Savannah in May, 1738, and returned to England in September following. Bishop Benson ordained him priest in January, 1739. He made several voyages to America, and traveled through nearly all the colonies. He went to the Bermudas in 1748. In 1769 he made his seventh and last voyage to America. After preaching in different parts of the country, he died suddenly at Newburyport, Massachusetts, September 30th, 1770, aged fifty-five. His powers of eloquence were wonderful, and his ministry was exceedingly fruitful. His voice was powerful. Dr. Franklin estimated that thirty thousand people might hear him distinctly when preaching in the open air. Of him Cowper wrote,

> " He loved the world that hated him ; the tear
> That dropped upon his Bible was sincere ;
> Assailed by scandal and the tongue of strife,
> His only answer was a blameless life ;
> And he that forged and he that threw the dart,
> Had each a brother's interest in his heart.
> Paul's love of Christ and steadiness unbribed
> Were copied close in him, and well transcribed ;
> He followed Paul, his zeal a kindred flame,
> His apostolic charity the same ;
> Like him, crossed cheerfully tempestuous seas,
> Forsaking country, kindred, friends, and ease ;
> Like him he labored, and like him content
> To bear it, suffer shame where'er he went.
> Blush, Calumny ! and write upon his tomb,
> If honest eulogy can spare thee room,
> The deep repentance of thy thousand lies,
> Which, aimed at him, have pierced th' offended skies,
> And say, blot out my sin, confessed, deplored,
> Against thine image in thy saint, oh Lord !"

DAVID BRAINERD was born at Haddam, Connecticut, April 20th, 1718. He entered Yale College in 1739 ; but, being expelled in 1742, on account of some indiscreet remarks respecting one of the tutors, he never obtained his degree. He immediately commenced the study of divinity. Toward the close of the year he was licensed to preach, and immediately afterward was appointed a missionary to the Indians. His first efforts were made among the Stockbridge Indians, about fifteen miles from Kinderhook, New York. There he lodged upon straw, and his food was the simple fare of the savages. After the Stockbridge Indians agreed to remove to Stockbridge, and place themselves under the instruction of Mr. Sergeant, Brainerd went to the Indians upon the Delaware. There he labored for a while, and then visited the Indians at Crossweeksung, or Crosswicks, in New Jersey, where he was very successful. He worked an entire reform in the lives of the savages at that place. In the summer of 1746, Mr. Brainerd visited the Indians upon the Susquehanna. The next spring, finding his health giving way, he traveled in New England. In July he halted at Northampton, and there, in the family of Jonathan Edwards, he passed the remaining weeks of his life. He died October 9th, 1747, aged twenty-nine years. His exertions in the Christian cause were of short continuance, but they were intense, incessant, and effectual.

OF THE REVOLUTION   337

Departure for Wyoming.   Nazareth.   Its Origin.   A chilling Mist.   Nap in the Coach.

CHAPTER XV.

" On Susquehanna's side, fair Wyoming !
    Although the wild flowers on thy ruined wall
And roofless homes a sad remembrance bring
    Of what thy gentle people did befall,
    Yet thou wert once the loveliest land of all
That see the Atlantic's wave their morn restore."
                                        CAMPBELL.

" Thou com'st in beauty on my gaze at last,
    ' On Susquehanna's side, fair Wyoming,'
Image of many a dream, in hours long past,
    When life was in its bud and blossoming,
And waters, gushing from the fountain spring
    Of pure enthusiast thought, dimm'd my young eyes,
As by the poet borne, on unseen wing,
    I breathed, in fancy, 'neath thy cloudless skies,
The summer's air, and heard her echoed harmonies."
                                        HALLECK.

LEFT Easton for the Valley of Wyoming, sixty miles distant, at three o'clock
in the morning.   The storm was over, and the broken clouds, flitting upon a
cool wind from the northwest, permitted a few gleams of moonlight to stray
down to earth.   Although there were but three passengers in the coach (two
ladies and an infant), I took a seat with the driver, for there were promises of
a bright morning and magnificent scenery.   The coachman was a good-natured
Pennsylvania Dutchman, rather taciturn, and such an adept in his profession
that his practiced ear detected the absence of a shoe from the foot of one of the
" leaders" when three miles from Easton.   A blacksmith by the road side was
aroused, the shoe was replaced, and within an hour we had ascended the fertile
slopes of the Delaware and Lehigh, to Nazareth, a Moravian village about half
way between Easton and the Wind-gap in the Blue Mountains.   The day had
not yet dawned, yet the snatches of moonlight enabled me to observe the uniform and neat appearance of the houses in the village.[1]   We were now high
among the hills, whence the mists from the rivers and valleys had rolled up
when the storm ceased at midnight, and I was glad to take shelter from the
chilling vapor within the coach.   The seats were spacious, and, having one in
exclusive possession, I made a couch of it, using the carpet bag of one of the
ladies for a pillow, and slept soundly for an hour.   When I awoke, the morning light was

---

[1] Nazareth is seven miles northwest of Easton.   It contains a church, a sisters' house, a large and flourishing seminary for boys, and the usual dead-house and cemetery peculiar to the sect.   The place was named,
and, it may be said, founded, by the Rev. George Whitefield, the eloquent cosmopolite preacher.   He had
labored in conjunction with the Moravians in Georgia.   When, about 1740, they refused to take up arms
for the governor of the province, and left Georgia for the more peaceful domain of William Penn, Whitefield
accompanied them.   He began to erect a large building " in the Forks of the Delaware" as a school for
negro children, while the Moravians, under Bishop Nischman, purchased the site and founded the town of
Bethlehem, about ten miles distant.   Whitefield named his domain, or manor, Nazareth.   He did not complete his building, but sold " the manor of Nazareth" to the Moravians, who finished the edifice.   It is still
standing, in the eastern border of the village.   The Moravian Sisters of Bethlehem wrought an elegant banner, and presented it to Count Pulaski.   A drawing of the banner, and the beautiful Consecration Hymn, written by Longfellow, will be found in another part of this work.

abroad, and we were within half a mile of the Wind-gap. I again mounted the driver's box, for all around us Nature was displaying her attractions in the plenitude of her magnificence and beauty. Before us, and in close proximity, were the Blue Mountains, their summits curtained in a white fog that was rising toward the loftier clouds. Behind us, far down into the valleys and intervales, orchards, corn-fields, forests, and meadows were spread out like a carpet of mellow tints, and on every side the gentle breeze was shaking the rain-drops from the boughs in diamond showers, glittering in the first rays of the morning sun. While the bleating of sheep and the bellowing of cattle reminded us of cultivated fields behind us, the whirring of the pheasant, the drumming of the partridge, and the whistling of the quail among the rocks and lofty evergreens around betokened the uncultivated wilderness.

The Wind-gap, unlike the far-famed Water-gap[1] in the same cluster of mountains, is a deep depression of the summit of the range, is quite level on both sides of the road for a considerable distance, and exhibits none of the majestic precipices of the latter. The earth is covered with masses of angular rocks, among which shoot up cedar and other trees and shrubs, chiefly of the coniferæ order ; but the road, by industry, is made quite smooth. The hills rise on each side of the Gap to an altitude of eight hundred feet, clothed and crowned with trees. It was through this pass in the mountains that two expert walkers crossed to a spur of the Pocono when measuring the extent of a district of country northwest of the Delaware, for the proprietors of Pennsylvania, in 1737. The Indians had agreed, for a certain consideration, to sell a tract of land included within prescribed points on the river, and extending back as far as a man could " walk in a day and a half." The proprietors immediately advertised for the most expert walkers in the province, and they performed a journey, in the day and a half, of eighty-six miles ! The Indians were greatly dissatisfied, for they had no idea that such a distance could be accomplished, and it included some of their finest lands. The walkers *ran* a considerable portion of the way. They ate as they traveled, and never stopped from sunrise until sunset. One old Indian said, bitterly, when complaining of the *cheat*, " No sit down to smoke—no shoot a squirrel, but lun, lun, lun, all day long." The Indians, supposing the walk would end not far from the Wind-gap, had collected there in great numbers ; but, to their astonishment, the walkers reached that point on the evening of the first day.

The turnpike road through the Wind-gap, and across the valleys and mountains, to Wilkesbarre, was made by Sullivan for the passage of his troops in 1779, when marching to join General Clinton on the Tioga. Before that time the pass was little more than a rough Indian war-path, and its obscurity made the hurried flight of the people from Wyoming over the solitary region more perplexing and dreadful than it would be now.

We descended from the Wind-gap, on the western side of the mountain, along a steep and winding road, skirting a precipice, crossed a beautiful mountain stream, and alighted at the Roscommon Tavern, among the hills, where we breakfasted at seven o'clock. At the table we were honored by the presence of one of the five candidates for the office of sheriff of Monroe county. He was out canvassing the district for votes, and a more earnest, intelligent, good-humored man I have seldom met. His strongest claim to the honors and emoluments of the office seemed to rest upon the fact that he was a representative of New England *pedagogueism* in the Wyoming Valley as early as " forty years ago ;" had taught the " young ideas" of the fathers of three Wilkesbarre lawyers " how to shoot," and, therefore, he assumed to have an undisputed right to the privilege of hanging the inhabitants of a neighboring county. He accompanied us to the next tavern, the proprietor of which, a fat little man, though already bearing upon his shoulders the responsibilities of a postmaster, was another aspirant ambitiously wheezing for the office of sheriff. Both were too good-natured to be made *rivals ;*

---

[1] The Water-gap is the passage through the Kittatinny or Blue Mountains of the Delaware River, about three miles from Stroudsburg. This village is upon the Delaware, twenty-four miles above Easton, and was the first settlement which the fugitives from Wyoming reached when fleeing from the valley in 1778 There was a fort there, called Hamilton, during the French and Indian war, and near the eastern end of the village Fort Penn was built during the Revolution.

they were only *different candidates* professing the same political faith.   We left them comparing notes over a glass of whisky, and in the course of a few hours we had crossed fertile little valleys and parallel ranges of mountains, and begun the toilsome ascent of the famous Pocono.   From base to summit, the distance, by the road, is about three miles, one third of which is a straight line up the mountain at an angle of thirty-five degrees.   Then our way was along the precipitous sides of the hills, from which we could look upon the tops of tall trees, hundreds of feet below.   It was noon when we reached the level summit, two thousand feet above tide water ; and there, three fourths of a mile from the eastern brow of the mountain, John Smith keeps a tavern, and furnished us with an excellent dinner.

The road upon the top of Pocono is perfectly level a distance of four miles ; and all the way to the Wilkesbarre Mountains, twenty miles, there is but little variation in the altitude.   On the left, near Smith's, is an elevation called the Knob, about two hundred feet above the general level, from the apex of which it is said the highest peaks of the Catskills, sixty miles distant, may be distinctly seen on a clear morning.   All around is a perfect wilderness as far as the eye can reach, and so trifling are the variations from a level, that the country appears like a vast plain.   The whole is covered with shrub oaks, from three to ten feet in height, from which rise lofty pines, cedars, and tamaracks, interspersed with a few birch and chestnut trees, and occasionally a mountain ash with its blazing berries.   The shrub oaks, at a distance, appeared like the soft light green grass of a meadow, and groups of lofty evergreens dotted the expanse like orchards upon a prairie.   Here and there a huge blasted pine, black and leafless, towered above the rest, a

> ' Stern dweller of the mountain ! with its feet
> Grasping the crag, and lifting to the sky
> Its haughty crest !'"

Vast cranberry marshes spread out upon this high, rolling table-land, and supply the surrounding settlements with an abundance of that excellent fruit.   Indeed, the whole region is almost a continuous morass, and the road, a large portion of the way, is a causeway made of logs.   Here the gray eagle wheels undisturbed, the bear makes his lair, and the wild deer roam in abundance.   These, with the flocks of pheasants, and the numerous rabbits that burrow upon this wild warren, invite the adventurous huntsman, willing to " camp out" in the wilderness.   No settlements enliven the way ; and the cabins and saw-mills of lumbermen, where the road intersects the streams, are the only evidences of a resident population, except three or four places where a few acres have been redeemed from the poverty of nature.   This wilderness extends more than a hundred miles between the Delaware and Susquehanna Rivers, and a death-like solitude broods over the region.

I kept my seat upon the driver's box all the way from the Wind-gap to Wilkesbarre, charmed by the romance of the scene, rendered still more wild and picturesque by the dark masses of cumulous clouds that overspread the heavens in the afternoon.   The wind blew very cold from the northwest, and the driver assured me that, during the hottest weather in summer, the air is cool and bracing upon this lofty highway.   Poor fellow, he was an emaciated, blue-lipped soldier, recently returned from the battle-fields of Mexico, where the *vomito* and *ague* had shattered a hitherto strong constitution, and opened his firm-knit system to the free entrance of diseases of every kind.   He was at Vera Cruz and Cerro Gordo.   He lay sick a whole summer at Perote, and now had resumed the whip with the feeble hope of regaining lost health.

We crossed the upper waters of the Lehigh at Stoddartsville, in the midst of the great lumber country, and reached the brow of the Wilkesbarre Mountains just before sunset.   There a scene of rare grandeur and beauty was revealed, heightened by contrast with the rugged and forbidding aspect of the region we had just traversed.   The heavy clouds, like a thick curtain, were lifted in the west to the apparent height of a celestial degree, and allowed the last rays of the evening sun to flood the deep valley below us with their golden light.   The natural beauties of the vale, reposing in shadow, were for a moment brought

out in bold outline ; and from our point of view we gazed upon a picture such as the painter's art can not imitate.   Like a thread of silver the Susquehanna appeared, in its winding
course, among the lofty, overshadowing trees, upon its margin, and the villages, hamlets,
green woodlands, rich bottoms, and fruitful intervales of Wyoming, twenty miles in extent,
and the purple mountains on its western borders were all included in the range of our vision.
The thought, impious though it may be, came into my mind, that if Satan, when he took
Immanuel to the top of an " exceeding high mountain," exhibited a scene like this, the temptation was certainly great.   Wilkesbarre,[1] apparently at our feet, was three miles distant,
and it was dark when we reached the Phœnix Hotel, upon the bank of the river.   It had
been a fatiguing day's journey of sixty miles ; but a supper of venison, warm biscuit, and
honey, and a comfortable bed, made me feel perfectly vigorous in the morning, and prepared
for a ramble over the historic portions of the valley.

September 16,   After an early breakfast I rode to the residence of Charles Miner, Esq., about
1848.   two miles from the village, expecting to rely chiefly upon his varied and extensive knowledge of the history of the valley for information concerning the localities of interest, but was disappointed.[2]   He was suffering from a severe attack of an epidemic fever
then prevailing in the valley, and was unable even to converse much, yet I have not forgotten the sincere regrets and kind wishes he expressed.   He referred me to several gentlemen
in the village, descendants of the first settlers in the valley, and to one of them (Mr. Lord
Butler, a grandson of Colonel Zebulon Butler) I am indebted for many kind services while
I remained there.   He accompanied me to the several localities of interest in the valley, and
furnished me with such facilities for acquiring information as only a stranger can appreciate.
We visited Kingston, Forty Fort, the monument, the chief battle-ground, Fort Wintermoot,
Monocasy Island, &c. ; but a record of the day's ramble will be better understood after a
consultation of the history, and we will, therefore, proceed to unclasp the old chronicle.

History and song have hallowed the Valley of Wyoming, and every thing appertaining to
it seems to be wrapped in an atmosphere of romance.   Its Indian history, too, long antecedent
to the advent of the whites there, is full of the poetry which clusters around the progress of
the aborigines.   Mr. Miner gives a graphic picture of the physical aspect of the valley.   " It
is diversified," he says, " by hill and dale, upland and intervale.   Its character of extreme
richness is derived from the extensive flats, or river bottoms, which, in some places, extend
from one to two miles from the stream, unrivaled in expansive beauty, unsurpassed in luxuriant fertility.   Though now generally cleared and cultivated, to protect the soil from floods
a fringe of trees is left along each bank of the river—the sycamore, the elm, and more especially the black walnut, while here and there, scattered through the fields, a huge shell-
bark yields its summer shade to the weary laborers, and its autumn fruit to the black and
gray squirrel, or the rival plow-boys.   Pure streams of water come leaping from the mountains, imparting health and pleasure in their course ; all of them abounding with the delicious trout.   Along those brooks, and in the swales, scattered through the uplands, grow

---

[1] This name is compounded of two, and was given in honor of *John Wilkes* and *Colonel Barrè*, two of the
ablest advocates of America, through the press and on the floor of the British House of Commons, during
the Revolution.

[2] Mr. Miner is the author of a " *History of Wyoming*," a valuable work of nearly six hundred pages, and
possessing the rare merit of *originality*, for a large proportion of its contents is a record of information obtained by him from the lips of old residents whose lives and memories ran parallel with the Revolutionary
history of the valley, and events immediately antecedent thereto.   He folded up little books of blank paper,
took pens and ink, and, accompanied by his daughter Sarah, who, though blind, was a cheerful and agreeable companion, and possessed a very retentive memory, visited thirty or forty of the old people who were
in the valley at the time of the invasion in 1778.   " We have come," he said to them, " to inquire about
old Wyoming ; pray tell us all you know.   We wish an exact picture, such as the valley presented sixty
years ago.   Give us its lights and shadows, its joys and sorrows."   At night, on returning home, he read
over to his daughter what he had taken down, and carefully corrected, by the aid of her memory, " any error
into which the pen had fallen."   In this way Mr. Miner collected a great amount of local history, which
must otherwise have perished with the source whence he derived it.   I shall draw liberally upon his interesting volume for many of my historic facts concerning Wyoming.

OF THE REVOLUTION. 341

Ancient Beauty and Fertility of Wyoming.   Campbell's "Gertrude of Wyoming."   Its Errors.   First Tribes in the Valley.

the wild plum and the butter-nut, while, wherever the hand of the white man has spared it, the native grape may be gathered in unlimited profusion. I have seen a grapevine bending beneath its purple clusters, one branch climbing a butter-nut, loaded with fruit, another branch resting upon a wild plum, red with its delicious burden ; the while, growing in the shade, the hazel-nut was ripening its rounded kernel.

"Such were the common scenes when the white people first came to Wyoming, which seems to have been founded by Nature, a perfect Indian Paradise. Game of every sort was abundant. The quail whistled in the meadow ; the pheasant rustled in its leafy covert ; the wild duck reared her brood and bent the reed in every inlet ; the red deer fed upon the hills ; while in the deep forests, within a few hours' walk, was found the stately elk. The river yielded at all seasons a supply of fish ; the yellow perch, the pike, the catfish, the bass, the roach, and, in the spring season, myriads of shad."[1]

Campbell, with a poet's license, sung,

"Delightful Wyoming ! beneath thy skies
    The happy shepherd swains had naught to do
But feed their flocks on green declivities,
    Or skim perchance, thy lake with light canoe,
From morn till evening's sweeter pastime grew,
    With timbrel, when beneath the forest's brow
Thy lovely maidens would the dance renew ;
    And aye those sunny mountains half way down
Would echo flageolet from some romantic town.

"Then, when of Indian hills the daylight takes
    His leave, how might you the flamingo see,
Disporting like a meteor on the lakes—
    And playful squirrel on his nut-grown tree :
And every sound of life was full of glee,
    From merry mock-bird's song, or hum of men ;
While hearkening, fearing naught their revelry,
    The wild deer arched his neck from glades, and then,
Unhunted, sought his woods and wilderness again."[2]

Wyoming, in the Delaware language, signifies "large plains." By what particular Indian nation or tribe it was first settled is not certainly known, but it is probable that the Delawares held dominion there long before the powerful confederacy of the Five Nations, by whom they were subjugated, was formed. The tribes known as the Wyoming Indians, unto whom Zinzendorf and his Moravian brethren preached the Gospel, and who occupied the plains when the white settlers from Connecticut first went there, were of the Seneca and

---

[1] Miner's *History of Wyoming*, preliminary chapter, p. xiv.
[2] *Gertrude of Wyoming.* This beautiful poem is full of errors of every kind. The "lakes," the "flamingo," and the "mock bird" are all strangers to Wyoming ; and the historical allusions in the poem are quite as much strangers to truth. But it is a charming poem, and hypercriticism may conscientiously pass by and leave its beauties untouched.

342   PICTORIAL FIELD-BOOK

Count Zinzendorf.   His Visit to Wyoming.   Jealousy of the Indians.   Attempt to murder him.   Providential Circumstance.

Oneida nations, connected by intermarriage with the Mingoes, and the subjugated Leni-Lenapes, or Delawares. As it is not my province to unravel Indian history, we will pass to a brief consideration of the white settlements there.

The first European whose feet trod the Valley of Wyoming was Count Zinzendorf, who, while visiting his Moravian brethren at Bethlehem and Nazareth, in 1742, extended his visits among the neighboring Indians. His warm heart had been touched by the accounts he had received of the moral degradation of the savages, and, unattended, except by an interpreter, he traversed the wilderness and preached salvation to the red men. In one of these excursions he crossed the Pocono, and penetrated to the Valley of Wyoming. With a missionary named

COUNT ZINZENDORF.[1]

Mack, and his wife, who accompanied him, he pitched his tent upon the western bank of the Susquehanna, a little below the present village of Kingston, at the foot of a high hill, and near a place in the river known as Toby's Eddy. A tribe of the Shawnees had a village upon the site of Kingston. They held a council to listen to the communications of the missionaries, but, suspicious of all white men, they could not believe that Zinzendorf and his companions had crossed the Atlantic for the sole purpose of promoting the spiritual welfare of the Indians. They concluded that the strangers had come to " spy out their country" with a view to dispossess them of their lands ; and, with such impressions, they resolved to murder the count. The savages feared the English, and instructed those who were appointed to assassinate Zinzendorf to do it with all possible secrecy. A cool September night was chosen for the deed, and two stout Indians proceeded stealthily from the town to the tent of the missionary. He was alone, reclining upon a bundle of dry weeds, engaged in writing, or in devout meditation. A blanket curtain formed the door of his tent, and, as the Indians cautiously drew this aside, they had a full view of their victim. The benignity of his countenance filled them with awe, but an incident (strikingly providential) more than his appearance changed the current of their feelings. The tent-cloth was suspended from the branch of a huge sycamore, in such a manner that the partially hollow trunk of the tree was within its folds. At its foot the count had built a fire, the warmth of which had aroused a rattlesnake in its den ; and at the moment when the savages looked into the tent the venomous reptile was gliding harmlessly across the legs of their intended victim, who did not see either the serpent or the lurking murderers. They at once regarded him as under the special protection of the Great Spirit, were

---

[1] Nicolas Lewis, Count Zinzendorf, was descended from an ancient Austrian family, and was the son of a chamberlain of the King of Poland. He was born in May, 1700, and was educated at Halle and Utrecht. When about twenty-one years of age, he purchased the lordship of Berthholdsdorp, in Lusatia. Some poor Christians, followers of John Huss, soon afterward settled upon his estate. Their piety attracted his attention, and he joined them. From that time until his death he labored zealously for the good of mankind. The village of Hernhutt was built upon his estate, and soon the sect spread throughout Bohemia and Moravia. He traveled through Germany, Denmark, and England, and in 1741 came to America, and preached at Germantown and Bethlehem. He returned to Europe in 1743, and died at Hernhutt in 1760. The Moravian missionaries were very successful in their operations. They established stations in various parts of Europe, in Greenland, in the West Indies, and in Georgia and Pennsylvania. Piety, zeal, benevolence, and self-denial always marked the Moravians, and at the present day they bear the character of "the best of people."

filled with profound reverence for his person, and, returning to the tribe, so impressed their fellows with the holiness of Zinzen-
dorf's character, that their enmity was changed to veneration. A successful mission was established there, which was continued until a war between the Shawnees and the Delawares destroyed the peace of the valley.[1]

VIEW NEAR TOBY'S EDDY.[2]

Not long afterward the war that ensued between the English and French drew the line of separation so distinctly between the Indian tribes that respectively espoused either cause, that the excitements of warlike zeal repressed the religious sentiments which the indefati-
gable missionaries were diffusing among the savages. The tribes in the interest of the French soon be-
gan to hover around the Moravian settlements. Gnadenhutten was destroyed, and the other settlements were menaced.[3]   For several years these pious missionaries suffered greatly, and the white settlements were broken up.   After the defeat of Brad-
dock in 1755, the Delawares went over to the French, and the frontiers of Pennsylvania and Virginia were terribly scourged by these new allies of the enemies of the English.

In 1753 an association was formed in Connecticut, called the Susquehanna Company, the object of which was to plant a colony in the Wyoming Valley, a region then claimed by Connecticut by virtue of its ancient unrepealed charter.[4]   To avoid difficulties with the

[1] This was originated in the following manner.   The Shawnees were a secluded clan, living, by permis-
sion of the Delawares, upon the western bank of the Susquehanna.   On a certain day, when the warriors of both tribes were engaged in the chase upon the mountains, a party of women and children of the Shaw-
nees crossed to the Delaware side to gather fruit, and were joined by some of the squaws and children of the latter.   At length a quarrel arose between two of the children about the possession of a grasshopper. The mothers took part respectively with their children, and the quarrel extended to all the women on both sides.   The Delaware squaws were more numerous, and drove the Shawnees home, killing several on the way.   The Shawnee hunters, on their return, espousing the cause of their women, armed themselves, and, crossing the river, attacked the Delawares; a bloody battle ensued, and the Shawnees, overpowered, retired to the banks of the Ohio, and joined their more powerful brethren.   How many wars between Chris-
tian nations have originated in a quarrel about some miserable grasshopper!

[2] This is a view upon a stream called Mud Creek, a few rods from its mouth, at Toby's Eddy, in the Sus-
quehanna, about a mile below Kingston.   It was pointed out to me as the place where, tradition avers, Count Zinzendorf erected his tent, and where the singular circumstance related in the text occurred.   It was near sunset on a mild day (September 16th, 1848) when I visited the spot, and a more inviting place for retirement and meditation can scarcely be imagined.   It is shaded by venerable sycamore, butternut, elm, and black walnut trees.   From the Eddy is a fine view of the plain whereon the Delawares had their village, and of the mountains on the eastern side of the valley.   The *eddy* is caused by a bend in the river.

[3] The Moravians had established six missionary settlements in the vicinity of the Forks of the Delaware, or the junction of the Delaware and Lehigh Rivers, viz., Nazareth, Bethlehem, Nain, Freidenshal, Ganden-
thaul, and Gnadenhutten.   The latter, the name of which in English is "Huts of Mercy," was founded chiefly for the accommodation and protection of those Indians who embraced the Christian faith.   Hence it was the first settlement attacked by the hostile savages.

[4] When the regions in the interior of America were unknown, the charters given to the colonists were generally very vague respecting their western boundary.   They defined the extent of each colony along the Atlantic coast, but generally said of the westward extent, "from sea to sea."   Such was the expression in the Connecticut charter, and Wyoming, lying directly west of that province, was claimed as a por-
tion of its territory.   The intervening portion of New York, being already in actual possession of the Dutch, was not included in the claim.

Indians, the agents of the company were directed to purchase the land of the Six Nations, the actual owners, though it was then in possession of the Delawares. A deputation for the purpose attended the great convention and Indian council which was held at Albany in 1754, and, notwithstanding the strong efforts made by the Governor of Pennsylvania, through his agents, to the contrary, the purchase was effected. The tract bargained for included the whole Valley of Wyoming and the country westward to the Allegany River. The Pennsylvanians were irritated at what they called an unfair and illegal encroachment of the Connecticut people, and in strong terms protested against the purchase, for they claimed that the whole country included therein was covered by the charter granted to William Penn. Here, then, was planted the seed which soon burst forth into a mature tree, and bore the apples of discord in abundance.

Another Connecticut association, called the Delaware Company, had purchased lands upon the Delaware River, at a place called Cushetunk. They commenced a settlement there in 1757, and the Susquehanna Company prepared to plant their colony in Wyoming the following year. But, owing to the unsettled state of the country, the French and Indian war then being in progress, the settlement was deferred until 1762, when about two hundred colonists pushed forward, and commenced building and planting near the mouth of Mill Creek, a litt.: above the present site of Wilkesbarre. The Indians, and among them their great chief Teedyuscung, were at first opposed to this settlement of the whites in the valley, but were soon reconciled, and lived in daily friendly intercourse with the new comers. The Pennsylvanians, however, determined to repel what they held to be a bold encroachment upon their rights. Proclamations were issued, and writs of ejectment were placed in the hands of the sheriff of Northampton county, within the limits of which Wyoming was situated; but the Yankees continued to build and plant. They brought their families into the valley, and new settlers were rapidly augmenting their numbers. An event now occurred which at one terrible blow cut off this flourishing settlement.

I briefly adverted, at the close of the last chapter, to the fact that a great council was held at Easton in 1758, where Teedyuscung, the Delaware chief, acted a conspicuous part. The Six Nations regarded the Delawares as subjects, and were jealous of the popularity and power of Teedyuscung. They could not brook his advancement, and in the autumn of 1763 a party of warriors descended the Susquehanna, and came to the valley upon a pretended visit of friendship. As previously concerted, they set fire to the house of Teedyuscung on a certain night, and the chief was burned in it; while, to crown their wicked act, they adroitly charged the deed upon the whites. The Delawares believed the tale. They loved their chief, and determined on revenge. At broad noon, on the 14th of October, they attacked and massacred thirty of the settlers in their fields.[1] The whole settlement was speedily alarmed, and men, women, and children fled to the mountains, from which they saw their houses plundered and their cattle driven away. At night the torch was applied to their buildings, and the lovely abode of several hundred peaceful dwellers in the morning was made a desolation. Over the wilderness of the Pocono they made their way to the Delaware, and so on to their homes in Connecticut, a distance of two hundred and fifty miles. The blow was as unexpected as it was merciless, for they regarded the Delawares as their friendly neighbors.[2]

The Susquehanna Company did not attempt a settlement again for several years; and in the mean time the proprietaries of Pennsylvania, taking advantage of an Indian council held at Fort Stanwix in 1768, made a direct purchase of the Wyoming Valley from the Six Nations, and took a deed from some of the chiefs A lease of the valley for seven years was given to three Pennsylvanians,[3] who established a trading house there, which they for-

---

[1] This is the testimony of current history. Mr Miner, on the contrary, is persuaded that the same hands that destroyed Teedyuscung—the Six Nations—perpetrated this outrage.

[2] Proud, Gordon, Chapman.

[3] Charles Stewart, Amos Ogden, and John Jennings. The latter was the sheriff of the county. Charles Stewart subsequently became a popular and efficient officer of the Pennsylvania line in the Continental army.

tified. Forty pioneers of the Susquehanna Company, prepared to act promptly, entered the valley in February, 1769, and closely invested the Pennsylvania garrison. There were but ten men in the block-house, but they had found means to send a message to Governor Penn, informing him of their situation. They did not wait for succor, however, but, under pretense of consulting about an amicable compromise, three of the Connecticut party were decoyed into the block-house, arrested by Sheriff Jennings, and sent to Easton Jail. The Connecticut immigrants increased rapidly, and Jennings called upon the *posse* of the county and several magistrates to assist in their arrest. Quite a formidable force marched to Wyoming, but the Connecticut people had not been idle. They too had erected a block-house, which they called Forty Fort. Jennings demolished its doors, and arrested thirty-one of the inmates, most of whom were taken to Easton Jail. They were admitted to bail, were reenforced by about two hundred from Connecticut, and, returning to Wyoming, built a fort, which they called Fort Durkee, in honor of the officer elected to its command. This fortification was about half a mile below Wilkesbarre, near the Shawnee Flats. They also built thirty log houses around it, furnished with loop-holes for musketry, and, the number of the settlers being three hundred able-bodied men, Jennings could make no further impression upon them. He reported to the Governor of Pennsylvania that the whole power of the county was inadequate to dislodge the Yankees.

For a short time hostilities ceased, and the Susquehanna Company sent commissioners to Philadelphia to endeavor to negotiate a compromise.[1] Governor Penn refused to treat with them, and sent an armed force to the valley, under the command of Colonel Francis. He demanded a surrender of Fort Durkee, but the order was not obeyed. He reconnoitered, and, finding the works too strong to be successfully assaulted, returned to Philadelphia, leaving Ogden, one of the lessees of the valley, with a small force in the neighborhood. A larger force was assembled under Sheriff Jennings, well armed, and provided with a six pound cannon. Captain Ogden, who was prowling about the settlement, hearing of the approach of Jennings, darted suddenly among the houses with forty men, and captured several inhabitants, among whom was Colonel Durkee. He was taken to Philadelphia, and closely imprisoned. Jennings, with two hundred armed men, appeared before the fort, and began the erection of a battery. The garrison, alarmed, proposed to surrender upon certain conditions, which were agreed to. The articles of capitulation were drawn up in due form and signed, but Ogden acted in bad faith, and the seventeen settlers who were allowed by the capitulation to remain in the valley and harvest their crops, were plundered of every thing and driven over the mountains.

In February, 1770, Lazarus Stewart led an armed party from Lancaster into the Valley of Wyoming, who were joined by another armed party from Connecticut. They captured Fort Durkee, and, proceeding to the house of Ogden (who was then absent), seized the cannon already mentioned. Captain Ogden, on hearing of these transactions, hastened to Wyoming with fifty men, and garrisoned his own house. A party of fifty Yankees was sent against him, and a skirmish ensued. Several Connecticut people were wounded, and one was killed. Colonel Durkee[2] had now been released, and had returned from Philadelphia. Under his command the Yankees commenced a regular siege upon the fortress of the Pennymites.[3] They mounted the four pound cannon upon the opposite side of the river, and for several days played upon Ogden's house. Receiving no succor from Governor Penn, he surrendered upon terms similar to those allowed the Yankees the year before. He was to with-

---

[1] Colonel Dyer, and Jedediah Elderkin, of Windham, Connecticut.

[2] John Durkee was a native of that portion of Norwich, Connecticut, called Bean Hill, and was generally called the "bold Bean Hiller." He left Wyoming and returned to Connecticut. When the Revolution broke out, he entered into the contest zealously. He was at Bunker Hill, and was commissioned a colonel in the Connecticut line. He was in the battle on Long Island, at Germantown, and other engagements. He died at his residence at Bean Hill in 1782, aged fifty-four years, and was buried with military honors.

[3] This civil commotion is usually termed the *Pennymite and Yankee war*. The former name was derived from John Penn, governor of Pennsylvania when hostilities commenced.

draw himself and all his men from the valley, except six, who were to remain and guard his property.   But the Yankees, imitating Ogden's bad faith with them, seized his property and burned his house as soon as he was gone.   Warrants were afterward issued by the Governor of Pennsylvania against Lazarus Stewart, Zebulon Butler, and Lazarus Young, for the crime of arson, but they were never harmed.

Governor Penn, fearing political outbreaks in his capital at that time, and unwilling to send any of the few troops away from Philadelphia, called upon General Gage, then in command at New York, for a detachment of his majesty's troops to restore order at Wyoming. Gage refused compliance, and the Pennsylvanians were obliged to rely upon their own resources.   It was autumn before another attempt was made against the Yankees.   Ogden, with only one hundred and forty men, marched by the Lehigh route, to take the settlers by surprise.   From the tops of the mountains he saw the people at work in groups in their fields, and, separating his force into parties equal in numbers to the unsuspecting farmers below, they rushed down upon them, made several prisoners, and sent them to Easton.   Ogden lay concealed in the mountains, awaiting another opportunity to assail the Yankees.   The latter sent messengers to solicit aid from their friends on the Delaware.   These fell into Ogden's hands, and, learning from them the exact position of Fort Durkee, he made a night attack upon it.   It was filled with women and children, and the garrison, too weak to defend it, surrendered unconditionally.   The fort and the houses of the settlement were plundered, and many of the principal inhabitants were sent prisoners to Easton and Philadelphia.

A small garrison was left by Ogden in Fort Durkee.   The Yankees having left the valley, they were not very vigilant.   On the night of the 18th of December, between twenty and thirty men, under Lazarus Stewart, reached the fort by stealth, and captured it, shouting, "Huzza for King George!"   The Pennymites were now, in turn, driven from the valley.   Stewart held possession of the fort until the middle of January following, when the sheriff of Northampton county, with a considerable force, arrived before it.   Captain Ogden and his brother Nathan accompanied the expedition.   A skirmish ensued at the fort, and Nathan Ogden was killed.[1]   Stewart perceived that he could not long hold out, and on the night of the 20th withdrew from the valley, leaving twelve men in the fort.   These were made prisoners and sent to Easton, and quiet again prevailed at Wyoming.

1770.

January, 1771.

For six months the Pennymites were undisturbed in the possession of the valley, and the number of the settlers of Ogden's party had increased to about eighty.   But their repose was suddenly broken by the descent from the mountains, on the 6th of July, of seventy armed men from Connecticut, under Captain Zebulon Butler, and a party under Lazarus Stewart, who had joined him.   Ogden had built another and a stronger fort, which he called Fort Wyoming.[2]   The invaders were almost daily re-enforced, and commenced several military works with a view of besieging Ogden and his party in the forts.   The besieged were well supplied with provisions, and, their works being strong, they defied the assailants.   Ogden, in the mean while, escaped from the fort by stratagem,[3] proceeded to Philadelphia, and succeeded in inducing the acting governor (Hamilton) to send a detachment of one hundred men to Wyoming.   The expedition was unsuccessful.   After prosecuting the siege until the 11th of August, Captain Butler sent to the garrison a formal summons to surrender.   The gar-

---

[1] A settler named William Speddy was recognized as the man who discharged the musket that killed Ogden, and in November he was tried for murder, at the Supreme Court held in Philadelphia.   He was acquitted.

[2] This fort stood upon the ground now occupied by the court-house in Wilkesbarre.   There was another fort on the bank of the river, a little below the Phœnix Hotel.   Traces of the ditches were visible when I visited the spot in 1848.

[3] Ogden prepared a light bundle that would float upon the water, on which he fastened a hat.   To this bundle he attached a cord several yards in length, and, entering the river, swam past the sentinels, drawing the bundle at the distance of the length of the cord behind him.   The hat was fired at several times, but Ogden escaped unhurt.

rison refused compliance.   Butler had no ordnance, and a colonist named Carey[1] made a cannon of a pepperidge log.   At the second discharge the cannon burst, but they had no further need of artillery, for the garrison surrendered.   On the 14th a detachment of sixty men from Philadelphia, to re-enforce the garrison, had arrived within two miles of the fort; but, hearing of the surrender, they retraced their steps.   Several persons were killed during the siege.   By the terms of the capitulation, Ogden and his party were all to leave the valley.   Thus closed the civil war in Wyoming for the year 1771, and the Yankees were left in possession of their much-coveted domain.

The settlement now increased rapidly, and the Susquehanna Company applied to the General Assembly of Connecticut to take them under its protection until the decision asked of the king should be made.   The Assembly advised them to organize a government by themselves.   Pursuant to this advice, the inhabitants of Wyoming established a thoroughly Democratic government.   "They laid out townships," says Chapman, "founded settlements, erected fortifications, levied and collected taxes, passed laws for the direction of civil suits, and for the punishment of crimes and misdemeanors, established a militia, and provided for the common defense and general welfare of the colony."   The supreme legislative power was vested directly in the people, and exercised by themselves in their primary meetings.   A magistracy was appointed; courts were instituted, having civil and criminal jurisdiction; and a high court of appeals, called the Supreme Court, was established, composed, like their Legislature, of the people themselves in primary assembly.   The government was well administered, the colony rapidly increased, the people were happy, and for two years the smiles of peace and prosperity gladdened the Valley of Wyoming.

During this season of repose the Assembly of Connecticut made an effort to adjust all difficulties between the settlers and the government of Pennsylvania.   Richard Penn was then governor of that province, and would enter into no negotiations on the subject.   The Connecticut Assembly, therefore, made out a case and sent it to England for adjudication.[2]   It was submitted to the ablest lawyers of the realm—Lord Thurlow, Wedderburne, Richard Jackson, and John Dunning—and their decision was in favor of the Susquehanna Company.

---

[1] Mr. Carey was a native of Dutchess county, New York, and went to Wyoming with his sons in 1769. His brother, Samuel Carey, was a distinguished Quaker preacher.   His sons became permanent settlers in Wyoming, and lived to a good old age.

[2] Colonel Eliphalet Dyer was sent to England as agent for the Connecticut Assembly.   He was one of the most eminent lawyers of that province.   His eloquence was of the most persuasive kind.   In allusion to this intellectual power, a wit wrote the following impromptu, while Dyer was advocating the cause of the Susquehanna Company on the floor of the Assembly chamber:

> "Canaan of old, as we are told,
>   When it did rain down manna,
> Wa'nt half so good, for heavenly food,
>   As Dyer makes Susquehanna."

This is the same Dyer alluded to in the amusing doggerel entitled "Lawyers and Bull-frogs," in which the people of Old Windham, in Connecticut, were interested.   The poem is printed in the Historical Collections of Connecticut, page 448.   The introduction avers that, after a long drought, a frog-pond became almost dry, and a terrible battle was fought one night by the frogs, to decide who should keep possession of the remaining water.   Many "thousands were found defunct in the morning."   There was an uncommon silence for hours before the battle commenced, when, as if by a preconcerted agreement, every frog on one side of the ditch raised the war-cry, *Colonel Dyer! Colonel Dyer!* and at the same instant, from the opposite side, resounded the adverse shout of *Elderkin too! Elderkin too!*   Owing to some peculiarity in the state of the atmosphere, the sounds seemed to be overhead, and the people of Windham were greatly frightened.   The poet says,

> "This terrible night the parson did fright
>   His people almost in despair;
> For poor Windham souls among the bean-poles
>   He made a most wonderful prayer.
> Lawyer Lucifer called up his crew;
> Dyer and Elderkin,* you must come too:
> Old Colonel Dyer you know well enough,
> He had an old negro, his name was Cuff."

---

* Jedediah Elderkin accompanied Colonel Dyer to Philadelphia in 1769, in behalf of the Susquehanna Company.

The settlement was now taken under the protection of Connecticut, and incorporated into that colony. The territory was erected into a chartered town called Westmoreland, and attached to Litchfield county; representatives from it were admitted to seats in the General Assembly, and Zebulon Butler and Nathan Denison were commissioned justices of the peace. Repose continued to reign in the valley, and unexampled prosperity blessed the settlement. A town immediately adjoining Wyoming Fort was planted by Colonel Durkee, and named Wilkesbarre; and the whole valley became a charming picture of active life and social happiness. The foot-prints of civil war were effaced, and the recollections of the gloomy past were obliterated. A dream of happiness lulled the people into the repose of absolute security. Isolated in the bosom of the mountains, and far removed from the agitations which disturbed the people upon the ocean coasts, they had heard little of the martial sound of preparations for the hostilities then elaborating in the imperial and colonial councils. They were enjoying, in full measure, the blessings of virtuous democracy, and felt none of the oppressions of Great Britain, then bearing with such heavy hand upon the commercial cities of America; yet they warmly sympathized with their suffering brethren, and their hearts and hands were open to the appeals of the patriots of the east.

Four years Wyoming enjoyed uninterrupted peace, when its repose was suddenly broken by an attack upon a branch of the colony, located about sixty miles below Wilkesbarre, by a body of Northumberland militia, who were jealous of the increasing prosperity of the Yankees. On the 28th of September, 1775, the unsuspecting inhabitants were suddenly assailed, several of them were killed, and the residue were sent to Sunbury and imprisoned. About the same time several boats from Wyoming, trading down the river, were plundered by the Pennsylvanians. The Continental Congress was then in session in Philadelphia, and the Connecticut people of Wyoming, preferring peaceful measures to a renewal of the civil war, petitioned that body for redress. Congress, " considering that the most perfect union between the colonies was essentially necessary for the preservation of the just rights of North America," adopted resolutions urging the governments of Pennsylvania and Connecticut to " take the most speedy and effectual steps to prevent hostilities" and to adjust difficulties.[1] But the lawless invaders had not yet learned to respect the voice of Congress. Its resolutions were unheeded, and the imprisoned settlers were more rigidly confined, under the apprehension that the exasperated people of Wyoming, now become numerous, might make a retaliatory movement against Sunbury. A proposition was made to raise a force, and march against Wyoming to subjugate it before the people could organize a military government. Governor Penn favored the design, and Colonel Plunkett, who was also a magistrate, was placed in command of the expedition. He was ostensibly vested with civil powers, and his force was called the *posse* of the county. Congress, still in session in Philadelphia, passed a resolution urging the immediate termination of all hostilities between the parties.[2] But the Pennsylvanians paid no attention to the resolution, and Plunkett advanced toward Wyoming. His progress was slow, for the river was much obstructed by ice; and before he came to the Nanticoke Rapids, at the south end of the valley, where he was obliged to leave his boats, the people had made ample preparations to receive him. The military were under the command of Colonel Zebulon Butler, and numbered about three hundred effective men.

December 20, 1775.

From the summit of a bold rock on the western side of the river, that overhung the road along which Plunkett was marching, a volley of musketry was discharged as he approached, and arrested his progress. By means of a bateau, which he caused to be brought above the rapids by land, his men attempted to cross the river, to march against Fort Wyoming on the eastern side. They were assaulted by an ambuscade on shore, and the whole invading force immediately retreated to their provision boats, moored below the rapids, where a council of war was held. This council wisely concluded that the chances of success were few, and the expedition was abandoned.

---

[1] Journals of Congress, vol. i., p. 215.   [2] Ibid., p. 279.

The war of the Revolution had now fairly commenced. The proprietary government of Pennsylvania was soon afterward virtually abolished, a constituent assembly was organized,[a] and the people and the governments of both colonies had matters of much [a 1777.] greater importance to attend to than disputes about inconsiderable settlements. Henceforth the history of Wyoming is identified with the general history of the Union. I have glanced briefly at the most important events connected with its early settlement, for they form an interesting episode in the general history of our republic, and exhibit prominently those social and political features which characterized the colonies when the war of independence broke out. Separate provinces, communities, and families, having distinct interests, and under no very powerful control from without, had learned independence of thought and action, self-reliance, patient endurance under the pressure of circumstances, and indomitable courage in the maintenance of personal and political rights, from the circumstances in which their relations to each other had placed them. It was in schools like that of the Pennymite war, the resistance of the New Hampshire Grants to the domination of New York, the opposition to the Stamp Act and kindred measures, and the Regulator movement in the Carolinas, that the people were tutored for the firm resistance which they made to British oppressions during the seven years of our struggle for political emancipation; and there is more of the true philosophy of our great Revolution to be learned by studying antecedent, but relative events, than in watching the progress of the war itself. We will now turn to a consideration of the events which occurred in Wyoming during our Revolution.

The defection of a large portion of the Six Nations, the coalition of the Delawares and Shawnees with the friends of the king westward of the Alleganies, and the menaces of the tribes bordering on Virginia, with whom Lord Dunmore, the royal governor of that province, had long tampered, seeking to bring their hatchets upon the frontier settlements of that rebellious state, gave the Continental Congress much uneasiness at the beginning of 1776. Thousands of mercenary Germans were preparing to come like " destroying locusts upon the east wind ;" the British Parliament had voted fifty-five thousand men for the American service ; loyalty to the crown was rife throughout the land ; and the dark cloud of savages upon the western border of the colonies, smarting under the wrongs inflicted by the white men for a century and a half, and without any definite ideas of the nature of the quarrel in question, or means of discriminating between the parties to the feud, were ready to raise the war-cry, and satiate their appetites for vengeance, rapine, and blood. Westmoreland, or Wyoming, was peculiarly exposed, lying upon the verge of the Indian country, and to the people of its lovely valley the conciliation of the Indians was a matter of vast importance. The council of Onondaga, the chief head of the Six Nations, made professions of peaceful intentions, but there was evident hypocrisy underlying the fair appearance of the surface, and occasional outrages upon the remote settlers had been committed without rebuke. On one occasion a man named Wilson, living within the limits of Westmoreland, had been cruelly treated by the Indians, and Colonel Zebulon Butler sent a messenger to ascertain the true intentions of the savages. A chief called John returned with the messenger, and, in a speech replete with Indian eloquence, disclaimed, in behalf of the Six Nations, all thoughts of hostility to the friends of Congress. The Rev. Mr. Johnson, the first pastor in Wyoming, acted as interpreter. " We are sorry," said the chief, " to have two brothers fighting with each other, and should be glad to hear that the quarrel was peaceably settled. We choose not to interest ourselves on either side. The quarrel appears to be unnecessary. We do not well understand it. We are for peace." He continued :

" Brothers, when our young men come to hunt in your neighborhood, you must not imagine they come to do mischief; they come to procure themselves provisions, also skins to purchase them clothing.

" Brothers, we desire that Wyoming may be a place appointed where the great men may meet, and have a fire, which shall ever after be called Wyomick, where you shall judge best how to prevent any jealousies or uneasy thoughts that may arise, and thereby preserve our friendship.

" Brothers, you see but one of our chiefs. You may be suspicious on that account ; but we assure you this chief speaks in the name of the Six Nations. We are of one mind.

" Brothers, what we say is not from the lips, but from the heart. If any Indians of little note should speak otherwise, you must pay no regard to them, but observe what has been said and written by the chiefs, which may be depended on.

" Brothers, we live at the head of these waters [Susquehanna]. Pay no regard to any reports that may come up the stream or any other way, but look to the head waters for truth ; and we do now assure you, as long as the waters run, so long you may depend on our friendship. We are all of one mind, and we are all for peace."

This was the strong language of assurance, and Colonel Butler, confident of its sincerity, wrote accordingly to Roger Sherman of the Connecticut Assembly. He mentioned in his letter that the Indians wanted an *American flag* as a token of friendship ; and the whole tone of his communication evinced a belief in the professed attachment of the savages to the republicans. But at that very time the Mohawks, Onondagas, and Senecas were leaguing against the patriots ; and already Brant and five hundred warriors had struck a severe blow of hostility to the republicans at the Cedars, on the St. Lawrence. The proposed council fire at Wyoming was doubtless intended as a pretense for assembling a large body of warriors in the heart of the settlement, to destroy it ; and the desire for an American flag was undoubtedly a wish to have it for a decoy when occasion should call for its use. Events soon occurred which confirmed these suspicions, and the people of Wyoming prepared for defense against their two-fold enemy, the Indians and the Tories.[1]

When the war broke out, the Connecticut Assembly prevented further immigration to Westmoreland. But people came there, from the Hudson and the Mohawk Valleys, having no sympathy with either of the parties in the " Pennymite war," and, as it appeared, no sympathy with the republicans. Almost every original settler had espoused the cause of the Whigs ; and the open expression of hostility to Congress by these interlopers, the most active of whom were the Wintermoots, Van Gorders, Van Alstyns, and a few other families, excited the indignation of the Wyoming people.[2] The recommendation of the Continental Congress, to organize committees of vigilance in every town, had been promptly acted upon in Wyoming, and these new comers, the avowed friends of the king, were soon subjected to the severest scrutiny of the committee there. The people of Wyoming, numbering nearly three thousand, and united in thought and action, were pursuing peacefully their various occupations. The sudden influx of strangers to them, not only in person but in political creed, justly excited suspicions that they were a colony of vipers, come to nestle among them for the purpose of disseminating the poison of Toryism. Influenced by these fears, several of the most suspicious of the interlopers were arrested and sent to Connecticut. This was an unwise act, although perhaps justifiable, and was one cause of subsequent disasters.

In the mean while two companies of regular troops, of eighty-two men each, had been raised in the valley, under a resolution of Congress, commanded by Captains Ransom and

---

[1] On the 10th of March, 1777, the following resolutions were adopted at a town meeting held at Wilkesbarre :

" *Voted,* That the first man that shall make fifty weight of good saltpetre in this town shall be entitled to a bounty of ten pounds lawful money, to be paid out of the town treasury.

" *Voted,* That the select-men be directed to dispose of the grain now in the hands of the treasurer or collector in such a way as to obtain powder and lead to the value of forty pounds lawful money, if they can do the same."

It was also subsequently voted to empower a committee of inspectors " to supply the soldiers' wives and the soldiers' widows with the necessaries of life." This was a noble resolution.

[2] Mr. Miner, in a letter to the late William L. Stone, mentions the fact that among the papers of Colonel Zebulon Butler he found a list of Tories who joined the Indians. The list contained sixty-one names, of which only three were those of New England men. Most of them were transient persons, who had gone to Wyoming as hunters and trappers. Six of them were of one family (the Wintermoots), from Minisink. Nine were from the Mohawk Valley, doubtless in the interest of the Johnsons, four from Kinderhook, and six from West Chester, New York. There were not ten Tory families who had resided two years in Wyoming.—See *Stone's History of Wyoming,* p. 181.

Durkee, and were attached to the Connecticut line.[1]   The Wintermoots, who had purchased land toward the head of the valley, and upon the old banks of the Susquehanna,[2] at a place where bubbled forth a large and living spring of pure water, erected a strong fortification known as Wintermoot's Fort.

SITE OF WINTERMOOT'S FORT.[4]

The town meeting alluded to, suspicious of the design of the Wintermoots, who had hitherto acted so discreetly that a charge of actual hostility to Congress could not properly be made against them, thought it best to counteract their apparent belligerence, and resolved that it had " become necessary for the inhabitants of the town to erect suitable forts as a defense against the common enemy." August 24, 1776. A fort was accordingly built, about two miles above Wintermoot's, under the supervision of the families of Jenkins and Harding, and called Fort Jenkins.[3]   Forty Fort (so called from the first forty Yankees, the pioneers of the Susquehanna settlers in Wyoming), then little more than a weak block-house, was strengthened and enlarged, and sites for other forts were fixed on, at Pittstown, Wilkesbarre, and Hanover.   It was agreed in town meeting that these several fortifications should be built by the people, " without either fee or reward from the town."

As we have observed in a former chapter, the tribes of the Six Nations which had receded from their solemn agreement of neutrality were not brought actively into the service of the king until the summer of 1777.   It was then that the people of Wyoming perceived, and fully appreciated, the perils attendant upon their isolation, and the attention of the Continental Congress was often called to their exposed situation.   While St. Leger was investing Fort Stanwix, some straggling parties of savages hung about and menaced Wyoming ; but, after the siege was raised, the people were not disturbed again during the remainder of the year and the following spring.   But early in the summer of 1778 the movements of Brant and his warriors, and the Johnsons and Butlers and their Tory legions, upon the upper waters of the Susquehanna, together with the actions of the Tories in the Valley of Wyoming, who were greatly exasperated on account of the harsh treatment of some of their number by the

---

[1] These two companies served with distinction at the skirmish on Millstone River, in New Jersey, on the 20th of January, 1777.   This occurred while the main army of the Americans were suffering from the smallpox at Morristown.   A line of forts had been established along the Millstone River, in the direction of Princeton.   One of these, at Somerset Court-house, was occupied by General Dickinson with these two regular companies and about three hundred militia.   A mill on the opposite bank of the stream contained considerable flour.   Cornwallis, then lying at New Brunswick, dispatched a foraging party to capture it.   The party consisted of about four hundred men, with more than forty wagons.   The British arrived at the mill early in the morning, and, having loaded their wagons with flour, were about to return, when General Dickinson, leading a portion of his force through the river, middle deep, attacked them with so much spirit, that they fled in haste, leaving the whole of their plunder, with their wagons, behind them.

[2] Along the western side of the Susquehanna, a large part of the way from the head of the valley to the village of Kingston, opposite Wilkesbarre, are traces of a more ancient shore than the present, when the river was broader and perhaps deeper than now.   The plain extending from the ancient shore to the foot of the mountain is a uniform level, several feet above the alluvial bottom between it and the present bank of the river.

[3] There was another fort, called Fort Jenkins, upon the Susquehanna, about half way between Wilkesbarre and Fort Augusta, or Sunbury.   The fort in question was about eight miles above Wilkesbarre.

[4] This view is from the ancient bed of the Susquehanna, looking west.   The building, formerly the property of Colonel Jenkins, and now owned by Mr. David Goodwin, is upon the site of old Fort Wintermoot, which was destroyed at the time of the invasion in 1778.   It is upon the ancient bank of the river, here from fifteen to twenty feet high, and about sixty rods from the stream in its present channel.

Whigs, greatly alarmed the people.   Several of the Loyalists had left and joined the forces under Colonel John Butler, and the people very properly apprehended their return with power sufficient to satisfy their manifest spirit of vengeance.   Early in May the savages had committed many robberies, and in June some murders, in the neighborhood of Tioga, and other points on the upper borders of Westmoreland.   The Indians were in considerable force at Conewawah (now Elmira, in Chemung county, New York), and were in constant communication with the Tory settlers, by runners, at Wyalusing and in the neighborhood of Tunkhannock, within the precincts of Westmoreland.   These circumstances were alarming ; yet the exposed territory, cut off as it was from immediate aid, if demanded, was weakened by drafts upon its able-bodied men for the Continental army, and demands upon its local treasury for the use of the Connecticut Assembly.   Mr. Miner has given, in a spirited historic "pen-and-ink sketch," a picture of the condition of Wyoming at the close of 1777, and at the opening of the active operations the following year.   He says, " Nearly all their able-bodied men were away in the service.   The remaining population, in dread of the savages, were building six forts or stockades, requiring great labor, 'without fee or reward.'   All the aged men out of the train bands, exempt by law from duty, were formed into companies to garrison the forts, one of the captains being also chief physician to the people and surgeon to the military.   Of the militia the whole were in constant requisition, to go on the scout and guard against surprise.   The small-pox pestilence was in every district.   A tax to go to Hartford was levied in the assessment of the year, of two thousand pounds,"[1] not in Continental bills of credit at their nominal value, but " lawful money of the state of Connecticut."

Such was the condition of Wyoming when, in June, 1778, an expedition of Tories and Indians was prepared to fall upon the defenseless inhabitants.   Congress was apprised of the dark design.   The officers and men in the army, from Wyoming, pleaded for their wives and little ones.   General Schuyler wrote a touching letter to Congress on the subject ; yet that body, always tardy in its movements, and at that time too much employed in sectional disputes and factious intrigues, left the settlement uncared for, and apparently unnoticed, except by the resolutions to permit the people to take measures for self-defense by raising troops among themselves, and finding " their own arms, and accouterments, and blankets."[2]   The heads of the families there exposed were cruelly detained in the ranks of the Continental army elsewhere, and thus, naked and helpless, the settlement presented an easy prey to the vultures that scented them from Niagara, and whose companions were then glutting their appetites in the Mohawk and Schoharie settlements.

A force, consisting of the Tory Rangers of Colonel John Butler, a detachment of Johnson's Royal Greens, and from five to seven hundred Indians, under the general command of Butler, and numbering in all about eleven hundred men, crossed the Genesee country from Niagara, and appeared at Tioga Point, in June, whence they embarked in canoes, and landed

---

[1] *History of Wyoming*, page 207.   Mr. Miner mentions an instance of the patriotism of the women of Wyoming, and the draft which the people made, under the pressure of circumstances, upon their undeveloped resources.   Gunpowder was very scarce at the time when the settlement was menaced by the enemy. The husbands, fathers, and brothers were away in the Continental ranks, and the females plowed, sowed, and reaped.   Nor was this all : they manufactured gunpowder for the feeble garrisons in the forts.   " They took up the floors of their houses, dug out the earth, put it in casks, and ran water through it, as ashes are leached.   They then took ashes in another cask, and made ley, mixed the water from the earth with weak ley, boiled it, and set it to cool, and the saltpetre rose to the top.   Charcoal and sulphur were then used, the mixture was pounded in an implement brought to the valley by Mr. Hollenback, and thus powder was produced for the public defense."—Page 212.

[2] See resolution of March 16th, 1778, in the Journals of Congress, vol. iv., p. 113.   This resolution authorized the raising of " one full company of foot in the town of Westmoreland."   Nothing further was done by Congress in behalf of the people there until the 23d of June following, when a resolution was passed to write to the two independent companies under Durkee and Ransom, then greatly reduced by battle and sickness, and permit them to return home for the defense of the settlement.   Congress also resolved to pay the officers and soldiers of the companies authorized to be raised by the resolution of the 16th of March preceding, for their arms and accouterments.   The sum of $1440 was granted to the Board of War, to be issued to Colonel Denison.   The Continental paper dollars were then rapidly depreciating, four of them being at that time worth only one in specie.

near the mouth of Bowman's Creek, on the west side of the river, about twenty miles above Wyoming.   They entered the valley through a notch from the west, not far from the famous Dial Rock,[1] and attacked the people near Fort Jenkins, three of whom were killed.[2]   Butler then made his head-quarters at Wintermoot's Fort, whence he sent out scouts and foraging parties.

July 2, 1778.

Virtually abandoned by Congress, the people had made all the preparations in their power to meet the invaders, of whose approach they had been informed.   A company of forty or fifty regulars (so called only because the raising of the company was authorized by Congress), and a few militia, under the general command of Captain Hewett, then recruiting in the valley, composed the military force to oppose the enemy.   Grandfathers and their aged sons, boys, and even women, seized such weapons as were at hand.   Colonel Zebulon Butler, then an officer in the Continental army, happening to be at home when the enemy entered the valley, was, by common consent, made commander-in-chief.   Forty Fort was made the place of general military rendezvous, and thither the women and children of the valley fled for safety.   Aged men garrisoned some of the smaller forts.   There were fearful odds, and no alternative was left but to fight or submit to the tender mercies of the Indians and the more savage Tories.   " Retirement or flight was alike impossible, and there was no security but in victory   Unequal as was the conflict, therefore, and hopeless as it seemed in the eye of

POSITION OF THE WYOMING FORTS.[4]

prudence, the young and athletic men fit to bear arms, and enlisted for their special defense, being absent with the main army, the inhabitants, looking to their dependent wives, mothers, sisters, and little ones, took counsel of their courage, and resolved to give the enemy battle."[3]

On the morning of the 3d of July a council of war was held in Forty Fort, to determine what action was proper.   Some, among whom were Colonels Butler and Denison and Lieutenant-colonel Dorrance, were in favor of a delay, hoping that a re-enforcement from General Washington's camp, then near New Brunswick, in New Jersey might reach them in time, or that Captain Spalding, who was on the march for the valley with his company, might arrive.   Others, having little hope

1778.

of succor, were anxious to meet the enemy at once.   While the debates were going on, five commissioned officers from the army arrived at Forty Fort.   Hearing of the anticipated in-

---

[1] Dial Rock, or Campbell's Rock, as it is sometimes called, is a high bluff at the junction of the Susquehanna and Lackawana Rivers.   Its name is derived from the circumstance that the rays of the sun first strike its western face at meridian, and the farmers in the valley have always an unerring indicator of noontide on clear days.

[2] The victims were all scalped.   The bodies were interred by their friends, and over the graves of two of the Harding family, who were killed, a stone was raised, many years afterward, on which is the following inscription : " Sweet is the sleep of those who prefer death to slavery."

[3] Wyoming Memorial to the Legislature of Connecticut.

[4] EXPLANATION OF THE PLAN.—The several divisions, Hanover, Wilkesbarre, Kingstown, &c., mark the districts into which the town of Westmoreland was divided ; in military language, the different *beats*.   *A* marks the site of Fort Durkee ; *B*, Wyoming or Wilkesbarre Fort; *C*, Fort Ogden ; *D*, village of Kingston ; *E*, Forty Fort.   [This in the early histories of the Revolution is called Kingston Fort.]   *F*, the battle-ground ; *G*, Wintermoot's Fort ; *H*, Fort Jenkins ; *I*, Monocasy Island ; *J*, the three Pittstown stockades. The dot below the G marks the place of Queen Esther's Rock.   The village of Troy is upon the battle-ground, and that of Wilkesbarre, upon the site of Wilkesbarre Fort and its ravelins.   The distances of the several points from the present bridge at Wilkesbarre are as follows : Fort Durkee, half a mile below, on the left bank.   Fort Ogden, three and a half miles above, and the Pittstown stockades, about eight miles, on the same side.   Forty Fort, three and a half miles ; the Monument, on the battle-ground, five and a half ; Queen Esther's Rock, six and a half ; Wintermoot's Fort and Fort Jenkins, eight miles above, on the west or right bank of the river.   Kingston is directly opposite Wilkesbarre, half a mile westwar l.

vasion, they had obtained permission to return home to protect their families. Already Fort Jenkins had been captured, four of the garrison slain, and three made prisoners, and the other stockade would doubtless share the same fate. Already a demand for the surrender of Forty Fort and the valley had been made by Colonel John Butler, and the tomahawks of the Indians were lifted above the heads of those families who had not succeeded in reaching the fort. Upon prompt action appeared to depend their salvation; and, influenced by the pleadings of the only hope of safety left—victory in battle—the majority decided to march at once against the invaders. The decision was rash, and the minority yielded with much reluctance.

About one o'clock in the afternoon the little army, consisting of about three hundred vigorous men, old men, and boys, divided into six companies and marched from the fort, leaving the women in the most painful anxiety. They were joined by the justices of the court and other civil officers, and marched up the river to Wintermoot's Fort, intending to surprise the enemy, but Colonel John Butler was too vigilant to be caught napping. He had news of their approach, and sent for the party then demolishing Fort Jenkins to join him immediately. When the patriots approached, the enemy was prepared to meet them. Colonel John Butler and his Rangers occupied the left, which rested upon the river bank near Wintermoots; and the right, extending into a marsh at the foot of the mountains on the western verge of the plain, was composed principally of Indians and Tories, under a celebrated Seneca chief named Gi-en-gwa-tah, which signifies *He who goes in the smoke*.[1] John-

---

[1] Until the late Mr. Stone made his researches for materials for his interesting biography of Joseph Brant, or Thayendanegea, it was believed that Brant and his Mohawk warriors were engaged in the invasion of Wyoming. Gordon, Ramsay, Thacher, Marshall, and Allen assert that he and John Butler were joint commanders on that occasion, and upon his memory rested the foul imputation of being a participant in the horrid transactions in Wyoming. Misled by history, Campbell, in his *Gertrude of Wyoming*, makes the Oneida say,

> "This is no time to fill the joyous cup;
> The mammoth comes—the foe—the monster Brant,
> With all his howling, desolating band."

And again:

> "Scorning to wield the hatchet for his tribe,
> 'Gainst Brant himself I went to battle forth,
> Accursed Brant! he left of all my tribe
> Nor man, nor child, nor thing of living birth.
> No! not the dog that watched my household hearth
> Escaped that night of blood upon the plains.
> All perish'd! I alone am left on earth!
> To whom nor relative nor blood remains—
> No, not a kindred drop that runs in human veins."

Brant always denied any participation in the invasion, but the evidence of history was against him, and the verdict of the world was, that he was the chief actor in the tragedy. From this aspersion Mr. Stone vindicated his character in his *Life of Brant*. A reviewer, understood to be Caleb Cushing, of Massachusetts, disputed the point, and maintained that Stone had not made out a clear case for the sachem. Unwilling to remain deceived, if he was so, Mr. Stone made a journey to the Seneca country, where he found several surviving warriors who were engaged in that campaign. The celebrated Seneca chief Kaoundoowand, better known as Captain Pollard, who was a young chief in the battle, gave Mr. Stone a clear account of the events, and was positive in his declarations that Brant and the Mohawks were not engaged in that campaign. The Indians were principally Senecas, and were led by Gi-en-gwa-tah, as mentioned in the text. John Brant, a son of the Mohawk sachem, while in England in 1823, on a mission in behalf of his nation, opened a correspondence with Mr. Campbell on the subject of the injustice which the latter had done the chief in his *Gertrude of Wyoming*. The result was a partial acknowledgment of his error by the poet, in the next edition of the poem that was printed. He did not change a word of the poem, but referred to the use of Brant's name there, in a note, in which he says, "His son referred to documents which completely satisfied me that the common accounts of Brant's cruelties at Wyoming, which I had found in books of travels, and in Adolphus's and other similar histories of England, were gross errors....... The name of Brant, therefore, remains in my poem a pure and declared character of fiction." This was well enough as far as it went; but an omission, after such a conviction of error, to blot out the name entirely from the poem, was unworthy of the character of an honest man; and the stain upon the poet's name will remain as long as the libel upon a humane warrior shall endure in the epic.

son's Greens, under Captain Caldwell,[1] formed on Butler's right, and Indian marksmen were placed at intervals along the line. Colonel Zebulon Butler commanded the right of the Americans, aided by Major Garratt. The left was commanded by Colonel Denison, of the Wyoming militia, assisted by Lieutenant-colonel Dorrance. The battle-ground was a level plain, partly cleared and cultivated, and partly covered by shrub oaks and yellow pines

As the Americans approached the lines of the enemy, they perceived Wintermoot's Fort in flames, fired, no doubt, to prevent its falling into the hands of the patriots, an event that seemed quite probable to the Tory leader, who was ignorant of the exact number of men marching against him. Captains Durkee and Ransom, and Lieutenants Ross and Wells, were sent forward to reconnoiter and select the position for battle. The Wyoming companies approached separately, and as they were wheeled into line, Colonel Zebulon Butler thus addressed them : " Men, yonder is the enemy. The fate of the Hardings tells us what we have to expect if defeated. We come out to fight, not only for liberty, but for life itself, and, what is dearer, to preserve our homes from conflagration, our women and children from the tomahawk. Stand firm the first shock, and the Indians will give way. Every man to his duty."[2]

At the conclusion of Colonel Butler's short address, the Americans opened the battle on the enemy's left. It was about four o'clock, the sky cloudless, and the heat quite oppressive. The Americans were ordered to advance a step at each fire. Soon the battle became general, and the British left, where Colonel John Butler, stripped of his feathers and other trap-

---

[1] It is uncertain whether either of the Johnsons was in this campaign. As they do not appear in any official connection, it is probable they were not.

[2] Zebulon Butler was one of the early settlers in the Wyoming Valley. He was a native of Lyme, New London county, Connecticut, and was born in 1731. On the breaking out of the French and Indian war he entered the army as an ensign. He was at Ticonderoga, Crown Point, and other places in Northern New York. He was also in the memorable expedition to Havana during that war, and rose to the rank of captain. He left the service at the peace in 1763. In 1769 he emigrated to Wyoming, and became one of the leading men in that settlement. Before he left Connecticut he was strongly imbued with feelings of hostility to the mother country, which the agitations of the Stamp Act had engendered, and when the Revolution broke out he was found an active patriot. He was appointed colonel in 1778. He accompanied Sullivan in his memorable Indian expedition in 1779, and served with distinction throughout the war. In 1787 he was made lieutenant of the new county of Luzerne, which office he held until its abrogation by the new Constitution in 1790. He died on the 28th of July, 1795, at his residence, about a mile and a half above Wilkesbarre, and his remains were buried in the grave-yard at the borough. " Among other marks of respect to his memory," says Mr. Minor, " a monody of a dozen verses was written, one of which was inscribed on his tombstone :

"Distinguished by his usefulness
At home and when abroad,
At court, in camp, and in recess,
Protected still by God."

Colonel Butler was thrice married. His first wife was Ellen Lord ; his second, the daughter of the Rev Mr. Johnson, of Wyoming (the Indian interpreter already mentioned) ; and the third was Miss Phœbe Haight, whom he married while he was on duty at West Point, near the close of the war. Colonel Butler was a well-educated and intelligent man, as his letters show. An autograph letter to General Washington,

kindly given me by his grandson, the Hon. Chester Butler, of Wilkesbarre, from which this fac-simile of his signature is copied, is a good specimen, not only of the chirography, but of the perspicuity, terseness, and comprehensive style that characterized the military dispatches of the Revolutionary officers. He was one of those reliable men whom Washington cherished in memory, and after the war he received tokens of the chief's regard. Activity, energy, and a high sense of honor were the distinguishing traits of Colonel Butler's character. He was not a relative of the Tory John Butler, as some have asserted.

pings, appeared, with a handkerchief tied round his head, earnestly cheering his men, began to give way. But a flanking party of Indians, which covered that wing of the enemy, and was concealed under some bushes upon the ancient river bank, kept up a galling fire. Cap tain Durkee was slain by one of their shots.[1] In the mean time the Indian sharp-shooters along the line kept up a horrid yell, the sound of which reached the ears of the women and children at the fort. For half an hour the battle was waged with unceasing energy on both sides, but the vastly superior numbers of the enemy began to manifest its advantage. The Indians on the American left, sheltered and half concealed by the swamp, succeeded in out-flanking Colonel Denison, and fell with terrible force upon his rear. He was thus exposed to the cross fire of the Tories and Indians. Perceiving this, he ordered his men to fall back in order to change his position. The order was mistaken for one to *retreat*. That word was uttered with fatal distinctness along the line, and his whole division fled in confusion at the moment when the British left was giving way. A few minutes more of firm resist-ance might have given victory to the republicans. The American Colonel Butler and Col-onel Dorrance used every exertion to rally the fugitives and retrieve the loss, but in vain. Colonel Butler, seemingly unconscious of danger, rode along the lines exposed to the fire of the contending parties, beseeching his troops to remain firm. " Don't leave me, my chil-dren," he exclaimed, " and the victory is ours !" But it was too late ; the Indians leaped forward like wounded tigers. Every American captain that led a company into action was slain at the head of his men. Longer resistance was vain, and the whole American line, broken, shattered, and dispersed, fled in confusion, some in the direction of Forty Fort, and

others toward Monocasy Island, nearly a mile distant, and the only point on the river that promised them an opportunity to escape. The scene that ensued was ter-rible indeed. A portion of the flanking party of Indians rushed forward to cut off the retreat to Forty Fort, while the rest of the invaders, following the main por-tion of the army, who fled through the fields of grain toward Mono-casy Island, slaughtered them by

THE SUSQUEHANNA AT MONOCASY ISLAND.[2]

scores. Many who could not swim, and hesitated upon the brink of the river, were shot down ; and others, who hid themselves in bushes upon the shore, were dragged out and shot or tomahawked, regardless of their cry for quarter. Many swam to Monocasy Island, whither their pursuers followed and hunted them like deers in cover. Others were shot while swim-ming ; and some, who were lured back to the shore by promises of quarter, were butchered. Only a few escaped to the eastern side of the river and fled in safety to the mountains.[3]

---

[1] Captain Robert Durkee was a younger brother of Colonel John Durkee. When the valley was men-aced, and he was refused permission to return home, he resigned his commission in the army, and hastened to the defense of his family. He was a volunteer in the battle where he lost his life.

[2] This view is from the left or eastern bank of the Susquehanna, opposite the center of Monocasy Island, looking up the river. Toward the foreground, on the right of the picture, a little beyond the bar-post, is seen a ravine, through which the fugitives who crossed the river in safety made their way. On the left are seen the upper end of Monocasy, and a sand-bar which divides the waters of the river. The distant hills on the left are those which bound the western side of the valley. From the head of Monocasy Island, across the sand-bar, the river is often fordable in summer to the eastern side.

[3] It would be neither pleasant nor profitable to relate the many instances of suffering on that occasion. All the horrors of war, although on a small scale, were exhibited on that memorable day ; and were the particulars chronicled, the most rapacious gourmand of horrors might be surfeited. I will mention one or two circumstances, which sufficiently exhibit the bestiality of human character developed by civil war, de-stroying or stifling every feeling of consanguineous affection or neighborly regard. One of the fugitives, named Pensu, hid h..nself among the willows upon Monocasy Island. His Tory brother, who had joined

Colonel Zebulon Butler escaped to Wilkesbarre Fort and Colonel Denison to Forty Fort, where the latter mustered the few soldiers that came in, placed sentinels, and prepared for a defense of the women and children collected there.

Darkness put an end to the pursuit, but not to the horrors. It was a dreadful night for Wyoming, for the enemy, elated by victory, held their fearful orgies upon the battle-field.

> "Whoop after whoop with rack the ear assail'd,
> As if unearthly fiends had burst their bar;
> While rapidly the marksman's shot prevail'd,
> And aye, as if for death, some lonely trumpet v ail'd."[1]

Many prisoners suffered the martyrdom of savage torture, while some of their friends on the opposite shore, near Pittston, powerless to help them, observed the dreadful proceedings by the light of the fires. Captain Bidlack was thrown, alive, upon the burning timbers of Wintermoot's Fort, where he was held down with pitchforks until he expired! Prisoners were arranged in circles around large stones, and, while strong Indians held them, they were dispatched with a tomahawk. One of these stones, called Queen Esther's Rock, is pointed out to the curious. It is upon the old river bank, about forty rods east of the main road, three miles above Forty Fort, and near the house that belonged to a Mr. Gay. Around it sixteen prisoners were arranged in a circle, and each was held by a savage. A half-breed Indian woman, called Queen Esther,[3] assumed

QUEEN ESTHER'S ROCK.[2]

the office of executioner, and, using a maul and tomahawk alternately as she passed around the

in the pursuit, found him there concealed, and recognized him. The fugitive cast himself at his brother's feet and begged his life, promising to serve him till death if he would spare him. But the brother was changed still to a demon. "Mighty well, you damned rebel!" he tauntingly replied, and instantly shot him dead! The Oneida *savage* mentioned in a previous chapter refused to imbrue his hands in his brother's blood. The worst passions raged with wild and desolating fury. All the sweet charities of life seemed extinguished. Lieutenant Shoemaker, one of the most generous and benevolent of men, whose wealth enabled him to dispense charity and do good, which was a delight to him, fled to the river, when Windecker, a man who had often fed at his board and drunk of his cup, came to the brink. "Come out, come out," he said; "you know I will protect you." How could Shoemaker doubt it? Windecker reached out his left hand as if to lead him, much exhausted, ashore, and dashed his tomahawk into the head of his benefactor, who fell back and floated away.—*See Miner*, p. 225.

[1] Gertrude of Wyoming.

[2] This view is near the ancient river bank, looking westward. The rock is a sort of conglomerate, a large proportion of which is quartz. Some of it is of a reddish color, which the credulous believe to be stains of blood still remaining. The rock projects only about eighteen inches above the ground, and its size is denoted by the figure standing beside it. In the distance, on the left, is seen the monument which has been erected to the memory of those who fell on the occasion. This scene includes a portion of the battle-ground. The little village of Troy also occupies a part of the field of conflict.

[3] Queen Esther, as she was called, was the celebrated Catharine Montour, whose residence was at Catharinestown, near the head of Seneca Lake, in New York. The town was named after her, and was the first of the Indian villages destroyed by Sullivan in 1779, after the battle of Chemung. She was a native of Canada, and her father was one of the French governors, probably Frontenac. She was made a captive during the wars between the Hurons and French and the Six Nations, and was carried into the Seneca country, where she married a young chief who was signalized in the wars against the Catawbas. He fell in battle, about the year 1730. Catharine had several children by him, and remained a widow. Her superior mind gave her great ascendency over the Senecas, and she was a queen indeed among them. She accompanied the delegates of the Six Nations to Philadelphia on several occasions, where her refinement of manners and attractive person made her an object of much regard, and she was greatly caressed by the ladies of that city. From the circumstance of her refinement of manners, Mr. Stone argues that she could not have been

ring, singing the death-song, deliberately murdered the prisoners in consecutive order as they were arranged.   The time was midnight, and, the scene being lighted up by a large fire burning near, she appeared like a very fury from Pandemonium while performing her bloody work.   With the death of each victim her fury increased, and her song rose clearer and louder upon the midnight air.   Two of the prisoners (Lebbeus Hammond and Joseph Elliot), seeing there was no hope, shook off the Indians who held them, and, with a desperate spring, fled to a thicket, amid the rifle-balls and tomahawks that were sent after them, and escaped.   Similar scenes were enacted on other portions of the battle-field on that dreadful night, but we will draw a vail before the revolting picture, and view occurrences at Forty Fort, where the hopes of the settlement were now centered.

Terrible were the suspense and anxiety of the people at the fort while the battle was in progress.   They could distinctly hear the firing, and, when the shots became fewer and nearer, hope departed, for they knew the Americans were dispersed and retreating.   At twilight Captain John Franklin arrived at Forty Fort, with the Hunterdon and Salem company, of thirty-five men.   It was a timely re-enforcement, and revived the hopes of the little remnant of Denison's force.   The night was spent in sleepless vigilance and alarm by those within the forts, while the people without were flying to the mountains and the wilderness July 4, beyond, under cover of the darkness.   Early the next morning a messenger was dis-1778. patched to Wilkesbarre Fort, to send up the cannon, and cause the whole settlement to concentrate for defense at Forty Fort.   But all was confusion.   The people were flying in dismay, and leaving their homes a prey to the invaders.   The messenger returned with his melancholy tidings just as another arrived from Colonel John Butler, demanding a surrender, and requesting Colonel Denison to come up to head-quarters, near the still burning ruins of Wintermoot's Fort, to agree on terms of capitulation.   Already the principal stockade at Pittston (Fort Brown) had surrendered, and, there being no hope of a successful defense, Colonel Denison complied.   Colonel Butler demanded the surrender of all the forts, and also of Colonel Zebulon Butler and his Continental troops (numbering only fifteen men) as prisoners of war.   Colonel Denison hastened back, by agreement, to consult with his brother officers.   He conferred with Colonel Zebulon Butler at Wilkesbarre Fort, and it was agreed that the latter and his men should immediately retire from the valley.   He placed Mrs. Butler behind him upon his horse, and that night they slept at Conyngham, in the Nescopeek Valley, twenty miles from Wilkesbarre.   Colonel Denison, on returning, reported to the British leader that the Continentals were beyond his command, and negotiations were opened without reference to them.   The terms were verbally agreed upon, but, there being no conveniences for writing at hand, the contracting parties went to Forty Fort, and, upon a table belonging to a Mr. Bennet, the terms of capitulation were drawn up and signed.[1]

---

guilty of the atrocities at Wyoming which history has attributed to her.   But Mr. Miner, whose means for correct information on points connected with the history of Wyoming were much superior to those of Mr. Stone, clearly fixes the guilt upon her.   She was well known to Colonel Denison and Colonel Franklin, and they both explicitly charge her with the deed.   Two of her sons accompanied her in the expedition, and it is said that her fury on the occasion was excited by the death of one of them, in the fight that occurred near Fort Jenkins on the 2d of July, the day before the battle of Wyoming.   She must have been then nearly eighty years of age.   One of General Sullivan's men, in his journal, cited by Minor, speaks of reaching "Queen Esther's plantation" [Sheshequin], where she "dwelt in retirement and sullen majesty.   The ruins of her palace," he said, "are still to be seen.   In what we supposed to be the chapel we found an idol, which might well be worshiped without violating the third commandment on account of its likeness to any thing in heaven or on earth.   About sunrise the general gave orders for Catharinestown to be illuminated, and accordingly we had a glorious bonfire of upward of thirty buildings."   One of the sons of Kate Montour, as she was familiarly called, was with Walter Butler at Cherry Valley, and with his own hands captured Mr. Cannon, the father of Mrs. Campbell, mentioned in our account of the invasion of that settlement.   The old man's life was spared, and he was taken to Niagara.   Kate Montour was there, and "was greatly enraged," says Stone, "because her son had not killed him outright."   This "exhibition of a savage temper" is in accordance with her acts at Bloody Rock.

[1] The following is a copy of the articles of capitulation, dated Westmoreland, July 4th, 1778:

"ART. 1st. That the inhabitants of the settlement lay down their arms, and the garrisons be demolished,

OF THE REVOLUTION   359

Surrender of the Fort.   Treaty Table.   Conduct of the Tories.   Bad Faith of the Indians.   The Treaty

Colonel Butler, ascertaining that there were several casks of whisky in the fort, ordered them to be rolled to the bank of the river and emptied, fearing that they might fall into the hands of the Indians and make them unmanageable.

THE "TREATY TABLE."[1]

Every thing being arranged, the two gates of the fort were thrown open. The arms of the patriots were piled up in the center, and the women and children retired within the huts that lined the interior of the stockade. At the appointed time the victors approached, with drums beating and colors flying. They came in two columns, whites and Indians. The former were led by Colonel John Butler, who entered the north gate, and the latter by Queen Esther, the bloody priestess of the midnight sacrifice. She was followed by Gi-en-gwa-tah, who, with his warriors, entered the south gate. The wily chief, fearing treachery, glanced quickly to the right and left as he entered. The Tories, with their natural instinct for plunder, immediately seized the piled arms. Butler ordered them to desist, and presented the muskets to the Indians. The inhabitants were then marked by the Indians with black paint in their faces, and ordered to carry a white cloth on a stick. These were badges which, the savages said, would insure their protection.

The terms of the capitulation were respected by the invaders, particularly the Indians, for a few hours only. Before night they spread through the valley, plundering the few people that were left, and burning the dwellings of those already gone to the wilderness. The village of Wilkesbarre, containing twenty-three houses, was burned, and the inhabitants, with others remaining in the valley, fled in dismay toward the mountains, whither a great number of their friends had gone during the night. Only one life[2] was taken after the surrender

---

" 2d. That the inhabitants occupy their farms peaceably, and the lives of the inhabitants be preserved entire and unhurt.

" 3d. That the Continental stores be delivered up.

" 4th. That Major Butler* will use his utmost influence that the private property of the inhabitants shall be preserved entire to them.

" 5th. That the prisoners in Forty Fort be delivered up, and that Samuel Finch, now in Major Butler's possession, be delivered up also.

" 6th. That the property taken from the people called Tories, up the river, be made good, and they to remain in peaceable possession of their farms, unmolested in a free trade in and throughout the state, as far as lies in my power.

" 7th. That the inhabitants that Colonel Denison now capitulates for, together with himself, do not take up arms during the present contest.

[Signed]

" NATHAN DENISON
JOHN BUTLER.

" Zarah Beech,   Samuel Gustin,
John Johnson,   William Caldwell."

[1] The table on which the capitulation was drawn up and signed was still in possession of a daughter of Mr. Bennet (Mrs. Myers) when I visited her in September, 1848. I shall have occasion to mention this venerable woman presently. The table is of black walnut, small, and of oval form, and was a pretty piece of furniture when new. It is preserved with much care by the family. The house of Mr. Bennet was near Forty Fort, and himself and family, with their most valuable effects, were within the stockade when it surrendered.

[2] This was Sergeant Boyd, a deserter from the British army. Standing in the gateway of the fort after the capitulation, Colonel Butler recognized him, and said, sternly, " Boyd, go to that tree !" " I hope," said

---

* In all accounts of the war John Butler is denominated a colonel, while here he gives what was doubtless his true title. Lord George Germaine, in a dispatch to Sir Henry Clinton, gives him the rank of lieutenant colonel. This capitulation was highly honorable, and certainly affords a plea in favor of the merciful character of Butler claimed for him by his friends. In the trans actions which subsequently took place he declared his inability to control the Indians. This may have been true. But no honorable man would have headed such an expedition ; and whatever may have been his efforts to allay the whirlwind of destruction which he had raised, history holds him responsible, next to his government, for the dreadful tragedy in Wyoming. The stories of his cruelties, set afloat by the flying fugitives from the valley, and incorporated in the histories of Gordon, Ramsay, and other early historians of the war, have been refuted by ample testimony, and proved to be the offspring of imaginations greatly excited by the terrors of the battle and flight. The story, that when Colonel Denison asked Butler upon what terms he would accept a surrender, he replied, " The hatchet," and tales of a kindred nature of cruelties permitted by him, have no foundation in truth.

360   PICTORIAL FIELD-BOOK

Flight of the People over the Pocono.   Incidents of the Flight.   Providential Aid of Mr. Hollenback.   Preservation of Papers.

of Forty Fort, but numbers of women and children perished in their flight in the great swamp on the Pocono Mountains, known as the *Shades of Death*, and along the wilderness paths by the way of the Wind-gap and Water-gap, to the settlements on the Lehigh and Delaware. So sudden was their departure, that scarcely a morsel of food was secured. Terrible indeed were the incidents of that flight, as related by the sufferers and their friends, and recorded by Chapman and Miner. "Tears gushed from the eyes of the aged widow of Mr. Cooper," says Mr. Miner, "when she related that her husband had lain on his face to lap up a little meal which a companion in their flight had spilled on the earth. Children were born, and several perished in the ' Dismal Swamp,' or ' Shades of Death,' as it is called to this day. Mrs. Treusdale was taken in labor ; daring to delay but a few minutes, she was seen with her infant moving onward upon a horse. Jabez Fish, who was in the battle, escaped ; but, not being able to join his family, was supposed to have fallen ; and Mrs. Fish hastened with her children through the wilderness. Overcome by fatigue and want, her infant died. Sitting down a moment on a stone, to see it draw its last breath, she gazed in its face with unutterable anguish. There were no means to dig a grave, and to leave it to be devoured by wolves seemed worse than death ; so she took the dead babe in her arms and carried it twenty miles, when she came to a German settlement. Though poor, they gave her food ; made a box for the child, attended her to the grave-yard, and decently buried it, kindly bidding her welcome until she should be rested.

" The wife of Ebenezer Marcy was taken in labor in the wilderness. Having no mode of conveyance, her sufferings were inexpressibly severe. She was able to drag her fainting steps but about two miles that day. The next, being overtaken by a neighbor with a horse, she rode, and in a week was more than a hundred miles with her infant from the place of its birth.

"Mrs. Rogers, from Plymouth, an aged woman, flying with her family, overcome by fatigue and sorrow, fainted in the wilderness, twenty miles from human habitation. She could take no nourishment, and soon died. They made a grave in the best manner they could. . . . . . . Mrs. Courtwright relates that she, then a young girl flying with her father's family, saw sitting by the road side a widow, who had learned the death of her husband. Six children were on the ground near her—the group the very image of despair, for they were without food. Just at that moment a man was seen riding rapidly toward them from the settlements. It was Mr. Hollenback.[1] Foreseeing their probable destitution, he had providentially loaded his horse with bread, and was hastening back, like an angel of mercy, to their relief. Cries and tears of gratitude and welcome went up to heaven. He imparted a morsel to each, and hastened on to the relief of others.

" The widow of Anderson Dana, Esq.,[2] and her widowed daughter, Mrs. Whiton, did not learn certainly the death of their husbands until they were at Bullock's, on the mountain, ten miles on their way. Many then heard the fate of their relatives, and a messenger brought to Mr. Bullock word that both his sons were dead on the field. Then were heard mourning and lamentation, with wringing of hands. Mrs. Dana had been extraordinarily careful. Not only had she provided food, but had taken a pillow-case of valuable papers (her husband being much engaged in public business), the preservation of which has thrown much light on our path of research. Depending chiefly on charity, the family sought their ancient home in

---

Boyd, imploringly, " your honor will consider me a prisoner of war." " Go to that tree, sir," shouted Butler. The sergeant obeyed, and a volley from some Indian marksmen laid him dead upon the spot.

[1] Mr. Hollenback survived the battle, and escaped by swimming the river at Monocasy Island. He crossed the mountains to the settlements in advance of the fugitives.

[2] Anderson Dana was from Ashford, Windham county, Connecticut. He was a lawyer of good attainments ; his talents and zeal, in the promotion of the welfare of the Wyoming settlement, obtained from the people their unanimous suffrage, and he was elected a member of the Connecticut Assembly. Returning home when Wyoming was threatened, he mounted his horse, and, riding from family to family throughout the valley, aroused the people to action, and, though exempt from military duty, hastened to the field and fell. His son-in-law, Stephen Whiton, but a few weeks married, also went into the battle and was slain.

Connecticut. These few instances, selected from a hundred, will present some idea of the dreadful flight."[1]

What a picture did that flight present! No embellishment of fancy is needed to give it effect. One hundred women and children, with but a single man to guide and protect them, are seen, in the wildest terror, hurrying to the mountains. "Let the mind picture to itself a single group, flying from the valley to the mountains on the east, and climbing the steep ascent; hurrying onward, filled with terror, despair, and sorrow; the affrighted mother, whose husband has fallen, with an infant on her bosom, a child by the hand, an aged parent slowly climbing the rugged steep behind them; hunger presses them severely; in the rustling of every leaf they hear the approaching savage; a deep and dreary wilderness before them, the valley all in flames behind; their dwellings and harvests all swept away in this spring flood of ruin, and the star of hope quenched in this blood shower of savage vengeance."[2]

From the settlements on the Delaware the fugitives made their way to Connecticut by various routes, and the tales of horror of a few who crossed the Hudson at Poughkeepsie were published in a newspaper printed there. The account of the atrocities therein related was repeated every where in America and in Europe, and, remaining uncontradicted, formed the material for the darkest chapter in the annals of the Revolution, as recorded by the earlier historians. No doubt the fugitives believed they were telling truths. The battle, the devastation of the valley, and the flight across the wilderness were matters of their own experience; and other refugees, joining them in their flight, added their various recitals to the general narrative of woe. We will not stop to detail what has been erroneously written. The pages of Gordon, Ramsay, and Botta will satisfy those who wish to "sup on horrors." The researches of Mr. Minor have obliterated half the stain which those recitals cast upon human nature, and we should rejoice at the result, for the honor of the race. It is but just to the memory of the dead to say, in passing, that the conduct of Colonels Zebulon Butler and Nathan Denison[3] on the occasion has been falsely represented, and injustice done to their characters. All that could be done was done by those brave and devoted men.

Our story of the disaster in Wyoming is almost ended. Although alarm and distress prevailed there until the close of the war, there were no hostilities of greater moment than the menaces of savages and a few skirmishes with marauders. But, before closing the historic tome, let us briefly glance at the events in the valley which followed the surrender of the forts and the flight of the people.

As we have seen, the terms of capitulation were broken by the invaders within a few hours after the treaty was signed, and the houses of the people and fields of waving grain were plundered and destroyed. The Indians began by breaking open the trunks and boxes in the huts of the surrendered fort. The town papers were scattered, and many valuable records were destroyed. Colonel Denison called upon Butler repeatedly to enforce the terms of capitulation by restraining the Indians. Butler did, indeed, attempt to restrain them, but they utterly disregarded his orders. At length, finding his authority set at naught, doubtless considering his own life in danger should he attempt harsh measures of control, and probably fearing greater enormities on the part of the Indians, Butler withdrew from the July 8, valley.[4] Gi-en-gwa-tah interposed his authority, and a greater part of the Indians 1778.

---

[1] *History of Wyoming*, p. 230.

[2] The *Hazleton Travelers*. This is not a volume, but a series of biographical and historical sketches by Charles Miner, Esq., in the form of colloquies between two travelers from Hazleton. They were published in the *Wyoming Republican* in 1837-8. They are admirably conceived and written, and contain vivid pictures of the character and sufferings of the people of Wyoming during the Revolution.

[3] Colonel Nathan Denison was a native of New London, Connecticut, and was one of the early settlers in Wyoming. He was well educated, and was an active man in the valley. After the close of the war he held several important offices under the authority of Pennsylvania. He died January 25th, 1809, aged sixty-eight years.

[4] Mr. Miner gives Colonel Butler full credit for humane intentions, and believes that he desired to regard faithfully the terms of the capitulation, and that he made the most earnest endeavors to prevent the pillage and murders which ensued. On the authority of a Mr. Finch, a prisoner at the time, who went over the

followed the leaders, with Queen Esther and her retinue in the van.   The appearance of the retiring enemy was extremely ludicrous, aside from the melancholy savageism that was presented.   Many squaws accompanied the invaders, and these brought up the rear.   Some had belts around their waists, made of scalps stretched upon small hoops ; some had on from four to six dresses of chintz or silk, one over the other ; and others, mounted on stolen horses, and seated, "not sidewise, but otherwise," had on their heads four or five bonnets, one within another.

As soon as Butler and the main body of the invaders left the valley, the Indians that remained, wholly uncontrolled, swept over the plains in small bands of from five to ten, and wantonly destroyed the crops, burned houses and barns, and treated the few remaining people most cruelly.[1]   Several murders were committed, and terror again reigned in the valley.   Colonel Denison, and all who remained at Forty Fort, fled, some down the river and some to the mountains.   Except a few who gathered about the fort at Wilkesbarre, the whole people abandoned the settlement.   It presented one wide scene of conflagration and ruin.

Captain Spalding was between the Pocono and Blue Mountains, nearly fifty miles from Wilkesbarre, on the day of the battle.   Apprised of the event by the flying settlers, he hastened forward, and when within twelve miles of the valley sent two scouts to reconnoiter.   From the brow of the mountain they saw the flames rising in all directions, and the valley in complete possession of the invaders.   The efforts of a single company would be vain, and Captain Spalding returned to Stroudsburg, to await the orders of Colonel Zebulon Butler, a August 3, who soon returned to Wyoming.   When the enemy had left the valley, Spalding 1778. marched thither, and took up his quarters at Wilkesbarre Fort,[a] which he strengthened.   Other means for the defense of the valley were adopted, and a few of those who had fled returned, with the hope of securing something that might be left of all their desolated possessions.   Some of them were waylaid and shot by straggling Indians and Tories.   There was no security ; throughout that fertile valley fire was the only reaper, and the luscious fruits fell to the earth ungathered.   Even the dead upon the battle-ground lay unburied until the autumn frosts had come ; and when their mutilated and shriveled bodies were collected and cast into one common receptacle of earth, but few could be identified.   October 22. That sad office was performed by guarded laborers, while parties of the enemy, like hungry vultures, scented their prey from afar, and hovered upon the mountains, ready to descend upon the stricken settlers when opportunity should offer.

Colonel Hartly, of the Pennsylvania line, joined Colonel Zebulon Butler, and an expedition was arranged to expel the marauders.   In September a detachment of one hundred and thirty men marched to Shesequin, Queen Esther's plantation, a beautiful plain on the east branch of the Susquehanna (now in Bradford county), where a battle ensued.   Several of

---

battle-ground with Mr. Miner in 1838, he says that Colonel Butler received a letter on the 5th, which hastened his departure from the valley.   It probably gave him notice of the approach of Captain Spalding or some other expected re-enforcements.   Mr. Miner tells an amusing anecdote of Finch.   They called together upon Mrs. Jenkins, an aged lady, more than eighty years old, who was a prisoner in Forty Fort.   She instantly recognized Finch, and said, with much archness and humor, " Oh, yes, Finch, to be sure I remember you.   An old squaw took you and brought you in.   She found you in the bushes, and, as she drove you along, patted you on the back, saying, ' My son, my son !' "   Finch did not relish the exposure as well as the by-standers.   He had been playing the hero in his account of the battle.   Mrs. Jenkins stripped him of his plumage, and he soon after left the valley.

[1] One illustrative instance I will mention.   From the farm of an old man named Weekes, seven persons, three of whom were his sons, one a grandson-in-law, two relatives, and the last a boarder, went out to the battle.   At night the whole seven lay dead on the field !   After the capitulation, a band of Indians came to his house and ordered him away.   "How can I ?" he said ; "my whole family you have killed.   How can I with fourteen grandchildren, all young and helpless."   They feasted on the food in his house ; and one of the Indians, taking the hat from the old man's head, and placing himself in a large rocking-chair which he had taken to the road, rocked with much glee.   They then informed him that he might have three days allowed him to prepare for departure, and the use of a pair of oxen and a wagon to carry away his grandchildren.   He departed, and the savages set fire to the building, and destroyed all that was left.   Over the rough country along the Lackawanna Mr. Weekes made his way to Orange county.—See Miner's *Wyoming*, p. 238, and *Hazleton Travelers*.

the Indians were killed, their settlement was broken up, and a quantity of plunder that had been taken from Wyoming was recovered. Returning to Wyoming, Colonel Hartly was called away, but left a garrison of one hundred men at Wilkesbarre Fort. Thus defended, although the season was much advanced, a few armed settlers plowed and sowed. Marauding parties of the enemy still hovered upon the mountains, and several of the whites were murdered in their fields, among whom was Jonathan Slocum, a member of the Society of Friends. The interesting story of the abduction of his little daughter, and her subsequent discovery among the Indians, will be related in the next chapter.

In March, 1779, the garrison at Wilkesbarre was menaced by a party of about two hundred and fifty Indians and painted Tories, who surrounded the fort. The discharge of a field piece drove them away, but, the garrison being too feeble to attempt a pursuit, the marauders carried off much plunder, not, however, without suffering considerably in some smart skirmishes with the inhabitants. In April a re-enforcement for the garrison, under Major Powell, while marching toward Wyoming, fell into an Indian ambuscade. April 30. Six of his men were killed, but the Indians were routed.

Toward the close of June, General Sullivan arrived in the valley, with his division of the army destined for the invasion of the Seneca country, the events of which have been narrated in a preceding chapter. The troops had rendezvoused at Easton, and marched to Wyoming by the way of the present turnpike. They arrived on the 23d of June, and encamped on the flats below Wilkesbarre. A large fleet of boats, that had been prepared in the lower waters of the Susquehanna, arrived, with provisions and stores, on the 24th. We have seen that Sullivan's movements were remarkably slow, and that the enemy became perfectly acquainted with his strength and his plans before he reached Tioga. The Indians, guided by the mind of Brant, tried to divert the attention of Sullivan by attacks upon his outposts.[1] Several of these occurred, but the American force was too large to be much affected by them , and on the 31st of July the tents were struck, and the whole army, with martial music and the thunder of cannon, moved up the Susquehanna, proceeding on the east side. 1779. As the fleet of boats approached Monocasy Island and the battle-ground, the lively music of fife and drum was changed to a solemn dirge, in honor of the patriot dead. The army encamped the first night a little above Pittston, near the confluence of the Susquehanna and Lackawanna Rivers. On the 5th it arrived at Wyalusing, on the 9th at Queen Esther's Plains (Shesequin), and on the 11th reached Tioga Point. The remainder August. of the story of the expedition has already been told.

As soon as the American army was gone, the Indians and Tories came prowling upon the borders of the valley, and, until peace was proclaimed, the settlers had not an hour of repose. " Revenge upon Wyoming," says Stone, " seemed a cherished luxury to the infuriated savages, hovering upon her outskirts upon every side. It was a scene of war, blood, and suffering. . . . . . . In the course of this harassing warfare there were many severe skirmishes, several heroic risings of prisoners upon their Indian captors, and many hair-breadth escapes."[2] It would require a volume to detail them, and the reader, desirous of more minute information, is referred to the works of Chapman, Miner, and Stone. I have other and broader regions to traverse and explore, and other pages of our wondrous history to open and recite. Let us close the book for the present, and ramble a while along the banks of the Susquehanna, where the tragedy we have been considering was enacted, but where now the smiles of peace, prosperity, and repose gladden the heart of the dweller and the stranger.

---

[1] The boldness of the Indians was remarkable. Although the Americans in camp were three thousand strong, they approached within two or three miles of the tents, and committed murders.

[2] History of Wyoming p. 206.

364   PICTORIAL FIELD-BOOK

Present Scenery in Wyoming.   Allusion to Campbell's Poem   Visit to Kingston and Forty Fort

CHAPTER XVI.

"I then but dream'd : thou art before me now
  In life, a vision of the brain no more.
I've stood upon the wooded mountain's brow,
  That beetles high thy lovely valley o'er.

    · · · · · ·

Nature hath made thee lovelier than the power
  Even of Campbell's pen hath pictured ; he
Had woven, had ne gazed one sunny hour
  Upon thy smiling vale, its scenery
With more of truth, and made each rock and tree
  Known like old friends, and greeted from afar ;
And there are tales of sad reality
  In the dark legends of thy border war,
With woes of deeper tint than his own Gertrude's are."

HALLECK.

MIST still reposed upon the waters, and veiled the fringe of trees along the Susquehanna, when, late in the morning, I left Wilkesbarre, in company with Mr. Lord Butler, to visit the celebrities of the valley. The poetry of the bard and the solemn prose of the historian awakened thoughts and associations which invested every venerable tree and antiquated dwelling, the plains, the river, and the mountains, with all the glowing characteristics of romance. The simple beauty of nature, though changed in feature, is as attractive as of old.

"But where are they, the beings of the mind,
  The bard's creations, molded not of clay,
Hearts to strange bliss and sufferings assign'd—
  Young Gertrude, Albert, Waldegrave—where are they ?

    · · · · · ·

            Waldegrave 'twere in vain
To point out here, unless in yon scarecrow
That stands full uniform'd upon the plain
To frighten flocks of crows and blackbirds from the grain.

"For he would look particularly droll
  In his ' Iberian boot' and ' Spanish plume,'
And be the wonder of each Christian soul,
  As of the birds that scarecrow and his broom.
But Gertrude, in her loveliness and bloom,
  Hath many a model here ; for woman's eye,
In court or cottage, wheresoe'er her home,
  Hath a heart-spell too holy and too high
To be o'er-praised, even by her worshiper—Poesy."

HALLECK.

We crossed the plain to Kingston, a pretty village about half a mile westward of Wilkesbarre, and then proceeded to the site of Forty Fort, three and a half miles above, which is reached by a road diverging toward the river from the main road to the head of the valley. It stood near the river bank, at a curve in the stream. Not a single trace of it is left, the spot having been long a common, perfectly smooth, and covered with a green sward. Near the site of the fort is a venerable house, one of the few that escaped the general conflagration, and close by is the residence of one of Mrs. Myers's family, in whose possession I found the *treaty table*, pictured in the last chapter. The venerable owner was not there, but I afterward saw her at the house of her son, near Kingston. A cottage and its garden occupy the bank of the river where the trembling families at Forty Fort stood and listened to the noise of the battle ; and from that point is a charming river view, bounded on the northwest by the lofty range of the Shawnee Mountains, through which the Susquehanna makes its way into the valley.

From Forty Fort we rode up to the monument, which is situated in a field a few rods east of the main road, near the pleasant little village of Troy, five and a half miles from Wilkesbarre. It is constructed of hewn blocks of granite, quarried in the neighborhood, is sixty two and a half feet in height, and stands upon the spot where the dead were buried in the autumn succeeding the battle.[1] On two marble tablets are engraved the names of those who fell, so far as could be ascertained, and also of those who were in the battle and survived. Another marble tablet contains an inscription, written by Edward Mallory, Esq.[2] This monument, like many others proposed to be erected to the memory of Revolutionary men or events, was tardily conceived and more tardily executed. It remained unfinished nearly forty years after the first movements were made toward raising money for the purpose. As early as 1809, Mr. Minor, the historian of the valley, wrote several essays intended to awaken public attention to the duty of erecting a monument, and in 1810 Charles F. Wells, Esq., wrote a stirring ode, concluding with the patriotic interrogation,

WYOMING MONUMENT

" O, when shall rise, with chisel'd head,
    The tall stone o'er their burial-place,
Where the winds may sigh for the gallant dead,
    And the dry grass rustle around its base ?"

---

[1] Professor Silliman visited many of the Revolutionary grounds about twenty years ago. In his Journal, vol. xviii., p. 310, in describing his visit to Wyoming, he says that a Mr. Perrin, one of those who assisted in the burial of the dead, went over the ground with him, and assured him that, owing to the intense heat and dryness of the air, the bodies were shriveled, dry, and quite inoffensive.

[2] The following is the inscription upon the monument :

Near this spot was fought,
On the afternoon of Friday, the third day of July, 1778,
THE BATTLE OF WYOMING,
In which a small band of patriot Americans,
Chiefly the undisciplined, the youthful, and the aged,
Spared, by inefficiency, from the distant ranks of the republic,
Led by Colonel Zebulon Butler and Colonel Nathan Denison
With a courage that deserved success,
Boldly met and bravely fought
A combined British, Tory, and Indian force
Of thrice their number.
Numerical superiority alone gave success to the invader,
And wide-spread havoc, desolation, and ruin
Marked his savage and bloody footsteps through the valley.
THIS MONUMENT,
Commemorative of these events,
And of the actors in them,
Has been erected
Over the bones of the slain,
By their descendants and others, who gratefully appreciate
The services and sacrifices of their patriot ancestors.

These appeals caused meetings to be held and resolutions to be adopted, but little more substantial was done until 1839, when a committee from Wyoming repaired to Hartford, to solicit pecuniary aid from the Legislature of Connecticut.   The committee set forth the claims of the Wyoming people upon Connecticut, in consideration of past allegiance and services.   A report was made, proposing a grant of three thousand dollars, but no further action was taken during that session.   In 1841 another petition was presented, and so ably was the matter conducted that the lower branch of the Legislature voted the appropriation asked for, by a large majority.   The Senate did not concur, and another failure was the consequence.   The ladies of Wyoming, doubtless feeling the truth of Dr. Clarke's assertion, that "in all benevolent or patriotic enterprises the services of one woman are equal to those of seven men and a half," resolved that the monument should be erected.   They formed a "Luzerne Monumental Association,"[1] solicited donations, held fairs, and by their energy obtained the necessary funds and erected a monument, commemorative alike of patriotic deeds and of female influence.   There is a world of philosophy (which solicitors of subscriptions would do well to observe) in the saying of Judge Halliburton's clock peddler, "The straight road to the *pockets* of the men is through the *hearts* of the women."

From the monument northward to the site of Wintermoot's Fort, a mile and a half, the road passes over the battle-ground ; but tillage has so changed the whole scene, that nothing remains as token or landmark of the fight, except the ancient river bank, and the tangled morass toward the mountains, through which the Indians made their way and fell upon Colonel Denison's rear.   The place was pointed out to me, upon the road side, where, tradition says, one of the Wyoming men, somewhat intoxicated, lagged behind and fell asleep, when the little band marched to the attack of the invaders.   When the retreat became general, and Colonel Zebulon Butler saw no other means of safety but flight, he put spurs to his horse. A swift-footed settler, hotly pursued by savages, caught the tail of Colonel Butler's horse as he passed by, and, with the tenacity of the witch that fastened upon the tail of Tam O'Shanter's mare, held on until he was far beyond danger.   As they passed the spot where the inebriate had just awaked, perfectly sober, the man at the tail shouted to him to shoot the pursuing savage.   He did so, and the Indian fell dead in the road.   Near the same spot Rufus Bennet was pursued by an Indian.   Both had discharged their pieces, and the savage was chasing with tomahawk and spear.   Richard Inman, one of five brothers who were in the battle, shot the Indian with his rifle, who fell dead within a few feet of his intended victim.[2]

Passing over the battle-ground, we visited the site of Wintermoot's Fort, a view of which is given on page 351, and, going down on the ancient bank of the Susquehanna, we came to Queen Esther's Rock, noticed and described on page 357.   There is a scow ferry near, by which we crossed to the eastern side of the river, along whose margin, skirted with lofty trees, we had a delightful ride to the ravine opposite Monocasy Island.   Here the road departs from the river bank, and passes among fertile intervales between that point and Wilkesbarre.   The wheat harvests were garnered, but the corn-fields and orchards were laden with the treas-

---

[1] The most active ladies in the association were descendants of those who suffered at the time of the invasion.   The names of the officers of the society are as follows : Mrs. Chester Butler, *President ;* Mrs. G. M. Hollenback and Mrs. E. Carey, *Vice-presidents ;* Mrs. J. Butler, Mrs. Nicholson, Mrs. Hollenback, Mrs. Lewis, Mrs. Ross, Mrs. Conyngham, Mrs. Beaumont, Mrs. Drake, Mrs. Bennet, Mrs. Carey, *Executive Committee ;* Miss Emily Cist, *Treasurer ;* Miss Gertrude Butler, *Secretary ;* Mrs. Donley, Mrs. L. Butler, *Corresponding Committee.*

[2] The Inman family were terrible sufferers.   Five brothers went to the field of battle.   Two others (for the father had seven sons) would have gone forth, but they had no arms.   Two were killed on the field, two escaped without injury, and the fifth, plunging into the waters under some willows on the river shore while heated by the exertions of the battle and the flight, took such a cold that in a few weeks he was in his grave. The remainder of the family fled with the rest of the settlement.   In the fall they ventured to return, and put in some winter grain.   A surviving son, a lad of nineteen years, while in the field, heard, as he supposed, some wild turkeys in the woods.   He went after them, shots were heard, but the boy never came back.   In the spring his body was found.   He had been murdered and scalped by the Indians.   Thus four sons of Elijah Inman perished within a few months.   One of the sons, Colonel Edward Inman, is still living, I believe, upon a fine farm a few miles below Wilkesbarre.

ures of the season, their abundance betokening the extreme fertility of the soil.   We passed the homestead of Colonel Butler, near which,

> " On the margin of yon orchard hill,
>   Are marks where time-worn battlements have been,
>   And in the tall grass traces linger still
>   Of arrowy frieze and wedged ravelin."

Near the entrance to the village, we came to the cemetery where repose many of the patriot dead of Wyoming.   There rest the remains of Colonel Butler and his wife.   The rude slab that first marked the bed of the hero had been removed, and in its place a neat white marble stone is laid, bearing the following inscription : " In memory of COLONEL ZEBULON BUTLER, of the Revolutionary army, who died July 28th, 1795, in the 64th year of his age ; and also in memory of Mrs. Phœbe H. Butler, his wife, who died January 19th, 1837, in the 82d year of her age."

It was late in the day when I reached my lodgings, and, wearied by the rambles of the morning, resolved to pass the remainder of the afternoon with the *Hazleton Travelers.* Their conversation was exclusively of those who acted and suffered at the time of the *massacre,* and I listened with intense interest to the recitals of the " knowing one."   I would gladly give the details here, if my space would allow, for they furnish one of the most interesting of those chapters in our Revolutionary history, showing the terrible cost at which our liberties were purchased.   Mr. Minor has made the record, and to it the reader is referred.

I passed the evening with the venerable Joseph Slocum, whose family was among the sufferers in the Wyoming Valley.   He related to me all the particulars of the capture and final discovery of his sister Frances, and other incidents connected with the sufferings of his family.   His father was a Quaker, and was distinguished for his kindness to the Indians.   He remained unharmed at the time of the invasion, and, while the torch was applied to the dwellings of others, his was left untouched.   But his son Giles was in the battle.   This doubtless excited the ire of the Indians, and they resolved on vengeance.   Late in autumn they were seen prowling about the house, which was situated about one hundred rods from the Wilkesbarre Fort.   A neighbor named Kingsley had been made a prisoner, and his wife and two sons had a welcome home in Mr. Slocum's family.   One morning the   November 2, two boys were grinding a knife near the house, when a rifle-shot and a shriek   1778. brought Mrs. Slocum to the door.   An Indian was scalping the eldest boy, a lad of fifteen, with the knife he had been grinding.   The savage then went into the house, and caught up a little son of Mrs. Slocum.   " See !" exclaimed the frightened mother, " he can do thee no good ; he is lame."   The Indian released the boy, took up her little daughter Frances, aged five years, gently in his arms, and, seizing the younger Kingsley, hastened to the mountains.   Two Indians who were with him carried off a black girl, about seventeen years old. Mr. Slocum's little daughter, aged nine years, caught up her brother Joseph (my informant), two and a half years old, and fled in safety to the fort, where an alarm was given, but the savages were beyond successful pursuit.

About six weeks afterward Mr. Slocum and his father-in-law, Ira Trip, were   December 16. shot and scalped by some Indians while foddering cattle near the house.   Again the savages escaped with their horrid trophies.   Mrs. Slocum, bereft of father, husband, and child, and stripped of all possessions but the house that sheltered her, could not leave the valley, for nine helpless children were yet in her household.   She trusted in the God of Elijah, and, if she was not fed by the ravens, she was spared by the vultures.   She mourned not for the dead, for they were at rest ; but little Frances, her lost darling, where was she ?   The lamp of hope kept on burning, but years rolled by, and no tidings of the little one came.   When peace returned, and friendly intercourse with Canada was established, two of the little captive's brothers started in search of her.   They traversed the wilderness to Niagara, offering rewards for her discovery, but all in vain.   They returned to Wyoming, convinced that the child was dead.   But the mother's heart was still the shrine of hope;

and she felt assured that Frances was not in the grave. Her soul appeared to commune with that of her child, and she often said, "I know Frances is living." At length the mother's heart was cheered; a woman (for many years had now passed, and Frances, if living, must be a full-grown woman) was found among the Indians, answering the description of the lost one. She only remembered being carried away from the Susquehanna. Mrs. Slocum took her home and cherished her with a mother's tenderness. Yet the mysterious link of sympathy which binds the maternal spirit to its offspring was unfelt, and the bereaved mother was bereaved still. "It may be Frances, but it does not seem so. Yet the woman shall be ever welcome," said Mrs. Slocum. The foundling also felt no filial yearnings, and, both becoming convinced that no consanguinity existed, the orphan returned to her Indian friends. From time to time the hope of the mother would be revived, and journeys were made to distant Indian settlements in search of the lost sister, but in vain. The mother went "down into the grave mourning," and little Frances was almost forgotten. Her brothers had become aged men, and their grandchildren were playing upon the very spot whence she had been taken.

In the summer of 1837, fifty-nine years after her capture, intelligence of Frances was received. Colonel Ewing, an Indian agent and trader, in a letter from Logansport, Indiana, to the editor of the Lancaster Intelligencer,[1] gave such information that all doubts respecting her identity were removed, and Joseph Slocum, with the sister who carried him to the fort, and yet survived, immediately journeyed to Ohio, where they were joined by their younger brother Isaac. They proceeded to Logansport, where they found Mr. Ewing, and ascertained that the woman spoken of by him lived about twelve miles from the village. She was immediately sent for, and toward evening the next day she came into the town, riding a spirited young horse, accompanied by her two daughters, dressed in full Indian costume, and the husband of one of them. An interpreter was procured (for she could not speak or understand English), and she listened seriously to what her brothers had to say. She answered but little, and at sunset departed for her home, promising to return the next morning. The brothers and sister were quite sure that it was indeed Frances, though in her face nothing but Indian lineaments were seen, her color alone revealing her origin.

True to her appointment, she appeared the following morning, accompanied as before. Mr. Joseph Slocum then mentioned a mark of recognition, which his mother had said would be a sure test. While playing one day with a hammer in a blacksmith's shop, Joseph, then a child two and a half years old, gave Frances a blow upon the middle finger of the left hand, which crushed the bone and deprived the finger of its nail. This test Mr. Slocum had withheld until others should fail. When he mentioned it, the aged woman was greatly agitated, and, while tears filled the furrows of her face, she held out the wounded finger. There was no longer a doubt, and a scene of great interest ensued. Her affections for her

---

[1] This letter was dated January 20th, 1835, a year and a half previous, and gave the following account: "There is now living near this place, among the Miami tribe of Indians, an aged white woman, who, a few days ago, told me that she was taken away from her father's house, on or near the Susquehanna River, when she was very young. She says her father's name was Slocum; that he was a Quaker, and wore a large-brimmed hat; that he lived about half a mile from a town where there was a fort. She has two daughters living. Her husband is dead. She is old and feeble, and thinks she shall not live long. These considerations induced her to give the present history of herself, which she never would before, fearing her kindred would come and force her away. She has lived long and happily as an Indian, is very respectable and wealthy, sober and honest. Her name is without reproach." The cause of the delay in the publication of the letter, and of its final appearance and effect, was not a little singular. Mr. Ewing sent it to the postmaster at Lancaster, with a request that he would have it published in a Pennsylvania paper. The postmaster, not acquainted with the writer, concluded that it was a hoax, and cast the letter among other papers, where it remained a year and a half. One day his wife, while engaged in arranging the office, saw the letter, and, having her feelings very much interested, sent it to the editor of the Intelligencer. It so happened that the issue of his paper in which the letter was published contained an important temperance document, and a large number of extra copies were printed for general distribution. One of these was sent to a gentleman in Wyoming, who, having heard the story of the "lost sister," and knowing Mr. Joseph Slocum, put the paper into his hands; and thus, by a series of providential circumstances, a clew to Frances was discovered.

OF THE REVOLUTION. 369

Interview between the "lost Sister" and her white Kindred.   Her Narrative.   Her Condition.   Children and Grandchildren

kindred, that had slumbered half a century, were aroused, and she made earnest inquiries after her father, mother, brothers, and sisters.   Her full heart—full with the cherished secrets of her history—was opened, and the story of her life freely given.   She said the sav-

FRANCES SLOCUM—MA-CON-A-QUA.[1]

ages (who were Delawares), after taking her to a rocky cave in the mountains, departed for the Indian country.   The first night was the unhappiest of her life.   She was kindly treated, being carried tenderly in their arms when she was weary. She was adopted in an Indian family, and brought up as their daughter.   For years she led a roving life, and loved it.   She was taught the use of the bow and arrow, and became expert in all the employments of savage existence.   When she was grown to womanhood both her Indian parents died, and she soon afterward married a young chief of the nation, and removed to the Ohio country.   She was treated with more respect than the Indian women generally ; and so happy was she in her domestic relations, that the chance of being discovered and compelled to return among the whites was the greatest evil that she feared, for she had

been taught that they were the implacable enemies of the Indians, whom she loved.   Her husband died, and, her people having joined the Miamies, she went with them and married one of that tribe.   The last husband was also dead, and she had been a widow many years Children and grandchildren were around her, and her life was passing pleasantly away When she concluded the narrative, she lifted her right hand in a solemn manner, and said, " All this is as true as that there is a Great Spirit in the heavens !"   She had entirely forgotten her native language, and was a pagan.   To her Christ and the Christian's Sabbath were unknown.

On the day after the second interview, the brothers and sister, with the interpreter, rode out to her dwelling.   It was a well-built log house, in the midst of cultivation.   A large herd of cattle and sixty horses were grazing in the pastures.   Every thing betokened plenty and comfort, for she was wealthy, when her wants and her means were compared.   Her annuity from government, which she received as one of the Miami tribe, had been saved, and she had about one thousand dollars in specie.   Her white friends passed several days very agreeably with her ; and subsequently her brother Joseph, with his daughter, the wife of

---

[1] This portrait I copied from a painting of life size in the possession of her brother, Mr. Joseph Slocum, of Wilkesbarre.   It was painted for him by an artist named Winter, residing at Logansport.   Her underdress is scarlet, and the mantle with the large sleeve is black cloth.   The Indians gave her the name of Ma-con-a-qua, a *Young Bear*.   The names of her children and grandchildren are as follows : Eldest daughter, Kich-ke-ne-che-quah, *Cut Finger ;* youngest daughter, O-saw-she-quah, *Yellow Leaf.*   Grandchildren : Kip-pe-no-quah, *Corn Tassel ;* Wap-pa-no-se-a, *Blue Corn ;* Kim-on-sa-quah, *Young Panther*

the Hon. Ziba Bennet of Wyoming, made her another visit, and bade her a last farewell. She died about four years ago, and was buried with considerable pomp, for she was regarded as a queen among her tribe.[1]

September 18, 1848. I passed a Sabbath in Wyoming. It was a dull and cheerless day. The mountains were hooded with vapor, and all day a chilly drizzle made the trees weep. But Monday morning dawned clear and warm, and in the course of the day I revisited Forty Fort and the battle-ground, ascended the mountain to Prospect Rock, to obtain another glorious view of the valley, peeped into the black caverns of the coal mines at the foot of the hills, and at noon took shelter from the hot sun in the shaded walks of Toby's Eddy, where Zinzendorf pitched his tent. Thence I rode to the residence of Mr. Myers, a son of the venerable lady already alluded to, where I passed an interesting hour with the living chronicle of the woes of Wyoming. I found her sitting in an easy chair, peeling apples, and her welcome was as cheerful and cordial as she could have given to a cherished friend. Her memory was clear, and she related the incidents of her girlhood with a perspicuity that evinced remarkable mental vigor. Although blindness has shut out the beautiful, and deprived her of much enjoyment, yet pious resignation, added to natural vivacity, makes her society extremely agreeable. " I am like a withered stalk, whose flower hath fallen," she said ; " but," she added, with a pleasant smile, " the fragrance still lingers." She was sixteen years old at the time of the invasion, and was in Forty Fort when it surrendered. Every minute circumstance there she remembered clearly, and her narrative of events was substantially the same as recorded in the last chapter. Her father's house was near the fort, and for a week after the surrender it was spared, while others were plundered and destroyed. Every morning when she arose her first thought was their house, and she would go early to see if it was safe. One morning as she looked she saw the flames burst through the roof, and in an hour it was a heap of embers. She remained two weeks in the valley after the surrender of the fort. The Indians kept her face painted and a white fillet around her head, as a protection against the tomahawks of strange savages, and she was treated very kindly by them. When Colonel Denison and others fled from the valley, she and her family accompanied them. After the savages left the valley, her family returned, and for seventy years she has enjoyed the sweets of peace and domestic happiness. Her maiden name was Bennet, and her family were conspicuous in the events at Wyoming during the Revolution.[2] She has been many years a widow. One of her sons was high sheriff of Luzerne county, another was a magistrate, and a daughter is the wife of the Rev. Dr. Peck, the editor of the Methodist Episcopal Review, published at the " Book Concern," in New York. She is yet living (November, 1849), at the ripe age of eighty-eight years, honored and beloved by all.

September 20. I returned to Wilkesbarre at sunset. The evening was as pleasant as June, and the moonlight scene from the upper piazza of the Phœnix, embracing the quiet-flowing Susquehanna, with its fringe of noble trees ; the sparkling of the lights at

---

[1] When the Miamies were removed from Indiana, the "lost sister" and her Indian relatives were exempted. The affecting story of her life was laid before Congress, and so eloquently did John Quincy Adams plead her cause, that he drew tears from the eyes of many members. Congress gave her a tract of land a mile square, to be held in perpetuity by her descendants, and there her children and grandchildren still dwell.

[2] Her brother Solomon was in the battle. In the spring succeeding the invasion, the father of Mrs. Myers, her brother (a lad), and Lebbeus Hammond (one of the two who escaped from Queen Esther at the bloody rock) were captured by a party of Indians while at work in the field, and hurried away to the north. It was evident that they were destined for torture, and, while the Indians were drinking at a spring on the third day of their journey into the wilderness, they concerted a plan for escape. Mr. Bennet, being old, was allowed to travel unbound, but the arms of Hammond and the boy were tied. There were six Indians in the party. At night all were laid down to sleep but Mr. Bennet and an Indian. The former brought in dry wood for the fire, and kept himself busy for some time. He then sat down by the fire, and, taking up a spear, he rolled it playfully on his thigh. The Indian finally began to nod, and the others were snoring soundly. Watching his opportunity, Bennet thrust the savage through with the spear, cut the cords that bound his son and Hammond, and the three attacked the sleeping savages. Five were killed, the other one escaped. The captives returned home, bringing, as trophies, the scalps of the slain savages.

Kingston, and the dark outline of the Shawnee Mountains, all hallowed by historic associa-tions, was one of great beauty and interest.   Let us employ the quiet hour in reminiscences of some stirring events that occurred, within trumpet call of our presence, after the Revolu-tion, for early on the morrow I must leave Wyoming, perhaps forever.

We have considered the civil war that disturbed Wyoming before the Revolution.   That great movement absorbed all lesser topics ; but as soon as the storm had subsided, and pri-vate interests again became paramount, old jealousies and animosities were resuscitated, and struggled into active life.   As soon as all fear of the Indians had subsided, Connecticut pour-ed hundreds of immigrants into this paradise of the Susquehanna.   The influx was regarded with jealousy by the Pennsylvanians, and it was not long before all the rancor of the Penny-mite and Yankee war was reproduced.

The Articles of Confederation, under which the general government of the United States was carried on, having made provision for the adjustment of difficulties that might arise be-tween states, and Connecticut insisting upon the maintenance of its jurisdiction over Wyo-ming, Pennsylvania applied to Congress to appoint a commission to hear the claimants by representatives, and to determine the question in dispute.   The commissioners met at Tren-ton, in New Jersey, toward the close of 1782, and, after a session of five weeks, decided, unanimously, that Connecticut had no right to the land in controversy, and that the juris-diction and pre-emption of all lands belonged to Pennsylvania.   The people of Wyoming appeared to be well satisfied with the decision, for, considering it a question of *jurisdiction* only, they deemed it a matter of little moment whether they rendered allegiance to Connec-ticut or Pennsylvania.   The Pennsylvanians, however, did not so construe the decision, but contended not only for *jurisdiction*, but for the *soil*, and steps were immediately taken for a sweeping ejectment of the Connecticut settlers.   In March ensuing, two companies were sent to garrison the fort at Wilkesbarre, under the pretext of affording protection to the peo-ple ; and the name of the fort was changed to Dickinson, in honor of the President of the Council of the State.   Pennsylvania had already appointed three commissioners to repair to Wyoming, to inquire into the state of affairs, and report proper measures to be adopted to-ward the settlers.   Their report proposed an entire surrender, on the part of the Wyoming people, of their tenures, and all claim to the soil then in their possession, with their improve-ments ; in lieu of which they were to receive an indefinite compensation, at the option of their oppressors, in the wild lands of some unknown region.   It was a most unjust and tyrannical measure, for the right to the soil had been purchased, not only with money, but with the dreadful sufferings of those about to be driven away.   This report of the commis-sioners, and the quartering of troops in the valley, now that the war was ended, and the spirit of tyrannical domination that characterized the soldiers, greatly exasperated the peo-ple, and they were upon the verge of open insurrection for several months.

Early in the autumn two special justices of the peace were appointed, who, in concert with the military, formed a tribunal for the adjudication of all questions arising under the civil law.   The real object of constituting this tribunal, sustained by military force, was ob-vious ; it was to dispossess the Connecticut people of their farms.   The tribunal became an instrument of cruelty and oppression, and a disgrace to the character of civilization.   The next year, according to Chapman, " the people were not only subject to insult, but their crops were destroyed in their fields, their cattle were seized and driven away, and 1783. in some instances their houses were destroyed by fire and the females rendered victims of licentiousness."   But why this rigorous treatment ?   " It was," says Pickering, " not only to strip the people of their possessions, but, by wearying them of their ' promised land,' drive them from the valley."   Although the inhabitants were greatly excited, they loved peace and order, and appealed to the Legislature of Pennsylvania for justice.   Their appeal was unnoticed, and they sent a memorial to Congress.   That body resolved[a] that a [a] January 23, committee of the states should hear both parties on the first Monday in June fol- 1784. lowing ; but neither Congress nor a committee of the states were in session at the time des-ignated, and the people were left without redress.

In the mean while a terrible scourge swept over the valley.   The winter had been intensely cold ; snow fell to a great depth, and the Susquehanna was bridged by ice of uncommon thickness.   The mountains, covered with forests, treasured up vast beds of snow among their rocks and in their deep ravines, from the action of the sun.   In March, 1784. a warm rain fell for nearly three days in succession.   The snow melted, and every mountain rivulet became a sweeping torrent, pouring its volume into the Susquehanna.   The ice in the river was broken up, and the huge masses, borne upon the flood, obstructed by trees, formed immense dams, spreading the waters of the swollen river over the plains.   At length the narrow Nanticoke pass at the lower end of the valley became blocked with the ice, and the water, flowing back, submerged the river flats, and filled all the lower intervales.   Houses and barns were uplifted on the bosom of the waters.   The people fled to the higher points in the valley, some to the mountains.   For several hours the waters continued to rise, until suddenly a dam in the mountain gorge, at the upper end of the valley, gave way, and down came the flood with fearful strength.   All the ice barriers in the valley were broken up, and the ponderous masses of ice, mingled with floating houses, barns, fences, drowned cattle and sheep, stacks of hay, furniture, and agricultural implements, were scattered over the plains,[1] or hurried forward to the broader expanse of the river below.   It was a scene of fearful grandeur, and to the poor settlers, shivering in the mountains, or huddled upon the little hills in the midst of the roaring floods, the star of hope seemed forever set.   The present was utter desolation—the future would unveil injustice and oppression.

As soon as the floods subsided the inhabitants returned, and with them came the soldiers, who snatched from them nearly all of the little food that had been saved, for they were "quartered upon the people."   Their rapacity and oppression were greater than ever, and the settlers, anxious to retrieve their farms from the ruin of the flood, were not allowed to work in peace, but were tormented by them continually.   At length the people resolved to oppose their oppressors by force, and armed for the purpose.   The magistracy, indignant at their presumption, sent out the soldiers to disarm them ; and in the process one hundred and fifty families, many of whom had lost portions of their household in the battle of Wyoming, were turned out of their newly-constructed dwellings, and compelled to fly on foot through the wilderness to the Delaware, a distance of eighty miles.   Houses were burned, and other atrocities were committed.   Ashamed of such conduct, the Legislature of Pennsylvania (which had refused to vote supplies to the sufferers by the flood), when the naked facts were known, endeavored to heal the wounds which, under its sanction, had been inflicted, and, in a measure, to wipe out the stain that rested upon the state authorities.   The troops were discharged, except a small guard left at Fort Dickinson, and a proclamation was issued, inviting the people who had been driven away to return.   Some of them did so, but the valley was allowed but a short season of repose.

So many of the discharged soldiers joined the guard at the Wilkesbarre Fort, that the people, alarmed, garrisoned Forty Fort.   A party of them, having occasion to visit their July 20, grain-fields below, were fired upon by a detachment of thirty from the other fort, and 1784. two promising young men were killed.   The people resolved on retaliation, and about midnight marched to Wilkesbarre Fort, to take the garrison by surprise.   The latter, informed of the movement, were prepared to receive them, and the settlers returned to Forty Fort with a stock of provisions.   On the 27th, the people, led by Colonel John Franklin, a native of Connecticut, invested the Wilkesbarre Fort, and made a formal summons for surrender.   Two hours were allowed the besieged for an answer.   Before one hour had elapsed information was received that a considerable re-enforcement for the garrison was approaching.   The siege was raised, and the besiegers returned to Forty Fort.   It was a false alarm ; the strangers, who were supposed to be the pioneers of a large number who were approaching,

---

[1] It is said that so huge were many of the masses of ice that were lodged in different portions of the valley, that it was the last of July before they were melted away.

were a committee appointed by the state council to proceed to Wyoming and disarm both parties. A conference was held, and such was the state of feeling that neither party would listen to the commissioners.

Stronger measures were now deemed necessary, and Colonel John Armstrong was sent with a considerable force to establish order in the valley. From Easton he sent forward a detachment, which was captured among the mountains on its way to Wyoming, by   August 2, a party of Connecticut people. Armstrong pushed forward, and on the 4th of Au-   1784. gust reached Wyoming, where his whole force numbered about four hundred men, including the garrison in Wilkesbarre or Dickinson Fort. He found Forty Fort too strong for success-ful attack, and resorted to stratagem. He professed pacific intentions, and proposed to the people of all parties to deliver up their arms at Fort Dickinson, and there reclaim any prop-erty which they might identify as their own. Numbers of the Connecticut people believed him sincere, went to the fort, delivered up their arms, and were captured. Forty of them were sent to the prison at Sunbury, and nearly as many to Easton. The jailer of the latter place was knocked down by a young man named Inman, and the whole party   [a] September 17. escaped.[a] They returned to the valley in company with about forty Vermont-ers, and, finding Armstrong and the few men left with him (for a large portion of his men had been discharged when the prisoners were sent to jail) harvesting the crops, they attacked them and drove them into Fort Dickinson. Forty Fort was again garrisoned by the people, and a plan was arranged for recovering the arms which they had surrendered. A block-house in which they were stored was attacked, and the arms recovered. Two men in the block-house were mortally wounded.

On hearing of this latter event, the executive council sent another expedition to Wyoming, under Armstrong, who was at the same time promoted to the office of adjutant general of the state. But the sympathies of the people of Pennsylvania began to be enlisted in favor of the Wyoming settlers, and they were regarded as a persecuted party. President Dickin-son also remonstrated with the Council and General Assembly, but to no purpose.[1] It so happened that about this time the Board of Censors held their septennial meeting. They called upon the Assembly for papers relative to Wyoming. The Assembly refused acqui-escence. A mandamus was issued, but the Assembly treated it with contempt. Thus treat-ed, and viewing affairs justly, the Censors openly espoused the cause of the Connecticut peo-ple, condemned all of the military proceedings, and passed a vote of censure upon the gov-ernment of the state. This strengthened the hands and hearts of the Wyoming people. They defied Armstrong and his troops; and as winter was approaching, food scarce, and not a recruit could be obtained, that officer discharged the garrison and returned to Philadelphia. Though relieved of the presence of the military, the condition of the settlers was indeed de-plorable. What the spring flood had spared was small, and the presence of the troops had prevented sowing and reaping. They appealed to Congress and to Connecticut for aid,[2] but they received little more than the cold charity of words—"Be ye clothed, and be ye fed"—without contributing to their necessities. The last military expedition against Wyoming had been accomplished, yet the question of possession was unsettled, and they had but little heart to improve their lands, not knowing how soon other efforts might be made to dispos-sess them. The population, however, increased rapidly, and for two years quiet prevailed

---

[1] Pennsylvania, under its first independent state Constitution, had no officer bearing the title of governor. The government of the commonwealth was vested in a House of Representatives, a president, and council. There was also a Board of Censors, elected by the people, who were to meet once in seven years, to inquire whether the Constitution had, in the mean while, been violated, and to transact other general supervisory business, such as trying impeachments, recommending the repeal of unwholesome laws, &c.

[2] In their appeal to the Connecticut Assembly they set forth that their "numbers were reduced to about two thousand souls, most of whom were women and children, driven, in many cases, from their proper hab-itations, and living in huts of bark in the woods, without provisions for the approaching winter, while the Pennsylvania troops and land claimants were in possession of their houses and farms, and wasting and de-stroying their cattle and subsistence."

1786. in Wyoming. On the petition of the people, the district of Wyoming and vicinity were formed into a new county, which they named Luzerne.[1]

About this time Colonel Timothy Pickering,[2] of Massachusetts, but then a resident of

Pennsylvania, visited Wyoming, and made himself thoroughly acquainted with the affairs of the valley. He became convinced that the settlers were satisfied with the political system of the state, and were ready to become obedient citizens of the commonwealth if they could be quieted in the possession of their farms. These views he communicated to Dr. Rush and other eminent men in Philadelphia, who, anxious to have an amicable adjustment of the difficulties, proposed to Mr. Pickering to accept of the five principal county offices, and remove to Wyoming ; for he, being a New England man, would doubtless exercise great influence over the people. He accepted the proposition and went to Wyoming, bearing to the Connecticut people the full assurance that the Pennsylvania Legislature would pass a law quieting them in their possessions.

Clothed with the necessary power, Colonel Pickering proceeded to hold elections and to organize the county. He succeeded in persuading the people to memorialize the Legislature for a compromise law, the chief provisions of which should be, that, in case the

---

[1] So called in honor of the Chevalier de Luzerne, the distinguished embassador from France to the United States during the latter years of the Revolution.

[2] Timothy Pickering was born in Salem, Massachusetts, on the 17th of July, 1745. He entered Harvard University at the age of fourteen years, and received collegiate honors in 1763. He was elected register of deeds in the county of Essex ; and before the Revolution he was a colonel of the Essex militia, and acquired a thorough knowledge of military tactics. When the town meeting was held at Salem in 1774, and an address voted to General Gage on the subject of the Boston Port Bill, Colonel Pickering was appointed to write the address and deliver it in person to the governor. For him is claimed the distinction of conducting the first resistance, in arms, to the power of the mother country. On Sunday, the 26th of February, 1775, an express arrived at Salem from Marblehead with the intelligence that British troops were landing from a transport, with the intention of marching through Salem to seize some military stores in the interior. The people were dismissed from their churches, and, led by Colonel Pickering, they opposed the progress of the British at a draw-bridge. A compromise was effected, the British were compelled to march back to Marblehead, and bloodshed was avoided.* When he heard of the battle of Lexington, Colonel Pickering marched, with his regiment, to intercept the enemy. In 1775 he was appointed a judge of the Court of Common Pleas for Essex. In the fall of 1776, with seven hundred Essex men, he performed duty under Washington, and was with the chief in his retreat across the Jerseys. He was engaged in the battles of Brandywine and Germantown, holding the office and rank of adjutant general. Congress appointed him a member of the Board of War with Gates and Mifflin ; and in 1780 he succeeded General Green as quartermaster general. At the close of the war he fixed his residence in Philadelphia, soon after which he was deputed to attempt the settlement of the troubles in Wyoming. He was a member of the convention called to revise the Constitution of Pennsylvania in 1790. Washington appointed him postmaster general in 1791, which office he held nearly four years, when, on the resignation of General Knox, he was appointed Secretary of War. In 1795 Washington made him his Secretary of State, which position he held until 1800, when he was removed by President Adams on political grounds. He was poor on leaving office, and, building a log house for his family upon some wild land that he owned in Pennsylvania, he commenced the arduous duties of clearing it for cultivation. Through the liberality of his friends, he was induced to return to

---

* Of this exploit, Trumbull, in his *M'Fingal*, wrote :

"Through Salem straight, without delay,
The bold battalion took its way ;
March'd o'er a bridge, in open sight
Of several Yankees arm'd for fight ;
Then, without loss of time or men,
Veer'd round for Boston back again,
And found so well their projects thrive,
That every soul got back alive !"

OF THE REVOLUTION. 375

New Difficulties in Wyoming.   John Franklin.   Arrest of Franklin.   Ethan Allen.

commonwealth would grant them the seventeen townships[1] which had been laid out, and on which settlements had been commenced previous to the decree of Trenton, they would, on their part, relinquish all their claims to any other lands within the limits of the Susquehanna purchase. The law was enacted, but new difficulties arose. Many of the best lands in these townships had been granted by the government of Pennsylvania to its own citizens, in the face of the claims of the Connecticut people. These proprietors must be satisfied. Commissioners were accordingly appointed, under the law, to go to Wyoming to examine and adjust claims on both sides.[2] They met in May, arranged the preliminaries, and adjourned until August. The law satisfied those within the seventeen townships, but the Connecticut 1787. people had extended settlements beyond these limits, and these, excluded from the benefits of the law, were much dissatisfied. It was also said that, pending the negotiations, the Susquehanna Company had been using great exertions to increase the number of settlers in the unincluded districts, and Colonel Pickering positively asserted that gratuitous offers of land were made to such as would come *armed*, " to man their rights."[3] The most active man in this alleged movement was John Franklin, whose great popularity enabled him to stir up a violent commotion among the " out-siders"—so violent that the commissioners were obliged to flee from the valley for personal safety. Chief-justice M'Kean issued a warrant for the arrest of Franklin, on the charge of high treason. But how should they catch him ? They could not trust the proper officer, the sheriff of Luzerne county, who was living in the midst of the *insurgents*, as they were called. Four strong, bold men, two of whom had served in the Revolutionary army, were selected for the purpose, and they repaired to Wyoming.[4]

Franklin was then thirty-five miles distant, exciting the people to armed resistance. Preparations were made for his safe-conduct to Philadelphia, and, on his return, he was arrested at the " Red House," near the river. It was with great difficulty that he was secured, and, as the people were assembling for his rescue, he would doubtless have escaped, had not Colonel Pickering immediately adopted.

THE "RED HOUSE."[5]

interfered. Observing the commotion from the window of his house, he sallied out with his pistols, and, presenting one to the breast of Franklin, kept him quiet while he was securely bound to a horse. Franklin was carried to Philadelphia and cast into prison.

The interference of Colonel Pickering greatly exasperated the people, and retaliatory measures were He was informed of the fact that a party was about to seize him,

his native state, out of debt, and a comfortable living in prospect. He was a United States senator in 1803, and again in 1805. He was a member of the Board of War in Massachusetts in 1812, and in 1814 was elected a member of the United States House of Representatives. He retired from public life in 1817, and died in Salem on the 29th of January, 1829, aged eighty-four years.

[1] These townships were Salem, Newport, Hanover, Wilkesbarre, Pittston, Westmoreland, Putnam, Braintree, Springfield, Claverack, Ulster, Exeter, Kingston, Plymouth, Bedford, Huntington, and Providence. These towns were represented as nearly square as circumstances would permit, and to be about five miles on a side, and severally divided into lots of three hundred acres each. Some of these lots were set apart as glebes, some for schools, and others for various town purposes.

[2] The commissioners were Timothy Pickering, William Montgomery, and Stephen Balliott.

[3] About this time " no little sensation was produced in the valley," says Minor, " by the appearance of the far-famed General Ethan Allen, from Vermont, arrayed in cocked hat and regimentals. The purpose of his visit was as well understood by Pickering as by Franklin and his associates. A grant of several thousand acres was made to him by the Susquehanna Company. How many men he was pledged to lead from the Green Mountains we have no means of ascertaining ; but it was not doubted that his object was to reconnoiter, and concert measures for early and decisive action."

[4] Three of these were Captain Lawrence Erbe, Captain Brady, and Lieutenant M'Cormick. The other name is not known.

[5] The " Red House" is situated upon the street in Wilkesbarre next the river, and about seventy-five rods below the bridge. It is the place where John Franklin was arrested. On his return from a political tour down the valley, he came up by the way of Hanover to Wilkesbarre. While standing near the ferry, an acquaintance came up to him and said, " A friend at the Red House wishes to speak to you." Franklin walked to the house, where a person caught him from behind, and attempted to pinion his hands. He was a powerful man, and shook off his captors ; but, a noose being thrown over his head, he was secured. They

and he fled to the mountains, whence he made his way to Philadelphia.   The partisans of Franklin now became alarmed.   They acknowledged their offense to the council, and prayed for pardon.   Under these circumstances, Pickering thought it safe for him to return to his family, particularly as the very people whose acts had driven him away had chosen him a delegate to the General Assembly during his exile !   He returned, but found many of the people still much exasperated against him, and he was often menaced.   Finally, one night

1778.   in June, fifteen ruffians, with painted faces, burst open the door of the room where himself and wife were sleeping, bound him with cords, and in the darkness of the night carried him up the valley.   For twenty days he was kept by them in the forest, and subjected to ill treatment in various forms.   Sometimes they threatened him with death ; then he was manacled and chained, and in this way the miscreants tormented him, and tried to wring from him a letter to the executive council recommending the discharge of Franklin. When this requirement was first proposed, and his own release promised on his compliance, Pickering promptly replied, " The executive council better understand their duty than to discharge a traitor to procure the release of an innocent man."   This determined tone and manner he preserved throughout.   They finally released him, and he found his way back to Wilkesbarre, where his death was considered a matter of certainty.   Haggard and unshaven, his wife regarded him with consternation, and his children fled from him affrighted.

This was the last scene in the drama of violence so long enacted in Wyoming.   Franklin was liberated on bail, and finally discharged ; and he and Pickering often met as friends in public life afterward.   The disputes about land titles and possessions in Wyoming remained unsettled for nearly fifteen years, while the population rapidly increased.   Ultimately the claims were all quieted by law, and for the last forty years the sweet vale of Wyoming has presented a beautiful picture of repose and prosperity.[1]   We will close the record and retire, for the moon has gone down behind the western hills, and chilly vapors are coming up from the bosom of the river.

September 20,   I left Wilkesbarre on the mail-coach early on Tuesday morning, for the Lack-
1848.   awanna Valley and the coal regions of Luzerne.   The whole of Wyoming was wrapped in a dense fog, and from the driver's box, where I had secured a seat, it was with difficulty that we could observe objects beyond the leaders.   The coveted pleasure of another view of the beautiful scenery as we passed along the uplands was denied ; but when we arrived at Pittston, the cool breeze that came through the mountain gateway of the Susquehanna, and from the valley of the Lackawanna, swept away the vapor, and revealed the rich plains at the head of the valley, the majestic curve of the river where it receives its tributary, and the grandeur of its rocky margins toward the north.   At the junction of the rivers we turned eastward, and in a few moments Wyoming and all its attractions were left behind, and scenery and associations of a far different cast were around us.

The Lackawanna River flows in a deep bed, and its valley, wider than Wyoming, is very rough and hilly, but thickly strewn with fertile spots.   Iron and anthracite every where abound ; and the latter is so near the surface in many places, that the farmers in autumn quarry out their winter's stock of fuel upon their own plantations with very little labor. Several iron manufactories are seated upon the river between its mouth and Carbondale, and little villages, brought forth and fostered by these industrial establishments, enliven the otherwise ungenial features of the route.   At one of these, called Hyde Park, we lunched and changed horses, receiving an addition to our company in the person of a tall, cadaverous Yankee lumberman, who, with a huge musk-melon and jack-knife in his hand, took a seat

---

then attempted to get him on horseback, when he cried out, " Help, help !   William Slocum ! where is William Slocum ?" and, drawing his pistols, discharged one, but without effect.   He was felled by a blow, and laid almost senseless.   It was seeding time, and nearly all the men were in the fields.   But the Yankee blood of Mrs. Slocum (the mother of the " lost sister") was up, and, seizing a gun, she ran to the door, exclaiming, " William !   Who will call William ?   Is there no *man* here ?   Will nobody rescue him ?"— *Miner.*   Colonel Pickering's dwelling was near the " Red House."   It is still standing, but so modernized that its original character is lost.

[1] Chapman. Gordon, Miner, Stone.

beside me on the driver's box.　Having satisfied his own appetite with the melon, he gener
ously handed the small remainder to the driver and myself; and the moment his jaws ceased
mastication, his tongue began to wag like a "mill-tail."　He discoursed fluently, if not wisely,
upon the general demerits of fever and ague, whose subject he had been for nearly a year, and
upon the particular productiveness of "Varmount."　"It's a garden of flowers," he said,
"while York state, and all 'tother side on't, is wild land, raisin' nothin' but snakes and agers."

> "Compared to New England, our horses are colts,
> Our oxen are goats, and a sheep but a lamb;
> The people poor blockheads and pitiful dolts—
> Mere Hottentot children, contrasted with them."

He was a capital specimen of the genus "brag," refined by superb Munchausen polish.　His
voice was a shrill falsetto, and, every word being audible to the passengers, we soon had a
laughing chorus within the coach that awoke the echoes of the hills.

　Approaching Carbondale, the road gently ascends a mountain ridge until all traces of cultivation disappear, and pines and cedars compose the forest.　From this rugged height it
winds along the steep acclivities; and the mining village, in the bosom of a deep, rocky intervale, may be seen below, at a distance of more than a mile.　It was about two o'clock
when we arrived at Carbondale.　Having two hours leisure before the departure of the mail-
coach for Honesdale and the Delaware, I applied to Mr. James Clarkson, the chief surveyor
at the mines, for permission to enter one of them.　It was cordially granted, and, in company with his assistant, Mr. Alexander Bryden, as guide, I entered the one wherein an appalling circumstance, resulting in the death of several miners, occurred on the morning of
the 12th of January, 1846.　Indications of danger were observed several months previously
in one of the chambers.　The pillars of coal and pine logs that supported the roof seemed to
be crushing beneath the superincumbent weight, and the chamber was abandoned.　Other
portions of the mine appeared to be safe, although in some cases the roof of slate was cracked.
Suddenly, at about eight o'clock on the morning in question, nearly sixty acres of the hill covering the mines sunk about two feet, crushing every thing beneath it, and producing a powerful concussion.　The fall was accompanied by a sound similar to distant thunder, and a
shock which was perceptible throughout the village.　Fortunately, a large portion of the
workmen were at breakfast.　Under or beyond the fallen body were about sixty men.　The
intelligence of the disaster rapidly spread, and general alarm pervaded the town.　There
were few who did not fear that some relative or friend was buried in the mine.　The scene
was exceedingly painful, and not easily described.　There were daughters, wives, and mothers at the mouth of the mine, in an agony of expectation that a loved one was lost, and for a
while it was difficult to enter to attempt a rescue of those within.　The superintendents and
others proceeded immediately, and at the risk of their own lives, to examine the bounds of
the destruction.　It was soon perceived that some, whose station must be within the limits
of the fall, were probably killed.

　Beyond the point where the roof was secure, some thirty or more of the men had escaped
immediate death, but their situation was truly horrible, having lost their lights, the roof
still cracking and breaking around them, and scarcely a hope left of escape from the spot.
Mr. Bryden, with courage sustained by love for his fellow-men, boldly entered the mine, and
endeavored to reach the point where the men were imprisoned.　He succeeded, after much
labor, and released them.　Informed that a man who had met with a serious accident had
been left in another chamber, Mr. Bryden directed his steps thitherward.　He found the
wounded man, and carried him upon his back to his companions.　Within five minutes after
Mr. Bryden left the chamber with his burden of life, the passage he had traversed was entirely closed by the crushed pillars of coal.

　Among those known to have been at about the center of the fall a short time before the
occurrence, was a young Scotchman named Hosea, another of the superintendents.　Diligent search was made for him on that and the succeeding day without success.　On the
third day, while a party were in search of him, he emerged from the mines unaided, having

dug his way out through fallen masses with his hands! The excitement relative to him had been extreme, and his sudden appearance, under the circumstances, produced great joy. He had been recently married. His young bride, having lost all hope of his recovery alive, was in a store purchasing mourning materials, when he was carried by homeward in a sleigh. The people flocked to his house, and saluted him as one risen from the dead. The hours he had spent entangled in the passages of the mines were horrible indeed. At one time he saw the glimmer of lights. He tried to make himself heard by the party carrying them, but was unsuccessful. He ran toward them, but, stumbling against a car, he fell senseless. When he revived, the lights had disappeared, and all was intense gloom. He scrambled over broken rocks and through narrow apertures, and finally reached one of the rail-roads and made his way out, having been forty-eight hours laboring, without food or drink, in removing the fallen masses. Fourteen perished by the disaster; the bodies of nine have been recovered, the remainder are still in the chambers—to them the "chambers of death." The air was expelled from the mine, when the superincumbent mass settled, with great force. A train of empty cars, drawn by a horse driven by a boy, was just entering when the event occurred. The boy and horse were instantly killed, and the train was shattered in pieces. The horse appeared to have been rolled over several times by the blast, and pieces of the harness were found thirty feet from his body.

It was into this mine, now considered perfectly safe, that Mr. Bryden conducted me. Seated upon a square block of wood on the bottom of one of a train of mine cars, in the attitude of a toad, each with a torch in his hand, we entered an aperture at the base of the mountain, by the side of the canal. The cars (five in a train), running upon iron rails, and drawn by a horse, are three feet long and two feet wide at top, tapering to the bottom. Thus boxed up, and our heads bowed in meek submission to the menaces of the low roof of the passage, we penetrated the mountain nearly half a mile, when we came to an inclined plane. There the horse that took us in was attached to a loaded train that had just descended, and went back to the entrance. The darkness was so profound, that objects could be seen by the light of our torches only a few feet from us, and on all sides were the black walls of anthracite, glistening in some places with water that trickled through the crevices. At the foot of the inclined plane we were one hundred and seventy feet beneath the surface of the earth. Up the rough steep, seven hundred and fifty feet, we clambered on foot, and, when half way to the summit, we saw the cables moving and heard the rumble of a descending train.[1] The passage is so narrow that there is very little space on each side of the cars. We were, therefore, obliged, for our safety, to seek out one of the slippery ledges of anthracite wide enough to sustain us, and, while thus "laid upon a shelf," the vehicles, with their burden, thundered by.

CARS ENTERING THE MINES.

A little beyond the inclined plane is the region of the fall. Here the roof is lower than in other parts. Crushed timbers and pulverized anthracite, the remains of the supporters of the chambers, are seen for some distance; and the filled-up avenues that led to other chambers, where some of the bodies remain buried, were pointed out to me. We at length reached the chambers where men were working, each with a lamp suspended by a hook from the front of his cap. So intense was the darkness, that, when a little distance from a workman, nothing of him could be seen but his head and shoulders below the lamp. The coal is quarried by blasting with powder; and the sulphurous vapor that filled the vaults, and the dull lights, with hideous-looking heads, apparently trunkless, beneath them, moving in the gloom, gave imagination free license to

---

[1] There is a double track upon the inclined plane, and, by means of cables and pulleys, the loaded train hauls up the empty one by force of gravity. From the main entrance many avenues are seen that extended to other chambers now exhausted. As fast as these avenues become useless, the rails are taken up, and they are filled with the slate or other impurities of the mines.

draw a picture of the palace of Pluto. Added to the sight was the feeling of awe which the apparent dangers of the place engendered, as the recollection of the tragedy just recorded was kept alive by the identification of localities connected with the event, by my guide. After collecting a few fossils,[1] we sought the " wind entrance," and, ascending a flight of steps about twenty-five feet, we stood high upon the mountain overlooking Carbondale, three quarters of a mile from the place of our entrance. Notwithstanding the air is comparatively pure within, except in the working chambers at the time of blast-

APPEARANCE OF THE CHAMBERS.[2]

ing, I breathed much freer when standing in the sunlight, and removed from all danger. Hastening down the mountain to the canal, I washed my fossils and hurried to the stage-office in the village, where I arrived just in time to hear the provoking rattle of the coach-wheels half a mile distant, on the road to Honesdale, leaving me to decide the question whether to remain over a day, or, departing at nine in the evening, ride all night. I chose the latter alternative, and passed the remainder of the afternoon among the mines and miners.

I left Carbondale at nine in the evening, and arrived at Cherry Hill, thirteen miles distant, at one in the morning. The road was exceedingly rough and the coach rickety. I had but a single fellow-passenger, and he was as deaf as a post. He was a grumbler of the first water, and his loud thoughts so amused me that I had no inclination to sleep. At Cherry Hill we awaited the coach from Honesdale. Informed that its arrival would be two hours later, we took beds; but the first dream had scarcely begun, when the wooden voice

[1] The coal is covered by a layer of slate, so even on its under surface that the roofs of the passages, when the coal has been removed, are quite smooth and flat. Upon this flat surface are impressions of stalks and leaves of plants of immense size, intermingled with those of the fern, of the size which now grow on the borders of marshes. Some of these fossil stalks found between the slate and the coal measure from ten to sixteen inches across (for they are all flattened, as if by pressure), and were evidently at least thirty feet long. They lie across each other in every direction, and in all cases the stalks are flattened. Many theories have been conceived to account for the origin of the coal and of the appearance of these fossils. The most plausible seems to be that the bed of coal was once a vast bed of *peat*, over which, in ages past, grew these mammoth ferns; that the slate that covers the upper stratum of coal was thrown up, in a semi-fluid state, from the bowels of the earth by volcanic action, and flowed over the fields of peat, casting down the ferns and other vegetables flat beneath the whelming mass, which, in time, became indurated, and was formed into slate. The huge stalks that have been found may have belonged to a species of water-lily that abounded when the mastodon and megatherium browsed in the marshes that now form the coal beds of the Lackawanna Valley.

[2] The miners, when they branch off from the main shaft or avenue, leave pillars of coal about eighteen feet square, to support the roof or mass above. These huge pillars were crushed by the great weight upon them, in the accident recorded.

NOTE.—The change which the Delaware and Hudson Canal and Mining Company has wrought in the physical features of this region is wonderful. Twenty years ago the whole country in the vicinity of Carbondale was an uninhabited wilderness; now fertile farms and thriving villages are there.* When Maurice Wurts, of Philadelphia, after spending years in exploring the country between the Lackawanna and the Hudson, presented his plan for the gigantic work now in progress, his friends looked upon him as nearly crazed, and, like Fulton, he was doomed to have hope long deferred. But there were some who comprehended the feasibility of the undertaking, and estimated correctly its golden promises of profit. The work was begun, and in 1829 seven thousand tons of anthracite coal were forwarded to New York. Wonderfully has the business increased. The company now employs between five and six thousand men and boys, over one thousand horses, and nearly nine hundred canal-boats, independent of the vessels at Rondout. Last year (1848) the company forwarded to market four hundred and fifty thousand tons of coal, and its monthly disbursements are about one hundred and fifty thousand dollars. At Carbondale there are nine mines or entrances; and about seven hundred men, chiefly Irish and Welsh, are employed under ground there. The coal is sent from Carbondale to Honesdale, a distance of sixteen miles, in cars upon an inclined plane, and there it is shipped for market upon the Delaware and Hudson Canal, the termination of which is upon the Hudson River, at Rondout, Ulster county.

* Carbondale contained about seven thousand inhabitants, and Honesdale about four thousand.

of a Dutch hostler broke our slumbers with the cry of " Stage !"   We were charged a quarter each for the privilege of warming a cold bed, which made the deaf grumbler swear like a pirate.   A young woman, unused to crowds, occupied a place by the side of the driver, and I was obliged to shrink into proper dimensions to share a seat within, with two elderly women who were by no means diminutive.   " I can't be squeezed, I can't be squeezed !" cried one of them, as I opened the coach-door to get in.   My size was magnified in the darkness to very improper dimensions, but the lady was pacified by a solemn assurance that what she saw was more than half overcoat.   Thus packed, we were trundled over one of the roughest roads in Pike county, and at six o'clock were set down at Decker's, among the Lackawanna Mountains, where we breakfasted.   Before reaching there, rain began to fall, and the delicate young lady, who occupied a seat with the driver for the sake of fresh air, implored shelter within.   Of course her petition was granted, but she proved a destroyer of the comfort of two of the passengers.   She was a plump Dutch girl, weighing nearly two hundred, and the two old gentlemen, who, in the plenitude of their good will and politeness, had offered her a seat upon their knees before she alighted from above, " worked their passage" down the rough mountain roads, for the horses were allowed a loose rein while the shower lasted.   One of the victims, whose obesity was conspicuous, declared that his gallantry could not have extended another rood, and that the announcement of the appearance of Decker's sign-post was as grateful to him as the " land ho !" is to the returning mariner.

At Decker's we changed coaches, horses, and drivers.   The former, like the morals of the latter, were very dilapidated.   A worse vehicle and more wicked driver than we were in the custody of I never encountered.   The rain fell copiously for two hours, and every passenger was subjected to the filthy drippings through the leaky roof of the coach, and the more filthy drippings of profanity and low slang from the lips of the driver, who was within speaking distance of a companion upon another stage.

Toward noon the clouds broke, and I escaped from my damp prison to the driver's box just as we reached the brow of the loftiest hill over which the road passes before descending to the Delaware Valley.   Twenty miles eastward loomed up the dark range of the Shawangunk Mountains ; on our right, far below, sparkled a beautiful bell-shaped lake fringed with evergreens, and, as far as the eye could reach, wooded hills stood " peeping over each others shoulders."   The scenery was as wild and more diversified than that of the Pocono.   Suddenly we came upon the brow of the mountain that overlooks the beautiful plain of Milford, on the Delaware, and in a few minutes we were rattling through the pretty village.   Milford is remarkable for the picturesque beauty of its own location and surrounding country, and for the size of one of its publicans, who died in 1841.[1]   Near it are the beautiful falls of the Sawkill, where,

> " Swift as an arrow from the bow,
>   Headlong the torrent leaps,
> Then tumbling round in dazzling snow
>   And dizzy whirls it sweeps ·
> Then shooting through the narrow aisle
> Of this sublime cathedral pile,
> Amid its vastness, dark and grim,
> It peals its everlasting hymn."
>   STREET.

---

[1] Milford has been settled about fifty years.   The chief business of the place is the lumber trade.   It is quite a large village, and, since 1814, has been the county seat of Pike.   In 1800 there were but two houses and a blacksmith's shop upon its site.   The plain was then covered with pines, hemlocks, and bushes.   The wadding of a hunter's gun set the brush on fire, and the plain was cleared for a great distance.   The buildings, however, remained untouched.   Some wag published an account of the fire, and said that it had " ravaged the town of Milford, and had left but two houses and a blacksmith's shop standing !"

The *publican* referred to was a tavern-keeper named Lewis Cornelius, whose dimensions were nearly as great as those of the famous Daniel Lambert.   His height was six feet ; in circumference at the waist, six feet two and a half inches ; circumference below the waist, eight feet two inches ; circumference of arm above the elbow, two feet two inches ; below the elbow, one foot nine inches ; at the wrist, one foot three inches ; of the thigh, four feet three inches ; of the calf of the leg, two feet seven inches ; weight, six hundred and forty-five and a half pounds, without any clothes.

But the pleasure of a visit thither were denied us by the urgent beck of time. It was after one o'clock, and we must be at Port Jervis, eight miles distant, at three, to enter the cars for the Hudson River, our point of destination.

The road from Milford to Port Jervis[1] passes along the margin of the Delaware Valley, sometimes beneath steep acclivities that seem ready to topple down. We crossed the river upon a bateau propelled by two strong men with poles, and guided by a rope stretched over the stream, and reached the rail-way station just as the last bell was ringing and a dark cloud began to pour out its contents. In a few minutes we were sweeping along the slopes of the Neversink Valley, and ascending, by a circuitous route, to the lofty passes among the Shawangunk Mountains.

The scenery here was indescribably grand. On the right the hills towered far above, and on the left, a thousand feet below, was the fertile valley of the Neversink lying in the shadows of the lofty hills on the west. The table-land upon the summit inclines gently to the eastward; and a little before sunset we passed through the fine grazing lands of Orange, lying between Middletown and Goshen, where the cow-herds furnish the materials for the far-famed *Goshen butter*. Westward of Middletown we passed near the historic ground of Minisink, and at twilight, descending the rugged slopes of Rockland along the winding course of a mountain stream, we passed by Ramapo and Tappan, places famous in our Revolutionary history. A visit there was reserved for another occasion, and, proceeding to Piermont, on the Hudson, the termination of the rail-road, I embarked for New York, and reached home at nine in the evening.

---

[1] Port Jervis was then (1848) the western terminus of travel on the New York and Erie Rail-road. It is situated on the eastern side of the Delaware, upon a small triangular plain at the mouth of the Neversink Creek, within the state of New York.

VIEW ON THE SHAWANGUNK MOUNTAINS.

CHAPTER XVII.

" I glory in the sages
     Who, in the days of yore,
In combat met the foemen,
     And drove them from the shore ;
Who flung our banner's starry field
     In triumph to the breeze,
.And spread broad maps of cities where
     Once waved the forest trees.
        Hurrah!

" I glory in the spirit
     Which goaded them to rise,
And form a mighty nation
     Beneath the western skies.
No clime so bright and beautiful
     As that where sets the sun ;
No land so fertile, fair, and free
     As that of Washington.
        Hurrah !"

                 GEORGE P. MORRIS.

O New England, the nursery of the Revolutionary spirit, I next turned my attention, and to that interesting field of research I proceeded, after visiting the battle-ground of Bennington, upon the Walloomscoick. I went up the Hudson on the morning of the 25th of September as far as Poughkeepsie,[1] where I passed the after- 1848. noon, and in the evening proceeded to Kingston, or Esopus, memorable in our Revolutionary annals for its destruction by the British.

Poughkeepsie is one of the finest villages in New York. It lies principally upon an elevated plain, half a mile from the east bank of the river, and in the midst of a region remarkable for its beauty and fertility. Although an old town, having been founded by the Dutch more than one hundred and fifty years ago, and lying directly in the path of travel between New York and Canada, it was spared the infliction of miseries which other places far more isolated suffered during the Revolution ; and it has but little history of general interest beyond the fact that a session of the state Legislature was held there in 1778, and that, ten years afterward, the state Convention to consider the Federal Constitution assembled there.

When the state government was organized, in 1777, by the adoption of a Constitution, the city of New York was in the possession of the enemy, and the first session of the Legislature under the new order of things was appointed to be held at Kingston, in July of that year. But the invasion of the state at several points—by Burgoyne on the north, by St. Leger and his Tory and Indian associates on the west, and by Sir Henry Clinton on the south —compelled Governor Clinton to prorogue that body until the 1st of September. Greater still, however, was the excitement in the state at that time, for Burgoyne was pressing tri umphantly toward Albany, and General Clinton was making active preparations to form a junction with him. No quorum was present until the 9th, and early in October, before any

---

[1] Poughkeepsie is a corruption of the Iroquois word Ap-o-keep-sinck, which signifies *safe harbor*. On an old map of the Hudson River in my possession it is spelled Pocapsey ; and I have heard many of the old inhabitants of Dutchess pronounce it as if so spelled, the *a* in the penultimate having the long sound, as in *ape*.

laws could be matured, the session was broken up, on the rapid approach of the enemy up

the Hudson, after the fall of the forts in the Highlands. Kingston was laid in ashes, and all was confusion. About the same time Burgoyne was conquered and captured, and Sir Henry Clinton retired to New York. As soon as the alarm had subsided, Governor Clinton called a meeting of the Legislature at Poughkeepsie. It assembled in the old stone building known as the Van Kleek House (then a tavern), early in January, 1778. Various acts, to complete the organization of the state government, were passed ; provisions were made for strengthening the civil and military powers of the state ; and it was during that session that the state gave its assent to the

February 6, 1778.

Articles of Confederation, the organic law of the Federal Union until our present Constitution was formed and adopted.

THE VANKLEEK HOUSE.[1]

This building was the meeting-place of the inhabitants to consult upon the public welfare, when the Boston Port Bill and kindred measures awakened a spirit of resistance throughout the country.[2] There the Committee of Correspondence of Dutchess held their meetings, and there the pledge to sustain the Continental Congress and the Provincial Assembly was signed by the inhabitants of Poughkeepsie, in June and July, 1775.[3]

---

[1] This is from a sketch which I made in 1835, a few weeks before the venerable building was demolished by the hand of improvement. It stood upon Mill Street, on the land of Matthew Vassar, Jr., a short distance from the Congregational Church. It was built by Myndert Vankleek, one of the first settlers in Dutchess county, in 1702, and was the first substantial house erected upon the site of Poughkeepsie. Its walls were very thick, and near the eaves they were pierced with lancet loop-holes for musketry. It was here that Ann Lee, the founder of the sect called Shaking Quakers, in this country, was lodged the night previous to her commitment to the Poughkeepsie jail, in 1776. She was a native of Manchester, England. During her youth she was employed in a cotton factory, and afterward as a cook in the Manchester Infirmary. She married a blacksmith named Stanley ; became acquainted with James and Jane Wardley, the originators of the sect in England, and in 1758 joined the small society they had formed. In 1770 she pretended to have received a revelation, while confined in prison on account of her religious fanaticism ; and so great were the spiritual gifts she was believed to possess, that she was soon acknowledged a spiritual *mother in Christ.* Hence her name of *Mother Ann.* She and her husband came to New York in 1774. He soon afterward abandoned her and her faith, and married another woman. She collected a few followers, and in 1776 took up her abode in the woods of Watervliet, near Niskayuna, in the neighborhood of Troy. By some she was charged with witchcraft ; and, because she was opposed to war, she was accused of secret correspondence with the British. A charge of high treason was preferred against her, and she was imprisoned in Albany during the summer. In the fall it was concluded to send her to New York, and banish her to the British army, but circumstances prevented the accomplishment of the design, and she was imprisoned in the Poughkeepsie jail until Governor Clinton, in 1777, hearing of her situation, released her. She returned to Watervliet, and her followers greatly increased. She died there in 1784, aged eighty-four years. Her followers sincerely believe that she now occupies that form or figure which John saw in his vision, standing beside the Savior. In a poem entitled " A Memorial to Mother Ann," contained in a book called "Christ's Second Appearing," the following stanza occurs :

"How much they are mistaken who think that mother's dead,
When through her ministrations so many souls are saved.
In union with the Father, she is the second Eve,
Dispensing full salvation to all who do believe."

[2] The city of New York elected James Duane, John Jay, Philip Livingston, Isaac Low, and John Alsop delegates to the first Continental Congress, in 1774. The Dutchess county committee, whose meetings upon the subject were held in the Van Kleek House, adopted those delegates as representatives for their district. —See *Journals of Congress*, i., 7.

[3] On the 29th of April, 1775, ten days after the skirmish at Lexington, a meeting of the inhabitants of

Huddlestone, the famous spy, who was captured upon Wild Boar Hill, near Yonkers, in West Chester county, was tried, condemned, and hung at Poughkeepsie in April, 1780. The place of his execution was upon a verge of the plain on which the town stands, known as Forbus's Hill. I have heard the late venerable Abel Gunn, of Poughkeepsie, who was a drum major in the Continental army, speak of Huddlestone and of his execution. He described him as a small man, with a large head and thick neck. He was accompanied to the scaffold by the county officers and a small guard of militia enrolled for the purpose.

The state Convention to consider the Federal Constitution assembled at the Vankleek House, in Poughkeepsie, on the 17th of June, 1788. There were fifty-seven delegates present, and Governor George Clinton was chosen the president of the Convention. In that Assembly were some of the most distinguished men of the Revolution, and the debates were of the most interesting character. In no state in the Union was hostility to the Federal Constitution more extensive and violent than in the state of New York. Forty-six of the fifty-seven delegates, including the governor, were anti-Federalists, or opposed to the Constitution. The principal advocates of the instrument were John Jay, Alexander Hamilton, and Robert Livingston. Mr. Hamilton had been a leading member of the National Convention that framed the Constitution, and also one of the principal writers of the *Federalist*.[1] He felt the responsibility of his situation, and the Convention readily acknowledged the value of his judgment. He was perfectly familiar with every topic included in the wide range which the debates embraced, and he was nobly sustained by his colleagues, Jay and Livingston. The hostile feelings of many of the anti-Federalists gradually yielded, and on the 26th of July the final question of ratification was carried in the affirmative by a majority of three votes.

A little more than a mile below Poughkeepsie, on the bank of the Hudson, is the residence of the late Colonel Henry A. Livingston, a grandson of Philip Livingston, one of the

the city of New York, called to consider the alarming state of public affairs, formed a general Association, or fraternized, to use a popular term, and adopted a pledge. The Association and pledge were approved by the Provincial Assembly, and copies of the latter were sent to every county in the state for signatures. The following was the form of the pledge :

"Persuaded that the salvation of the rights and liberties of America depend, under God, on the firm union of its inhabitants in a rigorous prosecution of the measures necessary for its safety ; and convinced of the necessity of preventing anarchy and confusion, which attend the dissolution of the powers of government, we, the freemen, freeholders, inhabitants of ——, being greatly alarmed at the avowed design of the ministry to raise a revenue in America, and shocked by the bloody scene now acting in MASSACHUSETTS BAY, do, in the most solemn manner, resolve never to become slaves ; and do associate, under all the ties of religion, honor, and love to our country, to adopt, and endeavor to carry into execution, whatever measures may be recommended by the CONTINENTAL CONGRESS, or resolved upon by our Provincial Convention for the purpose of preserving our CONSTITUTION, and opposing the execution of the several arbitrary ACTS of the British Parliament, until a reconciliation between Great Britain and America, on constitutional principles (which we most ardently desire), can be obtained ; and that we will in all things follow the advice of our General Committee respecting the purposes aforesaid, the preservation of peace and good order, and the safety of individuals and property."

The list of signers, and the names of those who refused to sign in Poughkeepsie, have been preserved. The number of signers was two hundred and thirteen ; the number who refused to sign was eighty-two. A list of the names of the signers, and those who refused to sign, in the various precincts in the county, may be found in Blake's *History of Putnam County*, p. 102–143 inclusive.

[1] When the Constitution, adopted by the National Convention, was submitted to the consideration of the people, extensive and violent opposition was observed, founded principally upon the undue jealousy with which the doctrine of state rights was regarded. The friends of the Constitution saw that general public enlightenment upon the subject was necessary to secure the ratification of the instrument by the requisite number of states to make it the organic law of the republic. To this end Jay, Hamilton, and Madison commenced a series of essays in explanation and vindication of the principles of government. They appeared successively every week in the New York papers, between October, 1787, and the spring of 1788. The whole work, which is called *The Federalist*, consists of eighty-five numbers. Mr. Jay wrote six numbers,* Mr. Madison twenty-five, and Mr. Hamilton the residue. They had a powerful effect upon the public mind and contributed largely to the success which finally crowned the efforts of the friends of the Constitution.

* Mr. Jay and other gentlemen armed and placed themselves under the command of Colonel Hamilton, to suppress a riot in New York known as *The Doctors' Mob*. He was nearly killed by a stone thrown by one of the rioters, and was confined to his bed for some time. He had written the fifth number of the Federalist essays when that event occurred. He recovered in time to write the sixty-fourth.

signers of the Declaration of Independence, and son of the late John H. Livingston, D.D., president of the College of New Brunswick.   It was built by his paternal grandfather, Henry Livingston, in 1714, and is a fine specimen of a country mansion of that period.   The situation is delightful, completely imbosomed in venerable trees, and far removed from the bustle of the highway.[1]   The late oc-

cupant, in the exercise of his good taste and patriotism, preserved the old mansion from the invasion of modern improvements, and kept up that generous hospitality which marked the character of the "gentleman of the old school."   Even the orifice in the side of the house, under the piazza, which was made by a cannon-ball fired from one of the British ships that conveyed the troops up the river, who burned Kingston, seventy-two years ago, is preserved with care, and shown to visitors as a token of the spite of the enemy against active Whigs.

THE LIVINGSTON MANSION.

The last time I visited the mansion the late proprietor was living, possessing apparently all the vigor and cheerfulness of a man of fifty, though then past three score and ten years.[2]   In the room which contained his valuable library I passed several hours, copying the portraits of John and Mary Livingston, the parents of Robert Livingston, the first emigrant of that name to America ; and also an interesting *genealogical tree*, illustrative of the family growth and connections, which Colonel Livingston kindly placed at my disposal.   I have referred to these before, and they will be found in another part of this work.

I left Poughkeepsie at ten in the evening, and reached Kingston village, ninety-three miles north of New York, a little past midnight.   The landing is upon a rocky island separated from the main land by a morass, crossed by a causeway.   It is nearly three miles from the village, which lies upon an elevated plain several miles in extent, and is surrounded by high hills on all sides except toward the Hudson.   On the northwest the Catskill range rises grand and beautiful, and far enough distant to present an azure hue.   I think I never saw a more imposing display of distant mountain scenery than is presented at Kingston, toward sunset, when the higher peaks and bold projections cast their long shadows over the agricultural districts below, reflecting, at the same time, from their southwestern declivities, the mellow light of departing day.

Kingston was settled by the Dutch as early as 1663, as appears from an account of troubles between the white settlers and the Indians there, and was called Wiltwyck—literally *Wild Witch*, or Indian Witch.   The Dutch built a redoubt upon the bank of the creek, near the ancient landing-place.   The creek was called Redoubt Kill, or Creek, and is now known by the corrupted name of Rondout Creek.[3]   The Esopus Indians then occupied the beautiful

---

[1] Since my visit the quiet and beauty of the place have been invaded by the Hudson River Rail-road, which passes within a few feet of the mansion, and in whose construction the beautiful cove has been destroyed, and some of the venerable willows, planted by the first owner, have been uprooted.   In our country the *beautiful* has but a feather's weight in the scale against the *useful.*

[2] Colonel Livingston died June 9th, 1849.   Although living in the retirement of a gentleman of wealth and leisure, he often consented to serve the public in offices requiring judgment, industry, and integrity. He was a member of the state Senate one term ; and it is a remarkable fact that he was never absent a day from his post in the Senate Chamber or in the hall of the Court of Errors.   He will long be remembered in Poughkeepsie as one of its best citizens.

[3] Benson's *Memoirs*, in the Collections of the New York Historical Society, vol. i., part ii., p. 119.

flats extending from the creek northward nearly to the present town of Saugerties, and, becoming dissatisfied with their white neighbors, resolved to destroy them. For this purpose they fell upon the settlement while the men were abroad in the fields, and killed or carried off sixty-five persons. The survivors retreated to the redoubt, and the Indians began to erect a stockade near it. A message was sent to Nieu Amsterdam (New York), and Governor Stuyvesant immediately forwarded a body of troops, under Martin Crygier, who drove the Indians back to the mountains. During the summer, parties of the Dutch made inroads among the hill fastnesses, destroyed the Indian villages and forts, laid waste and burned their fields and stores of maize, killed many of their warriors, released twenty-two of the Dutch captives, and captured eleven of the enemy. This chastisement caused a truce in December, and a treaty of peace in May following.

1663-4.

The Dutch settlement at Kingston received a valuable accession, toward the close of the century, by the arrival of a company of Huguenots,[1] who, after the revocation of the Edict of Nantes, fled from persecution to America. They were a fragment of the resolute Christian band of eight hundred thousand who escaped from France into Holland, Germany, Switzerland, and England. They settled in the fertile valleys of Ulster and Orange, but that repose which they coveted was a long time denied them, for the Indians, jealous of the encroachments of the pale faces, harassed them continually. The school of suffering in which they had been tutored before leaving Europe had given them patience and perseverance, and they succeeded in planting the Gospel of Peace in the midst of the heathen, and gave many hardy sons to do battle in the council and the field for American independence.

Kingston and the neighboring region suffered much from the Indians and Tories during the Revolution, for this was emphatically a Whig district; and when Kingston became so presumptuous as to harbor rebel legislators, it was marked for severe chastisement by the enemy.

In 1776, after the adoption of the Declaration of Independence, the General Assembly of New York changed its title from the "Provincial Congress of the colony" to the "Convention of the Representatives of the state of New York." The Assembly was to meet in the city of New York on the 8th of July, the special object of the session being the forming of a state Constitution. But before that day arrived, the fleet of Admiral Howe, with a British army, appeared near Sandy Hook, and the new Congress assembled at White Plains, in West Chester county, twenty-five miles from the city. At the moment of meeting it received intelligence of the adoption of the Declaration of Independence, and its first act was to approve that measure by a unanimous vote. On the 1st of August a committee was appointed to draw up and report a Constitution.[2] John Jay was the chairman of the committee, and the duty of drafting the instrument was assigned to him.

During the autumn the labors of the Convention were greatly disturbed by military events. The enemy had taken possession of New York city and island; had spread over the lower

---

[1] These people occupy a conspicuous place in the history of the sixteenth and seventeenth centuries, and, as will be observed hereafter, formed an essential element in the machinery of our Revolution, particularly in the Carolinas. On the 26th of August, 1572, the festival of St. Bartholomew, seventy thousand Protestants were butchered in France by royal and papal authority. Terrible persecutions continued until 1598, when Henry IV. issued an edict, called the Edict of Nantes, granting toleration to his Protestant subjects. For nearly a century this edict was in force, but in 1685 Louis XIV. revoked it, and persecutions began anew. This cruel and injudicious policy lost France eight hundred thousand of her best subjects, who were Protestants, fifty thousand of whom made their way to England, where they introduced silk weaving, the manufacture of jewelry, and other elegant employments then monopolized by France. Of those who settled in Ulster county the names of twelve are preserved, whose descendants are numerous, and among the most respectable citizens of that and Orange county. The following are the names: Lewis Dubois, Andre Lefevre, Louis Bevier, Hugues Frere [Frear], Christian Deyo, Jean Hasbrouck, Anthony Crispell, Isaac Dubois, Abraham Hasbrouck, Pierre Deyo, Abraham Dubois, Lyman Lefevre.

[2] The following are the names of the gentlemen who composed that committee: John Jay, John Sloss Hobart, William Smith, William Duer, Gouverneur Morris, Robert R. Livingston, John Broome, John Morris Scott, Abraham Yates, Jr., Henry Wisner, Sen., Samuel Townsend, Charles De Witt, and Robert Yates. James Duane was subsequently placed on the committee, and, Mr. Jay being absent when the draft of the Constitution was reported, it was submitted to the Assembly by him.—*Journal of the Convention*, p. 552 and 833.

part of West Chester county, and expelled the American troops, and Washington and his army had fled before them to the Delaware. The Convention migrated from place to place, and held brief sessions at Harlaem, White Plains, and Fishkill in Dutchess county. At the latter place the members armed themselves for defense against the British or Tories who should assail them.[1] Finally they retreated to Kingston, where they continued in session from February, 1777, until May of that year. There, undisturbed, the committee pursued its labors, and on the 12th of March reported the draft of a Constitution. It was under consideration more than a month, and was finally adopted on the 20th of April.

1777. It is a document of great merit, and exhibits a clear apprehension of the just functions of government, which distinguished the mind of its author. Its preamble sets forth explicitly the cause which demanded the erection of a new government; and its first article declared that no authority should be exercised in the state but such as should be derived from, and granted by, the people. Great wisdom was manifested in all its provisions for regulating the civil, military, and

"THE CONSTITUTION HOUSE," KINGSTON.[2]

judicial powers of the state. It was highly approved throughout the country, and English jurists spoke of it in terms of praise. Under it the government of the state was organized by an ordinance of the Convention, passed in May, and, as we have noticed, the first May 8, session of the Legislature was appointed to be held at Kingston in July.[3] This Con- 1777. stitution remained in force, with a few amendments, until 1823, when a new one was formed by a state Convention. This, in time, was submitted to the action of a Convention to revise it, and a third was formed and became law in 1846.

In the history of these movements toward perfecting the organic law of the state of New York is developed much of the philosophy of that progress which marks so distinctly the career of our republic. From the old Dutch laws, sometimes narrow and despotic, but marked by a sound and expansive policy, to the enlightened features of the Constitution of 1846, we may trace the growth of the benevolent principles of equality, and a correct appreciation in the public mind of human rights. " We may see," says Butler, " in the provisions of our several Constitutions, the effects of the intermixture of the different races : the Dutch; the English, Scotch, and Irish; the French, Swedes, and Germans; the Anglo-American from the eastern colonies, from whom our people have been derived. To this cause, and to the great number and diversity of religious sects and opinions which have flowed from it, may especially be ascribed the absolute freedom and perfect equality in matters of religion, and the utter separation of the Church from the State, secured by these instruments."[4]

---

[1] Lives of Gouverneur Morris and John Jay.

[2] This house, the property and residence of James W. Baldwin, Esq., was used for the session of the state Convention in 1777. It is built of blue limestone, and stands on the southwest corner of Maiden Lane and Fair Street. It is one of the few houses that survived the conflagration of the village.

[3] Popular elections for members of the Legislature were held in all the counties except New York, Kings, Queens, and Suffolk, which were then in possession of the enemy. George Clinton, then a brigadier general in the Continental army, was elected to the offices of governor and lieutenant governor. The former office he held by successive elections for eighteen years, and afterward for three years. Pierre Van Courtlandt, who was president of the Senate, became lieutenant governor; Robert R. Livingston was appointed chancellor; John Jay, chief justice; Robert Yates and John Sloss Hobart, judges of the Supreme Court; and Egbert Benson, attorney general.—Journals of the Convention, p. 916–918.

[4] Outline of the Constitutional History of New York, a discourse delivered at the annual meeting of the New York Historical Society, in 1847, by Benjamin F. Butler, late attorney general of the United States.

October 6,   Kingston (or Esopus), being the capital of the state when Sir Henry Clinton
1777.   gained possession of the forts in the Hudson Highlands, was marked by the conqueror for special vengeance.   Having demolished the *chevaux-de-frise* at Fort Montgomery,
the British fleet proceeded up the Hudson; the massive iron chain was not yet stretched
across the river at West Point.[1]   All impediments being removed, a flying squadron of light
frigates, under Sir James Wallace, bearing three thousand six hundred men, under the command of General Vaughan, sailed up the river.   They were instructed to scatter desolation
in their track, and well did they perform their mission.   Every vessel upon the river was
burned or otherwise destroyed; the houses of known Whigs, such as Henry Livingston, at
Poughkeepsie, were fired upon from the ships; and small parties, landing from the vessels,
desolated neighborhoods with fire and sword.   They penetrated as far northward as Kings-
1777.   ton, where they landed on the 13th of October.   The frigates were anchored a little
above the present landing on Kingston Point, and a portion of the invaders debarked
in the cove north of the steam-boat wharf.   Another division, in small boats, proceeded to
the mouth of Esopus (now Rondout) Creek, and landed at a place a little northeast of Rondout village, called Ponkhocken Point.   The people at the creek fled, affrighted, to Marbletown, seven miles southwest of Kingston, and their houses were destroyed.   The two divisions then marched toward the village, one by the upper road and the other by the Esopus
Creek Road.   Near the house of a Mr. Yeoman, who was in the army at Stillwater, they

THE YEOMAN HOUSE.[2]

seized a negro, and made him pilot them directly to the town.
The detachments joined upon a gentle eminence near the village, a few rods south of the Rondout Road, and, after a brief
consultation, proceeded to apply the torch.   Almost every
house was laid in ashes, and a large quantity of provisions
and stores situated there and at the landing was destroyed.
The town then contained between three and four thousand
inhabitants, many of whom were wealthy, and most of the
houses were built of stone.[3]   Warned of the approach of the
enemy, a few saved their most valuable effects, but many lost all their possessions, and were driven back upon the interior settlements upon the Wallkill.
Governor Clinton, with the members of the Legislature, was there, and efforts
were made to raise a sufficient number of militia for the protection of the town,
but without success.   The enemy, however, fearing their wanton cruelty would
bring the people in mass upon them, hastily retreated after destroying the village.   A detachment crossed the river and marched to Rhinebeck Flats,[4] two
miles eastward, where they burned several houses; and, after penetrating northward as far as Livingston's Manor, and burning some houses there, they rejoined
the main body, and the fleet returned to New York.

This wanton and apparently useless expedition excited great indignation.   It was supposed that the destination of the enemy was, according to arrangement, Albany, and a junction with Burgoyne, then hemmed in by Americans at Saratoga, and anxiously awaiting the

[1] A detail of this event, and a drawing of the remains of the chain now at West Point, may be found on
page 700 of this volume.

[2] This view is from the road, looking north.   An attempt was made by a soldier to burn this house, but
so rapid was the march of the invaders that the flames had made but little progress before the troops were
far on their road to the village.   A negro woman, who was concealed under some corn-stalks near, extinguished the flames.   The house is about half a mile from the river, on the right side of the road from the
landing to Kingston village.

[3] Governor Clinton, writing to Captain Machin on the subject of erecting works for the defense of Kingston, says, "I do not conceive it necessary to inclose the town, as the houses are stone, and will form (if the
windows are properly secured) good lines of defense."

[4] Rhinebeck Flats village is in Dutchess county, about seventeen miles north of Poughkeepsie.   It was
eminently a Whig place during the Revolution.   There was the residence of the widow of General Montgomery, who had been killed at Quebec two years before, and of many of her numerous relatives, the Livingstons, all of whom were friends of the patriot cause.

promised aid from Clinton.   When Vaughan and his troops were at Livingston's Mills (which they destroyed), a flood tide would have carried them to Albany in five hours ; and so completely had the army of Gates drained the country, in that vicinity, of men, that they might easily have burned the stores at Albany, and taken possession of that city.   Gates afterward declared that, had such an event occurred, he must have retreated into New England, and Burgoyne would have escaped.   But, instead of becoming honorable victors, Vaughan and his party appeared content to fulfill the office and earn the renown of successful marauders.   They may have thought that their operations would divert Gates's attention, and cause him to detach troops for the defense of the country below, and thus so weaken his force as to enable Burgoyne to conquer or escape.   But this effect was not produced, and the expedition was fruitless of good to the cause of the king.   Gates at that very time was making the most honorable propositions to Burgoyne for a surrender, and, when he heard of Vaughan's operations, he wrote that officer a letter replete with just severity.[1]

Kingston was the scene of the execution of several Loyalists during the Revolution, and there Sir Henry Clinton's spy, who was caught at New Windsor, with a dispatch for Burgoyne in a silver bullet (of which I shall hereafter write), was hung upon the limb of an apple-tree.   Several Tories saved their lives by consenting to enlist in the Continental army. October 12, 1777.

The depredations of the Indians and Tories in the Warwasing and Mamakating Valleys, and other portions of Ulster county, from 1778 till near the close of the war, will be noticed hereafter, in connection with the Minisink massacre.   Let us now make a flying visit to the Revolutionary localities in the vicinity of Kingston, and then pass on to the battle-ground of Bennington.

With the exception of the "Constitution House" (depicted on page 387) and two or three other stone buildings, and the venerable tomb-stones in the old Dutch burying-ground, Kingston presents little attraction to the seeker of Revolutionary relics.[2]   Its hills, and rich plains, and distant mountain scenery are still there, but greatly modified by cultivation.   I passed the morning in the village, with General Smith, and at about noon proceeded to Rondout. This thriving little village is nestled in a secluded nook near the mouth of the Rondout Creek, which here comes flowing through a deep and narrow gorge among the hills, and mingles its waters with the Hudson.   Mr. Gossman, the editor of the *Courier*, kindly offered to accompany me to points of interest connected with the Revolution, and I passed the remainder of the day in a pleasant ramble with him.   Crossing the creek in a skiff to its southwestern

---

[1] He concluded his letter by saying, "Is it thus that the generals of the king expect to make converts to the royal cause ?   Their cruelties operate as a contrary effect : independence is founded upon the universal disgust of the people.   The fortune of war has delivered into my hands older and abler generals than General Vaughan is reputed to be : their condition may one day become his, and then no human power can save him from the just vengeance of an offended people."   The friends of the king were also displeased at the movement.   One of the leading loyalists of New York, writing to Joseph Galloway, said, " Why a delay was made of seven days after Clinton had taken the forts, we are ignorant of.   The Highland forts were taken on the 6th of October ; Esopus was burned on the 13th ; Burgoyne's convention was signed on the 17th.   There was no force to oppose even open boats on the river.   Why, then, did not the boats proceed immediately to Albany ?   Had Clinton gone forward, Burgoyne's army had been saved.   Putnam could not have crossed to Albany.   The army amused themselves by burning Esopus, and the houses of individuals on the river bank."   Clinton and the brothers Howe seem to have been perfect malaprops, striking at the wrong time, and withholding a blow when most appropriate and promising the best success.

[2] In the old grave-yard rest the remains of some of the Huguenots and of many of their descendants ; and there repose the bodies of not a few who suffered during the war for independence.   Some of the earlier grave-stones are rude monuments.   One of them, at the head of the grave of Andries De Witt, is delineated in the engraving. The inscription is rudely carved.   The tall and slender slate stone is supported by a cedar post, which was probably set up when the stone was erected, yet it is perfectly preserved, and retains its odor.   I saw it there fifteen years ago, and then "the oldest inhabitant" remembered it from his boyhood.   The meaning of IVLY may need to be explained to young readers.   I was used for J and V for U in former times, and the letters, therefore, make the word JULY.

side, we called upon the venerable John Sleight, now eighty years old, who lives in the dwelling of his father, on the slope of a high hill near the water. He had a clear recollection of the landing of the British, and directed us to the different localities at the mouth of the creek. He said there were only three houses where Rondout now is, and they were burned. The occupants fled to Marbletown, and the few soldiers stationed at the redoubt on the hill, a little northeast of the village, with a single cannon, followed the flying inhabitants. The enemy did not cross the creek, and the house of Mr. Sleight was spared.

From the high hills a quarter of a mile from Mr. Sleight's we had a fine view of the land-

ing-places of both divisions of the enemy, as seen in the engraving. The water extending on the left is Rondout Creek, and that on the right and beyond the long point is the Hudson River, the spectator looking northeast. The high point on the left is the place where the redoubt was thrown up. The small building beyond, standing upon the water's edge, is upon Ponkhocken Point,[1] and in the cove between it and

VIEW AT THE MOUTH OF THE RONDOUT.

the redoubt is the place where the enemy landed. The long point in the distance is the present landing, immediately above which, in a sandy cove, the main division of the British army debarked. An amusing anecdote was related to me, connected with that event. Between the point and Ponkhocken are extensive flats, bare at low water, and yielding much coarse grass. When the enemy landed, some Dutchmen were at work just below the point, and were not aware of the fact until they saw the dreaded red-coats near them. It was low water, and across the flats toward Ponkhocken they fled as fast as their legs could carry them, not presuming to look behind them, lest, like Lot's wife, they might be detained. The summer hay-makers had left a rake on the marsh meadow, and upon this one of the fugitives trod. The handle flew up behind him, and gave him a severe blow on the back of his head. Not doubting that a "Britisher" was close upon his heels, he stopped short, and, throwing up his hands imploringly, exclaimed, "O, mein Cot! mein Cot! I kivs up. Hoorah for King Shorge!" The innocent rake was all the enemy that was near, and the Dutchman's sudden conversion to loyalty was known only to a companion in the race, who had outstripped him a few paces.

Passing along the river road to the upper point, we visited the landing-place of the British. A large portion of the cove is now filled by a mass of earth, rocks, and trees that slid down from the high shore a few years ago. The heaps of blue clay have the appearance of huge rocks, and will doubtless become such in time, by induration. Returning to Rondout, I rode over to Kingston at about sunset, passed the evening with Mr. Vanderlyn[2] the painter, and at midnight embarked in a steamer for Albany.

Sept. 27, 1848.   The morning was cold, and every thing without was white with hoar frost. I was in Troy a little after sunrise, and at eight o'clock, seated with the driver upon a mail-coach, was ascending the long hills on the road to Hoosick, in Rensselaer county,[3] about twenty-

---

[1] The ferry to Rhinebeck was from Ponkhocken Point until 1814, when the causeway was constructed at the upper point, and the ferry and landing established there.

[2] Mr. Vanderlyn was a native of Kingston. He resided many years in Europe, where he painted his large picture of the *Landing of Columbus*, for the rotunda of the Capitol at Washington. It was completed about three years ago (1846), and now occupies its appropriate place. He died in 1853.

[3] The original *Manor of Rensselaer*, or *Rensselaerwyck*, included all of Rensselaer county, except Hoosick,

OF THE REVOLUTION. 391

Ride to the Hoosick Valley.   Van Schaick's Mills.   Place of the Bennington Battle-ground.   Baume's Dispatch

five miles east of the Hudson.   The country is very elevated and hilly, and, when three miles east of Troy, the Green Mountains were seen in the distance.   Before the Hoosick Valley is reached, the country becomes extremely broken and picturesque.   We descended by a romantic mountain road into the valley, a little past noon, and halted at Richmond's, at Hoosick Four Corners.   This is the nearest point, on the turnpike, to the Bennington battle-ground.   The road thither skirted the Hoosick River northward for three miles, to the falls,[1] where we turned eastward, and passed through North Hoosick, situated at the junction of the Walloomscoick and White Creeks.   Here is still standing the old mill known as *Van Schaick's* in the Revolution.   It was occupied by a party of Americans when Baume and his Hessians approached ; and here the memorable battle of Bennington ended.   From this mill, along the hills and the valley on the right bank of the Walloomscoick, to the bridge near the house of Mr. Barnet, two miles above, is the scene of the battle ; and the hottest of the fight (which

VAN SCHAICK'S MILL.[3]

occurred when the Hessians retreated from the heights) took place between the little factory village of Starkville and the house of Mr. Taber.   These allusions will be better understood after consulting the history.

The conflict called the battle of Bennington[2] was a part of the operations connected with Burgoyne's invasion from Canada, in the summer and autumn of 1777.   The delay which he had experienced at Skenesborough and on his way to Fort Edward had so reduced his stores and provisions, that a re-

Schaghticoke, and Pittstown, and also the greater part of Albany county.   The city of Albany is near the center of the manor.   This domain was granted to Killian Van Rensselaer by patent from the States-General of Holland, after he had purchased the native right to the soil in 1641, and was twenty-four miles wide, on both sides of the river, and about forty-two miles long east and west.   When the English came into possession of the country, the right to his domain of the proprietor of Rensselaerwyck, who was called the *patroon,** was not questioned, and on the 4th of March, 1685, it was confirmed by letters patent under the great seal of the state of New York.

[1] At the Hoosick Falls is a manufacturing village containing about one hundred dwellings.   The river here falls about forty feet, and affords very extensive water power.   Near the factories I observed a handsome octagonal edifice, on the road side, on the front of which, in prominent letters, is the following :

"SACRED TO SCIENCE.
In sea, earth, and sky, what are untold
Of God's handiwork, both modern and old."

It contains, I was told, a large collection of natural curiosities, which the wealthy and tasteful proprietor takes pleasure in exhibiting freely.

[2] This battle was fought within the town of Hoosick, and five or six miles from Bennington.   At that time the boundary line between New York and New Hampshire (Vermont, as a state, not being then in existence) was at the Green Mountains, and Bennington was claimed to be within the borders of New York.

[3] This view is taken from the left bank of the Walloomscoick, a little below the bridge.   The mill belonged to a Whig named Van Schaick, who had joined General Stark's collecting forces at Bennington.   Lieutenant-colonel Baume wrote the following dispatch to Burgoyne from this place :

"Sancoik,† 14th August, 1777, 9 o'clock.

"SIR—I have the honor to inform your excellency that I arrived here at eight in the morning, having had intelligence of a party of the enemy being in possession of a mill, which they abandoned at our approach ;

* This title was given to those Dutch purchasers of lands who bought the soil fairly from the natives, and planted a colony. There were several patroon estates, but that of Van Rensselaer is the only one not disturbed by political changes.   This, however, is now on the verge of extinction, and, for several years past, *anti-rentism*, as the opposition to the patroon privilege is called, has been working a change in the public mind unfavorable to such vast landed monopolies.

† See note respecting this name on page 399.

plenishment was necessary. Informed that the Americans had a large quantity of these, and of cattle and horses, at Bennington and in the vicinity, he resolved, with the advice of Major Skene, to send a detachment of his army thither to capture them. Both Phillips and Reidesel, the most experienced of his generals, were opposed to the measure; but Burgoyne, actuated by an overweening confidence in his strength, and deceived as to the extent of the Royalist party in the colonies,[1] dispatched Lieutenant-colonel Baume thither with five hundred Hessians, Canadians, and Tories, and one hundred Indians. Burgoyne's instructions to the commander of the expedition, dated August 9th, 1777,[2] declared the objects to be to try the affections of the county, to disconcert the councils of the enemy, to mount Reidesel's dragoons, to complete Peters's corps [of Loyalists], and to obtain large supplies of cattle, horses, and carriages. Baume was directed " to scour the country from Rockingham to Otter Creek," to go down Connecticut River as far as Brattleborough, and return by the great road to Albany, there to meet General Burgoyne, and to endeavor to make the country believe his corps was the advanced body of the general's army, who was to cross Connecticut River and proceed to Boston. He ordered that " all officers, civil and military, acting under the Congress, should be made prisoners." Baume was also instructed " to tax the towns where they halted with such articles as they wanted, and take hostages for the performance, &c.; to bring all horses fit to mount the dragoons or to serve as battalion horses for the troops, with as many saddles and bridles as could be found." Burgoyne stipulated the number of horses to be brought at thirteen hundred at least, and more if they could be obtained, and directed them to be " tied in strings of ten each, in order that one man might lead ten horses." Dr. Thatcher, in his Journal, says, " This redoubtable commander surely must be one of the happiest men of the age, to imagine such prodigious achievements were at his command; that such invaluable resources were within his grasp. But, alas! the wisest of men are liable to disappointment in their sanguine calculations, and to have their favorite projects frustrated by the casualties of war. This is remarkably verified in the present instance."[3]

August, 1777.   With these full instructions, Baume left his encampment on the 13th, and the next day arrived at the mill on the Walloomscoick. He reached Cambridge on the evening previous, near which place an advanced guard of Tories and Indians attacked a small party of Americans who were guarding some cattle. The patriots, after delivering a well-directed fire, retreated to the woods, leaving five of their number behind, prisoners. Some horses were captured, but, according to a dispatch from Baume to Burgoyne, the Indians who secured them destroyed or drove away all that were not paid for in ready cash. In his whole expedition Burgoyne found the savages more trouble than profit. Let us leave the invader at " Sancoik's," while we take a retrospect of relative events on the part of the Americans.

On the evacuation of Ticonderoga, and the advance of Burgoyne toward the Hudson, the Eastern States were filled with alarm. Burgoyne's destination was not certainly known, and when he was at Skenesborough it was thought that Boston might be the point to which he would march. The whole frontier of New Hampshire and Massachusetts was uncovered,

---

out, in their usual way, fired from the bushes, and took their road to Bennington. A savage was slightly wounded; they broke down the bridge, which has retarded our march above an hour; they left in the mill about seventy-eight barrels of very fine flour, one thousand bushels of wheat, twenty barrels of salt, and about £1000 worth of pearlash and potash. I have ordered thirty provincials and an officer to guard the provisions and the pass of the bridge. By five prisoners taken here, they agree that from fifteen to eighteen hundred are at Bennington, but are supposed to leave it on our approach. I will proceed so far to-day as to fall on the enemy early to-morrow, and make such disposition as I may think necessary, from the intelligence I may receive. People [Tories] are flocking in hourly, but want to be armed. The savages can not be controlled; they ruin and take every thing they please.

"I am your excellency's most humble servant,
"F. BAUME."

[1] Major Skene assured him that " the friends to the British cause were as five to one, and that they wanted only the appearance of a protecting power to show themselves."—Gordon, ii., 242.

[2] The original of these instructions is in the archives of the Massachusetts Historical Society.

[3] Military Journal, p. 92.

and strenuous efforts were at once made for the defense of these states, particularly New Hampshire, which was lying nearest the scene of danger. The Committee of Safety of the New Hampshire Grants (now Vermont) wrote to the New Hampshire Committee of Safety at Exeter, apprising them of the pressing danger near, and imploring their assistance. The Provincial Assembly had finished their session, and had gone home, but a summons from the committee brought them together again in three days. Despondency seemed to pervade the whole convention when they met, until the patriotic John Langdon,[1] then Speaker of the Assembly, thus addressed them : " I have three thousand dollars in hard money. I will pledge my plate for three thousand more. I have seventy hogsheads of Tobago rum, which shall be sold for the most it will bring. These are at the service of the state. If we succeed in defending our firesides and homes, I may be remunerated ; if we do not, the property will be of no value to me. Our old friend Stark, who so nobly sustained the honor of our state at Bunker Hill, may be safely intrusted with the conduct of the enterprise, and we will check the progress of Burgoyne."

Langdon's patriotic spirit seemed to be infused into the Assembly, for the most energetic measures were planned and put in operation. The whole militia of the state was formed into two brigades. The first was placed under the command of William Whipple (one of the signers of the Declaration of Independence), and the second, of John Stark. They ordered one fourth part of Stark's brigade and one fourth of three regiments of Whipple's to march immediately, under the command of the former, to the frontiers of the state, and confront the enemy. The militia officers were empowered to disarm the Tories. A day of fasting and prayer was ordered and observed.

Stark was then a private citizen. He had been a brigadier with Washington at Trenton and Princeton, and, when the army went into winter-quarters at Morristown, returned to New Hampshire on a recruiting expedition. Having filled his regiments, he returned to Exeter to await orders, and there learned that several junior officers had been promoted by Congress, while he was left out of the list. Feeling greatly aggrieved, he resigned his commission and left the army, not, however, to desert his country in the hour of peril, for, like General Schuyler, he was active for good while divested of military authority. March, 1777. He was very popular, and the Assembly regarded him as a pillar of strength in upholding the confidence and courage of the militia of the state. That body offered him the command, and, laying aside his private griefs, he once more donned his armor and went to the field, stipulating, however, that he should not be obliged to join the main army, but hang upon the wing of the enemy on the borders of his state, strike when opportunity should offer, according to his own discretion, and be accountable to no one but the Assembly of New Hampshire.

Joy pervaded the militia when their favorite commander was announced as their chief, and they cheerfully flocked to his standard, which was raised, first at Charleston and then at Manchester, twenty miles north of Bennington, where Colonel Seth Warner, with his Green Mountain Boys was posted. This was only the remnant of the regiment that so gallantly opposed the enemy at Hubbardton on the 7th of July, and was then recruiting at

---

[1] John Langdon was born at Portsmouth, New Hampshire, in 1740. He received a mercantile education, and for several years prosecuted business upon the sea, and, when the Revolution broke out, was a leading merchant in Portsmouth. He espoused the republican cause, and was one of the party which removed the powder and military stores from Fort William and Mary, at New Castle, in 1774. He was a delegate in the Continental Congress in 1775 and 1776. For a short time he commanded a company of volunteers in Vermont and on Rhode Island. He was Speaker of the Provincial Assembly of New Hampshire, and Judge of the Court of Common Pleas in 1776 and 1777. He was Continental agent in New Hampshire in 1779, and was again elected a delegate to Congress in 1783. He served in the Legislature of his state for several years, and in 1788 was chosen President of New Hampshire. The next year he was elected a member of the United States Senate, and in 1794 was re-elected for another term of six years. From 1805 till 1811 he was four years governor of the state, and then retired into private life. He was of Jefferson's political school, and in 1812 the majority in Congress selected him for Vice-president of the United States, but he declined the honor. He died at Portsmouth, September 18th, 1819, aged seventy-eight years.

August, 1777. Manchester. There Stark met General Lincoln, who had been sent by General Schuyler, then in command of the Northern Department, to conduct him and his recruits to the Hudson. Stark positively refused to go, and exhibited the written terms upon which he had consented to appear in the field at all. His refusal was communicated to Congress, and that body resolved that the Assembly of New Hampshire should be informed that the instructions which they had given General Stark were " destructive of military subordination, and highly prejudicial to the common cause;" and the Assembly was desired " to instruct

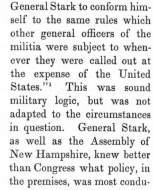

General Stark to conform himself to the same rules which other general officers of the militia were subject to whenever they were called out at the expense of the United States."[1] This was sound military logic, but was not adapted to the circumstances in question. General Stark, as well as the Assembly of New Hampshire, knew better than Congress what policy, in the premises, was most conducive to the general good, and the sequel proved that the apparent insubordination, which seemed so " highly prejudicial to the common cause," was productive of great benefits to the country. It was at this very juncture that Burgoyne was planning his expedition to Bennington, and on the day of the date of Baume's instructions Stark arrived at that place.

August 19.

August 9.

Informed of the presence of Indians at Cambridge, twelve miles north of Bennington, and of their attack upon the party of Americans there,[a] he detached Lieutenant-colonel Gregg, with two hundred men, to oppose their march. Toward night he received information that a large body of the enemy, with a train of artillery, was in the rear of the Indians, and in full march for Bennington. Stark immediately rallied his brigade, with all the militia that had collected at Bennington, and sent out an urgent call for the militia in the vicinity. He also sent an order to the officer in command of Colonel Warner's regiment, at Manchester, to march his men to Bennington immediately. The order was promptly obeyed, and they arrived in the night, thoroughly drenched with rain. On the morning of the 14th, about the time when Baume was at Van Schaick's Mills, Stark,[2] with his whole force, was moving forward to support Colonel Gregg. He was accompanied by Colonels Warner, Williams, and Brush. The regiment of the former was not with him ; they remained at Bennington, to dry themselves and prepare their arms for action. After marching about five miles, they met Gregg retreating, and the enemy within a mile

[a] August 13.

---

[1] Journals of Congress, vol. iii., 273.

[2] John Stark was the son of a native of Glasgow, in Scotland, and was born in Londonderry, New Hampshire, August 28th, 1728. His father removed to Derryfield (now Manchester), on the Merrimac, in 1736. While on a hunting expedition in 1752, young Stark was taken prisoner and carried off by a party of St. Francis Indians. He was redeemed by a Boston friend for the sum of one hundred and three dollars, to pay which he went on another hunting expedition on the Androscoggin. He served in Rogers's company of Rangers during the French and Indian war, and was made a captain in 1756. Repairing to Cambridge on hearing of the battle of Lexington, he received a colonel's commission, and on the same day enlisted eight hundred men. He fought bravely on Bunker Hill, his regiment forming a portion of the left of the American line, and its only defense being a rail inclosure covered with hay. He went to Canada in the Spring of 1776, and in the attack at Trenton commanded the van of the right wing. He was also in the battle of Princeton. In March, 1777, he resigned his commission, and retired to his farm. He commanded the New Hampshire militia at the battle of Bennington, in August, 1777, and in September enlisted a new and larger force, and joined the Continental army, under Gates, with the rank of major general. He served in Rhode Island in 1778 and 1779, and in New Jersey in 1780. In 1781 he had the command of the Northern Department at Saratoga. At the close of the war he left all public employments. In 1818 Congress voted him a pension of sixty dollars a month. He died on the 8th of May, 1822, in the ninety-third year of his age. He was buried on a small hill near the Merrimac, at Manchester, and over his remains is a granite obelisk, inscribed with the words Major General Stark. A costly monument is now in contemplation.

of him.   Stark immediately disposed his army for battle, and Baume and his men, halting advantageously upon high ground near a bend in the Walloomscoick River, began to intrench themselves.

Perceiving this, Stark fell back about a mile, to wait for re-enforcements and arrange a plan of attack. Baume, in the mean time, alarmed at the strength of the Americans, sent an express to Burgoyne for aid. Colonel Breyman was immediately dispatched with about five hundred men, but he did not arrive in time to render essential service.

The 15th was rainy, and both parties employed the time in preparing for battle. The Hessians and a corps of Rangers were strongly intrenched upon the high ground north of the Walloomscoick, and a party of Rangers and German grenadiers were posted at a ford (now the bridge near Mr. Barnet's), where the road to Bennington crossed the stream. Some Canadians, and Peters's corps of Tories, were posted on the south side of the river, near the ford.   At the foot of the declivity, on the east, near the mouth of a small creek, some chasseurs were posted, and about a mile distant from the main intrenchments on the height, on the south side of the river, Peters's American volunteers, or Tories, cast up a breast-work.   On the same side, upon the Bennington Road, Stark and the main body of his army were encamped.   The Walloomscoick, though called a river, is a small stream,

August, 1777.

Note.—The map here given is a copy, reduced, of one drawn by Lieutenant Durnford, and published in Burgoyne's "State of the Expedition," &c.   The Walloomscoick is there erroneously called Hosack (meaning Hoosick), that river being nearly three miles distant from the place of the Hessian intrenchments.   I would here remark that we are obliged to rely almost solely upon British authorities for plans of our Revolutionary battles.   They are, in general, correct, so far as relates to the disposition and movement of British troops, but are full of errors respecting the movements of the Americans, and also concerning the topography of the country, with which they were necessarily little acquainted.   It is too late now to correct many of these errors, for the living witnesses have departed, and the hearsay evidence of a younger generation is not sufficiently certain to justify any important corrections in the published plans of the battles.   I have, therefore, copied such maps as seemed most trustworthy, and endeavored, by slight alterations, and by descriptions in the text, to make them as correct as possible, as guides to a full understanding of the military operations of the time.   In this particular, as well as in local traditions, great caution is necessary in receiving testimony; and, where the subject has historical importance, I have uniformly rejected traditions, unless supported by other and concurrent authority, or the strongest probability.

The group upon this map, composed of a drum without a head, a musket, sword, and grenadier's cap, is a representation of those objects thus arranged and hanging over the door of the Massachusetts Senate Chamber at Boston.   They are trophies of the Bennington battle, and were presented by General Stark to the Commonwealth of Massachusetts.   The grenadier's cap is made of a coarse fabric resembling flannel, dyed red, and on the front is a large figured brass plate.   The drum is brass; the sword has an enormous brass guard and hilt; and the bayonet attached to the musket is blunted and bent.

every where fordable when the water is of ordinary depth.   Lying in the midst of high hills, its volume is often suddenly increased by rains.

Notwithstanding the rain fell copiously on the 15th, there was some skirmishing.   The Americans, in small parties, fell upon detachments of the enemy ; and so annoying did this mode of warfare become, that the Indians began to desert Colonel Baume, " because," as they told him, " the woods were filled with Yankees."   The Hessians continued their works upon the hill.   By night they were strongly intrenched, and had mounted two pieces of ordnance which they brought with them.

THE BENNINGTON BATTLE-GROUND.[1]

During the night of the 15th, Colonel Symonds, with a body of Berkshire militia, arrived. Among them was the Rev. Mr. Allen, of Pittsfield, whose bellicose ardor was of the most glowing kind.   Before daylight, and while the rain was yet falling, the impatient shepherd, who had many of his flock with him, went to Stark, and said, " General, the people of Berkshire have often been summoned to the field without being allowed to fight, and, if you do not now give them a chance, they have resolved never to turn out again."   " Well," said Stark, " do you wish to march now, while it is dark and raining ?"   " No, not just this moment," replied the minister of peace.   " Then," said the general, " if the Lord shall once more give us sunshine, and I do not give you fighting enough, I'll never ask you to come out again."   Sunshine did indeed come with the morrow, for at the opening of the dawn the clouds broke away, and soon all Nature lay smiling in the warm sunlight of a clear August morning ; and " fighting enough" was also given the parson and his men, for it was a day of fierce conflict.

August 16,   Early in the morning the troops of both parties prepared for action.   Stark had
1777.   arranged a plan of attack, and, after carefully reconnoitering the enemy at the dis-

---

[1] This view is from the hill on the southwest bank of the Walloomscoick, a little west of the road from the bridge to Starkville, looking northeast.   The road over this hill existed at the time of the battle, and is laid down on the map, page 395.   The river, which here makes a sudden bend, is seen at two points—near the cattle, and at the bridge, in the distance, on the right.   The house on the left, near the bridge, is Mr. Barnet's, and the road that crosses the center of the picture from right to left is the road from Bennington to Van Schaick's or North Hoosick.   It passes along the river flat, at the foot of the hills where the battle occurred.   The highest point on the distant hills, covered with woods, is the place where the Hessians were intrenched.   From that point, along the hills to the left, for about two miles, the conflict was carried on ; and upon the slopes, now cultivated, musket-balls and other relics of the battle have been plowed up.

tance of a mile, proceeded to act upon it.   Colonel Nichols, with two hundred men, was de
tached up the little creek that empties into the Walloomscoick above the bridge, to attack
the enemy's left in the rear, and Colonel Herrick was sent with three hundred to fall upon
the rear of their right, with orders to form a junction with Nichols before making a general
assault.   Colonels Hubbard and Stickney were ordered to march down the Walloomscoick
with two hundred men, to the right of the enemy, and with one hundred men in front, neai
Peters's intrenched corps, in order to divert Baume's attention to that point.   Thus arranged,
the action commenced at three o'clock in the afternoon, on the rear of the enemy's left, by
Colonel Nichols, who marched up from the deep-wooded valley, and fell furiously upon the
Hessian intrenchments.   At the same moment the other portions of the American army
advanced to the attack.   As soon as the first volley from Nichols's detachment was heard,
Stark, who remained with the main body at his camp, sprang to his saddle and gave the
word "Forward!"   They pressed onward to the hill above the Tory intrenchments, and
there the whole field of action was open to their view.   The heights were wreathed in the
smoke of the cannon and musketry, and along the slopes and upon the plains the enemy was
forming into battle order.[1]   The Americans rushed down upon the Tories, drove them across
the stream, and, following after them, the whole of both armies was soon engaged in the
fight.   "It lasted," says Stark, in his official account, "two hours, and was the hottest I
ever saw.   It was like one continued clap of thunder."   The Tories, who were driven across
the river, were thrown in confusion on the Hessians, who were forced from their breast-works
on the heights.   The Indians, alarmed at the prospect of being surrounded, fled at the commencement of the action, between the corps of Nichols and Herrick, with horrid yells and
the jingling of cow-bells, and the weight of the conflict finally fell upon the brave corps of
Reidesel's dragoons, led by Colonel Baume in person.   They kept their column unbroken,
and, when their ammunition was exhausted, were led to the charge with the sword.   But
they were finally overpowered, and gave way, leaving their artillery and baggage on the
field.   The Americans, like the dragoons, displayed the most indomitable courage.   With
their brown firelocks, scarce a bayonet, little discipline, and not a single piece of cannon, they
ventured to attack five hundred well-trained regulars, furnished with the best and most complete arms and accouterments, having two pieces of artillery, advantageously posted, and accompanied by one hundred Indians.   The mingled incentives of a defense of homes and promises of plunder[2] made the American militia fight with the bravery of disciplined veterans.

As soon as the field was won, the Americans dispersed to collect plunder.   This nearly
proved fatal to them, for at that moment Colonel Breyman arrived with his re-enforcements
for Baume.   They had approached within two miles before Stark was apprised of their proximity.   The heavy rain on the preceding day had kept them back, and, although their march
had been accelerated on hearing the noise of the battle just ended, they could not reach the
field in time to join in the action.   They met the flying party of Baume, which made a rally,
and the whole body pushed forward toward the abandoned intrenchments on the heights.
Stark endeavored to rally his militia, but they were too much scattered to be well arranged
for battle, and the fortunes of the day were, for a moment, in suspense.   Happily the corps
of Colonel Warner, which was left at Bennington in the morning, arrived at this juncture,
fresh and well armed, and fell vigorously upon the enemy.   Stark, with what men he had
been able to collect, pushed forward to his assistance.   The battle continued with obstinacy
until sunset.   It was a sort of running conflict, partly on the plains and partly on the hills,
from the heights to Van Schaick's, where the enemy made his last stand, and then fled toward the Hoosick.   The Americans pursued them until dark, and Stark was then obliged

---

[1] It was at this moment that Stark made the laconic speech to his men, which popular tradition has preserved: "See there, men! there are the red-coats.   Before night they are ours, or Molly Stark will be a
widow!"   This speech, it is said, brought forth a tremendous shout of applause from the eager troops,
which greatly alarmed the Loyalists in their works below.

[2] General Stark, in his orders in the morning, promised his soldiers all the plunder that should be taken
in the enemy's camp.—*Gordon*, ii., 244.

to draw off his men to prevent them from firing upon each other in the gloom of evening. Seven hundred of the enemy were made prisoners, among whom was Colonel Baume. He was wounded, and died soon afterward. "Another hour of daylight," said Stark, in his official report, "and I would have captured the whole body." Besides the prisoners, four pieces of brass cannon, two hundred and fifty dragoon swords, several hundred stand of arms, eight brass drums, and four ammunition wagons were secured. Two hundred and seven of the enemy were killed. The loss of the Americans was about one hundred killed, and as many wounded. General Stark had a horse killed under him, but was not injured himself. The total loss of the enemy in killed, wounded, and prisoners was nine hundred and thirty-four, including one hundred and fifty-seven Tories.[1]

This victory was hailed with great joy throughout the land. It was another evidence of the spirit and courage of the American militia when led to the field by a good commander.[2] It also crippled the strong arm of Burgoyne, and revived the spirits of the American army at Cohoes and Stillwater. The loud commendatory voice of the people forced Congress to overlook the insubordination of General Stark, which seemed so "highly prejudicial to the common cause," and on the 4th of October resolved, "That the thanks of Congress be presented to General Stark, of the New Hampshire militia, and the officers and troops under his command, for their brave and successful attack upon, and signal victory over, the enemy in their lines at Bennington; and that Brigadier Stark be appointed a brigadier general in the army of the United States."[3]

1777.

When I visited the Bennington battle-ground, every ancient resident in the vicinity, who had been familiar with the locality, had departed, and I was unable to find a person who could point out the exact place of the German intrenchments. A *vendue*, a few miles distant, had attracted the men from home; but, through the general familiarity with the scenes of Mr. Richmond, of Hoosick Four Corners, who accompanied me, and aided by the map of Lieutenant Durnford, which I had with me, the points of interest were easily recognized.

Ascending the rough hills northeast of Mr. Barnet's, we soon found, upon the highest knoll on the crown of the timbered heights, traces of the German intrenchments. Portions of the banks and ditches are quite prominent, and for several rods on all sides the timber is young, the spot having been cleared by the enemy. Descending the gentle slope northward, we emerged into cleared fields, whence we had a fine view of the valleys of the White Creek on the north and of the Walloomscoick[4] on the east. Here was the place where Colonel Nichols made his first attack upon the rear of the enemy's left. The view of the Walloomscoick Valley was one of the finest I ever beheld. From our point of vision it stretched away to the eastward, its extremity bounded by the lofty Green Mountains, about nine miles dis-

---

[1] Gordon, Ramsay, Thacher, Marshall, Allen, Burgoyne's Defense, Stedman, Everett's Life of Stark.

[2] There are several anecdotes related in connection with this battle, which exhibit the spirit of the people and the soldiers. Thacher says that an old man had five sons in the battle. On being told that one of them was unfortunate, he exclaimed, "What, has he misbehaved? Did he desert his post or shrink from the charge?" "Worse than that," replied his informant. "He was slain, but he was fighting nobly." "Then I am satisfied," replied the old man; "bring him to me." After the battle the body of his son was brought to him. The aged father wiped the blood from the wound, and said, while a tear glistened in his eyes. "This is the happiest day of my life, to know that my five sons fought nobly for freedom, though one has fallen in the conflict." This was an exhibition of old Spartan patriotism.

When Warner's regiment came into the field, Stark rode up and ordered a captain to lead his men into action. "Where's the colonel [Warner]? I want to see him first," he coolly replied. The colonel was sent for, and the captain, in a nasal tone, said, "Well, colonel, what d'ye want I should do?" "Drive those red-coats from the hill yonder," replied Warner. "Well, it shall be done," said the captain, and in an instant himself and men were on the run for the thickest of the battle.

[3] Journal of Congress, iii., 327. In passing the last clause of the resolution, the yeas and nays were required and taken. There was but one dissenting voice, Mr. Chase, of Maryland. The delegates from Virginia did not vote.

[4] This is said to be a Dutch word, signifying *Walloom's Patent*. It is variously spelled. On Durnford's map it is *Walmscock*. On Tryon's map of the state of New York, 1779, it is *Wallamschock;* and others spell it Wallamsac, Wolmseec, and Walmsook. The orthography which I have adopted is that which the New York records exhibit, and is doubtless correct.

tant, which formed a line of deeper blue than the sky, the tint broken a little by gray cliffs and bald summits reflecting occasional gleams of the evening sun. Through the rich inter-vales of the broad basin, the winding Walloomscoick, traversed by the highway, glistened at various points among the groves that shade its banks ; and the whole valley, dotted with farm-houses, presents one picture of peaceful industry. On the right, seven miles distant, and nestled among the hills near the Green Mountains, lies Bennington, the white spire of whose church was seen above the intervening forests. From the heights we could plainly discern a brick house in the valley, that belonged, during the Revolution, to a Tory named Mathews. It is remarkable only for its position, and the consequences which sometimes re-sulted therefrom. It stands upon the line between New York and Vermont, and in it cen-ter the corner points of four towns—Bennington, Shaftsbury, Hoosick, and White Creek ; also, those of the counties of Bennington, Washington, and Rensselaer. The occupant had only to step from one room to another, to avoid the operation of a legal process that might be issued against him in any one of the counties or four towns.

Descending the heights, we crossed the bridge at the old ford, near Barnet's, and went down the river, on its southern side, to Starkville. From the hill a few rods south of the place where Peters's Tories were intrenched (slight traces of the mounds were still visible) we had a fine view of the whole battle-ground. I tarried long enough upon the brow of the hill, near the river, to make the sketch on page 396. While thus engaged, a low bel-low, frequently repeated, attracted my attention, and, seeming to approach nearer, induced me to reconnoiter. Toward the foot of the hill a huge bull was pawing the earth, and mak-ing menacing advances up the slope. He had mistaken my cloak, fluttering in the wind, for a formal challenge to combat, and seemed about advancing to the charge. Regarding an honorable retreat as a wiser measure than the risk of a probable defeat, I gathered up my "implements of trade," and retired to the fence, thinking all the way of the similarly-chased negro's use of Henry Laurens's motto, "Millions for de fence." It was sunset when we reached Van Schaick's on our return, and I had barely light sufficient to complete the drawing of the old mill on page 391, for heavy clouds were gathering. The twilight was brief, and darkness was upon us when we arrived at Hoosick Four Corners.

There was an insurrectionary movement among the militia in this vicinity in 1781. Sit-uated above the north line of Massachusetts, the country was within the claimed jurisdiction of the New Hampshire Grants. The animosities between the state government of New York and the people of the Grants, which the active Revolutionary operations in that quarter had, for a time, quieted, now that those operations had ceased, were renewed in all their former vigor. So warm became the controversy, that, on the 1st of December, an insurrec-tion broke out in the regiments of Colonels John and Henry K. Van Rensselaer. The 1781. regiment of Colonel Peter Yates also became disaffected, and, indeed, a large portion of the militia between the Batten Kill and the Hoosick seemed disposed to take sides with the law-less people of the Grants, who disregarded the urgent demands of patriotism at that juncture. These disturbances arose in " Scaghticoke, St. Coych,[1] and parts adjacent." The insurgent regiments belonged to General Gansevoort's brigade. He heard of the defection on the 5th, and immediately directed Colonels Yates, Van Vechten, and Henry K. Van Rensselaer, whose regiments were the least tainted, to collect such troops as they could, and march to St. Coych, to quell the insurrection. An express was sent to Governor Clinton, at Poughkeepsie, who readily perceived that the movement had its origin among the people of the Grants. With his usual promptness, he ordered the brigade of General Robert Van Rensselaer to the as-sistance of Gansevoort, and gave the latter all necessary latitude in raising troops for the exi-gency. Gansevoort repaired to Saratoga, and solicited troops and a field piece from General Stark, who was stationed there. The latter declined compliance, on the plea that his troops were too poorly clad to leave their quarters at that season, and also that he thought it im-

---

[1] This place was Van Schaick's Mill, now North Hoosick. The name was variously written by the early historians—St. Coych, Sancoix, Saintcoix, &c.

proper to interfere without an order from General Heath, his superior. Governor Chittenden, of the Grants, had just addressed a letter to Stark, requesting him not to interfere ; and,
as his sympathies were with the Vermonters, that was doubtless the true cause of his withholding aid from Gansevoort. The latter, with what volunteers he could raise, pushed on
to St. Coych, where he discovered a motley force of about five hundred men, advancing to
sustain the insurgent militia. Having only eighty men with him, Gansevoort retired about
five miles, and attempted to open a correspondence with the leaders of the rebellion. He
1782. was unsuccessful, and the rebels remained undisturbed. Early in January following,
Washington wrote a calm and powerful letter to Governor Chittenden, which had great
effect in quelling disturbances there, and no serious consequences grew out of the movement.
September, I left Hoosick at nine on the morning of the 28th, on the Bennington mail-coach,
1848. for Troy. It was full inside, and the driver was flanked by a couple of passengers. The only vacant seat was one covered by a sheep-skin, upon the coach-roof—a delightful place on a pleasant morning, but now the lowering clouds betokened a storm. It
was "Hobson's choice," however, and, mounting the perch, I had a fine view of a portion
of the Hoosick Valley. The high hills that border it are cultivated to their summits, and
on every side large flocks of Saxony sheep were grazing.[1] As we moved slowly up the ravine, the clouds broke, the wind changed, and, when we reached the high rolling table-land
west of the valley, a bleak nor'wester came sweeping over the hills from the distant peaks
of the Adirondack and other lofty ranges near the sources of the Hudson. Detained on the
road by the cracking of an axle, it was nearly sunset when we reached Troy. I had intended to start for Connecticut that evening, but, as the cars had left, I rode to Albany, and departed in the early morning train for the Housatonic Valley and Danbury.

The country from Albany to the State Line,[2] where the Housatonic and Western Rail-roads
unite, is quite broken, but generally fertile. Sweeping down the valley at the rate of twenty
miles an hour, stopping for a few minutes only to take in wood and water, the traveler has
very little opportunity to estimate the character of the region through which he is passing.
The picture in my memory represents a narrow, tortuous valley, sometimes dwindling to a
rocky ravine a few rods wide, and then expanding into cultivated flats half a mile in breadth,
with a rapid stream, broken into riffs and small cascades, running parallel with our course,
and the whole surrounded on all sides by lofty hills, densely wooded with maples, oaks, hick-
ories, and chestnuts. At New Milford the narrow valley spreads out into a broad and beautiful plain, whereon the charming village stands. Thence to Hawleyville the country is
again very broken, but more generally redeemed from barrenness by cultivation.

At Hawleyville I left the rail-road, and took the mail-coach for Danbury, seven and a half
miles westward, where we arrived at two o'clock. This village, one of the oldest in the state,
is pleasantly situated upon a plain on the banks of a small stream, about twenty miles north
from Long Island Sound. Its Indian name was *Pahquioque*, and the first eight families
that settled there, in 1685, purchased the land from the aboriginal proprietors.[3] There is
nothing remarkable in its early history, aside from the struggles, privations, and alarms incident to a new Christian settlement in the midst of pagans. In truth, it seems to have
enjoyed more than ordinary prosperity and repose through the colonial period, but a terrible
blight fell upon it during our war for independence.

---

[1] Wool is the staple production of this region. The first flock of Saxony sheep in Hoosick was introduced
by a German named H. De Grove, about 1820. The price at which these sheep were then held was enormous, some bucks having been sold as high as five hundred dollars. But the great losses incurred in spec-
ulations in merino sheep, a few years previous, made people cautious, and the Saxony sheep soon commanded only their fair value. In 1845 the number of sheep of this fine breed in the town of Hoosick was fifty-
six thousand.

[2] The State Line station is upon the boundary between New York and Massachusetts, thirty-eight miles
from Albany and eleven from Pittsfield.

[3] Their names were Taylor, Bushnell, Barnum, Hoyt, two Benedicts, Beebe, and Gregory. They were all
from Norwalk, on the Sound, except Beebe, who came from Stratford.—See *Robbins's Century Sermon*, 1801.

OF THE REVOLUTION. 401

Tryon's Expedition to Danbury.   Trumbull's "M'Fingal."   Life of the Author.

CHAPTER XVIII.

" When Yankees, skill'd in martial rule,
First put the British troops to school;
Instructed them in warlike trade,
And new maneuvers of parade;
The true war-dance of Yankee reels,
And *manual exercise* of heels;
Made them give up, like saints complete,
The *arm* of flesh and trust the *feet*,
And work, like Christians undissembling,
Salvation out with fear and trembling."

TRUMBULL.[1]

 HE expedition to Danbury, in the spring of 1777, conducted by Governor Tryon, of New York, in person, was, in its inception, progress, and result, disgraceful to the British character, no less on account of the barbarity and savageism displayed than of the arrant cowardice that marked all the movements of the marauders. Sir William Howe did well for his own character, in disclaiming any approval of the acts of Tryon on that occasion, and in endeavoring to excuse the leader of the expedition by pleading the apparent necessity of such harsh measures. Every generous American should be ready to accord all the honor, skill, bravery, and humanity which often belonged to British officers during the war, for some of them, despite the relation which they held to our people struggling for freedom, demand our admiration and regard. But these very officers, guided by a false philosophy, and the instructions of ministers grossly ignorant of the temper and character of the colonists, planned and executed measures which every true Briton then condemned, and which every true Briton now abhors. The destruction of Danbury, and, two years later, of Norwalk and

---

[1] This is quoted from a political poem in three cantos, by John Trumbull, LL.D., called "M'Fingal," which gained for the author much celebrity in America and Europe. The first part of the poem was written in 1775, and published in Philadelphia, where the Continental Congress was then in session. Numerous editions appeared, and it was republished in England. It was not finished until 1782, when the whole was printed at Hartford, in three cantos. It is in the Hudibrastic strain, " and," says Griswold, " is much the best imitation of the great satire of Butler that has been written." The author was born in Waterbury, Connecticut, in 1750. So extraordinary was the development of his intellect, that he received lessons in Greek and Latin before he was six years old, and was pronounced fit to enter Yale College at the age of seven. He entered college at thirteen, and went successfully through the whole course of studies. In 1771 he and Timothy Dwight were elected tutors in Yale, and in 1773 he was admitted to the practice of the law. He went to Boston, entered the office of John Adams, and there, in the focus of Revolutionary politics, his republican principles had full play. He commenced the practice of law in New Haven toward the close of 1774, and there he wrote his " M'Fingal." He had already acquired considerable celebrity as a poet. He removed to Hartford in 1782. Joel Barlow, Colonel David Humphries, and Timothy Dwight were among his most intimate literary friends. He was one of the " four bards with Scripture names" whom a London satirist noticed, in some verses commencing,

"David and Jonathan, Joel and Timothy,
Over the water set up the hymn of the," &c.

In 1800 Trumbull was elected a member of the Legislature, and, the year following, a Judge of the Superior Court. He was Judge of the Supreme Court of Errors from 1808 to 1819. His poems were collected and published in 1820, and in 1825 he removed to Detroit, where he died in 1831, in the 81st year of his age.

Fairfield ; the massacre of Baylor's corps at Tappan and Wayne's detachment at Paoli, are among the records which Britons would gladly blot out.   Aside from the cold-blooded murder and incendiarism involved, there was cowardice displayed of the most abject kind.   In each case, when their work of destruction was effected, the troops displayed the

" Manual exercise of heels"

when fleeing back to their respective camps.

On Friday, the 25th of April, 1777, twenty-six sail of British vessels appeared off Norwalk Islands, standing in for Cedar Point.   It was a mild, sunny afternoon.   The inhabitants of Norwalk and Fairfield, aware of their approach, took measures for the defense of their respective towns.   But both villages were, at that time, spared.   A little before sunset about two thousand well-armed troops landed upon the long beach at the foot of the beautiful hill of Compo. on the eastern side of the Saugatuck River, and near its mouth.   They

Distant View of Compo.[1]

were commanded by Governor William Tryon, assisted by Generals Agnew and Sir William Erskine.   The expedition had been fitted out by Sir William Howe at New York, its ostensible object being the destruction of American military stores at Danbury.   The force marched about seven miles into the country that evening, where they rested until toward daylight.   Clouds had gathered during the night, and rain began to fall.   Resuming their march, they reached Reading, eight miles southeast of Danbury, at eight in the morning, where they halted and breakfasted.

General Silliman, who was attached to the Connecticut militia, was at his residence at Fairfield when the enemy landed.   He immediately sent out expresses to alarm the country and collect the militia.   The call was responded to,[2] and early the next morning he started in pursuit.   He reached Reading about noon, where his force amounted to five hundred men.   He was there joined by Generals Wooster and Arnold, with a small number of militia.   These officers, who were at New Haven, on hearing of the invasion, started immediately to the aid of Silliman.   The Americans continued the pursuit as far as Bethel, within four miles of Danbury.   They did not reach Bethel until eleven o'clock at night, owing to a heavy rain.   There they determined to halt and postpone their attack upon the enemy until he should attempt to return to his shipping.

April 26, 1777.   The British, piloted by two young men of Danbury—Stephen Jarvis and Eli Benedict—reached the village between one and two o'clock in the afternoon.   They

---

[1] This view is from the top of a high hill northeast of the dwelling of Mr. Ebenezer Smith, near Norwalk. Its long sand-bar is seen stretching into the Sound on the right, and over the lowest extremity of the point the shade trees of Fairfield are visible.   The water on the left is the mouth of the Saugatuck River, and that in the distance, on the right, is Long Island Sound.

[2] The people of this region were extremely patriotic, and never hesitated a moment when their country called.   Before actual hostilities commenced (March, 1775), a company of one hundred men was enlisted in Danbury, for the colonial service, and joined a regiment of Connecticut troops, under Colonel Waterbury They were engaged in active service until Montgomery reached Montreal, in December, when they returned home without the loss of a single man.   The last survivor, David Weed, died in Danbury, June 13th, 1842, aged ninety-four years.   When this little band of one hundred men left for Lake Champlain, their friends regarded them as lost.   When they all returned, many of those very friends were in their graves, swept away by a prevalent dysentery.

proceeded through Weston, by Reading Church, over Hoyt's Hill and through Bethel ;[1] and so expeditious was their march, that the people of Danbury were not warned of their approach until they were within eight miles of the town.   Then all was confusion and alarm. Although the chief object of the invaders—the capture or destruction of the military stores —was understood, the Revolutionary party felt a presentiment that the expedition was fraught with cruelty and woes.   Some fled, with the women and children and a few movable effects, to the woods and adjacent towns, while others remained to watch and guard the sick and aged who could not depart.   There was a small militia force of only one hundred and fifty in the town, under the Colonels Cook and Dimon, when the enemy approached[2]—too few to attempt resistance.   When Try-

on entered the village at the south end, Dimon and his troops, who were mostly without arms, retired across the Still River at the north, and, making a circuitous march under cover of night, joined the Americans at Bethel.[3]

Tryon established his head-quarters at the house of a Loyalist named Dibble, at the south end of the village, and near the public stores. Generals' Agnew and Erskine made their head-quarters in a house near the bridge, at the upper end of the main street, now owned by Mr. Knapp.   All the other houses in the village were filled with British troops at night.

HEAD-QUARTERS OF AGNEW AND ERSKINE.[4]

As soon as the enemy entered the town they began to insult and abuse the people, but com-

---

[1] At this place the enemy was brought to a halt by a single resolute American named Luther Holcomb. Wishing to give the people of Danbury as much time as possible to escape, or prepare for resistance, he rode to the brow of a hill over which the invaders were about to march, and, waving his hat, and turning, as if to address an army behind him, exclaimed, " Halt the whole universe ! break off into kingdoms !"   It was a mighty host whose obedience he evoked.   Tryon was alarmed.   He caused his army to halt, and, arranging his cannon so as to bear upon the supposed opponents, sent out flanking parties to reconnoiter. Finding himself in danger of being surrounded, Holcomb put spurs to his horse and retreated to Danbury.

[2] On hearing of the approach of the enemy, Colonel Cook sent to General Silliman for arms and ammunition.   The messenger was Lambert Lockwood, who, coming suddenly upon the British troops near Reading Church, was made a prisoner.   Tryon recognized him as a young man who had given him aid when his carriage broke down while passing through Norwalk.   On that account he took Lockwood under his protection, but, in his hasty retreat from Danbury, left him to take care of himself.   Tryon was writing a protection for him when he was informed that the Americans were coming.   The governor dropped his pen and seized his sword, and the protection remained unwritten.

[3] When the British approached, a citizen named Hamilton resolved to save a piece of cloth which was at a clothier's at the lower end of the village.   He had just mounted his horse with the cloth, and fastened one end to the saddle, when the British advanced guard appeared.   Three light horsemen started in pursuit of Hamilton, whose horse was less fleet than theirs.   Drawing near to him, one of the troopers exclaimed, " Stop, old daddy, stop !   We'll have you."   " Not yet," said Hamilton, and at that moment his roll of cloth unfurled, and, fluttering like a streamer behind him, so frightened the troopers' horses that the old man got several rods the start.   The chase continued through the town to the bridge at the upper end. Several times the troopers would attempt to strike, but the cloth was always in the way.   The pursuit was finally abandoned, and the old man escaped.

[4] This house is on the south bank of Still River, at the north end of the main street.   It was built by Benjamin Knapp, in 1770, and was owned by him at the time of the invasion.   His birth-place is also standing, on the north side of the river.   They were among the few houses not burned.   At the bridge seen on the right the British planted a cannon, and kept a strong guard there until their departure.   This house is now (1848) owned by Noah Knapp.

mitted no great excesses. Had the inhabitants who remained kept quiet, the town might have been saved from conflagration; but four men,[1] whose feelings were wrought to the highest pitch by the free use of liquor, madly placed themselves in a large and valuable dwelling near the court-house, belonging to Major Starr, and, as the van of the British army approached, fired upon them several times from the windows, without effect. The exasperated troops rushed into the house, seized the men, thrust them into the cellar, and burned the building over their heads. The unhappy men perished in the flames, victims of most egregious folly.

The public stores were now attacked. The Episcopal Church was filled with barrels of pork and flour as high as the galleries, and two other buildings were also filled with provisions. One of them, the barn of Mr. Dibble, is still standing, on the southwest side of Main Street, at the lower end 1848. of the town. The American commissioners made use of it without his consent. Being a Tory, his barn was spared, and all the stores in it were saved. Those in the church were taken into the street and destroyed. The liquors were freely used by the soldiery, and they passed the night in drinking and carousing.

DIBBLE'S BARN.

As yet, the torch had not been applied. The sky was cloudy and the night was intensely dark. Having marched a greater portion of the preceding night, the troops were much exhausted by fatigue and want of sleep. Those who remained awake were intoxicated, except a few sentinels. The force of two thousand men that landed at Compo was reduced, in reality, to three hundred; and could the American generals at Bethel have known the exact state of things in the hostile camp, they might have annihilated the invaders. Tryon was on the alert, and slept but little. He was apprised by a Tory scout of the gathering of the militia at Bethel. Knowing the present weakness of his army, he resolved on flight, and accordingly, before daylight on Sunday morning, his troops were put in marching order. April 27, 1777. Fire-brands were applied to every house in the village, except those belonging to Tories. These had been marked with a conspicuous cross the previous evening. At the dawn of day the enemy marched toward Ridgeway, while for miles around the country was illumined by the burning village.[2]

> "Through solid curls of smoke the bursting fires
> Climb in tall pyramids above the spires,
> Concentering all the winds, whose forces, driven
> With equal rage from every point of heaven,
> Wheel into conflict, round the scantling pour
> The twisting flames, and through the rafters roar;
> Suck up the cinders, send them sailing far,
> To warn the nations of the raging war."
>
> JOEL BARLOW.[3]

---

[1] Joshua Porter, Eleazer Starr, —— Adams, and a negro.

[2] Robbins's Century Sermon.

[3] This is quoted from the *Columbiad*, a long epic—the American Revolution its theme. The author was one of the poets of the Revolution whose writings have outlived them. Dwight, Trumbull, Humphries, Hopkins, and a few other men of literary reputation in Connecticut, were his friends and associates. He was a native of Reading, Connecticut, where he was born in 1755. He was the youngest in a family of ten. He graduated at Yale College in 1778. He recited an original poem on taking his bachelor's degree, but it possesses little merit. Four of his brothers were in the Continental army, and during his collegiate vacation he went to the field as chaplain. He was in the battle at White Plains, and displayed good courage in several minor engagements. He married the sister of the Hon. Abraham Baldwin, of New Haven, and in 1783 removed to Westford, where he commenced the publication of the "Mercury." He was admitted to the bar in 1785, and the same year, at the request of several Congregational ministers, prepared and published an enlarged and improved edition of Watts's version of the Psalms, and added to them a collection of hymns, several of them his own. His "*Vision of Columbus*" was published in 1787. It was dedicated to the unfortunate Louis XVI. In London and Paris it was reprinted, and received considerable applause. He was engaged, with the literary friends just named, in publishing a satirical poem called

Nineteen dwellings, the meeting-house of the New Danbury Society, and twenty-two stores and barns, with all their contents, were consumed. The exact amount of military stores that were destroyed is not known, but, from the best information that could be obtained, there were about three thousand barrels of pork, more than one thousand barrels of flour, four hundred barrels of beef, one thousand six hundred tents, and two thousand bushels of grain, besides many other articles, such as rum, wine, rice, army carriages, &c. A committee appointed to appraise the private losses estimated the whole amount at nearly eighty thousand dollars.

On inquiring for men of the Revolution in Danbury, I was referred to three, all of whom I had the pleasure of seeing. I first called upon the venerable Levi Osborn, then eighty-six years of age.[a] He resided in Danbury when the village was burned, and remained, amid the jeers of Tories and the insults of the invaders, to protect an aged and sick parent. He is a leader of the sect of Sandemanians, of the division known as "Osbornites."[1] His naturally strong mind was yielding to the pressure of bodily infirmities, yet he still lives, an honored representative of the men of 1776.

After sketching Knapp's house, printed on page 403, I walked down to the old burial-ground, toward the lower part of the village, where the remains of many of the men of the

a September, 1848.

the *Anarchiad*, which had considerable influence. In 1791 he published in London his "*Advice to the Privileged Orders*," and, the following year, *The Conspiracy of the Kings*. He had some correspondence with the French National Assembly, and, on going to Paris, was honored by the gift of citizenship, and made France his home. His time was devoted chiefly to commercial pursuits, by which he amassed a fortune. He traveled some on the Continent, and in Piedmont wrote a poem called "Hasty Pudding," the most popular of his writings. Returning to Paris in 1795, he was appointed by Washington consul at Algiers, with power to negotiate a treaty of commerce with the dey, and with Tunis and Tripoli. After an absence of seventeen years, he returned to the United States, and built a splendid mansion on the bank of the Potomac, near Washington, known afterward as "Kalorama." The *Columbiad*, the original *Vision of Columbus* greatly altered, was published in 1808, in a splendid quarto, richly illustrated. Its merits have been variously estimated, some regarding it as a fit companion of the *Iliad*, *Æneid*, and *Paradise Lost*, and others allowing it only a small share of merit. Mr. Barlow had prepared to write a history of the United States, in 1811, when the design was frustrated by his being appointed minister plenipotentiary to the French government. In the autumn of 1812 he was invited by the Duke of Bassano to a conference with Napoleon at Wilna, in Poland. He traveled thitherward without halting to rest. The fatigue and exposure brought on an inflammation of the lungs, which caused his death, at an obscure village near Cracow named Zarnowica, on the 2d of December, in the fifty-fourth year of his age. He has been charged with abjuration of Christianity, but the accusation rests solely upon inferences. In private life he was pure and greatly beloved, and his public career was without spot or blemish.—*Allen's Biographical Dictionary ; Griswold's American Poets.*

[1] This small sect derives its name from its founder, Robert Sandeman, a native of Perth, in Scotland. He came to America in 1764, and in Boston and Danbury organized societies in accordance with his peculiar religious notions. His doctrines were similar to those of Calvin, and his distinguishing tenet was, that "faith was a mere intellectual belief—a bare belief of the bare truth." Like other founders of sects, he claimed to belong to the only *true* Church. His followers meet on the Sabbath and Thursday afternoons of each week, and, seated around a large circular table, each with a copy of the Scriptures, the men read and comment on them as they are moved by desire. The females are silent. The attending congregation not members are mere spectators, and the worshipers seem not to notice their presence. They have prayer and singing, after which they go to the house of one of the members, and partake of a feast of love. Their morals are of the purest kind, and their influence in society is exceedingly salutary. The two divisions are known as the *Baptist Sandemanians* and the *Osbornites*. The former practice baptism, the latter do not. Of late years none have joined them, and death is reducing their number. There are a few in England. Mr. Sandeman died at Danbury in 1771, aged fifty-three years. His grave is marked by a handsome marble slab, bearing his name and an epitaph

Revolution rest, and among them those of the brave General Wooster, who fell, as we shall presently observe, while gallantly opposing Tryon and his marauders on their retreat from Danbury. Not even a rough stone of the field marked his grave, *and no person could then identify it !* The fact is a disgrace to the people, past and present, among whom he fell in battle ; and the government, whose representatives, with grateful appreciation of his services, long ago voted money to erect a monument to his memory,[1] is guilty of positive ingratitude in so long withholding the paltry sum, while the long grass is weaving a web of utter obscurity over his dust.

From the cemetery I strolled down the winding road along which Tryon entered Danbury, and, returning, called to see the venerable Joseph Dibble, then in his hundredth year.

He lives with a nephew, near the same spot where he resided when Danbury was burned. He is the Loyalist who, with his father, entertained Governor Tryon while he remained at Danbury. He was a Loyalist in principle, and adhered to the royal cause in accordance with his convictions of right as an order-loving, law-obeying citizen. He was not armed against his Whig neighbors, and took no part in the cruelties which his guest sanctioned, but simply gave " aid and comfort to the enemy" while there. But the outrages committed by the men whom he sheltered and fed drew upon himself much of the odium that belonged to them, and for many years he was greatly despised by the sufferers. One night he was taken from his bed by some of his neighbors in disguise, to a deep place in the little river near the village, where they ducked him several times during the darkness. He expected that they would leave him under water with the fishes at the last immersion, but there was as much funny mischief as serious malice in his tormentors, and, to his great joy, they released him on dry land just as the first hue of light in the east appeared. Time softened the asperities of feeling, and

---

[1] On the 17th of June, 1777, the Continental Congress adopted a resolution, " That a monument be erected to the memory of General Wooster, with the following inscription : ' In honor of David Wooster, brigadier general in the army of the United States. In defending the liberties of America, and bravely repelling an inroad of the British forces to Danbury, in Connecticut, he received a mortal wound on the 27th day of April, 1777, and died on the 2d day of May following. The Congress of the United States, as an acknowledgment of his merit and services, have caused this monument to be erected.' " *Resolved,* " That the executive power of the state of Connecticut requested to carry the foregoing resolution into execution, and that five hundred dollars be allowed for that purpose."—*Journals of Congress,* iii., 197.

It has been erroneously asserted that the money was subsequently put into the hands of General Wooster's son, and that it was squandered. This is not true, as the Journals of Congress will show. A bill for the purpose passed the House of Representatives in 1822, but, in consequence of the numerous similar petitions that were presented after the passage of the resolution by the Lower House, the Senate did not concur. Ezra Foote, Esq., a citizen of Danbury, aged eighty-four years, informed me that he could so nearly identify the grave of Wooster as to pronounce it with certainty to be one of two graves, situated, as I ascertained by measurement, twenty feet northeast of the grave of Sandeman. General Wooster was not in the Continental service at the time of his death. Conceiving himself neglected, he had resigned, and was appointed the first major general of militia in his native state. – See note 1, page 408.

OF THE REVOLUTION.   407

Tory Guides.   Night Ride toward Ridgefield.   Return to Danbury.   Ridgefield.   Military Movements.

for half a century he has lived among his old neighbors and their descendants, a worthy and respected citizen. The two guides who piloted the army to Danbury did not fare so well ; they were obliged to flee. After the war, Benedict returned to Danbury for the purpose of residing there, but the people at once prepared to ride him out of the town upon a rail, and he fled. Jarvis went to reside in Nova Scotia. Many years afterward he returned privately to Danbury, to visit his relations. His presence being known, some citizens prepared tar and feathers for him. They surrounded his father's house, and demanded his person. His sister concealed him in an ash-oven, where he lay until the search was over and the party gone, when he left the town, and never returned.

Mr. Dibble was too nearly a wreck to give me any clear account of Revolutionary matters in that vicinity, and it was with much difficulty that he could be made to understand my object in wishing to sketch his portrait and obtain his autograph. He was a bachelor, and assured me seriously that he intended to remain one all the days of his life. He lived almost three years longer, and died in the Summer of 1851.

I also called upon Ezra Foote, Esq., one of the patriarchs of the village. Although eighty-four years of age, his erect figure, firm voice, and clear, intelligent eye gave him the appearance of a man of sixty. After half an hour's pleasant and profitable conversation with him, on Revolutionary topics connected with the locality, I returned to the hotel, and prepared to depart for Ridgefield, nine miles distant, after supper. For two or three hours a strong southeast wind had been piling the driving scud from the ocean in huge cumulous masses along the northwestern horizon, and, when darkness came, it was intense. I had hired a conveyance, and a young man to accompany me from Danbury to Norwalk, by the way of Ridgefield, and, in the midst of the gloom and the rain that began to fall, we left the village. For a little while the beaten road was visible, but, when the light dust became wet with showers, not a trace of the track could be seen. The young man became alarmed, and urged me to turn back. I was too anxious to reach New Haven by Sunday to be easily persuaded, and, borrowing a tin lantern from a farmer whom he knew, we endeavored to grope our way. The perforations of the lantern were " like angels' visits, few and far between," and the light that stole through them was just enough to make " darkness visible." After tilting half over by the road side once or twice, and being assured by my companion that there was a " dreadful ugly place in Sugar Hollow, a mile or two beyond," I consented to turn back, on condition that he would be ready to start at peep of day. He promised, and at nine in the evening we were again in Danbury. At dawn we started for Ridgefield. The rain had ceased, and the clouds were dispersing. We had a delightful ride over the broken, but fertile country, and before ten o'clock I had visited the place where Wooster fell, and where Arnold made his escape, and made sketches of the localities. Let us for a moment follow the British on their departure from Danbury, and the Americans in their opposing maneuvers.

Tryon, doubtless fearing that he might be cut off on his retreat directly back to his shipping at Compo, marched toward Ridgeway, a parish in the town of Ridgefield, and north of that village. This movement was probably made to deceive the Americans into the belief that he intended to return by land through West Chester, and then, by a sudden turn, push for the shipping along the least guarded route. When this movement was made known to the American generals, they divided their forces into two parts. The largest division, consisting of about four hundred men, under Silliman and Arnold, proceeded to take post in front of the enemy, while Wooster, with the other division of two hundred, was left to hang upon and annoy their rear.

After proceeding to Ridgeway, the enemy turned southward toward Ridgefield,[1] their route from Danbury thus forming the two sides of a scalene triangle, of which the present direct

---

[1] The tract of land called Ridgefield was named by the Indians *Candatowa*, which signifies *high ground*. On some of the hills near the village Long Island and the Sound may be seen for a distance of forty miles. Twenty-five of the inhabitants of Norwalk purchased the ground of Catoonah, the chief sachem, in 1708, and the first settlement was made the following year.

April 27, road from village to village is the hypotenuse. This change of direction was made
1777. known to Wooster about nine in the morning, and, hastening forward, he came up
to them when within a few miles of Ridgefield. He attacked the rear-guard, and, after
a little skirmishing, took
forty prisoners. Thus he
harassed them, and kept
them in partial check, until they arrived within two
miles of Ridgefield meet-
ing-house, when another
smart skirmish ensued.
The ground is very bro-
ken, and well adapted for
such a sort of guerrilla
warfare as the American
militia kept up. While
the enemy were hidden
by a hill, near the present
road from Ridgefield to
Salem, Wooster encour-
aged his undisciplined army to push forward and

attack them on the flank.
The British made sever-
al discharges of artillery,
which caused the Amer-
ican column to break and
give way. Wooster en-
deavored to rally them.
exclaiming, "Come on,
my boys! Never mind
such random shots!"
While thus in the van,
urging his troops, a mus-
ket-ball took him obliquely in the side and broke
his back-bone. He fell
from his horse, and was
removed from the field to
Danbury, at which place
he died.[1]

General Arnold, informed of the change in the route of the enemy, made a forced march
across the country to Ridgefield village, where he arrived at about eleven o'clock in the
morning, with his force increased to about five hundred men. Across the upper end of the
main street he cast up a barricade of carts, logs, stones, and earth, which was flanked on the
right by a house and barn, and on the left by a ledge of rocks. Behind this barricade he
formed his men in battle order, and awaited the approach of the enemy. As soon as Tryon
discovered Arnold, he ordered General Agnew to advance with the main body in solid col-

---

[1] David Wooster was born in Stratford, Connecticut, on the 2d of March, 1710. He graduated at Yale
College in 1738, and the following year, when the Spanish war broke out, was made a lieutenant, and soon
afterward was promoted to the captaincy of the vessel built and armed by the colony as a *guarda costa*, or
coast guard. In 1740 he married the daughter of Rev. Thomas Clapp, president of Yale College. He was
a captain in Colonel Burr's regiment, which went on the expedition to Louisburg in 1745, from which place
he went to Europe, in command of a cartel ship. He was not permitted to land in France, but in England
he was received with distinguished honor. He was presented to the king, and became a favorite at court.
He was made a captain in the regular service, under Sir William Pepperel, and his likeness (from which
our engraving was copied) was published in the periodical magazines of that day. He was first a colonel
and then a brigadier in the French and Indian or Seven Years' War that ended in 1763. He espoused th
patriot cause, and was one of the principal conspirators against Ticonderoga in 1775, which resulted in its
capture by the provincials under Allen and Arnold. When the Continental army was organized, Wooster
was appointed one of the eight brigadiers, third in rank. He was in Canada in 1776, where he had the
chief command for a while. Returning to Connecticut, he was appointed the first major general of the militia of his state. In that capacity he was actively employed when Tryon's invasion occurred. He hastened
to the field, was fatally wounded, carried to Danbury, and expired on the 2d of May, at the age of sixty-
seven years. On the 27th of April, 1854, the corner-stone of a monument to be erected over the obscure
grave of the long-neglected Wooster was laid. When search was made for his grave, it was identified by
unmistakable evidences. With a skeleton was found some matted wire (the remains of epaulets), a portion
of a plume, and a leaden bullet. The latter was a smooth, English bullet, larger than those used by the
Americans. These were satisfactory evidence that the right grave had been opened. That bullet undoubtedly gave the death-wound to the patriot.* The bones were re-interred, with imposing ceremonies. The
Honorable Henry C. Deming was the Orator on the occasion.

---

* Colonel David Dimon, one of Wooster's subordinate officers at that time (mentioned on page 403), was a native of Fairfield, Connecticut, and was a brave and useful soldier. He was one of the volunteers who captured British stores at Turtle
Bay, New York, and one of Montgomery's staff in the expedition to Canada in 1775. He was active in the capture of St. John
on the Sorel, and Fort Chambly, after which he returned to Connecticut on public business, and was not with the army in its
defeat at Quebec. Colonel Dimon continued in active service until after Tryon's expedition to Danbury. He had the command
at the barricades in Ridgefield, and pursued the British to Compo. A fever, produced by exposure in the service, caused his
death in September following, when in the 36th year of his age

umn, while detachments were sent to outflank him and fall upon his rear. With only about

two hundred men, Arnold confronted nearly two thousand, who advanced, and delivered and received several fires. In this way the action continued nearly a quarter of an hour. Agnew succeeded in gaining the ledge of rocks. From that position a whole platoon of British infantry fired, with deliberate aim, at Arnold, who was not more than thirty yards distant. Not a bullet hit him, but his horse was

PLACE OF THE BARRICADE, RIDGEFIELD.[1]

pierced, and fell dead under him. Seeing their leader prostrate, the Americans fled. For a moment Arnold could not extricate his feet from the stirrups. Perceiving this, a Tory named Coon, from New Fairfield, rushed toward the general with his bayonet, to seize him. "Surrender! you are my prisoner!" shouted the Tory. "Not yet," exclaimed Arnold, as, springing to his feet, he drew his pistol, shot the Tory dead, and bounded toward a thick swamp near by, followed by a shower of bullets, and escaped. The number of Americans killed in this skirmish was between forty and fifty; of the enemy's loss no account was given. Colonel Gould, of Fairfield, was among the slain. He fell about eighty rods east of the house of Mr. Stebbins, seen in the engraving, and his body was carried to Fairfield.

Having repulsed the Americans, Tryon's army encamped upon high ground about a mile south of the Congregational Church in Ridgefield, until daylight the next morning, when they resumed their march toward Norwalk and Compo, through Wilton. April 28, 1777. Four dwellings were burned in Ridgefield, and other private property was destroyed when the marauders struck their tents. As they approached Norwalk, Tryon learned that Arnold was again in the saddle, and was rallying the scattered militia upon the road leading to Saugatuck Bridge. He filed off eastward, and forded the Saugatuck some distance above the bridge, where about five hundred Americans, under Colonel Huntingdon, were posted to oppose his passage. Small detachments of militia annoyed the British all the way from Wilton to the Saugatuck; and while the latter were pushing forward toward Compo and their shipping, on the east side of the creek, the former kept upon the west side, and galled them with cannon-shot and musket-balls. A small detachment of Americans forded the stream, picked off many of the rear-guard of the enemy, and returned without losing a man.

At the bridge was the battalion of the New York artillery, under Colonel John Lamb, with three field pieces, under Lieutenant-colonel Oswald. Perceiving the formidable force there collected, Tryon urged forward his men as fast as they could run, and they succeeded in passing by the bridge before the main body of the Americans could get over. Exposed to an enfilading fire, the enemy were partially checked, and for about fifteen minutes there was a sharp engagement at the bridge.[2] The Americans pushed across and followed the flying

[1] This view is at the north end of the main street. It was taken from the spot where, tradition asserts, Arnold's horse was killed, which is on the west side of the street, near a maple-tree, about one hundred yards southwest of the house of Samuel Stebbins, Esq., seen on the right in the picture. While making this sketch an old man (whose name I forgot to ask) came along, and informed me that on the day after the battle himself and some other boys skinned Arnold's horse, and discovered *nine bullet-holes in his hide.* The escape of the rider seemed miraculous.

[2] The bridge where the engagement took place was at the head of navigation in the Saugatuck, nearly

enemy to Compo, gaining the right flank of their rear in an advantageous position.   Here another hot skirmish ensued, and, but for a successful maneuver of Sir William Erskine, the exhausted Britons must all have been captured.   That officer landed some marines from the vessels, who furiously attacked the fatigued Americans in front, and drove them back some distance.   While this conflict was going on, the main body of the enemy embarked, amid a galling fire from Lamb's artillery.   The marines, by a sudden retrograde movement, took to their boats and reached their vessels.   At about sunset the fleet weighed anchor.

A large number of the Connecticut militia had collected at Compo, besides those actually enrolled in the special service on that day.   Many of them were without arms, others were insubordinate, and a good proportion of the new-comers behaved in the most cowardly manner.   Had they possessed a tithe of the courage of their leader, who was seen urging his men at points of most imminent danger, the exhausted troops of Tryon might have been made prisoners or destroyed.   Arnold knew this, and, unmindful of danger, urged on the militia by voice and example, until his horse was wounded in the neck and disabled.   The opportunity was not courageously improved, and the enemy escaped.

The loss of the Americans during the invasion was about one hundred men ; the enemy lost, in killed, wounded, and prisoners, about three hundred.   Tryon was slightly wounded. Colonel Lamb, while gallantly leading his men at Compo, received a violent contusion from a grape-shot.   Arnold was untouched, though a bullet wounded his horse, and another passed through the collar of his coat.   Congress, impressed with the brilliancy of his achievements, May 30, directed the quartermaster general[a] to " procure a horse and present the same, properly caparisoned, to Major-general Arnold, as a token of their approbation of his gallant conduct in the action against the enemy in the late enterprise to Danbury."[1]

It was a little after sunrise when we reached Ridgefield,[2] and, after sketching the place of the barricade in the village, we rode to the spot where General Wooster fell.   It is about

PLACE WHERE WOOSTER FELL.

a mile north of Mr. Stebbins's, at the forks of the road, one of which is the way from Ridgefield to North Salem.   For a long time tradition pointed to a large chestnut-tree as the place where the brave soldier was wounded.   The tree has been converted into rails, and the stump, almost decayed into dust, is flanked by the two thrifty sugar maples seen toward the left of the picture.   The taller tree is a locust.   It is to be hoped that some monument will be reared to mark the spot, before these mature and decay by age.   The owner of the land pointed out the locality to us, and expressed the patriotic opinion that " Congress ought to do something."   He had long contemplated the erection of a chestnut post at his own expense, but, having done that, the public would expect him " to paint some lettering on't," and he was not disposed to bear the whole burden himself.   Clearly right ; it would be asking too much of a single citizen.

Returning to the village, we breakfasted at ten at the tavern of Mr. Resseque, whose wife is the daughter of Mr. Keeler, the owner of the dwelling at the time of the invasion.   It is about half a mile south of the Congregational Church, where the British planted a cannon

---

three miles from the sea.   There is now a bridge upon the site, within the pleasant village of Westport (formerly called Saugatuck), which, at the time of the battle, contained only five houses.   Seven or eight men were killed near the present Congregational Church in Westport.   The smooth and really beautiful elevation of Compo is about two and a half miles south of the village, and commands a fine view of the Sound and of the distant shores of Long Island.

[1] Journals of Congress, iii., 158.

[2] Ridgefield is situated upon a high, rolling plain, and contains about sixty houses, on one street, within a mile.   Like Danbury, it is beautifully shaded with elms and sycamores.

after driving the Americans from the barricade. Near the northeast corner of the house is a four pound cannon-ball, lodged in one of the posts, where it has remained ever since the Revolution. Some Americans near the house were the objects at which some balls were discharged. One passed into the building, just over the north door, and, crossing a stair-case, hit a chimney and fell to the floor. A man was just ascending the stairs when the ball entered, with a terrible crash, and passed between his legs. Unhurt, but greatly fright-ened, he fell to the foot of the stairs, exclaiming, " I'm killed ! I'm a dead man !" and for some time he insisted that his legs were shot off. As soon as he was undeceived, he put them in requisition, and fled, as fast as they could carry him, toward Wilton. The house was set on fire, but the flames were extinguished by a Tory brother of Mr. Keeler, whose own property was endangered.

A few miles northeast from Ridgefield is the village of Reading,[1] distinguished as being the head-quarters of General Putnam in the winter of 1779. He occupied that position with General Poor's brigade of New Hampshire, two Connecticut brigades, Hazen's infantry corps, and a corps of cavalry under Shelden, for the purpose of covering the country from the British lines in New York, eastward along the Sound. Like many of the New England vil-lages, it is scattered, and beautifully shaded with elms, maples, and sycamores. Putnam's quarters were at a house situated on the Norwalk and Danbury Road, about three miles westward of the Congregational Church in Reading. During the winter a mutinous spirit pervaded the Connecticut troops. They were badly fed and clothed, and worse paid, for their small pittance, when received, consisted of the rapidly-depreciating Continental bills. Brooding over their hard lot, the Connecticut brigades finally resolved to march to Hartford and demand of the Assembly a redress of grievances. The second brigade had assembled under arms for that purpose, when in-formation of the movement reached Putnam. He immediately galloped to the encampment, and, in his uncouth, but earnest manner, thus ad-dressed them : " My brave lads, where are you going ? Do you intend

PUTNAM'S QUARTERS

to desert your officers, and to invite the enemy to follow you into the country ? Whose cause have you been fighting and suffering so long in ? Is it not your own ? Have you no prop-erty, no parents, wives, or children ? You have behaved like men so far ; all the world is full of your praise, and posterity will stand astonished at your deeds, but not if you spoil all at last. Don't you consider how much the country is distressed by the war, and that your officers have not been better paid than yourselves ? But we all expect better times, and that the country will do us ample justice. Let us all stand by one another, then, and fight it out like brave soldiers. Think what a shame it would be for Connecticut men to run away from their officers !" If this speech did not display the polished eloquence of Demosthenes, who made the Athenians cry out with one voice, " Let us go and fight Philip," it possessed the same spirit and produced a similar result. When Putnam concluded his short address, a loud cheer burst from the discontented regiments, and they returned to their quarters in good humor, resolved to suffer and fight still longer in the cause of liberty.

It was during Putnam's encampment at Reading, in 1779, that the famous event occur-red at West Greenwich, or Horseneck, in which the general was the principal actor. He was visiting his outposts at West Greenwich, and tarrying at the house of the late General Ebenezer Mead. Early on the morning of the 26th of March, while standing before a looking-glass, shaving, he saw the reflection of a body of " red-coats" marching up the road from the westward. He dropped his razor, buckled on his sword, and, half shaven, mounted his horse and hastened to prepare his handful of men to oppose the approaching enemy. They were a body of nearly fifteen hundred British regulars and Hessians, under Governor Tryon, who had marched from their lines in West Chester county, near King's

1779.

---

[1] The township derived its name from Colonel John Read, one of its most prominent settlers. His mon-ument is in a small burying-ground a little west of the town-house. He died in 1786, aged eighty five years.—Barber's *Historical Collections of Connecticut*.

412   PICTORIAL FIELD-BOOK

Tryon's Expedition to Horseneck.   Skirmish at Greenwich.   Defeat of the Americans.   Escape of Putnam.

Bridge, the previous evening, with the intention of surprising the troops and destroying the salt-works at Horseneck Landing. A scout of thirty men, under Captain Watson, who had been sent out by Putnam, discovered the enemy in the night at New Rochelle. At daylight they had advanced to Rye Neck, and there a slight skirmish ensued between the British advanced guards and Putnam's scouts. The latter retreated to Sawpits, on the Byram River, and thence to Horseneck, pursued by the enemy.

Putnam arranged his men (only one hundred and fifty in number) upon the brow of the hill, by the Congregational Church in the village. There he planted a battery composed of two old iron field pieces, and awaited the approach of the enemy. They moved up the road in solid column until almost within musket-shot, when detachments broke off and attempted to gain Putnam's flanks. At the same moment the British dragoons and some infantry prepared to charge. Perceiving this, and discovering the overwhelming numbers of the enemy, Putnam ordered a retreat, after a few discharges of the field pieces and some volleys of musketry. So near was the enemy, that the retreat of the Americans became a rout. The soldiers broke and fled singly to the adjacent swamps, while the general, putting spurs

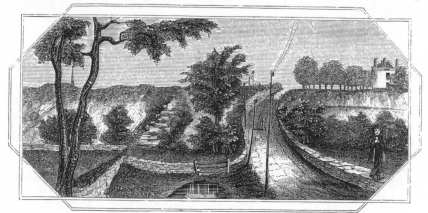

" PUTNAM'S HILL."

to his horse, sped toward Stamford, pursued by several of the dragoons. A quarter of a mile eastward of the Congregational Church is a steep declivity, on the brow of which the road turned northward, and passed, in a broad sweep, around the hill. Putnam perceived that his pursuers were gaining upon him, and, with the daring of desperation, left the road and wheeled his horse, while on a gallop, down the rocky height, making a zigzag course to the bottom, and reaching the road again in safety. The dragoons dared not follow, and, discharging their pistols at Putnam, without effect, rode back to the main army, and the general reached Stamford, five miles eastward, in safety.

Tryon plundered the inhabitants of every thing valuable, and, having destroyed a few salt a March 26, works, a small sloop and store, and damaged the houses of the Whigs, retreated to 1779. Rye the same evening,[a] and the next day reached King's Bridge. As soon as Putnam arrived at Stamford, he collected some militia and a few of his fugitives, and returned to attack the enemy on his retreat. He succeeded in taking thirty-eight prisoners and in recapturing a portion of the plunder, which he restored to the inhabitants. There were about twenty Americans killed. The loss of the British in killed is not recorded.

1848. I visited the scene of Putnam's exploit in June, previous to my journey to Danbury and Ridgefield, and made the accompanying sketch of " Putnam's Hill," as it is called. It is about five miles west from Stamford, on the main road to New York from Horseneck[1]

---

[1] This name was given to the peninsula extending into the Sound at Greenwich, from the circumstance that many horses used to be pastured upon it.

Landing. This sketch is taken from the road near the residence of the late General Ebenezer Mead, looking westward. The aspect of the place has materially changed since the Revolution. The old road, as I have mentioned, made a circuit northward around the hill. The present road, seen in the engraving, passes directly over the hill, being a causeway part of the distance, and a deep cut through the rocks on the brow of the eminence. On the hill, just south of the road, and in a line with the tall tree by the causeway, stood the old Episcopal Church; and it was for the accommodation of worshipers there, who lived eastward of the hill, that a flight of seventy rude stone steps was made. These are the steps so celebrated in the popular accounts of Putnam's exploit. They are now quite covered with earth and shrubbery, but their site is distinctly marked. I have given them more prominence than they really have, exhibiting them as they probably appeared when Putnam made his escape. Between the trees is seen the spire of the Congregational Church at Greenwich, standing upon the site of the one near which Putnam planted his battery. General Mead and others saw the descent of Putnam. He wheeled his horse from the road near the house of Dr. Mead, seen on the extreme right, and did not go down the steps at all (as popular tradition avers), except four or five of them near the bottom. As he hastened by toward Stamford, General Mead distinctly heard him cursing the British whom he had left behind. The feat was perilous, but, under the circumstances, not very extraordinary. I was told that in 1825 several of the dragoons in the escort of La Fayette to this place performed the same Let us resume our journey.

The ride from Ridgefield to Norwalk was very pleasant. The clouds were dispersed, and the air was almost sultry. The country was rough until we entered the valley of the Norwalk River, a region of great beauty and fertility. Our road lay along that winding stream, and, as we approached Norwalk, the transition from the open country to the populous town was almost imperceptible. Venerable elms and sycamores, planted by the early settlers, shaded handsome mansions thickly strewn along the winding road. These, the tolling of a bell, and the whistle of steam betokened a village near, and in a few minutes we reined up at the principal hotel in the compact street of a busy mart. We are again upon Revolutionary ground, the scene of another of Governor Tryon's marauding expeditions.[1]

After laying Fairfield in ashes, Governor Tryon and Brigadier-general Garth, with their troops, retreated to their vessels and crossed the Sound to Huntington Bay, Long Island, whence they sailed over to Norwalk on the night of the 11th of July, 1779. The main

FITCH'S POINT, THE LANDING-PLACE OF THE BRITISH.[2]

body landed at about nine o'clock in the evening, "in the 'Cow Pasture,' a peninsula on the

[1] Norwalk is situated near Long Island Sound, not far from the mouth of the Norwalk River (a small stream), and about forty-eight miles northeast from New York. It was among the earliest settlements in Connecticut, having been purchased of the natives in 1640. The bounds of the east tract, sold to Roger Ludlow, as described in the ancient records, were "from Norwalk River to Sawhatuc [Saugatuck] River, from sea, Indian one day walk in the country"—that is, one day's north walk into the country; hence the name of Norwalk. The articles given to the Indians for the tract were "eight fathoms wampum, six coats, ten hatchets, ten hoes, ten knives, ten scizers, ten juseharps, ten fathom tobaco, three kettles of six hands about, and ten looking-glasses." The articles given for the tract on the west side of the river, between it and Five Mile River, sold to Captain Patrick, were "of wampum ten fathoms, hatchets three, howes three, when ships come; six glasses, twelve tobacke pipes, three knives, ten drills, ten needles."—Barber's *Historical Collections ;* Hall's *Historical Records of Norwalk.*

[2] This view is from the west side of Gregory's Point, looking north-northwest. The promontory toward the left, covered with dark trees, is called Fort Point. There was an Indian fortification when the first set-

east side of the harbor, within a mile and a half of the bridge."[1]   They lay on their arms all night, awaiting the expected arrival of a company of Loyalists.   At dawn they marched toward the town, and were met by a company of about fifty Continental soldiers, under Captain Stephen Betts, who were posted upon an eminence known as *Gruman's Hill*, a little east of the road.   A skirmish ensued, but the little band of patriots were soon obliged to flee before overwhelming numbers, leaving four of their party dead.   The people, greatly alarmed, fled to Belden's Hill, five miles distant, during the night.   The Continentals and a few of the militia took post within "random cannon-shot upon the hills on the north," whence they annoyed the enemy exceedingly.   Tryon halted upon Gruman's Hill untill the other division landed at *Old Well*,[2] on the west side of the stream.   The two divisions joined, and soon drove nearly every Whig inhabitant from the village, dispersed the troops collected upon the hills, and seized one of their cannon.   The destruction of property then commenced. Governor Tryon thus coolly related the circumstances in his official dispatch to Sir Henry Clinton :   "After many salt-pans were destroyed, whale-boats carried on board the fleet, and the magazines, stores, and vessels set in flames, with the greater part of the dwelling-houses, the advanced corps were drawn back, and the troops retired in two columns to the place of our first debarkation, and, unassaulted, took ship, and returned to Huntington Bay."

While the village was burning, Tryon sat in a rocking-chair upon Gruman's Hill, and viewed the scene with apparent pleasure—a puny imitator of Nero, who fiddled while Rome was blazing.   It was a cruel and wanton destruction of property, and none but a small mind and spiteful heart could have conceived and consummated so foul an act.   Two houses of worship (Episcopal and Congregational), eighty dwellings, eighty-seven barns, twenty-two stores, seventeen shops, four mills, and five vessels were laid in ashes in the course of a few hours, and hundreds of women and children were driven to the woods for shelter.   Only six houses were spared.   One of them, now (1848) occupied by Ex-governor Bissell, was saved through the exertions of a maiden lady living with Mr. Belden, the then owner.   Governor Tryon had been Belden's guest one night, several years previous, and the lady went up to Gruman's Hill reminded him of the fact, and asked for and received a protection for the house.   Tryon sent a file of soldiers with her to guard it.   When the British left, most of the resident Tories went with them.   Among them was the Rev. Mr. Leamington, the Episcopalian minister.   He had continued praying for the "king and all others in authority," according to the Liturgy of his Church, until the people forbade him and threatened him with violence.

About five miles westward of Norwalk, on the main road to Stamford, is a Congregational Church more than one hundred years old.   Its pastor in 1781 was the Rev. Moses Mather.   On Sunday, the 22d of July, the church was surrounded by a party of Tories, under Captain Frost, just as the congregation were singing the first tune.   Dr Mather and the men of the congregation were taken to the banks of the Sound, thrust into boats, and conveyed across to Lloyd's Neck, on Long Island, whence they were carried to New York and placed in the Provost Jail.   Some died there.   Nineteen of the twenty-five prisoners were exchanged and returned to their families.   Peter St. John, one of the prisoners, wrote an account of the affair in doggerel verse.   Of the Provost he says .

DARIEN CHURCH.

"I must conclude that in this place
We found the worst of Adam's race ;

tlers arrived at Norwalk.   Further to the left, on the extreme edge of the picture, is seen one end of the rail-road bridge, which crosses Norwalk River.   The New York and New Haven Rail-road was then in progress of construction.   The point derives its name from its former proprietor, Governor Thomas Fitch, whose residence was Norwalk.   He was Governor of the colony of Connecticut, and his name is among the beloved of his generation.   He died July 18th, 1774, in the seventy-fifth year of his age.

[1] Tryon's official dispatch.

[2] This place is situated a little more than a mile from the center of the village of Norwalk.   It received its name from an *old well* from which, in ancient times, vessels engaged in the West Indian trade took their supplies of water.—*Barber.*

> Thieves, murderers, and pickpockets too,
> And every thing that's bad they'd do :
> One of our men found, to his cost,
> Three pounds York money he had lost ;
> His pockets picked, I guess before
> We had been there one single hour."

Dr. Mather was cruelly treated in the Provost, until his situation was made known to Mrs. Irving, mother of our distinguished writer, Washington Irving, who obtained permission to send him food and clothing. He was released at the close of the year.

The Rev. Edwin Hall, of the First Congregational Church, whose historical researches have made him familiar with localities of interest about Norwalk, kindly accompanied me as cicerone. We rode down to Gregory's Point, from which I sketched Tryon's landing-place, pictured on page 413. On the beautiful plain near by stood the ancient village, the first settlers having chosen the sea-washed level for their residences, in preference to the higher and rougher ground at the head of navigation, on which the present town is situated. The old village had gone into decay, and the new town was just beginning to flourish, when Tryon laid it in ruins. A little further seaward, upon a neck of land comprising Fitch's Point and an extensive salt meadow, is the *Cow Pasture*, so called from the circumstance that the cows belonging to the settlers were pastured there, under the direction of the town authorities.[1]

From Gregory's Point we rode over the hills to the estate of Mr. Ebenezer Smith, and from a high hill near his house I sketched the distant view of Compo, on page 402. From that eminence we obtained one of the most beautiful prospects of land and water imaginable. Southward was the broad mouth of the Norwalk River, with its beautiful green islands, and beyond was the heaving Sound, dotted with sails, and bounded by the wooded shores of Long Island in the distance. On the right were clustered the white houses of Norwalk, and on the left swelling Compo was stretched out, scarcely concealing the noble shade trees of Fairfield beyond.

GRUMAN'S HILL.

Returning along East Avenue to the village, I stopped near the residence of Mr. Hall, and made the accompanying sketch of Gruman's Hill. It is a high elevation, a little east of the avenue, partly covered by an orchard, and commanding a fine prospect of the village, harbor, and Sound. Tryon sat upon the summit of the hill, where the five Lombardy poplars are seen. The venerable Nathaniel Raymond, still living, when I was there (1848), near the Old Well, or West Norwalk Wharf (where he had dwelt from his birth, ninety-five years), remembers the hill being "red with the British." He was a corporal of the guard at the time, and, after securing his most valuable effects, and carrying his aged parents to a place of safety three miles

---

[1] The old records of the town, quoted by Mr. Hall, exhibit many curious features in the municipal regulations adopted by the early settlers. In 1665 it is recorded that " Walter Hait has undertaken to beat the drumm for meeting when all occasions required, for which he is to have 10s. Also, Thomas Benedict has undertaken to have the meeting-house swept for the yeere ensuing; he is to have 20s." Again : " At a town meeting in Norwalk, March the 20th, 1667, it was voted and ordered that it shall be left to the townsmen from yere to yere to appoint a time or day, at or before the 10th day of March, for the securing of the fences on both sides, and that they shall give notis to all the inhabitants the night before, and the drumb to be beten in the morning, which shall be accounted a sufficient warning for every man to secure his fence, or else to bear his own damages." Again : " At the same meeting (October 17th, 1667), voted and ordered that, after the field is cleared, the townsmen shall hier Steven Beckwith, or some other man, to fetch the cows out of the neck [the *Cow Pasture*]; and he that shall be hiered shall give warning by sounding a horne about twelve of the clock, that he that is to accompany him is to repaire to him."

distant, shouldered his musket, and was with the few soldiers whom Tryon boasted of having driven from the hills north of the town.   He says it was Saturday night when Tryon landed, and, like Danbury, the town was burned on Sunday.   Mr. Raymond was quite vigorous in body and mind, and Time seemed to have used him gently.   I desired to visit two other ancient inhabitants, but the hour for the arrival of the mail-coach for New Haven was near, and I hastened back to the hotel, whence I left for the east between three and four o'clock in the afternoon.

The coach, a sort of tin-peddler's wagon in form, was full, and, quite in accordance with my inclination, I took a seat with the driver.   It was a genial afternoon, and all things in nature and art combined to please and edify.   We reached Bridgeport, at the mouth of the Housatonic River, fourteen miles east of Norwalk, at sunset, and a more pleasing variety of beautiful scenery can nowhere be found than charmed us during that short journey.   We passed through Westport (old Saugatuck), Southport, and Fairfield, lovely villages lying upon estuaries of Long Island Sound, and all replete with historic interest.   Unlike most modern villages, with their rectangular streets, and exhibiting an ambitious imitation of large cities, the neat houses, embowered in shrubbery, are thinly scattered along winding avenues shaded by venerable trees, the ground on either side left undulating as the hand of Nature fashioned it.   Herein consists the great beauty of the New England villages, a beauty quite too often overlooked in other states in the process of laying out towns.   Nature and art have here wrought in harmony, and village and country are beautifully and healthfully blended.

I was informed, before leaving Norwalk, that the "Buckly House," the last relic of the Revolution in Fairfield, had fallen under the stroke of public improvement, and also that no living witness of the cruelty of Governor Tryon was there.   I therefore concluded to go directly through to New Haven that evening.   During a detention of the coach for half an hour at the post-office, in Fairfield, I made a rough sketch of the annexed view of the village Green, which I subsequently corrected by a picture in Barber's *Historical Collections of Connecticut*.   The view is from the eastern side of the Green, near the spacious new hotel that fronts upon it.   The jail on the left, the court-house in the center, and the church on the right were erected upon the foundations of those that were burned by the British in 1779, and in the same style of architecture.   Such being the fact, the Green, from our point of view, doubtless has the same general aspect that it presented before the marauder desolated it.   As the destruction of Fairfield was subsequent to the incursion of the enemy into New Haven, I shall give the record of its hard fate after noticing the movements of Tryon and his associates at the latter place.

THE GREEN, FAIRFIELD.

Immediately back of Fairfield village is the celebrated swamp where the warlike Pequots made their last stand against the English, in July, 1637.[1] . There they were overthrown

---

[1] The Pequots, or Pequods, were a formidable tribe of Indians, having at least seven hundred warriors. Their principal settlements were on a hill in Groton, Connecticut.   They were a terror to other tribes, and became a great annoyance to the Connecticut and Massachusetts settlements.   Governor Endicott, of the former province, had tried to treat with them, but in vain, and their bold defiance of the whites increased Early in 1637 they attacked the small English fort at Saybrook, murdered several women of Weathersfield, and carried away two girls into captivity.   The colonists mustered all their able men, and, being joined by portions of the Mohegans, Narragansets, and Niantic tribes, fell upon the Pequots in their retreat upon the Mystic River.   A warm battle ensued, and the Pequots were beaten.   They fought desperately, but were finally driven westward, and took shelter in the swamp near Fairfield.   Sassacus, their chief, escaped to the Mohawks, by whom he was afterward murdered.   The Indian name of Fairfield was Unguowa.   Mr. Ludlow, who accompanied the English troops, and was afterward Deputy-governor of the colony of Connecticut, pleased with the country in the neighborhood of the Sasco Swamp, began, with others, a plantation there, and called it their *fair field*.   Hence its name.

and annihilated, and the place has ever since been called the Pequot Swamp. They might have escaped had not one of their number, who loitered behind, been captured by Captain Mason, and compelled to disclose the retreat of his comrades. One hundred were made prisoners, the residue were destroyed. The fort at Mystic had previously been demolished, and they took refuge in this swamp.

We passed in sight of Greenfield Hill, near the village, renowned for its academy and church, wherein President Dwight, of Yale College, officiated as tutor and pastor for twelve years. The view from the hill is said to be exceedingly fine, and from the belfry of the church no less than seventeen houses of worship may be seen, in Fairfield and the adjacent villages. Dr. Dwight, while minister of Greenfield, wrote a poem called "Greenfield Hill." Referring to the view from the belfry, he exclaims,

> " Heavens, what a matchless group of beauties rare
> Southward expands ! where, crown'd with yon tall oak,
> Round Hill the circling land and sea o'erlooks ;
> Or, smoothly sloping, Grover's beauteous rise,
> Spreads its green sides and lifts its single tree,
> Glad mark for seamen ; or, with ruder face,
> Orchards, and fields, and groves, and houses rare,
> And scatter'd cedars, Mill Hill meets the eye ;
> Or where, beyond, with every beauty clad,
> More distant heights in vernal pride ascend.
> On either side a long, continued range,
> In all the charms of rural nature dress'd,
> Slopes gently to the main. Ere *Tryon* sunk
> To infamy unfathom'd, through yon groves
> Once glisten'd Norwalk's white ascending spires,
> And soon, if Heaven permit, shall shine again.
> Here, sky-encircled, Stratford's churches beam ;
> And Stratfield's turrets greet the roving eye.
> In clear, full view, with every varied charm
> That forms the finish'd landscape, blending soft
> In matchless union, Fairfield and Green's Farms
> Give luster to the day. Here, crown'd with pines
> And skirting groves, with creeks and havens fair
> Embellish'd, fed with many a beauteous stream,
> Prince of the waves, and ocean's favorite child,
> Far westward fading, in confusion blue,
> And eastward stretch'd beyond the human ken,
> And mingled with the sky ; there Longa's Sound
> Glorious expands."

The evening closed in, mild and balmy, before we reached Stratford, three miles eastward of Bridgeport, and the beautiful country through which we were passing was hidden from view. We crossed several small estuaries, and the vapor that arose from the grassy salt marshes was grateful to the nostrils. The warm land-breeze ceased at eight o'clock, and a strong wind from the ocean brought a chilling fog upon its wings, which veiled the stars, and made us welcome the sparkling lights of New Haven as we descended Milford Hill and crossed the broad salt marsh that skirts the western suburbs of the town. We arrived at the *Tontine* a little after nine, and supped with a keen appetite, for I had fasted since breakfast at Ridgefield at ten in the morning. It was Saturday night, and the weary journeys of the week made the privileges of the approaching day of rest appear peculiarly valuable.

> " The morning dawn'd with tokens of a storm—
> A ruddy cloud athwart the eastern sky
> Glow'd with the omens of a tempest near ;"

yet I ventured to stroll out to East Rock, two miles east-northeast of the city. Crossing the bridge at the factory owned by the late Eli Whitney, inventor of the cotton gin that bears his name, I toiled up the steep slope through the woods to the summit of the rock,

nearly four hundred feet above the plain below.   This rock is the southern extremity of the
Mount Tom range of hills.   It lies contiguous to a similar amorphous mass called West
Rock, and both are composed principally of hornblende and feldspar, interspersed with quartz
and iron.   The oxyd of iron, by the action of rains, covers their bare and almost perpendicular fronts, and gives them their red appearance, which caused the Dutch anciently to designate the site of New Haven by the name of *Red Rock*.   The fronts of these rocks are composed of assemblages of vast irregular columns, similar in appearance to the Palisades of the
Hudson, and, like them, having great beds of *debris* at their bases.   A view from either will
repay the traveler for his labor in reaching the summit.   That from the East Rock is particularly attractive, for it embraces the harbor, city, plain, and almost every point of historical interest connected with New Haven, or Quinnipiack, as the Indians called it.

> " I stood upon the cliff's extremest edge,
> And downward far beneath me could I see
> Complaining brooks that played with meadow sedge,
> Then brightly wandered on their journey free."
> WILLIS GAYLORD CLARKE.

Winding through the plain were Mill River and the Quinnipiack, spanned by noble bridges
near the city that lay stretched along the beautiful bay ; and

> " Beyond
> The distant temple spires that lift their points
> In harmony above the leaf-clad town—
> Beyond the calm bay and the restless Sound
> Was the blue island stretching like a cloud
> Where the sky stoops to earth : the Rock was smooth,
> And there upon the table-stone sad youths
> Had carved, unheeded, names, to weave for them
> That insect's immortality that lies
> In stone, for ages, on a showman's shelf."
> L. M. N.

East and West Haven, where the two divisions of the British invading force landed in 1779 ;
Fort Hale, whence they departed ; Neck Bridge, across Mill River, under which the fugitive
judges of King Charles I. were concealed ; and West Rock, where they " raised their Ebenezer" and dwelt in seclusion for some time, were all in full view.   With a spirit fraught
with reverence for the past, and with scenery hallowed by the presence of " young antiquity'
spread out before us, let us sit down a moment and listen to the teachings of the chronicler.
    In the summer of 1637 several wealthy and influential English gentlemen arrived at Bos
ton, preparatory to making a permanent location in wilderness America.   The young colony
of Massachusetts Bay regarded them with great favor, and various settlements coveted the
honor of numbering them among their proprietors.   But they determined to plant a distinct
colony, and, having heard of the beautiful country along the Sound, from Saybrook to the
Saugatuck, discovered by the English in their pursuit of the Pequots, they projected a settlement in that part of the land.   In the autumn a portion of them made a journey to Connecticut, to explore the harbors and lands along the coasts, who finally decided upon the beautiful plain on the Quinnipiack for settlement, and built a log hut there.[1]
    In the spring of 1638 the principal men of the new emigration to the colony—Rev. Mr.
Davenport, Mr. Pruden, and Samuel and Theophilus Eaton—with the people of their company, sailed from Boston for Quinnipiack.   They reached the haven in about a fortnight,
and their first Sabbath there was the 18th of April, 1638.   The people assembled under a
large oak, that stood where George and College Streets intersect ; and under its venerable
branches the New Haven and Milford Churches were afterward formed.   Designing to make
a large and flourishing settlement, founded on strict justice, they purchased the land of Mau-

---

[1] This was upon the corner of the present Church and George Streets, New Haven.—*Barber*.

OF THE REVOLUTION. 419

Organic Law of the New Haven Colony. The "Regicides." The Concealment. Friendship of Davenport. Narrow Escape.

maguin, the chief sachem of that region, on honorable terms, and entered into what they called a *plantation covenant* with each other. They laid out their town-plat in squares, designing it for an elegant city. They prospered for more than a year without any fixed laws, and in 1639 proceeded to lay the foundation of their civil and religious polity. Theophilus Eaton was chosen governor, and Mr. Davenport gave him a serious charge before all the people, from Deut., i., 16, 17. It was decreed by the freemen that there should be a general court annually in the plantation, on the last week in October. This was ordained a court of election, in which all the officers of the colony were to be chosen. This court determined that the Word of God should be the only rule for ordering the affairs of government in that commonwealth.

This was the original fundamental Constitution of New Haven, brief in words, but powerful in principle, for the Bible was the statute book. It exhibited the same general religious aspect in its external affairs as that of the Massachusetts colony. Seven pillars of the Church were chosen, and all government was originally in the Church. The members of the Church (none others being possessed of the elective franchise) elected the governor, magistrates, and all other officers. The magistrates were merely the assistants of the governor.[1] Thus the new colony, having its foundation laid upon divine laws and strong faith in man, began a glorious career; and the little settlement, ambitious of excellence, has grown to be, if not the largest, one of the most beautiful cities in the Western World. From the time of its foundation until the Revolution broke out, its history, like that of the other New England settlements, exhibits the ebbing and flowing of the tide of prosperity, under the influences of the laws of the supreme government and the pressure of Indian hostilities; sometimes burdened and cast down by the injustice of the former, and menaced with overthrow and ruin by the latter.

New Haven became famous as the "city of refuge" for three of the English regicides, or judges who condemned King Charles I. to death. They were Generals Goffe and Whalley, and Colonel Dixwell. Whalley was descended from a very ancient family, and was a relative of Oliver Cromwell. Goffe was the son of a Puritan divine, and married a daughter of Whalley. Dixwell was a wealthy country gentleman of Kent, and was a member of Parliament in 1654. On the restoration of Charles II. to the throne of his father, many of the judges were arrested; thirty were condemned to death, and ten were executed. The three above named escaped to New England. Goffe and Whalley arrived at Boston in July, 1660, and took up their residence in Cambridge. Feeling insecure there, they removed to New Haven, where their unaffected piety won for them the confidence and esteem of the people, and particularly of the minister, Mr. Davenport. Their apparent freedom from danger lasted but a few days. The proclamation of Charles, offering a large reward for their apprehension, and the news that pursuers were on the scent, reached them at the same time, and they were obliged to flee. They took shelter in a rocky cavern, on the top of West Rock, where they were supplied daily with food by their friends. They shifted their place of abode from time to time, calling each locality *Ebenezer*, and occasionally appeared publicly in New Haven. On one occasion they sat under the Neck Bridge, upon Mill River, when their pursuers passed over; and several times they came near falling into their hands. The people generally favored their escape, and for their lives they owed much to Mr. Davenport.[2]

[1] Trumbull's *History of Connecticut;* Barber's *History of New Haven.*
[2] About the time when the pursuers were expected at New Haven, Mr. Davenport preached publicly from the text, "Take counsel, execute judgment; make thy shadow as the night in the midst of the noon-day; *hide the outcasts; betray not him that wandereth.* Let mine outcasts dwell with thee, Moab; be thou a covert to them from the face of the spoilers." Isaiah, xvi., 3, 4. The sermon had the effect to put the whole town upon their guard, and made the people resolve on concealment of the "outcasts." The following anecdote is related of Goffe, while he was in Boston: A fencing-master erected a stage, and upon it he walked several days, defying any one to a combat with swords. Goffe wrapped a huge cheese in a napkin for a shield, and, arming himself with a mop filled with dirty water from a pool, mounted the stage and accepted the challenge. The fencing-master attempted to drive him off, but Goffe skillfully received the thrusts of

1675.

In the autumn they left New Haven and went to Hadley. While there, eleven years afterward, *King Philip's War* took place. While the people of the town were in their meeting-house, observing a fast, a body of Indians surrounded them. The continual expectation of such an event made the inhabitants always go armed to worship. They were so armed on this occasion, and sallied out to drive off the savages. At that moment there appeared in their midst a man of venerable aspect and singular costume, who placed himself at the head of the people, and, by causing them to observe strict military tactics, enabled them to disperse the assailants. The stranger then disappeared. The people believed an angel had been sent to lead them and effect a victory. The angel was General Goffe.

Colonel Dixwell was with Goffe and Whalley much of the time of their long exile. His latter years were passed in New Haven, where he called himself James Davids, Esq. He acknowledged his name and character before his death, which occurred in 1688, about a month previous to the arrest of Governor Andros in Boston. The governor was hated by the colonists, and when the news of the revolution in England, which Dixwell had predicted, reached Boston, the people seized the obnoxious chief magistrate and thrust him into prison.[1]

Goffe and Whalley died at Hadley, and it is supposed that their bodies were afterward secretly conveyed to New Haven. In the old burying-ground in that city, in the rear of the Center Church, are stones which bear the initials of the regicides. They are standing

separate; I have grouped them for convenience. The two marked E. W. are the head and foot stones of Whalley's grave; and the date, by an extension below the five, may read 1658 or 1678. He died about 1678. These stones are about two feet wide and high, and eight inches thick. Goffe's, marked 80 and M. G., is only ten inches high. The M, it is supposed, is an inverted W. Dixwell's stone, seen in front, is two and a half feet high and broad. It is a red stone; the others are a sort of dark blue stone. The reason given for inscribing only their initials on their stones is, a fear that some sycophant of royalty, "clothed with a little brief authority" in New England, might disturb their remains.[2]

New Haven was greatly agitated by proceedings growing out of the Stamp Act. It was among the earliest of the New England towns that echoed the voice of opposition raised by Boston against the oppression of the mother country, and the people were generally zealous in maintaining the liberty of action professed to be secured to them by disannulled charters. When Ingersoll, who was appointed stamp-master (or the agent of government to sell "stamped paper"), announced the reception of the objectionable articles, New Haven soon became in a state of actual rebellion. Ingersoll was menaced with every indignity, and even his life was proclaimed forfeit by some, if he persisted in exercising his new vocation. Finding

September 19, 1765.

his own town too warm for him, he proceeded toward Hartford. He was met near Weathersfield by a deputation of about five hundred men, and, when in the town, they demanded his resignation of the office. He refused acquiescence, on the reasonable plea that he awaited the action of the General Assembly of Connecticut, whose com-

---

his sword into the cheese. At the third lunge of his antagonist, Goffe held the sword fast in his soft shield long enough to smear the face of the fencing-master with the filthy mop. Enraged, the challenger caught up a broad-sword, when Goffe exclaimed, with a firm voice, "Stop, sir; hitherto, you see, I have only played with you, and not attempted to harm you; but if you come at me now with the broad-sword, know that I will certainly take your life." Goffe's firmness alarmed the fencing-master, who exclaimed, "Who can you be? You must be either Goffe, Whalley, or the devil, for there was no other man in England could beat me."

[1] Stiles's *History of the Regicides;* Barber's *History of New Haven.*

[2] A lineal descendant of Colonel Dixwell asked and received permission of the authorities of New Haven to disinter the remains of his ancestor, and bury them beneath a monument which he proposed to erect to his memory, on College Green, in the rear of the Center Church. They were accordingly removed in November 1849, and a neat monument, surrounded by an iron railing, is erected there.

mands in the premises he should implicitly obey.   But the people would listen to no legal excuses, and he, "thinking the cause not worth dying for," yielded to the menaces of the people, and signed a paper declaring his resignation of the office.   He was then forced to stand up and read it to the people.   Not content with this, they made him throw up his hat, cry out "Liberty and property," and give three cheers.   After dining, he was conducted to Hartford by a cavalcade of about one thousand, who surrounded the court-house, and caused him to read his resignation in the presence of the members of the Assembly.

The people were quite as much excited by joy when the news of the repeal of the noxious act reached them, in May, 1766.   The fact was thus announced on the 23d of May, by a New Haven newspaper : "Last Monday morning, early, an express arrived here with the charming news, soon after which many of the inhabitants were awakened with the noise of small arms from different quarters of the town ; all the bells were rung, and cannon roared the glad tidings.   In the afternoon the clergy publicly returned thanks for the blessing, and a company of militia were collected, under the principal direction of Colonel [afterward General] Wooster.   In the evening were illuminations, bonfires, and dances, all without any remarkable indecency or disorder.   The arrival of the regular post from Boston last night has completed our joy for the wise and interesting repeal of the Stamp Act.   Business will soon be transacted as usual in this loyal colony.   In short, every thing in nature seems to wear a more cheerful aspect than usual—to a great majority."

In all subsequent proceedings, in opposition to the unjust acts of the British government toward the colonies, New Haven was famed for its zeal and firmness ; and the people of Boston received its warmest sympathies and support in all the trials through which they had to pass, under the royal displeasure, from 1768 until 1776, when that city was purged of the enemies of freedom by the Continental army, under Washington.

ARNOLD'S RESIDENCE.[2]

New Haven was among the first of the New England towns that sent soldiers to the fields of the Revolution.   The news of the skirmish at Lexington reached New Haven at about noon the next day.   Benedict Arnold was then the captain of the Governor's Guards.   He summoned his corps, and proposed starting immediately for Lexington.   About forty of them consented to go.[1]   Arnold requested the town authorities to furnish the company with ammunition.   They refused, and the hot patriot marched his men to the house where the select-men were in session, formed a line in front, and sent in word that, if the keys of the

April 20, 1775.

---

[1] Among the members of the company who went with Arnold were Mr. Earl, a portrait painter, and Amos Doolittle, an engraver.   Mr. Earl made four drawings of Lexington and Concord, which were afterward engraved by Mr. Doolittle.   The plates were twelve by eighteen inches in size, and were executed with great dispatch, for in the Connecticut Journal of December 13th, 1775, is the following advertisement :

"THIS DAY PUBLISHED,

"And to be sold at the store of Mr. James Lockwood, near the college in New Haven, four different views of the battles of Lexington, Concord, &c., on the 19th of April, 1775.

"Plate I., the battle of Lexington.

"Plate II., a view of the town of Concord, with the ministerial troops destroying the stores.

"Plate III., the battle at the North Bridge, in Concord.

"Plate IV., the south part of Lexington, when the first detachment was joined by Lord Percy.

"The above four plates are neatly engraven on copper, from original paintings taken on the spot.

"Price, six shillings per set for plain ones, or eight shillings colored."

The engraving of the first of the above-named plates was Mr. Doolittle's earliest effort in that branch of art ; and it is not a little singular that his last day's labor with the burin was bestowed upon a reduced copy of the same picture, for Barber's History of New Haven, executed in 1832.   A copy of this print will be found on page 524.

[2] Arnold lived in Water Street, near the ship-yard.   The house is still standing (1848), on the left side of the street going toward the water   It is a handsome frame building, embowered in shrubbery.   In the

powder-house were not delivered to him within five minutes, he would order his company to break it open and help themselves. The keys were given up, the powder was procured, and soon the volunteers were on their march through Wethersfield and Pomfret, for Cambridge. At Pomfret they were joined by General Putnam, who left his plow in the furrow, and, on arriving at Cambridge, they took possession of the elegant mansion of Governor Oliver, who had fled from the vicinity. Arnold's corps made a fine appearance, and so correct was their discipline, that they were chosen to deliver to Governor Gage the body of a British officer who had died from wounds received at Lexington.

New Haven suffered equally with its sister towns of the sea-board during the whole war for independence, but the severest trial it endured was an invasion by a British force, under Governor Tryon of New York, and Brigadier-general Garth, in the summer of 1779. For some time the idea of a predatory war against the Americans had occupied the British commanders here. They finally decided upon the measure, and submitted their plans to the ministry at home. Wearied by fruitless endeavors to quell the rebellion, the king and his advisers readily consented to the prosecution of any scheme that promised success. Arthur Lee, the political spy abroad upon the movements of the British ministry, immediately forwarded to Governor Trumbull, of Connecticut, and the Committee for Foreign Affairs, information of the intended change in military operations. Under date of Paris, April 6th, 1779, he says, "I have received intelligence that it is determined in the British cabinet to send over immediate orders to New York for an expedition through the Sound, up Connecticut River. The enemy are to land at Wethersfield, and proceed by land to New Haven Bay, where they are to re-embark, after having plundered, burned, and destroyed all in their way." Adverse winds, and the capture of some of the papers sent by Lee, prevented the Americans from receiving timely warning.

Having received the ministerial instructions, Sir Henry Clinton proceeded to execute his orders. Governor Tryon was considered a very proper instrument to perform the nefarious service, and a force of twenty-six hundred men was put under his command, with Brigadier-general Garth as his lieutenant. These were placed upon two ships of war (the Camilla and Scorpion), with transports and tenders, forty-eight in number, commanded by Commodore Sir George Collier, and toward evening of the 3d of July they passed through Hell Gate into the Sound. On the 4th, while the patriots on land were celebrating the adoption of the Declaration of Independence, the two commanders joined in drawing up a proclamation and an address to the inhabitants of Connecticut, inviting and urging them to return to their allegiance, and promising ample protection in person and property to those who should remain peaceably in their dwellings, excepting the civil and military officers of the rebel government. This address was sent on shore and distributed, but, before the inhabitants had time to consult upon the public good, the enemy was among them.

SAVIN'S ROCK.[1]

July, 1779. Collier's fleet sailed up New Haven Bay on the night of the 4th, and early the next (Monday) morning landed in two divisions, those under Tryon at East Haven, and those under Garth at West Haven. The latter landed about sunrise, and im-

---

garret of the house the sign was found recently which hung over the door of Arnold's store, in Water Street. It was black, with white letters, and painted precisely alike on both sides. It was lettered

B, ARNOLD, DRUGGIST,
Bookseller, &c.,
FROM LONDON.
Sibi Totique.

The Latin motto may be rendered, *For himself* and *for the whole,* or *for all.* Arnold combined the selling of drugs and books in New Haven from 1763 to 1767.

[1] This is a view of the spot where Garth landed, in Orange, formerly West Haven. It is between three and four miles below New Haven, on the western side of the harbor entrance, and is a place of considerable resort in summer for the people of the city.

OF THE REVOLUTION.   423

Alarm in New Haven.   Bravery of the Militia.   Battle on Milford Hill.   West Bridge.   Death of Campbell.

mediately prepared to march upon the town. Information of the approach of the enemy having reached New Haven the previous evening, preparations had been made for defense. All, however, was confusion and alarm, and the care of families and property occupied those who otherwise might have made a successful stand against the invaders. Many of the inhabitants took refuge upon East Rock, where they remained until the departure of the enemy.

The first opposition to the invaders was made by twenty-five of the inhabitants of the town (some of whom were students of Yale College), under Captain Hillhouse, who met an advanced party of the enemy on Milford Hill. Already the West Bridge on the Milford

WEST BRIDGE AND MILFORD HILL.

Road had been destroyed, some field pieces taken thither, and slight breast-works thrown up Although there was but a handful of Americans, they were animated by such spirit, when they saw their homes and families in peril, that they drove the advancing enemy nearly back to their landing-place, and took one prisoner. The whole body of the invaders now moved forward, with strong flanking parties and two field pieces. The cannons of the Americans at West Bridge kept up such a brisk fire that the enemy dared not venture further upon that road, but moved along Milford Hill, northward to the Derby Road, to enter the town by that avenue. This movement required a circuitous march of several miles. The first attacking party of the Americans, continually augmenting, soon swelled to a hundred and fifty, and a sharp conflict ensued with the enemy's left flank, near the Milford Road. In this skirmish Major Campbell, the British adjutant, was killed. He

CAMPBELL'S MONUMENT.[2]

was singled out by a militia-man concealed behind a rock, and fell, pierced by a musket-ball

---

[1] This view is from the Milford Road, eastward of West Bridge. The high ground in the distance is Milford Hill, on which is seen the road, directly over the umbrella. A little to the right of the road is the spot where Major Campbell was buried. West Bridge is about a mile and a half from the central part of New Haven.

[2] This rude memorial was erected in 1831, by J. W. Barber, Esq., of New Haven, the historian of that city, and author of the *Historical Collections of Connecticut*, as a tribute of respect for a meritorious officer. It is about a foot and a half high. The site of Campbell's grave was pointed out to Mr. Barber by the late Chauncy Alling, who saw him buried. Several Americans, who were killed at the same time, were buried near. Their remains were afterward removed. Those of Adjutant Campbell rest undisturbed

near his heart. He was wrapped in a blanket, and carried upon a sheep-litter to a house near by, where he expired. He was buried in a shallow grave not far from the spot where he fell, on the summit of the high ground near the intersection of the Milford and West Haven Roads, in the southwest corner of a field known as *Campbell's Lot.*

After the skirmish, the British pressed onward toward the Derby Road. Eye-witnesses described their appearance from points near the city as very brilliant; Milford Hill seemed all in a blaze, from the mingled effects upon the eye of scarlet uniforms and glittering arms. The Americans annoyed them exceedingly all the way to Thompson's Bridge (now Westville), on the Derby Road, and the small force at West Bridge, under Captain Phineas Bradley, hastened to that point to oppose their passage. Bradley was too late; Garth had possession of the bridge and the fording-places of the stream, and, after a sharp skirmish of ten minutes, he drove the militia before him, and marched triumphantly into the town between twelve and one o'clock. He had been piloted all the way from the landing-place by a young Tory named William Chandler, who, with his father and family, left New Haven when the enemy departed.

Among those who went out to the West Bridge and beyond, to oppose the enemy, was the Rev. Dr. Daggett,[1] then late President of Yale College, and a warm republican. Armed with a musket, he joined his friends to oppose the common enemy. Near the West Bridge he was wounded and made a prisoner, and, but for the interference of young Chandler, the Tory guide, who had been a student in the college, he would doubtless have been murdered. He was cruelly injured with bayonets, and by a severe blow across the bowels with the butt of a musket, after he had surrendered and begged for quarters.[2] Yet his firmness did not forsake him. While abused and cursed, he was asked whether, if released, he would again take up arms against them, and replied, "I rather believe I shall if I get an opportunity."

As soon as the boats that conveyed the first division of the enemy to shore returned, the

LANDING-PLACE OF GENERAL TRYON.

second division, under Tryon, consisting chiefly of Hessians and Tories, landed, with two pieces of cannon, on the east side of the harbor, where the light-house now stands. They marched up and attacked the little fort on Black Rock (now Fort Hale), which was defended by a feeble garrison of only nineteen men, with three pieces of artillery. After a slight skirmish, the Americans were driven from the post. The enemy then pushed toward the town, while their shipping drew nearer and menaced the inhab-

---

[1] Naphtali Daggett was a native of Attleborough, Massachusetts. He graduated at Yale College in 1748, and in 1756 was appointed professor of divinity in that institution, which office he held until his death. He officiated as president of the college from 1766 until 1777, when he was succeeded by Dr. Stiles. He died November 25th, 1780, aged about sixty years.

[2] "I was insulted," says the doctor, in his account preserved in MS. in the office of the Secretary of State, at Hartford, "in the most shocking manner by the ruffian soldiers, many of which came at me with fixed bayonets, and swore they would kill me on the spot. They drove me with the main body a hasty march of five miles or more. They damned me, those that took me, because they spared my life. Thus, amid a thousand insults, my infernal drivers hastened me along, faster than my strength would admit in the extreme heat of the day, weakened as I was by my wounds and the loss of blood, which, at a moderate computation, could not be less than one quart. And when I failed, in some degree, through faintness, he would strike me on the back with a heavy walking-staff, and kick me behind with his foot. At length, by the supporting power of God, I arrived at the Green, New Haven. But my life was almost spent, the world around me several times appearing as dark as midnight. I obtained leave of an officer to be carried into the Widow Lyman's and laid upon a bed, where I lay the rest of the day and succeeding night, in such acute and excruciating pain as I never felt before."

itants with bombardment. At the bridge over Neck Creek (Tomlinson's Bridge) the Americans made some resistance with a field piece, but were soon obliged to yield to superior numbers and discipline. Before night the town was completely possessed by the invaders. Throughout the remainder of the day and night the soldiery committed many excesses and crimes, plundering deserted houses, ravishing unprotected women, and murdering several citizens, among whom were the venerable Mr. Beers, and an aged and helpless man named English.

The general movements of the enemy through the day could be seen by the fugitive inhabitants on East Rock, and gloomy indeed was the night they passed there. Families were separated, for the men were generally mustering from all parts of the adjacent country to expel the enemy. Anxiously their hearts beat for kindred then in peril, and eagerly their eyes were turned toward their homes, in momentary expectation of beholding them in flames.

It was Garth's intention to burn the town. He declared, in a note to Tryon, that the "conflagration it so richly deserved should commence as soon as he should secure the Neck Bridge." But during the night he changed his mind. Early on Sunday morning,[a] perceiving the militia collecting in large numbers, he called in his guards, and retreated to his boats. Part of his troops went on board the ships, and part crossed over to East Haven, where they joined Tryon's division. Toward that point the militia now directed their attention. In the afternoon, finding himself hard pressed by the citizen soldiers that were flocking to New Haven from the adjacent country, Tryon ordered a retreat to the shipping. Several buildings and some vessels and stores were set on fire at East Haven when they left. At five o'clock the fleet weighed anchor and sailed westward, carrying away about forty of the inhabitants of the town.

[a] July 7, 1779.

The appetite of Tryon and his troops for pillage and murder was not sated when, on the afternoon of the 7th, they embarked from Fort Rock, now Fort Hale.[1] Sailing down the Sound, they anchored off the village of Fairfield on the morning of the 8th. After a fog that lay upon the waters had cleared away, they landed a little eastward of Kensie's Point, at a place called the Pines, and marched immediately to the village. Dr. Timothy Dwight has given a graphic description of the destruction of the town. "On the 7th of July, 1779," he says, "Governor Tryon, with the army I have already mentioned, sailed from New Haven to Fairfield, and the next morning disembarked upon the beach. A few militia assembled to oppose them, and, in a desultory, scattered manner, fought with great intrepidity through most of the day. They killed some, took several prisoners, and wounded more. But the expedition was so sudden and unexpected, that efforts made in this manner were necessarily fruitless. The town was plundered; a great part of the houses, together with two churches, the court-house, jail, and school-houses, were burned. The barns had just been filled with wheat and other produce. The inhabitants, therefore, were turned out into the world almost literally destitute.

"Mrs. Burr, the wife of Thaddeus Burr, Esq., high sheriff of the county, resolved to continue in the mansion-house of the family, and make an attempt to save it from conflagration The house stood at a sufficient distance from other buildings. Mrs. Burr was adorned with all the qualities which give distinction to her sex; possessed of fine accomplishments, and a dignity of character scarcely rivaled; and probably had never known what it was to be treated with disrespect, or even with inattention. She made a personal application to Governor Tryon, in terms which, from a lady of her high respectability, could hardly have failed of a satisfactory answer from any person who claimed the title of a gentleman. The answer which she actually received was, however, rude and brutal. and spoke the want. not only of politeness and humanity, but even of vulgar civility. The house was sentenced to the flames, and was speedily set on fire. An attempt was made in the mean time, by some

---

[1] Fort Hale is situated upon an insulated rock, two miles from the end of Long Wharf, New Haven. It was named in honor of Captain Nathan Hale, one of the early Revolutionary martyrs. The Americans had a battery of three guns upon this point, which greatly annoyed the enemy when landing

of the soldiery, to rob her of a valuable watch, with rich furniture ; for Governor Tryon refused to protect her, as well as to preserve the house.　The watch had been already conveyed out of their reach ; but the house, filled with every thing which contributes either to
comfort or elegance of living, was laid in ashes.

"While the town was in flames a thunder-storm overspread the heavens, just as night
came on.　The conflagration of near two hundred houses illumined the earth, the skirts of
the clouds, and the waves of the Sound with a union of gloom and grandeur at once inexpressibly awful and magnificent.　The sky speedily was hung with the deepest darkness
wherever the clouds were not tinged by the melancholy luster of the flames.　The thunder
rolled above.　Beneath, the roaring of the fires filled up the intervals with a deep and hollow sound, which seemed to be the protracted murmur of the thunder reverberated from one
end of heaven to the other.　Add to this convulsion of the elements, and these dreadful effects of vindictive and wanton devastation, the trembling of the earth, the sharp sound of
muskets occasionally discharged, the groans here and there of the wounded and dying, and
the shouts of triumph ; then place before your eyes crowds of the miserable sufferers, mingled with bodies of the militia, and from the neighboring hills taking a farewell prospect of
their property and their dwellings, their happiness and their hopes, and you will form a just,
but imperfect, picture of the burning of Fairfield.　It needed no great effort of imagination
to believe that the final day had arrived, and that, amid this funereal darkness, the morning
would speedily dawn to which no night would ever succeed ; the graves yield up their inhabitants ; and the trial commence, at which was to be finally settled the destiny of man.

"The apology made by Governor Tryon for this Indian effort was conveyed in the following sentence : 'The village was burned, to resent the fire of the rebels from their houses, and
to mask our retreat.'　This declaration unequivocally proves that the rebels were troublesome to their invaders, and at the same time is to be considered as the best apology which
they are able to make.　But it contains a palpable falsehood, intended to justify conduct
which admits of no excuse, and rejects with disdain every attempt at palliation.　Why did
this body of men land at Fairfield at all ?　There were here no stores, no fortress, no enemy, except such as were to be found in every village throughout the United States.　It was
undoubtedly the original object of the expedition to set fire to this town, and the apology was
created after the work was done.　It was perfectly unnecessary to mask the retreat.　The
townsmen, and the little collection of farmers assembled to aid them, had no power to disturb it.　No British officer, no British soldier would confess that, in these circumstances, he
felt the least anxiety concerning any molestation
from such opposers.　The next morning the troops
re-embarked, and, proceeding to Green's Farms, set
fire to the church and consumed it, together with
fifteen dwelling-houses, eleven barns, and several
stores."[1]

The Hessians who accompanied Tryon were his
incendiaries.　To them he intrusted the wielding
of the torch, and faithfully they obeyed their master.
When the people fled from the town, not expecting
that their houses would be burned, they left most
of their furniture behind.　The distress was consequently great, for many lost every earthly possession.

THE BUCKLEY HOUSE.[2]

Among the buildings saved was that

---

[1] Dwight's *Travels in New England*, iii., 512.　According to a document in the office of the Secretary
of State of Connecticut, the number of buildings destroyed was ninety-seven dwellings, sixty-seven barns,
forty-eight stores, two school-houses, one county-house, two meeting-houses, and one Episcopal Church.

[2] This building stood upon the eastern side of the Green, fronting the church.　It was demolished three
or four years ago, having stood more than a century and a half.　The engraving is a copy, by permission
of the author, from Barber's *Historical Collections of Connecticut*, page 353.　Tryon lodged in the upper
room on the right of the main building.

of Mr. Buckley, pictured in the engraving. Tryon made it his head-quarters. The naval officer who had charge of the British ships, and piloted them to Fairfield, was Mrs. Buckley's brother, and he had requested Tryon to spare the house of his sister. Tryon acquiesced, and, feeling his indebtedness to her brother, the general informed Mrs. Buckley that if there was any other house she wished to save she should be gratified. After the enemy left, the enraged militia, under Captain Sturges, placed a field piece in front of the dwelling, and then sent Mrs. Buckley word that she might have two hours to clear the house, and leave it, or they would blow her to atoms. She found means to communicate a notice of her situation to General Silliman, who was about two miles distant. He immediately went to the town, and found one hundred and fifty men at the cannon. By threats and persuasion he induced them to withdraw. The next day Colonel Benjamin Tallmadge, with his regiment, arrived from White Plains, and, encamping on the smoking ruins, made Tryon's quarters his own.[1]

The cruelties committed upon helpless women and children, and the wanton destruction of property, at Fairfield, were worthy only of savages, and made the name of Tryon a synonym for every thing infernal. The passions of the soldiery were excited by strong drink, and murder, pillage, and brutal violence to women were their employment throughout the night. Like similar outrages elsewhere, these awakened the strongest feelings of hatred and revenge against the common enemy, and the pen, the pulpit, and the forum sent forth their righteous denunciations. Colonel David Humphreys, the soldier-poet of the Revolution, visited the scene of destruction soon after the event, and wrote the following elegy while on the spot ·

> " Ye smoking ruins, marks of hostile ire,
>   Ye ashes warm, which drink the tears that flow,
> Ye desolated plains, my voice inspire,
>   And give soft music to the song of woe.
> How pleasant, Fairfield, on the enraptured sight
>   Rose thy tall spires and oped thy social halls !
> How oft my bosom beat with pure delight
>   At yonder spot where stand thy darken'd walls !
> But there the voice of mirth resounds no more.
>   A silent sadness through the streets prevails ;
> The distant main alone is heard to roar,
>   The hollow chimneys hum with sudden gales—
> Save where scorch'd elms the untimely foliage shed,
>   Which, rustling, hovers round the faded green—
> Save where, at twilight, mourners frequent tread,
>   Mid recent graves, o'er desolation's scene.
> How changed the blissful prospect when compared,
>   These glooms funereal, with thy former bloom,
> Thy hospitable rights when Tryon shared,
>   Long ere he seal'd thy melancholy doom.
> That impious wretch with coward voice decreed
>   Defenseless domes and hallow'd fanes to dust ;
> Beheld, with sneering smile, the wounded bleed,
>   And spurr'd his bands to rapine, blood, and lust.
> Vain was the widow's, vain the orphan's cry,
>   To touch his feelings or to soothe his rage—
> Vain the fair drop that roll'd from beauty's eye,
>   Vain the dumb grief of supplicating age.
> Could Tryon hope to quench the patriot flame,
>   Or make his deeds survive in glory's page ?
> Could Britons seek of savages the same,
>   Or deem it conquest thus the war to wage ?

---

[1] Mrs. Buckley was not a friend of the enemy. According to her testimony, under oath, she was badly treated by the soldiery, notwithstanding she had a protection from General Garth, the second in command. They plundered her house, stripped her buckles from her shoes, tore a ring from her finger, and fired the house five times before leaving it.—See Hinman's *Historical Collections*, p. 620.

> Yes, Britons scorn the councils of the skies,
>   Extend wide havoc, spurn the insulted foes;
> The insulted foes to ten-fold vengeance rise,
>   Resistance growing as the danger grows.
> Red in their wounds, and pointing to the plain,
>   The visionary shapes before me stand;
> The thunder bursts, the battle burns again,
>   And kindling fires encrimson all the strand.
> Long, dusky wreaths of smoke, reluctant driven,
>   In black'ning volumes o'er the landscape bend:
> Here the broad splendor blazes high to heaven,
>   There umber'd streams in purple pomp ascend.
> In fiery eddies round the tott'ring walls,
>   Emitting sparks, the lighter fragments fly,
> With frightful crash the burning mansion falls,
>   The works of years in glowing embers lie.
> Tryon, behold thy sanguine flames aspire,
>   Clouds tinged with dies intolerably bright:
> Behold, well pleased, the village wrapp'd in fire,
>   Let one wide ruin glut thy ravish'd sight!
> Ere fades the grateful scene, indulge thine eyes,
>   See age and sickness tremulously slow
> Creep from the flames.   See babes in torture die,
>   And mothers swoon in agonies of woe.
> Go, gaze enraptured with the mother's tear,
>   The infant's terror, and the captive's pain;
> Where no bold bands can check thy cursed career,
>   Mix fire with blood on each unguarded plain!
> These be thy triumphs, this thy boasted fame!
>   Daughters of mem'ry, raise the deathless song,
> Repeat through endless years his hated name,
>   Embalm his crimes, and teach the world our wrong."

Large numbers of militia had collected in the neighborhood of Fairfield on the morning of the 9th, and at eight o'clock Tryon sounded a retreat to the shipping. His troops were galled very much by the militia, and it was noon before all were embarked. At three in the afternoon they weighed anchor and sailed over to Huntington, Long Island, whence they made a descent upon, and destroyed, Norwalk.

We will close the record and hasten from the mountain, for

> "'Tis Sabbath morn, and lingering on the gale
>   The mellow'd peals of the sweet bells arise,
> Floating where'er the restless winds prevail,
>   Laden with incense and with harmonies,"

and inviting me back to the city and the open sanctuary. I arrived in time for a luncheon breakfast, and to listen to an eloquent sermon in Trinity Church on the College Green, from a stripling deacon who had just taken orders. The afternoon was warm and lowery, the rain came pattering down in the evening, and the next morning a nor'easter was piping its melancholy notes among the stately elms of the city,[1] while the rain poured as if Aquarius had overturned his water-jar.

There was a lull in the storm about nine o'clock, and, accompanied by Mr. Barber, the artist-author, in a covered wagon, I visited some of the points of interest about the city. We first rode to the West Bridge on West River, near which the Americans made their first stand against General Garth, and in the midst of a heavy dash of rain made the sketch on page 423. Returning to the city, we visited the dwelling of Arnold, Neck Bridge, and the Cemetery. In the latter, a large and beautiful "city of the dead," lie many illustrious remains, among which are those of Colonel David Humphreys, one of Washington's aids.

---

[1] The fine elms which shade the public square and vicinity were planted by the Rev. David Austin and Hon. James Hillhouse. They are the pride of New Haven, and have conferred upon it the title of *The city of Elms.*

They lie near the southwestern part of the Cemetery, and over them stands a fine monument consisting of a granite obelisk and pedestal, about twelve feet in height. Upon two tablets of copper, inserted in the pedestal, is the following inscription, written by his friend, the author of M'Fingal : " David Humphreys, LL.D., Acad. Scient. Philad., Mass., et Connect., et in Angliâ Aquæ Solis, et Regiæ Societat. Socius. Patriæ et libertatis amore ac census, juvenis vitam reipub. integram consecravit. Patriam armis tuebatur, consiliis auxit, literis exornavit, apud exteras gentes concordiâ stabilivit. In bello gerendo maximi ducis Washington administer et adjutor ; in exercitu patrio Chiliarchus ; in republica Connecticutensi, militum evocatorum imperator ; ad aulam Lusitan. et Hispan. legatus. Iberia reversus natale solum vellere vere aureo ditavit. In Historia et Poesi scriptor eximius ; in artibus et scientiis excolendis, quæ vel decori vel usui inserviunt, optimus ipse et patronus et exemplar. Omnibus demum officiis expletis, cursuq ; vitæ feliciter peracto, fato cessit, Die XXI. Februar., Anno Domini

HUMPHREYS'S MONUMENT.

MDCCCXVIII. ; cum annos vixisset LXV."[1]

In the northeast section of the Cemetery is a dark stone, neatly carved with an ornamental border, sacred to the memory of Margaret, the first wife of Benedict Arnold, who died on the 19th of June, 1775, while her husband was upon Lake Champlain. Her maiden name was Mansfield, and by her Arnold had three sons. She was thirty-one years old when she died. She

is represented as a woman of the most fervent piety, exalted patriotism, gentleness of manners, and sweetness of disposition. These qualities are powerful checks upon unruly passions, particularly when exerted in the intimate relation of husband and wife. Had she lived until the close of the Revolution, far different might have been the fate of her husband, for there is little doubt that his resentments against Con-

gress and the managers of military affairs for two years previous to his treason were fostered

---

[1] Mr. Barber gives the following translation : " David Humphreys, doctor of laws, member of the Academy of Sciences of Philadelphia, Massachusetts, and Connecticut, of the Bath [Agricultural Society] and of the Royal Society of London. Fired with the love of country and of liberty, he consecrated his youth wholly to the service of the republic, which he defended by his arms, aided by his counsels, adorned by his learning, and preserved in harmony with foreign nations. In the field he was the companion and aid of the great Washington, a colonel in the army of his country, and commander of the veteran volunteers of Connecticut. He went embassador to the courts of Portugal and Spain, and, returning, enriched his native land with the true golden fleece.* He was a distinguished historian and poet ; a model and a patron of science, and of the ornamental and useful arts. After a full discharge of every duty, and a life well spent, he died on the 21st day of February, 1818, aged sixty-five years." To complete the brief biography given in this inscription, I will add that Colonel Humphreys was born in Derby, Connecticut, in 1753, and graduated at Yale College in 1771. He soon afterward went to reside with Colonel Phillips, of Phillips's Manor, New York. He joined the Continental army, and in 1778 was one of General Putnam's aids, with the rank of major. Washington appointed him his aid in 1780, and he remained in the military family of the chief until the close of the war. For his valor at Yorktown, Congress honored him with a sword. He accompanied Jefferson to Paris, as secretary of legation, in 1784. Kosciusko accompanied them. He was a member of the Legislature of Connecticut in 1786, and about that time he, Barlow, and Hopkins wrote the *Anarchiad*. From

---

* This is in allusion to the fact that Colonel Humphreys was the man who introduced *merino sheep* into the United States. He sent over from Spain a flock of one hundred in 1801.

by his intercourse with the Tory friends of his second wife, Margaret Shippen, of Philadelphia. Indeed, the Loyalists claimed him for a friend as early as December, 1778. Charles Stewart, writing to Joseph Galloway, said, "General Arnold is in Philadelphia. It is said that he will be discharged, being thought a pert Tory. Certain it is that he associates mostly with these people."

On leaving the Cemetery, we called upon the venerable Eneas Munson, M.D., a vigorous relic of the Revolution. He lived until August, 1852, when more than eighty-nine years of age. He was Dr. Thacher's assistant in the Continental army, and was present at the siege of Yorktown and the surrender of Cornwallis, in October, 1781. He was then a surgeon in Colonel Scammell's regiment, which, in that action, was attached to General Hamilton's brigade. During the siege Colonel Scammell was shot by a Hessian cavalry officer, while reconnoitering a small redoubt on a point of land which had been alternately in possession of the Americans and British. It was just at twilight, and, while making careful observ-them as a memorial of a brave and accomplished officer of the Revolution.

Eneas Munson [1]

ations, two Hessian horsemen came suddenly upon him, and presented their pistols. Perceiving that there was no chance for escape, he surrendered, saying, "Gentlemen, I am your prisoner." Either because they did not understand his words, or actuated by that want of humanity which generally characterized those mercenaries, one of them fired, and wounded the colonel mortally. He was carried to Williamsburg, and Dr. Munson was the first surgeon in attendance upon him. He died there on the 6th of October. Colonel Humphreys (to whose regiment Dr. Munson was attached after the death of Scammell) wrote the following poetic epitaph for the tomb of his friend. I do not know whether the lines were ever inscribed upon marble, or recorded by the pen of history. They were repeated to me by Dr. Munson, and I give

1788 until he was appointed minister to Portugal, in 1790, he resided with Washington at Mount Vernon. He was appointed minister plenipotentiary to Spain in 1794; married the daughter of a wealthy English gentleman at Lisbon in 1797; returned in 1801, and for ten years devoted his time to agriculture. In 1812 he took the command of the militia of Connecticut. His death was sudden, caused by an organic disease of the heart. His literary attainments were considerable. Besides several poems, he wrote some political pamphlets; and in 1788, while at Mount Vernon, completed a life of Putnam, a large portion of the material of which he received from the lips of the veteran.

[1] This portrait is from a Daguerreotype kindly lent me by Dr. Munson, with permission to copy it.

> " What though no friend could ward thine early fall,
> Nor guardian angels turn the treacherous ball ;
> Bless'd shade, be soothed !   Thy virtues all are known—
> Thy fame shall last beyond this mouldering stone,
> Which conquering armies, from their toils return,
> Read to thy glory while thy fate they mourn.''

A drawing of the place where Scammell was killed, and a biographical sketch of that officer, are given in the notice of my visit to Yorktown.   Dr. Munson died in October, 1852.

A few doors from Dr. Munson, in the same street, lived the almost centenarian, Nathan
Beers, who was paymaster in Scammell's regiment at Yorktown.   He was ninety-six years
old, and completely demented ; second childhood, with all its trials for the subject and his
friends, was his lot ; yet did I look with rev-
erence upon that thin visage and " lack-luster
eye," where once were indices of a noble mind
within.   A truer patriot never drew blade for
his country, and, above all, he was " an honest
man, the noblest work of God."   For years

SIGNATURE OF NATHAN BEERS AT 90.

he struggled with the misfortunes of life, and became involved in debt.   At length Congress
made a decision in his favor respecting a claim for a pension as paymaster in the Continental
army, and arrearages amounting to some thousands of dollars were awarded him.   There
was enough to give him a competence in his old age, but even this reward for public services he handed over to his creditors.   He has since gone to receive the final recompense of
the patriot and Christian.   He died on the 10th. of February, 1849, aged almost 98.

After a short visit to the Trumbull Gallery of Paintings and the Library of Yale College,[1] I
returned to my lodgings, and at four o'clock in the afternoon departed in the cars for Hartford.

---

[1] Yale College, aside from its intrinsic worth as a seminary of learning, is remarkable for the great number of the leading men of the Revolution who were educated within its walls.   That warm and consistent
patriot, President Daggett, gave a political tone to the establishment favorable to the republican cause, and
it was regarded as the nursery of Whig principles during the Revolution.   When New Haven was invaded
by Tryon, Yale College was marked for special vengeance, but, as we have seen, the invaders retreated hastily without burning the town.   There were very few among the students, during our war for independence,
who were imbued with Tory principles, and they were generally, if known, rather harshly dealt with.
One instance may suffice to show the spirit of the times.   In June, 1775, a student named Abiather Camp
was reported unfriendly to Congress.   A committee of investigation was appointed, who wrote a very polite
note to the young gentleman, setting forth the charges made against him, and demanding an explicit denial,
if the report was untrue.   The young scape-grace returned the following answer :

"New Haven, June 13, 1775.

" *To the Honorable and Respectable Gentlemen of the Committee now residing in Yale College :*

" May it please your honors, ham—ham—ham.

" Finis cumsistula, popularum gig—
A man without a head has no need of a wig.

" ABIATHER CAMP."

The insulted committee resolved to advertise Camp as an enemy to his country, and to treat him with all
possible scorn and neglect.   Such advertisement was posted upon the hall door.   He braved public opinion
until October, when he recanted, and publicly asked pardon for his offenses.
Yale College was founded by ten principal ministers in the colony, who met for the purpose, at New Haven, in 1700.   Each brought a number of books at their next meeting in 1701, and, presenting them to the
society, said, " I give these books for the founding of a college in the colony."   A proposition to found a college had been named fifty years before.   The first commencement was held at Saybrook, in 1702.   In 1717
the first college building was erected in New Haven.   It was seventy feet long and twenty-two wide.   From
time to time several liberal endowments have been made to the institution, the earliest and most munificent
of which was from Elihu Yale, in whose honor the college was named.   Among its distinguished benefactors
were Sir Isaac Newton, Dean Berkley, Bishop Burnet, Halley, Edwards, &c.   The present imposing pile
was commenced in 1750.   Additions have been made at different times, and it now consists of four spacious
edifices, each four stories high, one hundred and four by forty feet on the ground ; a chapel, lyceum, atheneum, chemical laboratory, dining-hall, and a dwelling-house for the president.

CHAPTER XIX.

"Land of the forest and the rock—
  Of dark blue lake and mighty river—
Of mountains rear'd aloft to mock
The storm's career, the lightning's shock:
  My own green land forever.

Oh! never may a son of thine,
Where'er his wandering steps incline,
Forget the sky which bent above
His childhood like a dream of love—
The stream beneath the green hill flowing—
The broad-armed trees above it growing—
The clear breeze through the foliage blowing,
Or hear, unmoved, the taunt of scorn
Breathed o'er the brave New England born."

WHITTIER

LTHOUGH much of the soil of New England is rough and sterile, and labor —hard and unceasing labor—is necessary to procure subsistence for its teeming population, in no part of our republic can be found stronger birth-place attachments. It is no sentiment of recent growth, springing up under the influence of the genial warmth of our free institutions, but ante-dates our Revolution, and was prominently manifest in colonial times. This sentiment, strong and vigorous, gave birth to that zealous patriot-ism which distinguished the people of the Eastern States during the ten years preceding the war for independence, and the seven years of that contest. Repub-licanism seemed to be indigenous to the soil, and the people appeared to inhale the air of freedom at every breath. Every where upon the Connecticut, and eastward, loyalty to the sovereign—a commendable virtue in a people governed by a right-eous prince—was changed by kingly oppression into loyalty to a high and holy prin-ciple, and hallowed, for all time, the region where it flourished. To a pilgrim on an errand like mine the rough hills and smiling valleys of New England are sanctuaries for patriot wor-ship; and as our long train swept over the sandy plain of New Haven, and coursed among the hills of Wallingford and Meriden, an emotion stirred the breast akin to that of the Jew of old when going up to Jerusalem to _the Great Feast._ A day's journey before me was Boston—the city of the pilgrims, the nursery of liberty cradled in the May Flower, the first altar-place of freedom in the Western World.

The storm, which had abated for a few hours at mid-day, came down with increased vio-lence, and the wind-eddies wrapped the cars in such wreaths of smoke from the engine, that only an occasional glimpse of the country could be obtained. It was almost dark when we October 2, reached Hartford, upon the Connecticut River, thirty-six miles northward of New 1848. Haven; where, sick and weary from the effects of exposure and fatigue during the morning, a glowing grate and an "old arm-chair" in a snug room at the "United States" were, under the circumstances, comforts which a prince might covet. Let us close the shut-ters against the impotent gusts, and pass the evening with the chroniclers of Hartford and its vicinage.

Hartford (Suckiag), and Wethersfield, four miles distant, were the earliest settlements in Connecticut. In 1633 the Dutch from Nieu Amsterdam went up the Connecticut River, and established a trading-house and built a small fort on the south side of the Mill River, at its junction with the Connecticut, near the site of Hartford.   The place is still known as Dutch Point.   About the same time William Holmes and others of the Plymouth colony sailed up the Connecticut, in a vessel having the frame of a dwelling on board, and, landing on the west side, near the present Windsor, erected the first house built in Connecticut.   The Dutch threatened to fire on them, but they were allowed to pass. by.   In 1635, John Steele and others, under the auspices of Rev. Thomas Hooker, of Cambridge, reached Holmes's residence, and began a settlement near.   Hooker and his wife, with about one hundred men, women, and children of his flock, left Cambridge the following year, and marched June, through the wilderness westward to the pioneer settlement, subsisting, on the journey, 1636 upon the milk of a herd of cows which they drove before them.   Over hills and mountains, through thickets and marshes, they made their way, with no guide but a compass, no shelter but the heavens and the trees, no bed save the bare earth, relying upon Divine Providence and their own indomitable perseverance for success.   The first house of worship was erected the previous year, and on the 9th of July, 1636, Mr. Hooker first preached, and administered the holy communion there.

The Dutch looked upon the new-comers as intruders, while the English settlers in turn regarded the Dutch in that light, because the whole country north of 40° belonged, by chartered rights, to the Plymouth and Massachusetts Companies.   Much animosity existed for several years, the Dutch refusing to submit to the laws framed by the

FIRST MEETING-HOUSE.[1]

English colony, and often threatening hostilities against them.   Finally, in 1654, an order arrived from Parliament requiring the English colony to regard the Dutch, in all respects, as enemies.   In conformity to this order, the Dutch trading-house, fort, and all their lands were sequestered for the benefit of the commonwealth.   The Dutch then withdrew.

The first court, or regularly organized government, in Connecticut, was held at Hartford in the spring of 1636.   The people were under the general government of Massachusetts, but were allowed to have minor courts of their own, empowered to make war or peace, and form alliances with the natives within the colony.   The English settlement was not fairly seated, before the Pequots, already mentioned, disturbed it with menaces of destruction. The Pequot war ensued in 1637, and, although it involved the colony in debt, and caused a present scarcity of provisions, it established peace for many years, and was ultimately beneficial.

In January, 1639, a convention of the free planters of Connecticut was held at Hartford, and a distinct commonwealth was formed.   They adopted a constitution of civil government, which was organized in April following, by the election of John Haynes governor, and six magistrates.   In 1642 their criminal code, founded upon Jewish laws as developed in the Scripture, was completed and entered on record.   By this code the death penalty was incurred by those guilty of worshiping any but the one triune God ; of witchcraft ; blasphemy ; willful murder, except in defense of life ; man-stealing ; false swearing, by which a man's life might be forfeited ; unchastity of various grades ; cursing or smiting of parents by a child over sixteen years of age, except when it could be shown that the child's training had been neglected or the parents were guilty of cruel treatment ; and of a stubborn disobedience of parents by a son over sixteen years of age.

The following year the colonies of Massachusetts, Plymouth, Connecticut (as Hartford was called), and New Haven confederated for their mutual safety and welfare, 1643. and called themselves the *United Colonies of New England* [2]   Each colony was author-

---

[1] This picture of the first house for Christian worship erected in Connecticut is copied from Barber's *Historical Collections.*   He obtained the drawing from an antiquary of Hartford, and believes it correct.

[2] The term New England was first applied by Captain John Smith, according to the dedicatory epistle to the " First Sermon preached in New England" by Robert Cushman.   " It was so called,'' says the address, " because of the resemblance that is in it of England, the native soil of Englishmen.   It being much what the same for heat and cold in summer and winter, it being champaign ground, but no high mountains, some-

434   PICTORIAL FIELD-BOOK

Conjunction of New Haven and Connecticut Colonies.   James II.   Quo Warranto.   Governor Andross.   The "Charter Oak."

ized to send two commissioners to meet annually in September, first at Boston, and then at Hartford, New Haven, and Plymouth, with power to make war and peace, and enact federal laws for the general good.   This union was productive of great benefit, for it made the united settlements formidable in opposition to their enemies, the Dutch and Indians.

In 1662, Charles II. granted a charter to the Connecticut colony, by which the New Haven colony was included within that of the former.   At first there was much dissatisfaction, but in 1655 the two colonies joined in an amicable election of officers, and chose John Winthrop for governor.

Charles was succeeded by his brother James, a bigoted, narrow-minded, and unjust prince. Many of his advisers were ambitious and unprincipled men, scheming for the consolidation of power in the person of the king.   Immediately on the accession of James, they arranged a plan for procuring a surrender of all the patents of the New England colonies, and forming the whole northern part of America into twelve provinces, with a governor general over a July, the whole.   Writs of *quo warranto* were accordingly issued,[a] requiring the several 1685. colonies to appear, by representatives, before his majesty's council, to show by what right they exercised certain powers and privileges.[1]   The colony of Connecticut sent an agent to England with a petition and remonstrances to the king.   The mission was vain, for already the decree had gone forth for annulling the charters.   Sir Edmund Andross was appointed the first governor general, and arrived at Boston in December, 1686.   He immediately demanded the surrender of the charter of Connecticut, and it was refused.   Nearly a

year elapsed, and meanwhile Andross began to play the tyrant.   His first fair promises to the people were broken, and, supported by royal authority, he assumed a dignity and importance almost equal to his master's, thoroughly disgusting the colonists.

In October, 1687, he went to Hartford with a company of soldiers while the Assembly was in session, and demanded an immediate surrender of their charter.   Sir Edmund was received with apparent respect by the members, and in his presence the subject of his demand was calmly debated until evening.   The charter was then brought forth and placed upon the table around which the members were sitting.   Andross was about to seize it, when the lights were suddenly extinguish-

THE CHARTER OAK.[2]

ed.   A large concourse of people had assembled without, and the moment the lights disap-

what like the soil in Kent and Essex; full of dales and meadow grounds, full of rivers and sweet springs, as England is.   But principally, so far as we can yet find, it is an island, and near about the quantity of England, cut out from the main land in America, as England is from Europe, by a great arm of the sea, which entereth in 40°, and runneth up north and west by west, and goeth out either into the South Sea or else into the Bay of Canada.   The certainty whereof and secrets of which we have not yet so found as that as eye-witnesses we can make narration thereof; but, if God give time and means, we shall, ere long, discover both the extent of that river, together with the secrets thereof, and so try what territories, habitations, or commodities may be found either in it or about it."   This address was written, and the sermon preached at Plymouth, in December, 1621.   By the *Bay of Canada* is meant the St. Lawrence, and by the "great arm of the sea," the Hudson River.   The explorations of Hendrick Hudson in 1609 seem not to have been known to the worthy divine, and he imagined a connection between the Hudson and St. Lawrence, by which New England was made an island.

[1] A writ of *quo warranto* issues against any person or corporation that usurps any franchise or liberty against the king without good title, and is brought against the usurpers to show by what right and title they hold and claim such franchise and liberty.—*Law Dictionary.*

[2] This venerable relic is still vigorous, and is a "gnarled oak" indeed.   It stands upon the northern slope of the Wyllys Hill, a beautiful elevation on the south side of Charter Street, a few rods east of Main Street. This engraving is from a sketch which I made of the tree from Charter Street, on the 3d of October, 1848. omitted the picket fence in front, in order to show the appearance of the whole trunk.   The opening of

peared they raised a loud huzza, and several entered the chamber.   Captain Wadsworth, of Hartford, seized the charter, and, unobserved, carried it off and deposited it in the hollow trunk of a large oak-tree fronting the house of Hon. Samuel Wyllys, then one of the magistrates of that colony.   The candles were relighted, quiet was restored, and Andross eagerly sought the coveted parchment.   It was gone, and none could, or would, reveal its hiding-place.   Sir Edmund stormed for a time, and threatened the colony with royal displeasure ; then quietly taking possession of the government, he closed the records of the court, October 31, or Assembly, with a simple annunciation of the fact.   1687.

The administration of Andross was short.   His royal master was driven from his 1688. throne and country the next year, and his minion in America was arrested, and confined in the Castle, near Boston, until February, 1689, when he was sent to England for trial.   Able jurists in England having decided that, as Connecticut had never given up her charter, it remained in full force, the former government was re-established.   From that time until the Revolution no important events of general interest occurred at Hartford.   A melancholy accident occurred there in May, 1766, on the occasion of rejoicings because of the repeal of the Stamp Act.   The day had been spent in hilarity.   Bells, cannons, and huzzas had testified the general and excessive joy, and great preparations were making for bonfires, fire-works, and a general illumination.   In the chamber of a brick school-house that stood where the Hartford Hotel was afterward built, a number of young men were preparing fire-works in the evening.   Under the house was a quantity of gunpowder, from which the militia had received supplies during the day.   The powder had been scattered from the building to the street.   Some boys accidentally set it on fire, and immediately the building was reduced to a ruin ; several of the inmates were killed, and many badly wounded.

The most important occurrences of general interest at Hartford, during the Revolution, were the two conferences between Washington and the Count de Rochambeau, the commander of the French army in America.   The first interview was on the 21st of September, 1780, the second on the 23d of May, 1781.   The French fleet, under the command of the Chevalier de Ternay, conveying the troops sent to our shores by Louis XVI. of France to aid us, arrived at Newport in July, 1780 ; and the conference of Washington with Rochambeau and Ternay, in September following, was to consult upon future operations.[1]   This interview resulted in the conclusion that the season was too far advanced for the allies to perform any thing of importance, and, after making some general arrangements for the next campaign, Washington returned to his camp at West Point, in the Hudson Highlands.   It was during his absence at Hartford that Arnold attempted to surrender West Point and its subordinate posts into the hands of the enemy.

The second conference between Washington and Rochambeau was at Wethersfield, four miles below Hartford.   Rochambeau and General the Marquis de Chastellux, with their suites, arrived at Hartford on the 21st of May, where they were met by Wash-   1781.

---

the cavity wherein the charter was concealed is seen near the roots.   The heavy wind that had been blowing for thirty hours had stripped the tree of a large portion of its autumnal leaves, and strewn the ground with acorns.   The trunk, near the roots, is twenty-five feet in circumference.   A daughter of Secretary Wyllys, writing to Dr. Holmes about the year 1800, says of this oak, " The first inhabitant of that name [Wyllys] found it standing in the height of its glory.   Age seems to have curtailed its branches, yet it is not exceeded in the height of its coloring or richness of its foliage. . . . . . . The cavity, which was the asylum of our charter, was near the roots, and large enough to admit a child.   Within the space of eight years that cavity has closed, as if it had fulfilled the divine purpose for which it had been reared."   The cavity within remains as large as anciently, but the orifice will hardly admit a hand.

[1] At that time the French fleet was blockaded in Narraganset Bay by a superior English squadron.   Ternay was quite dissatisfied with his situation, and wrote very discouraging letters to the Count de Vergennes, the French premier.   In one (written September 10th, 1780), from Newport, he said, " We are actually compelled to remain on a very strict defensive.   The English squadron is superior in number and in every other respect.   The fate of North America is yet very uncertain, and the Revolution is not so far advanced as it has been believed in Europe."   An account of the negotiations and other circumstances connected with the sending of troops from France to aid in the Revolution will be given in a future chapter, devoted to the subject of the diplomacy of the United States during the war for independence.

ington, and Generals Knox and Du Portail, and their suites.   The meeting was celebrated by discharges of cannon ; and, after partaking of refreshments, the officers, with several private gentlemen as an escort, rode to Wethersfield.   Washington lodged at the house of Mr.

Joseph Webb,[1] in Wethersfield, and there the conference was held.   The object of the interview was to concert a plan of operations for the ensuing campaign.   The minutes of the conference are in the form of queries by Rochambeau, which were answered by Washington.   The conclusion of the matter was an arrangement for the French army to march as speedily as possible to the Hudson River, and form a junction with the American army encamped there, for the purpose of making a demonstration upon the city of New York, if practicable.   An expedition southward seems to have been proposed by the French officers, but this idea was abandoned on account of the lateness of the season, and

THE WEBB HOUSE.[2]

the danger to which northern troops would be exposed in the Southern States in summer. It was also agreed to send to the West Indies for the squadron, under Count de Grasse, to sail immediately to Sandy Hook, and, forming a junction with the fleet under Count de Barras, confine Admiral Arbuthnot to New York Bay, and act in concert with the combined armies in besieging the city, then the strong-hold of the enemy.   The French troops consisted of about four thousand men, exclusive of two hundred that were to be left in charge of stores at Providence.   A circular letter was sent by Washington to the Eastern Legislatures, and to that of New Jersey, requesting them to supply as large a quota of Continental troops as possible.   Such a force as he felt sure could be mustered, Washington deemed adequate to undertake the siege of New York ; and, on his return from Wethersfield, he began his arrangements for the enterprise.   The two armies formed a junction near Dobbs's Ferry, at the beginning of July.   After several ineffectual attempts upon the upper end of York Island, circumstances caused Washington to abandon the enterprise.   The arrival of a reenforcement for Clinton in New York, the expressed determination of De Grasse to sail for the Chesapeake, and the peculiar situation of affairs in Virginia, where Cornwallis and La Fayette were operating against each other, induced Washington to march south with the combined armies.   The result was the siege of Yorktown and capture of Cornwallis.

The storm was raging as furiously as ever on the morning after my arrival in Hartford, and I abandoned the idea of visiting Wethersfield and Windsor.[3]   With a letter of introduction to the Rev. Thomas Robbins, the librarian of the Connecticut Historical Society, I vis-

---

[1] " May 18th.   Set out this day for the interview at Wethersfield with the Count de Rochambeau and Admiral Barras.   Reached Morgan's Tavern, forty-three miles from Fishkill Landing, after dining at Colonel Vanderburg's.   19th. Breakfasted at Litchfield, dined at Farmington, and lodged at Wethersfield, at the house of Mr. Joseph Webb."—Washington's Diary.   The Count Barras was prevented from attending the meeting by the appearance of a large British fleet, under Admiral Arbuthnot, off Block Island.   The residence of Colonel Vanderburg, where Washington dined, was at Poughquag, in Beekman, Dutchess county.

[2] This house is still standing (1848), in the central part of Wethersfield, a few rods south of the Congregational Church.

[3] Windsor is situated upon the Connecticut, a little above Hartford, at the mouth of the Farmington River. Here was planted the first English settlement in Connecticut, for here the first house was built.   It was the egg from which sprang Hartford and the Connecticut colony.   East Windsor, on the east side of the Connecticut, has a notoriety in our Revolutionary annals, on account of its being, for a short time, the quarters of a portion of the British and Hessian troops of Burgoyne's captured army, on their way to Boston ; also as the quarters of Governor Franklin, of New Jersey, and General Prescott, captured on Rhode Island, while prisoners in the hands of the Americans.   The events connected with the capture of these two persons will be noticed elsewhere.   They were confined, under a strong guard, in the house of Captain Ebenezer Grant, which, I was told, is still standing, a few rods south of the Theological Seminary.

OF THE REVOLUTION. 437

Connecticut Historical Society. Dr. Robbins's Library. Brewster's Chest. The Pilgrim Covenant. Names of the Pilgrims.

ited the room of that institution, situated in a fine edifice called the *Wadsworth Atheneum*. This building stands upon the site of the old Wadsworth Mansion, the place of Washington's first conference with Rochambeau. The cordial welcome with which I was received by Dr. Robbins was a prelude to many kind courtesies bestowed by him during a visit of three hours. He is a venerable bachelor of seventy-two years, and, habited in the style of a gentleman fifty years ago, his appearance carried the mind back to the time of Washington. The library of the society, valued at ten thousand dollars, is its property only in prospective; it belongs to Dr. Robbins, who has, by will, bequeathed it to the institution at his death. It contains many exceedingly rare books and MSS., collected by its intelligent owner during a long life devoted to the two-fold pursuits of a Christian pastor and a man of letters. There are many historical curiosities in the library-room, a few of which I sketched. The one in-

vested with the greatest interest was the chest of Elder Brewster, of the May Flower, brought from Holland in that Pilgrim ship. Near it stood a heavy iron pot that belonged to Miles Standish, the "hero of New England," one of the most celebrated of the Pilgrim passengers. The chest is of yellow Norway pine, stained with a color resembling London brown. Its dimensions are four feet two inches long, one foot eight inches broad, and two feet six inches high. The key, in size, has more the appearance of one be-

longing to a prison than to a clothing receptacle. The chest is a relic of much interest *per se*, but a fact connected with its history makes it an object almost worthy of reverence to a New Englander, and, indeed, to every American. Well-established tradition asserts that the solemn written compact made by the passengers of the May Flower previous to the landing of the Pilgrims was drawn up and signed upon the lid of this chest, it being the most convenient article at hand for the purpose. That compact, brief and general, may be regarded as the foundation of civil and religious liberty in the Western World, and was the first instrument of civil government ever subscribed as the act of the whole people.[1] It was conceived in the following terms:

"In the name of God, Amen. We whose names are under written, the Loyal Subjects of our dread Sovereign Lord King James, by the Grace of God of Great Britain, France, and Ireland, King, Defender of the Faith, &c., Having undertaken, for the Glory of God and the advancement of the Christian Faith, and Honor of our King and country, a Voyage to plant

[1] The harbor (Cape Cod) in which the May Flower anchored was ascertained to be north of the fortieth degree of latitude, consequently the proposed landing-place and settlement would be beyond the jurisdiction of the South Virginia Company, from whom these emigrants had received their charter. That instrument was, therefore, useless. Some of those who embarked from England had intimated that they would be under no law when ashore. The majority of the emigrants, concerned on account of this appearance of faction, thought proper to have recourse to natural law, and resolved that, before disembarkation, they should enter into an association, and bind themselves in a political body, to be governed by the majority. This was the origin of the compact. The following is a list of the signatures to the instrument: John Carver, William Bradford, Edward Winslow, William Brewster, Isaac Allerton, Miles Standish, John Alden, Samuel Fuller, Christopher Martin, William Mullins, William White,* Richard Warren, John Howland, Stephen Hopkins, Edward Tilley, John Tilley, Francis Cook, Thomas Rogers, Thomas Tinker, John Ridgedale, Edward Fuller, John Turner, Francis Eaton, James Chilton, John Crackston, John Billington, Moses Fletcher, John Goodman, Degory Priest, Thomas Williams, Gilbert Winslow, Edward Margeson, Peter Brown, Richard Britteridge, George Soule, Richard Clarke, Richard Gardiner, John Allerton, Thomas English, Edward Doty, Edward Leister. There were forty-one subscribers to the compact, each one placing opposite his name the number of his family. The whole number of souls was one hundred and one.—See Moore's *Memoirs of American Governors*, i., 25.

* Just previous to the landing of the Pilgrims, the wife of William White gave birth to a son, the first English child born in New England. From the circumstances of his birth he was named Peregrine. He died at Marshfield, July 22d, 1704, aged nearly eighty-four years. William White died soon after the seating of the colony, and his widow married Edward Winslow. This was the first English marriage in New England. It was a singular circumstance that Mrs. White was the first mother and the first bride in New England, and mother of the first native governor of the colony, who was also the sole bearer of the honor of commander-in-chief of the forces of the confederate colonies.—See *Baylies*, ii., 18.

438　　　　　　　　PICTORIAL FIELD-BOOK

Hand-writing of the Pilgrims.　　　　　Robinson's short Sword.　　　　　Ancient Chair.

the first Colony in the Northern parts of Virginia ; Do by these Presents, solemnly and mutually, in the Presence of God, and of one another, Covenant and Combine ourselves together into a Civil body Politic, for our better Ordering and Preservation, and Furtherance of the ends aforesaid ; and by Virtue hereof, to enact, constitute, and frame just and equal laws, ordinances, Acts, Constitutions, and Offices from Time to Time, as shall be thought most meet and convenient for the General Good of the Colony ; unto which we Promise all due Submission and Obedience.　In witness whereof we have hereunder subscribed our Names at Cape Cod, the eleventh of November, in the year of the Reign of our Sovereign Lord, King James, of England, France, and Ireland the Eighteenth, and of Scotland the Fifty-fourth, Anno Domini, 1620."

HAND-WRITING OF THE PILGRIMS.[1]

Another curious relic of the Pilgrims, preserved by Dr. Robbins, is a *mincing-knife*, made of the sword-blade that belonged to the Rev. Mr. Robinson, the pastor of the Pilgrims, at Leyden.　Mr. Robinson never came to New England, but remained at Leyden till his death in 1625.　His widow and family came over, bringing his effects, among which was his short sword, an article then generally worn by civilians as well as military men. His three sons were desirous of possessing this relic.　It being impossible for each to have it entire, it was cut into three pieces, and the sons, true to the impulses of New England thrift, each had his piece made into the *useful* implement here represented.

ANCIENT CHAIR.

Another interesting relic is a *chair* which was an heir-loom in the family of one of the earlier settlers of New Haven.　It is made wholly of turned wood (except the board bottom), fastened together by wooden pegs, and is similar, in appearance, to Governor Carver's chair, in the cabinet of the Massachusetts Historical Society.　Its existence is traced back to the thirteenth century.　The material is ash and its construction ingenious.

---

[1] These were copied from Russell's "Recollections of the Pilgrims."　He obtained them from old deeds and other documents.　The writers were members of the first Plymouth Church, and some of them were passengers in the May Flower.

The tavern sign of General Putnam, which hung before his door in Brooklyn, Connecticut, about the year 1768, is also preserved.[1] It is made of yellow pine, painted alike on both sides. The device is a full-length portrait of Wolfe, dressed in scarlet uniform, and, as a work of art, possesses much merit. The portrait of the young hero is quite correct. The background is a faint miniature copy of West's picture of *The Death of Wolfe*, painted by that artist during the first years of his residence in England. The sign-board is full of small punctures made by shot, the figure of Wolfe having been used as a target at some time.

Genl WOLFE

PUTNAM'S SIGN.

A drum, used to call the people to worship ; an ottoman, that belonged to Mrs. Washington ; the vest, torn and bloodstained, worn by Ledyard when massacred at Groton, and the wooden case in which the celebrated charter of Connecticut was sent over and kept, are in the collection. The latter is about three and a half feet long and four inches wide and deep, lined with printed paper, apparently waste leaves of a history of the reign of Charles I. In the center is a circular projection for the great seal, which was attached. I saw the charter itself in the office of the Secretary of State. It is written upon fine vellum, and on one corner is a beautifully drawn portrait of Charles, executed in India ink.

The storm abating a little at about noon, I rode down to Wethersfield and sketched the Webb House, returning in time to make the drawing of the Charter Oak pictured on page 434, the rain pouring like a summer shower, and my umbrella, held by a young friend, scarcely protecting my paper from the deluge. Pocketing some of the acorns from the venerable tree, I hastened back to my lodgings, and at a little past five in the evening departed for Boston. I passed the night at Springfield, ninety-eight miles west of Boston, and reached the latter place at one o'clock the next day. The city was enveloped in a cold mist that hung upon the skirts of the receding storm ; and, too ill to ramble for business or pleasure, even if fine weather had beckoned me out, I passed the afternoon and evening before a blazing fire at the *Marlborough*.

We are now upon the most interesting portion of the classic ground of the Revolution. Before noting my visit to places of interest in the vicinity, let us view the wide field of historic research here spread out, and study some of the causes which led to the wonderful effect of dismembering a powerful empire, and founding a republic, more glorious, because more beneficent, than any that preceded it.

---

[1] The following letter, in which Putnam alludes to the fact that he had kept tavern, I copied from the original in his hand-writing, now in possession of the Connecticut Historical Society :

"Brooklyn, Feb'y 18, 1782.

"GENTLEMEN—Being an Enemy to Idleness, Dissipation, and Intemperance, I would object against any measure that may be conducive thereto ; and as the multiplying of public houses where the public good does not require it has a direct tendency to ruin the morals of the youth, and promote idleness and intemperance among all ranks of people, especially as the grand object of those candidates for license is money, and where that is the case, men are not apt to be over-tender of people's morals or purses. The authority of this town, I think, have run into a great error in approbating an additional number of public houses, especially in this parish. They have approbated two houses in the center, where there never was custom (I mean traveling custom) enough for one. The other custom (or domestic), I have been informed, has of late years increased, and the licensing of another house, I fear, would increase it more. As I kept a public house here myself a number of years before the war, I had an opportunity of knowing, and certainly do know, that the traveling custom is too trifling for a man to lay himself out so as to keep such a house as travelers have a right to expect ; therefore I hope your honors will consult the good of this parish, so as only to license one of the two houses. I shall not undertake to say which ought to be licensed ; your honors will act according to your best information.   I am, with esteem, your honors' humble servant,
                                                                                "ISRAEL PUTNAM.

"*To the Hon'ble County Court, to be held at Windham on the 19th inst.*"

I have just mentioned the May Flower, and the solemn compact for the founding of a commonwealth, with a government deriving its powers from the consent of a majority of the governed, which was drawn up and signed in its cabin.   That vessel was truly the cradle of American liberty, rocked by the icy billows of Massachusetts Bay.   A glance at antecedent events, in which were involved the causes that led to the emigration to America of that body of Puritans called THE PILGRIMS, is profitable in tracing the remote springs of our Revolutionary movements in New England, for they contain the germs of our institutions.

1550.   Just three hundred years ago, when the exiled Hooper was recalled, and appointed Bishop of Gloucester, the Puritans had their birth as a distinct and separate religious body.   Henry VIII. quarreled with Pope Julius III. because he would not grant that licentious monarch a divorce from Catharine of Aragon, to allow him to marry the beautiful Anne Boleyn.   Henry professed Protestantism, abolished the pope's authority in England, and assumed to be himself the head of the Church.   He retained the title, "Defender of the Faith," which the pope had previously bestowed upon him in gratitude for his championship of Rome, for he had even written a book against Luther.   Thus, in seeking the gratification of his own unhallowed appetites, that monster in wickedness planted the seeds of the English Reformation.   The accession of Edward VI., a son of Henry by Jane Seymour, one of his six wives, led the way to the firm establishment of Protestantism in England.   The purity of life which the disciples of both Luther and Calvin exhibited won for them the esteem of the virtuous and good.   Yet the followers of these two reformers differed materially in the matter of rituals, and somewhat in doctrine.   Luther permitted the cross and taper, pictures and images, as things of indifference ; Calvin demanded the purest spiritual worship.   The reform having begun by decided opposition to the ceremonials as well as dogmas of the Papal Church, Calvin and his friends deemed it essential to the full completion of the work to make no concessions to papacy, even in non-essential matters.   The austere principle was announced; and Puritanism, which then had birth, declared that not even a ceremony should be allowed, unless it was enjoined by the Word of God.   Hooper, imbued with this spirit, refused a 1550.   for a time to be consecrated in the vestments required by law,[a] and the Reformed Church of England was shaken to its center by conflicting views respecting ceremonials.   Churchmen, or the Protestants who adhered to much of the Romish ceremonials, and the Puritans (first so called in derision) became bitter opponents.   During the reign of 1553-8.   Mary, a violent and bigoted papist, both parties were involved in danger.   The Puritans were placed in the greatest peril, because they were most opposed to papacy, and Hooper and Rogers, both Puritans, were the first martyrs of Protestant England.

Elizabeth, the youngest daughter of Henry VIII., succeeded Mary, and, though she professed Protestantism, long endeavored to retain in the Church of England the magnificent rituals of the Romish Liturgy.   She had in her private chapel images, the crucifix, and tapers ; she offered prayers to the Virgin ; insisted upon the celibacy of the clergy ; invoked the aid of saints, but left the doctrine of the real presence in the Eucharist, which some had been burned for denying, and some for asserting, as a question of national indifference.   With such views, Elizabeth regarded the Puritans with little favor, while they, having nothing to fear from earthly power, valuing, as they did, their lives as nothing in comparison with the maintenance of their principles, were bold in the annunciation of their views.   They claimed the right to worship according to the dictates of their own consciences, and denied the prerogative of the sovereign to interfere in matters of religious faith and practice.   They claimed the free exercise of private judgment in such matters ; and the Puritan preachers also promulgated the doctrine of civil liberty, that the sovereign was amenable to the tribunal of public opinion, and ought to conform in practice to the expressed will of the majority of the people.   By degrees their pulpits became the tribunes of the common people, and their discourses assumed a latitude in discussion and rebuke which alarmed the queen and the great body of Churchmen, who saw therein elements of revolution that might overturn the throne and bury the favored hierarchy in its ruins.   On all occasions the Puritan ministers were the bold asserters of that freedom which the American Revolution established.

Elizabeth had endeavored firmly to seat the national religion midway between the supremacy of Rome and the independence of Puritanism. She thus lost the confidence of both, and also soon learned herself to look upon both as enemies. Roman Catholic princes conspired against England, while Puritan divines were sapping the foundations of the royal prerogatives, and questioning the *divine right* of monarchs to govern. A convocation of the clergy was held; the "Thirty-nine Articles," which constitute the rule of faith of the English Church, were formed, and other methods were adopted, to give stability to the hierarchy; but nearly nine years elapsed before Parliament confirmed the Articles by act, and then not without some limitations, which the Puritans regarded as concessions to them.

Rigorous orders for conformity were now issued. The Puritans, thoroughly imbued with an independent spirit, assumed an air of defiance. Thirty London ministers refused subscription to the Articles, and some talked openly of secession. A separate congregation was at length actually formed. The government was alarmed, and several of the leading men and women were imprisoned for a year. Persecution begat zeal, and a party of Independents, or Separatists, appeared, under a zealous but shallow advocate named Brown. The great body of the Puritans desired reform, but were unwilling to leave the Church. The Independents denounced the Church as idolatrous, and false to Christianity and truth. Bitter enmity soon grew up between them, the Puritans reproaching the Separatists with unwise precipitancy, and they in return were censured for cowardice and want of faith.

Persecution now began in earnest. A court of high commission was established, for the detection and punishment of Non-conformists. Its powers were almost as absolute as those of the Inquisition. Parliament, particularly the House of Commons, in which was the leaven of Puritanism, disapproved of the commission, and a feeling of general dissatisfaction prevailed. Whitgift, archbishop of Canterbury, a man sincerely, but bigotedly, attached to the English Reformed Church, was at the head of the hierarchy, and assumed to control the entire body of the English Church. Conventicles were prohibited, yet, in a few years, it was asserted in Parliament that twenty thousand persons in England attended conventicles. Some were banished, others imprisoned, a few were hanged. The Separatists were nearly extinguished, while the more loyal branch of the Puritans still suffered contumely and persecution.

1583.

1593.

Elizabeth died, and the Puritans hailed the accession of James of Scotland, where independence of thought and action had taken deepest root, as a favorable event. It was thought that his education, the restraints from profligacy which the public morals of Scotland imposed, and his apparently sincere attachment to Protestantism, would guaranty to them fair toleration, if not actual power. But they were in error. He was thirty-six years old when he ascended the throne, and, in the freedom of self-indulgence which his new position afforded, exulted in gluttony, idleness, and licentiousness. Incapable of being a statesman, he aimed to be thought a scholar, and wrote books which courtiers lauded greatly, while wise men smiled and pitied. Bacon pronounced him incomparable for learning among kings; and Sully of France, who knew his worth, esteemed him "the wisest fool in Europe." A profligate dissembler and imbecile coward, he was governed entirely by self-interest, vanity, and artful men. He loved flattery and personal ease, and he had no fixed principles of conduct or belief. Such was the man upon whom the Puritans, for a moment, relied for countenance; but he had scarcely reached London before his conduct blighted their hopes. "No bishop, no king," was his favorite maxim; and in 1604 he said of the Puritans, "I will make them conform, or I will harrie them out of the land, or else worse; only hang them, that's all." During that year three hundred Puritan ministers were silenced, imprisoned, or exiled.

1603.

Among the exiled ministers at this period was John Robinson. Eminent for piety and courage, his congregation was greatly attached to him, and they contrived to have secret meetings every Sunday. But the pressure of persecution finally determined them to seek an asylum in Holland, "where, they heard, was freedom of religion for all men." Thither Mr. Robinson and his little flock, among whom was William Brewster (who afterward became a ruling elder in the Church), went into voluntary exile in 1608　They landed at Amsterdam, and then journeyed to Leyden, feeling that they were but PILGRIMS, with no particular abiding-place on earth.   They were joined by others who fled from persecution in England, and finally they established a prosperous church at Leyden.

While the Pilgrim Puritans were increasing in strength in Holland, and winning golden opinions from the Dutch on account of their purity of life and lofty independence of thought, companies were forming for settling the newly-discovered portions of America, north of the mouth of the Delaware.   Toward the Western World the eyes and hearts of the PILGRIMS 1617. were turned, and John Carver and Robert Cushman repaired to England, to obtain the consent of the Virginia Company to make a distinct settlement in the northern part of their territory.   Sandys, Southampton, and other liberal members of the House of Commons, prevailed upon the king to wink at their heresy.   A patent was granted in 1619, and James promised, not to aid them, but to let them alone.   This was all they required of his majesty.   Now another difficulty was to be removed : capital was needed.   Several London merchants advanced the necessary sums.   The famous Captain John Smith offered his services, but his religious views did not suit them.   His notions were too aristocratic, and he complained of their democracy—complained that they were determined " to be lords and kings of themselves."   They were, therefore, left " to make trial of their own follies."   In 1620 the PILGRIMS purchased two ships, the Speedwell, of sixty tons, and the May Flower, of one hundred and eighty tons ; and as many of the congregation at Leyden as could be accommodated in them left Delfthaven for Southampton, England.   There they were joined August 5, by a few others, and, with a fair wind, sailed for America.   But the captain of 1620. the Speedwell and his company, becoming alarmed, and pretending that the ship was unseaworthy, put back to Plymouth, and the May Flower, bearing one hundred and September 6, one men, women, and children, the winnowed remnants of the passengers in the 1620. two vessels, again spread her sails to an eastern breeze.   Their destination was the country near the Hudson, but adverse winds drove them upon the more northerly and barren coasts of Massachusetts Bay, after a boisterous voyage of sixty-three days.   Land was espied on the 9th of November, and two days afterward the May Flower was safely moored in Cape Cod Bay.   Before they landed, as we have already noticed, they formed themselves into a body politic by a solemn voluntary compact.   " In the cabin of the May Flower humanity recovered its rights, and instituted government on the basis of ' equal laws' for the general good."   John Carver was chosen governor for the year.   Democratic liberty and independent Christian worship were at once established in America.[1]

The ocean now lay between the PILGRIMS and the persecuting hierarchy, and the land of promise was before them.   Yet perils greater than they had encountered hovered around that bleak shore, already white with the snow of early winter.   But

> " They sought not gold nor guilty ease
>   Upon this rock-bound shore—
> They left such prizeless toys as these
>   To minds that loved them more.
> They sought to breathe a freer air,
>   To worship God unchain'd ;
> They welcomed pain and danger here,
>   When rights like these were gain'd."

Inspired with such feelings, the Pilgrims prepared to land.   The shallop was unshipped, but it needed great repairs.   More than a fortnight was employed by the carpenter in making it ready for sea.   Standish, Bradford, and others, impatient of the delay, determined to go ashore and explore the country.   They encountered many difficulties, and returned to the ship.   When the shallop was ready, the most bold and enterprising set out upon a cruise along the shore, to find a suitable place at which to land the whole company.   They explored every bay and inlet, and made some discoveries of buried Indian corn, deserted wig-

---

[1] Baem, Barlow, Hume, Hallam, Bancroft.

wams, and an Indian cemetery.   The voyage was fruitless of good, and they returned to
the May Flower.   Again Carver, Standish, Bradford, Winslow, and others, with eight or
ten seamen, launched the shallop in the surf.   The day was very cold, and the   December 6,
spray froze upon them and their clothes like iron mail.   They passed that night   1620.
at Billingsgate Point, at the bottom of Cape Cod Bay, on the western shore of Wellfleet
Harbor.   The company divided next morning, but united at evening, and encamped at
Namskeket, or Great Meadow Creek.   The next morning, as they arose from their knees
in the deep snow, when their matin devotions were ended, a flight of arrows and a war-whoop
announced the presence of savages.   They were of the Nauset tribe, and regarded the white
people as kidnappers.[1]   But the Indians made no further attacks, and the boat proceeded
along the coast a distance of some forty miles.   Suddenly a storm arose.   Snow and rain
fell copiously ;   the heavy swells snapped the rudder, and with oars alone they guided the
frail shallop.   Darkness came on and the storm increased.   As much sail as possible was
used to reach the shore ;   it was too much ;   the mast broke in three pieces, and the fragments,
with the sail, fell overboard.   Breakers were just ahead, but, by diligent labor with the oars,
they passed safely through the surf into a smooth harbor, landed, and lighted a fire.   At
dawn they discovered that they were upon an island, in a good harbor.[2]   There they passed
the day in drying their clothes, cleaning their arms, and repairing their shallop.   Night approached ;   it was the eve of the Christian Sabbath.   The storm had ceased, but snow nearly
eighteen inches in depth lay upon the ground.   They had no tent, no shelter but the rock.
Their ship was more than fifteen leagues away, and winter, with all its terrors, had set in.
Every personal consideration demanded haste.   But the next day was the Sabbath, and they
resolved to remain upon that bleak island and worship God, in accordance with their faith
and obligations as Christians.   In the deep snow they knelt in prayer ;   by the cold rock
they read the Scriptures ;   upon the keen, wintery air they poured forth their hymns of thanksgiving and praise.   In what bold relief does that single act present the Puritan character

> " And can we deem it strange
> That from *their* planting such a branch should bloom
> As nations envy ?
>
> .   .   .   .   .   .
>
> Oh ye who boast
> In your free veins the blood of sires like these,
> Lose not their lineaments.   Should Mammon cling
> Too close around your heart, or wealth beget
> That bloated luxury which eats the core
> From manly virtue, or the tempting world
> Make faint the Christian's purpose in your soul,
> Turn ye to Plymouth's beach, and on that rock
> Kneel in *their* footprints, and renew the vow
> They breathed to God."
>
> Mrs. Sigourney.

On Monday morning the exploring party pushed through the surf, and landed   December 22,
upon a rock on the main.[3]   The neighborhood seemed inviting for a settlement,   1620.
and in a few days the May Flower was brought around and moored in the harbor.   The
whole company landed near where the explorers stepped ashore :   the spot was called New

[1] The Indians of Cape Cod and the vicinity had experienced the treachery of the whites, for it must be
remembered that the Pilgrims were not the discoverers of that region.   Both French and English ships had
visited the coast.   Six years before the landing of the Pilgrims, an Englishman named Hunt had inveigled
several Indians on board a ship, and carried them to England.

[2] This island, within the entrance of Plymouth Harbor, has been called Clarke's Island ever since.   It
was so named from Clarke, the first man who stepped ashore from the shallop.   The cove in which they
were in such danger lies between the Gurnet Head and Saguish Point, at the entrance of Plymouth Bay.—
Moore, i., 35.   The May Flower afterward made two voyages from England to America, bearing Emigrants.

[3] A portion of this rock was conveyed to a square in the center of the town of Plymouth in 1774, where
it still remains, and is known as *The Forefathers' Rock*.

Plymouth, in memory of the hospitalities which they had received at Plymouth, in England, and in a few days they commenced the erection of dwellings. The exposure of the explorers, and of others who had reached the shore by wading, had brought on disease, and nearly one half of the company were sick when the first blow of the ax was struck in the primeval forest. Faith and hope nerved the arms of the healthy, and they began to build. " This was the origin of New England ; it was the planting of the New England institutions. Inquisitive historians have loved to mark every vestige of the Pilgrims ; poets of the purest minds have commemorated their virtues ; the noblest genius has been called into exercise to display their merits worthily, and to trace the consequences of their daring enterprise."[1]

The winter that succeeded the landing of the Pilgrims was terrible for the settlers. Many were sick with colds and consumptions, and want and exposure rapidly reduced the numbers of the colony. Governor Carver's son died soon after landing, and himself and his wife passed into the grave the next spring.[2] William Bradford was elected to fill his place. The living were scarcely able to bury the dead, and at one time there were only seven men capable of rendering any assistance. Forty-six of the one hundred died before April, yet not a murmur against Providence was heard.

The colonists had been apprehensive of an attack from the Indians, but not one approached the settlement until March, when a chief named Samoset boldly entered the rude town, exclaiming, in broken English, which he had learned from fishermen on the coast of Maine, " Welcome, Englishmen ! welcome, Englishmen !" He gave them much information, and told them of a pestilence that had swept off the inhabitants a few years before. This accounted for the deserted wigwams seen by the explorers. Samoset soon afterward visited the colony with Squanto, a chief who had been carried away by Hunt in 1614 ; and in April Massasoit, the chief of the Wampanoags, was induced to make the English a friendly visit. Treaties of amity were made, and, until the breaking out of King Philip's war, fifty years afterward, were kept inviolate. But Canonicus, a powerful chief of the Narragansets, who lived on the west side of the Narraganset Bay, regarded the English as intruders, and sent to them the ominous token of hostility, a bundle of arrows wrapped in a rattle-snake's skin. Governor Bradford[3] at once sent the skin back to Canonicus, filled with powder and shot. The chief understood the symbol, and, afraid of the deadly weapons in which such materials were used, sent them back ; the Narragansets were awed into submission. Massasoit, who lived at Warren, Rhode Island, remained the fast friend of the English, and his sons, Alexander and Philip (the celebrated King Philip), kept the bond of friendship unbroken until 1675.

After many difficulties, and receiving some accessions from immigration, the settlers pur-

---

[1] Bancroft, i., 313.

[2] John Carver was among the English emigrants to Leyden. He was chosen the first governor of the colony, by a majority of the forty-one male adults that sailed in the May Flower. There were twelve other candidates for the honor. On the 23d of March, 1621, a few laws were enacted, and Carver was regularly inaugurated governor of the new colony. He was taken suddenly ill in the fields, while laboring, on the 3d of April. A violent pain in his head ensued, and in a few hours he was deprived of the use of his senses. He lived but a few days, and his wife, overcome by grief, followed him to the grave in about six weeks. He was buried with all the honors the people could bestow. His broad-sword is preserved in the cabinet of the Massachusetts Historical Society.

[3] William Bradford, the second Governor of Plymouth Colony, was born at Ansterfield, in the north of England, in 1588. The first Puritan principles were instilled into his young mind by a minister named Richard Clifton, and when he was of legal age he was denounced as a Separatist. He followed Mr. Robinson to Holland, and came to America in the May Flower. While he was absent, with others, searching for a spot on which to land, his wife fell into the sea and was drowned. He was appointed governor on the death of Carver, being then only thirty-three years of age. His energy was of great value to the colony, and so much was he esteemed, that he was annually elected governor as long as he lived, except occasionally, when, " by importuning, he got off," as Winslow says, and another took his place pro tempore. His idea of public office was, " that if it was of any honor or benefit, others besides himself should enjoy it ; if it was a burden, others besides himself should help him to bear it." Present politicians consider such doctrine a " barbarous relic." Governor Bradford died in May, 1657, having served the colony as chief magistrate twenty-five years of the thirty of his residence in America.

chased the rights of the London merchants who had aided them with funds, for nine thousand dollars, and the colony thus severed the last link of pecuniary interest that bound it to Old England, beyond the claims of commercial transactions.   There was one drawback upon their prosperity—the non-existence of private property.   There was a community of interest in all the land and its products.   Thence arose, on the part of some, an unwillingness to labor, and of others the discontent which the industrious feel while viewing the idleness of the lazy, for whose benefit they are toiling.   It was now found necessary to enter into an agreement that each family should plant for itself, and an acre of land was accordingly assigned to each person in fee.   Under this stimulus, the production of corn became so great that from buyers the colonists became sellers to the Indians.[1]

Civil government being fully established to the satisfaction of all, and news of the fertility of the soil and the beauty of the climate having reached England, in the following autumn other adventurers prepared to come to America.   In the mean while Edward Winslow, one of the most accomplished of the colonists, made a journey to the residence of Massasoit to strengthen the friendship that existed, by presents, and by amicable agreements respecting future settlers that might come from England.[2] The visit was fruitful of good results.   Soon afterward Captain Standish[3] marched against the village of Corbitant, one of Massasoit's sachems, who held an interpreter in custody, and threatened the tribe with destruction.   The whole country was alarmed at this movement, and on the 13th of September, 1621, ninety petty sachems came to Plymouth and signed a paper acknowledging themselves loyal subjects of King James.

THE OLD COLONY SEAL.

New settlers now began to arrive, and new explorations of the coast were made.   Sixty adventurers from London, under the auspices of a merchant named Weston, began a plantation in the autumn of 1622, at Weymouth, twelve miles southeast from the present city of Boston, and the whole coast of Massachusetts Bay was explored.   They discovered a spacious harbor, studded with islands, and inclosing a peninsula remarkable for three hills, called by the natives Shawmut (sweet water).   This was the harbor and site of the city of Boston.[4]

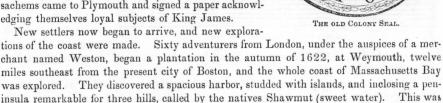

[1] Hildreth, i., 171.

[2] Edward Winslow was born in Worcestershire, England, in 1594.   While traveling on the Continent, he became acquainted with Mr. Robinson at Leyden, joined his congregation, sailed to America in the May Flower, and was one of the party that first landed on Plymouth Rock.   He made Massasoit a second visit, and found the sachem very sick, but by means of medicine restored him to health.   Grateful for his services, the chief revealed to Winslow a plot of some savages to destroy a small English settlement at Weymouth. Winslow went to England that fall, and in the spring brought over the first cattle introduced into the colony. He was appointed governor in 1633.   He was very active in the colony, and made several voyages to England in its behalf.   In 1655 he was appointed one of the commissioners to superintend the expedition against the Spaniards in the West Indies.   He died of fever on his passage, between Jamaica and Hispaniola, May 8th, 1655, aged sixty years.   His body was cast into the ocean.

[3] Miles Standish is called the "Hero of New England."   He served for some time in the English army in the Netherlands, and settled with Robinson's congregation at Leyden.   He was not a member of the Church—"never entered the school of Christ, or of John the Baptist."   He came to America in the May Flower, and was appointed military commander-in-chief at Plymouth.   His bold enterprises spread terror among the Indians, and secured peace to the colony.   In allusion to his exploit in killing Pecksuot, a bold chief, with his own hand, Mr. Robinson wrote to the governor, "O that you had *converted* some before you killed any!"   Standish was one of the magistrates of the colony as long as he lived.   He died at Duxbury in 1656, aged about seventy-two years.

[4] The Peninsula of *Shawmut* included between six and seven hundred acres of land sparsely covered by trees, and nearly divided by two creeks into three islands when the creeks were filled by the tides.   From the circumstance of the three hills, the English called the peninsula Tri-mountain, the modern Tremont. These three eminences have since been named Copp's, Fort, and Beacon Hills.   The name of Tri-mountain

In 1628 a company, under John Endicott, settled at Salem (Na-um-keag), and were joined by a few emigrants at Cape Ann, sixteen miles northward.   They received a charter from

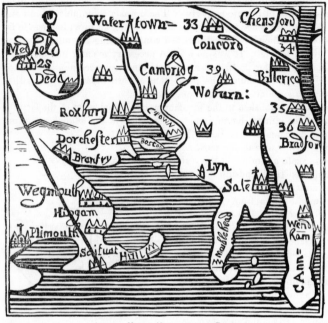

ANCIENT MAP OF MASSACHUSETTS BAY.[1]

the king, and were
incorporated by the
name of the "Govern-
or and Company of the
Massachusetts Bay in
New England."   In
1630 about three hun-
dred Puritan families,
under John Winthrop,
arrived, and joined the
Massachusetts Bay col-
ony.   They established
themselves at Dorches-
ter, Roxbury, Water-
town, and Cambridge.
A spring of pure and
wholesome water in-
duced some families
among whom was Mr
Winthrop, to settle up-
on Shawmut.   Win-
throp was the chosen
Governor of the colony
of Massachusetts Bay;
the whole government,
including   Plymouth,
was removed to the new settlement, and thenceforth Boston became the metropolis of New
England.

I have thus traced, with almost chronological brevity, the rise of the Puritans in England,
their emigration to America, and the progress of settlement, to the founding of Boston in 1630.
It is not within the scope of this work to give a colonial history of New England in all its
important details, and only so much of it will be developed as is necessary to present the links
of connection between the early history and the story of our Revolution.   That Revolution,
being a conflict of *principle*, had its origin more remote even than the planting of the New
England colonies.   The seed germinated when the sun of the Reformation warmed the cold
soil of society in Europe, over which the clouds of ignorance had so long brooded ; and its
blossoms were unfolded when the Puritans of England and the Huguenots of France boldly
asserted, in the presence of kingly power, the grand postulate of freedom—the SOCIAL AND
POLITICAL EQUALITY OF THE RACE.   These two sections of independent thinkers brought the
vigorous plant to America—the Puritans to New England, the Huguenots to the Carolinas.
The Covenanters of Scotland, and other dissenting communities, watered it during the reigns
of the Charleses and the bigot James II. ; and when the tactics of British oppression had
changed from religious persecution to commercial and political tyranny, it had grown a sturdy
tree, firmly rooted in a genial soil, and overshadowing a prosperous people with its beautiful
foliage.   The fruit of that tree was the American Revolution—the fruit which still forms
the nutriment that gives life and vigor to our free institutions.

was changed to Boston, as a compliment to the Rev. John Cotton, who emigrated from Boston, in Lincolnshire, England.

[1] This is a fac-simile of a map of Boston Harbor and adjacent settlements in 1667, and is believed to be
a specimen of the first engraving executed in America.   Instead of the top of the map being north, according to the present method of drawing maps, the right hand of this is north.

> " The Pilgrim *spirit* has not fled ;
> It walks in noon's broad light,
> And it watches the bed of the glorious dead,
> With their holy stars, by night.
> It watches the bed of the brave who have bled,
> And shall guard the ice-bound shore,
> Till the waves of the bay, where the May Flower lay,
> Shall foam and freeze no more."
>
> PIERPONT.

The persecutions of the Quakers, the proceedings against persons accused of witchcraft,[1] the disfranchisement of those who were not church members, and many other enactments in their civil code, considered alone, mark the Puritan as bigoted, superstitious, intolerant, unlovely in every aspect, and practically evincing a spirit like that of Governor Dudley, expressed in some lines found in his pocket after his death.

> " Let men of God in courts and churches watch
> O'er such as do a toleration hatch,
> Lest that ill egg bring forth a cocatrice,
> To poison all with heresy and vice.
> If men be left, and otherwise combine,
> My epitaph's, ' I died no libertine !' "

But when a broad survey is taken of the Puritan character, these things appear as mere blemishes—spots upon the sun—insects in the otherwise pure amber In religion and morality they were sincerely devoted to right—" New England was the colony of conscience."[2] Their worship was spiritual, their religious observances were few and simple. To them the

---

[1] A belief in witchcraft, or the direct agency of evil spirits through human instrumentality, was prevalent among all classes of Europe toward the close of the seventeenth century, and this superstition had a strong hold upon the metaphysical Puritans in America. A statute, enacted in the reign of Henry VIII., made it a capital offense for a person to practice the arts of witchcraft. The first James was a firm believer in witchcraft, and sanctioned some severe laws against its practitioners. Pretenders, called Witch-detectors, arose, and, during the commonwealth, traveled from county to county, in England, making accusations, in consequence of which many persons suffered death. The " Fundamentals" of Massachusetts contained a capital law against such offenses, founded upon the Scripture injunction, " Thou shalt not suffer a witch to live."—Exodus, xxii., 18. Increase Mather, father of the celebrated Cotton Mather, in a work called " Remarkable Providences," enumerated all the supposed cases of witchcraft that had occurred in New England. The high standing of the author turned public attention to the subject, and it was not long before a real witch was discovered in the person of an old woman at Newbury, whose house was alleged to be haunted. This was in 1686, and from that time until 1693, when King William's veto on the Witchcraft Act prevented any further trials, and all accused persons were released, the colonies were greatly agitated. Chief-justice Hale had given the weight of his opinion in England in favor of the delusion, and the Mathers, father and son, of Boston, eminent for their piety and learning, had written, and preached, and talked, and acted much under the belief in the reality of witchcraft. Cotton Mather published a book in 1692, called the " Wonders of the Invisible World," giving a full account of all the cases and trials, and stimulating the authorities to further proceedings. The delusion was now at its height, and no class of society was exempt from suspicion. The wife of Hale, minister of Beverly, was accused, at the very time when he was most active against others, and almost every ill-favored old woman was regarded as a servant of the devil. A son of Governor Bradstreet was accused, and had to flee for his life ; and even Lady Phipps, the wife of the Admiral Sir William, the newly-appointed Governor of Massachusetts, was suspected. When royal authority broke the spell, practical witchcraft ceased to act, and the people of Massachusetts recovered their senses. Mather, in his " Magnalia," confessed that things were carried a little too far in Salem, but never positively renounced his belief in the reality of witchcraft. His credulity had been thoroughly exposed by a writer named Calef, who addressed a series of letters to the Boston ministers on the subject. At first Mather sneered at him as a " weaver who pretended to be a merchant ;" but Calef laid his truths and sarcasms so strongly over the shoulders of Mather, that the latter called him a " coal from hell," to blacken his character, and afterward commenced a prosecution against him for slander.

The mischief wrought by this delusion was wide-spread and terrible. Society was paralyzed with alarm ; evil spirits were thought to overshadow the land ; every nervous influence, even every ordinary symptom of disease, was ascribed to demoniac power. When the royal veto arrived, twenty persons had been executed, among whom was a minister of Danvers named George Burroughs ; fifty-five had been tortured or terrified into a confession of witchcraft, one hundred and fifty were in prison, and two hundred more had been accused.

[2] John Quincy Adams.

elements remained but wine and bread ; they invoked no saints ; they raised no altar ; they adored no crucifix ; they kissed no book ; they asked no absolution ; they paid no tithes ; they saw in the priest nothing more than a man ; ordination was no more than an approbation of the officers, which might be expressed by the brethren as well as by the ministers ; the church, as a place of worship, was to them but a meeting-house ; they dug no grave in consecrated earth ; unlike their posterity, they married without a minister, and buried their dead without a prayer.   Witchcraft had not been made the subject of skeptical consideration, and, in the years in which Scotland sacrificed hecatombs to the delusion, there were but three victims in New England.

Rigorous in their moral and religious code, the Puritans were mild in their legislation upon other subjects.   For many crimes the death penalty was abolished, and the punishment for theft, burglary, and highway robbery was more mild than our laws inflict.   Divorce from bed and board was recognized by their laws as a barely possible event, but, during the first fifty years after the founding of New England, no record of such an occurrence is given.[1] Adultery was punished by death, the wife and paramour both suffering for the crime ; while the girl whom youth and affection betrayed was censured, but pitied and forgiven, and the seducer was compelled to marry his victim.   Domestic discipline was highly valued, and the undutiful child and faithless parent were alike punished.   Honest men were not imprisoned for debt until 1654 ; cruelty to animals was a civil offense, punishable by fine.   The people, united in endurance of hardships during the first years of settlement, were equally united when prosperity blessed them.   They were rich in affection for one another, and all around them were objects of love.   Their land had become a paradise of beauty and repose, and, even when the fires of persecution went out in England, none could be tempted to return thither, for they had found a better heritage.   Their morals were pure, and an old writer said, "As Ireland will not brook venomous beasts, so will not that land vile livers."   Drunkenness was almost unknown, and universal health prevailed.   The average duration of life in New England, as compared with Europe, was doubled, and no less than four in nineteen of all that were born attained the age of seventy years.   Many lived beyond the age of ninety, and a man one hundred years old when our Revolution broke out was not considered a wonder of longevity.

Such were the people who fostered the living principles of our independence—the parents of nearly one third of the present white population of the United States.   Within the first fifteen years—and there was never afterward any considerable increase from England—there came over twenty-one thousand two hundred souls.   Their descendants are now not far from four millions.   Each family has multiplied, on the average, to one thousand souls.   To New York and Ohio, where they constitute half the population, they have carried the Puritan system of free schools, and their example is spreading it throughout the civilized world.[2]

In 1634 the colony had become so populous that it was found inconvenient for all the freemen to assemble in one place to transact business.   By the general consent of the towns, the representative system was introduced, and to twenty-four representatives was delegated the power granted to the whole body of freemen by charter.   The appellation of general court was also applied to the representatives.   It was about this time that Hugh Peters, afterward Cromwell's secretary, and Henry Vane, afterward Sir Henry Vane, who was made governor, came to the colony, with a great number of immigrants.   It was about this time, also, that Roger Williams occasioned disturbances, and was banished.   These circumstances will be noticed hereafter.

In 1637 the Pequot war ensued ; and about 1640, persecutions having ceased in England, emigration to the colonies also ceased.   The Confederation was effected in 1643.   From that time the permanent prosperity of the colonies may be dated.[3]   Their commerce, which

---

[1] Trumbull's *History of Connecticut*, i., 283 ; Bancroft's *United States*, i., 465.

[2] Bancroft, i., 467–8.

[3] Captain Edward Johnson, in his "Wonder-working Providence of Zion's Savior in New England," writing in 1650, seven years after the union, says, "Good white and wheaten bread is no dainty, but every ordinary

first extended only to the Indians, and to traffic among themselves, expanded, and considerable trade was carried on with the West Indies.   Through this trade bullion was brought into New England, and " it was thought necessary, to prevent fraud in money," to establish a mint for coining shillings, sixpences, and threepences.   On the first coins the only inscription on one side was N. E., and on the other, XII., VI., or III.   In October, 1651, the court ordered that all pieces of money should have a double ring, with the inscription MASSACHUSETTS, and a tree in the center, on one side, and NEW ENGLAND, and the year of our Lord, on the other.   The first money was coined in 1652, and the date was not altered for thirty years.

THE "PINE-TREE SHILLING."[1]

In the year 1656 a few fanatics in religion, calling themselves Quakers, began to disturb the public peace, revile magistrates, and interfere with the public worship of the people. They assumed the name and garb of Quakers, but had no more the spirit and consistency of life of that pure sect than any monomaniac that might declare himself such.   The Quakers have ever been regarded, from their first appearance, as the most order-loving, peaceful citizens, cultivating genuine practical piety among themselves, and, with few exceptions, never interfering with the faith and practice of others, except by the reasonable efforts of persuasion.   Quite different was the character of some of those who suffered from the persecution of the Puritans.   They openly and in harsh language reviled the authorities in Church and State ; entered houses of worship, and denounced the whole congregation as hypocrites and an " abomination to the Lord," very much after the fashion of the wall-placarding and itinerant *prophets* of our day ; and shocked public morals by their indecencies.[2]   They were

man hath his choice, if gay clothing and a liquorish tooth after sack, sugar, and plums lick not away his bread too fast, all which are but ordinary among those that were not able to bring their own person over at their first coming.   There are not many towns in the country but the poorest person in them hath a house and land of his own, and bread of his own growing, if not some cattle.   Flesh is now no rare food, beef, pork, and mutton being frequent in many houses ; so that this poor wilderness hath not only equalized England in food, but goes beyond it in some places for the great plenty of wine and sugar which is ordinarily used, and apples, pears, and quince tarts, instead of their former pumpkin pies.   Poultry they have plenty."   At that time thirty-two trades were carried on in the colony, and shoes were manufactured for exportation.

[1] This is a fac-simile of the first money coined in America.   The mint-master, who was allowed to take fifteen pence out of every twenty shillings, for his trouble in coining, made a large fortune by it.   Henry Sewall, the founder of Newbury, in Massachusetts, married his only daughter, a plump girl of eighteen years.   When the wedding ceremony was ended, a large pair of scales was brought out and suspended.   In one disk the blushing bride was placed, and " pine tree shillings," as the coin was called, were poured into the other until there was an equipoise.   The money was then handed to Mr. Sewall as his wife's dowry, amounting to a handsome sum in those days.   There are a few pieces of this money still in existence.   One which I saw in the possession of a gentleman in New York was not as much worn as many of the Spanish quarters now in circulation among us.   The silver appeared to be very pure.

[2] Hutchinson mentions many instances of fanaticism on the part of the so-called Quakers.   Some at Salem, Hampton, Newbury, and other places, went into the meeting-houses in time of worship, called the ministers vile hirelings, and the people an abomination.   Thomas Newhouse went into the meeting-house at Boston with two glass bottles, and, breaking them in the presence of the whole congregation, exclaimed, " Thus will the Lord break you in pieces."   Mary Brewster went into meeting, having her face smeared with soot and grease ; another young married woman, Deborah Wilson, went through the streets of Salem perfectly naked, in emulation of the Prophet Ezekiel, as a sign of the nakedness of the land.   They were whipped through the streets at the tail of a cart.   Ann Hartley declared herself a prophetess, and had many followers who seceded from the congregation of Boston, and zealously propagated schism.   A Quaker woman entered a church in Boston, while the congregation were worshiping, clothed in sackcloth, with ashes on her head, her feet bare, and her face blackened so as to personify small-pox, the punishment with which she threatened the colony.—See Hutchinson's *History of Massachusetts*, i., 202–4.

Whipping was the usual punishment.   Marmaduke Stephenson, William Robinson, Mary Dyer, and William Leddra were hanged.   Mary Dyer was publicly whipped through the streets of Boston.   Dorothy Waugh was three times imprisoned, three times banished, and once whipped, and her clothes sold.   William Brand was four times imprisoned, four times banished, twice whipped, and branded.   John Copeland was seven times imprisoned, seven times banished, three times whipped, and had his ears cut off.   Christopher Holden was five times banished, five times imprisoned, twice whipped, and had his ears cut off.   These four were the leading characters who suffered in one year.—*New England's Ensigne*, p. 105.

first tenderly dealt with and kindly admonished.   Penalties ensued, and life was finally taken, before some of them would cease interference with the popular ceremonials of religion. The exercise of power to maintain subordination finally grew to persecution, and the benevolent Puritan became, almost from necessity, a persecutor.   Enactments for the preservation of good order were necessary, but the sanguinary laws against particular doctrines and tenets can not be defended.

The Quaker sect sprang up in England about 1650, under George Fox, and received their name from the peculiar shaking or quaking of their bodies and limbs while preaching.   They went further than the straitest Puritans in disregarding human authority when opposed to the teachings of the Bible, yet they were allowed full liberty of action during the protectorate of Oliver Cromwell.   They denounced war, persecution for religious opinions, and, above all, the slavish idolatry demanded by rulers in Church and State of those under their control. They condemned all ordained and paid priesthoods, refused to take oaths, and thus struck a direct blow at the hierarchy.   They differed from the Puritans in many things, and became noxious to them.   They derived their system of morals and politics chiefly from the New Testament, while the Puritans took theirs from the more sanguinary and intolerant codes of the old dispensation.   Laying aside the falsehoods of politeness and flattery, they renounced all titles, addressed all men, high or low, by the plain title of Friend, used the expressions yea and nay, and thee and thou ; and offices of kindness and affection to their fellow-creatures, according to the injunction of the Apostle James, constituted their practical religion. " The Quakers might be regarded as representing that branch of the primitive Christians who esteemed Christianity an entirely new dispensation, world-wide in its objects ; while the Puritans represented those Judaizing Christians who could not get rid of the idea of a peculiar chosen people, to wit, themselves."[1]

The English Puritans had warned their brethren in America against these " children of hell," and the first appearance in the colony of Mary Fisher and Ann Austin, who came from Barbadoes, and professed the new doctrine, greatly alarmed the New England theocracy. A special law was enacted, by which to bring a " known Quaker" into the colony was punishable with a fine of five hundred dollars, and the exaction of bonds to carry him back again. The Quaker himself was to be whipped twenty stripes, sent to the House of Correction, and kept there until transported.   The introduction of Quaker books was prohibited ; defending Quaker opinions was punishable with fine, and finally banishment ;' and in 1657 it was enacted that for every hour's entertainment given to a Quaker the entertainer should pay forty shillings.   It was also enacted that every male Quaker should lose an ear on the first conviction, and the other on a second ; and both males and females, on a third conviction, were to have their tongues bored through with a red-hot iron.   In 1658 the death penalty was enacted.   Under it those who should return to the colony a second time, after banishment, were to suffer death.   From unwillingness to inflict death, it was provided by a new law, in 1658, that any person convicted of being a Quaker should be delivered to the constable of the town, " to be stripped naked from the middle upward, and tied to a cart's tail, and whipped through the town, and thence be immediately conveyed to the constable of the next town toward the border of our jurisdiction, and so from constable to constable, to any the outermost town, and so to be whipped out of the colony. '   In case of return, this was to be twice repeated.   The fourth time the convict was to be branded with a letter R on the left shoulder, and after that, if incorrigible, to incur the death penalty.   Chiefly through the instrumentality of King William, these penal laws against the Quakers were abrogated by royal authority, and that sect became an important element in American society during the eighteenth century.   In Pennsylvania and New Jersey, as we shall hereafter see, the Quakers had a strong controlling influence during the Revolution.

In 1675 King Philip's war commenced, and almost all the Indians in New England were involved in it.   This will be noticed when we are considering my visit to the neighborhood

---

[1] Hildreth, i., 404.

OF THE REVOLUTION. 451

Arrival of Andross.   His Extortions.   Revolution in England.   Government of Massachusetts.   Hostilities with the French

of Mount Hope, the residence of the great sachem.   Upon the heels of this war, when the colonies were much distressed, the ministers of the second James conspired, as we have seen. to destroy popular government in America, and consolidate power in the throne.   A decision was procured in the High Court of Chancery, declaring the American charters forfeited, because of the alleged exercise of powers, on the part of the colonial governments, not recognized by those charters.   Sir Edmund Andross, who came with the title of governor gen eral, and empowered to take away their charters from the colonists, made Boston his head-quarters.   He came with the fair mask of kindness, which was soon cast off.   Fees 1687 of all officers were increased ; public thanksgivings without royal permission were forbidden . the press was restrained ; land titles were abrogated, and the people were obliged to petition for new patents, sometimes at great expense ; and in various ways Andross and others man aged to enrich themselves by oppressing and impoverishing the inhabitants.   The free spirit

THE BEACON.

of New England was aroused, and the people became very restive under the tyrant.   Secret meetings were held, in which the propriety of open resistance was discussed ; but before the people of Boston, aft erward so famous for their bold opposition to imperial power, lifted the arm of defiance, the news came that James was an exile, and that William and Mary were firmly seated on the throne of En- 1688. gland.   Boston was in great commotion.   People flocked in from the country, and cries of " Down with all tyrants" were mingled with the notes of joy rung out by the church-bells.   Andross, alarmed, fled to the fort,[1] but was soon arrested, imprisoned, and, as already no- 1689. ticed, sent home for trial.   A new charter was received in 1692, when the territories of Plymouth, Maine, and Nova Scotia were added to Massachusetts.   By that charter the governor was appointed by the crown, and a property qualification was necessary to procure the privilege of the elective franchise in choosing the members of the General Court or Assembly.   Such was the government that existed when the Revolution broke out.

About this time the French, who had settled upon the St. Law rence, began to excite the Northern and Eastern Indians against the English settlements in New England.   Dover and Salmon Falls in New Hampshire, Casco in Maine, and Schenectady in New York were desolated.   The colony fitted out a force, under General Win throp, to attack Montreal, and a fleet, under Sir William Phipps, to besiege Quebec.   The expedition was a failure, and for seven years, until the treaty of peace between France and England was concluded. the frontier was scourged by savage cruelties.   During this time military operations exhausted the treasury of Massachusetts, and 1690. the government emitted bills of credit, the first *paper money* issued in the American colonies.

From the beginning of the eighteenth century until the treaty of Paris, or, rather, of Fon tainbleau, in 1763, the New England colonies were continually agitated by successive wars

---

[1] The first fort was upon one of the three eminences in Boston, called Cornhill, from the circumstance that the first explorers found corn buried there.   The fort was completed in 1634.   It had complete com mand of the harbor.   It is now a green plat, two hundred feet in diameter, and called Washington Place The eminence is called Fort Hill.

Another of the eminences is called *Beacon Hill*, from the circumstance that on the top of it was a beacon pole, with a tar barrel at its apex, erected in 1635, which was to be fired, to give an alarm in the country, if Boston should be attacked by savages.   Upon a crane was suspended a basket containing some combusti bles for firing the barrel.   This beacon was blown down in 1789, and the next year a plain Doric column of brick and stone, incrusted with cement, was erected.   It was about sixty feet high, on an eight feet ped estal.   On the tablets of the pedestal were inscriptions commemorating the most important events from the passage of the Stamp Act until 1790.   This pedestal is preserved in the State House of Boston.   The mon ument stood a little north of the site of the present State House.   A view of the old beacon is given above.

452   PICTORIAL FIELD-BOOK

First American Paper money.   Prowess of Colonial Troops.   The French and Indian War.   The Revolutionary Era.

with the French and Indians, by jealousies concerning colonial rights, which acts of Parliament from time to time seemed to menace with subversion, and by the discontents arising

No (919) 20s

THIS Indented Bill of Twenty Shillings due from the Massachusets Colony to the Possessor shall be in value equal to money & shall be accordingly accepted by the Treasurer and Receivers subordinate to him in all Publick payments: and for any Stock at any time in the Treasury. Boston in New-England February the third 1690 By Order of the General Court

FAC-SIMILE OF THE FIRST AMERICAN PAPER MONEY.

from the avarice and misrule of royal governors sent over from England. For the wars they furnished full supplies of men and money, and it was chiefly by the prowess of colonial troops that French dominion in America was destroyed. During these wars the colonists discovered their own strength, and, doubtless, thoughts of independence often occupied the minds of many. The capture of Louisburg, the operations in Northern New York and upon Lake Ontario and the St. Lawrence, and the final passage of Quebec and Montreal into the hands of the English, have been noticed in former chapters. The campaign against the French posts on the Ohio and vicinity, when Washington first became distinguished as a military leader, will receive our attention hereafter.

We have now reached the borders of our Revolutionary era, and Boston, our point of view, where the first bold voice was heard and the first resolute arm uplifted against measures of the British Parliament that tended to abridge the liberties of the colonists, is a proper place whence to take a general survey of events immediately antecedent to, and connected with, that successful and righteous rebellion.

We have already observed, that after the expulsion of Andross a new charter was obtained by Massachusetts, but the governor thereafter was appointed by the crown. ^1688. This was the first link forged for the chain of absolutism with which England for nearly a century endeavored to enslave her American colonies. Such was the condition of all the colonies, except Connecticut and Rhode Island, whose original charters had never been surrendered. The other chartered communities were governed by men appointed by the king, but Connecticut and Rhode Island always enjoyed the democratic privilege of electing their own chief magistrates. These royal governors, by their exactions and their haughty disregard of public opinion in America, were greatly instrumental, it will be seen, in arousing the people to rebellion. Discontents, however, arising from an interference of the imperial government with the commerce of the colonies, had already begun to excite suspicions unfavorable to the integrity of the home government.

Among the first acts of Parliament, after the restoration of Charles II. in 1660, was the establishment of a board of commissioners, to have the general supervision of the commerce of the American colonies. This commission was afterward remodeled, and the *Board* ^1696. *of Trade and Plantations*, consisting of a president and seven members, known as LORDS OF TRADE, was established. This board had the general oversight of the commerce of the realm ; and, although its powers were subsequently somewhat curtailed, it exercised great influence, particularly in America, down to the time of the Revolution, and was the strong right arm of royalty here. It was the legalized spy upon all the movements of the people ; it watched the operations of the colonial assemblies ; and in every conceivable way it upheld the royal governors and the royal prerogatives. Under its auspices courts of vice-admiralty were established throughout the colonies, having powers similar to those of our United States District Courts, in which admiralty and revenue cases were tried without jury. These often exercised intolerable tyranny.

Previous to the establishment of the first commission, the acts of trade had so little ^1660. affected the colonists that they were hardly a subject of controversy ; but after the Restoration, the commercial restrictions, from which the New England colonies were exempt during the time of the commonwealth, were imposed with increased rigor. The harbors of the colonies were closed against all but English vessels ; such articles of American produce as were in demand in England were forbidden to be shipped to foreign markets ; the liberty of free trade among the colonies themselves was taken away, and they were forbidden to manufacture for their own use or for foreign markets those articles which would come in competition with English manufacturers. In addition to these oppressive commercial acts, a royal fleet arrived at Boston, bringing commissioners, who were instructed to hear ^1664. and determine all complaints that might exist in New England ; and they also had full power to take " such measures as they might deem expedient for settling the peace and security of the country on a solid foundation." The people justly regarded this commission as a prolific seed of tyranny planted among them. The colonists were alarmed, yet none but Massachusetts dared openly to complain. She alone, although professing the warmest loyalty to the king, openly asserted her chartered rights, and not only refused to acknowledge the authority of the commissioners, but protested against the exercise of their delegated powers within her domain. So noxious was the commission to the whole people, that it was soon abolished. In this boldness Massachusetts exhibited the germ of that opposition to royal authority for which she was afterward so conspicuous.

In 1672 the British Parliament enacted " that if any vessel which, by law, may trade in the plantations shall take on board any enumerated articles [mentioned in the act of 1660], and a bond shall not have been given with sufficient security to unlade them in England, there shall be rendered to his majesty, for sugars, tobacco, ginger, cocoa-nut, indigo, logwood, fustic, cotton, wool, the several duties mentioned in the law, to be paid in such places in the plantation, and to such officers as shall be appointed to collect the same ; and, for their better collection, it is enacted that the whole business shall be managed and the imposts shall be levied by officers appointed by the commissioners of imposts in England." This was the first act that imposed customs on the colonies alone ; this was the initial act of a series of like tenor, which drove them to rebellion.   The people justly complained, and as justly disregarded the law.   They saw in it a withering blight upon their infant commerce : they either openly disobeyed its injunctions, or eluded its provisions ; Barbadoes, Virginia, and Maryland, in particular, trafficked without restraint.

The colonies in general now began to regard the home government as an oppressor, and acted with a corresponding degree of independence.   Edward Randolph, afterward the surveyor general during the reign of William and Mary, writing to the commissioners of custom in 1676, iterated the declarations of the people that the law " made by Parliament obligeth them in nothing but what consists with the interests of the colonies ; *that the legislative power is and abides in them* SOLELY."   Governor Nicholson, of Maryland, writing

August 16.   in 1698, said, " I have observed that a great many people in all these colonies and provinces, especially those under proprietaries, and the two others under Connecticut and Rhode Island, think that no law of England ought to be in force and binding to them without their own consent ; for they foolishly say *they have no representative sent for themselves to the Parliaments of England;* and they look upon all laws made in England, that put any restraint upon them, to be great hardships."   Earlier than this the doctrine that the colonies should not be taxed without their consent was recognized by Lord Berkley and Sir George Cartwright, and not questioned by the king.   These distinguished men purchased

1664.   New Jersey of the Duke of York (afterward James II.), which he had taken from the Dutch by the authority of his brother Charles.

These "lords proprietors," for the better settlement of the pioneers, stipulated in their agreement with those who should commence plantations there that they (the proprietors) were " not to impose, or *suffer to be imposed*, any tax, custom, subsidy, tallage, assessment, or any other duty whatsoever, upon any color or pretense, upon the said province or inhabitants thereof, *other than what shall be imposed by the authority and consent of the General Assembly.*"[1]   In 1691 the New York General Assembly passed an act declaring " that no aid, tax, tallage, &c., whatsoever shall be laid, assessed, levied, or required of or on any of their majesties' [William and Mary] subjects within the provinces, &c., or their estates, in any manner of color or pretense whatsoever, but by the act and consent of the governor and council, and representatives of the people in General Assembly met and convened."   In 1692 the Massachusetts Legislature made a declaration in almost the same language, and almost all the colonies asserted, in some form, the same doctrine.   Thus we see that, nearly one hundred years before the Revolution, the fundamental principle upon which the righteousness of that rebellion relied for vindication—TAXATION AND REPRESENTATION ARE INSEPARABLE—was boldly asserted by the governed, and tacitly admitted by the supreme power as correct.

As early as 1729 the conduct of Massachusetts caused a suggestion in the House of Commons that it was the design of that colony " to shake off its dependency."   Governor Burnet, of New York, was appointed chief magistrate of the province in 1728.   The display that attended his reception at Boston, and the appearance of general prosperity on every hand, determined him to demand a fixed and liberal salary from the Assembly, a demand which had involved Shute, his predecessor, in continual bickerings with that body.   Burnet made the demand in his inaugural address, and the Assembly treated it in such a manner that immediately afterward the Council expressed their reprehension of the undutiful conduct of the members.   So bold was the Assembly in denying royal prerogatives and refusing obedience

1731.   to laws, that when Massachusetts petitioned the House of Commons, praying that they might be heard by counsel on the subject of grievances, that body resolved " That the petition was frivolous and groundless, a high insult upon his majesty's [George I.] government, and *tending to shake off the dependency of the said colony upon this kingdom, to which, in law and right, they ought to be subject.*"[2]

In 1739 a proposition was made to Sir Robert Walpole to tax the American colonies, but

---

[1] Smith's History of New Jersey, p. 517.   [2] Smith's History of New York, p. 75.

that statesman took an enlightened and liberal view, and said, smiling, " I will leave that to some of my successors who have more courage than I have, and are less friends to commerce than I am.   It has been a maxim with me, during my administration, to encourage the trade of the American colonies in the utmost latitude ; nay, it has been necessary to pass over some irregularities in their trade with Europe ; for, by encouraging them to an extensive growing commerce, if they gain five hundred thousand pounds, I am convinced that in two years afterward full two hundred and fifty thousand pounds of their gains will be in his majesty's exchequer, by the labor and produce of this kingdom, as immense quantities of every kind of our manufactories go thither ; and as they increase in their foreign American trade, more of our produce will be wanted.   This is taxing them more agreeably to their own Constitution and ours."   Had these views continued to prevail in the British cabinet, George III. might not have " lost the brightest jewel in his crown ;" had Walpole yielded, the republic of the United States might have existed almost half a century earlier.

Walpole's successors *were* " more courageous" than he, and " less friends to commerce," for in 1750 an act was passed, declaring " That from and after the 24th of June, 1750, no mill or other engine for slitting or rolling of iron, or any platting forge to work with a tilt-hammer, or any furnace for making steel, shall be erected, or, after such erection, continued, in any of his majesty's colonies in America."   The Navigation Act of 1660 was retained in full force.   Hatters were forbidden to have, at one time, more than two apprentices ; the importation of sugar, rum, and molasses was not allowed without the payment of considerable duties ; and the felling of pitch-pine-trees not within inclosures was prohibited.   True, these revenue laws were administered with much laxity, as Walpole acknowledged, and the colonies were not much oppressed by them, yet they practically asserted the right to tax the Americans—a right that was strenuously denied.   These things were, therefore, real griev ances, for they foreshadowed those intentions to enslave America which were afterward more boldly avowed.

I have noticed the Colonial Congress (page 303) held at Albany in 1754, when Dr. Franklin submitted a plan for the union of the colonies for the general good, and when Massachusetts, ever jealous of her rights, instructed her representatives to oppose any scheme for taxing them.   The war that had then just commenced (the Seven Years' War) soon diverted the attention of the colonists from the commercial grievances of which they complained, and as the common dangers multiplied, loyalty increased.   Cheerfully did they tax themselves. and contribute men, money, and provisions, for that contest.   They lost by the war twenty-five thousand of their robust young men, exclusive of sailors.   Upon application of Admiral Saunders, the squadron employed against Louisburg and Quebec was supplied with five hundred seamen from Massachusetts, besides many who were impressed out of vessels on the fishing banks.   During the whole war Massachusetts contributed its full quota of troops annually, and also, at times, furnished garrisons for Louisburg and Nova Scotia in addition.   That colony alone contributed more than five millions of dollars, in which sum is not included the expense of forts and garrisons on the frontiers.   Besides these public expenditures, there must have been almost an equal amount drawn from the people by extra private expenses and personal services.   The taxes imposed to meet the pressing demands upon all sides were enormous,[1] and men of wealth gave freely toward encouraging the raising of new levies.   This, it must be remembered, was the heavy burden laid upon one colony.   Other provinces contributed largely, yet not so munificently as Massachusetts.   Probably the Seven Years' War cost the aggregate colonies twenty millions of dollars, besides the flower of their youth ; and in return Parliament granted them, during the contest, at different periods, about five mill-

---

[1] Such was the assessment in Boston one year during the war, that, if a man's income was three hundred dollars, he had to pay two thirds, or two hundred dollars, and in that proportion.   If his house was valued at one thousand dollars, he was obliged to pay three hundred and sixty dollars.   He had also to pay a poll tax for himself, and for every male member of his family over sixteen years of age, at the rate of nearly four dollars each.   In addition to all this, he paid his proportion of excise on tea, coffee, rum, and wine, if he used them.—*Gordon.*

ions four hundred and nine thousand dollars.[1]   Yet the British ministry, in 1760, while the colonies were so generously supporting the power and dignity of the realm, regarded their services as the mere exercise of a duty, and declared that, notwithstanding grants of money had been made to them, they expected to get it all back, by imposing a tax upon them after the war, in order to raise a revenue.   Such was the language of Mr. Pitt in a letter to Lieutenant-governor Fauquier, of Virginia.   The war ended favorably to Great Britain, and Massachusetts and other colonies looked forward with the full hope of uninterrupted prosperity. New men were at the helm of State.   The old king was dead, and his grandson, the eldest son of the deceased Frederic, prince of Wales, had ascended the throne with the title of George III.   This was the prince who ruled Great Britain sixty years, in which time was included our war for independence.

October 26, 1760.

---

[1] Parliament subsequently voted one million of dollars to the colonies, but, on account of the troubles arising from the Stamp Act and kindred measures, ministers withheld the sum.—*Pictorial History of the Reign of George III.*, i., 36.

The following is a list of " The grants in Parliament for Rewards, Encouragement, and Indemnification to the Provinces in North America, for their Services and Expenses during the last [seven years] War :

" On the 3d of February, 1756, as a free gift and reward to the colonies of New England, New York, and Jersey, for their past services, and as an encouragement to continue to exert themselves with vigor, voted $575,000.

" May 19th, 1757.   For the use and relief of the provinces of North and South Carolina, and Virginia, in recompense for services performed and to be performed, $250,000.

" June 1st, 1758.   To reimburse the province of Massachusetts Bay their expenses in furnishing provisions and stores to the troops raised by them in 1756, $136,900.   To reimburse the province of Connecticut their expenses for ditto, $68,680.

" April 30th, 1759.   As a compensation to the respective colonies for the expenses of clothing, pay of troops, &c., $1,000,000.

" March 31st, 1760.   For the same, $1,000,000.   For the colony of New York, to reimburse their expenses in furnishing provisions and stores to the troops in 1756, $14,885.

" January 20th, 1761.   As a compensation to the respective colonies for clothing, pay of troops, &c., $1,000,000.

" January 26th, 1762.   Ditto, $666,666.

" March 15th, 1763.   Ditto, $666,666.

" April 22d, 1770.   To reimburse the province of New Hampshire their expenses in furnishing provisions and stores to the troops in the campaign of 1756, $30,045.   Total, $5,408,842."

In a pamphlet entitled *The Rights of* BRITAIN *and Claims of* AMERICA, an answer to the Declaration of the Continental Congress, setting forth the causes and the necessity of their taking up arms, printed in 1776, I find a table showing the annual expenditures of the British government in support of the civil and military powers of the American colonies, from the accession of the family of Hanover, in 1714, until 1775.   The expression of the writer is, " Employed in the defense of America."   This is incorrect, for the wars with the French on this continent, which cost the greatest amount of money, were wars for conquest and territory, though ostensibly for the defense of the Anglo-American colonies against the encroachments of their Gallic neighbors.   During the period alluded to (sixty years) the sums granted for the army amounted to $43,899,625 ; for the navy, $50,000,000 ; money laid out in Indian presents, in holding Congresses, and purchasing cessions of land, $30,500,000 ; making a total of $123,899,625.   Within that period the following bounties on American commodities were paid : On indigo, $725,110 ; on hemp and flax, $27,800 ; on naval stores imported in Great Britain from America, $7,293,810 ; making the total sum paid on account of bounties $8,047,320.   The total amount of money expended in sixty years on account of America $131,946,945.

GREAT SEAL OF GEORGE III . THE PURSE, AND CHANCELLOR'S MACE

OF THE REVOLUTION. 457

Death of George II. announced to his Heir.   Influence of the Earl of Bute.   Cool Treatment of Mr. Pitt.

CHAPTER XX.

"In a chariot of light from the regions of day
    The goddess of Liberty came,
Ten thousand celestials directed the way,
    And hither conducted the dame.
A fair budding branch from the garden above,
    Where millions with millions agree,
She brought in her hand as a pledge of her love,
    And the plant she named *Liberty Tree.*

"The celestial exotic struck deep in the ground,
    Like a native it flourish'd and bore;
The fame of its fruit drew the nations around,
    To seek out this peaceable shore.
Unmindful of names or distinction they came,
    For freemen, like brothers, agree;
With one spirit indued, they one friendship pursued,
    And their temple was *Liberty Tree.*

"But hear, O ye swains ('tis a tale most profane),
    How all the tyrannical powers,
Kings, Commons, and Lords, are uniting amain
    To cut down this guardian of ours.
From the east to the west blow the trumpet to arms,
    Through the land let the sound of it flee;
Let the far and the near all unite with a cheer
    In defense of our *Liberty Tree.*"

                THOMAS PAINE.

HE intelligence of the death of his grandfather was communicated to George, the heir apparent, on the morning of the 25th of October, while he was riding on horseback, near Kew Palace, with his inseparable companion, the Earl of Bute. William Pitt, afterward Earl of Chatham, was the prime minister of the deceased king. He immediately repaired to Kew, where the young sovereign (then in his twenty-third year) remained during the day and night. On the 26th George[1] went to St. James's, where Pitt waited upon him, and presented a sketch of an address to be pronounced by the monarch at a meeting of the Privy Council. The minister was politely informed that a speech was already prepared, and that every preliminary was arranged. He at once perceived that the courtier, Bute, the favorite of the king's mother, and his majesty's tutor and abiding personal friend, had made these arrangements, and that he would doubtless occupy a conspicuous station in the new administration.

1760.

Bute was originally a poor Scottish nobleman, possessed of very little general talent, narrow in his political views, but favored with a fine person and natural grace of manners. He was a favorite of George's father, and continued to be an inti-

GEORGE III.
AT THE TIME OF HIS ACCESSION.
From an anonymous print.

---

[1] George the Third was the son of Frederic, prince of Wales. His mother was the beautiful Princess Augusta, of Saxe Gotha. He was born in London on the 24th of May, 1738 He was married in

mate friend of the king's mother after Prince Frederic's death.   Indeed, scandal uttered some unpleasant suggestions respecting this intimacy, even after the accession of George. " Not contented with being wise," said Earl Waldegrave, " he would be thought a polite scholar and a man of great erudition, but has the misfortune never to succeed, except with

those who are exceedingly ignorant ; for his historical knowledge is chiefly taken from tragedies, wherein he is very deeply read, and his classical learning extends no further than a French translation."[1]   Such was the man whom the young monarch unfortunately chose for his counselor and guide, instead of the wise and sagacious Pitt, who had contributed, by his talents and energy, so much to the glory of England during the latter years of the reign of George II.   Like Rehoboam, George " forsook the counsel which the old men gave him, and took counsel with the young men that were brought up with him, that stood before him." It was a sad mistake, and clouds of distrust gathered in the morning sky of his reign.   The opinion got abroad that he would be ruled by the queen dowager and Bute, and that the countrymen of the earl, whom the English disliked, would be subjects of special favor.   Murmurs were heard in many quarters, and somebody had the boldness to put up a placard on the Royal Exchange, with these words : " No petticoat government—no Scotch minister—no Lord George Sackville."

Thus, at the very outset of his reign, the king had opponents in his own capital.   A general feeling of discontent pervaded the people as soon as it was perceived that Pitt, their favorite, was likely to become secondary among the counselors of the king, or, which seemed more certain, would leave the cabinet altogether.   The latter event soon followed. Disgusted by the assurance and ignorance of Bute, and the apathetic submission of George to the control of the Scotch earl, and perceiving that all his plans, the execution of which was pressing his country forward in a career of glory and prosperity, were thwarted by the

USUAL APPEARANCE OF THE KING ABOUT 1776.
From a sketch by Gear.

September, 1761, nearly a year after his accession, to the Princess Charlotte, of Mecklenberg Strelitz, daughter of the late duke of that principality.   Her character resembled that of her husband.   Like him, she was domestic in her tastes and habits, decorous, rigid in the observance of moral duties, and benevolent in thought and action.   George was remarkable for the purity of his morals ; even while a young man, in the midst of the licentious court of his grandfather, and through life, he was a good pattern of a husband and father.   He possessed no brilliancy of talents, but common sense was a prime element in his intellectual character.   He was tender and benevolent, although he loved money ; and his resentments against those who willfully offended him were lasting.   He was always reliable ; honest in his principles and faithful to his promises, no man distrusted him.   Their majesties were crowned on the 22d of September, 1761, soon after their marriage, and a reform in the royal household at once commenced.   Their example contributed to produce a great change in manners.   " Before their time," says M'Farland, " the Court of St. James had much of the licentiousness of the Court of Versailles, without its polish ; during their time it became decent and correct, and its example gradually extended to the upper classes of society, where it was most wanted."

For two years, from 1787 to 1789, his majesty was afflicted with insanity. The malady returned in 1801, and terminated his political life.   He died on the 29th of January, 1820, aged nearly eighty-two years, this being the sixtieth year of his reign.   His queen died in 1818.

QUEEN CHARLOTTE.
From a print by Worlidge

[1] Waldegrave's Memoirs

supple tools of the favorite, he resigned his office. The regrets of the whole nation followed him into retirement, while George, really esteeming him more highly than any other states man in his realm, in testimony of his appreciation of his services, granted a peerage to his lady, and a pension of fifteen thousand dollars.

Greater discontents were produced in the colonies by the measures which the new admin istration adopted in relation to them. By the advice of Bute, who was the real head of the government, George set about "a reformation of the American charters." Secret agents were sent to travel in the different colonies, to procure access to the leading men, and to col lect such information respecting the character and temper of the people as would enable min isters to judge what regulations and alterations could be safely made in the police and gov ernment of the colonies, in order to their being brought more effectually under the control of Parliament. The business of these agents was also to conciliate men of capital and station, hoping thereby to enlist a large number of dependents ; but herein they erred. Unlike men in a similar condition in England, the man of wealth here could influence very few ; and in New England such was the general independence of the people, that such agency was of no avail. The object of the agents was too apparent to admit of doubt ; the proposed reform was but another name for despotism, and the gossamer covering of deceit could not hide the intention of the ministry.

The first *reform* measure which aroused the colonies to a lively sense of their danger was the issuing of WRITS OF ASSISTANCE. These were warrants to custom-house offi cers, giving them and their deputies a general power to enter houses or stores where it might be suspected that contraband goods were concealed. The idea of such latitude being given to the "meanest deputy of a deputy's deputy" created general indignation and alarm. It might cover the grossest abuses, and no man's privacy would be free from the invasion of these ministerial hirelings. Open resistance was resolved upon. In Boston public meetings were held, and the voice of the fearless James Otis the younger called boldly upon the people to breast any storm of ministerial vengeance that might be aroused by opposition here. The Assembly sided with the people, and even Governor Bernard was opposed to the measure. Respectful remonstrances to Parliament and petitions to the king were sent, but without ef fect. That short-sighted financier, George Grenville, was Bute's Chancellor of the Excheq uer. An exhausted treasury needed replenishing, and ministers determined to derive a rev enue from the colonies, either by direct taxation or by impost duties, rigorously levied and col lected. They had also determined in council upon bringing about an entire subservience of the colonies, politically, religiously, and commercially, to the will of the king and Parliament.[1]

1761.

---

[1] Dr. Gordon says he was informed by Dr. Langdon, of Portsmouth, New Hampshire, that as the Rev. Mr. Whitfield was about leaving that place, he said to Dr. Langdon, and Mr. Haven, the Congregational min ister, "I can't, in conscience, leave this town without acquainting you with a secret. My heart bleeds for America. O poor New England ! There is a deep-laid plot against both your civil and religious liberties, and they will be lost. Your golden days are at an end. You have nothing but trouble before you. My information comes from the best authority in Great Britain. I was allowed to speak of the affair in general, but enjoined not to mention particulars. Your liberties will be lost."—*Gordon,* i., 102. It was known that, among other *reforms,* the Puritan, or dissenting, influence in religious matters was to be curtailed, if not de stroyed, by the establishment of Episcopacy in the colonies. The throne and the hierarchy were, in a meas ure, mutually dependent. In 1748 Dr. Secker, the archbishop of Canterbury, had proposed the establish ment of Episcopacy in America, and overtures were made to some Puritan divines to accept the miter, but without effect. The colonists, viewing Episcopacy in its worst light, as exhibited in the early days of the American settlements, had been taught to fear such power, if it should happen to be wielded by the hand of a crafty politician, more than the arm of civil government. They knew that if Parliament could create dioceses and appoint bishops, it would introduce tithes and crush heresy. For years controversy ran high upon this subject, much acrimony appeared on both sides, and art was brought in requisition to enforce ar guments. In the Political Register for 1769 is a picture entitled "*An Attempt to land a Bishop in Amer ica.*" A portion of a vessel is seen, on the side of which is inscribed *The Hillsborough.** She is lying be side a wharf, on which is a crowd of earnest people, some with poles pushing the vessel from her moorings. One holds up a book inscribed *Sidney on Government ;* another has a volume of *Locke's Essays ;* a third, in the garb of a Quaker, holds an open volume inscribed *Barclay's Apology ;* and from the mouth of a fourth

---

* Lord Hillsborough was then the Colonial Secretary, and it was presumed to be a plan of his to send a bishop to the colonies.

The idea of colonial subserviency was, indeed, general in England, and, according to Pitt, "even the chimney-sweepers of the streets talked boastingly of their *subjects* in America."[1] The admiralty undertook the labor of enforcing the laws, in strict accordance with the letter, and intrusted the execution thereof to the commanders of vessels, whose authoritative habits made them most unfit agents for such a service against such a people. Vessels engaged in contraband trade were seized and confiscated, and the colonial commerce with the West Indies was nearly annihilated.

GEORGE GRENVILLE.[2]

From causes never clearly understood, Lord Bute resigned the premiership on the 8th of April, 1763, and was succeeded by George Grenville, who, for a time, had fought shoulder to shoulder with Pitt, but had deserted him to take office under the Scotch earl. Grenville is represented as an honest statesman, of great political knowledge and indefatigable application ; but his mind, according to Burke, could not extend beyond the circle of official routine, and was unable to estimate the result of untried measures. He proved an unprofitable counselor for the king, for he began a political warfare against the celebrated journalist, John Wilkes, which resulted in the most serious partisan agitation throughout the kingdom ; and he originated the Stamp Act, by which Great Britain lost her American colonies.

is a scroll inscribed *No lords, spiritual or temporal, in New England.* Half way up the shrouds of the vessel is a bishop in his robes, his miter falling, and a volume of *Calvin's works,* hurled by one on shore, about to strike his head ; from his mouth issues a scroll inscribed, "*Lord, now lettest thou thy servant depart in peace.*" In the foreground is a paper inscribed, " *Shall they be obliged to maintain bishops that can not maintain themselves ?*" and near it is a monkey in the act of throwing a stone at the bishop. This print well illustrates the spirit of the times.

William Livingston, afterward governor of New Jersey, seems to have been one of the most eminent writers against Episcopacy, and Dr. Chandler and Samuel Seabury (afterward bishop) were among its chief supporters. An anonymous writer, whose alias was Timothy Tickle, Esq., wrote a series of powerful articles in favor of Episcopacy, in Hugh Gaines's New York Mercury, in 1768, supposed by some to be Dr. Auchmuty, of Trinity Church. The Synod of Connecticut passed a vote of thanks to Livingston for his essays, while in Gaines's paper he was lampooned by a shrewd writer in a poem of nearly two hundred lines. Livingston wrote anonymously, and the poet thus refers to the author :

> "Some think him a *Tindall,* some think him a *Chubb,*
> Some think him a *Ranter* that spouts from his *Tub ;*
> Some think him a *Newton,* some think him a *Locke,*
> Some think him a *Stone,* some think him a *Stock*—
> But a *Stock* he at least may thank Nature for giving,
> And if he's a STONE, I pronounce it a LIVING."

Episcopacy *was* introduced into America, took root, and flourished ; and when the Revolution broke out, seven or eight years afterward, there were many of its adherents found on the side of liberty, though, generally, so intimate was its relation, through the Mother Church, to the throne, its loyalty became a subject of reproach and suspicion, for the Episcopal clergy, as a body, were active or passive Loyalists.

[1] Parliamentary Debates, iii., 210.

[2] George Grenville was born in 1722, and in 1750 became a member of the House of Commons, where he was distinguished for his eloquence and general knowledge. He was made Treasurer of the Navy in 1754, and in 1760 was appointed Chancellor of the Exchequer. He became First Lord of the Treasury, or prime minister, in 1763, and the next year originated the famous Stamp Act. He resigned his office to Rockingham in 1765, and died on the 13th of November, 1770, aged fifty-eight years. He married the daughter of Sir William Wyndham. The late Marquis of Buckingham, who inherited the family estates in Buckinghamshire, was his eldest son.

Grenville found an empty treasury, and the national debt increased, in consequence of recent wars, to nearly seven hundred millions of dollars. To meet the current expenses of government, heavy taxation was necessary, and the English people were loudly complaining of the burden. Grenville feared to increase the weight, and looked to the American colonies for relief. He conceived the *right*[1] to draw a revenue from them to be undoubted, and, knowing their ability to pay, he formed a plan to tax them indirectly by levying new duties upon foreign articles imported by the Americans. A bill for levying these duties passed the House of Commons in March, 1764, without much notice, except from General Conway, who saw in it the seeds of further encroachments upon the liberties of the colonists. The Assembly of Massachusetts, acting in accordance with instructions given to the Boston representatives, had already denied the right to impose duties. Mr. Otis had published a pamphlet called "The Rights of the British Colonists asserted," which was highly approved here, and a copy was sent to the Massachusetts agent in England. In that pamphlet Mr. Otis used the strong language, "If we are not represented we are slaves!"

Thatcher, of Boston, also published a tract against Parliamentary taxation, and similar publications were made by Dulaney, the secretary of the province of Maryland, by Bland, a leading member of the House of Burgesses of Virginia, and "by authority" in Rhode Island.

On the 5th of May Mr. Grenville submitted to the House of Commons an act proposing a stamp duty,[2] at the same time assuring the colonial agents, with whom he had conferred, that he should not press its adoption that session, but would leave the scheme open for consideration. He required the colonies to pay into the treasury a million of dollars per annum, and he would leave it to them to devise a better plan, if possible, than the proposed stamp duty. The idea was not original with Mr. Grenville. It had been held out as early as 1739, by a club of American merchants, at the head of whom were Sir William Keith, governor of Pennsylvania, Joshua Gee, and others. In the colonial Congress at Albany, in 1754, a stamp act was talked of, and at that time Dr. Franklin thought it a just plan for taxing the colonies, conceiving that its operations would affect the several governments fairly and equally. Early in January (1764) Mr. Huske, a native of Portsmouth, New Hampshire, who had obtained a seat in Parliament, desirous of displaying his excessive loyalty, alluded to the proposition of a stamp duty made at the Albany Convention, and delighted the House by asserting the ability of the colonists to pay a liberal tax, and recommending the levying of one that should amount annually to two and a half millions of dollars.[3] With these precedents, and the present assurance of Huske, Grenville brought forward his bill. It was received, and, on motion of the mover, its consideration was postponed until the next session.

When the new impost law (which was, in fact, a continuation of former similar acts) and the proposed Stamp Act reached America, discontent was every where visible. Instead of being in a condition to pay taxes, the colonies had scarcely recovered from the effects of the late war; and the more unjust appeared the Stamp Act, when the previous act was about

1764.

---

[1] Early in March, 1764, it was debated in the House of Commons whether they had a *right* to tax the Americans, they not being represented, and it was determined unanimously in the affirmative. Of this vote, and the evident determination of ministers to tax the colonies, Mr. Mauduit, the agent of Massachusetts, informed the Assembly, and that body immediately resolved, "That the sole right of giving and granting the money of the people of that province was vested in them as the legal representatives; and that the imposition of taxes and duties by the Parliament of Great Britain, upon a people who are not represented in the House of Commons, is absolutely irreconcilable with their rights—That no man can justly take the property of another without his consent; upon which original principle the right of representation in the same body which exercises the power of making laws for levying taxes, one of the main pillars of the British Constitution, is evidently founded."

[2] It provided that every skin, or piece of vellum, or parchment, or sheet, or piece of paper used for legal purposes, such as bills, bonds, notes, leases, policies of insurance, marriage licenses, and a great many other documents, in order to be held valid in courts of law, was to be stamped, and sold by public officers appointed for that purpose, at prices which levied a stated tax on every such document. The Dutch had used stamped paper for a long time, and it was familiar to English merchants and companies, but in America it was almost wholly unknown.

[3] Gordon, i., 110; Jackson's letter to Lieutenant-governor Hutchinson, December 26th, 1765.

to intercept their profitable trade with the Spanish main and the West Indies, whence they derived much of their means to pay a tax. The *right* to tax them was also strenuously denied, and all the colonial Assemblies, wherever the subject was brought up, asserted their sole right to tax themselves. New England passed strong resolutions of remonstrance, and forwarded earnest petitions to the king to pause; and Virginia and New York adopted the same course, using firm, but respectful, language. They demonstrated, by fair argument, that the colonies were neither actually nor virtually represented in the British Parliament; they declared that they had hitherto supposed the pecuniary assistance which Great Britain had given them (the Parliamentary grants during the war) offered from motives of humanity, and not as the price of their liberty; and if she now wished a remuneration, she must make allowance for all the assistance she had received from the colonies during the late war, and for the oppressive restrictions she had imposed upon American commerce. They plainly told Great Britain that, as for her protection, they had full confidence in their own ability to protect themselves against any foreign enemy.

Remonstrances and petitions were sent by the colonies to their agents in London (some of whom had not opposed the Stamp Act), with explicit instructions to prevent, as far as they had power to act, the adoption of any scheme for taxing Americans. At this crisis Franklin was appointed agent for Pennsylvania; and other colonies, relying upon his skill and wisdom in diplomacy, his thorough acquaintance with government affairs, his personal influence in England, and, above all, his fearlessness, also intrusted him with the management of their affairs abroad. When he arrived in London, Grenville and other politicians waited upon him, and consulted him respecting the proposed Stamp Act. He told them explicitly that it was an unwise measure; that Americans would never submit to be taxed without their consent, and that such an act, if attempted to be enforced, would endanger the unity of the empire. Pitt, though living in retirement at his country seat at Hayes, was not an indifferent spectator, and he also consulted Franklin upon the important subject.

No doubt the expressed opinion of Franklin delayed, for a while, the introduction of the Stamp Act into the House of Commons, for it was not submitted until the 7th of February following. In the mean while respectful petitions and remonstrances were received from America, indicating a feeling of general opposition to ministers, and a determination not to be sheared by the " Gentle Shepherd."[1] The king, in his speech on the opening of Parliament, alluded to American taxation, and the manifest discontent in the colonies; yet, regardless of the visible portents of a storm, recommended the adoption of Grenville's scheme, and assured Parliament that he should use every endeavor to enforce obedience in America. The bill, containing fifty-five resolutions, was brought in, and Mr. Charles Townshend, the most eloquent man in the Commons, in the absence of Pitt, spoke in its favor, concluding with the following peroration: " And now will these Americans, children planted by our care, nourished up by our indulgence until they are grown to a degree of strength and opulence, and protected by our arms, will they grudge to contribute their mite to relieve us from the heavy weight of that burden which we lie under?" Colonel Barré arose, and, echoing Townshend's words, thus commented: " *They planted by your care!* No, your *oppressions* planted them in America. They fled from your tyranny, to a then uncultivated and inhospitable country, where they exposed themselves to almost all the hardships to which human nature is liable, and, among others, to the cruelties of a savage foe, the most subtle, and I will take upon me to say, the most formidable of any people upon the face of God's earth; yet, actuated by principles of true English liberty, they met all hardships with pleasure compared with those they suffered in their own

1765.

January 10, 1765.

February 7, 1765.

---

[1] In the course of a debate on the subject of taxation, in 1762, Mr. Grenville contended that the money was wanted, that government did not know where to lay another tax; and, addressing Mr. Pitt, he said, " Why does he not tell us where we can levy another tax?" repeating, with emphasis, " Let him tell me where—only tell me where!" Pitt, though not much given to joking, hummed in the words of a popular song, " Gentle shepherd, tell me where!" The House burst into a roar of laughter, and christened George Grenville THE GENTLE SHEPHERD.—*Pictorial History of the Reign of George III.*, i., 34.

OF THE REVOLUTION. 463

Barré's Speech rebuking Townshend.   His Defense of the Americans.   Effect of his Speech.   Passage of the Stamp Act.

country, from the hands of those who should have been their friends. *They nourished up by your indulgence!* They grew by your *neglect* of them. As soon as you began to care

COLONEL BARRÉ.[2]

about them, that care was exercised in sending persons to rule them in one department and another, who were, perhaps, the deputies of deputies to some members of this House, sent to spy out their liberties, to misrepresent their actions, and to prey upon them—men whose behavior on many occasions has caused the blood of those SONS OF LIBERTY[1] to recoil within them—men promoted to the highest seats of justice; some who, to my knowledge, were glad, by going to a foreign country, to escape being brought to the bar of public justice in their own. *They protected by your arms!* They have nobly taken up arms in your defense; have exerted a valor, amid their constant and laborious industry, for the defense of a country whose frontier was drenched in blood, while its interior parts yielded all its little savings to your emoluments. And believe me—remember I this day told you so—that same spirit of freedom which actuated that people at first will accompany them still; but

prudence forbids me to explain myself further. God knows I do not at this time speak from motives of party heat; what I deliver are the genuine sentiments of my heart. However superior to me, in general knowledge and experience, the respectable body of this House may be, I claim to know more of America than most of you, having seen and been conversant in that country. The people, I believe, are as truly loyal as any subjects the king has; but a people jealous of their liberties, and who will vindicate them if ever they should be violated. But the subject is too delicate; I will say no more." For a moment after the utterance of these solemn truths the House remained in silent amazement; but the utter ignorance of American affairs, and the fatal delusion wrought by ideas of royal power and colonial weakness, which prevailed in that assembly, soon composed their minds.[3] Very little debate was had upon the bill, and it passed the House after a single division, by a majority of two hundred and fifty to fifty. In the Lords it received scarcely any opposition. On the 22d of March the king cheerfully gave his assent, and the famous Stamp Act—the entering wedge for the dismemberment of the British empire—became a law. The protests of colonial agents, the remonstrances of London merchants trading with America, and the wise suggestions of men acquainted with the temper and resources of Americans were set at naught, and the infatuated ministry openly declared " that it was intended *to establish the power of Great Britain to tax the colonies*." " The sun of liberty is set," wrote Dr. Franklin to Charles Thom-

---

[1] This was the origin of the name which the associated patriots in America assumed when the speech of Barré reached the colonies, and organized opposition to the Stamp Act was commenced.

[2] Isaac Barré was born in 1727. His early years were devoted to study and military pursuits, and he attained the rank of colonel in the British army. Through the influence of the Marquis of Landsdowne he obtained a seat in the House of Commons, where he was ever the champion of American freedom. For several years previous to his death he was afflicted with blindness. He died July 1st, 1802, aged seventy-five years. Some have attributed the authorship of the celebrated *Letters of Junius* to Colonel Barré, the Marquis of Landsdowne, and Counselor Dunning, jointly, but the conjecture is unsupported by any argument.

[3] The apathy that prevailed in the British Parliament at that time respecting American affairs was astonishing, considering the interests at issue. Burke, in his Annual Register, termed it the " most languid debate" he had ever heard; and so trifling did the intelligent Horace Walpole consider the subject, that, in reporting every thing of moment to the Earl of Hertford, he devoted but a single paragraph of a few lines to the debate that day on America. Indeed, Walpole honestly confessed his total ignorance of American affairs.

son[1] the very night that the act was passed ; " the Americans must light the lamps of industry and economy."

When intelligence of the passage of the Stamp Act reached America, it set the whole country in a blaze of resentment. Massachusetts and Virginia—the *head* and the *heart* of the Revolution—were foremost and loudest in their denunciations, while New York and Pennsylvania were not much behind them in boldness and zeal. All the colonies were shaken, and from Maine to Georgia there was a spontaneous expression of determined resistance.

In October, 1764, the New York Assembly appointed a committee to correspond with their agent in Great Britain, and with the several colonial Assemblies, on the subject of opposition to the Stamp Act and other oppressive measures of Parliament.[2] In the course of their correspondence, early in 1765, this committee urged upon the colonial Assemblies the necessity of holding a convention of delegates to remonstrate and protest against the continued violation of their rights and liberties. Massachusetts was the first to act upon this suggestion. That action originated with James Otis, Jr., and his father, while visiting a sister of the former one evening at Plymouth.[3] The recommendation of the New York committee was the subject of conversation. It was agreed to propose action on the subject in the General Assembly, and on the 6th of June the younger Mr. Otis, who was a member of the Legislature, made a motion in the House, which was adopted, that " It is highly expedient there should be a meeting, as soon as may be, of committees from the Houses of Representatives, or burgesses, in the several colonies, to consult on the present circumstances of the colonies, and the difficulties to which they are, and must be, reduced, and to consider of a general address—to be held at New York the first Tuesday in October." The following circular letter was also adopted by the Assembly, and a copy ordered to be sent to the Speaker of each of the colonial Assemblies in America :

"Boston, June, 1765.

" SIR—The House of Representatives of this province, in the present session of general court, have unanimously agreed to propose a meeting, as soon as may be, of committees from the Houses of Representatives, or burgesses, of the several British colonies on this continent, to consult together on the present circumstances of the colonies, and the difficulties to which they are, and must be, reduced by the operation of the acts of Parliament for levying duties and taxes on the colonies ; and to consider of a general and united, dutiful, loyal, and humble representation of their condition to his majesty and to the Parliament, and to implore relief.

" The House of Representatives of this province have also voted to propose that such meeting be at the city of New York, in the province of New York, on the first Tuesday in October next, and have appointed a committee of three of their members to attend that service, with such as the other Houses of Representatives, or burgesses, in the several colonies, may think fit to appoint to meet them ; and the committee of the House of Representatives of this province are directed to repair to the said New York, on the first Tuesday in October next, accordingly ; if, therefore, your honorable House should agree to this proposal, it would

---

[1] Mr. Thompson was afterward the Secretary of the Continental Congress. In reply to Franklin's letter he said, " Be assured, we shall light torches of another sort," predicting the convulsions that soon followed.

[2] This committee consisted of Robert R. Livingston, John Cruger, Philip Livingston, William Bayard, and Leonard Lispenard. Mr. Cruger was then mayor of the city and Speaker of the Assembly.

[3] This sister was Mrs. Mercy Warren, wife of James Warren, Esq., of Plymouth, one of the members of the General Court. She wrote an excellent history of our Revolution, which was published in three volumes in 1805. She was born September 5th, 1728, at Barnstable, Massachusetts. Her youth was passed in the retirement of a quiet home, and reading, drawing, and needle-work composed the bulk of her recreations. She married Mr. Warren at the age of twenty-six. The family connections of both were extensive and highly respectable, and she not only became intimately acquainted with the leading men of the Revolution in Massachusetts, but was thoroughly imbued with the republican spirit. Her correspondence was quite extensive, and, as she herself remarks of her home, " by the Plymouth fireside were many political plans originated, discussed, and digested." She kept a faithful record of passing events, out of which grew her excellent history. She wrote several dramas and minor poems, all of which glow with the spirit of the times. Mrs. Warren died on the 19th of October, 1814, in the eighty-seventh year of her age.

be acceptable that as early notice of it as possible might be transmitted to the Speaker of the House of Representatives of this province."

This letter was favorably received by the other colonies, and delegates to the proposed Congress were appointed. They met in the city of New York on the first Monday in October. The time was earlier than the meeting of several of the colonial Assemblies, and, consequently, some of them were denied the privilege of appointing delegates. The Governors of Virginia, North Carolina, and Georgia refused to call the Assemblies together for the purpose. It was, therefore, agreed that *committees* from any of the colonies should have seats as delegates, and under this rule New York was represented by its corresponding committee. Nine of the thirteen colonies were represented, and the Assemblies of New Hampshire, Virginia, North Carolina, and Georgia wrote that they would agree to whatever was done by the Congress.[1]

The Convention was organized by the election, by ballot, of Timothy Ruggles, of Massachusetts, as chairman, and the appointment of John Cotten clerk. It continued in session fourteen consecutive days, and adopted a *Declaration of Rights*, a *Petition to the King*, and a *Memorial to both Houses of Parliament*, in all of which the principles that governed the leaders of the soon-following Revolution were clearly set forth. These documents, so full of the spirit of men determined to be free, and so replete with enlightened political wisdom, are still regarded as model state papers.[2]

All the delegates affixed their signatures of approval to the proceedings, except Mr. Ruggles, the president, and Mr. Ogden, of New Jersey, both of whom thus early manifested their defection from a cause which they afterward openly opposed. The conduct of the former drew down upon him a vote of censure from the Massachusetts House of Representatives, and he was reprimanded, in his place, by the Speaker. He and Otis were the leaders of the opposite parties, and as the Revolution advanced Ruggles became a bitter Tory.[3] Ogden was also publicly censured for his conduct on that occasion, was burned in effigy, and at the next meeting of the Assembly of New Jersey was dismissed from the Speaker's chair, which honorable post he held at the time of the Congress. The deputies of three of the colonies not having been authorized by their respective Assemblies to address the king and Parliament, did not sign the petition and memorial. All the colonies, by the votes of their respective Assemblies, when they convened subsequently, approved the measures adopted by the Congress; and before the day on which the noxious act was to take effect, America spoke with one voice to the king and his ministers, denouncing the measure, and imploring them to be just. November 1, 1765.

On the passage of the Stamp Act officers were appointed in the several colonies, to receive and distribute the stamped parchments and papers. The colonial agents in England were consulted, and those whom they recommended as discreet and proper persons were appointed. The agents generally had opposed the measure, but, now that it had become a law, they were disposed to make the best of it. Mr. Ingersoll, whom I have mentioned in

---

[1] The following delegates were present at the organization of the Convention:
Massachusetts.—James Otis, Oliver Partridge, Timothy Ruggles.
New York.—Robert R. Livingston, John Cruger, Philip Livingston, William Bayard, Leonard Lispenard.
New Jersey.—Robert Ogden, Hendrick Fisher, Joseph Borden.
Rhode Island.—Metcalf Bowler, Henry Ward.
Pennsylvania.—John Dickenson, John Morton, George Bryan.
Delaware.—Thomas M'Kean, Cæsar Rodney.
Connecticut.—Eliphalet Dyer, David Rowland, William S. Johnson.
Maryland.—William Murdock, Edward Tilghman, Thomas Ringgold.
South Carolina.—Thomas Lynch, Christopher Gadsden, John Rutledge.
[2] The Declaration of Rights was written by John Cruger; the Petition to the King, by Robert R. Livingston; and the Memorial to both Houses of Parliament, by James Otis.
[3] In Mrs. Warren's drama called *The Group*, Ruggles figures in the character of Brigadier Hate-All. He fought against the Americans, at the head of a corps of Loyalists, and at the close of the war settled in Nova Scotia, where he has numerous descendants.

466 PICTORIAL FIELD-BOOK

Franklin's Advice to Ingersoll.   Arrival of the Stamps.   Patrick Henry's Resolutions.   "Liberty Tree."   Effigies.

a former chapter as stamp-master in Connecticut, was in England at the time.   Franklin advised him to accept the office, adding, "Go home and tell your countrymen to get children as fast as they can"—thereby intimating that the colonists were too feeble, at that moment, to resist the government successfully, but ought to gain strength as fast as possible, in order to shake off the oppressions which, he foresaw, were about to be laid upon them.   But little did he and other agents suspect that the stamp-masters would be held in such utter detestation as they were, or that such disturbances would occur as followed, or they would not have procured the appointments for their friends.   The ministry, however, seem to have anticipated trouble, for a clause was inserted in the annual Mutiny Act, authorizing as many troops to be sent to America as ministers saw fit, and making it obligatory upon the people to find quarters for them.

During the summer and autumn the public mind was greatly disturbed by the arrival of vessels bringing the stamps, and the first of November was looked forward to with intense interest—by some with fear, but by more with firm resolution to resist the operations of the
May 30, oppressive act.   Virginia rang the alarum bell, by a series of resolutions drawn up
1765. by Patrick Henry, sustained by his powerful oratory, and adopted by the House of Burgesses.   Of these resolutions, and of Henry's eloquence on that occasion, I shall hereafter write.   So much did the notes of that alarum sound like the voice of treason, that a manuscript copy which was sent to Philadelphia, and another to New York, were handed about with great privacy.   In the latter city no one was found bold enough to print the resolutions, but in Boston they soon appeared in the Gazette of Edes and Gill, and their sentiments, uttered in the Assembly, were echoed back from every inhabited hill and valley in New England.

Before any stamps had arrived in America symptoms of an outbreak appeared in Boston.

"LIBERTY TREE."[2]

A large elm-tree, which stood at the corner of the present Washington and Essex Streets, opposite the Boylston Market, received the appellation of "Liberty Tree," from the circumstance that under it the association called SONS OF LIBERTY held meetings during the summer of 1765.   From a limb of this tree several of the Sons of Liberty[1] suspended two effigies early on the morning of the 14th of August.   One represented Andrew Oliver, secretary of the colony, and just appointed stamp distributor for Massachusetts; the other was a large *boot*, intended to represent Lord Bute, with a head and horns, to personify the devil peeping out of the top.   A great number of people were attracted to these effigies in the course of the day, the authorities in the mean while taking no public notice of the insult, for fear of serious consequences.   Indeed, Sir Francis Bernard, the royal governor, had thus far been almost non-committal on the subjects that were agitating the colonies, although he was strongly suspected of secretly encouraging the passage of the Stamp Act and kindred measures.   In the evening the effigies were cut down

1765

[1] John Avery, Jr., Thomas Crafts, John Smith, Henry Wills, Thomas Chace, Stephen Cleverly, Henry Ross, and Benjamin Edes.

[2] I am indebted to the Hon. David Sears, of Boston, for this sketch of the "Liberty Tree," as it appeared just previous to its destruction by the British troops and Tories, during the siege of Boston in August, 1775. Mr. Sears has erected a row of fine buildings upon the site of the old grove of elms, of which this tree was one; and within a niche, on the front of one of them, and exactly over the spot where the *Liberty Tree* stood, he has placed a sculptured representation of it, as seen in the picture.   From the time of the Stamp Act excitement until the armed possession of Boston by General Gage and his troops in 1774, that tree had been the rallying-place for the patriots, and had fallen, in consequence, much in disfavor with the friends of government.   It was inscribed "LIBERTY TREE," and the ground under it was called "LIBERTY HALL."   The

and carried in procession, the populace shouting, "Liberty and property forever! No stamps! No taxation without our consent!" They then proceeded to Kilby Street, and pulling down a small building just erected by Oliver, to be used, as they suspected, for selling stamps, they took a portion of it to Fort Hill and made a bonfire of it. The mob then rushed toward Oliver's house, beheaded his effigy before it, and broke all the front windows. His effigy was then taken to Fort Hill and burned. Returning to his house, they burst open the door, declaring their intention to kill him, and in brutal wantonness destroyed his furniture, trees, fences, and garden. Mr. Oliver had escaped by a rear passage, and the next morn- [a] August 15, ing,[a] considering his life in danger, he resigned his office. Four months afterward he was compelled by the populace to go under Liberty Tree, and there publicly read his resignation. In the evening the mob again assembled, and besieged the house of the late Chief-justice Hutchinson, now lieutenant governor of the province. They did but little damage, and finished their evening's orgies by a bonfire on the Common.

On the 25th the Rev. Jonathan Mahew, minister of the West Church in Boston, preached a powerful sermon against the Stamp Act, taking for his text, "I would they were even cut off which trouble you. For, brethren, ye have been called unto liberty :. only use not liberty for an occasion to the flesh, but by love serve one another."[1] On Monday evening following a mob collected in King Street, and, proceeding to the residence of Paxton, the marshal of the Court of Admiralty, menaced it. The owner assured them that the officer was not there, and, conciliating the populace by a present of a barrel of punch at a tavern near by, saved his premises from injury. Maddened with liquor, they rushed to the house of Story, registrar of the Admiralty, and destroyed not only the public documents, but his private papers. They next plundered the house of Hallowell, the controller of customs ; and, their numbers being considerably augmented and their excitement increased, they hurried to the mansion of Lieutenant-governor Hutchinson,[2] on North Square. Hutchinson and his family escaped

---

Essex Gazette of August 31st, 1775, in describing the destruction of the tree, says, "They made a furious attack upon it. After a long spell of laughing and grinning, sweating, swearing, and foaming with malice diabolical, they cut down the tree because it bore the name of liberty. A soldier was killed by falling from one of its branches during the operation." In a tract entitled "A Voyage to Boston," published in 1775 the writer thus alludes to the scene :

"Now shined the gay-faced sun with morning light,
All nature gazed, exulting at the sight,
When swift as wind, to vent their base-born rage,
The Tory Williams and the Butcher Gage
Rush'd to the tree, a nameless number near,
Tories and negroes following in the rear ;
Each, axe in hand, attack'd the honor'd tree,
Swearing eternal war with Liberty ;
Nor ceased his stroke till each repeating wound
Tumbled its honors headlong to the ground ;
But ere it fell, not mindless of its wrong,
Avenged, it took one destined head along.
A Tory soldier on its topmost limb ;
The genius of the Shade look'd stern at him,
And mark'd him out that self-same hour to dine
Where unsnuff'd lamps burn low at Pluto's shrine ;
Then tripp'd his feet from off their cautious stand ;
Pale turn'd the wretch—he spread each helpless hand,
But spread in vain—with headlong force he fell,
Nor stopp'd descending till he stopp'd in hell."

[1] Galatians, v., 12, 13.

[2] Thomas Hutchinson was born in 1711, and graduated at Harvard College in 1727. He studied English constitutional law, with a view to public employment. For ten years he was a member of the House of Representatives of Massachusetts, and three years its Speaker. He succeeded his uncle Edward as Judge of Probate in 1752 ; was a member of the Council from 1749 until 1756, and lieutenant governor from 1758 to 1771. He held the office of chief justice after the death of Sewall, in 1760. This office had been promised by Shirley to the elder Otis, and the appointment greatly displeased that influential family. Several acts of Hutchinson had made him unpopular with certain of the people. In 1748, the paper currency of the colony having depreciated to about an eighth of its original value, Hutchinson projected, and carried through the House, a bill for abolishing it, and substituting gold and silver. It was a proper measure, but displeased

in time to save their lives, for the mob were prepared, by liquor and other excitement, for any deed. It was now midnight. With yells and curses they entered, and by four o'clock in the morning "one of the best finished houses in the colony had nothing remaining but the bare walls and floors." Every thing but the kitchen furniture was taken from the dwelling or utterly destroyed. The rioters carried off between four and five thousand dollars in money, a large quantity of plate, family pictures, and clothing, and destroyed the fine library of the lieutenant governor, containing a large collection of manuscripts relating to the history of the colony, which he had been thirty years collecting. This loss was irreparable. The street in front of the house was next morning strewed with plate, rings, and money—destruction, not plunder, being the aim of the mob.

These proceedings were disgraceful in the extreme, and mar the sublime beauty of the picture exhibited by the steady and dignified progress of the Revolution. While no apology for mob rioters should be attempted, extenuating circumstances ought to have their due weight in the balance of just judgment. All over the land the public mind was excited against ministers and their abettors, and leading men in the colonies did not hesitate to recommend forcible resistance, if necessary, to the oppressions of the mother country. The principles underlying the violent movement in Boston were righteous, but the mass were too impatient for their vindication to await the effects of remonstrance and petition, argument and menace, employed by the educated and orderly patriots. As is commonly the fact, the immediate actors in these scenes were the dregs of the population. Yet it was evident that they had, in a degree, the sympathy of, and were controlled by, the great mass of the more intelligent citizens. The morning after the destruction of Hutchinson's house, a public meeting of leading men was held ; expressions of abhorrence for the act were adopted, and the lieutenant governor received a pledge from the meeting that all violence should cease, if he would agree not to commence legal proceedings. He acquiesced, and order was restored.

The disturbances thus begun in Boston were imitated elsewhere during the summer and autumn. These will be hereafter considered. It may properly be mentioned here that the opposition to the Stamp Act was not confined to the continental colonies. The people of the West India plantations were generally opposed to it, and at St. Kitts the stamp-master was obliged to resign. Canada and Halifax, on the continent, submitted, and remained loyal through the Revolution that followed.

Boston, our present point of view, kept up the spirit of liberty, but avoided acts of violence. A newspaper appeared under the significant title of "THE CONSTITUTIONAL COURANT, containing matters instructing to *liberty*, and no ways repugnant to *loyalty;* printed by *Andrew Marvel*, at the sign of the *Bribe Refused*, on *Constitution Hill, North America*." Its headpiece was a snake cut into eight pieces (see page 508), the head part having N. E., the in-

many. He also favored the law granting Writs of Assistance ; and on the bench, in the Council, and in the Assembly he was always found on the side of the ministry. These facts account for the violent feelings of the mob against him. In 1768 he was an active coadjutor of Governor Bernard in bringing troops to Boston, which made him still more unpopular. When Bernard left the province, in 1769, the government devolved wholly upon Hutchinson. In 1770 the *Boston massacre* occurred, and much of the responsibility of that outrage was laid upon him. He was appointed governor in 1771, and from that time until he left for England. in 1774, he was in continual trouble with the Assembly. The popular feeling against him was greatly increased by the publicity given to certain letters of his sent to ministers, in which he recommended stringent measures against the colonies. Toward the close of 1773 the destruction of tea in Boston Harbor was accomplished. The Sons of Liberty had then paralyzed the government, and there was not a judge or sheriff who dared to exercise the duties of his office against the wishes of the inflamed people. Hutchinson then resigned his office, and sailed for England in the spring of 1774. He died at Brompton, England, June rd, 1780, aged sixty-nine years.

itials of New England, inscribed upon it, and the other pieces the initials of the other colonies. Accompanying the device was the motto, JOIN OR DIE.

The morning of the 1st of November, the day appointed for the Stamp Act to take effect in America, was ushered in at Boston by the tolling of muffled bells, and the vessels in the harbor displaying their flags at half mast, as on the occasion of a funeral solemnity. On Liberty Tree were suspended two effigies, representing George Grenville and John Huske ; the latter the American member of Parliament whom I have mentioned as suggesting a heavy tax upon the colonies before the Stamp Act was proposed. A label, with a poetic inscription, was affixed to the breast of each.[1] The figures remained suspended until about three o'clock in the afternoon, when they were cut down in the presence of several thousand people of all ranks, who testified their approbation by loud huzzas. The effigies were placed in a cart, and taken to the court-house, where the Assembly were sitting, followed by a vast concourse in regular procession ; thence the people proceeded to the Neck, and hung the figures upon a gallows erected there. Speeches were made at the place of *execution*, and, after the lapse of an hour, they were taken down, torn in pieces, and the limbs thrown in the air. The people were now desired, by one of the leaders of the pageant, to go quietly home. They acquiesced, and Boston that night was remarkably tranquil.

The Stamp Act had now become a law. As none but stamped paper was legal, and as the people were determined not to use it, business was suspended.. The courts were closed, marriages ceased, vessels were delayed in the harbors, and the social and commercial operations of America were suddenly paralyzed. Few dared to think of positive rebellion ; the strong arm of government held the sword of power above them, and a general gloom overspread the colonies. Yet hope was not extinct, and it pointed out a peaceable, but powerful, plan for effecting a repeal of the noxious act. The commerce between Great Britain and the colonies had become very important, and any measure that might interrupt its course would be felt by a large and powerful class in England, whose influence was felt in Parliament. The expediency of striking a blow at the trade occurred to some New York merchants, and, accordingly, on the 31st of October, the day before the act went into operation, a meeting was held, and an agreement entered into not to import from England certain enumerated articles after the first day of January ensuing.[2] The merchants of Phil-

1765.

---

[1] The following are copies of the labels. On that representing Grenville, holding out a Stamp Act in his left hand :

> " YOUR Servant, Sirs ; do you like my Figure?
> YOU've seen one Rogue, but here's a bigger.
> Father of Mischief ! how I soar
> Where many a Rogue has gone before.
> Take heed, my Brother Rogues, take heed,
> In me your honest Portion read :
> Dear cousin PETER, no Excuse,
> Come dance with me without your shoes ,
> 'Tis G——le calls, and sink or swim,
> You'd go to h——l to follow him."

On the figure representing John Huske :

> *Quest.* " What, Brother H——ske ? why, this is bad !
> *Ans.* Ah, indeed ! but I'm a wicked Lad ;
> My Mother always thought me wild ;
> 'The Gallows is thy Portion, Child,'
> She often said : behold, 'tis true,
> And now the Dog must have his due ;
> For idle Gewgaws, wretched Pelf,
> I sold my Country, d——d myself ;
> And for my great, unequal'd Crime
> The D——l takes H——ske before his time.
> But if some Brethren I could name,
> Who shared the Crime, should share the shame,
> This glorious tree, though big and tall,
> Indeed would never hold 'em all !"

[2] The meeting was held at the house of George Burns, inn-keeper. As the agreement entered into there is a type of those adopted by the merchants and people of other colonies, I copy from the New York Mer-

adelphia readily responded to the measure, and on the 9th of December those of Boston entered into a similar agreement. Nor were the pledges confined to merchants alone, but the people in general ceased using foreign luxuries; articles of domestic manufacture came into general use, and the trade with Great Britain was almost entirely suspended.[1]

1765. In July the Marquis of Rockingham, an honorable and enlightened statesman, succeeded Grenville in the premiership. His cabinet was composed chiefly of the friends of America, and, for a while, the colonists hoped for justice. General Conway, who had raised the first voice of opposition to ministers in their relations to the colonies, was made one of the Secretaries of State, and Edmund Burke, one of the earliest friends of America, was Rockingham's private secretary. But the new ministry, against the determined will of the king and the influence of a strong power behind the throne, found it difficult to depart from the line of policy toward the colonies adopted by Grenville, and the hopes of the Americans faded in an hour.

A strange apathy concerning American affairs seemed still to prevail in England, notwithstanding every vessel from America carried tidings of the excited state of the people there.

December 17. Parliament met in December. The king, in his speech, mentioned that

CHARLES, MARQUIS OF ROCKINGHAM.
From an English print.

cury of November, 1765, the portion of the proceedings of the meeting containing the resolutions. These were, "*First*, That in all orders they send out to Great Britain for goods or merchandise of any nature, kind, or quality whatsoever usually imported from Great Britain, they will direct their correspondents not to ship them, unless the Stamp Act be repealed. It is, nevertheless, agreed that all such merchants as are owners of, and have, vessels already gone, and now cleared out for Great Britain, shall be at liberty to bring back in them, on their own accounts, crates and casks of earthen-ware, grindstones, and pipes, and such other bulky articles as owners usually fill up their vessels with. *Secondly*, It is further unanimously agreed that all orders already sent home shall be countermanded by the very first conveyance; and the goods and merchandise thereby ordered not to be sent, except upon the condition mentioned in the foregoing resolution. *Thirdly*, It is further unanimously agreed that no merchant will vend dry-goods or merchandise sent upon commission from Great Britain, that shall be shipped from thence after the first day of January next, unless upon the condition mentioned in the first resolution. *Fourthly*, It is further unanimously agreed that the foregoing resolutions shall be binding until the same are abrogated at a general meeting hereafter to be held for that purpose. In witness whereof we have hereunto respectively subscribed our names." [Here followed the names of more than two hundred of the principal merchants.] In consequence of the foregoing resolutions, the retail merchants of the city entered into an agreement not to buy or sell any goods shipped from England after the 1st of January.

This was the beginning of that system of non-importation agreements which hurled back upon England, with such force, the commercial miseries she had inflicted upon the colonies.

[1] The following extracts from a letter written by a gentleman in Newport, Rhode Island, to Hugh Gaine, the editor of the New York Mercury, and published in that paper early in 1768, will give the reader an idea of the industry of the colonists at that time: "Within eighteen months past four hundred and eighty-seven yards of cloth and thirty-six pairs of stockings have been spun and knit in the family of James Nixon of this town. Another family, within four years past, hath manufactured nine hundred and eighty yards of woolen cloth, besides two coverlids, and two bed-ticks, and all the stocking yarn for the family. Not a skein was put out of the house to be spun, but the whole performed in the family. We are credibly informed that many families in this colony, within the year past, have each manufactured upward of seven hundred yards of cloth of different kinds."

Another letter, dated at Newport, 1765, says, "The spirit of patriotism is not confined to the *sons* of America, but glows with equal fervor in the benevolent breasts of her daughters; one instance of which we think is worthy of notice. A lady of this town, though in the bloom of youth, and possessed of virtues and accomplishments, engaging, and sufficient to excite the most pleasing expectations of happiness in the married state, has declared that she should rather be an old maid than that the operation of the Stamp Act should commence in these colonies."

something had occurred in America which might demand the serious attention of the Legislature ; but that body almost immediately adjourned until after the Christmas holidays, and it was the 14th of January before they reassembled.   The king alluded to the disturbances in America, and assured the Houses that no time had been lost in issuing orders to the governors of the provinces, and to the commanders of the forces there, to use all the power of the government in suppressing riots and tumults.   Pitt, who was absent on account of gout when the passage of the Stamp Act was under consideration, was now in his place, and, leaning upon crutches, nobly vindicated the rights of the colonies.   After censuring ministers for their delay in giving notice of the disturbances in America, and animadverting severely upon the injustice of the Stamp Act, he proceeded to vindicate the Americans. " The colonists," he said, " are subjects of this kingdom, equally entitled with yourselves to all the natural rights of mankind and the peculiar privileges of Englishmen ; equally bound by its laws, and equally participating in the Constitution of this free country.   The Americans are the sons, not the bastards, of England.   Taxation is no part of the governing or legislative power.   Taxes are the voluntary gift or grant of the Commons alone. . . . . . . When, therefore, in this House we give and grant, we give and grant what is our own.   But in an American tax what do we do ?   We, your majesty's Commons for Great Britain, give and grant to your majesty, what ?   our own property ?   No ; we give and grant to your majesty the property of your majesty's Commons of America.   It is an absurdity in terms."

Grenville also censured ministers for their delay.   " The disturbances," he said, " began in July, and now we are in the middle of January ; lately they were only *occurrences;* they are now grown to *disturbances,* to *tumults* and *riots.*   I doubt they border on open rebellion ; and, if the doctrines of this day be confirmed, that name will be lost in revolution." And so it was.   Grenville also defended his own course, and dissented from Mr. Pitt respecting the right to tax the colonies.   He claimed obedience from America, because it enjoyed the protection of Great Britain.   " The nation," he said, " has run itself into an immense debt to give them protection ; and now they are called upon to contribute a small share toward the public expense—an expense arising from themselves—they renounce your authority, insult your officers, and break out, I might almost say, into open rebellion."   Fixing his eyes intently upon Pitt, he exclaimed, with great emphasis, " *The seditious spirit of the colonies owes its birth to factions in this House.   Gentlemen are careless of the consequences of what they say, provided it answers the purposes of opposition.*"

When Grenville ceased speaking, several members arose to their feet, among whom was Pitt.   There was a loud cry of " Mr. Pitt, Mr. Pitt," and all but he sat down.   He immediately fell upon Grenville, and told him that, since he had challenged him to the field, he would fight him on every foot of it.   " The gentleman tells us," he said, " that America is obstinate, America is almost in open rebellion.   I rejoice that America has resisted.   Three millions of people so dead to all the feelings of liberty as voluntarily to submit to be slaves, would have been fit instruments to make slaves of the rest."   Alluding to the alleged strength of Great Britain and the weakness of America, he said, " It is true, that in a good cause, on a good ground, the force of this country could crush America to atoms ; but on this ground, on this Stamp Act, many here will think it a crying injustice, and I am one who will lift up my hands against it.   In such a cause your success would be hazardous.   America, if she fall, would fall like the strong man ; she would embrace the pillars of the State, and pull down the Constitution along with her."[1]   Pitt concluded his speech with a proposition for an absolute and immediate repeal of the Stamp Act, at the same time recommending an act to accompany the repeal, declaring, in the most unqualified terms, the sovereign authority of Great Britain over her colonies.   This was intended as a sort of salvo to the national honor, necessary, as Pitt well knew, to insure the repeal of the act.   Burke, who had been elected to a seat in the House of Commons,[2] Conway, Barré, and others, seconded the views

---

[1] History Debates, &c., of the British Parliament, iv., 292–7.

[2] At this time Burke commenced his brilliant career as a statesman and an orator.   Dr. Johnson asserted

of Pitt, and with that great statesman were the principal advocates of a repeal. Chief-justice Pratt, now become Lord Camden, was the principal friend of the measure in the Upper House, but was opposed to the Declaratory Act proposed by Pitt. "My position is this," he said, in the course of debate; "I repeat it; I will maintain it to the last hour—taxation and representation are inseparable. The position is founded in the law of nature. It is more: it is itself an eternal law of nature."

1766.   On the 18th of March a repeal bill was passed by a large majority of the men who, a few months previous, were almost unanimously in favor of the Stamp Act. It was carried in the House of Commons by a vote of two hundred and seventy-five to one hundred and sixteen. It met strenuous opposition in the House of Lords, where it had a majority of thirty-four. Thirty-three peers entered a strong protest, in which they declared that "such a submission of king, Lords, and Commons, in so strange and unheard-of a contest," would amount to an entire surrender of British supremacy.

The change in the opinions of members of the House of Commons was wrought more by the petitions, remonstrances, and personal influence of the London merchants, than by appeals from America, or by disturbances there. Ministers would not receive the petitions of the colonial Congress held at New York, because that assembly had not been legally summoned to meet by the supreme power. It was the importunities of London merchants and tradesmen, suffering severely from the effects of the non-importation agreements, that wrought the wondrous change. Half a million of dollars were then due them from the colonies, and, under the existing state of things, not a dollar of it was expected to be paid. Their trade with the colonies was suddenly suspended, and nothing but bankruptcy and ruin was before them. London being the business heart of the kingdom, with a cessation of its pulsations paralysis spread to other portions. Nothing but a retraction could save England from utter commercial ruin, and, perhaps, civil war. These were the considerations which made the sensible men in Parliament retrace their steps. According to Pitt's recommendation, a Declaratory Act, which affirmed the right of Parliament "to bind the colonies in all cases whatsoever," accompanied the bill. The repeal of the Stamp Act became a law, by the reluctant signature of the king, on the day of its enactment.   March 18, 1766.

WILLIAM PITT.
From an English print

Great joy was manifested in London when the Repeal Act passed. Pitt had all the honor of the measure, and as he came out to the lobby of the House of Commons he was greeted by the crowd with the most extravagant demonstrations of joy. They clung about him like children upon a long-absent father. The ships in the river displayed their colors; houses at night, all over the city, were illuminated; and the most fulsome adulation was bestowed upon the king and Parliament for their goodness and wisdom!

Equally great was the joy that filled the colonies when intelligence of the repeal of the Stamp Act arrived. The Declaratory Act, involving, as it really did, the kernel of royal prerogatives which the colonists rejected, was, for the moment, overlooked, and throughout America there was a burst of loyalty and gratitude. New York voted statues to the king and to Pitt, both of which were presently erected;[1] Virginia voted a statue to the king;

---

that his two speeches on the repeal of the Stamp Act "were publicly commended by Mr. Pitt, and filled the town with wonder."

[1] The statue of the king was equestrian, and made of lead. It stood within the present inclosure at the foot of Broadway, New York, called the Bowling Green. The statue of Pitt was of marble, and stood at

Maryland passed a similar vote, and ordered a portrait of Lord Camden ; and the authorities of Boston ordered full-length portraits of Barré and Conway for Fanueil Hall.

The Repeal Act reached Boston at about noon on Friday, the 13th of May.   It was brought by the brig Harrison, a vessel belonging to John Hancock.   Great was the general joy.   The church-bells were immediately rung ; the colors of all the ships were hoisted ; cannons were discharged ; the Sons of Liberty gathered under their favorite tree, drank toasts, and fired guns ; and bonfires and illuminations enlivened the evening.   A general celebration was arranged by the select-men for the following Monday.   The dawn, bright and rosy, was ushered in by salvos of cannon, ringing of bells, and martial music.   Through the liberality of some citizens. every debtor in the jail was ransomed and set at liberty, to unite in the general joy.   "This charitable deed originated in a fair Boston nymph."   The whole town was illuminated in the evening.   On the Common the Sons of Liberty erected a magnificent pyramid, illuminated by two hundred and eighty lamps, the four upper stories of which were ornamented with figures of the king and queen, and "fourteen of the patriots who had distinguished themselves for their love of liberty."   On the four sides of the lower apartment were appropriate poetic inscriptions.[1]   "John Hancock, Esq.," says a newspaper of the day, from which I have drawn this account, "who gave a grand and elegant entertainment to the genteel part of the town, and treated the populace to a pipe of Madeira wine, erected at the front of his house, which was magnificently illuminated, a stage for the exhibition of his

1766.

---

the intersection of William and Wall Streets.   The mutilated remains of this statue are now within an iron railing of the Fifth Ward Hotel, on the corner of Franklin Street and West Broadway.   A sketch of the broken statue will be found on page 583, Vol. II.

[1] The following are the poetic inscriptions referred to.   They allude to emblematic figures on the lower story :

> " O thou whom next to Heaven we most revere,
> Fair Liberty ! thou lovely Goddess, hear !
> Have we not wooed thee, won thee, held thee long,
> Lain in thy Lap, and melted on thy Tongue—
> Through Death and Dangers, rugged Paths pursued,
> And led thee, smiling, to this SOLITUDE—
> Hid thee within our Hearts' most golden cell,
> And braved the Powers of Earth and Powers of Hell ?
> GODDESS ! we can not part, thou must not fly,
> Be SLAVES ! we dare to scorn it—dare to die."

> " While clanking Chains and Curses shall salute
> Thine ears, remorseless G——le, thine, O B——te,
> To you, bless'd PATRIOTS ! we our cause submit,
> Illustrious CAMBDEN, Britain's guardian, PITT !
> Recede not, frown not, rather let us be
> Deprived of being than of LIBERTY.
> Let Fraud or Malice blacken all our crimes,
> No disaffection stains these peaceful climes ;
> O save us, shield us from impending Woes,
> The Foes of Britain only are our Foes."

> " Boast, foul Oppression, boast thy transient Reign,
> While honest FREEDOM struggles with her Chain ,
> But now the Sons of Virtue, hardy, brave,
> Disdain to lose through mean Despair to save ;
> Aroused in Thunder, awful they appear,
> With proud Deliverance stalking in their rear :
> While Tyrant Foes their pallid Fears betray,
> Shrink from their Arms, and give their Vengeance way ;
> See, in the unequal War, OPPRESSORS fall,
> The Hate, Contempt, and endless Curse of all."

> " Our Faith approved, our LIBERTY restored,
> Our Hearts bend grateful to our sovereign Lord :
> Hail, darling monarch ! by this act endear'd,
> Our firm Affections are our best Reward ;
> Should Britain's self against herself divide,
> And hostile Armies form on either side—
> Should Hosts rebellious shake our Brunswick's Throne,
> And as they dared thy Parent, dare the Son,
> To this Asylum stretch thy happy Wing,
> And we'll contend who best shall love our KING."

fire-works." . . . . . . " Mr. Otis, and some other gentlemen who lived near the Common, kept open house the whole evening, which was very pleasant." At eleven o'clock, on a signal being given, a horizontal fire-wheel on the top of the pyramid was set in motion, "which ended in the discharge of sixteen dozen serpents in the air, which concluded the show. To the honor of the Sons of Liberty, we can with pleasure inform the world that every thing was conducted with the utmost decency and good order." His majesty's Council, by a previous invitation of the governor, met at the Province House in the afternoon, where many loyal toasts were drunk, and in the evening they went to the Common to see the fire-works. Past animosities were forgotten, and the night of the 16th of May was a happy one for Boston.

THE PROVINCE HOUSE.[1]

The glad sounds of rejoicing because of the repeal of the Stamp Act were not mellowed into the harmony of confident hope, before the ministry of England, by its unwise and unjust acts, again awakened loud murmurs of discontent throughout America. That germ of new oppressions, the Declaratory Act, which appeared so harmless, began to expand in the genial soil of ministerial culture. The House of Commons, by resolutions, demanded of the colonies restitution to the crown officers who had suffered loss by the Stamp Act riots. This was just, and the colonies complied; Massachusetts, however, in passing the Indemnification Bill, inserted a provision that a free pardon should be extended to all concerned. Much bad feeling was engendered by the insolent manner in which the settlement of the claims was demanded. Governor Bernard of Massachusetts was so peremptory and insulting, that the people of Boston flatly refused to pay; and it was not until the governor had lowered his authoritative tone very much that they complied.[2]

A new clause in the Annual Mutiny Act[3] was properly viewed as disguised taxation, and a measure calculated not only to strengthen the royal power in America, but to shift a heavy burden from the shoulders of the home government to those of the colonies. The clause provided that the British troops that might be sent here should be furnished with quarters, beer, salt, and vinegar at the expense of the people. It was a comparatively small tax, and easy to be borne, but it involved the same principles, substantially, that were avowed in the Stamp Act, and was more odious, because it was intended to make the people support bayonets sent to abridge their liberties. New York and Massachusetts refused to comply with its provisions, and opposition, as zealous as that against the Stamp Act, was soon aroused. The insolent soldiers met rebuffs at every corner, and at times serious outbreaks were apprehended in Boston, New York, and Philadelphia.

On the 2d of August, 1766, the Rockingham cabinet was suddenly dissolved. It was too liberal for " the king's friends," and was unable to stem the current of opposition flowing from royalty itself. The new cabinet was formed, by his majesty's commands, under the con-

---

[1] The Province House, the residence of the colonial governors, is still standing, in the rear of stores on Washington Street, opposite Milk Street. It is a large brick building, three stories high, and was formerly decorated with the king's arms richly carved and gilt. A cupola surmounted the roof. In front of the house was a pretty lawn with an iron fence, and on each side of the gate was a large oak-tree. The ground sloped, and in front were about twenty stone steps. Its grounds are now covered with buildings, and the house can not be seen without entering Province Court. The king's arms are in the cabinet of the Massachusetts Historical Society.

[2] The amount of indemnification claimed in Boston was as follows: Hutchinson, $12,000; Oliver, $646; Story, $255; Hallowell, $1446.

[3] The Mutiny Act granted power to every officer, upon obtaining a warrant from a justice, to break into any house, by day or by night, in search of deserters. Like the Writs of Assistance, these powers might be, and, indeed, were, used by unprincipled men for other than ostensible purposes; and the guaranty of the British Constitution that every man's house shall be his castle, and inviolate, was subverted.

trol of Mr. Pitt, just created Earl of Chatham.[1]   This honor was conferred on the 29th of July.   The transformation of the great Commoner into an earl was not more surprising than the curious medley of politicians that formed his cabinet, so diversified and discordant that neither party knew what confidence to repose in it.   " He made an administration so checkered and speckled," said Burke ; " he put together a piece of joinery so crossly indented and whimsically dove-tailed ; a cabinet so variously inlaid ; such a piece of diversified mosaic ; such a tesselated pavement without cement ; here a bit of black stone, and there a bit of white ; patriots and courtiers, king's friends and republicans ; Whigs and Tories ; treacherous friends and open enemies ; that it was, indeed, a very curious show, but utterly unsafe to touch and unsure to stand on.   The colleagues whom he had assorted at the same boards stared at each other, and were obliged to ask, ' Sir, your name ?'   ' Sir, you have the advantage of me.'   ' Mr. Such-a-one, I beg a thousand pardons.'   I venture to say it did so happen that persons had a single office divided between them, who had never spoken to each other in their lives until they found themselves they knew not how, pigging together, heads and points, in the same truckle-bed."[2]   Had the general direction of affairs been assumed by Pitt, even this incongruous cabinet might not have done much mischief ; but frequent and serious attacks of gout kept the great orator confined at Hayes, his country seat in Kent. " Having," said Burke, " put so much the larger part of his enemies and opposers into power, the confusion was such that his own principles could not possibly have any effect or influence in the conduct of affairs.   If ever he fell into a fit of the gout, or any other cause withdrew him from public cares, principles directly contrary to his own were sure to predominate. . . . . . . When his face was hid for a moment, his whole system was one wide sea without chart or compass."   It was during one of these attacks of illness that Grenville propos-   January, ed a tax of two millions of dollars upon America, for the support of troops, &c.   Charles 1767. Townshend, Pitt's chancellor of the Exchequer, upon whom devolved the duty of suggesting financial measures, agreed with Grenville as to the *right* thus to tax the colonies, but, in view of the late excitement produced by the Stamp Act, thought it inexpedient, at the same time pledging himself to the House to find a revenue in America sufficient to meet expenses.   This pledge he attempted to redeem in May, by asking leave to bring in a bill to impose a duty   May 13. upon paper, glass, painters' colors, lead, and tea imported by the Americans.   Leave was granted, and an act levying such duties became a law by royal assent on the 29th   1767. of June.   Another bill became a law on the 2d of July, which provided for taking off a shilling on a pound of the export tax on all black and single tea, and granting a drawback upon all teas exported to Ireland and America.   The object of this act was to encourage the exportation of tea to America, in the belief that the reduced price of the article would cause a great increase in the consumption, and, consequently, augment the revenue arising from it under the new act.   But in this ministers reckoned neither wisely nor well.

Another bill was passed, reorganizing the colonial custom-house system, and the establishment of a Board of Revenue Commissioners for America, to have its seat at Boston.   There was a provision in the first bill for the maintenance of a standing army in America, and enabling the crown, by sign manual, to establish *a general civil list* throughout every province, fixing the salaries of governors, judges, and other officers, such salary to be paid by the

---

[1] Three weeks before the installation of the new cabinet Pitt received an autograph letter from the king, commanding him to arrange a new administration.   Pitt spoke of his age and infirmities (he was then *fifty-eight*), and proposed taking to himself the office of the privy seal, which implied and necessitated his removal to the House of Lords !   The king was greatly astonished, but so desperately tangled were the public affairs, and so great seemed the necessity of having the powerful Pitt among his friends, that the king was obliged to yield.   The witty Lord Chesterfield, alluding to the ambition of Pitt to acquire a coronet, said, " Every body is puzzled to account for this step.   Such an event was, I believe, never heard or read of, to withdraw, in the fullness of his power and in the utmost gratification of his ambition, from the House of Commons (which procured him his power, and which could alone insure it to him), and to go into that *hospital of incurables*, the House of Lords, is a measure so unaccountable, that nothing but proof positive could make me believe it ; but so it is."   Chesterfield called it a " fall up stairs—a fall which did Pitt so much damage that he will never be able to stand upon his legs again."
[2] Speech on American Taxation.

crown.   Thus the executive and judicial officers, from whom the people were to expect good government and the righteous administration of laws, were made entirely independent of the people, and became, in fact, mere hireling creatures of the crown.   This had been the object of almost every minister from the time of Charles II.[1]

When intelligence of these acts reached America, the excitement throughout the colonies was as great as that produced by the Stamp Act, but action was more dignified and efficient. The royal governors and their retainers, elated with the prospect of being independent of the colonial Assemblies, eagerly forwarded the schemes of the ministry, and aided greatly in fostering opposition among the people.   The ministry seemed totally blind to every light of common sense, and disregarded the warnings of Lord Shelburne and others in Parliament, and the opinions of just observers in America.[2]

The colonists clearly perceived the intention of government to tax them in some shape, and took the broad ground asserted by Otis in his pamphlet, that " taxes on trade, if designed to raise a revenue, were just as much a violation of their rights as any other tax." The colonial newspapers, now increased to nearly thirty in number, began to be tribunes for the people, through which leading minds communed with the masses upon subjects of common interest. They teemed with essays upon colonial rights, among the most powerful of which were the " Letters of a Farmer of Pennsylvania to the Inhabitants of the British Colonies," written by John Dickinson,[3] and first published in the Pennsylvania Chronicle. They were twelve in number, and appeared during the summer and autumn of 1767.   Their effect, like that of the " Crisis," by Thomas Paine, a few years later, was wonderful in forming and controlling the will of the people, and giving efficiency to the strong right arm of action. In a style of great vigor, animation, and simplicity, Dickinson portrayed the unconstitutionality of the conduct of Great Britain, the imminent peril to American liberty which existed, and the fatal consequences of a supine acquiescence in min-

John Dickinson

---

[1] Gordon, i., 146.

[2] Gerard Hamilton (known as Single Speech Hamilton, because when a member of Parliament he made but one speech) was then in America, and, writing to Colcraft, a member from Lincolnshire, said, " In the Massachusetts government in particular there is an express law, by which every man is obliged to have a musket, a pound of powder, and a pound of bullets always near him ; so there is nothing wanting but knapsacks (or old stockings, which will do as well) to equip an army for marching, and nothing more than a Sartonius or a Spartacus at their head requisite to beat your troops and your custom-house officers out of the country, and set your laws at defiance."

[3] John Dickinson was born in Maryland, November 13th, 1732.   His father was Samuel Dickinson, first judge, in Delaware, of the Court of Common Pleas, about 1740.   His father was wealthy, and John had every means given him for acquiring learning which the colonies afforded.   He studied law in Philadelphia, and was for three years at the Temple in London.   He first appeared in public life as a member of the Pennsylvania Assembly in 1764.   He was a member from Pennsylvania of the " Stamp Act Congress" in 1765.   He soon afterward began his essays upon various political subjects, and his pen was never idle during the conflict that succeeded.   Dr. Franklin caused his " Letters of a Pennsylvania Farmer" to be republished in London in 1768, and in 1769 they were translated into French and published in Paris.   Mr. Dickenson was a member of the first Continental Congress in 1774.   He wrote the Declaration of the Congress of 1775, setting forth the causes and the necessity for war.   He was opposed to a political separation from Great Britain, and was intentionally absent from Congress when the final vote on the Declaration of Independence was taken on the 4th of July, 1776.   In 1777 he received the commission of brigadier general. In 1780 he took his seat in the Assembly of Delaware, and in 1782 was elected President of Pennsylvania. He was a member of the Convention that framed the Federal Constitution, and was its warm friend.   He

isterial measures—more fatal as precedents than by the immediate calamities they were calculated to produce.[1]   The people of Boston, at a public meeting, passed a vote of thanks to
Dickinson, and some who were afterward leading men of the Revolution composed the committee to write the letter.   In May, 1768, an association in Philadelphia, called the Society
of Fort St. David, presented an address to Mr. Dickinson, " in a box of heart of oak."   The
following inscriptions were neatly done upon it, in gold letters.   On the top was represented
the cap of liberty on a spear, resting on a cipher of the letters J. D.   Underneath the cipher,
in a semi-circular label, the words PRO PATRIA.   Around the whole, the following : " *The
gift of the Governor and Society of Fort St. David to the author of* THE FARMER'S LET-
TERS, *in grateful testimony to the very eminent services thereby rendered to this country,*
1768."   On the inside of the top was the following inscription : " *The liberties of the British colonies in America asserted with Attic eloquence and Roman spirit by John Dickinson, Esq., barrister at law.*"   Spirited resolutions were adopted by the colonial Assemblies,
denouncing the acts of Parliament, and new non-importation associations were formed, which
almost destroyed the commerce with England.

A special session of the Massachusetts Assembly was asked for in October, to " con- 1767.
sider the late acts of Parliament," but Governor Bernard unwisely refused to call one.
At the opening of the regular session, in December, a large committee was appointed to " consider the state of the province."   It elaborated several measures, the first of which was a
petition to the king, asserting the principles for which they were contending.   A bolder step,
and one that most displeased the British ministry, was now taken ; the Assembly February,
adopted a circular letter, to be addressed to all the colonies, imbodying the senti- 1768.
ments expressed in the petition to the king, and inviting their co-operation in maintaining
the liberties of America.   When intelligence of this letter reached the ministers, Lord Hillsborough, the colonial Secretary, sent instructions to Governor Bernard to call upon the General Assembly of Massachusetts to rescind its resolutions, and, in the event of non-compliance,
to dissolve that body.   But the Assembly, or House of Representatives, consisting of one
hundred and nine members, much the largest legislative Convention in America,[2] were not
easily frightened, and, instead of complying with the governor's demand, made that very demand a fresh cause of complaint.   Mr. Otis and Samuel Adams were the principal speakers
on the occasion.   The former made a speech which the friends of government pronounced
" the most violent, insolent, abusive, and treasonable declaration that perhaps ever was delivered."   " When Lord Hillsborough knows," said Otis, " that we will not rescind *our* acts,
he should apply to Parliament to rescind theirs.   *Let Britons rescind their measures, or
they are lost forever.*"   For nearly an hour he harangued the Assembly with words like
these, until even the Sons of Liberty trembled lest he should tread upon the domain of treason.
The House refused to rescind, passed resolutions denunciatory of this attempt to arrest free
discussion and expression of opinion, and then sent a letter to the governor, inform- June 30,
ing him of their action.   " If the votes of this House," they said, " are to be con- 1768.
trolled by the direction of a minister, we have left us but a vain semblance of liberty.   We
have now only to inform you that this House have voted not to rescind, and that, on a division on the question, there were ninety-two yeas and seventeen nays."   The seventeen
" rescinders" became objects of public scorn.   The governor, greatly irritated, proceeded to
dissolve the Assembly ; but, before the act was accomplished, that body had prepared a list
of serious accusations against him, and a petition to the king for his removal.   Thus Britain, through her representative, struck the first blow at free discussion in America.   Massachusetts, however, felt strong, for the answer to her circular letter from other colonies glowed with sympathy and assurances of support.

---

continued in public life, in various ways, until his death, which occurred at Wilmington on the 14th of February, 1808, at the age of seventy-five.
[1] American Portrait Gallery, vol. iii.
[2] About this time the debates in the Assembly began to be so interesting to the public at large, that a gallery was prepared for the use of spectators, which was usually crowded with citizens.

1767.
A new scene in the drama now opened.   The commissioners of customs had arrived in May, and were diligent in the performance of their duties.   The merchants were very restive under the strictness of the revenue officers, and these functionaries were exceedingly odious in the eyes of the people generally.   On the 10th of June the sloop Liberty, Nathaniel Bernard master, belonging to John Hancock, arrived at Boston with a cargo of Madeira wine.   It was a common practice for the tide-waiter, upon the arrival of a vessel, to repair to the cabin, and there to remain, drinking punch with the master, while the sailors were landing the dutiable goods.[1]   On the arrival of the *Liberty*, Kirke, the tidesman, went on board, just at sunset, and took his seat in the cabin as usual.   About nine in the evening Captain Marshall, and others in Hancock's employ, entered the cabin, confined Kirke below, and landed the wine on the dock without entering it at the custom-house, or observing any other formula.   Kirke was then released and sent ashore.   Captain Marshall died suddenly during the night, from the effects, it was supposed, of over-exertion in landing the wine.   In the morning the commissioners of customs ordered the seizure of the sloop, and Harrison, the collector, and Hallowell, the controller, were deputed to perform that duty.   Hallowell proceeded to place the broad arrow upon her (the mark designating her legal position), and then, cutting her moorings, he removed the vessel from Hancock's Wharf to a place in the harbor under the guns of the *Romney* ship of war.

This act greatly inflamed the people.   Already a crowd had collected to prevent the seizure ; but when the vessel was cut loose and placed under the protection of British cannon, a strong feeling of anger pervaded the multitude.   The assemblage of citizens became a mob, and a large party of the lower class, headed by Malcomb, a bold smuggler, pelted Harrison and others with stones, attacked the offices of the commissioners, and, dragging a custom-house boat through the town, burned it upon the Common.   The commissioners, alarmed for their own safety, applied to Governor Bernard for protection, but he told them he was utterly powerless.   They found means to escape on board the Romney, and thence to Castle William, a fortress upon Castle Island, in the harbor, nearly three miles southeast of the city, where a company of British artillery was stationed.[2]

The Sons of Liberty called a meeting at Faneuil Hall on the afternoon of the 13th.[3]   A large concourse assembled, and the principal business done was preparing a petition to the governor, asking him to remove the man-of-war from the harbor.   The Council passed resolutions condemnatory of the rioters, but the House of Representatives took no notice of the matter.   Legal proceedings were commenced against the leading rioters, but the difficulty of procuring witnesses, and the bad feeling that was engendered, made the prosecutors drop the matter in the following spring.

Alarmed by these tumultuous proceedings, the governor requested General Gage, then in New York, and captain general of all the British forces in America, to act upon a permission already given him by Lord Hillsborough, in a secret and confidential letter, to order some royal troops from Halifax to Boston.   Intelligence of this request leaked out, and the people of Boston were greatly irritated.   The arrival of an officer sent by Gage to prepare quarters for the coming troops occasioned a town meeting, and a committee, consisting of James Otis, Samuel Adams, John Hancock, and John Adams, was appointed to wait upon the governor, ascertain whether the report was true, and request him to call a special meeting of the Assembly.[a]   The governor frankly acknowledged that troops were about to be quartered in Boston, but refused to call a meeting of the Assembly until he should receive instructions from home.   Bernard was evidently alarmed ; he perceived the great popularity of the leaders who stood before him, and his tone was far more pacific

a September 12, 1768.

---

[1] Gordon.

[2] The present fort upon Castle Island is called Fort Independence, so named by the elder Adams while visiting it when he was President of the United States, in 1799.   It stands at the entrance of the harbor, and is one of the finest forts in America.

[3] The private meeting-place of the Sons of Liberty, according to John Adams, was the counting-room in Chase and Speakman's distillery, in Hanover Square, near the Liberty Tree.

than it had recently been. Nor did his pliancy end here; he actually stooped to the base alternative of endeavoring to make some of those leaders his friends by bribes. He gave

FANEUIL HALL.[1]

From an English print of the time

Hancock a commission honoring him with a seat in the Council, but the patriot tore the parchment into shreds in the presence of the people. He offered John Adams the lucrative office of advocate general, in the Court of Admiralty, but Adams hurled back the proffered patronage with disdain. Bernard also approached that sturdy representative of the Puritans, Samuel Adams, but found him, though poor in purse, as Hutchinson on another occasion said, "of such an obstinate and inflexible disposition that he could never be conciliated by any office or gift whatsoever."

The governor having peremptorily refused to convene the Assembly, the meeting recommended a convention of delegates from all the towns in the province, to meet in Boston within ten days. "A prevailing apprehension of war with France" was made the plausible pretense for calling the meeting; and they requested the people to act in accordance with a law of the colony, authorizing each one to provide himself with a musket and the requisite ammunition. Every town and district but one—more than a hundred in number[2]—sent a delegate. They met on the 22d, chose Mr. Thomas Cushing, late Speaker of the Assembly, as their chairman, and petitioned Governor Bernard to summon a Gen-   September

[1] Faneuil Hall has been denominated "the cradle of American liberty," having been the popular gathering-place of the Sons of Liberty during the incipient stages of the Revolution. It was erected in 1742, at the sole expense of Peter Faneuil, Esq., of Boston, and by him generously given to the town—the basement for a market, with a spacious and most beautiful hall, and other convenient rooms above, for public meetings of the citizens. It was burned in 1761, nothing but the brick walls remaining. The town immediately ordered it to be rebuilt. Mr. Faneuil had then been dead several years. The engraving shows it as it appeared during the Revolution. It was enlarged in 1805, by the addition of another story, and an increase of forty feet in its width. The hall is about eighty feet square, and contains some fine paintings of distinguished men. The lower part is no longer used as a market. The original vane, copied from that of the London Royal Exchange, still turns upon the pinnacle. It is in the form of a huge grasshopper (the crest of Sir Thomas Gresham), through whose munificence the Royal Exchange was built.

[2] At that time Massachusetts contained sixty-six regularly organized towns.

480 PICTORIAL FIELD-BOOK

eral Court. The governor refused to receive their petition, and denounced the Convention as treasonable, notwithstanding the conservatism which the delegates from the country infused into the proceedings.[1] They disclaimed all pretension to political authority, and professed to have met "in this dark and distressing time to consult and advise as to the best manner of preserving peace and good order." The governor warned them to desist from further proceedings, and admonished them to separate without delay. But the Convention, while it was moderate in its action, was firm in its assumed position. It remained in session four days, during which time a respectful petition to the king was agreed to; also a letter to De Berdt, the agent of the colony in England, the chief topic of which was a defense of the province against the charge of a rebellious spirit. They also adopted an address to the people, in which the alarming state of the country was set forth; but submission to legal authority and abstinence from violent tumults were strongly inculcated. This was the first of those popular assemblies in America which speedily assumed the whole political power in the colonies.

September 27, 1768. Two regiments of troops from Halifax, under Colonels Dalrymple and Carr, borne by a considerable fleet, arrived at Boston the day after the adjournment of the Convention. The people had resolved to oppose their landing. There was room for the troops in the barracks upon Castle Island, and the inhabitants insisted upon their being landed there. But the governor and General Gage determined to have the troops near at hand, and, pretending that the barracks were reserved for two other regiments, ordered by the home government from Ireland, proceeded to provide quarters in the town. The governor's Council refused to act in concert with him, and he took the responsibility upon himself. On Sunday morning the fleet sailed up the harbor,[2] invested the town, and, under cover

[1] The following is a copy of the governor's proclamation on the occasion. Being short, I give it entire, as a fair specimen of the mildest tone assumed by the royal representatives in America toward the people:

"*To the Gentlemen assembled at Faneuil Hall under the name of a Committee or Convention:*

"As I have lately received from his majesty strict orders to support his Constitutional authority within this government, I can not sit still and see so notorious a violation of it as the calling an assembly of people by private persons only. For a meeting of the deputies of the towns is an assembly of the representatives of the people to all intents and purposes; and it is not the calling it a Committee or Convention that will alter the nature of the thing. I am willing to believe that the gentlemen who so hastily issued the summons for this meeting were not aware of the high nature of the offense they were committing; and they who have obeyed them have not well considered of the penalties which they will incur if they should persist in continuing their session, and doing business therein. A present ignorance of the law may excuse what is past; a step further will take away that plea. It is, therefore, my duty to interpose this instant, before it is too late. I do, therefore, earnestly admonish you that instantly, and before you do any business, you break up this assembly, and separate yourselves. I speak to you now as a friend to the province and a well-wisher to the individuals of it. But if you should pay no regard to this admonition, I must, as governor, assert the prerogative of the crown in a more public manner. For assure yourselves (I speak from instruction) *the king is determined to maintain his entire sovereignty over this province*, and whoever shall persist in usurping any of the rights of it will repent of his rashness. FRA. BERNARD.

"Province House, Sept. 22d, 1768."

A respectful reply to this proclamation, signed by Mr. Cushing in behalf of the Convention, was sent to the governor, but he refused to receive the message.

[2] There were eight ships—the Beaver, Senegal, Martin, Glasgow, Mermaid, Romney, Launceston, and Bonetta. In the Boston *Journal of the Times* of September 29th, 1768, I find the following: "The fleet was brought to anchor near Castle William; that night there was throwing of sky-rockets, and those passing in boats observed great rejoicings, and that the *Yankee Doodle Song*✻ was the capital piece in the band

✻ This air, with quaint words about "Lydia Locket" losing "her pocket," was known in Cromwell's time. Our lyric poet, G. P MORRIS, ESQ., in the following pleasant song, in meter adapted to the air, gives a version of

THE ORIGIN OF YANKEE DOODLE.

Once on a time old Johnny Bull flew in a raging fury,
And swore that Jonathan should have no trials, sir, by jury;
That no elections should be held across the briny waters:
And now said he, "I'll tax the TEA of all his sons and daughters."
Then down he sate in burly state, and bluster'd like a grandee,
And in derision made a tune call'd "Yankee doodle dandy."
"Yankee doodle"—these are facts—"Yankee doodle dandy:
My son of wax, your tea I'll tax; you—Yankee doodle dandy."

of the guns of the ships, the troops, about seven hundred in number, landed with charged muskets, fixed bayonets, colors flying, drums beating, and every other military parade usual on entering a conquered city of an enemy. A part of the troops encamped on the Common, and part occupied Faneuil Hall and the town-house. Cannons were placed in front of the latter; passengers in the streets were challenged, and other aggravating circumstances attended the entrance of the troops. Every strong feeling of the New Englander was outraged, his Sabbath was desecrated, his worship was disturbed, his liberty was infringed upon. The people became greatly exasperated; mutual hatred, deep and abiding, was engendered between the citizens and the soldiers, and the terms *rebel* and *tyrant* were daily bandied between them.

All Americans capable of intelligent thought sympathized with Massachusetts, and the engine of non-importation agreements, which worked so powerfully against the Stamp Act, was put in motion with increased energy.[1] These associations became general in all the colonies, under the sanction of the Assemblies. An agreement, presented by Washington in the House of Burgesses of Virginia, was signed by every member, and the patriotism of the people was every where displayed by acts of self-denial.[2]

of music. . . . . . . We now behold Boston surrounded, at a time of profound peace, by about fourteen ships of war, with springs on their cables and their broadsides to the town! If the people of England could but look into the town, they would see the utmost good order and observance of the laws, and that this mighty armament has no other rebellion to subdue than what existed in the brain or letter of the inveterate G——r B——d and the detested commis——rs of c——s."

"October 3. In King [now State] Street, the soldiers being gathered, a proclamation was read, offering a reward of ten guineas to such soldier as should inform of any one who should attempt to seduce him from the service."

"October 6. In the morning nine or ten soldiers of Colonel Carr's regiment were severely whipped on the Common. To behold Britons scourged by negro drummers was a new and very disagreeable spectacle."

[1] The non-importation agreement of the people of Boston was, substantially, that they would not import any goods for the fall of 1768, except those already ordered; that they would not import any goods from Great Britain from the 1st of January, 1769, to the 1st of January, 1770, except salt, coals, fish-hooks and lines, hemp and duck, bar lead and shot, wool cards and card wires; that they would not import on their own account, or on commission, or purchase from any who should import, from any other colony in America, from January, 1769, to January, 1770, any tea, paper, glass, or painters' colors, until the act imposing duties on those articles should be repealed.

[2] A letter from Newport, published in a New York paper in January, 1768, remarks that, at an afternoon visit of ladies, "It was resolved that those who could spin ought to be employed in that way, and those who could not should reel. When the time arrived for drinking tea, bohea and hyperion were provided, and every one of the ladies judiciously rejected the poisonous bohea, and unanimously, to their very great honor, preferred the balsamic hyperion." The hyperion here spoken of was of domestic manufacture—the dried leaves of the raspberry plant.

John sent the tea from o'er the sea, with heavy duties rated;
But whether hyson or bohea I never heard it stated.
Then Jonathan to pout began—he laid a strong embargo—
"I'll drink no TEA, by Jove!" so he threw overboard the cargo.
Then Johnny sent a regiment, big words and looks to bandy,
Whose martial band, when near the land, play'd "Yankee doodle dandy."
    "Yankee doodle—keep it up—Yankee doodle dandy—
    I'll poison with a tax your cup; *you*—Yankee doodle dandy."

A long war then they had, in which John was at last defeated,
And "Yankee doodle" was the march to which his troops retreated.
Cute Jonathan, to see them fly, could not restrain his laughter;
"That tune," said he, "suits to a T. I'll sing it ever after."
Old Johnny's face, to his disgrace, was flush'd with beer and brandy,
E'en while he swore to sing no more this "Yankee doodle dandy."
    Yankee doodle—ho, ha, he—Yankee doodle dandy,
    We kept the tune, but not the tea—Yankee doodle dandy.

I've told you now the origin of this most lively ditty,
Which Johnny Bull dislikes as "dull and stupid"—what a pity!
With "Hail Columbia" it is sung, in chorus full and hearty—
On land and main we breathe the strain John made for his tea party.
No matter how we rhyme the words, the music speaks them handy,
And where's the fair can't sing the air of "Yankee doodle dandy!"
    Yankee doodle, firm and true—Yankee doodle dandy—
    Yankee doodle, doodle doo, Yankee doodle dandy.

Let us consider for a moment the acts of the British Parliament at this juncture. It assembled on the 8th of November. Pitt was ill at his country seat, Townshend was dead, and the Duke of Grafton, who had been 1768. one of the Secretaries of State in the Rockingham administration, was really at the head of this unpopular ministry. He was an able, straight-forward politician, a warm admirer and friend of Pitt, and a firm supporter of his principles.[1] The king, in his speech from the throne, alluded to fresh troubles in America, and denounced, in strong terms, the rebellious spirit evinced by Massachusetts. The response of ministers assured the king of their determination to maintain "the supreme authority of Great Britain over every part of the British empire." The address was adopted in the House of Lords, but met considerable opposition in the Commons, where the oppressive acts of the government toward America were severely criticised.

AUGUSTUS HENRY, DUKE OF GRAFTON.
From an English print.

Early in January the consideration of American affairs was taken up in Parliament. The petition from the Boston Convention was contemptuously rejected; the Lords recommended, in an address to the king, the transmission of instructions to the Governor of Massachusetts to obtain full information of all treasons, and to transmit the offenders to England, to be tried there under a statute of the 35th of Henry VIII., which provided for the punishment of treason committed out of the kingdom. The address was opposed in the Commons by Pownall (who had been Governor of Massachusetts[a]), Burke, Barré, and a 1757. Dowdeswell. The latter denounced the measure as "unfit to remedy the disorders," and as "cruel to the Americans and injurious to England." He also censured Hillsborough for taking the responsibility, during the recess of Parliament, of ordering colonial governors to dissolve the Assemblies. Burke thundered his eloquent anathemas against the measure. "At the request of an exasperated governor," he exclaimed, "we are called upon to agree to an address advising the king to put in force against the Americans the Act of Henry VIII. And why? Because you can not trust the juries of that country! Sir, that word must convey horror to every feeling mind. If you have not a party among two millions of people, you must either change your plan of government, or renounce the colonies forever." Even Grenville, the author of the Stamp Act, opposed the measure as futile and unjust. Yet the January 26, address and resolutions accompanying it were concurred in by a majority of one 1769. hundred and fifty-five against eighty-nine.[2]

On the 8th of February Mr. Rose Fuller moved to recommit the address, for he saw in the proposed rigor toward the Americans the portents of great evil to the nation. He alluded to the miserable attempts to collect a revenue in America, and the monstrous evils growing out of them. "As for money," he said, "all that sum might be collected in Lon-

---

In Boston a party of some forty or fifty young ladies, calling themselves Daughters of Liberty, met at the house of the Rev. Mr. Morehead, where they amused themselves during the day with spinning "two hundred and thirty-two skeins of yarn, some very fine, which were given to the worthy pastor, several of the party being members of his congregation." Numerous spectators came in to admire them. Refreshments were indulged in, and "the whole was concluded with many agreeable tunes, anthems, and liberty songs, with great judgment; fine voices performing, which were animated, in all their several parts, by a number of the Sons of Liberty." It is added that there were upward of one hundred spinners in Mr. Morehead's society.

[1] The Duke of Grafton was the nobleman to whom the celebrated "Junius" addressed eleven of his scorching letters. In these he is represented as a most unscrupulous libertine in morals. He succeeded his grandfather in the family honors in 1757. He died on the 11th of March, 1811, aged seventy-five years.

[2] Cavendish's Debates.

don at less than half the expense."[1]   Pownall, after alluding to the early settlement of America, the privations of the people, their virtues and courage, perseverance and enterprise, remarked, " But now that spirit, equally strong and equally inflamed, has but a slight and trifling sacrifice to make ; the Americans have not a country to leave, but a country to defend ; and have not friends and relatives to leave and forsake, but friends and relatives to unite with and stand by in one common union."   But all efforts to avert the evil were vain ; Mr. Fuller's motion was negatived by a majority of one hundred and sixty-nine against sixty-five.

Lord North had succeeded Charles Townshend as Chancellor of the Exchequer.   He began his long career of opposition to the Americans by offering a resolution, on the 14th

1769.

of March, that a respectful petition or remonstrance from the people of New York *should not be received*.   This proposition, which was adopted, called up Colonel Barré. He reminded the House that he had predicted all that would happen on the passage of the Stamp Act, and he now plainly warned ministers that, if they persisted in their wretched course of oppression, the whole continent of North America would rise in arms, and those colonies, perhaps, be lost to England forever.   But the British Legislature, blinded by ignorance of Americans when the Stamp Act was passed, seemed now still more blind, because of films of prejudice generated by a false national pride.   The motion of Lord North prevailed—the petition was refused acceptance.

Gage went to Boston in October, to enforce the requisitions of the Quartering Act.   But he found none to co-operate with him except Governor Bernard, whose zeal in

1768.

LORD NORTH.[2]

his majesty's service had procured him a baronetcy, at the king's expense.   The Council and the select-men declined to act, and Gage was obliged to hire houses for the troops, and provide many articles for them out of his own military chest. Thus matters remained until spring, when intelligence of the several acts of Parliament against Massachusetts aroused the fiercest sentiments of opposition, short of actual rebellion, throughout the colonies.   Legislative Assemblies spoke out boldly, and for this crime they were dissolved by royal governors.   Yet amid all the excitement the colonists held out the olive branch of peace and reconciliation.

The Massachusetts Assembly convened in May, and resolved that it was inconsistent with their dignity and freedom to deliberate in the midst of an armed force, and that the presence of a military and naval armament was a breach of privilege.   They refused to enter upon the business of supplies, or any thing else but a redress of grievances, and petitioned the governor to remove the troops from Boston.   He not only refused, but adjourned the Assembly to Cambridge, when he informed them that he was going to England to lay a statement of the affairs of the colony before the king.   The House unanimously voted a petition to his majesty, asking the removal of Bernard forever ; and also adopted a resolution, declaring that the establishment of a standing army in the colony, in time of peace, was an invasion of natural rights, a violation of the British Constitution, high-

May 31, 1769.

June 13.

[1] It has been said that when Charles Townshend's project of taxation was in agitation, the English merchants offered to pay the taxes, or an equivalent for them, rather than run the risk of provoking the Americans and losing their trade.—*Pictorial History of the Reign of George III.*, i., 72.

[2] Frederic, Earl of Guilford, better known as Lord North, was a man of good parts, sincerely attached to English liberty, and conscientious in the performance of all his duties.   Like many other statesmen of his time, he utterly misapprehended the character of the American people, and could not perceive the justice of their claims.   Devoted to his king and country, he labored to support the dignity of the crown and the unity of the realm, but in so doing he aided in bringing fearful misery upon the Americans for a time.   He was a persuasive orator, a fair logician, amiable in private life, and correct in his morals.   He was afflicted with blindness during the last years of his life.   He died July, 1792, aged sixty years.

ly dangerous to the people, and unprecedented.   The governor, finding the members incorri-
_{August 1,}   gible, dissolved the Assembly, and sailed for England,[1] leaving the colony in charge
_{1769.}   of his lieutenant, Thomas Hutchinson.

The effects of the non-importation agreements upon English commerce again brought ministers to their senses.   The English merchants were really more injured by the acts of Parliament than the Americans, and they joined their petitions with those of the colonists for a
repeal of the noxious acts.[2]   Under the direction of Lord North, Hillsborough sent a circular letter to the colonies, intimating that the duties upon all articles enumerated in the late
act would be taken off, as a measure of *expediency*, except on tea.   This would be a partial
relief from the burden, but not a removal of the cause of complaint.   The *principle* was the
same whether duties were exacted on one article or a dozen, and so long as the assumed right
of Parliament to tax the colonies was practically enforced in the smallest degree, so long the
Americans felt their rights infringed.   Principle, not expediency, was their motive of action,
and, therefore, the letter of Hillsborough had no effect in quieting the disturbed ocean of popular feeling.   The year 1769 closed without any apparent approximation of Great Britain
and her American colonies to a reconciliation.

---

[1] Francis Bernard was Governor of New Jersey after Governor Belcher, in 1756.   He succeeded Pownall as Governor of Massachusetts in 1760, and held the office nine years.   The first years of his administration were satisfactory to the inhabitants, but, associating himself with ministers in their taxation schemes,
he became odious to the Massachusetts people.   His first false step was the appointment of Hutchinson chief
justice instead of the elder Otis.   When difficulties arose under the Stamp Act and kindred measures, Bernard was unfit for his position, for he had no talent for conciliation, and was disposed to use British power
more prodigally than British justice in maintaining the supremacy of the laws.   He was created a baronet
in the summer of 1769.   He never returned to America after leaving it, and died in England in June, 1779.

[2] The exports from England to America, which in 1768 had amounted to $11,890,000, $660,000 being
in tea, had fallen in 1769 to $8,170,000, the tea being only $220,000.—*Murray's United States*, i., 352.

Pownall, in the course of a speech in Parliament, also showed that the total produce of the new taxes for
the first year had been less than $80,000, and that the expenses of the new custom-house arrangements had
reduced the net profits of the crown revenue in the colonies to only $1475, while the extraordinary military
expenses in America amounted, for the same time, to $850,000.—*Hildreth*, ii., 552.

CHAPTER XXI.

" There is a spirit working in the world,
    Like to a silent, subterranean fire ;
Yet, ever and anon, some monarch hurl'd
    Aghast and pale attests its fearful ire,
The dungeon'd nations now once more respire
    The keen and stirring air of liberty.
The struggling giant wakes, and feels he's free ;
By Delphi's fountain-cave that ancient choir
    Resume their song ; the Greek astonish'd hears,
And the old altar of his worship rears.
Sound on, fair sisters ! sound your boldest lyres—
    Peal your old harmonies as from the spheres.
Unto strange gods too long we've bent the knee,
·The trembling mind, too long and patiently."
GEORGE HILL.

" Grand jurors, and sheriffs, and lawyers we'll spurn ;
    As judges, we'll all take the bench in our turn,
And sit the whole term without pension or fee,
    Nor CUSHING nor SEWALL look graver than we.
Our wigs, though they're rusty, are decent enough ;
    Our aprons, though black, are of durable stuff;
    Array'd in such gear, the laws we'll explain,
That poor people no more shall have cause to complain."
HONEYWOOD'S " RADICAL SONG."

E have considered, in the preceding chapter, the most important events, during the first nine years of the reign of George III., having any bearing on the Revolution. We have seen the germs of oppression, planted at different times from the era of the Restoration, springing into life and vigor, and bearing the bitter fruit of tyranny ; and observed the bold freemen of America pruning its most noxious branches, and trampling in the dust its " apples of Sodom." We have seen the tide of British power swelling high, and menacing, and beheld the firm rock of sound principles fearlessly breasting its billows, and hurling them back toward their source. We have seen a loyal people, warmly attached to the person of their sovereign, and venerating the laws of their fatherland, goaded, by ministerial ignorance and haughty indifference respecting the claims of right when interfering with expediency, to the assumption of manly defiance both of king and Parliament, until hireling butchers, with pike and bayonet, were seated in their midst to " harass the people and eat out their substance." We now behold them pressed to the alternative TO FIGHT OR BE SLAVES.

For several years the newspaper press had been rapidly growing in political importance, and the vehicle of mere general news became the channel of political and social enlightenment. In proportion to the development of its power and the creation of public opinion favorable to its views, was the increase of its boldness, and at the beginning of 1770 the American press was not only united in sentiment, but almost as fearless in the expression of political and religious opinions as the newspapers of the present day. American liberty was its theme, and almost every sheet, whether newspaper, almanac, tract, or hand-bill, issued at this time, was tinctured if not absolutely pervaded, by the absorbing topic. I have before me a copy of Bickerstaff's Boston Almanac for 1770, the title-page of which is here given, with a fac-simile of the engraving that adorns it. The portrait of Otis is supported on one side by Liberty, and on the other by Hercules, or Perseverance. At the feet of the latter, uncoiling, preparatory to striking a blow, is the venomous *rattlesnake*, an emblem used on some of the colonial flags when the war began. This was significant of the intention of America, under the guidance of the Spirit of Liberty, *to persevere, and strike a deadly blow, if necessary.* The poetry and maxims of the almanac are replete with political sentiments favorable to freedom ; and its pages contain the celebrated " *Massachusetts Song of Liberty,*" which became almost as popular throughout the colonies as did Robert Treat Paine's " Adams and Liberty" at a later day.[1] It is believed to have been written by Mrs. Mercy Warren.

B I C K E R S T A F F ' S

BOSTON ALMANACK,

For the Year of our LORD 1770. Being the fecond Year after Leap Year.

The Hon. JAMES OTIS, jun. Esq;

B O S T O N :

Printed by MEIN and FLEEMING, and to be SOLD by JOHN MEIN, at the LONDON BOOK-STORE, North-fide of KING-STREET.

[Price feven Coppers fingle, and 25 s. Old Tenor, or 3 s. 4. Lawful the Dozen.]

Party lines began now to be strictly drawn, and the old names of Whig and Tory, used in England toward the close of the seventeenth century, and recently revived, were adopted here, the former being assumed by those who opposed Parliamentary taxation, and the latter applied to those who favored it.[2] In Boston the wound inflicted by Bernard, in the introduction of soldiers, was daily festering. A weekly paper, the " Journal of the Times," fostered the most bitter animosity against the soldiers, by the publication of all sorts of stories concerning them, some true, but many more false and garbled. Daily quarrels between citizens and soldiers occurred upon the Common and in the streets ; and

---

[1] We give on the following page a copy of the Massachusetts Song of Liberty, with the music, as printed in the *Boston Almanac.*

[2] See note, page 71.

the fact that Mr. Otis had been severely beaten with fists and canes, in a coffee-house, by

THE MASSACHUSETTS SONG OF LIBERTY.

FAC-SIMILE OF THE MUSIC.

" Come swallow your bumpers, ye *Tories*, and roar,
  That the Sons of fair Freedom are hamper'd once more;
  But know that no *Cut-throats* our spirits can tame,
  Nor a host of *Oppressors* shall smother the flame.
    " *In Freedom we're born, and, like Sons of the brave,*
      Will never surrender,
      But swear to defend her,
      And scorn to survive, if unable to save.

" Our grandsires, bless'd heroes, we'll give them a tear,
  Nor sully their honors by stooping to fear;
  Through deaths and through dangers their *Trophies* they won,
  We dare be their *Rivals*, nor will be outdone.
    " *In Freedom we're born, &c.*

" Let tyrants and minions presume to despise,
  Encroach on our RIGHTS, and make FREEDOM their prize;
  The fruits of their rapine they never shall keep,
  Though vengeance may nod, yet how short is her sleep.
    " *In Freedom we're born, &c.*

" The tree which proud *Haman* for *Mordecai* rear'd
  Stands recorded, that virtue endanger'd is spared;
  That *rogues*, whom no bounds and no laws can restrain,
  Must be stripp'd of their honors and humbled again.
    " *In Freedom we're born, &c.*

" Our wives and our babes, still protected, shall know
  Those who dare to be free shall forever be so;
  On these arms and these hearts they may safely rely
  For in freedom we'll live, or like *Heroes* we'll die.
    " *In Freedom we're born, &c.*

" Ye insolent *Tyrants!* who wish to enthrall;
  Ye *Minions*, ye *Placemen, Pimps, Pensioners*, all;
  How short is your triumph, how feeble your trust,
  Your honor must wither and nod to the dust.
    " *In Freedom we're born, &c.*

" When oppress'd and approach'd, our KING we implore,
  Still firmly persuaded our RIGHTS he'll restore;
  When our hearts beat to arms to defend a just right,
  Our monarch rules there, and forbids us to fight.
    " *In Freedom we're born, &c.*

" Not the glitter of arms nor the dread of a fray
  Could make us submit to their chains for a day;
  Withheld by affection, on *Britons* we call,
  Prevent the fierce conflict which threatens your fall.
    " *In Freedom we're born, &c.*

" All ages shall speak with amaze and applause
  Of the prudence we show in support of our cause:
  Assured of our safety, a BRUNSWICK still reigns,
  Whose free loyal subjects are strangers to chains.
    " *In Freedom we're born, &c.*

" Then join hand in hand, brave AMERICANS all,
  To be free is to live, to be slaves is to fall;
  Has the land such a dastard as scorns not a LORD,
  Who dreads not a fetter much more than a sword?
    " *In Freedom we're born,*" *&c.*

one of the commissioners of customs and his friends,[1] produced the utmost excitement, and it was with great difficulty that open hostility was prevented. Numerous fights with straggling soldiers occurred, and a crisis speedily arrived.

While the non-importation agreements were generally adhered to faithfully, there were a few merchants who, loving mammon more than liberty, violated their obligations. In Boston they coalesced with the military officers, and many of the proscribed articles were imported in the names of the latter, ostensibly for the use of the soldiers. Many goods were January 23, brought in and sold under this cover. This fact became known, and a meeting 1770. of citizens was held at Faneuil Hall to consider it. Spirited resolutions were adopted, among which was one agreeing not only "totally to abstain from the use of tea" (the excepted article mentioned in Hillsborough's letter), and from other of the enumerated articles, but that they would use all proper measures to prevent a violation of the non-importation pledges. From that time TEA was a proscribed article, and the living principle of opposition to British oppression was strongly manifested by the unanimity with which the pleasant beverage was discarded.

February 9.   Early in February the females of Boston made a public movement on the subject of non-importation, and the mistresses of three hundred families subscribed their names to a league, binding themselves not to drink any tea until the Revenue Act was February 12. repealed. Three days afterward the *young ladies* followed the example of the matrons, and multitudes signed a document in the following terms : " We, the daughters of those patriots who have, and do now, appear for the public interest, and in that principally regard their posterity—as such, do with pleasure engage with them in denying ourselves the drinking of foreign tea, in hopes to frustrate a plan which tends to deprive a whole community of all that is valuable in life." All classes were thoroughly imbued with patriotism, and even the children were sturdy asserters of natural rights.[2]

Disregarding these expressions of public sentiment, a few merchants in Boston continued to sell the proscribed articles. Among them were Theophilus Lillie and four others, who were particularly bold in their unpopular conduct. To designate his store as one to be February 22, shunned, a mob, consisting chiefly of half-grown boys, raised a rude wooden head 1770. upon a pole near Lillie's door, having upon it the names of the other importers. A hand was attached to it, with the dexter finger pointing to Lillie's establishment. The merchant was greatly irritated. One of his friends, named Richardson, a stout, rough man, tried to persuade a countryman to prostrate the pageant by running his wagon against it.

---

[1] Robinson, one of the commissioners, had made such representations of Mr. Otis in Britain as provoked him to make a publication in the Boston Gazette on the subject. For some expression used in that article Robinson attempted to pull Otis's nose at a coffee-house. An affray ensued, in which Mr. Otis was so severely beaten that he was obliged to leave the city and retire to his country residence. From the injuries then received he never thoroughly recovered. Heavy damages (£2000) were awarded him against Robinson for the assault, but Otis generously forgave his assailant, and refused to take the money.

[2] While the king's troops were in Boston, an incident occurred that evinced the bold spirit of even the little boys. In the winter they were in the habit of building little hills of snow, and sliding down them to the pond on the Common, for amusement. The English soldiers, to provoke them, would often beat down these hills. On one occasion, having rebuilt their hills, and finding, on their return from school, that they were again demolished, several of the boys determined to wait upon the captain and complain of his soldiers. The officer made light of it, and the soldiers became more troublesome than ever. At last a meeting of the larger boys was held, and a deputation was sent to General Gage, the commander-in-chief. He asked why so many children had called upon him. " We come, sir," said the tallest boy, " to demand satisfaction." " What !" said the general, " have your fathers been teaching you rebellion, and sent you to exhibit it here ?" " Nobody sent us, sir," replied the boy, while his eyes flashed and cheek reddened at the imputation of rebellion ; " we have never injured or insulted your troops, but they have trodden down our snow-hills and broken the ice on our skating-grounds. We complained, and they called us young rebels, and told us to help ourselves if we could. We told the captain of this, and he laughed at us. Yesterday our works were destroyed the third time, and we will bear it no longer." The nobler feelings of the general's heart were awakened, and, after gazing upon them in silent admiration for a moment, he turned to an officer by his side, and said, " The very children here draw in a love of liberty with the air they breathe. You may go, my brave boys, and be assured, if my troops trouble you again, they shall be punished."—*Lossing's* " 1776," p. 90.

The man was a patriot, and refused, and Richardson attempted to pull it down himself. The mob pelted him with dirt and stones, and drove him into Lillie's house. Greatly exasperated, Richardson brought out a musket and discharged it, without aim, into the crowd. A lad named Christopher Gore (afterward Governor of the Commonwealth[a]) was slightly wounded, and another, Christopher Snyder, son of a poor widow, was killed. The mob seized Richardson and an associate named Wilmot, and carried them to Faneuil Hall, where they were examined and committed for trial. Richardson was found guilty of murder, but Lieutenant-governor Hutchinson refused to sign his death warrant. After two years' imprisonment, he was pardoned by the king.

[a] 1809.

The murder of the boy produced a great sensation throughout the country, and in Boston it was made the occasion of a most solemn pageant. His coffin, covered with inscriptions, such as " Innocence itself is not safe," and others of like tenor, was taken to Liberty Tree, where a great concourse assembled, and thence followed the remains to the grave. In that procession between four and five hundred school-boys took the lead. Six of Snyder's playfellows supported the coffin ; after them came the relatives and friends of the deceased, and nearly fifteen hundred of the inhabitants. The bells of the city were tolled, and those of the churches in the neighboring towns. The newspapers were filled with accounts of the murder and the funeral, and little Christopher Snyder was apotheosized as the *first martyr* in the cause of American liberty.

A more serious occurrence took place a few days afterward. A soldier, passing the rope-walk of John Grey, got into a quarrel with the workmen, and was severely beaten. He went to the barracks, and, returning with some comrades, they beat the rope-makers, and chased them through the streets. A large number of the people assembled in the afternoon, determined to avenge the workmen, but were stopped by the military. It was Friday, and the act of vengeance was deferred until Monday, so as not to disturb the Sabbath. On the evening of Monday, between six and seven o'clock, about seven hundred men, with clubs and other weapons, assembled in King (now State) Street, shouting, " Let us drive out these rascals ! They have no business here—drive them out !" The mob speedily augmented in numbers, and about nine o'clock an attack was made upon some soldiers in Dock Square, the mob shouting, " Town born, turn out ! Down with the bloody backs !" at the same time tearing up the market-stalls. The fearful cry of " Fire, fire !" was echoed through the town, and the inhabitants poured into the streets in terror and confusion. The whole city was in commotion, and before midnight the shouts of the multitude, the ringing of the alarum bells as if a great conflagration was raging, and the rattle of musketry, produced a fearful uproar. Two or three leading citizens endeavored to persuade the mob to disperse, and had, in a measure, secured their respectful attention, when a tall man, dressed in a scarlet cloak, and wearing a white wig, suddenly appeared among them, and commenced a violent harangue against the government officers and soldiers. He concluded his inflammatory speech by a loud shout, " To the main guard ! to the main guard !" The populace echoed the shout with fearful vehemence, and, separating into three divisions, took different routes toward the quarters of the main guard. As one of these divisions was passing the custom-house, a boy came up, and, pointing to the sentinel on duty there, cried out, " That's the scoundrel who knocked me down."[1] Instantly a score of voices shouted, " Let us knock *him* down ! Down with the bloody back ! kill him ! kill him !" The sentinel loaded his musket, the mob in the mean while pelting him with pieces of ice and other missiles, and finally attempting to seize him. He ran up the custom-house steps, but, unable to procure admission, called to the main guard for assistance. Captain Preston, the officer of the day,

March 5, 1770.

---

[1] This boy was an apprentice to a barber named Piemont, at whose shop some of the British officers were in the habit of shaving. One of them had come there some months previous to dress by the quarter, whose bill Piemont promised to allow to the boy who shaved him, if he behaved well. The quarter had expired, but the money could not be got, although frequently asked for. The last application was made on that evening, and, as the boy alleged, the officer knocked him down in reply to the " dun." The sentry he pointed out as the man that abused him.—See " *Traits of the Tea Party.*"

detailed a picket guard of eight men with unloaded muskets, and sent them to the relief of the sentinel. As they approached, the mob pelted them more furiously than they had the sentinel, and a stout mulatto named Attucks, who was at the head of a party of sailors, shouted, "Let us fall upon the nest! The main guard! the main guard!" The soldiers now loaded their guns. Attucks dared them to fire; and the mob pressed so closely upon them that the foremost were against the points of their bayonets. The soldiers, perfectly understanding the requirements of discipline, would not fire without orders. Emboldened by what seemed cowardice, or, perhaps, by a knowledge of the law which restrained soldiers from firing upon their fellow-citizens without orders from the civil magistrates, Attucks and the sailors gave three loud cheers, beat the muskets of the soldiers with their clubs, and shouted to the populace behind them, "Come on! don't be afraid of 'em—they daren't fire! knock 'em over! kill 'em!" At that moment Captain Preston came up, and endeavored to appease the excited multitude. Attucks aimed a blow with a club at Preston's head, which was parried with his arm, and, descending, knocked the musket of one of the soldiers to the ground. The bayonet was seized by the mulatto, and the owner of the musket was thrown down in the struggle. Just then voices in the crowd behind Preston cried, "Why don't you fire? why don't you fire?" The word fire fell upon the ears of Montgomery, the soldier struggling with Attucks, and as he rose to his feet he fired, and shot the mulatto dead. Immediately five other soldiers fired at short intervals; three of the populace were instantly killed, five dangerously wounded, and a few slightly hurt.[1]

The mob instantly dispersed. It was near midnight; the ground was covered with snow the air was clear and frosty, and the moon, in its first quarter, gave just sufficient light to reveal the dreadful scene. It was a fearful night for Boston. A cry, "The soldiers are rising! To arms! to arms! Turn out with your guns!" resounded through the streets, and the town drums beat their alarum call. Captain Preston also ordered his drums to beat to arms, and in a short time Colonel Dalrymple, the commander of the troops in the absence of Gage, with Lieutenant-governor Hutchinson, at the head of a regiment, was on the spot. Order was at length restored, and the streets were quiet before dawn. Captain Preston, in the mean time, had been arrested and put in prison, and during the next forenoon the eight soldiers were also committed, under a charge of murder.

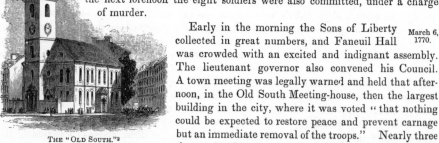

Early in the morning the Sons of Liberty collected in great numbers, and Faneuil Hall was crowded with an excited and indignant assembly. The lieutenant governor also convened his Council. A town meeting was legally warned and held that afternoon, in the Old South Meeting-house, then the largest building in the city, where it was voted "that nothing could be expected to restore peace and prevent carnage but an immediate removal of the troops." Nearly three thousand voices were unanimous in its favor. A committee of fifteen, with Samuel Adams as chairman, was appointed to present the resolution

March 6, 1770.

THE "OLD SOUTH."[2]

---

[1] Crispus Attucks, Samuel Gray, and James Caldwell were killed on the spot; Samuel Maverick and Patrick Carr received mortal wounds, of which the former died the next morning, and Carr on Wednesday of the next week.

[2] This venerable and venerated edifice, that stood through all the storms of the Revolution, and yet remains, stands on the corner of Washington and Milk Streets. It is of brick, and was erected in 1729–30, upon the site of an edifice built by the Pedo-baptists in 1669. The ancient church was of cedar, two stories high, with a steeple, gallery, and pews. The "Old South" was the famous gathering-place of the people during the excitements of 1773. The British troops occupied it as a circus for the drill of cavalry in 1775, after removing all the wood-work within, except the eastern gallery and the pulpit and sounding board. The British officers felt no compunctions in thus desecrating a *Presbyterian chapel*. It was repaired in 1782, and remains a fine model of our early church architecture. This view is from Washington Street.

to the acting governor and his Council, and to Colonel Dalrymple.   These officers were assured by Royal Tyler, one of the committee, that the people were determined to remove the troops out of town by force, if they would not go voluntarily.   " They are not such people," he said, " who formerly pulled down your house, that conduct these measures, but men of estates, men of religion.   The people," he continued, " will come in to us from all the neighboring towns ; we shall have ten thousand men at our backs, and your troops will probably be destroyed by the people, be it called rebellion or what it may."

Hutchinson and Dalrymple were in a dilemma.   They equally feared the popular indignation and the censure of ministers, and each endeavored to make the other responsible for the concessions which they saw must inevitably be made.   Hutchinson would not promise the committee that more than one regiment of the troops should be removed ; their report to the meeting was, therefore, quite unsatisfactory.   In the afternoon another committee was appointed, consisting of seven of the former deputation,[1] who bore the following resolution to the lieutenant governor : " It is the unanimous opinion of this meeting that the reply made to the vote of the inhabitants, presented to his honor this morning, is by no means satisfactory, and that nothing else will satisfy them but a total and immediate removal of all the troops."   Samuel Adams again acted as chairman.   Hutchinson denied that he had power to grant their request ; Adams in a few words proved to him that he had power conferred by the charter.   The governor consulted with Dalrymple in a whisper, and then made the offer again to remove one regiment.   The patriots were not to be trifled with.   Adams, seeming not to represent, but to personify, the universal feeling, stretched forth his arm, as if it had been upheld by the strength of thousands, and, with unhesitating promptness and dignified firmness, replied, " Sir, if the lieutenant governor or Colonel Dalrymple, or both together, have authority to remove *one* regiment, they have authority to remove *two ;* and nothing short of a total evacuation of the town, by all the regular troops, will satisfy the public mind or preserve the peace of the province."

The officers were abashed before this plain committee of a democratic assembly.   They knew the danger that impended ; the very air was filled with breathings of suppressed indignation.   They receded, fortunately, from the arrogance they had hitherto maintained.   Their reliance on a standing army faltered before the undaunted, irresistible resolution of free, unarmed citizens.[2]   Hutchinson consulted his Council.   The concession was agreed upon—the lieutenant governor, Council, and Dalrymple consenting to bear mutually the responsibility of the act—and the people were assured of the immediate removal of the troops. On Monday following the troops were conducted to Castle William, and Boston be- March 12, came quiet. 1770.

The obsequies of the victims murdered on the night of the 5th were performed on the 8th.[3] The hearses met upon the spot in front of the custom-house, where the tragedy occurred, and thence the procession, in platoons six deep, marched to the Middle Burial-ground, wherein the bodies were deposited.   As on the occasion of the burial of young Snyder, the bells of Boston and adjacent towns tolled a solemn knell, and again a cry of vengeance burst over the land.   The story of the " Boston massacre," as it was called, became a tale of horror, which every where excited the most implacable hatred of British domination ; and the justifiable act of the soldiers, in defending their lives against a lawless mob, was exaggerated into an unprovoked assault of armed mercenaries upon a quiet and defenseless people.

Captain Preston and the eight soldiers, after the lapse of several months, were put upon their trial before Judge Lynde for murder.[4]   John Adams, an eminent lawyer, one of the

---

[1] The committee consisted of Samuel Adams, John Hancock, William Molineux, William Phillips, Joseph Warren, Joshua Henshaw, and Samuel Pemberton.

[2] Snow's *History of Boston.*

[3] Attucks and Caldwell had no relatives, and were friendless.   Their bodies were borne from Faneuil Hall.   Maverick, only seventeen years of age, was borne from the house of his mother, in Union Street, and Gray from that of his brother, in Royal Exchange Lane.

[4] Captain Preston's trial commenced on the 24th of October, and lasted until the 30th.   The trial of the soldiers commenced on the 27th of November, and ended on the 5th of December.   So searching was the

leaders in the attempt to procure the removal of the troops, and greatly esteemed by the people for his patriotism, was solicited to undertake their defense.   It was a severe ordeal for his independence of spirit, yet he did not hesitate.   At the risk of losing the favor and esteem of the people, he appeared as the advocate of the accused, having for his colleague Josiah Quincy, another leading patriot, whose eloquent voice had been often heard at assemblies of the Sons of Liberty.   Robert Treat Paine, afterward one of the signers of the Declaration of Independence, conducted the prosecution, with great reputation, in the absence of the attorney general.   A Boston jury was empanneled, and, after a fair trial, Captain Preston and six of the soldiers were adjudged not guilty.   The other two, Montgomery and Killroy, who were known to have fired their muskets, were found guilty of manslaughter only.   They were branded in the hand, in open court, and discharged.   This trial, when all the circumstances are considered, exhibits one of the most beautiful of the many pictures of justice and mercy that characterized the Revolution, and silenced forever the slander of the British ministry who favored the revival of the Act of Henry VIII., that American jurors might not be trusted.

March 5, 1770.   On the very day of the " Boston massacre" Lord North asked leave to bring in a bill in the House of Commons, repealing the duties upon glass, &c., mentioned in Hillsborough's circular, but retaining the three per cent. duty upon tea.   This duty was small, and was avowedly a " pepper-corn rent;" to save the national honor.   North's proposition met with little favor from either party.   The friends of America asked for a repeal of the whole act, and the friends of government opposed a partial repeal as utterly fruitless of good.   The bill, however, after encountering great opposition in both Houses, and particularly in the House of Lords, was carried, and received the royal assent on the 12th of April.

When the intelligence of this act reached the colonies, it was regarded with very little favor.   The same unrighteous principle was practically asserted, and the people felt that very little concession was made.   But they were beginning, toward the close of 1770, to be less faithful in observing the non-importation agreements ; and in October, at a meeting of the Boston merchants, it was resolved, in consequence of the almost universal violation of these agreements in New York, to import every thing but TEA.   The Philadelphia and Charleston merchants followed their example, and that lever of coercion in the hands of the colonists, operating upon Parliament through English merchants, was almost wholly abandoned, much to the chagrin of the leading patriots.   These associations, while they had a favorable political effect upon the colonies, were also instrumental in producing social reforms of much value.   Many extravagant customs, such as pageantries at funerals, displays of costly finery at balls and parties, and kindred measures, involving great expenditure of time and money, were discontinued ; new sources of wealth and comfort to be derived from home industry were developed ; and, better than all, lessons of the strictest economy were learned.   The infant manufactories of America received a strong impulse from the agreements, and homemade articles, first worn from necessity, became fashionable.   The graduating class at Cambridge took their degrees in homespun suits, in 1770.

For two years very little occurred to disturb the tranquillity of Boston.   The brutal attack of Robinson had deprived the patriots of the services of James Otis, for insanity clouded his active mind and terminated his public career.[1]   But new men, equally patriotic stood

examination of witnesses by Mr. Quincy, that Mr. Adams was obliged to ask him to desist, for he was eliciting from them facts that were not only irrelevant to the case in hand, but dishonorable to the town.

[1] James Otis, Jr., was the son of Colonel James Otis, of Barnstable, Massachusetts, where he was born February 5th, 1725.   He graduated at Harvard College in 1743.   He studied law with Mr. Gridley, then the first lawyer in the province, and commenced the practice of his profession at Plymouth at the age of twenty-one years.   In 1761 he distinguished himself by his plea in opposition to the Writs of Assistance.   His antagonist on that occasion was his law tutor, Mr. Gridley.   Of his speech at that time John Adams said, " James Otis was a flame of fire. . . . . . American independence was then and there born.   Every man of an immense crowded audience appeared to me to go away as I did

ready to take his place. John Adams, then in the vigor of life, and rapidly rising in public estimation, was chosen to fill his place in the House of Representatives. He, Samuel Adams, John Hancock, Joseph Warren (a young physician), Josiah Quincy, and Dr. Benjamin Church were the leaders in private meetings, now beginning to be held, in which schemes for public action were planned. These men were exceedingly vigilant, and noticed every infringement of natural or chartered rights on the part of government and its agents. In the House of Representatives they originated almost every measure for the public good, and the people esteemed them as the zealous guardians of their rights and privileges. When Hutchinson removed the General Court to Cambridge, they protested, contending that it March 31, could be held, legally, only at Boston ; and in all the struggles between the Assem- 1770. bly and the governor, during his administration, these men were foremost in defense of popular rights.

Lieutenant-governor Hutchinson received the appointment of governor in the spring of 1771. About the same time Dr. Franklin was chosen agent for Massachusetts, Dennis de Berdt being dead. When the Assembly convened in May, the subject of taxing the May 25, salaries of crown officers, that of removing the General Court back to Boston, and 1771. kindred topics, produced considerable excitement in that body. Hutchinson told them that he had been instructed not to give his consent to any act taxing the income of the crown officers, and he positively refused to adjourn the Assembly to Boston. The consequence was, that the Court was prorogued without making any provision for the public expense.

The next year Parliament, by special act, made the governors and judges of the colonies quite independent of the colonial Assemblies for their salaries ; and Hutchinson 1772. informed the Massachusetts Assembly that henceforth his salary would be paid by the crown. The Assembly at once denounced the measure as a violation of the charter, and no better than a standing bribe of six thousand six hundred and sixty-six dollars a year from the crown to the governor. Other colonial Assemblies took umbrage, and made similar denunciations, and again the public mind was agitated.

---

ready to take up arms against Writs of Assistance." Otis was elected to the Legislature in 1762, and was a member of the Stamp Act Congress held at New York in 1765. That year he wrote his celebrated pamphlet in defense of colonial rights. He held the office of judge advocate, but in 1767 resigned, and renounced all offices under government, because of encroachments upon the rights of the people. Brutally beaten by a commissioner of customs in the autumn of 1769, he was obliged to retire to his country residence. The injuries he received left their effects upon his mind, and from that time his reason was shattered. The great man, though in ruins, lived nearly thirteen years, when, on the 23d of May, 1782, while standing in the door of Mr. Osgood's house in Andover, he was killed by lightning. He had often expressed a desire to be thus deprived of life when it should please God to call him. In a commemorative ode, written at the time by the Hon. Thomas Dawes, the following lines occur :

> " Yes, when the glorious work which he begun
> Shall stand the most complete beneath the sun—
> When peace shall come to crown the grand design,
> His eyes shall live to see the work divine—
> The heavens shall then his generous spirit claim,
> In storms as loud as his immortal fame.
> Hark ! the deep thunders echo round the skies !
> On wings of flame the eternal errand flies ;
> One chosen, charitable bolt is sped,
> And Otis mingles with the glorious dead."

Mr. Otis was a scholar as well as a statesman. He was complete master of classical literature,* and no American at that time possessed more extensive knowledge. He may be justly ranked among the founders of our republic, for he was truly the master of ceremonies in laying the corner-stone. He lived to see the work nearly completed, and beheld the wing of peace spread over the land.

---

* The following anecdote is related of Mr. Otis as illustrative of his ready use of Latin even during moments of mental aberration. Men and boys, heartless and thoughtless, wou'd sometimes make themselves merry at his expense when he was seen in the streets afflicted with lunacy. On one occasion he was passing a crockery store, when a young man, who had a knowledge of Latin, sprinkled some water upon him from a sprinkling-pot with which he was wetting the floor of the second story, at the same time saying, *Pluit tantum, nescio quantum, Scis ne tu ?* " It rains so much, I know not how much. Do you know ?" Otis immediately picked up a missile, and, hurling it through the window of the crockery store, it smashing every thing in its way, exclaimed, *Fregi tôt, nescio quot, Scis ne tu ?* " I have broken so many, I know not how many. Do you know ?"

In the midst of this effervescence a circumstance occurred which augmented intensely the flame of rebellion burning in the hearts of the people.   By it Boston was thrown into a violent commotion, and it was with great difficulty that the people were restrained from enacting anew the violence against Hutchinson in 1765.   In October a town meeting was held, at which a large committee, composed of the popular leaders, was appointed to draw up a statement of the rights of the colonies, and to communicate and publish the same to the several towns of the province.   This paper contained a list of all the grievances which Massachusetts had suffered since the accession of the reigning sovereign, and condemned a plan, said to have been in agitation for a long time, to establish bishops in America.   It was the boldest exposition of the grievances and rights of the colonies yet put forth, and, by its suggestion, Committees of Correspondence, such as were soon afterward organized in Virginia, were appointed in the several towns.[1]   This paper was republished by Franklin in London, January, with a preface of his own, and produced a great sensation.   At the opening of the 1773. next session of the Legislature Hutchinson denounced the Boston address as seditious and traitorous, and violent discussions ensued.

Just at this moment, when the public mind was greatly inflamed against Hutchinson, the Assembly received a communication from Dr. Franklin, inclosing several letters written by Hutchinson and others[2] to Thomas Whately, a member of Parliament, then out of office, wherein they vilified the character of several of the popular leaders, advised the immediate adoption of coercive measures, and declared that there " must be an abridgment of what are called English liberties."   By what means Franklin obtained possession of these letters is not certainly known, for he was too honorable to divulge the names of parties concerned.[3] They were sent to the Rev. Dr. Cooper, of Boston, and by him handed to Mr. Cushing, the Speaker of the Assembly.   After having been shown privately to leading men for several months, they were made public.   The town was at once in a violent ferment.   A committee was appointed to wait upon the governor, and demand an acknowledgment or denial of the genuineness of the letters.   He owned them as his, but declared that they were quite confidential.   This qualification was not considered extenuating, and the Assembly adopted a petition to the king for the removal of Governor Hutchinson and Lieutenant-governor Oliver, as public slanderers, and enemies to the colony, and, as such, not to be tolerated.

This petition was sent to Franklin, who was instructed to present it in person, if possible. This request could not be granted.   He sent the petition to Lord Dartmouth, then at his country seat, who presented it to the king.   After considerable delay, Franklin was informed that his majesty had referred it to his Privy Council.[4]   The publication of the letters produced excitement in England, and Franklin, to defend innocent parties, frankly took upon

---

[1] Dr. Gordon says (i., 207) that the system of Committees of Correspondence originated with James Warren, who suggested them to Samuel Adams while the latter was passing an evening with the former at Plymouth.   Adams, pleased with the suggestion, communicated it to the leading patriots at the next secret caucus, and that powerful engine in the Revolution was speedily put in motion.

JAMES WARREN was an active patriot.   He was descended from one of the first settlers at Plymouth, and was greatly esteemed for his personal worth.   He was chosen a member of the General Court of Massachusetts in 1760, and, though not a brilliant orator, was a deep and original thinker.   He was for many years Speaker of the House of Representatives.   At the close of the war he retired from public duties, and died at Plymouth, November 27th, 1808, aged eighty-two years.   He was the husband of Mercy Warren, the historian.

[2] The names of the several writers were Andrew Oliver, Charles Paxton, Thomas Moffatt, Robert Auchmuty, Nathaniel Rogers, and George Rome.   Mr. Whately was dead when the letters were given to Franklin.

[3] The late Dr. Hosack, of New York, in his memoir of Dr. Hugh Williamson, published in 1823, asserts that the papers were put into Franklin's hands by that gentleman, without any suggestion on his part.   Williamson obtained them by stratagem from the office of Mr. Whately, brother of the late Thomas Whately, then dead.   Mr. Whately suspected that Lord Temple, Pitt's brother-in-law, who had asked permission to examine the papers of Secretary Whately, was the man who abstracted them, and placed them in Franklin's hands.   Whately charged the act upon Temple, and a duel was the result, in which the former was wounded.   Of this affair Franklin knew nothing until it was over.   In justice to others, he took the responsibility upon himself, as mentioned in the text.

[4] The Privy Council consists of the cabinet and thirty-five peers.

OF THE REVOLUTION. 495

Franklin before the Privy Council.   Wedderburne's Abuse.   Franklin's Vow.   New Taxation Scheme.   East India Company.

himself the whole responsibility of sending them to America.   He was accordingly summoned before the Council, where he appeared without a legal adviser.   Finding
Wedderburne, the solicitor general, re-
tained as counsel for Hutchinson, Franklin asked
and obtained leave to have counsel also.   He employed Mr. Dunning, one of the ablest Constitu
tional lawyers of the day, and toward the close of
February the case was brought before the Privy
Council.   The solicitor general made a bitter attack upon Franklin, accusing him of dishonor in
procuring private letters clandestinely, and charging him with duplicity and wily intrigue.   The
philosophic statesman received this tirade of abuse
in silence, and without any apparent emotion, for
he was conscious that he had violated no rule of
honor or integrity.   The accusations and pleadings of Wedderburne had their effect, however.
His abuse greatly pleased the peers, and the petition was dismissed as "groundless, scandalous,
and vexatious."   A few days afterward Franklin
received a notice of his dismissal from the responsible and lucrative office of postmaster general for
the colonies.   This was an act of spite which recoiled fearfully upon ministers.[2]

LORD DARTMOUTH.[1]
From an English print.

January 29, 1774.

Early in 1773 a new thought upon taxation made its advent into the brain of Lord North.
The East India Company,[3] feeling the effects of the colonial smuggling trade, and of the non
importation agreements, requested the government to take off the duty of three per cent. a
pound on their tea, levied in America.   Already seventeen millions of pounds had accumulated in their stores in England, and they offered to allow government to retain six pence
upon the pound as an exportation tariff, if they would take off the three-pence duty.   Here
was a fair and honorable opening not only to conciliate the colonies, but to procure, without expense, double the amount of revenue.   But the ministry, deluded by false views of
national honor, would not take advantage of this excellent opportunity to heal the dissensions
and disaffection in the colonies, but stupidly favored the East India Company, and utterly

[1] Lord Dartmouth succeeded the Earl of Hillsborough in the office of Secretary of State for the colonies,
and as head of the Board of Trade, in 1772.   Dartmouth was considered rather friendly to the colonies, and
he and Franklin had ever been on terms of amity.

[2] On returning to his lodgings that night, Franklin took off the suit of clothes he had worn, and declared
that he would never wear it again until he should sign the degradation of England and the independence of
America.   He kept his word, and more than ten years afterward, when, on the 3d of September, 1783, he
signed a definitive treaty of peace with Great Britain, on the basis of absolute independence for America, he
wore the same suit of clothes for the first time after his vow was uttered.

[3] The East India Company, still in existence, is a joint-stock company, originally established to carry on
a trade by sea, between England and the countries lying eastward of the Cape of Good Hope.   It was constituted by royal charter in 1600, and enjoyed the monopoly of the trade in those remote regions until 1688,
when another corporation was chartered.   The two united in 1702, and the monopoly thus granted to them
was continued, by successive acts of Parliament, until 1804.   It then received some important modifications,
and the charter was renewed for twenty years.   In 1833 an act was passed extending the charter, but abolishing the monopoly of the China trade, which the company had enjoyed nearly two hundred and fifty years.
This company planted the British empire in India.   It first established armed factories, and for many years
competed with the French for the trade and political influence in the surrounding districts.   Under the pretense of securing honest trade, they subdued small territories, until Lord Clive, the governor general of the
company in India, by several victories, established British power there, and obtained a sway over some of
the fairest portions of the Mogul empire.   At the present time the British Indian empire comprises the
whole of Hindostan, from the Himalaya Mountains to Cape Comorin, with a population of more than one
hundred and twenty millions!   At the time under consideration the East India Company was at the height
of its success, commercial and political.

neglected the feelings of the Americans.   It was a sacrifice of principle to mammon which produced a damage that no subsequent act could repair.

1773.   On the 10th of May a bill was passed, allowing the company to export tea to America on their own account, without paying export duty.   Ships were immediately laden with the article, and in a few weeks several large vessels, bearing the proscribed plant, were crossing the Atlantic for American ports.   Agents or consignees were appointed in the several colonies to receive it, and the ministry fondly imagined that they had at last outwitted the vigilant patriots.

Information of this movement had been received in the colonies, and, before the company's vessels arrived, preparations were made in the chief cities to prevent the landing of the cargoes.   Public meetings were held, and the consignees were called upon to resign.   In Boston the consignees were known to the public ; they were all friends of Governor Hutchinson. Two were his sons, and one (Richard Clarke[1]) was his nephew.   They were summoned to November 3,   attend a meeting of the Sons of Liberty, convened under Liberty Tree, and re-
1773.   sign their appointments,[2] but they contemptuously refused to comply.   This meeting was announced by the town-crier in the streets, and by the ringing of bells for an hour. About five hundred persons assembled at the tree, from the top of which, fastened to a pole, a large flag was unfurled.   Two days afterward a legal town meeting was held, at which John Hancock presided.[3]   They adopted as their own the sentiments of eight resolutions passed at a public meeting in Philadelphia a month before, and appointed a committee to wait upon the consignees and request them to resign.   These gentlemen equivocated, and the meeting voted their answer " unsatisfactory and daringly affrontive."   On the 18th an-
November,   other meeting was held, and a committee appointed again to wait upon the con-
1773.   signees.   Their answer this time was more explicit.   " It is out of our power to comply with the request of the town."   In the evening the house of Richard Clarke and his sons, in School Street, was surrounded by a crowd.   A pistol was fired among them from the dwelling, and was responded to by the populace breaking the windows.

The meeting, on receiving the reply of the consignees, broke up without uttering a word. This was ominous ; the consignees were alarmed, for it was evident that the people had determined to stop talking, and henceforth to act.   The governor called a meeting of the Council, and asked advice respecting measures for preserving the peace.   A petition was presented by the consignees, asking leave to resign their appointments into the hands of the governor

---

[1] John Singleton Copley, the eminent painter, and father of Lord Lyndhurst, married a daughter of Richard Clarke.   Both Copley and his father-in-law became early refugee Loyalists, and fled to England, where the latter was pall-bearer at Governor Hutchinson's funeral in 1780.

[2] The following is a copy of the hand-bill that advertised the meeting :

" *To the Freemen of this and the neighboring Towns.*

" GENTLEMEN—You are desired to meet at the Liberty Tree this day at twelve o'clock at noon, then and there to hear the persons to whom the TEA shipped by the East India Company is consigned, make a public resignation of their offices as consignees, upon oath ; and also swear that they will reship any teas that may be consigned to them by the said company, by the first vessel sailing to London.   O. C., *Sec'y.*

" Boston, November 3, 1773.

" ☞ *Show me the man that dare take this down !*"

The following hand-bill was also circulated about the same time :

" The true Sons of Liberty and supporters of the non-importation agreement are determined to resent any or the least insult or menace offered to any one or more of the several committees appointed by the body at Faneuil Hall, and chastise any one or more of them as they deserve ; and will also support the printers in any thing the committee shall desire them to print.

" ☞ As a warning to any one that shall affront as aforesaid, upon sure information given, one of these advertisements will be posted up at the door of the dwelling-house of the offender."

These placards, and others given in connection with the tea excitement, I copied from originals preserved by the Massachusetts Historical Society, in tome marked *Proclamations.*

[3] On the 12th the captain general of the province issued an order for the Governor's Cadets (Bostonians) to stand ready to be called out for the purpose of aiding the civil magistrates in keeping the peace.   John Hancock was colonel of this regiment.

and Council, and praying them to take measures for the safe landing of the teas.   The prayer was refused on the part of the Council, and the consignees, for safety, withdrew to the castle.

While the Council was thus declining to interfere, one of the ships (the Dartmouth, Captain Hall) came to anchor near the castle.   A meeting of the people of Boston and the neighboring towns was convened at Faneuil Hall,[1] which being too small for the assembly, it adjourned to the Old South Meeting-house.   They resolved "that the tea shall not be landed ; that no duty shall be paid ; and that it shall be sent back in the November 29 1773. same bottom."   They also voted " that Mr. Roch, the owner of the vessel, be directed not to enter the tea at his peril ; and that Captain Hall be informed, and at his peril, not to suffer any of the tea to be landed."   The ship was ordered to be moored at Griffin's Wharf,[2] and a guard of twenty-five men was appointed to watch her.   The meeting received a letter from the consignees, offering to store the teas until they could write to England and receive instructions, but the people were determined that the pernicious weed should not be landed.   The offer was rejected with disdain.   The sheriff then read a proclamation by the governor, ordering the meeting to disperse ; it was received with hisses.   A resolution was then passed, ordering the vessels of Captains Coffin and Bruce, then hourly expected with cargoes of tea, to be moored at Griffin's Wharf; and, after solemnly agreeing to carry their resolves into execution at any risk, and thanking their brethren from the neighboring towns, the meeting was dissolved.

From that time until the 14th every movement on the part of the people relating to the tea was in charge of the Boston Committee of Correspondence.   The December, 1773. two vessels alluded to arrived, and were moored at Griffin's Wharf, under charge of the volunteer guard, and public order was well observed.   On the 14th another meeting was held in the Old South,[3] when it was resolved to order Mr. Roch to apply immediately for a clearance for his ship, and send her to sea.   The governor, in the mean while, had taken measures to prevent her sailing out of the harbor.   Under his direction, Admiral Montague fitted out two armed vessels, which he stationed at the entrance of the harbor ; and Colonel Leslie, in command of the castle, received Hutchinson's written orders not to allow any vessel to pass the guns of the fortress outward, without a permission signed by himself.

On the 16th several thousand people (the largest meeting ever to that time December, 1773. known in Boston) collected in the Old South and vicinity.   Samuel Phillips Savage, of Weston, presided.   The youthful Josiah Quincy was the principal speaker, and, with words almost of prophecy, harangued the multitude of eager and excited listeners.   " It is not, Mr. Moderator," he said, " the spirit that vapors within these walls that must stand us in stead.   The exertions of this day will call forth events which will make a very different spirit necessary for our salvation.   Whoever supposes that shouts and hosannas will terminate the trials of this day entertains a childish fancy.   He must be grossly ignorant of the importance and value of the prize for which we contend ; we must be equally ignorant of the power of those who have combined againt us ; we must be blind to that malice, inveteracy, and insatiable revenge which actuate our enemies, public and private, abroad and in

---

[1] The following is a copy of the hand-bill announcing the meeting.   The Dartmouth arrived on Sunday, and this placard was posted all over Boston early on Monday morning :

" Friends ! Brethren ! Countrymen !—That worst of plagues, the detested TEA shipped for this port by the East India Company, is now arrived in the Harbor ; the Hour of Destruction, or manly opposition to the Machinations of Tyranny, stares you in the Face ; every Friend to his Country, to himself, and to Posterity is now called upon to meet at *Faneuil Hall*, at nine o'clock THIS DAY (at which time the bells will ring), to make united and successful resistance to this last, worst, and most destructive measure of administration.

" Boston, November 29, 1773."

[2] This was a little south of Fort Hill, near the present Liverpool Dock.

[3] The notice for the meeting was as follows :

" Friends ! Brethren ! Countrymen !—The perfidious arts of your restless enemies to render ineffectual the resolutions of the body of the people, demand your assembling at the Old South Meeting-house precisely at two o'clock this day, at which time the bells will ring."

our bosoms, to hope that we shall end this controversy without the sharpest, the sharpest conflicts—to flatter ourselves that popular resolves, popular harangues, popular acclamations, and popular vapor will vanquish our foes.   Let us consider the issue.   Let us look to the end.   Let us weigh and consider before we advance to those measures which must bring on the most trying and terrible struggle this country ever saw.''[1]

When Mr. Quincy closed his harangue (about three o'clock in the afternoon), the question was put, "Will you abide by your former resolutions with respect to not suffering the tea to be landed?"   The vast assembly, as with one voice, gave an affirmative reply.   Mr. Roch, in the mean while, had been sent to the governor, who was at his country house at Milton, a few miles from Boston, to request a permit for his vessel to leave the harbor.   A demand was also made upon the collector for a clearance, but he refused until the tea should be landed. Roch returned late in the afternoon with information that the governor refused to grant a permit until a clearance should be exhibited.   The meeting was greatly excited ; and, as twilight was approaching, a call was made for candles.   At that moment a person disguised like a Mohawk Indian raised the war-whoop in the gallery of the Old South, which was answered from without.   Another voice in the gallery shouted, "Boston Harbor a tea-pot to-night !   Hurra for Griffin's Wharf !''   A motion was instantly made to adjourn, and the people, in great confusion, crowded into the streets.   Several persons in disguise were seen crossing Fort Hill in the direction of Griffin's Wharf, and thitherward the populace pressed.

Concert of action marked the operations at the wharf ; a general system of proceedings had doubtless been previously arranged.   The number of persons disguised as Indians was fifteen or twenty, but about sixty went on board the vessels containing the tea.   Before the work was over, it was estimated that one hundred and forty were engaged.   A man named Lendall Pitts seems to have been recognized by the party as a sort of commander-in-chief, and under his directions the Dartmouth was first boarded, the hatches were taken up, and her cargo, consisting of one hundred and fourteen chests of tea, was brought on deck, where the boxes were broken open and their contents cast into the water.   The other two vessels (the *Eleanor*, Captain James Bruce, and the *Beaver*, Captain Hezekiah Coffin) were next boarded, and all the tea they contained was thrown into the harbor.   The whole quantity thus destroyed within the space of two hours was three hundred and forty-two chests.

It was an early hour on a clear, moonlight evening when this transaction took place, and the British squadron was not more than a quarter of a mile distant.   British troops, too, were near, yet the whole proceeding was uninterrupted.   This apparent apathy on the part of government officers can be accounted for only by the fact alluded to by the papers of the time, that something far more serious was expected on the occasion of an attempt to land the tea, and that the owners of the vessels, as well as the public authorities, felt themselves

---

[1] Josiah Quincy was born in Boston, February 23d, 1744.   As a student he was remarkably persevering, and with unblemished reputation he graduated at Harvard in 1763.   He pursued legal studies under the celebrated Oxenbridge Thacher, of Boston.   The circumstances of the times turned his thoughts to political topics. and he took sides with Otis, Adams, and others, against the aggressive policy of Britain.   As early as 1768 he used this bold language : "Did the blood of the ancient Britons swell our veins, did the spirit of our forefathers inhabit our breasts, should we hesitate a moment in preferring death to a miserable existence in bondage?"   In 1770 he declared, "I wish to see my countrymen break off—*off forever !* all social intercourse with those whose commerce contaminates, whose luxuries poison, whose avarice is insatiable, and whose unnatural oppressions are not to be borne."   Mr. Quincy was associated with John Adams in the defense of the perpetrators of the "Boston massacre" in 1770, and did not by that defense alienate the good opinion of the people.   In February, 1771, he was obliged to go to the south on account of a pulmonary complaint.   At Charleston he formed an acquaintance with Pinckney, Rutledge, and other patriots, and, returning by land, conferred with other leading Whigs in the several colonies.   Continued ill health, and a desire to make himself acquainted with English statesmen, induced him to make a voyage to England in 1774, where he had personal interviews with most of the leading men.   He asserts that, while there, Colonel Barré, who had traveled in America, assured him that such was the ignorance of the English people, two thirds of them thought the Americans were all negroes !   Becoming fully acquainted with the feelings and intentions of the king and his ministers, and hopeless of reconciliation, Mr. Quincy determined to return and arouse his countrymen to action.   He embarked for Boston, with declining health, in March, and died when the vessel was in sight of land, April 26th, 1775, aged thirty-one years.

placed under lasting obligations to the *rioters* for extricating them from a serious dilemma.[1] They certainly would have been worsted in an attempt forcibly to land the tea.   In the

actual result the vessels and other property were spared from injury ; the people of Boston, having carried their resolution into effect, were satisfied ; the courage of the civil and military officers was unimpeached, and the "national honor" was not compromised. None but the East India Company, whose property was destroyed, had reason for complaint.   As soon as the work of destruction was completed, the active party marched in perfect order into the town, preceded by drum and fife, dispersed to their homes, and Boston, untarnished by actual mob or riot,[2] was never more tranquil than on that bright and frosty December night.

A large proportion of those who were engaged in the destruction of the tea were disguised, either by a sort of Indian costume or by blacking their faces.   Many, however, were fearless of consequences, and boldly employed their hands without concealing their faces from the bright light of the moon. The names of fifty-nine of the participators in the act have been preserved,[3] but only one of the men, so far as is known, is still living.   This is DAVID KINNISON, of Chicago, Illinois, whose portrait and sign manual are

here given.   The engraving is from a Daguerreotype from life, taken in August, 1848, when

[1] A " Bostonian," in his " Traits of the Tea Party," on the authority of G. R. T. Hewes, one of the survivors, says that Admiral Montague was at the house of a Tory named Coffin during the transaction, and that, when the party marched from the wharf, he raised the window and said, " Well, boys, you've had a fine, pleasant evening for your Indian caper, haven't you ?   But mind, you have got to pay the fiddler yet !" " Oh, never mind !" shouted Pitts, the leader ; " never mind, squire ! just come out here, if you please, and we'll settle the bill in two minutes."   The populace raised a shout, the fifer struck up a lively air, and the admiral shut the window in a hurry.

[2] Some, whose acquisitiveness overmatched their patriotism, were pretty severely handled during the destruction of the cargoes.   One Charles O'Connor was detected filling his pockets and "the lining of his doublet" with tea while assisting to throw the broken chests overboard.   He was completely stripped of his clothes and kicked ashore.   A man was found at South Boston a few days afterward, with part of a chest of tea, which he had carried away from the harbor.   He had sold some.   They made him give up the money, and then, taking the remainder of the chest, they made a bonfire of it on the common, in front of Mr. Hancock's house.   Some of the tea is preserved at Harvard College.

[3] The following is a list of those known to have been engaged in destroying the tea :

George R. T. Hewes,* Joseph Shed, John Crane, Josiah Wheeler, Thomas Uranu, Adam Colson, Thomas Chase, S. Cooledge, Joseph Payson, James Brewer, Thomas Bolter, Edward Proctor, Samuel Sloper, Thomas Gerrish, Nathaniel Green, Thomas Mellville, Henry Purkett,* Edward C. How, Ebenezer Stevens, Nicholas Campbell, John Russell, Thomas Porter, William Hurdley, Benjamin Rice, Samuel Gore, Nathaniel Frothingham, Moses Grant, Peter Slater,* James Starr, Abraham Tower, Isaac Simpson,* Joseph Eayres, Joseph Lee, William Molineux, Paul Revere, John Spurr, Thomas Moore, S. Howard, Mathew Loring, Thomas Spear, Daniel Ingollson, Jonathan Hunnewell,* John Hooten,* Richard Hunnewell, William Pierce,* William Russell, T. Gammell, Mr. M'Intosh,* Dr. Young, Mr. Wyeth, Edward Dolbier, Mr. Martin, Samuel Peck, Lendall Pitts, Samuel Sprague,* Benjamin Clarke, John Prince,* Richard Hunnewell, Jr., David Kinnison.*   Many of these were merely lads at the time.

* These were living in 1836.   All are now in the grave.   Mr. Kinnison died in 1851, at the age of 115 years.

the veteran was one hundred and eleven years and nine months old. He was alive a few weeks since (January, 1850), in his one hundred and fourteenth year. Through the kindness of a friend at Chicago, I procured the Daguerreotype, and the following sketch of his life from his own lips. The signature was written by the patriot upon the manuscript.

DAVID KINNISON was born the 17th of November, 1736, in Old Kingston, near Portsmouth, province of Maine. Soon afterward his parents removed to Brentwood, and thence in a few years to Lebanon (Maine), at which place he followed the business of farming until the commencement of the Revolutionary war. He is descended from a long-lived race. His great-grandfather, who came from England at an early day, and settled in Maine, lived to a very advanced age; his grandfather attained the age of one hundred and twelve years and ten days; his father died at the age of one hundred and three years and nine months; his mother died while he was young.

He has had four wives, neither of whom is now living; he had four children by his first wife and eighteen by his second; none by the last two. He was taught to read after he was sixty years of age, by his granddaughter, and learned to sign his name while a soldier of the Revolution, which is all the writing he has ever accomplished.

He was one of seventeen inhabitants of Lebanon who, some time previous to the "Tea Party," formed a club which held *secret* meetings to deliberate upon the grievances offered by the mother country. These meetings were held at the tavern of one "Colonel Gooding," in a private room hired for the occasion. The landlord, though a true American, was not enlightened as to the object of their meeting. Similar clubs were formed in Philadelphia, Boston, and the towns around. With these the Lebanon Club kept up a correspondence. They (the Lebanon Club) determined, whether assisted or not, to destroy the tea at all hazards. They repaired to Boston, where they were joined by others; and twenty-four, disguised as Indians, hastened on board, twelve armed with muskets and bayonets, the rest with tomahawks and clubs, having first agreed, whatever might be the result, to stand by each other to the last, and that the first man who faltered should be knocked on the head and thrown over with the tea. They expected to have a fight, and did not doubt that an effort would be made for their arrest. "But" (in the language of the old man) "we cared no more for our lives than three straws, and determined to throw the tea overboard. We were all captains, and every one commanded himself." They pledged themselves in no event, while it should be dangerous to do so, to reveal the names of the party—a pledge which was faithfully observed until the war of the Revolution was brought to a successful issue.

Mr. Kinnison was in active service during the whole war, only returning home once from the time of the destruction of the tea until peace had been declared. He participated in the affair at Lexington, and, with his father and two brothers, was at the battle of Bunker Hill, all four escaping unhurt. He was within a few feet of Warren when that officer fell. He was also engaged in the siege of Boston; the battles of Long Island, White Plains, and Fort Washington; skirmishes on Staten Island, the battles of Brandywine, Red Bank, and Germantown; and, lastly, in a skirmish at Saratoga Springs, in which his company (scouts) were surrounded and captured by about three hundred Mohawk Indians. He remained a prisoner with them one year and seven months, about the end of which time peace was declared. After the war he settled at Danville, Vermont, and engaged in his old occupation of farming. He resided there eight years, and then removed to Wells, in the state of Maine, where he remained until the commencement of the last war with Great Britain. He was in service during the whole of that war, and was in the battles of Sackett's Harbor and Williamsburg. In the latter conflict he was badly wounded in the hand by a grape-shot, the only injury which he received in all his engagements.

Since the war he has lived at Lyme and at Sackett's Harbor, New York. At Lyme, while engaged in felling a tree, he was struck down by a limb, which fractured his skull and broke his collar-bone and two of his ribs. While attending a "training" at Sackett's Harbor, one of the cannon, having been loaded (as he says) "with rotten wood," was discharged. The contents struck the end of a rail close by him with such force as to carry it around, breaking and badly shattering both his legs midway between his ankles and knees. He was confined a long time by this wound, and, when able again to walk, both legs had contracted permanent " fever sores." His right hip has been drawn out of joint by rheumatism. A large scar upon his forehead bears conclusive testimony of its having come in contact with the heels of a horse. In his own language, he " has been completely bunged up and stove in."

When last he heard of his children there were but seven of the twenty-two living. These were scattered abroad, from Canada to the Rocky Mountains. He has entirely lost all traces of them, and knows not that any are still living.

Nearly five years ago he went to Chicago with the family of William Mack, with whom he is now living. He is reduced to extreme poverty, and depends solely upon his pension of ninety-six dollars per annum for subsistence, most of which he pays for his board. Occasionally he is assisted by private donations. Up to 1848 he has always made something by labor. " The last season," says my informant, " he told me he gathered one hundred bushels of corn, dug potatoes, made hay, and harvested oats. But now he finds himself too infirm to labor, though he thinks he could walk twenty miles in a day by ' *starting early*.' "

He has evidently been a very muscular man. Although not large, his frame is one of great power. He boasts of " the strength of former years." Nine years ago, he says, he lifted a barrel of rum into a wagon with ease. His height is about five feet ten inches, with an expansive chest and broad shoulders. He walks somewhat bent, but with as much vigor as many almost half a century younger. His eye is usually somewhat dim, but, when excited by the recollection of his past eventful life, it twinkles and rolls in its socket with remarkable activity. His memory of recent events is not retentive, while the stirring scenes through which he passed in his youth appear to be mapped out upon his mind in unfading colors. He is fond of martial music. The drum and fife of the recruiting service, he says, " daily put new life into him." " In fact," he says, " it's the sweetest music in the world. There's some sense in the drum, and fife, and bugle, but these pianos and other such trash I can't stand at all."

Many years ago he was troubled with partial deafness; his sight also failed him somewhat, and he was compelled to use glasses. Of late years both hearing and sight have returned to him as perfectly as he ever possessed them. He is playful and cheerful in his disposition. " I have seen him," says my informant, " for hours upon the side-walk with the little children, entering with uncommon zest into their childish pastimes. He relishes a joke, and often indulges in ' cracking one himself.' "

At a public meeting, in the summer of 1848, of those opposed to the extension of slavery, Mr. Kinnison took the stand and addressed the audience with marked effect. He declared that he fought for the " freedom of all," that freedom ought to be given to the " black boys," and closed by exhorting his audience to do all in their power to ABOLISH SLAVERY.

The portrait of another member of the " Boston Tea Party," GEORGE ROBERT TWELVE HEWES, is preserved. I have copied it, by permission, from the " Traits of the Tea Party, and Memoir of Hewes." He was born in Boston, on the 5th of September, 1742. His early opportunities for acquiring education were very small. To Mrs. Tinkum. wife of the town-crier, he was indebted for his knowledge of reading and writing.　Farming, fishing, and shoe-making seem to have been the chief employment of his earlier years. In 1758 he attempted to enlist in the army to serve against the French, but did not " pass muster ;" he was equally unsuccessful in attempts to join the navy, and then resumed shoe-making.　In the various disturbances in Boston from the time of the passage of the Stamp Act, Hewes, who was both excitable and patriotic, was generally concerned.　He was among the foremost in the destruction of the tea at Boston.　When the Americans invested the city, and many patriots were shut up under the vigilant eyes of the British officers, Hewes was among them.　He managed to escape, and entered the naval service of the colonies as a privateer, in which he was somewhat successful.　Afterward he joined the army, and was stationed for a time at West Point, under General M'Dougal.　He was never in any land battle, except with the *Cow Boys* and *Skinners*, as they were called, of the *neutral ground* of West Chester.　After the Revolution he returned to Boston, and again engaged in business upon the sea.　He, like Kinnison, was one of the thousands of that time utterly unknown to the world, except within the small love-circle of family relationship and neighborly regard ; and even this present slight embalming of their memory would not have occurred, had not the contingency of great longevity distinguished them from other men.　Although personally unknown, their *deeds* are felt in the political blessings we enjoy.　When the Bunker Hill Monument was completed and was dedicated, on the 17th of June, 1843, Mr. Hewes, then one hundred and one years old, was there, and honored by all.　Returning to the residence of his son, at Richfield, in Otsego county, New York, some sixty miles west of the Hudson, he soon went down into the grave, when more than a century old, " a shock of corn fully ripe."

1773.　The events of the 16th of December produced a deep sensation throughout the British realm.　They struck a sympathetic chord in every colony, and even Canada, Halifax, and the West Indies had no serious voice of censure for the Bostonians.　But the ministerial party here and the public in England were amazed at the audacity of the American people ; and the friends of the colonists in Parliament were, for a moment, silent, for they had no excuse to make in behalf of their transatlantic friends for destroying private property. But with the intelligence of the event went an intimation that the town of Boston was ready to pay the East India Company for the tea, and so the question rested at once upon its original basis—the right of Great Britain to tax the colonies.　Ministers were bitterly indignant, and the House of Lords was like a " seething caldron of impotent rage."　The alleged honesty of the Americans was entirely overlooked, and ministers and their friends saw nothing but open rebellion in the Massachusetts colony.　Strange as it may appear, the king 1774.　did not send a message to Parliament on the subject until the 7th of March, several weeks after the disturbances at Boston were known to government.　Then he detailed the proceedings, and his message was accompanied by a variety of papers, consisting of letters from Hutchinson, Admiral Montague, and the consignees of the tea ; the dispatches of several colonial governors (for menaces of similar violent measures had been uttered in other colonies) ; and some of the most exciting manifestoes, hand-bills, and pamphlets put forth by the Americans.　The king, in his message, called upon Parliament to devise means immediately to suppress these tumultuous proceedings in the colonies.

On the receipt of the message and the accompanying papers in the House of Commons, an address of thanks to the king, and of assurances that he should be sustained in his efforts to preserve order in America, was proposed.　This proposition, with the message and papers, produced great excitement, and the House became, according to Burke, " as hot as Faneuil Hall or the Old South Meeting-house at Boston."　The debate that ensued was excessively stormy.　Ministers and their supporters charged open rebellion upon the colonies, while the opposition denounced, in the strongest language which common courtesy could tolerate, the foolish, unjust, and wicked course of the government.　They reviewed the past ; but ministers, tacitly acknowledging past errors, objected to retrospection, and earnestly pleaded for strict attention to the momentous present.　They asked whether the colonies were or were not longer to be considered dependent upon Great Britain, and, if so, how far and in what manner. If it was decided not to give them up to independence, then ministers were ready to act efficiently.   This question they wished settled as preliminary to further action.   The appeal struck upon a tender chord, and awakened national sympathies; the address was adopted by an overwhelming majority, without a division.

Feeling his position strengthened by this vote, Lord North brought forth the first of his vigorous schemes for subjugating the colonies and punishing the town of Boston.   On the 14th of March he offered a bill which provided for the removal of customs, courts of justice, and government officers of every kind from Boston to Salem; and that "the landing, discharging, and shipping of wares and merchandise at Boston, or within the harbor thereof," should be discontinued.   It provided, also, that when the Bostonians should fully submit, the king should have the power to open the port.[1]   This was the famous *Boston Port Bill*, an act which crushed the trade of the city, and brought the greatest distress upon its inhabitants.   Lord North justified the harsh measure, by asserting that Boston was the center of rebellious commotion in America, "the ringleader in every riot, and set always the example which others followed."   He thought that to inflict a signal penalty upon that city would strike at the root of the evil, and he referred to precedents where whole communities

1774.

had been punished for the crimes of some of their members.   The most violent language was used, by some of the supporters of the ministers, against the Americans.   "They are never actuated by decency or reason; they always choose tarring and feathering as an argument," said Mr. Herbert.   Mr. Van, another ministerial supporter, denounced the people of Boston as utterly unworthy of civilized forbearance.   "They ought to have their town knocked about their ears and destroyed!" he exclaimed, and concluded his tirade of abuse by quoting the factious cry of old Roman orators, "Delenda est Carthago."[2]   Mr. Rose Fuller proposed the imposition of a fine; and even Barré and Conway, the undaunted friends of America, approved of the measure as lenient, and affecting only a single town.   They voted for the bill, and for this apparent disaffection the people of Boston removed their portraits from Faneuil Hall.   But Burke, who at that time began his series of splendid orations in favor of

EDMUND BURKE.[3]
From an English print.

American liberty, denounced the whole scheme as essentially unjust, by confounding and pun-

---

[1] The celebrated Charles James Fox, son of Lord Holland, made his first speech in Parliament on this bill.   It was a strange beginning of his brilliant career.   *He objected to the power vested in the British crown to reopen the port of Boston.*   Neither party supported his suggestion.

[2] "*Carthage must be destroyed.*"   This phrase was often used by Roman orators to excite the people to the utter destruction of Carthage, then the rival of the great city.   During the revolutionary mania among the French this sentiment was often quoted as a threat against England.

[3] Edmund Burke, one of England's greatest statesmen, was born in Carlow, in Ireland, January 1st, 1730.   He was educated at Dublin, and took his bachelor's degree in 1749.   In 1753, having been unsuccessful in his application for the logic professorship at Glasgow, he went to London and entered at the Middle Temple.   He early employed his pen in literature and his eloquence in politics.   His first literary production of note was an essay on the *Vindication of Natural Society*, in imitation of Bolingbroke's style.   In 1757 he published his essay on the *Sublime and Beautiful*.   In 1758 he and Dodswell commenced the Annual Register, which acquired great celebrity.   He accompanied Gerard (or Single Speech) Hamilton to Ireland in 1761, and, by the interposition of that gentleman, obtained a pension of fifteen hundred dollars on the Irish Establishment.   On his return he was introduced to the Marquis of Rockingham, who made him his secretary, and procured his election to a seat in the House of Commons.   There he eloquently and efficiently pleaded the cause of the Americans.   On the downfall of North's administration he became pay-master

504   PICTORIAL FIELD-BOOK

Opposition in Parliament to the Boston Port Bill.   Passage of the Bill.   Goldsmith's "Retaliation."   Epitaph for Burke.

ishing the innocent with the guilty. "It is wished, then," he said, "to condemn the accused without a hearing, to punish indiscriminately the innocent with the guilty! You will thus irrevocably alienate the hearts of the colonies from the mother country. Before the adoption of so violent a measure, the principal merchants of the kingdom should at least be consulted. The bill is unjust, since it bears only upon the city of Boston, while it is notorious that all America is in flames; that the cities of Philadelphia, of New York, and all the maritime towns of the continent, have exhibited the same disobedience. You are contending for a matter which the Bostonians will not give up quietly. They can not, by such means, be made to bow to the authority of ministers; on the contrary, you will find their obstinacy confirmed and their fury exasperated. The acts of resistance in their city have not been confined to the populace alone, but men of the first rank and opulent fortune in the place have openly countenanced them. One city in proscription and the rest in rebellion can never be a remedial measure for general disturbances. Have you considered whether you have troops and ships sufficient to reduce the people of the whole American continent to your devotion? It was the duty of your governor, and not of men without arms, to suppress the tumults. If this officer has not demanded the proper assistance from the military commanders, why punish the innocent for the fault and the negligence of the officers of the crown? The resistance is general in all parts of America; you must, therefore, let it govern itself by its own internal policy, or make it subservient to all your laws, by an exertion of all the forces of the kingdom. These partial counsels are well suited to irritate, not subjugate." Pownall, Johnstone (late Governor of Florida), Dodsworth, Fox, and others followed Burke on the same side, but argument was of no avail. Without a division, the bill 1774. passed by an almost unanimous vote, and on the 31st of March it became a law by the royal assent.

---

general, and obtained a seat in the Council. His great speeches against Warren Hastings, when on trial before the House of Commons, were such as the British Legislature had never before heard. He retired from Parliament in 1794, on a pension of six thousand dollars. During his political career he wrote much, and his compositions rank among the purest of the British classics. He died on the 8th of July, 1797, in the seventieth year of his age.

Goldsmith, in his *Retaliation,** wrote the following epitaph for Burke. It was written in 1776, when Burke was in the midst of his career.

> "Here lies our good Edmund, whose genius was such,
> We scarcely can praise it or blame it too much;
> Who, born for the universe, narrow'd his mind,
> And to party gave up what was meant for mankind.
> Though fraught with all learning, yet straining his throat
> To persuade Tommy Townshend† to lend him a vote;
> Who, too deep for his hearers, still went on refining,
> And thought of convincing while they thought of dining.
> Though equal to all things, for all things unfit:
> Too nice for a statesman, too proud for a wit;
> For a patriot too cool; for a drudge, disobedient,
> And too fond of the *right* to pursue the *expedient*.
> In short, 'twas his fate, unemploy'd or in place, sir,
> To eat mutton cold and cut blocks with a razor."

---

* The history of this poem is a "curiosity of literature." Goldsmith had peculiarities which attracted attention, and it was proposed, at a club of literary men, of which he was a member, to write characters of him in the shape of epitaphs. Dean Barnard, Cumberland, Garrick, and others complied. Garrick wrote the following couplet:

> "Here lies poor Goldsmith, for shortness call'd Noll;
> Who wrote like Apollo, and talk'd like *poor poll.*"

Goldsmith felt called upon for retaliation, and at the next meeting produced the poem from which the following is an extract. It contained epitaphs for several of the club, and he paid off his friend Garrick with compound interest. These lines occur in Garrick's epitaph:

> "Of praise a mere glutton, he swallow'd what came
> And the puff of a dunce he mistook it for fame,
> Till his relish grew callous, almost to disease;
> Who pepper'd the highest was surest to please."

But he generously added,

> "But let us be candid, and speak out our mind—
> If dunces applauded, he paid them in kind."

† Afterward Lord Sydney.

Another bill soon followed, "for better regulating the government of Massachu- March 28.
setts Bay." It was tantamount to an abrogation of the charter of that colony. It
gave to the crown the appointment of counselors and judges of the Supreme Court, and the
nomination of all other officers, military, executive, and judicial, was given to the governors,
independently of any approval by the Council. The sheriffs were empowered to select jurors, a duty before performed by the select-men of the towns. All town meetings, except for
elections, were prohibited. This bill, so manifestly hostile to the freedom of British subjects,
elicited a warm debate, and Burke and Barré opposed it with all their might. "What can
the Americans believe," said Burke, "but that England wishes to despoil them of all liberty,
of all franchise, and, by the destruction of their charters, to reduce them to a state of the
most abject slavery? ...... As the Americans are no less ardently attached to liberty than
the English themselves, can it ever be hoped that they will submit to such exorbitant usur
pation, to such portentous resolutions?" Pownall warned ministers to pause. He alluded
to that powerful engine, the Committees of Correspondence, then unceasingly working in the
colonies, and assured ministers that their harsh measure would drive the people to the calling of a general Congress, and perhaps a resort to arms. All opposition was fruitless, and the
bill passed the House by the overwhelming majority of two hundred and thirty-nine against
sixty-four. Lord Shelburne and others vehemently denounced it in the Upper House, and
eleven peers signed a protest in seven long articles.

North had begun to work the lever of oppression so forcibly that it seemed not easy for
him to desist. A third bill was introduced, intended to protect the servants of roy- April 21,
alty in America against the verdicts of colonial juries. It provided for the trial in 1774.
England of all persons charged in the colonies with murders committed in support of government. It was suggested by a retrospect of the "Boston massacre," and was a most unjust
and insulting comment upon the verdict in favor of Captain Preston and his soldiers. It
was more—it guarantied comparative safety to those who might shoot a *rebel* in the name
of the king. This measure was bitterly denounced by the opposition leaders. "This," said
Colonel Barré, "is, indeed, the most extraordinary resolution ever heard in the Parliament
of England. It offers new encouragement to military insolence, already so insupportable.
...... By this law Americans are deprived of a right which belongs to every human creature—that of demanding justice before a tribunal of impartial judges. Even Captain Preston, who, in their own city of Boston, had shed the blood of citizens, found among them a
fair trial and equitable judges." Alderman Sawbridge was more bold and recriminating in
his denunciations of the measure. He called it "ridiculous and cruel;" asserted that it
was meant to enslave the Americans, and expressed an ardent hope that they would not admit the execution of any of these destructive bills, but nobly refuse them all. "If they do
not," he said, "they are the most abject slaves upon earth, and nothing the ministers can
do is base enough for them." Again remonstrance was vain, and the bill passed the House
by a majority of one hundred and twenty-seven to forty-four; in the Lords, by forty-nine to
twelve. Eight peers entered a strong protest against it. It became a law by royal assent
on the 20th of May.

A fourth bill, for quartering troops in America, was also brought in, and took the course
of others. Rose Fuller, who generally supported ministers, attempted to break the severity
of the several enactments, and produce a reconciliation with the colonies, by proposing a repeal of the act imposing the duty on tea. His proposition was negatived by a large majority. On the annunciation of the result, Mr. Fuller uttered these remarkable words: "I will
now take my leave of the whole plan; you will commence your ruin from this day! I am
sorry to say that not only the House has fallen into this error, but the people approve of the
measure. The people, I am sorry to say, are misled. But a short time will prove the evil
tendency of this bill. If ever there was a nation rushing headlong to ruin, it is this."

Evidently anticipating rebellion in America, and distrustful of the loyalty of the newly-
acquired colony of Quebec, or Canada, a fifth act was brought forward by ministers, making
great concessions to the Roman Catholic population of that province. This law, known as

the Quebec Act, has already been noticed in detail on pages 156–7.[1] Let us now turn our eyes back to the colonies, and observe the spirit of the people of Boston on hearing of the plans maturing for their enslavement and ruin.

May 13. Intelligence of the passage of the Boston Port Bill reached Massachusetts in May. Already the Assembly had taken high, but correct ground on the subject of the sal-

1774. aries of crown officers in the colonies. In January that body resolved that it was in-cumbent upon the judges to determine at once whether they would receive their sala-ries direct from the crown, or depend therefor upon the votes of the Assembly. Chief-jus-tice Oliver was questioned upon this point, and replied that he should hereafter look to the crown for the emoluments of office. The Assembly then resolved, by a majority of sixty-nine to nine, " That Peter Oliver hath, by his conduct, proved himself an enemy to the Con-stitution of the province, and is become greatly obnoxious to the good people of it ; that he ought to be removed from the office of chief justice ; and that a remonstrance and petition to the governor and Council, for his immediate removal, be prepared." They also resolved to impeach the chief justice. The governor not only refused to remove him, but declared the acts of the Assembly unconstitutional.[2]

Fortunately for Hutchinson's personal safety, but much to his chagrin, his recall accom-panied the Port Bill, and General Gage was appointed his successor. Thus far, in all mat-ters relative to the agitations in the colonies, Gage had behaved so discreetly that he enjoyed a considerable share of public confidence and esteem, and in proportion as the people of Bos-ton detested Hutchinson they were disposed to respect the new governor. Hutchinson, de-prived of the shield of delegated power, so much feared the resentment of the Boston popu-lace, that he retired to his country house at Milton, where he remained in seclusion until a

June 1, favorable opportunity offered for him to leave the province. It is an erroneous be-
1774. lief that the people were unanimous in opposition to government and in support of re-publican views. For a while, when the issue came, the parties were very nearly balanced in Boston ; and during the whole time of its occupancy by the British troops, until the evac-uation in 1776, a large portion of the inhabitants were loyal. Before Hutchinson departed, one hundred and twenty merchants of Boston, and many lawyers, magistrates, and principal gentlemen of that town, and Salem, and Marblehead, signed an address to him, in which they expressed entire approbation of his public conduct, and affectionate wishes for his pros-perity. These " addressors" were afterward obliged to recant. Some who would not left the province, and were the earliest of the *refugee Loyalists.*

General Gage, doubtful what reception he should meet at Boston, proceeded with great caution. Four additional regiments were ordered to the rebellious town, but he went thither from New York unattended by any military except his staff. On the day when he

---

[1] A fact not noticed in the former consideration of the Quebec Act is worthy of record, as showing the actual despotic tendency of Parliamentary enactments at that time. By a provision of the act in question, the total revenue of the province of Canada was consigned, in the first instance, to a warrant from the Lord of the Treasury, for the purpose of pensioning judges during pleasure, and the support of a civil list, totally unlimited. This first Lord of the Treasury, or prime minister, was thus in actual possession of the whole revenue of the province, and unrestrained in its expenditure, except by general instructions to use it " to defray the expenses of the administration of justice, and to support civil government in the colonies." Sim-ilar despotic ingredients were profusely sprinkled throughout the whole batch of measures brought forward by Lord North to rule the Americans. The superficial observer is apt to consider the zeal of the Ameri-cans against Parliamentary measures highly intemperate and sometimes censurable, for apparently trifling causes aroused the most violent action. But the colonists clearly perceived the huge monster of despotism artfully covered under a fair guise, and what seemed but an insect, magnified by the microscope of preju-dice, *they* knew to be the germ of a monster reality. The three per cent. duty on tea, considered alone, was but a grain of sand as an obstacle to friendly feelings, but the principle that slept there was a tower-ing Alp.

[2] Peter Oliver, brother of Andrew Oliver, the stamp-master already noticed, was born in 1713, and gradu-ated at Harvard in 1730. He was appointed judge of the Superior Court in 1756, and became chief justice when his brother-in-law, Hutchinson, was appointed governor. He was impeached by the Massachusetts Assembly in 1774. Judge Oliver soon afterward went to England. He died at Birmingham in October, 1791, aged nearly seventy-nine years.

OF THE REVOLUTION. 507

Arrival of General Gage in Boston.   Meeting in Faneuil Hall.   Excitement among the People.   Newspaper Devices.

entered the harbor the town was greatly excited, news of the Port Bill having just May 13,
arrived. He landed at Long Wharf, and was received with much respect by the 1774.
immense crowd of people that met him. He was entertained by the magistrates and others at a public dinner, and on that
evening Hutchinson was burned in
effigy on the Common, in front of
John Hancock's mansion.

The next day a numerously attended town meeting, at which Samuel
Adams presided, was held in Faneuil
Hall to consider the Port Bill. The
people were, indeed, at their " wits'
end." The decree had gone forth to
blight the town ; a governor, commissioned to execute the ministerial
will, was present, and soldiers were
on their way to support his authority. The meeting voted "That it is
the opinion of the town that, if the
other colonies come into a joint reso-

HANCOCK'S HOUSE, BOSTON.[1]

lution to stop all importation from, and exportation to, Great Britain, and every part of the
East Indies, till the act be repealed, the same will prove the salvation of North America
and her liberties ; and that the impolicy, injustice, inhumanity, and cruelty of the act exceed all our powers of expression ; we, therefore, leave it to the just censure of others, and
appeal to God and the world." Paul Revere, an artist and mechanic of Boston, and one of
the most active patriots, was sent to New York and Phila-
delphia to invoke sympathy and co-operation. A vast number of copies of the act, printed with heavy black lines around
it, and some of them having the sepulchral device of skull
and cross-bones rudely engraved as a head-piece, were scattered over the country, and cried in cities and villages as the
" Barbarous, cruel, bloody, and inhuman murder !"[2] The
whole country was inflamed, and every where the most lively sympathy for the people of Boston was awakened. Orators at public gatherings, ministers in the pulpits, and the
newspaper press throughout the land, denounced the oppression laid upon Boston as a type of what was in store for the
whole country Some of the newspapers placed at their head
the significant device used during the Stamp Act excitement,
a serpent cut in ten pieces, with the inscription " *Join or
die!* or " *Unite or die!*"[3] The cause of Boston became the

[1] This is a substantial stone building, situated upon Beacon Street, fronting the Common. It was erected by Thomas Hancock, an uncle of Governor Hancock, in 1737. The present proprietor is a nephew of
the governor.

[2] The engraving is a fac-simile, one fourth the size of the original, of a device upon one of these papers.
Over the skull is a rude resemblance of a crown, and beneath the bones that of the Cap of Liberty, denoting
that all was death and destruction between the crown and liberty. This device is supposed to be the work
of Paul Revere, who engraved the pictures of the naval investment of Boston in 1768, and the *Boston Massacre* in 1770. Revere was a very ingenious man, an active patriot, and, as grand master of the Masonic
fraternity in Massachusetts, had extensive influence. He was a co-worker with Samuel Adams, Joseph
Warren, and other compatriots in setting the ball of the Revolution in motion.

[3] The cut upon the next page is a fac-simile of one of those illustrations. I copied it from the *Pennsylvania Journal*, 1774, where it appeared for nearly a year, or until the colonies were fairly *united* by a
Continental Congress. The loyal papers loudly condemned the use of the device. A writer in *Rivington's*

cause of all the colonies, and never were the British ministry really weaker in their government relations to America than when Lord North was forging, as he vainly thought, the fetters of majestic law to bind the colonies indissolubly to the throne. In honorable concession alone lay his real strength, but of these precious locks the Delilah of haughty ambition had shorn him, and when he attempted to put forth his power, he found himself "like other men," weak indeed!

Royal Gazette,[1] who called it a "scandalous and saucy reflection," was answered as follows by a correspondent of the Journal:

"*To the Author of the Lines in Mr. Rivington's Paper, on the Snake depicted in some of the American Newspapers.*

"That New England's abused, and by sons of sedition,
Is granted without either prayer or petition;
And that 'tis 'a scandalous, saucy reflection,
That merits the soundest, severest correction,'
Is readily granted. 'How came it to pass?'
Because she is pester'd by snakes in the grass,
Who, by lying and cringing, and such like pretensions,
Get places *once* honor'd disgraced with pensions.
And you, Mr. Pensioner, instead of repentance
(If I don't mistake you), have wrote your own sentence;
For by such *snakes* as this New England's abused,
And the head of the serpents, 'you know, must be bruised."

               "NEW JERSEY."

---

[1] Rivington was the "king's printer" in New York city. His office was at the southeast corner of Pearl and Wall Streets. He had the entire confidence of the British authorities, and held the "rebels" in great contempt. He was a caustic writer, and his remarks were often remembered with bitterness for years. The following anecdote is illustrative of this fact:

Among those who cherished very hostile feelings toward Rivington was that dare-devil, General Ethan Allen, of Vermont, who swore he would "lick Rivington the very first opportunity he had." Rivington himself, aware of his intentions, gave a most humorous description of his interview with Allen, showing, at the same time, his exceeding cleverness and tact, which may even at this day be profitable to his editorial brethren. Rivington was a fine, portly-looking man, dressed in the extreme of fashion—curled and powdered hair, claret-colored coat, scarlet waistcoat trimmed with gold lace, buckskin breeches, and top boots—and kept the very best society.

The clerk below stairs saw Allen coming at a distance. "I was sitting," said Rivington, "after a good dinner, alone, with my bottle of Madeira before me, when I heard an unusual noise in the street, and a huzza from the boys. I was in the second story, and, stepping to the window, saw a tall figure in tarnished regimentals, with a large cocked hat and an enormous long sword, followed by a crowd of boys, who occasionally cheered him with huzzas, of which he seemed insensible. He came up to my door and stopped. I could see no more. My heart told me it was Ethan Allen. I shut down my window, and retired behind my table and bottle. I was certain the hour of reckoning had come. There was no retreat. Mr. Staples, my clerk, came in paler than ever, and clasping his hands, said, 'Master, he is come!' 'I know it.' 'He entered the store, and asked "if James Rivington lived there." I answered, "Yes, sir." "Is he at home?" "I will go and see, sir," I said; and now, master, what is to be done? There he is in the store, and the boys peeping at him from the street.' I had made up my mind. I looked at the bottle of Madeira—possibly took a glass. 'Show him up,' said I; 'and if such Madeira can not mollify him, he must be harder than adamant.' There was a fearful moment of suspense. I heard him on the stairs, his long sword clanking at every step. In he stalked. 'Is your name James Rivington?' 'It is, sir, and no man could be more happy than I am to see Colonel Ethan Allen.' 'Sir, I have come—' 'Not another word, my dear colonel, until you have taken a seat and a glass of old Madeira.' 'But, sir, I don't think it proper—' 'Not another word, colonel. Taste this wine; I have had it in glass for ten years. Old wine, you know, unless it is originally sound, never improves by age.' He took the glass, swallowed the wine, smacked his lips, and shook his head approvingly. 'Sir, I come—' 'Not another word until you have taken another glass, and then, my dear colonel, we will talk of old affairs, and I have some droll events to detail.' In short, we finished two bottles of Madeira, and parted as good friends as if we never had cause to be otherwise."

OF THE REVOLUTION. 509

General Gage at Boston.   Proceedings of the Massachusetts Assembly.   Proposition for a General Congress.

CHAPTER XXII.

Scene IV. In Boston, while the Regulars were flying from Lexington.

LORD BOSTON, *surrounded by his Guards and a few Officers.*

Lord Boston. If Colonel Smith succeeds in his embassy, and I think there's no doubt of it, I shall have the pleasure this evening, I expect, of having my friends Hancock and Adams's good company ; I'll make each of them a present of a pair of handsome iron ruffles, and Major Provost shall provide a suitable entertainment for them in his apartment.

Officer. Sure they'll not be so unpolite as to refuse your excellency's kind invitation.

Lord Boston. Should they, Colonel Smith and Major Pitcairn have my orders to make use of all their rhetoric and the persuasive eloquence of British thunder.

Enters a messenger in haste.

I bring your excellency unwelcome tidings—

Lord Boston. For Heaven's sake ! from what quarter ?

Messenger. From Lexington plains.

Lord Boston. 'Tis impossible !

Messenger. Too true, sir.

Lord Boston. Say—what is it ?   Speak what you know.

Messenger. Colonel Smith is defeated and fast retreating.

Lord Boston. Good God ! what does he say ?   Mercy on me !

Messenger. They're flying before the enemy.

Lord Boston. Britons turn their backs before the Rebels ! the Rebels put Britons to flight !   Said you not so ?

Messenger. They are routed, sir ; they are flying this instant ; the provincials are numerous, and hourly gaining strength ; they have nearly surrounded our troops.   A re-enforcement, sir, a timely succor, may save the shattered remnant.   Speedily ! speedily, sir ! or they're irretrievably lost.

"The FALL OF BRITISH TYRANNY, OR AMERICAN LIBERTY TRIUMPHANT."[1]

ENERAL GAGE soon became a tyrant in the eyes of the people of Boston.   However humane were his intentions, the execution of his commission necessarily involved harsh and oppressive measures.   Pursuant to the provisions of the Port Bill, he proceeded, after the appointment of the members of the Council (see *note* 1, next page), to transfer the government offices to Salem, and on the 31st of May the Assembly held its final session in Boston.   By proclamation, Gage adjourned the House until the 7th of June, and ordered the next meeting at Salem.   Anticipating this measure, the House appointed two members of the Assembly—Samuel Adams and James Warren—to act in the interim, as the exigencies of the case might require.   These, with a few others already named, held private conferences, and arranged plans for the public good.   On the third evening after the adjournment of the Assembly, their plans were matured.   The suggestions of New York and other places, as well as the hints thrown out by Pownall in the House of Commons respecting a general Congress, were favorably considered.   A plan was arranged for a Continental Congress ; they also matured measures for making provisions for supplying funds and munitions of war, prepared an address to the other colonies, inviting their co-operation in the measure of a general Congress, and drew up a non-importation agreement.

June 1, 1774.

---

[1] This is a well-written drama, published by Styner and Cist, Philadelphia, in 1776.   Its sub-title is, "A tragi-Comedy of Five Acts, as lately planned at the Royal Theatrum Pandemonium at St. James's. The principal place of action, in America."   It is dedicated "To Lord Boston [General Gage], Lord Kidnapper [Dunmore, governor of Virginia], and the innumerable and never-erding class of Macs and Donalds upon Donalds, and the remnant of the gentlemen Officers, Actors, Merry Andrews, Strolling Players, Pi-

These several propositions and plans were boldly laid before the General Court when it
June 7, reopened at Salem.   The few partisans of the crown in that Assembly were filled
1774.   with amazement and alarm at the boldness of the popular leaders; and as rank
treason was developed in the first acts of the majority, a partisan of government determined,
if possible, to put a stop to further rebellious pro-
ceedings.   Feigning sudden illness, he was allowed to leave the Assembly.   He went immediately to the governor and acquainted him
with the proceedings in progress.[2]   Gage sent
his secretary to dissolve the Assembly by proc-
June 17. lamation, but the patriots were too
vigilant for him.   The doors of the
Assembly were locked, and the keys were safely deposited in Samuel Adams's pocket.   The
secretary read the proclamation on the stairs,
but it was unheeded by the patriots within.
They proceeded to adopt and sign a "Solemn
League and Covenant," in which all former
non-importation agreements and cognate undertakings were concentrated, and a committee
was appointed to send the covenant, as a circular, to every colony in America.[3]   They also
adopted the other plans matured by Adams and
others, and a resolution that "a meeting of
committees, from the several colonies on this

continent, is highly expedient and necessary, to consult upon the present state of the country, and the miseries to which we are and must be reduced by the operation of certain acts
of Parliament, and to deliberate and determine on wise and proper measures to be recom-

---

rates, and Buccaneers in America."   As most of the real names of the *dramatis personæ* are familiar to the
readers of the few preceding chapters, I give the list as printed in the copy of the drama before me.

Lord Paramount	BUTE.	Charley	JENKINSON.
Lord Mocklaw	MANSFIELD.	Brazen	WEDDEBURNE.
Lord Hypocrite	DARTMOUTH.	Colonel	BARRÉ.
Lord Poltroon	SANDWICH.	Lord Boston	GAGE.
Lord Catspaw	NORTH.	Admiral Tombstone	GRAVES.
Lord Wisdom	CHATHAM.	Elbow Room	HOWE.
Lord Religion	BISHOP OF ST. ASAPH.	Mr. Caper	BURGOYNE.
Lord Justice	CAMDEN.	Lord Kidnapper	DUNMORE.
Lord Patriot	WILKES.	General Washington.	
Bold Irishman	BURKE.	General Lee.	Officers, soldiers, sailors, ne-
Judas	HUTCHINSON.	General Putnam.	groes, &c., &c.

[1] The political complexion of the new Council did not please Gage.   He exercised the prerogative given
to him by the charter to the fullest extent in rejecting thirteen of the elected counselors.   The remainder
were not much more agreeable to him.

[2] General Gage was then residing at the house of Robert Hooper, Esq., in Danvers, about four miles
from Salem.

[3] All who felt an attachment to the American cause were called upon to sign it; and the covenanters
were required to obligate themselves, in the presence of God, to cease all commerce with England, dating
from the last of the ensuing month of August, until the late wicked acts of Parliament should be repealed
and the Massachusetts colony reinstated in all its rights and privileges; to abstain from the use of any British goods whatsoever; and to avoid all commerce or traffic with those who refused to sign the League.
Finally, it was covenanted that those who refused to sign the League should be held up to public scorn
and indignation by the publication of their names.   The articles of the League were transmitted by circulars to all the other provinces, with invitations to the inhabitants to affix their names thereto.   Philadelphia alone, as a city, did not accept the invitation to join in such a measure, preferring to refer the matter
to a general Congress, and agreeing to execute faithfully all measures therein agreed upon.

[4] A biographical sketch of this distinguished patriot will be found among those of the signers of the Declaration of Independence printed in the Supplement.

mended to all the colonies for the recovery and re-establishment of our just rights and liberties, civil and religious, and the restoration of union and harmony between Great Britain and America, which is most ardently desired by all good men." They designated the 1st of September as the time, and Philadelphia as the place of meeting. Thomas Cushing, the Speaker of the Assembly, James Bowdoin, many years a member of the Council, Samuel Adams, John Adams, and Robert Treat Paine, were chosen delegates. A treasurer was appointed, and the towns were called upon to pay their respective shares of the sum of two thousand five hundred dollars, voted to the delegates in payment of their expenses. The whole business being ended, the Assembly adjourned indefinitely, and thus ended the last session of the Assembly of Massachusetts Bay, under a royal governor.

Gage was greatly irritated by the proceedings of the Assembly, and the acts of the people of Boston in sustaining these traitorous measures. He refused to receive the answer of the General Court to his address, and issued a strong proclamation in denunciation of the *League* as an unlawful combination, hostile to the crown and Parliament, and ordering the magistrates to apprehend and bring to trial all who should be guilty of signing it. The people laughed at his proclamation, defied the pliant magistrates, and signed the League by thousands. Uncompromising hostility was aroused, and the arm of bold defiance was uplifted, even in the midst of distress and the menaces of foreign bayonets.

At noon on the 1st of June the port of Boston was closed to all vessels that wished to enter, and, after the 14th, all that remained were not allowed to depart. The two 1774. regiments ordered to Boston by Gage had arrived, and were encamped on the Common. Soon afterward, these being re-enforced by several regiments from Halifax, Quebec, New York, and Ireland, the town became an immense garrison. The utter prostration of all business soon produced great distress in the city. The rich, deprived of their rents, became straitened, and the poor, denied the privilege of labor, were reduced to beggary. All classes felt the scourge of the oppressor, yet the fortitude and forbearance of the inhabitants were most remarkable. The sympathy of the people abroad was commensurate with the sufferings of the patriots, and from every quarter came expressions of friendship and substantial tokens of attachment to the sufferers. The people of Georgia sent the Bostonians sixty-three barrels of rice, and seven hundred and twenty dollars in specie. Wheat and other grain were forwarded to them from different points ; Schoharie, in New York, alone sending five hundred and twenty-five bushels of wheat. The city of London, in its corporate capacity, subscribed one hundred and fifty thousand dollars for the relief of the poor of Boston. The people of Marblehead and Salem offered the Boston merchants the free use of wharves and stores, for they scorned to enrich themselves at the expense of their oppressed neighbors. A committee was appointed in Boston to receive and distribute donations, and, in the midst of martial law, the suffering patriots were bold and unyielding.

General Gage was warned to relax the rigor of his military rule, or open rebellion would ensue. He affected to disregard these warnings, yet he employed precautionary measures. Boston is situated upon a peninsula, at that time connected with the continent by a narrow strip of land called the Neck. Convinced that hostilities must ensue unless the home government should recede, and relying more upon soldiers than upon conciliatory deeds, Gage moved in subserviency to this reliance, and stationed a strong guard of armed men upon the Neck. He gave as a reason for this measure the shallow pretext that he wished to prevent desertions from his ranks. The people readily interpreted the meaning of his movement, and saw at once that the patriots of Boston were to be cut off from free communication with those in the country, and that arms and ammunition were not to be transported from the city to the interior. For the first time the free intercourse of New Englanders was interrupted, and the lightning of rebellion, that had for years been curbed within the hearts of the people, leaped forth in manifestations which alarmed the hitherto haughty hirelings of royalty. The members of the new Council, appointed by the governor under the act which changed, and indeed abrogated, the charter of Massachusetts, who had accepted office, were treated with disdain at every step, and a large proportion of them were forced to resign.

512   PICTORIAL FIELD-BOOK

Peaceable Resistance of the People.   Preparations for War.   Recantation of the Hutchinson Addressors.

VIEW OF BOSTON FROM DORCHESTER HEIGHTS IN 1774.[1]

The courts of justice were suspended; the attorneys who had issued writs of citation were compelled to ask pardon in the public journals, and promise not to expedite others until the laws should be revoked and the charter re-established. The people occupied the seats of justice, that no room might be left for judges. When invited to withdraw, they answered that they recognized no other tribunals and no other magistrates than such as were established by ancient laws and usage.[2]

Persuaded that war was inevitable, the people, throughout the province, began to arm themselves and practice military tactics daily. Every where the fife and drum were heard, and fathers and sons, encouraged by the gentler sex, took lessons together in the art of war. The forge and hammer were busy in making guns and swords, and every thing bore the animated but gloomy impress of impending hostility. The zeal of true patriots waxed warmer; the fears of the timid and lukewarm assumed the features of courage; the avowed friends of government became alarmed, and those *Addressors*, as they were called, who signed an address to Hutchinson on his departure, were obliged to make public recantations in the newspapers.[3] Some of the Boston clergy (particularly Dr. Cooper, the person who

---

[1] This picture is from an English print of the time. Then the principal portion of the town was upon the eastern slope and flats. There were a few houses upon the higher ground in the vicinity of Beacon Hill, around the Common, among which was that of John Hancock. In this picture, Beacon Hill is designated by the pole, which, with its barrel, is noticed in a preceding chapter. The peninsula originally contained about seven hundred acres. The hills have been razed and the earth carried into the water, by which means the peninsula is so enlarged that it now comprises about fourteen hundred acres.

[2] Otis's *Botta*, i., 124.

[3] There were many persons of some significance who were willing, at this stage of the controversy, to offer conciliatory measures, and they even gave encouragement to General Gage and his government. One hundred and twenty merchants and others of Boston signed an address to General Gage, expressing a willingness to pay for the tea destroyed. It is averred, also, that some of the wealthiest people of Boston actually endeavored to raise money to pay the East India Company for the tea, but the attempt failed. There were some others who protested against the course of the Committee of Correspondence and the action of a large portion of the ministers of the Gospel, who, they averred, were unduly exciting the people, and urging them headlong toward ruin. But these movements were productive only of mischief. They made the colonists more determined, and deluded the home government with the false idea that the most respectable portion of the people were averse to change or revolution. The following is a copy of the recantation, signed by a large number of the addressers: "Whereas we, the subscribers, did some time since sign an address to Governor Hutchinson, which, though prompted to by the best intentions, has, nevertheless, given great offense to our country; We do now declare, that we desire, so far from designing, by that action, to

OF THE REVOLUTION. 513

Spirit of the American Press.   Zeal of the Committees of Correspondence.   Their importance.   Fortification of Boston Neck.

first received Hutchinson's letters from Franklin) were very active in promoting hostility to the rulers, and the press exerted its power with great industry and effect.[1]

The *Massachusetts Spy* and the *Boston Gazette* were the principal Whig journals, and through the latter, Otis, Adams, Quincy, Warren, and others communed with the public, in articles suited to the comprehension of all.   Epigrams, parables, sonnets, dialogues, and every form of literary expression remarkable for point and terseness, filled these journals.   The following is a fair specimen of logic in rhyme, so frequently employed at that day.   I copied it from Anderson's *Constitutional Gazette*,[2] published in New York in 1775.   That paper was the uncompromising opponent of Rivington's (Tory) Gazette, published in the same city:

> " THE *Quarrel with America fairly Stated.*
>
> " Rudely forced to drink tea, Massachusetts in anger
> Spills the tea on John Bull—John falls on to bang her;
> Massachusetts, enraged, calls her neighbors to aid,
> And give Master John a severe bastinade.
> Now, good men of the law! pray, who is in fault,
> The one who begun, or resents the assault?"

The Boston Committee of Correspondence were busy night and day preparing the people of the province for energetic action, and it needed but a slight offense to sound the battle cry and invoke the sword of rebellion from its scabbard.[3]

Alarmed at the rebellious spirit manifested on all sides, Gage removed the seat of government from Salem back to Boston, and began to fortify the Neck.   The   August, 1774.

VIEW OF THE LINES ON BOSTON NECK.
From an English print published in 1777

work went on slowly at first, for British gold could not buy Boston carpenters, and workmen had to be procured from other places.   The people viewed these warlike preparations with indignation, which was heightened by an injudicious act of Gage in sending a detach-

show our acquiescence in those acts of Parliament so universally and justly odious to all America, that, on the contrary, we hoped we might, in that way, contribute to their repeal; though now, to our sorrow, we find ourselves mistaken.   And we do now further declare, that we never intended the offense which this address has occasioned; that, if we had foreseen such an event, we should never have signed it; as it always has been and now is our wish to live in harmony with our neighbors, and our serious determination is to promote, to the utmost of our power, the liberty, the welfare, and happiness of our country, which is inseparably connected with our own."   The Committee of Correspondence declared the recantation satisfactory, and recommended the signers of it as true friends to America.

[1] There were five newspapers printed in Boston in 1774, as follows: the *Boston Post*, on Monday morning, by Thomas and John Fleet; the *Boston News-Letter*, by Margaret Draper (widow of Richard Draper) and Robert Boyle; the *Massachusetts Gazette and Boston Post Boy and Advertiser*, by Mills and Hicks; the *Boston Gazette and Country Journal*, by Edes and Gill; and the *Massachusetts Spy*, by Isaiah Thomas.—See Thomas's *History of Printing.*

[2] Anderson was the father of Dr. Alexander Anderson of New York, the earliest wood-engraver, as a distinct art, in America.   Now (1855), at the age of eighty years, he uses the graver with all the skill and vigor of earlier manhood.

[3] The committee of 1774 consisted of Samuel Adams, John Hancock, James Bowdoin, John Adams, William Phillips, Joseph Warren, and Josiah Quincy.   The importance of these committees of correspondence may be understood by the estimate placed upon them by a Tory writer over the signature of *Massachusettensis*.   " This," he said, " is the foulest, subtlest, and most venomous serpent ever issued from the egg of sedition.   *It is the source of the rebellion.*   I saw the small seed when it was implanted; it was a grain of mustard.   I have watched the plant until it has become a great tree.   The vilest reptiles that crawl upon the earth are concealed at the root; the foulest birds of the air rest upon its branches.   I now would induce you to go to work immediately with axes and hatchets and cut it down, for a two-fold reason: because it is a pest to society, and lest it be felled suddenly by a stronger arm, and crush its thousands in its fall."

September 1, 1774.   ment of troops to seize a quantity of gunpowder belonging to the province, stored at Charlestown and Cambridge. This act greatly exasperated the people, and large numbers assembled at Cambridge, determined upon attacking the troops in Boston. About the same time, intelligence went abroad that the ships of war in Boston harbor were bombarding the town and the regular troops were massacring the people, sparing neither age nor sex. The news spread rapidly, and the thrill of horror produced by the report was succeeded by a cry of vengeance. In less than thirty-six hours the country for more than one hundred and seventy miles in extent was aroused. From the shores of Long Island to the green hills of Berkshire, "To arms! to arms!" was the universal shout. Instantly, on every side, men of all ages were seen cleansing and burnishing their weapons, furnishing themselves with provisions and warlike stores, and preparing for an immediate march; gentlemen of rank and fortune exhorting and encouraging others by voice and example. The roads were soon crowded with armed men, marching for Boston with great rapidity, but without noise or tumult. Full thirty thousand men were under arms and speeding toward the town; nor did they halt until well assured that the report was untrue.[1]

September 3.

At a convention of delegates from the several towns in Suffolk county, to which Boston belonged, held on the 6th of September, it was resolved that no obedience was due to any part of the late acts of Parliament. Collectors of taxes, and other officers holding public money, were recommended to retain the funds in their hands until the old charter was restored; that persons who had accepted seats in the Council had violated the duty they owed to their country; that those who did not resign by the 20th of September should be considered public enemies; that the Quebec Act, establishing Romanism in Canada, was dangerous to Protestantism and liberty, and that they were determined to act on the defensive only so long as just reason required. They also recommended the people to seize and keep as a hostage any servant of the crown who might fall in their way, when they should hear of a patriot being arrested for any political offense. They drew up an address to General Gage, telling him frankly that they did not desire to commence hostilities, but that they were determined not to submit to any of the late acts of Parliament; they also complained loudly of the fortifications upon the Neck.

1774.

Gage denounced the convention as treasonable, and, in reply to their address, declared that he should take such measures for the safety of his troops and the friends of government as he thought proper, at the same time assuring them that the cannon placed in battery on the Neck should not be used except to repel hostile proceedings. Unlike Governor Carleton of Canada, he had no word of kindness or act of conciliation for the patriots,[2] and they, in turn, reviled the governor and set his power at naught. Tarring and feathering and other violent acts became common, and the Tories or friends of government in the surrounding country were obliged to seek refuge in Boston. The eight military companies in the town, composed of citizens, were mostly broken up. John Hancock had been commander of a corps called the Governor's Independent Cadets. General Gage had dismissed him, and the company, indignant at the affront, appointed a committee, on the 14th of August, to

---

[1] See Hinman's *Historical Collections from Official Records*, &c., *of Connecticut.*

It was believed by some, that the rumor of the bombardment at Boston was set afloat by some of the leading patriots, to show General Gage what multitudes of people would rise up to crush his troops if he dared to abuse his power by committing the least act of violence.

[2] The kindness which Governor Carleton manifested toward the American prisoners captured at Quebec and the Cedars in 1776, did more to keep down rebellion in that province than any severe measures could have effected. Lamb says, that "in the spring of 1776, Governor Carleton addressed the prisoners with such sweetness and good-humor as was sufficient to melt every heart. 'My lads,' he said, 'why did you come to disturb an honest man in his government that never did any harm to you in his life? I never invaded your property, nor sent a single soldier to disturb you. Come, my boys, you are in a very distressing situation, and not able to go home with any comfort. I must provide you with shoes, stockings, and warm waistcoats. I must give you some victuals to carry you home. Take care, my lads, that you do not come here again, lest I should not treat you so kindly."—Lamb's *Journal of the American War*, p. 89: Dublin, 1809.

wait on the governor at Salem, and return him their standard, "as they had almost unanimously disbanded themselves."[1]

The day before the meeting of the Suffolk convention, the general Continental Congress met in Philadelphia,

September 5, 1774.

and as soon as information of its firm proceedings reached Massachusetts, the patriots assumed a bolder tone. Gage summoned the House of Representatives to meet at Salem, to proceed to business according to the new order of things under the late act of Parliament. Town meetings were held, but so revolutionary were their proceedings, that Gage countermanded his order for the Assembly. His right to countermand was denied, and most of the members elect, to the number of ninety, met at Salem on the day appointed.

October 5.

Gage, of course, was not there, and as nobody appeared to open the court or administer the oaths, they resolved themselves into a provincial Congress, adjourned to Concord, and there organized by choosing John Hancock president, and

JOHN HANCOCK.[2]

---

[1] I copy from the *Massachusetts Spy* of September, 1774, the following lampoon in rhyme :

"*A sample of gubernatorial eloquence, as lately exhibited to the company of cadets*

"Your Colonel H—n—k, by neglect
Has been deficient in respect;
As he my sovereign toe ne'er kissed,
'Twas proper he should be dismissed;
I never was and never will
By mortal man be treated ill.
I never was nor ever can
Be treated ill by mortal man.
Oh had I but have known before
That temper of your factious corps,
It should have been my greatest pleasure
To have prevented that bold measure.
To meet with such severe disgrace—
My standard flung into my face !
Disband yourselves ! so cursed stout !
Oh had I, had I, *turned you out !*"

This is given as a specimen of the fearlessness of the press at that time, for it must be remembered that the *Spy* was printed in Boston, then filled with armed troops employed to put down rising rebellion. Gage's proclamations were paraphrased in rhyme, and otherwise ridiculed. One of these, now before me, commences,

"Tom Gage's Proclamation,
Or blustering Denunciation
(Replete with Defamation),
Threatening Devastation
And speedy Jugulation
Of the New English Nation,
Who shall his pious ways shun."

It closes with

"Thus graciously the war I wage,
As witnesseth my hand—
TOM GAGE.

"By command of *Mother Carey.*
"THOMAS FLUCKER, *Secretary.*"*

[2] A biographical sketch of Mr. Hancock will be found among those of the signers of the Declaration of Independence, in the Supplement.

---

* Flucker was Secretary of Massachusetts under Gage. Henry (afterward general) Knox, of the Revolution, married his

Benjamin Lincoln, afterward a revolutionary general, secretary.   A committee, appointed to consider the state of the province, prepared an address to Gage, which the Congress adopted, and then adjourned to Cambridge, where another committee was sent to present the address to the governor.   In that address they protested against the fortification of the Neck, and complained of the recent acts of Parliament, while they expressed the warmest loyalty to the king and the government.   Gage replied, as he did to the Suffolk committee, that his military preparations were made only in self-defense, and were justified by the war-like demonstrations on every hand.   He concluded by pronouncing their Assembly illegal, and in contravention of the charter of the province, and warned them to desist.

The denunciations of Gage had no other effect than to increase the zeal of the patriots. The Provincial Congress proceeded to appoint a Committee of Safety, at the head of which was John Hancock, giving it power to call out the militia.   A committee was appointed to provide ammunition and stores, and the sum of sixty-six thousand dollars was appropri-
October 26, ated for the purpose.   Provision was also made for arming the people of the
1774.   province.   They appointed Henry Gardner treasurer of the colony, under the title of *receiver general*, into whose hands the constables and tax-collectors were directed to pay all public moneys which they received.   Jedediah Preble, Artemus Ward, and Seth Pome-roy, were appointed general officers of the militia.[1]   The first did not accept the appoint-ment, and Ward and Pomeroy alone entered upon the duty of organizing the military. Ammunition and stores were speedily collected at Concord, Woburn, and other places. Mills were erected for making gunpowder ; manufactories were set up for making arms, and great encouragement was given to the production of saltpeter.

The Provincial Congress disavowed any intention to attack the British troops, yet took
November 10. measures to cut off their supplies from the country.   Gage issued a proclama-tion, denouncing their proceedings, to which no attention was paid ; and as the recommendations of the Provincial Congress had all the authority of law, he was unsupport-ed except by his troops, and a few officials and their friends in the city.   Apprehending that the people of Boston might point the cannons upon the fortifications about the town upon himself and troops, he caused a party of sailors to be landed by night from a ship of war in the harbor, who spiked all the guns upon the battery at Fort Hill.

At a session of the Provincial Congress of Massachusetts, convened on the 23d of No-vember, it was voted to enrol twelve thousand minute men—volunteers pledged to be ready to enter the field at a minute's notice—and an invitation was sent to Connecticut and Rhode Island to follow this example, and increase the number of minute men to twenty thousand.   They elected the same delegates to the general Congress, to meet again in May, 1775 ; appointed Colonel Thomas and Colonel Heath additional generals ; and adopted measures for the formation of a new Provincial Congress, to meet early in the ensuing year. They then adjourned to attend the general thanksgiving, held according to their own ap-pointment.[2]   When the year 1774 closed, the colonies were on the verge of open insurrec-tion.   Let us turn for a moment to view the progress of events in England.

When the colonial agents there observed the manifest improbability of a reconciliation and the certainty of an appeal to arms, they were exceedingly active in their efforts to mold the popular opinion in favor of the colonies.   The various addresses put forth by the

---

[1] For a sketch of the life of General Ward, see *antè*, page 190.   Pomeroy was in the battle of Lake George, in 1755, and was the soldier of that name whom Everett supposes to have shot Baron Dieskau. See page 109.

[2] This appointment was always made by the governor, as at the present day, but the patriots had abso-lutely discarded his authority.

---

daughter Lucy, in opposition to the wishes of her father, who desired a more advantageous match for her.   Knox was a young bookseller in Boston, and Miss Flucker, who possessed considerable literary taste, became acquainted with him while visiting his store to purchase articles in his line.   A sympathy of taste, feeling, and views produced mutual esteem, which soon ripened into love.   Her friends looked upon her as one ruined in prospects of future social esteem and personal happiness, in wedding one who had espoused the cause of rebellion ; but many of those very friends, when the great political change took place, were outcasts and in poverty, while Lucy Knox was the center of the first social circle in America.

Continental Congress were printed and industriously circulated. Dr. Franklin and other friends of America traversed the manufacturing towns in the north of England, and by personal communications enlightened the people upon the important questions at issue. The inhabitants of those districts were mostly Dissenters, looking upon the Church of England as an oppressor; and, by parity of simple reasoning, its main pillar, the throne, was regarded equally as an instrument of oppression. They were, therefore, eager listeners to the truths respecting human rights which the friends of republicanism uttered, and throughout Yorkshire, Lancashire, Durham, and Northumberland, the people became much excited.

ADAM SMITH.[1]
From a medallion by Tassie.

Ministers were alarmed, and concerted measures to counteract the effects produced by these itinerant republicans. Adam Smith, the author of " The Wealth of Nations," Wedderburne, the solicitor general, and other friends of the ministry, wielded their pens vigorously; and, at their solicitation, Dr. Roebuck, of Birmingham, a very popular man among the manufacturing population, followed in the wake of Franklin and his friends, and endeavored to apply a ministerial antidote to their republican poison. In this he was measurably successful, and the districts were quieted.

Parliament assembled on the 30th of November. The king informed them that America was 1774. on the verge of open rebellion. When the usual address to the king was proposed in the House of Commons, the opposition offered an amendment, asking his majesty to lay before Parliament all letters, orders, and instructions relating to American affairs, as well as all the intelligence received from the colonies. Lord North opposed the amendment, because it made the first advances toward a reconciliation, and therefore was inconsistent with the dignity of the government! The address was replete with assurances of support for the king and ministers in all measures deemed necessary to maintain government in the colonies, or, in other words, in drawing the sword, if necessary, to bring the Americans to the feet of royal authority. A debate, characterized by considerable bitterness, ensued, but the amendment was rejected, and the loyal address was adopted by a vote of two hundred and sixty-four against seventy-three. Similar action was had in the House of Lords, and an address was carried by a vote of sixty-three to thirteen. Nine peers signed a sensible protest, which concluded with these words: " Whatever may be the mischievous designs or inconsiderate temerity which leads others to this desperate course, we wish to be known as persons who have ever disapproved of measures so pernicious in their past effects and future tendencies; and who are not in haste, without inquiry and information, to commit ourselves in declarations which may precipitate our country into all the calamities of a civil war."

Franklin and his associates caused strong remonstrances and petitions to be sent in from the northern manufacturing districts; and respectful petitions were also sent in from London, Liverpool, Manchester, Bristol, and other large towns, praying for a just and conciliatory course toward America. These petitions were referred to an inactive committee—" a committee of oblivion," Burke called it—while a few counter petitions, procured by Roebuck, were acted upon immediately. Petitions from Americans, and even one from Ja-

[1] Adam Smith was born at Kirkaldy, in Scotland, in 1723. At the age of three years he was carried off by some gipsies, but soon afterward was recovered. He was educated at Oxford, and was designed for the Church. He became an infidel in religious views, and of course turned his attention to other than clerical duties. He was the friend of Hume, Gibbon, and several of the most distinguished infidel writers of France. He wrote much, but the work on which his reputation rests is his " Inquiry into the Nature and Cause of the Wealth of Nations," published in 1771. It was for a long time the ablest work on political economy in the English language. He died in 1790, as he had lived, a contemner of Christianity.

maica, in favor of the colonies, were treated with disdain, and the Americans had every reason to believe that government was anxious to light up the flame of war, with the expectation of at once crushing the spirit of independence in the West by a single tread of its iron heel of power.

1775.   Parliament, which adjourned until after the Christmas holidays, reassembled on the 20th of January.   Greatly to the astonishment of every one, Lord Chatham (Pitt) was in his place in the Upper House on the following day.   It was understood that he had washed his hands of American affairs, and that he would probably not be seen in Parliament during the session.   It was a mistake, and the great statesman opened the business of the session by proposing an address to the king, asking him to " immediately dispatch orders to General Gage to remove his forces from Boston as soon as the rigors of the season would permit."   " I wish, my lords," he said, " not to lose a day in this urgent, pressing crisis.   An hour now lost may produce years of calamity.   For my part, I will not desert, for a single moment, the conduct of this weighty business.   Unless nailed to my bed by extremity of sickness, I will give it my unremitted attention.   I will knock at the door of this sleeping and confounded ministry, and will rouse them to a sense of their impending danger.   When I state the importance of the colonies to this country, and the magnitude of danger from the present plan of misadministration practiced against them, I desire not to be understood to argue for a reciprocity of indulgence between England and America.   I contend not for indulgence, but justice to America ; and I shall ever contend that the Americans owe obedience to us in a limited degree."   After stating the points on which the su premacy of the mother country was justly predicated, the great orator continued : " Resistance to your acts was necessary as it was just ; and your vain declarations of the omnipotence of Parliament, and your imperious doctrines of the necessity of submission, will be found equally incompetent to convince or to enslave your fellow-subjects in America, who feel that tyranny, whether ambitioned by an individual part of the Legislature or the bodies who compose it, is equally intolerable to British subjects."   He then drew a picture of the condition of the troops in Boston, suffering from the inclemencies of winter, insulted by the inhabitants, wasting away with sickness and pining for action ; and finally, after alluding to the wisdom of the late Congress and the approval of their acts by the people, he exclaimed, " I trust it is obvious to your lordships that all attempts to impose servitude upon such men, to establish despotism over such a mighty continental nation, must be vain— must be fatal.   We shall be forced ultimately to retract ; let us retract while we can, not when we must. . . . . . To conclude, my lords, if the ministers thus persevere in misadvising and misleading the king, I will not say that they *can* alienate the affections of his subjects from his crown, but I will affirm that they will make the crown not worth his wearing.   I will not say that the king is betrayed, but I will pronounce that the kingdom is undone."

Chatham's motion was negatived by a vote of sixty-eight to eighteen.   Not at all discouraged, he immediately presented a bill, in which it was proposed to renounce the power of taxation, demand of the Americans an acknowledgment of the supreme authority of Great Britain, and invite them to contribute, voluntarily, a specified sum annually, to be employed in meeting the charge on the national debt.   This accomplished, it proposed an immediate repeal of all the objectionable acts of Parliament passed during the current reign, and then in force.[1]   This, of course, ministers regarded as a concession to the colonies quite as injurious to national honor as any thing yet proposed, and more humiliating, even, than Dr. Tucker's propositions, then attracting much attention, that Parliament should, by solemn act, separate the colonies from the parent government, and disallow any application for restoration to the rights and privileges of British subjects, until, by humble petition, they should

[1] These were ten in number : the *Sugar Act*, the two *Quartering Acts*, the *Tea Act*, the *Act suspending the New York Legislature* (hereafter to be noticed), the two *Acts for the Trial in Great Britain of Offenses committed in America*, the *Boston Port Bill*, the *Act for Regulating the General Government of Massachusetts*, and the *Quebec Act*

OF THE REVOLUTION.   519

Virtual Declaration of War against the Colonists.   Warm Debates in Parliament.   Chatham and Franklin.   Gibbon and Fox.

ask for pardon and reinstatement.[1]   Chatham's proposition received very little favor in the House of Lords, though loudly applauded by the more intelligent people without,[2] and it was negatived, on the motion of the Earl of Sandwich to "reject the bill now and forever," by a vote of sixty-one against thirty-two.

The ministry, governed by the ethics of the lion (without his magnanimity), "might makes right," followed up their foolish rejection of the olive branch, by proposing measures tantamount to an actual declaration of war upon the American colonists, as rebels.   On the 2d of February, North proposed the first of a series of coercive measures.   He moved, in the Commons, for an address to the king, affirming that the province of Massachu- 1775. setts was in a state of rebellion; that Great Britain would not relinquish an iota of her sovereign rule in the colonies, and urging his majesty to take effectual meas- ures for enforcing obedience to the laws.   The address concluded with the usual resolution to support him with their "lives and fortunes."

EDWARD GIBBON.

On introducing the motion, North intimated that a part of his plan was to materially increase the military forces in America, and to restrain the entire commerce of New England with Great Britain, Ireland, and the West Indies.   Fox moved an amendment, censuring the ministry and praying for their removal.   Dunning and the great Thurlow engaged in the debate on the side of the opposition, which became very warm.   Fox's amendment was negatived by a vote of three hundred and four against one hundred and five, and North's motion prevailed by a majority of two hundred and ninety-six to one hundred and six in the Commons, and in the Upper House by eighty-seven to twenty-seven; nine peers protesting.[3]

---

[1] Josiah Tucker, D.D., dean of Gloucester, was an able English divine, and son of Abraham Tucker, author of *The Light of Nature Pursued*, a work in nine octavo volumes.   Dr. Tucker was a famous pamphleteer at the time of our Revolution.   He was the only friend of the British ministry who wrote in favor of the independence of the colonies.

[2] The corporation of the city of London passed a vote of thanks to him, and Franklin (to whom Chatham submitted the bill before offering it in the Senate) sent forth an address to the people of England, and to his own countrymen there, in which he portrayed the wickedness of rejecting this plan of reconciliation, the only feasible one that had been offered for years.   Franklin and other agents asked to be examined at the bar of the House of Commons touching the demands of the general Congress; but even this *courtesy*, for it could be called nothing more, was roughly denied.

[3] Gibbon the historian, author of the *Decline and Fall of the Roman Empire*, who had then a seat in Parliament, writing to his friend Sheffield, said, "We voted an address of 'lives and fortunes,' declaring Massachusetts Bay in a state of rebellion; more troops, but, I fear, not enough, to go to America, to make an army of ten thousand men at Boston; three generals, Howe, Clinton, and Burgoyne!   In a few days we stop the ports of New England.   I can not write volumes, but I am more and more convinced that, with firmness, all may go well; *yet I something doubt.*"

Gibbon was very much disposed to take sides with the Americans, and it is said that he publicly declared at Brooke's Coffee-house, that "there was no salvation for England, unless six of the heads of the cabinet council were cut off and laid upon the tables of the houses of Parliament as examples."   Gibbon had his price, and, within a fortnight after the above expression was uttered, took office under that same cabinet council, with a liberal salary and promise of a pension.   His mouth was thus stopped by the sugar-plums of patronage.   So says Bailey, author of "Records of Patriotism and Love of Country," page 169.   Bailey also gives the following poem, which he asserts was written by Fox:

> "King George, in a fright, lest Gibbon should write
>   The story of Britain's disgrace,
> Thought no means more sure his pen to secure
>   Than to give the historian a place.
> But his caution is vain, 'tis the curse of his reign
>   That his projects should never succeed·
> Though he write not a line, yet a cause of *decline*
>   In the author's example we read.

In the debate on this bill the celebrated John Wilkes, then a member of Parliament, formerly editor of the North Briton, a radical paper, who had given the government a world

JOHN WILKES.

of trouble during a portion of the first eight years of the reign of George III., took a conspicuous part in favor of the Americans.   He declared that a proper resistance to wrong was *revolution*, and not *rebellion*, and intimated that if the Americans were successful, they might, in after times, celebrate the revolution of 1775 as the English did that of 1688.   Earnest recommendations to pursue milder measures were offered by the opposition, but without effect.   It was voted that two thousand additional seamen and one thousand four hundred soldiers should be sent to America.

A few days afterward Lord North brought forth another bill, providing for the destruction of the entire trade of the New England colonies, and of their fisheries.[2]   It had a clause, excepting those individuals from the curse who should produce a certificate from their respective governors testifying to their general good conduct, and who should acknowledge the supremacy of the British Parliament.   In addition to the opposition which the bill received in the Commons, the merchants of London presented an earnest remonstrance against it,[3] and so did the Quakers in behalf of their brethren in Nantucket, but without effect.   It passed by a majority of one hundred and eighty to fifty-eight.   Fresh intelligence from America, representing the general adhesion to the Continental Congress, arrived at this juncture, and another bill was speedily passed, in the form of an amendment, including all the colonies in the Restraining Act, except New York and North Carolina, where loyalty seemed to predominate.

February 10, 1775.

March 8.

March 21.

While the Restraining Act was under consideration, North astonished all parties by offering what he pretended to be a conciliatory bill.   It proposed that when the proper authorities, in any colony, should offer, besides maintaining its own civil government, to raise

The first volume of Gibbon's Rome was published in 1776, and the sixth and last on his fifty-first birthday, in 1788.   His bookseller, Mr. Cadell, on that day gave him forty thousand dollars.   Gibbon died in January, 1794.

[1] This fearless political writer was born in 1727.   He became a member of Parliament in 1757.   In the forty-fifth number of the " North Briton," published in 1763, he made a severe attack on government, for which he was sent to the Tower.   On account of a licentious essay on woman he was afterward expelled from the House of Commons.   Acquitted of the charge for which he was committed to the Tower, he prosecuted Mr. Wood, the Under Secretary, received five thousand dollars damages, and then went to Paris. He returned to England in 1768, sent a letter of submission to the king, and was soon afterward elected to a seat in Parliament for Middlesex.   The seat was successfully contested by another.   He was then elected alderman of London, and the same year obtained a verdict of twenty thousand dollars against the Secretary of State for seizing his papers.   He was sheriff in 1771, and in 1774 was elected lord mayor, and took his seat in Parliament for Middlesex.   He was made Chamberlain of London in 1779, and soon afterward retired from the field of party politics.   He died at his seat in the Isle of Wight in 1797, aged seventy years. The likeness here given is copied from a medal struck in his honor.   The obverse side has a pyramid upon a pedestal, beside which stands a figure of Time inscribing upon the pyramid the number 45.   On the pedestal are the words *Magna Charta*, and beneath, IN MEMORY OF THE YEAR MDCCLXVIII.   Wilkes had a most forbidding countenance, but his manners were pleasing.   In his private character he was licentious, yet his talents and energy employed upon the popular side made him the idol of the people.

[2] According to testimony produced in Parliament, about 400 ships, 2000 fishing shallops, and 20,000 men were thus employed in the British Newfoundland fisheries.

[3] The people of New England were, at that time, indebted to the merchants of London nearly five million dollars.   With the destruction of the trade of the colonists, all hope of collecting even a small share of this sum would be lost.

a certain revenue and place it at the disposition of Parliament, it would be proper to forbear imposing any tax, except for the regulation of commerce. The ministerial party opposed it because it was conciliatory, and the opposition were dissatisfied with it because it proposed to abate but a single grievance, and was not specific. To his great astonishment, the minister found himself in the midst of a cross-fire from both parties; yet he stood his ground well, and adroitly carried the proposition through. Although he acknowledged that it was really a cheat with a fair exterior of honesty, and intended to sow division in the councils of the colonies, heedless members of Parliament gave it support, and the bill was passed by a vote of two hundred and seventy-four to eighty-eight.

On the heel of this bill Burke proposed a conciliatory plan, and five days afterward Mr. Hartley offered a mild scheme, similar to Chatham's; but they were negatived by large majorities. The " lord mayor, aldermen, and livery of London," urged by the merchants, who were smarting under the effects of the lash applied to the Americans, addressed the king in condemnation of the late measures toward the colonies. They were sternly rebuked by his majesty, who expressed his astonishment that any of his subjects presumed to be abettors of the rebels. It was obvious that March 22.

April 10, 1775.

> " King, Commons, and Lords were uniting amain
> To cut down this guardian of ours,"

and Franklin, abandoning all hope of reconciliation, sailed for America.

For more than ten years the colonies had complained of wrongs, petitioned for redress, and suffered insults. Forbearance was no longer a virtue, and, turning their backs upon Great Britain, they prepared for war. In this movement Massachusetts took the lead. The Provincial Congress ordered the purchase of ammunition and stores for an army of fifteen thousand men. They called upon the Congregational clergy to preach liberty from their pulpits, and hearty responses were given. " The towns, which had done so fearlessly and so thoroughly the preparatory work of forming and concentrating political sentiment, came forward now to complete their patriotic actions by voting money freely to arm, equip, and discipline ' Alarm List Companies;' citizens of every calling appeared in their ranks; to be a private in them was proclaimed by the journals an honor; to be chosen to office in them, a mark of the highest distinction. In Danvers, the deacon of the parish was elected captain of the minute men, and the minister his lieutenant. The minute men were trained often, the towns paying the expense; and the company, after its field exercises, would sometimes repair to the meeting-house to hear a patriotic sermon, or partake of an entertainment at the town-house, where zealous sons of liberty would exhort them to prepare to fight bravely for God and their country. Such was the discipline—so free from a mercenary spirit, so full of inspiring influences—of the early American soldiery. And thus an army, in fact, was in existence, ready at a moment's call, for defensive purposes, to wheel its isolated platoons into solid phalanxes, while it presented to an enemy only opportunity for an inglorious foray upon its stores."[1]

Had the counsels of inflamed zeal and passion—inflamed by the most cruel and insulting oppression—prevailed, blood would have been shed before the close of 1774. Troops continued to arrive at Boston,[2] and the insolence of the soldiery increased with their numbers

---

[1] Frothingham's *Siege of Boston*, p. 42.

[2] In November, 1774, there were eleven regiments of British troops, besides the artillery, in Boston. In December, 500 marines landed from the Asia man-of-war, and, at the close of the month, all the troops ordered from the Jerseys, New York, and Quebec had arrived. A guard of 150 men was stationed at the lines upon the Neck. The army was brigaded. The first brigadier general was Earl Percy, Moncrief his brigade major; the second general was Pigott, his major, Small; third general, Jones, his major, Hutchinson, son of the late governor. The soldiers were in high spirits, and the officers looked with contempt upon the martial preparations of the people. "As to what you hear of their taking arms to resist the force of England," wrote an officer, in November, 1774, "it is mere bullying, and will go no further than words, whenever it comes to blows, he that can run the fastest will think himself best off. Believe me, any two regiments here ought to be decimated, if they did not beat, in the field, the whole force of the Massachusetts province."

and strength; but the Americans were determined that when collision, which was inevitable, should take place, the first blow should be struck by the British troops, and thus make government the aggressor. The occasion was not long delayed. General Gage discovered that the patriots were secretly conveying arms and ammunition out of Boston. In carts, beneath loads of manure, cannon balls and muskets were carried out; and powder, concealed in the panniers of the market-women, and cartridges in candle-boxes, passed unsuspected by the guard upon the Neck.[1] On discovering these movements, and learning that some brass cannon and field-pieces were at Salem, Gage sent a detachment of troops to seize them. They were repelled by the people under Colonel Timothy Pickering, without bloodshed, as we have noticed on page 374. This movement aroused the utmost vigilance throughout the country. At a special session of the Connecticut Assembly, Colonel Wooster was commissioned a major general, and Joseph Spencer and Israel Putnam were appointed brigadiers. Elbridge Gerry, a merchant of Marblehead, and afterward a signer of the Declaration of Independence, was at the head of the Massachusetts Committee of Supply, and under his directions munitions of war were rapidly accumulated, the chief deposit of which was at Concord, about twenty miles from Boston. Meanwhile, Sewall, the attorney general of the province, wrote a series of powerful articles, calling upon the people to cease resistance; and, greatly to the alarm of the patriots lest there should be defection in their strong-hold, Governor Trumbull, of Connecticut, soon afterward offered to mediate between General Gage and the people of Boston, for the sake of preventing hostilities. Timothy Ruggles, president of the "Stamp Act Congress," got up counter associations against those of the patriots, and a small number at Marshfield and other places signed the agreement, calling themselves the "Associated Loyalists." But John Adams promptly replied to Judge Sewall; Governor Trumbull's apparent conservatism was soon understood to be but a testimony against government, to prove that offers of reconciliation had been made and rejected; the patriots made the "Associated Loyalists" recant, and the republicans assumed a bolder tone than ever of defiance and contempt.

March, 1775.

When spring opened, Gage's force amounted to about three thousand five hundred effective men. He determined, with this force, to nip the rebellion in the bud, and his first active movement was an attempt to seize or destroy the stores of the patriots at Concord, which were under the charge of Colonel James Barrett. Officers in disguise were sent to make sketches of the roads, and to ascertain the state of the towns. Bodies of troops were occasionally marched into the country, and a general system of reconnoissance around Boston was established. The ever-vigilant patriots were awake to all these movements. A night-watch was established at Concord, and every where the minute men were ready with burnished muskets, fixed bayonets, and filled cartouches.

Early in April, many who had taken a prominent part in the revolutionary proceedings at Boston, apprehending arrest, and probable transportation to England for trial, left the town.[2] Among those who remained was Dr. Joseph Warren, and he kept the patriots continually advised of the movements of Gage and his troops. Samuel Adams and John Hancock, who were members of the Provincial Congress, were particularly obnoxious to General Gage, and, as it appeared afterward, he had resolved to arrest them on their return to the

---

[1] On the 18th of March the discovery was made, and the guard at the Neck seized 13,425 musket cartridges and a quantity of balls. In doing this, a teamster was severely handled. This circumstance, the oration of Dr. Joseph Warren, in the "Old South," on the anniversary of the Massacre (March 5th), the tarring and feathering of a citizen of Billerica, charged with tempting a soldier to desert, and an assault upon the house of John Hancock, greatly excited the people.

[2] "A daughter of liberty, unequally yoked in point of politics, sent word by a trusty hand to Mr. Samuel Adams, residing, in company with Mr. Hancock, at Lexington, that the troops were coming out in a few days. Upon this, their friends in Boston were advised to move out their plate, &c., and the Committee of Safety voted that all the ammunition be deposited in nine different towns, and that other articles be lodged, some in one place and some in another; so, as to the 15 medicine-chests, 2000 iron pots, 2000 bowls, 15,000 canteens, and 1000 tents; and that the six companies of matrosses be stationed in different towns."
--Gordon, i., 309.

city. Fortunately, they were persuaded to remain at Lexington, at the house of the Reverend Jonas Clark.

On Tuesday night, the 18th of April, Gage sent eight hundred British troops, light infantry and grenadiers, under Lieutenant-colonel Smith, aided by Major Pitcairn, to 1775. destroy the stores at Concord. They embarked at the Common, and, landing at Phipps's Farm, marched with great secrecy, arresting every person they met on the way, to prevent intelligence of their expedition being given.

They left Boston at about midnight, Gage supposing the movement to be a profound secret; but the patriots had become aware of the expedition early in the evening. As Lord Percy was crossing the Common, about nine o'clock, he joined a group of persons, one of whom said, "The British troops will miss their aim." "What aim?" inquired Percy, who was Gage's confidant in the matter. "The cannon at Concord," replied the man.

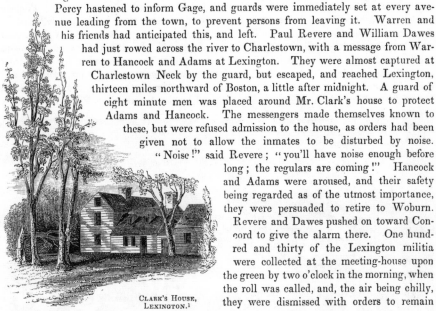

Percy hastened to inform Gage, and guards were immediately set at every avenue leading from the town, to prevent persons from leaving it. Warren and his friends had anticipated this, and left. Paul Revere and William Dawes had just rowed across the river to Charlestown, with a message from Warren to Hancock and Adams at Lexington. They were almost captured at Charlestown Neck by the guard, but escaped, and reached Lexington, thirteen miles northward of Boston, a little after midnight. A guard of eight minute men was placed around Mr. Clark's house to protect Adams and Hancock. The messengers made themselves known to these, but were refused admission to the house, as orders had been given not to allow the inmates to be disturbed by noise. "Noise!" said Revere; "you'll have noise enough before long; the regulars are coming!" Hancock and Adams were aroused, and their safety being regarded as of the utmost importance, they were persuaded to retire to Woburn. Revere and Dawes pushed on toward Concord to give the alarm there. One hundred and thirty of the Lexington militia were collected at the meeting-house upon the green by two o'clock in the morning, when the roll was called, and, the air being chilly, they were dismissed with orders to remain

CLARK'S HOUSE, LEXINGTON.[1]

within drum-beat.

The midnight march of the British regulars was performed in silence, and, as they supposed, in secret. But vigilant eyes were upon them. Messrs. Gerry, Orne, and Lee, members of the Provincial Congress, were at Menotomy (West Cambridge), and saw them passing; and, as they approached Lexington, the sound of bells and guns warned them that their expedition was known.[2]

Colonel Smith detached six companies under Major Pitcairn, with orders to press on to

[1] This building was standing when I visited Lexington in 1848. It was built by Thomas Hancock, Esq., of Boston, as a parsonage for his father, the Reverend John Hancock, of Lexington, about 130 years ago. Mr. Hancock was a minister at Lexington fifty-two years, and was succeeded by the Reverend Jonas Clark, the occupant of the house at the time of the skirmish at Lexington. Mr. Clark lived in the house fifty-two years. The room in which the two patriots, Samuel Adams and John Hancock, were sleeping on the night before the skirmish at Lexington, is retained in its original condition. The wainscoting is of Carolina pine, and the sides of the room are covered with a heavy paper, with dark figures, pasted upon the boards in rectangular pieces about fourteen inches square. In an adjoining room is one of those ancient fire-places, ornamented with pictorial tiles, so rarely found in New England.

[2] These three patriots had a narrow escape. They saw the head of the column pass by. Just before the rear-guard had come up, a detachment was sent to search the house where they were staying. They escaped to the fields by a back door, where they kept in concealment until the house was searched and the troops moved on.

524   PICTORIAL FIELD-BOOK

The British Troops and Minute Men at Lexington.   Conduct of Major Pitcairn.   Battle on Lexington Common.

Concord and secure the two bridges; at the same time he sent a messenger to Boston for re-enforcements. Pitcairn advanced rapidly toward Lexington by the light of a waning moon, capturing several persons on the way. One, named Bowman, escaped, and, hasten‐ ing on horseback to Lexington, notified Captain Parker, commander of the minute men, of the approach of the enemy. It was now between four and five o'clock in the morning. The bells were rung, guns were fired, and the drums were beaten. About one hundred of the militia were speedily collected upon the green, armed with loaded muskets, but in much confusion and alarm, for the number of the approaching regulars was unknown. In the gray of the early morning the scarlet uniforms of the troops appeared, and an overwhelming force halted, within a few rods of the meeting-house, and loaded their pieces. The militia, undismayed, stood firm. They had been ordered not to draw a trigger until fired upon by the enemy, and for a moment silence and hesitation prevailed, for neither party seemed will‐ ing to become the aggressor. The parley with judgment was but for a moment. Pitcairn and other officers galloped forward, waving their swords over their heads, and followed by their troops in double-quick time. They shouted, " Disperse, you villains ! lay down your arms ! Why don't you disperse, you rebels ? disperse !" In rushing forward the troops became confused. As the patriots did not instantly obey the command to lay down their arms, Pitcairn wheeled his horse, and, waving his sword, gave orders to press forward and surround the militia. At the same moment some random shots were fired by the British, but without effect, which were promptly returned by the Americans. Pitcairn then drew

SKIRMISH AT LEXINGTON.[1]

his pistol and discharged it, at the same moment giving the word *fire!* A general dis‐ charge of musketry ensued ; four patriots were killed, and the remainder were dispersed. Finding themselves fired upon while retreating, several of them halted, and returned the shots, and then secured themselves behind stone walls and buildings. Three British sol‐ diers, and Pitcairn's horse, were wounded, while eight Americans were killed : four on the

---

[1] This is the picture alluded to on page 421, from the one drawn by Earl, and engraved by Doolittle in 1775. The largest building in the picture is the meeting-house, and the officer on horseback in front of it is Major Pitcairn. The figures in the foreground are the provincial militia. The dwelling with the two chimneys, on the left (which is still standing), was Buckman's Tavern. The position of the monument since erected upon Lexington Green, is about where the provincials on the left are seen dispersing. The merit of this picture consists in its truthfulness in depicting the appearance of the spot at the time of the engagement.

ground, near the spot where the monument stands, and four others while escaping over the fences.[1]

As soon as the patriots dispersed, the detachment of regulars, joined by Colonel Smith and his party, pushed on toward Concord, six miles distant. Confident of success, the whole party were in high spirits. But Concord had been aroused, and a formidable body of militia had collected to receive the invaders. We have noticed that Revere and Dawes started from Lexington to alarm the country toward Concord. They met Dr. Samuel Prescott, and, while in conference with him, some British officers came upon them. Revere and Dawes were made prisoners, but Prescott escaped over a wall, and reached Concord about two in the morning. The bells were rung, and before daylight the people were under arms. When the guns at Lexington were heard in the morning, the Committee of Safety, and the principal citizens of Concord, had assembled, and arranged a plan of reception for the British troops. The military operations were under the able management of Colonel James Barrett,[2] while the whole male population, and some women, aided in removing the stores to a place of safety in distant woods

SIGNATURE OF COLONEL BARRETT.

The militia of Lincoln and other places hastened to join those of Concord, and the whole paraded on the Common. Guards were stationed at the North and South Bridges, and in the center of the town, all under the command of Captain Jonathan Farrar.

At about seven o'clock the British column was seen advancing on the Lexington Road. Some companies of militia that had marched down that road returned in haste and reported the number of the British as three times that of the Americans. These companies, with those in the town, fell back to an eminence some eighty rods from the center of the village, where they were joined by Colonel Barrett, and were formed into two battalions. They had hardly formed, before the glittering of the bayonets and flashing of the red uniforms of the British in the bright morning sun were seen, but a quarter of a mile distant, rapidly advancing. A short consultation was held. Some were for making a desperate stand upon the spot, while others proposed a present retreat, until re-enforced by the neighboring militia. The latter council prevailed, and the provincials retired to the high ground over the North Bridge, about a mile from the Common.

The British troops entered Concord in two divisions : one by the main road, the other on the hill north of it. Colonel Smith and Major Pitcairn, who had immediate command of the grenadiers and light infantry, remained in the town, but detached six companies under Captain Parsons to secure the bridges, prevent the militia from crossing them, and to ferret out and destroy the secreted stores, information concerning which had been given by Captain Beeman of Petersham, and other Tories. Captain Lawrie, with three companies, was stationed on the North Bridge, while Parsons, with the other three companies, marched to destroy the stores at the residence of Colonel Barrett. Captain Pole, with a party, took post at the South Bridge, and destroyed what few stores were found in that vicinity ; but so

---

[1] The names of the slain are recorded on the monument erected to their memory on the green at Lexington. A picture of the monument and a copy of the inscription may be found on page 553. Captain Jonas Parker was among the slain. He had repeatedly said that he never would run from the British. He was wounded at the first fire, but, continuing to discharge his gun. without retreating, was killed by a bayonet.

[2] Colonel Barrett had been a captain in the provincial army during the French and Indian war. He was with Shirley at Oswego, and afterward accompanied Abercrombie to Ticonderoga and Amherst to Crown Point. Becoming aged, he resigned his commission. When the Massachusetts militia were organized at the beginning of 1775, Captain Barrett was solicited to take command of a regiment, but declined on account of his age. "We don't want active service, we want your advice," said his earnest townsmen. Thus urged, and actuated by patriotic zeal, he took the command. Colonel Barrett died at about the close of the war. These facts I obtained from his grandson, Major Barrett, eighty-seven years old when I visited him in 1848.

COLONEL BARRETT'S HOUSE.[1]

diligently had the people worked in concealing the stores that the object of the expedition was almost frustrated.   The British broke open about sixty barrels of flour in the center of the town, but nearly half of that was subsequently saved. They knocked off the trunnions of three iron twenty-four pound cannons, burned sixteen new carriage wheels, and a few barrels of wooden trenchers and spoons, cut down the liberty-pole and set the court-house on fire.   The flames were extinguished by a Mrs. Moulton, before much damage was done.   About five hundred pounds of balls were thrown into the mill-pond and wells.

While the British were thus engaged, the number of the militia was rapidly increasing by accessions of minute men from Carlisle, Chelmsford, Weston, Littleton, and Acton neighboring towns, and before ten o'clock the force amounted to nearly four hundred men Joseph Hosmer, acting as adjutant, formed them into proper line as fast as they arrived on the field, westerly of the house since owned by Joseph Buttrick.   Most of the operations of the British, within the town, could be seen from this point, and when the fires in the center of the village were lighted the people were greatly excited.   Many of the prominent citizens, and the Committee of Safety, were with the militia, and, after a brief consultation, and a stirring appeal from the brave Hosmer, it was resolved to dislodge the enemy at the North Bridge.   "I haven't a man that's afraid to go," said the intrepid Captain Isaac Davis; and, wheeling into marching order, they were joined by other companies, and pushed forward toward the bridge, under the command of Major John Buttrick, of Concord.

BATTLE GROUND AT CONCORD.[2]

[1] This sketch is from the road leading to the village of Concord by the way of the North Bridge.   The house was erected about eighty years ago, by Colonel Barrett, and is now owned by his kinsman, Prescott Barrett.

[2] This view, looking southeast, is from the road leading to the village by the way of the North Bridge.

The Acton company, under Davis, was in front, followed by those of Captains Brown, Miles, and Nathan Barrett, and by others whose commanders' names are not recorded, in all nearly three hundred effective men. They marched in double file, with trailed arms. The British guard were on the west side of the river, but, on seeing the Americans approaching, they crossed over, and commenced taking up the planks of the bridge. Major Buttrick called to them to desist, and urged his men forward to arrest the destruction of the bridge. The enemy formed for action, and when the Americans were within a few rods of the river, they were fired upon by some of the regulars. The first shots were ineffectual, but others that followed were fatal. One of the Acton company was wounded,[1] and Captain Isaac Davis and Abner Hosmer, of the same company, were killed. " Fire, fellow-soldiers ! for God's sake, fire !" shouted Buttrick, on seeing his companions fall, and immediately a full volley was given by the provincials. Three of the British were killed, and several wounded and made prisoners. Some other shots were fired, but in a few minutes Lawrie ordered a retreat, and the provincials took possession of the bridge. Two of the British soldiers killed were left on the ground, and were buried by the provincials. Their graves are a few feet from the monument. Another, who was not yet dead, was dispatched by a blow from a hatchet in the hands of a young provincial who had more zeal than humanity. This circumstance gave rise to the horrible story sent abroad by the British and Tories, that the militia " killed and *scalped* the prisoners that fell into their hands."

PLAN OF THE MOVEMENTS AT CONCORD.[2]

Colonel Smith, in the village, on hearing the firing at the bridge, sent a re-enforcement. These met the retreating detachment of Lawrie, but, observing the increasing force of the militia, wheeled, and joined in the retreat. In the mean time, the party under Captain Parsons returned from Colonel Barrett's, and were allowed by the provincials to cross the river at the North Bridge, where the skirmish had just occurred, unmolested. It may be asked why the militia did not cut them off, which they might easily have done. It must be remembered that war had not been declared, and that the people had been enjoined to make Great Britain the aggressor, they acting only on the defensive. The militia at Concord had not yet heard of the deaths at Lexington ; *their* volley that had just slain three of the king's troops was fired purely in self-defense, and they hesi-

to the residence of Mr. Prescott Barrett. The point from which the sketch was made is upon an elevation a little north of that where the militia assembled under Colonel Barrett. The stream of water is the Concord, or Sudbury River. The site of the North Bridge is at the monument seen in the center of the picture. The monument stands upon the spot where the British were stationed, and in the plain, directly across the river from the monument, is the place where Davis and Hosmer, of the American militia, were killed. The house, the roof and gable of which are seen in the distance, just on the left of the largest tree, was the residence of the Reverend Dr. Ripley (afterward a chaplain in the army) at the time of the skirmish. It is upon the road leading to Concord village, which lies nearly half a mile beyond.

[1] He was a fifer, named Blanchard. One of the Concord minute men, named Brown, was also slightly wounded. The ball that wounded them passed under the arm of Colonel Robinson, who, by request, accompanied Major Buttrick.

[2] This plan I have copied from Frothingham's interesting work, *History of the Siege of Boston,* p. 70.

EXPLANATION OF THE PLAN.—1. Lexington Road ; 2. Hills and high land where the liberty pole stood ; 3. Center of the town, and main body of the British ; 4. Road to the South Bridge ; 5, 5, 5. Road to the North Bridge and to Colonel Barnett's, two miles from the center of the town ; 6. High ground a mile north of the meeting-house, where the militia assembled ; 7. Road along which they marched to dislodge the British at North Bridge ; 8. Spot where Davis and Hosmer fell ; 9. Reverend Mr. Emerson's house ; 10. Bridges and roads made in 1793, when the old roads with dotted lines were discontinued ; 11. The monument. The arrows show the return of Captain Parsons, after the firing at the North Bridge ; 12 is the place where re-enforcements met him.

tated, for the moment, to act on the offensive by renewing the combat. This is the explanation given by their cotemporaries.

Observing the rapid augmentation of the militia, Colonel Smith thought it prudent to return with his troops to Boston as speedily as possible. A little after twelve o'clock they
commenced their retreat toward Lexington, the main column covered by strong flanking
guards. They soon perceived that the whole region was in arms, and minute men were
collecting from all points. The cautious counsels at Concord, not to attack the enemy
without further provocation, were disregarded, and at Merriam's Corner, a company of provincials under Captain Brooks (afterward the distinguished colonel at Saratoga, and Governor of Massachusetts), secreted behind barns and fences, made a destructive assault upon
the retreating enemy. A volley was fired in return, but not a militia-man was injured.
This example was followed along the whole line of march to Lexington, and the British
were terribly galled all the way. From every house, barn, and stone wall guns were fired
with sure aim, and many of the regulars were slain. At Hardy's Hill there was a severe
skirmish, and at almost every wooded defile numbers of the enemy were picked off by the
concealed marksmen. All military order among the provincials was at an end, and each
fought according to the dictates of his own judgment. Some of them were killed by the
flankers, who came suddenly upon them behind the walls; but the number of the militia
slain was comparatively small. Colonel Smith was severely wounded in the leg at Fiske's
Hill, near Lexington; and near the battle ground of the morning, at Lexington meeting-
house, several of the British soldiers were shot. Greatly fatigued by the night's march and
the day's adventures, and worried on every side by the militia, that seemed, to use the expression of one of their officers, "to drop from the clouds," the whole body of eight hundred
men, the flower of the British army at Boston, must have surrendered to the provincials in
an hour had not relief arrived.

An express was sent from Lexington to General Gage, early in the morning, acquainting
him with the rising of the militia, and praying for a strong re-enforcement. At nine o'clock
three regiments of infantry, and two divisions of marines, amounting to about nine hundred
men, with two field-pieces, under Lord Percy, left Boston and marched toward Lexington.
They passed through Roxbury, the bands playing *Yankee Doodle* in derision, it being employed as a sort of "Rogue's March" when offending soldiers were drummed out.[1] Vague

---

[1] Gordon relates that a shrewd boy in Roxbury made himself extremely merry when he heard the tune
of Yankee Doodle, and by his antics attracted the attention of Lord Percy. He asked the boy why he was
so merry. "To think," said the lad, "how you will dance by-and-by to *Chevy Chase*." Percy was often
much influenced by presentiments, and the remarks of the boy worried him all day. It may be asked why
was Earl Percy troubled, and what connection had the name of Chevy Chase with him. The answer is in
the fact that Percy was a son of the Duke of Northumberland, a lineal descendant of Earl Percy, one of
the heroes of the battle of Chevy Chase, and who was there slain. There was great rivalry between the
houses of Percy and Douglas, the former an English borderer and the latter a Scotch borderer. Percy was
determined to have a field fight with his rival, and so vowed publicly that he would "take pleasure in the
border woods three days, and slay the Douglas's deer." Earl Douglas heard the vaunt. "Tell him," he
said, "he will find *one* day more than enough." Percy's aim was the armed encounter thus promised. He
appeared at Chevy Chase with his greyhounds and fifteen hundred chosen archers. After taking his sport
at the Douglas's expense, gazing on a hundred dead fallow deer and harts, tasting wine and venison cooked
under the greenwood tree, and saying the Douglas would not keep his word, when

> "Lo! yonder doth Earl Douglas come,
>   His men in armor bright;
> Full twenty hundred Scottish spears
>   All marching in our sight.
> All men of pleasant Tiviot-dale,
>   Fast by the River Tweed.
> 'O cease your sport!' Earl Percy said,
>   'And take your bows with speed.'

Soon after this,

> "The battle closed on every side,
>   No slackness there was found;
> And many a gallant gentleman
>   Lay gasping on the ground."

rumors of the skirmish at Lexington had reached the people there, and this movement confirmed their worst fears. No sooner had the British troops passed by, than the minute men assembled, and, along the whole march, vigilant corps of militia were gathering, and hovered around the little army of Percy, ready to strike a blow whenever it might be effectual.

Percy's brigade met the wearied troops between two and three o'clock, about half a mile from the Lexington meeting-house. He formed a hollow square, planted his cannon for its defense on the high ground near Munroe's Tavern, and received within it the worn-out companies of Colonel Smith. Many of the soldiers fell upon the ground, completely overcome. They "were so much exhausted with fatigue that they were obliged to lie down for rest on the ground, their tongues hanging out of their mouths, like those of dogs after a chase."[1] Percy dared not halt long, for the woods were swarming with minute men. After partaking of a little refreshment and brief rest, the united forces resumed their march toward Boston, marking their retreat by acts of vengeance, aside from the more dignified use of ball and bayonet. Three houses, two shops, and a barn, were laid in ashes in Lexington, and many buildings were destroyed or defaced, and helpless persons abused on the route. But prompt and terrible retribution instantly followed. As soon as Percy renewed the retreat, the provincials again attacked his forces from concealed points, until they arrived at West Cambridge, where a hot skirmish ensued. General Heath and Dr. Warren were active in the field, and in this foray Warren barely escaped with his life, a musket ball having knocked a pin out of an ear-curl of his hair. The British kept the militia at bay, and committed many atrocious acts. Percy tried to restrain his soldiers, but in vain. Houses were plundered, property destroyed, and several innocent persons were murdered. This conduct greatly inflamed the militia, and

"Again the conflict glows with rage severe,
And fearless ranks in combat mix'd appear."

"Indignation and outraged humanity struggled on the one hand, veteran discipline and desperation on the other."[2] The contest was brief, and the enemy, with their wounded, pressed on toward Boston. The Cambridge bridge had been taken up, and they were obliged to go by the way of Charlestown. They took the road that winds around Prospect Hill, while the main body of the provincials, unawed by the field-pieces, hung close upon their rear.

The situation of the British regulars was now critical, for their ammunition was almost exhausted, and a strong force was marching upon them from Roxbury, Dorchester, and Milton. Colonel Pickering, in the mean time, with seven hundred of the Essex militia, threatened to cut off their retreat to Charlestown. Another short but warm engagement occurred at the base of Prospect Hill, but the regulars reached Charlestown in safety. By command of General Heath the pursuit was now suspended.

Throughout the day Charlestown had been in the greatest excitement. Dr. Warren rode through in the morning, proclaiming the bloodshed at Lexington. Many of the people had seized their muskets, and hastened to the country to join their brethren. The schools were

---

The mail-clad leaders combated hand to hand, until the blood dropped from them like rain. "Yield thee, Percy," cried Douglas, "I shall freely pay thy ransom, and thy advancement shall be high with our Scottish king."

"'No, Douglas,' quoth Earl Percy, then,
'Thy proffer I do scorn;
I would not yield to any Scot
That ever yet was born.'"

Douglas almost immediately dropped, struck to the heart with an arrow. "Fight on, my merry men," he cried with his dying breath. Percy took his hand, and said, "Earl Douglas, I would give all my lands to save thee." At that moment an arrow pierced Percy's heart, and both leaders expired together.—See Knight's *Old England*, Scott's *Castle Dangerous*, and the ballad of *Chevy Chase*.

[1] Stedman's *History of the American War*, i., 118.
Stedman was a British officer, and accompanied Earl Percy in this expedition. He highly praises Percy, but says that Colonel Smith's conduct was much censured.
[2] Everett's *Lexington Address*.

dismissed; the shops were closed; and when it was ascertained that the British were retreating and must pass through the town, many of the inhabitants prepared to leave and to carry with them their most valuable effects. When the firing at Cambridge was heard, the people rushed toward Charlestown Neck, to flee to the country. There they met the retreating troops, and were obliged to fly back, panic-stricken, to their houses. A report got abroad that the British were slaughtering women and children in the streets. Terror every where prevailed, and a large number of the defenseless people passed the night in the clay-pits back of Breed's Hill. The alarm was false; not an individual was harmed in Charlestown. Percy ordered the women and children into their houses, and demanded nothing but refreshments for his troops. The main body occupied Bunker Hill that night, and a strong line was formed upon Charlestown Neck. A re-enforcement was sent over from Boston, guards were stationed in various parts of the town, the wounded were conveyed to the hospitals in the city, and that night all was quiet in the neighborhood. General Pigot assumed command at Charlestown the next morning, and before noon the crest-fallen troops returned to their quarters in Boston. Thus ended the first act in the bloody tragedy of the American Revolution.[1] During the day the British lost sixty-five killed, one hundred and eighty wounded, and twenty-eight made prisoners; in all two hundred and seventy-three. The provincials lost fifty-nine killed, thirty-nine wounded, and five missing; in all one hundred and three.[2]

The events of the 19th of April, 1775, were of vast importance, considered in their relation to subsequent scenes and results. On that day the life of the first British soldier, sent hither to oppress a people panting for the privileges of freedom, was sacrificed—on that day the first American, aroused by armed invasion to the necessity of resistance, fell in defense of the dearest rights guaranteed to him by the British Constitution[3]—on that day "the scabbard" was indeed "thrown away,"[4] and a war of seven years' duration began—and on that day the jubilee trumpet was sounded, proclaiming "Liberty throughout all the land unto all the inhabitants thereof."[5] The events of that day formed the first disruption of the chrysalis of old political systems, whence speedily came forth a noble and novel creature, with eagle eye and expansive wings, destined speedily to soar far above the creeping reptiles of despotism that brood amid the crumbling relics of old dynasties. They formed the significant prelude to that full diapason, whose thundering harmony, drawn forth by the magic touch of the spirit of Freedom, filled the nations with wonder, and ushered in the New Era so long predicted and so long hoped for.

The military events of the day, compared with the movements of armies in the great contests of war at other times, were exceedingly insignificant in themselves; but the temper shown by the provincials, and the vulnerable character of the British soldiery, as exhibited in the various skirmishes and in the retreat, had a great and abiding effect upon the minds of both parties. The haughty boasts of English officers, that three regiments might march unmolested throughout the continent, and that the Americans were "sorry poltroons, their courage displayed to its utmost in tarring and feathering individuals," were silenced, and Gage, in alarm, called upon the ministry to send large re-enforcements. The patriots, on the other hand, learned their strength when united; that British troops were not invincible, and that the true spirit and courage of men resolved on freedom animated and nerved

---

[1] Gordon, Stedman, Stiles, Ripley, Shattuck, Clarke, Frothingham, &c.

[2] The following officers and citizens of note were among the slain: Justice Isaac Gardner, of Brookline; Captain Isaac Davis, of Acton; Captain Jonathan Wilson, of Bedford; Lieutenant John Baron, and Sergeant Elisha Mills, of Needham; and Deacon Josiah Haynes, of Sudbury. The estimated value of property destroyed by the invaders is as follows: In Concord, $1375; in Lexington, $8305; in Cambridge, $6010. A list of the killed, wounded, and missing is given on page 532.

[3] It will be seen hereafter that the first life sacrificed in defense of liberty in America was upon the Alamance, in North Carolina, in 1771. In that event, however, the militia were in open and armed rebellion against the royal authority, and were the actual aggressors.

[4] John Wilkes, in his speech in Parliament, already alluded to, asked, significantly, "Who can tell whether, in consequence of this very day's violent and mad address [to the king], *the scabbard may not be thrown away by them as well as by us?*"

[5] Levit. xxv., 10.

the militia. Britons were alarmed; Americans were elated. Individual wrongs were adopted by the whole people as their own, and every man slain at Lexington, Concord, and Menotomy or West Cambridge, lived again in the strong arms of a thousand determined patriots. In Massachusetts, in particular, ties of consanguinity, property, marriage, manners, religion, social circumstances, and general equality, made whole communities weep over a single victim, and the hearts of the people of the whole province were made to bleed when the first martyrs in the cause of American Independence were laid in the grave.[1] Linked with that grief was the buoyant sentiment expressed by Percival:

> "O it is great for our country to die, where ranks are contending!
>   Bright is the wreath of our fame, glory awaits us for aye—
> Glory that never is dim, shining on with light never ending—
>   Glory that never shall fade—never, O never! away.
>
> *   *   *   *   *   *   **
>
> "O then, how great for our country to die, in the front rank to perish!
>   Firm, with our breast to the foe, victory's shout in our ear.
> Long they our statues shall crown, in songs our memory cherish;
>   We shall look forth from our heaven, pleased the sweet music to hear."

The Provincial Congress of Massachusetts was immediately summoned, and met at Watertown, seven miles west of Boston, on the 22d of April. Dr. Joseph Warren was chosen president, and Messrs. Gerry, Church, and Cushing were appointed a committee to draw up a "narrative of the massacre."[2] A committee on depositions was also formed, and many affidavits were taken at Lexington and Concord. When all necessary information was collected, a communication, giving a minute account of the whole affair, was drawn up and ordered to be sent to Arthur Lee, the colonial agent in England. An address "To the Inhabitants of Great Britain" was also prepared and sent with the other papers, and was first published in the London Chronicle of May 30th, 1775. The address was firm but respectful. While its signers asserted their continued loyalty to the sovereign, and their readiness to "defend his person, family, crown and dignity," they boldly exhibited their manhood in declaring that they would no longer submit to the tyrannical rule of a weak and wicked ministry. The Honorable Richard Derby, of Salem, was engaged by the committee to fit out his vessel as a packet, and take the dispatches to London. He arrived there on the 29th of May, ten days before Gage's dispatches reached government. The ministry were confounded, and affected to disbelieve the statements that appeared in the London Chronicle of the 30th; but, in a few days, they were obliged to acknowledge the truth of the report.[3]

(margin: 1775.)

(margin: April 25.)

(margin: 1775.)

---

[1] In Lexington, Concord, Danvers, and West Cambridge, monuments have been erected in memory of the slain. The two former will be noticed presently, in connection with an engraving of each. The monument at West Cambridge has been completed since my visit there in 1848. Beneath it rest the remains of twelve persons who were killed in the skirmish there. The names of only three are known: Jason Russel, Jason Winship, and Jabez Wyman. The monument is a simple granite obelisk, nineteen feet high The funds for its erection were furnished by the voluntary contributions of the citizens of West Cambridge.

[2] The first accounts of the events at Lexington and Concord were published in the newspapers and in handbills. One of the latter, preserved in the library of the Massachusetts Historical Society, has the figures of forty coffins at the head.

[3] Dartmouth, the Secretary of State for the colonies, issued the following card on the 30th: "A report having been spread, and an account having been printed and published, of a skirmish between some of the people in the province of Massachusetts Bay and a detachment of his majesty's troops, it is proper to inform the public that no advice has, as yet, been received in the American department of any such event."

Arthur Lee was in London, narrowly watching every movement of government, and transmitting secret intelligence to the Committee of Correspondence of Boston, and to his brother, Richard Henry Lee, member of the Continental Congress. He was the agent of the Massachusetts colony at that time, and issued the following card, over his proper signature:

"As a doubt of the authenticity of the account from Salem, touching an engagement between the king's troops and the provincials, in the Massachusetts Bay, may arise from a paragraph in the Gazette of this evening, I desire to inform all those who wish to see the original affidavits which confirm that account, that they are deposited at the Mansion House, with the Right Honorable the Lord Mayor, for their inspection.   ARTHUR LEE."

The dispatches of Gage were published on the 10th of June, and London was almost as much excited as Boston.   Gage's report confirmed every important circumstance mentioned by the patriots, and the metropolis was soon enlivened by placards, lampoons, and doggerel verse.   The retreat of the British from Lexington was regarded as a defeat and a flight, and at every corner ministers heard revilings concerning "the great British army at Boston that had been beaten by a FLOCK OF YANKEES!"

NOTE.—The following list of the names of the first martyrs in the cause of American liberty, is given in the eighteenth volume of the Massachusetts Historical Collections:

LEXINGTON.—*Killed:* Jonas Parker, Robert Monroe, Samuel Hadley, Jonathan Harrington, Jr., Isaac Muzzy, Caleb Harrington, John Brown, Jedediah Moore, John Raymond, Nathaniel Wyman, 10.   *Wounded:* John Robbins, Solomon Pierce, John Tidd, Joseph Comee, Ebenezer Monroe, Jr., Thomas Winship, Nathaniel Farmer, Prince Estabrook, Jedediah Monroe, Francis Brown, 10.

CONCORD.—*Wounded:* Charles Miles, Nathan Barrett, Abel Prescott, Jr., Jonas Brown, George Meriot, 5.

CAMBRIDGE.—*Killed:* William Marcy, Moses Richardson, John Hicks, Jason Russell, Jabez Wyman, Jason Winship, 6.   *Wounded:* Samuel Whittemore, 1.   *Missing:* Samuel Frost, Seth Russell, 2.

NEEDHAM.—*Killed:* John Bacon, Elisha Mills, Amos Mills, Nathaniel Chamberlain, Jonathan Parker, 5.   *Wounded:* Eleazer Kingsbury, —— Tolman, 2.

SUDBURY.—*Killed:* Josiah Haynes, Asahel Reed, 2.   *Wounded:* Joshua Haynes, Jr., 1.

ACTON.—*Killed:* Isaac Davis, Abner Hosmer, James Hayward, 3.   *Wounded:* Luther Blanchard, 1.

BEDFORD —*Killed:* Jonathan Wilson, 1.   *Wounded:* Job Lane, 1.

WOBURN.—*Killed:* Daniel Thompson, Asahel Porter, 2.   *Wounded:* George Reed, Jacob Bacon, —— Johnson, 3.

MEDFORD.—*Killed:* Henry Putnam, William Polly, 2.

CHARLESTOWN.—*Killed:* James Miller, Edward Barber, 2.

WATERTOWN.—*Killed:* Joseph Coolidge, 1.

FRAMINGHAM.—*Wounded:* Daniel Hemminway, 1.

DEDHAM.—*Killed:* Elias Haven, 1.   *Wounded:* Israel Everett, 1.

STOW.—*Wounded:* Daniel Conant, 1

ROXBURY.—*Missing:* Elijah Seaver, 1.

BROOKLINE.—*Killed:* Isaac Gardner, 1.

BILLERICA.—*Wounded:* John Nichols, Timothy Blanchard, 2.

CHELMSFORD.—*Wounded:* Aaron Chamberlain, Oliver Barron, 2.

SALEM.—*Killed:* Benjamin Pierce, 1.

NEWTON.—*Wounded:* Noah Wiswell, 1.

DANVERS.—*Killed:* Henry Jacobs, Samuel Cook, Ebenezer Goldthwait, George Southwick, Benjamin Deland, Jotham Webb, Perley Putnam, 7.   *Wounded:* Nathan Putnam, Dennis Wallace, 2.   *Missing:* Joseph Bell, 1.

BEVERLY.—*Killed:* Reuben Kerryme, 1.   *Wounded:* Nathaniel Cleves, Samuel Woodbury, William Dodge, 3.

LYNN.—*Killed:* Abednego Ramsdell, Daniel Townsend, William Flint, Thomas Hadley, 4.   *Wounded:* Joshua Felt, Timothy Monroe, 2.   *Missing:* Josiah Breed, 1.

TOTAL: Killed, 49; Wounded, 39; Missing. 5=93.

OF THE REVOLUTION. 533

Preparations for Raising an Army in Massachusetts.   Zeal of the Committee of Safety.   Circular of the Provincial Congress

CHAPTER XXIII.

" A viceroy, I, like monarchs, stay
Safe in the town; let others guide the fray.
A life like mine is of no common worth;
'Twere wrong, by Heaven! that I should sally forth.
A random bullet, from a RIFLE sent,
Might pierce my heart, and ruin NORTH's intent.
   *   *   *   *   *   *   *
Ye souls of fire, who burn for chief command,
Come! take my place in this disastrous land.
To wars like these I bid a long good night;
Let NORTH and GEORGE themselves such battles fight."
GAGE'S SOLILOQUY, BY PHILIP FRENEAU, 1775

" In their ragged regimentals
Stood the old Continentals,
    Yielding not,
When the grenadiers were lunging,
And like hail fell the plunging
    Cannon shot;
    Where the files
    Of the isles
From the smoky night encampment bore the banner of the rampant unicorn,
And grummer, grummer, grummer rolled the roll of the drummer, through the morn. '
KNICKERBOCKER MAGAZINE.

HE events of the 19th of April, like an electric shock, thrilled every nerve through the heart-confederated American colonies, and all over the land there was a cry *to arms !* In Massachusetts there was no more hesitation. Who shall be the aggressor? was an answered question. Who shall be the conqueror? was the great problem before them. It was for Massachusetts to lead the van in the contest, and her people readily stepped forth to the duty, knowing that the warm sympathy and generous aid of the sister colonies were enlisted for the war. The reassembled Provincial Congress voted to raise an army of thirteen thousand six hundred men. The Committee of Safety labored day and night, with a zeal worthy of the glorious cause in which they were engaged. Circulars were sent out by both bodies, calling upon the people to form an army as speedily as possible ; and the other New England colonies were solicited to forward as many troops as they could spare,[1] in order to

---

[1] The Provincial Congress of Massachusetts sent the following letter to the several committees of safety in the province :

" *In Congress at Watertown, April 30th,* 1775.

" GENTLEMEN,—The barbarous Murders on our innocent Brethren on Wednesday the 19th Instant, has made it absolutely necessary that we immediately raise an army to defend our Wives and our Children from the butchering Hands of an inhuman Soldiery, who, incensed at the Obstacles they meet with in their bloody progress, and enraged at being repulsed from the Field of Slaughter, will, without the least doubt, take the first Opportunity in their Power to ravage this devoted Country with Fire and Sword. We conjure you, therefore, that you give all Assistance possible in forming an Army. Our all is at Stake. Death and Devastation are the certain Consequences of Delay; every Moment is infinitely precious; an Hour lost may deluge your Country in Blood, and entail perpetual Slavery upon the few of your Posterity who may survive the Carnage. We beg and entreat you, as you will answer it to your Country, to your own Consciences, and, above all, as you will answer to God himself, that you will hasten and encourage, by all possible Means, the Enlistment of Men to form the Army, and send them forward to Head-quarters at Cambridge, with that expedition which the vast Importance and instant Urgency of the affair demands.

" JOSEPH WARREN, *President,* P.T."

make up a united force of thirty thousand men.   These official appeals were scarcely necessary, for as soon as the intelligence of bloodshed went abroad, the people had rushed toward Boston from all quarters, and by the 21st it was estimated that twenty thou- April,
sand men were collected in the neighborhood of that city.   General Ward, by virtue 1775.
of a previous appointment, took command on the 20th, and in the afternoon held a council
of war with the officers present.[1]   Of course all was confusion ; for the people came, some
with arms in their hands, and some having none, with the inquiry marked on every countenance, What can I do ?   A partial organization was effected, and preparations were made
to besiege Boston.   Among those who hastened thither was the veteran Putnam, then an
old man of sixty years, who, it is said, left his plow in the furrow, and in his working
dress, mounted one of his horses, and hastened toward Cambridge at the head of a large
body of Connecticut volunteers.   Colonel (afterward general) John Stark was also there,
with a crowd of New Hampshire volunteers, and all were active and ardent.   In the course
of a few days the troops were tolerably well officered, their pay was agreed upon, and thirty
thousand were enrolled.   But great numbers returned home ; some to attend to pressing
private affairs, and others to make permanent arrangements to join the army.   The number was thus suddenly much reduced, and the important pass of Boston Neck was defended
for nine consecutive days and nights by only six or seven hundred men under Colonel Robinson, of Dorchester.   The ranks were soon afterward well filled, and preparations for a
regular siege of the city commenced.
Cambridge was made the head-quarters, and a line of cantonments was
formed nearly twenty miles in extent,
the left leaning upon the River Mystic and the right upon Roxbury, thus
completely inclosing the town.

On the 5th of May, the Provincial Congress resolved " that
General Gage has, by the late transactions and many other means, utterly disqualified himself from serving
this colony as governor, or in any
other capacity ; and that, therefore,
no obedience is in future due to him ;
but that, on the contrary, he ought to
be considered and guarded against as
an unnatural and inveterate enemy to
the country."   Previous to this renunciation of allegiance, they had
prepared for the payment of the army,
by authorizing the issue of bills of
credit, or paper money, to the amount
of three hundred and seventy-five thousand dollars, in sums small enough to
be used as a circulating currency, and
directed the receiver general to borrow that amount, upon those notes,

REVERSE OF A MASSACHUSETTS TREASURY NOTE.[2]

---

[1] The officers who composed the council were Generals Ward, Heath, and Whitcombe ; Colonels Bridge,
Frye, James Prescott, William Prescott, Bullard, and Barrett; and Lieutenant-colonels Spaulding, Nixon,
Whitney, Mansfield and Wheelock.   Colonels Learned and Warner arrived the next day.

[2] This is a fac simile of the device on the back of one of the first of the Massachusetts treasury notes or
bills of credit.   The literal translation of the Latin inscription is " He seeks by the Sword calm repose under the
auspices of Freedom."   In other words, to use a phrase of the present time, they were determined " to con-

bearing an interest of six per cent.   They also forwarded dispatches to the general   May 3, 1775.
Congress which was to assemble on the 10th, suggesting the necessity for making
provision for a large army, to oppose the expected troops from Great Britain.

While these transactions were taking place without Boston, General Gage was pursuing
a course of rigorous surveillance over the people within the city.   By his orders all   April 19, 1775.
intercourse with the country was cut off, and none were allowed to leave the town
without his permission first obtained.   This measure exposed the people to great distress,
for their accustomed supply of provisions and fuel was thus cut off.   They at once felt all
the horrors of civil war gathering around them—visions of famine, rapine, and blood clouded their thoughts, and all the miseries which gloomy anticipation delineate began to be felt.
Gage himself became uneasy.   Boston was surrounded by an exasperated multitude, armed
and ready for combat at the least provocation ; and he was justly apprehensive that, should
an assault commence from without, the patriots within would rise upon his troops.   In this
exigency he so far receded from his haughty demeanor toward the municipal authorities as
to seek an interview with the selectmen.   It was obtained, and he assured them that no
violence should be done to the town, provided the people would behave peaceably.   A town
meeting was held on the 22d, and an agreement was entered into between the selectmen
and Gage, " That, upon the inhabitants in general lodging their arms in Faneuil Hall, or
any other convenient place, under the care of the selectmen, marked with the names of the
respective owners, all such inhabitants that are inclined might leave the town, with their
families and effects, and those who remained might depend upon the protection of the governor ; and that the arms aforesaid, at a suitable time, should be returned to the owners."[1]
This measure was sanctioned by the Committee of Safety sitting at Cambridge, and the arrangement was carried out in good faith for a short time, until the removal became so general as to alarm the Tories and the governor himself.[2]   The Tories, about this time, were
excessively loyal.   Two hundred of them were enrolled as a military corps under Timothy
Ruggles, and, offering their services to General Gage, were put on duty.   They thought
the arrangement Gage had agreed to was unwise, for they apprehended that, when the patriots had all left the town with their effects, they would not scruple to burn it.   They remonstrated with Gage, and their importunities and his own fears became more potent than
his sense of honor.   Obstructions were thrown in the way of removals, until, finally, passes
were denied, or so framed that families would have to be separated, and property left behind.   Gage, finally, would not allow women and children to leave Boston, but kept them
there as a sort of hostages, or pledges of good behavior on the part of the patriots.   This
exhibition of bad faith disgusted and exasperated the people as much as any of his previous acts.

quer a peace."   The face of the bill has a neatly-engraved border of scroll-work; and on the left of the
brace where the names of the committee are signed, is a circle with a ship within it.   The following is a
copy of one of the notes :

"Colony of the Massachusetts Bay, } August 18, 1775.

"The Possessor of this Bill shall be paid by the Treasurer of this colony, TWENTY FOUR SHILLINGS,
Lawful Money, by the 18th day of August, 1778, which Bill shall be received for the aforesaid sum, in all
payments at the Treasury and in all other Payments by order of the General Assembly.

" Committee, {

[1] The following is a copy of one of the passes granted to the inhabitants who left.   It is copied from one
preserved in the cabinet of the Massachusetts Historical Society .

"Boston, May, 1775.

" Permit ——— ———, together with his family, consisting of ——— persons, and ——— effects, to
pass ——— ———, between sunrise and sunset.
                              By order of his Excellency the Governor.
" No Arms nor Ammunition is allowed to pass."

[2] Under this arrangement, 1778 fire-arms, 634 pistols, 273 bayonets, and 38 blunderbusses, were deposited with the selectmen.   The same day (April 27th) the Provincial Congress recommended to the inhabitants of the sea-ports the removal of their effects, &c.   Gordon, i., 336.

May 1, 1775.   The Provincial Congress of Massachusetts, in the mean time, made provision for five thousand poor people expected from Boston, who were unable to help themselves. Each town had a proportion allotted to it, and thus much suffering was prevented, while the feelings of the beneficiaries were tenderly respected by the declaration of the resolution that they were not to be numbered with the town paupers. The same provision was also made for the suffering inhabitants who remained in Charlestown, unable to remove from the danger that menaced them. So great were the alarm and distress in that thriving suburban village of Boston, that it was almost deserted. Its population of two thousand seven hundred was reduced to about two hundred.

While Massachusetts was thus exercising its patriotism and humanity, preparatory to the approaching contest, the other colonies were alive with zeal. The Rhode Island Assembly voted an army of observation of fifteen hundred men, and appointed Nathaniel April 25. Greene, a young iron master, and a Quaker by birthright, but recently disowned because of his military propensities, commander-in-chief, with the rank of brigadier. His colonels were Varnum, Hitchcock, and Church. The Connecticut Assembly voted to raise six regiments of a thousand men each; and Wooster, Putnam, and Spencer, already April 26. commissioned as generals, were each to have a regiment. The others were to be placed under the command of Hinman, Waterbury, and Parsons. Already, as we have noticed, New Hampshire volunteers had flocked to Cambridge, with the gallant Stark, who was commissioned a colonel. Under the direction of the Committee of Safety of that colony, they were supplied with necessaries until the meeting of the Provincial Congress of their own province in May. That body resolved to raise two thousand troops in addition May 17. to those already in the field, and Nathan Folsom was appointed commander-in-chief, with the rank of brigadier. They were organized into three regiments; and two additional regiments were placed under the command of Stark and James Reed. The latter, and Enoch Poor, were commissioned colonels. New Hampshire and Rhode Island both also issued bills of credit. Although other colonies did not send soldiers to Boston, all, with the exception of New York, approved of the action of the general Continental Congress, and expressed the warmest sympathy for New England.

On the 19th of May, the Provincial Congress of Massachusetts clothed the Committee of Safety, then sitting at Cambridge, with full power to regulate the movements of the gathering army.[1] General Ward, as we have seen, was appointed captain general; John Thomas was made lieutenant general; and Richard Gridley, the commissioned commander of an artillery corps authorized to be raised, was appointed chief engineer, assisted by Henry Knox, late commander of an artillery corps in Boston. To promote rapid enlistments, a resolution had been previously adopted, promising a captain's commission to every one who should raise a company of fifty-nine men, and a colonel's commission to each who should raise a regiment of ten companies. The form of the commissions of the several officers was adopted, the pay of officers and soldiers was fixed, and other provisions for organizing the army were arranged.

At the beginning of June the combined forces amounted to about sixteen thousand men,[2] really united only in respect to the common cause which brought them together, for each colony had absolute control over its respective troops. But by common consent, sanctioned by the several colonial authorities, obedience was rendered to General Ward as captain general. Ward, as well as Putnam, Thomas, Stark, Pomeroy, Prescott, and Gridley, had been educated in the military art in the practical school of the French and Indian war; and the militia that had assembled, familiar with their names and deeds, placed the utmost confidence in their skill and valor.

---

[1] The Committee of Safety consisted of John Hancock, Joseph Warren, Benjamin Church, Benjamin White, Joseph Palmer, Richard Devens, Abraham Watson, John Pigeon, Azor Orne, Benjamin Greenleaf, Nathan Cushing, and Samuel Holten. Hancock was necessarily absent, being a delegate to the Continental Congress.

[2] Massachusetts furnished 11,500; Connecticut, 2300; New Hampshire, 1200; and Rhode Island, 1000.

The British force in Boston had increased, in the mean while, by fresh arrivals from England and Ireland, to ten thousand men. The Cerberus man-of-war arrived on the 25th of May, with Generals Howe,[1] Clinton, and Burgoyne, three officers experienced in the military tactics of Europe, but little prepared for service here. They were surprised at the aspect of affairs, and Gage was reproached for his apparent supineness.[2] However, unity of action was necessary, and the new-comers heartily co-operated with Gage in his plans, such as they were, for dispersing the rebel host that hemmed him in. He issued a proclamation on the 12th of June, insulting in words and menacing in tone. It declared martial law ; pronounced those in arms and their abettors "rebels, parricides of the Constitution," and offered a free pardon to all who would forthwith return to their allegiance, except John Hancock and Samuel Adams, who were outlawed, and for whose apprehension as traitors a reward was offered.[3] This proclamation, so arrogant and insulting, served only to exasperate the people. In the mean while, several skirmishes had occurred between parties of the British regulars and the provincials, upon some of the cultivated islands that dot the harbor of Boston. Each party were employed in carrying off to their respective camps the live stock upon the islands, and on one occasion quite a severe action occurred upon Hog Island, which continued until late at night. One or two armed vessels in the harbor were engaged in the foray. A considerable number of the provincials were killed. Toward morning a British schooner got aground. The Americans boarded her, stripped her of every thing valuable, and returned to camp in triumph. In the course of these depredations the owners were completely despoiled ; several hundred cattle, sheep, and lambs having been carried off by both parties, without leave or remuneration.[4] In the attendant skirmishes the Americans were generally most successful, and they served to initiate the raw militia into the preliminary dangers of a battle.

But little progress had been made at this time, by the Americans, in erecting fortifications. Some breast-works had been thrown up at Cambridge, near the foot of Prospect Hill, and a small redoubt had been formed at Roxbury. The right wing of the besieging army, under General Thomas, was at Roxbury, consisting of four thousand Massachusetts troops, including four artillery companies, with field-pieces and a few heavy cannon. The Rhode Island forces, under Greene, were at Jamaica Plains, and near there was a greater part of General Spencer's Connecticut regiment. General Ward commanded the left wing at Cambridge, which consisted of fifteen Massachusetts regiments, the battalion of artillery under Gridley, and Putnam's regiment, with other Connecticut troops. Most of the Connecticut forces were at Inman's farm. Paterson's regiment was at the breast-work on Prospect Hill, and a large guard was stationed at Lechmere's Point. Three companies of Gerrish's regi-

[1] General Howe was a brother of the young Lord Howe who was killed at Ticonderoga in 1758. In the address of the Continental Congress to the people of Ireland, adopted on the 28th of July, 1775, the addressers say, "America is amazed to find the name of Howe in the catalogue of her enemies. She loved his brother."

[2] The newly-arrived generals were so assured, before leaving England, that they would have no occasion to draw the sword in support of ministerial measures, that they had prepared to amuse themselves with fishing and other diversions, instead of engaging in military service. It seems that the whole affair of the 19th of April was kept a profound secret from all his officers by Gage, except those immediately employed in it and Lord Percy, until the skirmish had ensued at Lexington, and a re-enforcement was called for. When General Haldimand, afterward Governor General of Canada, who was with Gage, was asked how the sortie happened, he said that the first he knew of it was from his barber, who came to shave him.

[3] It has been related that when John Hancock placed his bold signature to the Declaration of Independence, on the 4th of July, 1776, he remarked, "There ! John Bull can read that name without spectacles. Now let him double his reward !"

[4] It was in reference to these expeditions on the part of the British, that Freneau, the stirring song-writer of the Revolution, in his "Gage's Soliloquy," thus wrote :

> "Let others combat in the dusty field ;
> Let petty captains scorn to live or yield ;
> I'll send my ships to neighboring isles, where stray
> Unnumbered herds, and steal those herds away.
> I'll strike the women in this town with awe,
> And make them tremble at my MARTIAL LAW."

ment were at Chelsea; Stark's regiment was at Medford, and Reid's at Charlestown Neck,
with sentinels reaching to Penny Ferry and Bunker Hill

It was made known to the Committee of Safety that General Gage had fixed upon the night of the 18th of June to take possession of and fortify Bunker Hill and Dorchester Heights. This brought matters to a crisis, and measures were taken to perfect the blockade of Boston. The Committee of Safety ordered Colonel Prescott, with a detachment of one thousand men, including a company of artillery, with two field-pieces, to march at night and throw up intrenchments upon Bunker Hill, an eminence just within the peninsula of Charlestown, and commanding the great northern road from Boston, as well as a considerable portion of the town. To make the relative position of the eminences upon the Charlestown peninsula and the Neck, to Boston, more intelligible to the reader, I have copied from Frothingham's *History of the Siege of Boston*, by permission of the author, the annexed sketch, communicated to him, in a manuscript of 1775, from Henry Stevens, Esq. I also quote from Mr. Frothingham's work a description of the localities about Bunker Hill. The peninsula of Charlestown is opposite the north part of Boston, and is about a mile in length from north to south. Its greatest breadth, next to Boston, is about half a mile. It is connected with the main land by a narrow isthmus or neck. The Mystic River, half a mile wide, is on the east, and the Charles River, here formed into a large bay, is on the west, a part of which, by a dam stretching in the direction of Cobble Hill, is a mill-pond. [See map, page 543.] In 1775, an artificial causeway [4] was so low as to be frequently overflowed by the tides. The communication with Boston was by

a ferry, where Charles River bridge is, and with Malden by another, called Penny Ferry, where Malden Bridge now is. Near the Neck, on the main land, was a large green, known as the Common. Two roads ran by it: one in a westerly direction, as now, by Cobble Hill (M'Lean Asylum), Prospect Hill, and Inman's Woods, to Cambridge Common; the other in a northerly direction, by Plowed Hill (Mount Benedict) and Winter Hill, to Medford—the direct road to West Cambridge not having been laid out in 1775. Bunker Hill begins at the isthmus, and rises gradually for about three hundred yards, forming a round, smooth hill, sloping on two sides toward the water, and connected by a ridge of ground on the south with the heights now known as Breed's Hill. This was a well-known public place, the name, "Bunker Hill," being found in the town records and in deeds from an early period. Not so with "Breed's Hill," for it was not named in any description of streets previous to 1775, and appears to have been called after the owners of the pastures into which it was divided, rather than by the common name of Breed's Hill. Thus, Monument Square was called Russell's Pasture; Breed's Pasture lay further south, and Green's Pasture was at the head of Green Street. The easterly and westerly sides of this height were steep. On the east, at its base, were brick-kilns, clay-pits, and much sloughy land. On the west side, at the base, was the most settled part of the town [5]. Moulton's Point, a name coeval with the settlement of the town, constituted the southeastern corner of the peninsula. A part of this tract formed what is called Morton's Hill. Bunker Hill was one hundred and ten feet high, Breed's Hill sixty-two

CHARLESTOWN IN 1775.[1]

---

[1] No. 1 is Bunker Hill; 2, Breed's Hill; 3, Moulton's Point; 4, a causeway near the Neck, at the foot of Bunker Hill; 5, Charlestown, at the foot of Breed's Hill. Charlestown Neck is on the extreme left.

feet, and Moulton's Hill [3] thirty-five feet.   The principal street of the peninsula was Main Street, which extended from the Neck to the ferry.   A road ran over Bunker Hill, around Breed's Hill, to Moulton's Point.   The westerly portions of these eminences contained fine orchards.[1]

A portion of the regiments of Prescott,[2] Frye, and Bridge, and a fatigue party of two hundred Connecticut troops with intrenching tools, paraded in the Cambridge camp at six o'clock in the evening.   They were furnished with packs and blankets, and ordered to take provisions for twenty-four hours.   Samuel Gridley's company of artillery joined them, and the Connecticut troops were placed under the command of Thomas Knowlton, a captain in Putnam's regiment, who was afterward killed in the battle on Harlem Heights.   After an impressive prayer from the lips of President Langdon, of Harvard College, Colonel Prescott and Richard Gridley, preceded by two servants with dark lanterns, commenced their march, at the head of the troops, for Charlestown.   It was about nine o'clock at night, the sky clear and starry, and the weather very warm.   Strict silence was enjoined, and the object of the expedition was not known to the troops until they arrived at Charlestown Neck, where they were joined by Major Brooks, of Bridge's regiment, and General Putnam.   A guard of ten men was placed in Charlestown, and the main body marched over Bunker Hill.   A council was held, to select the best place for the proposed fortification.   The order was explicit, to fortify Bunker Hill; but Breed's Hill being nearer Boston, and appearing to be a more eligible place, it was concluded to proceed to fortify it, and to throw up works, also, on Bunker Hill, to cover a retreat, if necessary, across Charlestown Neck.   Colonel Gridley marked out the lines of the proposed fortifications, and, at about midnight, the men, having thrown off their packs and stacked their arms, began their perilous work—perilous, because British sentinels and British ships-of-war were almost within sound of their picks.[3]

> " No shout disturbed the night,
>   Before that fearful fight;
>   There was no boasting high—
>   No marshaling of men,
>   Who ne'er might meet again—
>   No cup was filled and quaffed to Victory !

(margin note: June 16, 1775.)

---

[1] Frothingham, page 129.

[2] William Prescott was born at Groton, Massachusetts, in 1726.   His father was for some years a counselor of Massachusetts, and his mother was a daughter of another counselor.   He was a lieutenant of foot under General Winslow, at the capture of Cape Breton, where he was distinguished for his bravery.   He inherited a large estate, and resided at Pepperell while the Revolution was ripening.   He had command of a regiment of minute men, and when the news of the affair at Lexington reached him, promptly marched thither at the head of as many as he could collect.   His known military talents caused him to be selected by General Ward for the important duty of fortifying Bunker Hill; and in the memorable engagement that occurred there on the 17th of June, 1775, he was the chief in command, and was greatly distinguished by his bravery and skill.   That evening, although repulsed, and his troops greatly fatigued and much dispirited, he solicited from the Committee of Safety permission to make an attempt to retake the peninsula of Charlestown.   It was a movement too perilous, and the gallant soldier was obliged to rest.   He continued in the service through 1776, and served as a volunteer under Gates until the surrender of Burgoyne in 1777.   From 1786 until his death he was an acting magistrate in his native town.   He died in Pepperell on the 13th of October, 1795, aged sixty-nine.   William H. Prescott, of Boston, the eminent historian, is a grandson of Colonel Prescott.   He married a grand-daughter of Captain Linzee, who commanded the sloop of war *Falcon*, that cannonaded the works on Breed's Hill on the 17th of June, 1775.   The swords then used by Colonel Prescott and Captain Linzee, the respective grandfathers of the historian and his wife, are now in Mr. Prescott's possession, and are crossed, in a conspicuous place, in his valuable library at Boston.

[3] The following are the names of the British vessels then in the harbor of Boston, which took part in the battle that ensued : *Somerset*, 68 guns, 520 men, Captain Edward Le Cras; *Cerberus*, 36 guns, Captain Chads; *Glasgow*, 24 guns, 130 men, Captain William Maltby; *Lively*, 20 guns, 130 men, Captain Thomas Bishop; *Falcon*, Captain Linzee; *Symmetry*, transport, 18 nine pounders.   See the *British Annual Register* for 1775.   The Falcon lay off Moulton's, or Morton's, Point; the Lively lay opposite the present navy-yard; the Somerset was at the ferry; the Glasgow was near Cragie's Bridge; and the Cerberus and several floating batteries were within gunshot of the American works.—*Frothingham.*

> No plumes were there,
> No banners fair,
>   No trumpets breathed around ;
>   Nor the drum's startling sound
> Broke on the midnight air."—JOHN NEAL.

Officers and men labored together with all their might, with pickaxes and spades, and were cheered on in their work by the distant signals of safety—" All's well !"—that came from the shipping, and the sentinels at the foot of Copp's Hill. It proclaimed that they were still undiscovered ; and at every cry of " All's well !" they plied their tools with increased vigor. When the day dawned, at about four o'clock, they had thrown up intrenchments six feet high ; and a strong redoubt, which was afterward the admiration of the enemy, loomed up on the green height before the wondering eyes of the astonished Britons like a work of magic. The British officers could hardly be convinced that it was the result of a few hours' labor only, but deemed it the work of days. Gage saw at once how foolish he had been in not taking possession of this strong point, as advised, while it was in his power to do so.

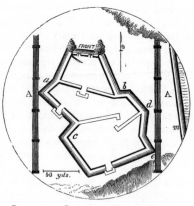

PLAN OF THE REDOUBT ON BREED'S HILL.[1]

The fortification was first discovered at dawn, by the watchmen on board the Lively. Without waiting for orders, the captain put springs upon his cables, and opened a fire on the American works. The noise of the cannon aroused the sleepers in Boston, and when the sun arose on that bright morning, every eminence and roof in the city swarmed with people, astonished at the strange apparition upon Breed's Hill. The shots from the Lively did no harm, and, defended by their intrenchments, the Americans plied their labor in strengthening their works within, until called to lay aside the pick and shovel for gun and knapsack.

Admiral Graves, the naval commander at Boston, ordered the firing to cease ; but it was soon renewed, not only by the shipping, but from a battery of six guns upon Copp's Hill in the city. Gage summoned a council of war early in the morning. As it was evident that the Americans were rapidly gaining strength, and that the safety of the town was endangered, it was unanimously resolved to send out a force to drive them from the peninsula of Charlestown and destroy their works on the heights. It was decided, also, to make the attack in front, and preparations were made accordingly. The drums beat to arms, and Boston was soon in a tumult. Dragoons galloping, artillery trains rumbling, and the marching and countermarching of the regulars and loyalists, together with the clangor

June 17, 1775.

---

[1] This plan is copied from an English drawing of the time, first published in the *London Gentleman's Magazine* for 1775.

EXPLANATION.—A A represents the situation of two strong fences, composed of stones and rails ; *a* and *b*, two well-contrived flanks, so arranged that their fires crossed within twenty yards of the face of the redoubt ; *c*, another well-arranged flank ; *d*, a bastion, with its flanks *e* and *b* ; *m*, a small portion of a trench, that extended from the eastern side of the redoubt to a slough at the foot of the hill toward the Mystic River. On the southeast side of the redoubt was a deep hollow. Two cannons were placed in embrasures at the front of the redoubt, in the two salient angles of which were large apple-trees.

This redoubt was eight rods square. The Bunker Hill Monument now occupies its center. The eastern side commanded an extensive field. On the north side was an open passage-way, and the breastwork upon the eastern side extended about one hundred yards north. This trench was incomplete when the battle began. Between the south end of the breast-work and the redoubt was a sally-port, protected by a blind, and on the inside of the parapet were steps of wood and earth for the men to mount and fire. Between the slough and the rail fence on the east was an open space, and this was the weakest part of the lines. Such were the American works of defense when the battle of the 17th of June commenced.

of the church bells, struck dismay into many a heart before stout in the presence of British protectors.   It is said that the danger which surrounded the city converted many Tories into patriots ; and the selectmen, in the midst of that fearful commotion, received large accessions to their list of professed friends from the ranks of the timid loyalists.

Toward noon, between two and three thousand picked men, from the British army, under the command of General Sir William Howe and General Pigot, embarked in twenty-eight barges, part from the Long Wharf and some from the North Battery, in Boston, and landed at Morton's, or Moulton's Point,[1] beyond the eastern foot of Breed's Hill, covered by the guns of the Falcon and other vessels.

> " About two thousand were embarked to go
> 'Gainst the redoubt and formidable foe.
> The Lively's, Falcon's, Fame's, and Glasgow's roar,
> Covered their landing on the destined shore."[2]

The Americans had worked faithfully on their intrenchments all the morning, and were greatly encouraged by the voice and example of Prescott, who exposed himself, without care, to the random shots of the battery on Copp's Hill.[3]   He supposed, at first, that the enemy would not attack him, but, seeing the movements in the city, he was convinced to the contrary, and comforted his toiling troops with assurances of certain victory.   Confident of such a result himself, he would not at first send to General Ward for a re-enforcement ; but between nine and ten o'clock, by advice of his officers, Major Brooks was dispatched to head-quarters for that purpose.   General Putnam had urged Ward early in the morning to send fresh troops to relieve those on duty ; but only a portion of Stark's regiment was allowed to go, as the general apprehended that Cambridge would be the principal point of attack.   Convinced otherwise, by certain intelligence, the remainder of Stark's regiment, and the whole of Reed's corps, on the Neck, were ordered to re-enforce Prescott. At twelve o'clock the men in the redoubt ceased work, sent off their intrenching tools, took some refreshments, hoisted the New England flag, and prepared to fight. The intrenching tools were sent to Bunker Hill, where, under the direction of General Putnam, the men began to throw up a breast-work.   Some of the more timid soldiers made the removal of the tools a pretext for leaving the redoubt, and never returned.

THE NEW ENGLAND FLAG.[4]

It was between twelve and one o'clock when the Brit-

[1] This is written Morton, Moreton, and Moulton, by different authors.   Morton is the proper name.

[2] From "The American War," a poem in six books, published in London, 1786.

[3] A soldier (Asa Pollard, of Billerica) who had ventured outside of the redoubt, was killed by a cannon ball.   The circumstance so alarmed those within, that some of them left the hill.   Prescott, to inspire his men with confidence, walked leisurely around the works upon the parapet, in full view of the British officers in Boston.   Gage, who was reconnoitering the works through a glass, saw his tall and commanding form, and asked Counselor Willard, who stood near him, who it was.   Willard, recognizing his brother-in-law, said, "That is Colonel Prescott."   "Will he fight?" inquired Gage.   "Yes, sir," replied Willard ; "he is an old soldier, and will fight as long as a drop of blood remains in his veins."   "The works must be carried immediately," responded Gage, as he turned upon his heel to give orders.

[4] This is copied from an old Dutch work, preserved in the library of the New York Historical Society, containing pictures of the flags of all nations.   In the original, a divided sphere, representing the earth, is in the quarter where I have placed the *pine-tree*.   I have made the alteration in the device, because in the flag raised upon the bastion of the redoubt on Breed's Hill, the *pine-tree* occupied the place of the *sphere*, the more ancient device.   The question has been unsettled respecting the flag used on that occasion, as cotemporary writers are silent on the subject.   An intelligent old lady (Mrs. Manning) whom I saw between the Brandywine and Kennet Square, in Pennsylvania, informed me that her father, who was in the battle, assisted in hoisting the standard, and she had heard him speak of it as a "noble flag."   The ground was blue, and one corner was quartered by the red cross of St. George, in one section of which was the pine-tree.   This was the New England flag, as given in the sketch.   Doubtless there were many other flags belonging to the several regiments.   Botta says of Dr. Warren, during the retreat, "Finding the corps

ish troops, consisting of the fifth, thirty-eighth, forty-third, and fifty-second battalions of infantry, two companies of grenadiers, and two of light-infantry, landed, their rich uniforms and arms flashing and glittering in the noonday sun, making an imposing and formidable display.   General Howe reconnoitered the American works, and, while waiting for re-enforcements, which he had solicited from Gage, allowed his troops to dine.   When the intelligence of the landing of the enemy reached Cambridge, two miles distant, there was great excitement in the camp and throughout the town.   The drums beat to arms, the bells were rung, and the people and military were speedily hurrying in every direction.   General Ward used his own regiment, and those of Paterson and Gardner and a part of Bridge's, for the defense of Cambridge.   The remainder of the Massachusetts troops were ordered to Charlestown, and thither General Putnam conducted those of Connecticut.

At about two o'clock the re-enforcement for Howe arrived, and landed at the present navy-yard.   It consisted of the forty-seventh battalion of infantry, a battalion of marines, and some grenadiers and light infantry.   The whole force (about four thousand men) was commanded and directed by the most skillful British officers then in Boston ;[1] and every man preparing to attack the undisciplined provincials was a drilled soldier, and quite perfect in the art of war.   It was an hour of the deepest anxiety among the patriots on Breed's Hill.   They had observed the whole martial display, from the time of the embarkation until the forming of the enemy's line for battle.   For the Americans, as yet, very little succor had arrived.   Hunger and thirst annoyed them, while the labors of the night and morning weighed them down with excessive fatigue.   Added to this was the dreadful suspicion that took possession of their minds, when only feeble re-enforcements arrived, that treachery had placed them there for the purpose of sacrifice.   Yet they could not doubt the patriotism of their principal officers, and before the action commenced their suspicions were scattered to the winds by the arrival of their beloved Dr. Warren and General Pomeroy.[2]   Warren, who was president of the Provincial Congress, then sitting at Watertown, seven miles distant, informed of the landing of the enemy, hastened toward Charlestown, though suffering from sickness and exhaustion.   He had been commissioned a major general four days before.   Putnam, who was at Cambridge, forwarding provisions and re-enforcements to Charlestown, tried to dissuade him from going into the battle.   Warren was not to be diverted from his purpose, and mounting a horse, he sped across the Neck and entered the redoubt, amid the loud cheers of the provincials, just as Howe gave orders to advance.   Colonel Prescott offered the command to Warren, as his superior, when the latter replied, " I am come to fight as a volunteer, and feel honored in being allowed to serve under so brave an officer."

While the British troops were forming, and preparing to march along the Mystic River for the purpose of flanking the Americans and gaining their rear, the artillery, with two field-pieces, and Captain Knowlton, with the Connecticut troops, left the redoubt, took a

he commanded hotly pursued by the enemy, despising all danger, he stood alone before the ranks, endeavoring to rally his troops, and encouraging them by his own example.   He reminded them of the mottoes inscribed on their ensigns, on one side of which were these words, '*An appeal to Heaven,*' and on the other, ' *Qui transtulit, sustinet ;*' meaning, that the same providence that brought their ancestors through so many perils to a place of refuge, would also deign to support their descendants."   Botta often exhibits more poetry than truth in his brilliant narrative.   After the battle under consideration, and while Putnam commanded on Prospect Hill, a flag with the inscription above given was presented to him, and was first unfurled on the 18th of July ensuing.   The author of " The Veil Removed" properly treats the assertion of Botta as a fiction, and sarcastically remarks that, " instead of such a sentimental allusion to Latin mottoes, the only command, when their ammunition was spent, must have been *Sauve qui peut,* ' Save himself who can.' "   Qui transtulit, sustinet, is the motto in the seal of Connecticut.

[1] The most distinguished British officers that accompanied General Howe were General Pigot ; Colonels Nesbit, Abercrombie, and Clark ; Majors Butler, Williams, Bruce, Spendlove, Smelt, Mitchell, Pitcairn, Short, Small, and Lord Rawdon.

[2] General Pomeroy left Cambridge when he heard the first sound of the cannon.   The veteran borrowed a horse from General Ward, to ride to Charlestown, but, observing that the guns of the Glasgow raked the Neck by an enfilading fire, he was afraid to risk the borrowed animal.   Leaving him in charge of a sentry, he walked across the Neck, and, with a borrowed musket, joined the troops at the rail fence as a volunteer. He was well known, and a loud huzza welcomed him to the post of danger.

position near Bunker Hill, and formed a breast-work seven hundred feet in length, which served an excellent purpose. A little in front of a strong stone and rail fence, Knowlton built another, and between the two was placed a quantity of new-mown grass. This apparently slight breast-work formed a valuable defense to the provincials.

It was now three in the afternoon. The provincial troops were placed in an attitude of defense, as the British column moved slowly forward to the attack. Colonel Prescott and the original constructors of the redoubt, except the Connecticut troops, were within the works. General Warren also took post in the redoubt. Gridley and Callender's artillery companies were between the breast-works and rail fence on the eastern side. A few troops, recalled from Charlestown after the British landed, and a part of Warner's company, lined the cart-way on the right of the redoubt. The Connecticut and New Hampshire forces were at the rail fence on the west of the redoubt; and three companies were stationed in the Main Street at the foot of Breed's Hill.

Before General Howe moved from his first position, he sent out strong flank guards, and directed his heavy artillery to play upon the American line. At the same time a blue flag was displayed as a signal, and the guns upon Copp's Hill, and the ships and floating batteries in the river, poured a storm of round shot upon the redoubt. A furious cannonade was opened at the same moment upon the right wing of the provincial army at Roxbury, to prevent re-enforcements being sent by General Thomas to Charlestown. Gridley[1] and Callender, with their field-pieces, returned a feeble response to the heavy guns of the enemy.

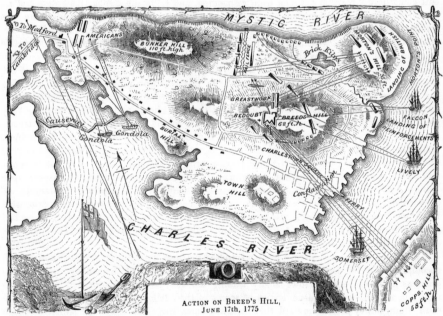

ACTION ON BREED'S HILL,
JUNE 17th, 1775

Gridley's guns were soon disabled; while Callender, who alleged that his cartridges were too large, withdrew to Bunker Hill. Putnam was there, and ordered him back to his first position. He disobeyed, and nearly all his men, more courageous than he, deserted him In the mean while, Captain Walker, of Chelmsford, with fifty resolute men, marched down the hill near Charlestown, and greatly annoyed the enemy's left flank. Finding their posi-

---

[1] Captain Samuel Gridley was a son of Richard Gridley, the engineer. He was quite inefficient, and had received his appointment solely in compliment to his father.

tion very perilous, they marched over to the Mystic, and did great execution upon the right flank. Walker was there wounded and made prisoner, but the greater part of his men succeeded in gaining the redoubt.

Under cover of the discharges of artillery, the British army moved up the slope of Breed's Hill toward the American works, in two divisions, General Howe with the right wing, and General Pigot with the left. The former was to penetrate the American lines at the rail fence ; the latter to storm the redoubt. They had not proceeded far before the firing of their artillery ceased, in consequence of discovering that balls too large for the field-pieces had been sent over from Boston. Howe ordered the pieces to be loaded with grape ; but they soon became useless, on account of the miry ground at the base of the hill. Small arms and bayonets now became their reliance.

Silently the British troops, burdened with heavy knapsacks, toiled up the ascent toward the redoubt, in the heat of a bright summer's sun. All was silent within the American intrenchments, and very few provincials were to be seen by the approaching battalions ; but within those breast-works, and in reserve behind the hills, crouched fifteen hundred determined men, ready, at a prescribed signal, to fall upon the foe. The provincials had but a scanty supply of ammunition, and, to avoid wasting it by ineffectual shots, Prescott gave orders not to fire until the enemy were so near that the whites of their eyes could be seen. "Then," he said, "aim at their waistbands ; and be sure to pick off the commanders, known by their handsome coats !" The enemy were not so sparing of their powder and ball, but when within gunshot of the apparently deserted works, commenced a random firing. Prescott could hardly restrain his men from responding, and a few did disobey his orders and returned the fire. Putnam hastened to the spot, and threatened to cut down the first man who should again disobey orders, and quiet was restored. At length the enemy reached the prescribed distance, when, waving his sword over his head, Prescott shouted " FIRE !" Terrible was the effect of the volley that ensued. Whole platoons of the British regulars were laid upon the earth, like grass by the mower's scythe. Other deadly volleys succeeded, and the enemy, disconcerted, broke, and fled toward the water. The provincials, joyed at seeing the regulars fly, wished to pursue them, and many leaped the rail fence for the purpose ; but the prudence of the American officers kept them in check, and in a few minutes they were again within their works, prepared to receive a second attack from the British troops, that were quickly rallied by Howe. Colonel Prescott praised and encouraged his men, while General Putnam rode to Bunker Hill to urge on re-enforcements. Many had arrived at Charlestown Neck, but were deterred from crossing by the enfilading fire of the Glasgow and two armed gondolas near the causeway. Portions of regiments were scattered upon Bunker Hill and its vicinity, and these General Putnam, by entreaties and commands, endeavored to rally. Colonel Gerrish, who was very corpulent, became completely exhausted by fatigue ; and other officers, wholly unused to warfare, coward-like kept at a respectful distance from danger. Few additional troops could be brought to Breed's Hill before the second attack was made.

The British troops, re-enforced by four hundred marines from Boston, under Major Small, accompanied by Dr. Jeffries, the army surgeon, advanced toward the redoubt in the same order as at first, General Howe boldly leading the van, as he had promised.[1] It was a mournful march over the dead bodies of scores of their fellow-soldiers ; but with true English courage they pressed onward, their artillery doing more damage to the Americans than at the first assault. It had moved along the narrow road between the tongue of land and Breed's Hill, and when within a hundred yards of the rail fence, and on a line with the breast-works, opened a galling fire, to cover the advance of the other assailants. In the mean while, a carcass, and some hot shot, were thrown from Copp's Hill into Charlestown,

---

[1] Clarke, an officer in the marines, relates that, just before commencing the first march toward the redoubt, General Howe made a short speech, in which he said, "If the enemy will not come out of their intrenchments, we must drive them out, at all events, otherwise the town of Boston will be set on fire by them. *I shall not desire one of you to go a step further than where I go myself at your head.*"

which set the village on fire.[1] The houses were chiefly of wood, and in a short time nearly two hundred buildings were in flames, shrouding in dense smoke the heights in the rear whereon the provincials were posted. Beneath this veil the British hoped to rush unobserved up to the breast-works, scale them, and drive the Americans out at the point of the bayonet. At that moment a gentle breeze, which appeared to the provincials like the breath of a guardian angel—the first zephyr that had been felt on that sultry day—came from the west, and swept the smoke away seaward, exposing to the full view of the Americans the advancing columns of the enemy, who fired as they approached, but with little execution. Colonels Brener, Nixon, and Buckminster were wounded, and Major Moore was killed. As before, the Americans reserved their fire until the British were within the prescribed distance, when they poured forth their leaden hail with such sure aim and terrible effect that whole ranks of officers and men were slain. General Howe was at the head, and once he was left entirely alone, his aids and all about him having perished. The British line recoiled, and gave way in several parts, and it required the utmost exertion in all the remaining officers, from the generals down to the subalterns, to repair the disorder which this hot and unexpected fire had produced.[2] All their efforts were at first fruitless, and the troops retreated in great disorder to the shore.

General Clinton, who had beheld the progress of the battle with mortified pride, seeing the regulars repulsed a second time, crossed over in a boat, followed by a small re-enforcement, and joined the broken army as a volunteer. Some of the British officers remonstrated against leading the men a third time to certain destruction ; but others, who had ridiculed American valor, and boasted loudly of British invincibility, resolved on victory or death. The incautious loudness of speech of a provincial, during the second attack, declaring that the ammunition was nearly exhausted, gave the enemy encouraging and important information. Howe immediately rallied his troops and formed them for a third attack, but in a different way. The weakness of the point between the breast-work and the rail fence had been discovered by Howe, and thitherward he determined to lead the left wing with the artillery, while a show of attack should be made at the rail fence on the other side. His men were ordered to stand the fire of the provincials, and then make a furious charge with bayonets.

So long were the enemy making preparations for a third attack, that the provincials began to imagine that the second repulse was to be final. They had time to refresh themselves a little, and recover from that complete exhaustion which the labor of the day had produced. It was too true that their ammunition was almost exhausted, and being obliged to rely upon that for defense, as comparatively few of the muskets were furnished with bayonets, they began to despair. The few remaining cartridges within the redoubt were distributed by Prescott, and those soldiers who were destitute of bayonets resolved to club their arms, and use the breeches of their guns when their powder should be gone. The loose stones in the redoubt were collected for use as missiles if necessary, and all resolved to fight as long as a ray of hope appeared.

During this preparation on Breed's Hill, all was confusion elsewhere. General Ward was at Cambridge, without sufficient staff officers to convey his orders. Henry (afterward general) Knox was in the reconnoitering service, as a volunteer, during the day, and upon his reports Ward issued his orders. Late in the afternoon, the commanding general dispatched his own, with Paterson's and Gardner's regiments, to the field of action ; but to the raw recruits the aspect of the narrow Neck was terrible, swept as it was by the British

---

[1] A carcass is a hollow case formed of ribs of iron, covered with cloth, or sometimes iron, with holes in it. Being filled with combustible materials, it is thrown from a mortar into a besieged place, by which means buildings are set on fire. The burning of Charlestown had been resolved upon by Gage some time before, in the event of the Americans taking possession of any of the hills belonging to it. "This resolution was assigned by a near female relative of the general to a gentlewoman with whom she had become acquainted at school, as a reason why the other, upon obtaining a pass to quit Boston, should not tarry at her father's (Mr. Cary's) house in Charlestown."—*Dr. Gordon*, i., 352.

[2] Stedman, i., 127.

cannon. Colonel Gardner succeeded in leading three hundred men to Bunker Hill, where Putnam set them intrenching, but soon ordered them to the lines. Gardner was advancing boldly at their head, when a musket ball éntered his groin and wounded him mortally.[1] His men were thrown into confusion, and very few of them engaged in the combat that followed, until the retreat commenced. Other regiments failed to reach the lines. A part of Gerrish's regiment, led by Adjutant Christian Febiger, a Danish officer, who afterward accompanied Arnold to Quebec, and was distinguished at Stony Point, reached the lines just as the action commenced, and effectually galled the British left wing. Putnam, in the mean time, was using his utmost exertions to form the confused troops on Bunker Hill, and get fresh corps with bayonets across the Neck.

All was order and firmness at the redoubt on Breed's Hill, as the enemy advanced. The artillery of the British swept the interior of the breast-work from end to end, destroying many of the provincials, among whom was Lieutenant Prescott, a nephew of the colonel commanding. The remainder were driven within the redoubt, and the breast-work was abandoned. Each shot of the provincials was true to its aim, and Colonel Abercrombie, and Majors Williams and Speedlove fell. Howe was wounded in the foot, but continued fighting at the head of his men. His boats were at Boston, and retreat he could not. His troops pressed forward to the redoubt, now nearly silent, for the provincials' last grains of powder were in their guns. Only a ridge of earth separated the combatants, and the assailants scaled it. The first that reached the parapet were repulsed by a shower of stones. Major Pitcairn, who led the troops at Lexington, ascending the parapet, cried out, " Now for the glory of the marines !" and was immediately shot by a negro soldier.[2] Again numbers of the enemy leaped upon the parapet, while others assailed the redoubt on three sides. Hand to hand the belligerents struggled, and the gun-stocks of many of the provincials were shivered to pieces by the heavy blows they were made to give. The enemy poured into the redoubt in such numbers that Prescott, perceiving the folly of longer resistance, ordered a retreat. Through the enemy's ranks the Americans hewed their way, many of them walking backward, and dealing deadly blows with their musket-stocks. Prescott and Warren were the last to leave the redoubt. Colonel Gridley, the engineer, was wounded, and borne off safely.[3] Prescott received several thrusts from bayonets and rapiers in his clothing, but escaped unhurt. Warren was the last man that left the works. He was a short distance from the redoubt, on his way toward Bunker Hill, when a musket ball passed through his head, killing him instantly. He was left on the field, for all were flying in the greatest confusion, pursued by the victors, who remorselessly bayoneted those who fell in their way.

Major Jackson had rallied Gardner's men upon Bunker Hill, and pressing forward with

---

[1] I have before me a drama, bearing the autograph of General James Abercrombie, entitled " THE BATTLE OF BUNKER HILL; a dramatic piece in five acts, in heroic measure : by a gentleman of Maryland." Printed at Philadelphia, by Robert Bell, in 1776. Colonel Gardner is one of the *dramatis personæ*, and is made to say, at the moment of receiving the wound,

> "A musket ball, death-winged, hath pierced my groin,
> And widely oped the swift current of my veins.
> Bear me, then, soldiers, to that hollow space
> A little hence, just on the hill's decline.
> A surgeon there may stop the gushing wound,
> And gain a short respite to life, that yet
> I may return, and fight one half hour more.
> Then shall I die in peace, and to my GOD
> Surrender up the spirit which he gave."

[2] Major Pitcairn was carried by his son to a boat, and conveyed to Boston, where he soon died. He left eleven children. The British government settled a pension of one thousand dollars a year upon his widow.

[3] Colonel Richard Gridley, the able engineer and brave soldier in this battle, was born in Boston in 1721. He served as an engineer in the reduction of Louisberg in 1745, and entered the British army as colonel and chief engineer in 1755. He was engaged in the expedition to Ticonderoga in 1756, and constructed Fort George, on Lake George. He served under Amherst in 1758, and was with Wolfe, on the Plains of Abraham, the following year. He was appointed chief engineer of the provincial army near Boston in 1775. He died at Stoughton, on the 20th of June, 1796, aged seventy-five years.—*Curwen.*

three companies of Ward's, and Febiger's party of Gerrish's regiment, poured a destructive fire upon the enemy between Breed's and Bunker Hill, and bravely covered the retreat from the redoubt. The Americans at the rail fence, under Stark, Reed, and Knowlton, re-enforced by Clark's, Coit's, and Chester's Connecticut companies, and a few other troops, maintained their ground, in the mean while, with great firmness, and successfully resisted every attempt of the enemy to turn their flank. This service was very valuable, for it saved the main body, retreating from the redoubt, from being cut off. But when these saw their brethren, with the chief commander, flying before the enemy, they too fled. Putnam used every exertion to keep them firm. He commanded, pleaded, cursed and swore like a madman, and was seen at every point in the van, trying to rally the scattered corps, swearing that victory should crown the Americans.[1] "Make a stand here," he exclaimed; "we can stop them yet! In God's name, fire, and give them one shot more!" The gallant old Pomeroy, also, with his shattered musket in his hand, implored them to rally, but in vain. The whole body retreated across the Neck, where the fire from the Glasgow and gondolas slew many of them. They left five of their six field-pieces, and all their intrenching tools, upon Bunker Hill, and they retreated to Winter Hill, Prospect Hill, and to Cambridge. The British, greatly exhausted, and properly cautious, did not follow, but contented themselves with taking possession of the peninsula. Clinton advised an immediate attack upon Cambridge, but Howe was too cautious or too timid to make the attempt. His troops lay upon their arms all night on Bunker Hill, and the Americans did the same on Prospect Hill, a mile distant. Two British field-pieces played upon them, but without effect, and both sides feeling unwilling to renew the action, hostilities ceased. The loss of the Americans in this engagement was one hundred and fifteen killed and missing, three hundred and five wounded, and thirty who were taken prisoners; in all four hundred and fifty. The British loss is not positively known. Gage reported two hundred and twenty-six killed, and eight hundred and twenty-eight wounded; in all ten hundred and fifty-four. In this number are included eighty-nine officers. The Provincial Congress of Massachusetts, from the best information they could obtain, reported the British loss at about fifteen hundred. The battle, from Howe's first attack until the retreat, occupied nearly two hours. The number of buildings consumed in Charlestown, before midnight, was about four hundred; and the estimated loss of property (most of the families, with their effects, having moved out) was nearly six hundred thousand dollars.

The number engaged in this battle was small, yet cotemporary writers and eye-witnesses represent it as one of the most determined and severe on record. There was absolutely no victory in the case. The most indomitable courage was displayed on both sides; and when the provincials had retired but a short distance, so wearied and exhausted were all that neither party desired more fighting, if we except Colonel Prescott, who earnestly petitioned to be allowed to lead a fresh corps that evening and retake Breed's Hill. It was a terrible day for Boston and its vicinity, for almost every family had a representative in one of the two armies. Fathers, husbands, sons, and brothers were in the affray, and deep was the mental anguish of the women of the city, who, from roofs, and steeples, and every elevation, gazed with streaming eyes upon the carnage, for the battle raged in full view of thousands of interested spectators in the town and upon the adjoining hills.[2] In contrast with the terrible scene were the cloudless sky and brilliant sun.

---

[1] It is said that, for the foul profanity in which the brave old general indulged on that occasion, he made a sincere confession, after the war, before the church of which he was a member. "It was almost enough to make an angel swear," he said, "to see the cowards refuse to secure a victory so nearly won!"

[2] "In other battles," said Daniel Webster, in an article published in the North American Review for October, 1818, "the *recollection* of wives and children has been used as an excitement to animate the warrior's breast and to nerve his arm. Here was not a mere recollection, but an actual *presence* of them, and other dear connections, hanging on the skirts of the battle, anxious and agitated, feeling almost as if wounded themselves by every blow of the enemy, and putting forth, as it were, their own strength, and all the energy of their own throbbing bosoms, into every gallant effort of their warring friends."

548   PICTORIAL FIELD-BOOK

Reflections on the Battle.   Burgoyne's Opinion of the Conflict.   The Character of Warren.

"The heavens, the calm pure heavens, were bright on high;
　Earth laughed beneath in all its freshening green;
The free, blue streams sang as they wandered by;
　And many a sunny glade and flowery scene
Gleamed out, like thoughts of youth, life's troubled years between,"
                                        WILLIS GAYLORD CLARK.

while upon the green slopes, where flocks were quietly grazing but a few hours before, WAR
had reared its gory altars, and the earth was saturated with the blood of its victims.   Fearfully augmented was the terror of the scene, when the black smoke arose from Charlestown
on fire, and enveloped the redoubt on the summit of Breed's Hill, which, like the crater of
a volcano, blazed and thundered in the midst of the gloomy curtain that veiled it.

"Amazing scenes! what shuddering prospects rise!
What horrors glare beneath the angry skies!
The rapid flames o'er Charlestown's heights ascend;
To heaven they reach! urged by the boisterous wind.
The mournful crash of falling domes resound,
And tottering spires with sparkles reach the ground.
One general burst of ruin reigns o'er all;
The burning city thunders to its fall!
O'er mingled noises the vast ruin sounds,
Spectators weep! earth from her center groans!
Beneath prodigious unextinguished fires
Ill-fated Charlestown welters and expires."
                                        EULOGIUM ON WARREN, 1781.

"It was," said Burgoyne, who, with Gage and other British officers, was looking on from a
secure place near Copp's Hill in Boston, "a complication of horror and importance, beyond
any thing that ever came to my lot to witness.   Sure I am that nothing ever can or has

been more dreadfully ter-
rible than what was to
be seen or heard at this
time."   But it is profit-
less to dwell upon the
gloomy scene.   Time
hath healed the grief
and heart-sickness that
were born there; and
art, in the hands of busy
men, has covered up for-
ever all vestiges of the
conflict.

Many gallant, many
noble men perished on
the peninsula upon that
sad day; but none was
so widely and deeply
lamented, because none
was so widely and truly
loved, as the self-sacri-
ficing and devoted War-
ren.   He was the imper-
sonation of the spirit of

generous and disinterest-
ed patriotism that inspired the colonies.   In ev-
ery relation in life he was
a model of excellence.
"Not all the havoc and
devastation they have
made has wounded me
like the death of War-
ren," wrote the wife
of John Adams,   July 5,
three weeks aft-   1775.
erward.   "We want
him in the Senate; we
want him in his profes-
sion; we want him in
the field.   We mourn
for the citizen, the sen-
ator, the physician, and
the warrior."   General
Howe estimated his in-
fluence, when he declar-
ed to Dr. Jeffries, who
recognized the body of

---

[1] Joseph Warren, son of a Massachusetts farmer, was born in Roxbury in 1740, and graduated at Harvard College in 1759.   He studied the science of medicine under Dr. Lloyd, and rapidly rose to the head,
or, at least, to the front rank of that profession in Boston.   Sentiments of patriotism seemed to form a part

Warren on the field the next day, that his death was worth, to the British, five hundred of the provincial privates.   Eulogy and song have aided history in embalming his memory with the

of his moral nature, and courage to avow them was always prompting him to action.   He became necessarily a politician, at a time when all men were called upon to act in public matters, or be looked upon as drones.   He was one of the earliest members of the association in Boston known as the Sons of Liberty, and from 1768 was extremely efficient in fostering the spirit of rational liberty and independence in the wide and influential circle in which he moved.   His mind, suggestive and daring, planned many measures, in secret caucus with Adams and others, for resisting the encroachments of British power.   In 1771 he delivered the oration on the anniversary of the Boston Massacre.   He solicited the honor of performing a like duty on the 5th of March, 1775, in consequence of a threat of some of the British officers that they would take the life of any man who should dare to speak on that occasion.   The old South meeting-house was crowded on the appointed day, and the aisles, stairs, and pulpit were filled with armed British soldiers. The intrepid young orator entered a window by a ladder, back of the pulpit, and, in the midst of a profound silence, commenced his exordium in a firm tone of voice.   His friends, though determined to avenge any attempt at assassination, trembled for his safety.   He dwelt eloquently upon the early struggles of the New England people, their faith and loyalty, and recounted, in sorrowful tones, the oppressions that had been heaped upon them.   Gradually he approached the scene on the 5th of March, and then portrayed it in such language and pathos of expression, that even the stern soldiery that came to awe him wept at his words.   He stood there in the midst of that multitude, a striking symbol of the revolt which he was leading, firm in the faith of that sentiment, "Resistance to tyrants is obedience to God."   Looking at him, it might be said, as Magoon remarks, in classic quotation,

"Thou hast seen Mount Athos;
While storms and tempests thunder at its brows
And oceans beat their billows at its feet,
It stands unmoved, and glories in its height.
Such is that haughty man; his towering soul,
Mid all the shocks and injuries of fortune,
Rises superior, and looks down on Cæsar."

When John Hancock went to the Continental Congress, Warren was elected to fill his place as president of the Provincial Congress.   Four days previous to the action on Breed's Hill, that body gave him the commission of major general, and he was the only officer of that rank engaged in the conflict; yet he was without command, and fought as a volunteer.   "He fell," as Everett has beautifully expressed it, "with a numerous band of kindred spirits—the gray-haired veteran, the stripling in the flower of youth—who had stood side by side on that dreadful day, and fell together, like the beauty of Israel in their high places!"   Warren's body was identified, on the morning after the battle, by Dr. Jeffries, who was his intimate acquaintance.   He was buried where he fell, and the place was marked.   After the evacuation of Boston in 1776, his remains were disinterred, and, on the 8th of April, were carried in procession from the Representatives' chamber to King's Chapel, and buried with military and masonic honors.   The Reverend Dr. Cooper offered prayers, and Perez Morton pronounced an oration on the occasion.   Warren's remains now rest beneath St. Paul's Church.   He was Grand Master of Freemasons for North America at the time of his death.   A lodge in Charlestown erected a monument to his memory in 1794, on the spot where he fell.   It was composed of a brick pedestal eight feet square, rising ten feet from the ground, and supporting a Tuscan pillar of wood eighteen feet high.   This was surmounted by a gilt urn, bearing the inscription " J. W., aged 35," entwined with masonic emblems.   On the south side of the pedestal was the following inscription

WARREN'S MONUMENT

"Erected A.D. MDCCXCIV.,
By King Solomon's Lodge of Free-masons,
constituted in Charlestown, 1783,
In Memory of
MAJOR-GENERAL JOSEPH WARREN
and his associates,
who were slain on this memorable spot June 17,
1775.
None but they who set a just value upon the blessings of liberty are worthy to enjoy her.   In vain we toiled, in vain we fought; we bled in vain, if you, our offspring, want valor to repel the assault of her invaders.
Charlestown settled, 1628.   Burned, 1775.   Rebuilt, 1776."

This monument stood forty years, and then was removed to give place to the present granite structure, known as Bunker Hill Monument.   A beautiful model of Warren's monument stands within the colossal obelisk, from which I made the accompanying sketch.

immortality that rests upon the spot where he fell.   He was a hero in the highest sense of the term, and so were Prescott and other compatriots in the struggle ; but all were not heroes who surrounded them.   Unused to war ; some entirely ignorant of the sound of a cannon ; inferior, by two thirds, in number, and vastly so in discipline, to the enemy, the wonder is that the provincials fought so well, not that so many used their heels more expertly than their hands.   Many officers, chosen by the men whom they commanded, were totally unfitted in knowledge and spirit for their stations, and a few exhibited the most arrant cowardice.   They were tried by court martial, and one was cashiered for disobedience and for being a poltroon.[1]   But they have all passed away ; let us draw the curtain of charity around their resting-places, remembering that

> " Hero *motives*, placed in judgment's scale,
> Outweigh all *actions* where the heart is wrong."

Here let us close the volume of history for a time, and while the gentle breeze is sweeping the dust and smoke of battle from Bunker Hill,[2] and the tumult of distress and alarm is subsiding in Boston, let us ride out to Lexington and Concord, to visit those places consecrated by the blood of the first patriot martyrs.   We have had a long, but, I trust, profitable consultation of the records of the past.   I have endeavored to point out for consideration the most prominent and important links in the chain of events, wherein is remarkably manifested the spirit of true liberty which finally wrought out the independence of these American states.   In brief outlines I have delineated the features of those events, and traced the progress of the principles of freedom from the little conventicles of despised and persecuted, but determined men, toward the close of the sixteenth century, who assembled to assert the most undoubted natural right, that of worshiping God as the conscience of the creature shall dictate, to the uprising of nearly two millions of the same people in origin and language, in defiance of the puissance of the mightiest arm upon earth ; and the assembling of a council in their midst, of which the great Pitt was constrained to say, " I must declare and avow that in all my reading and study—and it has been my favorite study ; I have read Thucydides, and have studied and admired the master states of the world—that for solidity of reasoning, force of sagacity, and wisdom of conclusion, under such a complication of circumstances, no nation or body of men can stand in preference to the general Congress of Philadelphia."

On the 8th of April, 1777, Congress, by resolution, ordered " that a monument be erected to the memory of General Warren, in the town of Boston, with the following inscription :

In honor of
Joseph Warren,
Major General of Massachusetts Bay.
He devoted his life to the liberties
Of his country ;
And in bravely defending them, fell
An early victim,
In the battle of Bunker Hill,
June 17th, 1775.
The Congress of the United States,
As an acknowledgment of his services,
Have erected this monument to his memory.

Congress also ordered " that his eldest son be educated at the expense of the United States."*   The patriotic order for the erection of a monument has never been obeyed.

[1] This was Captain Callender.   The court sentenced him to be cashiered, and, in an order of July 7th, Washington declared him to be " dismissed from all further service in the Continental army."   Callender felt much aggrieved, and, confronting the charge of cowardice, remained in the army as a volunteer, and fought so bravely at the battle of Long Island, the next year, that Washington commanded his sentence to be erased from the orderly-book.

[2] This battle should properly be called the battle of Breed's Hill, for there the great events of the day occurred.   There was much fighting and slaughter upon Bunker Hill, where Putnam chiefly commanded, but it was not the main theater of action.

CHAPTER XXIV.

" How suddenly that straight and glittering shaft
Shot thwart the earth ! in crown of living fire
Up comes the day ! As if they conscious quaff'd
The sunny flood, hill, forest, city spire
Laugh in the waking light."
RICHARD H. DANA.

" War, fierce war, shall break their forces ;
Nerves of Tory men shall fail ;
Seeing Howe, with alter'd courses,
Bending to the Western gale.
Thus from every bay of ocean
Flying back with sails unfurl'd,
Toss'd with ever-troubled motion,
They shall quit this smiling world."
MILITARY SONG, 1776.[1]

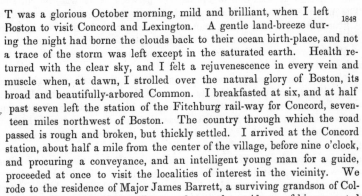

T was a glorious October morning, mild and brilliant, when I left
Boston to visit Concord and Lexington. A gentle land-breeze dur-   1848
ing the night had borne the clouds back to their ocean birth-place, and not
a trace of the storm was left except in the saturated earth. Health returned with the clear sky, and I felt a rejuvenescence in every vein and
muscle when, at dawn, I strolled over the natural glory of Boston, its
broad and beautifully-arbored Common. I breakfasted at six, and at half
past seven left the station of the Fitchburg rail-way for Concord, seventeen miles northwest of Boston. The country through which the road
passed is rough and broken, but thickly settled. I arrived at the Concord
station, about half a mile from the center of the village, before nine o'clock,
and procuring a conveyance, and an intelligent young man for a guide,
proceeded at once to visit the localities of interest in the vicinity. We
rode to the residence of Major James Barrett, a surviving grandson of Colonel Barrett, about two miles north of the village, and near the residence of his venerated
October,   ancestor. Major Barrett was eighty-seven years of age when I visited him, and
1848.   his wife, with whom he had lived nearly sixty years, was eighty. Like most .of
the few survivors of the Revolution, they were remarkable for their mental and bodily vigor.
Both, I believe, still live. The old lady—a small, well-formed woman—was as
1850.   sprightly as a girl of twenty, and moved about the house with the nimbleness of foot
of a matron in the prime of life. I was charmed with her vivacity, and the sunny radiance
which it seemed to shed throughout her household ; and the half hour that I passed with
that venerable couple is a green spot in the memory.
Major Barrett was a lad of fourteen when the British incursion into Concord took place.
He was too young to bear a musket, but, with every lad and woman in the vicinity, he labored in concealing the stores and in making cartridges for those who went out to fight.
With oxen and a cart, himself, and others about his age, removed the stores deposited at
the house of his grandfather into the woods, and concealed them, a cart-load in a place, under pine boughs. In such haste were they obliged to act on the approach of the British

---

[1] This song of forty-eight lines, by an anonymous writer, is entitled " A Military Song, by the Army, on
General Washington's victorious entry into the town of Boston."

from Lexington, that, when the cart was loaded, lads would march on each side of the oxen and goad them into a trot.   Thus all the stores were effectually concealed, except some carriage-wheels.   Perceiving the enemy near, these were cut up and burned; so that Parsons found nothing of value to destroy or carry away.

From Major Barrett's we rode to the monument erected at the site of the old North Bridge, where the skirmish took place, and I sketched, on my way, the residence of Colonel Barrett, depicted on page 526.   The road crosses the Concord River a little above the site of the North Bridge.   The monument stands a few rods westward of the road leading to the village, and not far from the house of the Reverend Dr. Ripley, who gave the ground for the purpose.   The monument is constructed of granite from Carlisle, and has an inscription upon a marble tablet inserted in the eastern face of the pedestal.[1]   The view is from the green shaded lane which leads from the highway to the monument,

MONUMENT AT CONCORD.

looking westward.   The two trees standing, one upon each side, without the iron railing, were saplings at the time of the battle; between them was the entrance to the bridge. The monument is reared upon a mound of earth a few yards from the left bank of the river. A little to the left, two rough, uninscribed stones from the field mark the graves of the two British soldiers who were killed and buried upon the spot.

We returned to the village at about noon, and started immediately for Lexington, six miles eastward.

Concord is a pleasant little village, including within its borders about one hundred dwellings.   It lies upon the Concord River, one of the tributaries of the Merrimac, near the junction of the Assabeth and Sudbury Rivers.   Its Indian name was Musketaquid.   On account of the peaceable manner in which it was obtained, by purchase, of the aborigines, in 1635, it was named Concord.   At the north end of the broad street, or common, is the house of Colonel Daniel Shattuck, a part of which, built in 1774, was used as one of the depositories of stores when the British invasion took place.   It has been so much altered, that a view of it would have but little interest as representing a relic of the past.

The road between Concord and Lexington passes through a hilly but fertile country.   It is easy for the traveler to conceive how terribly a retreating army might be galled by the fire of a concealed enemy.   Hills and hillocks, some wooded, some bare, rise up every where, and formed natural breast-works of protection to the skirmishers that hung upon the flank and rear of Colonel Smith's troops.   The road enters Lexington at the green whereon the old meeting-house stood when the battle occurred.   The town is upon a fine rolling plain, and is becoming almost a suburban residence for citizens of Boston.   Workmen were inclosing the Green, and laying out the grounds in handsome plats around the monument,

---

[1] The following is a copy of the inscription:

HERE,
On the 19th of April, 1775,
was made the first forcible resistance to
BRITISH AGGRESSION.
On the opposite bank stood the American
militia, and on this spot the first of the enemy fell
in the WAR OF THE REVOLUTION,
which gave Independence to these United States.
In gratitude to God, and in the love of Freedom,
This Monument was erected,
A.D. 1836.

OF THE REVOLUTION.   553

The Lexington Monument.   The "Clark House" and its Associations.   Tradition of the Surprise   Abijah Harrington.

which stands a few yards from the street. It is upon a spacious mound ; its material is granite, and it has a marble tablet on the south front of the pedestal, with a long inscription.[1] The design of the monument is not at all graceful, and, being surrounded by tall trees, it has a very " dumpy" appearance. The people are dissatisfied with it, and doubtless, ere long, a more noble structure will mark the spot where the curtain of the revolutionary drama was first lifted.

After making the drawings here given, I visited and made the sketch of " Clark's House," printed on page 523. There I found a remarkably intelligent old lady, Mrs. Margaret Chandler, aged eighty-three years. She has been an occupant of the house, I believe, ever since the Revolution, and has a perfect recollection of the events of the period. Her version of the escape of Hancock and Adams is a little different from the published accounts, which I have adopted in the historical sketch. She says that on the evening of the 18th of April, some

MONUMENT AT LEXINGTON.[2]

British officers, who had been informed where these patriots were, came to Lexington, and inquired of a woman whom they met, for " Mr. Clark's house." She pointed to the parsonage ; but in a moment, suspecting their design, she called to them and inquired if it was Clark's *tavern* that they were in search of. Uninformed whether it was a *tavern* or a *parsonage* where their intended victims were staying, and supposing the former to be the most likely place, the officers replied, " Yes ; Clark's tavern." " Oh," she said, " Clark's tavern is in that direction," pointing toward East Lexington. As soon as they departed, the woman hastened to inform the patriots of their danger, and they immediately arose and fled to Woburn. Dorothy Quincy, the intended wife of Hancock, who

NEAR VIEW OF THE MONUMENT.

was at Mr. Clark's, accompanied them in their flight. Paul Revere soon afterward arrived, and the events already narrated then occurred.

I next called upon the venerable Abijah Harrington, who was living in the village. He was a lad of fourteen at the time of the engagement. Two of his brothers were among the

---

[1] The following is a copy of the inscription :
" Sacred to the Liberty and the Rights of Mankind ! ! !   The Freedom and Independence of America— sealed and defended with the blood of her sons—This Monument is erected by the Inhabitants of Lexington, under the patronage and at the expense of the Commonwealth of Massachusetts, to the memory of their Fellow-citizens, Ensign Robert Monroe, Messrs. Jonas Parker, Samuel Hadley, Jonathan Harrington, Junr., Isaac Muzzy, Caleb Harrington, and John Brown, of Lexington, and Asahel Porter, of Woburn, who fell on this Field, the first victims of the Sword of British Tyranny and Oppression, on the morning of the ever-memorable Nineteenth of April, An. Dom. 1775. The Die was Cast ! ! !   The blood of these Martyrs in the Cause of God and their Country was the Cement of the Union of these States, then Colonies, and gave the Spring to the Spirit, Firmness, and Resolution of their Fellow-citizens. They rose as one man to revenge their Brethren's blood, and at the point of the Sword to assert and defend their native Rights. They nobly dared to be Free ! ! !   The contest was long, bloody, and affecting. Righteous Heaven approved the Solemn Appeal ; Victory crowned their Arms, and the Peace, Liberty, and Independence of the United States of America was their glorious Reward. Built in the year 1799."

[2] This view is from the Concord Road, looking eastward, and shows a portion of the inclosure of the Green. The distant building seen on the right is the old " Buckman Tavern," delineated in Doolittle's engraving on page 524. It now belongs to Mrs. Merriam, and exhibits many scars made by the bullets on the morning of the skirmish.

554   PICTORIAL FIELD-BOOK

Incidents of the Battle at Lexington.   Jonathan Harrington and his Brother.   Anniversary Celebration at Concord in 1850.

minute men, but escaped unhurt. Jonathan and Caleb Harrington, near relatives, were killed. The former was shot in front of his own house, while his wife stood at the window in an agony of alarm. She saw her husband fall, and then start up, the blood gushing from his breast. He stretched out his arms toward her, and then fell again. Upon his hands and knees he crawled toward his dwelling, and expired just as his wife reached him.

Caleb Harrington was shot while running from the meeting-house. My informant saw almost the whole of the battle, having been sent by his mother to go near enough, and be safe, to obtain and convey to her information respecting her other sons, who were with the minute men. His relation of the incidents of the morning was substantially such as history has recorded. He dwelt upon the subject with apparent delight, for his memory of the scenes of his early years, around which cluster so much of patriotism and glory, was clear and full. I would gladly have listened until twilight to the voice of such experience, but time was precious, and I hastened to East Lexington, to visit his cousin, Jonathan Harrington, an old man of ninety, who played the fife when the minute men were marshaled on the Green upon that memorable April morning. He was splitting fire-wood in his yard with a vigorous hand when I rode up ; and as he sat in his rocking-chair, while I sketched his placid features, he appeared no older than a man of seventy. His brother, aged eighty-eight, came in before my sketch was finished, and I could not but gaze with wonder upon these strong old men, children of one mother, who were almost grown to manhood when the first battle of our Revolution occurred! Frugality and temperance, co-operating with industry, a cheerful temper, and a good constitution, have lengthened their days, and made their protracted years hopeful and happy.[1] The aged fifer apologized for the rough appearance of his signature, which he kindly wrote for me, and charged the tremulous motion of his hand to his labor with the ax. How tenaciously we cling even to the appearance of vigor, when the whole frame is tottering to its fall ! Mr. Harrington opened the ball of the Revolution with the shrill war-notes of the fife, and then retired from the arena. He was not a soldier in the war, nor has his life, passed in the quietude of rural pursuits, been distinguished except by the glorious acts which constitute the sum of the achievements of a GOOD CITIZEN.

I left Lexington at about three o'clock, and arrived at Cambridge at half past four. It was a lovely autumnal afternoon. The trees and fields were still green, for the frost had

---

[1] The seventy-fifth anniversary of the battles of Lexington and Concord was celebrated at the latter place on the 19th of April, 1850. In the procession was a carriage containing these venerable brothers, aged, respectively, nearly ninety-one and ninety-three ; Amos Baker, of Lincoln, aged ninety-four ; Thomas Hill, of Danvers, aged ninety-two ; and Dr. Preston, of Billerica, aged eighty-eight. The Honorable Edward Everett, among others, made a speech on the occasion, in which he very happily remarked, that " it pleased his heart to see those venerable men beside him ; and he was very much pleased to assist Mr. Jonathan Harrington to put on his top coat a few minutes ago. In doing so, he was ready to say, with the eminent man of old, 'Very pleasant art thou to me, my brother Jonathan !' " He died in March, 1854.

OF THE REVOLUTION. 555

Ride to Cambridge.   Early History of the Town.   Washington's Head-quarters.

not yet been busy with their foliage and blades. The road is Macadamized the whole distance ; and so thickly is it lined with houses, that the village of East Lexington and Old Cambridge seem to embrace each other in close union.

Cambridge is an old town, the first settlement there having been planted in 1631, cotemporaneous with that of Boston. It was the original intention of the settlers to make it the metropolis of Massachusetts, and Governor Winthrop commenced the erection of his dwelling there. It was called New Town, and in 1632 was palisaded. The Reverend Mr. Hooker, one of the earliest settlers of Connecticut, was the first minister in Cambridge. In 1636, the General Court provided for the erection of a public school in New Town, and appropriated two thousand dollars for that purpose. In 1638, the Reverend John Harvard, of Charlestown, endowed the school with about four thousand dollars. This endowment enabled them to exalt the academy into a college, and it was called Harvard University in honor of its principal benefactor.

Cambridge has the distinction of being the place where the first printing-press in America was established. Its proprietor was named Day, and the capital that purchased the materials was furnished by the Reverend Mr. Glover. The first thing printed was the " Freeman's Oath," in 1636 ; the next was an almanac ; and the next the Psalms, in meter.[1] Old Cambridge (West Cambridge, or Menotomy, of the Revolution), the seat of the University, is three miles from West Boston Bridge, which connects Cambridge with Boston. Cambridgeport is about half way between Old Cambridge and the bridge, and East Cambridge occupies Lechmere's Point, a promontory fortified during the siege of Boston in 1775.

Arrived at Old Cambridge, I parted company with the vehicle and driver that conveyed me from Concord to Lexington, and hither ; and, as the day was fast declining, I hastened to sketch the head-quarters of Washington, an elegant and spacious edifice, standing in the midst of shrubbery and stately elms, a little distance from the street, once the highway from Harvard University to Waltham. At this mansion, and at Winter Hill, Washington passed most of his time, after taking command of the Continental army, until the evacuation of Boston in the following spring. Its present owner is HENRY WADSWORTH LONGFELLOW, professor of modern languages in Harvard University, and widely known in the world of literature as one of the most gifted men of the age. It is a spot worthy of the residence of an American bard so endowed, for the associations which hallow it are linked with the noblest themes that ever awakened the inspiration of a child of song.

WASHINGTON'S HEAD-QUARTERS.

" When the hours of Day are number'd,
    And the voices of the Night
Wake the better soul that slumber'd
    To a holy, calm delight ;
Ere the evening lamps are lighted,
    And, like phantoms grim and tall,
Shadows from the fitful fire-light
    Dance upon the parlor wall,"—LONGFELLOW,

[1] Records of Harvard College.

then to the thoughtful dweller must come the spirit of the place and hour to weave a gor-geous tapestry, rich with pictures, illustrative of the heroic age of our young republic. My tarry was brief and busy, for the sun was rapidly descending—it even touched the forest tops before I finished the drawing—but the cordial reception and polite attentions which I received from the proprietor, and his warm approval of, and expressed interest for the suc-cess of my labors, occupy a space in memory like that of a long, bright summer day.

This mansion stands upon the upper of two terraces, which are ascended each by five stone steps. At each front corner of the house is a lofty elm—mere saplings when Wash-ington beheld them, but now stately and patriarchal in appearance. Other elms, with flowers and shrubbery, beautify the grounds around it ; while within, iconoclastic innovation has not been allowed to enter with its mallet and trowel to mar the work of the ancient builder, and to cover with the vulgar stucco of modern art the carved cornices and paneled wainscots that first enriched it. I might give a long list of eminent persons whose former presence in those spacious rooms adds interest to retrospection, but they are elsewhere iden-tified with scenes more personal and important. I can not refrain, however, from noticing the visit of one, who, though a dark child of Africa and a bond-woman, received the most polite attention from the commander-in-chief. This was PHILLIS, a slave of Mr. Wheatley, of Boston. She was brought from Africa when between seven and eight years old. She seemed to acquire knowledge intuitively ; became a poet of considerable merit, and corre-sponded with such eminent persons as the Countess of Huntingdon, Earl of Dartmouth, Rev-erend George Whitefield, and others. Washington invited her to visit him at Cambridge, which she did a few days before the British evacuated Boston ; her master, among others, having left the city by permission, and retired, with his family, to Chelsea. She passed half an hour with the commander-in-chief, from whom and his officers she received marked attention.[1]

---

[1] Phillis wrote a letter to General Washington in October, 1775, in which she inclosed a poem eulogistic of his character. In February following the general answered it. I give a copy of his letter, in illustration of the excellence of the mind and heart of that great man, always so kind and courteous to the most hum-ble, even when pressed with arduous public duties.

" Cambridge, February 28, 1776.

" MISS PHILLIS,—Your favor of the 26th of October did not reach my hands till the middle of Decem-ber. Time enough, you will say, to have given an answer ere this. Granted. But a variety of import-ant occurrences, continually interposing to distract the mind and withdraw the attention, I hope will apol-ogize for the delay, and plead my excuse for the seeming, but not real neglect. I thank you most sincerely for your polite notice of me in the elegant lines you inclosed ;[*] and however undeserving I may be of such encomium and panegyric, the style and manner exhibit a striking proof of your poetical talents ; in honor of which, and as a tribute justly due to you, I would have published the poem, had I not been apprehensive that, while I only meant to give the world this new instance of your genius, I might have incurred the im-putation of vanity. This, and nothing else, determined me not to give it a place in the public prints. If you should ever come to Cambridge, or near head-quarters, I shall be happy to see a person so favored by the Muses, and to whom nature has been so liberal and beneficent in her dispensations. I am, with great respect, your obedient, humble servant,   GEO. WASHINGTON."

---

[*] "I have not been able to find," says Mr. Sparks, "among Washington's papers, the letter and poem addressed to him." Her lines " On the Death of Whitfield," " Farewell to America," and kindred pieces, exhibit considerable poetic talent. The follow-ing is a specimen of her verse, written before she was twenty years of age. It is extracted from a poem on "Imagination.'

" Though winter frowns, to fancy's raptured eyes
The fields may flourish and gay scenes arise ;
The frozen deeps may break their iron bands,
And bid their waters murmur o'er their sands ;
Fair Flora may resume her fragrant reign,
And with her flowery riches deck the plain ;
Sylvanus may diffuse his honors round,
And all the forests may with leaves be crown'd ;
Showers may descend, and dews their gems disclose,
And nectar sparkle on the blooming rose."

In 1773, when she was at the age of nineteen, a volume of her poems was published in London, dedicated to the Countess of Huntingdon. They give evidence of quite extensive reading and remarkable tenacity of memory, many of them abounding with fine allusions to freedom, her favorite theme. After the death of her master, in 1776, she married a man of her own color, but who was greatly her inferior. His name was Peters. She died in Boston, in extreme poverty, on the 5th of December, 1784, aged nearly thirty-one years.

A few rods above the residence of Professor Longfellow is the house in which the Brunswick general, the Baron Riedesel, and
his family were quartered, during the
stay of the captive army of Burgoyne
in the vicinity of Boston.   I was not
aware, when I visited Cambridge, that
the old mansion was still in existence;
but, through the kindness of Mr. Longfellow, I am able to present the features of its southern front, with a description.   In style it is very much
like that of Washington's head-quarters, and the general appearance of
the grounds around is similar.   It is
shaded by noble linden-trees, and

THE RIEDESEL HOUSE, CAMBRIDGE.[1]

adorned with shrubbery, presenting to the eye all the attractions noticed by the Baroness of
Riedesel in her charming Letters.[2]   Upon a window-pane on the west side of the house

[1] This is from a pencil sketch by Mr. Longfellow.   I am also indebted to him for the fac-simile of the
autograph of the Baroness of Riedesel.   It will be perceived that the *i* is placed before the *e* in spelling the
name.   I have heretofore given it with the *e* first, which is according to the orthography in Burgoyne's
State of the Expedition, &c., wherein I supposed it was spelled correctly.   This autograph shows it to be
erroneous.   Mr. Longfellow's beautiful poem, "The Open Window," refers to this mansion.

[2] She thus writes respecting her removal from a peasant's house on Winter Hill to Cambridge, and her
residence there :

"We passed three weeks in this place, and were then transferred to Cambridge, where we were lodged
in one of the best houses of the place, which belonged to Royalists.   Seven families, who were connected
by relationship, or lived in great intimacy, had here farms, gardens, and splendid mansions, and not far off
orchards, and the buildings were at a quarter of a mile distant from each other.   The owners had been in
the habit of assembling every afternoon in one or another of these houses, and of diverting themselves with
music or dancing, and lived in affluence, in good humor, and without care, until this unfortunate war at once
dispersed them, and transformed all their houses into solitary abodes, except two, the proprietors of which
were also soon obliged to make their escape.

"On the 3d of June, 1778, I gave a ball and supper, in celebration of my husband's birth-day.   I had
invited all our generals and officers, and Mr. and Mrs. Carter.   General Burgoyne sent us an apology, after
he had made us wait for him till eight o'clock.   He had always some excuse for not visiting us, until he
was about departing for England, when he came and made me many apologies, to which I made no other
reply than that I should be extremely sorry if he had put himself to any inconvenience for our sake.   The
dance lasted long, and we had an excellent supper, to which more than eighty persons sat down.   Our
yard and garden were illuminated.   The king's birth-day falling on the next day, it was resolved that the
company should not separate before his majesty's health was drank; which was done, with feelings of the
liveliest attachment to his person and interests.   Never, I believe, was 'God Save the King' sung with
more enthusiasm, or with feelings more sincere.   Our two eldest girls were brought into the room to see

The following curious attestation of the genuineness of the poems of Phillis is printed in the preface to the volume.   Many of
the names will be recognized as prominent in the Revolution.

"To THE PUBLIC.—As it has been repeatedly suggested to the publisher, by persons who have seen the manuscript, that
numbers would be ready to suspect they were not really the writings of Phillis, he has procured the following attestation from
the most respectable characters in Boston, that none might have the least ground for disputing their original: 'We, whose
names are underwritten, do assure the world that the poems specified in the following page were (as we verily believe) written
by Phillis, a young negro girl, who was, but a few years since, brought an uncultivated barbarian from Africa, and has ever
since been, and now is, under the disadvantage of serving as a slave in a family in this town.   She has been examined by some
of the best judges, and is thought qualified to write them.

"'His Excellency THOMAS HUTCHINSON, *Governor.*
"'The Hon. ANDREW OLIVER, *Lieut. Governor*

"'The Hon. Thomas Hubbard,
The Hon. John Erving,
The Hon. James Pitts,
The Hon. Harrison Gray,
The Hon. James Bowdoin,
John Hancock, Esq.,
Joseph Green, Esq.,
Richard Carey, Esq.,

The Rev. Charles Chauncey, D.D.,
The Rev. Mather Byles, D.D.,
The Rev. Edward Pemberton, D.D.,
The Rev. Andrew Eliot, D.D.,
The Rev. Samuel Cooper, D.D.,
The Rev. Mr. Samuel Mather,
The Rev. Mr. John Moorhead,
Mr. John Wheatley (her master).' "

may be seen the undoubted autograph of the accomplished general, inscribed with a diamond point. It is an interesting memento, and is preserved with great care. The annexed is a fac simile of it.

During the first moments of the soft evening twilight I sketched the "Washington elm," one of the ancient *anakim* of the primeval forest, older, probably, by a half century or more, than the welcome of Samoset to the white settlers. It stands upon Washington Street, near the westerly corner of the Common, and is distinguished by the circumstance that, beneath its broad shadow, General Washington first drew his sword as commander-in-chief of the Continental army.[a1] Thin lines of clouds, glowing in the light of the setting sun like bars of gold, streaked the western sky, and so prolonged the twilight by reflection, that I had ample time to finish my drawing before the night shadows dimmed the paper.

a July 3, 1775.

Early on the following morning I procured a chaise to visit Charlestown and Dorchester Heights. I rode first to the former place, and climbed to the summit of the great obelisk that stands upon the site of the redoubt upon Breed's Hill. As I ascended the steps which lead from the street to the smooth gravel-walks upon the eminence whereon the "Bunker Hill Monument" stands, I experienced a feeling of disappointment and regret, not easily to be expressed. Before me was the great memento, huge and grand—all that patriotic reverence could wish—but the ditch scooped out by Prescott's toilers on that starry night in June, and the mounds that were upheaved to protect them from the shots of the astonished Britons, were effaced, and no more vestiges remain of the handiwork of those in whose honor and to whose memory this obelisk was raised, than of Roman conquests in the shadow of Trajan's Column—of the naval battles of Nelson around his monument in Trafalgar Square, or of French victories in the Place Vendôme. The fosse and the breast-works were all quite prominent when the foundation stone of the monument was laid,

BUNKER HILL MONUMENT.[2]

the illumination. We were all deeply moved, and proud to have the courage to display such sentiments in the midst of our enemies. Even Mr. Carter* could not forbear participating in our enthusiasm."—*Letters and Memoirs relating to the War of American Independence, and the Capture of the German Troops at Saratoga: By Madame De Riedesel.*

[1] This important event is recorded on page 564, where a picture of the tree is given.

[2] This monument stands in the center of the grounds included within the breast-works of the old redoubt on Breed's Hill. Its sides are precisely parallel with those of the redoubt. It is built of Quincy granite, and is two hundred and twenty-one feet in height. The foundation is composed of six courses of stones, and extends twelve feet below the surface of the ground and base of the shaft. The four sides of the foun-

* Mr. Carter was the son-in-law of General Schuyler. Remembering the kindness which she had received from that gentleman while in Albany, the baroness sought out Mr. and Mrs. Carter (who were living in Boston) on her arrival at Cambridge. "Mrs. Carter," she says, "resembled her parents in mildness and goodness of heart, but her husband was revengeful and false." The patriotic zeal of Mr. Carter had given rise to foolish stories respecting him. "They seemed to feel much friendship for us," says Madame De Riedesel; ' though, at the same time, this wicked Mr. Carter, in consequence of General Howe's having burned several villages and small towns, suggested to his countrymen to cut off our generals' heads, to pickle them, and to pu' them in small barrels, and, as often as the English should again burn a village, to send them one of these barrels; but that cru elty was not adopted."

and a little care, directed by good taste, might have preserved them in their interesting state of half ruin until the passage of the present century, or, at least, until the sublime centenary of the battle should be celebrated. Could the visitor look upon the works of the patriots themselves, associations a hundred-fold more interesting would crowd the mind, for wonderfully suggestive of thought are the slightest relics of the past when linked with noble deeds. A soft green-sward, as even as the rind of a fair apple, and cut by eight straight gravel-walks, diverging from the monument, is substituted by art for the venerated irregularities made by the old mattock and spade. The spot is beautiful to the eye untrained by appreciating affection for hallowed things; nevertheless, there is palpable desecration that may hardly be forgiven.

The view from the top of the monument, for extent, variety, and beauty, is certainly one of the finest in the world. A "York shilling" is charged for the privilege of ascending the monument. The view from its summit is "a shilling show" worth a thousand miles of travel to see. Boston, its harbor, and the beautiful country around, mottled with villages, are spread out like a vast painting, and on every side the eye may rest upon localities of great historical interest. Cambridge, Roxbury, Chelsea, Quincy, Medford, Marblehead, Dorchester, and other places, where

dation extend about fifty feet horizontally. There are in the whole pile ninety courses of stone, six of them below the surface of the ground, and eighty-four above. The foundation is laid in lime mortar; the other parts of the structure in lime mortar mixed with cinders, iron filings, and Springfield hydraulic cement. The base of the obelisk is thirty feet square; at the spring of the apex, fifteen feet. Inside of the shaft is a round, hollow cone, the outside diameter of which, at the bottom, is ten feet, and at the top, six feet. Around this inner shaft winds a spiral flight of stone steps, two hundred and ninety-five in number. In both the cone and shaft are numerous little apertures for the purposes of ventilation and light. The observatory or chamber at the top of the monument is seventeen feet in height and eleven feet in diameter. It has four windows, one on each side, which are provided with iron shutters. The cap-piece of the apex is a single stone, three feet six inches in thickness and four feet square at its base. It weighs two and a half tons.

Almost fifty years had elapsed from the time of the battle before a movement was made to erect a commemorative monument on Breed's Hill. An association for the purpose was founded in 1824; and to give eclat to the transaction, and to excite enthusiasm in favor of the work, General La Fayette, then "the nation's guest," was invited to lay the corner-stone. Accordingly, on the 17th of June, 1825, the fiftieth anniversary of the battle, that revered patriot performed the interesting ceremony, and the Honorable Daniel Webster pronounced an oration on the occasion, in the midst of an immense concourse of people. Forty survivors of the battle were present; and on no occasion did La Fayette meet so many of his fellow-soldiers in our Revolution as at that time. The *plan* of the monument was not then decided upon; but one by Solomon Willard, of Boston, having been approved, the present structure was commenced, in 1827, by James Savage, of the same city. In the course of a little more than a year, the work was suspended on account of a want of funds, about fifty-six thousand dollars having then been collected and expended. The work was resumed in 1834, and again suspended, within a year, for the same cause, about twenty thousand dollars more having been expended. In 1840, the ladies moved in the matter. A fair was announced to be held in Boston, and every female in the United States was invited to contribute some production of her own hands to the exhibition. The fair was held at Faneuil Hall in September, 1840. The proceeds amounted to sufficient, in connection with some private donations, to complete the structure, and within a few weeks subsequently, a contract was made with Mr. Savage to finish it for forty-three thousand dollars. The last stone of the apex was raised at about six o'clock on the morning of the 23d of July, 1842. Edward Carnes, Jr., of Charlestown, accompanied its ascent, waving the American flag as he went up, while the interesting event was announced to the surrounding country by the roar of cannon. On the 17th of June, 1843, the monument was dedicated, on which occasion the Honorable Daniel Webster was again the orator, and vast was the audience of citizens and military assembled there. The President of the United States (Mr. Tyler), and his whole cabinet, were present.

In the top of the monument are two cannons, named, respectively, "Hancock" and "Adams," which formerly belonged to the Ancient and Honorable Artillery Company. The "Adams" was burst by them in firing a salute. The following is the inscription upon the two guns:

"SACRED TO LIBERTY.

"This is one of four cannons which constituted the whole train of field-artillery possessed by the British colonies of North America at the commencement of the war, on the 19th of April, 1775. This cannon and its fellow, belonging to a number of citizens of Boston, were used in many engagements during the war. The other two, the property of the government of Massachusetts, were taken by the enemy.

"By order of the United States in Congress assembled, May 19th, 1788."

> " The old Continentals,
>   In their ragged regimentals,
>   Falter'd not,"

and the numerous sites of small fortifications which the student of history can readily call to mind.   In the far distance, on the northwest, rise the higher peaks of the White Mountains of New Hampshire ; and on the northeast, the peninsula of Nahant, and the more remote Cape Anne may be seen.   Wonders which present science and enterprise are developing and forming are there exhibited in profusion.   At one glance from this lofty observatory may be seen seven rail-roads,[1] and many other avenues connecting the city with the country ; and ships from almost every region of the globe dot the waters of the harbor. Could a tenant of the old grave-yard on Copp's Hill, who lived a hundred years ago, when the village upon Tri-mountain was fitting out its little armed flotillas against the French in Acadia, or sending forth its few vessels of trade along the neighboring coasts, or occasionally to cross the Atlantic, come forth and stand beside us a moment, what a new and wonderful world would be presented to his vision !   A hundred years ago !

> " Who peopled all the city streets
>   A hundred years ago ?
> Who fill'd the church with faces meek
>   A hundred years ago ?"

They were men wise in their generation, but ignorant in practical knowledge when compared with the present.   In their wildest dreams, incited by tales of wonder that spiced the literature of their times, they never fancied any thing half so wonderful as our mighty dray-horse,

> " The black steam-engine ! steed of iron power—
> The wond'rous steed of the Arabian tale,
> Lanch'd on its course by pressure of a touch—
> The war-horse of the Bible, with its neck
> Grim, clothed with thunder, swallowing the way
> In fierceness of its speed, and shouting out,
> ' Ha ! ha !'[2]   A little water, and a grasp
> Of wood, sufficient for its nerves of steel,
> Shooting away, ' Ha ! ha !' it shouts, as on
> It gallops, dragging in its tireless path
> Its load of fire."   STREET.

I lingered in the chamber of the Bunker Hill monument as long as time would allow, and descending, rode back to the city, crossed to South Boston, and rambled for an hour among the remains of the fortifications upon the heights of the peninsula of Dorchester. The present prominent remains of fortifications are those of intrenchments cast up during the war of 1812, and have no other connection with our subject than the circumstance that they occupy the site of the works constructed there by order of Washington.   These were greatly reduced in altitude when the engineers began the erection of the forts now in ruins, which are properly preserved with a great deal of care.   They occupy the summits of two hills, which command Boston Neck on the left, the city of Boston in front, and the harbor on the right.   Southeast from the heights, pleasantly situated among gentle hills, is the village of Dorchester, so called in memory of a place in England of the same name, whence many of its earliest settlers came.   The stirring events which rendered Dorchester Heights famous will be noticed presently.

I returned to Boston at about one o'clock, and passed the remainder of the day in visiting places of interest within the city—the old South meeting-house, Faneuil Hall, the Province House, and the Hancock House, all delineated and described in preceding pages.   I am

---

[1] When I visited Boston, in 1848, it was estimated that two hundred and thirty trains of cars went daily over the roads to and from Boston, and that more than six millions of passengers were conveyed in them during the preceding year.

[2] Job, xxxix., 24, 25.

indebted to John Hancock, Esq., nephew of the patriot, and present proprietor and occupant of the "Hancock House," on Beacon Street, for polite attentions while visiting his interesting mansion, and for information concerning matters that have passed under the eye of his experience of threescore years. He has many mementoes of his eminent kinsman, and among them a beautifully-executed miniature of him, painted in London, in 1761, while he was there at the coronation of George III. He also owns the original portrait of Governor Hancock, of which the engraving on page 515 is a copy.

Near Mr. Hancock's residence is the State House, a noble structure upon Beacon Hill, the corner-stone of which was laid in 1795, by Governor Samuel Adams, assisted by Paul Revere, master of the Masonic grand lodge. There I sketched the annexed picture of the colossal statue of Washington, by Chantrey, which

WASHINGTON.[2]

stands in the open center of the first story; also the group of trophies from Bennington, that hang over the door of the Senate chamber.[1] Under these trophies, in a gilt frame, is a copy of the reply of the Massachusetts Assembly to General Stark's letter, that accompanied the presentation of the trophies. It was written fifty years ago.

After enjoying the view from the top of the State House a while, I walked to Copp's Hill, a little east of Charlestown Bridge, at the north end of the town, where I tarried until sunset in the ancient burying-ground. The earliest name of this eminence was Snow Hill. It was subsequently named after its owner, William Copp.[3] It came into the possession of the Ancient and Honorable Artillery Company by mortgage, and when, in 1775, they were forbidden by Gage to parade on the Common, they went to this, their own ground, and drilled in defiance of his threats. The fort, or battery, that was built there by the British, just before the battle of Bunker Hill, stood near its southeast brow, adjoining the burying-ground. The remains of many eminent men repose in that little cemetery. Close by the entrance is the vault of the Mather family. It is covered by a plain, oblong structure of brick, three feet high and about six feet long, upon which is laid a heavy brown stone slab, with a tablet of slate, bearing the names of the principal tenants below.[4]

MATHERS' VAULT.

Oct. 7, 1848.
I passed the forenoon of the next day in the rooms of the Massachusetts Historical Society, where every facility was afforded me by Mr. Felt, the librarian, for examining the assemblage of things curious collected there.[5] The printed books and manuscripts, relating principally to American his-

---

[1] See map on page 395.

[2] This is a picture of Chantrey's statue, which is made of Italian marble, and cost fifteen thousand dollars.

[3] On some of the old maps of Boston it is called *Corpse Hill*, the name supposed to have been derived from the circumstance of a burying-ground being there.

[4] The following is the inscription upon the slate tablet: "The Reverend Doctors Increase, Cotton, and Samuel Mather were interred in this vault.

"INCREASE died August 27, 1723, Æ. 84.
Cotton   "   Feb.   13, 1727, "   65.
Samuel   "   Jan.   27, 1785, "   79."*

[5] This society was incorporated in February, 1794. The avowed object of its organization is to collect, preserve, and communicate materials for a complete history of this country, and an account of all valuable efforts of human industry and ingenuity from the beginning of its settlement. Between twenty and thirty octavo volumes of its "Collections" have been published.

---

* The library of Dr. Samuel Mather was burned at Charlestown, when it was destroyed by the British in 1775.

tory, are numerous, rare, and valuable.   There is also a rich depository of the autographs of the Pilgrim fathers and their immediate descend-ants.   There are no less than twenty-five large folio volumes of valuable manuscript letters and other documents; besides which are six thick quarto manuscript volumes—a comment-ary on the holy Scriptures—in the hand-writing of Cotton Mather.   From an autograph letter of that singular man the annexed fac-simile of his writing and signature is given.   Among the portraits in the cabinet of the society are those of Governor Winslow,

While I was preaching at a private fast (kept for a possessed young woman,)— on mark 9. 28, 29. — ye Devil in ye Danish flew upon me, & tore ye loaf, as it is now torn, over against ye Text; Nov. 29. 1692.

Cotton Mather.

MATHER'S WRITING.

supposed to have been painted by Vandyke, Increase Mather, and Peter Faneuil, the founder of Faneuil Hall.

I had the pleasure of meeting, at the rooms of the society, that indefatigable antiquary,

SPEAKER'S DESK AND WINSLOW'S CHAIR.[1]

Dr. Webb, widely known as the American correspondent of the "Danish Society of Northern Antiquarians" at Copenha-gen.   He was sitting in the chair that once belonged to Gov-ernor Winslow, writing upon the desk of the speaker of the colonial Assembly of Massachusetts, around which the warm debates were carried on concerning American liberty, from the time when James Otis denounced the Writs of Assistance, un-til Governor Gage adjourned the Assembly to Salem, in 1774. Hallowed by such associations, the desk is an interesting relic. Dr. Webb's familiarity with the collections of the society, and his kind attentions, greatly facilitated my search among the six thousand articles for things curious connected with my subject, and made my brief visit far more profitable to myself than it would otherwise have been.   Among the relics preserved are the chair that belonged to Governor Carver, very similar in its appearance to

PHILIP'S SAMP-PAN.

the ancient one delineated on page 438; the sword of Miles Standish; the huge key of Port Royal gate; a *samp-pan*, that belonged to Metacomet, or King Philip; and the sword reputed to have been used by Captain Church when he cut off that unfortunate sachem's head. The dish is about twelve inches in diameter, wrought out of an elm knot with great skill.   The sword is very rude, and was doubtless made by a blacksmith of the colony.   The handle is a roughly-wrought piece of ash, and the guard is made of a wrought-iron plate.   The circumstances connected with the death of Philip will be noticed hereafter.

I lingered in the rooms of the society, copying and sketching, with busy hands, until after one o'clock.   An urgent call beckoning me homeward, I de-parted in the cars for Norwich and New-London between two and three o'clock in the afternoon, regretting that my tarry in the city of the Pilgrims was necessarily so brief, and that I was obliged to forego the pleasures of a visit to the neighboring villages, all of which are associated with events of the Revolution.   Before departure let us revert to the history of Boston subse-quent to the battle of Bunker Hill.   That event was but the beginning of the stirring scenes of the siege, which terminated in success for the Americans.

CHURCH'S SWORD.

---

[1] This desk is made of ash.   The semicircular front is about three feet in diameter   The chair, which belonged to Governor Winslow, is of English oak.   It was made in 1614.

On the 15th of June, 1775, two days before the Bunker Hill battle, the Continental Congress, in session in Philadelphia, resolved " That a general be appointed to command all the Continental forces, raised or to be raised for the defense of American liberty ;" also, " That five hundred dollars per month be allowed for the pay and expenses of the general."[1] The most difficult question then to be decided was the choice of the man for the responsible office. Military men of much experience were then in the field at the head of the army beleaguring Boston, and by the common consent of the New England colonies General Artemus Ward was the commander-in-chief. It was conceded that he did not possess all the requisites of a skillful and judicious commander, so essential for the service ; yet, it being doubtful how the New England people, and particularly the soldiery, would relish the supercession of General Ward by another, Congress was embarrassed respecting a choice. The apparent difficulty was soon overcome by the management of the New England delegation. The subject of the appointment had been informally discussed two or three days before, and John Adams had proposed the adoption of the provincial troops at Boston as a CONTINENTAL ARMY. At the conclusion of his remarks, he expressed his intention to propose a member from Virginia for the office of generalissimo. All present understood the person alluded to to be Colonel George Washington, whose commanding military talents, as displayed in the service of Virginia, and his capacity as a statesman, as exhibited in the Congress of 1774, had made him exceedingly popular throughout the land. Acting upon this suggestion, Thomas Johnson, a delegate from Maryland, nominated Colonel Washington, and by a unanimous vote he was elected commander-in-chief. On the opening of the session on the following morning, President Hancock communicated to Washington, officially, a notice of his appointment. He rose in his place, and signified his acceptance in a brief and truly patriotic reply.[2] Richard Henry Lee, Edward Rutledge, and John Adams were appointed a committee to draught a commission and instructions for the general ; these were given to him four days afterward.[3] Four major generals, eight brig-

July 17, 1775.

---

[1] Journals of Congress, i., 111, 112.

[2] The following is a copy of his reply :

" Mr. President,—Though I am truly sensible of the high honor done me in this appointment, yet I feel great distress, from a consciousness that my abilities and military experience may not be equal to the extensive and important trust. However, as the Congress desire it, I will enter upon the momentous duty, and exert every power I possess in their service, and for the support of the glorious cause. I beg they will accept my most cordial thanks for this distinguished testimony of their approbation. But, lest some unlucky event should happen unfavorable to my reputation, I beg it may be remembered, by every gentleman in this room, that I this day declare, with the utmost sincerity, I do not think myself equal to the command I am honored with. As to pay, sir, I beg leave to assure the Congress that, as no pecuniary consideration could have tempted me to accept the arduous employment at the expense of my domestic ease and happiness, I do not wish to make any profit from it. I will keep an exact account of my expenses. Those, I doubt not, they will discharge, and that is all I desire."

His expressions of distrust in his own ability to perform the duties imposed by the acceptance of the appointment were heartfelt and sincere. In a letter to his wife, dated the day after his appointment, he said, " You may believe me, my dear Patsy [the familiar name of Martha], when I assure you, in the most solemn manner, that, so far from seeking the appointment, I have used every endeavor in my power to avoid it, not only from my unwillingness to part with you and the family, but from a consciousness of its being a trust too great for my capacity ; and that I should enjoy more real happiness in one month with you at home than I have the most distant prospect of finding abroad, if my stay were to be seven times seven years." Washington was at this time forty-three years of age.

[3] His commission was in the following words :

" To GEORGE WASHINGTON, ESQ.—We, reposing special trust and confidence in your patriotism, valor, conduct, and fidelity, do, by these presents, constitute and appoint you to be general and commander-in-chief of the army of the United Colonies, and of all the forces now raised, or to be raised by them, and of all others who shall voluntarily offer their services, and join the said army for the defense of American liberty, and for repelling every hostile invasion thereof ; and you are hereby vested with full power and authority to act as you shall think for the good and welfare of the service. And we do hereby strictly charge and require all officers and soldiers under your command to be obedient to your orders, and diligent in the exercise of their several duties. And we do also enjoin and require you to be careful in executing the great trust reposed in you, by causing strict discipline and order to be observed in the army, and that the soldiers be duly exercised, and provided with all convenient necessaries. And you are to regulate your

adiers, and one adjutant general were appointed,[1] and the pay of the several officers was agreed upon.[2]

Washington left Philadelphia for the camp at Cambridge on the 21st of June, where he arrived on the 2d of July. He was every where greeted with enthusiasm   1775. by crowds of people, and public bodies extended to him all the deference due to his exalted rank. He arrived at New York on the 25th, escorted by a company of light horse from Philadelphia. Governor Tryon arrived from England on the same day, and the same escort received both the distinguished men. There Washington first heard of the battle of Bunker Hill. He held a brief conference with General Schuyler, and gave that officer directions concerning his future operations. Toward evening, on the 26th, he left New York, under the escort of several military companies, passed the night at Kingsbridge, at the upper end of Manhattan or York Island, and the next morning, bidding adieu to the Philadelphia light horse, pressed on toward Boston. He reached Watertown on the morning of the 2d of July. The Provincial Congress of Massachusetts, presided over by James Warren, was in session, and voted him a congratulatory address. Major-general Lee, who

accompanied him, also received an address from that body. They arrived at Cambridge at two o'clock in the afternoon, and Washington established his head-quarters at the house prepared for him, delineated on page 555.

On the morning of the 3d of July, at about nine o'clock, the troops at Cambridge were drawn up in order upon the Common to receive the commander-in-chief. Accompanied by the general officers of the army who were present, Washington walked from his quarters to the great elm-tree that now stands at the north end of the Common, and, under the shadow of its broad covering, stepped a few paces in front, made some remarks, drew his sword, and formally took command of the Continental army.

THE WASHINGTON ELM.[3] That was an auspicious act for America; and the love and reverence which all felt for him on that occasion never waned during the eight long years of the conflict. When he resigned that commission into the hands of Congress at Annapolis, not a blot was visible upon the fair escutcheon of his character; like Samuel, he could boldly "testify his integrity"[4] in all things.

conduct in every respect by the rules and discipline of war (as here given you), and punctually to observe and follow such orders and directions, from time to time, as you shall receive from this or a future Congress of these United Colonies, or committee of Congress. This commission is to continue in force until revoked by this or a future Congress. Signed,   JOHN HANCOCK, *President.*"

The original of this commission, with other relics of the illustrious chief, is carefully preserved in a glass case, in a room of the Patent Office building at Washington City.

[1] The names of these several officers are contained in a note on page 190.

[2] The pay of the several officers was as follows, per month: major general, $166, and when acting in a separate department, $330; brigadier general, $125; adjutant general, $125; commissary general, $80; quarter-master general, $80; his deputy, $40; paymaster general, $100; his deputy, $50; chief engineer, $60; three aids-de-camp for the general, each, $33; his secretary, $66; commissary of the musters, $40.

[3] The house seen in this sketch is one of the oldest in Cambridge, having been built about 1750. It has been in the possession of the Moore family about seventy-five years. Since I visited Cambridge I have been informed that a Mrs. Moore was still living there, who, from the window of that house, saw the ceremony of Washington taking command of the army.   [4] 1 Samuel, xii., 3.

Washington called a council of war on the 9th. It was composed of the major generals and the brigadiers, and the object of the council was to consult upon future operations. The commander-in-chief found himself at the head of an army composed of a mixed multitude of men of every sort, from the honest and intelligent citizen, possessed of property and station, to the ignorant knave, having nothing to lose, and consequently every thing to gain. Organization had been effected in a very slight degree, and thorough discipline was altogether unknown. Intoxication, peculation, falsehood, disobedience, and disrespect were prevalent, and the punishments which had been resorted to were quite ineffectual to produce reform.[1] It was estimated by the Council that, from the best information which could be obtained, the forces of the enemy consisted of eleven thousand five hundred effective men, while the Americans had only about fourteen thousand fit for duty.[2] It was unanimously decided by the Council to maintain the siege by strengthening the posts around Boston, then held by the Americans, by fortifications and recruits. It was also agreed that, if the troops should be attacked and routed by the enemy, the places of rendezvous should be Wales's Hill, in the rear of the Roxbury lines; and also that, at the present, it was "inexpedient to fortify Dorchester Point, or to oppose the enemy if he should attempt to take possession of it."

Some riflemen from Maryland, Virginia, and Western Pennsylvania, enlisted under the orders of Congress, and led by Daniel Morgan, a man of powerful frame and sterling courage, soon joined the camp.[3] Upon their breasts they wore the motto "LIBERTY OR DEATH." A large proportion of them were Irishmen, and were not very agreeable to the New Englanders. Otho Williams, afterward greatly distinguished, was lieutenant of one of the Maryland companies. Both these men rose to the rank of brigadier.

The first care of the commander-in-chief was to organize the army.[4] He arranged it into three grand divisions, each division consisting of two brigades, or twelve regiments, in

July, 1775.

---

[1] These punishments consisted in pecuniary fines, standing in the pillory, confinement in stocks, riding a wooden horse, whipping, and drumming out of the regiment.

[2] The following return of the army was made to Adjutant-general Gates on the 19th of July:

Colonies.	No. of regiments.	Commissioned officers and staff.	Non-commissioned officers.	Rank and file.					Total.
				Present fit for duty.	Sick present.	Sick absent.	On furlough.	On command.	
Massachusetts	26	789	1,326	9,396	757	450	311	774	11,688
Connecticut	3	125	174	2,105	212	2	14		2,333
New Hampshire...	3	98	160	1,201	115	20	49	279	1,664
Rhode Island	3	107	108	1,041	24	18	2		1,085
Total........	35	1,119	1,768	13,743	1,108	490	376	1,053	16,770

[3] These men attracted much attention, and on account of their sure and deadly aim, they became a terror to the British. Wonderful stories of their exploits went to England, and one of the riflemen, who was carried there a prisoner, was gazed at as a great curiosity.

[4] The following general order was issued on the 4th of July, the day after Washington took command of the army:

"The Continental Congress having now taken all the troops of the several colonies, which have been raised, or which may be hereafter raised for the support and defense of the liberties of America, into their pay and service, they are now the troops of the UNITED PROVINCES OF NORTH AMERICA; and it is hoped that all distinction of colonies will be laid aside, so that one and the same spirit may animate the whole, and the only contest be, who shall render, on this great and trying occasion, the most essential service to the great and common cause in which we are all engaged. It is required and expected that exact discipline be observed, and due subordination prevail through the whole army, as a failure in these most essential points must necessarily produce extreme hazard, disorder, and confusion, and end in shameful disappointment and disgrace. The general most earnestly requires and expects a due observance of those articles of war, established for the government of the army, which forbid profane cursing, swearing, and drunkenness; and in like manner, he requires and expects of all officers and soldiers, not engaged on actual duty, a punctual attendance on divine service, to implore the blessings of Heaven upon the means used for our safety and defense."

This brief order may be regarded as a model. In a few words, it evokes harmony, order, the exercise of patriotism, morality, sobriety, and an humble reverence for and reliance upon Divine Providence. It includes all the essential elements of good government. These principles were the moral bonds of union that kept the little Continental army together during the dreary years of its struggle for the mastery.

which the troops from the same colony, as far as practicable, were brought together.   The right wing, under Major-general Ward, consisted of two brigades, commanded by Generals Thomas and Spencer,[1] and was stationed at Roxbury and its southern dependencies.   The left wing was placed under the command of General Lee, and consisted of the brigades of Sullivan and Greene.   The former was stationed upon Winter Hill; the latter upon Prospect Hill.   The center, stationed at Cambridge, was commanded by General Putnam, and consisted of two brigades, one of which was commanded by Heath, and the other by a senior officer, of less rank than that of brigadier.   Thomas Mifflin, who accompanied Washington from Philadelphia as aid-de-camp, was made quarter-master general.   Joseph Trum

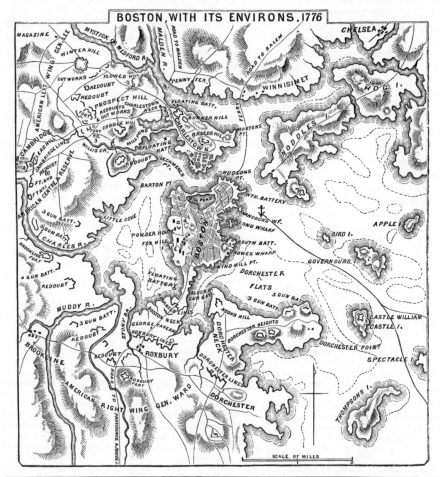

BOSTON, WITH ITS ENVIRONS, 1776

---

[1] JOSEPH SPENCER served as a major and colonel during the Seven Years' War.   He was a native of East Haddam, in Connecticut, where he was born in 1714.   He was with the Continental army in the expedition against Rhode Island, in 1778, and assisted in Sullivan's retreat.   He soon afterward resigned his commission, and left the army, when he was chosen to be a delegate in Congress from his native state.   He died at East Haddam in January, 1789, aged seventy-five years.   General Seth Pomeroy, who was appointed with Spencer and others, refused to serve, and Spencer took rank next to Putnam in the army at Boston.   This removed, in a degree, the difficulty that was apprehended in settling the rank of some of the officers.   By this arrangement, General Thomas, who was Ward's lieutenant general, was made the first brigadier.

bull, a son of the patriot governor of Connecticut, was appointed commissary general, and upon Joseph Reed, of Philadelphia, was bestowed the post of secretary to the commander-in-chief.   In the course of a few months Reed returned to Philadelphia, and was succeeded in office by Robert H. Harrison, a Maryland lawyer.

The relative position of the belligerent armies was, according to a letter written by Washington to the President of Congress, on the 10th of July, as follows : the British were strongly intrenched on Bunker Hill, about half a mile from the chief place of action on the 17th of June, with their sentries extending about one hundred and fifty yards beyond the narrowest point of Charlestown Neck.   Three British floating batteries were in the Mystic River near Bunker Hill, and a twenty-gun ship was anchored below the ferry-place between Boston and Charlestown.   They had a battery upon Copp's Hill in Boston, and the fortifications upon the Neck, toward Roxbury, were strengthened.   Until the 7th, the British advance guards occupied Brown's Buildings, about a mile from Roxbury meeting-house.   On that day a party from General Thomas's camp surprised the guard, drove them in, and burned the houses.   The bulk of the army, commanded by General Howe, lay upon Bunker Hill ; and the light horse, and a corps of Tories, remained in Boston.

The Americans had thrown up intrenchments on Winter and Prospect Hills, in full view of the British camp, which was only a mile distant.   Strong works were also thrown up at Roxbury, two hundred yards above the meeting-house.   Strong lines were made across from the Charlestown Road to the Mystic River, and by connecting redoubts, there was a complete line of defense from that river to Roxbury.[1]

A letter written by the Reverend William Emerson, a chaplain in the army, a few days after Washington's arrival, gives the following life-like picture of the camp : "New lords, new laws.   The generals, Washington and Lee, are upon the lines every day.   New orders from his excellency are read to the respective regiments every morning after prayers.   The strictest government is taking place, and great distinction is made between officers and soldiers.   Every one is made to know his place, and keep in it, or to be tied up and receive thirty or forty lashes, according to his crime.   Thousands are at work every day from four till eleven o'clock in the morning.   It is surprising how much work has been done.   The lines are extended almost from Cambridge to the Mystic River ; so that very soon it will be morally impossible for the enemy to get between the works, except in one place, which is supposed to be left purposely unfortified, to entice the enemy out of their fortresses.   Who would have thought, twelve months past, that all Cambridge and Charlestown would be covered over with American camps, and cut up into forts and intrenchments, and all the lands, fields, and orchards laid common—horses and cattle feeding in the choicest mowing land, whole fields of corn eaten down to the ground, and large parks of well-regulated locusts cut down for fire-wood and other public uses.   This, I must say, looks a little melancholy.   My quarters are at the foot of the famous Prospect Hill, where such preparations are made for the reception of the enemy.   It is very diverting to walk among the camps.   They are as different in their form as the owners are in their dress, and every tent is a portraiture of the temper and taste of the persons who encamp in it.   Some are made of boards, and some of sail-cloth ; some partly of one and partly of the other.   Again, others are made of stone or turf, brick or brush.   Some are thrown up in a hurry ; others are curiously wrought with doors and windows, done with wreaths and withes, in the manner of a basket.   Some are your proper tents and marquees, looking like the regular camp of the enemy.   In these are the Rhode Islanders, who are furnished with tent equipage and every thing in the most exact English style.   However, I think this great variety rather a beauty than a blemish in the army."[2]

While Washington was organizing the Continental army, Congress was active in the

_____

[1] The reader will more clearly understand the relative position of the hostile forces and their respective fortifications, by a careful examination of the map on the preceding page.   It shows the various works thrown up during the summer and autumn of 1775, and at the beginning of 1776.

[2] Spark's *Life and Writings of Washington* (Appendix), iii., 491.

adoption of measures to strengthen his hands, and to organize civil government. Acting upon the suggestion of the Provincial Congress of New York, we have already observed June 23, (*ante*, page 316) that Congress authorized the emission of bills of credit. Articles 1775. of war were agreed to on the 30th of June, and on the 6th of July a Declaration was issued, setting forth the cause and necessity for taking up arms. A firm but respectful petition to the king was drawn up by John Dickinson, the author of "Letters of a Pennsylvania Farmer," &c., and adopted on the 8th; and addresses to the inhabitants of Great Britain, Ireland, Canada, and Jamaica, were adopted in the course of the month. The Indians were not overlooked; it was important to secure their neutrality at least; and three boards for Indian affairs were constituted: one for the Six Nations and other northern tribes; a second for the Cherokees, at the South; and a third for the intervening nations, on the borders of Pennsylvania and Virginia. Already some Stockbridge Indians, from Massachusetts, near the New-York line, the last remnant of the tribes of Western New England, were in the camp at Boston; and Kirtland, the missionary among the Six Nations of New York, was making overtures to the Oneidas and the Mohawks. Congress also established a post-office system of its own, extending in its operations from Falmouth (now Portland, Maine) to Savannah, and westward to remote settlements. Dr. Franklin was appointed post-master general.[1] An army hospital for the accommodation of twenty thousand men was established. At its head was placed Dr. Benjamin Church, of Boston, till this time a brave and zealous compatriot of Warren and his associates. Soon after his appointment he was detected in secret correspondence with Gage. He had intrusted a letter, written in cipher, with his mistress, to be forwarded to the British commander. It was found upon her; she was taken to head-quarters, and there the contents of the letter were deciphered, and the defection of Dr. Church established. He was found guilty, by a court martial, of criminal correspondence with the enemy. Expulsion from the House of Representatives of Massachusetts, and close confinement in Norwich Jail, in Connecticut, by order of the general Congress, speedily followed. His health failing, he was allowed to leave the country. He sailed for the West Indies; but the vessel that bore him was never afterward heard from. His place in the hospital was filled by Dr. John Morgan, one of the founders of the Medical School in Philadelphia. Church was the first traitor to the American cause.

The New England colonies, sustained by the presence of a strong army, labored energetically in perfecting their civil governments. Connecticut and Rhode Island, as we have observed, were always democratic, and through the energy of Trumbull, the governor of the former, that colony took an early, bold, and commanding stand for freedom. Nor was the latter colony much behind her democratic colleague. Benning Wentworth, governor of New Hampshire, having lost all political power, shut himself up, for two months, in Fort William and Mary at Portsmouth, during which time his house was pillaged by a mob. He prorogued the Assembly in July, and then fled to Boston for safety. Massachusetts organized a House of Representatives under the original charter; and as, according to the provisions of that charter, the executive authority devolved upon the Council in the absence 1775. of the governor and his lieutenant, that body, chosen on the 21st of July, assumed such authority. Such continued to be the government of the colony until the adoption of a state constitution in 1780. A single executive committee was constituted, vested with all the powers hitherto exercised by the several committees of correspondence, inspection, and safety. This consolidation produced far greater efficiency. Of the civil and military operations of other colonies I shall write hereafter; for the present, let us view the progress of events at Boston.

---

[1] In the General Post-office at Washington city I saw, several years ago, the book in which Franklin kept his post-office accounts. It is a common, half-bound folio, of three quires of coarse paper, and contained all the entries for nearly two years. The first entry was November 17, 1776. Now more than fifteen hundred of the largest-sized ledgers are required annually for the same purpose; the number of contractors and other persons having accounts with the office being over thirty thousand. There are about one hundred clerks employed in the department.

During the remainder of the summer, and throughout the autumn, the belligerents continually menaced each other, but neither appeared ready for a general engagement. The British were awaiting re-enforcements, and the Americans were too feeble in men, discipline, and munitions of war, to make an assault with a prospect of success. Several skirmishes occurred, and on two or three occasions a general battle was apprehended.

The declaration of Congress, setting forth the causes and the necessity for taking up arms, was read by President Langdon,[1] of Harvard, before the army at Cambridge, on the 15th of July. On the 18th, it was read to the division under General Thomas, at Roxbury, and also to the troops under Putnam, upon Prospect Hill. At the close of the reading a cannon was fired, three hearty cheers were given by the army, and the flag that was presented to Putnam a few days before was unfurled.[2] " The Philistines on Bunker Hill," said the *Essex Gazette*, in its account of the affair, " heard the shouts of the Israelites, and being very fearful, paraded themselves in battle array." The 20th was observed as a day of fasting by the whole army. On the 30th (Sunday), five hundred British troops marched over Charlestown Neck, and built a slight breast-work ; at the same time a British floating battery was rowed up the Charles River. Another party of troops sallied out toward Roxbury, drove in the American sentinels, and set fire to a tavern. Frequent excursions were made by both parties to the islands in the harbor, and skirmishes, sometimes severe, were the consequences. These things kept the two armies on the alert, and disciplined them in habits of vigilance.

British cruisers kept the New England coast, from Falmouth to New London, in a state of continual alarm. They were out in every direction, seeking plunder and endeavoring to supply the camp with fresh provisions. Lieutenant Mowatt, commander of a British brig, made a descent upon Gloucester, Cape Anne, and attempted to land. He was repulsed, after he had thrown several bombs into the town without serious effect. Sto- August 13. nington, in Connecticut, was bombarded for a day ; two men were killed, and September 30. the houses were much shattered. In October, Mowatt was sent to Falmouth (now Portland, in Maine), to obtain a supply of provisions from the inhabitants, and to demand a surrender of their arms. They refused obedience, and boldly defied him ; whereupon, after giving time sufficient for the women and children to leave the town, he bombarded and set it on fire. It contained about five hundred buildings, and presently a large portion of them were in flames. One hundred and thirty-nine houses, and two hundred and seventy-eight stores and other buildings were destroyed ; but the resolute inhabitants October 7. maintained their ground, repulsed the enemy, and prevented his landing. Bristol, on the east side of Narragansett Bay, and other towns in the neighborhood, were visited in like manner by the depredators. These wanton cruelties excited intense indignation, and the American troops that environed Boston could hardly be restrained from attacking the oppressors of their countrymen.

The Americans, as a countervailing measure, fitted out cruisers, and in a short time each colony had a navy board. These privateers became very formidable to the enemy, and the extent of British depredations along the coast was greatly lessened. Washington sent out five or six armed vessels to intercept supplies coming into the port of Boston, and some important captures were made. Some of the American naval officers proved very inefficient. Captain Manly, almost alone, at that time, sustained the character of a bold and skillful commander, and he and his crew did good service to the cause. They bravely maintained their position off Boston Harbor, and in the course of a few weeks captured three valuable

---

[1] Reverend Samuel Langdon was a native of Boston, and graduated at Harvard in 1740. He succeeded Mr. Locke as president of that institution, in 1774. On account of a lack of urbanity, he was disliked by the students, who made his situation so disagreeable that he resigned the presidency in 1780. In 1781, at Hampton Fall, New Hampshire, he resumed his ministerial labors, in which he continued faithful until his death. This event occurred on the 29th of November, 1797, at the age of seventy-four.

[2] This was the flag before alluded to, which bore on one side the motto " *An appeal to Heaven*," and on the other " *Qui transtulit, sustinet*."

vessels, one of which was laden with heavy guns, mortars, and intrenching tools—a valuable prize for the Americans at that time. Only thirteen days before, Washington wrote to Congress, "I am in very great want of powder, lead, mortars, indeed most sorts of military stores." Captain Manly supplied him more promptly and bountifully than Congress could do. The finest of the mortars was named Congress, and placed in the artillery park at Cambridge.

Manly soon became a terror to the British, and the Falcon sloop-of-war, Captain Linzee, was sent out to attempt to seize him. He was chased, in company with a schooner, into Gloucester Harbor. The schooner was seized by the enemy. Manly ran his brig ashore. Linzee fired more than three hundred guns, and sent barges of armed men to take the brig; but the crew and the neighboring militia behaved so bravely that Linzee was repulsed, having lost nearly half his men. Manly's vessel was got off without much damage, and was soon cruising again beneath the pine-tree flag.[1]

THE PINE-TREE FLAG.[2]

1775. Early in August, Washington discovered that a great mistake had been made in reporting to him the condition of the commissariat, in the article of powder. "Our situation," he said, in a letter to Congress, "in the article of powder, is much more alarming than I had the most distant idea of." "Instead of three hundred quarter-casks," wrote Reed, "we have but thirty-two barrels." Powder-mills were not yet in successful operation in the province, and great uneasiness prevailed lest the enemy should become acquainted with their poverty. Vessels were fitted out, on private account, to go to the West Indies for a supply of powder. The Provincial Congress of Massachusetts passed a law prohibiting a waste of powder in shooting birds or for sports of any kind, and every precaution was adopted to husband the meager supply on hand.

August 12.

Although Washington did not feel strong enough to make an assault upon Boston, he was prepared to receive an attack from the enemy, and was anxious for such an event. For weeks it had been rumored that the British intended to make a sortie in full force; and, finally, the 25th of August was designated as the day selected for the demonstration. It was understood that Earl Percy was to have the command of Boston Neck, where he expected to retrieve the honors which he lost in his retreat from Lexington. In the mean while, the British were daily practicing the maneuvers of embarking and debarking, and every movement indicated an intention to make an effort to break up the circumvallating line of provincials that hemmed them so closely in.

1775. On Saturday night, the 26th of August, General Sullivan, with a fatigue party of one thousand men, and a guard of two thousand four hundred, marched, in imitation of the feat of Prescott's, to Plowed Hill (now Mount Benedict), within point blank shot of

---

[1] Bradford's *History of Massachusetts*, page 75.
[2] This engraving is a reduced copy of a vignette on a map of Boston, published in Paris in 1776. The *London Chronicle*, an anti-ministerial paper, in its issue for January, 1776, gives the following description of the flag of an American cruiser that had been captured: "In the Admiralty office is the flag of a provincial privateer. The field is white bunting; on the middle is a green pine-tree, and upon the opposite side is the motto, '*Appeal to Heaven.*' "

the enemy's batteries on Bunker Hill, and before morning cast up such intrenchments as afforded excellent protection against the cannons of the British. Washington hoped this maneuver would bring on a general action, and he rejoiced to hear the cannonade that opened upon the American works in the morning, from Bunker Hill and a ship and two floating batteries in the Mystic. More than three hundred shells were thrown by the enemy on that occasion.[1] On account of the scarcity of powder the cannonade was not returned. A nine pounder, planted on a point at the Ten Hills Farm, played so effectually against the floating batteries that one of them was sunk and the other silenced. The British cannonade ceased at night. In the morning, troops were observed to be drawn up on Bunker Hill, as if for marching. Washington now expected an attack, and sent five thousand men to Plowed Hill[2] and to the Charlestown Road. It was a bold challenge for the enemy, but he prudently refused to accept it. For several days he fired a few cannon shots against the American works, but, perceiving them to be ineffectual, he ceased all hostilities on the 10th of September. It was about this time that the Continental army received seven hundred pounds of powder from Rhode Island ; " probably a part," says Gordon, " of what had been brought from Africa."[3]

The close investment of Boston by troops on land and privateers at sea began to have a serious effect upon the officers, troops, and people in the city.[4] They had an abundance of salt provision, but, being unaccustomed to such diet, many fell sick. Gage, doubtless, spoke in sentiment, if not in words, as Freneau wrote :

> " Three weeks, ye gods ! nay, three long years it seems
> Since *roast beef* I have touched, except in dreams.
> In sleep, choice dishes to my view repair ;
> Waking, I gape, and champ the empty air.
> Say, is it just that I, who rule these bands,
> Should live on husks, like rakes in foreign lands ?
> Come, let us plan some project ere we sleep,
> And drink destruction to the rebel sheep.
> On neighboring isles uncounted cattle stray ;
> Fat beeves and swine—an ill-defended prey—
> These are fit 'visions for my noonday dish ;
> These, if my soldiers act as I could wish,
> In one short week would glad your maws and mine ;
> On mutton we will sup—on roast beef dine."
> MIDNIGHT MUSINGS ; OR, A TRIP TO BOSTON, 1775.

In daily apprehension of an attack from the provincials, and the chances for escape hourly diminishing, they exerienced all the despondency of a doomed people. Gage was convinced that the first blow against American freedom had been struck in the wrong place, and that the position of his troops was wholly untenable. He had been re-enforced since the battle of Bunker Hill, but the new-comers were a burden rather than an aid ; for he had the sagacity to perceive that twice the number of troops then under his command were insufficient to effectually disperse the Continental army, backed, as it was, by other thousands ready to step from the furrow to the intrenchment when necessity should call. Idleness begat vice, in various forms, in his camp, and inaction was as likely as the weapons of his enemy to decimate his battalions.[5] Much annoyance to the British officers was produced by the cir-

---

[1] During this cannonade, Adjutant Mumford, of Colonel Varnum's Rhode Island regiment, and another soldier, had their heads shot off, and a rifleman was mortally wounded.

[2] Bunker Hill, Plowed Hill, and Winter Hill are situated in a range from east to west, each of them on or near the Mystic River.

[3] Early in 1775, two vessels, laden with New England rum, sailed from Newport to the coast of Africa. The rum was exchanged, at the British forts, for powder ; and so completely did this traffic strip the fortresses of this article, that there was not an ounce remaining that could be taken from the use of the garrisons. This maneuver produced a seasonable supply for the provincials.

[4] The number of inhabitants in Boston, on the 28th of July, was six thousand seven hundred and fifty-three. The number of the troops was thirteen thousand six hundred.

[5] Most of the soldiers were encamped on the Common, which was not, as now, shaded by large trees,

culation of hand-bill addresses among the soldiers. They found their way into the British camp; how, no one could tell.[1] They were secret and powerful emissaries; for the soldiers pondered much, in their idle moments, upon the plain truths which these circulars contained.

1775.   Every thing now betokened ruin to the royal cause. Even as early as the 25th of June, Gage said, in a letter to Dartmouth, when giving an account of the battle of the 19th, " The trials we have had show the rebels are not the despicable rabble too many have supposed them to be; and I find it owing to a military spirit encouraged among them for a few years past, joined with an uncommon degree of zeal and enthusiasm, that they are not otherwise." Toward the close of July he wrote despairingly to Lord Dartmouth. After averring that the rebellion was general, he said, " This province began it—I might say this town; for here the arch rebels formed their scheme long ago." He spoke of the disadvantageous position of the troops, and suggested the propriety of transferring the theater of operations to New York, where " the friends of government were more numerous."

The few patriots who remained in Boston were objects of continual suspicion, and subject to insults daily. They were charged with sketching plans of the military works, telegraphing with the provincials by signals from steeples, and various other acts, for which some were thrown into prison. At length provisions became so scarce, and the plundering expeditions sent out by Gage to procure fresh food were so unsuccessful,[2] that the commander determined to make arrangements for the removal of a large number of the inhabitants from the town. It was notified that James Urquhart, the town major, would receive the names July 24,   of those who wished to leave. Within two days more than two thousand names 1775.   were handed in, notwithstanding there was a restriction that no plate was to be carried away, and no more than five pounds in cash by each person. Many people of property, who would gladly have left, were unwilling to do so, for they knew that what property remained would become a prey to the soldiery. Of those who departed, many women quilted silver spoons into their garments. Coin was smuggled out of the city in the same way. These refugees landed principally at Chelsea, and scattering over the country, were all re-

---

but exposed to the heat of the summer sun. " It is not to be wondered," said a letter-writer, in August, " that the fatigue of duty, bad accommodations, and the use of too much spirits, should produce fever in the camp. The soldiers can not be kept from rum. Six-pence will buy a quart of West India rum, and four-pence is the price of a quart of New England rum. Even the sick and the wounded have often nothing to eat but salt pork and fish."

[1] I saw one of these hand-bills among the Proclamations, &c., in the Massachusetts Historical Society. It was an address to the soldiers who were about embarking for America, and was printed in London. The writer, in speaking of the course of the provincials, emphasizes, by italics, printed in a single conspicuous line, the expression,

" *Before God and man they are right !*"

On the back of this address is the following endorsement, which was evidently printed in this country, the type and ink being greatly inferior to the other. It alludes to the two camps: the one on Prospect Hill, under Putnam; the other on Bunker Hill, under Howe.

PROSPECT HILL.	BUNKER HILL.
I. Seven dollars a month.	I. Three-pence a day.
II. Fresh provisions, and in plenty.	II. Rotten salt pork.
III. Health.	III. The scurvy.
IV. Freedom, ease, affluence, and a good farm.	IV. Slavery, beggary, and want.

[2] One of these, in August, was quite successful. In the neighborhood of New London, a small British fleet obtained eighteen hundred sheep and more than one hundred head of oxen. Frothingham (page 236) quotes a letter from Gage to Lord Dartmouth, in which this important fact is announced. This letter was published, and in the anti-ministerial *London Chronicle* the following impromptu appeared:

" In days of yore the British troops
     Have taken warlike kings in battle;
But now, alas! their valor droops,
     For Gage takes naught but—harmless cattle.

" Britons, with grief your bosoms strike!
     Your faded laurels loudly weep!
Behold your heroes, Quixotte like,
     Driving a timid flock of—sheep!'

OF THE REVOLUTION. 573

Council of War.   Situation of the Army.   Washington's Complaints.   Gage recalled.   His Life and Character.

ceived with the open arms of hospitality every where, except a few Tories who ventured to leave the city. These were treated with bitter scorn, and there were many martyrs for opinion's sake. This measure was a great relief to Gage ; and the capture, about that time, of an American vessel laden with fresh provisions, made food quite plentiful in the city for a while.

The inactive and purely defensive policy pursued by both armies became exceedingly onerous to Washington, and he resolved, if expedient, to endeavor to put an end to it. Congress, too, became impatient, and requested Washington to attack the enemy if he perceived any chance for success. The commander-in-chief, accordingly, called a council of war on the 11th of September. In view of the rapid approach of the time when the term of enlistment of many of the troops would expire, and also of the general unfavorable condition of the army, Washington desired to make an immediate and simultaneous attack upon the city and the camp of the enemy on Bunker Hill. But his officers dissented ; and the decision of the Council was " that it is not expedient to make the attempt at present." Ten days afterward, Washington wrote a long letter to the President of Congress, in which, after making a statement which implied a charge of neglect on the part of that body, he drew a graphic picture of the condition of the army. " But my situation," he said, " is inexpressibly distressing, to see the winter fast approaching upon a naked army, the time of their service within a few weeks of expiring, and no provisions yet made for such important events. Added to these, the military chest is totally exhausted ; the paymaster has not a single dollar in hand ; the commissary general assures me that he has strained his credit for the subsistence of the army to the utmost ; the quarter-master general is in precisely the same situation ; and the greater part of the troops are in a state not far from mutiny, upon a deduction from their stated allowance. I know not to whom I am to impute this failure ; but I am of opinion that, if the evil is not immediately remedied, and more punctuality observed in future, the army must absolutely break up." Thus we perceive, that within three months after his appointment to the chief command, Washington had cause to complain of the tardy movements of the general Congress. Throughout the war, that body often pressed like a dead weight upon the movements of the army, embarrassing it by special instructions, and neglecting to give its co-operation when most needed. It was only during the time when Washington was invested with the powers of a military dictator, that his most brilliant military achievements were accomplished.

It was in September that the expedition to Quebec, under Arnold, by the way of the Kennebec, was planned. This important measure, and the progress and result of the expedition, have already been noticed on pages 190 to 194 inclusive.

Convinced of the inefficiency of Gage, and alarmed at the progress of the rebellion, the king summoned that officer to England to make a personal explanation of the state of affairs at Boston. Gage sailed on the 10th of October, leaving affairs in the hands of General Howe.[1] Before his departure, the Mandamus Council, a number of the prin-

1775

1775

---

[1] Thomas Gage, the last royal governor of Massachusetts, was a native of England, and was an active officer during the Seven Years' War. He was appointed Governor of Montreal in 1760, and, at the departure of Amherst from America, in 1763, was commissioned commander-in-chief of the British forces in America. He superseded Hutchinson as Governor of Massachusetts, and had the misfortune to enter upon the duties of his office at a time when it became necessary for him, as a faithful servant of his king, to execute laws framed expressly for the infliction of chastisement upon the people of the capital of the colony over which he was placed. From that date his public acts are interwoven with the history of the times. He possessed a naturally amiable disposition, and his benevolence often outweighed his justice in the scale of duty. Under other circumstances his name might have been sweet in the recollection of the Americans; now it is identified with oppression and hatred of freedom. He went to England in the autumn of 1775, where he died in April, 1787. Gage expected to return to America and resume the command of the army ; but ministers determined otherwise, and appointed General Howe in his place. The situation was offered to the veteran Oglethorpe, the founder of Georgia, but as he would not accept the commission unless he could go to the Americans with assurances from gov-

cipal inhabitants of Boston, and several who had taken refuge in the country, in all about seventy persons, addressed him in terms of loyal affection, amounting to panegyric. It was certainly unmerited; for his civil administration had been weak, and his military operations exceedingly inefficient. This was felt by all parties. His departure was popular with the army; and the provincials, remembering the spirit displayed by General Howe in the battle on Breed's Hill, anticipated a speedy collision. Howe was superior to Gage in every particular, and possessed more caution, which was generally founded upon logical deductions from fact. Governed by that caution, he was quite as unwilling as Gage to attack the Americans. He remembered the disparity in numbers on the 17th of June, and the bravery of the provincials while fighting behind breast-works cast up in a single night. He properly argued that an army of the same sort of men, fifteen thousand strong, intrenched behind breast-works constructed by the labor of weeks, was more than a match for even his disciplined troops of like number, and prudently resolved to await expected re-enforcements from Ireland before he should attempt to procure that "elbow-room" which he coveted.[1] In the mean while, he strengthened his defenses, and prepared to put his troops into comfortable winter quarters. He built a strong fort on Bunker Hill,[2] and employed six hundred men in making additional fortifications upon Boston Neck. In the neighborhood of the haymarket, at the south end of the city, many buildings were pulled down, and works erected in their places. Strong redoubts were raised upon the different eminences in Boston, and the old South meeting-house was stripped of its pews and converted into a riding-school for the disciplining of the cavalry.[3] This last act took place on the 19th of October, and the desecration greatly shocked the feelings of the religious community. On

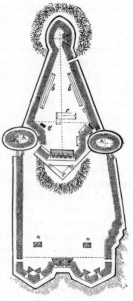

BRITISH FORT ON BUNKER HILL

October, 1775.   the 28th, Howe issued three proclamations, which created much indignation, and drew forth retaliatory

ernment that strict justice should be done them, the post was assigned to Howe. This was a tacit admission, on the part of ministers, that justice to the Americans formed no part of their scheme.

[1] It is said that both officers and soldiers regarded the Americans with a degree of superstitious fear, for many highly exaggerated tales of their power had been related. Dr. Thatcher says (Journal, p. 38) that, according to letters written by British officers from Boston, some of them, while walking on Beacon Hill in the evening, soon after the arrival of Gage, were frightened by noises in the air, which they took to be the whizzing of bullets. They left the hill with great precipitation, and reported that they were shot at with air-guns. The whizzing noise which so much alarmed these valiant officers was no other than the whizzing of bugs and beetles while flying in the air. Trumbull, in his M'Fingall, thus alludes to this ludicrous circumstance:

> "No more the British colonel runs
> From whizzing beetles as air-guns;
> Thinks horn-bugs bullets, or, through fears,
> Mosquitoes takes for musketeers;
> Nor 'scapes, as if you'd gain'd supplies
> From Beelzebub's whole host of flies.
> No bug these warlike hearts appals;
> They better know the sound of balls."

[2] This was a well-built redoubt. The parapet was from six to fifteen feet broad; the ditch from fourteen to eighteen feet wide, and the banquet about four feet broad. The galleries and parapet before them were raised about twenty feet high, and the merlons at the six-gun battery in the center were about twelve feet high. *a a*, two temporary magazines; *b b*, barracks; *c*, guard-houses; *d*, magazine; *e*, advanced ditch; *h h*, bastions.

[3] A Mr. Carter, quoted by Frothingham, writing on the 19th of October, says, "We are now erecting redoubts on the eminences on Boston Common; and a meeting-house, where sedition has been often preached, is clearing out to be made a riding-school for the light dragoons." Gordon says, "In clearing every thing away, a beautiful carved pew, with silk furniture, formerly belonging to a deceased gentleman [Dea-

measures from Washington. The first forbade all persons leaving the town without permission, under pain of military execution ; the second prohibited persons who were permitted to go from carrying with them more than twenty-five dollars in cash, under pain of forfeiture—one half of the amount to be paid to the informer ; and the third ordered all the inhabitants within the town to associate themselves into military companies. Washington retaliated by ordering General Sullivan, who was about departing for Portsmouth, New Hampshire, to seize all officers of government unfriendly to the patriots. Similar orders were sent to Governor Trumbull, of Connecticut, and Deputy-governor Cooke, of Rhode Island.

While Howe was thus engaged, Washington was not idle. A committee of Congress, consisting of Dr. Franklin, Thomas Lynch, and Benjamin Harrison (father of the late President Harrison), arrived at head-quarters on the 18th of October, to confer with the commander-in-chief respecting future operations. Deputy-governor Griswold and Judge Wales, of Connecticut ; Deputy-governor Cooke, of Rhode Island ; several members of the Massachusetts Council, and the President of the Provincial Congress of New Hampshire, were present at the conference, which lasted several days, and such a system of operations was matured as was satisfactory to General Washington.[1] A plan was agreed upon for an entirely new organization of the army, which provided for the enlistment of twenty-six regiments of eight companies each, besides riflemen and artillery. Already measures had been adopted to organize a navy. As early as June, Rhode Island had fitted out two armed vessels to protect the waters of that colony ; Connecticut, at about the same time, 1775. one or two armed vessels ; and, on the 26th of June, the Provincial Congress of Massachusetts resolved to provide six armed vessels. None of the latter had been got in readiness as late as the 12th of October, as appears by a letter from Washington to the President of the Continental Congress.

Having received no instructions from Congress on the subject, Washington took the responsibility, under his general delegated powers, of making preparations to annoy the enemy by water. Agents were appointed to superintend the construction of vessels, and to furnish supplies. Captain Broughton, of Marblehead, received a naval commission from Washington, dated September 2d, 1775, the first of the kind issued by the Continental Congress through its authorized agent. Before the close of October, six vessels of small size[2] had been

armed and manned, and sent to cruise within the capes of Massachusetts Bay. Two strong floating batteries were launched, armed, and manned in the Charles River ; and, on the 26th of October, they opened a fire upon Boston that produced great alarm and damaged several houses. The six schooners commissioned by Wash-

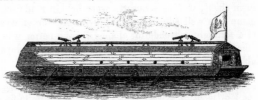

AMERICAN FLOATING BATTERY.[3]

con Hubbard] in high estimation, was taken down and carried to Mr. John Armory's house, by the order of an officer, who applied the carved work to the erection of a hog-stye."

[1] While Dr. Franklin was at head-quarters, the Provincial Congress of Massachusetts paid him the remaining moneys due him for services as agent for the colony in England, amounting to nine thousand two hundred and seventy dollars. Five hundred dollars had been sent to him from London as a charitable donation for the relief of the Americans wounded in the skirmishes at Lexington and Concord, and for the widows and orphans of those who were killed. This sum he paid over to the proper committee.

[2] The names of five of these vessels were Hannah, Harrison, Lee, Washington, and Lynch. The six commanders were Broughton, Selman, Manly, Martindale, Coit, and Adams.

[3] I am indebted to the kindness of Peter Force, Esq., of Washington city (editor of "The American Archives"), for this drawing of one of the American floating batteries used in the siege of Boston. It is copied from an English manuscript in his possession, and is now published for the first time. I have never met with a description of those batteries, and can judge of their construction only from the drawing. They appear to have been made of strong planks, pierced, near the water-line, for oars ; along the sides, higher up, for light and musketry. A heavy gun was placed in each end, and upon the top were four swivels. The

576   PICTORIAL FIELD-BOOK

Vessels of War authorized by Congress.   Letters of Marque and Reprisal.   Condition of the Army before Boston.

ington, and the floating batteries, sailed under the pine-tree flag. The Continental Congress
authorized two vessels to be fitted out and manned;[a] afterward two others, one
of twenty and one of thirty-six guns, were ordered.[b] On the 28th of November.
a code of naval regulations was adopted. On the 1st of February following (1776), the
navy, if so it might be properly called, was formed into a new establishment, being composed
of four vessels—the Hancock, Captain Manly; the Warner, Captain Burke; the Lynch,
Captain Ayres; and the Harrison, Captain Dyer. Captain Manly was the commodore of
the little fleet.[1] In November, the Massachusetts Provincial Congress issued letters of
marque and reprisal, and established courts of admiralty. Such was the embryo of the navy
of the United States. A more detailed account of the organization of the navy and its operations during the Revolution, will occupy a chapter in another portion of this work. I have
mentioned here only so much as related to operations connected with the siege of Boston.

The term of enlistment of many of the troops was now drawing to a close, and Washington felt great apprehensions for the result. Nearly six months had elapsed since the battle
of Bunker Hill, yet nothing had been done, decisively, to alter the relations in which the
belligerents stood toward each other. The people began to murmur, and the general Congress fretted. New enlistments were accomplished tardily, and in December not more than
five thousand recruits had joined the army. It became excessively weakened in numbers
and spirit, and as the cold increased, want of comfortable clothing and fuel became an almost
insupportable hardship. Many regiments were obliged to eat their provisions raw, for the
want of wood to cook them. Fences, and the fruit and shade trees for more than a mile
around the camp, were used for fuel. The various privations in the camp produced frequent
desertions. The Connecticut troops demanded a bounty, and being refused, resolved to leave
the camp in a body on the 6th of December. Measures were taken to prevent the movement, yet many went off and never returned. The commander-in-chief was filled with the
greatest anxiety. Still, he hopefully worked on in preparation for action, either offensive
or defensive. A strong detachment under Putnam broke ground at Cobble Hill (now
M'Lean Asylum); the works on Lechmere's Point were strengthened, and a call that was
made upon the New England militia to supply the places of the troops that left the army
in its hour of peril, was nobly responded to.

At the close of the year most of the regiments were full; and about ten thousand minute
men, chiefly in Massachusetts, were held in ready reserve to march when called upon. The
camp was well supplied with provisions;[2] order was generally observed, and in the course
of a fortnight a wonderful change for the better was wrought. The ladies of several of the
officers arrived in camp; and the Christmas holidays were spent at Cambridge quite agreeably, for hope gave joy to the occasion.[3]

[a] October 13, 1775.
[b] October 30.

---

ensign was the pine-tree flag, according to Colonel Reed, who, in a letter from Cambridge to Colonels Glover
and Moylan, dated October 20th, 1775, said, "Please to fix some particular color for a flag, and a signal
by which our vessels may know one another. What do you think of a flag with a white ground, a tree in
the middle, the motto 'Appeal to Heaven?' This is the flag of our floating batteries."

[1] Sparks's *Life and Writings of Washington*, iii., 516.

[2] The rations for the soldiers were as follows: corned beef and pork four days in the week, salt fish one
day, and fresh beef two days. Each man had a pound and a half of beef, or eighteen ounces of pork a day;
one quart of strong beer, or nine gallons of molasses, to one hundred men per week; six pounds of candles
to one hundred men per week; six ounces of butter, or nine ounces of hogs' lard per week; three pints of
beans or pease, per man, a week, or vegetables equivalent; one pound of flour per day, and hard bread to
be dealt out one day in the week.

[3] Mrs. Washington arrived on the 11th of December, accompanied by her son, John Parke Custis, and his
wife. Some persons thought her in danger at Mount Vernon, as Lord Dunmore was making the most determined hostile movements against republicanism in Virginia. It was feared that he might attempt to
seize the person of Lady Washington, to be held as a hostage. As the commander-in-chief could not leave
the army, she was requested to pass the winter with him at Cambridge. The expenses incurred by the
occasional visits of Mrs. Washington to the camp during the war were charged to the government. Washington was careful to call attention to this fact, and in the rendition of his accounts for settlement he refers
to it, and expresses a hope that the charges will be considered right, inasmuch as he had not visited his
home during his time of service, a privilege which he was allowed by the terms of his appointment.

OF THE REVOLUTION. 577

First unfurling of the Union flag.   Return of Colonel Knox, with heavy artillery.

CHAPTER XXV.

" When Freedom, from her mountain height,
    Unfurl'd her standard to the air,
She tore the azure robe of night,
    And set the stars of glory there.
She mingled with its gorgeous dyes
The milky baldric of the skies,
And striped its pure celestial white
With streakings of the morning light;
Then from his mansion in the sun
She call'd her eagle-bearer down,
And gave into his mighty hand
The symbol of her chosen land."

               JOSEPH RODMAN DRAKE.

N the first of January, 1776, the new Continental army was organized, and on that day the UNION FLAG OF THIRTEEN STRIPES was unfurled, for the first time, in the American camp at Cambridge. On that day the king s speech (of which I shall presently write) was received in Boston, and copies of it were sent, by a flag, to Washington. The hoisting of the Union ensign was hailed by Howe as a token of joy on the receipt of the gracious speech, and of submission to the crown.[1] This was a great mistake, for at no time had Washington been more determined to attack the king's troops, and to teach oppressors the solemn lesson that " Resistance to tyranny is obedience to God."

After the arrival of Colonel Knox with military stores from the north, whither he had been sent in November, the commander-in-chief resolved to attack the enemy, either by a general assault, or by bombardment and cannonade, notwithstanding the British force was then nearly equal to his in numbers, and greatly superior in experience. Knox brought with him from Fort George, on forty-two sleds, eight brass mortars, six iron mortars, two iron howitzers, thirteen brass cannons, twenty-six iron cannons, two thousand three hundred pounds of lead, and one

[1] Washington, in a letter to Joseph Reed, written on the 4th of January, 1776, said, " The speech I send you. A volume of them was sent out by the Boston gentry, and, farcical enough, we gave great joy to them without knowing or intending it; for on that day, the day which gave being to the new army, but before the proclamation came to hand, we had hoisted the *Union flag*, in compliment to the United Colonies.

* This flag bore the device of the English *Union*, which distinguishes the Royal Standard of Great Britain. It is composed of the cross of St. George, to denote England, and St. Andrew's cross, in the form of an X, to denote Scotland. This device was placed in the corner of the Royal Flag, after the accession of James the Sixth of Scotland to the throne of England as James the First. A picture of this device may be seen on page 321, Vol. II. It must be remembered that at this time the American Congress had not declared the colonies "free and independent" states, and that even yet the Americans proffered their warmest loyalty to British justice, when it should redress their grievances. The British ensign was therefore not yet discarded, but it was used upon their flags, as in this instance, with the field composed of thirteen stripes, alternate red and white, as emblematic of the union of the thirteen colonies in the struggle for freedom. Ten months before, "a Union flag with a red field" was hoisted at New York, upon the Liberty-pole on the "Common," bearing the inscription—"George Rex, and the Liberties of America," and upon the other side, " No Popery." It was this British *Union*, on the American flag, which caused the misapprehension of the British in Boston, alluded to by Washington. It was a year and a half later (and a year after the colonies were declared to be independent states), that, by official orders, "thirteen white stars upon a blue field" was a device substituted for the British *Union*, and then the " stripes and stars" became our national banner.

barrel of flints.   In the harbor of Boston the enemy had several vessels of war,[1] and upon Bunker Hill his works were very strong.

Washington's plan depended, in its execution, upon the weather, as it was intended to pass the troops over to Boston, from Cambridge, on the ice, if it became strong enough. The Neck was too narrow and too well fortified to allow him to hope for a successful effort to enter the town by that way.   The assault was to be made by the Americans in two divisions, under Brigadiers Sullivan and Greene, the whole to be commanded by Major-general Putnam.   Circumstances prevented the execution of the plan, and January passed by without any decisive movement on the part of either army.   The American forces, however, were daily augmenting, and they were less annoyed by the British cannon than they had been, for Howe was more sparing of powder than Gage.[2]

The Provincial Congress of Massachusetts, at its winter session, organized the militia of the province anew.   John Hancock, James Warren, and Azor Orne were appointed major generals, and thirteen regiments were formed.   A new emission of paper money, to a large amount, was authorized, and various measures were adopted to strengthen the Continental army.   Early in February, ten of the militia regiments arrived in camp ; large supplies of ammunition had been received ; intense cold had bridged the waters with ice, and Washington was disposed to commence operations immediately and vigorously.   He called a council February, 1776. of war on the 16th, to whom he communicated the intelligence, derived from careful returns, that the American army, including the militia, then amounted to a little more than seventeen thousand men, while that of the British did not much exceed five thousand fit for duty.   Many of them were sick with various diseases, and the small-pox was making terrible havoc in the enemy's camp.[3]   Re-enforcements from Ireland, Halifax, and New York were daily expected by Howe, and the present appeared to be the proper moment to strike.   But the council again decided against attempting an assault, on account of the supposed inadequacy of the undisciplined Americans for the task.   They estimated the British forces at a much higher figure ; considered the fact that they were double officered and possessed ample artillery, and that the ships in the harbor would do great execution upon an army on the ice, exposed to an enfilading fire.   It was resolved, however, to bombard and cannonade the town as soon as a supply of ammunition should arrive, and that, in the mean time, Dorchester Heights and Noddle's Island (now East Boston) should be taken possession of and fortified.   The commander-in-chief was disappointed at this decision, for he felt confident of success himself.   "I can not help acknowledging," he said, in a letter February 18, 1776. to Congress, "that I have many disagreeable sensations on account of my situation ; for, to have the eyes of the whole Continent fixed with anxious expectation of hearing of some great event, and to be restrained in every military operation for the want of the necessary means for carrying it on, is not very pleasing, especially as the means

---

But behold ! it was received in Boston as a token of the deep impression the speech had made upon us, and as a signal of submission.   So we hear by a person out of Boston last night.   By this time, I presume, they begin to think it strange that we have not made a formal surrender of our lines."   The principal flag hitherto used by the army was plain crimson.   Referring to the reception of the king's speech, the Annual Register (1776) says, "So great was the rage and indignation [of the Americans], that they burned the speech, changed their colors from a plain red ground which they had hitherto used, to a flag with thirteen stripes, as a symbol of the number and union of the colonies."   The blue field in one corner, with thirteen stars, was soon afterward adopted ; and by a resolution of the Continental Congress, already referred to, passed on the 14th of June, 1777,[*] this was made the national flag of the United States.

[1] The Boyne, sixty-four guns ; Preston, fifty guns ; Scarborough, and another sloop, one of twenty and the other of sixteen guns, and the Mercury.

[2] From the burning of Charlestown to Christmas day, the enemy had fired more than two thousand shot and shells, one half of the former being twenty-four pounders.   They hurled more than three hundred bombs at Plowed Hill, and one hundred at Lechmere's Point.   By the whole firing on the Cambridge side they killed only seven men, and on the Roxbury side just a dozen !—Gordon, i., 418.

[3] Quite a number of people, sick with this loathsome disease, were sent out of Boston ; and General Howe was charged with the wicked design of attempting thus to infect the American army with the malady.

used to conceal my weakness from the enemy conceal it also from our friends, and add to their wonder." In the midst of these discouragements Washington prepared for a bombardment. The British troops in Boston were beginning to be quite contented with their lot, and Howe felt almost as secure as if he was on the shores of Old England. He wrote to Dartmouth that he was under no apprehension of an attack from the rebels; and so confident were the Tories of the triumph of British arms, that Crean Brush, a conceited and sycophantic Loyalist from New York, offered to raise a body of volunteers of three hundred men, to " occupy the main posts on the Connecticut River, and open a line of communication westward toward Lake Champlain," after " the subduction of the main body of the rebel force."[1]   The enemy had also procured a plentiful supply of provisions, and the winter, up to the 1st of February, was tolerably mild. " The bay is open," wrote Colonel Moylan, from Roxbury. " Every thing thaws here except Old Put. He is still as hard as ever, crying out, ' Powder! powder! ye gods, give me powder!'"   The British officers established a theater; balls were held, and a subscription had been opened for a masquerade, when Washington's operations suddenly dispelled their dream of security, and called them to lay aside the " sock and buskin," the domino, and the dancing-slipper, for the habiliments of real war. They had got up a farce called " Boston Blockaded;"[2] they were now called to perform in the serio-comic drama of Boston bombarded, with appropriate costume and scenery.

The design of Washington to fortify Dorchester Heights was kept a profound secret, and, to divert the attention of Howe, the Americans opened a severe bombardment and cannonade, on the night of the 2d of March, from the several batteries at Lechmere's Point, Roxbury, Cobble and Plowed Hills, and Lamb's Dam. Several houses in the city were shattered, and six British soldiers killed. The fire was returned with spirit, but without serious effect. In the course of the bombardment, the Americans burst the " Congress' thirteen inch mortar, another of the same size, and three ten inch mortars.

On Sunday and Monday nights a similar cannonade was opened upon the city. At seven o'clock on Monday evening, General Thomas, with two thousand men, and intrenching tools, proceeded to take possession of Dorchester Heights. A train of three hundred carts, laden with fascines and hay, followed the troops. Within an hour, marching in perfect silence, the detachment reached the heights. It was separated into two divisions, and upon the two eminences already mentioned they commenced throwing up breastworks. Bundles of hay were placed on the town side of Dorchester Neck to break the rumble of the carts passing to and fro, and as a defense against the guns of the enemy, if they should be brought to bear upon the troops passing the Neck. Notwithstanding the moon was shining brightly and the air was serene, the laborers were not observed by the British sentinels. Under the direction of the veteran Gridley, the engineer at Bunker Hill, they worked wisely and well. Never was more work done in so short a time, and at dawn two forts were raised sufficiently high to afford ample protection for the forces within. They presented a formidable aspect to the alarmed Britons. Howe, overwhelmed with astonishment, exclaimed, " I know not what I shall do. The rebels have done more in one night than my whole army would have done in a month." They had done more than merely raise embankments; cannons were placed upon them, and they now completely commanded the town, placing Britons and Tories in the utmost peril.

January 10, 1776.

1776.

March 3, 4, 1776.

[1] Frothingham; from manuscripts in the office of the Secretary of State of Massachusetts.

[2] This play was a burletta. The figure designed to represent Washington enters with uncouth gait, wearing a large wig, a long, rusty sword, and attended by a country servant with a rusty gun. While this farce was in course of performance on the evening of the 8th of January (1776), a sergeant entered suddenly, and exclaimed, " The Yankees are attacking our works on Bunker Hill!" The audience thought this was part of the play, and laughed immoderately at the idea; but they were soon undeceived by the voice of the burly Howe shouting, " Officers, to your alarm-posts!" The people dispersed in great confusion. The cause of the fright was the fact that Majors Knowlton, Carey, and Henly had crossed the milldam from Cobble Hill, and set fire to some houses in Charlestown occupied by British soldiers. They burned eight dwellings, killed one man, and brought off five prisoners.

The morning on which these fortresses were revealed to the enemy was the memorable 5th of March, the anniversary of the *Boston Massacre*.[1] The associations connected with the day nerved the Americans to more vigorous action, and they determined to celebrate and signalize the time by an act of retributive vengeance. Howe saw and felt his danger ; and his anxiety was augmented when Admiral Shuldham assured him that the British fleet in the harbor must be inevitably destroyed when the Americans should get their heavy guns and mortars upon the heights. Nor was the army in the city secure. It was therefore re-solved to take immediate measures to dislodge the provincials. Accordingly, two thousand four hundred men were ordered to embark in transports, rendezvous at Castle William, and, under the gallant Earl Percy, make an attack that night upon the rebel works.[2] Wash-ington was made acquainted with this movement, and, supposing the attack was to be made immediately, sent a re-enforcement of two thousand men to General Thomas. Labor con-stantly plied its hands in strengthening the works. As the hills on which the redoubts were reared were very steep, rows of barrels, filled with loose earth, were placed outside the breast-works, to be rolled down upon the attacking column so as to break their ranks ; a measure said to have been suggested by Mifflin. All was now in readiness. It was a mild, sunny day. The neighboring heights were crowded with people, expecting to see the bloody trag-edy of Breed's Hill acted again. Washington himself repaired to the intrenchments, and encouraged the men by reminding them that it was the 5th of March. The commander-in-chief and the troops were in high spirits, for they believed the long-coveted conflict and victory to be near.

While these preparations were in progress on Dorchester Heights, four thousand troops, in two divisions, under Generals Sullivan and Greene, were parading at Cambridge, ready to be led by Putnam to an attack on Boston when Thomas's batteries should give the signal. They were to embark in boats in the Charles River, now clear of ice, under cover of three floating batteries, and, assaulting the city at two prominent points, to force their way to the works on the Neck, open the gates, and let in the troops from Roxbury.

Both parties were ready for action in the afternoon ; but a furious wind that had arisen billowed the harbor, and rolled such a heavy surf upon the shore where the boats of the en-emy were obliged to land, that it was unsafe to venture. During the night the rain came down in torrents, and a terrible storm raged all the next day. Howe abandoned his plan, and Washington, greatly disappointed, returned to his camp, leaving a strong force to guard the works on Dorchester Heights.

The situation of Howe was now exceedingly critical. The fleet and army were in peril, and the loyal inhabitants, greatly terrified, demanded that sure protection which Howe had March, so often confidently promised. . He called a council of officers on the 7th, when it 1776. was resolved to save the army by evacuating the town. This resolution spread great consternation among the Tories in the city, for they dreaded the just indignation of the patriots when they should return. They saw the power on which they had leaned as almost invincible growing weak, and quailing before those whom it had affected to despise. They well knew that severe retribution for miseries which they had been instrumental in inflict-ing, surely awaited them, when British bayonets should leave the peninsula and the excited patriots should return to their desolated homes. The dangers of a perilous voyage to a strange land seemed far less fearful than the indignation of the oppressed Americans, and the Loyalists resolved to brave the former rather than the latter. They began, therefore to prepare for a speedy departure ; merchandise, household furniture, and private property of every kind were crowded on board the ships. Howe had been advised by Dartmouth, in

[1] The day, usually observed in Boston, was now commemorated at Watertown, notwithstanding the ex-citing events occurring in the city and vicinity. The Reverend Peter Thacher delivered an oration on the occasion.—*Bradford*, 94.

[2] Three weeks previously, suspecting that the Americans were about to take possession of Dorchester Neck, Howe sent a detachment from Castle William, under Lieutenant-colonel Leslie, and some grenadiers and light infantry, under Major Musgrove, to destroy every house and other cover on the peninsula. They passed over on the ice, executed their orders, and took six of the American guard prisoners.

November, to evacuate Boston, but excused himself by pleading that the shipping was inadequate.   He was now obliged to leave with less, and, in addition to his troops, take with him more than one thousand refugee Loyalists, and their effects.   Ammunition and warlike magazines of all kinds were hurried on board the vessels; heavy artillery, that could not be carried away, was dismounted, spiked, or thrown into the sea, and some of the fortifications were demolished.   The number of ships and transports was about one hundred and fifty; but these were insufficient for the conveyance of the multitude of troops and inhabitants, their most valuable property, and the quantity of military stores to be carried away.[1]

The few patriots who remained in Boston now felt great anxiety for the fate of the town.   They saw the preparations for departure, and were persuaded that the enemy, smarting under the goadings of disappointed pride and ambition, would perform some signal act of vengeance before leaving—probably set fire to the city.[2]   Actuated by these surmises (which were confirmed by the threat of Howe that he would destroy the town if his army was molested in departing), and by the fearful array of ships which the admiral had arranged around the city, a delegation of the most influential citizens communicated with the British commander, through General Robertson.   The conference resulted in a promise, on the part of Howe, that, if Washington would allow him to evacuate quietly, the town should be spared.   A communication to this effect, signed by four leading men—John Scollay, Timothy Newell, Thomas Marshall, and Samuel Austin—was sent to the camp at Roxbury without any special address.   It was received by Colonel Learned, who carried it to Washington.   The commander-in-chief observed, that as it was an unauthenticated paper, without an address, and not obligatory upon General Howe, he would take no notice of it.   Learned communicated this answer to the persons through whom the address from Boston was received.   Although entirely non-committal, it was received as a favorable answer, and both parties tacitly consented to the arrangement.

Washington, however, did not relax his vigilance, and continued his preparations for an assault upon Boston if the enemy did not speedily leave.   A battery was placed near the water on Dorchester Neck on the 9th, to annoy the British shipping.   On the same night a detachment marched to Nooks' Hill, a point near the city completely commanding it, and planted a battery there.   A fire imprudently kindled revealed their labor in progress to the enemy.   A severe cannonade was immediately opened upon the patriots from the British batteries in the city.   This was a signal for a general discharge of cannons and mortars from the various American batteries, and until dawn there was a continual roar of heavy guns.   More than eight hundred shot were fired during the night.   It was a fearful hour for the people of Boston, and all the bright anticipations of a speedy termination of the dreadful suspense in which for months they had lingered were clouded.   But the belligerents were willing to avoid bloodshed   Washington determined to have possession of Boston at all events, but preferred to take it peaceably; while Howe, too cautious to risk a general action, and desirous of employing his forces in some quarter of the colonies where better success might be promised, withheld his cannonade in the morning, and hastened his preparations for evacuation. *(March, 1776.)*

And now a scene of great confusion ensued.   Those who were about to leave and could not carry their furniture with them, destroyed it; the soldiers broke open and pillaged many stores; and Howe issued an order to Crean Brush,[3] who had fawned at his feet ever since the siege began, to seize all clothing and dry goods not in possession of Loyalists, and place

---

[1] General Howe's official account.

[2] Congress gave Washington instructions in the Autumn to destroy Boston if it should be necessary to do so in order to dislodge the enemy.   This instruction was given with the full sanction of many patriots who owned much property in the city.   John Hancock, who was probably the largest property holder in Boston, wrote to Washington, that, notwithstanding such a measure would injure him greatly, he was anxious the thing should be done, if it would benefit the cause.   Never were men more devoted than those who would be the greatest sufferers.

[3] This order, which is dated March 10th, 1776, is in the office of the Secretary of State of Massachusetts, and bears Howe's autograph.—*Frothingham.*

them on board two brigantines in the harbor. This authorized plunder caused great distress, for many of the inhabitants were completely stripped. Shops and dwellings were broken open and plundered, and what goods could not be carried away were wantonly destroyed. March 12. These extremes were forbidden in general order the next day, but the prohibition was little regarded.

On the 15th, the troops paraded to march to the vessels, the inhabitants being ordered to remain in their houses until the army had embarked. An easterly breeze sprang up, and the troops were detained until Sunday, the 17th. In the mean while, they did much mischief by destroying and defacing furniture, and throwing valuable goods into the river. They acted more like demons than men, and had they not been governed by officers possessed of some prudence and honor, and controlled by a fear of the Americans, the town would doubtless have suffered all the horrors of sack and pillage.

Early on Sunday morning, the embarkation of the British army and of the Loyalists commenced. The garrison on Bunker Hill left it at about nine o'clock. Washington observed these movements, and the troops in Cambridge immediately paraded. Putnam with six regiments embarked in boats on the Charles River, and landed at Sewall's Point. The sentinels on Bunker Hill appeared to be at their posts, but, on approaching, they were observed to be nothing but effigies ; not a living creature was within the British works. With a loud shout, that startled the retreating Britons, the Americans entered and took possession. When this was effected, the British and Tories had all left Boston, and the fleet that was to convey them away was anchored in Nantasket Roads, where it remained ten days.[1] A detachment of Americans entered the city, and took possession of the works and the military stores that were left behind.[2] The gates on Boston Neck were unbarred, and General Ward, with five thousand of the troops at Roxbury, entered in triumph, Ensign Richards bearing the Union flag. General Putnam assumed the command of the whole, and in the name of the *Thirteen United Colonies* took possession of all the forts and other defenses which the a March 18, retreating Britons had left behind.[a] On the 20th, the main body of the army, 1776. with Washington at the head, entered the city, amid the joyous greetings of hundreds, who for ten months had suffered almost every conceivable privation and insult. Their friends from the country flocked in by hundreds, and joyful was the reunion of many families that had been separated more than half a year. On the 28th, a thanksgiving sermon was preached by the Reverend Dr. Elliot, from the words of Isaiah, "Look upon Zion, the city of our solemnities : thine eye shall see Jerusalem a quiet habitation, a tabernacle that shall not be taken down : not one of the stakes thereof shall be removed, neither shall any of the cords thereof be broken."[3] It was a discourse full of hope for the future, and con-

---

[1] The whole effective British force that withdrew, including seamen, was about eleven thousand. The Loyalists, classed as follows, were more than one thousand in number : 132 who had held official stations , 18 clergymen; 105 persons from the country ; 213 merchants ; 382 farmers, traders, and mechanics : total 924. These returned their names on their arrival at Halifax, whither the fleet sailed. There were nearly two hundred more whose names were not registered. It was a sorrowful flight to most of them ; for men of property left all behind, and almost every one relied for daily food upon rations from the army stores. The troops, in general, were glad to depart. Frothingham (page 312) quotes from a letter written by a British officer while lying in the harbor. It is a fair exhibition of the feelings of the troops : "Expect no more letters from Boston ; we have quitted that place. Washington played upon the town for several days. A shell which burst while we were preparing to embark did very great damage. Our men have suffered. We have one consolation left. You know the proverbial expression, 'Neither Hell, Hull, nor Halifax can afford worse shelter than Boston.' To fresh provision I have for many months been quite an utter stranger. An egg was a rarity. The next letter from Halifax."

[2] So crowded were the vessels with the Loyalists and their effects that Howe was obliged to leave some of his magazines. The principal articles which were left at Castle Island and Boston were 250 pieces of cannon, great and small; four thirteen and a half inch mortars ; 2500 chaldrons of sea coal ; 2500 bushels of wheat ; 2300 bushels of barley ; 600 bushels of oats ; 100 jars of oil, containing a barrel each, and 150 horses. Some of the ordnance had been thrown into the water, but were recovered by the Americans. In the hospital at Boston a large quantity of medicine was left, in which it was discovered that white and yellow arsenic was mixed ! The object can be easily guessed.—*Gordon*, ii., 32.

[3] Isaiah, xxxiii., 20.

firmed the strong faith of the hundreds of listeners in the final triumph of liberty in America.

Sadness settled upon the minds of the people when the first outburst of joyous feeling had subsided, for Boston, the beautiful city—the metropolis of New England—was a desolation. Many of the finest houses were greatly injured ; shade-trees were cut down ; churches were disfigured ; ornamental inclosures were broken or destroyed ; and the public buildings were shamefully defaced. The spacious old South meeting-house, as we have seen, was changed into a riding-school ; and in the stove that was put up within the arena were burned, for kindling, many rare books and manuscripts of Prince's fine library. The parsonage house belonging to this society was pulled down for fuel. The old North Chapel was demolished for the same purpose, and the large wooden steeple of the West Church was converted to the same use. Liberty Tree, noticed on page 466, vol. i., furnished fourteen cords of wood. Brattle Street and Hollis Street churches were used for barracks, and Faneuil Hall was converted into a neat theater.[1] A shot from the American lines, which struck the tower of Brattle Street Church, was picked up, and subsequently fastened at the point where it first struck, and there it remains.

Ignorant of the destination of Howe, and supposing it to be New York, Washington sent off five regiments, and a portion of the artillery, under General Heath, for that city. They marched to New London, where they embarked, and proceeded to New York through the Sound. On the departure of the main body of the British fleet from Nantasket Roads, Washington ordered the remainder of the army to New York, except five regiments, which were left for the protection of Boston, under General Ward. Sullivan marched on the 27th ; another brigade departed on the 1st of April ; and the last brigade, under Spencer, marched on the 4th. Washington, also, left Cambridge for New York on that day. March 18, 1776. April 4.

A portion of the British fleet, consisting of five vessels, still lingered in the harbor, and was subsequently joined by seven transports, filled with Highlanders. The people of Boston were under great apprehension of Howe's return. All classes of people assisted in building a fortification on Noddles Island (now East Boston) and in strengthening the other defenses. These operations were carried on under the general direction of Colonel Gridley. In May, Captain Mugford, of the schooner Franklin, a Continental cruiser, captured the British ship Hope, bound for Boston, with stores, and fifteen hundred barrels of powder. On the 19th, the Franklin and Lady Washington started on a cruise, but got aground at Point Shirly. Thirteen armed boats from the British vessels attacked them, and a sharp engagement ensued. Captain Mugford, while fighting bravely, received a mortal wound. His last words were those used nearly forty years afterward by Lawrence, " Don't give up the ship! You will beat them off !" And so they did. The cruisers escaped, and put to sea. May 17.

In June, General Lincoln proposed a plan for driving the British fleet from the harbor. It was sanctioned by the Massachusetts Assembly, and was put in execution on the 14th. He summoned the neighboring militia, and, aided by some of General Ward's regular troops, took post on Moon Island, Hoff's Neck, and at Point Anderton. A large force also collected at Pettick's Island, and Hull ; and a detachment with two eighteen pounders and a thirteen inch mortar took post on Long Island. Shots were first discharged at the enemy from the latter point. The fire was briskly returned ; but the commander, Commodore Banks, perceiving the perilous situation of his little fleet, made signals for weighing anchor. After blowing up the light-house, he spread his sails and went to sea, leaving Boston harbor and vicinity entirely free from an enemy, except in the few dissimulating Tories who lurked in secret places. Through a reprehensible want of foresight, no British cruisers were left in the vicinity to warn British ships of the departure of the troops and fleet. The consequence was, that several store-ships from England soon afterward arrived, and, sailing into the harbor

---

[1] Frothingham, page 328.

584   PICTORIAL FIELD-BOOK

Capture of Campbell and Store-ships.   Effect of the Evacuation of Boston.   Medal awarded to Washington

without suspicion, fell into the hands of the Americans. In this way, Lieutenant-colonel Campbell and seven hundred men were made prisoners in June.

The evacuation of Boston diffused great joy throughout the colonies, and congratulatory addresses were received by Washington and his officers from various legislative bodies, assemblages of citizens, and individuals. The Continental Congress received intelligence of the evacuation, by express, on the 25th of March, and immediately, on motion of John Adams, passed a vote of thanks to the commander-in-chief and the soldiers under his command, and also ordered a gold medal to be struck and presented to the general. John Adams, John Jay, and Stephen Hopkins were appointed a committee to prepare a letter of thanks and a proper device for the medal.[1]

The intelligence of this and other events at Boston within the preceding ten months produced great excitement in England, and attracted the attention of all Europe. The British Parliament exhibited violent agitations, and party lines began to be drawn almost as definitely among the English people, on American affairs, as in the colonies. In the spring, strong measures had been proposed, and some were adopted, for putting down the rebellion, and these had been met by counter action on the part of the American Congress.[2] During the summer, John Wilkes, then Lord Mayor of London, and his party, raised a storm of indignation against government in the English capital. He presented a violent address to the king in the name of the livery of London,

GOLD MEDAL AWARDED TO WASHINGTON.[3]

---

[1] Journals of Congress, ii., 104.

[2] Congress issued a proclamation, declaring that "whatever punishment shall be inflicted upon any persons in the power of their enemies for favoring, aiding, or abetting the cause of American liberty, shall be retaliated in the same kind, and in the same degree, upon those in their power, who had favored, aided, or abetted, or shall favor, aid, or abet the system of ministerial oppression." This made the Tories and the British officers cautious in their proceedings toward patriots in their power.

[3] This drawing is the size of the medal. It was struck in Paris, from a die cut by Duvivier. The device is a head of Washington, in profile, with the Latin legend "GEORGIO WASHINGTON, SUPREMO DUCI EXERCITUUM ADSERTORI LIBERTATIS COMITIA AMERICANA;" "The American Congress to George Washington, commander-in-chief of its armies, the assertors of freedom." Reverse: troops advancing toward a town; others marching toward the water; ships in view; General Washington in front, and mounted, with his staff, whose attention he is directing to the embarking enemy. The legend is "HOSTIBUS PRIMO FUGATIS;"

in which it was asserted that it was plainly to be perceived that government intended to establish arbitrary rule in America without the sanction of the British Constitution, and that they were also determined to uproot the Constitution at home, and to establish despotism upon the ruins of English freedom. The address concluded by calling for an instant dismissal of the ministers. The king was greatly irritated, and refused to receive the address, unless presented in the corporate capacity of " mayor, aldermen, livery," &c. This refusal Wilkes denounced as a denial of the right of the city to petition the throne in any respectful manner it pleased ; " a right," he said, " which had been respected even by the accursed race of Stuarts." Another address, embodying a remonstrance and petition, was prepared, and inquiry was made of the king whether he would receive it while sitting on the throne, it being addressed by the city in its corporate capacity. The king replied that he would receive it at his next levee, but not on the throne. One of the sheriffs sent by Wilkes to ask the question of his majesty, assured the king that the address would not be presented except when he was sitting upon the throne. The king replied that it was his prerogative to choose *where* he would receive communications from his subjects. The livery of London declared this answer to be a denial of their rights, resolved that the address and remonstrance should be printed in the newspapers, and that the city members in the House of Commons should be instructed to move for " an impeachment of the evil counselors who had planted popery and arbitrary power in America, and were the advisers of a measure so dangerous to his majesty and to his people as that of refusing to hear petitions."[1] The common council adopted a somewhat more moderate address and remonstrance, which the king received, but whether sitting upon the throne or at his levee is not recorded.[2]

On the 23d of August, the government, informed of the events of the 17th of June at Charlestown, issued a proclamation for suppressing rebellion, preventing seditious correspondences, et cetera. Wilkes, as lord mayor, received orders to have this proclamation read in the usual manner at the Royal Exchange. He refused full obedience, by causing it to be read by an inferior officer, attended only by a common crier ; disallowing the officers the use of horses, and prohibiting the city mace to be carried before them. The vast assembly that gathered to hear the reading replied with a hiss of scorn.

1775.

A few days afterward the respectful petition of the Continental Congress was laid before the king by Richard Penn. Earl Dartmouth soon informed Penn that the king had resolved to take no notice of it; and again the public mind was greatly agitated, particularly in London, at what was denominated " another blow at British liberty." The strict silence of ministers on the subject of this petition gave color to the charge that they had a line of policy marked out, from which *no action* of the Americans could induce them to deviate short of absolute submission. The Duke of Richmond determined to have this silence broken, and procured an examination of Governor Penn before the House of Lords. That examination brought to light many facts relative to the strength and union of the colonies which ministers would gladly have concealed. It revealed the truth that implicit obedience

---

" The enemy for the first time put to flight." The exergue under the device—" Bostonium recuperatum XVII MARTII MDCCLXXVI;" "Boston recovered, 17th March, 1776."

[1] Pictorial History of England, v., 235.

[2] It was about this time that the celebrated John Horne Tooke, a vigorous writer and active politician, was involved in a proceeding which, in November, 1775, caused him to receive a sentence of imprisonment for one year, pay a fine of one thousand dollars, and find security for his good behavior for three years. His alleged crime was " a libel upon the king's troops in America." The libel was contained in an advertisement, signed by him, from the Constitutional Society (supposed to be revolutionary in its character), respecting the Americans. That society called the Lexington affair a " *murder*," and agreed that the sum of five hundred dollars should be raised " to be applied to the relief of the widows, orphans, and aged parents of our beloved American fellow-subjects" who had preferred death to slavery. This was a set-off against subscriptions then being raised in England for the widows and orphans of the British soldiers who had perished. The sum raised by this society was sent to Dr. Franklin, who, as we have seen, paid it over to the proper committee, when he visited the army at Cambridge, in October, under the direction of Congress. Out of the circumstance of Horne Tooke's imprisonment arose his letter to Counselor Dunning, which formed the basis of his subsequent philological work, *The Diversions of Purley*, published in 1780.

to Congress was paid by all classes of men ; that in Pennsylvania alone there were twenty thousand effective men enrolled for military service, and four thousand minute men ; that the Pennsylvanians perfectly understood the art of making gunpowder ; that the art of casting cannon had been carried to great perfection in the colonies ; that small arms were also manufactured in the best manner ;[1] that the language of Congress was the voice of the people ; that the people considered the petition as an olive branch ; and that so much did the Americans rely upon its effect, that if rejected, or treated with scorn, they would abandon all hope of a reconciliation.

On the 11th of October an address, memorial, and petition, signed by eleven hundred and seventy-one "gentlemen, merchants, and traders of London," was laid before his majesty, in which it was charged that all the troubles in America, and consequent injury to trade, arose from the bad policy pursued by Parliament ; and the new proposition which had just leaked out, to employ foreign soldiers against the Americans, was denounced in unmeasured terms. A counter petition, signed by nine hundred and twenty citizens of London, was presented three days afterward, in which the conduct of the colonists was severely censured. This was followed by another on the same side, signed by ten hundred and twenty-nine persons, including *the livery of London*, who, a few months previously, under Wilkes, had spoken out so boldly against government. This address glowed with loyalty to the king and indignation against the *rebels !* Like petitions from the provincial towns, procured by ministerial agency, came in great numbers, and the government, feeling strengthened at home, contemplated the adoption of more stringent measures to be pursued in America. Suspected per-

sons in England were closely watched, and several were arraigned to answer various charges against them.[2] Lord North became the idol of the government party, and, in addition to being *fêted* by the nobility, and thoroughly bespattered with fulsome adulation by corporate bodies and the ministerial press, the University of Oxford had a medal struck in his honor.

MEDAL STRUCK IN HONOR OF LORD NORTH.

1775.   Parliament assembled on the 26th of October, much earlier than common, on account of the prevalent disorders. The king, in his speech at the opening,[3] after mentioning the rebellious position of the American colonies, expressed (as he had done before) his determination to act decisively. He alleged that the course of government hitherto had been moderate and forbearing ! but now, as the rebellion seemed to be general, and the ob-

---

[1] I have in my possession a musket manufactured here in 1774, that date being engraved upon the breech. It is quite perfect in its construction. It was found on the battle field of Hubbardton, in Vermont, and was in the possession of the son of an American officer (Captain Barber) who was in that action. See page 146, of this volume.

[2] On the 23d of October (1775), Stephen Sayre, a London banker, an American by birth, was arrested on a charge of high treason, made against him by a sergeant in the Guard (also a native of America), named Richardson. He charged Sayre with having asserted that he and others intended to seize the king on his way to Parliament, to take possession of the town, and to overturn the present government. Sayre was known to be a friend to the patriots, and on this charge Lord Rochford, one of the secretaries of state, caused his papers to be seized and himself to be arrested. Sayre was committed to the Tower, from which he was released by Lord Mansfield, who granted a writ of habeas corpus. Sayre was subsequently tried and acquitted. He prosecuted Lord Rochford for seizing his papers, and the court awarded him a conditional verdict of five thousand dollars damages. The conditions proved a bar to the recovery of the money, and Sayre was obliged to suffer a heavy pecuniary loss in costs, besides the personal indignity.

[3] This is the speech alluded to in the beginning of this chapter, which the British officers in Boston supposed had produced a determination on the part of the Americans to submit.

jects of the insurgents an independency of empire, they must be treated as rebels. He informed Parliament that he had increased the naval establishment, and greatly augmented the land forces, " yet in such a manner as to be least expensive or burdensome to the kingdom." This was in reference to the employment of German troops, which I shall presently notice. He professed a desire to temper his severity with mercy, and for this purpose proposed the appointment of commissioners to offer the olive branch of peace and pardon to all offenders among " the unhappy and deluded multitude" who should sue for forgiveness, as well as for whole communities or provinces. He also expressed a hope that his friendly relations with other European governments would prevent any interference on their part with his plans.[1]

The address of Parliament responsive to the king's speech was, of course, but an echo of that document. It was firmly opposed by all the old leaders of opposition, and the management of the summer campaign in America was severely commented upon. Ministers were charged with placing their sovereign in a most contemptible position before the world, and with wresting from him the scepter of colonial power in the West. " They have acted like fools in their late summer campaign," said Colonel Barré. " The British army at Boston," he said, " is a mere wen—an excrescence on the vast continent of America. Certain defeat awaits it. Not the Earl of Chatham, nor Frederic the Great, nor even Alexander the Great, ever gained so much in one campaign as ministers have lost." " They have lost a whole continent," said Fox ; and at the same time he characterized North as " the blundering pilot who had brought the vessel of state into its present difficulties." " It is a horrible idea, that the Americans, our brethren, shall be brought into submission to ministerial will by fleets and armies," said General Conway ; and other members were equally severe upon ministers. In the Upper House, the Duke of Grafton, Lords Shelburne, Camden, Richmond, Gower, and Cavendish, and the Marquis of Rockingham, took decided ground against ministers. Chatham was very ill, and could not leave his country seat. The Duke of Grafton, one of the minority, was bold in his denunciations, and in the course of an able speech declared that he had been greatly deceived in regard to the Americans, and that nothing short of a total repeal of every act obnoxious to the colonists passed since 1763 could now restore peace. The Cabinet, of course, did not concur with his grace, and he resigned the seals of office, and took a decided stand with the opposition.[2] Dr. Hinchcliffe, bishop of Peterborough, followed Grafton, and also became identified with the opposition. Thurlow and Wedderburne were North's chief supporters. The address was carried in both houses by large majorities.

Burke again attempted to lead ministers into a path of common sense and common justice, by proposing a conciliatory bill. It included a proposition to repeal the Boston Port Bill ; a promise not to tax America ; a general amnesty ; and the calling of a Congress by royal authority for the adjustment of remaining difficulties. North was rather pleased with the proposition, for he foresaw heavy breakers ahead in the course

November 16,
1775.

---

[1] The king did not reckon wisely when he relied upon the implied or even expressed promises of non-intervention on the part of other powers. He had made application to all the maritime powers of Europe to prevent their subjects from aiding the rebel colonies by sending them arms or ammunition ; and they all professed a friendship for England, while, at the same time, she was the object of their bitterest jealousy and hate, on account of her proud commercial eminence and political sway. The court of Copenhagen (Denmark) had issued an edict on the 4th of October against carrying warlike articles to America. The Dutch, soon afterward, took similar action ; the punishment for a violation of the edict being a fine of only four hundred and fifty dollars, too small to make shipping merchants long hesitate about the risk where such enormous profits were promised. In fact, large quantities of gunpowder were soon afterward shipped to America from the ports of Holland in glass bottles invoiced " gin." France merely warned the people that what they did for the Americans they must do upon their own risk, and not expect a release from trouble, if they should get into any, by the French admiralty courts. Spain flatly refused to issue any order.

[2] His office of Lord of the Privy Seal was given to Lord Dartmouth, and the office of that nobleman was filled by his opponent, Lord George Germaine—" the proud, imperious, unpopular Sackville." Germaine had taken an active part in favor of all the late coercive measures, and he was considered the fit instrument to carry out the plans of government toward the Americans, in the capacity of Colonial Secretary.

of the vessel of state; but he had abhorred concession, and this appeared too much like it. A large majority voted against Burke's proposition.

Lord North introduced a bill a few days afterward, prohibiting all intercourse

November 22. or trade with the colonies till they should submit, and placing the whole country under martial law. This bill included a clause, founded upon the suggestion in the king's speech, to appoint resident commissioners, with discretionary powers to grant pardons and effect indemnities.[1] The bill was passed by a majority of one hundred and ninety-two to sixty-four in the Commons, and by seventy-eight to nineteen in the House of Lords. Eight peers protested. It became a law by royal assent on the 21st of December.

Having determined to employ sufficient force to put down the rebellion, the next necessary step was to procure it. The Committee of Supply proposed an augmentation of the navy to twenty-eight thousand men, and that eighty ships should be employed on the American station. The land forces necessary were estimated at twenty-five thousand men. The king, as Elector of Hanover, controlled the troops of that little kingdom. Five regiments of Hanoverian troops were sent to Gibraltar and Minorca, to allow the garrisons of English troops there to be sent to America. It was also proposed to organize the militia of the kingdom, so as to have an efficient force at home while the regulars should go across the Atlantic. For their support while in actual service it was proposed to raise the land-tax to four shillings in the pound. This proposition touched the pockets of the country members of Parliament, and cooled their warlike ardor very sensibly.

The peace establishment at home being small, it was resolved, in accordance with suggestions previously made, to employ foreign troops. The king wrote an autograph letter to the States General of Holland, soliciting them to dispose of their Scotch brigade for service against the Americans. The request was nobly refused. A message was sent to the Parliament of Ireland requesting a supply of troops; that body complied by voting four thousand men for the American service. They servilely agreed to send men to butcher their brethren and kinsmen for a consideration; while the noble Hollanders, with a voice of rebuke, dissented, and refused to allow their soldiers to fight the strugglers for freedom, though strangers to them in blood and language.[2]

The king was more successful with some of the petty German princes. He entered into a treaty with the Landgrave of Hesse-Cassel, the Duke of Brunswick, the Prince of Hesse, and the Prince of Waldeck, for seventeen thousand men, to be employed in America. On the 29th of February, 1776, Lord North moved " that these treaties be referred to the Committee of Supply." A most vehement debate ensued in the House of Commons. Ministers pleaded necessity and economy as excuses for such a measure. " There was not time to fill the army with recruits, and hired soldiers would be cheaper in the end, for, after the war, if native troops were employed, there would be nearly thirty battalions to claim half pay." Such were the ostensible reasons; the real object was, doubtless, not so much economy, as the fear that native troops, especially raw recruits, unused to the camp, might affiliate with the insurgents. The opposition denounced the measure as not merely cruel toward the Americans, but disgraceful to the English name; that England was degrading herself by applying to petty German princes for succors against her own subjects; and that nothing would so effectually bar the way for reconciliation with the colonists as this barbarous prep-

---

[1] This bill became a law, and under that clause General Howe, and his brother, Lord Howe, were appointed commissioners.

[2] I can not forbear quoting the remarks of John Derk van der Chapelle, in the Assembly of the States of Overyssel, against the proposition. " Though not as principals, yet as auxiliaries our troops would be employed in suppressing (what some please to call) a rebellion in the American colonies; for which purpose I would rather see janisaries hired than troops from a free state. In what an odious light must this unnatural civil war appear to all Europe—a war in which even savages (if credit can be given to newspaper information) refuse to engage. More odious still would it appear for a people to take a part therein who were themselves once slaves, bore that hateful name, but at last had spirit to fight themselves free. But, above all, it must appear superlatively detestable to me, who think the Americans worthy of every man's esteem, and look upon them as a brave people, defending, in a becoming, manly, and religious manner, those rights which, as men, they derive from God, and not from the Legislature of Great Britain."

aration to enslave them. It was also intimated that the soldiers to be hired would desert as soon as they reached America; for their countrymen were numerous in the colonies, were all patriots, and would have great influence over them;[1] that they would accept land, sheathe their swords, and leave the English soldiers to do the work which their German masters sent them to perform. On the other hand, ministers counted largely upon the valor of their hirelings, many of whom were veterans, trained in the wars of Frederic the Great, and that it would be only necessary for these blood-hounds to show themselves in America to make the rebellious people lay down their arms and sue for pardon. The opposition, actuated by a sincere concern for the fair fame of their country, pleaded earnestly against the consummation of the bargain, and used every laudable endeavor to arrest the incipient action. But opposition was of little avail; North's motion for reference was carried by a majority of two hundred and forty-two to eighty-eight.

Another warm debate ensued when the committee reported on the 4th of March; and in the House of Lords the Duke of Richmond moved not only to countermand 1776. the order for the mercenaries to proceed to America, but to cease hostilities altogether. The Earl of Coventry maintained that an acknowledgment of the independence of the colonies was preferable to a continuance of the war. "Look on the map of the globe," he said; "view Great Britain and North America; compare their extent, consider the soil, rivers, climate, and increasing population of the latter; nothing but the most obstinate blindness and partiality can engender a serious opinion that such a country will long continue under subjection to this. The question is not, therefore, how we shall be able to realize a vain, delusive scheme of dominion, but how we shall make it the interest of the Americans to continue faithful allies and warm friends. Surely that can never be effected by fleets and armies. Instead of meditating conquest and exhausting our strength in an ineffectual struggle, we should, wisely abandoning wild schemes of coercion, avail ourselves of the only substantial benefit we can ever expect, the profits of an extensive commerce, and the strong support of a firm and friendly alliance and compact for mutual defense and assistance."[2] This was the language of wise and sagacious statesmanship—of just and honorable principles—of wholesome and vigorous thought; yet it was denounced as treasonable in its tendency, and encouraging to rebellion. The report recommending the ratification of the bargain was adopted, and the disgraceful and cruel act was consummated. The Landgrave of Hesse-Cassel agreed to furnish twelve thousand one hundred and four men; the Duke of Brunswick, four thousand and eighty-four; the Prince of Hesse, six hundred and sixty-eight, and the Prince of Waldeck, six hundred and seventy; making in all seventeen thousand five hundred and twenty-six soldiers, including the officers. Perceiving the stern necessity which compelled the British government to negotiate with them, these dealers in fighting machines drove a hard bargain with Lord George Germaine and Lord Barrington, making their price in accordance with the principle of trade, where there is a small supply for a great demand. They asked and received thirty-six dollars for each man, and in addition were to receive a considerable subsidy. The whole amount paid by the British government was seven hundred and seventy-five thousand dollars! The British king also guarantied the dominions of these princes against foreign attack. It was a capital bargain for the sellers; for, while they pocketed the enormous poll-price for their troops, they were released from the expense of their maintenance, and felt secure in their absence. Early in the spring these mercenaries, with a considerable number of troops from England and Ireland, sailed for America, under convoy of a British fleet commanded by Admiral Lord Howe.[3] The fierce German

[1] It was estimated that, when the Revolution broke out, there were about one hundred and fifty thousand German emigrants in the American colonies, most of whom had taken sides with the patriots.

[2] Cavendish's Debates.

[3] Admiral Howe, who was a man of fine feelings, hesitated long before he would accept the command of the fleet destined to sail against his fellow-subjects in America. In Parliament, a few days before he sailed, he spoke with much warmth upon the horrors of civil war, and "declared that he knew no struggle so painful as that between a soldier's duties as an officer and a man. If left to his own choice, he should decline serving; but if commanded, it became his duty, and he should not refuse to obey." General Conway said

warriors—fierce, because brutish, unlettered, and trained to bloodshed by the continental butchers—were first let loose upon the patriots in the battle of Long Island,[1] and thenceforth the *Hessians* bore a prominent part in many of the conflicts that ensued.

During the residue of the session of Parliament under consideration, American affairs occupied a good portion of the time of the Legislature, but nothing of great importance was done. The Duke of Grafton made an unsuccessful attempt to have an address to the king adopted, requesting that a proclamation might be issued to declare that if the colonists should, within a reasonable time, show a willingness to treat with the commissioners, or present a petition, hostilities should be suspended, and their petition be received and respected. He assured the House that both France and Spain were arming; and alarmed them by the assertion that " two French gentlemen had been to America, had conferred with Washington at his camp, and had since been to Philadelphia to confer with Congress.[2] The duke's proposition was negatived.

A very brief official announcement of the evacuation of Boston appeared in the London Gazette of the 3d of May, 1776.[3] Ministers endeavored to conceal full intelligence of the transaction, and assumed a careless air, as if the occurrence were of no moment. But Colonel Barré would not allow them to rest quietly under the cloak of mystery, but moved in the House of Commons for an address to his majesty, praying that copies of the dispatches of General Howe and Admiral Shuldham might be laid before the House. There, and in the House of Lords, the ministry were severely handled. Lord North declared that the army was not compelled to abandon Boston, when he well knew to the contrary ; and Lord George Germaine's explanation was weak and unsatisfactory. The thunders of Burke's eloquent denunciations were opened against the government, and he declared that " every measure which had been adopted or pursued was directed to impoverish England and to emancipate America ; and though in twelve months nearly one thousand dollars a man had been

---

a war with our fellow-subjects in America differed very widely from a war with foreign nations, and that before an officer drew his sword against his fellow-subjects he ought to examine well his conscience whether the cause were just. Thurlow declared that such sentiments, if once established as a doctrine, must tend to a dissolution of all governments.—*Pictorial History of England*, v., 248.

[1] I intended to defer a notice of these German troops (generally called *Hessians*, because the greater portion came from Hesse and Hesse-Cassel) until the battle of Long Island should be under consideration ; but the action relative to their employment occupies such a conspicuous place in the proceedings of the session of Parliament, where the most decided hostile measures against America were adopted, that here seemed the most appropriate place to notice the subject in detail. See note 2, page 164, vol. ii.

[2] Some time in the month of November, 1775, Congress was informed that a foreigner was in Philadelphia who was desirous of making to them a confidential communication. At first no notice was taken of it, but the intimation having been several times repeated, a committee, consisting of John Jay, Dr. Franklin, and Thomas Jefferson, was appointed to hear what he had to say. They agreed to meet him in a room in Carpenters' Hall, and, at the time appointed, they found him there—an elderly, lame gentleman, and apparently a wounded French officer. He told them that the French king was greatly pleased with the exertions for liberty which the Americans were making ; that he wished them success, and would, whenever it should be necessary, manifest more openly his friendly sentiments toward them. The committee requested to know his authority for giving these assurances. He answered only by drawing his hand across his throat, and saying, " Gentlemen, I shall take care of my head." They then asked what demonstrations of friendship they might expect from the King of France. " Gentlemen," he answered, " if you want arms, you shall have them ; if you want ammunition, you shall have it ; if you want money, you shall have it." The committee observed that these were important assurances, and again desired to know by what authority they were made. " Gentlemen," said he, again drawing his hand across his throat, " I shall take care of my head ;" and this was the only answer they could obtain from him. He was seen in Philadelphia no more.—See *Life of John Jay, written by his son, William Jay*.

[3] The official announcement in the Gazette was as follows : " General Howe, commander-in-chief of his majesty's forces in North America, having taken a resolution on the 7th of March to remove from Boston to Halifax with the troops under his command, and such of the inhabitants, with their effects, as were desirous to continue under the protection of his majesty's forces ; the embarkation was effected on the 17th of the same month, with the greatest order and regularity, and without the least interruption from the rebels When the packet came away, the first division of transports was under sail, and the remainder were preparing to follow in a few days, the admiral leaving behind as many men-of-war as could be spared from the convoy for the security and protection of such vessels as might be bound to Boston."

spent for salt beef and sour-krout,[1] the troops could not have remained ten days longer if the heavens had not rained down manna and quails."

The majority voted down every proposition to elicit full information respecting operations in America, and on the 23d of May his majesty, after expressing a hope " that his rebellious subjects would yet submit," prorogued Parliament.   1776.

The evacuation of Boston was approved by the king and his ministers, and on the day when the announcement of the event was made in London, Lord George Germaine   May 3, wrote to Howe, deploring the miscarriage of the general's dispatches for the minis-   1776. ters,[2] praising his prudence, and assuring him that his conduct had " given the fullest proofs of his majesty's wisdom and discernment in the choice of so able and brave an officer to command his troops in America."

Thus ended the SIEGE OF BOSTON, where the first decided triumph of American arms over the finest troops of Great Britain was accomplished.   The departure of Howe was regarded in England as a flight; the patriots viewed it as a victory for themselves.   Confidence in their strength to resist oppression was increased ten-fold by this event, and doubt of final and absolute success was a stranger to their thoughts.   " When the siege of Boston commenced, the colonies were hesitating on the great measures of war ; were separated by local interests ; were jealous of each other's plans, and appeared on the field, each with its independent army under its local colors.   When the siege of Boston ended, the colonies had drawn the sword and nearly cast away the scabbard.   They had softened their jealousy of each other ; they had united in a political association ; and the Union flag of thirteen stripes waved over a Continental army."[3]

Few events of more importance than those at other large sea-port towns occurred at Boston after the flight of the British army.   The Americans took good care to keep their fortifications in order, and a full complement of men to garrison them sufficiently.[4]   This fact

[1] A Dutch or German dish, made of cabbage.

[2] It appears that Howe sent dispatches to England on the 23d of October, 1775, by the hands of Major Thompson, and those were the last from him that reached the ministry before the army left Boston for Halifax.   Major Thompson was afterward the celebrated philosopher, Count Rumford.   He was a native of Woburn, in Massachusetts, and was born on the 26th of March, 1753.   He early evinced a taste for philosophy and the mechanic arts, and obtained permission to attend the philosophical lectures of Professor Winthrop at Cambridge.   He afterward taught school at Rumford (now Concord), New Hampshire, where he married a wealthy young widow.   In consequence of his adhesion to the British cause, he left his family in the autumn of 1775, went to England, and became a favorite of Lord George Germaine, who made him under secretary in the Northern Department.   Near the close of the Revolution he was sent to New York, where he commanded a regiment of dragoons, and returning to England, the king knighted him.   He became acquainted with the minister of the Duke of Bavaria, who induced him to go to Munich, where he became active in public affairs.   The duke raised him to a high military rank, and made him a count of the empire.   He added to his title the place of his marriage, and became Count Rumford.   He was in London in 1800, and projected the Royal Institution of Great Britain.   His wife, whom he abandoned, died in 1794 in New Hampshire.   Count Rumford died August 20th, 1814, aged sixty-one years.   His scientific discoveries have made his name immortal.   He bequeathed fifty thousand dollars to Harvard College.

[3] Frothingham, page 334.

[4] With the exception of Dorchester, Bunker Hill, and Roxbury, I believe there are few traces of the fortifications of the Revolution that can be certainly identified; and so much altered has been the fortress on Castle Island that it exhibits but little of the features of 1776.   Every year the difficulty of properly locating the several forts becomes greater, and therefore to preserve, in this work, a record of those landmarks by which they may be identified, I condense from Silliman's Journal for 1822 an interesting article on the subject which was communicated by J. Finch, Esq., with such references as later writers have made.   A recurrence to the map on page 566, vol. i., will assist the reader.

I. BREED'S HILL and BUNKER HILL.—These works were on the summits and slopes of the hills, looking toward Boston.   Bunker Hill Monument now stands upon the spot where Prescott's redoubt was thrown up.

II. PLOWED HILL.—This fort was upon the summit of the eminence, commanding the Mystic River and the Penny Ferry.   It was in a direct line from Charlestown Neck to Winter Hill, further northward.

III. COBBLE or BARRELL'S HILL.—In consequence of its strength, the fort on this hill was called Putnam's impregnable fortress.   This was on the north side of Willis's Creek, in full view of Bunker and Breed's Hills, and commanding the whole western portion of the peninsula of Charlestown.

IV. LECHMERE'S POINT was strongly fortified at a spot one hundred yards from West Boston Bridge

seemed to be well known to the enemy; for while Newport and the places adjacent suffered from the naval operations of British vessels, Boston Harbor was shunned by them. Some

There was a causeway across the marsh, and a line of works along Willis's Creek to connect with those on Cobble Hill.

V. WINTER HILL.—The works at this point, commanding the Mystic and the country northward from Charlestown, were more extensive than any other American fortification around Boston. There rested the left wing of the army under General Lee, at the time of the siege of Boston. There was a redoubt near, upon the *Ten Hill Farm*, that commanded the Mystic; and between Winter and Prospect Hills was a redoubt, where a quarry was opened about the year 1819. This was called *White House Redoubt*, in the rear of which, at a farm-house, Lee had his quarters.

VI. PROSPECT HILL has two eminences, both of which were strongly fortified, and connected by a rampart and fosse, or ditch. These forts were destroyed in 1817. There is an extensive view from this hill.

VII. THE CAMBRIDGE LINES, situated upon Butler's Hill, consisted of six regular forts connected by a strong intrenchment. These were in a state of excellent preservation when Mr. Finch wrote. The *Second Line of Defense* might then be traced on the College Green at Cambridge.

VIII. A SEMICIRCULAR BATTERY, with three embrasures, was situated on the northern shore of Charles River, near its entrance into the bay. It was rather above the level of the marsh.

IX. BROOKLINE FORT, on Sewall's Point, was very extensive. The ramparts and irregular bastion, which commanded Charles River, were very strong. The fort was nearly quadrangular.

X. There was a *battery* on the southern shore of Muddy River, with three embrasures. Westward of this position was a redoubt; and between Stony Brook and Roxbury were three others.

XI. ROXBURY.—There were strong fortifications at this point, erected upon eminences which commanded Boston Neck, sometimes called Roxbury Neck. About three quarters of a mile in advance of these redoubts were THE ROXBURY LINES, situated northward of the town. There were two lines of intrenchments, which extended quite across the peninsula; and the ditch, filled at high water, made Boston an island. The works thrown up by Gage when he fortified Boston Neck were near the present Dover Street.

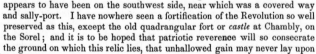

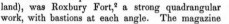

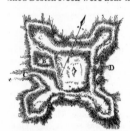

Upon a higher eminence, in the rear of the Roxbury lines (at present [1850] west of Highland Street, on land owned by the Honorable B. F. Copeland), was Roxbury Fort,[2] a strong quadrangular work, with bastions at each angle. The magazine

ROXBURY FORT.[1]

appears to have been on the southwest side, near which was a covered way and sally-port. I have nowhere seen a fortification of the Revolution so well preserved as this, except the old quadrangular fort or *castle* at Chambly, on the Sorel; and it is to be hoped that patriotic reverence will so consecrate the ground on which this relic lies, that unhallowed gain may never lay upon the old ramparts the hand of demolition.

GROUND PLAN OF THE FORT.[3]

The history of the construction of *Roxbury Fort* is somewhat obscure. It is known to have been the first regular work erected by the Americans when they nearly circumvallated Boston. Tradition avers, that when the Rhode Island "Army of Observation," which hastened toward Boston, under Greene, after the skirmishes at Lexington and Concord, encamped at Jamaica Plains, a detachment was sent forward and commenced this redoubt at Roxbury. General Ward, who, by common consent, was captain-general of the accumulating forces, ordered them to desist, as he was about to commence a regular line of fortifications under the direction of Gridley. The Rhode Islanders, acknowledging no authority but their own Provincial Assembly, proceeded in their work; and when Washington took command of the army, he regarded this fort as the best and most eligibly located of all the works then in course of construction. During the siege

---

[1] This view is from the southwest angle of the fort. In the foreground a portion of the ramparts is seen. These are now overgrown, in part, with shrubbery. On the right is seen the house of Mr. Benjamin Perkins, on Highland Street, and extending across the picture, to the left, is the side of the fort toward Boston, exhibiting prominent traces of the embrasures for the cannons. It was a foggy day in autumn when I visited the fort, in company with Frederic Kidder, Esq., of Boston, to whose courtesy and antiquarian taste I am indebted for the knowledge of the existence of this well-preserved fortification. No distant view could be procured, and I was obliged to be content with the above sketch, made in the intervals of "sun and shower." The bald rocks on which the fort stands are huge bowlders of *pudding-stone*, and upon three sides these form natural revetments, which would be difficult for an enemy to scale. The embankments are from eight to fifteen feet in height, and within, the *terre-plein*, on which the soldiers and cannons were placed, is quite perfect.

[2] See map on page 566, vol. i.

[3] This is a ground plan of the fort as it now appears. A is the parade; B, the magazine; C, the sally-port D, the side toward Boston.

of the Tories who went with Howe to Halifax returned, and cast themselves upon the clemency of the new government.   Those who possessed influence that might be dangerous were immediately arrested and thrown into prison, where they were confined for several months, until satisfactory arrangements were made for their release.

Boston was the place whither the captured troops of Burgoyne were sent in 1777, to embark for England on parole.[1]   They entered Cambridge on the 7th of November, during the prevalence of a severe northeast storm.   A graphic description of the appearance of the Hessians is given in a letter from Mrs. Winthrop to Mrs. Warren, printed on page 82.   Speaking of the British portion of the captive army, the same writer says : " Their baggage-wagons were drawn by poor half-starved horses ; but to bring up the rear was a noble-looking guard of American, brawny, victorious yeomanry, who assisted in bringing these sons of slavery to terms.   Some of our wagons, drawn by fat oxen, driven by joyous-looking Yankees, closed the cavalcade.   The generals and other officers went to Bradish's, where they quarter at present.   The privates trudged through thick and thin to the hills, where we thought they were to be confined ; but what was our surprise when, in the morning, we beheld an inundation of these disagreeable objects filling our streets."   These captive troops were quartered in some of the best private houses, and the students of Harvard College were dismissed to make room for these foreign soldiers.   Alluding to this fact, Mrs. Winthrop writes, " Is there not a degree of unkindness in loading poor Cambridge, almost ruined before this great army seemed to be let loose upon us ?[2] . . . . . . Surprising that our general [Gates], or any of our colonels, should insist on the first university in America being disbanded for their genteel accommodation, and we, poor oppressed people, seek an asylum in the woods against a piercing winter. . . . . . General Burgoyne dined on Sunday in Boston with General ——.   He rode through the town properly attended, down Court Street and through the Main Street, and on his return walked to Charlestown ferry, followed by as great a number of spectators as ever attended a pope."   There must have been a great contrast between the feelings of Burgoyne at that time and when he walked the same streets two years before, a general covered with fresh laurels won upon the Spanish Peninsula.[3]   The captive army were sent to Charlottesville, in Virginia, at the beginning of 1779.

of Boston, ROXBURY FORT was considered superior to all others for its strength and its power to annoy the enemy.

XII. DORCHESTER HEIGHTS.—The ancient fortifications there are covered by the remains of those erected in 1812, and have little interest except as showing the locality of the forts of the Revolution.

XIII. At NOOK'S HILL, near South Boston Bridge, the last breast-work was thrown up by the Americans before the flight of the British.   It was the menacing appearance of this suddenly-erected fort that caused Howe to hasten his departure.   The engineers employed in the construction of these works were Colonel Richard Gridley, chief; Lieutenant-colonel Rufus Putnam, Captain Josiah Waters, Captain Baldwin, of Brookfield, and Captain Henry (afterward general) Knox, assistants.   These were the principal works erected and occupied by the Americans at Boston.   When Mr. Finch wrote in 1822, many of these were well preserved, and he expressed a patriotic desire that they should remain so.   But they are gone, and art has covered up the relics that were left.   But it is not yet too late to carry out a portion of his recommendation, by which to preserve the identity of some of the localities.   "The laurel, planted on the spot where Warren fell, would be an emblem of unfading honor; the white birch and pine might adorn Prospect Hill ; at Roxbury, the cedar and the oak might yet retain their eminence ; and upon the heights of Dorchester we would plant the laurel, and the finest trees which adorn the forest, because there was achieved a glorious victory, without the sacrifice of life !"

[1] I have before me the original *paroles of honor*, signed by all the surviving officers of Burgoyne's captured army.   They are the property of J. Wingate Thornton, Esq., of Boston, who kindly placed them in my hands for use.   The paroles are dated at Cambridge, December 13th, 1777.   One is signed by 185 English officers, headed by Burgoyne ; the other by 95 German officers, headed by Riedesel, the Brunswick general.   Their names may be found in the Supplement, page 672.

[2] This sudden influx menaced the country about Boston with famine, for the five thousand prisoners of war had to be fed.   Every article rapidly rose in price ; wood was sold at twenty-seven and a half dollars a cord.

[3] When Burgoyne left Boston for England, General Phillips was left in chief command of the captive troops, quartered on Prospect Hill.   He was a conceited, irritable person, and often his haughty pride made him forget the relation in which he stood to the victorious Americans, whom he had been taught to despise. On one occasion, one of his officers was returning from Boston, with two females, to the British camp, and refused to answer the challenge of the sentinel.   He was shot dead, and the act was justified by the rules

In July, 1779, the State of Massachusetts fitted out an expedition at Boston to go against the British troops at Penobscot, a small town on the east side of Penobscot River in Maine. The enemy were estimated to be one thousand strong.   Fifteen hundred men were ordered to be raised for the expedition, but only about nine hundred were actually employed, and some of these were pressed into the service.   Some were conveyed thither by a fleet, consisting of several sloops of war, carrying from sixteen to twenty-eight guns, one of thirty-two guns, seven armed brigs, and twenty-four other vessels, which served as transports.   Other portions of the militia marched from the lower counties of Maine.   Commodore Salstonstall commanded the fleet, and Generals Lovell and Wadsworth led the land forces.   A disagreement arose between the commanders of the fleet and army, which greatly weakened the power of the expedition   It was agreed, however, to attack the enemy.   The American land force debarked, and rushed to the assault of the fort up a steep declivity, in the face of a storm of shot from the enemy.   The marines did not come to their support, and a large naval re-enforcement for the British arriving at that moment, the assailants were repulsed and forced to abandon the expedition.   The Americans destroyed many of their vessels to prevent them from falling into the hands of the enemy, and in scattered detachments, the troops, marines, and sailors, made their way back to their homes, suffering great hardships in their route through the almost unbroken wilderness.   It was a most unfortunate affair The General Court of Massachusetts instituted an inquiry, which resulted in censuring the naval commander, and commending Lovell and Wadsworth.[1]

Here let us close the chronicles of Boston.   Henceforth we shall only refer to them incidentally, as the elucidation of prominent events elsewhere shall make this necessary.   We have seen the discontents of the colonies ripen into open rebellion in this hot-bed of patriotism ; we have seen a Continental army organized, disciplined, and prepared for action, and those yeomanry and artisans, drawn from the fields and workshops, piling, with seeming Titan strength, huge fortifications around a well-disciplined British army, and expelling it from one of the most advantageous positions on the continent. ˙ Let us now proceed to places where other scenes in the great drama were enacted.

of war.   General Phillips was greatly enraged, and wrote the following impudent letter to General Heath, the commanding officer :

"Cambridge, June 17, 1778.

" Murder and death have at length taken place.   An officer, riding out from the barracks on Prospect Hill, has been shot by an American sentinel.   I leave the horrors of that bloody disposition, which has joined itself to rebellion in these colonies, to the feelings of all Europe.   I do not ask for justice, for I believe every principle of it has fled from this province.   I *demand* liberty to send an officer to General Sir Henry Clinton, by way of the head-quarters of General Washington.   WM. PHILLIPS, *Major General."*

This was strange language for a prisoner of war to use toward his keeper !   Before the insulting note had been received by Heath, the sentry had been put under guard to await the decision of a jury of inquest. Heath had also written a polite note to Phillips, informing him of the fact.   As I have observed before, the haughty insolence of the British functionaries, civil and military, toward the Americans, did more to engender hatred and foster the rebellion than any other single cause.   Phillips's conduct is a fair picture, among many others, of the haughty bearing of the Britons in authority.   I have before me an autograph letter to General Heath, written at about the same time, by Lieutenant Kingston, Burgoyne's deputy adjutant general.   It is marked by flippant insolence, although a little more polite than Phillips's letter.

[1] Peleg Wadsworth was a native of Massachusetts, and graduated at Harvard College in 1769.   After his unsuccessful attempt against the British fort at Penobscot in 1779, where his bravery was acknowledged, he was sent to command in the district of Maine, whither he took his family.   In February, 1781, a party of the enemy captured him in his own house, and conveyed him to the British quarters at Bagaduce or Castin.   In company with Major Burton, he effected his escape from the fort in June, crossed the Penobscot in a canoe, and traveled through the wilderness to his home.   Of his capture, sufferings, and escape, Dr. Dwight has given a long and interesting account in the second volume of his *Travels in New England.*   For many years Wadsworth was a member of Congress from Cumberland district.   He died at Hiram, in Maine, in November, 1829, aged eighty years.   His son, Lieutenant Henry Wadsworth, was blown up in a fire-ship in the harbor at Tripoli in September, 1804.—*Allen's American Biography.*

CHAPTER XXVI.

"Day wanes; 'tis autumn's eventide again;
And, sinking on the blue hill's breast, the sun
Spreads the large bounty of his level blaze,
Lengthening the shades of mountains and tall trees,
And throwing blacker shadows o'er the sheet
Of the dark stream, in whose unruffled tide
Waver the bank-shrub and the graceful elm,
As the gray branches and their trembling leaves
Catch the soft whispers of the evening air."

GEORGE LUNT.

T was in the afternoon of a warm, bright day in October, that I left Boston for Norwich and New London, upon the Thames, in Connecticut, where I purposed to pass two or three days in visiting the interesting localities in their respective neighborhoods. I journeyed upon the great Western rail-way from Boston to Worcester, forty-four miles westward, where the Norwich road branches off in the direction of Long Island Sound, and courses down the beautiful valleys of the French and Quinebaug Rivers. Every rood of the way is agreeably diversified. Hill and mountain, lake and streamlet, farm-house and village, charmed the eye with a kaleidoscope variety as our train thundered over the road at the rate of thirty miles an hour. Yet memory can fix upon only a few prominent points, and these appear to make the sum of all which the eye gazed upon. Thus I remember the sweet Lake Cochituate, whose clear waters now bless the city of Boston with limpid streams. I remember it stretching away north from the rail-way, pierced with many green headlands, and rippled by the wings of waterfowl. Thus, too, I remember the beautiful little Mashapaug,[1] lying in a bowl of the wooded hills of Killingly, sparkling in the slant rays of the evening sun as we swept by and became lost among the rugged heights and dark forests at twilight.

The Quinebaug is dotted with pretty factory villages at almost every rift in its course; and, as we halted a moment at the stations, the serried lights of the mills, and the merry laughter of troops of girls just released from labor, joyous as children bursting from school, agreeably broke the monotony of an evening ride in a close car. We reached the Shetucket Valley at about half past seven o'clock, and at eight I was pleasantly housed at the Mer-

---

[1] This sheet of water is now known by the unpoetical name of Alexander's Lake, from the circumstance that a Scotchman, named Neil Alexander, settled there, and owned all the lands in the vicinity in the year 1720. The Indians, who called it Mashapaug, had a curious tradition respecting the origin of the lake. I quote from *Barber's Historical Collections of Connecticut*, p. 431 : "In ancient times, when the red men of this quarter had long enjoyed prosperity, that is, when they had found plenty of game in the woods and fish in the ponds and rivers, they at length fixed the time for a general *powwow*—a sort of festival for eating, drinking, smoking, singing, and dancing. The spot chosen for this purpose was a sandy hill, or mountain, covered with tall pines, occupying the situation where the lake now lies. The *powwow* lasted four days in succession, and was to continue longer, had not the Great Spirit, enraged at the licentiousness that prevailed there, resolved to punish them. Accordingly, while the red people, in immense numbers, were capering about on the summit of the mountain, it suddenly gave way beneath them and sunk to a great depth, when the waters from below rushed up and covered them all, except *one good old squaw*, who occupied the peak which now bears the name of Loon's Island. Whether the tradition is entitled to credit or not, we will do it justice by affirming that in a clear day, when there is no wind, and the surface of the lake is smooth, the huge trunks and leafless branches of *gigantic pines* may be occasionally seen in the deepest part of the water, some of them reaching almost to the surface, in such huge and fantastic forms as to cause the beholder to startle !"

chants' Hotel in Norwich, a city beautifully situated at the confluence of the Yantic and Shetucket Rivers, whose wedded waters here form the broad and navigable Thames.

Early in the morning I started in search of celebrities, and had the good fortune to meet with Edwin Williams, Esq., the widely-known author of the "Statesman's Manual" and other standard works. Norwich is his birth-place, and was his residence during his youth, and he is as familiar with its history and topography as a husbandman is with that of his farm. With such a guide, accompanied by his intelligent little son, an earnest delver among the whys and wherefores in the mine of knowledge, I anticipated a delightful journey of a day. Nor was I disappointed; and the pleasures and profit of that day's ramble form one of the brightest points in my interesting tour. I procured a span of horses and a barouche to convey us to Lebanon, twelve miles northward, the residence of Jonathan Trumbull, the patriot governor of Connecticut during the Revolution. While the hostler is harnessing our team, let us open the chronicles of Norwich and see what history has recorded there.

Like that of all the ancient New England towns, the Indian history of Norwich, commencing with the advent of the English in that neighborhood about 1643, is full of romance, and woos the pen to depict it; but its relation to my subject is only incidental, and I must pass it by with brief mention.

Norwich is in the midst of the ancient Mohegan country, and Mohegan was its Indian name. Uncas was the chief of the tribe when the English first settled at Hartford, and built a fort at Saybrook, at the mouth of the Connecticut River. He formed a treaty of amity with the whites; and so fair were his broad acres upon the head waters of the Pequot River, now the Thames, that the sin of covetousness soon pervaded the hearts of the Puritan settlers. Wawekus Hill, now in the center of Norwich, was a famous observatory for his warriors, for eastward of them were the powerful Narragansets, sworn enemies of the Mohegans, and governed by the brave Miantonŏmoh, also a friend of the white men. In the spring of 1643 the flame of war was lighted between these powerful tribes, and Miantonŏmoh led his warriors to an invasion of the Mohegan country. His plans were secretly laid, and he hoped to take Uncas by surprise. For this purpose six hundred of his bravest warriors were led stealthily, by night marches, toward the head waters of the Pequot. At dawn, one morning, they were discovered at the Shetucket Fords, near the mouth of the Quinebaug, by some of the vigilant Mohegan scouts upon the Wawekus. From the rocky nooks near the falls of the Yantic, a canoe, bearing a messenger with the intelligence, shot down the Thames to Shantock Point, where Uncas was strongly fortified. With three or four hundred of his best warriors he marched to meet Miantonŏmoh. They confronted at the Great Plains, a mile and a half below Norwich, on the west side of the Thames. A fierce conflict ensued. The advantage gained by Uncas by strategy[1] was maintained, and the Narragansets were put to flight, closely pursued by the Mohegans. Through tangled woods and over rocky ledges, across the Yantic, and over the high plain of Norwich toward the Shetucket Fords, the pursued and pursuers swept like a blast. Two swift-footed Mohegans pursued Miantonŏmoh with unwearied pertinacity, and finally outstripped him, he being encumbered with a heavy corselet. They impeded his progress, but did not attempt to seize him, that honor being reserved for their chief. As soon as Uncas touched Miantonŏmoh, the latter halted and sat down in silence. He was conducted in triumph to Shantock, where Uncas treated him with generous kindness and respect. The conflict had been brief, but thirty of the Narragansets were slain. Among the prisoners were a brother of the captive king, and two sons of Canonicus, his uncle.

Uncas, probably fearing that the Narragansets would make an attempt to recapture their

---

[1] When Uncas saw the superior number of Miantonŏmoh's warriors, he sent a messenger to that chief to say, in the name of Uncas, "Let us two fight single-handed. If you kill me, my men shall be yours; if I kill you, your men shall be mine." Miantonŏmoh, suspecting treachery, disdainfully rejected the proposition. Uncas then fell on his face, a signal previously agreed upon with his warriors, who, with bent bows, rushed upon the Narragansets, who were carelessly awaiting the result of the conference, and thus put them to flight

chief, sent him to Hartford, and surrendered him into the custody of the English, agreeing to be governed in his future conduct toward his prisoner by their advice. Miantonōmoh was imprisoned until September, when the commissioners of the United Colonies, at their meeting in Boston, after debating the question whether it would be lawful to take the life of Miantonōmoh, referred his case to an ecclesiastical tribunal, composed of five of the principal ministers of the colonies. Their decision was in favor of handing him over to Uncas for *execution, without torture*, within the dominions of that sachem. Delighted with the verdict of his Christian allies, the equally savage Mohegan, with a few trusty followers, conducted Miantonōmoh to the spot where he was captured, and, while marching unsuspicious of present danger, a brother of Uncas, at a sign from that chief, buried his hatchet in the head of the royal prisoner. Uncas cut a piece of flesh from the shoulder of the slain captive and ate it, saying, "It is very sweet; it makes my heart strong." Satisfied revenge made it sweet; and no doubt his heart felt stronger when he saw his powerful enemy lying dead at his feet. The whole transaction was base treachery and ingratitude. Miantonōmoh had been the firm friend of the whites on Rhode Island, and his sentence was a flagrant offense against the principles of common justice and Christianity. He was buried where he was slain, and from these circumstances the place has since been called the Sachem's Plain.[1]

The Narragansets, burning with revenge, and led by Pessacus, a brother of Miantonōmoh, invaded the Mohegan country in the spring of 1645. Plantations were laid waste, and Uncas, with his principal warriors, was driven into his strong fortress at Shantock. There he was closely besieged, but found means to send a messenger to Captain Mason, the destroyer of the Pequots, then commanding the fort at Saybrook. As in duty bound, that officer sent succor to his ally, not in men, for they were not needed, but in provisions. Thomas Leffingwell, a young man of undaunted courage, paddled a canoe up the Pequot at night, laden with many hundred weight of beef, corn, pease, &c., and deposited them safely within the fort at Shantock. This timely relief was made known to the besiegers by hoisting a piece of beef upon a pole above the ramparts of the fort. Unable to break down the fortress, the Narragansets raised the siege and returned to their own country. This invasion was repeated, and with almost fatal effect to Uncas. The English saved him, and, finally, after nearly twenty years of strife, the hatchet was buried between these tribes.

UNKOS,

his mark

OWANEKO,

his mark.

ATTAWAUHOOD,

his mark.

SIGNATURES OF UNCAS AND HIS SONS.[2]

1645. It was in the midst of these hostilities that the younger Winthrop and others commenced a settlement at Pequot Harbor, now New London; and in 1659 Uncas and his two sons signed a deed at Saybrook, conveying a tract of land, "lying at the head of the Great River," nine miles square, to Thomas Leffingwell and others, for a value consideration of about three hundred and fifty dollars. Leffingwell had thirty-five associates, and there founded the city of Norwich, at the head of the plain now known as the *old town*, or *up town*. It is not my province to trace the progress of settlement, but simply to note the prominent points

[1] The spot where Miantonōmoh was buried is a little northward of the village of Greenville, on the west bank of the Shetucket, and about a mile and a half from Norwich. A pile of stones was placed upon his grave, and for many years a portion of his tribe came, in the season of flowers, and mourned over his remains, each one adding a stone to the tumulus. At length their visits ceased, and the voice of tradition being seldom heard at that isolated spot, the proprietor of the land, ignorant of the fact that the pile of stones was sepulchral and sacred to patriotism, used them in the construction of the foundation of a barn. On the 4th of July, 1841, the people of Greenville celebrated, by a festival, the erection of a monument to Miantonōmoh, on the spot where he was slain. It is a block of granite eight feet high, and about five feet square at the base, bearing the inscription

MIANTONŌMOH.
1643.

I did not visit the spot, but, from description, I think the initial letter I, at the beginning of this chapter, is a fair representation of it.

[2] Owaneko was a bold warrior in his youth, and was distinguished in King Philip's War. In maturity.

in the colonial history of a people who were among the earliest and most ardent supporters of the Revolution.[1]

1659.   It was a charming spot where the Puritan settlers founded the city of Norwich, a name given to it in honor of the English birth-place of some of them.   " Birds and animals of almost every species belonging to the climate were numerous to an uncommon degree ; and the hissing of snakes, as well as the howling of wolves and bears must soon have become familiar to their ears.   To complete the view, it may be added, that the streams swarmed with fish and wild fowl ; in the brooks and meadows were found the beaver and the otter, and through the whole scene stalked at intervals the Indian and the deer."[2]   The planting of this settlement greatly pleased Uncas, but irritated the Narragansets ; the former regarding it with pleasure, as the latter did with anger, as a barrier to the meditated invasions of the Mohegan country by the tribe of Miantonōmoh.   Uncas remained a firm friend to the whites until his death, which occurred soon after the close of King Philip's War, probably in 1683.   He died at Mohegan (Norwich), and was interred in the burial-ground of his family, situated upon the high plain just above the falls of the Yantic.   The royal cemetery has been inclosed, and a granite monument erected therein to the memory of the celebrated sachem.

UNCAS'S MONUMENT.[3]

November 1, 1660.   The first male white child born in Norwich was Christopher Huntington, afterward recorder of the town.   The name of Huntington is intimately connected with the whole history of that settlement, and is prominent in our revolutionary annals.   Several of that name were engaged in the army, and one Samuel Huntington, was President of Congress.   Indeed, the whole population seemed to be

1765.   thoroughly imbued with the spirit of freedom, and from the Stamp Act era until the close of the war for independence, almost every patriotic measure adopted was an act of the town, not of impromptu assemblages of the friends of liberty or of committees.[4]   Like

having lost the stimulus of war, " he used to wander about with his blanket, metonep, and sandals, his gun, and his squaw," says Miss Caulkins, " to beg in the neighboring towns, quartering himself in the kitchens and outhouses of his white friends, and presenting to strangers, or those who could not well understand his imperfect English, a *brief*, which had been written for him by Mr. Richard Bushnell.   It was as follows

> " ' Oneco king, his queen doth bring
>   To beg a little food ;
> As they go along their friends among
>   To try how kind, how good.
> Some pork, some beef, for their relief ;
>   And if you can't spare bread,
> She'll thank you for your pudding, as they go a gooding,
>   And carry it on her head.' "

[1] The reader is referred to a well-written volume of 360 pages, *A History of Norwich, Connecticut, from its Settlement in* 1660, *to January*, 1845 : *by Miss F. M. Caulkins*.   It is carefully compiled from the town records, old newspapers, and well-authenticated traditions, many of the latter being derived from then living witnesses of the scenes of the Revolution.   I am indebted to this valuable little work for much interesting matter connected with Norwich.   [2] Miss Caulkins, page 40.

[3] This monument is on the south side of Prospect Street, and stands within a shaded inclosure surrounded by a hedge of prim, upon the estate of Judge Goddard.   The obelisk is a single block of granite, and, with the pedestal, is about twenty feet high.   The monument was erected by the citizens of Norwich.   The foundation-stone was laid by President Jackson, while visiting Norwich during his Eastern tour in 1832.   Several small tomb-stones of those of the royal line of Uncas are within the inclosure.   The name has now become extinct, the last Uncas having been buried there about the beginning of the present century.   A descendant of Uncas, named Mazeon, was buried there in 1827, on which occasion the wife of Judge Goddard (he being absent) invited the remnant of the Mohegan tribe, then numbering about sixty, to partake of a cold collation.

[4] On the 7th of April, 1765, on the receipt of intelligence of the passage of the Stamp Act, the people, in town-meeting assembled, voted unanimously " that the town clerk shall proceed in his office as usual, and the town will save him harmless from all damage that he may sustain thereby."

OF THE REVOLUTION. 599

Norwich Liberty Tree. Celebration under it. Honors to John Wilkes. Patriotic Town Meeting. Benevolence of the People.

those of Boston, the people of Norwich had their *Liberty Tree,* under which public meetings were held in opposition to the Stamp Act.   It was brought from the forest, and erected in the center of the open plain.   Ingersoll, the stamp distributor for Connecticut, was burned in effigy upon the high hill overlooking the plain, just above the site of the old meeting-house.   The repeal of the Stamp Act was celebrated, on the first anniversary of the event, on the 18th of March, 1767, with great festivity, under *Liberty Tree,* which was decked with standards and appropriate devices, and crowned with a Phrygian cap.   A tent, or booth, was erected under it, called a pavilion.   Here, almost daily, people assembled to hear news and encourage each other in the determination to resist every kind of oppression.[1]

The inhabitants of Norwich entered heartily into the scheme of non-importation from Great Britain.   The pledge was generally signed, and almost all were strictly faithful.   On the 7th of June, 1768, an entertainment was given at Peck's tavern,[2] to celebrate the election of John Wilkes to a seat in Parliament.   Every thing was arranged in excellent taste. All the table furniture, such as plates, bowls, tureens, tumblers, and napkins, were marked " 45," the number of the *North Briton,* Wilkes's paper, that drew down upon his head the ire of the British government, and, consequently, as a *persecuted patriot,* obtained for him a seat in the House of Commons.   The Tree of Liberty was decorated with new banners and devices, among which was a flag inscribed " No. 45, WILKES AND LIBERTY."   Another celebration was held there in September, avowedly to ridicule the commissioners of customs at Boston ; and in various ways the people manifested their defiance of British power, where it wielded instruments of oppression.   The margins of their public records, for a series of years, were emblazoned with the words LIBERTY ! LIBERTY ! LIBERTY !   Every man was a self-constituted member of the committee of vigilance, and none could drink tea, or use other proscribed articles with impunity.   Some who offended were forced publicly to recant. The conduct of such persons was under the special inspection of the Sons of Liberty, of whom Captain Joseph Trumbull, eldest son of Governor Trumbull, was one of the most active.

On the 6th of June, 1774, a town meeting was held in Norwich, to take into consideration " the melancholy state of affairs."   Honorable Jabez Huntington was chosen moderator ; a series of resolutions, drawn up by Captain Trumbull and Samuel Huntington, were adopted,[3] and a standing committee of correspondence, composed of some of the leading patriots of the town, was appointed.[4]   The people of Boston, in their distress, consequent upon the closing of the port,[a] received substantial testimonies of the sympathy of those of   [a] June 1 Norwich ;[5] and when the rumor which went abroad that the British soldiers were massacring the people of Boston, reached Norwich, a multitude gathered around the   September 3, Liberty Tree, and the next morning (Sunday) four hundred and sixty-four men,   1774.

---

[1] Miss Caulkins, page 208.

[2] This building, though somewhat altered, is yet standing on one side of the green in the upper town, not far from the court-house.   Belah Peck, Esq., son of the proprietor of the house at that time, and then a half-grown boy, was yet living.   I met him upon the road, when returning from Lebanon, sitting in his wagon as erect as most men at seventy.   He died toward the close of 1850, in the ninety-fifth year of his age.

[3] One of these resolutions, looking favorably to a general Congress, was as follows : " That we will, to the utmost of our abilities, assert and defend the liberties and immunities of British America ; and that we will co-operate with our other brethren, in this and the other colonies, in such reasonable measures as shall, in *general Congress or otherwise,* be judged most proper to release us from burdens we now feel, and secure us from greater evils we fear will follow from the principles adopted by the British Parliament respecting the town of Boston."   This was one of the earliest movements in the colonies favorable to a general Congress.

[4] The committee consisted of Captain Jedediah Huntington, C. Leffingwell, Dr. Theophilus Rogers, Captain William Hubbard, and Captain Joseph Trumbull.   Captain Huntington was afterward aid to General Washington, and brigadier general in the Continental army.   Captain Trumbull was made a commissary in the army.

[5] The inhabitants of Norwich sent cash, wheat, corn, and a flock of three hundred and ninety sheep, for the relief of the suffering poor of Boston.   This liberality was greatly applauded in the public prints of the day.   A further instance of the liberal devotion of the people of Norwich to the cause may be mentioned. The Connecticut Gazette for January, 1778, published at New London, says, " On the last Sabbath of December, 1777, a contribution was taken up in the several parishes of Norwich for the benefit of the officers

a large proportion of them well mounted, started for the oppressed city, under Major John Durkee. The report proved to be false; but the following year, when the skirmish at Lex ington inflamed all Anglo-America, a large proportion of these same men hastened to Cam bridge, and Durkee and others were in the battle of Bunker Hill.[1] A company of one hund red choice men, raised by Durkee in Norwich, marched thither under Lieutenant Joshua Huntington, and were annexed to Putnam's brigade.

In the spring of 1776, the Continental army that left Boston for New York after the British evacuation of the former place, passed through Norwich to embark for New London. There General Washington met Governor Trumbull by appointment, and both dined together at the table of Colonel Jedediah Huntington. The dwelling of that active patriot, pictured in the engraving, is well preserved in its original character. It is in the present possession of his nieces, the daughters of Colonel Ebenezer Huntington. Its roof at different times sheltered several of the foreign officers—La Fayette, Steuben, Pulaski, the Duke de Lauzun, and the Marquis de Chastellux. While Lauzun's legion was cantoned at Leb

RESIDENCE OF GENERAL HUNTINGTON

anon, in the winter of 1780–81, General Huntington invited that nobleman and his officers to a banquet at his house. The noble and brilliant appearance of these men when they rode into the town attracted great attention. After the dinner was over, the whole party went into the yard, now adorned with flowering shrubs, and gave three loud huzzas for liberty !

Our vehicle is at the door ; let us take the reins and depart for Lebanon.

Before leaving Norwich, we called upon Jonathan G. W. Trumbull, Esq., a grandson of the patriot governor of that name, who kindly furnished us with a letter of introduction to " the oldest inhabitant" of Lebanon, Captain Hubbard Dutton. Mr. Trumbull is a lineal descendant, through his grandmother, of the Reverend John Robinson, the Puritan divine whose flock were the PILGRIM FATHERS. Among other relics, Mr. Trumbull showed us a

---

and soldiers who belonged to said town, when they collected 386 pairs of stockings, 227 pairs of shoes, 118 shirts, 78 jackets, 48 pairs of overalls, 208 pairs of mittens, 11 buff caps, 15 pairs of breeches, 9 coats, 22 rifle frocks, 19 handkerchiefs, and £258 17s. 8d. [about $1295], which was forwarded to the army. Also collected a quantity of pork, cheese, wheat, rye, Indian corn, sugar, rice, flax, wood, &c., &c., to be distributed to the needy families of the officers and soldiers. The whole amounted to the sum of £1400," or about $7000.

[1] This was the Colonel Durkee engaged in affairs at Wyoming, and known as " the bold Bean Hiller ' See note. page 345,

[2] This pleasant mansion is situated in Old Norwich, or "up town," a few rods eastward of that of Governor Huntington. The original owner, Jedediah Huntington, was one of five sons of General Jabez Huntington, who were in the Continental army at different times during the war. He was born at Norwich, August 15, 1745, and graduated at Harvard College in 1763. The address which he delivered upon that occasion was "the first *English* oration ever heard upon the commencement boards" of that institution. When opposition to British rule began, young Huntington was aroused, and at once espoused the cause of the colonists. He was an active Son of Liberty, and was one of the earliest captains of militia in his native town. He raised a regiment, and with it joined the Continental army in 1775. In 1777, Congress commissioned him a brigadier, which office he held until the close of the war. Washington highly esteemed him, and appointed him collector of the port of New London in 1789. He resided there until his death, which occurred on the 25th of September, 1818. His first wife was daughter of Governor Trumbull. She died at Dedham, while her husband was on his way to Cambridge, in 1775. His second wife was sister to the late Bishop Moore of Virginia. She died in 1831.

Benjamin Huntington, of another family, was the first mayor of Norwich, and was a representative in the Continental Congress from 1784 to 1787 inclusive ; also during Washington's administration. His son Benjamin married a daughter of General Jedediah Huntington, who became the mother of Huntington, our distinguished artist. He was at one time one of the most eminent of New York brokers. He died on the 3d of August, 1850, at the age of seventy-three years.

silver cup, with a richly-wrought handle, and bearing the initials I. R., which belonged to Mr. Robinson. It is properly preserved as a most precious heir-loom.

The road to Lebanon passes through a broken but fertile country, every where thoroughly cultivated where tillage is practicable. We passed through Old Norwich and over Bean Hill, but, mistaking the Colchester road for the Lebanon turnpike, found ourselves at Fitchville, in Bozrah, nearly two miles from our most direct way.[1] The ride along the high banks of the winding Yantic, coursing in a deep bed among stately trees, was ample compensation for the loss of time, and we had no inclination to chide the road-fork that deceived us.

The gentle hills rise one above another toward Lebanon, until they are lost in a high, rolling plain, on which the old town is situated. The land throughout that region has ever been held in the highest estimation for its fertility ; and around Lebanon, the focus of Connecticut patriotism and vigilance during the Revolution, cluster associations of the deepest interest. Here was the residence of Governor Trumbull, whose name and deeds are worthily associated with those of Washington, on the records of our war for independence. No man during that contest acted with more

---

[1] The origin of this name is a little amusing. A plain man, who lived where Fitchville now is, was not remarkable for quoting Scripture correctly. On one occasion, in quoting the passage from Isaiah, " Who is this that cometh from Edom, with dyed garments from Bozrah," &c., he stated that the *Prophet Bozrah* said thus and so. He was afterward called the Prophet, and the place of his residence *Bozrah*. When the town was incorporated, that name was given to it.—*Barber*, 302.

[2] Jonathan Trumbull was born at Lebanon, Connecticut, on the 10th of June (O. S.), 1710. He graduated at Harvard in 1727, and commenced the study of theology with the Reverend Solomon Williams, of Lebanon. The death of an elder brother, who was engaged in a mercantile business with his father at Lebanon, caused him to become a merchant instead of a clergyman. At the age of twenty-three he was elected a member of the Connecticut Assembly, where his business capacities raised him rapidly in public estimation. He was elected lieutenant governor of the colony in 1766, and by virtue of that office became chief justice of the Superior Court. His first bold step in opposition to Great Britain was in refusing to take the oath enjoined in 1768, which was an almost unconditional submission to all the power claimed by Parliament ; nor would he be present when others, more timorous than he, took it. Because of his firmness he was chosen governor of the colony in 1769, and he has the proud distinction of being the only colonial governor at the commencement of the Revolution who espoused the cause of the colonies. He was considered the whig leader in New England while the Adamses and Hancock were legislating in the Continental Congress ; and during the whole contest no man was more implicitly relied upon as a firm, consistent, and active friend of liberty than Governor Trumbull. " General Washington relied on him," says Sparks, " as one of his main pillars of support." In 1783, when peace for the colonies returned, Governor Trumbull, then seventy-three years old, declined a re-election to the office of governor, which he had held fourteen consecutive years. He retired from public life, but did not live long to enjoy the quiet he so much coveted in the bosom of his family. He was seized with a malignant fever in August, 1785, and on the 17th of that month died. His son was afterward Governor of Connecticut, and in 1849 his grandson filled that responsible office.

The Marquis de Chastellux, who came to America with Rochambeau in 1780, has left behind him a charming, life-like description of his sojourn here. He thus pleasantly alludes to Governor Trumbull. " I have already painted Governor Trumbull. At present you have only to represent to yourself this little old man, in the antique dress of the first settlers in this colony, approaching a table surrounded by twenty huzzar officers, and, without either disconcerting himself or losing any thing of his formal stiffness, pronouncing, in a loud voice, a long prayer in the form of a *benedicite*. Let it not be imagined that he excites the laughter of his auditors ; they are too well trained ; you must, on the contrary, figure to yourself twenty *Amens*.

602 PICTORIAL FIELD-BOOK

Character and Services of Governor Trumbull.   His Dwelling and War Office.   Settlement of Lebanon.   Lauzun

energy, or plied his talents and resources with more industry than he. During the whole war, the responsible duties and services of governor of the state rested upon him, yet he performed immense labors in other departments of the field to which he was called, notwithstanding he was more than threescore years old. His correspondence was very extensive, and he sat in council no less than one thousand days during the war. Washington never applied to him for supplies of any kind without receiving an immediate response. It is a fact worthy of record that, although Connecticut can not point to any brilliant battle field within her borders, she furnished for that war more troops and supplies than any other colony, except Massachusetts. If the old *war office* of Governor Trumbull, yet standing at Lebanon, had a tongue to speak, it might tell

GOVERNOR TRUMBULL'S WAR OFFICE.[1]

of many a scheme elaborated there, which, in its consummation, may have been the act that turned the scale of destiny in favor of the Americans. There the illustrious owner discussed with Washington, Franklin, Rochambeau, and others, the gravest questions which then occupied the attention of two hemispheres. Such a spot is like consecrated ground, and the shoes of irreverence should never press the green-sward around it.

THE TRUMBULL HOUSE.

We dined at the upper end of the village, and then proceeded to visit the relics of the era of the Revolution which remain. I have called Lebanon an old town. A portion of the tract was purchased about 1698, of *Owaneko*, the son of *Uncas*. There were several tracts purchased by the whites in the vicinity, all of which were united in the year 1700. The village is situated principally upon a street thirty rods wide, and more than a mile in length. Several well-built houses erected before or about the time of the Revolution yet remain. Among them is that of Governor Trumbull. It is a substantial frame building, and is now (1849) owned by Mrs. Eunice Mason, a widow eighty years of age. We were denied the pleasure of an interview with her on account of her feeble health. The house is on the west side of the street, near the road running westward to Colchester. Sixty or seventy rods southwest from the Trumbull House is the "barrack lot," the place where Lauzun's legion of cavalry were encamped.[2] His corps consisted of about five hundred horsemen. Rocham-

[1] This was the building in which Governor Trumbull transacted his public business. It formerly stood near his dwelling, but is now several rods northwest of it, on the same side of the Common. For many years it was occupied as a post-office. This sketch was taken from the open field in the rear, looking north.

[2] The Duke de Lauzun was an accomplished, but exceedingly voluptuous and unprincipled man. His personal beauty, talents, wit, wealth, and bravery were passports to the friendship of men who abhorred his profligacy. Why he espoused the cause of the Americans it is not easy to determine, unless, surfeited with sensual indulgences, he was desirous of engaging in new excitements, where he might regain the waning vigor of his body. His conduct here made him very popular. After his return to Europe he became acquainted with Talleyrand, and accompanied him on a mission to England in 1792. There one of his familiar associates was the Prince of Wales, afterward George IV. On the death of his uncle, the Duke de Biron, Lauzun succeeded to the title. He became involved in the stormy movements of the French Revolution, and being found guilty of secretly favoring the Vendeans, was executed on the 31st of December, 1793. Two officers in his regiment in America, named Dillon, brothers, also suffered death by the guillotine.

beau was there, with five regiments, for about three weeks, in the winter of 1780, and while he tarried Washington arrived, stayed a few days, and reviewed the French troops. A French soldier was shot for desertion, a few rods north of the " barrack lot."

Nearly opposite the Trumbull mansion is the old tavern kept during the Revolution by Captain Alden. It is famous generally as a place of rendezvous of the French officers, for drinking and playing, and more particularly as the house where General Prescott, the British officer who was captured on Rhode Island, stopped to dine, while on his way, under an escort, to Washington's camp, and received a horsewhipping from the landlord.[1] Of the remarkable circumstances of Prescott's capture I shall hereafter write. Mr. Wattles, the present proprietor of the old tavern, is a descendant of Captain Alden. While making the annexed sketch we were joined by Captain Dutton, the venerable citizen to whom we bore a letter of introduction, but who was ab-

THE ALDEN TAVERN.

sent from home when we arrived in the village. He has a distinct recollection of all the revolutionary events about Lebanon and vicinity, and could direct us to every spot made memorable by those events.

On the corner of the road leading from Lebanon to Windham is the house once occupied by William Williams, one of the signers of the Declaration of Independence. It has been slightly modified, but its general appearance is the same as it was during the Revolution Its present occupant is Mr. Simeon Peckam. A biographical sketch of Mr. Williams will be found among those

THE WILLIAMS HOUSE.

THE TRUMBULL VAULT.[2]

of the Signers, in another portion of this work, and the most prominent events of his life are also noticed in his epitaph, given on the next page.

We will pass on to the sacred inclosure containing the vault of the Trumbull family. It is in a cemetery a little eastward of the village, and near the Windham Road — a cemetery which probably contains the remains of more distinguished men of the Revolution than any other in the country. In the Trumbull tomb are the remains of two governors of Connecticut, the first commissary general of the United States, and a signer of the Declaration of Independence.

[1] While at table, Mrs. Alden brought on a dish of succotash (boiled beans and corn), a dish much valued in America. Prescott, unused to such food, exclaimed indignantly, " What! do you treat me with the food of hogs?" and taking the dish from the table, strewed the contents over the floor. Captain Alden, being informed of this, soon entered with a horsewhip, and flogged the general severely. After Prescott was exchanged and restored to his command on Rhode Island, the inhabitants of Newport deputed William Rotch, Dr. Tupper, and Timothy Folger to negotiate some concerns with him in behalf of the town. They were for some time refused admittance to his presence, but the doctor and Folger finally entered the room. Prescott stormed with great violence, until Folger was compelled to withdraw. After the doctor had announced his business, and Prescott had become calm, the general said, " Was not my treatment to Folger very uncivil?" " Yes," replied the doctor. " Then," said Prescott, " I will tell you the reason; he looked so much like a d—d Connecticut man that horsewhipped me, that I could not endure his presence."
—*Thatcher's Journal*, p. 175.

[2] The marble monument standing in front of the tomb is in memory of William Williams, a signer of the

604   PICTORIAL FIELD-BOOK

Return to Norwich.   Destruction of the Yantic Falls.   Birth-place of Arnold.   Inscription upon the Trumbull Monument.

The day was waning when I finished my sketches, and bidding Lebanon and its interesting associations adieu, we returned to Norwich, stopping for a few minutes at the Sachem's Burial-ground, on the verge of the city, to delineate the monument of Uncas, printed on page 30.

On the following morning, accompanied by Mr. Williams and his son in a light dearborn, I proceeded to visit the many points of historic interest within and around Norwich. We went to the plain and the upper town by the road that passes along the margin of the Yantic, to the once romantic falls near the mouth of that river. The natural beauties of this cascade were half hidden and defaced long ago by towering factories; but the chief spoiler was *public improvement*, which, with pick and powder-blast, hammer and trowel, has digged down the crown of the waterfall, and bridged it by a rail-way viaduct. A curve of a few rods might have spared the beautiful Yantic Falls; but what right has Nature to intrude her charms in the way of the footsteps of Mammon? I saw at the house of Mr. Trumbull in Norwich, a fine picture of these romantic falls, painted by the eminent artist JOHN TRUMBULL, a son of the patriot governor, before a layer of brick or the sound of an ax had desecrated the spot. It was, indeed, a charming scene.

BIRTH-PLACE OF BENEDICT ARNOLD.

About half way between Norwich city and the upper town, on the right or south side of the road, was the birth-place of Benedict Arnold, depicted in the annexed engraving. The view is from the road, looking southeast. The house had had some slight additions to its size since Arnold played in its garden in petticoats and bib, yet its general appearance was the same as at that time. Several circumstances bord-

Declaration of Independence, and bears the following inscription: "The remains of the Honorable WILLIAM WILLIAMS are deposited in this tomb. Born April 8th, 1731; died the 2d of August, 1811, in the 81st year of his age. A man eminent for his virtues and piety. For more than 50 years he was constantly employed in public life, and served in many of the most important offices in the gift of his fellow-citizens. During the whole period of the Revolutionary war, he was a firm, steady, and ardent friend of his country, and in the darkest times risked his life and wealth in her defense. In 1776 and 1777 he was a member of the American Congress, and as such signed the Declaration of Independence. His public and private virtues, his piety and benevolence, will long endear his memory to his surviving friends; above all, he was a sincere Christian, and in his last moments placed his hope, with an humble confidence, in his Redeemer. He had the inexpressible satisfaction to look back upon a long, honorable, and well-spent life."

On the pedestal upon the top of the tomb are the following inscriptions: "Sacred to the memory of Jonathan Trumbull, Esq., who, unaided by birth or powerful connections, but blessed with a noble and virtuous mind, arrived to the highest station in government. His patriotism and firmness during 50 years' employment in public life, and particularly in the very important part he acted in the American Revolution, as Governor of Connecticut, the faithful page of history will record. Full of years and honors, rich in benevolence, and firm in the faith and hopes of Christianity, he died, August 9, 1785, Ætates 75."

"Sacred to the memory of Madam Faith Trumbull,* the amiable lady of Governor Trumbull, born at Duxbury, Mass., A.D. 1718. Happy and beloved in her connubial state, she lived a virtuous, charitable, and Christian life at Lebanon, in Connecticut, and died lamented by numerous friends A.D. 1780, aged 62 years."

"Sacred to the memory of Joseph Trumbull, eldest son of Governor Trumbull, and first commissary general of the United States of America; a service to whose perpetual cares and fatigues he fell a sacrifice A.D. 1778, aged 42 years. Full soon, indeed! may his person, his virtues, and even his extensive benevolence be forgotten by his friends and fellow-men. But blessed be God! for the Hope that in his presence he shall be remembered forever."

"To the memory of Jonathan Trumbull, Esq.,† late Governor of the State of Connecticut. He was born March 26th, 1740, and died August 7th, 1809, aged 69 years. His remains were deposited with those of his father."

* Her maiden name was Robinson, and she was a lineal descendant of the Reverend Mr. Robinson, pastor at Leyden of many of the Pilgrim Fathers.
† Son of the first governor

ering upon the marvelous, and viewed with a little superstition, gave the house an unpleasant notoriety, and for many years it was untenanted, because it was haunted! by what or whom rumor never deigned to reveal.   When I visited it, only two or three rooms were occupied, the others being empty and locked.   The room in which Arnold was born, in the southwest corner of the second story, was occupied, and the people seemed to be familiar with the traditions respecting the boyhood of that distinguished man.   Arnold was blessed with a mother (Hannah King, of Norwich), who was, says her epitaph, "A pattern of patience, piety, and virtue," but her lessons seem to have been fruitless of good effect upon the headstrong boy.[1]   He was wayward, disobedient, unscrupulous, and violent—traits of character which finally worked his ruin.   He even attempted *murder*, while a young man residing at Norwich, by shooting a youthful Frenchman, who paid court to Arnold's sister, Hannah, by whom his love was reciprocated.   Young Arnold disliked him, and finding persuasion powerless on the mind of his sister to induce her to break off her engagement with the foreigner, vowed vengeance upon him if he ever caught him in the house again.   The opportunity occurred, and Arnold discharged a loaded pistol at him as he escaped from a window, fortunately without effect.   The young man left the place forever, and Hannah Arnold lived the life of a maiden.   Arnold and the Frenchman afterward met at Honduras They fought a duel, in which the latter was severely wounded.

When a mere boy, Arnold's courage was remarkable, and among his playmates he was a perfect despot.   A ringleader in every mischievous sport, he often performed astonishing feats of daring.   On a gala-day, he set a field-piece upright, poured powder into it, and dropped from his own hand a firebrand into the muzzle.   On another occasion, at the head of a number of boys, he rolled away some valuable casks from a ship-yard at Chelsea,[2] to make a thanksgiving bonfire.   An officer, sent by the owner to recover them, arrested the casks on their way.   The stripling Arnold was enraged, and, taking off his coat upon the spot, dared the constable, a stout man, to fight him!   Such was the boyhood of one of the most intrepid generals of our Revolution—such was the early type of the unscrupulous, violent man whose memory is black with the foulest treason.[3]   We have met him in preceding

---

[1] Miss Caulkins publishes the following letter from Mrs. Arnold to Benedict, while he was at school in Canterbury.   It exhibits the character of his mother in strong contrast with his own in after life.

"Norwich, April 12, 1754.

"DEAR CHILD,—I received yours of the 1st instant, and was glad to hear that you was well.   Pray, my dear, let your first concern be to make your peace with God, as it is of all concerns of the greatest importance.   Keep a steady watch over your thoughts, words, and actions.   Be dutiful to superiors, obliging to equals, and affable to inferiors, if any such there be.   Always choose that your companions be your betters, that by their good examples you may learn.

"From your affectionate mother,   HANNAH ARNOLD.

"P.S.—I have sent you 50s.   Use it prudently, as you are accountable to God and your father.   Your father and aunt join with me in love and service to Mr. Cogswell and lady, and yourself.   Your sister is from home."

[2] Chelsea is the old port of Norwich.   The houses cluster chiefly at the mouth of the Shetucket.

[3] Oliver Arnold, a cousin of Benedict, and also a resident of Norwich, was the reputed author of the following scorching acrostic, written after the treason of his kinsman.   It is bad poetry and worse sentiment.

> "Born for a curse to virtue and mankind,
> Earth's broadest realm ne'er knew so black a mind.
> Night's sable veil your crimes can never hide,
> Each one so great, 'twould glut historic tide.
> Defunct, your cursed memory will live,
> In all the glare that infamy can give.
> Curses of ages will attend your name,
> Traitors alone will glory in your shame.

> "Almighty vengeance sternly waits to roll
> Rivers of sulphur on your treacherous soul;
> Nature looks shuddering back with conscious dread
> On such a tarnish'd blot as she has made.
> Let hell receive you riveted in chains,
> Doom'd to the hottest focus of its flames!"

The author of the above had a peculiar talent for making extempore verses.   Joel Barlow once met him

pages in his glorious career as a bold patriot; we shall meet him again presently amid the scenes of his degradation.

Leaving the Arnold House, we rode to the upper town, and halted at the spacious mansion of Charles Spaulding, Esq., formerly the residence of Governor Samuel Huntington, who was also a signer of the Declaration of Independence, and President of Congress. It was considered the finest dwelling in Norwich when occupied by the governor, and now presents an excellent specimen of the architecture of that era. Surrounded by shade-trees and adorned with shrubbery, it is a summer residence to be coveted by those who love spacious rooms and a quiet location. I saw in the possession

GOVERNOR HUNTINGTON'S MANSION.

of Mrs. Spaulding an autograph letter of General Washington, written to Governor Huntington, then President of Congress. It has never been published, and as its purport is of an interesting public nature, I give a copy of it here.[1]

"Head-quarters, New Windsor, 10th April, 1781.

"SIR,

"I beg leave to introduce to your excellency Colonel Menonville, deputy adjutant general to the French army. This gentleman, who is charged by his excellency the Count de Rochambeau with matters respecting a contract entered into by Dr. Franklin, in behalf of the United States, for the supply of a quantity of provision, will, through your excellency, lay his business generally before Congress.

"He will also, agreeably to the wishes of Count Rochambeau, make an application for some heavy iron cannon for the use of the works at Newport, which he understands were imported into New Hampshire for the use of the seventy-four gun ship now upon the stocks. The brass artillery at present in them are the artillery of siege, and must be removed should the army remove. If there are such cannon in New Hampshire, and there is no probability of their being soon wanted for the purpose for which they were intended, I think a part of them can not be better applied.

"I recommend Colonel Menonville to your excellency's personal attention as a gentleman of peculiar merit.

"I have the honor to be, with great respect, your excellency's most obedient and humble servant,   GEO. WASHINGTON.

"His Excellency the President of Congress."

In the rear of the Huntington mansion is the cemetery of the first Congregational society of Norwich. Within it lie the remains of many of the early inhabitants of the town, and

---

in a book-store in New Haven, and asked him for a specimen of his talent. Arnold immediately repeated the following:

"You've proved yourself a sinful cre'tur;
You've murder'd Watts and spoil'd the meter;
You've tried the Word of God to alter,
And for your pains deserve a halter."

To understand the witty sarcasm of these lines, it must be remembered that Barlow, at that time, was enjoying much notoriety by a publication of a revised and altered edition of Watts's Psalms and Hymns.

[1] The only letter written by Washington at this date, and published in his "Life and Writings" by Sparks, was addressed to the Count de Rochambeau, on the subject of an expedition to Penobscot. See Sparks, viii., 8.

OF THE REVOLUTION. 607

Family Vault of Governor Huntington.　　Tomb of General Jabez Huntington.　　His five Sons.　　The old Burying-ground

upon the steep southern slope of a hill is the family vault of Governor Huntington.　It is
substantially built of brick.　On the
front, over the entrance, is an inscribed
marble tablet.[1]　The tomb is somewhat dilapidated, and the ground overgrown with brambles.　In the southern portion of the cemetery, separated
from the others by a stone fence, is the
family vault of General Jabez Huntington,[2] formerly one of the leading

GOVERNOR HUNTINGTON'S TOMB.

men of Norwich, and peculiarly honored in contributing five hardy sons to the Continental
army.　Jedediah was a brigadier general ; Andrew was a commissary ; Joshua and Ebenezer were colonels.　Zachariah, the youngest, was still living with his son, Thomas M. Huntington, Esq., a few rods north of the residence of General Jedediah Huntington, pictured on
page 32.　We called to see him, but indisposition prevented his receiving visitors.　He
was then nearly eighty-six years of age.　He was drafted in the militia in 1780, but saw
little of active military service.[3]

General Jabez Huntington's tomb, like that of the governor, is constructed of brick, having
an inscribed marble tablet in front ;[4] but, un-
like the other, it was not covered with brambles, nor was there a blade of grass upon the
old graves that surround it.　The ground had
been burned over to clear it of bushes and bri-
ers, and the ancient tomb-stones were shamefully blackened by fire.　A few yards from
Huntington's tomb is the more humble grave
of Diah Manning, who was a drummer in the
Continental army.　He was the jailer at Norwich during the French Revolution.　When

GENERAL HUNTINGTON'S TOMB

Boyer, afterward President of Hayti, was brought to Norwich, among other French prisoners, in 1797, he was treated with great kindness by Manning.　The prisoner did not forget
it, and when President of St. Domingo, he sent presents to Manning's family.

Leaving the ancient cemetery, we returned to the city, and called upon the almost centenarian Captain Erastus Perkins, residing on Shetucket Street.　He is yet living (1850),
in the ninety-ninth year of his age.　We found him quite strong in body and mind.　Many
scenes of his early years are still vivid pictures in his memory, and he was able to reproduce
them with much interest.　He said he distinctly remembered the circumstance of quite a
large body of men going from Norwich to New Haven, in 1765, to assist in compelling In-

---

[1] The following is a copy of the inscription : "SAMUEL HUNTINGTON, Esq., Governor of Connecticut,
having served his fellow-citizens in various important offices, died the 5th day of January, A.D. 1796, in the
65th year of his age."

"His consort, Mrs. Martha Huntington, died June 4th, A.D. 1794, in the 57th year of her age."

A portrait and biographical sketch of Governor Huntington will be found among those of the signers of
the Declaration of Independence, in another part of this work.

[2] Jabez Huntington was born in Norwich, in 1719.　He graduated at Yale College in 1741, and soon
afterward entered into mercantile business.　At one time himself and sons owned and fitted out at the port
of Norwich twenty vessels for the West India trade.　In 1750 he was elected a member of the Connecticut
Assembly, was speaker for several years, and also a member of the Council.　He lost nearly half his property by the capture of his vessels when the Revolution broke out.　He was an ardent patriot, a very active
member of the Council of Safety, and held the office of major general in the militia.　He died at Norwich
in 1786.

[3] General Zachariah Huntington is no more.　He died in June, 1850, at the age of eighty-eight.　Thus
one after another of those whom I visited has since gone to rest in the grave.

[4] The following is a copy of the inscription : "The family tomb of the Honorable Jabez Huntington,
Esq., who died October 5, 1786, aged 67 years."

gersoll, the stamp distributor, to resign his office.   Captain Perkins went to Roxbury in 1775, and was a sutler in Colonel Huntington's regiment at the time of the battle of

^{1848.} Bunker Hill.   He was in New York about two years ago, and pointed out the spot in Wall Street where he stood and saw Washington take the oath as President of the United States, sixty-one years before.   For many years Captain Perkins was surveyor of the port of Norwich, and throughout a long life has preserved the esteem of its citizens He is now the honored head of five generations.[1]   A few friends of his youth are still living in Norwich, but most of that generation have long since departed.   I was informed by Dr. W. P. Eaton that, the day before I visited Norwich, Captain Perkins and three other men were in his store, whose united ages were three hundred and fifty-seven years—an average of eighty-nine !

Toward evening we strolled up the Shetucket to Greenville, visited the extensive paper and cotton mills there, and returning, crossed, at Chelsea, to the Preston side of the river, and ascended by a winding road to the lofty summit of Tory Hill, so called from the cir- cumstance that it was the confiscated property of a Tory of the Revolution.   A magnificent prospect opens to the view from that bald, rocky pinnacle.   Southward was visible the dark line of Long Island Sound ; on the west, half hidden by groves, rolled the Thames ; north- ward and eastward lay a vast amphitheater of cultivated hills, and the valleys of the Yantic, Quinebaug, and the Shetucket, and at our feet was Norwich city, in crescent form, clasping a high, rocky promontory, like the rich setting of a huge emerald, for in the midst rose the towering Wawekus, yet green with the lingering foliage of summer.   A more picturesque scene than this grand observatory affords need not be sought for by the student and lover of nature.   There we lingered until the sun went down behind the hills that skirt the great Mohegan Plain, and in the dim twilight we made our way back to the city.   Between eight and nine o'clock in the evening I bade my kind friend Mr. Williams[2] adieu, and left Nor-

---

[1] It is a rather singular fact that Captain Perkins and his wife were both born on Sunday.   Their first child was born on Sunday.   They had one born on every day of the week—the first on Sunday morning, and the last on Saturday evening ; and the head of each of the five generations of which he is the eldest was born on Sunday.

[2] Mr. Edwin Williams, and his elder brother, Mr. Joseph Williams, of Norwich, are sons of General Jo- seph Williams, who, though a young man, was an active patriot during the Revolutionary war.   He was a merchant, and, in connection with his partner, William Coit, whose daughter he married, was engaged in fitting out armed vessels from Norwich and New London.   In one of these he made a voyage to the West Indies.   The vessel was pursued by a British armed ship, and an action ensued in which the American vessel was the winner.   General Williams spent much of the latter portion of his life in organizing and disciplin- ing the militia of New London county ; and until his death he was extensively engaged as a shipping and importing merchant.   He died in October, 1800, aged forty-seven years.

Mrs. Russell Hubbard, of Norwich, daughter of General Williams, permitted me to have a copy of a letter of his, written in 1776, from near New York, to his business partner, Mr. Coit.   Young Williams had ac- companied the Connecticut Continental troops to New York, taking with him a supply of articles adapted to the use of the army.   He was then only twenty-three years of age.   The letter is interesting, as exhib iting a feature in the business life of the day, and the perfect coolness with which trade was carried on in the midst of the most imminent peril.   The letter is written on the blank leaf of an account book.

"New York, seven miles from the city, September 8, 1776.

"DEAR SIR,

"Ever since I wrote you by Mr. Walden we have been in confusion.   The enemy opened two batteries opposite to our fort at Hell Gate last Saturday evening, and began cannonading and bombarding early on Sunday morning.   They fired several shot into the house where we kept our store.   We thought it prudent to move a little back, which we have done, but have not got clear of their shot ; they are flying about us continually.   We have about £140 in value on hand, besides money that I have purchased since I came here with what was on hand before.

"The enemy are now landing on the island between Hell Gate and the main, and 'tis supposed they mean to make a push for Kingsbridge, and cut us off from the main ; but I believe they can not do it, as we are prepared for them at Kingsbridge ; but I make no doubt we shall soon have an engagement.

"Colonel Sergeant, Dr. Hamans, and I, have sent what money we have to West Chester by Dr. Hamans's boy.   I have sent about £150.   It will not do to move our stores till the regiment is obliged to go, as they can not do without some necessaries here.

wich, in the cars, for Allyn's Point, seven miles below, whence I embarked for New London, eight miles further down the Thames, arriving there at ten.

New London is pleasantly situated upon a rocky slope on the right bank of the Thames, three miles from Long Island Sound, and one hundred and thirty-four miles eastward of New York city. From the high ground in the rear of the city, whereon many fine resi dences are built, a very extensive view of the Sound and the surrounding country is obtained Its earliest Indian name was *Nameaug ;* but the first English settlers, John Winthrop and others, called it Pequot, from the people who had inhabited the country on the banks of the Pequot or Thames River. By an act of the Assembly of Connecticut, in March, 1658, it was named New London, to perpetuate in America the title of the capital of England. The river was also named Thames, by the same authority and for a similar reason. The harbor is one of the best in the United States. It is commanded by forts Griswold and Trumbull,

situated, the former upon its east bank, at Groton, and the latter upon the west. The fortifications are upon the sites of those of the same name which were erected there in the time of the Revolution.

NEW LONDON HARBOR.

New London and Norwich were intimately associated in all political matters when the controversy with Great Britain arose. The latter, included within New London county, was regarded as the chief place ; while the former, being the port of entry, became the point of most importance when British fleets and armies came to subdue the Americans. From an early period the harbor of New London was a favorite resort for vessels navigating the Sound, on account of the depth of water and its sheltered position. Here the brigantines and other vessels of the famous buccaneers sometimes sought shelter from storms ; and it is believed that therein lay the vessel of the notorious Captain Kidd about the time when his treasures were concealed on Gardiner's Island, on the opposite side of the Sound. Great efforts were made by the commanders of British ships to obtain possession of the city and harbor during the Revolution, and for a long time a fleet of some thirty vessels hovered along the coast in the vicinage, chiefly in Gardiner's Bay and the neighborhood of Fisher's Island. But the vigilant authorities and people of Connecticut kept them at bay. From the time of the Bunker Hill battle until the town was burned by British troops, headed by the then traitor, Benedict Arnold, a strong military force was kept there, and every attention was paid to fortifying the harbor. September 6, 1781.

In 1774 the people of New London held a town meeting, and passed strong resolutions in reference to the oppressive acts of the British Parliament. After expressing their sincere loyalty to the king, they resolved that " the cause of Boston is the common cause of all the North American colonies ;" that a *union* of all the colonies was of the greatest importance ; that they earnestly wished for, and would promote, the assembling June 22.

" I shall send Isaac* out to-day. If we are taken or killed, you can send for the money I have sent out. I would not have this stop your sending the goods I wrote for, as far as it will do to come by water.
" From your humble servant,
" JOSEPH WILLIAMS.

" P.S.—Commandant Serjeant tells me he has just received intelligence that our Congress has appointed a committee to wait on Lord Howe."†

---

* He was a brother of the writer of the letter, and was then about fifteen years old. He served his country during a greater portion of the war, and was finally captured by the English and pressed into their naval service, in which he lost a leg. So grea was his hatred of the English, that he engaged in the French marine service during the French Revolution, in consequence of which he was tried for violating the United States laws of neutrality, was found guilty, and fined and imprisoned. He died at Preston, when about eighty years of age. General Williams had two other brothers in the Continental army—Frederic, who died or was killed in New York in 1776, and was buried in St. Paul's church-yard ; and Benjamin, who lost his life in the Jersey prison-ship, in 1781, at the age of twenty-three.

† The conference of this committee with Lord Howe was held on the 11th of September, 1776, at the house of Colonel Billop, yet standing at the southwest end of Staten Island. A drawing of the building will be found on page 609, vol. ii.

of a general Congress ; and that they would religiously observe and abide by the resolves of such a body. They also appointed a committee of correspondence for the town.[1]

NEW LONDON HARBOR, LOOKING NORTH.[2]

In 1775 the erection of two forts for the defense of the harbor of New London was begun, one upon the rocky extremity of a peninsula on the west side of the Thames, about a mile below the city, and the other upon Groton Hill, on the opposite side of the harbor. The former, when completed, was called Fort Trumbull, and the latter Fort Griswold. Several vessels of the little naval armament of Connecticut were fitted out at New London ; and into that port a number of prizes captured by American cruisers were taken, and their cargoes disposed of.[3] In 1777, a frigate of thirty-six guns, ordered by the Continental Congress to be built in Connecticut, was constructed in the Thames, between New London and Norwich, under the direction of Captain Joshua Huntington. Several small armed vessels on private account sailed from this port, and greatly annoyed the enemy upon the coast, capturing their provision vessels, and injuring transports that happened to be separated from convoys. These things so irritated the British commanders here, that New London was marked for special vengeance, and Benedict Arnold was the chosen instrument to execute it.

I have already alluded to the junction of the American and French armies upon the Hudson, in the summer of 1781, and their departure for Virginia—the original design of attacking New York city having been abandoned, in consequence of the reception, by Clinton, of re-enforcements from abroad, and the intelligence that the Count de Grasse might not be expected from the West Indies in time for such an operation.[4] When Sir Henry Clinton became certain of the destination of the allied armies, and perceived that they were too far on their way for him to hope to overtake them in pursuit, he dispatched Arnold, who had just returned from a predatory expedition in Virginia, to make like demonstrations upon the New England coast. Clinton's hoped-for result of this measure was to deter Washington from his purpose of pushing southward, or, at least, to make him weaken his army by sending back detachments for the defense of the New England frontier upon the Sound. But he failed to effect his purpose, and the expedition of Arnold was fruitful only of misery for a few inhabitants, and of abundant disgrace and contumely for the perpetrators of the outrage.

At daybreak on the morning of the 6th of September, 1781, a British fleet, under Captain Beasly, consisting of twenty-four sail, bearing a considerable land and marine force under the general command of Benedict Arnold, appeared off the harbor of New London, having left the eastern end of Long Island the evening previous. A large proportion of the land forces consisted of Tories and some Hessians, the instruments employed when any thing cruel

---

[1] This committee consisted of Richard Law, Gurdon Salstonstall, Nathaniel Shaw, Jr., Samuel H. Parsons, and Guy Richards. The little village of Groton, opposite, also held a town meeting the week previous, and, after passing similar resolutions, appointed a committee of correspondence.—See Hinman's *Historical Collections*, p. 52–56.

[2] This little sketch shows the relative position of the forts. Fort Trumbull is seen on the left of the picture, and Fort Griswold, with the Groton Monument, is on the extreme right.

[3] The following are the names of the war-vessels in the service of the State of Connecticut during the Revolution : Brigs Minerva, American, Silliman ; ship Oliver Cromwell ; frigates Trumbull, Bourbon ; schooners Spy, Defense ; sloops Dolphin, Mifflin, Resistance, Schuyler, Stark, Young Cromwell, Confederacy, Count de Grasse, Tiger, Alliance, Phœnix ; and row-galleys Shark, Whiting, Crane, The Guilford, New Defense, Putnam, and Revenge. [4] See page 436, vol. i.

was to be performed.[1] They landed in two divisions of about eight hundred each : one on the east or Groton side of the Thames, commanded by Lieutenant-colonel Eyre, and the other on the New London side, led by the traitor general, who debarked in the cove at Brown's

Farm, near the light-house. The militia hastened in small parties to oppose them, but were too few to produce much effect other than wounding some of the enemy on their march toward the town. The advance battery, situated about half way be-

VIEW OF THE LANDING-PLACE OF ARNOLD.[2]

tween Fort Trumbull and the light-house, in which were eight pieces of cannon, as well as the fort itself, was too feebly manned to offer resistance, and the troops of each evacuated, and crossed over to the stronger post of Fort Griswold, on Groton Hill. The city was thus left exposed to the enemy, whose great weapon of destruction was the torch. First, the stores upon the wharves were set on fire, and then the dwellings on Mill Cove were consumed. Nearly the whole town was laid in ashes, and several vessels were burned.[3] Many inhabitants in comfortable circumstances were now houseless and wanderers, reduced to absolute beggary. None were permitted to save their furniture, and the soldiery were allowed free scope for brutality and plunder. It is said that Arnold stood in the belfry of a church,

---

[1] The division under Arnold consisted of the 38th regiment of regulars, the Loyal Americans, the American Legion, refugees, and a detachment of fifty Yagers. Colonel Eyre's was composed of the 40th and 54th regiments, the third battalion of Jersey volunteers, and a detachment of Yagers and artillery.

[2] This sketch is from the west side of the cove in which the troops under Arnold landed. In the distance, on the extreme right, is the point where the division under Eyre debarked, and near the center is seen the monument on Groton Hill, near Fort Griswold. The shores of the cove are sandy, but the projections which form them are bold promontories of granite rock.

[3] The buildings burned in this expedition were 65 dwelling-houses containing 97 families, 31 stores, 18 shops, 20 barns, and 9 public and other buildings, among which were the court-house, jail, and church ; in all 143. Fifteen vessels with the effects of the inhabitants escaped up the river. The value of property destroyed was estimated at $485,980. This was the estimate of the committee which was appointed by the General Assembly of Connecticut, after the war, to ascertain the amount of loss sustained by the several towns in the state by conflagrations during the predatory inroads of the enemy. In 1793, the Assembly granted to the sufferers five hundred acres of land, lying within the precincts of the Western Reserve, in Ohio, and now included in the counties of Huron and Erie, and a small part of Ottawa. This tract is known as the "Fire Lands." I have noticed on page 371, vol. i., the settlement, by commissioners, who met at Trenton in 1782, of the question of jurisdiction over the Valley of Wyoming, and that it was decided in favor of Pennsylvania. Although Connecticut acquiesced in that decision, that state still claimed a right to the country westward of Pennsylvania, in extent north and south equal to its own limits in that direction and indefinitely westward, according to the letter of its charter. Connecticut, however, waived this claim by a sort of compromise, in 1786, by ceding to the United States all the lands thus included within its charter limits westward of Pennsylvania, except the reservation of a tract one hundred and twenty miles in length, adjoining that state. This tract was called the *Western Reserve*. After giving the half million of acres to the sufferers of Danbury, Fairfield, Norwalk, New Haven, and New London, the remainder was sold in 1795, and the proceeds were used as a school fund, for the support of schools in the state. Congress confirmed the title of Connecticut to the *Reserve* in 1800. It now forms a part of the State of Ohio, and is settled chiefly by New England people.

while the town was burning, and looked upon the scene with the apparent satisfaction of a Nero. Had he been content to be a traitor merely, the extenuating circumstances that have been alleged in connection with his treason might have left a feeling of commiseration in the bosoms of the American people; but this murderous expedition against the neighbors of his childhood and youth, and the wanton destruction of a thriving town, almost in sight of the spire of the church wherein he was baptized, present an act of malice too flagrant to be overlooked even by "meek-eyed pity" or loving charity. It was his last prominent blow against his country, and was such a climax to his treachery, that Britons, who "accepted the treason, but despised the traitor," shunned him as a monster of wickedness.

When the enemy landed, alarm-guns were fired; and before noon, while the town was burning, the militia collected in large numbers. Perceiving his peril, Arnold hastily retreated to his boats, closely pursued by the armed inhabitants. Five of the enemy were killed, and about twenty wounded. The Americans lost four killed, and ten or twelve wounded, some of them mortally.

When Fort Trumbull was evacuated, Arnold sent an order to Lieutenant-colonel Eyre to take immediate possession of Fort Griswold, in order to prevent the American shipping from leaving the harbor and sailing up the river. The militia hastily collected for the defense of the fort to the number of one hundred and fifty-seven—so hastily that many of them were destitute of weapons. Colonel William Ledyard was the commander of the fortress. The enemy approached cautiously through the woods in the rear, and captured a small advanced battery. Colonel Eyre then sent Captain Beckwith, with a flag, to demand a surrender of the fort, which was peremptorily refused.[1] An assault was begun; the American flag on the southwest bastion was shot down, and an obstinate battle of about forty minutes ensued, during which the British were repulsed, and were on the point of fleeing back to their shipping. The attack was made on three sides, the fort being square, with flanks. There was a battery between the fort and the river, but the Americans could spare no men to work it. The enemy displayed great coolness and bravery in forcing the pickets, making their way into the fosse, and scaling the revetment, in the face of a severe fire from the little garrison. When a sufficient number had obtained entrance thus far, they forced their way through the feebly-manned embrasures, and decided the conflict with bayonets, after a desperate struggle with the handful of determined patriots, many of whom were armed only with pikes. The fort was surrendered unconditionally. Colonel Eyre was wounded near the works, and died within twelve hours afterward on ship-board. Major Montgomery was pierced through with a spear, in the hands of a negro, and killed as he mounted the parapet, and the command devolved upon Major Bromfield. The whole loss of the British was two commissioned officers and forty-six privates killed, and eight officers (most of whom afterward died), with one hundred and thirty-nine non-commissioned officers and privates, wounded. The Americans had not more than a dozen killed before the enemy carried the fort. When that was effected, Colonel Ledyard ordered his men to cease firing and to lay down their arms, relying upon the boasted generosity of Britons for the cessation of bloodshed. But instead of British regulars, led by honorable men, his little band was surrounded by wolf-like Tories, infernal in their malice, and cruel even to the worst savagism, and also by the hired assassins, the German Yagers. They kept up their fire and bayonet thrusts upon the unarmed patriots, and opening the gates of the fort, let in blood-thirsty men that were without, at the head of whom was Major Bromfield, a New Jersey Loyalist. "Who commands this garrison?" shouted Bromfield, as he entered. Colonel Ledyard, who was standing near, mildly replied, "I did, sir, but you do now," at the same time handing his sword to the victor. The Tory miscreant immediately murdered Ledyard by running him through the body with the weapon he had just surrendered![2] The massacre continued in all parts

---

[1] There were several hundreds of the people collected in the vicinity, and an officer had been sent out to obtain re-enforcements. Upon these Colonel Ledyard relied; but the officer became intoxicated, and the expected aid did not arrive.

[2] Colonel Ledyard was a cousin of John Ledyard, the celebrated traveler, who was a native of Groton

of the fort, until seventy men were killed, and thirty-five mortally or dangerously wounded.[1] The enemy then plundered the fort and garrison of every thing valuable. Their appetite for slaughter not being appeased, they placed several of the wounded in a baggage-wagon, took it to the brow of the hill on which the fort stands, and sent it down with violence, intending thus to plunge the helpless sufferers into the river. The distance was about one hundred rods, the ground very rough. The jolting caused some of the wounded to expire, while the cries of agony of the survivors were heard across the river, even in the midst of the crackling noise of the burning town! The wagon was arrested in its progress by an apple-tree, and thus the sufferers remained for more than an hour, until their captors stretched them upon the beach, preparatory to embarkation. Thirty-five of them were paroled and carried into a house near by, where they passed the night in great distress, a burning thirst being their chief tormentor. Although there was a pump in a well of fine water within the fort, the wounded were not allowed a drop with which to moisten their tongues, and the first they tasted was on the following morning, when Fanny Ledyard, a niece of the murdered colonel, came, like an angel of mercy, at dawn, with wine, and water, and chocolate. She approached stealthily, for it was uncertain whether the enemy had left. Fortunately, they had sailed during the night, carrying away about forty of the inhabitants prisoners.[2] Thus ended the most ignoble and atrocious performance of the enemy during the war, and the intelligence of it nerved the strong arms of the patriots in the conflict at Yorktown, in Virginia, a few weeks later, which resulted in the capture of the British army of the South under Cornwallis.

During the war between the United States and Great Britain, from 1812 to 1815, New London was several times menaced with invasion by the enemy. In May, 1813, as Commodore Decatur, then in command of the *United States*, with his prize, the *Macedonian*, fitted out as an American frigate, was attempting to get to sea, he was chased by a British squadron under Commodore Hardy, and driven into New London, where he was blockaded for some time. On one occasion the town and neighborhood were much alarmed on account of a report that the enemy were about to bombard the place. A considerable military force was stationed there, and preparations were made to repel the invaders. The forts were well garrisoned with United States troops, and the militia turned out in great numbers. The enemy, however, did not attempt an attack, and, becoming wearied of watching Decatur, the British squadron put to sea, soon followed by our gallant commodore. Since that time no event has disturbed the repose or retarded the progress of New London. The whaling business, and other commercial pursuits, have poured wealth into its lap, and spread its pleasant dwellings over more than thrice its ancient area.

The most prominent point of attraction to the visitor at New London is the Groton Monument, on the eastern side of the Thames, which, standing upon high ground, is a conspicuous object from every point of view in the vicinity. I crossed the Thames early on the

---

His niece, Fanny, mentioned in the text, was from Southold, Long Island, and was then on a visit at the house of her uncle. The vest worn by Colonel L. on that occasion (as I have already noticed) is preserved in the cabinet of the Connecticut Historical Society.

[1] Arnold, in his dispatch to Sir Henry Clinton, gave the impression that the killed were victims of honorable strife. Of course he knew better, for his dispatch was written two days after the event, and every circumstance must have been known by him. Hear him: "I have inclosed a return of the killed and wounded, by which your excellency will observe that our loss, though very considerable, is short of the enemy's, who lost most of their officers, among whom was their commander, Colonel Ledyard. *Eighty-five men were found dead in Fort Griswold*, and sixty wounded, most of them mortally. Their loss on the opposite side (New London) must have been considerable, but can not be ascertained."

[2] See Arnold's *Dispatch to Sir H. Clinton;* Gordon, iii., 249; Sparks's *Life of Arnold; The Connecticut Journal*, 1781; *Narrative of Stephen Hempstead.* Mr. Hempstead was a soldier in the garrison at the time of the massacre, and was one of the wounded who were sent down the declivity in the baggage-wagon, suffered during the night, and experienced the loving kindness of Fanny Ledyard in the morning. His narrative was communicated to the Missouri Republican in 1826, at which time he was a resident of that state. Mr. Hempstead was a native of New London, and entered the army in 1775. He was at Dorchester during the siege of Boston, was in the battle of Long Island, and also in the engagement on Harlem Heights, where he had two of his ribs broken by a grape-shot.

October 12, morning after my arrival, and ascended to Fort Griswold, now a dilapidated for-
1848. tress, without ordnance or garrison, its embankments breaking the regular outline
of Groton Hill, now called Mount Ledyard.
A little northward of the fort rises a granite
monument, one hundred and twenty-seven feet
high, the foundation-stone of which is one
hundred and thirty feet above tide-water. It
was erected in 1830, in memory of the patriots who fell in the fort in 1781. Its pedestal, twenty-six feet square, rises to the height
of about twenty feet, and upon it is reared an
obelisk which is twenty-two feet square at the
base, and twelve feet at the top. It is ascended within by one hundred and sixty-eight
stone steps; and at the top is a strong iron
railing for the protection of visitors. Marble
tablets with inscriptions are placed upon the
pedestal.[2] The cost of its erection was eleven

MONUMENT AT GROTON.[1]

thousand dollars, which amount was raised by a lottery authorized by the state for that
purpose.

I paid the tribute-money of a "levy," or York shilling, to a tidy little woman living in the
stone building seen at the right of the monument, which procured for me the ponderous key
of the structure, and, locking myself in, I ascended to the top, with the privilege of gazing
and wondering there as long as I pleased. It was a toilsome journey up that winding stair-
case, for my muscles had scarcely forgotten a similar draught upon their energies at Breed's
Hill; but I was comforted by the teachings of the new philosophy that the *spiral* is the
only true ascent to a superior world of light, and beauty, and expansiveness of vision;[3] and
so I found it, for a most magnificent view burst upon the sight as I made the last upward
revolution and stood upon the dizzy height. The broad, cultivated hills and valleys; the
forests and groves slightly variegated by the pencil of recent frost; the city and river at my
feet, with their busy men and numerous sails; the little villages peeping from behind the
hills and woodlands in every direction, and the heaving Sound glittering in the southern horizon, were all basking in the light of the morning sun, whose radiance, from that elevation,
seemed brighter than I had ever seen it. It was a charming scene for the student of nature, and yet more charming for the student of the romance of American history. At the

---

[1] This is a view from the southwest angle of old Fort Griswold, looking northeast. The embankments
of the fort are seen in the foreground; near the figure is the well, the same mentioned by Mr. Hempstead
in his narrative; and just beyond this is the old entrance, or sally-port, through which the enemy, under
Bromfield, entered the fort.

[2] Over the entrance of the monument is the following inscription:

This Monument
was erected under the patronage of the State of Connecticut, A.D. 1830,
and in the 55th year of the Independence of the U. S. A.,
. In memory of the brave Patriots
who fell in the massacre at Fort Griswold, near this spot,
on the 6th of September, A.D. 1781,
when the British under the command of
the traitor Benedict Arnold,
burned the towns of New London and Groton, and spread
desolation and woe throughout this region.

On the south side of the pedestal, toward the fort, on a large tablet, are the names of the eighty-five persons who were killed in the fort, over which is the following:
"Zebulon and Naphtali were a people that jeoparded their lives until the death in the high places of the
field.—*Judges*, 5 *chap.*, 18 *verse*."

[3] See Swedenborg's *Views of the Spiritual World*, and *Revelations* of Davis, the clairvoyant.

base of the monument were the ruined fortifications where patriot blood flowed in abundance ; and at a glance might be seen every locality of interest connected with the burning of New London and the massacre at Groton.   Here was Fort Griswold ; there were Fort Trumbull and the city ; and yonder, dwindling to the stature of a chessman, was the lighthouse, by whose beacon the arch-traitor and his murderous bands were guided into the harbor.

Let us turn back two centuries, and what do we behold from this lofty observatory ? The Thames is flowing in the midst of an unbroken forest, its bosom rippled only by the zephyr, the waterfowl, or the bark canoe.   Here and there above the tree tops curls of blue smoke arise from the wigwams of the savages, and a savory smell of venison and fish comes up from the Groton shore.   Around us spreads the broad fair land known as the Pequot country, extending from the Nahantic, on the west, to the dominion of the Narragansets— the Rhode Island line—on the east, and northward it interlocks with that of the Mohegans, where Uncas, the rebel sachem, afterward bore rule.[1]   On yonder hill, a little southeast from our point of view, crowned with the stately oak and thick-leaved maple, is the royal residence of Sassacus, the prince of the Pequots.   Haughty and insolent, he scorns every overture of friendship from the whites, and looks with contempt upon the rebellious doings of Uncas.   Near by is his strong fort upon the Mystic River, and around him stand seven hundred warriors ready to do his bidding.   The English are but a handful, what has he to fear ?   Much, very much !

It is the season of flowers.   The white sails of vessels flutter in Narraganset Bay (now the harbor of Newport), and Captain Mason and seventy-seven well-armed men kneel upon their decks in devotion, for it is the morning of the Christian Sabbath.   On Tuesday they land.   Miantonōmoh, the chief sachem, gives them audience, and a free passport through his country.   Nor is this all ; with two hundred of his tribe, Miantonōmoh joins the English on their march of forty miles through the wilderness toward the Mystic River ; and the brave Niantics and the rebellious Mohegans, led by Uncas, swell the ranks, until five hundred savage "bowmen and spearmen" are in the train of Captain Mason.

It is a clear moonlight night.   Sheltered by huge rocks on the shore of the Mystic sleeps the little invading army,[2] while the unsuspecting Pequots in their fort near by are dancing and singing, filled with joy, because they have seen the pinnaces of the English sail by without stopping to do them harm, and believe that the Pale-faces dare not come nigh them. Little do they think that the tiger is already crouching to spring upon his prey !   On that high hill, upon the right, is the Pequot fort.[3]   It is early dawn, and the little army June 5, is pressing on silently up the wooded slope.   The Narragansets and Niantics, seized 1637. with fear, are lagging, while the eager English and Mohegans rush up to the attack.[4]   All but a sentinel are in a deep sleep.   Too late he cries, "*Owanux! Owanux!*"   "Englishmen ! Englishmen !"   The mounds are scaled ; the entrance is forced ; the palisades are

----

[1] Uncas was of the royal blood of the Pequots, and a petty sachem under Sassacus.   When the English first settled in Connecticut, he was in open rebellion against his prince.   To save himself and be revenged on his adversary, he sought and obtained the alliance of the English, and when the Pequot nation was destroyed, Uncas became the powerful chief of that tribe of Pequots called the Mohegans, from the circumstance of their inhabiting the place called Mohegan, now Norwich.

The Pequot country comprised the present towns of Waterford, New London, and Montville, on the west side of the Thames, and Groton, Stonington, and North Stonington, on the east of that river.   Windham, and a part of Tolland county, on the north, was the Mohegan country.

[2] These are called *Porter's Rocks*, and are situated near Portersville, on the west side of the Mystic. They are on the shore, about half a mile south of the residence of Daniel Eldridge.—See Barber's *Hist. Coll. of Conn.*, p. 313.

[3] This hill, eight miles northeast from New London, is known at the present day by the name of Pequot Hill.   It is a spot of much interest, aside from the commanding view obtained from its summit, as the place where the first regular conflict between the English and the natives of New England took place.   Such was the terror which this event infused into the minds of the Indian tribes, that for nearly forty years they refrained from open war with the whites, and the colonies prospered.

[4] Sassacus was the terror of the New England coast tribes.   A belief that he was in the fort on Pequot Hill was the cause of the fear which seized the Narragansets.   "Sassacus is in the fort !   Sassacus is all one god !" said Miantonōmoh ; "nobody can kill him."

broken down ; the mattings of the wigwams and the dry bushes and logs of the fort are set on fire, and seven hundred men, women, and children, perish in the flames or by the sword ! It is a dreadful sight, this slaughter of the strong, the beautiful, and the innocent ; and yet, hear the commander of the assailants impiously exclaiming, " God is above us !   He laughs his enemies and the enemies of the English to scorn, making them as a fiery oven.   Thus does the Lord judge among the heathen, filling the place with dead bodies !"[1]

From the other fort near the Pequot (Thames), where dwells Sassacus, three hundred warriors approach with horrid yells and bent bows.   But the English are too skillful, and too strongly armed with pike, and gun, and metal corselet, for those bare-limbed warriors, and they are scattered like chaff by the whirlwind of destruction.   The English make their way to Groton ; and yonder, just in time to receive them, before the remnant of the Pequots can rally and fall upon them, come their vessels around the remote headland.   With a fair breeze, many of the English sail for Saybrook, making the air vocal with hymns of praise and thanksgiving.   Others, with the Narragansets, march through the wilderness to the Connecticut River, and then, in happy reunion, warriors, soldiers, ministers, and magistrates join in a festival of triumph ![2]

Stately and sullen sits Sassacus in his wigwam on yonder hill, as the remnant of his warriors gather around him and relate the sad fortunes of the day.   They charge the whole terrible event to his haughtiness and misconduct, and tearing their hair, and stamping on the ground, menace him and his with destruction.   But hark ! the blast of a trumpet startles them ; from the head waters of the Mystic come two hundred armed settlers from Massachusetts and Plymouth to seal the doom of the Pequots.   Despair takes possession of Sassacus and his followers, and burning their wigwams and destroying their fort, they flee across the Pequot River westward, pursued by the English.   What terrible destruction is wrought by the new invaders !   Throughout the beautiful country bordering on the Sound wigwams and corn-fields are destroyed, and helpless men, women, and children are put to the sword. With Sassacus at their head, the doomed Pequots fly like deer pursued by hounds, and take shelter in Sasco Swamp, near Fairfield, where they all surrender to the English, except the chief and a few men who escape to the Mohawks.   The final blow is struck which annihilated the once powerful Pequots, and the great Sassacus, the last of his royal race in power except Uncas, falls by the hand of an assassin, among the people who opened their protecting arms to receive him.[3]

The dark vision of cruelty melts away ; smiling fields, and laden orchards, and busy towns, the products of a more enlightened and peaceful Christianity than that of two centuries back, are around me.   Russet corn-fields cover the hill—the royal seat of Sassacus—and in the bright harbor where the little English pinnaces, filled with bloody men, were just an-

---

[1] See Captain Mason's *Brief History of the Pequot War*, published in Boston in 1738, from which the principal facts in this narrative are drawn.   It makes one shudder to read the blasphemous allusions to the interposition of God in favor of the English which this narrative contains, as if

"The poor Indian, whose untutor'd mind
Sees God in clouds or hears him in the wind,"

was not an object of the care and love of the Deity.   Happily, the time is rapidly passing by when men believe that they are doing God service by slaughtering, maiming, or in the least injuring with vengeful feelings any of his creatures.

[2] The English lost only two men killed and sixteen wounded, while the Indians lost nearly six hundred men and seventy wigwams.

[3] The ostensible cause of this destructive war upon the Pequots was the fact that in March of that year, Sassacus, jealous of the English, had sent an expedition against the fort at Saybrook.   The fort was attacked, and three soldiers were killed.   In April they murdered several men and women at Wethersfield, carried away two girls, and destroyed twenty cows.   The English, urged by fear and interest, resolved to chastise them, and terrible indeed was the infliction.   " There did not remain a sannup or a squaw, a warrior or a child of the Pequot name.   A nation had disappeared in a day !"   The Mohegans, under Uncas, then became the most powerful tribe in that region, and soon afterward, as we have seen, they and the Narragansets, who assisted in the destruction of the Pequots, began a series of long and cruel wars against each other.

chored, spreads many a sail of peaceful commerce. The sun is near the meridian ; let us descend to the earth.

From the monument, after sketching the picture on page 46, I returned to the village of Groton, on the river bank, and visited the patriarch-*ess* of the place, Mrs. Anna Bailey, familiarly known as " Mother Bailey." Her husband, Captain Elijah Bailey, who died a few weeks previous to my visit, was appointed postmaster of the place by President Jefferson, and held the office until his death, a lapse of forty years. He was a lad about seventeen years old when New London was burned, and was in Fort Griswold just previous to the attack of Colonel Eyre. Young Bailey and a man named Williams were ordered by Ledyard to man a gun at the advanced redoubt, a little southeast of the fort. They were directed, in the event of not being able to maintain their ground, to retreat to the fort. They soon found it necessary to abandon their piece. Williams fled to the fort and got within ; but young Bailey, stopping to spike the gun, lost so much time, that when he knocked at the gate it was close barred, for the enemy were near. He leaped over the fence into a corn-field, and there lay concealed until the battle and massacre in the fort ended. " He was courting me at that very time, boy as he was," said Mrs. Bailey, who

MRS. BAILEY.[1]

related this circumstance to me. She was then a girl six weeks older than her lover, and remembers every event of the " terrible day." I was agreeably surprised on being introduced to Mrs. Bailey, expecting to find a common, decrepit old woman. She sat reading her Bible, and received me with a quiet ease of manner, and a pleasant countenance, where, amid the wrinkles of old age, were lingering traces of youthful beauty. I had been forewarned that, if I wished to find any favor in her sight, I must not exhibit the least hue of Whiggery in politics—a subject which engrosses much of her thoughts and conversation. Her husband had been a Democrat of the old Jefferson school ; and she possessed locks of hair, white, sandy, and grizzled, from the heads of Presidents Jackson and Van Buren, and of Colonel Richard M. Johnson, all of whom had honored her house by personal visits. With such precious mementoes, how could she be other than a Democrat ? Almost the first words she uttered on my entrance were, " What are Cass's prospects in New York ?" Forewarned, forearmed, I summoned to the support of my conscience all the possibilities in his favor, and told her that Mr. Cass would doubtless be elected President—at any rate, *he ought to be.* These words unlocked her kind feelings, and I passed an hour very agreeably with her. Her mind was active, and she related, in an interesting manner, many reminiscences of her youth and womanhood, among which was the following, in which she was the chief heroine. When the British squadron which drove Decatur into the harbor of New London, in 1813, menaced the town with bombardment, the military force that manned the forts were deficient in flannel for cannon cartridges. All that could be found in New London was sent to the forts, and a Mr. Latham, a neighbor of Mrs. Bailey, came to her at Groton seeking for more. She started out and collected all the little petticoats of children that she could find in town. " This is not half enough," said Latham, on her return. " You

---

[1] While making this sketch, I remarked to Mrs. Bailey (and with sincerity, too) that I saw in her features evidence that Captain Bailey was a man of good taste. She immediately comprehended my meaning and the compliment, and replied, with a coquettish smile, " I was never ashamed of my face, and never mean to be." She lived happily with her husband for seventy years. Since the above was put in type, she has died. Her clothes took fire, and she was burned to death on the 10th of January, 1851, aged about 89

shall have mine too," said Mrs. B., as she cut with her scissors the string that fastened it, and taking it off, gave it to Latham. He was satisfied, and hastening to Fort Trumbull, that patriotic contribution was soon made into cartridges. "It was a heavy new one, but I didn't care for that," said the old lady, while her blue eyes sparkled at the recollection. "All I wanted was to see it go through the Englishmen's insides!" Some of Decatur's men declared that it was a shame to cut that petticoat into cartridge patterns; they would rather see it fluttering at the mast-head of the *United States* or *Macedonian*, as an ensign under which to fight upon the broad ocean! This and other circumstances make Mrs. Bailey a woman of history; and, pleading that excuse, I am sure, if she shall be living when this page shall appear, that she will pardon the liberty I have taken. I told her that the sketch of her which she allowed me to take was intended for publication.

I recrossed the Thames to New London, and after an early dinner rode down to the light-house, near which Arnold landed, and made the drawing printed on page 43. Returning along the beach, I sketched the outlines of Fort Trumbull and vicinity, seen on page 42, and toward evening strolled through the two principal burial-grounds of the city. In the ancient one, situated in the north part of the town, lie the remains of many of the first settlers. In the other, lying upon a high slope, westward of the center of the city, is a plain monu-

BISHOP SEABURY'S MONUMENT.[1]

ment of Bishop Seabury, whose name is conspicuous in our Revolutionary annals as that of an unwavering Loyalist. I shall have occasion to notice his abduction from West Chester county, and imprisonment in Connecticut, as well as his general biography, when I write of the events at White Plains.

We will now bid adieu to New London, not forgetting, however, in our parting words, to note the fact so honorable to its name and character, that the first printing-press in Connecticut was established there, according to Barber, forty-five years before printing was executed in any other place in the colony. Thomas Short, who settled in New London in 1709, was the printer, and from his press was issued *The Saybrook Platform*,[2] in 1710, said to be the first book printed in the province. Short died in 1711, and there being no printer in the colony, the Assembly procured Timothy Green, a descendant of Samuel Green, of Cambridge, the first printer in America, to settle at New London. Samuel Green, the publisher of the "Connecticut Gazetteer" until 1845, the oldest newspaper in the state, is a descendant of this colonial printer.

Business demanding my presence at home, I left New London at ten in the evening, in the "Knickerbocker," and arrived in New York at nine the following morning.

[1] The following is the inscription upon the slab: "Here lieth the body of SAMUEL SEABURY, D.D., bishop of Connecticut and Rhode Island, who departed from this transitory scene February 25th, Anno Domini 1796, in the 68th year of his age, and the 12th of his Episcopal consecration.

"Ingenuous without pride, learned without pedantry, good without severity, he was duly qualified to discharge the duties of the Christian and the bishop. In the pulpit he enforced religion; in his conduct he exemplified it. The poor he assisted with his charity; the ignorant he blessed with his instruction. The friend of men, he ever designed their good; the enemy of vice, he ever opposed it. Christian! dost thou aspire to happiness? Seabury has shown the way that leads to it."

[2] This was a Confession of Faith or Articles of Religion arranged in 1708. Yale College was first established at Saybrook, and fifteen commencements were held there. To educate young men of talents and piety for the ministry was the leading design of the institution. The founders, desirous that the Churches should have a public standard or Confession of Faith, according to which the instruction of the college should be conducted, such articles were arranged and adopted after the commencement at Saybrook in 1708, and from that circumstance were called the *Saybrook Platform*. The standards of faith of the Congregational and Presbyterian Churches are substantially the same as the *Saybrook Platform*.

CHAPTER XXVII

"I've gazed upon thy golden cloud
    Which shades thine emerald sod;
Thy hills, which Freedom's share hath plow'd,
Which nurse a race that have not bow'd
    Their knee to aught but God.
And thou hast gems, ay, living pearls,
    And flowers of Eden hue;
Thy loveliest are thy bright-eyed girls,
Of fairy forms and elfin curls,
    And smiles like Hermon's dew.
They've hearts, like those they're born to wed,
    Too proud to nurse a slave.
They'd scorn to share a monarch's bed,
And sooner lay their angel head
    Deep in their humble grave."
                                    HUGH PETERS.

"Ye say they all have pass'd away,
    That noble race and brave;
That their light canoes have vanish'd
    From off the crested wave;
That mid the forests where they warr'd
    There rings no hunter's shout;
But their name is on your waters,
    Ye may not wash it out."
                                    MRS. SIGOURNEY.

O the land of the Narragansets and Wampanoags—the land of Massasoit and Philip, of Canonicus and Miantonōmoh—the land of Roger Williams and toleration—the Rhode Island and Providence plantations of colonial times, I next turned my attention. On a clear frosty evening, the moon in its wane and the winds hushed, I went up the Sound in the steam-boat Vanderbilt. We passed through the turbulent eddies of Hell Gate at twilight, and as we entered the broader expanse of water beyond Fort Schuyler, heavy swells, that were upheaved by a gale the day before, came rolling in from the ocean, and disturbed the anticipated quiet of the evening voyage. It was to end at Stonington[1] at midnight, so I paced the promenade deck in the biting night air to keep off sea-sickness, and was successful. We landed at Stonington between twelve and one o'clock, where we took cars for Providence, arriving there at three. Refreshed by a few hours' sleep, and an early breakfast at the "Franklin," I started upon a day's ramble with Mr. Peeks, of Providence, who kindly offered to accompany me to memorable places around that prosperous city. We first visited the most interesting, as well as one of the most ancient, localities connected with the colonial history of Rhode Island, the rock on which Roger Williams first landed upon its shores. It is reached

October 19, 1848.

---

[1] Stonington is a thriving town, situated upon an estuary of Long Island Sound, and about midway between the mouths of the Mystic and Pawcatuc Rivers. It was settled by a few families about 1658. The first *squatter* was William Cheeseborough, from Massachusetts, who pitched his tent there in 1649. It has but little Revolutionary history except what was common to other coast towns, where frequent alarms kept the people in agitation. It suffered some from bombardment in 1813, by the squadron under Sir Thomas Hardy, which drove Decatur into the harbor of New London. The enemy was so warmly received, that Hardy weighed anchor, and made no further attempts upon the coast of Connecticut.

620   PICTORIAL FIELD-BOOK

Roger Williams's Rock.   "Water Lots."   Proposed Desecration.   Arrival of Roger Williams.   His Character

from the town by the broad avenue called Power Street, which extends to the high bank of the Seekonk or Pawtucket River, and terminates almost on a line with the famous rock, some sixty feet above high water mark. The town is rapidly extending toward the Seekonk, and the hand of improvement was laying out broad streets near its bank when I was there. The channel of the Seekonk here is narrow, and at low tide broad flats on either side are left bare. I was informed that a proposition had been made to dig down the high banks and fill in the flats to the edge of the channel, to make "desirable water lots," the "Roger Williams' Rock" to be in the center of the public square, though at least thirty feet below the surface ! Mosheim informs us that when the Jews attempted to rebuild Jerusalem, in the time of Julian, the workmen

LANDING-PLACE OF ROGER WILLIAMS.[1]

were prevented from labor by the issuing of fire-balls from the earth with a horrible noise, and that enterprise, undertaken in opposition to the prophecy of Jesus, was abandoned.[2] Should mammon attempt the desecrating labor of covering the time-honored rock on the shore of old Seekonk, who can tell what indignant protests may not occur ?

Here is a mossy spot upon the patriarch's back ; let us sit down in the warm sunlight and wind-sheltered nook, and glance at the record.

A few months after the arrival of Winthrop and his company at Boston, and before Hooker and Cotton, afterward eminent ministers in the colony, had sailed from England, there landed February 5, 1631. at Nantasket an enlightened and ardent Puritan divine, young in years (for he was only thirty-one), but mature in judgment and those enlightened views of true liberty of conscience, which distinguish the character of modern theological jurisprudence from the intolerance of the seventeenth century. He was a fugitive from English persecution ; but his wrongs had not clouded his accurate understanding. In the capacious recesses of his mind he had resolved the nature of intolerance, and he alone had arrived at the great principle which is its sole effectual remedy. He announced his discovery under the simple proposition of sanctity of conscience. The civil magistrate should restrain crime, but never control opinion ; should punish guilt, but never violate the freedom of the soul.[3] This was a wonderful discovery in modern science ; too wonderful for the hierarchy of England, or the magistrates and ministers of the Puritan colony of America. They could not comprehend

---

[1] This view is on the left bank of the Seekonk, looking south. The point on which the figure stands is the famous rock, composed of a mass of dark slate, and rising but little above the water at high tide. The high banks are seen beyond, and on the extreme left is India Point, with the rail-road bridge near the entrance of the river into Narraganset Bay.

[2] Mosheim's *Church History* (external), part i., chap. i., sec. xiv.

[3] Bancroft, i., 367.

its beauty or utility; and as it had no affinity with their own narrow views of the dignity of the human soul, they pronounced it heresy, as soon as the discoverer began to make a practical development of his principles.   Yet they perceived, with a yearning affection for its truth, that it would quench the fires of persecution, abrogate laws making non-conformity a felony, abolish tithes, and all forced contributions to the maintenance of religion, and protect all in that freedom of conscience to worship God as the mind should dictate, for which they had periled their lives and fortunes in the wilderness.   Still, its glory was too brilliant; it dazzled their vision; the understanding could not comprehend its beneficent scope; they looked upon it with the jealous eye of over-cautiousness, and, true to the impulses of human nature, what they could not *comprehend*, they *rejected*.   This great apostle of toleration and intellectual liberty was ROGER WILLIAMS.

The New England Churches had not renounced the use of coercion in religious matters, and Williams, so soon as his tolerant views were made known, found himself regarded with suspicion by the civil and religious authorities.   Disappointed, yet resolutely determined to maintain his principles, he withdrew to the settlement at Plymouth, where he remained two years, and by his charity, virtues, and purity of life, won the hearts of all.   The people of Salem called him to be their minister, a movement which made the court of Boston marvel. Being an object of jealousy, and now having an opportunity to speak in the public ear, he was in perpetual collision with the clergy.   The magistrates insisted on the presence of every man at public worship.   Williams reprobated the law.   To compel men to unite with those of a different creed he regarded as an open violation of their natural rights; to drag to public worship the irreligious and unwilling seemed only like requiring hypocrisy.   This doctrine alarmed both magistrates and clergy, and they began to denounce Williams.   In proportion to the severity of their opposition his zeal was kindled, and so earnest did he become in enforcing his tolerant views, that intolerance and fanaticism marked his own course.   He denounced King James as a liar; declared that the settlers had no right to the lands they occupied, these belonging to the aborigines; raised a tumult about the red cross of St. George in the banner;[a][1] at last boldly denounced the Churches of New England as anti-Christian, and actually excommunicated such of his parishioners as held intercourse   [a] 1634. with them.   The vision of that great mind which saw general principles of righteousness in a clear light, became clouded in his practical endeavors to bring the power of those principles to bear upon society.   When weak and persecuted, the scope of his vision of intellectual liberty and Christian charity embraced the earth; when in power and strong, it contracted to the small orbit of his parish at Salem—himself the central sun of light and goodness. Such is the tendency of all human minds under like circumstances; and Roger Williams, great and good as he was, was not an exception.

The magistrates were greatly irritated; some of Williams's language was construed as treasonable and schismatic, and he was arraigned before the General Court at Boston on this charge.   There he stood alone in defense of his noble principles; for his congregation, and even the wife of his bosom, could not justify all his words and acts.   Yet he was undaunted, and declared himself "ready to be bound, and banished, and even to die in New England," rather than renounce the truth whose light illuminated his mind and conscience. He was allowed to speak for himself before the court, and also to dispute upon religious points with the Reverend Mr. Hooker.   Every effort to "reduce him from his errors" was unavailing, and the court, composed of all the ministers, proceeded to pass sentence   October, of banishment upon him.   He was ordered to leave the jurisdiction of the colony   1635.

---

[1] The preaching of Williams warmed the zeal of Endicott, then one of the board of military commissioners for the colony, and afterward governor.   The banner of the train-bands at Salem had the cross of St. George worked upon it.   Endicott, determining to sweep away every vestige of what he deemed popish or heathenish superstition, caused the cross to be cut out of the banner.   The people raised a tumult, and the court at Boston, mercifully considering that Endicott's intentions were good, though his act was rash, only "adjudged him worthy admonition, and to be disabled for one year from bearing any public office."—Savage's *Winthrop*, i., 158; Moore's *Colonial Governors*, i., 353.

within six weeks. He obtained leave to remain until the rigors of winter had passed, but, continuing active in promoting his peculiar views, the court determined to ship him immediately for England. He was ordered to Boston for the purpose of embarking. He refused obedience, and, hearing that a warrant had been issued for his arrest, set out, with a few followers, for the vast unexplored wilds of America, with an ambitious determination to found a new colony, having for its foundation the sublime doctrine of liberty of conscience in all its plenitude, and the equality of opinions before the law. In the midst of deep snows and bit-
January, ing winds they journeyed toward Narraganset Bay. "For fourteen weeks he was
1636. sorely tossed in a bitter season, not knowing what bread or bed did mean."[1] He describes himself, in a letter to Mason, "as plucked up by the roots, beset with losses, distractions, miseries, hardships of sea and land, debts and wants." He at last found refuge and hospitality from the Indian sachem Massasoit, whom he had known at Plymouth ; and in the spring, under a grant from that sachem, commenced a settlement at Seekonk,[2] on the east side of the Seekonk or Pawtucket River, just within the limits of the Plymouth colony. Many of the ministers in that colony wrote him friendly letters, for he was personally beloved by all. Winslow, who was then governor, wrote a letter to Williams, in which he claimed Seekonk as a part of the Plymouth domain, and suggested his removal beyond the jurisdiction of that colony to prevent difficulty. Williams heeded the advice of Winslow,
June, 1636. and, entering a canoe with five others, paddled down the Seekonk almost to its mouth, and landed upon the west side of the river, upon the bare rock, delineated on page 52. He crossed over to the west side of the peninsula, and upon that shore, at the head of the bay, commenced a new settlement. He obtained from Canonicus and Miantonômoh, principal chiefs of the Narragansets, a grant of land for the purpose. He named his new settlement PROVIDENCE, "in commemoration of God's providence to him in his distress." "I desired," he said, "it might be for a shelter for persons distressed for conscience." And so it became, for men of every creed there found perfect freedom of thought. Although every rood of land belonged to Williams, by right of deed from the Narraganset sachems, not a foot of it did he reserve for himself. He practiced his holy precepts, and "gave away his lands and other estates to them that he thought most in want, until he gave away all."[3] Nor was there any distinction made among the settlers, "whether servants or strangers ;" each had an equal voice in the affairs of government, and the political foundation of the settlement was a pure democracy. The Massachusetts people believed that the fugitives "would have no magistrates," and must necessarily perish politically, yet they thrived wonderfully. The impress of that first system is yet seen upon the political character of Rhode Island, for "in no state in the world, not even in the agricultural state of Vermont, have the magistrates so little power, or the representatives of the freemen so much."[4] Such was the planting of the first and only purely democratic colony in America ; and its founder, though persecuted and contemned, maintained, in the opinion of all good men, that high character which Cotton Mather and others were constrained to award him, as "one of the most distinguished men that ever lived, a most pious and heavenly-minded soul."[5]

The Christian charity of Roger Williams was remarkably displayed soon after his banishment from Massachusetts. In 1637, when the Pequots were attempting to induce the Narragansets to join them in a general war upon the whites, and particularly against the

---

[1] *Massachusetts Historical Collections*, i., 276.

[2] Seekonk is the Indian name for the wild or black goose with which the waters in that region originally abounded. The town is the ancient Rehoboth, first settled by William Blackstone, an English non-conformist minister, a few months previous to the arrival here of Roger Williams. Blackstone was the first white man who lived upon the peninsula of Shawmut, where Boston now stands. Williams's plantation was on the little Seekonk River, the navigable portion of which is really an arm of Narraganset Bay.
Although Williams was the real founder of Rhode Island, Blackstone was the first white settler within its borders. He had no sympathy with Williams, and continued his allegiance to Massachusetts, though without its jurisdiction.

[3] Backus's *History of New England*, i., 290.

[4] Bancroft, i., 380.   [5] Callender's *Historical Discourse*.

Massachusetts people, Mr. Williams informed the latter of the fact. They solicited his mediation, and, forgetting the many injuries he had received from those who now needed his favor, he set out on a stormy day, in a poor canoe, upon the rough bay, and through many dangers repaired to the cabin of Canonicus. The Pequots and Narragansets were already assembled in council. The former threatened him with death, yet he remained there three days and nights. "God wonderfully preserved me," he said, "and helped me to break in pieces the designs of the enemy, and to finish the English league, by many travels and changes, with the Narragansets and Mohegans against the Pequots." This alliance we noticed in the last chapter. Notwithstanding this great service, the Massachusetts court would not revoke Williams's sentence of banishment.

ROGER WILLIAMS'S SIGNATURE.[1]

Let us now close the volume for a time, and visit other places of historic interest.

Leaving the Seekonk, we walked to the site of the encampment of the French army in the autumn of 1782, while on its march to Boston for embarkation. It had remained in Virginia after the battle of Yorktown, in the autumn of 1781, until the summer of 1782, when it joined Washington and his army on the Hudson. The place of its encampment there was near Peekskill. The order and discipline of this army, and its uniform respect for property—the soldiers not even taking fruit from the trees without leave—were remarkable, and on their march northward Rochambeau and his officers received many congratulatory addresses.[2] The army remained at Peekskill until October, when it commenced its march for Boston, going by the way of Hartford and Providence. Count de Rochambeau accompanied it to the latter place, where he took his leave of the troops and returned to Washington's head-quarters. The army had received orders to sail to the West Indies in the French fleet of fifteen sail of the line and four frigates, then lying in the harbor of Boston, in the event of the evacuation of New-York or Charleston by the British. The Baron de Viomenil was ordered to accompany the troops as commander instead of Rochambeau. The latter, with several other officers, returned from Rhode Island to Virginia, and at Norfolk embarked for France.

October 22, 1782.

---

[1] ROGER WILLIAMS was born in Wales, in 1599, and was educated at Oxford. He became a minister in the Church of England, but his views of religious liberty made him a non-conformist, and he came to America. Bold in the annunciation of his tenets respecting the perfect liberty of mind and conscience, he was banished from Massachusetts, and planted a colony at the head of Narraganset Bay, now the city of Providence. In 1639 he embraced the doctrines of the Baptists, and being baptized by one of his brethren, he baptized ten others. Doubts as to the correctness of his principles arose in his mind, and he finally concluded that it would be wrong to perform the rite of baptism without a revelation from Heaven. The Church which he had formed was accordingly dissolved. He went to England in 1643, as agent for the colony, and obtained a charter, with which he returned in September, 1644. This charter was granted on the 14th of March, and included the shores and islands of Narraganset Bay, west of Plymouth and south of Massachusetts, and as far as the Pequot River and country, to be known as the PROVIDENCE PLANTATIONS. He landed at Boston, but was not molested on account of being under sentence of banishment, for he brought with him recommendatory letters from influential members of Parliament. He went to England again for the colony in 1651, where he remained until 1654. He was chosen president of the government on his return, which office he held until 1657, when Benedict Arnold was appointed. In 1672 he held a dispute with the Quakers for three days at Newport, of which he wrote an account.* He died in April, 1683, aged eighty-four years.

[2] At Philadelphia, a deputation of Quakers waited upon Rochambeau, and one of them, in behalf of the others, said, "General, it is not on account of thy military qualities that we make thee this visit; those we hold in little esteem; but thou art the friend of mankind, and thy army conducts itself with the utmost order and discipline. It is this which induces us to render thee our respects."

---

* The title of the pamphlet containing the account (which was published in 1676) was, "George Fox digged out of his Burrows." it being written against Fox and Burrows, two eminent Quakers. An answer to it was published in 1679, entitled "A New England Fire-brand Quenched."

The French troops arrived at Providence in November, and to give color to the pretext that they marched eastward to go into winter quarters, made excavations, in which to find protection from the cold, instead of pitching their tents, as a moving army would do.   The object was to allow the expedition to the West Indies—where a brisk naval warfare was in progress between the French and British—to remain a secret even to the suspicions of the English.   After remaining about a fortnight at Providence the troops marched toward Boston, where they arrived early in December.[1]   On the 24th of that month the French fleet sailed from Boston for St. Domingo, with all the troops except Lauzun's legion, the army having been in the United States two and a half years.[2]

The place of the encampment at Providence is in a field of cold, wet land, rough and rocky, a mile and a half east-northeast from Market Square in the city.   It lies on the northeast side of Harrington's Lane, at the head of Greene Lane, which latter runs parallel with Prospect Street.   We passed on our way along the brow of Prospect Hill, whence we had a fine view of the city and surrounding country, including northward the spires of Pawtucket, and southward the blue waters of Narraganset Bay.   The encampment was on the western slope of the northern termination of Prospect Hill.   Several shallow pits and heaps of stones, with some charcoal intermingled (the remains of the temporary dwellings of the French soldiers), are yet to be seen.   It was a sheltered position, and favorable for a winter encampment

1848.

HOPKINS'S MONUMENT.

The ground is full of small surface springs, which, with the wash from the cultivated hills above, will soon obliterate every trace of the encampment.

About a quarter of a mile westward of the camp ground is the "North Burying-ground," belonging to the city.   It has been beautified within a few years by graveled foot-paths and carriage-ways, fine vaults, handsome monuments and inclosures.   Its location is such that it may be made a beautiful cemetery, though small.   Not far from the south entrance is a marble monument about nine feet high, erected to the memory of Stephen Hopkins, for a long time colonial governor of Rhode Island, and one of the signers of the Declaration of Independence.   On the southern side of the obelisk is the name of HOPKINS in large letters.   The inscriptions are upon three sides of the pedestal.[3]

In the northeast part of the burial-ground is a granite ob-

[1] Soon after their arrival, Governor John Hancock and the Council gave a public dinner to the commanding general, Viomenil, and his officers, and to the commander of the fleet, Vaudreuil, and his officers.

[2] The *Magnifique*, a French seventy-four gun ship, one of the fleet, having been lost in Boston Harbor by accident, Congress, in testimony of their sense of the generosity of the French king, had resolved, more than three months before (September 3), to present the *America*, a seventy-four gun ship, to the French minister, the Chevalier de Luzerne, for the service of his king.—See *Journals of Congress*, viii., 343.

[3] The following are the inscriptions :

NORTH SIDE.—"Sacred to the memory of the illustrious STEPHEN HOPKINS, of Revolutionary fame, attested by his signature to the Declaration of our National Independence.   Great in council, from sagacity of mind ; magnanimous in sentiment, firm in purpose, and good as great, from benevolence of heart, he stood in the first rank of statesmen and patriots.   Self-educated, yet among the most learned of men, his vast treasury of useful knowledge, his great retentive and reflective powers, combined with his social nature, made him the most interesting of companions in private life."

WEST SIDE.—"His name is engraved on the immortal records of the Revolution, and can never die.   His titles to that distinction are engraved on this monument, reared by the grateful admiration of his native state in honor of her favorite son."

SOUTH SIDE.—Born March 7, 1707.   Died July 13, 1785."

A biography and portrait of this venerated patriot will be found among those of the signers of the Declaration of Independence, in another part of this work.   The fac-simile of his signature here given is a copy of his autograph in my possession, attached to the commission of Captain Ephraim Wheaton, issued in June, 1761.   Mr. Hopkins was then Governor of Rhode Island, and in that capacity signed the instrument.   It is attested by HENRY WARD, secretary.   Mr. Ward was one of the delegates from Rhode Island to the

elisk erected to the memory of Nicholas Cooke, who was Governor of Rhode Island from 1775 until 1778, and an active and efficient patriot until his death, which occurred before the independence of his country was secured by treaty.[1]

GOVERNOR COOKE'S MONUMENT.

His biography is briefly inscribed upon his monument in the following words :

" NICHOLAS COOKE, born in Providence, February 3d, 1717 ; Died September 14th, 1782. Unanimously elected Governor of Rhode Island in 1775, he remained in office during the darkest period of the American Revolution. He merited and won the approbation of his fellow-citizens, and was honored with the friendship and confidence of Washington." This is the inscription upon the east side, immediately above which, in raised letters, is the name COOKE. On the west is the following :

" Hannah Sabine, relict of Nicholas Cooke, born in Killingly, Connecticut, March 13th, 1722 ; died in Providence, March 22d, 1792."

This monument is about twenty feet high, composed of a single block. The sketch of it here given is from the cemetery, looking eastward, and includes in the distance the French camp-ground just mentioned. The most remote of the two fields seen between the trees on the right, is the one wherein the remains of the encampment are to be seen.

On the road leading from the cemetery to the town is a brick building, with a hip-roof, which La Fayette occupied as head-quarters, while in Providence a short time in 1778. He had been sent by Washington with two thousand men to assist Sullivan in the siege of Newport. The house is well preserved, but changed somewhat in its external appearance.

On our way into the town we passed along Benefit Street, on the east side of which, in a vacant lot, upon the slope of a steep hill, near the mansion of the father of Governor Dorr, is a living water-fountain, called *Roger Williams's Spring.* Tradition asserts that here, in the cool shade of sycamores (of which the huge trees that now overshadow it are the sprouts), Williams first reposed after his journey, and that here his first tent was pitched, at twilight, on a beautiful evening in June. It is a pleasant spot now, even with the pent-up city around it ; it must then have been a delicious resting-place for the weary exile, for below him were the bright waters of the Narraganset, beyond which arose the gentle slopes and more lofty hills of the fair land of Canonicus, his friend and protector.

" Stamp Act Congress" in 1765. This signature of Hopkins exhibits the same tremulousness of hand which is seen in that attached to the Declaration of Independence, written fifteen years afterward, and is a proof, if evidence were wanting, that it was not the effect of fear, but "shaking palsy," that makes the patriot's sign-manual to our National Document appear so suspiciously crooked.

SIGNATURE OF STEPHEN HOPKINS.

[1] Mr. Cooke was deputy governor in 1775. When the Assembly, or House of Magistrates of the colony, voted to raise an army of fifteen hundred men, Joseph Wanton, then the Governor of Rhode Island, his deputy, and others in the government, were opposed to the measure. The people were displeased, yet Wanton, who had been chief magistrate since 1769, was rechosen governor in May ; but, failing to appear and take the prescribed oath, the Assembly directed that the deputy governor should perform the duties of chief magistrate. Mr. Cooke became convinced that the warlike measures of the Assembly were correct, and entered heartily into all their views. Wanton appeared in June, and demanded that the oath of office should be administered to him, but, as he had not given satisfaction to the Assembly, his request or demand was not complied with.

Within the city, on the east side of Market Square, stands the old tavern, with moss-grown roof, where many a grave and many a boisterous meeting were held by the freemen of the Providence Plantations during the Stamp Act excitement, and the earlier years of the war of the Revolution. There the Sons of Liberty met and planned their measures in opposition to the British ministry. From the same balcony were read the proclamation announcing the accession of George III. to the throne in 1760; the odious Stamp Act in 1765; the bill for its repeal in 1766; and the Declaration of Independence in 1776. That balcony seemed to be the forum of the people; and many excited audiences have crowded Market Square, in front of it, to listen to patriotic speeches.

OLD TAVERN IN PROVIDENCE.[1]

The people of Providence, and particularly the matrons and maidens, cheerfully acquiesced in the demands made upon their self-denial by the non-importation agreements, and foreign tea was discarded as if it had been a poisonous drug.[2] In 1773, when it was ascertained that the ships of the East India Company, heavily laden with tea, were about to sail for America, the people of Providence were among the first to express their disapprobation; and on one occasion the town crier, with a drum, patroled the streets in the evening, announcing that a bonfire of *tea* would be made in Market Square at ten o'clock at night, and requesting those who possessed and repudiated the article to cast it upon the heap. At the appointed hour the square was crowded, and the old tavern front and its neighbors were brilliantly illuminated by the glow of the burning tea, aided by other combustibles, while shouts long and loud went up as one voice from the multitude. This was but a prelude to the united and vigorous action of the people when the war notes from Lexington aroused the country; and until the close of the contest Providence was a " nest of rebels against the king."

I concluded the labors and pleasures of the day by making the above sketch, and in the evening attended, by invitation, a meeting of the Rhode Island Historical Society, over which Albert G. Greene, Esq., presided, the venerable president, John Howland, then ninety-one years of age, being absent. Their rooms are in a small but convenient building near Brown University, and contain about five thousand volumes of books and pamphlets, many of them very rare. The meeting was one of much interest, especially to Rhode Islanders, for Professor Gammel, of the University, made a verbal communication on the subject of important manuscripts concerning the early history of New England, which are in the British colonial office. He imparted the gratifying intelligence that J. Carter Brown, Esq., of Providence,

---

[1] This view is from the market, looking north. The building stands on the east side of the square, and parallel with its front commences North Main Street. In the yard on the right is a venerable horse-chestnut tree, standing between the house and the Roger Williams' Bank. In former times, a balcony extended across the front. The door that opened upon it is still there, but the balcony is gone. The roof is completely overgrown with moss, and every appearance of age marks it.

[2] On the 12th of June, 1769, twenty-nine young ladies, daughters of the first citizens of Providence, met under the shade of the sycamores at the Roger Williams' Spring, and there resolved not to drink any more tea until the duty upon it should be taken off. They then adjourned to the house of one of the company (Miss Coddington), where they partook of a frugal repast, composed in part of the " delicious Hyperion,' a tea of domestic manufacture.—See note on page 481

with an enlightened liberality worthy of all praise, had made arrangements to have all the manuscripts in question copied at his own expense, under the direction of Mr. Stephens, the eminent agriculturist, then in Europe.[1] The manuscripts relate to New England history, from 1634 to 1720, and consist of more than four hundred pieces, about two hundred and fifty of which have special reference to the Rhode Island and Providence Plantations. Among them is a minute account of all the transactions relating to Captain Kidd, the noted pirate. Already two thousand four hundred pages of copies, beautifully written by one hand, on vellum foolscap, had been forwarded to Mr. Brown, a few of which were exhibited by Professor Gammel.

1848

Moon and stars were shining brightly when we left the Society's rooms, and afforded a fine field of view through a large telescope that was standing under the porch of the college. The professor having it in charge kindly allowed me a glance at our celestial neighbors. The moon was gibbous, and brilliant as molten silver appeared its ragged edges. Saturn was visible, but the earth being upon the plane of its rings, they could not be seen. Some double stars, even of the seventeenth magnitude, were pointed out ; and over the whole field of view, those distant worlds, that appear like brilliant points to the unaided vision, were seen glowing in all the beautiful colors of the emerald, the ruby, the sapphire, and the topaz. While gazing upon them, it seemed to me as if

> " Their silver voices in chorus rang,
>   And this was the song the bright ones sang .
>
> " Away ! away ! through the wide, wide sky—
>   The fair blue fields that before us lie.
>   Each sun with the worlds that round it roll ;
>   Each planet poised on her turning pole ;
>   With her isles of green and her clouds of white,
>   And her waters that lie like fluid light.
>
> " For the Source of Glory uncovers his face,
>   And the brightness o'erflows unbounded space ;
>   And we drink, as we go, the luminous tides,
>   In our ruddy air and our blooming sides.
>   Lo ! yonder the living splendors play ;
>   Away ! on our joyous path, away !
>
>   .   .   .   .   .   .
>
> " Glide on in your beauty, ye youthful spheres,
>   To weave the dance that measures the years.
>   Glide on in the glory and gladness sent
>   To the farthest wall of the firmament—
>   The boundless, visible smile of Him,
>   To the veil of whose brow our lamps are dim."
>   BRYANT'S "SONG OF THE STARS."

On the morning of the 21st, I procured a sort of pinnace, and a boatman to manage it, and with a stiff, cold breeze from the northwest, sailed down the Narraganset Bay[2] to Gaspee Point, a place famous in our Revolutionary annals as the scene of a daring act on the part of the people of Rhode Island. The Point is on the west side of the bay, about six miles below Providence, and consists, first, of a high jutting bank, and then a sandy beach stretching into the bay, almost uncovered at low tide, but completely submerged at high water. The bay is here about two miles wide, and the low bare point extends at least half a mile from the bank, its termination marked by a buoy. The navigation of this section of the bay is dangerous on account of the sand-bars, and also of submerged rocks, lying just below the surface at low water. Two of them, in the vicinity of Field's Point, are marked by strong stone towers about thirty feet high, both of which are

October,
1848.

---

[1] Mr. Brown is a son of Nicholas Brown, whose liberal endowment of the college at Providence, and active influence in its favor, caused the faculty to give his name to the institution. It is called Brown University.

[2] The northern portion of the bay is quite narrow, and from the Pawtuxet to its head is generally called Providence River.

above Gaspee Point. The tide was ebbing when we arrived at the Point, and anchoring our vessel, we sought to reach the shore in its little skiff—a feat of no small difficulty on account of the shallowness of the water. I waited nearly an hour for the ebbing tide to leave the Point bare, before making my sketch.

STONE TOWER.

The historical incident alluded to was the burning of the Gaspee, a British armed schooner, in 1772. She first appeared in the waters of Narraganset Bay in March, having been dispatched thither by the commissioners of customs at Boston to prevent infractions of the revenue laws, and to put a stop to the illicit trade which had been carried on for a long time at Newport and Providence. Her appearance disquieted the people, and her interference with the free navigation of the bay irritated them. Deputy-governor Sessions, residing at Providence, wrote in behalf of the people there to Governor Wanton[1] at Newport, expressing his opinion that the commander of the Gaspee, Lieutenant Duddington. had no legal warrant for his proceedings. Governor Wanton immediately dispatched

GASPEE POINT.[2]

a written message, by the high sheriff, to Duddington, in which he required that officer to produce his commission without delay. This the lieutenant refused to do, and Wanton made a second demand for his orders. Duddington, apparently shocked at the idea that a colonial governor should claim the right to control, in any degree, the movement of his majesty's officers, did not reply, but sent Wanton's letters to Admiral Montague at Boston.

[1] Joseph Wanton was a native of Newport, Rhode Island. He graduated at Harvard in 1751. In 1769 he was elected Governor of Rhode Island, which office he held by re-election until 1775, when his opposition to the views of the people, and his neglect to take the oath of office at the proper time, made the Assembly declare his place vacant. His deputy, Nicholas Cooke, performed the duties of governor. The confidence of the people in his attachment to American liberty was doubtless shaken by his appointment, under the great seal of England, to inquire into the affair of the Gaspee. But in that he acted as a conscientious man, and there was evidently a desire on his part that the incendiaries of that vessel should not be known, although he labored with apparent zeal to discover them. He was regarded as a Loyalist during the remainder of his life. He died at Newport in 1782.

[2] This view is from the bank of the cove just below the Point, looking northeast, showing its appearance at low water when the clam-fishers are upon it. The buoy is seen beyond the extreme end of the Point on the right. The bank is about fifteen feet high. In front of Pawtuxet, about a mile above, are the remains of breast-works, thrown up during the war of 1812. There are also breast-works at Field's Point, two miles below Providence, where is a flag-staff. There is the quarantine ground.

That functionary, forgetting that the Governor of Rhode Island was elected to office by the voice of a free people—that he was the chief magistrate of a colony of free Englishmen, and not a creature of the crown—wrote an insulting and blustering letter to Governor   April 6, Wanton in defense of Duddington, and in reprehension of his opponents.   In it he   1772. used these insulting words : " I shall report your two insolent letters to my officer [Duddington] to his majesty's secretaries of state, and leave them to determine what right you have to demand a sight of all orders I shall give to all officers of my squadron ; and I would advise you not to send your sheriff on board the king's ship again on such ridiculous errands."   To this letter Governor Wanton wrote a spirited reply.   " I am greatly   May 8, obliged," he said, " for the promise of transmitting my letters to the secretaries of   1772. state.   I am, however, a little shocked at your impolite expression made use of upon that occasion.   In return for this good office, I shall also transmit your letter to the Secretary of State, and leave to the king and his ministers to determine on which side the charge of insolence lies.   As to your advice not to send a sheriff on board any of your squadron, please to know, that I will send the sheriff of this colony at any time, and to any place within the body of it, as I shall think fit."   On the 20th of May, Governor Wanton, pursuant to a vote of the Assembly, transmitted an account of the matter to the Earl of Hillsborough ; but, before any reply could be received, the Gaspee became a wreck, under the following circumstances :

On the 9th of June, 1772, Captain Lindsey left Newport for Providence, in his packet,[1] at about noon, the wind blowing from the South.[2]   The Gaspee, whose commander did not discriminate between the well-known packets and the strange vessels that came into the harbor, had often fired upon the former, to compel their masters to take down their colors in its presence—a haughty marine Gesler, requiring obeisance to its imperial cap.   As Captain Lindsey, on this occasion, kept his colors flying, the Gaspee gave chase, and continued it as far as Namquit (now Gaspee) Point.   The tide was ebbing, but the bar was covered.   As soon as Lindsey doubled the Point, he stood to the westward.   Duddington, commander of the Gaspee, eager to overtake the pursued, and ignorant of the extent of the submerged Point from the shore, kept on a straight course, and in a few minutes struck the sand.   The fast ebbing tide soon left his vessel hopelessly grounded.   Captain Lindsey arrived at Providence at sunset, and at once communicated the fact of the grounding of the Gaspee to Mr. John Brown, one of the leading merchants of that city.   Knowing that the schooner could not be got off until flood-tide, after midnight, Brown thought this a good opportunity to put an end to the vexations caused by her presence.   He ordered the preparation of eight of the largest long-boats in the harbor, to be placed under the general command of Captain Whipple, one of his most trusty ship-masters ; each boat to have five oars, the row-locks to be muffled, and the whole put in readiness by half past eight in the evening, at Fenner's Wharf, near the residence of the late Welcome Arnold.   At dusk, a man named Daniel Pearce passed along the Main Street, beating a drum, and informing the inhabitants that the Gaspee lay aground on Namquit Point ; that she could not get off until three o'clock in the morning ; and inviting those who were willing to engage in her destruction to meet at the house of James Sabine, afterward the residence of Welcome Arnold.   The boats left Providence between ten and eleven o'clock, filled with sixty-four well-armed men, a sea captain in each boat acting as steersman.   They took with them a quantity of round paving-stones.   Between one and two in the morning they reached the Gaspee, when a sen-   June 9, tinel on board hailed them.   No answer being returned, Duddington appeared in   1772. his shirt on the starboard gunwale, and waving the boats off, fired a pistol at them.   This

---

[1] This packet was called the Hannah, and sailed between New York and Providence, touching at Newport.

[2] Cooper, in his *Naval History*, i., 81, says that the Hannah was " favored by a fresh southerly breeze." The details here given are taken chiefly from a statement by the late Colonel Ephraim Bowen, of Providence, who was one of the party that attacked the Gaspee.   Colonel Bowen says the wind was from the North.   The circumstances of the chase, however, show that it must have been from the South.

discharge was returned by a musket from one of the boats.[1]   Duddington was wounded in the groin, and carried below.   The boats now came alongside the schooner, and the men boarded her without much opposition, the crew retreating below when their wounded commander was carried down.   A medical student among the Americans dressed Duddington's wound,[2] and he was carried on shore at Pawtuxet.   The schooner's company were ordered to collect their clothing and leave the vessel, which they did ; and all the effects of Lieutenant Duddington being carefully placed in one of the American boats to be delivered to the owner, the Gaspee was set on fire and at dawn blew up.[3]

June 12.   On being informed of this event, Governor Wanton issued a proclamation, ordering diligent search for persons having a knowledge of the crime, and offering a reward of five hundred dollars " for the discovery of the perpetrators of said villainy, to be paid immediately upon the conviction of any one or more of them."   Admiral Montague also made endeavors to discover the incendiaries.   Afterward the home government offered a reward of five thousand dollars for the leader, and two thousand five hundred dollars to any person who would discover the other parties, with the promise of a pardon should the informer be an accomplice.   A commission of inquiry, under the great seal of England, was established, which sat from the 4th until the 22d of January, 1773.[4]   It then adjourned until the 26th of May, when it assembled and sat until the 23d of June.   But not a solitary clew to the identity of the perpetrators could be obtained, notwithstanding so many of them were known to the people.[5] The price of treachery on the part of any accomplice would have been exile from home and country ; and the proffered reward was not adequate to such a sacrifice, even though weak moral principles or strong acquisitiveness had been tempted into compliance.   The commissioners closed their labors on the 23d of June, and further inquiry was not attempted.[6]

SIGNATURES OF THE COMMISSIONERS.

---

[1] Thomas Bucklin, a young man about nineteen years of age, fired the musket.   He afterward assisted in dressing the wound which his bullet inflicted.

[2] This was Dr. John Mawney.   His kindness and attention to Duddington excited the gratitude of that officer, who offered young Mawney a gold stock-buckle ; that being refused, a silver one was offered and accepted.

[3] The principal actors in this affair were John Brown, Captain Abraham Whipple, John B. Hopkins, Benjamin Dunn, Dr. John Mawney, Benjamin Page, Joseph Bucklin, Turpin Smith, Ephraim Bowen, and Captain Joseph Tillinghast.   The names were, of course, all kept secret at the time.

[4] The commission consisted of Governor Joseph Wanton, of Rhode Island ; Daniel Horsmanden, chief justice of New York ; Frederic Smyth, chief justice of New Jersey ; Peter Oliver, chief justice of Massachusetts ; and Robert Auchmuty, judge of the Vice-admiralty Court.

[5] The drum was publicly beaten ; the sixty-four boldly embarked on the expedition without disguise ; and it is asserted by Mr. John Howland (still living), that on the morning after the affair, a young man, named Justin Jacobs, paraded on the " Great Bridge," a place of much resort, with Lieutenant Duddington's gold-laced beaver on his head, detailing the particulars of the transaction to a circle around him.

[6] See *Documentary History of the Destruction of the Gaspee*, by the Honorable William R. Staples ; Providence, 1845.   In a song written at the time, and composed of fifty-eight lines of doggerel verse, is ingeniously given the history of the affair.   It closes with the following allusion to the rewards offered :

After finishing my sketch of Namquit, or Gaspee Point (page 60), we embarked for Providence, the wind blowing a gale from the northwest. It was with much difficulty that we managed our vessel ; and before we reached the harbor we were drenched with the spray that dashed over the gunwale from the windward. In company with Mr. Weeden I visited the fine library of the Athenium Association,[1] and afterward had the pleasure of a brief interview, at his residence, with the venerable Mr. Howland, president of the Historical Society. So clear and vigorous was his well-cultivated mind, that I regretted the brevity of my visit, made necessary by the near approach of the hour of departure of the steam-packet, in which I was to proceed to Newport. Mr. Howland passed his ninety-first birth-day a few days before I saw him. He was a soldier early in the war for independence, having been drafted as a minute man in the winter of 1775, to go to Newport. He was afterward attached to the Rhode Island regiment under Colonel Lippincott, and joined the Continental army under Washington at Kingsbridge, at the upper end of York or Manhattan Island. He was in the retreat to White Plains in the autumn of 1776, and was engaged in the skirmish at Chatterton's Hill. He related an amusing circumstance which occurred during that retreat. While the Americans halted upon Chatterton's Hill, the British, in close pursuit, rested, for a short time, upon another eminence close by. An Irishman, one of Colonel Lippincott's servants, who was called "Daddy Hall," seemed quite uneasy on account of the presence of the enemy. He had charge of the colonel's horse, and frequently exclaimed, "What are we doing here ? Why do we stop here ? Why don't we go on ? I don't believe the colonel knows that the red-coated rascals are so near." Paymaster Dexter,[2] seeing the perturbation of the poor fellow, said, " Daddy Hall, you're afraid ! you're a trembling coward !" The Milesian's ire was aroused at these words, and looking the paymaster in the face with a scornful curl of his lips, he said, " Be jabers ! no, Maisther Dexther, I'm not afeerd more nor yez be ; but faith ! ye'll find yourself that one good pair of heels is worth two of hands afore night ; if ye don't, call Daddy Hall a spalpeen." And so he did ; for before sunset the Americans were flying before their pursuers, more grateful to heels than hands for safety.

Mr. Howland accompanied Washington in his retreat across New Jersey, and was in the division of Cadwallader, at Bristol, which was to go over the Delaware on the night when Washington crossed that river, and surprised the Hessians at Trenton. The ice prevented ; but they crossed the next day, and were stationed at Crosswicks for a day or two. Mr. Howland was among those at Trenton who were driven across the Assanpink by the British on the evening of the 2d of January, the night before the battle of Princeton. The bridge across the Assanpink was much crowded, and Mr. Howland remembers having his arm scratched by one of Washington's spurs as he passed

December 25, 1776.

1777.

"Now, for to find these people out.
King George has offered very stout,
One thousand pounds to find out one
That wounded William Duddington.
One thousand more he says he'll spare,
For those who say the sheriff's were.
One thousand more there doth remain
For to find out the leader's name ;
Likewise five hundred pounds per man
For any one of all the clan.
But let him try his utmost skill,
I'm apt to think he never will
Find out any of those hearts of gold,
Though he should offer fifty-fold."

[1] Mr. Weeden was formerly librarian of the institution. It is situated in a handsome building on the east side of Benefit Street, and contains about five thousand volumes, among which is a copy of the great work on Egypt, arranged under the superintendence of Denon, and published by Napoleon at the expense of the government of France. This copy belonged to Prince Polignac, the minister of Charles X. Many of the plates were colored by his direction. It is a beautiful copy, bound in morocco.

[2] I was informed, after leaving Providence, that Mr. Dexter was yet living in the northern part of the town, at the age of ninety-two years.

by the commander in the crowd, who sat upon his white horse at the south end of the bridge. He performed the dreary night march through the snow toward Princeton, and was in the battle there on the following morning. His term of service expired while the American army was at Morristown, whither it went from Princeton. From Morristown, himself and companions made their way on foot, through deep snows, back to Providence, crossing the Hudson River at King's Ferry (Stony Point), and the Connecticut at Hartford. Gladly would I have listened until sunset to the narrative of his great experience, but the first bell of the packet summoned me away.

I left Providence at three o'clock in the Perry, and arrived at Newport, thirty miles distant, at about five, edified on the way by the conversation of the venerable William Cranston, of Attlebury, Massachusetts, then eighty-one years of age, who was a resident of Newport during the Revolution. The bald appearance of Rhode Island, relieved only by orchards, which showed like dark tufts of verdure in the distance, with a few wind-mills and scattered farm-houses, formed a singular and unfavorable feature in the view as we approached Newport; while upon small islands and the main land appeared the ruins of forts and batteries, indicating the military importance of the waters we were navigating. This was

> " Rhode Island, the land where the exile sought rest;
> The Eden where wandered the Pilgrim oppress'd.
> Thy name be immortal! here man was made free,
> The oppress'd of all nations found refuge in thee.
>
> " There Freedom's broad pinions our fathers unfurl'd,
> An ensign to nations and hope to the world;
> Here both Jew and Gentile have ever enjoy'd
> The freedom of conscience in worshiping God."
>   ARTHUR A. ROSS.

The fair promises of a pleasant morrow, sweetly expressed by a bright moonlight evening, October 22, were not realized, for at dawn heavy rain-drops were pattering upon my window, 1848. and the wind was piping with all the zeal of a sudden "sou'easter." I had intended to start early for the neighborhood of Quaker Hill, toward the north end of the island, the scene of conflict in 1778; but the storm frustrated my plans, and I passed the day in visiting places of interest in the city and its immediate vicinity. The object of greatest attraction to the visitor at Newport is the Old Tower, or wind-mill, as it is sometimes called. It stands within a vacant lot owned by Governor Gibbs, directly in front of his fine old mansion, which was erected in 1720, and was then one of the finest dwellings in the colony. It is a brick building, covered with red cedar. The main object in the picture is a representation of the tower as it appeared at the time of my visit. On the right of it is seen the residence of Governor Gibbs,[1] surrounded by shade-trees and flowering shrubs in abundance. I passed the stormy morning under its roof; and to the proprietor I am indebted for much kindness during my visit at Newport, and for valuable suggestions respecting the singular relic of the past that stands upon his grounds, mute and mysterious as a mummy. On the subject of its erection history and tradition are silent, and the object of its construction is alike unknown and conjectural. It is a huge cylinder, composed of unhewn stones —common granite, slate, sandstone, and pudding-stone—cemented with coarse mortar, made of the soil on which the structure stands, and shell lime. It rests upon eight round columns, a little more than three feet in diameter, and ten feet high from the ground to the spring of the arches. The wall is three feet thick, and the whole edifice, at the present time, is twenty-four feet high. The external diameter is twenty-three feet. Governor Gibbs informed me that, on excavating at the base of one of the pillars, he found the soil about four feet deep, lying upon a stratum of hard rock, and that the foundation of the column, which rested upon this rock, was composed of rough-hewn spheres of stone, the lower ones about four feet in circumference. On the interior, a little above the arches, are small square

---

[1] Mr. Gibbs was Governor of Rhode Island in 1819.

OF THE REVOLUTION.   633

Old Tower at Newport.   Its former Appearance.   Attempt to destroy it.   Obscurity of its Origin

niches, in depth about half the thickness of the wall, designed, apparently, to receive floor-timbers.   In several places within, as well as upon the inner surface of some of the columns,

OLD TOWER AT NEWPORT.

are patches of stucco, which, like the mortar, is made of coarse sand and shell lime, and as hard as the stones it covers.   Governor Gibbs remembers the appearance of the tower more than forty years ago, when it was partially covered with the same hard stucco upon its exterior surface.   Doubtless it was originally covered within and without with plaster, and the now rough columns, with mere indications of capitals and bases of the Doric form, were handsomely wrought, the whole structure exhibiting taste and beauty.   During the possession of Rhode Island by the British, in the Revolution, the tower was more perfect than now, having a roof, and the walls were three or four feet higher than at present.[1]   The British used it for an ammunition magazine, and when they evacuated the island, they attempted to demolish the old " mill" by igniting a keg of powder within it !   But the strong walls resisted the Vandals, and the only damage the edifice sustained was the loss of its roof and two or three feet of its upper masonry.   Such is the Old Tower at Newport at the present time.   Its early history is yet unwritten, and may forever remain so.[2]

---

[1] Governor Gibbs showed me a Continental bill of the denomination of five dollars (not signed), which his son found in a crevice in the tower.

[2] There has been much patient investigation, with a great deal of speculation, concerning this ancient edifice, but no satisfactory conclusion has yet been obtained.   Of its existence prior to the English emigration to America there is now but little doubt; and it is asserted that the Indians, of whom Mr. Coddington and other early settlers upon Aquitneck (now Rhode Island) solicited information concerning the structure, had no tradition respecting its origin.   Because it was called a "mill" in some old documents, some have argued, or, rather, have flippantly asserted, that it was built by the early English settlers for a wind-mill.   Thus Mr. Cooper disposes of the matter in his preface to *Red Rover*.   A little patient inquiry would have given him a different conclusion; and if the structure is really ante-colonial, and perhaps ante-Columbian, its history surely is worthy of investigation.   That it was converted into and used for a wind-mill by some of the early settlers of Newport, there is no doubt, for it was easily convertible to such use, although not by a favorable arrangement.   The English settlement upon the island was commenced in 1636, at the north end, and in 1639 the first house was erected on the site of Newport, by Nicholas Easton.   Mention is made in the colonial records of the erection of a wind-mill by Peter Easton, in 1663, twenty-five years after the founding of Newport; and this was evidently the *first* mill erected there, from the fact that it was considered of sufficient importance to the colony to induce the General Court to reward Mr. Easton for his enterprise, by a grant of a tract of fine land, a mile in length, lying along what is still known as *Easton's*

634   PICTORIAL FIELD-BOOK

First Wind-mill at Newport.   Inquiries respecting the Tower.   "Antiquitates Americana."   Inscription on Dighton Rock

The rain ceased at ten o'clock, and a westerly wind dispersed the clouds, but made the day unpleasant by its blustering breath.   I sketched the house on the corner of Spring and Peck-

Beach.   That mill was a wooden structure, and stood upon the land now occupied by the North Burying-ground, in the upper suburbs of Newport.   The land on which the Old Tower stands once belonged to Governor Benedict Arnold, and in his will, bearing the date of 1678, forty years after the settlement, he mentions the " stone mill," the tower having evidently been used for that purpose.   Its form, its great solidity, and its construction upon columns, forbid the idea that it was originally erected for a mill; and certainly, if a common wind-mill, made of timber, was so highly esteemed by the people, as we have seen, the construction of such an edifice, so superior to any dwelling or church in the colony, would have received special attention from the magistrates, and the historians of the day.   And wherefore, for such a purpose, were the foundation-stones wrought into spheres, and the whole structure stuccoed within and without?

When, in 1837, the Royal Society of Northern Antiquaries of Copenhagen published the result of their ten years' investigations concerning the discovery of America by the Northmen in the tenth century, in a volume entitled "Antiquitates Americana," the old "mill" at Newport, the rock inscription at Dighton, in Massachusetts, and the discovery of skeletons, evidently of a race different from the Indians,* elicited the earnest attention of inquirers, as subjects in some way connected with those early discoveries.   Dr. Webb (whom I have mentioned as extending to me his friendly services at the rooms of the Historical Society of Massachusetts), who was then a resident of Providence, and secretary to the Rhode Island Historical Society, opened a correspondence with Charles C. Rafn, the secretary to the Royal Society of Copenhagen.   Dr. Webb employed Mr. Catherwood to make drawings of the "mill," and these, with a particular account of the structure, he transmitted to Professor Rafn.   Here was opened for the society a new field of inquiry, the products of which were published, with engravings from Mr. Catherwood's drawings.   According to Professor Rafn, the architecture of this building was in the ante-Gothic style, which was common in the north and west of Europe from the eighth to the twelfth century.   "The circular form, the low columns, their thickness in proportion to their distance from each other, and the entire want of ornament," he says, "all point out this epoch."   He imagines that it was used for a baptistry, and accounts for the absence of buildings of a similar character by the abundance of wood in America.   The brevity of the sojourn of the Northmen here was doubtless another, and perhaps principal reason, why similar structures were not erected.   The fact that the navigators of Sweden, Norway, and Iceland visited and explored the American coast as far as the shores of Connecticut, and probably more southerly, during the tenth and eleventh centuries (five hundred years before the voyages of Columbus), appears to be too well attested to need further notice here.   For the proofs, the reader is referred to the interesting work alluded to, "Antiquitates Americana."

The inscription upon the rock at Dighton has given rise to much speculation and to many theories.   The

INSCRIPTION ON DIGHTON ROCK.

rock lies upon the east side of Taunton River, between high and low water marks, so that it is covered and exposed at every ebb and flow of the tide.   It is an insulated mass of fine-grained granite, or grunstein, lying northwest and southeast on the sands of the river.   Its length is eleven feet, and its height four and a half feet.   It has a regular surface and nearly smooth, whereon the inscription is carved.   The inscription presents four parts or divisions, and evidently refers to a combat.   On the left is a figure armed with a bow and arrow, and may represent an Indian.   Next to it is an inscription composed of Runic or Phœnician characters, doubtless a history of the event there partially pictured.   Further to the right is a vessel, and on the extreme right are two figures, differing from the one on the left, without bows and arrows, and evidently connected with the vessel.   These and the vessel doubtless indicate them as voyagers from a distant land.†   Between the figures and the boat are Runic or Phœnician characters.   The question arises, By whom was the inscription made?   The Phœnician characters seem to be proof that those ancient navigators visited the American coast and made this record of combat

* Dr. J. C. V. Smith, of Boston, has written an account of a remarkable stone cemetery, discovered about fifty years ago on Rainsford Island, in Boston Bay, which contained a skeleton and sword-hilt of iron.   Dr. Webb has also published an interesting account of a skeleton discovered at Fall River, in Massachusetts, on or near which were found a bronze breast-plate, bronze tubes belonging to a belt, &c., none of which appear to be of Indian, or of comparatively modern European manufacture.   Drs. Smith and Webb both concluded that these skeletons were those of Scandinavian voyagers.

† Kendall, in his Travels, published in 1809, describes this rock and the inscription, and gives the following Indian tradition : "Some ages past, a number of white men arrived in the river in a bird [sailing vessel], when the white men took Indians into the bird as hostages.   They took fresh water for their consumption at a neighboring spring, and while procuring it, the Indians fell upon and murdered some of them.   During the affray, thunder and lightning issued from the bird, and frightened the Indians away.   Their hostages, however, escaped."   The thunder and lightning spoken of evidently refers to fire-arms, and, if the tradition is true, the occurrence must have taken place as late as the latter part of the fourteenth century, for gunpowder, for warlike purposes, was not used in Europe previous to 1350.   In a representation of the battle of Cressy (which was fought in 1343) upon a manuscript Froissart, there are no pictures of fire-arms, and probably they were not in common use at that time ; there is a piece of ordnance at Amberg, in Germany, on which is inscribed the year 1303.   Roger Bacon, who died in 1292, was acquainted with gunpowder, and the Chinese and other Eastern nations were familiar with it long before that time.

OF THE REVOLUTION.   635

Prescott's Head-quarters in Newport.   Old Cemetery.   Perry's Monument.   Runic Inscriptions elsewhere.

ham Streets, now owned by Mr. Joshua
Sayre, which was occupied as his city
head-quarters by the petty tyrant, General Prescott, while he was in command
of the British troops on Rhode Island.
His acts will be noted presently. About
noon I strolled up to the cemetery in
the northern part of the city, where lie
the remains of a great multitude of the
early inhabitants of Newport. Workmen were employed in regulating it, by

placing the old
grave - stones
upright, and
painting them
so as to bring
out their half-

PRESCOTT'S HEAD-QUARTERS.

effaced inscriptions, and in beautifying the grounds in various ways.
There, beneath a broad slab of slate, repose the bodies of John and
William Cranston, father and son, who were governors of Rhode
Island—the former in 1679, the latter from 1698 to 1726. Near
by is the tomb of William Jefferay, who, tradition says, was one of
the judges of Charles I. It is covered by a large slab of graywacke, ornamented, or, rather, disfigured, at the head, by a representation of a skull and cross-bones, below which is a poetic epitaph.
He died January 2d, 1675. On the top of the slope on which a
portion of the cemetery lies, is a granite obelisk, erected to the memory of Commodore Perry, by the State of Rhode Island, at a cost
of three thousand dollars. It is formed of a single stone, twenty-
three feet in height, standing upon a square pedestal ten feet high,

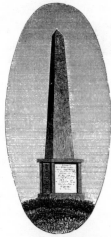

PERRY'S MONUMENT.

with the Indians; and hence some reject the opinion of others that the rock was inscribed by the hand of a
Scandinavian. When we remember that the Phœnicians were for many ages in the undisputed possession
of the traffic of the Baltic, around which clustered the Scandinavian nations, and that Runic, or ancient German inscriptions, in Phœnician characters, have been discovered in abundance in all the countries formerly
occupied by these nations, the inference is plainly correct, that the Scandinavians received their alphabet
from the Phœnicians.* In the *Journal des Debats* of Paris, a letter was published, dated Copenhagen,
February 5, 1850, in which it is mentioned that Dr. Pierre André Munch, professor at the University of
Christina, then in Copenhagen, had just presented to the Society of Northern Antiquaries an extremely curious manuscript, in a state of excellent preservation, which he discovered and obtained during his voyage,
in 1849, to the Orkney Isles. This manuscript, which the professor refers to the ninth and tenth centuries,
contains several episodes, in the Latin language, on the history of Norway, presenting some important facts,
heretofore entirely unknown, which illustrate the obscure ages that in Norway preceded the introduction of
Christianity. Dr. Munch also presented to the society several fac-similes of Runic inscriptions, which he
discovered in the Orkney Isles and in the north of Scotland. It is probable these discoveries may cast some
light upon the obscure subject under consideration. In the record of the voyages to America of the Northmen, a severe combat with the natives (*skrellings*) is mentioned, and various circumstances show that in the
vicinity of this inscription the battle occurred. Is it not reasonable to infer that those Scandinavians, acquainted with the Phœnician alphabet, made a record of the battle upon the rock, by a mingling of alphabetical characters and pictorial hieroglyphics? And may not the same people have reared the Old Tower
at Newport, in the vicinity, for a baptistry, with a view of erecting a church, and making a permanent settlement there? for it must be remembered that at that time those Northern nations were nominal Christians.
The records of their voyages were compiled by Bishop Thorlack, of Iceland, a grandson of Snorre,† son of
Gudrida, who was born in Wineland, or Massachusetts, in 1008. The subject is one of great interest, and
worthy of further and more minute inquiries than have yet been made.

* On this point consult Schlegel's fourth lecture on *The History of Literature.*
† The late Bertel Thorwalsden, the greatest sculptor of our time, was a lineal descendant of Snorre.

636   PICTORIAL FIELD-BOOK

'Tonomy Hill.   Hubbard's House and Mill.   Inscription on Perry's Monument.

having white marble tablets. It is inclosed by an iron railing, and has an imposing appearance.[1]

About a mile and a half northward of Newport rises a bold, rocky eminence, called "'Tonomy Hill" (the first word being an abbreviation of Miantonōmoh), celebrated as the seat

TOP OF 'TONOMY HILL.[2]

of the Narraganset sachem of that name, and the commanding site of a small fort or redoubt during the war of the Revolution. Thitherward I made my way from the old cemetery, passing several wind-mills that were working merrily in the stiff breeze which swept over the island from the west. The absence of streams of sufficient strength to turn water-wheels is the cause of the retention of these ancient mills, which give Rhode Island an Old England appearance. One of them, standing near the junction of the main road and the lane leading up to "'Tonomy Hill," is a patriarch among the others, for its sails revolved when the Gaspee lorded over the waters of the Narraganset. It is invested with associations of considerable interest. The mill and the old house near by were owned by a man named Hubbard. When the British took possession

HUBBARD'S HOUSE AND MILL.[1]

[1] The inscriptions upon the monument are as follows :

EAST SIDE.—" Oliver Hazard Perry. At the age of 27 years he achieved the victory of Lake Erie, September 10, 1813."

NORTH SIDE.—" Born in South Kingston, R. I., August 23d, 1785. Died at Port Spain, Trinidad, August 23d, 1819, aged 34 years."

WEST SIDE.—"His remains were conveyed to his native land in a ship of war, according to a resolution of Congress, and were here interred, December 4, 1826."

SOUTH SIDE.—" Erected by the State of Rhode Island."

[2] This view is from the north side of the hill, looking south. The wall appearance is a steep precipice of huge masses of pudding-stone, composed of pebbles and larger smooth stones, ranging in size from a pea to a man's head. It is a very singular geological formation. In some places the face is smooth, the stones and pebbles appearing as if they had been cut with a knife in a pasty or semi-fluid state. On the top of this mound are traces of the breast-works that were thrown up, not high, for the rocks formed a natural rampart, on all sides but one, against an enemy . Here Miantonōmoh had his fort, and here his councils were held when he planned his expeditions against the Mohegans. The observatory is a strong frame, covered with lattice-work. On the right is seen the city of Newport in the distance.

[3] The house and the mill are covered with shingles instead of clap-boards. This view is from the lane, looking east. The ocean is seen in the distance, on the left.

of Rhode Island, Prescott turned many of the families of the Whigs (and there were but few others) out of their houses, to take shelter in barns and other coverts, while his soldiers occupied their comfortable dwellings. Mr. Hubbard and his family were thus driven from their house, and compelled to live for nearly two years in their mill, while insolent soldiery, ignorant and vile, occupied their rooms. The family of Mr. Hubbard took possession of the house on the evening after the evacuation, but all was desolation, the enemy having broken or carried away every article the family had left there.

'Tonomy Hill is said to be the highest land upon the island, except Quaker Hill, toward the northern end. On its southern slope is the mansion of Mr. Hazzard, where families from a distance have a pleasant home during the warm season, while the younger fashionables are sporting at the Ocean House on the shore. On the top of the hill Mr. Hazzard has erected an observatory, seventy feet high, over a cellar which was dug by the Indians, and in which is a living spring of water. The hill is two hundred and seventy feet above the bay, and the top of the observatory commands one of the most beautiful panoramic views in the world. Stretching away northward was seen Narraganset Bay, broken by islands and pierced by headlands, and at its remote extremity the spires of Providence were glittering in the sun. On its western shore were glimpses of Warwick, Greenwich, and Wickford, and on the east were seen Warren and Bristol, and the top of Mount Hope, the throne of King Philip. On the south and west were the city and harbor of Newport, the island of Canonicut with its ruined fort, and the smaller islands in the harbor, with the remains of fortifications. Beyond the city, looking oceanward with a spy-glass over the ramparts of Fort Adams, was seen the dim outline of Block Island, like a mist lying upon the waters. There rolled the dark and boundless Atlantic, with no limit but the blue horizon, no object but a few sails. Turning the glass a little more eastward, there was a faint apparition of Gayhead, on Martha's Vineyard, and of some of the islands in Buzzard's Bay. The cultivated fields of more than one half of Rhode Island, upon which I stood, were spread out like a map around me, rich in Nature's bounties and historical associations. From our lofty observatory, let us take a field survey with the open chronicle before us.

We have seen Roger Williams expelled from Massachusetts because of alleged heresy. The rulers of that colony had scarcely recovered their equanimity, before similar difficulties arose from an unexpected quarter. Mrs. Anne Hutchinson, a Lincolnshire lady of good birth, education, and great energy of character, had been leavened by the tolerant principles of Williams before he left, and assumed the right to discuss religious dogmas and to detect the errors of the clergy. A privilege had been granted to hearers, at the end of sermons, to ask questions "wisely and sparingly." Mrs. Hutchinson put so many searching questions upon abstruse points in theology, in a manner which convinced the ministers that she well understood the subject, that they were greatly annoyed. She held conferences at her own house every Sabbath evening, which were fully attended, and her brother-in-law, a minister named Wheelwright, who was of the same mind with her, drew crowds to his chapel every Sunday. Henry Vane, a young man of splendid talents, heir to a princely fortune, and son to Charles the First's chief secretary, had just arrived in the colony, and took up his residence with the Reverend Mr. Cotton, who treated Mrs. Hutchinson's views with gentleness, if not with favor. Vane (afterward Sir Henry Vane) was elected governor the following year, and being imbued with the spirit of toleration, was on terms of intimacy with Mrs. Hutchinson. The ministers were alarmed; their churches were thinned, while the chapel of Mr. Wheelwright could not contain the hundreds that flocked to hear him. A clamor was raised by the old party of ministers and their friends, and the next year Mr. Winthrop was elected governor, and Vane soon afterward returned to England.

A general synod of ministers now assembled at Salem, consisting of the preach-   August 30, ers, deputies from the congregations, and magistrates, and after a session of three   1637. weeks, marked by stormy debates, unanimously passed sentence of censure against Mr. Wheelwright, Mrs. Hutchinson, and their adherents. Continuing to hold her conferences, Mrs. Hutchinson was ordered to leave the colony within six months; and a similar command was given to Mr. Wheelwright, Mr. Aspinwall, and others. They, like the Tories in the Revolution, were required to deliver up their arms. With their departure ended the Antinomian strife in Massachusetts. Wheelwright and his friends went to the banks of the Piscataqua, and founded the town of Exeter at its head waters; but the larger number of Mrs. Hutchinson's friends, led by John Clarke and William Coddington, proceeded southward, designing to make a settlement on Long Island, or with the Swedes on the Delaware. On their way through the wilderness Roger Williams gave them a hearty welcome, and by his influence and the name of Henry Vane as their friend, obtained for them from Miantonōmoh, chief of the Narragansets, a gift of the beautiful island of Aquitneck.[1] A deed signed by Canonicus and Miantonōmoh was given them in March, 1638. Naming the beautiful land the *Isle of Rhodes*, because they fancied that it resembled the island of that name in the eastern Mediterranean, they bound themselves as a community of freemen, by these solemn words, to found a new state, appealing to the great Searcher of Hearts for aid in the faithful performance of their promises:

" We, whose names are underwritten, do swear solemnly, in the presence of the Great Jehovah, to incorporate ourselves into a body politic; and as he shall help us, will submit our persons, lives, and estates unto the Lord Jesus Christ, the King of kings and Lord of lords, and to all those most perfect laws of his, given us in his most holy word of truth, to be guided and judged thereby."

This was a simple declaration, but a broad and sure foundation upon which to build a state. Mr. Clarke and eighteen others began their new settlement at Pocasset (Portsmouth), on the north part of the island; borrowed the forms of the administration of laws from the Jews; elected Coddington "judge in the new Israel," and prospered greatly. Soon after the arrival of these pioneers, Mrs. Hutchinson, with her children, made her way through the wilderness to the settlement of Roger Williams, and paddling down the Narraganset in a canoe, joined her friends on Rhode Island. She had been left a widow, but blessed with affectionate children. Her powerful mind continued active; young men from the neighboring colony were converted to her doctrines, and so great became her influence that "to the leaders of Massachusetts it gave cause of suspicion of witchcraft," and they sought to ensnare her. Rhode Island seemed no longer a place of safe refuge for her, and the whole family removed into the territory of the Dutch, in the neighborhood of Albany. The Indians and Keift, the Dutch governor, were then at enmity. The former regarded all white people as enemies, and Mrs. Hutchinson and her whole family, except one child, were murdered by the savages, and their dwelling burned.[2]

So rapid was the increase of the Rhode Island settlement at Pocasset, that another town was projected. Newport was founded in 1639. Settled by persecuted men holding the same liberal views, the republic of Roger Williams at Providence, and that upon Aquitneck, governed by no other than the Divine laws of the Bible, felt themselves as one political community, and were so regarded by the other colonies. Under the pretense that the Providence and Rhode Island Plantations had no charter, and were claimed by Plymouth and Massachusetts, they were excluded from the confederacy that was formed in 1643. Perceiving the disadvantages of an entire independency of the imperial government, Roger Williams proceeded to England, and in March, 1644, through the influence of his personal character, and of Henry Vane, obtained a free charter of incorporation from Parliament, then waging a fierce war with King Charles the First. The two plantations were united by it under the same government, and the signet for the state was ordered to be a "sheafe of arrows," with the motto "AMOR VINCET OMNIA"—*Love is all powerful.*

In 1647, the General Assembly of the several towns met at Portsmouth, and organized the government by the choice of a president and other officers. They adopted a code of

---

[1] This Indian name of Rhode Island is variously spelled: Aquiday, Aquitnet, and Aquitneck. It is a Narraganset word, signifying *peaceable isle.*

[2] Bancroft, i., 388, 393. Winthrop, i., 296. Callender, Gorton, in Hutchinson's History of Massachusetts, i., 73.

OF THE REVOLUTION. 639

oleration in Rhode Island.   Separation and Reunion of the Plantations.   Newport.   Destruction of the Sloop Liberty.

laws by which entire freedom of thought in religious matters, as well as a democracy in civil affairs, was guarantied.   Churchmen, Roman Catholics, Quakers, were all tolerated ; and none were excluded from the ballot-box on account of their religious opinions.   Consequently, many Quakers settled in Rhode Island, and they have ever formed a large and influential class of the population.

The two plantations were separated for a brief time, when, in 1651, Mr. Coddington was appointed by the supreme authority of England, Governor of Rhode Island alone.   The people, alarmed at the apparent danger of having their freedom abridged by depriving them of the choice of their own rulers, sent Roger Williams to England, who obtained a revocation of the appointment.   Mr. Coddington retired to private life, the Plantations were reunited, and from that time until the Revolution they were prosperous and happy, disturbed only by the alarms produced by King Philip's War, to be noticed presently, and the distant conflicts with the French and Indians during the first half of the eighteenth century.   A charter of incorporation was obtained in 1663 from Charles II., by which the province was constituted a body politic, by the name of " The Governor and Company of the Rhode Island and Providence Plantations in New England, in America."   Under this charter the state has been governed until the present time.   Rhode Island quietly submitted to the brief usurpation of Andross, and its charter was undisturbed.   On his imprisonment, the people assembled at Newport, resumed their former charter privileges, and re-elected the officers whom that petty tyrant had displaced.

The fine harbor of Newport and its healthy location made that place one of the most important sea-port towns on the American coast ;[1] and soon after the Revolution it was said that if New York continued to increase as rapidly as it was then growing it would soon rival Newport in commerce !   The navies of all Europe might safely ride at anchor in its deep and capacious harbor, and for a long time Newport was regarded as the future commercial metropolis of the New World.   During the wars with the French, English and colonial privateers made Newport their chief rendezvous.   In the course of one year, more than twenty prizes, some of them of great value, were sent into that harbor.   1745.

During all the occurrences preliminary and relative to the Revolution, the people of Rhode Island, thoroughly imbued with the principles of freedom, took a firm stand against British oppression, and were ever bold in the annunciation and maintenance of their political views. Indeed, Newport was the scene of the first overt act of popular resistance to royal authority other than the almost harmless measures of opposition to the Stamp Act in 1765.   This was the destruction of the British armed sloop Liberty, which the commissioners of customs had sent to Narraganset Bay on an errand similar to that of the Gaspee subsequently. This vessel was boarded, her cable cut, and having drifted to Goat Island, she was there scuttled and set on fire, after her stores and armaments had been thrown   July, 1769 overboard.[2]

---

[1] Dr. Benjamin Waterhouse, in an article published in the *Boston Intelligencer*, in 1824, says, "The island of Rhode Island, from its salubrity and surpassing beauty, before the Revolutionary war so sadly defaced it, was the chosen resort of the rich and philosophic from nearly all parts of the civilized world.   In no spot of the thirteen, or, rather, twelve colonies, was there concentrated more individual opulence, learning, and liberal leisure."   "In 1769," says Mr. Ross, " Newport rivaled New York in foreign and domestic navigation.   The inhabitants of New Haven, New London, &c., depended entirely upon Newport for a market to supply themselves with foreign goods, and here they found a ready market for the produce of their own state."—See *Historical Discourse* by Reverend Arthur A. Ross of Newport : 1838, page 29.

[2] A sloop and a brig belonging to Connecticut had been seized and brought into Newport.   The wearing apparel and sword of the captain of the brig were put on board the Liberty, and going for them he was violently assaulted.   As his boat left the sloop a musket and brace of pistols were discharged at him.   This act greatly exasperated the people of Newport.   They demanded of Captain Reid, of the Liberty, that the man who fired on Captain Packwood, of the brig, should be sent ashore.   The request was denied, or rather, a wrong man was sent each time, until the populace determined not to be trifled with longer.   A number of them went on board, cut her cables, and set her adrift, with the result mentioned in the text. Her boats were dragged up the Long Wharf, thence to the Parade, through Broad Street, at the head of which, on the Common, they were burned.   The "Newport Mercury," of July 31, 1769, contained this announcement : " Last Saturday the sloop Liberty was floated by a high tide, and drifted over to Goat Island,

The first warlike menace made against Rhode Island was in the autumn of 1775. We have already noticed the alacrity with which the people armed and hastened toward Boston when they received intelligence of the affair at Lexington. Admiral Wallace commanded a small British fleet in the harbor of Newport during that summer, and the people became convinced that it was his intention to carry off the live stock from the lower end of the island, with which to supply the British army at Boston. Accordingly, on a dark night in September, some of the inhabitants went down and brought off about one thousand sheep and fifty head of cattle. Three hundred minute men drove up to Newport a large number more, and Wallace was foiled in his attempts at plunder. Enraged, he threatened the town with destruction. He laid the people under contributions to supply his fleet with provisions, and, to enforce the demand, he cut off their supplies of fuel and provisions from the main. The inhabitants were greatly alarmed, and about one half of them left the town, among whom were the principal merchants, with their families. By consent of the state government and the Continental Congress, a treaty was entered into. The people agreed to supply

October 1, 1775. the fleet with beer and fresh provisions, and Wallace removed all restrictions upon their movements. He then sailed up the bay to Bristol, and demanded from the inhabitants there three hundred sheep. They refused compliance, and the town was bom-

October 7. barded, the assault commencing at about eight o'clock in the evening. The rain was pouring in torrents. The house of Governor Bradford, with some others, was burned, and in the midst of the darkness women and children fled to the open fields, beyond the reach of the invaders' missiles, where they suffered dreadfully. This Wallace was the same officer who was afterward sent up the Hudson River to plunder and destroy, laying Kingston in ashes, and desolating the farms of innocent men because they loved freedom better than tyranny and misrule.[1] He was a commissioned pirate in the Narraganset Bay, and for a month reveled in the wanton destruction of property. Every American vessel that came into Newport harbor was captured and sent into Boston. He burned and plundered the dwellings upon the beautiful island of Providence, in the bay; and at the close of No-

1775. vember passed over to Canonicut, and destroyed all the buildings near the ferry. These outrages aroused the vengeance of the people, and the few Tories upon the island who favored the marauders were severely dealt with. Washington, then at Boston, sent General Charles Lee, with some riflemen, to their assistance. Lee arrested all the Tories he could find, deprived them of their arms, and imposed upon them the severest restrictions.

Wallace maintained possession of the harbor until the spring of 1776. On the 6th of April, American troops, with two row-galleys, bearing two eighteen pounders each, arrived from Providence. The British fleet was then anchored about a mile above Newport. Two eighteen pounders, brought by the provincial troops, were planted on shore in view of the enemy, and without any works to protect them. These, commanded by Captain Elliot, with the row-galleys, under Captain Grimes, promised Wallace such great and immediate danger, that he weighed anchor and left the harbor with his whole squadron without firing a shot. Soon afterward, the Glasgow, of twenty-nine guns, came into the harbor and anchored near Fort Island, having been severely handled in an engagement with Admiral Hopkins off Block Island.[2] Colonel Richmond, the same evening, ordered several pieces of heavy artil-

---

and is grounded near the north end, near the place where the pirates were buried. What this prognosticates we leave to the determination of astrologers." The same paper observed, August 7, "Last Monday evening, just after the storm of rain, hail, and lightning, the sloop Liberty, which we mentioned in our last as having drifted on Goat Island near where the pirates were buried, was discovered to be on fire, and continued burning for several days, until almost entirely consumed."—See Ross's Discourse.

[1] See page 388.

[2] This engagement occurred on the same day when Wallace left Newport. Hopkins, with his little fleet, was on a cruise eastward, having left the Capes of the Delaware in February, visiting the Bermudas, and was now making his way toward Massachusetts Bay. On the 4th of April (1776) he fell in with a British schooner on the east end of Long Island, and took her. About one in the morning of the 6th he fell in with the Glasgow, of twenty-nine guns and one hundred and fifty men. The American brigantine Cabot, Captain Hopkins, Junior, and the Columbus, Captain Whipple, raked her as she passed. The American brig Annadona and sloop Providence were also in the engagement, yet the Glasgow escaped and fled into

lery to be brought to bear upon the Glasgow from Brenton's Point, where a slight breast-work was thrown up. On the following morning such a vigorous fire was opened from this battery upon the Glasgow and another vessel, that they cut their cables and went to sea.

A few days after these events, the British ship of war Scarborough, of twenty guns and two hundred and twenty-five men, and the Scymetar, of eighteen guns and one hundred and forty men, came into the harbor with two prize ships, and anchored a little south of Rose Island. The Americans resolved to attempt the rescue of the prizes. The Washington galley, Captain Hyers, attacked the Scarborough, and at the same time Captain Grimes and his men, of the Spitfire galley, boarded one of the prizes and took it. The guns upon the North Battery and upon Brenton's Point were well manned, to give aid if necessary. The Scarborough attempted to recapture her prize, and the other schooner in her custody tried to get under the protecting wing of that vessel ; but the hot cannonade from the Washington and the North Battery arrested the progress of both, and the schooner was captured and sent to Providence. The Scarborough and Scymetar now came to anchor between Canonicut, and Rose Island ; but a battery upon the former, unknown to the enemy, poured such a shower of well-directed balls upon them, that, finding no safe place in the harbor, they determined to take refuge in the broad expanse of the ocean. As they passed out of the harbor, they were terribly galled by a cannonade from Brenton's Point and Castle Hill.[1] For eight days War held a festival upon the waters of Newport Harbor, yet in all that time the Americans did not lose a man, and had only one slightly wounded !

The summer of 1776 was a season of comparative quiet for the people of Rhode Island. They were active, however, in fitting out privateers, and in preparations for future invasions.[2] Early in the fall intelligence reached them that the British fleet and army, which had been so roughly received and effectually repulsed at Charleston, in South Carolina, were on the way to take possession of Rhode Island. These forces arrived on the 26th of December, the day on which Washington crossed the Delaware and accomplished his brilliant achievement at Trenton. The squadron was commanded by Sir Peter Parker, and the land forces, consisting of about an equal number of British and Hessians, in all between eight and ten thousand men, were commanded by General Clinton and Earl Percy. The squadron sailed up on the west side of Canonicut, crossed the bay at the north point of the island, and landed the troops in Middletown, about four and a half miles above Newport. They were encamped upon the southern slope of two hills (Gould's and Winter's), except a few who landed at Coddington's Cove and marched into Newport. When the enemy entered the harbor, there were two Rhode Island frigates (the Warren and Providence) and several privateers at anchor. These, with the weak land force, were insufficient to make a successful resistance, and the island was left at the mercy of the invaders.[3] The American frigates and privateers fled up the bay to Providence, whence, taking advantage of a northeast gale, and eluding the vigilance of the blockading squadron, they escaped, and went to sea. A system of general plunder of the inhabitants was immediately commenced by the troops, and, after one week's encampment, the British soldiers were unceremoniously quartered in the houses of the inhabitants, from ten to forty in each, according to the size and convenience of the edifice. The beautiful Aquitneck, or *Isle of Peace*, soon became the theater of discord, misery, and desolation.

April 15.

Newport Harbor, whither Hopkins thought it not prudent to follow. Of the American navy of the Revolution and its operations in general I have given an account in the Supplement, page 637.

[1] These localities will be better understood by reference to the map of Narraganset Bay on page 648.

[2] These privateers captured about seventy-five prizes (some of them very valuable) during the season and sent them to Providence, New London, and one or two other ports.

[3] On hearing of the approach of the enemy, the people of the island drove large quantities of sheep and cattle from it, crossing to the main at Howland's Ferry.

642   PICTORIAL FIELD-BOOK

Condition of Rhode Island in 1777.   Re-encampment of the British.   General Prescott.   His Character

CHAPTER XXVIII.

"The winds of March o'er Narraganset's Bay
    Move in their strength; the waves with foam are white;
O'er Seekonk's tide the waving branches play;
    The winds roar o'er resounding plain and height.
'Twixt sailing clouds, the sun's inconstant ray
    But glances on the scene, then fades from sight.
The frequent showers dash from the passing clouds;
The hills are peeping through their wintery shrouds."
                                DURFEE'S "WHAT CHEER?"

EAR after year the free dwellers upon Rhode Island had beheld a scene like that described by the poet, and more cruel wintery storms, piling their huge snow-drifts, had howled around their dwellings, but never in their history had the March winds and April floods appeared to them so cheerless and mournful as in the spring of 1777. They had cheerfully brooked all the sufferings attendant upon a new settlement, and gladly breasted the tempest on land or sea in pursuit of wealth or social enjoyment, while freedom was their daily companion and solace: but now the oppressor was in their midst; his iron heel was upon their necks; their wives and daughters were exposed to the low ribaldry, profanity, and insults of an ignorant and brutal soldiery; their peaceful dwellings were made noisy barracks; their beautiful shade-trees, pleasant groves, and broad forests were destroyed, and the huge right arm of general plunder was plying its strength incessantly. Enslaved and impoverished, the bright sun and warm south winds, harbingers of on-coming summer and the joyous season of flowers, brought no solace to them, but were rather a mockery. At home all was desolation; abroad all was doubt and gloom.

1777.   Early in May the British troops left the houses of the inhabitants and returned to their camp. This was some relief, yet plunder and insolence were rife. General Clinton, with nearly half of the invading army, soon afterward left the island for New York, and the command of those who remained to hold possession devolved upon Major-general Prescott, infamous in the annals of that war as one of the meanest of petty tyrants when in power, and of dastards when in danger. He had been nurtured in the lap of aristocracy, and taught all its exclusive precepts. Possessing a narrow mind, utterly untutored by benevolence or charity; a judgment perverse in the extreme; a heart callous to the most touching appeals of sympathy, but tender when avarice half opened its lips to plead, he was a most unfit commander of a military guard over people like those of Rhode Island, who could appreciate courtesy, and who might be more easily conquered by kindness than by the bayonet. He was a tyrant at heart, and, having the opportunity, he exercised a tyrant's doubtful prerogatives.[1]

---

[1] Mr. Ross, in his *Historical Discourse*, mentions several circumstances illustrative of Prescott's tyranny. His habit while walking the streets, if he saw any of the inhabitants conversing together, was to shake his cane at them, and say, "Disperse, ye rebels!" He was also in the habit, when he met citizens in the streets, of commanding them to take off their hats, and unless the order was instantly complied with, it was enforced by a rap of his cane. One evening, as he was passing out of town to his country quarters, he overtook a Quaker, who did not doff his hat. The general, who was on horseback, dashed up to him, pressed him against a stone wall, knocked off his hat, and then put him under guard. Prescott caused many citizens of Newport to be imprisoned, some of them for months, without any assigned reason. Among others thus deprived of liberty, was William Tripp, a very respectable citizen. He had a large and interesting family, but the tyrant would not allow him to hold any communication with them, either written or verbal

Incensed by the conduct of Prescott, the inhabitants devised several schemes to rid themselves of the oppressor. None promised success, and it was reserved for Lieutenant-colonel Barton, of Providence,[1] to conceive and execute one of the boldest and most hazardous enterprises undertaken during the war. It was accomplished on the night of the 10th of July, 1777. At that time General Prescott was quartered at the house of a Quaker named Overing, about five miles above Newport, on the west road leading to the ferry, at the north part of the island. Barton's plan was to cross Narraganset Bay from the main, seize Prescott, and carry him to the American camp. It was a very hazardous undertaking, for at that time there were three British frigates, with their guard-boats, lying east of Prudence Island, and almost in front of Prescott's quarters. With a few chosen men, Colonel Barton embarked in four whale-boats, with muffled oars, at Warwick Point, at nine o'clock in the evening, and passed unobserved over to Rhode Island, between the islands of Prudence and Pa-

The first intelligence he received from them was by a letter, baked in a loaf of bread, which was sent to him by his wife. In this way a correspondence was kept up during his confinement of many months. During his incarceration, his wife sought an audience with the general to intercede for the liberty of her husband, or to obtain a personal interview with him. She applied to a Captain Savage, through whom alone an interview with the general could be obtained. She was directed to call the following day, when the *savage* by name and nature, echoing his master's words, roughly denied her petition for an interview with the general, and with fiendish exultation informed her, as he shut the door violently in her face, that he expected her husband would be hung as a rebel in less than a week!

I was informed that when Prescott took possession of his town quarters, he had a fine sidewalk made for his accommodation some distance along Pelham and up Spring Street, for which purpose he took the door-steps belonging to other dwellings. The morning after the evacuation, the owners of the steps hastened to Prescott's quarters, each to claim his door-stone. It was an exciting scene, for sometimes two or three persons, not positive in their identification, claimed the same stone. Prescott's fine promenade soon disappeared, and like Miss Davidson's

> "Forty old bachelors, some younger, some older,
> Each carrying a maiden home on his shoulder,"

the worthy citizens of Newport bore off their long-abased door-steps.

[1] William Barton was a native of Providence, Rhode Island. He was appointed to the rank of lieutenant colonel in the militia of his state, and held that position when he planned and executed the expedition for the abduction of General Prescott. For that service Congress honored him by the presentation of a sword, and also by a grant of land in Vermont. By the transfer of some of this land he became entangled in the toils of the law, and was imprisoned for debt in Vermont for many years, until the visit of La Fayette to this country in 1825. That illustrious man, hearing of the incarceration of Colonel Barton and its cause, liquidated the claim against him, and restored his fellow-soldier to liberty. It was a noble act, and significantly rebuked the Shylock who held the patriot in bondage, and clamored for "the pound of flesh." This circumstance drew from Whittier his glorious poem, *The Prisoner for Debt*, in which he exclaims,

> "What has the gray-hair'd prisoner done?
> Has murder stain'd his hands with gore?
> Not so; his crime's a fouler one:
> *God made the old man poor.*
> For this he shares a felon's cell,
> The fittest earthly type of hell!
> For this, the boon for which he pour'd
> His young blood on the invader's sword,
> And counted light the fearful cost—
> His blood-gain'd liberty is lost.
>
> . . . .
>
> Down with the law that binds him thus!
> Unworthy freemen, let it find
> No refuge from the withering curse
> Of God and human kind!

644   PICTORIAL FIELD-BOOK

Expedition to capture Prescott.   Prescott's Quarters.   A Sentinel deceived.   Names of Barton's Men.

PRESCOTT'S HEAD-QUARTERS.[2]

tience.[1] They heard the cry, "All's well!" from the guard-boats of the enemy, as they passed silently and unobserved, and landed in Coddington's Cove, at the mouth of a small stream which passed by the quarters of Prescott. Barton divided his men into several squads, assigning to each its duty and station, and then, with the strictest order and profound silence, they advanced toward the house. The main portion of the expedition passed about midway between a British guard-house and the encampment of a company of light horse, while the remainder was to make a circuitous route to approach Prescott's quarters from the rear, and secure the doors. As Barton and his men approached the gate, a sentinel hailed them twice, and then demanded the countersign. "We have no countersign to give," Barton said, and quickly added, "Have you seen any deserters here to-night?" The sentinel was misled by this question, supposing

> Open the prisoner's living tomb,
> And usher from its brooding gloom
> The victims of your savage code
> To the free sun and air of God!
> No longer dare, as crime, to brand
> The chastening of the Almighty's hand!"

Colonel Barton was wounded in the action at Bristol Ferry in 1778, and was disabled from further service during the war. He died at Providence in 1831, aged eighty-four years. The portrait here given is from a painting of him executed soon after the close of the Revolution, and now in possession of his son, John B. Barton, Esq., of Providence, who kindly allowed me to make a copy.

[1] Mr. Barton, by request, furnished me with the following list of the names of those who accompanied his father on the perilous expedition:

OFFICERS.—Andrew Stanton, Eleazer Adams, Samuel Potter, John Wilcox.

NON-COMMISSIONED OFFICERS.—Joshua Babcock and Samuel Phillips.

PRIVATES.—Benjamin Pren, James Potter, Henry Fisher, James Parker, Joseph Guild, Nathan Smith, Isaac Brown, Billington Crumb, James Haines, Samuel Apis, Alderman Crank, Oliver Simmons, Jack Sherman, Joel Briggs, Clark Packard, Samuel Cory, James Weaver, Clark Crandall, Sampson George, Joseph Ralph, Jedediah Grenale, Richard Hare, Darius Wale, Joseph Denis, William Bruff, Charles Hassett, Thomas Wilcox, Pardon Cory, Jeremiah Thomas, John Hunt, Thomas Austin, Daniel Page (a Narraganset Indian). Jack Sisson* (black), and —— Howe, or Whiting, boat-steerer.

[2] This house is on the east side of the west road, about a mile from the bay. The view is from the road where the small stream crosses, after leaving the pond seen in the picture. It is a beautiful summer resi-

---

* In Allen's *American Biography*, the name of the black man is written Prince, and he says that he died at Plymouth in 1821, aged seventy-eight years. The name given by Mr. Barton must be correct, for he has the original paper of his father.

them to be friends, and was not undeceived until his musket was seized, and himself bound and menaced with instant death if he made any noise. The doors had been secured by the division from the rear, and Barton entered the front passage boldly. Mr. Overton sat alone, reading, the rest of the family being in bed. Barton inquired for General Prescott's room. Overton pointed upward, signifying that it was directly over the room in which they were standing. With four strong men, and Sisson, a powerful negro who accompanied them, Barton ascended the stairs and gently tried the door. It was locked; no time was to be lost in parleying; the negro drew back a couple of paces, and using his head for a battering-ram, burst open the door at the first effort. The general, supposing the intruders to be robbers, sprang from his bed, and seized his gold watch that was hanging upon the wall. Barton placed his hand gently upon the general's shoulder, told him he was his prisoner, and that perfect silence was now his only safety. Prescott begged time to dress, but it being a hot July night, and time precious, Barton refused acquiescence, feeling that it would not be cruel to take him across the bay, where he could make his toilet with more care, at his leisure. So, throwing his cloak around him, and placing him between two armed men, the prisoner was hurried to the shore. In the mean time, Major Barrington, Prescott's aid, hearing the noise in the general's room, leaped from a window to escape, but was captured. He and the sentinel were stationed in the center of the party. At about midnight captors and prisoners landed at Warwick Point, where General Prescott first broke the silence by saying to Colonel Barton, "Sir, you have made a bold push to-night." "We have been fortunate," coolly replied Barton. Captain Elliot was there with a coach to convey the prisoners to Providence, where they arrived at sunrise. Prescott was kindly treated by General Spencer and other officers, and in the course of a few days was sent to the head-quarters of Washington, at Middlebrook on the Raritan. On his way the scene occurred in the Alden Tavern at Lebanon, mentioned on page 603. Prescott was exchanged for General Charles Lee[1] in April following, and soon afterward resumed his command of the British troops on Rhode Island. This was the same Prescott who treated Colonel Ethan Allen so cruelly when that officer was taken prisoner near Montreal in the autumn of 1775. July 11, 1777. 1778.

On account of the bravery displayed and the importance of the service in this expedition, Congress, having a "just sense of the gallant behavior of Lieutenant-colonel Barton, and the brave officers and men of his party, who distinguished their valor and address in making prisoner of Major-general Prescott, of the British army, and Major William Barrington, his aid-de-camp,"[2] voted Barton an elegant sword; and on the 24th of December following, he was promoted to the rank and pay of colonel in the Continental army.[3] July 25, 1777.

General Sullivan was appointed to the command of the American troops in Rhode Island in the spring of 1778, at about the time when Prescott resumed his command of the enemy's forces. The latter, incensed and mortified by his capture and imprisonment, determined to gratify his thirst for revenge. Under pretense of an anticipated attack upon the island, he sent a detachment of five hundred men up the bay on the 24th of May, to destroy the American boats and other property that fell in their way. At daylight the next morning they landed between Warren and Bristol, and proceeded in two divisions to execute their orders. One party, who proceeded to the Kickemuet River, destroyed seventy flat-bottomed boats and a state galley; the other burned the meeting-house and a number of dwellings at Warren, and plundered and abused the inhabitants in various ways. The females were robbed of their shoe-buckles, finger-rings, and other valuables, and live stock were driven away for the use of the British army. They then proceeded to Bristol, and fired 1778

---

dence, the grounds around it being finely shaded by willows, elms, and sycamores. The present occupant kindly showed me the room in which Prescott was lying at the time of his capture. It is on the second floor, at the southwest corner of the house, or on the right as seen in the engraving. It is a well-built frame house, and was probably then the most spacious mansion on the island out o. Newport.

[1] General Lee had been captured at Baskingridge, in New Jersey, in December, 1776, while passing from the Hudson to join Washington on the Delaware.

[2] Journals of Congress, iii., 241.   [3] Ibid., 459.

the Episcopal church (mistaking it for a dissenters' meeting-house), burned twenty-two dwellings, and carried off considerable plunder. A few days afterward, another marauding party of a hundred and fifty burned the mills at Tiverton, and attempted to set fire to and plunder the town, but a resolute band of twenty-five men kept them at bay, effectually disputing their passage across the bridge. Satisfied with this great display of prowess and vengeance, Prescott refrained from further hostile movements, until called upon to defend himself against the combined attacks of an American army and a French fleet.

I have noticed on pages 86 and 87, *ante,* the treaty of alliance and commerce concluded between the United States and France on the 6th of February, 1778.[1] Pursuant to the stipulations of that treaty, a French squadron for the American service was fitted out at Toulon, consisting of twelve ships of the line, and four frigates of superior size. Count d'Estaing, a brave and successful naval officer, was appointed to the command, and on the 13th of April the fleet sailed for America. Silas Deane, one of the American commissioners, and M. Gerard, the first appointed French minister to the United States, came passengers in the Languedoc, D'Estaing's flag-ship. Authentic information of the sailing of this expedition reached the British cabinet on the 4th of May. Some of the ministers being out of town, a cabinet council was not held until the 6th, when it was determined speedily to dispatch a powerful squadron, then at Portsmouth, to America. On the 20th, Admirals Byron and Hyde Parker, with twenty-two ships of the line, weighed anchor. Doubtful of the destination of D'Estaing, and not knowing that Deane and Gerard were with him, ministers countermanded the order for sailing, and the squadron, overtaken by an express, returned to Plymouth, where it remained until the 5th of June, when it again sailed under the command of Admiral Byron alone.[3]

Estaing

The conduct of the French government, in thus openly giving aid, by treaty and arms, to the revolted colonies, aroused the ire, not only of ministers, but of the people of Great Britain, in whose bosoms the embers of ancient feuds were not wholly extinct. In Parliament, which was just on the eve of adjournment, ministers moved an appropriate address to the king. The opposition proposed an amendment requesting his majesty to dismiss the ministry! A furious debate arose, but the original address was carried by a majority of two hundred and sixty-three against one hundred and thirteen in the Commons, and an equally

---

[1] The French envoy, De Noailles (uncle of La Fayette's wife), delivered a rescript to Lord Weymouth on the 17th of March, in which he informed the British court of the treaty. While in it he professed in the name of the government a desire to maintain amicable relations with Great Britain, and declared that the "court of London" would find in his communication "new proofs of his majesty's [Louis XVI.] constant and sincere disposition for peace," he plainly warned it that his sovereign, "being determined to protect effectually the lawful commerce of his subjects, and to maintain the dignity of his flag, had, in consequence, taken effectual measures, in concert with the Thirteen United and Independent States of America." This note greatly incensed the British ministry, for they considered it more than half ironical in language, and intentionally insulting in spirit. Orders were issued for the seizure of all French vessels in English ports A similar order was issued by the French government. War thus actually commenced between the two nations, though not formally declared.

[2] Charles Henry Count d'Estaing was a native of Auvergne, in France. He was under the famous Count Lally, governor general of the French possessions in the East Indies, in 1756. He was taken prisoner by the English, but escaped by breaking his parole. He was commander at the taking of Grenada after his services in America. He became a member of the Assembly of Notables in the French Revolution, and, being suspected of unfriendliness to the Terrorists, was guillotined on the 29th of April, 1793.

[3] Admiral Byron carried with him to Earl Howe, the naval commander on the American coast, a permit for that officer to return to England, pursuant to his own urgent request. Byron became his successor in the chief command.

decided majority in the Upper House. Parliament soon afterward adjourned, and did not meet again until November, when the king, in his speech at the opening, directed the attention of the Legislature to the conduct of France. After speaking of the good faith of Great Britain, and the quiet then prevailing in Europe, he said, "In a time of profound peace, without pretense of provocation or color of complaint, the court of France hath not forborne to disturb the public tranquillity, in violation of the faith of treaties and the general rights of sovereigns ; at first by the clandestine supply of arms and other aid to my revolted subjects in North America ; afterward by avowing openly their support, and entering into formal engagements with the leaders of the rebellion ; and at length by committing open hostilities and depredations on my faithful subjects, and by an actual invasion of my dominions in America and the West Indies." He alluded to the want of success in America, the means that had been put forth to suppress the rebellion, the complete failure of the commissioners to conclude a peace, and the evident preparations for hostilities which Spain was making. He closed his address by calling upon Parliament to put forth their utmost energies which the crisis demanded, assuring them that his cordial co-operation would always be extended, and informed them that he had called out the militia for the defense of the country. In fact, the king carefully avoided casting censure upon ministers for the late miscarriages in America, and, by implication, fixed the blame upon the commanders in that service. The address was warmly opposed in both houses, and in the Commons the king was accused of falsehood—uttering "a false, unjust, and illiberal slander on the commanders in the service of the crown ; loading them with a censure which ought to fall on ministers alone." Yet ministers were still supported by pretty large majorities in both houses, while the war-spirit, renewed by the French alliance, was hourly increasing among the multitude without.[1]

After a voyage of eighty-seven days, the French squadron arrived on the coast, and anchored at the entrance of Delaware Bay. Howe, with his fleet, had, fortunately for himself, left the Delaware a few days before, and was anchored off Sandy Hook, to co-operate with the British land forces under Clinton, then proceeding from Philadelphia to New York.[2] On learning this fact, Deane and Gerard proceeded immediately up the Delaware to Philadelphia, where Congress was then in session.[3] After communicating with that body, D'Estaing weighed anchor and sailed for Sandy Hook. Howe was within the Hook, in Raritan or Amboy Bay,[4] whither D'Estaing could not with safety attempt to follow him with his large vessels, on account of a sand-bar extending to Staten Island from Sandy Hook.[5] He anchored near the Jersey shore, not far from the mouth of the Shrewsbury River.

On the 22d of July, D'Estaing sailed with his squadron, at the urgent request of Washington, to co-operate with General Sullivan, then preparing to make an attempt

July 8, 1778.

1778.

---

[1] Lossing's "1776," p. 274.

[2] It was during this progress of the British army toward New York that the Americans, under the immediate command of Washington, pursued and overtook them near Monmouth court-house, in New Jersey, where a severe battle occurred on the 28th of June, 1778.

[3] Congress had sat at York, in Pennsylvania, from the time of the entrance of the British into Philadelphia in the autumn of 1777, until the 30th of June, 1778, after the evacuation of that city by the enemy under Clinton.

[4] Howe's fleet consisted of only six 64 gun ships, three of 50, and two of 40, with some frigates and sloops. Several of D'Estaing's ships were of great bulk and weight of metal, one carrying 90, another 80, and six 74 guns each. Had D'Estaing arrived a little sooner, and caught Howe's fleet in the Delaware, he might easily have captured or destroyed it ; and doubtless the land forces of the enemy would have shared the fate of those under Burgoyne at Saratoga.

[5] Sandy Hook, in form and extent, has been greatly changed since the time in question. According to a map, in my possession, of the State of New York, published under the direction of Governor Tryon, in 1779, Sandy Hook was a low point, extending northward from the Highlands of Neversink or Navesink. The sandy bar on which the Ocean House, at the mouth of the Neversink River, now stands, forming a sound many miles in extent, was not then in existence ; and it was not until the sea made a breach across the neck of Sandy Hook in 1778, that there was a passage within it along the base of the Highlands from the Raritan or Amboy Bay. Now the water is from thirty to forty feet in depth in the main ship channel, immediately above the east beacon on Sandy Hook, quite sufficient to allow ships as heavy as D'Estaing's to enter.

to expel the enemy from Rhode Island. In consequence of the failure, on the part of General Spencer, to carry out the plan of an expedition against the British on Rhode Island in 1777, Congress ordered an inquiry into the cause. This expedition was arranged by General Spencer at considerable expense, and with fair promises of success. The Americans September, 1777. were stationed at Tiverton, near the present stone bridge, and had actually embarked in their boats to cross over to Rhode Island to surprise the enemy, when Spencer prudently countermanded the order. He had ascertained that the British commander was apprised of his intentions, and seeing no effort on the part of the enemy to oppose his

OPERATIONS UPON RHODE ISLAND IN 1778.[5]

landing, apprehended some stratagem that might be fatal. Such, indeed, was the fact. The British had determined to allow the Americans to land and march some distance upon the island, when they would cut off their retreat by destroying their boats, and thus make them captives. General Spencer, indignant at the censure implied in the proposed inquiry of Congress, resigned his commission, and General Sullivan was appointed in his place.[1]

The French fleet appeared off the harbor of Newport on the 29th of July, and 1778. the next morning, to the great joy of the inhabitants, the vessels of the allies were anchored near Brenton's Reef, where General Sullivan had a conference with the admiral, and a plan of operations was agreed upon. One of the ships ran up the channel west of Canonicut, and anchored at the north point of that island.

Washington had directed Sullivan to call upon Rhode Island, Massachusetts, and Connecticut for five thousand militia. The call was made, and promptly responded to. The Massachusetts militia marched under John Hancock as general;[2] and so great was the enthusiasm engendered by the presence of the French squadron, that thousands of volunteers, gentlemen and others, from Boston, Salem, Newburyport, Portsmouth, &c., engaged in the service.[3] Two brigades of Continental infantry, under La Fayette, were sent from the main army; and the whole force, ten thousand strong, was arranged in two divisions, under the immediate command of Generals Greene[4] and La Fayette.

On the morning of the 5th of August, D'Es-

---

[1] Joseph Spencer was born at East Haddam, in Connecticut, in 1714. He was a major in the colonial army in 1756, and was one of the first eight brigadiers appointed by the Continental Congress in 1775. He was appointed a major general in August, 1776, and in 1777 was in command of the American forces on Rhode Island. After his resignation he was elected a delegate to Congress from his native state. He died at East Haddam in January, 1789, aged seventy-five years.

[2] Hildreth, iii., 252.   [3] Gordon, ii., 369.

[4] General Greene was then the quarter-master general of the Continental army. His prudence, military skill, and the fact that he was a Rhode Islander, induced Washington to dispatch him to that field of operations at that time.

[5] The letters upon the map indicate the position of the following named objects: A, head-quarters of Prescott when he was captured; C D, the two British lines across the island, the former extending from

taing commenced operations. Two of his vessels approached to the attack of four British frigates (the Orpheus, Lark, Juno, and Cerberus) and some smaller vessels, lying near Prudence Island. Unable to fight successfully or to escape, the enemy set fire to all these vessels, and soon afterward sunk two others (the Flora and Falcon), to prevent their falling into the hands of D'Estaing. Unfortunately, the American troops were not quite prepared to co-operate with the French fleet. Although Sullivan had every thing in readiness at Providence, a delay in the arrival of troops prevented his departure for Rhode Island, and it was nearly a week before he was prepared to make a descent upon it. This delay was the occasion of great difficulty, and proved fatal to the enterprise.

On the 10th, according to agreement, the whole American force, in two divisions, crossed from Tiverton in eighty-six flat-bottomed boats,[1] prepared under the direction of the energetic Major Talbot, and landed on the north end of the island, where it was to be joined by four thousand marines from the French squadron. The British had just been re-enforced, and were about six thousand strong, under the immediate command of Sir Robert Pigot. They abandoned their works on the north part of the island when the Americans landed, and retired within their strongly-intrenched lines about three miles above Newport. Perceiving this movement, Sullivan ordered the Americans to advance, without waiting for the landing of the French troops. They moved from the ferry, and in the afternoon encamped upon the high ground known as Quaker Hill, between ten and eleven miles north of Newport. August, 1778.

Within five days after D'Estaing left Sandy Hook, four British men-of-war had arrived singly at New York. With this re-enforcement Howe determined to proceed to the relief of his majesty's army on Rhode Island. He appeared off Newport harbor with a fleet of twenty-five sail on the afternoon of the 9th; and the next morning, D'Estaing, instead of landing his marines according to agreement, spread his sails to a favorable breeze, and sailed out of the harbor, under a severe cannonade from the British batteries, to attack Admiral Howe. It was about eight o'clock in the morning when the French fleet went out into the open sea, and all that day the two naval commanders contended for the weather-gage.[2] This maneuvering prevented an engagement. The next morning the wind had increased to a gale, and a violent tempest, that raged for nearly forty-eight hours,[3] separated the belligerents. Two of the French ships were dismasted, and the count's flag-ship lost her rudder and all her masts. In this condition she was borne down upon by a British frigate under full sail, from which she received a broadside, but with little damage. Another of the French disabled vessels was attacked in the same way, the assailants sheering off after firing a single broadside; but the junction of six sail of the French squadron on the 14th prevented other attacks on the crippled ships. On the 16th, the French seventy-four gun ship Cæsar and the British fifty gun ship Iris had a August, 1778. August 10, 1778.

---

[1] Tonomy Hill, H, and the latter crossing the slope near Rose Island, near Newport; E, the American lines between Quaker and Turkey Hills and Butts's Hill, at the north end of the island; F, the position of the Americans, with their batteries, when preparing to attack the British lines and waiting for D'Estaing; G, Barker's Hill, fortified by the British; H, 'Tonomy Hill; O, the west or Narraganset passage of the bay; P, the middle; and Q, the east or Seaconet passage. The Bristol Ferry, across which the Americans retreated, is named on the map. It was at the narrowest place, a line to the right of the word Butts. There were fortifications upon Gold, Rose, Goat, and Contour Islands, as well as upon Canonicut, ruins of which are still visible. The short double lines upon the map, immediately above the letter N in Newport, mark the site of the present Fort Adams, the Castle Hill of the Revolution, and opposite, upon a point of Canonicut, is the Dumplings Fort, or Fort Canonicut, now a picturesque ruin.

[1] These boats were capable of bearing one hundred men each. They were fitted out with great dispatch, and Talbot, who directed the operations, became so wearied by over-exertions, that he slept soundly, for a long time, under one of them, while the hammers of the caulkers, who were at work by candle-light, were rattling over his head.—Tuckerman's *Life of Talbot*, p. 47.

[2] A ship is said to have the weather-gage when she is at the windward of another vessel. In naval engagements, obtaining the weather-gage is an important desideratum for the contending squadrons.

[3] This storm is still spoken of by the older inhabitants of Newport as "the great storm," accounts of which they had received from their parents. So violent was the wind, that the spray was brought by it from the ocean, and incrusted the windows in the town with salt.

severe engagement for an hour and a half, in which both vessels were much injured. This ended the contest, and D'Estaing, with his disabled vessels, appeared off the harbor of New-port on the 20th.

The Americans, greatly disappointed and chagrined by the abandonment of them by their allies, nevertheless continued their preparations for attack with vigor. They had suffered much from the gale and the rain. On the night of the 12th, not a tent or marquee could be kept standing. Several soldiers perished, many horses died, and all the powder delivered to the troops was ruined by the rain. The troops were in a deplorable state when the storm ceased on the 14th, yet their courage and ardor were not abated. On the August, 1778. 15th, in expectation of the speedy return of the French squadron, as promised by the admiral, they marched forward in three divisions, took post within two miles of the en-emy's lines, commenced the erection of batteries, and soon afterward opened a fire of balls and bombs upon the British works.[1] On the night of the reappearance of D'Estaing, Gen-erals Greene and La Fayette proceeded to visit him on board his vessel, to consult upon measures proper to be pursued. They urged the count to return with his fleet into New-port harbor; for the British garrison, disappointed and dispirited on account of not receiving provision and ammunition from Howe, would doubtless surrender without resistance. D'Es-taing was disposed to comply, but his officers insisted upon his adherence to the instructions of his government to put into Boston harbor for repairs in the event of injuries being sustained by his vessels. Such injuries had been sustained in the late gale and partial engagement, and, overruled by his officers, he refused compliance, sailed for Boston, and left the Americans to take care of themselves.[2] Greene and La Fayette returned on the night of the 21st with a report of the resolution of the French admiral, and the next day Generals Sullivan and Hancock sent letters of remonstrance to him. A protest against the count's taking the fleet to Boston, signed by all the general officers except La Fayette, was sent to him, declaring such a measure derogatory to the honor of France, contrary to the intentions of its monarch, destructive to the welfare of the United States, and highly injurious to the alliance formed between the two nations.[3] D'Estaing affected to be offended at this protest, and returned August 23, 1778. a spirited answer, just as he weighed anchor for Boston, which drew from Sulli-van a sarcastic reflection, in general orders, the following morning.[4] From Bos-ton the count wrote an explanatory and vindicatory letter to Congress, in which he com-plained of the protest and of Sullivan's ungenerous innuendoes. The whole matter was final-ly amicably adjusted.

Disgusted at what they deemed the perfidy of the French commander, and despairing

---

[1] General Sullivan quartered about five miles from Newport, at what is now called the Gibb's Farm La Fayette quartered on the east side of the island, at what was then called the Boller Garden Farm; and Greene had his quarters in Middletown, on the farm now owned by Colonel Richard K. Randolph.—Ross's *Historical Discourse*, page 53.

[2] It is asserted that D'Estaing was disliked by his officers, not on account of personal considerations, but from the fact that he had been a land officer, and they considered it an affront that he was placed over them. They therefore cast every impediment in his way, where opportunities were presented in which he might gain personal distinction. In the case in question, all his officers insisted upon his proceeding to Boston, and entered into a formal protest against his remaining at Newport.

[3] This protest was signed by John Sullivan, Nathaniel Greene, John Hancock, J. Glover, Ezekiel Cor-nell, William Whipple, John Tyler, Solomon Lovell, and John Fitzconnel.

[4] "The general can not help," said Sullivan, in his orders, "lamenting the sudden and unexpected de-parture of the French fleet, as he finds it has a tendency to discourage some who placed great dependence upon the assistance of it, *though he can by no means suppose the army or any part of it endangered by this movement.*" Sullivan was doubtless correct in his opinion, intimated in the last clause, that the French al-liance was of little advantage to the Americans, as will be hereafter seen. This same Admiral d'Estaing subsequently abandoned the Americans at the South, at a most critical juncture, under pretense that he must seek *safe winter quarters,* although it was then only in the month of October! The English and Americans were both duped by "his most Christian majesty" of France; and, as I have elsewhere said, a balance-sheet of favors connected with the alliance will show not the least preponderance of service in favor of the French, unless the result of the more vigorous action of the Americans, caused by the hopes of success from that alliance, shall be taken into the account.

of success, between two and three thousand of the American volunteers left for home on the 24th and 25th. The American force was thus reduced to about the number of that of the enemy. Under these circumstances, an assault upon the British lines was deemed hazardous, and a retreat prudent. La Fayette was dispatched to Boston, to solicit the return of D'Estaing to Newport, but he could only get a promise from that officer to march his troops by land to aid the Americans in the siege, if requested. It was too late for such a movement.

On the night of the 28th, the Americans commenced a retreat with great order and secrecy, and arrived at the high grounds at the north end of the island, with all their artillery and stores, at three the next morning. Their retreat having been discovered by the enemy, a pursuit was undertaken. The Americans had fortified an eminence called Butts's Hill, about twelve miles from Newport. Here they made a stand, and at daylight called a council of war. General Greene proposed to march back and meet the enemy on the west road, then approaching in detachments, and consisting only of the Hessian chasseurs and two Anspach regiments under Lossberg. On the east road was August. 1778.

SCENE OF THE ENGAGEMENT ON RHODE ISLAND, AUG. 29, 1778.
From a print in the Gentleman's Magazine, 1778.

General Smith, with two regiments and two flank companies. To the former were opposed the light troops of Lieutenant-colonel Laurens, and to the latter those of Colonel Henry B. Livingston. Greene's advice was overruled, and the enemy were allowed to collect in force upon the two eminences called respectively Quaker and Turkey Hill.[1] A large detachment of the enemy marched very near to the American left, but were repulsed by Glover, and driven back to Quaker Hill. About nine o'clock the British opened a severe cannonade upon the Americans from the two hills, which was returned from Butts's Hill with spirit. Skirmishes continued between advanced parties until near ten, when two British sloops of war and other armed vessels, having gained the right flank of the Americans, began a fire upon that point simultaneously with a furious attack there by the land forces of the enemy. This attempt to gain the rear of the Americans, and cut off a retreat, brought on an almost general action, in which from twelve to fifteen hundred of the patriots were at one time engaged. The enemy's line was finally broken, after a severe engagement, in attempts to take the redoubt on the American right, and they were driven back in great confusion to Turkey Hill, leaving many of their dead and wounded in the low grounds between the contending armies, where the hottest of the battle occurred. This was between two and three o'clock in the afternoon of a very sultry day, and a number on both sides perished from the effects of the heat and fatigue. A cannonade was kept up by both parties until sunset, when the battle ceased. The skirmishing and more general action continued seven hours without intermission, and the most indomitable courage was evinced by both parties. The Americans had thirty killed, one hundred and thirty-two wounded, and forty-

[1] The three eminences, Butts's, Quaker, and Turkey Hill, are seen in the picture, the former on the left, its slopes covered with the American tents, Quaker Hill in the center, and Turkey Hill on the right. The house in the fore-ground, on the right, belonged to a Mr. Brindley, now near the site of the residence of Mr. Anthony.

four missing. The British lost, in killed and wounded, two hundred and ten, and twelve missing.

So nearly matched were the belligerents, that both willingly rested in their respective camps during the night, and the next morning each seemed reluctant to renew the battle. Sullivan had good cause to refrain from another engagement, for at break of day a messenger arrived from Providence, informing him that Howe had again sailed for Newport, was seen off Block Island the day before, and probably, before night, would be in Newport harbor.[1] Under these circumstances, Sullivan thought it prudent to evacuate Rhode Island, a measure concurred in by his officers. There were difficulties in the way, for the first indications of a retreat on the part of the Americans would bring the repulsed enemy upon them in full force. The sentinels of the two armies were only four hundred yards apart, and the greatest caution was necessary to prevent information of Sullivan's design from reaching Sir Robert Pigot. Fortunately, Butts's Hill concealed all movements in the rear of the American camp. During the day, a number of tents were brought forward by the Americans and pitched in sight of the enemy, and the whole army were employed in fortifying the camp. This was intended to deceive the British, and was successful. At the same time, and, indeed, during the engagement of the previous day, the heavy baggage and stores were falling back and crossing Bristol ferry to the main. At dark the tents were struck, fires were lighted in front at various points, the light troops, with the baggage, marched down to the ferry, and before midnight the whole American army had crossed in flat-bottomed boats to the main, in good order, and without the loss of a man. During the retreat, La Fayette arrived from Boston, whither, as we have seen, he had been sent to persuade D'Estaing to proceed with his squadron to Newport again. He was greatly mortified at being absent during the engagement.[2] Anticipating that a battle would take place, he traveled from Rhode Island to Boston, nearly seventy miles, in a little more than seven hours, and returned in six and a half.[3] Although denied the laurels which he might have won in battle, he participated in the honors of a successful retreat.

The evacuation of Rhode Island was a mortifying circumstance to General Sullivan, for Newport had been almost within his grasp, and nothing could have saved the British army

August 29.

August 30, 1778.

---

[1] The fleet of Lord Howe had on board Sir Henry Clinton, with four thousand troops destined for Rhode Island; but on approaching Newport, and hearing of the retreat of Sullivan (for the fleet did not arrive until the 31st, the day after) and the sailing of the disabled French squadron to Boston, Howe changed his course, and sailed for the latter port, where he arrived on the 1st of September. Perceiving no chance of success in attacking D'Estaing, Howe prudently withdrew, after throwing the town of Boston into the greatest consternation, and, with the disappointed Sir Henry Clinton, sailed for New York. On the way, Clinton ordered his marauding officer, General Grey, to land with the troops at New Bedford, on the west side of the Acushnet River, and proceed to destroy the shipping in the harbor. They landed upon Clark's Neck, at the mouth of the river, and between six o'clock in the evening on the 5th of September and twelve the next day, destroyed about seventy sail of vessels, many of them prizes taken by American privateers, and several small craft; burned the magazine, wharves, stores, warehouses, vessels on the stocks, all the buildings at M'Pherson's wharf, the principal part of the houses at the head of the river, and the mills and houses at Fairhaven, opposite. The amount of property destroyed was estimated at $323,266. Grey and his troops then embarked, and proceeded to Martha's Vineyard, where they destroyed several vessels, and made a requisition for the militia arms, the public money, three hundred oxen, and ten thousand sheep. The defenseless inhabitants were obliged to comply with the requisition, and the marauders returned to New York with a plentiful supply of provisions for the British army.

[2] La Fayette had advised a retreat from Newport six days before. On the 24th he gave his opinion in writing, as follows: "I do not approve of continuing the siege. The time of the militia is out, and they will not longer sacrifice their private interests to the common cause. A retreat is the wisest step." Writing to Washington after the retreat, he expressed his mortification, and said, "That there has been an action fought where I could have been, and was not, will seem as extraordinary to you as it seems to myself." He arrived while the army was retreating, and brought off the rear guard and pickets in the best manner. His feelings were soothed by the resolutions of Congress, adopted on the 19th of September, thanking General Sullivan and those under his command for their conduct in the action and retreat, and specially requesting the president to inform the marquis of their due sense of his personal sacrifice in going to Boston, and his gallantry in conducting the pickets and out-sentries in the evacuation.—*Journals of Congress*, iv., 378.

[3] Gordon, ii., 376.

from capitulation had D'Estaing co-operated. Policy, at that time, dictated the course of Congress in withholding the voice of censure, but the people unhesitatingly charged the failure of the expedition upon the bad conduct of the French. The retreat was approved of by Congress, in a resolution adopted on the 9th of September. It was not unanimously agreed to, and an unsuccessful attempt was made to reconsider it. With this event 1778. closed the Eastern campaign, neither party in the contest having gained any thing.[1]

The British held possession of Rhode Island until the autumn of 1779, when Sir Henry Clinton, desirous of making a further demonstration at the South, and apprehending an attack upon New York from the combined forces of the American and French, supposed to have been concerted between Washington and D'Estaing, dispatched a number of transports to bring off the troops from Newport to strengthen his position at head-quarters. They embarked on the 25th of October, leaving Rhode Island in possession of the Americans, after an occupation of three years by the enemy. During their stay, they had 1779. desolated the island. Only a single tree of the ancient forest is left, a majestic sycamore, standing near the bank of the Seaconet channel, on the eastern side of the island. When they left, they burned the barracks at Fort Adams and the light-house upon Beavertail Point. They also carried away with them the town records. These were greatly injured by being submerged in the vessel that bore them, which was sunk at Hell Gate. They were recovered and sent back to Newport, but were of little service afterward. This event produced some embarrassment in respect to property, but they were as nothing compared to the sufferings of the impoverished inhabitants when they returned to their mutilated dwellings and desolated farms. The winter of 1779–80 was a terrible one for the people of Rhode Island.[2]

It is proper to remark, that after Sir Robert

ANCIENT SYCAMORE.[3]

Pigot superseded Prescott in command of the British forces in Rhode Island, the people were greatly relieved of the annoyances they had been subject to under the rule of the latter. Private property was respected, plunder ceased, the people were treated with respect, and, when the evacuation took place, no violence marked the departure of the enemy. General Gates was then at Providence with a small force, and kept a vigilant eye upon the movements of the British,[4] anticipating predatory excursions along the coast; but General Pigot

[1] Washington, in a letter to Brigadier-general Nelson of Virginia, written on the 20th of August, says: "It is not a little pleasing nor less wonderful to contemplate that, after two years' maneuvering, and undergoing the strangest vicissitudes that perhaps ever attended any one contest since the creation, both armies are brought back to the very point they set out from, and that the offending party in the beginning is now reduced to the use of the spade and pickaxes for defense. The hand of Providence has been so conspicuous in all this, that he must be worse than an infidel that lacks faith, and more wicked, that has not gratitude enough to acknowledge his obligations."—Sparks's *Life and Writings of Washington*, vi., 36.

[2] This was the severest winter ever experienced in America. Narraganset Bay was frozen over; and the reader will remember the fact already mentioned, that the Bay of New York was so firmly bridged that troops and heavy field-pieces crossed from the city to Staten Island. The British having destroyed the trees on Rhode Island, fuel was very scarce. It was sold in Newport for twenty dollars a cord. Food, also, was very scarce; corn sold at four silver dollars a bushel, and potatoes at two dollars. A tax of ten thousand dollars was levied for the relief of the poor, and Tiverton and neighboring towns contributed generously to their aid.—Ross's *Historical Discourse*, p. 59.

[3] This tree stands, solitary and peerless, within a few rods of the water. It is upon the land of Mr. Thomas R. Hazzard, and between his fine mansion and the river. It is thirty-two feet in circumference within twelve inches of the ground. It is yet vigorous, though storms have riven some of its topmost branches. When I made the sketch it was leafless, the autumn winds having defoliated it.

[4] During the occupation of the island by the British, after the retreat of Sullivan, Gates was in constant

was no marauder, and scorned to do, even under command, what Tryon, Wallace, and Grey seemed to take great delight in.

Early in the summer of 1779 the Marquis de La Fayette obtained leave of absence for one year, and returned to France.   But this absence was not a season of idleness among his old associates, or of forgetfulness of the Americans on the part of La Fayette.   On the contrary, the chief design of his visit to his native country was to enlist the sympathies of his people and government more warmly in the cause of the Americans, and to procure for them more substantial aid than they had hitherto received.   After passing a few days with his beautiful and much loved wife, he addressed a long letter to the Count de Vergennes, one of the French ministers, on the subject of furnishing an army, well-appointed in every particular, to fight in America.   In making such a request, a soul less ardent and hopeful than the youthful general's would not have perceived the least probability of success.   He was acting without instructions from the American Congress, or even its sanction or the full approval of Washington.   It seemed but too recently that French and American troops were battling in opposition in the Western World, to hope that they would freely commingle, though Britons were still the foes of the French.   La Fayette, however, understood French character better than Washington and Congress did, and he *knew* that success would attend the measure.   "He had that interior conviction which no argument or authority could subdue, that the proposed expedition was practicable and expedient, and he succeeded in imparting his enthusiasm to the ministers."[1]   He was only twenty-two years old, and held a subordinate rank in the army of his king; he, therefore, had no expectation of being commander of any force that might be sent; his efforts were disinterested.[2]   Nothing could divert him from his object, and, with a joyful heart, he returned to America the following

May, 1780.   spring, bearing to the patriots the glad tidings that a French squadron, with an army of more than four thousand men, admirably officered and equipped, and conveying money for the United States Treasury, was about to sail for our shores.   The marquis also brought a commission from Louis XVI. for Washington, appointing him lieutenant general of the armies of France, and vice-admiral of its fleets.   This was a wise measure, and operated, as intended, to prevent difficulties that might arise respecting official etiquette. It was stipulated that the French should be considered as auxiliaries, and always cede the post of honor to the Americans.   Lieutenant-general the Count de Rochambeau, the commander of the French expedition, was to place himself under the American commander-in-chief, and on all occasions the authority of Washington was to be respected as supreme. This arrangement secured the best understanding between the two armies while the allies remained in America.[3]

---

receipt of intelligence respecting the movements of the enemy, by means of secret letters and a sort of telegraphic communication.   Lieutenant Seth Chapin employed a woman, residing in Newport, to write down every thing of importance, and conceal the letter in a hole in a certain rock.   By setting up poles, as if to dry clothes, and by other signals agreed upon, the lieutenant was informed of the presence of a letter in the secret post-office, and of perfect safety in coming to receive it.   He would then row across from the opposite shore of Little Compton, get the packet, and send it off to Gates.   After the evacuation, the lieutenant and his aids received one thousand five hundred dollars, Continental money, for their services, the whole amount being worth then only about seventy dollars in specie.

[1] Everett's *Eulogy on La Fayette.*

[2] At the request of Count de Vergennes, La Fayette drew up a statement containing a detailed plan of the proposed expedition.   It is a paper of great interest, and exhibits genius of the highest order, of which a general of threescore might be proud.   The number and disposition of the troops, the character of the officers proper to accompany them, the appointments of the fleet and army, the time of embarkation, proper place for landing, and the probable service to which the fleet and army would be called, were all laid out with a minuteness and clearness of detail which seemed to indicate almost an intuitive knowledge of the future.   The whole expedition was arranged in accordance with the plan of the marquis.

[3] This arrangement was conceived by La Fayette, and he made it a fundamental point.   Not content with soliciting troops for America, La Fayette requested large supplies of clothing, guns, and ammunition for the Republican army.   They were promised, but only a part were sent.   Such was the importunity of La Fayette, and such the disinterested enthusiasm with which he represented the wants and claims of his Republican friends, that the old Count Maurepas, who was then prime minister, said one day in the Coun-

Great was the joy of the American Congress produced by the tidings brought by La Fayette, and assurance possessed the minds of that assembly that the next campaign would secure peace and independence to the States. Although policy forbade giving publicity to the fact that aid from abroad was near at hand, sufficient information leaked out to diffuse among the people pleasant hopes for the future. The return of La Fayette was hailed with delight. Congress, by resolution,[a] testified their satisfaction at his return, and accepted with pleasure a tender of the further services of so gallant and meritorious an officer.[1] Three days afterward[b] Congress resolved that bills be immediately drawn on Dr. Franklin for twenty-five thousand dollars, and on Mr. Jay for the same amount, payable at sixty days' sight; and that the money be applied solely to the bringing of the army into the field, and forwarding them supplies in such a manner as the exigency and nature of the service shall require. Also, that the States of Virginia, Maryland, Delaware, Pennsylvania, New Jersey, New York, Connecticut, Rhode Island, Massachusetts Bay, and New Hampshire, be most earnestly called upon to pay into the Continental treasury, within thirty days, ten millions of dollars. It was also resolved that the Legislatures, from New Hampshire to Virginia, be requested to invest their executive authority, or some other persons, with such powers as would enable them, on the application of the committee at the head-quarters of the army, to draw forth the resources of the state.[2] The Carolinas and Georgia were exempt from the requisition, because they were then bearing the heavy burden of an active campaign within their own limits. Congress thus began to prepare for the most energetic co-operation with the allies when they should arrive.

a May 15, 1780.

b May 19.

The French fleet, under the command of Admiral de Ternay, sailed from Brest early in April, and appeared off the coast of Virginia on the 4th of July.[3] On the evening of the 10th it entered Newport harbor, on which occasion the town was brilliantly illuminated, and every demonstration of joy was made by the inhabitants. General Heath, then in command on Rhode Island, was present to receive Rochambeau and his troops on landing, and to put them in possession of the batteries upon the island. On the 24th, the General Assembly, then in session, presented complimentary addresses to Rochambeau and Ternay; and General Washington, having heard of their arrival, recommended, in general orders at his camp in the Hudson Highlands, to the officers of the American army, to wear cockades of black and white—the *ground* being of the first color, and the *relief* of the second —as a compliment to, and a symbol of friendship and affection for their allies.[4] The American cockade, at that time, was black; the French white.

1780.

As soon as intelligence was received of the arrival of the allies, La Fayette set out for Newport, under instructions from Washington, to concert measures with Rochambeau for future operations. The French troops were pleasantly encamped southeast of Newport, but they were not suffered to remain quiet. When intelligence of the sailing of Ternay from Brest reached the British cabinet, they dispatched Admiral Graves, with six ships of the line, to re-enforce Admiral Arbuthnot, the successor of Byron, then commanding the squadron on the American coast. Graves arrived at New York three days after Ternay entered New-

---

cil, "It is fortunate for the king that La Fayette does not take it into his head to strip Versailles of its furniture, to send to his dear Americans, as his majesty would be unable to refuse it." La Fayette purchased, on his own account, a large quantity of swords and other military equipages, which he brought with him and presented to the officers of the light infantry whom he commanded during the campaign.—See Appendix to vol. vii. of Sparks's *Life and Writings of Washington*, where will be found interesting documents relating to this expedition.

[1] *Journals of Congress*, vi., 49. While in France, La Fayette was presented with an elegant sword, prepared there under the directions of Franklin, by order of Congress. Franklin sent it to the marquis from Passy, by his grandson. An account of this sword, and drawings will be found on page 119, vol. ii.

[2] *Journals of Congress*, vi., 50, 51.

[3] The fleet consisted of two ships of eighty guns each, one of seventy-four, four of sixty-four, two frigates of forty, a cutter of twenty, a hospital-ship, pierced for sixty-four, a bomb-ship, and thirty-two transports. The land forces consisted of four regiments, a battalion of artillery, and the legion of the Duke de Lauzun, amounting in all to about six thousand men.

[4] Thacher, p. 200. Gordon, iii., 65.

July 13, 1780.
  port harbor.   The English fleet, now stronger than the French, proceeded immediately to attempt a blockade of the latter in Narraganset Bay.   On the 19th, four
British ships, the advance sail of the fleet rendezvousing at Block Island, appeared off Newport.   The next morning, as soon as the wind would permit, three French frigates went in
pursuit of them, but, falling in with nine or ten ships of the enemy that were approaching,
made sail for the harbor, under full chase.

    Intelligence was received that General Clinton, lately returned to New York from the
South, was preparing to proceed in person, with a large part of his army, to attack Rhode
Island.   Menaced by sea and land, General Heath called earnestly upon Rhode Island,
Massachusetts, and Connecticut for troops, and his requisition was promptly complied with ,
so promptly, that, before any enemy appeared, the allied forces felt quite competent to oppose
the largest army that Clinton could possibly bring into the field.   Sir Henry actually sailed
from New York with eight thousand troops, but proceeded no further than Huntington Bay,
in Long Island Sound.   Informed there of the fortified position of the French at Newport,
the rapid gathering of the militia, and the approach of Washington toward New York city,
Clinton abandoned the expedition and returned to his head-quarters.

    While these events were taking place on our coast, the French and English fleets were
striving for the mastery in the West Indies.   The former was commanded by Admiral de
Guichen, the latter by Admiral Rodney.   It was the understanding when Ternay and Rochambeau left France, that they were to be joined at Rhode Island by the squadron of De
Guichen.   Events unforeseen prevented this junction.   The arrival of Rodney at St. Lucie,
and subsequent maneuvers and encounters, detained De Guichen in the West Indies until
July 5.
  July ; and five days before Ternay arrived at Newport, De Guichen left St. Domingo for Europe, his ships having suffered greatly in the engagements, and the land
troops which they carried having been terribly diminished by sickness.   The failure of this
co-operation, the great number of invalids among the French troops at Newport, and the
expectation of an attack there, or an attempt to blockade the squadron, made it inexpedient
to break up the encampment on Rhode Island and attempt any operations at a distance.   It
was concluded to pass the winter there.   Lauzun and his legion, as we have seen, were cantoned at Lebanon, in Connecticut.   Three thousand five hundred militia were kept under
arms at Newport, to assist in guarding the French squadron, and the allies became a burden, rather than an aid, to the Americans.   The conference between Washington and Rochambeau, and the final departure of the French troops in 1781, to form a junction with the
American army on the Hudson, have been noticed on page 436.

    The Chevalier de Ternay died at Newport soon after the arrival of the fleet, and was
buried with distinguished honors in Trinity Church-yard, where a slab was afterward erected
March, 1781.
  to his memory.   Admiral de Barras succeeded him in command early in the following spring, about which time Washington arrived at Newport, and held a conference
with Rochambeau.   The town was illuminated on the occasion of his visit, and from that
time until the departure of the allies, quiet prevailed on Rhode Island.   Active military operations ceased there, and, until the close of the war, the people were undisturbed, except
by occasional menaces from English vessels in pursuit of American privateers, of which a
large number hailed from Narraganset Bay, or made its waters their place of refuge when
in danger upon the coast.[1]   Newport suffered terribly during the war.   Its population of
eleven thousand in 1774, was reduced to about six thousand in 1782 ; and, according to an

---

[1] It is believed that Newport furnished more seamen for the naval service of the United States during
the Revolution than any other port on the continent, except Boston.   At least one thousand men were
shipped for service in the navy from that port, one half of whom fell into the hands of the enemy and died
in prison-ships.   The naval commanders in the war who belonged to Rhode Island were John Grimes, Benjamin Pierce, Joseph Gardiner, William Dennis, James Godfred, Remembrance Simmons, Thomas Stacy,
Oliver Read, Captain Bently, Samuel Jeffers, John Coggeshall, William Finch, Captain Jaques, James Phillips, Ezekiel Burroughs, John Murphy, Isaac Frabor, William Ladd, Joseph Sheffield, and Captain Gazzee.
These either sailed from Newport previous to its possession by the enemy, or subsequently from other ports
of New England.—*Ross*, page 62.   Silas Talbot, also, belonged to Rhode Island.

estimate of a committee of the General Assembly, appointed for the purpose, the value of private property destroyed was six hundred and twenty-four thousand dollars, silver money.

The sun has gone down behind Conannicut and the hills of the Narraganset country; the broad sails of the wind-mills are still; the voices of the milkers come up from the neighboring farm-yard, and twilight is spreading its mysterious veil over the bay, the islands, and the ocean. Let us descend from our observatory on the hill of Miantonōmoh and return to the city, and in the morning visit the places hallowed by events just viewed in the speculum of history.

The morning of the 23d was cold and blustering; the ground was hard frozen, ice covered the surface of the pools, and the north wind was as keen as the breath of December. I started early in a light rockaway for the battle-ground at the north end of the island, making a brief call on the way (or, rather, out of the way) upon Mr. Nathaniel Greene, a grandson of the eminent general of the Revolution who bore that name. He resides about three miles above Newport, and kindly furnished me with explicit directions respecting the localities I was about to visit. About a mile north of his estate I came to the head-quarters of Prescott, printed on page 76, which I sketched in haste, for my fingers were too soon benumbed with cold to hold the pencil expertly. Twelve miles from Newport I came to the residence of Mr. Anthony, which is, I believe, the "Brindley House" in the picture on page 83. An introductory line from his brother, David Anthony, Esq., was a key to his generous hospitality; and after accompanying me to the top of Butts's Hill, and pointing out the places of interest included in the view from its summit, he kindly invited me to dine with him when my sketching should be finished, an invitation heartily accepted, for a ride of twelve miles in the cold morning air was a whetstone to my usually good appetite.

QUAKER HILL, FROM THE FORT ON BUTTS'S HILL.

The remains of the old fort on Butts's Hill, the embankments and fossé, with traces of the hastily-constructed ravelins, are well preserved. Even the ruts made by the carriage-wheels of the cannons, at the embrasures (for the ordnance was composed of field-pieces), were visible. The banks, in some places, are twenty feet high, measuring from the bottom of the fossé. Fortunately for the antiquary, the works were constructed chiefly upon a rocky ledge, and the plow can win no treasure there; the banks were earth, and afford no quarry for wall builders, and so the elements alone have lowered the ramparts and filled the ditches. Southward from this eminence, I had a fine view of Quaker and Turkey Hills—indeed, of the whole battle-ground. Sitting upon the exterior slope of the southern parapet, and sheltered from the wind by a clump of bushes and the remains of one of the bastions, I sketched the above view, which includes all the essential portions of the field of conflict. The eminence in the center, on which stands a wind-mill, is Quaker Hill; that on the right is Turkey Hill, on the northern slope of which is seen the west road. In the hollow at the foot of these hills the hottest of the battle was waged. On the left is seen the little village of Newton, beyond which is the Eastern or Seaconet Channel, stretching away to the ocean, and bounded on the left by the cultivated slopes of Little Compton. The undulations in the foreground are the embankments of the fort.

658   PICTORIAL·FIELD-BOOK

North View from Butts's Hill.   The Narraganset Country.   Massasoit and his Sons.   King Philip.

Northward the view is more extensive, and in some respects more interesting. The houses near the center of the picture mark the site of the old Bristol ferry, over which the

VIEW NORTHWARD FROM BUTTS'S HILL.

Americans, under Sullivan, retreated to the main land. A little to the left, lying upon the east shore of the Narraganset, was Bristol; beyond was a glimpse of Warren; and in the far distance, directly over the steam-boat seen in the picture, the church spires of Providence were visible. On the right the high promontory of Mount Hope loomed up; and turning eastward, beyond the limits of the sketch, stood Tiverton and its old stone bridge, already mentioned. I could find no sheltered nook in making the sketch; upon the bleak summit of the hill I plied the pencil, until I could hold it no longer; but the drawing was finished.

From this eminence the vision takes in some of the most interesting portions of the Narraganset country and of the domains of Massasoit, the fast friend of the English. There were old Pocasset and Pokanoket, and, more conspicuous and interesting than all, was Mount Hope, the royal seat of King Philip, the last of the Wampanoags. It is too cold to turn the leaves of the chronicle here; let us wrap our cloaks around us, and, while gazing upon the beautiful land over which that great sachem held sway, read the records upon the tablets of memory, brief but interesting, concerning "King Philip's War."

> "'Tis good to muse on nations pass'd away
>   Forever from the land we call our own;
> Nations as proud and mighty in their day,
>   Who deem'd that everlasting was their throne.
> An age went by, and they no more were known!
>   Sublimer sadness will the mind control,
> Listening time's deep and melancholy moan;
>   And meaner griefs will less disturb the soul;
> And human pride falls low at human grandeur's goal."
>   ROBERT C. SANDS.

We have observed how Massasoit, the sagamore of the Wampanoags, whose dominions extended from Narraganset Bay to that of Massachusetts, presenting the hand of friendship and protection to the white settlers, remained faithful while he lived. His residence was near Warren, on the east side of the Narraganset; and so greatly was his friendship prized by the PILGRIM FATHERS, that Winslow and others made a long journey to visit him when dangerously ill.[a] Recovering, he entered into a solemn league of friendship with the whites, and faithfully observed it until his death, which occurred thirty-two years afterward.[b] Alexander, his eldest son, succeeded him, and gave promise of equal attachment to the whites; but his rule was short; he died two years after the death of his father, and his brother[1] Pometacom or Metacomet, better known as King Philip, became the head of his nation. He was a bold, powerful-minded warrior, and al-

[a] March, 1623.

[b] 1655.

---

[1] Bancroft and Hildreth say nephew. Earlier historians disagree. Prince and Trumbull say he was grandson to Massasoit, and Hutchinson and Belknap call him his son. Governor Prince, it is said, named Alexander and Philip after the great Macedonians, in compliment to Massasoit, indicating his idea of their character as warriors. They were doubtless sons of Massasoit.

OF THE REVOLUTION. 659

Jealousy of King Philip.   Treaties with the Whites.   Curtailment of his Domains.   His chief Captains.   John Eliot.

ready his keen perception gave him uneasiness respecting the fate of his race. Year after year the progress of settlement had curtailed the broad domains of the Wampanoags, until now they possessed little more than the nar·row tongues of land at Pocanoket and Pocasset, now Bristol and Tiverton; yet Philip renewed the treaties made with Massasoit, and kept them faithfully a dozen years; but spreading settlements, reducing his domains acre by acre, breaking up his hunting-grounds, diminishing the abundance of his fisheries, and menacing his nation with the fate of the landless, stirred up his savage patriotism, and made him resolve to sever the ties that bound him, with fatal alliance, to his enemies. His residence was at Mount Hope; and there, in the solitude of the primeval forest, he called his warriors around him, and planned, with consummate skill, an alliance of all the New England tribes against the European intruders.[1]

1662.

PORTRAIT AND SIGN-MANUAL OF KING PHILIP.[2]

For years the pious Eliot[3] had been preaching the gospel among the New England tribes;

[1] The number of Indians in New England at that time has been variously estimated. Dr. Trumbull, in his History of the United States (i., 36), supposes that there were thirty-six thousand in all, one third of whom were warriors. Hutchinson (i., 406) estimates the fighting men of the Narragansets alone at two thousand. Hinckley says the number of Indians in Plymouth county in 1685, ten years after Philip's war, was four thousand. Church, in his History of King Philip's War, published in Boston in 1716, estimated the number of Indian warriors in New England, in the commencement of that war, at ten thousand. Bancroft (ii., 94) says there were probably fifty thousand whites and hardly twenty-five thousand Indians in New England, west of the Piscataqua; while east of that stream, in Maine, were about four thousand whites and more than that number of red men.

[2] I copied this and the annexed marks of Philip's chief captains, from an original mortgage given by the sachem, to Constant Southworth, on land four miles square, lying south of Taunton. The mortgage is dated October 1, 1672. It was drawn up by Thomas Leonard, and is signed by himself, Constant Southworth, and Hugh Cole. It was acknowledged before, and signed by, John Alden.* This interesting document is in the possession of that intelligent antiquary, S. G. Drake, Esq., of Boston, to whose kindness I am indebted for these signatures. No. 1 is the sign of MUNASHUM, alias NIMROD; No. 2, of WONCKOMPAWHAN; No. 3, of Captain ANNAWAN, the "next man to Philip," or his chief warrior.

No. 1.   No. 2.   No. 3

[3] John Eliot, usually called the Apostle of the Indians, was minister of Roxbury, Massachusetts. He was born in Essex county, England, in 1604, and came to America in 1631. Educated thoroughly at Cambridge University, he soon obtained great influence among the settlers. Touched by the ignorance of the Indians respecting spiritual things, his heart yearned to do them good, and for many years he labored assiduously among them, with great success. He founded, at Natick, the first Indian church in America, in 1660. The next year he published the New Testament in the Indian language, and in a few years the whole Bible and other books. He died May 20th, 1690, aged about eighty-six. The venerable apostle was buried in the Ministers' Tomb,† in the first burying-ground at Roxbury, which is situated on the east side of the great avenue across the Neck to Boston. The residence of Eliot was opposite the house of Governor Thomas Dudley, on the other side of the brook. Dudley's mansion was taken down in 1775, and a redoubt was erected upon the spot. The site is now occupied by the Universalist church. Reverend Dr. Putnam, of Roxbury, is the fifth pastoral successor of the apostle in the first church. The remains of

* Alden was a passenger in the May Flower, and one of the immortal FORTY-ONE who signed the instrument of civil government, given on pages 437 and 438, vol. i., of this work, where also is the signature of Southworth.

† In 1724-5, a citizen of Roxbury, named William Bowen, was made prisoner by the Turks. The people of his town raised a sum of money sufficient for his ransom. Before it could be applied they received intelligence of his death. The money was then appropriated to the building of a tomb for the ministers of the church.

no pains were spared to teach them to read and write; and in a short time a larger proportion of the Massachusetts Indians could do so than, recently, of the inhabitants of Russia.[1] Churches were gathered among the natives; and when Philip lifted the hatchet, there were four hundred " praying Indians," as the converts were called, who were firmly attached to the whites; yet Christianity hardly spread beyond the Indians on Cape Cod, Martha's Vineyard, and Nantucket, and the seven feeble villages around Boston. Philip, like Red Jacket of our days, opposed meddling with the religion of his fathers, and, two years before the war, boldly and openly, at the head of seven hundred warriors, boasted of his own and their attachment to the ancient belief.

HANDWRITING OF ELIOT AND GOOKIN.

A " praying Indian" named John Sassamon, who had been educated at Cambridge, and employed as a teacher, had fled to Philip on account of some misdemeanor, and became a sort of secretary to the sachem. Being persuaded to return to the whites, he accused Philip of meditated treason. For this he was waylaid by the savages, and slain. Three of Philip's men, suspected of the murder, were tried by a jury of half English and half Indians, convicted, and hanged. The evidence on which they were convicted was slender, and the Wampanoags were greatly irritated. Philip was cautious; his warriors were impetuous. Overruled by their importunities, and goaded by a remembrance of the wrongs and humiliations he had suffered from the English,[2] he trampled solemn treaties beneath his feet, and lighted the flame of war. Messengers were sent to other tribes, to arouse them to co-operation, and, with all the power of Indian eloquence, Metacomet exhorted his followers to curse the white men, and swear eternal hostility to the pale faces.

> " Away! away! I will not hear
> Of aught but death or vengeance now;
> By the eternal skies I swear
> My knee shall never learn to bow!
> I will not hear a word of peace,
> Nor clasp in friendly grasp a hand
> Link'd to the pale-brow'd stranger race,
> That work the ruin of our land.

his predecessors all lie in the Ministers' Tomb. The commissioners of the Forest Hills Cemetery have designated the heights on its western border as the *Eliot Hills*, and there the citizens of Roxbury are about to erect a beautiful monument to the memory of the apostle.

DANIEL GOOKIN, whose signature is given above, was the friend of, and a zealous co-worker with, Mr. Eliot. He came to Virginia, from England, in 1621. He went to Massachusetts with his family in 1644, and settled in Cambridge. He was soon called to fill civil and military offices, and in 1652 was appointed superintendent of the Indians. This office he held until his death, in 1687, at the age of seventy-five years. Gookin wrote an historical account of the New England Indians, and was the firm friend of the red man through life. His remains are in the old burying-ground at Cambridge. Lieutenant Gookin of our Revolutionary army was his lineal descendant.

[1] Bancroft, ii., 94.

[2] In 1671, Philip was suspected of secret plottings against the English, and, notwithstanding his asseverations to the contrary, was ordered to give up his fire-arms to the whites. This was a fortunate occurrence for the English; for, had the Indians possessed those arms in the war that ensued, their defeat would have been doubtful.

> " Before their coming, we had ranged
>   Our forests and our uplands free ;
> Still let us keep unsold, unchanged,
>   The heritage of Liberty.
> As free as roll the chainless streams,
>   Still let us roam our ancient woods ;
> As free as break the morning beams,
>   That light our mountain solitudes.
>
> " Touch not the hand they stretch to you ;
>   The falsely-proffer'd cup put by ;
> Will you believe a coward true ?
>   Or taste the poison'd draught, to die ?
> Their friendship is a lurking snare ;
>   Their honor but an idle breath ;
> Their smile the smile that traitors wear ;
>   Their love is hate, their life is death.
>
>   .   .   .   .   .
>
> " And till your last white foe shall kneel,
>   And in his coward pangs expire—
> Sleep—but to dream of brand and steel ;
> Wake—but to deal in blood and fire."
>
>   C. SHERRY.

Although fierce and determined when once aroused, no doubt Philip was hurried into this war against his best judgment and feelings, for his sagacity must have forewarned him of failure. The English were well armed and provisioned ; the Indians had few guns, and their subsistence was precarious. " Phrensy prompted their rising. It was but the storm in which the ancient inhabitants of the land were to vanish away. They rose without hope, and therefore they fought without mercy. For them as a nation there was no to-morrow."[1]

Bancroft has given a condensed, yet perspicuous and brilliant narrative of this war. "The minds of the English," he says, " were appalled by the horrors of the impending conflict, and superstition indulged in its wild inventions. At the time of the eclipse of the moon, you might have seen the figure of an Indian scalp imprinted on the center of its disk. The perfect form of an Indian bow appeared in the sky. The sighing of the wind was like the whistling of bullets. Some distinctly heard invisible troops of horses gallop through the air, while others formed the prophecy of calamities in the howling of the wolves.[2]

" At the very beginning of danger, the colonists exerted their wonted energy. Volunteers from Massachusetts joined the troops from Plymouth, and, within a week from the commencement of hostilities, the insulated Pokanokets were driven from Mount Hope, and in less than a month Philip was a fugitive among the Nipmucks, the interior tribes of Massachusetts. January 29, 1675. The little army of the colonists then entered the territory of the Narragansets, and from the reluctant tribe extorted a treaty of neutrality, with a promise to give up every hostile Indian. Victory seemed promptly assured ; but it was only the commencement of horrors. Canonchet, the chief sachem of the Narragansets, was the son of Miantonōmoh ; and could he forget his father's wrongs ? And would the tribes of New England permit the nation that had first given a welcome to the English to perish unavenged ? Desolation extended along the whole frontier. Banished from his patrimony,

---

[1] Bancroft, ii., 101.

[2] Cotton Mather, in his *Magnalia*, ii., 486, says, " Yea, and now we speak of things *ominous*, we may add, some time before this [the execution of three Indians for the murder of Sassamon], in a clear, still, sunshiny morning, there were divers persons in Malden who heard in the air, on the southeast of them, a *great gun* go off, and presently thereupon the report of *small guns*, like musket shot, very thick discharging, as if there had been a battle. This was at a time when there was nothing visible done in any part of the colony to occasion such noises ; but that which most of all astonished them was the flying of *bullets*, which came singing over their heads [beetles ? See page 574, vol. i.], and seemed very near to them ; after which the sound of *drums*, passing along westward, was very audible ; and on the same day, in Plymouth colony, in several places, invisible troops of horse were heard riding to and fro." No credence is to be attached to this book of Mather's.

where the Pilgrims found a friend, and from his cabin, which had sheltered the exiles, Philip and his warriors spread through the country, arousing their brethren to a warfare of extermination.

"The war, on the part of the Indians, was one of ambush and surprise. They never once met the English in open field; but always, even if eight-fold in number, fled timorously before infantry. But they were secret as beasts of prey, skillful marksmen, and in part provided with fire-arms, fleet of foot, conversant with all the paths of the forest, patient of fatigue, mad with passion for rapine, vengeance, and destruction, retreating into swamps for their fastnesses, or hiding in the green-wood thickets, where the leaves muffled the eyes of the pursuers. By the rapidity of their descent, they seemed omnipotent among the scattered villages, which they ravaged like a passing storm; and for a full year they kept all New England in a state of terror and excitement. The exploring party was waylaid and cut off, and the mangled carcasses and disjointed limbs of the dead were hung upon the trees to terrify pursuers. The laborer in the field, the reapers as they went forth to harvest, men as they went to mill, the shepherd's boy among the sheep, were shot down by skulking foes, whose approach was invisible. Who can tell the heavy hours of woman? The mother, if left alone in the house, feared the tomahawk for herself and children; on the sudden attack, the husband would fly with one child, the wife with another, and perhaps only one escape; the village cavalcade, making its way to meeting on Sunday, in files on horseback, the farmer holding the bridle in one hand and a child in the other, his wife seated on a pillion behind him, it may be with a child in her lap, as was the fashion of those days, could not proceed safely; but, at the moment when least expected, bullets would whiz among them, discharged with fatal aim from an ambuscade by the wayside. The red men hung upon the skirts of the English villages 'like the lightning on the edge of the clouds.'

"What need of repeating the same tale of horrors? Brookfield was set on
^{a August 12.} fire,^a and rescued only to be abandoned. Deerfield was burned.^b Hadley,
^{b September 11} surprised during a time of religious service,[1] was saved only by the daring of Goffe, the regicide, now bowed with years, a heavenly messenger of rescue, who darted from his hiding-place, rallied the disheartened, and, having achieved a safe defense, sank away in his retirement, to be no more seen. The plains of Northfield were wet with the blood of
^{a September 23} Beers^a and twenty of his valiant associates. Lathrop's company of young men, the very flower of Essex, culled out of the towns of that county, were
^{b September 28.} butchered;^b hardly a white man escaped; and the little stream whose channel became red with their life currents, is called Bloody Brook to this day."

The Narragansets played false to the white men, and in winter sheltered the foe that wasted their settlements. It was resolved to treat them as enemies, and through the deep snows of December, a thousand men, levied by the united colonies, marched to the great fort of the tribe.[2] Its feeble palisades quickly yielded, and fire and sword soon "swept away the humble glories of the Narragansets. Their winter stores, their wigwams, and all the little comforts of savage life, were destroyed; and more, their old men, their women, their babes, perished by hundreds in the fire."[3] It was a terrible blow for the Indians. Cold, hunger, and disease followed, and were the powerful allies of the English in the decimation of the tribe. Yet Canonchet did not despair, and he fought gallantly, until, being taken prisoner by the English, he was put to death.

In the spring, the spirit of revenge and retaliation began its work. Weymouth,
^{1676.} Groton, Medfield, Lancaster, and Marlborough, in Massachusetts, were laid in ashes,

---

[1] See page 420, of this vol.

[2] The fort was situated upon an island containing four or five acres, imbosomed in a swamp. The island was encompassed by high and strong palisades, with *abatis* outside, and there three thousand of the Narragansets were collected to pass the winter. This swamp is a short distance southwest of Kingston village, in the township of Kingston, Washington county, Rhode Island. The Stonington and Providence rail-way passes along the northern verge of the swamp.

[3] Bancroft, ii., 105.

Warwick and Providence, in Rhode Island, were burned; and every where the isolated dwellings of adventurous settlers were laid waste. But as the season advanced, and more remote tribes came not to re-enforce them, the Indians, wasted and dispirited, abandoned all hopes of success. Strifes arose among them. The Connecticut Indians charged their misfortunes upon Philip, and so did the Narragansets. The cords of alliance were severed. Some surrendered to avoid starvation; other tribes wandered off and joined those of Canada; while Captain Church, the most famous of the English partisan warriors, went out to hunt and destroy the fugitives.[1] During the year, between two and three thousand Indians were killed or submitted. Philip was chased from one hiding-place to another; and although he had vainly sought the aid of the Mohawks, and knew that hope was at an end, his proud spirit would not listen to words of peace; he cleft the head of a warrior who ventured to propose it. At length, after an absence of a year, he resolved, as it were, to meet his destiny. He returned to the beautiful land where his forefathers slept, the cradle of his infancy, and the nestling-place of his tribe. Once he escaped narrowly, leaving   August, 1676. his wife and only son prisoners. This bereavement crushed him. "My heart breaks," cried the chieftain, in the agony of his grief; "now I am ready to die." His own followers now began to plot against him, to make better terms for themselves. In a few days he was shot by a faithless Indian, and Captain Church cut off his head with his own sword. The captive orphan was transported to an island of the ocean. So perished the princes of the Pokanokets. Sad to them had been their acquaintance with civilization. The first ship that came on their coast kidnapped men of their kindred; and now the harmless boy, who had been cherished as an only child and the future sachem of their tribes—the last of the family of Massasoit—was sold into bondage, to toil as a slave under the suns of Bermuda.[2] Of the once prosperous Narragansets of old, the chief tribe of New England, hardly one hundred remained. The sword, famine, fire, and sickness had swept them from the earth. "During the whole war the Mohegans remained faithful to the English, and not a drop of blood was shed on the happy soil of Connecticut. So much the greater was the loss in the adjacent colonies. Twelve or thirteen towns were destroyed. The disbursements and losses equaled in value half a million of dollars—an enormous sum for the few of that day. More than six hundred men, chiefly young men, the flower of the country, of whom any mother might have been proud, perished in the field. As many as six hundred houses were burned. Of the able-bodied men in the colony, one in twenty had fallen; and one family in twenty had been burned out. The loss of lives and property was, in proportion

---

[1] Benjamin Church was born at Duxbury, in 1639. He was the first white settler at Seaconnet, or Little Compton. He was the most active and noted combatant of the Indians during King Philip's war, and when Philip was slain, Church cut off his head with his own hands. The sword with which he performed the act is in the cabinet of the Massachusetts Historical Society (see page 562, *ante*). In 1689, Church was commissioned by President Hinckley, of Plymouth, and the governors of Maine and Massachusetts, commander-in-chief of a force sent against the Eastern Indians. He continued making expeditions against them until 1704. In his old age he was corpulent. A fall from his horse was the cause of his death, which occurred at Little Compton, January 17, 1718, at the age of seventy-seven years. Under his direction his son prepared a history of the Indian wars, which was published in 1716.

[2] The disposal of this child was a subject of much deliberation. Several of the elders were urgent to put him to death. It was finally resolved *to be merciful*, and send him to Bermuda, to be sold into slavery. Such was the fate of many Indians, a fate to them worse than death. During the war the government of Plymouth gave thirty shillings for every head of an Indian killed in battle, and Philip's brought the same price. Their living bodies brought a high price in Bermuda, and probably more living Indian heads went thither than dead ones to the market at Plymouth. Witamo, the squaw sachem of Pocasset, shared in the disasters of Philip. She was drowned while crossing a river in her flight. Her body was recovered, and the head cut off and stuck upon a pole at Taunton, amid the jeers of the whites and the tears of the captive Indians. The body of Philip was beheaded and quartered, according to the sentence of the English law against traitors. One of his hands was given to the Indian who had shot him, and on the day appointed for a public thanksgiving, his head was carried in triumph into Plymouth. What a mockery of Christianity! Men, guilty of gross injustice to a race that had befriended them, lifting their hands toward heaven reeking with the blood of those they had injured, and singing *Te Deum Laudamus*, or praising God for his providential care! No Providence for the poor Indian, because he had neither cunning, skill, nor gunpowder!

to numbers, as distressing as in the Revolutionary war. There was scarce a family from which Death had not selected a victim."[1] Thus ended the first general Indian war in New England. Righteousness, sitting upon the throne of judgment, has long since decided the question of equity ; and we, viewing the scene at a distance, can not fail to discern the true verdict against the avaricious white man.

Those dark days of distress and crime are passed away forever. The splendors of an October sun, which then shed a radiance over the forests and the waters, beautiful as now, no longer light up the ambuscade of the red men, or the hiding-places of the pale-faces lurking for blood From the bald eminence on which I stand, the land of Philip and Canonchet, of Witamo and Miantonŏmoh, and the broad waters where they sported in peace, are spread out to the eye beautiful as the " Happy Valley," and upon the whole domain rest the beneficent influences of love, harmony, righteousness, and peace. Let us, then, endeavor to forget the gloomy past, and leave upon memory only the bright vision of the present.

The vision was bright indeed, but it was the sheen of the glacier. The unclouded sun and the uncurbed north wind wrestled for the mastery. The latter was the victor, and, until I was warmed at the table of Mr. Anthony, I could not fully comprehend the charms which I had beheld while half frozen among the mounds of the old fortress on the hill.

I returned to Newport by the way of Vaucluse, on the eastern road, where I sketched the great sycamore pictured on page 653, which is standing upon the bank of the Seaconnet or Eastern Channel. Near the mouth of this passage, a little below Vaucluse, occurred one of those events, characterized by skill and personal bravery, which make up a large portion of the history of our war for independence. In order to close up this channel, when the French fleet appeared off Newport, the British converted a strong vessel of two hundred tuns into a galley, and named it *Pigot*, in honor of the commander on Rhode Island. Its upper deck was removed, and on its lower deck were placed twelve eight-pounders, which belonged to the Flora, that was sunk in Newport harbor, and also ten swivels. Thus armed, she was a formidable floating battery. Major Silas Talbot, whose exploits had already won the expressed approbation of Congress, proposed an expedition to capture or destroy this vessel, for it effectually broke up the local trade of that section. General Sullivan regarded his scheme as impracticable, but finally consented to give Talbot permission to make the attempt. A draft of men for the purpose was allowed, and with sixty resolute patriots, Talbot sailed from Providence in a coasting sloop called the *Hawk*, which he had fitted out for the purpose. Armed with only three three-pounders, besides the small arms of his men, he sailed by the British forts at Bristol Ferry, and anchored within a few miles of the *Pigot*. Procuring a horse on shore, he rode down the east bank and reconnoitered. The galley presented a formidable appearance, yet the major was not daunted. At nine o'clock in the evening, favored with a fair wind, and accompanied by Lieutenant Helm, of Rhode Island, and a small re-enforcement, Talbot hoisted the anchor of the *Hawk*, and with a kedge-anchor lashed to the jib-boom to tear the nettings of the *Pigot*, he bore down upon that vessel. It was a very dark night in October. Under bare poles he drifted past
1778.   Fogland Ferry fort without being discovered, when he hoisted sail and ran partly under the stern of the galley. The sentinels hailed him, but, returning no answer, a volley of musketry was discharged at the *Hawk* without effect. The anchor tore the nettings and grappled the fore-shrouds of the *Pigot*, enabling the assailants to make a free passage to her deck. With loud shouts, the Americans poured from the *Hawk*, and drove every man of the *Pigot* into the hold, except the commander, who fought desperately alone, with no other mail than shirt and drawers, until he perceived that resistance was useless. The *Pigot* was surrendered, with the officers and crew. Her cables were coiled over the hatchways, to secure the prisoners below, and, weighing anchor, Talbot, with his prize, entered the harbor of Stonington the next day. This bold adventure was greatly applauded, and, on the 14th of November following, Congress complimented Talbot and his men, and presented him with

---

[1] Bancroft, ii., 108, 109.

a commission of lieutenant colonel in the army of the United States.[1] He was afterward transferred to the navy, in which service we shall meet him again.

I reached Newport at four o'clock, and at sunset was on board the *Empire State*, a noble Sound steam-boat (which was partially destroyed by fire a few weeks afterward), bound for New York. We passed old Fort Canonicut and Fort Adams, and out of the harbor at twilight; and at dark, leaving the Beaver-tail light behind, we were breasting the moon-lit waves of the ocean toward Point Judith. I now bade a final adieu to New England, to visit other scenes hallowed by the struggle of our fathers for liberty. Often since has the recollection of my visit there come up in memory like a pleasant dream; and never can I forget the universal kindness which I received during my brief tarry among the people of the East.

CANONICUT, OR DUMPLINGS FORT

> " They love their land because it is their own,
>   And scorn to give aught other reason why;
>   Would shake hands with a king upon his throne,
>   And think it kindness to his majesty;
>   A stubborn race, fearing and flattering none.
>   Such are they nurtured, such they live and die,
>   All, but a few apostates, who are meddling
>   With merchandise, pounds, shillings, pence, and peddling;
>
> " Or, wandering through the Southern countries, teaching
>   The A B C from WEBSTER's spelling-book;
>   Gallant and godly, making love and preaching,
>   And gaining, by what they call ' hook and crook,'
>   And what the moralists call overreaching,
>   A decent living.   The Virginians look
>   Upon them with as favorable eyes
>   As GABRIEL on the Devil in Paradise.
>
> " But these are but their outcasts.   View them near,
>   At home, where all their worth and pride are placed;
>   And there their hospitable fires burn clear,
>   And there the lowliest farm-house hearth is graced
>   With manly hearts; in piety sincere;
>   Faithful in love, in honor stern and chaste,
>   In friendship warm and true, in danger brave,
>   Beloved in life, and sainted in the grave."
>   HALLECK'S "CONNECTICUT."

---

[1] See Tuckerman's *Life of Talbot; Journals of Congress*, iv., 471.

666   PICTORIAL FIELD-BOOK

The Hudson Highlands.   Newburgh.   The Indian Summer.   Its character

CHAPTER XXIX.

" By wooded bluff we steal, by leaning lawn,
 By palace, village, cot, a sweet surprise
At every turn the vision breaks upon;
 Till to our wondering and uplifted eyes
The Highland rocks and hills in solemn grandeur rise.

" Nor clouds in heaven, nor billows in the deep,
 More graceful shapes did ever heave or roll;
Nor came such pictures to a painter's sleep,
 Nor beam'd such visions on a poet's soul!
The pent-up flood, impatient of control,
 In ages past here broke its granite bound,
Then to the sea in broad meanders stole,
 While ponderous ruin strew'd the broken ground,
And these gigantic hills forever closed around."

          Theodore S. Fay.

VERY place made memorable by Revolutionary events has an interest
in the mind and heart of the American, and claims the homage of regard from the lover of freedom, wheresoever he may have inspired his
first breath. But there are a few localities so thickly clustered with associations of deep interest, that they appear like fuglemen in the march of
events which attract the historian's notice. Prominent among these are the
Highlands, upon the Hudson, from Haverstraw to Newburgh, the scenes of
councils, battles, sieges, triumphs and treason, in all of which seemed to be
involved for the moment, the fate of American liberty. Thitherward I journeyed
at the commencement of our beautiful Indian summer,[1] the season

     " When first the frost
Turns into beauty all October's charms;
When the dread fever quits us; when the storms
Of the wild equinox, with all its wet,
Has left the land as the first deluge left it,
With a bright bow of many colors hung
Upon the forest tops,"
        Brainerd.

and rambled for a week among those ancient hills and the historic grounds adjacent. I arrived at Newburgh on the morning of the 25th of October. The town is pleasantly
1848. situated upon the steep western bank of the Hudson, sixty miles from New York, and
in the midst of some of the finest scenery in the world, enhanced in interest to the student
of history by the associations which hallow it. In the southern suburbs of the village, on
the brow of the hill, stands the gray old fabric called " The Hasbrouck House," memorable

---

[1] The week or ten days of warm, balmy weather in autumn, immediately preceding the advent of winter
storms, when, as Irving says of Sleepy Hollow, a "drowsy, dreamy influence seems to hang over the land
and pervade the very atmosphere," appears to be peculiar to the United States, and has attracted the attention of travelers and philosophers. It is called *Indian summer*, because it occurs at a season when the
natives gathered in their crops of maize or Indian corn. The atmosphere is smoky, and so mellows the
sunlight that every object wears the livery of repose, like the landscapes of Southern Italy. The cause of
the warmth and other peculiarities of this season is an unexplained question. It is the season when the
fallen leaves of our vast forests begin to decay. As decadence is slow combustion, may not the heat evolved
in the process produce the effects noticed ?

as the head-quarters of Washington at the close of the Revolution.   From the rickety piazza or *stoop* on the river front may be seen the historic grounds of Fishkill, New Windsor, Plumb Point, Pollopel's Island, and the Beacon Hills; and through the mighty gateway in the Highlands, whose posts are Breakneck and Butter Hills, in altitude fifteen hundred feet, appear glimpses of distant West Point and the amphitheater of mountains which surround it.   Let us take a peep

WASHINGTON'S HEAD-QUARTERS AT NEWBURGH.[1]

within the venerable mansion; and as the morning sun is shining pleasantly upon the porch, we will there sit down, and glance over the pages of the old clasped volume, the *vade mecum* and Mentor of our journey.

The front door opens into a large square room, which was used by Washington for his public audiences, and as a dining hall.   It is remarkable for the fact that it has seven doors, and only one window.   Of the two doors on the left in the picture, the nearest one to the spectator was the entrance to the chief's sitting-room; the other, to his bed-room.   There is no plaster ceiling above; the heavy beams, nine inches wide and fourteen deep, completely exposed, give it a strong as well as antique appearance.   Properly taken care of,

---

[1] This view is from the northeast, comprising the north gable and east or river front.   The house is substantially built of stone, and is now (1850) just one hundred years old.   This remark applies only to the portion containing the large room with seven doors, and the two bed-rooms on the north of it.   This portion was built in 1750.   Afterward a kitchen was built on the south end, and in 1770 an addition was made to it, on the west side, of the same length and height of the old part.   The dates of the first and last additions are cut in the stones of the building.   The fire-place in the large room is very spacious, "in which," says Mr. Eager, "a small bullock might have been turned upon a spit."*   The house has been in the possession of the Hasbrouck family (one of the oldest of the Huguenot families in the county) from the time of its erection until recently, when it was purchased by the State of New York for the purpose of preserving it as a relic of the Revolution.   It is placed in charge of the trustees of the village of Newburgh, who are required to expend a certain amount in repairs, ornamenting the grounds, &c.   The family residing in the house is employed for the purpose of receiving and attending visitors.   The house has been thoroughly repaired since the above sketch was made, under the direction of an advisory committee for its restoration and the embellishment of the grounds.   Some of the modern alterations within have been changed, and the whole appearance of the edifice is now as much like that of the era of the Revolution as it is possible to make it.   Interesting ceremonies were had upon the occasion of its dedication, on the 4th of July, 1850.   There was a civic and military procession.   The ceremonies on the green before the house were opened with prayer by Reverend Doctor Johnson, and an address by J. J. Monell, Esq., of Newburgh.   While a choir was singing the following last stanza of a beautiful ode, written by Mrs. Monell,

"With a prayer your faith expressing,
Raise our country's flag on high;
Here, where rests a nation's blessing,
Stars and stripes shall float for aye!
Mutely telling
Stirring tales of days gone by,"

major-general Scott, who was present, hoisted the American flag upon a lofty staff erected near.   The Declaration of Independence was read by Honorable F. J. Betts, after which Honorable J. W. Edmonds pronounced an oration, marked by evidences of much historic research.   Henceforth this venerated relic belongs to the people of New York; and doubtless its cabinet of Revolutionary remains, already begun, will be augmented by frequent donations, until a museum of rare interest shall be collected there.

---

* *History of Orange County.*

this relic of the Revolution may remain another century. The timbers are sound, the walls massive, and the roof and weather-boards were well preserved.

THE DINING-HALL, OR ROOM WITH SEVEN DOORS.[1]

Lady Washington was a resident of the "Hasbrouck House" during the summer of 1783, and, in gratification of her taste for gardening, a large space in front of the house was cultivated by her. Mr. Eager, the historian of Orange county, informed me that within his remembrance the brick borders of her flower-beds remained. Washington, with his lady, left there about the middle of August, to attend upon Congress, then in session at Princeton, New Jersey, leaving the portion of the Continental army then in service under the command of General Knox. The commander-in-chief did not return to Newburgh, but made his head-quarters, for a few days in November, at West Point, from whence he repaired to New York and took possession of that city on its evacuation by the British troops.

1783.

November 25, 1783.

Orange county was among the first settled portions of the State of New York. It was organized in 1683; its name was given in honor of William, prince of Orange, afterward King of England. The first permanent settlers in the county were Germans, and their original location was in the present town of Newburgh, at a place called by the Indians Quassaic, on a creek of that name, a little below the village. They obtained a patent from Queen Anne, in 1719, for twenty-one hundred and ninety acres, extending north from the Quassaic Creek, and proceeded to lay out a village which they called New Burgh or New

---

[1] In the December number of the New York Mirror for 1834, is an interesting account of this old building, by Gulian C. Verplanck, Esq. He relates the following anecdote connected with this room, which he received from Colonel Nicholas Fish, father of the late governor of the State of New York. Just before La Fayette's death, himself and the American minister, with several of his countrymen, were invited to dine at the house of that distinguished Frenchman, Marbois, who was the French secretary of legation here during the Revolution. At the supper hour the company were shown into a room which contrasted quite oddly with the Parisian elegance of the other apartments where they had spent the evening. A low boarded, painted ceiling, with large beams, a single small, uncurtained window, with numerous small doors, as well as the general style of the whole, gave, at first, the idea of the kitchen, or largest room of a Dutch or Belgian farm-house. On a long rough table was a repast, just as little in keeping with the refined kitchens of Paris as the room was with its architecture. It consisted of a large dish of meat, uncouth-looking pastry, and wine in decanters and bottles, accompanied by glasses and silver mugs, such as indicated other habits and tastes than those of modern Paris. "Do you know where we now are?" said the host to La Fayette and his companions. They paused for a few minutes in surprise. They had seen something like this before, but when and where? "Ah! the seven doors and one window," said La Fayette, "and the silver camp-goblets, such as the marshals of France used in my youth! We are at Washington's head-quarters on the Hudson, fifty years ago!"

The view here given is from the west door of the dining-hall, looking out of the east door upon the Hudson, the green fields of Fishkill, and the North Beacon of the Highlands, whereon the Americans lighted watch-fires when occasion demanded it. The fire-place on the right is within the area of the room, having a heavy hewn stone for a *back-log*. The visitor may stand there, and look up the broad-mouthed chimney to the sky above.

Town. Five hundred acres were reserved as glebe land, and under favorable auspices the village of Newburgh was founded. The Germans in time became dissatisfied, sold out their patent and dispersed, some going to Pennsylvania, and others to the Mohawk country. Some English, Irish, New Englanders, and a few Huguenots from Ulster filled their places, and flourishing settlements were soon planted along the river, or upon the rich bottoms of the water-courses. They also spread interiorly, and Goshen, Minisink, Wawarsing, and other thriving towns started up in the midst of the red men. The ante-revolutionary history of this section of the state is full of stirring incidents, for the wily Indian, properly suspicious of the pale faces, was ever on the alert to do them damage; and the privations, alarms, and sufferings of those who opened the fertile bosom of the country to the sun and rain, and spread broad acres of cultivation where the deer grazed in shady solitudes, compose a web of romance wonderful indeed. And when the Revolution broke out, and the savages of the Mohawk Valley and of Western New York were let loose upon the remote settlements, the people of Orange county were intense sufferers, particularly those upon its frontier settlements, in the direction of the wilderness. The Tories and their savage associates spread terror in every direction, and in Wawarsing and vicinity many patriots and their families were the victims of ambuscade or open attack. But I will not repeat a tale of horror such as we have already considered in viewing the history of the Mohawk Valley. The atrocities committed in Orange county were but a counterpart in character and horror of the former.[1] Strong houses were barricaded and used as forts; the people went armed by day, and slept armed at night; and almost hourly murder and rapine stalked boldly abroad. It was a time of darkest misery; and not until the Indian power of the West was broken, and the Tories failed to receive their aid, was the district blessed with quiet.

The invasion of Minisink,[2] alluded to in a former chapter, was one of those prominent links in the chain of Indian and Tory depredations, that I may not pass it over with only brief mention. Here let us consider it. There were very few engaged in the battle that ensued, yet that few fought with wonderful valor, and suffered a terrible slaughter.

Count Pulaski and his legion of cavalry were stationed, during a part of the winter of 1778–9, at Minisink. In February, he was ordered to South Carolina, to join the army under Lincoln. The settlement was thus left wholly unprotected, which being perceived by Brant, the accomplished Mohawk warrior, he resolved to make a descent upon it. During the night of the 19th of July, at the head of sixty Indians, and twenty-seven Tories disguised as savages, he stole upon the little town, and before the people were aroused   1779. from their slumbers he had fired several dwellings. With no means for defense, the inhabitants sought safety in flight to the mountains, leaving their pretty village and all their worldly goods a spoil to the invaders. Their small stockade fort, a mill, and twelve houses and barns were burned, several persons were killed, some taken prisoners, the orchards and plantations were laid waste, cattle were driven away, and booty of every kind was carried to Grassy Brook, on the Delaware, a few miles above the mouth of the Lackawaxen, where the chief had left the main body of his warriors. When intelligence of this invasion reached Goshen, Doctor Tusten, colonel of the local militia, issued orders to the officers of his regiment to meet him at Minisink the next day, with as many volunteers as they could muster. The call was promptly responded to, and one hundred and forty-nine hardy men were gathered around Tusten the following morning. Many of these were principal gentlemen of the vicinity. A council was held, and it was unanimously determined to pursue the invaders.

---

[1] For details of the trials of the settlers, and the atrocities committed by the Indians and Tories in this section, see a pamphlet published at Rondout, entitled "THE INDIANS; or, Narratives of Massacres, &c., in Wawarsing and its Vicinity during the American Revolution."

[2] Minisink was one of the most ancient settlements in Orange county. It was in existence as a white settlement as early as 1669, when a severe battle was fought with the Indians on the 22d of July, ninety years, to a day, previous to the conflict in question. From that time until the Revolution it was often the scene of strife with the red men, and almost every dell, and rock, and ancient tree has its local tradition. The place of the ancient settlement is situated about ten miles northwest of Goshen, among the Shawangunk Mountains, between the Wallkill and the Navasink Valleys.

Colonel Tusten, who well knew the skill, prowess, caution, and craftiness of Brant, opposed the measure, as a hazardous undertaking with so small a force. He was overruled, and the debates of the council were cut short by Major Meeker, who mounted his horse, flourished his sword, and shouted, " Let the *brave* men follow me ; the *cowards* may stay behind !" These words ignited the assembly, and the line of march was immediately formed. They traveled seventeen miles, and then encamped for the night. The next morning, Colonel Hathorn, of the Warwick militia, with a small re-enforcement, joined them. He was Tusten's senior officer, and took the command. They resumed their march at sunrise, and at Half-way Brook came upon the Indian encampment of the previous night ; the smoldering watch-fires were still smoking. The number of these fires indicated a large savage force, and the two colonels, with the more prudent of the company, advocated, in council, a return, rather than further pursuit. But excited bravado overcame prudence, and a large majority determined to pursue the Indians ; the minority yielded, and the march was resumed.

A scouting party, under Captain Tyler, was sent forward upon the Indian trail. The pursuers were discovered, and a bullet from an unseen foe slew the captain. There was momentary alarm ; but the volunteers pressed eagerly onward, and at nine in the morning they hovered upon the high hills overlooking the Delaware near the mouth of the Lacka-waxen. The enemy were in full view below, marching in the direction of a fording-place. Hathorn determined to intercept them there, and disposed his men accordingly. The intervening hills hid the belligerents from each other. Brant had watched the movements of his pursuers, and comprehending Hathorn's design, he wheeled his column, and thridding a deep and narrow ravine which the whites had crossed, brought his whole force in the rear of the Americans. Here he formed an ambuscade, and deliberately selected his battle ground.

The volunteers were surprised and disappointed at not finding the enemy where they expected to, and were marching back when they discovered some of the Indians. One of them, mounted on a horse stolen at Minisink, was shot by a militia-man. This was a signal for action, and the firing soon became general. It was a long and bloody conflict. The Indians were greatly superior in numbers, and a detachment of Hathorn's troops, consisting of one third of the whole, became separated from the rest at the commencement of the engagement. Closer and closer the savages pressed upon the whites, until they were hemmed within the circumference of an acre of ground, upon a rocky hill that sloped on all sides. The ammunition of the militia was stinted, and they were careful not to fire at random and without aim. Their shots were deadly, and many a red man was slain. The conflict began at eleven o'clock, and continued until the going down of the sun, on that long July day. At twilight the battle was yet undecided, but the ammunition of the whites being exhausted, a party of the enemy attacked and broke their hollow square at one corner. The survivors of the conflict attempted to retreat. Behind a ledge of rocks, Doctor Tusten had been dressing the wounds of the injured during the day. There were seventeen men under his care when the retreat commenced. The Indians fell upon them furiously, and all, with the Doctor, were slain. Several who attempted to escape by swimming across the Delaware were shot by the Indians ; and of the whole number that went forth, only about thirty returned to relate the dreadful scenes of the day.[1] This massacre of the wounded is one of the darkest stains upon the memory of Brant, whose honor and humanity were often more conspicuous than that of his Tory allies. He made a weak defense of his conduct by asserting that he offered the Americans good treatment if they would surrender ;

July 22, 1779.

---

[1] The place of conflict is about two miles from the northern bank of the Delaware, and the same distance below the *Lechawachsin* or Lackawaxen River. It is about three miles from the Barryville station, on the New York and Erie rail-road. The battle ground and the adjacent region continue in the same wild state as of old, and over the rocky knolls and tangled ravines where the Indians and the Goshen militia fought, wild deer roam in abundance, and a panther occasionally leaps upon its prey. The place is too rocky for cultivation, and must ever remain a wilderness. At the Mohackamack Fork (now Port Jervis, on the Delaware) was a small settlement, and a block-house, called Jersey Fort.

OF THE REVOLUTION. 671

Brant's Defense.   Effect of the Massacre.   Salvation of Major Wood.   Interment of the Remains of the Slain.   Monument.

that he warned them of the fierceness of the thirst for blood that actuated his warriors, and that he could not answer for their conduct after the first shot should be fired ; and that

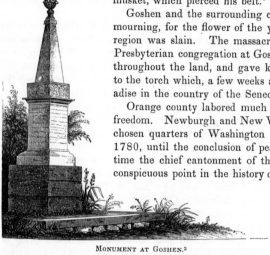

his humane proposition was answered by a bullet from an American musket, which pierced his belt.[1]

Goshen and the surrounding country was filled with the voice of mourning, for the flower of the youth and mature manhood of that region was slain. The massacre made thirty-three widows in the Presbyterian congregation at Goshen. At the recital, a shudder ran throughout the land, and gave keenness to the blade and fierceness to the torch which, a few weeks afterward, desolated the Indian paradise in the country of the Senecas and Cayugas.

Orange county labored much and suffered much in the cause of freedom. Newburgh and New Windsor, within it, having been the chosen quarters of Washington at different times, from December, 1780, until the conclusion of peace in 1783, and a portion of that time the chief cantonment of the American army, the county is a conspicuous point in the history of the war. At the close of 1780,

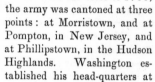

the army was cantoned at three points : at Morristown, and at Pompton, in New Jersey, and at Phillipstown, in the Hudson Highlands. Washington established his head-quarters at

MONUMENT AT GOSHEN.[2]

[1] During the battle, Major Wood, of Goshen, made a masonic sign, by accident, which Brant, who was a Free-mason, perceived and heeded. Wood's life was spared, and as a prisoner he was treated kindly, until the Mohawk chief perceived that he was not a Mason. Then, with withering scorn, Brant looked upon Wood, believing that he had obtained the masonic sign which he used, by deception. It was purely an accident on the part of Wood. When released, he hastened to become a member of the fraternity by whose instrumentality his life had been spared. The house in which Major Wood lived is yet standing (though much altered), at the foot of the hill north of the rail-way station at Goshen. The house of Roger Townsend, who was among the slain, is also standing, and well preserved. It is in the southern part of the village. The *Farmers' Hall Academy*, an old brick building, two stories high, and now used for a district school-house, is an object of some interest to the visitor at Goshen, from the circumstance that there Noah Webster, our great lexicographer, once taught school. An old gentleman of the village informed me that he had often seen him at twilight on a summer's evening in the grove on the hill northward of the rail-way station, gathering up the manuscripts which he had been preparing in a retired spot, after school hours.

[2] In 1822, the citizens of Orange county collected the bones of those slain in the battle of Minisink, which had been left forty-three years upon the field of strife, and caused them to be buried near the center of the green at the foot of the main street of the village. On that occasion there was a great gathering of people, estimated at fifteen thousand in number. The cadets from West Point were there, under the command of the late General Worth, then a major. The corner-stone was laid by General Hathorn, one of the survivors of the battle, then eighty years of age. He accompanied the act with a short and feeling address. A funeral oration was pronounced by the Reverend James R. Wilson, now of Newburgh. Over these remains a marble monument was erected. It stands upon three courses of brown freestone, and a stone pavement a few feet square, designed to be surrounded by an iron railing. In consequence of neglecting to erect the railing, the monument has suffered much from the prevailing spirit of vandalism which I have already noticed. Its corners are broken, the inscriptions are mutilated, and the people of Goshen are made to feel many regrets for useless delay in giving that interesting memorial a protection. On the east side of the pedestal is the following inscription :

"ERECTED by the inhabitants of Orange county, 22d July, 1822. *Sacred* to the memory of their fellow-citizens who fell at the battle of MINISINK, 22d July, 1779."

Upon the other three sides of the pedestal are the following names of the slain :
" Benjamin Tusten, colonel ; Bezaleel Tyler, Samuel Jones, John Little, John Duncan, Benjamin Vail, captains ; John Wood, lieutenant ; Nathaniel Finch, adjutant ; Ephraim Mastin, Ephraim Middaugh, ensigns ; Gabriel Wisner, Esq., Stephen Mead, Mathias Terwilliger, Joshua Lockwood, Ephraim Ferguson, Roger Townsend, Samuel Knapp, James Knapp, Benjamin Bennet, William Barker, Jonathan Pierce, James Little, Joseph Norris, Gilbert Vail, Abraham Shepperd, Joel Decker, Nathan Wade, Simon Wait, —— Tallmadge, Jacob Dunning, John Carpenter, David Barney, Jonathan Haskell, Abraham Williams,

New Windsor in December, 1780, where he remained until June, 1781, when the French, who had quartered during the winter at Newport and Lebanon, formed a junction with the Americans on the Hudson. In April, 1782, he established his head-quarters at Newburgh, two miles above the village of New Windsor, where he continued most of the time until November, 1783, when the Continental army was disbanded.

For a short time in the autumn of 1782, while the head-quarters of Washington were at Newburgh, the main portion of the army was encamped at Verplanck's Point, in pursuance of an engagement with Rochambeau to form a junction of the American and French forces at that place, on the return of the latter from Virginia. The allies marched eastward late in autumn, when the American army crossed the Hudson at West Point, traversed the mountains, and arrived in the township of New Windsor on the 28th of November, 1782. where it was hutted for the winter. The main portion of the army was encamped in the neighborhood of Snake Hill; of this we will write presently. Washington continued his head-quarters at the stone house at Newburgh; Generals Knox and Greene, who had the immediate command of the chief forces and of the artillery, were quartered at the house of John Ellison (now Captain Charles Morton's), in the vicinity of the main camp near Snake Hill; Gates and St. Clair, with the hospital stores, were at Edmonston's, at The Square; La Fayette was at William Ellison's, near by; and the Baron Steuben was at the house of Samuel Verplanck, on the Fishkill side of the river.

At Newburgh occurred one of the most painful events in the military life of Washington. For a long time the discontents among the officers and soldiers in the army respecting the arrearages of their pay and their future prospects, had been increasing, and in the spring of 1783 became alarmingly manifest. Complaints were frequently made to the commander-in-chief. Feeling the justice of these complaints, his sympathy was fully alive to the interests of his companions in arms. Colonel Nicola, an experienced officer, and a gentleman possessed of much weight of character, was usually the medium for communicating to him, verbally, their complaints, wishes, and fears. In May, Colonel Nicola addressed a letter to Washington, the tenor of which struck harshly upon the tenderest chord in that great man's feelings. After some general remarks on the deplorable condition of the army, and the little hope they could have of being properly rewarded by Congress, the colonel entered into a political disquisition on the different forms of government, and came to the conclusion that republics are, of all others, the least susceptible of stability, and the least capable of securing the rights, freedom, and power of individuals. He therefore inferred that America could never become prosperous under such a form of government, and that the English government was nearer perfection than any other. He then proceeded to express his opinion that such a government would be the choice of the people, after due consideration, and added, " In this case it will, I believe, be uncontroverted, that the same abilities which have led us through difficulties apparently insurmountable by human power to victory and glory—those qualities, that have merited and obtained the universal esteem and veneration of an army—would be most likely to conduct and direct us in the smoother paths of peace. Some people have so connected the idea of tyranny and monarchy as to find it very difficult to separate them. It may, therefore, be requisite to give the head of such a constitution as I propose some title apparently more moderate; but, if all other things were once adjusted, I believe strong arguments might be produced for admitting the title of KING, which I conceive would be attended with some national advantage." How amazingly Colonel Nicola, and those officers and civilians (and they, doubtless, were not a few) whom he represented, misapprehended the true character of Washington, may be readily inferred from the prompt and severe rebuke which they received from his hand. The commander-in-chief replied as follows:

James Mosher, Isaac Ward, Baltus Nierpos, Gamaliel Bailey, Moses Thomas, Eleazer Owens, Adam Embler, Samuel Little, Benjamin Dunning, Samuel Reed."

"SIR,—With a mixture of great surprise and astonishment, I have read with attention the sentiments you have submitted to my perusal. Be assured, sir, no occurrence in the course of this war has given me more painful sensations than your information of there being such ideas existing in the army as you have expressed, and which I must view with abhorrence and reprehend with severity. For the present, the communication of them will rest in my own bosom, unless some further agitation of the matter shall make a disclosure necessary. I am much at a loss to conceive what part of my conduct could have given encouragement to an address which to me seems big with the greatest mischiefs that can befall my country. If I am not deceived in the knowledge of myself, you could not have found a person to whom your schemes are more disagreeable. At the same time, in justice to my own feelings, I must add, that no man possesses a more serious wish to see ample justice done to the army than I do ; and, as far as my power and influence, in a constitutional way, extend, they shall be employed to the utmost of my abilities to effect it, should there be any occasion. Let me conjure you, then, if you have any regard for your country, concern for yourself or posterity, or respect for me, to banish these thoughts from your mind, and never communicate, as from yourself or any one else, a sentiment of the like nature. I am, &c."[1]

In this affair the disinterested patriotism of Washington shone with its brightest luster. At the head of a victorious army ; beloved and venerated by it and by the people ; with personal influence unbounded, and with power in possession for consummating almost any political scheme not apparently derogatory to good government, he receives from an officer whom he greatly esteems, and who speaks for himself and others, an offer of the scepter of supreme rule and the crown of royalty ! What a bribe ! Yet he does not hesitate for a moment ; he does not stop to revolve in his mind any ideas of advantage in the proposed scheme, but at once rebukes the author sternly but kindly, and impresses his signet of strongest disapprobation upon the proposal. History can not present a parallel.

The apprehensions which this event produced in the mind of Washington, though allayed for a while, were painfully revived a few months later. The same circumstances of present hardship and gloomy prospects that disturbed the army when Nicola addressed Washington, not only continued to exist, but reasons for discontent daily increased. After the return of the army from Verplanck's Point, and their settlement in winter quarters in the neighborhood of Newburgh and New Windsor, the officers and soldiers had leisure to reflect upon their situation and prospects. Expecting a dissolution of the Revolutionary government when peace should be established, and a thorough reorganization of civil and military affairs, they apprehended great difficulties and losses in the adjustment of their claims, particularly those appertaining to the long arrearages of their pay. They were aware of the poverty of the treasury and the inefficiency of the existing government in commanding resources for its replenishment ; a condition arising from the disposition of individual states to deny the right of Congress to ask for pecuniary aid from their respective treasuries in satisfying public creditors. This actual state of things, and no apparent security for a future adjustment of their claims, caused great excitement and uneasiness among the officers and soldiers, and in December they addressed a memorial to Congress on the subject of their grievances.[2] A committee, composed of General M'Dougal, Colonel Ogden, and Colonel Brooks, were appointed to carry the memorial to Philadelphia, lay it before Congress, and explain its import. Congress appointed a committee, consisting of a delegate from each state, to consider the memorial. The committee reported, and, on the 25th of January, Congress passed a series of resolutions, which were not very satisfactory. In 1783.

1782.

---

[1] Sparks's *Life and Writings of Washington*, viii., 300, 302. Washington's letter to Colonel Nicola is dated at Newburgh, 22d May, 1782.

[2] This memorial comprehended five different articles : 1. Present pay ; 2. A settlement of the accounts of the arrearages of pay, and security for what was due ; 3. A commutation of the half-pay authorized by different resolutions of Congress, for an equivalent in gross ; 4. A settlement of the accounts of deficiencies of rations and compensation ; 5. A settlement of the accounts of deficiencies of clothing and compensation

regard to present pay, the superintendent of finance was directed to make "such payment and in such measure as he shall think proper," as soon as the state of public finances would permit. In relation to arrearages and the settlement of accounts, it was resolved "that the several states be called upon to complete, without delay, the settlements with their respect-

ive lines of the army, up to the 1st day of August, 1783, and that the superintendent of finance be directed to take such measures as shall appear to him most proper for effecting the settlement from that period." Concerning security for what should be found due on such settlement, Congress declared, by resolution, that they would "make every effort in their power to obtain from the respective states substantial funds, adequate to the object of funding the whole debt of the United States, and will enter upon an immediate and full consideration of the nature of such funds, and the most likely mode of obtaining them."[1]

In these resolutions, Congress, feeble in actual power and resources, made no definite promises of present relief or future justice; and when General Knox, who had been appointed by the army to correspond with their committee, reported the facts, the discon- February 8, tent and dissatisfaction was quite as 1783.

great as before the action of Congress. Some thought it necessary to further make known their sentiments and enforce their claims, and to this end it was deemed advisable to act with energy. A plan was arranged among a few "for assembling the officers, not in mass, but by representation; and for passing a series of resolutions, which, in the hands of their committee, and of their auxiliaries in Congress, would furnish a new and powerful lever" of operation. Major John Armstrong,[2] General Gates's aid-de-camp, a young officer of six-and-

---

[1] *Journals of Congress*, viii., 82. The remainder of the report was referred to a committee consisting of Messrs. Mann, Osgood, Fitzsimmons, Gervais, Hamilton, and Wilson.

[2] John Armstrong was born at Carlisle, in Pennsylvania, on the 25th of November, 1758. He was the youngest of two sons of General John Armstrong, of Carlisle, distinguished by his services in the French and Indian war in 1756. In 1775, at the most critical period of the American Revolution, young Armstrong, then a student of Princeton College, joined the army as a volunteer in Potter's Pennsylvania regiment. He was soon after appointed aid-de-camp by General Hugh Mercer, and remained with him till the connection was severed on the bloody field of Princeton by the death of his chief. He subsequently occupied the same position in the family of Major-general Gates, and served through the campaign which ended in the capture of Burgoyne. In 1780 he was made adjutant general of the Southern army, but falling sick of fever on the Pedee, was succeeded by Colonel Otho Williams, a short time previous to the defeat at Camden. Resuming his place as aid, he remained with General Gates till the close of the war. He was the author of the celebrated *Newburgh Addresses*, the object of which has been greatly misrepresented, and very generally misunderstood. They were intended to awaken in Congress and the States a sense of justice toward its creditors, particularly toward the army, then about to be disbanded without requital for its services, toils, and sufferings. General Washington, in 1797, bore testimony to the patriotic motives of the author.

Armstrong's first civil appointments were those of Secretary of the State of Pennsylvania, and adjutant general, under Dickenson's and Franklin's administrations; posts which he continued to occupy till 1787, when he was chosen a member of the old Congress. In the autumn of the same year, he was appointed by Congress one of the three judges for the Western Territory; this appointment he declined, and having married, in 1789, a sister of Chancellor Livingston, of New York, removed to that state. Here he purchased a farm, and devoted himself to agricultural pursuits; and, though offered by President Washington, in 1793, the place of United States supervisor of the collection of internal revenue in the State of New York, he declined this and other invitations to public office, until, in the year 1800, he was elected United States senator by an almost unanimous vote of botn houses of the Legislature. Having resigned in 1802, he was again

twenty, and possessing much ability, was chosen to write an address to the army suited to the subject ; and this, with an anonymous notification of a meeting of the officers, was circulated privately.[1]   The address exhibits superior talents, and was calculated to make a deep impression upon the minds of the malcontents.   Referring to his personal feelings, and his sacrifices for his country, the writer plays upon the sensibilities of his readers, and prepares their minds for a relinquishment of their faith in the justice of their country, already weakened by circumstances.   " Faith," he says, " has its limits as well as temper, and there are points beyond which neither can be stretched without sinking into cowardice or plunging into credulity.   This, my friends, I conceive to be your situation ; hurried to the verge of both, another step would ruin you forever.   To be tame and unprovoked, when injuries press hard upon you, is more than weakness ; but to look up for kinder usage, without one manly effort of your own, would fix your character, and show the world how richly you deserved the chains you broke."   He then takes a review of the past and present — their wrongs and their complaints — their petitions and the denials of redress — and then says, "If this, then, be your treatment while the swords you wear are necessary for the defense of America, what have you to expect from peace, when your voice shall sink, and your strength dissipate by division ; when those very swords, the instruments and companions of your glory, shall be taken from your sides, and no remaining mark of military distinction left but your wants, infirmities, and scars ?   Can you, then, consent to be the only sufferers by the Revolution, and, retiring from the field, grow old in poverty, wretchedness, and contempt ?   Can you consent to wade through the vile mire of dependency, and owe the miserable remnant of that life to charity, which has hitherto been spent in honor ?   If you can, go, and carry with you the jest of Tories and the scorn of Whigs ; the ridicule, and, what is worse, the pity of the world !   Go, starve, and be forgotten."

The writer now changes from appeal to advice.   " I would advise you, therefore " he says, " to come to some final opinion upon what you can bear and what you will suffer.   If your determination be in proportion to your wrongs, carry your appeal from the justice to the fears of government.   Change the milk-and-water style of your last memorial ; assume

---

elected in 1803, and, the year following, appointed by Mr. Jefferson minister plenipotentiary to France ; which post, at a very critical period of our relations with that country, he filled with distinguished ability for more than six years, discharging incidentally the functions of a separate mission to Spain with which he was invested.

In 1812 he was appointed a brigadier general in the United States army, and commanded in the city of New York until called by Mr. Madison, in 1813, to the War Department.   This office he accepted with reluctance, and with little anticipation of success to our arms.   In effecting salutary changes in the army, by substituting young and able officers for the old ones who had held subordinate stations in the army of the Revolution, he made many enemies.   The capture of the city of Washington in 1814 led to his retirement from office.   Public opinion held him responsible for this misfortune, but, as documentary history has shown, without justice.   No man took office with purer motives, or retired from it with a better claim to have faithfully discharged its duties.

General Armstrong died at his residence at Red Hook, N. Y., on the 1st of April, 1843, in the eighty-fifth year of his age.   He was among the remarkable men of a remarkable generation.   The productions of his pen entitle him to rank with the ablest writers of his time and country.   These consist of a voluminous correspondence, diplomatic and military ; a valuable treatise on agriculture, the result of some experience and much reading ; and "Notices of the War of 1812," a work written with great vigor of style. The portrait of General Armstrong, printed on the preceding page, is from a painting in possession of his daughter, Mrs. William B. Astor, drawn from life by John Wesley Jarvis.

[1] This notice was circulated on the 10th of March, 1783.   It was in manuscript, as well as the anonymous address that followed.   The originals were carried by a major, who was a deputy inspector under Baron Steuben, to the office of Barber, the adjutant general, where, every morning, aids-de-camp, majors of brigades, and adjutants of regiments were assembled, all of whom, who chose to do so, took copies and circulated them.   Among the transcribers was the adjutant of the commander-in-chief's guard, who probably furnished him with the copies that were transmitted to Congress.   The following is a copy of the anonymous notification :

"A meeting of the field officers is requested at the Public Building on Tuesday next at eleven o'clock. A commissioned officer from each company is expected, and a delegate from the medical staff.   The object of this convention is to consider the late letter of our representatives in Philadelphia, and what measures (if any) should be adopted to obtain that redress of grievances which they seem to have solicited in vain."

a bolder tone, decent, but lively, spirited, and determined ; and suspect the man who would advise to more moderation and longer forbearance.[1] Let two or three men who can feel as well as write, be appointed to draw up *your last remonstrance*—for I would no longer give it the suing, soft, unsuccessful epithet of *memorial*." He advises them to talk boldly to Congress, and to warn that body that the slightest mark of indignity from them now would operate like the grave, to part them and the army forever ; " that in any political event, the army has its alternative. If peace, that nothing shall separate you from your arms but death ; if war, that, courting the auspices and inviting the direction of your illustrious leader you will retire to some unsettled country, smile in your turn, ' and mock when their fear cometh on.' Let it represent, also, that should they comply with the request of your late memorial, it would make you more happy, and them more respectable."

A copy of these papers was put into the hands of the commander-in-chief on the day of their circulation, and he wisely determined to guide and control the proceedings thus begun, rather than to check and discourage them by any act of severity. In general orders the March 11, next morning, he referred to the anonymous papers and the meeting. He express-
1783. ed his disapprobation of the whole proceeding as disorderly ; at the same time, he requested that the general and field officers, with one officer from each company, and a propei representation of the staff of the army, should assemble at twelve o'clock on Saturday the 15th, at the New Building (at which the other meeting was called), for the purpose of hearing the report of the committee of the army to Congress. He requested the senior officer in rank (General Gates) to preside at the meeting. On the appearance of this order, the writer of the anonymous address put forth another, rather more subdued in its tone, in which he sought to convince the officers that Washington approved of the scheme, the time of meeting only being changed. The design of this interpretation the commander-in-chief took care to frustrate, by conversing personally and individually with those officers in whose good sense and integrity he had confidence. He impressed their minds with a sense of the danger that must attend any rash act at such a crisis, inculcated moderation, and exerted all

---

[1] This sentence, particularly alluded to by Washington in his address to the officers, was the one which drew down upon the head of the writer the fiercest anathemas of public opinion, and he alone has been held responsible for the suggestion that the army should use its power to intimidate Congress. Such a conclusion is unwarrantable. It is not likely that a young man of twenty-six, acting in the capacity of aid, should, without the promptings of men of greater experience who surrounded him, propose so bold a measure. It is well known, too, that many officers, whose patriotism was never suspected, were privy to the preparation of the address, and suggested many of its sentiments; and there can be no reasonable doubt that General Gates was a prominent actor. Nor was the idea confined to that particular time and place. General Hamilton, one of the purest patriots of the Revolution, wrote to Washington from Philadelphia, a month before (February 7, 1783), on the subject of the grievances of the army, in which he held similar language. After referring to the deplorable condition of the finances, the prevailing opinion in the army "that the disposition to recompense their services will cease with the necessity for them," and lamenting "that appearances afford too much ground for their distrust," he held the following language : "It becomes a serious inquiry, What is the true line of policy ? *The claims of the army, urged with moderation but with firmness*, may operate on those weak minds which are influenced by their apprehensions more than by their judgments, so as to produce a concurrence in the measures which the exigencies of affairs demand. They may add weight to the applications of Congress to the several states. So far, a useful turn may be given to them."* What was this but " carrying their appeal from the *justice* to the *fears* of government ?" Hamilton further remarked, that the difficulty would be " to keep a *complaining* and *suffering* army within the bounds of moderation ;" and advised Washington not to discountenance their endeavors to procure redress, but, " by the intervention of confidential and prudent persons, to *take the direction of them*." Hamilton was at that time a member of Congress. In a letter to him, written on the 12th of March, Washington remarked that all was tranquillity in the camp until after the arrival from Philadelphia of "a certain gentleman" (General Walter Stewart), and intimated that the discontents in the army were made active by members of Congress, who wished to see the delinquent states thus forced to do justice. Hamilton, in reply, admitted that he had urged the propriety " of uniting the influence of the public creditors" (of whom the soldiers were the most meritorious) "and the army, to prevail upon the states to enter into their views."† But, while Hamilton held these views, he deprecated the idea of the army turning its power against the civil government. " There would be no chance of success," he said, "without having recourse to means that would reverse our Revolution."‡

---

* See the *Life of Hamilton*, by his son, John C. Hamilton, ii., 47.   † Ibid., ii., 71.   ‡ Ibid., ii., 158.

OF THE REVOLUTION.

677

Meeting called by Washington.　Major Burnet's Recollections.　Washington's Address to the Officers.

his powers of argument to appease their discontents. They were thus prepared to deliberate in the proposed convention without passion, and under a deep sense of the responsibilities which rested upon them as patriots and leaders.

The meeting was held pursuant to Washington's orders. There was a full attendance of officers, and deep solemnity pervaded the assembly when the commander-in-chief stepped forward upon the platform to read an address which he had prepared for the occasion.[1] This address, so compact in construction of language; so dignified and patriotic; so mild, yet so severe, and, withal, so vitally important in its relation to the well-being of the unfolding republic and the best interests of human freedom, I here give entire, in a foot-note, for a mere synopsis can not do it justice.[2]

---

[1] Major Robert Burnet, of Little Britain, Orange county, who was one of the officers present, informed me that the most profound silence pervaded the assembly when Washington arose to read his address. As he put on his spectacles,* he said, "You see, gentlemen, that I have not only grown *gray* but *blind* in your service." This simple remark, under such circumstances, had a powerful effect upon the assemblage. Humphreys, in his *Life of Putnam*, mentions this circumstance; so, also, does Mr. Hamilton, in the *Life* of his father.

[2] "GENTLEMEN,—By an anonymous summons, an attempt has been made to convene you together; how inconsistent with the rules of propriety, how unmilitary, and how subversive of all order and discipline, let the good sense of the army decide. In the moment of this summons, another anonymous production was sent into circulation, addressed more to the feelings and passions than to the reason and judgment of the army. The author of the piece is entitled to much credit for the goodness of his pen, and I could wish he had as much credit for the rectitude of his heart; for, as men see through different optics, and are induced by the reflecting faculties of the mind to use different means to attain the same end, the author of the address should have had more charity than to mark for suspicion the man who should recommend moderation and longer forbearance; or, in other words, who should not think as he thinks, and act as he advises.

"But he had another plan in view, in which candor and liberality of sentiment, regard to justice, and love of country have no part; and he was right to insinuate the darkest suspicion to effect the blackest design. That the address is drawn with great art, and is designed to answer the most insidious purposes : that it is calculated to impress the mind with an idea of premeditated injustice in the sovereign power of the United States, and rouse all those resentments which must unavoidably flow from such a belief; that the secret mover of this scheme, whoever he may be, intended to take advantage of the passions while they were warmed by the recollection of past distresses, without giving time for cool, deliberate thinking, and that composure of mind which is so necessary to give dignity and stability to measures, is rendered too obvious, by the mode of conducting the business, to need other proofs than a reference to the proceedings.

"Thus much, gentlemen, I have thought it incumbent on me to observe to you, to show upon what principles I opposed the irregular and hasty meeting which was proposed to have been held on Tuesday last, and not because I wanted a disposition to give you every opportunity, consistent with your own honor and the dignity of the army, to make known your grievances. If my conduct heretofore has not evinced to you that I have been a faithful friend to the army, my declaration of it at this time would be equally unavailing and improper. But, as I was among the first who embarked in the cause of our common country; as I have never left your side one moment, but when called from you on public duty; as I have been the constant companion and witness of your distresses, and not among the last to feel and acknowledge your merits; as I have ever considered my own military reputation as inseparably connected with that of the army; as my heart has ever expanded with joy when I have heard its praises, and my indignation has arisen when the mouth of detraction has been opened against it, it can scarcely be supposed, at this last stage of the war, that I am indifferent to its interests. But how are they to be promoted? The way is plain, says the anonymous addresser. "If war continues, remove into the unsettled country; there establish yourselves, and leave an ungrateful country to defend itself." But who are they to defend? Our wives, our children, our farms, and other property which we leave behind us? or, in this state of hostile separation, are we to take the two first (the latter can not be removed), to perish in a wilderness, with hunger, cold, and nakedness?

"If peace takes place, never sheathe your swords," says he, "until you have obtained full and ample justice. This dreadful alternative of either deserting our country in the extremest hour of her distress, or turning our arms against it—which is the apparent object—unless Congress can be compelled into instant compliance, has something so shocking in it, that humanity revolts at the idea. My God! what can this writer have in view by recommending such measures? Can he be a friend to the army? Can he be a friend to this country? Rather, is he not an insidious foe? some emissary, perhaps, from New York, plotting the

---

* It is said that the identical spectacles used by Washington during the Revolution are now (1850) in the possession of an aged lady, named Marsh, who resides in Detroit, Michigan. They came to her from a deceased relative, who exchanged spectacles with the general. "They are of a heavy silver frame," says the Detroit Advertiser, "with very large, round glasses, and apparently constructed after the style we have been accustomed to see, in the books, upon the nose of Red Riding Hood's grandmother.'

After reading the address, Washington retired without uttering a word, leaving the officers to deliberate without restraint. Their conference was brief; their deliberations short. They passed resolutions, by unanimous vote, thanking their chief for the course he had pursued; expressing their unabated attachment to his person and their country; declaring their unshaken confidence in the good faith of Congress, and their determination to bear with patience their grievances, until in due time they should be redressed.[1] These proceedings were

---

ruin of both, by sowing the seeds of discord and separation between the civil and military powers of the Continent? And what a compliment does he pay to our understandings, when he recommends measures, in either alternative, impracticable in their nature?

"But, here, gentlemen, I will drop the curtain, because it would be as imprudent in me to assign my reasons for this opinion, as it would be insulting to your conception to suppose you stood in need of them. A moment's reflection will convince every dispassionate mind of the physical impossibility of carrying either proposal into execution. There might, gentlemen, be an impropriety in my taking notice, in this address to you, of an anonymous production; but the manner in which that performance has been introduced to the army, the effect it was intended to have, together with some other circumstances, will amply justify my observations on the tendency of that writing.

"With respect to the advice given by the author, to suspect the man who shall recommend moderate measures and longer forbearance, I spurn it, as every man, who regards that liberty and reveres that justice for which we contend, undoubtedly must; for, if men are to be precluded from offering their sentiments on a matter which may involve the most serious and alarming consequences that can invite the consideration of mankind, reason is of no use to us. The freedom of speech may be taken away, and dumb and silent we may be led, like sheep, to the slaughter. I can not, in justice to my own belief, and what I have great reason to conceive is the intention of Congress, conclude this address, without giving it as my decided opinion that that honorable body entertains exalted sentiments of the services of the army, and, from a full conviction of its merits and sufferings, will do it complete justice; that their endeavors to discover and establish funds for this purpose have been unwearied, and will not cease till they have succeeded, I have not a doubt. But, like all other large bodies, where there is a variety of different interests to reconcile, their determinations are slow. Why, then, should we distrust them, and, in consequence of that distrust, adopt measures which may cast a shade over that glory which has been so justly acquired, and tarnish the reputation of an army which is celebrated through all Europe for its fortitude and patriotism? And for what is this done? To bring the object we seek nearer? No; most certainly, in my opinion, it will cast it at a greater distance. For myself (and I take no merit in giving the assurance, being induced to it from principles of gratitude, veracity, and justice, a grateful sense of the confidence you have ever placed in me), a recollection of the cheerful assistance and prompt obedience I have experienced from you under every vicissitude of fortune, and the sincere affection I feel for an army I have so long had the honor to command, will oblige me to declare, in this public and solemn manner, that in the attainment of complete justice for all your toils and dangers, and in the gratification of every wish, so far as may be done consistently with the great duty I owe my country, and those powers we are bound to respect, you may freely command my services to the utmost extent of my abilities.

"While I give you these assurances, and pledge myself in the most unequivocal manner to exert whatever ability I am possessed of in your favor, let me entreat you, gentlemen, on your part, not to take any measures, which, viewed in the calm light of reason, will lessen the dignity and sully the glory you have hitherto maintained. Let me request you to rely on the plighted faith of your country, and place a full confidence in the purity of the intentions of Congress, that, previous to your dissolution as an army, they will cause all your accounts to be fairly liquidated, as directed in the resolutions which were published to you two days ago, and that they will adopt the most effectual measures in their power to render ample justice to you for your faithful and meritorious services. And let me conjure you, in the name of our common country, as you value your own sacred honor, as you respect the rights of humanity, and as you regard the military and national character of America, to express your utmost horror and detestation of the man who wishes, under any specious pretenses, to overturn the liberties of our country, and who wickedly attempts to open the flood-gates of civil discord, and deluge our rising empire in blood.

"By thus determining and thus acting, you will pursue the plain and direct road to the attainment of your wishes; you will defeat the insidious designs of our enemies, who are compelled to resort from open force to secret artifice; you will give one more distinguished proof of unexampled patriotism and patient virtue rising superior to the pressure of the most complicated sufferings; and you will, by the dignity of your conduct, afford occasion for posterity to say, when speaking of the glorious example you have exhibited to mankind, 'Had this day been wanting, the world had never seen the last stage of perfection to which human nature is capable of attaining.'—*Journals of Congress*, viii., 180–183.

[1] One of the resolutions is expressed in the following strong language:

"*Resolved unanimously*, That the officers of the American army view with abhorrence and reject with disdain the infamous propositions contained in a late anonymous address to the officers of the army, and resent with indignation the secret attempts of some unknown persons to collect the officers together in a manner totally subversive of all discipline and good order."

signed by General Gates, as president of the meeting; and on the 18th, Washing- ton, in general orders, expressed his entire satisfaction. All the papers relating to the affair were transmitted to Congress, and entered at length upon their Journals.[1] March, 1783.

It was in this old building at Newburgh, on the porch of which we are sitting, that Washington wrote his address to the officers, on the occasion just considered; and here, also, he penned his admirable circular letter addressed to the governors of all the states, on dis- banding the army. This was his last official communication with these function- aries. "This letter," says Sparks, "is remarkable for its ability, the deep interest it manifests for the officers and soldiers who had fought the battles of their country, the soundness of its principles, and the wisdom of its counsels. Four great points he aims to enforce, as essential in guiding the deliberations of every public body, and as claiming the serious attention of every citizen, namely, an indissoluble union of the states; a sacred re- gard to public justice; the adoption of a proper military peace establishment;[2] and a pacific and friendly disposition among the people of the states which should induce them to forget local prejudices, and incline them to mutual concessions for the advantage of the community. These he calls the pillars by which alone independence and national character can be sup- ported. On each of these topics he remarks at considerable length, with a felicity of style and cogency of reasoning in all respects worthy of the subject. No public address could have been better adapted to the state of the times; and coming from such a source, its in- fluence on the minds of the people must have been effectual and most salutary."[3] The Legislatures that were then in session passed resolves highly commendatory of the public acts of the commander-in-chief; and he received letters from several of the governors, ex- pressing their thanks and gratitude for his long and successful services in the cause of his country. June 8, 1783.

Many of the troops now went home on furlough, and Washington, having leisure, pro-

---

At that time the author of the anonymous addresses was unknown except to a few; and for forty years there was no certainty in the public mind that Major Armstrong was the writer. That he was generally suspected of being the author, among those who were acquainted with his abilities, is evident from a letter to him written by Colonel Timothy Pickering, in after years, in which he says, that so certain was he, at the time, of the identity of the author, that he endorsed the copy of the address which he received, "Writ- ten by Major John Armstrong, Jr." An article appeared in the January number of the *United States Magazine* for 1823, in which the author, understood to be General Armstrong, avowed himself the writer of the Newburgh Addresses. The article in question contains a history of the event we have been just con- sidering, and defends the course of the writer on that occasion with the plea that apparent urgent necessity justified the act. Subsequent events proved the writer to be mistaken in his views, and his proposition to be highly dangerous to the common good. General Armstrong has, consequently, been greatly censured, and his patriotism has been questioned by writers and speakers who have judged him by results instead of by the circumstances in which he was placed. I can see no reason to doubt the purity of his motives and the sincerity of his patriotism. Other men, as we have noticed in a preceding note, who were far above suspicion, held similar views. Unfortunately for his reputation, in this particular, he was the aid-de-camp and confident of Gates, whose ambition had made him a plotter against Washington. In fact, the com- mander-in-chief plainly alluded to Gates, when, writing to Hamilton concerning the scheme, he said that some believed it to be "the illegitimate offspring of a person in the army."

It appears that the first president was made acquainted with the authorship of these addresses toward the close of his second administration, some fourteen years after they were penned. His estimate of the motives of the writer may be understood by the following letter, addressed to Armstrong:

"Philadelphia, February 23d, 1797.

"SIR,—Believing that there may be times and occasions on which my opinion of the anonymous letters and the author, as delivered to the army in the year 1783, may be turned to some personal and malignant purpose, I do hereby declare, that I did not, at the time of writing my address, regard you as the author of said letters; and further, that I have since had sufficient reason for believing that the object of the author was just, honorable, and friendly to the country, though the means suggested by him were certainly liable to much misunderstanding and abuse.

"I am, sir, with great regard, your most obedient servant,   GEORGE WASHINGTON."

[1] *Journals of Congress,* vol. viii.
[2] Washington proposed the establishment of a military academy at West Point as early as April, 1783 His proposition will be hereafter noticed.
[3] Sparks's *Life and Writings of Washington,* i., 395.

680   PICTORIAL FIELD-BOOK

Washington's Tour to the Northern Battle Fields.   Called to Princeton.   A Statue ordered by Congress.   General Clinton.

ceeded up the Hudson with Governor Clinton to visit the principal fields of military operations at the north. He passed over the battle ground at Stillwater, with Generals Schuyler and Gansevoort, and extended his journey as far northward as Ticonderoga and Crown Point, and westward to Fort Schuyler (now Rome), on the Mohawk. He returned to Newburgh after an absence of nineteen days, where he found a letter from the President of Congress requesting his attendance upon that body, then in session at Princeton, in New Jersey. While he was awaiting the convalescence of Mrs. Washington, and preparing to go, Congress conferred upon the chief the distinguished honor of voting, unanimously, that an equestrian statue of him should be executed by the best artist in Europe, under the direction of the minister of the United States at the court of Versailles, and erected at the place where the residence of Congress should be established.[1] Like other similar memorials authorized by Congress to be made in honor of their servants, this statue has never been constructed.

Upon the lawn before us, now covered with the matted and dull-green grass of autumn, Washington parted with many of his subalterns and soldiers forever, on the day he left the army to attend upon Congress at Princeton. It was an affecting prelude to the final parting with his official companions in arms at Fraunce's tavern, in New York, a few months subsequently, and furnishes a noble subject for the pencil of art. The scenery is beautiful and grand, and here I would fain loiter all the day, musing upon the events which hallow the spot; but the sun has climbed high toward meridian, and I must hasten away to adjacent localities, all of which are full of interest.

August 18, 1783.

I left Newburgh toward noon, and rode down to New Windsor, two miles below, along a fine sandy road upon the beach. The little village, once the rival of Newburgh, is nestled in a pleasant nook near the confluence of Chambers's Creek with the Hudson, on the western rim of the bay. Its sheltered position and fertile acres wooed the exploring emigrants from Ireland, who were seeking a place whereon to pitch their tents on the banks of the Hudson, and here some of them sat down. Among them was Charles Clinton; and at a place called Little Britain, a few miles interior, were born his four sons; two of whom, James and George, were distinguished men of the Revolution. The former was a major general in the army, and the latter a brigadier, and Governor of New York during the contest.

1731.

New Windsor claims the distinction of being the birth-place of Governor Dewitt Clinton, a son of General James Clinton;

[1] The following is a description of the proposed statue, as given in the resolution of Congress adopted on the 7th of August, 1783:

"*Resolved,* That the statue be of bronze: the general to be represented in a Roman dress, holding a truncheon in his right hand, and his head encircled with a laurel wreath. The statue to be supported by a marble pedestal, on which are to be represented, in basso relievo, the following principal events of the war, in which General Washington commanded in person, viz., the evacuation of Boston; the capture of the Hessians at Trenton; the battle of Princeton; the action of Monmouth; and the surrender of York. On the upper part of the front of the pedestal to be engraved as follows: The United States in Congress assembled, ordered this statue to be erected in the year of our Lord 1783, in honor of George Washington, the illustrious commander-in-chief of the armies of the United States of America, during the war which vindicated and secured their liberty, sovereignty, and independence."

[2] A biographical sketch of General Clinton may be found on page 272, *ante,* and also a brief notice of his father on page 255.

but evidence is adduced to prove that a violent snow storm, which detained his mother at "the Fort," in Deerpark, the residence of her brother, deprived the village of the intended honor.[1] Although denied the distinction of the paternity of a great man, it can boast the residence, for a time, of one of the smallest of women, beautiful, witty, and good. The name of this "pretty, charming little creature" was Anna Brewster; her height, in womanhood, three feet; her symmetry of form perfect; her face sweet and intelligent; her mind active and pure; her extraction truly noble, for her ancestor was Elder Brewster, of the May Flower. Too little to be wooed, too wise to be won, she was loved and admired by every body. She lived a charming maiden until she was seventy-five years old, when she died. Fifty years before, a rustic poet, inspired by her charms during an evening 1844. passed in her company, portrayed her character in verse.[2] Mrs. Washington, pleased with the sprightly little maiden, invited her, on one occasion, to visit her at head-quarters while the chief was at New Windsor,[3] but she declined, believing it to be curiosity rather than respect that prompted the invitation. It was a mistake; but she had through life such a dignified self-respect, that it repelled undue familiarity, and closed all opportunities for the indulgence of prying curiosity.

From New Windsor I rode to Plum Island, or Plum Point, the fine estate of Philip A. Verplanck, Esq. At high tide, this alluvial height, which rises about one hundred and twenty feet above the Hudson, is an island, approached by a narrow causeway from the main, which bridges a rivulet, with a heavy stone arch. Murderer's Creek washes its southwestern border, and a marsh and rivulet inclose it upon the land side. Upon a broad, level table-land of some thirty-five acres in extent, stands the mansion of Mr. Verplanck, noted for the beauty and grandeur of the scenery which encompasses it. Accompanied by the proprietor, I strolled down the winding pathway to the base of the steep river bank, where, overgrown by a new forest, are well-preserved remains of a fortification, erected there

REMAINS OF FORTIFICATIONS AT PLUM POINT.[4]

[1] See Eager's *History of Orange County*, page 630.

[2] His poetic effort produced the following

"ACROSTIC.

"A pretty, charming little creature,
N eat and complete in every feature,
N ow at New Windsor may be seen,
A ll beauteous in her air and mien.
B irth and power, wealth and fame,
R ise not to view when her we name:
E very virtue in her shine,
W isely nice, but not o'er fine.
S he has a soul that's great, 'tis said,
T hough small's the body of this maid:
E 'en though the casket is but small,
R eason proclaims the jewel's all."

October 8, 1794.

[3] Washington established his head-quarters at New Windsor village, first on the 23d of June, 1779, and again toward the close of 1780, where he remained till the summer of 1781. He lived at a plain Dutch house, long since decayed and demolished. In that humble tenement Lady Washington entertained the most distinguished officers and their ladies, as well as the more obscure who sought her friendship. On leaving New Windsor in June, 1781, Washington established his quarters, for a short time, at Peekskill.

[4] This view is from the interior of the redoubt looking eastward upon the river. In the distance is seen Pollopel's Island, near the upper entrance to the Highlands, beyond which rise the lofty Beacon Hills, whereon alarm-fires often gleamed during the war.

partly at an early period of the war, and partly when the American army was in the vicinity. It was a redoubt, with a battery of fourteen guns, and was designed to cover strong *chevaux-de-frise* and other obstructions placed in the river, and extending from the flat below Murderer's Creek to Pollopel's Island.[1] It would also rake the river channel at the opening in the Highlands. The *chevaux-de-frise* were constructed under the superintendence of Captain Thomas Machin, in the summer of 1778. Had they and the strong redoubt on Plum Point been in existence a year sooner, the marauding expedition of Vaughan and Wallace, up the Hudson, could not have occurred. The remains of this battery, the old Continental road, and the cinders of the forges, extend along the river bank several hundred feet. The embrasures are also very prominent.

Mr. Verplanck pointed out the remains of the cellar of a log-house, which stood a little above the battery, and belonged to a man named M'Evers, long before the Revolution. M'Evers was a Scotchman, and when about to emigrate to America, he asked his servant, Mike, if he would accompany him. Mike, who was faithful, and much attached to his master, at once consented to go, saying, in illustration of the force of his love, "Indeed, gude mon, I'll follow ye to the gates o' hell, if ye gang there yersel'." The voyage was long and tempestuous, and instead of entering New York harbor by the Narrows, the vessel sailed through Long Island Sound and the East River. At the whirlpool called *Hellgate*, the ship struck upon the *Hog's Back* with a terrible crash. The passengers, in affright, rushed upon deck, and none was more appalled than Mike. "What place is it?" he exclaimed. "*Hellgate*," was the short reply of a sailor. "God ha' mercy on me!" groaned Mike; "I promised my master I'd follow him to the *gate* o' hell, but I didna' say I'd gang *through* with him!" The vessel floated off with the tide, arrived safely in New York, and Mike lived to be a gardener on Plum Point.

A pleasant ride of about three miles westward from Plum Point placed me at the residence of Charles F. Morton, Esq., a picturesque old mansion on the south side of the New Windsor road. It was built about 1735[2] by John Ellison, one of the first settlers in New Windsor. The material is stone, and its dormer windows and spacious and irregular roof give it the appearance of a large cottage in rural England. A living stream passes through a rocky glen within a few yards of it. Just below is the old mill, erected more than a hundred

HEAD-QUARTERS OF GREENE AND KNOX.[3]

years ago by the first proprietor; nor has the monotonous music of its stones and hopper yet ceased.

This old mansion was the head-quarters of Generals Greene and Knox while Washington was domiciled at the Hasbrouck House in Newburgh, and it was from hence that the com-

---

[1] According to a survey made by Henry Wisner and Gilbert Livingston in the autumn of 1776, the channel of the river, wherein these *chevaux-de-frise* were placed, was about fifty feet deep, and eighty chains, or about five thousand two hundred and eighty feet broad. The channel east of Pollopel's Island was not deep enough for the passage of ships of war.

[2] One of the fire-places has a cast-iron back, on which, in raised letters, is the date 1734.

[3] This view is from the turnpike road, looking southeast. The water in front is a mill-pond, over the dam of which passes a foot-bridge. The mill is hidden by the trees in the ravine below. This side was originally the rear of the house, the old Goshen road passing upon the other side. The old front is a story and a half high. Captain Morton, the proprietor, is a son of the late General Jacob Morton, of New York city.

mander-in-chief, accompanied by those generals, after taking some refreshments, rode to the "New Building," to attend the meeting of officers convened by Washington on account of the anonymous addresses just considered. Here the accomplished Lucy Knox gave her choice *soirées*, graced by the presence of Mrs. Washington, and other ladies of taste and refinement with which that region abounded; and here, if tradition is truthful, Washington opened a ball on one occasion, having for his partner Maria Colden, then one of the pretty belles of Orange county.[1]

I dined with Mr. Morton in the old drawing-room, which, with the other apartments, is preserved by him, with scrupulous care, in the original style. The ceilings are high, and the wainscoting displays architectural taste. The heavy window-sashes, with their small squares of glass, remain; very few of the panes have been broken and replaced since the Revolution. On one of them, inscribed by a diamond, are the names of three young ladies of the "olden time" (Sally Janson, Gitty Winkoop, and Maria Colden), one of whom was the reputed partner of Washington at the ball. May not these names have been written on that occasion? Believing it probable, I copied the signatures, and present them here for the gratification of the curious and the sentimental.

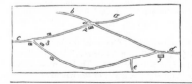

In October, 1777, the vicinage we are now considering was the scene of much commotion. Forts Clinton and Montgomery, among the Hudson Highlands, fell beneath one heavy blow, suddenly and artfully dealt by a British force from New York, and the smitten garrisons were scattered like frightened sheep upon the mountains; not, however, until they had disputed the possession of the fortresses with the besiegers long and desperately. General James Clinton and his brother George were in command of the fortresses, and escaped up the river. At a place afterward called *Washington Square*,[2] about four

October 6, 1777.

---

[1] I was informed by the venerable Mrs. Hamilton that Washington *never danced*. He often attended balls by invitation, and sometimes *walked* the figures, but she never saw him attempt to dance. Probably no lady of that day, if we except Mrs. Knox, was more often at parties and social gatherings with Washington than Mrs. Hamilton.

It may not be inappropriate here to give a copy of a letter on the subject of dancing, written by Washington a short time before his death. It was in reply to an invitation from a committee of gentlemen of Alexandria to attend the dancing assemblies at that place. I copied it from the original in the Alexandria Museum.

"*To Messrs. Jonathan Swift, George Deneale, William Newton, Robert Young, Charles Alexander, Jr., James H. Hoole, Managers.*

"Mount Vernon, 12th November, 1799.

"GENTLEMEN,—Mrs. Washington and myself have been honored with your polite invitation to the assemblies of Alexandria this winter, and thank you for this mark of your attention. But, alas! our dancing days are no more. We wish, however, all those who have a relish for so agreeable and innocent an amusement all the pleasure the season will afford them; and I am, gentlemen,

"Your most obedient and obliged humble servant,
"GEO. WASHINGTON."

[2] "The Square" is a small district of country, and so called from the fact that the public roads ran in such a drection as to form a diamond-shaped inclosure, as seen in the diagram, in which *a* is the road to Newburgh; *b*, to Goshen; *c*, to Little Britain; and *d*, to New Windsor. 1 denotes the house of Mrs. Falls; 2, the quarters of St. Clair and Gates;* and, 3, the quarters of La Fayette.

* There are two ancient houses at this angle of "The Square," but I could not ascertain which was occupied by those officers. It is probable, however, that the one on the northwest side of the road, which is supposed to have been Edmonston's, was the one.

miles west of the village of New Windsor, Governor Clinton established his head-quarters at the house of a Mrs. Falls, and there the dispersed troops were collected, preparatory to their marching for the defense of Kingston.

At about noon on the 10th of October, 1777. a horseman, apparently in great haste, approached the disordered camp. The sentinel on duty challenged him, when he replied, "I am a friend, and wish to see General Clinton." The horseman was a messenger, bearing a secret dispatch from Sir Henry Clinton to Burgoyne, the latter being then hedged round by the Americans at Saratoga. The messenger supposed the American forces in the Highlands to be utterly broken and destroyed, and having never heard of a *general* Clinton[2]

MRS. FALLS'S.[1]

in the patriot army, he believed himself to be among his friends. He was conducted to Clinton's quarters, and, when ushered into his presence, he perceived his mistake. "I am lost!" he exclaimed, in a half subdued voice, and immediately cast something into his mouth and swallowed it. Suspicion was aroused, and he was arrested. Dr. Moses Higby, who was then residing near Mrs. Falls's, was summoned. He administered to the prisoner a powerful dose of tartar emetic, which soon brought from his stomach a silver bullet of an oval form. Though closely watched, the prisoner succeeded in swallowing it a second time. He now refused the emetic, but yielded when Governor Clinton threatened to hang him upon a tree and search his stomach by the aid of the surgeon's knife. The bullet again appeared. It was a curiously-wrought hollow sphere, fastened together in the center by a compound screw. Within it was found a piece of thin paper, on which was written the following note :[3]

"Fort Montgomery, October 8, 1777.

" *Nous y voici,*[4] and nothing now between us and Gates. I sincerely hope this little success of ours may facilitate your operations. In answer to your letter of the 28th of September, by C. C.,[5] I shall only say, I can not presume to order, or even advise, for reasons obvious. I heartily wish you success.

"Faithfully yours,   H. CLINTON.

"GEN. BURGOYNE."

The prisoner's guilt was clear ; *out of his own mouth* he was condemned. Governor Clinton soon afterward marched to Esopus, or Kingston, taking the spy with him. At Hurley, a few miles from Kingston, he was tried, condemned, and hanged upon an apple-tree near the old church, while the village of Esopus was in flames, lighted by the marauding enemy.[6]

---

[1] This house, now (1850) owned by Mr. Samuel Moore, is a frame building, and stands on the right side of the New Windsor road, at the southeastern angle of "The Square." It is surrounded by locust and large balm-of-Gilead trees. There Major Armstrong wrote the famous *Newburgh Addresses,* and there those in the secret held their private conferences.

[2] The British officers in this country adhered pertinaciously to the resolution of not dignifying the *rebel* officers with their assumed titles. They were called Mr. Washington, Mr. Clinton, Mr. Greene, &c. It is amusing to look over the Tory newspapers of the day, particularly Rivington's Gazette, and observe the flippant and attempted witty manner in which the American generalissimo was styled *Mister* Washington.

[3] Letter of Governor Clinton to the Council of Safety, dated "Head-quarters, Mrs. Falls's, 11th October, 1777."

[4] "Here we are." I copied this note from a transcript in the handwriting of Governor Clinton, which is among the manuscripts of General Gates in the library of the New York Historical Society. It is endorsed "Sir Henry Clinton to J. Burgoyne, 8th of October, 1777, found in a silver bullet." That identical bullet was, a few years ago, in the possession of the late General James Tallmadge, executor of the will of Governor George Clinton. It is now the property of one of Clinton's descendants.

[5] Captain Campbell. See page 79, vol. i.

[6] The name of the spy was Daniel Taylor. He was a sergeant in the British service. The father of the

Leaving Mr. Morton's, I proceeded to visit the site of the "New Building," or *Temple*, as it was called, where the meeting of officers was held. It is in a field now belonging to Mr. William M·Gill (formerly to the late Jabez Atwood), upon a commanding eminence about one hundred rods east of the road to Newburgh, and two miles northward of Morton's. The day was foggy and drizzly, and the distant scenery was entirely hidden from view; but, on a second visit, upon a bright summer day, with some Newburgh friends, I enjoyed the magnificent prospect to be obtained from that observatory. On the southeast loomed the lofty Highlands, cleft by the Hudson; North and South Beacons, and Butter Hill, rising above their hundred lesser companions, were grouped in a picture of magnificence and beauty. Glittering in meridian sunlight were the white houses of Cornwall and Canterbury; and far up the slopes of the

THE TEMPLE.[1]

mountains, stretching westward to Woodcock Hill, yellow grain-fields and acres of green maize variegated the landscape. In the far distance, on the northwest, was the upper Shawangunk range, and an occasional glimpse was caught of the blue high peaks of the Catskills, sixty miles northward. Across the meadows westward we could distinctly trace the line of

the old causeway, constructed while the army was encamped there; and in the groves which skirt the slopes (whither we soon afterward went) we found the remains of several huts that were built for the use of the soldiers.

The *Temple* was a large, temporary structure, erected by command of Washington for the several purposes of a chapel for the army, a lodge-room for the fraternity of Free-masons which existed

VIEW OF THE CAMP GROUND.[2]

late Judge Woodward, of the Supreme Court of the State of New York, acted as judge-advocate on the occasion. On page 389, *ante*, I have alluded to this occurrence, and remarked that Kingston was the place of the execution of the spy. Hurley was then included in the township of Kingston.

[1] This view is from the site of the *Temple*, looking southeast. In the distance is seen the opening of the Highlands into Newburgh Bay. On the right is Butter Hill, and near it is the village of Cornwall. The form and appearance of the *Temple* was drawn from the description given by Major Burnet, and doubtless has a general resemblance to the original.

[2] This is from a painting by Tice, in my possession. The land on which the encampment on the west side of the meadow was, is now owned chiefly by Gilbert Tompkins and Nathaniel Moore. This view is from the land of Mr. Tompkins, looking east-southeast. On the slopes seen in the foreground, and on the margin of the meadow beyond, Van Cortlandt's New York regiment, and the Maryland and Virginia troops were encamped. On the east side of the meadow, upon the most distant elevation in the middle ground, the New England troops were stationed. On the slope toward the right of that elevation stood the *Temple*. In the distance is seen the upper entrance of the Hudson into the Highlands. The meadow was formerly called Beaver Dam Swamp, from the circumstance that beavers constructed dams at the lower extremity, causing the waters to overflow the low grounds. The Americans built a causeway across, and a stone dike, or *levee*, on the west side, to protect their parade. I saw the remains of this causeway; its site is marked by the light line across the flat. About a quarter of a mile north of the site of the *Temple* is an ancient stone house, seen in the picture, the only dwelling near in the time of the war. It was built by Samuel P. Brewster in 1768, as appears from an inscribed stone in the front wall. It was owned by a Mr. Moore. Its present occupant is Francis Weyant

686   PICTORIAL FIELD-BOOK

The Temple as described by Major Burnet.   Two living Patriots.   Visit to Major Burnet.

among the officers, and for public meetings of various kinds.   When erected, it was called *The Temple of Virtue;* when dedicated, the suffix was properly omitted, and it was named simply *The Temple.*   The orgies held on the occasion of its dedication disrobed it of its mantle of purity.   It was described to me by Major Burnet, who is still living (1851) in the neighborhood, as a structure of rough-hewn logs, oblong square in form, one story in height, a door in the middle, many windows, and a broad roof.   The windows were square, unglazed, and about the size of ordinary port-holes in a man-of-war.   There was a small gallery, or raised platform, at one end, for speakers and presiding officers.   We traced, near an old apple-tree in Mr. M'Gill's field, evident lines of the foundation of the building.   It must have been some eighty feet long and forty wide.   On the crown of the hill northward are traces of fire-places, and there, at the beginning of the present century, a long building was standing.   Some have supposed this to have been the *Temple;* it was only the barracks for the New England troops stationed there.   In a few years those faint land-marks and that old apple-tree will be no more seen.   The spot is consecrated by one of the loftiest exhibitions of true patriotism with which our Revolutionary history abounds.   There love of country, and devotion to exalted principles, achieved a wonderful triumph over the seductive power of self-love and individual interest, goaded into rebellion against higher motives by the lash of apparent injustice and personal suffering.   It is, indeed, a hallowed spot ; and if the old stone house at Newburgh is worthy of the fostering regard of the state because it was the head-quarters of the beloved Washington, surely the site of the *Temple,* where he achieved his most glorious victory, deserves some monument to perpetuate the memory of its place and associations.

At Little Britain, a few miles from the *Temple,* and within a quarter of a mile of each other, reside two of the sons of Orange county, who loved and served Washington and their country in the war for independence. These are ROBERT BURNET and USUAL KNAPP. Of the once long list of Revolutionary pensioners in Orange county, these only remain, honored living witnesses of the prowess of those who wrestled successfully for freedom.   I left the *Temple* field on the occasion of my first visit with the intention of seeing these patriot fathers, but missing the proper road, and the night shadows coming thickly with the fog and rain, I made my way back to Newburgh.

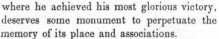

Kind friends afterward procured likenesses and autographs of both for me.[1]   Better than this, I subsequently enjoyed the pleasure of a personal interview with Major Burnet at his residence.   It was on the occasion of my second visit to the camp ground.   At dark, on that August 1, 1850. sultry day, we made our way up a green lane, flanked by venerable willows—a few cast down by a recent tornado—and sat down in the spacious hall of the old soldier's man-

---

[1] I am indebted to Mr. Charles U. Cushman, of Newburgh, for a daguerreotype, from life, of Major Burnet, from which the picture above was copied.   The likeness of Mr. Knapp is from an excellent painting of the almost centenarian's head, by Mr. Charles W. Tice, an accomplished self-taught artist of Newburgh, who kindly furnished me with a copy for my use.

OF THE REVOLUTION. 687

Public Life of Major Burnet and Sergeant Knapp.   Washington's Letter to Greene.

sion. He had just retired to his bed-room, but soon appeared, standing before us as erect and manly as if in the prime of his life, although then in his ninetieth year.

The father of Major Burnet was a Scotchman, his mother a native of Ireland. He was a lieutenant in Captain Stevens's company, and commanded Redoubt No. 3, at West Point, at the time of Arnold's defection. He afterward attained to the rank of major in the service, and was one of the delegates who attended the meeting of officers at the *Temple*.[1] He continued in the army, under the immediate command of the chief, until the disbanding of the forces in 1783. When the Americans marched into the city of New York as the British evacuated it, he commanded the rear guard. He told me that he remembered distinctly the dignified appearance of Washington, when, with Governor November 25, 1783. Clinton and other civil and military officers, he stood in front of an old stone house,[2] about two miles below Kingsbridge, while the troops, with uncovered heads, passed by. He saw Cunningham, the wicked provost-marshal at New York, strongly guarded by his friends, in the march to the place of embarkation, while the exasperated populace were eager to seize and punish him according to his deservings.

Major Burnet was also present when Washington finally parted with his officers at Fraunce's[3] tavern, in New York. How could the heart do otherwise than beat quick and

strong with deep feeling, while conversing face to face with one who grasped the hand of the chief on that occasion, so pathetically described by Marshall and others! The lips of the patriot quivered with emotion while speaking of that scene, and I perceived my own eye dimmed with the rheum of sympathetic sentiment. Major Burnet has seen, what few men in modern times have beheld, the living representatives of seven generations of his kindred : his great-grandfather, grandfather, father, himself, his children, grandchildren, and great-grandchildren.[4]

It was late when we said farewell to Major Burnet — too late to visit his neighbor, Mr. Knapp, who was ninety-one years of age, and quite feeble. From another I learned the principal events of his public life, and obtained his autograph, a facsimile of which is here given, with his portrait. Mr. Knapp was born in Connecticut, in 1759. He joined the army when about eighteen years of age. His first experience in warfare was in the battle at White Plains ; afterward he served under General Wooster in the skirmish at Ridgefield.[5] When La Fayette

---

[1] Washington, in a letter to General Greene, dated "Newburgh, 6th February, 1782," refers to Mr. Burnet as follows : "I intended to write you a long letter on sundry matters ; but Major Burnet came unexpectedly at a time when I was preparing for the celebration of the day, and was just going to a review of the troops previous to the *feu de joie*.* As he is impatient, from an apprehension that the sleighing may fail, and as he can give you the occurrences of this quarter more in detail than I have time to do, I will refer you to him."

[2] This stone house is yet standing. A drawing of it may be found in another part of this work. It has other interesting reminiscences.

[3] This tavern, now (1850) the Broad Street Hotel, is well preserved. It stands on the corner of Broad and Pearl Streets. A drawing of it may be found on page 633, vol. ii.

[4] Died Dec. 1, 1854, aged 92 years and 9 months.   [5] See page 408.

---

* The anniversary of the signing of the treaty of alliance between the United States and France is here alluded to.

enrolled his corps of light infantry, Mr. Knapp became a member, and with them fought in the battle at Monmouth, in June, 1778.[1] He was soon afterward chosen a member of the *Commander-in-chief's Guard*, and served faithfully as a sergeant therein for more than two years. He left the service in 1782, bearing the approbation of Washington. He is believed to be the only surviving member of that well-disciplined corps of the Revolution, WASHINGTON'S LIFE GUARD.[2] Although feeble in body, I was informed that his mind was

---

[1] Many of the muskets which belonged to that corps are now preserved in the *Relic Room* of the Head-quarters at Newburgh. La Fayette purchased them with his own money in France, and presented them to his favorite corps.

[2] *The Commander-in-chief's Guard*, commonly called *The Life Guard*, was a distinct corps of superior men, attached to the person of the commander-in-chief, but never spared in battle. It was organized in 1776, soon after the siege of Boston, while the American army was encamped upon York or Manhattan Island, near the city of New York. It consisted of a major's command—one hundred and eighty men. Caleb Gibbs, of Rhode Island, was its first chief, and bore the title of *captain commandant*. He held that office until the close of 1779, when he was succeeded by William Colfax, one of his lieutenants. Gibbs's lieutenants were Henry P. Livingston, of New York, William Colfax, of New Jersey, and Benjamin Goymes, of Virginia. Colonel Nicholas, of Virginia, was a lieutenant under Colfax. The latter officer remained in command of the corps until the disbanding of the army in 1783. The terms of enlistment into the *Guard* were the same as those into any other corps of the regular army, except in the matter of qualification. They were selected with special

SIGNATURES OF THE OFFICERS OF WASHINGTON'S LIFE GUARD.*

reference to their physical, moral, and intellectual character; and it was considered a mark of peculiar distinction to belong to the *Commander-in-chief's Guard*. From George W. P. Custis, Esq., of Arlington House, Virginia, I learned many particulars respecting this corps. Mr. Custis is a grandson of Lady Washington, and the adopted son of the general. He was acquainted with several of the officers and privates of the *Guard*, distinctly remembers their uniform, and is familiar with their history. He owns a flag which once belonged to the *Guard*. It is now in the museum at Alexandria, on the Potomac, where I sketched the annexed representation of it. The flag is white silk, on which the device is neatly painted. One of the *Guard* is seen holding a horse, and is in the act of receiving a flag from the

BANNER OF WASHINGTON'S LIFE GUARD.

Genius of Liberty, who is personified as a woman leaning upon the Union shield, near which is the American eagle. The motto of the corps, "CONQUER OR DIE," is upon a ribbon. The uniform of the *Guard* consisted of a blue coat with white facings, white waistcoat and breeches, black half gaiters, a cocked hat with a blue and white feather. They carried muskets, and occasionally side arms.

The corps varied in numbers at different periods. At first it consisted of one hundred and eighty men. During the winter of 1779–80, when the American army under Washington was cantoned at Morristown, in close proximity to the enemy, it was increased to two hundred and fifty. In the spring it was reduced to its original number; and in 1783, the last year of service, it consisted of only sixty-four non-commissioned officers and privates. Care was always taken to have all the states, from which the Continental army was supplied with troops, represented in this corps.

Peter Force, Esq., of Washington City, kindly allowed me to copy the names of the *Guard*, contained in an original Return in his possession, bearing the date of March 2, 1783. It is signed by Colfax, and on the back is an endorsement in the handwriting of Washington, a fac simile of which is given on the next page. I found in the archives of the State Department another Return, dated June 4th, 1783.† It is one of the last Re-

---

* I copied these signatures from the original oaths of allegiance, signed at Valley Forge, in the spring of 1778, by each officer of the Continental army, and of the militia then in service there. These oaths are carefully preserved in the archives of the State Department at Washington City.

† The following are the names of the non-commissioned officers and privates, from the various states, who constituted the *Commander-in-chief's Guard* on the 4th of June, 1783:

NEW HAMPSHIRE.—Ebenezer Carlton and Samuel Smith, *privates*.

quite active and clear respecting the war-scenes of his youth.   He delights "to fight his battles o'er again," and is pleased when,

> "With cherub smile, the prattling boy,
>   Who on the vet'ran's breast reclines,
> Has thrown aside the favorite toy,
>   And round his tender finger twines
> Those scattered locks, that, with the flight
> Of *ninety* years are snowy white;
> And, as a scar arrests his view,
> He cries, 'Grandpa, what wounded you?'"
>
>   HANNAH F. GOULD.

Broad flashes of sheet lightning, and rumbling thunder, on the van of an approaching shower, made us use the whip freely when we left the dark lane of the patriot. We reached Newburgh at eleven o'clock, wearied and supperless, the tempest close upon us, but in time to escape a drenching. This, be it remembered, was on the occasion of my second visit to the camp ground in New Windsor, in the fervid summer time. Let us resume our narrative of the autumnal tour.

The mist and clouds were gone the next morning. At six o'clock I crossed the Hudson to Fishkill landing, and at half past seven breakfasted at the village, five miles eastward. The air was a little frosty, but as soon as the sun appeared above the hills, the warm breath and soft light of the Indian summer spread their genial influence over the face of nature, and awakened corresponding delight in the heart and mind of the traveler. The country through which the highway passes is exceedingly picturesque. It skirts the deep, rich valleys of Matteawan and Glenham, where flows a clear stream from a distant mountain lake and bubbling spring,[1] turning, in its course, many mill-wheels and thousands of spindles set up along its banks. On the south the lofty range of the eastern Highlands, rocky and abrupt near their summits, come down with gentle declivities, and mingle their rugged forms with the green undulations of the valley. Up their steep slopes, cultivated

October 26, 1848.

turns made to the commander-in-chief, for the army was disbanded soon afterward. The roll is precisely the same as that in possession of Mr. Force, with the exception of the omission of the names of John Dent, *corporal*, and Samuel Wortman, *private*, in the June Return. Dennis Moriarty, who was a *corporal* in March, appears as a *private* in June. The latter Return is signed by Colfax, with his certification that "The above list includes the whole of the Guard." It is endorsed, "Return of the non-commissioned officers and privates in the Commander-in-chief's Guard, who are engaged to serve during the war."

Return of the Com^n in Chiefs Guard 2^d March 1783

I have been thus particular respecting this corps, because history is almost silent upon the subject, and because the living witnesses, now almost extinct, will take with them the unwritten records of the *Guard* into the oblivion of the grave.

[1] The chief sources of this beautiful stream are Whaley's Pond, situated high among the broken hills of the eastern Highlands, on the borders of Pawlings, and a spring at the foot of the mountains in the Clove in Beekman.

MASSACHUSETTS.—John Phillips, *sergeant;* John Herrick, *corporal;* Isaac Manning, *fifer;* Joseph Vinal, John Barton, Joel Crosby, *privates.*

RHODE ISLAND.—Davis Brown, *sergeant;* Randall Smith, Reuben Thompson, William Tanner, Solomon Daley, *privates.*

CONNECTICUT.—Elihu Hancock, *corporal;* Diah Manning [see notice of him on page 607], *drum major;* Jared Goodrich and Frederic Park, *fifers;* Peter Holt, Jedediah Brown, Levi Dean, James Dady, Henry Wakelee, Elijah Lawrence, *privates.*

NEW YORK.—John Robinson, Jacob Schriver, Edward Wiley, John Cole, *privates.*

NEW JERSEY.—Jonathan Moore, Benjamin Eaton, Stephen Hetfield, Lewis Campbell, Samuel Bailey, William Martin, Laban Landor, Robert Blair, Benjamin Bonnel, *privates;* John Fenton, *drummer.*

PENNSYLVANIA.—William Hunter and John Arnold, *sergeants;* Enoch Wills, *corporal;* Cornelius Wilson, *drummer;* Charles Dougherty, William Karnahan, Robert Findley, John Dowthar, John Patton, Hugh Cull, James Hughes, John Finch, Dennis Moriarty, John Montgomery, Daniel Hymer, Thomas Forrest, William Kennessey, Adam Foutz, George Fisher, *privates.*

MARYLAND.—Edward Weed, Jeremiah Driskel, Thomas Gillen, *privates.*

VIRGINIA.—Reaps Mitchell, *sergeant;* Lewis Flemister, William Coram, William Pace, Joseph Timberlake, *privates.*

fields have crept like ivy upon some gray old tower; and there, tinted with all the glories of autumn, they seemed to hang in the soft morning sunlight like rich gobelins in the chamber of royalty.

Fishkill village lies pleasantly in the lap of a plain near the foot of the mountains, and is a place of much interest to the student of our history. Securely sheltered by high mountains from invasion from below, and surrounded by a fertile country, it was chosen as a place of safe depository for military stores; for the confinement of Tory prisoners and others captured by strategy or in partisan skirmishes upon the *Neutral Ground*, in West Chester;

THE WHARTON HOUSE.

and, for a while, as the place of encampment of a portion of the Continental army, and the quiet deliberations of the state Legislature.[1] The barracks were about half a mile south of the village, extending along the line of the road, from the residence of Isaac Van Wyck, branches eastward from the turnpike.

Esq., to the foot of the mountains. The headquarters of the officers were at Mr. Van Wyck's, then the property of a Mr. Wharton. From this circumstance it is known as "The Wharton House." The burial-place of the soldiers is at the foot of the mountains, where a road

Enoch Crosby

This vicinity is the scene of many of the most thrilling events portrayed by Cooper in his "*Spy; a Tale of the Neutral Ground.*" In the Wharton House, Enoch Crosby, the alleged *reality* of the novelist's *fictitious* Harvey Birch, was subjected to a mock trial by the Committee of Safety, and then confined in irons in the old Dutch church in the village. Crosby engaged in the "secret service" of his country in the autumn of 1776, and eminent were his personal achievements in making revelations to his Whig friends of the movements and plans of the Tories. At that period, secret enemies were more to be feared than open foes among these, in West Chester and the southern portions of Dutchess, Crosby mingled freely, for a long time, without incurring their distrust. While on one of his excursions, he solicited lodgings for the night at the house of a woman who proved to be a Tory. From her he learned that a company of Loyalists were forming in the neighborhood to march to

---

[1] The Marquis de Chastellux, who visited Fishkill in the autumn of 1780, says, in his interesting narrative, "This town, in which there are not more than fifty houses in the space of two miles, has been long the principal depôt of the American army. It is there they have placed their magazines, their hospitals, their work-shops, &c.; but all these form a town of themselves, composed of handsome large barracks, built in the wood at the foot of the mountains; for the Americans, like the Romans in many respects, have hardly any other winter quarters than wooden towns or barricaded camps, which may be compared to the *hiemalia* of the Romans."—*Travels in North America*, i., 54.

The war-sword of Washington, carefully preserved in a glass case in the National Museum at Washington City, was manufactured by J. Bailey, in Fishkill, and bears his name. His shop was yet in existence when I was there, but used as a stable. It was demolished in 1849. A drawing of the sword, and of the staff which Franklin bequeathed to Washington, may be found in another part of this work.

[2] This picture is from a sketch from life by Captain H. L. Barnum, the author of a small, thin volume, entitled *The Spy Unmasked*, dedicated to James Fennimore Cooper, Esq. It contains the memoirs of Enoch Crosby, who, the author asserts, was the original of Mr. Cooper's "Harvey Birch." The narratives were taken from Crosby's own lips, in short-hand, by Captain Barnum. Attempts have been made to cast discredit upon the work; but Doctor White, of Fishkill, who kindly accompanied me to the localities in that vicinity, assured me that his father, an aged man still living, was well acquainted with Crosby, and says the narrative of Barnum is substantially correct. Enoch Crosby was a native of Harwich, Barnstable county, in Massachusetts, where he was born on the 4th of January, 1750. During his infancy his parents went to

New York and join the British army.

DUTCH CHURCH, FISHKILL.[2]

He became excessively loyal, and, agreeing to enlist with them, he obtained the unbounded confidence of the captain, who revealed to him all his plans. That night, when all was quiet, Crosby left his bed stealthily, hastened to White Plains, where the Committee of Safety resided,[1] communicated the secrets of the expedition to them, and was back to his lodgings, unobserved, before daylight. At Crosby's suggestion, a meeting of the company was held the following evening, and while in session, the house was surrounded by a band of Whigs, sent for the purpose by the Committee of Safety, and the inmates were all made prisoners. They were conveyed to Fishkill, and confined in manacles in the old stone church, one of the relics of the Revolution yet remaining. The Committee of Safety, who had come up to try them, were at the Wharton House. After an examination, the prisoners were all remanded to prison, Crosby among the

the State of New York, and settled in Southeast, in Dutchess (now Putnam) county. In the midst of the noble and picturesque scenery of that region his childhood was passed. He learned the trade of a shoemaker. When the Revolution broke out, he laid aside his lapstone and last, and shouldered a musket. He was then residing at Danbury, and was one of the hundred men before mentioned, who, in 1775, marched to Lake Champlain, and were engaged in the battles in that quarter until Quebec was stormed. After his return, Crosby remained quiet for a while, and then became engaged in the "secret service." He caused many Tory companies to fall into the hands of the Whigs, and on such occasions he was usually captured, suffered imprisonment, but was generally allowed to escape. At length his successful exits from durance excited the suspicion of the Tories, and Crosby, deeming it unsafe to mingle with them longer, joined the detachment of the Continental army under Heath, then stationed in the Highlands. When his term of service expired, he returned to Southeast, where he cultivated a small farm, until his death in 1834. Captain Barnum asserts that the *plan* of Cooper's *Spy* was conceived at the house of John Jay, at Bedford, in West Chester county. Mr. Jay was one of the Committee of Safety who employed Crosby, and was necessarily acquainted with his exploits. Crosby was a witness at a court in New York city in 1827, and was recognized by an old gentleman, who introduced him to the audience as the original of "Harvey Birch."* The fact became noised abroad. The *Spy*, dramatized, was then in course of performance at one of the theaters; Crosby was invited to attend; his acceptance was announced; and that evening a crowded audience greeted the old soldier. Our gifted countrywoman, Miss Anne C. Lynch, has written thus doubtingly,

"ON A PICTURE OF HARVEY BIRCH.

"I know not if thy noble worth
My country's annals claim,
For in her brief, bright history,
I have not read thy name.

"I know not if thou e'er didst live,
Save in the vivid thought
Of him who chronicled thy life,
With silent suffering fraught.

"Yet in thy history I see
Full many a great soul's lot,
Who joins the martyr-army's ranks,
That the world knoweth not."

[1] The Committee of Safety then consisted of Messrs. Jay, Platt, Duer, and Sackett, distinguished patriots during the Revolution.

[2] This is from a pencil sketch by Miss Newlin, taken from the yard, looking southwest, the same point

* In a monthly historical work, published at Concord, New Hampshire, in 1823, by Jacob B. Moore, Esq., late librarian of the New York Historical Society, is a brief biographical sketch of David Gray, who was a "spy" of the "Neutral Ground." The writer says, "The incidents of his life correspond in many particulars with the character of Harvey Birch, in the popular novel of the 'Spy.'" This was written six years before the publication of "The Spy Unmasked."

rest.   By apparent accident he was left alone with the committee a few minutes, and a plan of escape was devised.   He effected it through a window at the northwest corner of the church, which was hidden by a willow.   On reaching the ground, he divested himself of his loose manacles ; and with the speed of a deer he rushed by the sentinels, and escaped unhurt to a swamp, followed by three or four bullets, fired at random in the gloom.   He was made a prisoner, with Tories, twice afterward, but managed to escape.

Several British and Hessian soldiers were at one time prisoners in the old stone church. The former were captured by stratagem at Teller's Point, near the mouth of the Croton River ; the latter were stragglers, who fell in with a party of Loyalists near Yonkers, on the Neutral Ground.   The British soldiers were captured by Crosby and a few men who composed part of a detachment under Colonel Van Cortlandt, then stationed on the east side of the Hudson to watch operations upon the Neutral Ground.   While they were near Teller's Point, a British sloop of war sailed up the river and cast anchor in the channel opposite. Crosby and six others proceeded to the Point, five of whom, with himself, concealed themselves in the bushes ; the other, dressed in infantry uniform, paraded the beach.   The officers on the vessel observed him, and eleven men were dispatched in a boat to capture him. When the Englishmen landed, the American took to his heels.   Unsuspicious of danger, they followed, when Crosby and his five men, making a noise in the bushes as if half a regiment was there, rushed out and bade the enemy surrender.   Deceived and alarmed, they complied without firing a shot.   The next day they were prisoners in the stone church in Fishkill.

Before visiting the Wharton House, I called upon the Reverend Mr. Kip, the pastor of the old church.   He kindly allowed me to examine the records of the society, which, until a late period, were made in the Dutch language.   They extend back to 1730, at which time, and for many years afterward, the church at Fishkill and another at Poughkeepsie were united, with the title of " The Parish Church at Fishkill and Poughkeepsie."   I could find no account of the building of the church, but there is reason to believe that it was erected about the year 1725.   Mr. Kip showed me a silver tankard, belonging to the communion-service of the church, which was presented to the society by Samuel Verplanck, Esq., chiefly

for the purpose of commemorating, by an inscription upon it, a resident Norwegian, who died at the extraordinary age of six score and eight years.[1]

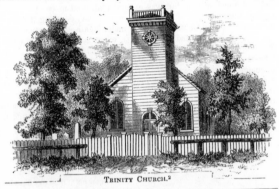

I passed half an hour at the Wharton House, and, returning to the village, sketched the old English church (now called Trinity) by the way.   It stands upon the west side of the road, in the suburbs of the village, and in form is about the same as it was when it was used as an hospital for the

TRINITY CHURCH.[2]

of view from whence I made a drawing, less pleasing to myself than the one kindly furnished me by the fair artist.   The church is built of rough-hewn stone, stuccoed on three sides.

[1] The following is a copy of the inscription : " Presented by Samuel Verplanck, Esq., to the First Reformed Dutch Church in the town of Fishkill, to commemorate Mr. Englebert Huff, by birth a Norwegian, in his lifetime attached to the life guards of the Prince of Orange, afterward King William III. of England. He resided for a number of years in this country, and died, with unblemished reputation, at Fishkill, 21st of March, 1765, aged 128 years."

It is related of Huff, that when he was a hundred and twenty years old he made love to a pretty girl of twenty.   She already had an accepted lover of her own age, and of course rejected the suit of the Nestor. The old suitor was indignant at the refusal.   He thought he had the best right to claim the heart and hand of the maiden, for he had a hundred years more experience than " the foolish boy," and knew better how to treat a wife than the interfering stripling.

[2] This picture is also from a pencil sketch by Miss Newlin.

OF THE REVOLUTION. 693

Printing of the first Constitution of the State of New York.   Head-quarters of Baron Steuben.   Anecdote of the Baron.

sick, and as a meeting-place of the flying Legislature of New York, when it adjourned from White Plains to Fishkill. According to the records, the session here commenced on the 3d of September, 1776. A few years since, while digging a grave in the yard, the sexton discovered a skeleton, with bits of scarlet cloth and a brass button, the remains, doubtless, of a British soldier, who was buried in his uniform.

An interesting bibliographic fact, connected with Fishkill, was communicated to me by Gulian C. Verplanck, Esq. I have already noticed the harassing circumstances under which the first republican Constitution of the State of New York was elaborated, discussed, and adopted;[1] the Legislature retiring before the approach of British bayonets, first to Harlem, then to Kingsbridge, Yonkers, White Plains, Fishkill, and Kingston. "The Constitution of the State of New York," says Mr. Verplanck, "was printed in 1777, and was the *first*, as well as the *most important* book, ever printed in the state. The people could find but *one press* in their domain with which to print this work of their representatives. It was done at Fishkill, by Samuel Loudon, who had been a Whig editor and printer in the city of New York, and who had retired with his press to Fishkill, where was the chief deposit of stores, hospitals, &c., of the northern army of the United States."[2] Mr. Verplanck possesses a copy of this precious piece of American typography. They have become almost as scarce as the Sibylline Books, and quite as relatively valuable, for the principles therein embodied foreshadowed the destiny of the commonwealth. Unlike Tarquin the Proud, the possessor values it above all price.

I left the village toward noon, and, taking a more northerly route for the ferry, visited the residence of the late Judge Verplanck, situated in a beautiful, isolated spot, about a mile from the east bank of the Hudson, and two miles northeast of Fishkill landing. It is approached from the highway by a winding carriage track which traverses a broad, undulating lawn, shaded by venerable trees. The old mansion is of stone, a story and a half high, with dormer windows, and in the style of the best class of Dutch-built houses erected one hundred years ago. It was owned by Samuel Verplanck, Esq., during the Revolution. An addition, two stories high, has been erected at the north end. I sketched only the ancient edifice. This house is remarkable, in connection with my subject, as the head-quarters

THE VERPLANCK HOUSE.

of the Baron Steuben when the American army was encamped in the vicinity of Newburgh,[3] and also as the place wherein the celebrated *Society of the Cincinnati* was organized in 1783. The meeting for that purpose was held in the large square room on the north side of the passage.[4] The room is carefully preserved in its original style. 1782–1783.

---

[1] See page 387, this volume.   [2] I have a public document, printed there by Loudon, in 1776.
[3] An anecdote illustrative of Steuben's generous character is related, the scene of which was at Newburgh, at the time of the disbanding of the army. Colonel Cochrane, whom I have mentioned in a former chapter, was standing in the street, penniless, when Steuben tried to comfort him by saying that better times would come. "For myself," said the brave officer, "I can stand it; but my wife and daughters are in the garret of that wretched tavern, and I have nowhere to carry them, nor even money to remove them." The baron's generous heart was touched, and, though poor himself, he hastened to the family of Cochrane, poured the whole contents of his purse upon the table, and left as suddenly as he had entered. As he was walking toward the wharf, a wounded negro soldier came up to him, bitterly lamenting that he had no means with which to get to New York. The baron borrowed a dollar, and handing it to the negro, hailed a sloop and put him on board. "God Almighty bless you, baron!" said the negro, as his benefactor walked away. Many similar acts hallow the memory of the Baron Steuben.
[4] The following record of the proceedings at the final meeting of the convention I copied from the orig-

" While contemplating a final separation of the officers of the army," says Doctor Thacher, " the tenderest feelings of the heart had their afflicting operation.   It was at the suggestion of General Knox, and with the acquiescence of the commander-in-chief, that an expedient was devised by which a hope was entertained that their long-cherished friendship and social intercourse might be perpetuated, and that at future periods they might annually communicate, and revive a recollection of the bonds by which they were connected."[1]   Pursuant to these suggestions, the officers held a meeting.   A committee, consisting of Generals

inal manuscript in the possession of Peter Force, Esq., of Washington City, and print it here as an interesting scrap in the history of the closing scenes of the Revolution.

" Cantonment of the American Army, 19th June, 1783.

" At a meeting of the general officers, and the gentlemen delegated by the respective regiments, as a convention for establishing the Society of the Cincinnati, held by the request of the president, at which were present Major-general Baron de Steuben, president ; Major-general Howe, Major-general Knox, Brigadier-general Paterson, Brigadier-general Hand, Brigadier-general Huntington, Brigadier-general Putnam, Colonel Webb, Lieutenant-colonel Huntington, Major Pettengill, Lieutenant Whiting, Colonel H. Jackson, Captain Shaw, Lieutenant-colonel Hull, Lieutenant-colonel Maxwell, and Colonel Cortlandt, General Baron de Steuben acquainted the convention that he had, agreeably to their request at the last meeting, transmitted to his excellency the Chevalier de la Luzerne, minister plenipotentiary from the court of France, a copy of the institution of the Society of the Cincinnati, with their vote respecting his excellency and the other characters therein mentioned, and that his excellency had returned an answer declaring his acceptance of the same, and expressing the grateful sense he entertains of the honor conferred on himself and the other gentlemen of the French nation by this act of the convention.

" *Resolved*, That the letter of the Chevalier de la Luzerne be recorded in the proceedings of this day, and deposited in the archives of the society, as a testimony of the high sense this convention entertain of the honor done to the society by his becoming a member thereof.

(Here follows the letter.)

" The baron having also communicated a letter from Major l'Enfant, inclosing a design for the medal and order containing the emblems of the institution,

" *Resolved*, That the bald eagle, carrying the emblems on its breast, be established as the *order* of the society, and that the ideas of Major l'Enfant respecting it and the manner of its being worn by the members, as expressed in his letter, hereto annexed, be adopted.   That the order be of the same size, and in every other respect conformable to the said design, which for that purpose is certified by the Baron de Steuben, president of this convention, and to be deposited in the archives of the society, as the original from which all copies are to be made.   Also that silver medals, not exceeding the size of a Spanish milled dollar, with the emblems, as designed by Major l'Enfant and certified by the president, be given to each and every member of the society, together with a diploma, on parchment, whereon shall be impressed the exact figures of the order and medal, as above mentioned, any thing in the original institution respecting gold medals to the contrary notwithstanding.

(Here follows Major l'Enfant's letter.)

" *Resolved*, That the thanks of this convention be transmitted by the president to Major l'Enfant for his care and ingenuity in preparing the aforementioned designs, and that he be acquainted that they cheerfully embrace his offer of assistance, and request a continuance of his attention in carrying the designs into execution, for which purpose the president is desired to correspond with him.

" *Resolved*, That his excellency the commander-in-chief be requested to officiate as president general, until the first general meeting, to be held in May next.

" That a treasurer general and a secretary general be balloted for, to officiate in like manner.

" The ballots being taken, Major-general M'Dougall was elected treasurer general, and Major-general Knox secretary general, who are hereby requested to accept said appointments.

" *Resolved*, That all the proceedings of this convention, including the institution of the society, be recorded from the original papers in his possession by Captain Shaw, who at the first meeting was requested to act as secretary, and that the same, signed by the president and secretary, together with the original papers, be given into the hands of Major-general Knox, secretary general to the society, and that Captain North, aid-de-camp to the Baron de Steuben, and acting secretary to him as president, sign the said records.

" The dissolution of a very considerable part of the army, since the last meeting of this convention, having rendered the attendance of some of its members impracticable, and the necessity for some temporary arrangements, previous to the first meeting of the general society, being so strikingly obvious, the convention found itself constrained to make those before mentioned, which they have done with the utmost diffidence of themselves, and relying entirely on the candor of their constituents to make allowance for the measure.

" The principal objects of its appointment being thus accomplished, the members of this convention think fit to dissolve the same, and it is hereby dissolved accordingly.

" STEUBEN, *Major General, President.*"

[1] *Military Journal* p. 317.

Knox, Hand, and Huntington, and Captain Shaw, was appointed to revise the proposals for the institution. Another meeting was held on the 13th of May, at the quarters of Steuben (Verplanck's), when the committee reported. A plan, in the following words, was adopted,[1] and the society was duly organized :

"It having pleased the Supreme Governor of the universe, in the disposition of human affairs, to cause the separation of the colonies of North America from the domination of Great Britain, and, after a bloody conflict of eight years, to establish them free, independent, and sovereign states, connected by alliances, founded on reciprocal advantages, with some of the greatest princes and powers of the earth :

"To perpetuate, therefore, as well the remembrance of this vast event, as the mutual friendships which have been formed under the pressure of common danger, and in many instances cemented by the blood of the parties, the officers of the American army do hereby, in the most solemn manner, associate, constitute, and combine themselves into one society of friends, to endure so long as they shall endure, or any of their eldest male posterity, and in failure thereof, the collateral branches, who may be judged worthy of becoming its supporters and members.[2]

"The officers of the American army, having generally been taken from the citizens of America, possess high veneration for the character of that illustrious Roman, LUCIUS QUINTIUS CINCINNATUS, and being resolved to follow his example, by returning to their citizenship, they think they may with propriety denominate themselves the

SOCIETY OF THE CINCINNATI.

"The following principles shall be immutable, and form the basis of the Society of the Cincinnati :

"An incessant attention to preserve inviolate those exalted rights and liberties of human nature for which they have fought and bled, and without which the high rank of a rational being is a curse instead of a blessing.

"An unalterable determination to promote and cherish, between the respective states, that unison and national honor so essentially necessary to their happiness and the future dignity of the American empire.

"To render permanent the cordial affection subsisting among the officers, this spirit will dictate brotherly kindness in all things, and particularly extend to the most substantial acts of beneficence, according to the ability of the society, toward those officers and their families who unfortunately may be under the necessity of receiving it.

"The general society will, for the sake of frequent communications, be divided into state societies, and these again into such districts as shall be directed by the state society.

"The societies of the districts to meet as often as shall be agreed on by the state society ; those of the state on the 4th day of July annually, or oftener if they shall find it expedient ; and the general society on the first Monday in May annually, so long as they shall deem it necessary, and afterward at least once in every three years.

---

[1] This document, according to Colonel Timothy Pickering, was drawn up by Captain Shaw, who was the secretary of the committee.

[2] This clause gave considerable alarm to the more rigid Whigs, because of the recognition of the right of primogeniture in membership succession. Judge Ædanus Burke, of South Carolina, attacked it with much vehemence, as an incipient order of nobility, and an attempt to establish the pretensions of the military to rank above the mass of citizens. The objection was groundless, for no civil, military, political, or social prerogative was claimed. On the other hand, the King of Sweden (Gustavus Adolphus III.) declined permitting the few officers in the French army who were his subjects to wear the order of the Cincinnati, on the ground that the institution had a republican tendency not suited to his government. On this subject, Washington, in a letter to Rochambeau, written in August, 1784. said, " Considering how recently the King of Sweden has changed the form of the government of that country, it is not so much to be wondered at that his fears should get the better of his liberality as to any thing which might have the semblance of republicanism ; but when it is further considered how few of his nation had, or could have, a right to the order, I think he might have suffered his complaisance to have overcome them."—See Sparks's *Life and Writings of Washington*, ix., 56.

"At each meeting, the principles of the institution will be fully considered, and the best measures to promote them adopted.

"The state societies will consist of all the members residing in each state respectively, and any member removing from one state to another is to be considered in all respects as belonging to the society of the state in which he shall actually reside.[1]

SOCIETY OF THE CINCINNATI.—MEMBERS' CERTIFICATE.[2]

[1] This clause is omitted by Dr. Thacher and others. I find it in a manuscript copy of the Constitution of the society, and records of the proceedings at its formation, among the papers of Colonel Richard Varick, in the handwriting of General William North.

[2] This engraving is a fac simile of a certificate, about one fourth the size of the original, which is thirteen inches and a half in breadth, and twenty inches in length. The originals are printed on fine vellum. The plate was engraved in France by J. J. le Veau, from a drawing by Aug. le Belle. I am indebted to the late James G. Wilson, son of Ensign Wilson, named in the certificate, for the use of the original in making this copy. The former was engraved on copper; this is engraved on wood. The design represents American liberty as a strong man armed, bearing in one hand the Union flag, and in the other a naked sword. Beneath his feet are British flags, and a broken spear, shield, and chain. Hovering by his side is the eagle, our national emblem, from whose talons the lightning of destruction is flashing upon the British lion. Britannia, with the crown falling from her head, is hastening toward a boat to escape to a fleet, which denotes the departure of British power from our shores. Upon a cloud, on the right, is an angel blowing a trumpet, from which flutters a loose scroll. Upon the scroll are the sentences *Palam nuntiata libertatis,** A.D. 1776. *Fœdus sociale cum Gallia,* A.D. 1778. *Pax: libertas parta,* A.D. 1783 : " Independence declared, A.D. 1776. Treaty of alliance with France declared, A.D. 1778. Peace ! independence obtained, A.D. 1783."

Upon the medallion on the right is a device representing Cincinnatus at his plow, a ship on the sea, and a walled town in the distance. Over his head is a flying angel, holding a ribbon inscribed *Virtutis præmium* : " Reward of virtue." Below is a heart, with the words *Esto perpetua :* " Be thou perpetual." Upon the rim is the legend, *Societas Cincinnatorum Instituta A.D. MDCCLXXXIII. :* " Society of the Cincinnati, instituted 1783." The device upon the medallion on the left is Cincinnatus with his family, near his house. He is receiving a sword and shield from three senators ; an army is seen in the distance. Upon the rim are the words *Omnia relinquit servare rempublicam :* " He abandons every thing to serve his country" (referring to Cincinnatus).

* There is a fact connected with this sentence worthy of notice. In the earlier impressions from the plate, taken previous to the year 1785, the sentence is *Palam nuntiata libertas,* not *libertatis.* Some person, who doubtless supposed the original word to be incorrect, caused the letters *t i s* to be crowded into the space occupied by the final *s* in *libertas.* I have the authority of one of our most learned Latin critics, to whom the question was submitted, for saying that the original word was correct, and that the alteration renders the sentence ungrammatical and totally incorrect, thereby destroying its meaning. Do any of our historical antiquaries know by whose authority the alteration was made ?

"The state societies to have a president, vice-president, secretary, treasurer, and assistant treasurer, to be chosen annually by a majority of votes at the stated meeting.

"In order to obtain funds which may be respectable, and assist the unfortunate, each officer shall deliver to the treasurer of the state society one month's pay, which shall remain forever to the use of the state society. The interest only of which, if necessary, to be appropriated to the relief of the unfortunate.

"The society shall have an *order*, by which its members shall be known and distinguished, which shall be a medal of gold, of a proper size to receive the emblems, and be suspended by a deep blue ribbon, two inches wide, edged with white, descriptive of the union of America with France."

I am indebted to the kindness of Colonel Joseph Warren Scott, of New Brunswick, New Jersey, now (1850) the president of the society of that state, for the following information respecting the successive presidents general of the institution. General Washington was the first president general, and continued in office until his death, in December, 1799. In May, 1800, General Alexander Hamilton was elected as his successor. He was killed in a duel with Aaron Burr in 1804, and, at the next general meeting, General Charles Cotesworth Pinckney, of South Carolina, was elected as his successor. He died in August, 1825. At a special meeting of the society, held at Philadelphia in November, 1826, Major-general Thomas Pinckney was elected president general.[1] At his death, Colonel Aaron Ogden, of New Jersey, was elected to fill his place. He held the office until his decease in April, 1838, when General Morgan Lewis, of New York, became his successor. General Lewis died on the 7th of May, 1844, in his ninetieth year, and the venerable Major Popham, also of New York, was elected as his successor at the general meeting in November following. Major Popham died in the summer of 1848, and, at the meeting in November of that year, General Dearborn, the present incumbent, was elected to supply the vacancy. Such is the brief history of a society over which the venerated Washington first presided.

I left the interesting mansion wherein the society was organized at noon, and reached Newburgh in time to dine and embark at half past one for West Point, eight miles below.

ORDER OF THE CINCINNATI.[2]

[1] "At that meeting," says Colonel Scott, in a letter to me dated July 9, 1850, "delegates attended from Massachusetts, Rhode Island, Connecticut, New York, New Jersey, Maryland, and South Carolina. Colonel Ogden and myself were delegates from New Jersey. At that meeting it was ascertained that all the officers of the society but one had departed this life. The survivor was Major Jackson, of Pennsylvania. These communications were given and received in sadness, and a respectful and affectionate notice was taken of those who had left us forever."

[2] This was drawn from an original in the possession of Edward Phalon, Esq., of New York. The engraving is the exact size of the original. The leaves of the sprigs of laurel are of gold, and green enamel; the head and tail of the eagle gold, and white enamel; and the sky in the center device blue enamel. The device and motto are the same as upon the medallion on the right of the certificate.

CHAPTER XXX.

" What though no cloister gray nor ivyed column
   Along these cliffs their somber ruins rear;
What though no frowning tower nor temple solemn
   Of despots tell, and superstition here;
What though that moldering fort's fast-crumbling walls
Did ne'er inclose a baron's bannered halls,

" Its sinking arches once gave back as proud
   An echo to the war-blown clarion's peal—
As gallant hearts its battlements did crowd
   As ever beat beneath a breast of steel,
When herald's trump on knighthood's haughtiest day
Called forth chivalric hosts to battle-fray."
                             C. F. HOFFMAN.

" Low sunk between the Alleghanian hills
   For many a league the sullen waters glide,
   And the deep murmur of the crowded tide
With pleasing awe the wondering voyager fills.
   On the green summit of yon lofty clift
A peaceful runnel gurgles clear and slow,
   Then down the craggy steep-side dashing swift,
Tumultuous falls in the white surge below."
                  MARGARETTA V. FAUGERES.[1]

N the midst of wild mountain scenery, picturesque but not magnificent when compared with the White Mountains of New Hampshire, the Adirondack and Catskill range in New York, or the Alleghanies in Western Pennsylvania and Virginia, is a bold promontory called West Point, rising more than one hundred and fifty feet above the waters of the Hudson, its top a perfectly level and fertile plateau, and every rood hallowed by associations of the deepest interest. West Point! What a world of thrilling reminiscences has the utterance of that name brought to ten thousand memories in times past, now, alas! nearly all slumbering in the dreamless sleep of the dead! How does it awaken the generous emotions of patriotic reverence for the men, and things, and times of the Revolution, in the bosoms of the present generation! Nor is it by the associations alone that the traveler is moved with strong emotions when approaching West Point; the stranger, indifferent to our history and of all but the present, feels a glow of admira-

---

[1] Mrs. Faugeres was the grand-daughter of Brandt Schuyler, and daughter of Mrs. Anne Eliza Bleecker, one of the notable sufferers from the invasion of Burgoyne in 1777. Mrs. Bleecker was then living, with her husband, about eighteen miles from Albany. Mr. Bleecker went to that city to make arrangements for moving his family thither. While absent, Mrs. Bleecker heard of the approach of Burgoyne and his horde of savages, and, leading her eldest child by the hand, and bearing her youngest in her arms, she started on foot for Albany. After a wearisome journey of a day, and a night passed in a wretched garret, she started forward with her precious charge, and soon met her husband, with whom she returned to the city. Her babe died a few days afterward, and within a month her mother expired in her arms, at Red Hook, in Dutchess county. Her husband was afterward captured by a party of Tories. This event, and his sudden restoration when she thought him dead, so overpowered her, that her constitution sunk beneath the shocks, and she died in the autumn of 1783. Margaretta (afterward Mrs. Faugeres) was the "sweet sister" alluded to in the following lines, extracted from a poem written by Mrs. Bleecker on the death of her child:

tion as he courses along the sinuous channel of the river or climbs the rough hills that embosom it.   The inspiration of nature then takes possession of his heart and mind, and

> " When he treads
> The rock-encumbered crest, and feels the strange
> And wild tumultuous throbbings of his heart,
> Its every chord vibrating with the touch
> Of the high power that reigns supreme o'er all,
> He well may deem that lips of angel-forms
> Have breathed to him the holy melody
> That fills his o'erfraught heart."
>
> BAYARD TAYLOR.

The high plain is reached by a carriage-way that winds up the bank from the landing ; the visitor overlooking, in the passage, on the right, the little village of Camptown, which comprises the barracks of United States soldiers and a few dwellings of persons not immediately connected with the military works.   On the left, near the summit, is " the Artillery Laboratory," and near by, upon a little hillock, is an obelisk erected to the memory of Lieutenant-colonel Wood.[1]   On the edge of the cliff, overlooking the steam boat landing, is a spacious hotel, where I booked myself as a boarder for a day or two.   A more delightful spot, particularly in summer, for a weary traveler or a professed lounger, can not easily be found, than the broad piazza of that public dwelling presents.   Breezy in the hottest weather, and always enlivened by pleasant company, the sojourner need not step from beneath its shadow to view a most wonderful variety of pleasing objects in nature and art.   Upon the grassy plain before him are buildings of the military establishment—the Academic Halls, the Philosophical and Library buildings, the Observatory, the Chapel, the Hospital, the Barracks and Mess Hall of the cadets, and the beautifully shaded dwellings of the officers and professors that skirt the western side of the plateau at the base of the hills.   On the parade, the cadets, in neat uniform, exhibit their various exercises, and an excellent band of music delights the ear.   Lifting the eyes to the westward, the lofty summit of Mount Independence, crested by the gray ruins of Fort Putnam, and beyond it the loftier apex of Redoubt Hill, are seen.   Turning a little northward, Old Cro' Nest and Butter Hill break the horizon nearly half way to the zenith ; and directly north, over Martelaer's Rock or Constitution Island, through the magnificent cleft in the chain of hills through which the Hudson flows, is seen the bright waters of Newburgh Bay, the village glittering in the sunbeams, and the beautiful, cultivated slopes of Dutchess and Orange.   The scenery at the eastward is better comprehended and more extensive as seen from Fort Putnam, whither we shall presently climb.

I passed the remainder of the afternoon among the celebrities clustered around the plain.   I first visited the Artillery Laboratory, where are deposited several October 26, 1848. interesting trophies and relics of the Revolution.   In the center of the court is a group of great interest, consisting of a large brass mortar, mounted, which was taken from the English when Wayne captured Stony Point ; two small brass mortars, taken from Burgoyne at Saratoga, and a portion of the famous chain which the Americans stretched across the river at West Point to obstruct the passage of the vessels of the enemy.   The large mortar

---

> "Rich in my children, on my arms I bore
> My living treasures from the scalper's power.
> When I sat down to rest beneath some shade,
> On the soft grass how innocent she play'd,
> While her sweet sister from the fragrant wild
> Collects the flowers to please my precious child."

[1] The following is the inscription on this monument :
" To the memory of Lieutenant-colonel E. D. WOOD, of the corps of engineers, who fell while leading a charge at the sortie of Fort Erie, Upper Canada, 17th of September, 1814, in the 31st year of his age.   He was exemplary as a Christian, and distinguished as a soldier.   A pupil of this institution,* he died an honor to his country.   This memorial was erected by his friend and commander, Major-general JACOB BROWN."

* Military Academy at West Point.

has a caliber of ten and a half inches; the smaller ones, of four inches and three quarters. The former is emblazoned with the English coat of arms, beneath which is engraved "*As-chaleh, fecit*, 1741." There are twelve links, two clevises, and a portion of a link of the

GREAT CHAIN AND MORTARS

great chain remaining. The links are made of iron bars, two and a half inches square, average in length a little over two feet, and weigh about one hundred and forty pounds each. The chain was stretched across the river at the narrowest point between the rocks just below the steam-boat landing, and Constitution Island opposite. It was fixed to huge blocks on each shore, and under the cover of batteries on both sides of the river. The remains of these are still visible. "It is buoyed up," says Doctor Thacher, writing in 1780, "by very large logs of about sixteen feet long, pointed at the ends, to lessen their opposition to the force of the current at flood and ebb tide. The logs are placed at short distances from each other, the chain carried over them, and made fast to each by staples. There are also a number of anchors dropped at proper distances, with cables made fast to the chain, to give it greater stability."[1] The history of this chain will be noted presently.

Near this group is a cannon, by the premature discharge of which, in 1817, a cadet named Lowe was killed. There is a beautiful monument erected to his memory in the cemetery of the institution. I observed several long French cannons, inscribed with various dates; and among others, two brass field-pieces, of British manufacture, bearing the monogram of the king, "G. R.," and the inscription "*W. Bowen, fecit*, 1755." These were presented to General Greene by order of Congress, as an inscription among the military emblems avers.[2]

At the northeast corner of the plain, a little eastward of the hotel, are mounds denoting the ramparts of old Fort Clinton. Among these mounds stands the monument erected to the memory of KOSCIUSZKO. It is made of white marble, and is a conspicuous object to travelers upon the river. On one side of the pedestal, in large letters, is the name KOSCI-

[1] *Military Journal*, page 211.
[2] The inscription is as follows:

"Taken from the British army, and presented, by order of the United States in Congress assembled, to Major-general Greene, as a monument* of their high sense of the wisdom, fortitude, and military talents which distinguished his command in the Southern department, and of the eminent services which, amid complicated dangers and difficulties, he performed for his country. October yᵉ 18th, 1783."

* To the dishonor of our country, it must be said that these two brazen cannons form the only "monument" ever made to the memory of that great commander. Savannah, in Georgia, has a ward and a square bearing his name, and in the center of the latter is the foundation-stone of an *intended* monument to his memory. This and the corner-stone of a monument to Pulaski were laid by La Fayette in 1825. For a further notice of this matter, See page 514, vol. ii.

uszko; and on the other is the brief inscription, "*Erected by the Corps of Cadets*, 1828." The monument was completed in 1829, at a cost of five thousand dollars. A drawing of it forms a portion of the vignette of the map printed on page 137. From this monument the view of the river and adjacent scenery, especially at the northward, is very fine, and should never be unobserved by the visitor.

VIEW FROM FORT CLINTON, LOOKING NORTH.

Emerging from the remains of Fort Clinton, the path, traversing the margin of the cliff, passes the ruins of a battery, and descends, at a narrow gorge between huge rocks, to a flight of wooden steps. These terminate at the bottom upon a grassy terrace a few feet wide, over which hangs a shelving cliff covered with shrubbery. This is called Kosciuszko's Garden, from the circumstance of its having been a favorite resort of that officer while stationed there as engineer for a time during the Revolution. In the center of the terrace is a marble basin, from the bottom of which bubbles up a tiny fountain of pure water. It is said that the remains of a fountain constructed by Kosciuszko was discovered in 1802, when it was removed, and the marble bowl which now receives the jet was placed there. It is a beautiful and romantic spot, shaded by a weeping willow and other trees, and having seats provided for those who wish to linger. Upon a smooth spot, high upon the rocks and half overgrown with moss, are slight indications of written characters. Tradition says it is the remains of the name of Kosciuszko, inscribed by his own hand; but I doubt the report, for he possessed too much common sense to be guilty of such folly as

KOSCIUSZKO'S GARDEN.

the mutilated benches around the fountain exhibit; his name was already upon the tablet of Polish history,

KOSCIUSZKO'S SIGNATURE.

and his then present deeds were marking it deep upon that of our war for independence.

The sun had gone down behind the hills when I ascended from the garden to the plain. The cadets were performing their evening parade, and, as the last rays left Bear Hill and the Sugar Loaf, the evening gun and the tattoo summoned them to quarters. During the twilight hour, I strolled down the road along the river bank, half a mile beyond the barracks, to Mr. Kingsley's Classical School, situated upon a commanding eminence above the road leading to Buttermilk Falls. Near his residence was a strong redoubt, called Fort Arnold, one of the outposts of West Point in the Revolution. I was informed that the remains are well preserved; but it was too dark to distinguish an artificial mound from a natural hillock, and I hastened back to my lodgings.

Unwilling to wait until the late hour of eight for breakfast the next morning, I arose at dawn, and before sunrise I stood among the ruins of Fort Putnam, on the pinnacle of Mount Independence, nearly five hundred feet above the river.

I had waked
From a long sleep of many changing dreams,
And now in the fresh forest air I stood

Nerved to another day of wandering.

.   .   .   .

               The sky bent round
The awful domes of a most mighty temple,
Built by Omnipotent hands for nothing less
Than infinite worship.   Here I stood in silence ;
I had no words to tell the mingled thoughts
Of wonder and of joy that then came o'er me
Even with a whirlwind's rush."

                      JAMES G. PERCIVAL.

Around me were strewn mementoes of the Revolution.   My feet pressed the russet turf upon the ramparts of a ruined fort.   Eastward, behind which were glowing the splendors of approaching day, stretched a range of broken hills, on whose every pinnacle the vigilant patriots planted batteries and built watch-fires.   At their feet, upon a fertile terrace almost a mile in breadth, was the " Beverly House," from which Arnold escaped to the Vulture ; old Phillipstown, around which a portion of the Revolutionary army was cantoned in 1781,[1] and intermediate localities, all rich with local traditions and historic associations.   On the left, over Constitution Island, arose the smoke of the furnaces and forges at Cold Spring, a thriving village at the river terminus of a mountain furrow that slopes down from the eastern hills.   A little beyond, and beneath the frowning crags of Mount Taurus,[2] appeared "Under Cliff," the country seat of George P. Morris, Esq., lying like a pearl by the side of a sleeping giant, and just visible in the fading shadows of the mountains.   Nowhere in our broad land is there a more romantic nook, or more appropriate spot for the residence of an American song-writer than this,

        " Where Hudson's waves o'er silvery sands
          Winds through the hills afar,
        And Cro' Nest like a monarch stands
          Crown'd with a single star."

                      MORRIS.

Hark ! the sunrise gun on the plain below hath spoken !   How eagerly its loud voice is caught up by echo and carried from hill to hill !   The Sugar Loaf answers to Redoubt Mountain, and Anthony's Nose to Bear Mountain and the Dunderberg, and then there is only a soft whisper floating away over the waters of the Haverstraw.   The reveille is beating ; the shrill notes of the fife, and the stirring music of the cornet-players, come up and fill the soul with a martial spirit consonant with the place and its memories.   Here, then, let us sit down upon the lip of this rock-fountain, within the ruins of the fort, and commune a while with the old chronicler.

    The importance of fortifying the Hudson River at its narrow passes among the High-

---

[1] It was here that the general inoculation of the soldiers of the Continental army was performed by Doctors Cochrane, Thacher, Munson, and others, as mentioned on page 307, vol. i.

[2] This, in plain English and common parlance, is *Bull Hill.* I feel very much disposed to quarrel with my countrymen for their want of taste in giving names to localities. They have discarded the beautiful "heathenish" names of the Indian verbal geographies, and often substituted the most commonplace and inappropriate title that human ingenuity, directed earthward, could invent—Bull Hill ! Crow's Nest ! Butter Hill ! ! Ever blessed be the name and memory of JOSEPH RODMAN DRAKE, whose genius has clothed these Highland cones, despite their vulgar names, with a degree of classic interest, by thus summoning there, with the herald voice of imagination,

        "Ouphe and goblin ! imp and sprite !
          Elf of eve and starry fay !
        Ye that love the moon's soft light,
          Hither, hither wend your way.
        Twine ye in a jocund ring ;
          Sing and trip it merrily ;
        Hand to hand and wing to wing,
          Round the wild witch-hazel tree !"

            THE CULPRIT FAY, CANTO XXXVI.*

---

* This beautiful poem was written *con amore*, during a brief ramble of the author among the Hudson Highlands.

lands was suggested to the Continental Congress by the Provincial Assembly of New York at an early period of the war. On the 6th of October, 1775, the former directed the latter to proceed to make such fortifications as they should deem best.[1] On the 18th of November, Congress resolved to appoint a commander for the fortress, with the rank of colonel, and recommended the New York Assembly, or Convention, to empower him to raise a body of two hundred militia from the counties of Dutchess, Orange, and Ulster, and a

INTERIOR OF FORT PUTNAM.[2]

company of artillery from New York city, to garrison them. The Convention was also recommended to forward from Kingsbridge such ordnance as they should think proper.[3] That body had already taken action. On the 18th of August, a committee was appointed to superintend the erection of forts and batteries in the vicinity of West Point.[4] They employed Bernard Romans, an English engineer (who, at that time, held the same office in the British army), to construct the works; and Martelaer's Rock (now Constitution Island), opposite West Point, was the chosen spot for

the principal fortification. Romans commenced operations on the 29th of August, and on the 12th of October he applied to Congress for a commission, with the rank and pay of colonel. It was this application which caused the action of Congress on the 18th of November. In the mean while, Romans and his employers quarreled, and the commission was never granted; the work was soon afterward completed by others. The fort was named *Constitution*, and the island has since borne that title.[5] The fort and its outworks were quite extensive, though the main fortress was built chiefly of perishable materials, on account of the apparent necessity for its speedy erection. The whole cost was about twenty-five thousand dollars. The remains of the fort and surrounding batteries are scattered over the island. Near the highest point on the western end are the

PLAN OF FORT CONSTITUTION.[6]

---

[1] *Journals of Congress*, i., 199.

[2] This little sketch is a view of the remains of the casemates, or vaults, of Fort Putnam. There were nine originally, but only six remain in a state of fair preservation. They were built of brick and covered with stone; were twelve feet wide and eighteen feet deep, with an arched roof twelve feet high. Each one had a fire-place, and they seem to have been used for the purposes of barracks, batteries, and magazines. In the center of the fort is a spring, that bubbles up in a rocky basin. The whole interior is very rough, it being the pinnacle of a bald, rocky elevation.

[3] *Journals of Congress*, i., 223.

[4] The committee consisted of Isaac Sears, John Berrien, Colonel Edward Fleming, Anthony Rutger, and Christopher Miller. Fleming and Rutger declined the appointment, and Captain Samuel Bayard and Captain William Bedlow were appointed in their places.

[5] This island belonged to the widow of Captain Ogilvie, of the British army, and her children, during the Revolution, as appears by a correspondence between the New York Committee of Safety and Colonel Beverly Robinson. The committee supposed that the island belonged to Robinson, and applied to him for its purchase. In his reply, he mentioned the fact of its belonging to Mrs. Ogilvie, and added, "Was it mine, the public should be extremely welcome to it. The building of the fort there can be no disadvantage to the small quantity of arable land on the island." Robinson afterward chose the royal side of the political question, and held the commission of a colonel in the British army.

[6] This plan of Fort Constitution is from Romans's report to the Committee of Safety of New York, on the 14th of September, 1775, and published in the *American Archives*, iii., 735.

EXPLANATION.—*a*, guard-room and store-house; *b*, barracks; *c*, block-house and main guard; *d*, magazine; *e*, the gateway; 1, a battery of four four-pounders; 2, three twelve-pounders; 3, three twelve-pounders and one nine-pounder; 4, five eighteen-pounders; 5, four twelve-pounders; 6, three eighteen-pounders; 7 and 8, one each, nine and twelve-pounder; 9, one four-pounder.

704   PICTORIAL FIELD-BOOK

New Forts in the Highlands proposed.   West Point selected.   Radière and other Engineers from France

well-preserved remains of the magazine, the form of which is given in the annexed diagram. It is upon a high rock, accessible only on one side. The whole wall is quite perfect, except

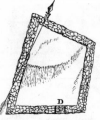

at the doorway, D, where a considerable portion has fallen down and blocked up the entrance.

PLAN OF THE MAGAZINE.

After the capture of Forts Clinton and Montgomery, near the lower entrance to the Highlands, in 1777, and the abandonment of Fort Constitution by the Americans a few days afterward, public attention was directed to the importance of other and stronger fortifications in that vicinity. On the 5th of November, Congress appointed General Gates to command in the Highlands, or rather that post was connected with the Northern department. Gates was made president of the Board of War about that time, and never entered upon the prescribed duties in the Highlands. Anxious to have those passes strongly guarded, Washington requested General Putnam to bestow his most serious attention upon that important

December 2, 1777.

subject. He also wrote to Governor Clinton, at the same time, desiring him to take the immediate supervision of the work ; but his legislative duties, then many and pressing, made it difficult for him to comply. Clinton expressed his willingness to devote as much time as possible to the matter, and also made many valuable suggestions respecting the proposed fortifications. He mentioned West Point as the most eligible site for a strong fort.

Duty calling General Putnam to Connecticut, and General Parsons not feeling himself authorized to progress with the works, but little was done until the arrival of General

a 1778.

b January.

M'Dougal, who took command on the 20th of March following.[a] In the mean while, several officers examined various localities in the neighborhood,[b] and all were in favor of erecting a strong fort on West Point, except La Radière, a French engineer.[1] A committee of the New York Legislature, after surveying several sites, unanimously recommended West Point as the most eligible. Works were accordingly commenced there,

La Radière

under the direction of Kosciuszko, who had been appointed to succeed Radière in the Highlands, his skill being quite equal, and his manners more acceptable to the people. Kosciuszko arrived on the 20th of March, and the works were pushed toward completion with

1778.

much spirit. The principal redoubt, constructed chiefly of logs and earth, was completed before May, and named Fort Clinton. It was six hundred yards around within the walls. The embankments were twenty-one feet at base, and fourteen feet high. There were barracks and

WEST POINT IN 1780.[2]

---

[1] The American commissioners in France were instructed by Congress to procure some good engineers for the Continental army. Franklin and Deane contracted with four officers of this description, who had served in such capacity, under commissions, in the French army, namely, Duportail, Laumoy, Radière, and Gouvion. These officers came to the United States with the knowledge and approbation of the French government, and were the only ones engaged by the express authority of Congress. The Chevalier Duportail was appointed colonel of engineers, Laumoy and Radière lieutenant colonels, and Gouvion major. Duportail was afterward promoted to a brigadier, Laumoy and Radière to colonels, and Gouvion to a lieutenant colonel. Radière died in the service at the beginning of 1780. See *Journals of Congress*, iii., 224, 322, 403.

le Ch.~ Duportail

[2] This view is from a print published in the *New York Magazine* for 1790. It was taken from Constitution Island. On the left is seen a portion of old Fort Constitution. The great chain, four hundred and fifty yards in length, and covered by a strong battery, is seen stretched across the river, immediately below Fort Clinton, the structure on the high point. In the distance, on the left, two mountain summits are seen, crowned with fortifications. These were the North and Middle Redoubts. Upon the range of the Sugar Loaf Mountain, higher than these, and hidden, in the view, by Fort Clinton, was another redoubt, called the South Battery. The view on page 708 I sketched from the same spot whence this was taken.

huts for about six hundred men.[1]   The cliff on which Fort Clinton was erected rises one hundred and eighty-eight feet above the river, and is more elevated than the plain in the

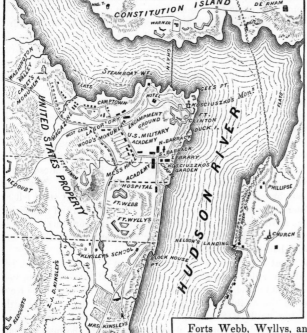

WEST POINT.

1/2 mile

rear.   The only accessible point from the river was at the house and dock, on the water's edge, seen in the engraving. That point is now a little above the steam-boat landing. This weak point was well defended by palisades.

To defend Fort Clinton, and more thoroughly to secure the river against the passage of an enemy's fleet, it was thought advisable to fortify the heights in the neighborhood. The foundation of a strong fort was accordingly laid on Mount Independence, and, when completed, it was named *Putnam*, in honor of the commander of the post. On eminences south of it, Forts Webb, Wyllys, and other redoubts were constructed ; and at the close of 1779, West Point was the strongest military post in America.   In addition to the batteries that stood menacingly upon the hill tops, the river was obstructed by an enormous iron chain, the form and size of which is noted on page 132.   The iron of which this chain was constructed was wrought from ore of equal parts, from the Stirling and Long Mines, in Orange county.   The chain was manufactured by Peter Townshend, of Chester, at the Stirling Iron Works, in the same county, which were situated about twenty-five miles back of West Point.[2]   The general superintendent of the work, as engineer, was Captain Thomas Machin, who afterward assisted in the engineering operations at York-

---

NOTE.—This map exhibits all of the most important localities at West Point during the Revolution and at the present time.   It will be seen that the Hudson River rail-road crosses the cove and Constitution Island a little eastward of the ruins of the main fortress, on that side of the river.   The island is owned by Henry W. Warner, Esq., and upon the eminence where the ravelins of the fort were spread is his beautiful country seat, called " Wood Crag."   The kitchen part of his mansion is a portion of the barracks erected there in the autumn of 1775.

[1] Letter of General Putnam to the commander-in-chief, January, 1778.   In this letter, Putnam gives, in a few words, a picture of the terrible privations which the soldiers in the Highlands were enduring, while those at Valley Forge were also suffering intensely.   " Dubois's regiment," he says, " is unfit to be ordered on duty, there being not one blanket in the regiment.   Very few have either a shoe or a shirt, and most of them have neither stockings, breeches, or overalls.   Several companies of enlisted artificers are in the same situation, and unable to work in the field.

[2] The Stirling Works are still in operation.   They are situated on the outlet of Stirling Pond, about five

town, when Cornwallis was captured.　The chain was completed about the middle of April, 1778, and on the 1st of May it was stretched across the river and secured.[1]

When Benedict Arnold was arranging his plans to deliver West Point and its dependencies into the hands of the enemy, this chain became a special object of his attention; and it is related that, a few days before the discovery of his treason, he wrote a letter to André, in a disguised hand and manner, informing him that he had weakened the obstructions in the river by ordering a link of the chain to be taken out and carried to the smith, under a pretense that it needed repairs.　He assured his employer that the link would not be returned to its place before the forts should be in possession of the enemy.　Of the treason of Arnold I shall write presently.

West Point was considered the keystone of the country during the Revolution, and there a large quantity of powder, and other munitions of war and military stores, were collected. These considerations combined, made its possession a matter of great importance to the enemy, and hence it was selected by Arnold as the prize which his treason would give as a bribe.　When peace returned, it was regarded as one of the most important military posts in the country, and the plateau upon the point was purchased by the United States government.　Repairs were commenced on Fort Putnam in 1794, but little was done.　Not being included in the government purchase, the owner of the land on which the fort stood felt at liberty to appropriate its material to his private use, and for years the work of demolition was carried on with a Vandal spirit exercised only by the ignorant or avaricious.　It was not arrested until Congress purchased the Gridly Farm (see the map), on which the fort stood, in 1824, when the work had become almost a total ruin.

The Military Academy at West Point was established by an act of Congress, which became a law on the 16th of March, 1802.　Such an institution, at that place, was proposed by Washington to Congress in 1793; and earlier than this, even before the war of the Revolution had closed, he suggested the establishment of a military school there.[2]　But little progress was made in the matter until 1812, when, by an act of Congress, a corps of engineers and of professors were organized, and the school was endowed with the most attractive features of a literary institution, mingled with that of the military character.　From that period until the present, the academy has been increasing in importance, in a military point of view.　Over three thousand young men have been educated there, and, under the superintendence of Major Delafield, who was appointed commandant in 1838, it continues to flourish.　The value of the instruction received there was made very manifest during the late war with Mexico; a large portion of the most skillful officers of our army, in that conflict, being graduates of this academy.

The bell is ringing for breakfast; let us close the record and descend to the plain.

---

miles southwest of the Sloatsburg station, on the Erie rail-way.　They are owned by descendants of Peter Townshend, and have now been in operation about one hundred years, having been established in 1751, by Lord Stirling (the Revolutionary general) and others.

[1] Gordon and other early writers have promulgated the erroneous opinion that this chain was constructed in 1777, and was destroyed by the British fleet that passed up the Hudson and burned Kingston in October of that year.　Misled by these authorities, I have published the same error in my *Seventeen Hundred and Seventy-six*.　Documentary evidence, which is far more reliable than the best tradition, shows that the chain was constructed in the spring of 1778.　Colonel Timothy Pickering, accompanied by Captain Machin, arrived at the house of Mr. Townshend late on a Saturday night in March of that year, to engage him to make the chain.　Townshend readily agreed to construct it; and in a violent snow-storm, amid the darkness of the night, the parties set out for the Stirling Iron Works.　At daylight on Sunday morning the forges were in operation.　New England teamsters carried the links, as fast as they were finished, to West Point, and in the space of six weeks the whole chain was completed.　It weighed one hundred and eighty tons.

[2] In the spring of 1783, Washington communicated a request to all his principal officers, then in camp at Newburgh, and also to Governor Clinton, to give him their views in reference to a peace establishment, which must soon be organized.　They complied, and, from their several letters, Washington compiled a communication to Congress, extending to twenty-five folio pages.　In that communication, the commander-in-chief opposed the proposition of several officers to establish military academies at the different arsenals in the United States, and recommended the founding of one at West Point.　For his proposed plan in outline, see *Washington's Life and Writings*, viii., p. 417, 418.

The winding road from Fort Putnam to the plain is well wrought along the mountain side, but quite steep in many places.   A little south of it, and near the upper road leading to the stone quarries and Mr. Kingsley's, are the ruins of Fort Webb, a strong redoubt.

built upon a rocky eminence, and designed as an advanced defense of Fort Putnam.   A short distance below this, on another eminence, are the remains of Fort Wyllys, a still stronger fortification.   I visited these before returning to the hotel, and from the broken ramparts of Fort Webb sketched this distant view of Fort Putnam.

After a late breakfast, I procured the service of a water-

RUINS OF FORT PUTNAM, AS SEEN FROM FORT WEBB.

man to convey me in his skiff to Constitution Island, and from thence down to Buttermilk Falls,[1] two miles below West Point.   I directed him to come for me at the island within an hour and a half, but, either forgetting his engagement or serving another customer, it was almost noon before I saw him, when my patience as well as curiosity was quite exhausted. I had rambled over the island, making such sketches as I desired, and for nearly an hour I sat upon a smooth bowlder by the margin of the river, near the remains of the redoubt made to cover and defend the great chain at the island end.   On the southeast side of a small marshy cove, clasping a rough rock, a good portion of the heavy walls of Fort Constitution remain. The outworks are traceable several rods back into the stinted forest.   The sketch on the next page is from the upper edge of the cove, and includes, on the left, a view of the re-

---

[1] These falls derive their name from the milky appearance of the water as it rushes in a white foam over the rocks in a series of cascades.

mains of the redoubt across the river, the site of Fort Clinton, the chain, and Kosciuszko's monument, and, in the distance, Fort Hill, in the neighborhood of Ardenia and the Robinson House.

From Constitution Island we proceeeded along under the high cliffs of West Point to Buttermilk Falls. There was a strong breeze from the south that tossed our little craft about like an egg-shell, and my cloak was well moistened with the spray before reaching the landing. There, in a little cottage, overhung by a huge cliff that seemed ready to tumble down, lived a boatman, named Havens, seventy-nine years old. For more than fifty years himself and wife have lived there under the rocks and within the chorus of the cascades. He was too young to remember the stirring scenes of the Revolution, but immediate subsequent events were fresh in his recollection. He was engaged in removing powder from Fort Clinton, at West Point, when

VIEW FROM CONSTITUTION ISLAND.

1807. the Clermont, Fulton's experiment boat, with its bare paddles, went up the river, exciting the greatest wonder in its course. After I had passed a half hour pleasantly with this good old couple, the veteran prepared his little boat and rowed me across to " Beverly Dock" (the place from whence Arnold escaped in his barge to the Vulture), where he agreed to await my return from a visit to the Robinson House, three quarters of a mile distant. The path lay along the border of a marsh and up a steep hill, the route which tradition avers Arnold took in his flight. Two of the old willow trees, called " Arnold's willows," were yet standing on the edge of the morass, riven and half decayed.

The Robinson House, formerly owned by Colonel Beverly Robinson, is situated upon a fertile plateau at the foot of Sugar Loaf

ARNOLD'S WILLOW.

Mountain, one of the eastern ranges of the Highlands, which rises in conical form to an elevation of eight hundred feet above the plain. This mansion, spacious for the times, is at present occupied by Lieutenant Thomas Arden, a graduate of West Point, who, with commendable taste, preserves every part of it in its original character. The lowest building, on the left, was the farm-house, attached to the other two which formed the family mansion. Here Colonel Robinson lived in quiet, but not in retirement, for his house had

THE ROBINSON HOUSE.[1]

[1] This house, the property of Richard D. Arden, Esq. (father of the proprietor), is now called Beverly, the Christian name of Colonel Robinson. The dock built by Colonel R., and yet partially in existence, is Beverly Dock. The fine estate of Mr. Arden he has named Ardenia.

This view is from the lawn on the south side of the house. The highest part, on the right, was the portion occupied by Arnold. On the extreme right is an ancient cherry-tree, which doubtless bore fruit during the Revolution. This mansion was the country residence of Colonel Beverly Robinson, who married a daughter of Frederic Phillipse, the owner of an immense landed estate on the Hudson. Colonel Robinson was a son of John Robinson, who was president of the Council of Virginia on the retirement of Governor Gooch in 1734 He was a major in the British army under Wolfe at the storming of Quebec in 1759. He emi

too wide a reputation for hospitality to be often without a guest beneath its roof. There Generals Putnam and Parsons made their head-quarters in 1778–9. Dr. Dwight, then a chaplain in the army, and residing there, speaks of it as a most delightful spot, "surrounded by valuable gardens, fields, and orchards, yielding every thing which will grow in this climate." But the event which gives the most historic importance to this place was the treason of Arnold, which we will here consider.

When the British evacuated Philadelphia in the spring of 1778, Arnold (whose leg, wounded at the battle of Stillwater the previous autumn, was not yet healed) was appointed by Washington military governor of the city, having in command a small detachment of troops. After remaining a month in Philadelphia, Arnold conceived the project of quitting the army and engaging in the naval service. He applied to Washington for advice in the matter, expressing his desire to be appointed to a command in the navy, and alleging the state of his wounds as a reason for desiring less active service than the army, yet a service more fitted to his genius than the inactive one he was then engaged in. Washington answered him with caution, and declined offering an opinion. As no further movement was made in the matter, it is probable that the idea originated with Arnold alone; and, as he could not engage the countenance of Washington, he abandoned it.

Fond of show, and feeling the importance of his station, Arnold now began to live in a style of splendor and extravagance which his income would not allow, and his pecuniary embarrassments, already becoming troublesome to him, were soon fearfully augmented. The future was all dark, for he saw no honorable means for delivering himself from the dilemma. No doubt, dreams of rich prizes filled his mind while contemplating a command in the navy, but these

---

grated to New York, and became very wealthy by his marriage. The mansion here delineated was his residence when the war of the Revolution broke out, and, loving quiet, he refrained from engaging in the exciting events of the day. He was opposed to the course of the ministry during the few years preceding

the war, joined heartily in carrying out the spirit of the non-importation agreements, but, opposed to any separation of the colonies from the parent country, he took sides with the Loyalists when the Declaration of Independence was promulgated. He removed to New York, and there raised a military corps called the Loyal American Regiment, of which he was commissioned the colonel. His son, Beverly, was commissioned its lieutenant colonel. It is supposed that he was Arnold's correspondent and confidant in his preliminary acts of treason, and that the intentions of the traitor were known to him before any intimation of them was made to Sir Henry Clinton. Robinson figures publicly in that affair, and his country mansion was the head-quarters of the recusant general while arranging the crowning acts of his treachery.

At the conclusion of the war, Colonel Robinson and a portion of his family went to England, where he remained until his death, which occurred at Thornbury in 1792, at the age of 69 years. His wife died in 1822, at the age of 94. Colonel Robinson and Washington were personal friends before the war, and it is asserted that, at the house of the former, the Virginian colonel, while on his way to Boston in 1756, to consult General Shirley on military affairs, saw and

"fell in love" with Miss Mary Phillipse, a sister of Mrs. Robinson. It is also said that Washington made a proposition of marriage to her, but she refused him, telling him frankly that she loved another. The favored suitor was Roger Morris, one of Washington's companions in arms in the battle of the Great Meadows, where Braddock was killed. Morris was that general's aid-de-camp. A portrait of this lady may be found on page 626, vol. ii.

The miniature from which this likeness of Colonel Robinson was copied is in the possession of his grandson, Beverly Robinson, Esq., of New York. It was painted by Mr. Plott in 1785, when Colonel Robinson was sixty-two years old. The letter from which I copied his signature was written in 1786. The last surviving son of Colonel Robinson (Sir Frederick Philipse Robinson), died at his residence, at Brighton, England, on the 1st of January, 1852, at the age of 87 years.

being dissipated, he saw the web of difficulty gathering more closely and firmly around him. He had recently married Miss Margaret Shippen, daughter of Edward Shippen, one of the disaffected or Tory residents of Philadelphia. She was much younger than he, and he loved her with passionate fondness—a love deserved by her virtues and solidity of understanding. In addition to these advantages, she was beautiful in person and engaging in her manners. When the British troops entered Philadelphia, a few months previously, her friends had given them a cordial welcome ; therefore the marriage of Arnold with a member of such a family excited great surprise, and some uneasiness on the part of the patriots. "But he was pledged to the republic by so many services rendered and benefits received, that, on reflection, the alliance gave umbrage to no one."[1]

Arnold resided in the spacious mansion that once belonged to William Penn,[2] and there he lived in a style of luxury rivaled by no resident in Philadelphia. He kept a coach-and-four, servants in livery, and gave splendid banquets. Rather than retrench his expenses and live within his means, he chose to procure money by a system of fraud, and prostitution of his official power,[3] which brought him into collision with the people, and with the president and Council of Pennsylvania. The latter preferred a series of charges against him, all implying a willful abuse of power and criminal acts. These were laid before Congress. A committee, to whom all such charges were referred, acquitted him of criminal designs.

The whole subject was referred anew to a joint committee of Congress, and the Assembly and Council of Pennsylvania. After proceeding in their duties for a while, it was thought expedient to hand the whole matter over to Washington, to be submitted to a military tribunal. Four of the charges only were deemed cognizable by a court martial, and these were transmitted to Washington. Arnold had previously presented to Congress large claims against the government, on account of money which he alleged he had expended for the public service in Canada. A part of his claim was disallowed ; and it was generally believed that he attempted to cheat the government by false financial statements.

Arnold was greatly irritated by the course pursued by Congress and the Pennsylvania Assembly, and complained, probably not without cause (for party spirit was never more rife in the national Legislature than at that time), of injustice and partiality on the part of

BENEDICT ARNOLD.[4]

---

[1] *American Register*, 1817, ii., 31.

[2] A view of this mansion, which is still standing, may be found on page 95, vol. ii.

[3] Under pretense of supplying the wants of the army, Arnold forbade the shop-keepers to sell or buy ; he then put goods at the disposal of his agents, and caused them to be sold at enormous profits, the greater proportion of which he put into his own purse. "At one moment he prostituted his authority to enrich his accomplices ; at the next, squabbled with them about the division of the prey." His transactions in this way involved the enormous amount of one hundred and forty thousand dollars.

[4] Benedict Arnold was born in Norwich, Connecticut, on the 3d of January, 1740. He was a descendant of Benedict Arnold, one of the early governors of Rhode Island. He was bred an apothecary, under the brothers Lathrop of Norwich, who were so much pleased with him as a young man of genius and enterprise, that they gave him two thousand dollars to commence business with. From 1763 to 1767, he combined the business of druggist and bookseller in New Haven. Being in command of a volunteer company there when the war broke out, he marched to Cambridge, and thenceforth his career is identified with some of the bravest exploits of the Revolution, until his defection in 1780. In preceding chapters his course and character have been incidentally noticed, and it is unnecessary to repeat them here. On going over to the enemy, he received the commission of brigadier general in the British army, together with the price of his treason. After the war he went to England, where he chiefly resided until his death. He was engaged in trade in St. John's, New Brunswick, from 1786 till 1793. He was fraudulent in his dealings, and became so unpopular, that in 1792 he was hung in effigy by a mob. He left St. John's for the West In-

the former, in throwing aside the report of their own committee, by which he had been acquitted, and listening to the proposals of men who, he said, were moved by personal enmity, and had practiced unworthy artifices to cause delay. After the lapse of three months, the Council of Pennsylvania were not ready for the trial, and requested it to be put off, with the plea that they had not collected all their evidence. Arnold considered this a subterfuge, and plainly told all parties so. He was anxious to have the matter settled, for he was unemployed; for on the 18th of March, 1779, after the committee of Congress had reported on the charges preferred by the Council of Pennsylvania, he had resigned his commission. He was vexed that Congress, instead of calling up and sanctioning the first report, should yield to the solicitations of his enemies for a military trial.[1]

The day fixed for the trial was the 1st of June; the place, Washington's head-quarters at Middlebrook. The movements of the British prevented the trial being held, and it was deferred until the 20th of December,[a] when the court assembled for the purpose, at Morristown.[2] The trial commenced, and continued, with slight interruptions, until the 26th of January,[b] when the verdict was rendered. Arnold made an elaborate defense, in the course of which he magnified his services, asserted his entire innocence of the criminal charges made against him, cast reproach, by imputation, upon some of the purest men in the army, and solemnly proclaimed his patriotic attachment to his country. "The boastfulness and malignity of these declarations," says Sparks, "are obvious enough; but their consummate hypocrisy can be understood only by knowing the fact that, at the moment they were uttered, he had been eight months in secret correspondence with the enemy, and was prepared, if not resolved, when the first opportunity should offer, to desert and destroy his country."

[a] 1779.

[b] 1780.

Arnold was acquitted of two of the four charges; the other two were sustained in part. The court sentenced him to the mildest form of punishment, a simple reprimand by the commander-in-chief.[3] Washington carried the sentence into execution with all possible delicacy;[4] but Arnold's pride was too deeply wounded, or, it may be, his treasonable schemes were too far ripened, to allow him to take advantage of the favorable moment to regain the confidence of his countrymen and vindicate his character. He had expected from the court a triumphant vindication of his honor; he was prepared, in the event of an unfavorable verdict, to seek revenge at any hazard.

dies in 1794, but, finding a French fleet there, and fearing a detention by them, the allies of America, he sailed for England. He died in Gloucester Place, London, June 14th, 1801, at the age of sixty-one. His wife died at the same place, on the 14th of June, 1804, aged forty-three. Arnold had three children by his first wife, and four by his second, all boys.

[1] Sparks's *Life and Treason of Arnold*, 131, 133.

[2] Arnold continued to reside in Philadelphia after resigning his command. No longer afraid of his power, the people testified their detestation of his character by various indignities. One day he was assaulted in the streets by the populace. He complained to Congress, and asked a guard of twenty men to be placed around his residence. Congress declined to interfere, and this added another to the list of his alleged grievances. In the mean while, Arnold devised several schemes by which to relieve himself of his pecuniary embarrassments. He proposed to form a settlement in Western New York for the officers and soldiers who had served under him. He also conceived the idea of joining some of the Indian tribes, and, uniting many of them in one, become a great and powerful chief among them.

[3] Colonel Philip Van Cortlandt, of West Chester county, recorded the following in his diary: "General Arnold being under arrest for improper conduct in Philadelphia while he commanded there, I was chosen one of the court martial, Major-general Howe, president. There were also in that court four officers who had been at Ticonderoga when Colonel Hazen was called on for trial, &c. We were for cashiering Arnold, but the majority overruled, and he was finally sentenced to be reprimanded by the commander-in-chief. Had all the court known Arnold's former conduct as well as myself, he would have been dismissed the service."

[4] "When Arnold was brought before him," says M. de Marbois, "he kindly addressed him, saying, ' Our profession is the chastest of all. Even the shadow of a fault tarnishes the luster of our finest achievements. The least inadvertence may rob us of the public favor, so hard to be acquired. I reprimand you for having forgotten that, in proportion as you had rendered yourself formidable to our enemies, you should have been guarded and temperate in your deportment toward your fellow-citizens. Exhibit anew those noble qualities which have placed you on the list of our most valued commanders. I will myself furnish you, as far as it may be in my power, with opportunities of regaining the esteem of your country.' "

In manifest treason there was great danger, and, before proceeding to any overt acts of that nature, Arnold tried other schemes to accomplish his desire of obtaining money to meet the claims of his creditors and the daily demands of his extravagant style of living. He apparently acquiesced in the sentence of the court martial, and tried to get Congress to adjust his accounts by allowing his extravagant claims. This he could not accomplish, and he applied to M. de Luzerne, the French minister, who succeeded Gerard, for a loan, promising a faithful adherence to the king and country of the embassador. Luzerne admired the military talents of Arnold, and treated him with great respect; but he refused the loan, and administered a kind though keen rebuke to the applicant for thus covertly seeking a bribe.[1] He talked kindly to Arnold, reasoned soundly, and counseled him wisely. But words had no weight without the added specific gravity of gold, and he left the French minister with mingled indignation, mortification, and shame. From that hour he doubtless resolved to sell the liberties of his country for a price.

Hitherto the intimacy and correspondence of Arnold with officers of the British army had been without definite aim, and apparently incidental. His marriage with the daughter of Mr. Shippen (who was afterward chief justice of Pennsylvania) was no doubt a link of the greatest importance in the chain of his treasonable operations. That family was disaffected to the American cause. Shippen's youngest daughter, then eighteen years of age, remarkable, as we have observed, for her beauty, gayety, and general attractions, had been admired and flattered by the British officers, and was a leading personage in the splendid *fête* called the *Mischianza*, which was given in honor of Sir William Howe when he was about leaving the army for Europe. She was intimate with Major André, and corresponded with him after the British army had retired to New York. This was the girl who, attracted by the station, equipage, and brilliant display of Arnold, gave him her hand; this was the girl he loved so passionately. From that moment he was peculiarly exposed to the influence of the enemies of his country, and they, no doubt, kept alive the feelings of discontent which disturbed him after his first rupture with the authorities of Pennsylvania. His wife may not have been his confidant; but through her intimacy with Major André his correspondence with Sir Henry Clinton was effected. Whether she was cognizant of the contents of the letters of her husband is not known; probably she was not.

West Point was an object of covetous desire to Sir Henry Clinton. Arnold knew that almost any amount of money and honors would be given to the man who should be instrumental in placing that post in the hands of the enemy. He resolved, therefore, to make this the subject of barter for British gold. Hitherto he had pleaded the bad state of his wounds in justification of comparative inaction; now they healed rapidly. Though he could not endure the fatigues of active service on horseback, he thought he might fulfill the duties of commander at West Point. Hitherto he was sullen and indifferent; now his patriotism was aroused afresh, and he was eager to rejoin his old companions in arms. He was ready to make the sacrifice of domestic ease for an opportunity to again serve his bleeding country. With language of such import he addressed his friends in Congress, particularly General Schuyler, and others who he knew had influence with Washington. He intimated to Schuyler his partiality for the post at West Point. He also prevailed upon Robert R. Livingston, then a member of Congress from New York, to write to Washington and suggest the expe-

---

[1] M. de Marbois, who was the secretary of the French legation, has preserved a vivid picture of this interview in his account of the treason of Arnold, an excellent translation of which may be found in the *American Register*, 1817. He says Luzerne listened to Arnold's discourse with pain, but he answered with frankness. "You desire of me a service," he said, "which it would be easy for me to render, but which would degrade us both. When the envoy of a foreign power gives, or, if you will, lends money, it is ordinarily to corrupt those who receive it, and to make them the creatures of the sovereign whom he serves; or, rather, he corrupts without persuading; he buys and does not secure. But the firm league entered into between the king and the United States is the work of justice and the wisest policy. It has for its basis a reciprocal interest and good will. In the mission with which I am charged, my true glory consists in fulfilling it without intrigue or cabal, without resorting to any secret practices, and by the force alone of the condition of the alliance."

diency of giving Arnold the command of that station. Livingston cheerfully complied, but his letter had no appearance of being suggested by Arnold himself. Scarcely had Livingston's letter reached the camp, before Arnold appeared there in person. Under pretense of having private business in Connecticut, he passed through the camp, to pay his respects to the commander-in-chief. He made no allusion to his desire for an appointment to the command of West Point, and pursued his journey. On his return, he again called upon Washington at his quarters, and then suggested that, on joining the army, the command of that post would be best suited to his feelings and the state of his health. Washington was a little surprised that the impetuous Arnold should be willing to take command where there was no prospect of active operations. His surprise, however, had no mixture of suspicion. Arnold visited and inspected all the fortifications, in company with General Robert Howe and then returned to Philadelphia.

Having resolved to join the army, Arnold applied to Congress for arrearages of pay, to enable him to furnish himself with a horse and equipage. Whether his application was successful no record explains. He reached the camp on the last day of July, while the army was crossing the Hudson from the west side, at King's Ferry (Verplanck's Point). 1780.
On the arrival of the French at Newport, Sir Henry Clinton made an effort to attack them before they could land and fortify themselves. The result we have already considered. This movement caused Washington, who was encamped between Haverstraw and Tappan, to cross the river, with the intention of attacking New York in the absence of Clinton. Arnold met Washington on horseback, just as the last division was crossing over, and asked if any place had been assigned to him. The commander-in-chief replied that he was to take command of the left wing, the post of honor. Arnold was disappointed, and perceiving it, Washington promised to meet him at his quarters, and have further conversation on the subject. He found Arnold's heart set upon the command of West Point. He was unable to account for this strange inconsistency with his previous ambition to serve in the most conspicuous place. Still he had no suspicion of wrong, and he complied with Arnold's request. The instructions which gave him command of " that post and its dependencies, in which all are included from Fishkill to King's Ferry,"[1] were dated at Peekskill on the 3d of August, 1780. Arnold repaired immediately to the Highlands, and established his quarters at Colonel Robinson's house. Sir Henry Clinton having abandoned his expedition against the French at Newport, the American army retraced its steps, and, crossing the Hudson, marched down to Tappan and encamped, where it remained for several weeks. General Greene commanded the right wing, and Lord Stirling the left; six battalions of light infantry, stationed in advance, were commanded by La Fayette.

Thus far Arnold's plans had worked admirably. He had now been in correspondence with Sir Henry Clinton for eighteen months,[2] both parties always writing over fictitious names, and, for a great portion of the time, without a knowledge, on the part of the British commander, of the name and character of the person with whom he was in communication. Arnold corresponded with Clinton through the hands of Major André. Writing in a dis-

---

[1] *Sparks's Life and Writings of Washington,* viii., 139.

[2] It is not positively known how early Arnold's correspondence with officers of the British army commenced, or at what precise period he first conceived the idea of betraying his country. The translator of the Marquis de Chastellux's *Travels in North America,* an English gentleman of distinction, and a resident here during our Revolution, says (i., page 97), " There is every reason to believe that Arnold's treachery took its date from his connection with Lieutenant *Hele,* killed afterward on board the *Formidable,* in the West Indies, and who was undoubtedly a very active and industrious spy at Philadelphia in the winter of 1778, whither he was sent for that purpose in a pretended flag of truce, which being wrecked in the Delaware, he was made prisoner by Congress, a subject of much discussion between them and the commander at New York. That the intended plot was known in England, and great hopes built upon it long before it was to take place, is certain. General Mathews and other officers, who returned in the autumn of 1780, being often heard to declare ' that it was all over with the rebels; that they were about to receive an irreparable blow, the news of which would soon arrive, &c., &c.' Their silence, from the moment in which they received an account of the failure of the plot and the discovery of the traitor, evidently pointed out the object of their allusions."

guised hand, he clothed his meaning in the ambiguous style of a commercial correspondence, and affixed to his letters the signature of GUSTAVUS. André signed his JOHN ANDERSON. He was an aid-de-camp of the commander-in-chief of the British forces, and was afterward the adjutant general of the British army. He enjoyed the unbounded confidence of Sir Henry Clinton, and to him, when the name and station of Arnold became known, was

FAC SIMILE OF ARNOLD'S DISGUISED HANDWRITING.

FAC SIMILE OF A PORTION OF ONE OF ANDRÉ'S LETTERS.[1]

intrusted the delicate task of consummating the bargain with the traitor. Even while the name of Arnold was yet concealed, Clinton was confident that his secret correspondent was an officer of high rank in the American army; and before Arnold was tried by a court martial, the British general was convinced that he was the man. That trial lessened his value in the estimation of Clinton; but when Arnold obtained the command of West Point, the affair assumed greater magnitude and importance.

The general plan of operations agreed upon for placing West Point in possession of the enemy was, for Sir Henry Clinton to send a strong force up the Hudson at the moment when the combined French and American armies should make an expected movement against New York. This movement was really a part of Washington's plan for the autumn campaign, and Sir Henry Clinton was informed of it by Arnold. It was concluded that West Point and its dependencies would be the depositories of a great portion of the stores and ammunition of the allied armies. It was rumored that the French were to land on Long Island, and approach New York in that direction, while Washington was to march with the main army of the Americans to invade York Island at Kingsbridge. At this juncture, a flotilla under Rodney, bearing a strong land force, was to proceed up the Hudson to

---

[1] This is a portion of a concluding sentence of a letter from André to Colonel Sheldon, which will be mentioned presently.

the Highlands, when Arnold, under pretense of a weak garrison, should surrender the post and its dependencies into the hands of the enemy.   In this event, Washington must have retreated from Kingsbridge, and the French on Long Island would probably have fallen into the hands of the British.   With a view to these operations, the British troops were so posted that they could be put in motion at the shortest notice ; while vessels, properly manned, were kept in readiness on the Hudson River.

It was now necessary that Clinton should be certified of the identity of General Arnold and his hidden correspondent, in order that he might make himself secure against a counterplot.   A personal conference was proposed, and Arnold insisted that the officer sent to confer with him should be Adjutant-general Major Andrè.[1]   Clinton, on his part, had already fixed upon Andrè as the proper person to hold the conference.   It must be borne in mind that Andrè did not seek the service, though, when engaged in it, he used his best endeavors, as in duty bound, to carry out its objects.

As money was the grand lure that made Arnold a traitor, he felt it necessary to have an understanding respecting the reward which he was to obtain.   Under date of August 30th, he wrote to Andrè in the feigned hand and style alluded to, and said, referring to himself in the third person, " He is still of opinion that his first proposal is by no means unreasonable, and makes no doubt, when he has a conference with you, that you will close with it.   He expects, when you meet, that you will be fully authorized from your house ; that the risks and profits of the copartnership may be fully understood.   *A speculation of this kind might be easily made with ready money.*"   Clinton understood this hint, and Andrè was authorized to negotiate on that point.

Arnold's first plan was to have the interview at his own quarters in the Highlands, Andrè to be represented as a person devoted to the American interest, and possessing ample means for procuring intelligence from the enemy.   This was a safe ground for Arnold to proceed upon, for the employment of secret agents to procure intelligence was well known.[2]   He dispatched a letter to Andrè informing him of this arrangement, and assuring him that if he could make his way safely to the American outposts above White Plains, he would find no obstructions thereafter.   Colonel Sheldon was then in command of a detachment of cavalry stationed on the east side of the Hudson.   His head-quarters, with a part of the detachment, was at Salem, and those of his lieutenant (Colonel Jameson) and of Major Tallmadge, with the remainder of the corps, were at North Castle.   Arnold gave Sheldon notice that he expected a person from New York, with whom he would have an interview at the colonel's quarters, to make important arrangements for receiving early intelligence from the enemy.   He requested Sheldon, in the event of the stranger's arrival, to send information of the fact to his quarters at the Robinson House.   Arnold's plan was not entirely agreeable to Andrè, for he was not disposed to go within the American lines and assume the odious character of a spy.   He accordingly wrote the following letter to Colonel Sheldon, signed JOHN ANDERSON, which, he knew, would be placed in Arnold's hands.   It proposed a meeting at Dobbs's Ferry, upon the Neutral Ground.   " I am told that my name is made known to you, and that I may hope your indulgence in permitting me to meet a friend near your outposts.   I will endeavor to obtain permission to go out with a flag, which will be sent to Dobbs's Ferry on Monday next, the 11th instant, at twelve o'clock, when I shall be happy to meet Mr. G———.   Should I not be allowed to go, the officer who is to command the escort—between whom and myself no distinction need be made—can speak in the affair.

1780.

September, 1780.

---

[1] Sir Henry Clinton's letter to Lord George Germain.

[2] In this connection it may be mentioned, that when Arnold was about to proceed to the Highlands, he went to La Fayette, and requested him to give him the names of spies which the marquis had in his employ in New York, suggesting that intelligence from them might often reach him more expeditiously by the way of West Point.   La Fayette objected, saying that he was in honor bound not to reveal the names of spies to any person.   The object which Arnold had in view became subsequently obvious.

Let me entreat you, sir, to favor a matter so interesting to the parties concerned, and which is of so private a nature that the public on neither side can be injured by it." This letter puzzled Colonel Sheldon, for he had never heard the name of JOHN ANDERSON, nor had Arnold intimated any thing concerning an escort. He supposed, however, that it was from the person expected by Arnold. He therefore inclosed it to the general, telling him that he (Sheldon) was too unwell to go to Dobbs's Ferry, and expressing a hope that Arnold would meet Anderson there himself. Andrè's letter puzzled Arnold too, for he found it difficult to explain its meaning very plausibly to Colonel Sheldon. But the traitor contrived, with consummate skill, to prevent the mystery having any importance in the mind of that officer.

MAP SHOWING THE SCENE OF ARNOLD'S TREASON.[2]

Arnold left his quarters on the 10th, went down the river in his barge to King's Ferry, and passed the night at the house of Joshua Hett Smith, near Haverstraw,[1] who afterward acted a conspicuous part in the work of treason, he being, as is supposed, the dupe of Arnold. Early in the morning the traitor proceeded toward Dobbs's Ferry, where Andrè and Colonel Beverly Robinson had arrived. As Arnold approached that point, not having a flag, he was fired upon by the British gun-boats stationed near, and closely pursued. He escaped to the opposite side of the river, and the conference was necessarily postponed. Having gone down the river openly in his barge, Arnold deemed it necessary to make some explanation to General Washington, and accordingly he wrote a letter to him, in which, after mentioning several important matters connected with the command at West Point, he incidentally stated that he had come down the river to establish signals as near the enemy's lines as possible, by which he might receive information of any movements of a fleet or troops up the Hudson. This letter was

---

[1] This house is yet standing. A drawing of it is presented on page 152. It is about two miles and a half below Stony Point, on the right side of the road leading to Haverstraw.

There has ever been a difference of opinion concerning the true character of Smith; some supposing him to have been a Tory, and acting with a full knowledge of Arnold's instructions; others believing him to have been the traitor's dupe. Leake, in his *Life of John Lamb* (p. 256), says that Arnold often visited Smith to while away tedious hours; and that Colonel Lamb, while in command at West Point, was frequently invited to visit him, but invariably declined, notwithstanding Mrs. Smith and Mrs. Lamb were nearly related. Colonel Lamb said he knew Smith to be a Tory, and he would not visit his own father in a similar category. There is evidence that he was a Whig. See William Smith's letter on page 724.

[2] This map includes the Hudson River and its shores from Dobbs's Ferry to West Point, and exhibits a chart of the whole scene of Arnold's treason, and of the route, capture, and execution of the unfortunate Andrè. The thin lines upon the map indicate the public roads. By a reference to it, in perusing the narrative, the reader will have a clear understanding of the matter.

dated at "Dobbs's Ferry, September 11th," and on that night he returned to his quarters at the Robinson House.

It was now necessary to make arrangements for another interview. No time was to be lost; no precautionary measure was to be neglected. Arnold knew that Washington was preparing to go to Hartford, to hold a conference with the newly-arrived French officers, and that the proper time to consummate his plans would be during the absence of the commander-in-chief. As Washington would cross the Hudson at King's Ferry, it was very necessary, too, that no movement should be made until his departure that might excite his suspicions.

Two days after Arnold returned to his quarters, he found means to send a communication to Andrè, which, as usual, was couched in commercial language. $\quad$ September 13, 1780. He cautioned Andrè not to reveal any thing to Colonel Sheldon. "I have no confidant," he said; "I have made one too many already, who has prevented some profitable speculation." He informed Andrè that a person would meet him on the west side of Dobbs's Ferry, on Wednesday, the 20th instant, and that he would conduct him to a place of safety, where the writer would meet him. "It will be necessary," he said, "for you to be in disguise. I can not be more explicit at present. Meet me, if possible. You may rest assured that, if there is no danger in passing your lines, you will be perfectly safe where I propose a meeting." Arnold also wrote to Major Tallmadge, at North Castle, instructing him, if a person by the name of John Anderson should arrive at his station, to send him without delay to head-quarters, escorted by two dragoons.

Sir Henry Clinton, who was as anxious as Arnold to press the matter forward, had sent Colonel Robinson up the river on board the Vulture, with orders to proceed as high as Teller's Point. Robinson and Arnold seem to have had some general correspondence previous to this time, and it is believed (as I have mentioned on a preceding page) that the former was made acquainted with the treasonable designs of the latter some time before the subject was brought explicitly before Sir Henry Clinton. As Arnold was occupying Colonel Robinson's confiscated mansion, a good opportunity was afforded him to write to the general without exciting suspicion, making the burden of his letters the subject of a restoration of his property. This medium of communication was now adopted to inform General Arnold that Robinson was on board the Vulture. Robinson wrote to General Putnam, pretending a belief that he was in the Highlands, and requesting an interview with him on the subject of his property. This letter was covered by one addressed to Arnold, requesting him to hand the inclosed to General Putnam, or, if that officer had gone away, to return it by the bearer. "In case General Putnam shall be absent," he said, "I am persuaded, from the humane and generous character you bear, that you will grant me the favor asked." These letters were sent, by a flag, to Verplanck's Point, the Vulture then lying about six miles below. On the very day that Washington commenced his journey to Hartford, Arnold $\quad$ September 18. had come down to the Point, a few hours before the arrival of the chief at the ferry on the opposite shore, and received and read Colonel Robinson's letter. He mentioned the contents to Colonel Lamb and others, with all the frankness of conscious integrity. The commander-in-chief and his suite crossed the river in Arnold's barge[1] soon afterward, and the latter accompanied them to Peekskill. Arnold frankly laid the letter before Washing-

---

[1] Sparks (*American Biography*, vol. iii., from which a large portion of these details are drawn) says that two incidents occurred during this passage across the river, which, though almost unnoticed at the time, afterward, when the treachery was known, assumed some importance. The Vulture was in full view, and while Washington was looking at it through a glass, and speaking in a low tone to one of his officers, Arnold was observed to appear uneasy. Another incident was remembered. There was a daily expectation of the arrival of a French squadron on the coast, under Count de Guichen. La Fayette, alluding to the frequent communications by water between New York and the posts on the Hudson, said to Arnold, "General, since you have a correspondence with the enemy, you must ascertain, as soon as possible, what has become of Guichen." Arnold was disconcerted, and demanded what he meant; but immediately controlling himself, and the boat just then reaching the shore, nothing more was said. No doubt, for a moment, Arnold thought his plot was discovered.—Page 186.

ton, and asked his advice.   His reply was, that the civil authority alone could act in the matter, and he did not approve of a personal interview with Robinson.   This frankness on the part of Arnold effectually prevented all suspicion, and Washington proceeded to Hartford, confident in the integrity of the commandant of West Point.

Arnold dared not, after receiving this opinion from Washington, so far disregard it as to meet Robinson, but it gave him an opportunity to use the name of the commander-in-chief in his reply, which he openly dispatched by an officer in a flag-boat to the Vulture.   He September, informed Colonel Robinson that on the night of the 20th he should send a person 1780. on board of the Vulture, who would be furnished with a boat and a flag of truce ; and in a postscript he added, "I expect General Washington to lodge here on Saturday next, and I will lay before him any matter you may wish to communicate."   This was an ingenuous and safe way of informing the enemy at what time the commander-in-chief would return from Hartford.

Arnold's communication was sent to Sir Henry Clinton, and the next morning André proceeded to Dobbs's Ferry, positively instructed by his general not to change his dress, go within the American lines, receive papers, or in any other way act in the character of a spy. It was supposed that Arnold himself would visit the Vulture ; but he had arranged a plan for effecting a meeting involving less personal hazard.   Joshua Hett Smith, just mentioned, who lived about two miles below Stony Point, had been employed by General Robert Howe, when in command of West Point, to procure intelligence from New York.   Smith occupied a very respectable station in society, and could command more valuable aid, in the business in question, than any other person.   To him Arnold went with a proposition to assist him in his undertaking, without, as Smith alleged, revealing to him his real intentions.   He flattered him with expressions of the highest confidence and regard, and informed him that he was expecting a person of consequence from New York with valuable intelligence from the enemy, and he wanted Smith's service in bringing him within the American lines. While at Smith's on this business, Arnold was joined by his wife with her infant child, who had come on from Philadelphia.   There she remained all night, and the next morning her husband went with her, in his barge, to head-quarters.

Arnold made his arrangements with Smith to have his meeting with André (whom he had resolved should be brought on shore from the Vulture) take place at his house, in the event of the conference being protracted.   Smith, accordingly, took his family to Fishkill to visit some friends, and returning, halted at the Robinson House, and arranged with Arnold a plan of operations.   The general gave him the customary pass for a flag of truce, sent an order to Major Kierse, at Stony Point, to supply Smith with a boat whenever he should want one, and directed Smith to proceed to the Vulture the following night and bring on shore the person who was expected to be there.   Smith failed in his endeavors to make the arrangements, and did not visit the Vulture at the time he was directed to.   Samuel Colquhon, one of his tenants, to whom he applied for assistance as boatman, refused to go. Smith sent Colquhon to Arnold with a letter, informing him of his failure.   The messenger, September 21. by riding all night, reached the Robinson House at dawn.   Early in the forenoon, Arnold himself went down the river to Verplanck's Point, and thence to Smith's house.   At Verplanck's, Colonel Livingston handed him a letter which he had just received for him from Captain Sutherland of the Vulture.   It was a remonstrance against an alleged violation of the rules of war by a party on Teller's Point.[1]   The letter was in the handwriting of André, though signed by Sutherland.   Arnold at once perceived the main object of this secretaryship to be, to inform him that André was on board the Vulture.

Arnold now hastened to make arrangements to bring André ashore.   He ordered a skiff

---

[1] A flag of truce was exhibited at Teller's Point, inviting, as was supposed, a pacific intercourse with the ship.   A boat, with another flag, was sent off, but as soon as it approached the shore it was fired upon by several armed men who were concealed in the bushes.   On account of this outrage, Captain Sutherland sent a letter of remonstrance to Colonel Livingston, "the commandant at Verplanck's Point."   The letter was dated "morning of the 21st of September."

to be sent to a certain place in Haverstraw Creek, and then proceeded to Smith's house. Every thing was made ready, except procuring two boatmen, and this was found a difficult matter. The voyage promised many perils, for American guard-boats were stationed at various places on the river. These, however, had been ordered not to interfere with Smith and his party. Samuel Colquhon and his brother Joseph were again solicited to accompany Smith, but both positively refused at first to go; they yielded only when Arnold himself threatened them with punishment. At near midnight the three men pushed off from shore with muffled oars. It was a serene, starry night; not a ripple was upon the Hudson, not a leaf was stirred by the breeze. Silently the little boat approached the Vulture, and when near, the sentinel on deck hailed them. After making some explanations and receiving some rough words, Smith was allowed to go on board. In the cabin he found Beverly Robinson and Captain Sutherland. These officers and Major André were the only persons in the ship who were privy to the transactions in progress. Smith bore a sealed letter from Arnold to Beverly Robinson, in which the traitor said, "This will be delivered to you by Mr. Smith, who will conduct you to a place of safety. Neither Mr. Smith nor any other person shall be made acquainted with your proposals. If they (which I doubt not) are of such a nature that I can officially take notice of them, I shall do it with pleasure. I take it for granted that Colonel Robinson will not propose any thing that is not for the interest of the United States as well as himself." This language was a guard against evil consequences in the event of the letter falling into other hands. Smith had also two passes, signed by Arnold, which Robinson well understood to be intended to communicate the idea that the writer expected André to come on shore, and to secure the boat from detention by the water-guard.[1]

Major André was introduced to Smith, and both descended into the boat. They landed at the foot of a great hill, called Long Clove Mountain, on the western shore of the Hudson, about two miles below Haverstraw. This place had been designated by Arnold for the meeting, and thither he had repaired from Smith's house. Arnold was concealed in the thick bushes, and to the same place Smith conducted André. They were left alone, and for the first time the conspirators heard each other's voice; for the first time Arnold's lips uttered audibly the words of treason. There, in the gloom of night, concealed from all human cognizance, they discussed their dark plans, and plotted the utter ruin of the patriot cause. When, at the twilight of an autumn day, I stood upon that spot, in the shadow of the high hills, and the night gathering its veil over the waters and the fields, a superstitious dread crept over me lest the sentence of *anathema, maranatha*, should make the spot as unstable as the earth whereon rested the tents of the rebellious Korah, Dathan, and Abiram.

The hour of dawn approached, and the conference was yet in progress. Smith came, and warned them of the necessity for haste. There was much yet to do, and André reluctantly consented to mount the horse rode by Arnold's servant, and accompany the general to Smith's house, nearly four miles distant.[2] It was yet dark, and the voice of a sentinel, near

---

[1] These passes, which are still in existence, are as follows:

"Head-quarters, Robinson House, September 20, 1780.

"Permission is given to Joshua Smith, Esquire, a gentleman, Mr. John Anderson, who is with him, and his two servants, to pass and repass the guards near King's Ferry at all times.

"B. Arnold, *M. Gen'l.*"

"Head-quarters, Robinson House, September 21, 1780.

"Permission is granted to Joshua Smith, Esq., to go to Dobbs's Ferry with three Men and a Boy with a Flag to carry some Letters of a private Nature for Gentlemen in New York, and to Return immediately.

"B. Arnold, *M. Gen'l.*

"N.B.—He has permission to go at such hours and times as the tide and his business suits.

"B. A."

[2] The fact that Arnold had provided a spare horse (for there was no necessity for a servant to accompany him to the place of meeting), is evidence that he expected a longer conference than the remainder of the night would afford. Furthermore, convicted as Arnold is of innate wickedness, it may not be unjust to suppose that he was prepared, after getting André within the American lines, to perform any act of dishonor to extort a high price for his treason, or to shield himself from harm if circumstances should demand it.

the village of Haverstraw, gave André the first intimation that he was within the American lines. He felt his danger, but it was too late to recede. His uniform was effectually concealed by a long blue surtout, yet the real danger that environed him, he being within the enemy's lines without a flag or pass, made him exceedingly uneasy. They arrived at Smith's house at dawn, and at that moment they heard a cannonade in the direction of the Vulture. Colonel Livingston had been informed that the vessel lay so near the shore as to be within cannon shot. Accordingly, during the night, he sent a party with cannon from Verplanck's Point, and at dawn, from Teller's

SMITH'S HOUSE.[1]

Point, they opened a fire upon the Vulture, of such severity that the vessel hoisted her anchors and dropped farther down the river.[2] This movement André beheld with anxiety ; September 22, but, when the firing ceased, his spirits revived. During that morning the whole 1780. plot was arranged, and the day for its consummation fixed. André was to return to New York, and the British troops, already embarked under the pretext of an expedition to the Chesapeake, were to be ready to ascend the river at a moment's warning. Arnold was to weaken the various posts at West Point by dispersing the garrison. When the British should appear, he was to send out detachments among the mountain gorges, under pretense of meeting the enemy, as they approached, at a distance from the works. As we have noticed, a link from the great chain at Constitution Island was to be removed. The river would be left free for the passage of vessels, and the garrison, so scattered, could not act in force ; thus the enemy could take possession with very little resistance. All the

[1] This view is from the slope in front of the house. The main building is of stone ; the wings are wood. The piazza in front of the main building, and the balustrades upon the top, are the only modern additions ; otherwise the house appears the same as when Arnold and André were there. It stands upon a slope of *Treason Hill*, a few rods west of the road leading from Stony Point to Haverstraw, and about half way between the two places. It was in a room in the second story that the conspirators remained during the day of their arrival. The present owner of the house and grounds is Mr. William C. Houseman.

[2] Colonel Livingston, on perceiving the position of the Vulture, conceived a plan for destroying her. He asked Arnold for two pieces of heavy cannon for the purpose, but the general eluded the proposal on frivolous pretenses, so that Livingston's detachment could bring only one four-pounder to bear upon her. He had obtained some ammunition from Colonel Lamb, from West Point, who sent it rather grudgingly, and with an expressed wish that there might not be a wanton waste of it. "Firing at a ship with a four-pounder," he said, "is, in my opinion, a waste of powder." Little did he think what an important bearing that cannonade was to have upon the destinies of America. It was that which drove the Vulture from her moorings, and was one of the causes of the fatal detention of André at Smith's house. The Vulture was so much injured that, had she not got off with the flood, she must have struck. Colonel Livingston saw Arnold pass Verplanck's in his barge when he escaped to the Vulture ; and he afterward declared that he had such suspicion of him that, had his guard-boats been near, he would have gone after him instantly, and de manded his destination and errand.

HENRY LIVINGSTON, who commanded at Stony Point at the time of Arnold's treason, was born at the Livingston Manor, in Columbia county, New York, January 19th, 1752. He married in Canada at an early age, and while residing there became familiar with the French language. He was among the first who took up arms against Great Britain. He accompanied Montgomery to St. John's, Montreal, and Quebec. He assisted in the capture of the fort at Chambly, and otherwise distinguished himself in that campaign. He was a lieutenant colonel in the army at Stillwater, and was present at the capture of Burgoyne. At the close of the war he was made a brigadier general, and throughout a long life maintained the highest confidence and respect of his countrymen. The Marquis de Chastellux, who breakfasted with him at Verplanck's Point on one occasion, says of him, in his Journal (i., 94), "This is a very amiable and well-informed young man." He died at his residence, Columbia county, May 26th, 1823, at the age of seventyone years.

plans being arranged, Arnold supplied Andrè with papers explanatory of the military condition of West Point and its dependencies.[1] These he requested him to place between his

---

[1] These documents, with five of the passes given by Arnold on this occasion, are now preserved in the Library of the State of New York, at Albany, having been purchased from the family of a lineal descendant of Governor George Clinton. They were in my custody a few weeks, when I had the opportunity of comparing the following copies, previously made, with the originals, and found them correct. These manuscripts, though somewhat worn, are quite perfect. Those written upon one side of the paper only have been pasted upon thicker paper for preservation. The others yet exhibit the wrinkles made by Andrè's foot in his boot. The following are true copies of the several papers:

"West Point, September 5th, 1780.

"*Artillery Orders.*—The following disposition of the corps is to take place in Case of an alarm:

"Capt. Dannills with his Comp'y at Fort Putnam, and to detach an Officer with 12 men to Wyllys's Redoubt, a Non Commissioned Officer with 3 men to Webb's Redoubt, and the like number to Redoubt No. 4.

"Capt. Thomas and Company to repair to Fort Arnold.

"Captain Simmons and Company to remain at the North and South Redoubts, at the East side of the River, until further Orders.

"Lieutenant Barber, with 20 men of Capt. Jackson's Company, will repair to Constitution Island; the remainder of the Company, with Lieut. Mason's, will repair to Arnold.

"Capt. Lieut. George and Lieut. Blake, with 20 men of Captain Treadwell's Company, will Repair to Redoubt No. 1 and 2; the remainder of the Company will be sent to Fort Arnold.

"Late Jones's Company, with Lieut. Fisk, to repair to the South Battery.

"The Chain Battery, Sherburn's Redoubt, and the Brass Field pieces, will be manned from Fort Arnold as Occation may require.

"The Commissary and Conductor of Military stores will in turn wait upon the Commanding Officer of Artillery for Orders.

"The artificers in the garrison (agreeable to former Orders) will repair to Fort Arnold, and there receive further Orders from the Command'g Officer of Artillery.

"S. BAUMAN, *Major Comm't Artillery.*"

This document gave the British full information of what would be the disposition of the Americans on the occasion; and as Sir Henry Clinton and many of his officers were acquainted with the ground, they would know at what particular points to make their attacks. This and the following document are in Arnold's handwriting:

"*Estimate of Forces at W'st Point and its Dependencies, September 13, 1780.*

"A brigade of Massachusetts Militia, and two regiments of Rank and File New Hampshire, Inclusive of 166 Batteaux Men at Verplanck's and Stony Points	992
"On command and Extra Service at Fishkills, New Windsor, &c., &c., who may be called in occationally	852
"3 regiments of Connecticut Militia, under the com'd of Colonel Wells, on the lines near N. Castle	488
"A detachment of New York levies on the lines	115
	Militia, 2447
"Colonel Lamb's Regiment	167
"Colonel Livingston's, at Verplank and Stoney Pts.	80
	Continent: 247
"Colonel Sheldon's Dragoons, on the lines, about one half mounted	142
"Batteaux Men and Artificers	250
	Total, 3086."

The following document is in the handwriting of Villefranche, a French engineer:

"*Estimate of the Number of Men necessary to Man the Works at West Point and in the Vicinity.*

"Fort Arnold	620	Redoubt No. 2	150	Redoubt No. 7	78
— Putnam	450	ditto 3	120	North Redoubt	120
— Wyllys	140	ditto 4	100	South Redoubt	130
— Webb	140	ditto 5	139		
Redoubt No. 1	150	ditto 6	110	Total,	2438

Villefranche, Engineer

N.B.—The Artillery Men are not Included in the above Estimate."

722   PICTORIAL FIELD-BOOK

Return of the Ordnance in the different Forts at West Point.   Arnold's Description of the Works.

stockings and feet, and in the event of accident, to destroy them. He then gave him a pass, a fac simile of which is printed on the next page, and bidding Andrè adieu, Arnold went

The following table is in the handwriting of Bauman, Major Commandant of Artillery :

"RETURN OF THE ORDNANCE IN THE DIFFERENT FORTS, BATTERIES, &C., AT WEST POINT AND ITS DEPENDENCIES, SEPT. 5, 1780."

Column groups: Garrison / Traveling / Stocked Carriages (caliber in pounders), Mortars (in Inches), Howitzers (in Inches).

Calibers	Metal	24	18	12	9	9	6	.		4	3	0		5½	4¾		8	Total
Fort Arnold	Brass	..	..	..	..	..	..	..	..	..	..	..	1	5	5	1	..	23
	Iron	1	6	..	..	1	..	..	..	..	..	3	..	..	..	..	..	
Fort Putnam	Brass	..	..	..	..	..	..	2	..	..	..	..	..	..	4	..	..	14
	Iron	..	5	..	2	..	..	..	..	..	..	..	..	..	..	..	..	
Constitution Island	Iron	..	..	..	4	..	1	5	..	..	..	..	..	..	..	..	..	10
South Battery	Iron	..	4	..	1	..	..	..	..	..	..	..	..	..	..	..	..	5
Chain Battery	Iron	..	..	..	1	2	..	..	..	..	..	..	..	..	..	..	..	3
Lanthorn Battery	Iron	..	..	..	..	2	..	..	..	..	..	..	..	..	..	..	..	2
Webb's Redoubt	Iron	..	..	..	1	..	2	..	..	1	..	..	..	..	..	..	..	4
Sherman's Redoubt	Iron	..	..	..	..	..	2	3	..	..	..	..	..	..	..	..	..	5
Megg's Redoubt	Iron	..	..	..	..	..	..	..	1	..	1	..	..	..	..	..	..	2
South Redoubt	Iron	..	..	..	1	..	..	4	..	..	..	..	..	..	..	..	..	5
North Redoubt	Iron	..	3	..	3	..	..	..	..	..	..	..	..	..	..	..	..	6
Wyllys's Redoubt	Iron	..	..	2	..	..	..	..	..	..	..	..	3	..	..	..	..	5
Rocky Hill, No. 4	Iron	..	..	..	..	..	..	..	2	..	..	..	..	..	..	..	..	2
" No. 1	Iron	..	..	..	1	..	4	..	..	..	..	..	..	..	..	..	..	5
" No. 2	Iron	..	..	..	..	..	..	..	2	..	..	..	..	..	..	..	..	2
Verplanck's Point	Brass	..	..	..	..	..	..	..	..	..	..	..	..	..	2	1	..	3
Stony Point	Iron	..	..	1	..	..	2	..	..	..	..	..	2	..	..	..	1	4
Total		1	18	3	14	5	9	14	5	2	1	3	6	5	11	2	1	100

N.B.—The following ordnance not distributed :

No. 6	iron	12 pounder.
4	"	9 "
1	"	6 "
1	"	4 "
2	"	3 "
14		

3	brass	24 pounders.
7	"	12 "
1	"	8-inch howitzer.
11		

J. Bauman, Major Com[mandan]t of Artillery

The following description of the works at West Point and its dependencies is in the handwriting of Arnold, endorsed " Remarks on Works at West Point, a copy to be transmitted to his Excellency General Washington. Sep'r. 1780."

"Fort Arnold is built of Dry Fascines and Wood, is in a ruinous condition, incompleat, and subject to take Fire from Shells or Carcasses.

"Fort Putnam, Stone, Wanting great repairs, the wall on the East side broke down, and rebuilding From the Foundation; at the West and South side have been a Chevaux-de-Frise, on the West side broke in many Places. The East side open; two Bomb Proofs and Provision Magazine in the Fort, and Slight Wooden Barrack.—A commanding piece of ground 500 yards West, between the Fort and No. 4—or Rocky Hill.

up the river, in his own barge, to head-quarters, fully believing that no obstacle now interposed to frustrate his wicked scheme. Andrè passed the remainder of the day alone, and

Head Quarters Robinsons
Horn Sep.ʳ 22ᵈ 1780

Permit Mr. John Anderson to pass the
Grounds to the White Plains, or below
it He Chuses. He being on Public
Business by my Direction

B. Arnold M. Genl

as soon as evening came, he applied to Smith to take him back to the Vulture. Smith positively refused to go, and pleaded illness from ague as an excuse. If he quaked, it was probably not from ague, but from fear, wrought by the firing upon the Vulture; for he offered to ride half the night with Andrè, on horseback, if he would take a land route. Having no other means of reaching the vessel, Andrè was obliged to yield to the force of circumstances. He con-

---

"Fort Webb, built of Fascines and Wood, a slight Work, very dry, and liable to be set on fire, as the approaches are very easy, without defenses, save a slight Abattis.

"Fort Wyllys, built of stone 5 feet high, the Work above plank filled with Earth, the stone work 15 feet. the Earth 9 feet thick.—No Bomb Proofs, the Batteries without the Fort.

"Redoubt No. 1. On the South side wood 9 feet thick, the Wt. North and East sides 4 feet thick, no cannon in the works, a slight and single Abattis, no ditch or Pickett. Cannon on two Batteries. No Bomb Proofs.

"Redoubt No. 2. The same as No. 1. No Bomb Proofs.

"Redoubt No. 3, a slight Wood Work 3 Feet thick, very Dry, no Bomb Proofs, a single Abattis, the work easily set on fire—no cannon.

"Redoubt No. 4, a Wooden work about 10 feet high and fore or five feet thick, the West side faced with a stone wall 8 feet high and four thick. No Bomb Proof, two six pounders, a slight Abattis, a commanding piece of ground 500 yards Wt.

"The North Redoubt, on the East side, built of stone 4 feet high; above the Stone, wood filled in with Earth, Very Dry, no Ditch, a Bomb Proof, three Batteries without the Fort, a poor Abattis, a Rising piece of ground 500 yards So., the approaches Under Cover to within 20 yards.—The Work easily fired with Faggots diptd in Pitch, &c.

"South Redoubt, much the same as the North, a Commanding piece of ground 500 yards due East—3 Batteries without the Fort."

The "Artillery Orders" of September 5, 1780; the estimate of forces at West Point; estimate of men to man the works, by Villefranche; the "Return" of Bauman; the description of the works at West Point and vicinity, and a copy of a council of war held at Washington's quarters, September 6, 1780, are the papers which were taken from Andrè's stocking. The latter document, which set forth the weakness, wants, and gloomy prospects of the American army, was a statement made by Washington to the council. It is too long for insertion here. Preserved among these papers are five passes, signed by Arnold, a memo-

sented to cross King's Ferry to Verplanck's Point, and make his way back to New York by land.   He had been prevailed upon by Arnold, in the event of his taking a land route (which had been talked of), to exchange his military coat for a citizen's dress.   This act, and the receiving of papers from Arnold, were contrary to the express orders of Sir Henry Clinton, but André was obliged to be governed by the unforeseen circumstances in which he was placed. Smith agreed to attend him on the way as far as the lower outposts of the American lines. September,   A little before sunset, on the evening of the 22d, accompanied by a negro servant, 1780.   they crossed King's Ferry.   At dusk, they passed through the works at Verplanck's Point, and turned their faces toward White Plains.   While they are pursuing their route toward the Neutral Ground, let us consider events at the Robinson House, and then resume our own journey.   We shall overtake the travelers presently, when the concluding portion of the narrative of Arnold's treason will be given.

---

randum, which, from its ambiguity, is unintelligible,* and the following letter from Joshua Smith to his brother Thomas, after his arrest on suspicion of being an accomplice with Arnold :

"Robinson House, Sept. 25th, 1780.

"DEAR BROTHER,—I am here a prisoner, and am therefore unable to attend in person.   I would be obliged to you if you would deliver to Captain Cairns, of Lee's Dragoons, a British uniform Coat, which you will find in one of the drawers in the room above stairs.† I would be happy to see you.   Remember me to your family.

"I am affectionately yours,

Joshua H. Smith

I have before me three interesting MS. letters, written by Smith and his two brothers, at about this time. The first is from the Tory Chief Justice Smith, of New York, to his brother Thomas; the second is from Thomas to Governor Clinton, covering the one from Judge Smith; and the third is from Joshua H. Smith, written in the jail at Goshen.   See Note * on page 752.

"New York, 12th October, 1780.

"DEAR SIR,—You will naturally suppose us in great anxiety for our brother Joshua, though General Arnold assured us that he knew nothing of *his* designs, and that he has written to General Washington more than once asserting his, and the innocence of several others still more likely to be suspected, from their connections with him, while in his confidence.   Joshua meets with a faithful reward from his old friends.   God Almighty protect him.   I hope his relations, at least, have not deserted him in his afflictions.   Our last accounts were, that he was still in the hands of the army, which appears strange to all here that have just views of civil liberty, or know any thing of Thomas Smith, Esq., that that model for a Constitution poor Joshua helped to frame at Kingston,‡ as an improvement upon that under which we were all born.

"Your friends here would be all well, if they thought you were so.   Our sister, Livingston, has spent several weeks with us, and will return sooner than we wish.

"Your son's health seems at length to be established, and he seems inclined to winter in South Carolina.   I have suspended my assent to the voyage till I know your opinion ; which ought to come soon, to avoid the danger of a winter voyage.

"Commend me to all friends.   I add no more, from an attention to your condition in an angry and suspicious hour.   God preserve you and yours through the storm, which I hope is nearly over.

"Ever most affectionately yours,   WILLIAM SMITH."
"16th October, 1780.

"DEAR SIR,—The inclosed was this moment delivered me by Mrs. Hoffman, who came out in a Flag via Elizabeth Town, as I wish to receive no letters from my brother but such as are subject to public inspection.   I have taken the liberty to inclose it for your perusal.   The situation in which the unhappy affair of my brother Joshua has placed me and all the family, calls for the greatest care to avoid suspicion.   I am yours, with esteem and affection,   THOMAS SMITH.

"His Excellency Governor CLINTON.

"P.S. I should be glad, if your house at Windsor is not engaged, to hire it, as I am determined to quit this place."

"Goshen, Orange County, 19th Nov., 1780.

"SIR,—In pursuance of a warrant of the Commissioners of Conspiracy, I was on the 12th day of this instant committed to the close custody of the sheriff of this County.   My long and severe confinement before and during my trial by the court-martial has greatly impaired my health, and I find my constitution much shattered.   I have been subject to repeated attacks of a bilious colic and an intermittent fever ; and am advised that a close confinement will soon terminate my existence, unless I can be permitted to use some exercise.   I have, therefore, to request some indulgence on this head, in compassion to my distressed situation.

"As I have never been officially acquainted with the sentence of the court-martial, I have also to request your Excellency to favor me with a copy of it by Major Hatfield, and thereby much oblige,

"Your Excellency's most obedient and distressed humble servant,

"JOSHUA H. SMITH."

"His Excellency GEORGE CLINTON, Esq., &c., &c.

---

* Copy of the memorandum :
<blockquote>
"Hennisut
Elijah Hunter
Mr. I. Johnson, B. R——r
Mr. J. Stewart, to the care of Joshua Smith, Esq., to be left at Head Q'rs.
Isaac Adams, 5 ,, 5 ,, 5."
</blockquote>
This was Major André's coat, which that officer exchanged with Smith for a citizen's dress-coat, as mentioned in the text. See page 387 of this volume.

OF THE REVOLUTION. 725

Arnold's Composure in Presence of his Aids.   Washington's Return from Hartford.   His Approach to Arnold's Quarters

CHAPTER XXXI.

" Here onward swept thy waves,
When tones, now silent, mingled with their sound,
And the wide shore was vocal with the song
Of hunter chief or lover's gentle strain.
Those pass'd away—forgotten as they pass'd ;
But holier recollections dwell with thee.
Here hath immortal Freedom built her proud
And solemn monuments.   The mighty dust
Of heroes in her cause of glory fallen,
Hath mingled with the soil, and hallow'd it.
Thy waters in their brilliant path have seen
The desperate strife that won a rescued world,
The deeds of men who live in grateful hearts,
And hymn'd their requiem."

ELIZABETH F. ELLET.

ITH such consummate art had General Arnold managed his scheme of villainy thus far, that not a suspicion of his defection was abroad. He returned to his quarters at the Robinson House, as we have observed, toward evening, and after passing a half hour with his wife and child, and one or two domestics, he conversed freely with his aids-de-camp, Majors Varick[1] and Franks, concerning the important information he was expecting to receive from New York, through a distinguished channel which he had just opened. This was on the 22d; the 24th was the day fixed upon for the ascent of the river by the British, and the surrender of West Point into the hands of the enemy. Yet, September, 1780. with all this guilt upon his soul, Arnold was composed, and the day on which his treason was to be consummated, no change was observed in his usual deportment.

Washington returned from Hartford on the 24th, by the upper route, through Dutchess county to Fishkill, and thence along the Highland road by Philipstown.   Soon after leaving Fishkill, he met Luzerne, the French minister, with his suite, on his way to visit Rochambeau.   That gentleman induced the commander-in-chief to turn back and pass the night with him at Fishkill.   Washington and his suite were in the saddle before dawn, for he was anxious to reach Arnold's quarters by

SIGNATURES OF ARNOLD'S AIDS.

---

[1] Richard Varick, who, before the close of the war, was promoted to colonel, was a sterling patriot. He admired Arnold as a soldier; and when that officer's defection became known, Varick was almost insane for a day or two, so utterly contrary to the whole life of Arnold appeared the fact. Varick became one of Washington's military family near the close of the war, as his recording secretary. He was mayor of the city of New York from 1791 to 1801. On the death of John Jay, he was elected president of the American Bible Society, which office he held until his death, which occurred at Jersey City, July 30th, 1831, at the age of seventy-nine years.

breakfast time, and they had eighteen miles to ride. The men, with the baggage, started earlier, and conveyed a notice to Arnold of Washington's intention to breakfast with him. When opposite West Point, the commander-in-chief turned his horse down a lane toward the river. La Fayette, perceiving it, said, "General, you are going in a wrong direction; you know Mrs. Arnold is waiting breakfast for us, and that road will take us out of the way." Washington answered, good-naturedly, "Ah, I know you young men are all in love with Mrs. Arnold, and wish to get where she is as soon as possible. You may go and take your breakfast with her, and tell her not to wait for me, for I must ride down and examine the redoubts on this side of the river,[1] and will be there in a short time." The officers, however, did not leave him, except two aids-de-camp, who rode on, at the general's request, to make known the cause of the delay.

Breakfast was waiting when the officers arrived, and as soon as it was ascertained that the commander-in-chief and the other gentlemen would not be there, Arnold, his family, and the aids-de-camp sat down to breakfast. Arnold appeared somewhat moody. The enemy had not appeared according to arrangements, and Washington had returned at least two days sooner than he anticipated. While they were at table, Lieutenant Allen came with a letter for Arnold. The general broke the seal hastily, for he knew by the superscription that it was from Colonel Jameson, stationed at one of the outposts below. The letter was, indeed, from that officer; but, instead of conveying the expected intelligence that the enemy were moving up the river, it informed him that *Major Andrè, of the British army, was a prisoner in his custody*[2] Arnold's presence of mind did not forsake him, and, although agitated, his emo-

THE BREAKFAST ROOM.[3]

tion was not sufficiently manifest to excite the suspicion of those around him. He informed the aids-de-camp that his immediate attendance was required at West Point, and desired them to say to General Washington, when he arrived, that he was unexpectedly called over the river, and would soon return. He ordered a horse to be made ready, and then leaving the table, he went up to Mrs. Arnold's chamber, and sent for her.[4] There was no time to be lost, for another messenger might speedily arrive with evidence of his treason. In brief and hurried words he told her that they must instantly part, perhaps forever, for his life depended on reaching the enemy's lines without detection. Horror-stricken, the poor young creature, but one year a mother and not two a bride, swooned and sunk senseless upon the floor. Arnold dared not call for assistance, but kissing, with lips blasted by words of guilt and treason, his boy, then sweetly sleeping in angel innocence and purity,[5] he rushed from the room, mounted a horse belonging

---

[1] These redoubts were upon the point, near the rail-way tunnel above Garrison's Landing.

[2] This letter was written on the 23d, two days before. The circumstances of the arrest of Andrè are detailed on page 752 to 758 inclusive.

[3] This is a view of the room in the Robinson House in which Arnold was at breakfast when he received Colonel Jameson's letter announcing the arrest of Andrè. It is preserved in its original style, which is quite antique. The ceiling is low; the heavy beams are bare; the fire-place surrounded with neat panel-work, without a mantel-shelf. The door on the right opens into a small room which Arnold used as an office; the windows on the left open upon the garden and lawn on the south, from whence I made the sketch of the house printed on page 708.

[4] This chamber is also preserved in its original character. Even the panel-work over the fire-place has been left unpainted since the Revolution, in order to preserve some inscriptions made upon it with a knife. There is carved in bold letters, "G. WALLIS, Lieut. VI. Mass. Reg't."

[5] This was the only child of Arnold by his second wife, born in the United States. His name was James Robertson. He entered the British army, and rose to the rank of colonel of engineers. He was stationed at Bermuda from 1816 to 1818, and from the last-named year until 1823 was at Halifax, and the command-

to one of the aids of Washington, and hastened toward the river, not by the winding road that led to the " Beverly Dock," but along a by-way down a steep hill, which is yet called *Arnold's Path*.   At the dock he entered his barge, and directed the six oarsmen to push out into the middle of the stream, and pull for Teller's Point.[1]

Arnold's oarsmen, unconscious of the nature of the general's errand, had their muscles strengthened by a promise of two gallons of rum, and the barge glided with unusual speed. He told them he was going on board the Vulture with a flag, and was obliged to make all possible haste, as he wished to return in time to meet General Washington at his quarters. When he passed Verplanck's Point, he displayed a white handkerchief, which, as a signal of amity, answered for both Colonel Livingston at the Point, and Captain Sutherland of the Vulture, which lay in sight a few miles below.   They reached the Vulture without interruption, and, after having introduced himself to Captain Sutherland, Arnold sent for the coxswain, and informed him that he and his oarsmen were prisoners.   They indignantly asserted their freedom to depart, alleging truly, as they supposed, that they had come on board under the protection of a flag.   Arnold coolly replied that they must remain on board.   Captain Sutherland would not interfere with Arnold's commands, but, despising his meanness, he gave the coxswain a parole to go on shore and get such things as he wanted.   This was done, and, when the Vulture arrived in New York, Sir Henry Clinton set them all at liberty.   In this transaction, the inherent meanness of Arnold's spirit was conspicuous, and made the British officers regard him with scorn as a reptile unworthy of that esteem which a high-souled traitor—a traitor because of great personal wrongs—might claim.

Washington arrived at Robinson's house shortly after Arnold had left.   Informed that he had gone to West Point, the commander-in-chief took a hasty breakfast, and concluded not to wait, but go directly over and meet Arnold there.   Hamilton remained behind, and it was arranged that the general and his suite should return to dinner.   While crossing the river in a barge, Washington expressed his expectation that they would be greeted with a salute, as General Arnold was at the Point ; but, to his surprise, all was silent when they approached the landing-place.   Colonel Lamb, the commanding officer, who came strolling down a winding path, was much confused when he saw the barge touch the shore.   He apologized to Washington for the apparent neglect of courtesy, alleging his entire ignorance of his intended visit.   The general was surprised, and said, " Sir, is not General Arnold here ?"   " No, sir," replied Colonel Lamb, " he has not been here these two days, nor have I heard from him within that time."   This awakened the suspicions of Washington.   He proceeded, however, to inspect the several works at West Point, and at about noon returned to the Beverly Dock, from whence he had departed.

While ascending from the river, Hamilton was seen approaching with hurried step and anxious countenance.   He conversed with Washington in a low tone, and returned with him into the house, where he laid several papers, the damning evidence of Arnold's guilt, before him.   These consisted of the documents given in a preceding chapter, which Arnold had placed in Andrè's hands.   They were accompanied by a letter from Colonel Jameson, and one from Andrè himself.   Jameson, uninformed of the return of Washington from Hartford, had dispatched a messenger thither, with the papers, to the commander-in-chief.   After rid-

---

ing officer of engineers in Nova Scotia and New Brunswick.   While thus in command, he was at St. John's, and, on going into the house built by his father, in King Street (which is still standing), wept like a child. His wife was a Miss Goodrich, of the Isle of Wight.   He is a small man, his eyes of remarkable sharpness, and in features bears a striking resemblance to his father.   A gentleman who has been in service with him, and is intimately acquainted with him, speaks of him in terms of high commendation, and relates that he expressed a desire to visit the United States.   Since the accession of Queen Victoria, he has been one of her majesty's aids-de-camp.   In 1841, he was transferred from the engineer's corps, and is now (1846) a major general, and a knight of the royal Hanoverian Guelphic order.—See Sabine's *Biographical Sketches of American Loyalists*.

[1] The coxswain on the occasion was James Larvey.   The aged Beverly Garrison, whom I saw at Fort Montgomery, knew him well.   He said Larvey always declared that, had he been aware of Arnold's intention, he would have steered to Verplanck's Point, even if the traitor had threatened to blow his brains out.

ing almost to Danbury, the messenger heard of the return of Washington by the upper road, and, hastening back, took the nearest route to West Point through Lower Salem, where André was in custody. He thus became the bearer of André's letter to Washington.[1] He arrived at the Robinson House four hours after the departure of Arnold, and placed the papers in the hands of Hamilton.

Washington called in Knox and La Fayette for counsel. "Whom can we trust now?" said the chief, with calmness, while the deepest feeling of sorrow was evidently at work in his bosom. The condition of Mrs. Arnold, who was quite frantic with grief and distress in another room, awakened his liveliest sympathies. He believed her innocent of all previous knowledge of her husband's treasonable designs, and this gave keenness to the pang which her sorrows created.[2] Yet he maintained his self-possession, and calmly said, when dinner was announced, "Come, gentlemen, since Mrs. Arnold is unwell, and the general is absent, let us sit down without ceremony."

As soon as the contents of the papers were made known, Washington dispatched Hamilton on horseback to Verplanck's Point, that preparations might be made there to stop the traitor. But Arnold had got nearly six hours' the start of him, the tide was ebbing, and the six strong oarsmen, prompted by expected reward, had pulled with vigor. When Hamilton arrived at the Point, a flag of truce was approaching from the Vulture to that post. The bearer brought a letter from Arnold to Washington, which Hamilton forwarded to the commander-in-chief, and then wrote to General Greene at Tappan, advising him to take precautionary measures to prevent any movement of the enemy in carrying out the traitor's projects. The failure of the plot was not known to Sir Henry Clinton until the arrival of the Vulture at New York the next morning, and then he had no disposition to venture an attack upon the Americans in the Highlands, now thoroughly awake to the danger that had threatened.

Arnold's letter to Washington was written to secure protection for his wife and child. "I have no favor to ask for myself," he said; "I have too often experienced the ingratitude of my country to attempt it; but, from the known humanity of your excellency, I am induced to ask your protection for Mrs. Arnold from every insult and injury that a mistaken vengeance of my countrymen may expose her to. It ought to fall only on me. She is as good and innocent as an angel, and is incapable of doing wrong." In this letter Arnold avowed his love for his country, and declared that that sentiment actuated him in his present

---

[1] This letter of André's is a model of frankness, and exhibits the highest regard for truth and honor. After revealing his name and character, and relating the circumstances under which he was lured within the American lines without his knowledge or consent, and mentioning his capture, he says, "Thus, as I have had the honor to relate, was I betrayed (being adjutant general of the British army) into the vile condition of an enemy in disguise within your posts." He disavowed any intention of being a spy, and asked, as a favor, that he should not be branded as such, he "being involuntarily an impostor." He further requested the privilege of sending an open letter to Sir Henry Clinton, and another to a friend, for linen; and concluded by intimating that there were several American prisoners who were taken at Charleston for whom he might be exchanged.

[2] "She, for a considerable time," says Hamilton, in a vivid description of the scene, "entirely lost herself. The general went up to see her. She upbraided him with being in a plot to murder her child. One moment she raved; another, she melted into tears. Sometimes she pressed her infant to her bosom, and lamented its fate, occasioned by the imprudence of its father, in a manner that would have pierced insensibility itself. All the sweetness of beauty, all the loveliness of innocence, all the tenderness of a wife, and all the fondness of a mother, showed themselves in her appearance and conduct. We have every reason to believe that she was entirely unacquainted with the plan, and that the first knowledge of it was when Arnold went to tell her he must banish himself from his country and from her forever. She instantly fell into convulsions, and he left her in that situation."

Mr. Leake, the biographer of Colonel John Lamb, basing his opinion upon information received from Arnold's sister Hannah, in 1801, regards this scene as only a trick to deceive, and believes that Arnold's wife was the chief instrument in bringing about the defection of her husband. Hannah Arnold averred that the traitor's wife received a pension from the Queen of England during her life.—See *Life of John Lamb*, by Isaac Q. Leake, p. 270. I can not but regard the inference of Mr. Leake as untenable. It was certainly consoling to the feelings of Hannah Arnold to believe that the influence of another, and not his own base principles, was the source of the defection and disgrace of her brother.

conduct. "In short," says Sparks, "the malignant spirit, impudence, and blunted moral feeling shown in this letter were consistent with his character. Attachment to his wife was the only redeeming quality which seemed not to be extinguished."[1]

Washington also received a letter from Beverly Robinson, dated on board the Vulture, demanding, in mild terms, the release of André, claiming it as equitable, he being on shore with a flag of truce at the request of General Arnold. Robinson attempted to influence the mind of the chief by referring to their former friendship, but the letter had not the least effect upon Washington's firmness of purpose. He was ignorant of the extent of defection, and his thoughts and efforts were first directed to measures of security. He had a most delicate task to perform. He might suspect the innocent, and give his confidence to the unworthy. He resolved, as the least dangerous course, to confide unreservedly in all his officers, and this resolution, promptly acted upon, had a very salutary effect.[2]

Washington sent orders to General Greene, directing him to put the left wing of the army, near Tappan, in motion as soon as possible, and march toward King's Ferry. It was midnight when the express reached Greene's quarters; before dawn the whole division was upon the march. The commander-in-chief also dispatched a letter to Colonel Jameson, directing him to send André to Robinson's house under a strong guard. This messenger also reached his destination at Lower Salem, at midnight. André was aroused, and, although the rain was falling fast, and the night was exceedingly dark, a guard, under Major Tallmadge, set off with the prisoner immediately. They rode all night, and arrived at Robinson's house at dawn on the 26th. André was taken over to West Point the same evening, and on the morning of the 28th was conveyed, under a strong escort of cavalry, to Tappan, where he was tried and convicted as a spy. This event will be noticed September, 1780.

in connection with the details of his capture. For the present, my tour leads me to the consideration of other important transactions within cannon-echo of the *Sugar Loaf,* at whose base we are standing, and up whose steep sides I was desirous of climbing, to view the prospect so glowingly depicted by the pen of Dr. Dwight;[3] but recollecting that the venerable boatman was awaiting my

VIEW AT BEVERLY DOCK.[4]

return, I exchanged a hasty adieu with Lieutenant Arden, and hastened back to the Beverly Dock by way of *Arnold's Path.* There I found the old waterman quietly

---

[1] Inclosed in the letter to Washington was one for Mrs. Arnold, who, when thus made acquainted of her husband's safety, became more quiet. She was treated with great tenderness by Washington, and was soon afterward sent to New York under an escort, and joined her husband. Her affection survived his honor, and through all his subsequent career she exemplified the character of a true woman's love, which often "Clings like ivy to a worthless thing."

[2] The position of Colonel Livingston at Verplanck's Point, with some circumstances that appeared suspicious, made him liable to be distrusted, for it might fairly be presumed that he was directly or indirectly concerned in Arnold's movements. By a brief letter, Washington ordered Livingston to come to head-quarters immediately. Conscious of his integrity, that officer promptly obeyed, but he expected his conduct would be subjected to a strict investigation. Washington made no inquiries. He told him that he had more explicit orders to give than he could well communicate by letter, and that was the object of calling him to the Highlands. "It is a source of gratification to me," said the commander-in-chief, "that the post was in the hands of an officer so devoted as yourself to the cause of your country." Washington's confidence was not misplaced, for there was not a purer patriot in that war than Henry Livingston.

[3] Dwight's *Travels in New England.*

[4] This view is taken from the Hudson River rail-road, looking north. The dock, covered with cord wood, is seen near the point on the left. It is at the termination of a marsh, near the point of a bold, rocky promontory, through which is a deep rock cutting for the road. The distant hills on the extreme left are on the

fishing, and apparently unconscious that two hours had elapsed since we parted. He locked his oars, and in a few minutes we were at the foot of Buttermilk Falls. I clambered up the steep, rough road under the cliff, to the village, dined at a late hour upon cold mutton and stale bread, and in a light wagon, procured with difficulty for the occasion, set off, with a boy driver, for Fort Montgomery, about four miles below. For half the distance the road (which is the old military one of the Revolution) was smooth ; the residue of the way was as rough as rocks and gulleys could make it. On every side huge bowlders, many of them ten feet in diameter, lie scattered over the bare flat rocks, like fruit shaken from a tree in autumn. They become more numerous toward the base of the steep mountain range on the west, where they lie in vast masses, like mighty pebbles rolled up by the waves upon the shore. Here the geologist has a wonderful page spread out for his contemplation.

Within a short distance of Fort Montgomery, we turned up a rough mountain road to visit an old lady named Rebecca Rose, eighty years of age, who lived close by Fort Montgomery at the time it was taken by the enemy. I found her upon a bed of sickness, too feeble then to converse, but at a subsequent visit she was well and communicative. She was a child only seven or eight years old, and has no distinct recollection of events at the taking of the forts, except her care and anxiety in concealing her rag babies in a sap trough, while her parents were hiding their property in the woods. Her father was a tanner and shoemaker, in the employ of the garrison at the two forts. The British tried to frighten him into the performance of the duty of a guide for them, by twice hauling him up to an apple-tree with a halter around his neck. He resolutely defied them, and they passed on. From the cottage of Mrs. Rose, among the hills, is one of the most magnificent views of rock and forest, cliff and river, imaginable ; overlooking Forts Montgomery and Clinton, the Race flanked by Anthony's Nose and the Dunderberg, and the fertile hills of West Chester in the distance.

Near Mrs. Rose lived an old soldier who was wounded at the siege of Fort Montgomery. I found him living with his daughter, a little plump widow of fifty, in a cottage beside a clear stream that comes leaping down from the hills. He was a private in Captain De Vere's company, Colonel Dubois's regiment, and was bayoneted in the thigh when the enemy made their way over the ramparts of Fort Montgomery and fought the garrison hand to hand. Although nearly ninety years old, he was vigorous and talked sensibly. I asked the privilege of sketching his portrait, which he readily granted, and I was about unlocking my port-folio for the purpose, when his daughter, resting upon a broom handle, and assuming the shrewd look of a speculator, inquired, " What'll ye give ?" " For what ?" I inquired. " For daddy's likeness," she answered. Unacquainted with the market value of such commodities, and being doubtful as to the present sample possessing much intrinsic worth, I made the indefinite offer of " What is right." " No, no," she said, tuning her voice to a higher key, and beginning to sweep the floor vigorously, " you sha'n't look at him till you tell me what you'll give. We've been cheated enough a'ready. Two scamps come along here last week, and told my darter they'd make a likeness on her for their breakfasts, and they on'y guv her a nasty piece of black paper, that had a nose no more like sis's than that tea-pot spout. No, sir ; give me a half a dollar, or clear out quick !" The more fortunate silhouettists had evidently ruined my prospects for a gratuitous sitting of the old soldier ; and feeling very doubtful whether the demanded half dollar, if paid, would add a mite to his comforts, I respectfully declined giving the price. The filial regard of the dear woman was terribly shocked, and she called me a cheat and other hard names. I shook hands with the old " Continentaler" as I rose to depart, and turning quietly to the dame, who was yet sweeping around the room in a towering passion, invited her to sit for her portrait ! This produced a climax ; she seized the broom by the brush ; I saved my head by closing the door between us. I walked off unscathed and much amused, in the midst of a perfect

west side of the Hudson ; and through the gorge formed for the road may be seen the military edifices of West Point.

OF THE REVOLUTION.   731

Sites of Forts Clinton and Montgomery.   Lake Sinnipink.   Beverly Garrison.

shower of grape-shot from her tongue-battery, compelled to content myself with a pen and ink sketch of the hornet instead of the one I had asked for.

VIEW NEAR FORT MONTGOMERY.[2]

We descended the hills, and proceeded to the site of Fort Montgomery, a rough promontory on the north side of Peploap's, or Poplopen's, Kill.[1] It terminates in a steep cliff at the mouth of the stream, and was an admirable situation for a strong fortress to command the river. Almost the entire line of the fortifications may be traced upon the brow of the cliff, which is rocky, and bare of every thing but stinted grass and dwarf cedars. More than half way down to the water's edge are the remains of the two-gun-battery which was placed there to cover the chain and *chevaux de frise* which were stretched across the river from the upper side of Poplopen's Kill to Anthony's Nose.

We crossed to the southern side of the stream, and clambered up a winding and romantic pathway among cedars, chestnuts, and sassafras, to the high table land whereon stood Fort Clinton, within rifle shot of Fort Montgomery. A fine mansion, belonging to Mrs. Pell, with cultivated grounds around it, occupy the area within the ravelins of the old fort. The banks of the fortress have been leveled, its fossé filled up, and not a vestige of it remains. About a quarter of a mile west of Mrs. Pell's is Lake Sinnipink, a small sheet of crystal water, surrounded by the primitive forest, and as wild in its accompaniments as when the Indian cast his bait in its deep waters. From its western rim rises the highest peak of Bear Mountain to an altitude of more than a thousand feet. The lake itself is one hundred and twenty-three feet above the river.

Near the north end of Lake Sinnipink, on the river slope of the hills, stands the cottage of the aged Beverly Garrison, a hale old man of eighty-seven years. He was a stout lad of fourteen when the forts were taken. His father, who worked a great deal for Beverly Robinson, and admired him, named this boy in honor of that gentleman. When the British approached the

LAKE SINNIPINK, OR BLOODY POND.[3]

---

[1] This *kill*, or *creek*, is the dividing line between the towns of Monroe and Cornwall, in Orange county. Its correct orthography is uncertain. Upon a map of the State of New York made in 1779 it is called *Coplap's Kill ;* in the British plan of the engagements there, of which the map given on page 166 is a copy, it is spelled Peploap's ; Romans, who was engaged in the construction of the forts, wrote it Pooploop's.

[2] This view is from an eminence near the mountain road, about three quarters of a mile in the rear of Fort Montgomery. In the distance, the cultivated slopes of West Chester, between Peekskill and Verplanck's Point, are seen. On the left is the high, rocky promontory called Anthony's Nose ; on the right is the Dunderberg, with a portion of Beveridge's Island ; the buildings in the center of the picture, owned by Mrs. Pells indicate the site of Fort Clinton ; toward the right is seen the deep ravine through which flows Poplopen's Creek, and on the extreme right, partly hidden by the tree in the foreground, and fronting the river, is the site of Fort Montgomery. The scenery from this point of view is indeed magnificent This picture is from a pencil sketch by Tice, who accompanied me to the spot.

[3] This view is from the outlet of the lake, within a few rods of the spot where a large number of the Americans and British were slain in a preliminary skirmish on the afternoon when the forts were taken. The bodies were thrown into the lake, and from that circumstance it was afterward called Bloody Pond.

forts, Beverly and his father, who was wagon-master at Fort Montgomery, were ordered to take a large iron cannon to the outworks on the neck of the promontory. While thus engaged, they were made prisoners; but Beverly, being a boy, was allowed his liberty. He told me that he was standing on the ramparts of Fort Montgomery on the morning when Arnold passed by, in his barge, fleeing to the Vulture, and that he recognized the general, as well as Larvey, his coxswain. He also informed me that a Tory, named Brom Springster, piloted the enemy over the Dunderberg to the forts. Brom afterward became a prisoner to the patriots,

but his life was spared on condition that he should pilot Wayne on his expedition over the same rugged hills to attack Stony Point. Mr. Garrison remembered the famous Irish woman called *Captain Molly*, the wife of a cannonier, who worked a field-piece at the battle of Monmouth, on the death of her husband. She generally dressed in the petticoats of her sex, with an artilleryman's coat over. She was in Fort Clinton, with her husband, when it was attacked. When the

Americans retreated from the fort, as the enemy scaled the ramparts, her husband dropped his match and fled. Molly caught it up, touched off the piece, and then scampered off. It was the last gun fired by the Americans in the fort. Mrs. Rose (just mentioned) remembers her as *Dirty Kate*, living between Fort Montgomery and Buttermilk Falls, at the close of the war, where she died a horrible death from the effects of a syphilitic disease. I shall have occasion to refer to this bold camp-follower, whom Washington honored with a sergeant's commission for her bravery on the field of Monmouth, nearly nine months afterward, when reviewing the events of that battle.

Here, by the clear spring which bubbles up near the cottage of the old patriot, and in the shadow of Bear Mountain, behind which the sun is declining, let us glance at the Revolutionary history of this region.

Forts Clinton and Montgomery were included in the Highland fortifications ordered to be constructed in 1775–6. These, like Fort Constitution, were commenced by Bernard Romans, assisted by skillful French engineers, and were finally completed under the superintendence of Captain Thomas Machin. Fort Montgomery was of sufficient size to accommodate eight hundred men; Fort Clinton was only about half as large. They were built of stones and earth, and were completed in the spring of 1776. Pursuant to a recommendation of Romans, made the previous autumn, preparations were made to place obstructions in the river from the mouth of Poplopen's, or Peploap's Kill, to Anthony's Nose, opposite. These obstructions, which were not completed until the autumn of 1777, just before the forts were attacked, consisted of a vrey strong boom, and heavy iron chain.[1] The latter, eighteen ▬▬▬▬▬▬▬▬▬▬ in length, was hundred feet ▬▬▬▬▬▬▬▬▬▬ buoyed up by heavy spars, connected by iron links, and also by large rafts of timber. It was believed that these obstructions, covered by the guns of the fort, and accompanied by several armed vessels, would be sufficient to effectually prevent the enemy from ascending the river. The result, however, was otherwise.

---

[1] Generals Knox and Greene visited Fort Montgomery in the spring of 1777, in company with Generals Wayne, M'Dougal, and Clinton. They made a joint report to Washington, in which they recommended the completion of the obstructions substantially as they were afterward done. The boom and the *chevaux de frise* so obstructed the current of the river (here very strong), that the water was raised two or three feet above them, and pressed upon them heavily. Twice the chain was parted by this pressure: first, a swivel. which came from Ticonderoga, was broken; and the second time a clevis, which was made at Poughkeepsie. gave way.

When Burgoyne found himself environed with difficulties at Saratoga, and perceived the rapid augmentation of the American army under Gates, he dispatched messengers to Sir Henry Clinton, then commanding at New York in the absence of General Howe,[1] urging him to make a diversion in his favor, and join him, if possible, with a force sufficient to scatter the half-disciplined provincials. Clinton was eager to comply; but a re-enforcement of troops from Europe, expected for several weeks, was still delayed. This force, amounting to almost two thousand men, under General Robertson, arrived at the beginning of October. Having sailed in Dutch bottoms, they were three months on the voyage. The first battle of Stillwater had now been fought, and the second was nigh at hand. Putnam was in the Highlands, with fifteen hundred men; his head-quarters were at Peekskill. Washington had drawn upon Putnam, toward the close of September, for twenty-five hundred troops, to aid in defending Philadelphia and the works on the Delaware, then menaced by the enemy.[2] Their places were supplied by militia of New York and Connecticut; but, apprehending no hostile movement up the Hudson, Putnam had discharged about one thousand of them, leaving his effective force only fifteen hundred strong. Forts Clinton and Montgomery, commanded by the brothers James and George Clinton, were feebly garrisoned; in both fortresses there were not more than six hundred men, chiefly militia from Dutchess and Ulster. There was a fortification near Peekskill, called Fort Independence, which was also feebly garrisoned; in fact, the Highland posts were almost defenseless against a respectable demonstration on the part of the enemy.

On the arrival of re-enforcements, Sir Henry Clinton prepared for an expedition up the Hudson, partly for the purpose of destroying American stores at Peekskill, but chiefly to make a diversion in favor of Burgoyne. On Saturday evening, the 4th of October, he proceeded up the river in flat boats and transports, with about five thousand men, and landed at Tarrytown, nearly thirty miles from New York.[3] This was a feint to deceive General Putnam into the belief that Peekskill was his destination. To strengthen this belief, and to divert Putnam's attention from the Highland forts, Clinton proceeded on Sunday, with three thousand troops, to Verplanck's Point, eight miles below Peekskill, where he debarked. General Putnam fell back, on his approach, to the high ground in the rear of Peekskill, and sent a messenger to Governor Clinton, desiring him to send to his aid as many troops as he could spare from the forts. The militia in the vicinity rallied around Putnam, and he had about two thousand men, on the afternoon of the 5th, to dispute the progress of the enemy up the Hudson, either by land or water. Sir Henry Clinton perceived that his stratagem was successful, and the next morning, under cover of a fog, he passed two thousand of his troops over to Stony Point, whence they made their way among the tangled defiles and lofty crags of the Dunderberg to Forts Clinton and Montgomery, twelve miles distant. The transports were anchored near Stony Point, and the corps of Loyalists, under Colonels Bayard and Fanning, remained at Verplanck's Point. A detachment was left near Stony Point, to guard the pass and preserve a communication with the fleet. Three frigates, the Tartar, Preston, and Mercury, proceeded up the river to a position between what is now known as Caldwell's Landing and Fort Independence, and within cannon-shot of the latter.

Governor Clinton received advices on Sunday night of the arrival of the enemy's ships and transports at Tarrytown, and, on Monday morning, a scouting party of one hundred

---

[1] General Howe was now in Pennsylvania. His army was encamped at Germantown, and being in possession of Philadelphia, he had established his headquarters in that city.

[2] When this requisition was made, Putnam was preparing a plan for attacking the enemy at four different points: Staten Island, Long Island, Paulus's Hook, and New York. He relied upon the militia of Connecticut, New York, and New Jersey, to accomplish his designs. Fortunately, Washington made his requisition in time to prevent what must have proved a disastrous expedition.

[3] Colonel Luddington was posted at Tarrytown with about five hundred militia. Clinton sent a flag with a peremptory summons for them to surrender themselves prisoners of war. While parleying with the flag, the enemy endeavored to surround the militia, which Luddington perceiving, he ordered a retreat. The British then returned to their shipping.

734　　　　　　　PICTORIAL FIELD-BOOK

Governor Clinton informed of the Landing of the British.　　　A reconnoitering Party.　　　Skirmish near Doodletown.

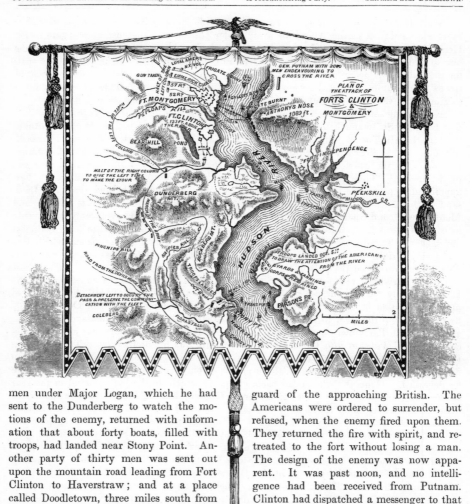

men under Major Logan, which he had sent to the Dunderberg to watch the motions of the enemy, returned with information that about forty boats, filled with troops, had landed near Stony Point. Another party of thirty men was sent out upon the mountain road leading from Fort Clinton to Haverstraw; and at a place called Doodletown, three miles south from the fort, they fell in with the advanced guard of the approaching British. The Americans were ordered to surrender, but refused, when the enemy fired upon them. They returned the fire with spirit, and retreated to the fort without losing a man. The design of the enemy was now apparent. It was past noon, and no intelligence had been received from Putnam. Clinton had dispatched a messenger to that officer, requesting him to send him a strong

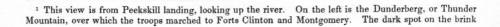

VIEW FROM PEEKS KILL LANDING.[1]

---

[1] This view is from Peekskill landing, looking up the river. On the left is the Dunderberg, or Thunder Mountain, over which the troops marched to Forts Clinton and Montgomery. The dark spot on the brink

re-enforcement to defend the forts.   The messenger, whose name was Waterbury, treacherously delayed his journey, and the next day deserted to the enemy.   In the mean while, Putnam, astonished at hearing nothing further from the enemy, rode to reconnoiter, and did not return to his head-quarters, near Continental Village, until after the firing was heard on the other side of the river.   Colonel Humphreys, who was alone at head-quarters when the firing began, urged Colonel Wyllys, the senior officer in camp, to send all the men not on duty to Fort Montgomery.[1]   He immediately complied, but it was too late.   It was twilight before they reached the river, and the enemy had then accomplished their purpose.

The British army, piloted by a Tory, traversed the Dunderberg in a single column, and at its northern base separated into two divisions.   One division, under Lieutenant-colonel Campbell, consisting of nine hundred men, was destined for the attack on Fort Montgomery ; the other, under the immediate command of Sir Henry Clinton, and consisting of an equal number, was to storm Fort Clinton.   There was a large body of Hessians in each division. Governor Clinton, on hearing of the attack upon his scouts near Doodletown, sent out a detachment of more than one hundred men, under Colonels Bruyn and M‘Claghrey,[2] with a brass field-piece and sixty men, to an advantageous post on the road to Orange furnace.   As the enemy approached, another detachment of one hundred men was sent to the same point, but they were pressed back by the bayonets of a superior force, and retreated to a twelve-pounder in the rear, leaving their guns (which they spiked) in possession of the assailants. With the second cannon they did great execution, until it bursted, when they retreated to Fort Montgomery, followed by Emerick's corps of chasseurs, a corps of Loyalists and New York volunteers, and the fifty-second and fifty-seventh British regiments, under Campbell. The pursued kept up a galling fire with small-arms while on their retreat, and slew many of the enemy.

Sir Henry Clinton, in the mean while, made his way toward Fort Clinton with much difficulty, for upon a narrow pass between the Sinnipink Lake at the foot of Bear Mountain and the high river bank was a strong *abatis*.[3]   This was overcome after much hard fighting, and at about four o'clock both forts were invested by the enemy.   Sir Henry Clinton sent a flag, with a summons for both garrisons to surrender prisoners of war within five minutes, or they would all be put to the sword.   Lieutenant-colonel Livingston was sent by Governor Clinton to receive the flag, and to inform the enemy that the Americans were determined to defend the forts to the last extremity.   The action was immediately renewed

of the river, upon the extreme left, shows the place of the coffer-dam made by the deluded seekers after Captain Kidd's treasure.   At the water's edge, on the right, is seen the grading of the Hudson River railroad, in course of construction when the sketch was made.   The dark mountain on the right is Anthony's Nose.   Intermediately, and projecting far into the river, is a high, sandy bluff, on which stood Fort Independence.   Further on is Beveridge's Island ; and in the extreme distance, behind the flag-staff, is seen Bear Mountain.   Between the point of Fort Independence and the rock cutting of the rail-road is the mouth of the Peek's Kill, or Peek's Creek.   The *Plan* of the attack here given is copied from the narrative of Stedman, a British officer, and appears to be mainly correct.   The reader may correct the slight errors by the text.

[1] See Humphreys's *Life of Putnam*.   This detachment seems to have been mistaken by Stedman for the whole army under Putnam, for on his map, at the top, he says, " General Putnam with 2000 men endeavoring to cross the river."

[2] In connection with a notice of Colonel M‘Claghrey, who was made a prisoner at the capture of the fort, Mr. Eager, in his *History of Orange County*, makes a slight error.   He says he was taken to New York, and confined in the Hospital.   In the room above him, he affirms, was Colonel Ethan Allen, who had been a prisoner in the hands of the British since the autumn of 1775.   The floor between them was full of wide cracks, through one of which M‘Claghrey, who had heard of the capture of Burgoyne, passed a scrap of paper to Allen, on which he had written the information.   Allen immediately went to his window, and called out to some British officers passing in the street, " Burgoyne has marched to Boston to the tune of Yankee Doodle."   " For this and other offenses, we believe," says Mr. Eager, " Allen was sent to England in chains."   Quite the contrary.   He was sent to England in irons two years before, and had returned to New York, where he was admitted to his parole.   In January, 1777, he was ordered to reside on Long Island ; and in August following he was sent to the provost jail, where he remained until exchanged in May, 1778.

[3] These *abatis* were placed on the margin of the outlet of Lake Sinipink, near its center, the place from which the view on page 731 was sketched

with great vigor on both sides. The British vessels under Commodore (afterward Admiral) Hotham approached within cannon shot of the forts, and opened a desultory fire upon them, and on some American vessels lying above the *chevaux de frise*.[1] At the same time, Count Grabowski, a brave Pole, and Lord Rawdon, led the grenadiers to the charge on Fort Montgomery. The battle continued until twilight, when the superior number of the assailants obliged the patriots at both forts to give way, and attempt a scattered retreat or escape. It was a cloudy evening, and the darkness came on suddenly. This favored the Americans in their flight, and a large proportion of those who escaped the slaughter of the battle made their way to the neighboring mountains in safety. The brothers who commanded the forts escaped. General James Clinton was severely wounded in the thigh by a bayonet, but escaped to the mountains, and reached his residence in Orange county, sixteen miles distant, the next day, where he was joined by his brother George, and about two hundred of the survivors of the battle. Lieutenant-colonels Livingston, Bruyn, and Claghery, and Majors Hamilton and Logan, were made prisoners. The loss of the Americans in killed, wounded, and prisoners, was about three hundred; that of the British about one hundred and forty in killed and wounded, among whom were Colonel Campbell and Count Grabowski.[2]

Above the boom the Americans had two frigates, two galleys, and an armed sloop. On the fall of the forts, the crews of these vessels spread their sails, and, slipping their cables, attempted to escape up the river, but the wind was adverse, and they were obliged to abandon them. They set them on fire when they left, to prevent their falling into the hands of the enemy. "The flames suddenly broke forth, and, as every sail was set, the vessels soon became magnificent pyramids of fire. The reflection on the steep face of the opposite mountain, and the long train of ruddy light which shone upon the water for a prodigious distance, had a wonderful effect; while the ear was awfully filled with the continued echoes from the rocky shores, as the flames gradually reached the loaded cannons. The whole was sublimely terminated by the explosions, which left all again in darkness."[3] Early in the morn-

October 7, 1777. ing, the obstructions in the river, which had cost the Americans a quarter of a million of dollars, Continental money, were destroyed by the British fleet. Fort Constitution, opposite West Point, was abandoned, and the enemy had a clear passage up the Hudson. Vaughan and Wallace sailed up the river upon their marauding expedition, and, as we have before noticed, burned Kingston, or Esopus. It was deemed too late to assist Burgoyne by a junction with him, for on that very day the second battle of Stillwater, so disastrous to that commander, was fought; ten days afterward he and his whole army were captives. Yet the fall of the Highland forts was a serious blow to the Americans, for quite a large quantity of ordnance and ammunition was collected there.[4]

---

[1] An account in the *Annual Register* for 1778 says that the British galleys approached so near the forts that the men could touch the walls with their oars! Both forts were upon a precipice more than one hundred feet above the water, rather beyond the reach of oars of ordinary length.

[2] Count Grabowski fell at the foot of the ramparts of Fort Montgomery, pierced by three bullets. He gave his sword to a grenadier, with a request that he would convey it to Lord Rawdon, with the assurance of the owner that he died as a brave soldier ought to.—*Stedman*, i., 362. A pile of stones still marks the burial-place of the count.

[3] Stedman, i., 364.

[4] The Americans lost 67 cannons in the forts, and over 30 in the vessels, making a total of more than 100 pieces. Also, 54 casks, 11 half barrels, and 12,236 pounds of loose powder, exclusive of what was in the vessels. There were also 1852 cannon cartridges, and 57,396 for muskets. Also, 9530 round cannon shot, 886 double-headed, 2483 grape and case, and 36 cwt. of langridge; 1279 pounds of musket balls, 116 pounds of buck shot, and 5400 flints. In addition to these were stores of various kinds, such as gun-carriages, port-fires, tools, &c., in great plenty

It was almost sunset when I left the ruins of Fort Montgomery to seek for a waterman to carry me to Peekskill, on the east side of the river, four miles distant. The regular ferryman was absent on duty, and after considerable search, I procured, with difficulty, the services of a fisherman to bear me to the distant village. We embarked at twilight—a glorious Indian summer twilight—the river as calm as a lake of the valley.

> "The Dunderberg sat silently beneath
> The snowy clouds, that form'd a vapory wreath
>   Above its peak. The Hudson swept along
> Its mighty waters—oh! had I a pen
> Endued with master gifts and genius, then
>   Might I aspire to tell its praise in song."
>
> THOMAS MACKELLAR.

The boat was a scaly affair, and the piscatory odor was not very agreeable; nevertheless, I had no alternative, and, turning my eyes and nose toward the glowing heavens, I tried to imagine myself in a rose-scented caique in the Golden Horn. I had half succeeded, when three or four loud explosions, that shook the broad mountains and awoke an hundred echoes, broke the charm, and notified me that I was in a fisherman's shallop, and a little too near for safety to St. Anthony's Nose,[1] where the constructors of the Hudson River rail-road, then working day and night, were blasting an orifice through that nasal feature of the Highlands. We sheered off toward the Dunderberg, and, shooting across Peekskill Bay, with the tide flowing strongly down its eastern rim, I landed in time for a warm supper at the "Atlantic."

Early on the morning of the 27th I made the sketch from Peekskill landing printed on page 166, and then walked up to the village on the slopes and hills, by a   October, 1848. steep winding way that overlooks a deep ravine, wherein several iron founderies are nestled. The town is romantically situated among the hills, and from some of its more prominent points of view there are magnificent prospects of the river and Highland scenery in the vicinity. Here, spreading out south and east for miles around, was the ancient manor of Cortlandt,[2] stretching along and far above the whole eastern shore of Haverstraw Bay, and extending back to the Connecticut line. The manor house, near the mouth of the Croton River, is yet standing. Within Peekskill village, opposite the West Chester County Bank, is the old Birdsall residence, a part of which, as seen in the picture upon the next page, is a grocery store. This building was erected by Daniel Birdsall, one of the founders of the village. His store was the first one erected there.[3] The owner and occupant, when I visited it, was a son of

---

[1] This is a high rocky promontory, rising to an altitude of twelve hundred and eighty feet above the level of the river, and situated directly opposite Fort Montgomery. The origin of its name is uncertain. The late proprietor of the land, General Pierre Van Cortlandt, says, that before the Revolution, as Captain Anthony Hogans, the possessor of a remarkable nose, was sailing near the place, in his vessel, his mate looked rather quizzically first at the hill, and then at the captain's nose. The captain comprehended the silent allusion, and said, "Does that look like my nose? If it does, call it Anthony's Nose, if you please." The story got abroad on shore, and it has since borne that name. Washington Irving, in his *authentic* history of New York, by Diedrich Knickerbocker, gives it an earlier origin. He says that while the fiery-nosed Anthony Van Corlear, the trumpeter of one of the Dutch governors, was standing one morning upon the deck of an exploring vessel, while passing this promontory, a ray of the sun, darting over the peak, struck the broad side of the trumpeter's nose, and, glancing off into the water, killed a sturgeon! What else could the hill be called, under the circumstances, but *Anthony's Nose?*

[2] The Courtlandts, or Van Courtlandts, are descended from a noble Russian family. The orthography, in the Dutch language, is properly *korte-landt*, meaning *short land*, a term expressing the peculiar form of the ancient duchy of Courland in Russia. This domain constituted a portion of Livonia, but was conquered by the Teutonic knights in 1561, and subsequently became a fief of Poland. It remained a short time independent, under its own dukes, after the fall of that power, but in 1795 it was united to Russia. The dukes of Courland were represented in 1610 by the Right Honorable Steven Van Cortlandt, then residing at Cortlandt, in South Holland. He was the father of Oloff Stevenson Van Cortlandt, the first lord of the manor, of that name, on the Hudson.

[3] The first settlement at Peekskill commenced one mile north of the present village, near the head waters of the creek. The name is derived from John Peek, one of the early Dutch navigators, who, mistaking the creek for the course of the river, ran his yacht ashore where the first settlement was commenced. The settlement of the present village was commenced in 1764.—Bolton's *History of West Chester*, i., 63.

the first owner, and was then eighty years of age.   His lady, many years his junior, kindly showed me the different apartments made memorable by the presence and occupancy of dis-tinguished men in the Revolution.   It was occupied

THE BIRDSALL HOUSE.

by Washington when the head-quarters of the army were there ; and the rooms are pointed out which were used by the chief and La Fayette as sleeping apartments.   Chairs, a table, and an old clock which has told the hours for more than eighty years, are still there ; and in the parlor where Whitefield once preached, I sat and sketched one of the pieces of this venerable furniture.   This old mansion, projecting into and marring the regularity of the street, is an eyesore to the villagers, and when the present owner shall depart, no doubt this relic will be removed by the desecrating hand of improvement.

On leaving the Birdsall House, I proceeded to visit another octogenarian named Sparks, whose boyhood and long life have been passed in Peekskill.   I found him sitting in the sun, upon his stoop, reading a newspaper without glasses, and his little grandson, a fair-haired child, playing at his feet.   For an hour I sat and listened to his tales of the olden times, and of scenes his eyes had witnessed.   He had often seen Washington and his suite at the Birdsall House, and well remembers Putnam, Heath, M'Dougall, and other officers whose quarters were at Peekskill.   He never became a soldier, and saw only one battle during the war.   That occurred near the Van Cortlandt House, two miles east of Peekskill, between some American pickets at the foot of Gallows Hill, and a picket guard of the enemy at the base of the eminences opposite.   They were too near each other to keep quiet, and a skir-mish at length ensued.   " They made a great smoke and noise," said Mr. Sparks, " but nobody was hurt except by fright."   Pointing to a huge oak standing near the Peekskill Academy on Oak Hill, and in full view of our resting-place, he related the circumstance of the execution of a British spy, named Daniel Strang, upon that tree.   He was a Tory, and was found lurking about the American army at Peekskill with enlisting orders sewed up in his clothes.   I left the vigorous old man to enjoy the warm sunlight and his newspaper alone, and procuring a conveyance, rode out to Van Cortlandt's house ; the church-yard, where rest the remains of one of Andrè's captors ; Gallows Hill, famous as the camping-ground of Putnam for a short period during the Revolution, and to Continental Village, the scene of one of Tryon's marauding expeditions.

Van Cortlandt's house is situated in the midst of one of the fine estates of that family.[1] It is a brick mansion, and was erected in 1773.   It stands in the center of a pleasant lawn, shaded by locust trees, on the north side of the post-road.   It was occupied by Washington, for a brief space, as head-quarters ; and there the Van Cortlandt family resided in safety,

---

[1] General Philip Van Cortlandt was the last possessor of the manor house, near Croton, by entail.   He was born in the city of New York on the 1st of September, 1749, and was reared at the manor house.   At nineteen, he commenced business as a land surveyor, but when the Revo-lution broke out, agreeing in sentiment with his father, Honorable Pierre Van Cortlandt, he joined the Re-publican army.   His Tory relatives tried to dissuade him from his purpose, and Governor Tryon forwarded him a major's commission in the Cortlandt militia.   He tore it in pieces, and accepted a lieutenant col-onel's commission in the Continental army.   He was appointed a colonel in 1776, and in that capacity served at the battles of Stillwater.   He also served against the Indians on the New York frontier in 1778, and in 1779–80 was a member of the court martial convened for the trial of Arnold.   He commanded a regiment of militia under La Fayette in 1781, and for his gallant conduct at the siege of Yorktown he was promoted to a brigadier's command.   Seven hundred of the British and Hessian prisoners of war after-ward intrusted to his care while on their march from Charlottesville to Fredericktown, in Maryland.   He was for sixteen years a member of Congress, but in 1811 declined a re-election.   General Van Cortlandt accompanied La Fayette in his tour through the United States in 1824.   He died at the manor house, at Croton, November 21st, 1831, at the age of eighty-two.   With him expired the property entail.

while desolation was rife around them. When I visited the mansion, General Pierre Van Cortlandt, the late owner (brother of General Philip Van Cortlandt, of the manor house), had been dead but a few months. Many of the family portraits were yet there, some of them more than one hundred years old. They have since been removed to the old manor house at Croton. The mansion which we are considering was occupied for a while by General M‘Dougall's advanced guard, when the British took possession of Peeks-kill in March, 1777, an event that will be noticed presently. The old oak tree is standing in a field a little eastward of the house, which was used for the purpose of a military whip-ping-post during the encampment there. It is green and vigorous, and so regular are its branches, that, when in full foliage, its form, above the trunk, is a perfect sphere. October, 1848.

Upon a knoll, a little eastward of Van Cortlandt's house, is an ancient wooden church, erected in 1767 for worship, according to the rituals of the Church of England. Within

PAULDING'S MONUMENT, AND ST. PETER'S CHURCH.[1]

its grave-yard, which spreads over the knoll westward, is the monument erect-ed to the memory of John Paulding, one of the captors of Andrè, by the cor-poration of the city of New York. The monument is constructed of West Ches ter marble, in the most simple form, consisting of a pedestal surmounted by a cone. It is massive, and so con structed as to last for ages. The base of the pedestal covers a square of seven feet, and is surrounded by a strong iron railing. The height is about thirteen feet. One side of the monument ex hibits a representation, in low relief, of the face of the medal voted by Con gress to each of the captors of Andrè ; the other side exhibits the reverse of the medal. The main inscription is upon the western panel of the pedestal.[2]

From the old church-yard I rode to the summit of Gallows Hill, a lofty ridge on the north, and bared of trees by the hand of cultivation. It is famous as a portion of the camp-ground of the division of the American army under Putnam in 1777, and also as the place where a spy was executed, from which circumstance the hill derives its name. Leaving my vehicle at the gate of a farm-house by the road side, I crossed the fields to the place designated by tradition as the spot where the old chestnut-tree stood, near which the spy was hanged. It is about one hundred rods west of the road, on the southeastern slope of the hill, and is marked by a huge bowlder lying upon the surface, by the side of which is the decayed trunk

[1] The site of this church and the grave-yard was a gift of Andrew Johnson, of Perth Amboy, New Jer-sey. The parish was called St. Peter's ; and this and the parish of St. Philip, in the Highlands, were en dowed with two hundred acres of land by Colonel Beverly Robinson.

[2] The following are the inscriptions :

NORTH SIDE.—"Here repose the mortal remains of JOHN PAULDING, who died on the 18th day of Feb-ruary, 1818, in the 60th year of his age."

WEST SIDE.—"On the morning of the 23d of September, 1780, accompanied by two young farmers of the county of West Chester (whose names will one day be recorded on their own deserved monuments), he intercepted the British spy, Andrè. Poor himself, he disdained to acquire wealth by the sacrifice of HIS COUNTRY. Rejecting the temptation of great rewards, he conveyed his prisoner to the American camp ; and, by this act of noble self-denial, the treason of Arnold was detected ; the designs of the enemy baffled ; West Point and the American Army saved ; and these United States, now by the grace of God Free and Independent, rescued from most imminent peril."

SOUTH SIDE.—"The Corporation of the city of New York erected this tomb as a memorial sacred to PUBLIC GRATITUDE."

The monument was erected in 1827 ; the cone was placed on the pedestal on the 22d of November of that year, in the presence of a large concourse of citizens, who were addressed by William Paulding, then Mayor of New York. A copy of the medal presented to the captors of Andrè may be found on page 773

of a chestnut, as seen in the picture,[1] said to be a sprout of the memorable tree.   The name of
the spy was Edmund Palmer.   He was an athletic young
man, connected by nature and affection with some of the
most respectable families in West Chester, and had a wife
and children.   He was arrested on suspicion, and enlisting
papers, signed by Governor Tryon, were found upon his person.   It was also ascertained that he was a lieutenant in
a Tory company.   These and other unfavorable circumstances made it clear that he was a spy, and on that charge he
was tried, found guilty, and condemned to be hung.   His young
wife pleaded for his life, but the dictates of the stern policy of war made Putnam inexorable.   Sir Henry Clinton sent a flag to the American commander,
claiming Palmer as a British officer, and menacing the Republicans with his severest wrath if he was not delivered up.   Putnam's sense of duty was as deaf to the
menaces of the one as to the tears of the other, and he sent to Clinton the following laconic reply :

"Head-quarters, 7th August, 1777.

" SIR,—Edmund Palmer, an officer in the enemy's service, was taken as a spy, lurking
within our lines.   He has been tried as a spy, condemned as a spy, and shall be executed
as a spy ; and the flag is ordered to depart immediately.   ISRAEL PUTNAM.

" P.S.—He has been accordingly executed."

From the top of Gallows Hill there is a glorious prospect of the surrounding country, particularly southward, in which direction the eye takes in glimpses of Peekskill village, the
river and its rocky shores on the west, and the fertile estates of West Chester as far as the
high grounds of Tarrytown.   On the southeast of the ridge is the beautiful undulating
Peekskill Hollow, and on the north, between it and the rough turrets of the Highland towers, is scooped the Canopus Valley, deep and rich, wherein is nestled Continental Village,
the scene of one of Tryon's desolating expeditions.   We are upon historic ground ; let us
open the chronicle for a few moments.

In view of the relative position of the belligerent armies at the opening of 1777, Peekskill was regarded by the commander-in-chief as a very important post.   Believing that the
chief design of the next campaign would be, on the part of the enemy, to accomplish a junction of the forces under Sir William Howe at New York and an army preparing in Canada
March 12,   for invasion, Washington wrote, in a letter to General Schuyler, as follows : " Un-
1777.   der these considerations, I can not help thinking much too large a part of our force
is directed to Ticonderoga.   Peekskill appears to me a much more proper place, where, if
the troops are drawn together, they will be advantageously situated to give support to any
of the Eastern or Middle States.   Should the enemy's design be to penetrate the country up
the North River, they will be well posted to oppose them ; should they attempt to penetrate into New England, they will be well stationed to cover it ; if they **move** westward,
the Eastern and Southern troops can easily form a junction ; and besides, it will oblige the
enemy to have a much stronger garrison at New York."[2]   With these views, the commander-in-chief determined to collect a respectable force at Peekskill.   This was done as speedily
as possible, and General Heath, of Massachusetts, was placed in command.   This officer
was obliged to return to his state, and the command devolved upon General M'Dougall.[3]

---

[1] Near this bowlder a gallows, rudely constructed of logs, was erected, on which the spy was hung.   It
remained there for several years afterward, an object of superstitious dread to the country people who were
obliged to pass it in the night.   [2] Sparks's *Washington*, iv., 359.

[3] Alexander M'Dougall was the son of a Scotchman from the
Lowlands, who came to America about twenty years before the
Revolution broke out, and commenced business in the city of
New York.   The date of his birth is not known.   He became a zealous Whig during the years immedi-
ately preceding the Revolution, and when the war broke out he joined the army.   In August, 1776, he was

Cattle and military stores, in large quantities, were collected at Peekskill and in the vicinity; and the post, not being very strongly manned, attracted the attention of the enemy. Sir William Howe projected a scheme to capture or destroy them. Stratagem was a part of his plan. He caused a conversation on the subject to be held in the hearing of an American officer who had been captured at Fort Washington, in which it was arranged that an excursion was to be made into the country by three divisions: one to go up the Sound and land at Mamaroneck, another to march up the center road by Kingsbridge, and a third to go up the Hudson and land at Tarrytown. The officer was soon afterward released, and escorted with a flag to the American lines. The object was to have him report the conversation, and thus draw off General M‘Dougall's attention from the real point of attack. M‘Dougall had only two hundred and fifty effective men, too few to attempt opposition. He immediately commenced sending his stores to Forts Clinton and Montgomery for safety, but before he had accomplished his design, ten sail of British vessels appeared off Tarrytown, and two went up to Haverstraw Bay, at a point twelve miles below Peekskill. March 22, 1777. The next day the whole fleet anchored in Peekskill Bay; and at one o'clock, five hundred men, in eight flat-boats, under the command of Colonel Bird, landed at Lent's Cove, on the south side of the bay. They had four pieces of light artillery, drawn by the sailors. General M‘Dougall retreated to Gallows Hill and vicinity, giving directions for destroying such stores as could not be removed. At the same time, he sent a dispatch to Lieutenant-colonel Willett, at Fort Constitution, to leave a subaltern's command there, and hasten to his assistance. The British held possession of the town until next day, March 24. when a detachment advanced toward the Highlands. These were attacked by Colonel Willett, and a smart skirmish ensued. The detachment retreated back to the main body of the enemy, and in the evening, favored by the light of the moon, they all embarked and sailed down the river. Their object, the destruction of the stores, was partially accomplished, but not by their own hands. They had nine of their number killed in the skirmish with Willett, and four at the verge of the creek, while attempting to burn some boats. The Americans had one man killed by a cannon shot.[1] Two or three houses were burned, and about forty sheep, furnished by the Tories, were carried off.

Near the banks of Canopus Creek, and overlooked by Gallows Hill, is Continental Village. It is about three miles from Peekskill, at the main entrance to the Highland passes northward. There, in 1777, were constructed barracks sufficient to accommodate two thousand men. A large number of cattle, and a great quantity of military stores under the charge of Major Campbell, were collected there. Two small redoubts were erected on the high ground, for the double purpose of protecting the public property and guarding the mountain road. Hither, on the morning of the 9th of October, three days after the capture of Forts Clinton and Montgomery, General Tryon was detached with Emerick's chasseurs and other Germans, with a three-pounder, to destroy the settlement. He accomplished the object most effectually. The barracks, and nearly every house in the little village, together with the public stores, were consumed, and many of the cattle were slaughtered. The inhabitants fled to the hills, while the few troops that were left when Putnam and the main force retired to Fishkill on the fall of the mountain fortresses, were compelled to fly for safety. In a few hours the smiling little valley was a scene of utter desolation.[2] Gen-

---

appointed a brigadier, and in October, 1777, he was promoted to the rank of major general. He commanded in the action near White Plains, and was in the battle at Germantown in the autumn of 1777. In 1781 he was elected to a seat in the Continental Congress, and was afterward a member of the New York State Senate. He died June 8, 1786.

[1] *General M‘Dougall's MS. Letter* of March 29, 1777, quoted by Sparks.

[2] The feelings of Tryon toward the Republicans may be learned from a letter of his, written a few weeks after this transaction, in reply to one of remonstrance on the part of General Parsons. "I have," he says, "the candor enough to assure you, as much as I abhor every principle of inhumanity or ungenerous conduct, I should, were I in more authority, burn every committee-man's house within my reach, as I deem those agents the wicked instruments of the continued calamities of this country; and in order sooner to purge this country of them, I am willing to give twenty-five dollars for every acting committee-man who shall be delivered up to the king's troops."

eral Parsons[1] marched down from Fishkill with two thousand men a few days afterward, and took possession of Peekskill. From that time it was the scene of no stirring military events, other than those incident to the brief encampment of regiments or divisions of the American army.

Sam'l H. Parsons

After sketching the only prominent object on the site of poor Palmer's gallows, I resumed the reins, and, when part way down the northern slope of the ridge, turned up a green lane near the Soldier's Spring[2] to the farm-house of Mr. Lent, to inquire for an aged couple of that name. Informed that they lived at a little village called Oregon, a mile and a half distant, I returned to Peekskill Hollow, and proceeded thither. My journey was fruitless of information. They were, indeed, a venerable pair ; one aged eighty-four, and the other eighty-three years.

After dinner at Peekskill, I rode down to Verplanck's Point, eight miles below.[3] It was October 27, 1848. a lovely afternoon ; a fine road amid ever-varying scenery, and every rock, and knoll, and estuary of the river clustered over with historic associations, made the journey of an hour one of great pleasure and interest. Verplanck's Point is the termination of a peninsula of gently rolling land, gradually ascending from the neck toward the shore, where it ends in a bluff, from thirty to fifty feet high. Here, during the memorable season 1836. of land and town speculation, when the water-lot mania emulated that of the tulip and the South Sea games, a large village was mapped out, and one or two fine mansions were erected. The bubble burst, and many fertile acres there, where corn and potatoes once yielded a profit to the cultivator, are scarred and made barren by intersecting streets, not *de*populated, but *un*populated, save by the beetle and grasshopper. On the brow of

---

In allusion to this and kindred expeditions, Trumbull makes Malcom say,

"Behold, like whelps of Britain's lion,
Our warriors, Clinton, Vaughan, and Tryon,
March forth with patriotic joy
To ravish, plunder, and destroy.
Great gen'rals, foremost in their nation,
The journeymen of Desolation !
Like Sampson's foxes, each assails,
Let loose with fire-brands in their tails,
And spreads destruction more forlorn
Than they among Philistines' corn."
M'FINGAL, CANTO IV.

[1] SAMUEL HOLDEN PARSONS was a native of Connecticut, and one of a committee of correspondence in that state before the commencement of the war. He was appointed a brigadier general by Congress in August, 1776, and served his country faithfully during the contest. Under his direction, the successful expedition of Colonel Meigs against the enemy at Sag Harbor, on Long Island, in 1777, was sent out. He was appointed a commissioner to negotiate with the Western Indians in 1785. In 1787, he was appointed one of the judges of the Northwestern Territory. He was drowned in the Ohio, in December, 1789.

[2] This is a little fountain bubbling up by the road side, and named *The Soldier's Spring*, from the circumstance that an American soldier, while retreating before the enemy, stooped at the fountain to quench his thirst. While so doing, a cannon ball, that struck the hills above him, glanced obliquely, hit and shattered his thigh, and left him dying beside the clear waters. He was conveyed in a wagon that passed soon afterward, to Fishkill, where he expired.

[3] This was the point off which Henry Hudson's vessel, the *Half Moon*, came first to anchor after leaving the mouth of the river. The Highland Indians, filled with wonder, came flocking to the ship in boats, but their curiosity ended in a tragedy. One of them, overcome by acquisitiveness, crawled up the rudder, entered the cabin window, and stole a pillow and a few articles of wearing apparel. The mate saw the 'hief pulling his bark for land, and shot at and killed him. The ship's boat was sent for the stolen articles, and when one of the natives, who had leaped into the water, caught hold of the side of the shallop, his hand was cut off by a sword, and he was drowned. This was the first blood shed by these voyagers. Intelligence of this spread over the country, and the Indians hated the white man, afterward, intensely.

The exceedingly tortuous creek which traverses the marsh southward of Verplanck's Point was called, by the Indians, Meahagh, and this was the name which they gave to the peninsula. It was purchased of the Indians by Stephanus Van Cortlandt in 1683. From him it passed into the possession of his son Johannes, whose only daughter and heiress, Gertrude, married Philip Verplanck, from whom it acquired its present appellation

the Point, near the western extremity, and overlooking the water, a small fortification, called Fort Fayette, was erected   It was an eligible site for a fort; and, in connection with the fortress on the rocky promontory opposite, was capable of being made a formidable defense at this, the lower gate of the Hudson Highlands.   These two promontories make the river

VIEW OF VERPLANCKS PT.

quite narrow, and, if well fortified, might defy the passage of any number of hostile vessels.[1] The site of Fort Fayette is distinctly traceable in the orchard upon the high grounds in the rear of Mr. Bleakly's store upon the wharf.   The mounds and fossé of the main fort, as it was enlarged and strengthened by the British, and also the embankments of the smaller outworks, are quite prominent in many places.

The small forts at Verplanck's and Stony Points were captured by the enemy commanded by Sir Henry Clinton in person, on the 1st of June, 1779.   The garrison of Stony Point consisted of only about forty men, and that at Verplanck's of seventy men, commanded by Captain Armstrong.   As these forts secured a free communication between the troops of New England and those of the central and southern portions of the confederacy, Clinton determined to dislodge the Americans therefrom.   Accordingly, on the 30th of May, he sailed up the river with a strong force, accompanied by General Vaughan; the flotilla was commanded by Admiral Collier.   They landed in two divisions on the morning of the 31st, the one under Vaughan, on the east side, eight miles below Verplanck's, and the other under Clinton, on the west side, a little above Haverstraw.   The garrison at Stony Point retired to the Highlands on the approach of the enemy, and the fort changed masters without bloodshed.   The next morning, the guns of the captured fortress, and the cannons and mortars dragged up during the night, were pointed toward Fort Fayette opposite, and a heavy cannonade was opened upon it.   Unable to make a respectable resistance to this assault, and attacked in the rear by Vaughan's division, the little garrison surrendered themselves prisoners of war.[2]   The loss of these forts was greatly lamented by Washington,

May, 1779

---

[1] This map shows the relative position of Verplanck's and Stony Points, and of the forts in the time of the Revolution.   A represents the position and form of the fort on Stony Point; B, General Wayne's right column, and C his left column, when he stormed the ramparts and fort; and D shows the site of Fort Fayette, on the east side of the river.

[2] The following were the terms of capitulation:

"On the glacis of Fort Fayette, June 1st, 1779.

"His excellency Sir Henry Clinton and Commodore Sir George Collier grant to the garrison of Fort La Fayette terms of safety to the persons and property (contained in the fort) of the garrison, they surrendering themselves prisoners of war.   The officers shall be permitted to wear their side-arms.

"JOHN ANDRÈ, Aid-de-camp."

and his first care was to make an effort to recover them, for West Point was now in danger. The main body of the American army was moved from Middlebrook toward the Highlands, and Washington established his quarters at Smith's Clove, far in the rear of Haverstraw.[1] Sir Henry Clinton gave orders for the immediate strengthening of the forts, and to guard the detachments left for the purpose, he descended the river with his army only as far as Phillipsburgh, now Yonkers.

REAR VIEW AT STONY POINT.[2]

On the 23d of June, Washington established his head-quarters at New Windsor, leaving General Putnam in command of the main army at Smith's Clove. General M'Dougall was transferred to the command at West Point; the garrisons at Constitution Island, and at the redoubts opposite West Point, were strengthened; the road to Fish-kill was well guarded, and three brigades were placed under the command of General Heath, who had lately been ordered from Boston. On the 1st of July, General Wayne was appointed to the command of the light infantry of the line, and was stationed in the vicinity of the Dunderberg, between Fort Montgomery and the main army at the Clove. The British had now greatly enlarged and strengthened the two forts in question, well supplied them with ammunition and stores, and had them strongly garrisoned. The force at Stony Point consisted of the seventeenth regiment of foot, the grenadier companies of the seventy-first, and some artillery; the whole under the command of Lieutenant-colonel Johnson of the seventh. The garrison at Verplanck's was commanded by Lieutenant-colonel Webster, and was quite equal in force to that at Stony Point. Several small British vessels of war were anchored in the bay within close cannon shot of the forts. Such was the situation of the two armies, when the attack of the Americans under Wayne and Howe upon Stony Point and Verplanck's Point was planned and executed by order of Washington.

1779.   On the morning of the 15th of July, all the Massachusetts light infantry were marched to the quarters of Wayne at Sandy Beach, fourteen miles from Stony Point. At meridian on that exceedingly sultry day, the whole body moved through narrow defiles, over rough crags, and across deep morasses, in single file, and at eight in the evening rendezvoused a mile and a half below Stony Point. There they remained until General Wayne and several officers returned from reconnoitering the works of the enemy, when they were formed into column, and moved silently forward under the guidance of a negro slave belonging to a Captain Lamb who resided in the neighborhood.[3]

The position of the fortress was such that it seemed almost impregnable. Situated upon a huge rocky bluff, an island at high water, and always inaccessible dry-shod, except across

---

[1] Smith's Clove extends northward from the Ramapo Valley, not far from Turner's station on the Erie ail-road.

[2] This sketch presents a rear view of the old embankments of the fort, and of the light-house, which is seen vy all travelers upon the river, just before entering the Highlands. The beacon stands exactly in the center if the fort, upon the site of the magazine. There was a covered way toward the water on the north side of the hill, and about twenty yards in the rear are some prominent remains of the ravelins which extended across the point.

[3] Mr. Ten Eyck, the old ferryman at Stony Point, informed me that he knew this negro well. His name was Pompey, and for his services on that night his master gave him a horse to ride, and never exacted any labor from him afterward. Pompey's master was a warm Whig, and himself was a shrewd negro. Soon after the enemy took possession of the Point, Pompey ventured to go to the fort with strawberries to sell. He was kindly received; and as the season advanced, and berries and cherries became plentiful, he carried on an extensive traffic with the garrison, and became a favorite with the officers, who had no suspicion that he was regularly reporting every thing to his Whig master. Finally, Pompey informed them that his master would not allow him to come with fruit in the daytime, for it was hoeing-corn season. Unwilling to lose their supply of luxuries, the officers gave Pompey the countersign regularly, so that he could pass the sentinels in the evening. He thus possessed a knowledge of the countersign on the night of the attack, and made good use of it. That countersign was, "The fort's our own," and this was the watch-word of the Americans when they scaled the ramparts.

a narrow causeway in the rear, it was strongly defended by outworks and a double row of *abatis*. Upon three sides of the rock were the waters of the Hudson, and on the fourth was a morass, deep, and dangerous. But Wayne was not easily deterred by obstacles; and tradition avers, that while conversing with Washington on the subject of this expedition, he remarked, with emphasis, "General, I'll storm hell if *you* will only plan it." He possessed the true fire of the flint, and was always governed by the maxim, "Where there's a will there's a way." He resolved to storm the fort at all hazards, and only waited for the ebbing of the tide, and the deep first slumber of the garrison, to move toward the fortress.

GENERAL WAYNE.[1]

[1] ANTHONY WAYNE was born in the township of Eastown, in Chester county, Pennsylvania, on the 1st of January, 1745. He was educated in Philadelphia, and having studied mathematics with care, he opened a surveyor's office in his native town. He was sent to Nova Scotia in 1765, to locate a grant of land from the crown to several gentlemen in Pennsylvania. They made Wayne superintendent of the settlement. This post he held until 1767, when he returned home, married a young lady in Philadelphia, and resumed his profession as surveyor. In 1773, he was appointed a representative to the general Assembly of his state. He quitted the council for the field in 1775, where he was appointed a colonel in the Continental army, and went to Canada with General Thomas. At the close of the campaign there in 1776, he was promoted to brigadier general. He was with the commander-in-chief at Brandywine, Germantown, and Monmouth, in all of which engagements he was distinguished for his valor. The capture of Stony Point raised him to the highest mark in the admiration of his countrymen. In 1781, he went with the Pennsylvania line to the South, and in Virginia co-operated with La Fayette. After the capture of Cornwallis, he was sent to conduct the war in Georgia, and was very successful. As a reward for his services, the Legislature of Georgia made him a present of a valuable farm. He was a member of the Pennsylvania Convention that ratified the Federal Constitution. In 1792, he succeeded St. Clair in the command of the army to be employed against the Western Indians, and gained a great victory over them in the battle of the Miamis, in August, 1794. He concluded a treaty with the Indians in August, 1795. While engaged in the public service, and returning home from the West, he was seized with the gout, and died in a hut at Presque Isle, in December, 1796, aged fifty-one years. He was buried, at his own request, under the flag-staff of the fort, on the shore of Lake Erie, from whence his remains were conveyed in 1809, by his son, Colonel Isaac Wayne, to Radnor church-yard, in Delaware county. The venerable church, near which the body of the hero lies, was erected in 1717. The Pennsylvania State Society of the Cincinnati caused a handsome monument of white marble to be erected over his remains, upon which are the following inscriptions:

NORTH FRONT.—"Major-general ANTHONY WAYNE was born at Waynesborough,* in Chester county, State of Pennsylvania, A.D. 1745. After a life of honor and usefulness, he died in December, 1796, at a military post on the shore of Lake Erie, commander-in-chief of the army of the United States. His military achievements are consecrated in the history of his country and in the hearts of his countrymen. His remains are here interred."

SOUTH FRONT.—"In honor of the distinguished military services of Major-general ANTHONY WAYNE, and as an affectionate tribute of respect to his memory, this stone was erected by his companions in

WAYNE'S MONUMENT.

arms, the Pennsylvania State Society of the Cincinnati, July 4, A.D. 1809, thirty-fourth anniversary of the independence of the United States of America; an event which constitutes the most appropriate eulogium of an American soldier and patriot."

* This is an error. His birth-place was about a mile and a quarter south of the Paoli tavern

It was half past eleven o'clock at night when the Americans commenced their silent march toward the fort. All the dogs in the neighborhood had been killed the day before, that their barking might not give notice of strangers near. The negro, with two strong men disguised as farmers, advanced alone. The countersign was given to the first sentinel, on the high ground west of the morass, and while he was conversing with Pompey, the men seized and gagged him. The silence of the sentinel at the causeway was secured in the same manner, and as soon as the tide ebbed sufficiently, the whole of Wayne's little army, except a detachment of three hundred men under General Muhlenburg, who remained in the rear as a reserve, crossed the morass to the foot of the western declivity of the

VIEW OF STONY POINT FROM THE SOUTHWEST.[1]

promontory, unobserved by the enemy. The troops were now divided into two columns; the van of the right, consisting of one hundred and fifty volunteers, under Lieutenant-colonel De Fleury, and that of the left, of one hundred volunteers, under Major Stewart, each with unloaded muskets and fixed bayonets. An *avant-guard* of twenty picked men for each company, under Lieutenants Gibbon and Knox, preceded them, to remove the *abatis* and other obstructions. These vans composed the forlorn hope on that memorable night.

At a little past midnight the advanced parties moved silently to the charge, one company on the southern, and the other toward the northern portion of the height. They were followed by the two main divisions; the right, composed of the regiments of Febiger and Meigs, being led by General Wayne in person. The left was composed of Colonel Butler's regiment, and two companies under Major Murfey. The Americans were undiscovered until within pistol shot of the pickets upon the heights, when a skirmish ensued between the sentinels and the advanced guards. The pickets fired several shots, but the Americans, true to orders, relied entirely upon the bayonet, and pressed forward with vigor. The garrison was aroused from their slumbers, and instantly the deep silence of the night was broken by the roll of the drum, the loud cry *To arms! to arms!* the rattle of musketry from the ramparts and behind the *abatis*, and the roar of cannon, charged with the deadly grape-shot, from the embrasures.[2] In the face of this terrible storm, the Americans forced their way, at

---

[1] This view shows a large portion of the morass, and the place where the assaulting party divided and prepared for an attack upon the fort, which was situated where the light-house is seen. The place of the causeway is on the left, denoted by the cattle. When I made this sketch it was quite high water, and the morass, there about one hundred feet wide, was almost covered. There was another place near the river shore, on the right, where the Point was accessible at times. It is distinguished in the sketch by the narrow strip of land extending nearly across the mouth of the morass. Upon this the enemy had dug pits and placed sharpened stakes within them, so that, had the Americans attempted to reach the Point by that way many would have been impaled. The position of the Americans in the attack, and of the outworks and the *abatis*, will be better understood by a reference to the map on a preceding page.

[2] Major (afterward General) Hull says in his Memoir, "At about half past eleven o'clock, the two columns commenced their march in platoons. The beach was more than two feet deep with water, and before the right column reached it we were fired on by the out-guards, which gave the alarm to the garrison. We were now directly under the fort, and, closing in a solid column, ascended the hill, which was almost perpendicular. When about half way up, our course was impeded by two strong rows of *abatis*, which the forlorn hope had not been able entirely to remove. The column proceeded silently on, and, clearing away the *abatis*, passed to the breast-work, cut and tore away the pickets, cleared the chevaux de frise at the sally-port, mounted the parapet, and entered the fort at the point of the bayonet. Our column on the other side en-

the point of the bayonet, through every obstacle, until the van of each column met in the center of the works, where each arrived at the same time.[1]   At the inner *abatis*, Wayne was struck upon the head by a musket ball, which brought him upon his knees.   His two brave aids, Fishbow and Archer, raised him to his feet, and carried him gallantly through the works.   Believing himself mortally wounded, the general exclaimed, as he arose, " March on ! carry me into the fort, for I will die at the head of my column !"   But the wound was not very severe, and he was able to join in the loud huzzas that arose when the two columns met as victors within the fort.   Colonel De Fleury first entered the works, and struck the British standard with his own hands.   The garrison surrendered at discretion as prisoners of war, and that brilliant achievement was rendered the more glorious for the clemency which the victors exercised toward the vanquished.   Not a life was taken after the flag was struck and the garrison had pleaded for quarters.   Wayne had but fifteen killed and eighty-three wounded ; the British had sixty-three killed ;[2] and Johnson, the commander, with five hundred and forty-three officers and men, were made prisoners.   The ships of the enemy lying in the river in front of Stony Point slipped their cables and moved down to a place of security.   Before daylight, Wayne sent to the commander-in-chief the brief but comprehensive reply, of which a fac simile is here given :

tered the fort at the same time.   Each of our men had a white paper in his hat, which in the darkness distinguished him from the enemy ; and the watch-word was, ' *The fort's our own !* '"   Some authors have asserted that bomb-shells were thrown by the British, but such, probably, was not the fact.   No official account that I have seen mentions the use of shells.

[1] Wayne's official dispatch, dated at Stony Point, July 17, 1779.

[2] This is the number given in the American account.   Colonel Johnson, in his official dispatch, says he had only twenty killed.

At dawn the next morning the cannons of the captured fort were turned upon the enemy's works at Verplanck's Point under Colonel Webster, and a desultory bombardment was kept up during the day. Major-general Robert Howe had been sent to attack Fort Fayette, but on account of delays, and some misconceptions of Washington's orders, he did not make the attack in time to dislodge the garrison. News of Webster's critical situation and the capture of Stony Point was speedily communicated to Sir Henry Clinton, and he immediately sent relief to the menaced garrison at Verplanck's. Howe withdrew, and the enterprise was abandoned.

Washington, clearly perceiving the danger of attempting to retain the post at Stony Point

GOLD MEDAL AWARDED BY CONGRESS TO GENERAL WAYNE.[1]

with so few troops as could be employed in the service, concluded to order an evacuation, and a destruction of the works after the ordnance and stores should be removed. This was accordingly done on the night of the eighteenth. All that was originally intended July, 1779. was accomplished, namely, the destruction of the works and the seizure of the artillery and stores. A large portion of the heavy ordnance was placed upon a galley to be conveyed to West Point. As soon as the vessel moved, a cannonade from Verplanck's and the British shipping was commenced upon it. A heavy shot from the Vulture struck it below water-mark, and the galley went down at the point just above Caldwell's Landing, where speculation recently made credulity seek for treasures in a sunken vessel alleged to have belonged to the famous Captain Kidd. If, as asserted, a cannon was drawn up from a vessel lying at the bottom of the river there, it was doubtless one of the pieces taken from Stony Point, and the " ship's timbers" there discovered are the remains of the old galley. The " treasures," if secured, would be of little worth in these " piping times of peace."

The British repossessed themselves of Stony Point on the 20th, but they had little of value left them but the eligible site for a fortification.

The storming and capture of Stony Point, regarded as an exhibition of skill and indomitable courage, was one of the most brilliant events of the war. General Wayne, the leader

---

[1] This is a representation of the medal, the size of the original. On one side is a device representing an Indian queen crowned, a quiver on her back, and wearing a short apron of feathers. A mantle hangs from her waist behind, the upper end of which appears as if passed through the girdle of her apron, and hangs gracefully by her left side. With her right hand she is presenting a wreath to General Wayne; in her left she is holding up a mural crown toward his head. At her feet, on the left, an alligator is lying. The American shield is resting against the animal. Over the figure is the legend "ANTONIO WAYNE DUCI EXERCITUS," and beneath, "COMITIA AMERICANA;" "The American Congress to General Anthony Wayne." On the reverse is a fort on the top of a hill; the British flag flying; troops in single file advancing up the hill, and a large number lying at the bottom. Artillery are seen in the foreground, and six vessels in the river. The inscription is, "STONY POINT EXPUGNATUM, XV. JUL. MDCCLXXIX.;" "Stony Point captured, July 15, 1779."

of the enterprise, was every where greeted with rapturous applause.[1] Congress testified their grateful sense of his services by a vote of thanks " for his brave, prudent, and soldierly conduct." It was also resolved that a medal of gold, emblematical of this action, should be struck, and presented to General Wayne. Thanks were also presented by Congress to Lieutenant-colonel De Fleury[2] and Major Stewart, and a medal of silver was ordered to be struck

MEDAL AWARDED TO LIEUTENANT-COLONEL DE FLEURY.[3]

and presented to each. The conduct of Lieutenants Gibbon and Knox was warmly applauded, and brevets of captain was given to each, and to Mr. Archer, the volunteer aid of Wayne, who was the bearer of the general's letter to Washington on the occasion. Pursuant to the recommendation of the commander-in-chief, and in fulfillment of promises made by Wayne before the assault, with the concurrence of Washington, Congress resolved, " That the value of the military stores taken at Stony Point be ascertained and divided among the gallant

---

[1] General Charles Lee, who was not on the most friendly terms with Wayne, wrote to him, saying, " I do most seriously declare that your assault of Stony Point is not only the most brilliant, in my opinion, throughout the whole course of the war, on either side, but that it is the most brilliant I am acquainted with in history ; the assault of Schiveidnitz, by Marshal Laudon, I think inferior to it." Dr. Rush wrote, saying, " Our streets rang for many days with nothing but the name of General Wayne. You are remembered constantly next to our good and great Washington, over our claret and Madeira. You have established the national character of our country ; you have taught our enemies that bravery, humanity, and magnanimity are the national virtues of the Americans."

[2] De Fleury was descended from Hercule Andre de Fleury, a French nobleman, who was the preceptor of the grandson of Louis XIV. during the latter years of the life of that monarch. He was afterward made cardinal and prime minister. The subject of our sketch came to America soon after the news of the revolt reached France. Washington received him kindly, obtained for him a commission, and he proved to be a brave and worthy soldier. Educated as an engineer, his talents were brought into requisition here. In that capacity he was acting at the time of the engagement at Fort Mifflin, on the Delaware. He was at the battle of Brandywine, and for his gallantry there Congress gave him a horse. He returned to France soon after the capture of Stony Point.

[3] This is a representation of the medal, the size of the original. The device is a helmeted soldier, standing against the ruins of a fort. His right hand is extended, holding a sword upright ; the staff of a stand of colors is grasped by his left ; the colors are under his feet, and he is trampling upon them. The legend is, " VIRTUTIS ET AUDACIÆ MONUM ET PRÆMIUM. D. D. FLEURY EQUITI GALLO PRIMO MUROS RESP. AMERIC. D. D. ;" " A memorial and reward of valor and daring. The American Republic has bestowed (this medal) on Colonel D. de Fleury, a native of France, the first over the walls (of the enemy)." On the reverse are two water batteries, three guns each ; a fort on a hill, with a flag flying ; a river in front, and six vessels before the fort. The legend is, " AGGERES PALUDES HOSTES VICTI ;" " Mountains, morasses, foes, overcome." Exergue, " STONY PT. EXPUGN., XV. JUL., MDCCLXXIX. ;" " Stony Point stormed, 15th of July, 1779."

This identical silver medal was found by a boy while digging in a garden at Princeton, New Jersey, toward the close of April, 1850, and was deposited in the bank at that place for the inspection of the curious. How the medal came there is uncertain. De Fleury returned to France before the medal was struck, and it probably was never in his possession. Congress was afterward in session at Princeton, and the medal may have been lost by the secretary, in whose custody it properly belonged until delivered to the recipient of the honor.

troops by whom it was reduced, in such manner and proportions as the commander-in-chief shall prescribe."[1]

MEDAL AWARDED TO MAJOR STEWART.[2]

[1] See *Journals of Congress*, v., 226, 227.   The following rewards were promised : To the first man who entered the enemy's works, five hundred dollars; to the second, four hundred; to the third, three hundred; to the fourth, two hundred; to the fifth, one hundred : being fifteen hundred dollars in the aggregate.   The ordnance and other stores were estimated at one hundred and fifty-eight thousand six hundred and forty dollars in value, which amount was divided among the troops in proportion of officers and privates.—Sparks's *Washington*, vi., 540.

[2] This represents the medal the size of the original.   The device is America personified by an Indian queen, who is presenting a palm branch to Major Stewart.   A quiver is at her back; her left hand is resting on the American shield, and at her feet is an alligator crouchant.   The legend is, " JOANNI STEWART COHORTIS PRÆFECTO, COMITIA AMERICANA;" "The American Congress to Major John Stewart."   On the reverse is a fortress on an eminence.   In the foreground an officer is cheering on his men, who are following him over *abatis* with charged bayonets, the enemy flying.   Troops in single file are ascending to the fort on one side; others are advancing from the shore; ships are in sight.   The inscription is, " STONY POINT OPPUGNATUM XV. JUL. MDCCLXXIX.;" "Stony Point attacked 15th of July, 1779."

I believe there is no biography of Major Stewart.   Professor Wyatt, in his *Memoirs of American Generals, Commodores,* &c., says he was killed by a fall from his horse, near Charleston, South Carolina.

Lieutenant James Gibbon, who commanded one of the "forlorn hopes," was finally promoted to major. He died at Richmond, Virginia, on the first of July, 1834, in the seventy-seventh year of his age.   His remains were interred with military honors.

CHAPTER XXXII.

" From Cain to Catiline, the world hath known
  Her traitors—vaunted votaries of crime—
Caligula and Nero sat alone
  Upon the pinnacle of vice sublime ;
But they were moved by hate, or wish to climb
  The rugged steeps of Fame, in letters bold
To write their names upon the scroll of Time ;
  Therefore their crimes some virtue did enfold—
But Arnold ! thine had none—'twas all for sordid gold !"

Estelle Anna Lewis.

HE localities more immediately associated with the brief career of Andrè during his hapless connection with Arnold, now commands our attention, for toward Haverstraw I next journeyed. It was three o'clock in the afternoon when I crossed the ferry at Verplanck's Point in a small row-boat This was the old King's Ferry of the Revolution, where the good Wash ington so often crossed, and where battalion after battalion of troops, royal, French, and American, at various times spanned the Hudson with their long lines of flat-boats, for it was the main crossing-place of armies moving between the Eastern and Middle States. It was here, too. that a portion of the forces of Burgoyne crossed the Hudson when on their march from Massachusetts to Virginia. The landing-place on the Stony Point side, in former times, was in the cove at the opening of the marsh, on the north of the promontory ; now the western terminus of the ferry is a little above, at the cottage of Mr Tenyck, the jolly old ferryman, who has plied the oar there, almost without inter-

The Ferryman.

mission, ever since 1784. He was sitting upon his doorstone when his son moored the boat at its rock-fastening ; and, as we ascended the bank, the old man held up a bottle of whisky, and proffered a draught as a pledge of welcome to the " millionth man" that had crossed his ferry. Preferring milk to whisky, I sat down under the rich-leaved branches of a maple, and regaled myself with that healthful beverage. While the veteran and two of his neighbors were enjoying the aqua vitæ, I sketched the old King's Ferry sign-board, with its device, which was nailed to a sapling near, and then, accompanied by the old man and his companions, started for a ramble over the rough site of the fort on Stony Point. Upon its ancient mounds I sat and listened for an hour to the adventurous tales of the octogenarian, until the long shadows of the mountains warned me that the day was fast waning, when I hastened to make the drawings upon pages 744 and 746. At sunset, accompanied by

KING'S · FERRY.

one of the men as bearer of my light baggage, I started on foot for the neighborhood of Haverstraw. The road passes through a truly romantic region, made so by nature, history, and tradition. I stopped often to view the beautiful river prospect on the southeast. while the outlines of the distant shores were imperceptibly fading as the twilight came on. At dusk we passed an acre of ground, lying by the roadside on the right, which was given

752 PICTORIAL FIELD-BOOK

"God's Acre." Benson's Tavern. Interview with a Builder of Stony Point Fort. View from Smith's House

many years ago for a neighborhood burial-place. Its numerous white slabs proclaimed an already populous city of the dead, and ere long another generous hand should donate an acre near for the same purpose.

> " I like that ancient Saxon phrase which calls
> The burial-ground *God's Acre !* It is just;
> It consecrates each grave within its walls,
> And breathes a benison o'er the sleeping dust.
> *God's Acre !* Yes, that blessed name imparts
> Comfort to those who in the grave have sown
> The seed that they had garner'd in their hearts,
> Their bread of life, alas ! no more their own."
>
> LONGFELLOW.

It was quite dark when we reached the tavern of Mr. Benson, near Sampsonville, about three miles below Stony Point. Haverstraw was two miles distant, and, wearied with the rambles of the day, I halted at Benson's until morning. After an early breakfast I proceeded to the foot of Torn Mountain, a little northwest of Haverstraw, to visit a man named Allison, who was eighty-eight years old. I had been informed of his vigor of body and mind, and was much disappointed on finding him in bed, feeble and sinking from the effects of a fall. Our conversation was brief, but his short communications were interesting. He was a young man of eighteen when the fort at Stony Point was built, and assisted in carrying material for its construction from the main. In company with many others in the neighborhood not allowed to join in Wayne's expedition, he hung upon the rear of the little army on that eventful night ; and when the shout of victory arose from the fort, his voice was among the loudest in the echo that was sent back by the yeomanry gathered upon the neighboring hills. He gave me a minute account of the movements of the Americans before crossing the morass, and told me of a black walnut-tree still standing by the roadside between Haverstraw and Stony Point, under which the negro, Pompey, took charge, as pilot, of Wayne's assaulting force. I had intended, on leaving Mr. Allison, to go down near the river bank, where Arnold and André met ; but the hour was approaching at which I had promised myself to return to Verplanck's Point, so I postponed my visit to this interesting spot until a subsequent date.

On my return toward Stony Point, I tarried at and sketched Smith's House, delineated on page 720. It is in the present possession of William C. Houseman, whose good taste has adorned the grounds around it with fine shrubbery. It is located upon the brow of an eminence, known, for obvious reasons, as Treason Hill, and commands an extensive view of the Hudson and the country beyond.[1] From the window in the second story, where, tradition avers, André looked with anxious eyes for the appearance of the Vulture, I made the drawing printed on the opposite page. Between the foreground and the river is seen the broad alluvial flat in the rear of Haverstraw, and on the brink of the water is the village. The headland on the left is Teller's Point, and the highest ground on the extreme right is Torn Mountain, extending down to the verge of Haverstraw Bay, where it is called

[1] The Marquis de Chastellux, in his *Travels in North America* (i., 98, 99), says, " My thoughts were occupied with Arnold and his treason when my road brought me to Smith's farm-house, where he had his interview with André, and formed his horrid plot . . . . Smith, who was more than suspected, but not convicted of being a party in the plot, is still in prison,* where the law protects him against justice. But his home seems to have experienced the only chastisement of which it was susceptible ; it is punished by solitude ; and is, in fact, so deserted, that there is not a single person to take care of it, although it is the mansion of a large farm."

* Joshua Hett Smith, implicated in Arnold's treason, was a brother of the Tory chief justice, William Smith, and a man of considerable influence. The part which he had acted with Arnold made him strongly suspected of known participation in his guilt. He was arrested at Fishkill, in Dutchess county, and was taken to the Robinson House a few hours previous to the arrival of André. There Smith was tried by a military court and acquitted. He was soon afterward arrested by the civil authority of the state, and committed to the jail at Goshen, Orange county, whence he escaped, and made his way through the country, in the disguise of a woman, to New York. He went to England with the British army at the close of the war, and in 1808 published a book in London, entitled *An Authentic Narrative of the Causes which led to the Death of Major André* ; a work of very little reliable authority, and filled with abuse of Washington and other American officers. Smith died in New York in 1818.

the Hook Mountain.   The vessel in the river denotes the place where the Vulture lay at anchor.

Half a mile above the Smith House, on the right of the road to Stony Point, is the huge black walnut-tree mentioned by Mr. Allison. I procured a branch from it, large and straight enough for a *maul-stick*, and then plodded on in the warm sun, to the ferry.   The old waterman, though nearly eighty years of age, rowed his boat across with a vigorous hand, and at one o'clock I left Verplanck's for Tarrytown, a village on the eastern bank of the Hudson, twenty-seven miles above New

VIEW FROM SMITH'S HOUSE.

York, and memorable as the place where Major André was captured.

The village of Tarrytown lies scattered over the river front of the Greenburgh Hills, and presents a handsome appearance from the water.   It is upon the site of an Indian village called Alipconck, which, in the Delaware language, signifies the *Place of Elms*.   The Dutch, who settled there about 1680, called the place Tarwe Town, or "wheat town," probably from the abundant culture of that grain in the vicinity.[1]   The salubrity of its climate, and the commanding river view in front, has always made it a desirable place of residence.   During the Revolution it was the theater of many stormy scenes, consisting chiefly of skirmishes between the lawless bands of marauders known by the distinctive appellation of *Cow-boys* and *Skinners*.[2]   These infested the Neutral Ground[3] in West Chester, and made it a political and social hell for the dwellers.   Many left it, and allowed their lands to become a waste, rather than remain in the midst of perpetual torments.

The place where André was captured is upon the turnpike on the northeast verge of the village, three quarters of a mile from the river, and near the academy of Mr. Newman.   A few yards south of the academy, a small stream crosses the road and runs through a deep ravine riverward.   The marshy and thickly-wooded glen into which it poured was known as Wiley's Swamp.   A little south of this stream, on the west side of the road, is a dwarf cedar, near which (indicated, in the picture, by the spot where the figure sits) are the remains of a tree, said to be that of the stately white-wood under whose shadow the captors of André caused him to strip, and then made the momentous discovery of the papers in his

[1] Bolton.   Irving, in his *Legend of Sleepy Hollow*, says, " This name was given, we are told, in former days, by the good housewives of the adjacent country, from the inveterate propensity of their husbands to linger about the village tavern on market days."

[2] The party called *Cow-boys* were mostly Refugees belonging to the British side, and engaged in plundering the people near the lines of their cattle and driving them to New York.   Their vocation suggested their name.   The *Skinners* generally professed attachment to the American cause, and lived chiefly within the patriot lines ; but they were of easy virtue, and were really more detested by the Americans than their avowed enemies, the *Cow-boys*.   They were treacherous, rapacious, and often brutal.   One day they would be engaged in broils and skirmishes with the *Cow-boys ;* the next day they would be in league with them in plundering their own friends as well as enemies.   Oftentimes a sham skirmish would take place between them near the British lines ; the *Skinners* were always victorious, and then they would go boldly into the interior with their booty, pretending it had been captured from the enemy while attempting to smuggle it across the lines.   The proceeds of sales were divided between the parties.   See Sparks's *Life of Arnold*, 218–21 inclusive.

[3] The Neutral Ground, thirty miles in extent along the Hudson, and embracing nearly all West Chester county, was a populous and highly cultivated region, lying between the American and British lines.   Being within neither, it was called the Neutral Ground.   The inhabitants suffered dreadfully during the war, for they were sure to be plundered and abused by one party or the other.   If they took the oath of fidelity to the American cause, the *Cow-boys* were sure to plunder them ; if they did not, the *Skinners* would call them Tories, seize their property, and have it confiscated by the state.

stocking.[1] By a spring in the grove, just over the fence on the left, the young men were card-playing when their victim approached. We will not anticipate the history in the description, but here resume the narrative of events connected with Andrè's capture and trial, from the time we left him and Smith to pursue their journey from Verplanck's Point toward the Neutral Ground.

VIEW OF THE PLACE WHERE ANDRE WAS CAPTURED.

It was after dark   September 22, 1780. when Andrè and Smith left Verplanck's Point. They took the road toward White Plains, and met with no interruption until hailed by a sentinel near Crompond, a little village eight miles from Verplanck's Point.[2] He belonged to a party under Captain Boyd. That vigilant officer made many and searching inquiries of the travelers, and would not be satisfied that all was right until he procured a light and examined the pass from Arnold, which they assured him they possessed.

During the investigation Andrè was uneasy, but the pass being in explicit terms, and known to be genuine, Captain Boyd was readily persuaded that all was correct. The captain apologized for the strictness of his scrutiny, and manifested much concern for their safety on account of the prevalence of *Cow-boys* in the neighborhood. He advised them to remain till morning; but Smith assured him that their business was urgent, and it was necessary for them to proceed immediately toward White Plains. The captain magnified the dangers to which they were exposed, and Smith, taking counsel of his fears, was disposed to tarry. Andrè was differently inclined, and it was a long time before he could be persuaded to turn back and take lodging at the cottage of Andreas Miller. The travelers slept in the same bed, and, according to Smith's account, it was a weary and restless night for Andrè. He was up at dawn, and at an early hour they were again in the saddle. As they approached Pine's Bridge, and Andrè was assured that they were beyond patrolling parties, his taciturnity and gloom were exchanged for garrulity and cheerfulness, and he conversed in an almost playful manner upon poetry, the arts, literature, and common topics. Near Pine's Bridge[3] they parted company, after partaking of a frugal breakfast with Mrs. Sarah Underhill, whose grandson, I believe, still owns the house. Smith proceeded to Fishkill by the way of the

---

[1] "This tree towered like a giant," says Irving, in his Sketch Book, "above all the other trees of the neighborhood, and formed a kind of landmark. Its limbs were gnarled and fantastic, large enough to form trunks for ordinary trees, twisting down almost to the earth, and rising again into the air." The trunk was twenty-six feet in circumference, and forty-one feet in length. It was struck by lightning on the same day that intelligence of Arnold's death arrived at Tarrytown, a coincidence which many thought remarkable.

[2] Here, at the parsonage, the Yorktown Committee of Public Safety met; and members of the Provincial Congress assembled there to grant commissions to officers. Colonel Robertson, who commanded a regiment of Loyalists, was ordered to destroy that post; and, piloted thither by a Tory named Caleb Morgan, he burned the parsonage in the autumn of 1776.

[3] This bridge, situated in the southeast corner of Yorktown, spanned the Croton River. At this place the great dam connected with the Croton aqueduct is situated, and the present bridge crosses the lake above it, a little eastward of the Revolutionary structure. Here the Americans generally kept a strong guard, as it was the chief point of communication between the lines.

OF THE REVOLUTION.   755

Volunteer Expedition against the *Cow-boys*.   Arrest of Major Andrè.   Discovery of Papers in his Stockings.

Robinson House, where he pleased Arnold by communicating the particulars of the journey and the place where he left Andrè. It is not at all probable that Smith, at this time, was acquainted with the real name and mission of Andrè, for he knew him only as Mr. Anderson.

Andrè, being told that the *Cow-boys* were more numerous on the Tarrytown road, took that direction, contrary to the advice of Smith and others, for these marauders were his friends, and from them he had nothing to fear.

On the morning when Andrè crossed Pine's Bridge, a little band of seven volunteers went out near Tarrytown to prevent cattle being driven to New York, and to arrest any suspicious characters who might travel that way. John Yerks (who was living in the town of Mount Pleasant in 1848) proposed the expedition the day before, and first enlisted John Paulding, John Dean,[1] James Romer, and Abraham Williams. They were at North Salem, and Paulding procured a permit from the officer commanding there, at the same time persuading his friend, Isaac Van Wart, to accompany them. On their way toward Tarrytown they were joined by David Williams. They slept in a hay barrack at Pleasantville that night, and the next morning early they arrived near Tarrytown. Four of the party agreed to watch the road from a hill above, while Paulding, Van Wart, and David Williams were to lie concealed in the bushes by the stream near the post-road. Such was the position of the parties when Andrè approached. The circumstances of the capture are minutely narrated in the testimony of Paulding and Williams, given at the trial of Smith, eleven days afterward. The testimony was written down by the judge-advocate on that occasion, from whose manuscript Mr. Sparks copied it, as follows:[2] " Myself, Isaac Van Wart, and David Williams were lying by the side of the road about half a mile above Tarrytown, and about fifteen miles above Kingsbridge, on Saturday morning, between nine and ten o'clock, the 23d of September. We had lain there about an hour and a half, as near as I can recollect, and saw several persons we were acquainted with, whom we let pass. Presently, one of the young men who were with me said, ' There comes a gentleman-like looking man, who appears to be well dressed, and has boots on, and whom you had better step out and stop, if you don't know him.' On that I got up, and presented my firelock at the breast of the person, and told him to stand, and then I asked him which way he was going. ' Gentlemen,' said he, ' I hope you belong to our party.' I asked him what party. He said, ' The Lower Party.' Upon that I told him I did.[3] Then he said, ' I am a British officer, out in the country on particular business, and I hope you will not detain me a minute ,' and, to show that he was a British officer, he pulled out his watch. Upon which I told him to dismount. He then said, ' My God! I must do any thing to get along,' and seemed to make a kind of laugh of it, and pulled out General Arnold's pass, which was to John Anderson, to pass all guards to White Plains and below. Upon that he dismounted. Said he, ' Gentlemen, you had best let me go, or you will bring yourselves into trouble, for your stopping me will detain the general's business ;' and said he was going to Dobbs's Ferry to meet a person there and get intelligence for General Arnold. Upon that I told him I hoped he would not be offended ; that we did not mean to take any thing from him ; and I told

---

[1] While strolling among the ancient graves in the Sleepy Hollow church-yard, a little north of Tarrytown, at the time of my visit there, I was joined by an elderly gentleman, a son of Mr. Dean. He pointed out a brown freestone at the head of his father's grave, on which is the following inscription : " In memory of John Dean. He was born September 15th, A.D. 1755, and died April 4th, A.D. 1817, aged 61 years, 6 months, and 20 days.

> "A tender father, a friend sincere,
> A tender husband slumbers here ;
> Then let us hope his soul is given
> A blest and sure reward in heaven."

By his side is the grave of his father, who was buried eighty years ago.

[2] See Sparks's *Life and Treason of Arnold, Am. Biog.*, iii., 223–226.

[3] " Paulding had effected his escape," says Bolton (i., 224), " only three days previously, from the New York Sugar House, in the dress of a German Yager. General Van Cortlandt says that Paulding wore this dress on the day of the capture, which tended to deceive Andrè, and led him to exclaim, ' Thank God ! I am once more among friends.' "

him there were many bad people on the road, and I did not know but perhaps he might be one."

When further questioned, Paulding replied, that he asked the person his name, who told him it was John Anderson; and that, when Anderson produced General Arnold's pass, he should have let him go, if he had not before called himself a British officer. Paulding also said, that when the person pulled out his watch, he understood it as a signal that he was a British officer, and not that he meant to offer it to him as a present.

All these particulars were substantially confirmed by David Williams, whose testimony in regard to the searching of André, being more minute than Paulding's, is here inserted.

" We took him into the bushes," said Williams, " and ordered him to pull off his clothes, which he did; but, on searching him narrowly, we could not find any sort of writings. We told him to pull off his boots, which he seemed to be indifferent about; but we got one boot off, and searched in that boot, and could find nothing. But we found there were some papers in the bottom of his stocking next to his foot; on which we made him pull his stocking off, and found three papers wrapped up. Mr. Paulding looked at the contents, and said he was a spy. We then made him pull off his other boot, and there we found three more papers at the bottom of his foot within his stocking.

" Upon this we made him dress himself, and I asked him what he would give us to let him go. He said he would give us any sum of money. I asked him whether he would give us his horse, saddle, bridle, watch, and one hundred guineas. He said ʻYes,' and told us he would direct them to any place, even if it was that very spot, so that we could get them. I asked him whether he would not give us more. He said he would give us any quantity of dry goods, or any sum of money, and bring it to any place that we might pitch upon, so that we might get it. Mr. Paulding answered, ʻNo, if you would give us ten thousand guineas, you should not stir one step.' I then asked the person who had called himself John Anderson if he would not get away if it lay in his power. He answered, ʻYes, I would.' I told him I did not intend he should. While taking him along, we asked him a few questions, and we stopped under a shade. He begged us not to ask him questions, and said when he came to any commander he would reveal all.

" He was dressed in a blue over-coat, and a tight body-coat, that was of a kind of claret color, though a rather deeper red than claret. The button-holes were laced with gold tinsel, and the buttons drawn over with the same kind of lace. He had on a round hat, and nankeen waistcoat and breeches, with a flannel waistcoat and drawers, boots, and thread stockings."

André was conducted to North Castle, the nearest military post, and there, with all the papers found upon his person, he was delivered up to Lieutenant-colonel Jameson, the officer in command. With an obtuseness of perception most extraordinary and unaccountable, Jameson resolved to send the prisoner immediately to Arnold! He knew a portion of the papers to be in the undisguised handwriting of General Arnold, and it is most extraordinary that the circumstances under which they were found should not have awakened a suspicion of the fidelity of that officer.

COLONEL JAMESON'S HEAD-QUARTERS.

Washington afterward said, in allusion to Jameson's conduct, that, either on account of his " egregious folly or bewildered conception, he seemed lost in astonishment, and not to know what he was doing." There can be no doubt of the purity of his intentions, but who can respect his judgment? He penned a letter to Arnold, saying that he sent a certain Mr. Anderson forward under the charge of Lieutenant Allen and a guard, who had been taken while on his way to New York. " He had a passport," said Jameson, " signed in your name, and a parcel of papers, taken from under

<hr>

[1] This is a view of the out-buildings of Mr. Sands, at North Castle, situated a few yards from his residence. The lowest building, on the left, is the dwelling, now attached to the barn of Mr. Sands, which Jameson used as his head-quarters. In that building André was kept guarded until sent to West Point.

his stockings, which I think of a very dangerous tendency." He described the papers, and informed Arnold that he had sent them to Washington.

Major Benjamin Tallmadge, next in command to Jameson, was on duty below White Plains on that day, and did not return until evening. When informed of the circumstances, he was filled with astonishment at the folly of Jameson, and boldly expressed his suspicions of Arnold's fidelity. He offered to take upon himself the entire responsibility of proceeding on that ground, if Jameson would allow it. The latter refused to sanction any action that should imply a distrust of Arnold. Tallmadge then earnestly besought him to have the prisoner brought back. To this he reluctantly consented, but insisted that his letter to Arnold should be forwarded, and that the general should be informed why the prisoner was not sent on. This was the letter which Arnold received in time to allow him to make his escape to the Vulture. September 23, 1780.

Jameson sent an express after Lieutenant Allen, with orders to conduct his prisoner back to head-quarters at North Castle. As soon as Tallmadge saw him, and observed his manner and gait while pacing the room, he was convinced that he was a military man; and, joining this belief with other circumstances,[1] his suspicions of Arnold's treachery were fully confirmed to his own mind. He partially imbued Jameson with the same opinions, and that officer agreed, with Tallmadge, that it was advisable to keep their prisoner in close custody until orders should be received from Arnold or Washington. Andrè was accordingly removed, under an escort commanded by Major Tallmadge, to Colonel Sheldon's quarters at North Salem, as a more secure place. They arrived there at about eight in the morning. Andrè was introduced to Mr. Bronson, who was attached to Sheldon's regiment, and that gentleman kindly offered to share his little room with the prisoner. Learning that the papers found on his person had been sent to General Washington, he wrote, in Bronson's room, a letter to the American chief, in which he frankly avowed his name and rank, and briefly related the circumstances connected with his present situation. This letter he handed to Major Tallmadge to read, who was greatly astonished to find that the prisoner in his custody was the adjutant general of the British army. The letter was sealed and sent to Washington. From that hour the prisoner's mind seemed relieved.[2]

---

[1] Eight or nine days previous to the capture, Major Tallmadge received a letter from Arnold of similar import to the one Colonel Sheldon received from him, in which he requested, if a man by the name of Anderson should come within the lines, to have him sent to head-quarters with two horsemen. This incident was strongly in favor of Tallmadge's suspicions.

[2] The following is a copy of the letter:

"Salem, September 24th, 1780.

"Sir,—What I have as yet said concerning myself was in the justifiable attempt to be extricated. I am too little accustomed to duplicity to have succeeded.

"I beg your excellency will be persuaded that no alteration in the temper of my mind, or apprehension for my safety, induces me to take the step of addressing you, but that it is to rescue myself from an imputation of having assumed a mean character for treacherous purposes or self-interest; a conduct incompatible with the principles that actuate me, as well as with my condition in life. It is to vindicate my fame that I speak, and not to solicit security. The person in your possession is Major John Andrè, adjutant general to the British army.

"The influence of one commander in the army of his adversary is an advantage taken in war. A correspondence for this purpose I held, as confidential (in the present instance), with his excellency Sir Henry Clinton. To favor it, I agreed to meet, upon ground not within the posts of either army, a person who was to give me intelligence. I came up in the Vulture man-of-war for this effect, and was fetched by a boat from the ship to the beach. Being here, I was told that the approach of day would prevent my return, and that I must be concealed until the next night. I was in my regimentals, and had fairly risked my person.

"Against my stipulations, my intention, and without my knowledge beforehand, I was conducted within one of your posts. Your excellency may conceive my sensation on this occasion, and must imagine how much more must I have been affected by a refusal to reconduct me back the next night as I had been brought. Thus become a prisoner, I had to concert my escape. I quitted my uniform, and was passed another way in the night, without the American posts, to neutral ground, and informed I was beyond all armed parties, and left to press for New York. I was taken at Tarrytown by some volunteers. Thus, as I have had the honor to relate, was I betrayed (being adjutant general of the British army) into the vile condition of an enemy in disguise within your posts.

Pursuant to an order from General Washington, André was conducted to West Point, September, where he remained until the morning of the 28th, when he was conveyed in a 1780. barge to Stony Point, and from thence conducted, under a strong escort, to Tappan, about two miles westward of the present Piermont, the Hudson River terminus of the New York and Erie rail-road.   Major Tallmadge, who commanded the escort, and rode by André's side all the way, has left, in a communication to Mr. Sparks, an interesting account of the events of that day's march.   As he and André were about the same age, and held the same rank in the respective armies, they agreed on a cartel, by the terms of which each one was permitted to put any question to the other not involving a third person.   In the course of conversation, thus made as unreserved as possible, André informed Tallmadge that he was to have taken a part in the attack on West Point, if Arnold's plan had succeeded, and that the only reward he asked was the military glory to be won by such service to his king.   He had been promised, however, the rank and pay of a brigadier general if he had succeeded.   In reply to André's earnest inquiries respecting the probable result of his capture, Tallmadge frankly reminded him of the character and fate of the unfortunate Captain Hale.   "But you surely do not consider his case and mine alike?" said André.   "Yes, precisely similar," replied Major Tallmadge, "and similar will be your fate."   André became troubled in spirit, and from that time until the hour of his execution his most poignant sorrow arose from the reflection that he was branded with the odious name of a spy.[1]

As soon as Washington had completed all necessary arrangements for the security of September 29. West Point, he hastened to the army at Tappan.   The next day after his arrival he summoned a board of general officers, and directed them to examine into the case of Major André and report the result.   He also directed them to give their opinion as to the light in which the prisoner ought to be regarded, and the punishment that should be inflicted.   We shall visit Tappan presently, and then the events in the last scene of this drama shall be rehearsed; for the present, let us stroll about Tarrytown during the remainder of this pleasant afternoon.

After sketching a view of the spot where André was captured, I walked to the famous

ANCIENT DUTCH CHURCH.[2]

old Dutch church of Sleepy Hollow, standing by the side of the post-road, about a mile northward. I can not better describe its location than by quoting the language of Mr. Irving concerning it.   "The sequestered situation of the church," he says, "seems always to have made it a favorite haunt of troubled spirits.   It stands on a knoll, surrounded by locust-trees and lofty elms, from among which its decent white-washed walls shine modestly forth, like Christian purity beaming through the shades of retirement.   A gentle slope descends to it from a silver sheet of water,

"Having avowed myself a British officer, I have nothing to reveal but what relates to myself, which is true on the honor of an officer and a gentleman.   The request I have to make to your excellency, and I am conscious I address myself well, is, that in any rigor policy may dictate, a decency of conduct toward me may mark that, though unfortunate, I am branded with nothing dishonorable, as no motive could be mine but the service of my king, and as I was involuntarily an impostor.   Another request is, that I may be permitted to write an open letter to Sir Henry Clinton, and another to a friend for clothes and linen.

"I take the liberty to mention the condition of some gentlemen at Charleston, who, being either on parole or under protection, were engaged in a conspiracy against us.   Though their situation is not similar, they are objects who may be set in exchange for me, or are persons whom the treatment I receive might affect.   It is no less, sir, in a confidence of the generosity of your mind, than on account of your superior station, that I have chosen to importune you with this letter.

"I have the honor to be, with great respect, sir, your excellency's most obedient and most humble servant,
"JOHN ANDRÉ, Adjutant General."

[1] See Sparks's Amer. Biog., iii., 255-259.
[2] This view is from the church-yard, looking southwest.   The porch seen on the right fronts upon the

bordered by high trees, between which peeps may be caught of the blue hills of the Hudson.   To look upon its grass-grown yard, where the sunbeams seem to sleep so quietly, one would think that there, at least, the dead might rest in peace.   On one side of the church extends a woody dell, along which laves a large brook among broken rocks and trunks of fallen trees.   Over a deep black part of the stream, not far from the church, was formerly thrown a wooden bridge.   The road that led to it, and the bridge itself, were thickly shaded by overhanging trees, which cast a gloom about it, even in the daytime, but occasioned a fearful darkness at night."[1]

It was at this bridge, in the dark glen near the church, that poor Ichabod Crane had his terrible encounter with the headless horseman of Sleepy Hollow.[2]   The road still " leads through a sandy hollow, shaded by trees for about a quarter of a mile," but " the bridge famous in goblin story" is no more.   The present structure is a few yards westward of the site of the old one ; and although not so shaded in cavernous gloom, is quite as romantic in its situation.   From its planks there is a fine view of Castle

BRIDGE OVER SLEEPY HOLLOW CREEK.

Philipse, as the ancient manor house of Frederic Philipse was called, from the circumstance of its being originally fortified against the Indians.   It is a spacious and substantial stone building, and near it is the old mill, whose wheel turned in the same place during the Revolution.   The dam forms a pleasant little lake extending back almost to the bridge.

Upon the slopes and the brow of the hill eastward of the old church is the Tarrytown cemetery, extending down to the ancient burial-ground.   It is susceptible of being made one of the most attractive burial-places in this country, for, aside from the beauties of nature there spread out, associations of the deepest interest give a charm to the spot.   The Receiving Tomb, constructed of light stone, is near the top of the hill ; and around it for many

COMMUNION-TABLE.

highway, and is a modern addition, the ancient entrance being on the south side. This is believed to be the oldest church in existence in this state, having been erected, according to an inscription upon a stone tablet upon its front, by Vredryck Flypsen (Frederic Philips) and Catharine his wife, in 1699.   It is built of brick and stone, the former having been imported from Holland for the express purpose.   The old flag-shaped vane, with the initials of the founder cut out of it, yet turns upon its steeple, and in the little tower hangs the ancient bell, bearing this inscription : " SI. DEUS. PRO. NOBIS. QUIS. CONTRA. NOS. 1685"—

THE VANE.

" If God be for us, who can be against us !"   The pulpit and communion-table were imported from Holland ; the latter alone has escaped the ruthless hand of modern improvement.   [1] *Legend of Sleepy Hollow.*

[2] Ichabod, according to Irving, in the *Legend*, returning from a late evening tarry with Katrina Van Tassel, on his lean steed Gunpowder, was chased by a huge horseman, without a head, from the André tree to the bridge.   "He saw the walls of the church dimly gleaming under the trees beyond.   He recollected the place where Brom Bones's ghostly competitor had disappeared.   'If I can but reach that bridge,' thought Ichabod, 'I am safe.'   Just then he heard the black steed panting and blowing close behind him ; he even fancied that he felt his hot breath.   Another convulsive kick in the ribs, and old Gunpowder sprang upon the bridge ; he thundered over the resounding planks ; he gained the opposite side ; and now Ichabod cast a look behind, to see if his pursuer should vanish, according to rule, in a flash of fire and brimstone.   Just then he saw the goblin rising in his stirrups, and in the very act of hurling his head at him.   Ichabod endeavored to dodge the horrible missile, but too late ; it encountered his cranium with a terrible crash ; he was tumbled headlong into the dust, and Gunpowder, the black steed, and the goblin rider, passed like a whirlwind."

A shattered pumpkin was found on the road the next day, but Ichabod had gone to parts unknown. Brom Bones, his rival, soon afterward led the pretty Katrina to the altar.   The good country people always maintained that Ichabod was spirited away by the *headless horseman*, who was the ghost of a Hessian soldier, whose body, deprived of its caput by a cannon-ball, was sleeping in the church-yard near.

760   PICTORIAL FIELD-BOOK

Greenburgh on the Nepera.   Van Wart's Monument.   *Sunnyside*, the Residence of Washington Irving.

rods, where the hand of improvement had not yet effaced them, might be seen vestiges of a small fortification, thrown up there during the war.

I passed the night at Tarrytown, and the next morning rode out to the beautiful Saw-mill Valley, to visit the burial-ground at Greenburgh, wherein repose the remains of Isaac Van Wart, one of the captors of Andrè. The ground is attached to the Presbyterian church, and is near the lovely Nepera, or Saw-mill River. Over the remains of the patriot is a handsome marble monument, erected to his memory by the citizens of West Chester county, in 1829. Its completion was celebrated by a large concourse of people assembled there on the 11th of June of that year. General Aaron Ward, of Sing Sing, was the orator on the occasion. Mr. Van Wart was an efficient officer of that church for many years, and acted as chorister up to the

RECEIVING TOMB.

time of his death. On returning to Tarrytown, I rode down to *Sunnyside*, the residence of Washington Irving, situated upon the river bank, about two miles below. It is reached from the post-road by a winding carriage-way, that cleaves rich cultivated fields and pleasant woodlands. Desirous of passing an hour at Dobbs's Ferry, and of crossing the Hudson at Tappan in season to visit places of note there, I enjoyed the friendly greeting of the gifted proprietor but a few moments, and then pursued my journey. I subsequently visited *Sunnyside*, and made the sketch given on the opposite page. It was in leafy June, and a

1850.

lovelier day never smiled upon the Hudson and its green banks. Close by Mr. Irving's residence, a prospective village[1] had recently burst into existence, almost as suddenly as the leaves had unfolded from the buds in the adjacent groves; and a rail-way station, with its bustle and noise, was upon the river margin, within bird-call of the once secluded Wolfert's Roost. I strolled along the iron way to a stile, over which I clambered, and, ascending the bank by a shaded pathway, was soon seated in the elegant little parlor at *Sunnyside*, where the kindest courtesy makes the stranger-visitor feel that he is indeed upon the sunny side of humanity, and in the warmest glow of that generous feeling which illumines every pen-stroke of Geoffrey Crayon. Beautified and enriched by the hand of nature, hallowed by the voice of traditionary history speaking out from the old walls and umbrageous trees, and consecrated by the presence of true genius, *Sunnyside* has a charm for the American mind as bewitching and

VAN WART'S MONUMENT.[2]

Dearman; afterward altered to Irvington.

[2] The following are the inscriptions upon this monument:

NORTH SIDE.—"Here repose the mortal remains of ISAAC VAN WART, an elder in the Greenburgh church, who died on the 23d of May, 1828, in the 69th year of his age. Having lived the life, he died the death, of the Christian."

SOUTH SIDE.—"The citizens of the county of West Chester erected this tomb in testimony of the high sense they entertained for the virtuous and patriotic conduct of their fellow-citizen, as a memorial sacred to public gratitude."

EAST SIDE.—"Vincit, Amor Patriæ. Nearly half a century before this monument was built, the conscript fathers of America had, in the Senate chamber, voted that ISAAC VAN WART was a faithful patriot, one in whom the love of country was invincible, and this tomb bears testimony that the record is true."

WEST SIDE.—"Fidelity. On the 23d of September, 1780, ISAAC VAN WART, accompanied by JOHN PAULDING and DAVID WILLIAMS, all farmers of the county of West Chester, intercepted Major Andrè, on his return from the American lines in the character of a spy, and, notwithstanding the large bribes offered them for his release, nobly disdained to sacrifice their country for gold, secured and carried him to the commanding officer of the district, whereby the dangerous and traitorous conspiracy of Arnold was brought to light, the insidious designs of the enemy baffled, the American army saved, and our beloved country free."

classic as were the groves where Orpheus piped and Sappho sang to the Acadians of old. As I sat beneath a spreading cedar sketching the unique villa, and scolded without stint by a querulous matronly cat-bird on one side and a vixen jenny-wren on the other, and observed the "lord of the manor" leading a little fair-haired grand-nephew to the river brink in search of daisies and butter-cups, I could not repress the thoughts so beautifully expressed in his own little story of *The Wife:* "I can wish you no better lot than to have a wife and children. If you are prosperous, they are to share your prosperity; if otherwise, they are to comfort you. . . . Though all abroad is darkness and humiliation, yet there is still a little world of love at home [for the husband] of which he is the monarch."[1]

VIEW OF "SUNNYSIDE," THE RESIDENCE OF WASHINGTON IRVING.

The residence of Mr. Irving is upon the site of the famous "Wolfert's Roost" of the olden time. It was built by Wolfert Ecker, an ancient burgher of the town, and afterward came into the possession of Jacob Van Tassel, one of the "race of hard-headed, hard-handed, stout-hearted Dutchmen, descended of the primitive Netherlanders." Van Tassel was the owner when the Revolution broke out, and was a stanch Whig. His house was in the midst of the debatable region called the Neutral Ground, and in the broad waters of the Tappan Sea[2] in front, British vessels were almost constantly anchored. The Republican propensities of Van Tassel were well known, and as the Roost was a place of general ren-

---

[1] *Sketch Book.*
[2] *Tappaan Zee*, or Tappan Sea, was the name given by the Dutch to the expansion of the Hudson at this place.

dezvous for the American water-guards[1] and land-scouts, he was made liable to attacks from the enemy.   He pierced his old mansion with musketry loop-holes, and took other measures for defense.   His garrison, *per se*, consisted of his stout-hearted wife and a redoubtable sister, Nochie Van Wurmer, a match, as he said, for the " stoutest man in the country."   His ordnance was a goose gun " of unparalleled longitude," capable of doing great execution. He was in league with many ardent Whigs in his vicinity, who had sworn eternal hostility to the *Cow-boys* and *Skinners* who infested the region, and the Roost was their head-quarters.   Van Tassel frequently joined his companions in distant expeditions.   On one of these occasions, while far away from his castle, an armed vessel came to anchor off the Roost. The garrison consisted of only Jacob's spouse, his sister Nochie, a blooming daughter, and a brawny negro woman.   A boatful of armed men put off from the vessel toward the Roost. The garrison flew to arms.   The goose gun, unfortunately, was with its owner.   Broomsticks, shovels, and other missiles were seized, and a vigorous defense was made ; but, alas ! it was all in vain.   The house was sacked, plundered, and burned ; and as the marauders were about departing, they seized the pretty " Laney Van Tassel, the beauty of the Roost," and endeavored to bear her to the boat.   Mother, aunt, and Dinah flew to the rescue, and a fierce struggle ensued all the way to the water's edge.   A voice from the frigate ordered the spoilers to leave the prize behind, " and the heroine of the Roost escaped with a mere rumpling of the feathers."[2]   Soon after this event Van Tassel fell into the hands of the enemy, was sent to New York, and there remained a prisoner until near the close of the war.[3] His house was rebuilt upon the ruins of the Roost and that phœnix, modified and enlarged, is the present mansion at Sunnyside.

From Mr. Irving's I rode down to Dobbs's Ferry, two or three miles below.   This is a small village, lying pleasantly upon the river slope, and along a ravine of the Greenburgh

Hills, at the mouth of the Wysquaqua Creek.   It derives its name from the ancient family of Dobbs, who owned the property here, and first established a ferry.   It is a place memorable 1698. in the annals of the Revolution, not for sanguinary battles, but for the relative importance of its location in the movements of armies.   Upon the high bank immediately above the rail-way station at the lower landing are remains of the first fort erected there.   It was built at the beginning of 1776, and in October of that year Colonel Sargent strongly garrisoned it, by order of General Heath.[4]   Several other strong redoubts were thrown

VIEW FROM THE RUINS OF THE OLD FORT.[5]

---

[1] The water-guards were resolute men, well armed with muskets, and skillful with the oar, who, in small vessels technically called *whale-boats* (sharp, canoe-shaped boats), lurked in the coves and behind the headlands of the river, to obtain information of the approach or position of vessels of the enemy.   With muffled oars, they often reconnoitered the British ships at night, and sometimes cut off boats that ventured from them toward the shore.

[2] *Knickerbocker Magazine.*

[3] There were a number of the Van Tassels living in the vicinity of the Greenburgh church.   In November, 1777, a party of Chasseurs, under Captain Emerick, went up from Kingsbridge, surprised the Van Tassels, burned their houses, stripped the women and children of their clothing, and carried off Peter and Cornelius Van Tassel prisoners.   In retaliation for the outrage, the patriots fitted out an expedition at Tarrytown under the command of Abraham Martlingh, which proceeded down the river in boats, passed the water-guards of the enemy in safety, landed a little below Spuyten Devil Creek, set fire to General Oliver de Lancey's house, and returned without losing a man.   General De Lancey was a most active and bitter Loyalist.   He will come under our observation in a conspicuous manner hereafter. See page 624, vol. ii.

[4] The garrison consisted of five hundred infantry, forty light horse, a company of artillery, with two twelve-pounders under Captain Horton, and Captain Crafts with a howitzer.

[5] This view is from the bank immediately above the rail-way station, looking northwest.   In the foreground is seen the wagon-road, passing by, on an arch of masonry, over the rail-way.   On the left is the wharf.   Toward the right, in the distance, is seen the long pier and village of Piermont ; and at the **ex**

up in the vicinity, remains of which are still visible. One, a little southwest of the residence of Mr. Stephen Archer (the ancient mansion of Van Brugh Livingston), appears to have been equally strong with the one just mentioned. A few rods north of this mansion, in a locust grove, on the west of the post-road, are very prominent remains of a strong redoubt. They extended through the adjoining garden, but there the mounds have been leveled and the fossé filled up. These forts commanded the ferry to Paramus (now Sneeden's) landing on the Jersey shore, and also the passage of the river. They often greatly annoyed the British shipping while passing and repassing.

In this vicinity the British portion of the enemy rendezvoused

a October 28, 1776.   after the battle of White Plains,a before march-

b November 16.   ing against Fort Washington ;b and at Hastings, one mile below, a British force of six thousand men, under Corn-

November 18.   wallis, embarked in boats, and, crossing over to Paramus, marched to the attack of Fort Lee, and

THE LIVINGSTON MANSION.[1]

then commenced the pursuit of Washington and his broken army through the Jerseys. Here, in January, 1777, the division of the American army under Lincoln was encamped for a brief space. Here was the spot selected by Arnold for his first conference with Andrè in 1780 ; and here, on the night of the 3d of August, 1781, while the American army lay in the neighborhood, and the chief's head-quarters were at the Livingston mansion, a skirmish ensued between some guard-boats of the enemy and the little garrison of the fort on the river bank.

After viewing the remains of the old forts, and passing a pleasant half hour with Mr Archer (a member of the society of Friends) upon the shaded porch of the Livingston Mansion, I crossed the Hudson in a small boat to Sneeden's, and proceeded on foot to Tappan, a distance of about two miles, where I arrived in time to sketch the head-quarters of Washington, printed on page 196, and to visit the place of Andrè's execution.

Tappan village lies in the bosom of a fertile, rolling valley, not far from the head of the deep gorge which terminates on the Hudson at Piermont. Southwest of the village is a lofty ridge, on which the American army lay encamped. Upon its gentle slope toward the road to old Tappan, Major Andrè was executed. Travelers passing up the Hudson, and viewing with astonishment the mighty amorphous wall of the *Palisades*, along the western shore, have no idea of the beauty and fertility of the country in the rear. The Palisades, so bare and precipitous in front, present a heavily-wooded slope in the rear, reaching down into a plain of great fertility. This plain extends, with a slight variance from a level, from Tappan to Bergen Point, a distance of twenty-seven miles, and is watered by the Hackensack and its tributaries. It was a country noted for the abundance of its forage at the time of the Revolution, and was an eligible place for an army to encamp. After visiting the interesting localities in the neighborhood, I walked to Piermont, about two miles distant, where I arrived in time to embark in the boat of the Erie Rail-road Company, at eight o'clock, for New York. Though "wearied and worn" with the day's ramble, let us turn to history a while before retiring to rest.

Tappan, lying upon one of the great lines of communication from the East, by way of

treme right, in the distance, is the mountain near the foot of which Ardrè and Arnold first met. Piermont is the port of Tappan, the place where Andrè was executed. The sketch here presented was made when I visited Dobbs's Ferry in the autumn of 1849, after the rail-way was finished.

[1] This is a view from the lawn on the north side. It is embowered in trees and shrubbery, and is one of the most pleasantly-located mansions in the country, overlooking interesting portions of the Hudson River. Within its walls many of the leading men of the Revolution were entertained. It was the head-quarters of Washington, when he abandoned an attempt to capture New York city, changed his plans, and marched his whole army to Virginia to capture Cornwallis. There, at the close of the war, Washington, Governor Clinton, and General Sir Guy Carleton, and their respective suites, met to make arrangements for the evacuation of the city of New York by the British. Washington and Clinton came down the river from West Point in a barge ; Carleton ascended in a frigate. Four companies of American Infantry performed the duty of guards on that occasion.

King's Ferry, was made a place of considerable importance as a camping-ground; its position among the hills, and yet contiguous to the river, being very favorable. When, in September, 1778, Cornwallis had possession of the Hudson portion of New Jersey, foraging parties were sent in this direction, as well as scouts, to ascertain the condition of the posts at West Point. General Knyphausen, with a large force, was at the same time on the east side of the Hudson, at Dobbs's Ferry, and Washington believed that an expedition up the river was intended. Lieutenant-colonel Baylor, with a regiment of light horse, was sent to watch the movements of the enemy, and to intercept their scouts and foragers. He made his head-quarters at old Tappan, and there lay in a state of such unsoldierly insecurity, that Cornwallis was led to form a plan for taking his whole corps by surprise.[1] General Grey,

September 27, with some light infantry and other troops, was sent, at night, to approach Tap-
1778.   pan on the west, while a corps from Knyphausen's division was to approach from the east, and thus surround and capture not only the sleepers in Baylor's camp, but a body of militia, under Wayne, who were stationed near. Some deserters from the enemy gave the militia timely warning; but Baylor's troops, who lay unarmed in barns,[2] were not apprised of the proximity of the enemy. At midnight, Grey approached silently, cut off a sergeant's patrol of twelve men without noise, and completely surprised the troop of horse. Unarmed, and in the power of the enemy, they asked for quarter, but this was inhumanly refused by Grey, who, like Tryon, was a famous marauder during the war.[3] On this occasion he gave special orders not to grant any quarter. Many of the soldiers were bayoneted in cold blood. Out of one hundred and four persons, sixty-seven were killed or wounded. Colonel Baylor was wounded and made prisoner, and seventy horses were butchered.

The event of the most importance which occurred at Tappan was the trial and execu-
1850.   tion of Major André. He was confined, while there, in the old stone mansion, now occupied as a tavern, and called the "76 STONE HOUSE." Its whole appearance has been materially changed. The room wherein the unfortunate prisoner was confined, and which was kept with care in its original condition more than half a century, has been enlarged and *improved* for the purposes *of a ball-room!* I was there a few years ago, when the then owner was committing the sacrilege, and he boasted, with great satisfaction, that he had received a "whole dollar for the old lock that fastened up Major Andrew!" Sen-

timent does not obey the laws of trade —it seems to cheapen with a decrease of supply. The sign-board is now the only evidence that there is any on hand at the "76 Stone House." The trial took place in the old Dutch church, which was torn down in 1836. Upon its site another and larger one of brick has been erected. It stands within a few yards of the house where André was confined. Washington's head-quarters were in the old stone building now occupied by Samuel S Verbryck, situated near the road from Sneeden's Landing, within a few rods of its junction with the main street

WASHINGTON'S HEAD-QUARTERS AT TAPPAN.[4]

[1] Gordon, ii., 391.

[2] The encampment, on the night in question, was about two and a half miles southwest of Tappan village, near the Hackensack River.

[3] General Grey, on account of his common practice of ordering the men under his command to take the flints out of their muskets, that they might be confined to the use of the bayonet, acquired the name of *the no-flint general.*

[4] This view is from the yard, near the well. The date of its erection (1700) is made by a peculiar arrangement of the bricks in the front wall. In the large room called "Washington's quarters" the fire

of the village.   It was then owned by John de Windt, a native of St. Thomas's, West Indies, and grandfather of Mrs. Verbryck, who now resides there.

I have mentioned that, on the arrival of Washington at Tappan, he ordered a court of inquiry.   This court, consisting of fourteen general officers,[1] was convened at Tappan on the

JOHN ANDRÈ.
From a Miniature, by himself

29th of September, and on that day Major Andrè was arraigned before it and examined.   John Laurance,[2] afterward a distinguished legislator and jurist, was judge advocate.   Andrè made a plain statement of the facts we have been considering; acknowledged and confirmed the truthfulness of his statements in his letter to General Washington from Salem; confessed that he came ashore from the Vulture *in the night, and without a flag;* and answered the query of the Board, whether he had any thing further to say respecting the charges preferred against him, by remarking, "I leave them to operate with the Board, persuaded that you will do me justice."   He was remanded

1780.

MAJOR ANDRE.[3]
From a Pencil Sketch.

to prison, and, after a long and careful deliberation, the Board reported, "That Major Andrè, adjutant general of the British army, ought to be considered as a spy from the enemy, and that, agreeably to the law and usage of nations, it is their opinion he ought to suffer death."   On the next day Washington signified his approval of the decision as follows:

place is surrounded by Dutch pictorial tiles illustrative of Scripture scenes.   Indeed, the whole house remains in precisely the same condition, except what the elements have changed externally, as it was when the chief occupied it.   When I visited it, Mrs. Verbryck's sister, an old lady of eighty, was there.   She said she remembered sitting often upon Washington's knee.   She was then ten years old.

[1] The following are the names of the officers who composed the court martial on that occasion: Major-generals *Greene, Stirling, St. Clair, La Fayette, R. Howe,* and the Baron *Steuben;* and Brigadiers *Parsons, James Clinton, Knox, Glover, Paterson, Hand, Huntington,* and *Stark.*   General *Greene* was president of the board, and *John Laurance* judge-advocate general.

[2] Mr. Laurance was a native of Cornwall, England, where he was born in 1750.   He held the rank of colonel in the Continental army, and was highly esteemed by the commander-in-chief.   Colonel Laurance was a representative for New York in the first Congress held after the adoption of the Federal Constitution, and retained a seat therein during President Washington's first administration.   On his retiring from office, Washington appointed him a judge of the District Court of New York.   He was elected to the United States Senate in 1796, and served four years, when he resigned his seat and retired to private life.   He died at No. 356 Broadway, New York, in November, 1810, in the sixtieth year of his age.   Judge Laurance married a daughter of General Alexander M'Dougall, of the Continental army, who, with Sears, Willett, Lamb, and others, early and earnestly opposed the British government in its aggressive acts.   An interesting sketch of the public life of Judge Laurance, from the pen of Edwin Williams, Esq., was published in a New York journal in February, 1851.

[3] This is a fac simile of a pencil sketch which I received from London with the drawing of Andrè's monument in Westminster Abbey, printed on page 767.   I do not know from what picture the artist copied, but, considering the channel through which I received it, I think it may be relied on as a correct profile.

JOHN ANDRÈ was a native of London, where he was born in 1751.   His parents were from Geneva, in Switzerland, and at that place he was educated.   He returned to London before he was eighteen years of age, and entered the counting-house of a respectable merchant, where he continued nearly four years

"Head-quarters, September 30, 1780.

" The commander-in-chief approves of the opinion of the Board of general officers respecting Major Andrè, and orders that the execution of Major Andrè take place to-morrow at five o'clock P.M."

Possessing a literary taste and promising genius, he became acquainted with several of the writers of the day, among whom was Miss Anna Seward, the daughter of a clergyman in Litchfield. Miss Seward had a cousin named Honora Sneyd, a charming girl of whom Andrè became enamored.* His attachment was reciprocated by the young lady, and they made an engagement for marriage. The father of the girl interposed his authority against the match, and the marriage was prevented. Four years afterward, Honora was wedded to Richard Lovell Edgeworth,† father of the late Maria Edgeworth, the novelist, by a former wife. Until that event occurred, Andrè had cherished the hope that some propitious circumstance might effect their reunion. The portal of hope was now closed, and, turning from commercial pursuits, he resolved to seek relief from the bitter associations of his home amid the turmoils of war. He entered the army which came to America in 1775. He was taken prisoner at St. John's, on the Sorel, when that post was captured by Montgomery, and was sent to Lancaster, in Pennsylvania. In a letter written to a friend from that place, he said, " I have been taken prisoner by the Americans, and stripped of every thing except the picture of Honora, which I concealed in my mouth. Preserving that, I yet think myself fortunate." This picture had been delineated by his own hand from the living features of his beloved, at the time of his first acquaintance with her at Buxton, in 1769. The bravery and talents of Andrè secured for him the affectionate regards of his commander, Sir Henry Clinton, and he raised him to the duty of adjutant general of the British army in America, with the rank of major. His future career was full of brilliant promises, when Arnold, the wily serpent, crept into the paradise of his purity and peace, and destroyed him. He was not yet thirty years old when he suffered the death of a spy.

Major Andrè possessed a graceful and handsome person, with rare mental accomplishments. He was passionately fond of the fine arts, and his journal, kept during his life in America, was enriched by many drawings of such objects of interest as attracted his attention. While here, he wrote several poetical pieces for the loyal newspapers; and it is a singular fact that the last canto of his satirical poem, called THE COW CHASE, was published in Rivington's Royal Gazette, in New York, on the 23d of September, 1780, the day of his capture. It ends with the following stanza :

" And now I've closed my epic strain,
    I tremble as I show it,
Lest this same warrio-drover, Wayne,
    Should ever catch the poet !"‡

His memory has been embalmed in verse by his friend, Miss Seward;§ and his king testified his admiration of his character and genius by the erection of a beautiful monument to his honor in Westminster Abbey, near the *Poets' Corner*. The monument is in relief against the wall, and is about seven and a half feet in height. It is composed of a sarcophagus, elevated on a molded paneled base and plinth, and was executed in statuary marble by P. M. Van Gelder, from a design by Robert Adam. On the front of the sarcophagus is a *basso relievo*, in which is represented General Washington and officers in a tent at the moment when

---

* Miss Seward, in her poem entitled " The Anniversary," thus alludes to her cousin :

" Why fled ye all so fast, ye happy hours,
That saw Honora's eyes adorn these bowers ?
These darling bowers that much she loved to hail,
The spires she called The Ladies of the Vale !"

† Mr. Edgeworth was educated partly at Trinity College, Dublin, and partly at Oxford. Before he was twenty, he ran off with Miss Elers, a young lady of Oxford, to whom he was married at Gretna Green. He embarked in a life of gayety and dissipation. In 1770 he succeeded to his Irish property. During a visit to Litchfield soon afterward, he saw Honora Sneyd, loved her, and married her after the death of his wife. Honora died six years afterward of consumption, when he married her sister. —Chambers's *Cyclopedia of English Literature*, ii., 568.

‡ This satirical poem was written at General Clinton's head-quarters, now No. 1 Broadway, New York. It is not a little singular that Wayne commanded the division of the army at Tappan when Andrè was executed.

§ In Ainsworth's Magazine of a recent date I find the following record of *A dream realized* : " Major Andrè, the circumstances of whose lamented death are too well known to make it necessary for me to detail them here, was a friend of Miss Seward's, and, previously to his embarkation for America, he made a journey into Derbyshire to pay her a visit, and it was arranged that they should ride over to see the wonders of the Peak, and introduce Andrè to Newton, her minstrel, as she called him, and to Mr. Cunningham, the curate, who was also a poet.

" While these two gentlemen were awaiting the arrival of their guests, of whose intentions they had been apprised, Mr. Cunningham mentioned to Newton that, on the preceding night, he had a very extraordinary dream, which he could not get out of his head. He had fancied himself in a forest; the place was strange to him ; and, while looking about, he perceived a horseman approaching at great speed, who had scarcely reached the spot where the dreamer stood, when three men rushed out of the thicket, and, seizing his bridle, hurried him away, after closely searching his person. The countenance of the stranger being very interesting, the sympathy felt by the sleeper for his apparent misfortune awoke him ; but he presently fell asleep again, and dreamed that he was standing near a great city, among thousands of people, and that he saw the same person he had seen seized in the wood brought out and suspended to a gallows. When Andrè and Miss Seward arrived, he was horror-struck to perceive that his new acquaintance was the antitype of the man in the dream."

The youth, candor, and gentlemanly bearing of Andrè during the trying scenes of his examination made a deep impression upon the court; and had the decision of those officers been in consonance with their feelings instead of their judgments and the stern necessities imposed by the expedients of war, he would not have suffered death. When the decision of the court was made known to him, the heroic firmness of his mind challenged the admiration of all. He exhibited no fear of death, but the *manner* was a subject that gave him uneasiness; he wished to die as a *soldier*, not as a *spy*. Tender of the feelings of his commander, he obtained permission of Washington to write to Sir Henry Clinton, for the purpose of assuring him that the dilemma in which he found himself September 29. was not attributable to the duty required of him by his general. In that letter he implied a presentiment of his fate, and said, " I have a mother and two sisters, to whom the value of my commission would be an object, as the loss of Grenada has much effected their income."[1]

There could be no question among military men as to the *equity* of Andrè's sentence, and

ANDRÈ'S MONUMENT IN WESTMINSTER ABBEY

the chief had received the report of the court of inquiry; at the same time a messenger has arrived with the letter from Andrè to Washington, petitioning for a soldier's death (see page 770). On the right is a guard of Continental soldiers. and the tree on which Andrè was executed. Two men are preparing the prisoner for execution, while at the foot of the tree, Mercy, accompanied by Innocence, is bewailing his fate. On the top of the sarcophagus is the British lion, and the figure of Britannia, who is lamenting the fate of the accomplished youth. Upon a panel is the following inscription : " Sacred to the memory of Major JOHN ANDRÈ, who, raised by his merit at an early period of life to the rank of adjutant general of the British forces in America, and employed in an important but hazardous enterprise, fell a sacrifice to his zeal for his king and country, on the 2d of October, A.D. 1780, universally beloved and esteemed by the army in which he served, and lamented even by his FOES. His gracious sovereign, KING GEORGE THE THIRD, has caused this monument to be erected." On the base of the pedestal upon which the sarcophagus rests has subsequently been inscribed the following : " The remains of MAJOR JOHN ANDRÈ were, on the 10th of August, 1821, removed from Tappan by JAMES BUCHANAN, Esq., his majesty's consul at New York, under instructions from his Royal Highness, the DUKE OF YORK; and with the permission of the Dean and Chapter, finally deposited in a grave contiguous to this monument, on the 28th of November, 1821."*

The king settled a pension upon the family of Andrè; and, to wipe out the imputed stain produced by his death as a spy, the honor of knighthood was conferred upon his brother. A certified copy of Andrè's will is in the office of the Surrogate of New York. It is dated at Staten Island, 7th of June, 1777, and signed " JOHN ANDRÈ, captain in the 26th regiment of foot." The date of probate is October 12, 1780, ten days after his execution. The will is sworn to October 9, 1781, before Carey Ludlow, Esq., then Surrogate of New York. By his will, Andrè gave the bulk of his property to his three sisters (Maria, Anna Marguerite, and Louisa) and his brother, each $3500, on condition that they pay to his mother, Mary Louise Andrè, each $50 a year. Anna Marguerite Andrè—" the tuneful Anna," as Miss Seward called her—his last surviving sister, lived a maiden, and died in London in 1848, at the age of ninety years. Andrè's watch was sold for the benefit of his captors. It was bought by Colonel William S. Smith, of the Continental army, for thirty guineas, and, through General Robertson, he generously transmitted it to Andrè's family. His commission was sold by Sir Henry Clinton for the benefit of his mother and sisters.

[1] Colonel Hamilton, who was the bearer of the request from Andrè to Washington asking his permission to send this open letter to Clinton, observes, in an account which he gave to Colonel Laurens, that Andrè seemed to foresee the result of the proceedings in which he was concerned. " There is only one thing which disturbs my tranquillity," he said to Hamilton. " Sir Henry Clinton has been too good to me ; he has been lavish of his kindness; I am bound to him by too many obligations, and love him too well, to bear the thought that he should reproach himself, or others should reproach him, on the supposition of my having conceived myself obliged, by his instructions, to run the risk I did. I would not for the world leave a sting in his mind that should imbitter his future days."

* An account of this transaction may be found on page 773.

yet there was a general desire on the part of the Americans to save his life. Washington was deeply impressed with this feeling, and was ready to employ any measure to effect it consistent with his public duty.[1] The only mode to save Andrè was to exchange him for Arnold, and hold the traitor responsible for all the acts of his victim. This could hardly be expected, for Sir Henry Clinton was a man of nice honor; nor would the American commander make a formal proposition of this kind. It was, however, determined that an opportunity for such an arrangement should be offered, and a plan for that purpose was conceived. Washington

placed a packet of papers, directed to Sir Henry Clinton, in the hands of a trusty officer of the New Jersey line, Captain Aaron Ogden, containing an official account of the trial of Andrè, the decision of the Board of inquiry, and the letter written by Andrè to his general. Ogden was directed to go to General La Fayette for further instructions, after he should arrange his escort of men, known for their tried fidelity. La Fayette was in command of the light infantry, stationed nearest to the British lines. He instructed Ogden to travel so slowly, that when he should reach Paulus's Hook (now Jersey City), it might be so late that he would be invited to stay all night. He was then to communicate to the commandant of the post, as if incidentally, the idea of an exchange of Andrè for Arnold. Every thing occurred as was an-

[1] Never was a sympathy more real, or feeling more genuine, than that exhibited by the American officers on this occasion; and yet the prejudiced M'Farland, after quoting from a letter of La Fayette to his wife, in which he expressed his sympathy for Andrè, says, "Some of the American generals, too, *lamented*, but kept twisting the rope that was to hang him;" and then falsely adds, "There are accounts which say that the deep sympathy and regret was all a farce, and that Andrè, who was a wit and a poet, was most cordially hated by the Americans on account of some witticisms and satirical verses at their expense."—*Pictorial History of the Reign of George III.*, i:, 434.

The London *General Evening Post* for November 14th, 1780, in an article abusive of Washington, gives a pretended account of Andrè's "last words," in which the unfortunate man is made to say, "Remember that I die as becomes a British officer, while the manner of my death must reflect disgrace on your commander." Andrè uttered no sentiment like this. Miss Seward, his early friend, on reading this account, wrote thus in her "Monody on Major Andrè:"

> "Oh Washington! I thought thee great and good,
> Nor knew thy Nero-thirst for guiltless blood!
> Severe to use the pow'r that Fortune gave,
> Thou cool, determin'd murderer of the brave!
> Lost to each fairer virtue, that inspires
> The genuine fervor of the patriot fires!
> And you, the base abettors of the doom,
> That sunk his blooming honors in the tomb,
> Th' opprobrious tomb your harden'd hearts decreed
> While all he asked was as the brave to bleed!"

[2] Aaron Ogden was born the 3d of December, 1756, at Elizabethtown, New Jersey. He graduated at Princeton in 1773. He was nurtured in the love of Whig principles, and took an active part in the early struggles of the patriots. In the winter of 1775–6, he was one of a party who boarded and captured a vessel lying off Sandy Hook, named *Blue Mountain Valley*, and carried her safely into Elizabethport. Mr. Ogden received an appointment in the first New Jersey regiment in the spring of 1777, and continued in the service until the close of the war. He was in the battle of Brandywine in the autumn of 1777; was brigade major in a portion of the advanced corps of General Lee at Monmouth in the summer of 1778, and served as assistant aid-de-camp to Lord Stirling during that memorable day. He was aid-de-camp to General Maxwell in the expedition of Sullivan against the Indians in 1779, and was in the battle at Springfield, in New Jersey, in 1780, where he had a horse shot under him. On the resignation of Maxwell, Ogden was appointed to a captaincy of light infantry under La Fayette, and was serving in that capacity when called upon to perform the delicate service mentioned in the text. He afterward accompanied La Fayette in his memorable campaign in Virginia in 1781. At the siege of Yorktown, Captain Ogden and his company gallantly stormed the left redoubt of the enemy, for which he was "honored with the peculiar appro-

ticipated. The commandant received Ogden courteously, sent the packet across the river, asked him to stay all night, and in the course of the evening André became the subject of conversation. Ogden, in reply to the commandant's question, "Is there no way to spare André's life?" assured him that, if Sir Henry Clinton would give up Arnold, André might be saved. He informed him, however, that he had no assurance to that effect from Washington, but that he had reason to know that such an arrangement might be effected. The commandant immediately left the company, crossed the river, and had an interview with Clinton. Sir Henry promptly refused compliance, for honor would not allow the surrender of a man who had deserted from the Americans and openly espoused the cause of the king. This decision was communicated to Ogden, and he prepared to return to the camp. At dawn, on mustering his men, a sergeant was missing—he had deserted to the enemy during the night. No time could be lost in searching for the deserter, and Ogden returned to Tappan without him.[1]

October 1, 1780.

Great was the distress of Sir Henry Clinton on reading Washington's dispatch and the letter of André. He immediately summoned a council of officers, and it was resolved that a deputation of three persons should proceed to the nearest American outpost, open a communication with Washington, and, presenting proofs of the innocence of André, endeavor to procure his release. Toward noon on the 1st of October, General Robertson, Andrew Elliott, and William Smith, the deputation appointed by Clinton, accompanied by Beverly Robinson as a witness in the case, arrived at Dobbs's Ferry, in the Greyhound schooner, with a flag of truce. A request for a parley had been sent by Clinton to Washington, by Captain Ogden, in the morning. General Greene was deputed by the chief to act in his behalf, and he was already at the ferry when the Greyhound came to anchor. General Robertson, with great courtesy of manner and flattering words, opened the conference, and was proceeding to discuss the subject at issue, when Greene politely interrupted him by saying, "Let us understand our position. I meet you only as a private gentleman, not as an officer, for the case of an acknowledged spy admits of no discussion." With this understanding the conference proceeded; but Robertson produced nothing new calculated to change Greene's opinion respecting the justice of the sentence of the prisoner. A letter from Arnold to Washington, which had been kept in reserve, was now produced and read. The deputies believed that this would have the desired effect, and kept it back until verbal arguments should fail. Had their words been full of persuasion and convincing facts, this letter, so hypocritical, malignant, and impudent, would have scattered all favorable impressions in the mind of Greene to the winds. The traitor menaced Washington with dreadful retaliation if André should be slain, and in prospective charged upon the commander-in-chief the guilt of causing torrents of blood to flow.[2] "It is hardly possible," says Sparks, "that this letter could have been read by Sir Henry Clinton, although written at his request, with

---

bation of Washington." He applied himself to the study of the law after the war, and rose rapidly in his profession. He was appointed one of the electors of president and vice-president in 1800, a state senator in 1801, and in 1812 he was elected governor of New Jersey. He died in April, 1839, at the age of eighty-three years.

[1] The desertion of the sergeant was arranged by Washington, without the knowledge of Ogden. The object was to obtain information of much importance. A paper had been intercepted in which was found the name of General St. Clair, so relatively connected with other particulars as to excite a suspicion that he was concerned in Arnold's treason. The intelligent sergeant soon ascertained that there were no grounds for such suspicion, and that the paper in question was designed by the enemy to fall into Washington's hands, and excite jealousy and ill feelings among the American officers. The papers were traced to a British emissary named Brown. The sergeant found means to convey this intelligence to Washington.

[2] "If, after this just and candid representation of Major André's case," wrote Arnold, "the board of general officers adhere to their former opinion, I shall suppose it dictated by passion and resentment; and if that gentleman should suffer the severity of their sentence; I shall think myself bound by every tie of duty and honor to retaliate on such unhappy persons of your army as may fall in my power, that the respect due to flags and the law of nations may be better understood and observed."

What could have been more injudicious than holding such language to Washington, under the circumstances? and as to the "respect due to flags," the traitor well knew that in no part of the transaction had André been under such protection.

a view of operating on the judgment and clemency of Washington.   Could any language written by an individual have a more opposite tendency?   Disgust and contempt were the only emotions it could excite; and it was at least an evidence that neither the understanding or the heart of the writer had been improved by his political change.   Hitherto he had discovered acuteness and mental resources, but in this act his folly was commensurate with his wickedness."[1]

The conference ended at sunset, and Greene returned to Tappan.   Robertson expressed his confidence in Greene's candor in communicating the substance of their discussion to Washington; informed him that he should remain on board the Greyhound all night, and expressed a hope that in the morning he might take Major André back with him, or at least bear to his general an assurance of his ultimate safety.   At an early hour the next morn-
October 2,   ing the commissioners received a note from Greene, stating that the opinion and
1780.   decision of Washington were unchanged, and that the prisoner would be executed that day.   Robertson was overwhelmed with astonishment and grief.   He had written to Clinton the evening before, expressing his belief that André was safe.   The wish was father to the thought, for he had no reasonable warrant for such a conclusion, except in the known clemency of General Washington.   Reluctant to return without some word of consoling hope for Clinton, Robertson wrote a letter to Washington, recapitulating the points discussed at the conference; but it was of no avail.   No new fact was presented; no new phase was exhibited.   Sir Henry Clinton also wrote a long letter to Washington, offering some important prisoners in exchange; but it was too late.   Let us turn from the contemplation of their noble efforts to save the prisoner, to the victim himself.

I have said that André had no fear of death, but the *manner* was a subject that disturbed him.   When the sentence of the Board was communicated to him, he evinced no surprise or evident emotion; he only remarked, that, since he was to die, there was still a choice in the mode, which would make a material difference in his feelings.   He was anxious to be shot—to die the death of a soldier—and for this privilege he importuned Washington, in a letter written the day before his execution.[2]   He pleaded with a touching yet manly earnestness for this boon, but it could not be granted by the customs of war.   Unwilling to wound his feelings by a positive refusal, no answer was returned either to his verbal solicitation or his letter, and he was left the consoling hope that his wish might possibly be gratified.

The 1st of October, at five o'clock in the afternoon, had been fixed for the time of his

---

[1] *Life of Arnold, Amer. Biog.*, iii., 275.

[2] The following is a copy of his letter: the original is at Charlottesville, Virginia.

"SIR,—Buoyed above the terror of death by the consciousness of a life devoted to honorable pursuits, and stained with no action that can give me remorse, I trust that the request I make to your excellency at this serious period, and which is to soften my last moments, will not be rejected.   Sympathy toward a soldier will surely induce your excellency, and a military tribunal, to adapt the mode of my death to the feelings of a man of honor.   Let me hope, sir, that if aught in my character impresses you with esteem toward me, if aught in my misfortunes marks me as the victim of policy and not of resentment, I shall experience the operation of these feelings in your breast by being informed that I am not to die on a gibbet.

"I have the honor to be, your excellency's most obedient and most humble servant,

"JOHN ANDRÉ."

This letter has been thus beautifully paraphrased, in verse, by N. P. Willis:

"It is not the fear of death
   That damps my brow;
It is not for another breath
   I ask thee now;
I can die with a lip unstirr'd,
   And a quiet heart—
Let but this prayer be heard
   Ere I depart.

'I can give up my mother's look—
   My sister's kiss;
I can think of love—yet brook
   A death like this!

I can give up the young fame
   I burn'd to win;
All—but the spotless name
   I glory in.

"Thine is the power to give,
   Thine to deny,
Joy for the hour I live,
   Calmness to die.
By all the brave should cherish,
   By my dying breath,
I ask that I may perish
   By a soldier's death."

execution, but, in consequence of the protracted conference at Dobbs's Ferry, it was postponed until the next day.   Andrè had procured his military suit, and in calmness counted

MAJOR ANDRÈ.
From a Pen-and-ink Sketch by himself.[1]

the speeding hours of his life, talking with self-possession to those who visited him, and even
indulging in the practice of his favorite accomplishment.   On the morning of the day fixed
for his execution, he sketched with a pen a likeness of himself, sitting by a table,   October 1,
of which a fac simile is here given.   The original is now in the *Trumbull Gal-*   1780.
lery at Yale College.   It will be seen that there is a strong resemblance in the features of
this sketch to those in the portrait on page 197.

Major Andrè was executed at Tappan, at twelve o'clock, on the 2d of October, 1780.[2]
Doctor Thacher, then a surgeon in the Continental army, and present on the occasion, has
left the following account in his Journal : " Major Andrè is no more among the living.   I
have just witnessed his exit.   It was a tragical scene of the deepest interest. . . . . . The

[1] I copied this fac simile from one in Sparks's *Life and Treason of Arnold*, where is given the following
extract from a letter, written by Ebenezer Baldwin to the president of Yale College, and dated at New
Haven, August 8th, 1832 :
"It affords me pleasure, as agent of Mr. Jabez L. Tomlinson, of Stratford, and of Mr. Nathan Beers [see
page 431, this volume, for a notice of Mr. Beers], of this city, to request your acceptance of the accompanying miniature of Major JOHN ANDRÈ.   It is his likeness, seated at a table, in his guard-room, and drawn
by himself, with a pen, on the morning of the day fixed for his execution.   Mr. Tomlinson informs me that
a respite was granted until the next day, and that this miniature was in the mean time presented to him
(then acting as officer of the guard) by Major ANDRÈ himself.   Mr. Tomlinson was present when the sketch
was made, and says it was drawn without the aid of a [looking] glass.   The sketch subsequently passed
into the hands of Mr. Beers, a fellow-officer of Mr. Tomlinson, on the station, and from thence was transferred to me.   It has been in my possession several years."

[2] His executioner was a Tory named Strickland, who resided in the Ramapo Valley.   He was in confinement at Tappan, and was set at liberty on condition that he should perform the office of hangman.   Ben
jamin Abbot, a drum-major, who died at Nashua, New Hampshire, in June, 1851, at the age of 92 years,
played the dead march on that occasion.

principal guard-officer, who was constantly in the room with the prisoner, relates, that when the hour of execution was announced to him in the morning, he received it without emotion, and, while all present were affected with silent gloom, he retained a firm countenance, with calmness and composure of mind. Observing his servant enter his room in tears, he exclaimed, 'Leave me, until you can show yourself more manly.' His breakfast being sent to him from the table of General Washington, which had been done every day of his confinement, he partook of it as usual, and, having shaved and dressed himself, he placed his

hat on the table, and cheerfully said to the guard-officers, 'I am ready at any moment, gentlemen, to wait on you.' The fatal hour having arrived, a large detachment of troops was paraded, and an immense concourse of people assembled. Almost all our general and field officers, excepting his excellency[1] and his staff, were present on horseback. Melancholy and gloom pervaded all ranks, and the scene was awfully affecting. I was so near, during the solemn march to the fatal spot, as to observe every movement, and to participate in every emotion the melancholy scene was calculated to produce. Major Andrè walked from the stone house in which he had been confined between two of our subaltern officers, arm-in-arm. The eyes of the immense multitude were fixed on him, who, rising superior to the fears of death, appeared as if conscious of the dignified deportment he displayed. He betrayed no want of fortitude, but

PLACE OF EXECUTION.[2]

retained a complacent smile on his countenance, and politely bowed to several gentlemen whom he knew, which was respectfully returned. It was his earnest desire to be shot, as being the mode of death most conformable to the feelings of a military man, and he had indulged the hope that his request would be granted. At the moment, therefore, when suddenly he came in view of the gallows, he involuntarily started backward and made a pause. 'Why this emotion, sir?' said an officer by his side. Instantly recovering his composure, he said, 'I am reconciled to my death, but I detest the mode.' While waiting, and standing near the gallows, I observed some degree of trepidation—placing his foot on a stone and rolling it over, and choking in his throat as if attempting to swallow. So soon, however, as he perceived that things were in readiness, he stepped quickly into the wagon, and at this moment he appeared to shrink; but, instantly elevating his head with firmness, he said, 'It will be but a momentary pang;' and, taking from his pocket two white handkerchiefs, the provost marshal, with one, loosely pinioned his arms, and with the other the victim, after taking off his hat and stock, bandaged his own eyes with perfect firmness, which melted the hearts and moistened the cheeks not only of his servant, but of the throng of spectators. The rope being appended to the gallows, he slipped the noose over his head, and adjusted it to his neck, without the assistance of the awkward executioner. Colonel Scammel now informed him that he had an opportunity to speak, if he desired it. He raised the

[1] It is said that Washington never saw Major Andrè, having avoided a personal interview with him from the beginning.

[2] The place of Andrè's execution is now designated by a stone, lying on the right of a lane which runs from the highway from Tappan village to old Tappan, on the westerly side of a large peach orchard owned by Dr. Bartow, about a quarter of a mile from Washington's head-quarters. The stone is a small bowlder, on the upper surface of which is inscribed "ANDRÈ EXECUTED OCT. 2d, 1780." It is about three feet in length. This stone was placed there and inscribed in 1847, by a patriotic merchant of New York. A more elegant and durable monument should be erected upon the spot.

handkerchief from his eyes, and said, 'I pray you to bear me witness that I meet my fate like a brave man.' The wagon being now removed from under him, he was suspended, and instantly expired. It proved, indeed, 'but a momentary pang.' He was dressed in his royal regimentals and boots. His remains, in the same dress, were placed in an ordinary coffin, and interred at the foot of the gallows;[1] and the spot was consecrated by the tears of thousands. Thus died, in the bloom of life, the accomplished Major Andrè, the pride of the royal army, and the valued friend of Sir Henry Clinton."[2]

The captors of Andrè (Paulding, Williams,[3] and Van Wart), were nobly rewarded by Congress for their fidelity. In a letter to the president of Congress, Washington said, October 7, "Their conduct merits our warmest esteem; and I beg leave to add, that I think 1780. the public would do well to allow them a handsome gratuity. They have prevented, in all probability, our suffering one of the severest strokes that could have been meditated against us." Pursuant to this recommendation, Congress adopted a resolution November 3, expressive of the public sense of the virtuous and patriotic conduct of the "three 1780. young volunteer militia-men," and ordered "that each of them receive annually, out of the public treasury, two hundred dollars in specie, or an equivalent in the current money of these states PATRIÆ, 'the during life, love of country conquers,' and that the and forward Board of War them to the procure for commander-each of them in-chief, who a silver med-is requested to al, on one side present the of which shall same, with a be a shield copy of this with this in-resolution and scription; FI-the thanks of DELITY; and Congress, for on the other their fidelity, the follow-and the emi-ing motto: nent service VINCIT AMOR

THE CAPTORS' MEDAL.

[1] In a subsequent publication by Doctor Thacher, entitled *Observations relating to the Execution of Major Andrè*, he says that the regimentals of that officer were given to his servant. His remains were taken up in 1831 by Mr. Buchanan, the British consul at New York, removed to England, and deposited near his monument in Westminster Abbey. As no metallic buttons were found in his grave, it is evident he had been stripped of his regimentals before burial. He was interred in an open field then belonging to a Mr. Mabie.

Mr. Buchanan published an interesting account of the disinterment in 1831. It was done by command of the Duke of York. On opening the grave, the moldering coffin was found about three feet below the surface. The roots of a peach-tree, which some sympathizing hand had planted at the head of his grave, had twined like a net-work around the young hero's skull. A leather string, which he had used for tying his hair, was perfect; this Mr. Buchanan sent to Andrè's surviving sisters. While a prisoner after his capture at St. John's in 1775, Andrè parted with his watch. This was also obtained and sent to his sisters. Two small cedars were growing by the grave. A portion of one of these was sent to England with the remains, and Mr. Buchanan suggested to the duke the propriety of having a snuff-box made of some of the wood, as a present for the Reverend Mr. Demarest, of Tappan, who greatly assisted the consul in the disinterment. The duke had an elegant box made, lined with gold, and inscribed "From his royal highness the Duke of York to the Reverend Mr. Demarest." Mr. Buchanan received a silver inkstand, inscribed "The surviving sisters of Major Andrè to James Buchanan, Esq., his majesty's consul, New York." They also sent a silver cup, with a similar inscription, to Mr. Demarest.

[2] *Military Journal*, p. 222, 223.

[3] DAVID WILLIAMS was born in Tarrytown, October 21st, 1754. He entered the army in 1775, was under Montgomery at St. John's and Quebec, and continued in the militia service until 1779. He took an active part against the *Cow-boys* and *Skinners* on the Neutral Ground. He was not in regular service when he joined in the expedition the day before the capture of Andrè. After the war, he married a Miss Bene-

they have rendered their country."[1] The medals were afterward given to the three individuals by Washington himself, at head-quarters, and the captors enjoyed the annuity during their lives.[2]

Commensurate with the strong feeling of sympathy evinced for André was the sentiment of indignant hatred and disgust of Arnold, and it was the ardent desire of Washington and his compatriots to obtain possession of the person of the arch-traitor and punish him as his wickedness deserved. Various plans were arranged, secret and open, to capture him, and several expeditions were formed for that avowed object. One, while the army was yet at Tappan, and the tears of sympathy for poor André were hardly dry upon the cheeks of the soldiers, was almost successful. It was known only to Washington, Major Henry Lee, and Sergeant Champe, the latter the principal actor in the movement.

Washington had learned that Arnold's quarters in New York were next door to those of Sir Henry Clinton (now No. 3 Broadway), and that he seemed to feel so secure with his new friends that his usual caution was but little exercised. The chief conceived a plan for abducting the traitor and bringing him to the American camp. The principal difficulty appeared to be to procure the proper instruments for such an enterprise. Recent events had made the commander-in-chief suspicious, for he knew not where smaller traitors might be lurking. He sent for Major Henry Lee, the commandant of a brave legion of cavalry; a man in whose patriotism, prudence, and judgment he knew he could confide. Already he had intrusted to this officer the delicate service of ascertaining the truth of many flying rumors that other officers of high rank were likely to follow Arnold's example. To him Washington disclosed his wishes. "I have sent for you, Major Lee," he said, "in the expectation that you have in your corps individuals capable and willing to undertake an indispensable, delicate, and hazardous project. Whoever comes forward on this occasion will lay me under great obligations personally, and in behalf of the United States I will reward him amply. No time is to be lost; he must proceed, if possible, to-night." The nature of the service was disclosed to Lee, and he promptly replied to his commander that he had no doubt his legion contained many men daring enough to undertake any enterprise, however perilous; but for the service required there was needed a combination of talent rarely found in the same individual.[3] Lee suggested a plan which was highly approved of by Washing-

---

dict, and settled in Schoharie county. He died at Broome, in that county, on the 2d day of August, 1831, at the age of seventy-seven. His remains were interred, with military honors, at Livingstonville, in the presence of a large concourse of citizens. His widow, I believe, is yet living with her son at Broome, at the age of ninety-four. Ten years after the death of her husband, she obtained a continuance of his pension, which had been stopped at his death, receiving $2000 at once. Congress has been repeatedly petitioned for an appropriation to erect a monument to Williams, but without success. See Simms's *Schoharie County*.

[1] *Journals of Congress*, vi., 154.

[2] In 1817, Mr. Paulding applied to Congress for an augmentation of his annuity. Major Tallmadge, who was then a member of the House of Representatives, strongly opposed the prayer of the petitioner, on the ground that he and his companions had been more than compensated for the *real patriotism* which they exercised on the occasion of making Major André a prisoner. The statements of André, at the time, impressed Tallmadge with the belief that the plunder of a traveler was their first incentive to arrest his progress, and that, could they have been certified of their prisoner's ability to perform his promises of large pay for his release, they would not have detained him. André solemnly asserted that they first ripped up the housings of his saddle and the cape of his coat, in search of money, but finding none, one of the party said, "He may have it [money] in his boots." The discovery of the papers there concealed gave them the first idea that he might be a spy. Major André was of opinion that if he could have given them a small sum in specie at first, they would have let him pass; but he only had a small amount in Continental bills, which was given him by Smith. While we may not claim entire purity of intent on the part of the captors when they first arrested the progress of André, we can not doubt the strength of their patriotism to withstand the lure of large bribes after they discovered his real character. For particulars on this point, see a small volume, entitled *Vindication of the Captors of Major André*, published in New York in 1817; also Walsh's *American Register*, vol. ii., 1817. In this volume of the *Register* may be found a translation of Marbois's *Complot du Arnold*.

[3] In addition to the capture of Arnold, the emissary was to be commissioned to ferret out information touching the alleged defection of other officers of the Continental army. Already, as we have noticed, a sergeant under the command of Captain Ogden had been employed for such a purpose, and satisfied Washington of the innocence of one general officer who was accused.

ton. He named Champe, the sergeant major of his cavalry, as every way well qualified for the service, but he was afraid his sense of personal honor would not allow him to take the first step in the perilous expedition—desertion—for he was anxiously awaiting a vacancy in the corps to receive a promised commission.[1]

Lee sent instantly for Champe, communicated to him the wishes of Washington, and depicted, with all the earnestness and eloquence of which he was master, the glory that awaited him, if successful. Champe listened with the deepest attention, his countenance evincing the greatest excitement of feeling. He expressed himself charmed with the plan, and its proposed beneficial results; declared that he was ready to embark in any enterprise for his country's good, however perilous, which did not involve his honor; but the idea of desertion to the enemy, and hypocritically espousing the cause of the king, were obstacles in his way too grave to be disregarded, and he prayed to be excused. Lee combated these scruples with every argument calculated to impress the heart of a brave soldier. He spoke of the personal honor which success promised; the honor of the corps to which he belonged; the great service which he would perform for his beloved commander-in-chief, and the plaudits of his countrymen. He told him that desertion, by request of his general, for a laudable purpose, carried with it no dishonor, and that the stain upon his character would remain only until prudence should allow the publication of the facts. After long persuasion, the sergeant major consented to undertake the mission, and preparations were immediately made.

Washington had already drawn up instructions. These were read to Champe, and he carefully noted their import in such a way that their true meaning could not be understood by another. He was to deliver letters to two individuals in New York, unknown to each other, who had long been in the confidence of the general. He was to procure such aid in bringing Arnold away as his judgment should dictate; and he was strictly enjoined to forbear killing the traitor under any circumstances.[2] These preliminaries being settled, the difficulties that lay in his way between the camp and the enemy's outposts at Paulus's Hook, were next considered. There were many pickets and patrols in the way, and straggling parties of American irregulars often ventured almost to Bergen Point in search of booty or an adventure. Major Lee could offer the sergeant no aid against these dangers, lest he should be involved in the charge of favoring his desertion, and Champe was left to his own resources. All that Lee could do was to delay pursuit as long as possible, after it should be ascertained that the sergeant major had deserted.

At eleven o'clock at night, Champe took his cloak, valise, and orderly-book, October 20, mounted his horse secretly, and with three guineas in his pocket, which were given 1780. him by Lee, "put himself on fortune." Lee immediately went to bed, but not to sleep. Within half an hour, Captain Carnes, the officer of the day, came to him in haste, and informed him that one of the patrols had fallen in with a dragoon, who, on being challenged, put spurs to his horse and escaped. Lee complained of fatigue and drowsiness, pretended to be half asleep, and thus detained the captain some minutes before he seemed fairly to understand the object of that officer's visit. He ridiculed the idea that one of his own dragoons had deserted, for such an event had occurred but once during the whole war. The captain was not to be convinced by such arguments, but immediately mustering the whole squadron of horse, by Lee's reluctant order, satisfied both himself and his commander that *one* had deserted, and that he was no less a personage than Champe, the sergeant major, who had decamped with his arms, baggage, and orderly-book. Captain Carnes ordered an

---

[1] JOHN CHAMPE was a Virginian. "He was a native of Loudon county," says Lee, in his *Memoirs*, "and at this time twenty-three or twenty-four years of age; enlisted in 1776; rather above the common size; full of bone and muscle; with a saturnine countenance, grave, thoughtful, and taciturn, of tried courage and inflexible perseverance, and as likely to reject an overture, coupled with ignominy, as any officer in the corps."—*Memoirs*, p. 272.

[2] Lee made an arrangement with Mr. Baldwin, of Newark, to aid Champe. With him the sergeant was to have daily intercourse, as if by accident, and through him Lee was to receive communications from his sergeant major. He agreed to pay Baldwin, if successful, one hundred guineas, five hundred acres of land, and three negroes.

immediate pursuit. Lee made as much delay in the preparation as possible, and when all was ready, he ordered a change in the command, giving it to Lieutenant Middleton, a young man whose tenderness of disposition would cause him to treat Champe leniently, if he should be overtaken. By parleying and other delays, Champe got an hour the start of his pursuers.

It was a bright starry night, and past twelve o'clock, when Middleton and his party took the saddle and spurred after the deserter. A fall of rain at sunset had effaced all tracks in the road, and thus favored the pursuit, for the single foot-prints of the dragoon's horse were easily traced and recognized.[1] Often, before dawn, when coming to a fork or a cross-road, a trooper would dismount to examine the track. Ascending an eminence at sunrise near the "Three Pigeons,"[2] a tavern a few miles north of the village of Bergen, they descried from its summit the deserting sergeant, not more than half a mile in advance. The pursuers were discovered by Champe at the same moment, and both parties spurred onward with all their might. They were all well acquainted with the roads in the vicinity. There was a short cut through the woods to the bridge below Bergen, which left the great road a little below the Three Pigeons. There Middleton divided his party, sending a detachment by the short road to secure the bridge, while himself and the others pursued Champe to Bergen. He now felt sure of capturing the deserter, for he could not reach Paulus's Hook without crossing the bridge in question. The two divisions met at the bridge, but, to their great astonishment, Champe had eluded their vigilance, and was not to be found. He, too, was acquainted with the short cut, and shrewdly considered that his pursuers would avail themselves of it. He therefore wisely determined to abandon his design of going to the British post at Paulus's Hook, and seek refuge on board one of two of the king's galleys which were lying in the bay in front of the little settlement of Communipaw, about a mile from Bergen.

Middleton retired hastily from the bridge to Bergen, and inquired if a dragoon had been seen there that morning. He was answered in the affirmative, but no one knew which way he went from the village. The beaten track no longer gave a legible imprint of his horse's shoes, and for a moment his pursuers were foiled. The trail was soon discovered on the road leading to Bergen. The pursuit was vigorously renewed, and in a few moments Champe was discovered near the water's edge, making signals to the British galleys. He had lashed his valise, containing his clothes and orderly-book, upon his back. When Middleton was within a few hundred yards of him, Champe leaped from his horse, cast away the scabbard of his sword, and with the naked blade in his hand, he sped across the marsh, plunged into the deep waters of the bay, and called to the galleys for help. A boat filled with strong oarsmen responded to his call, and he was soon on board the galley, with all the evidences of the sincerity of his desertion in his possession. The captain of the galley gave him a letter to Sir Henry Clinton, in which the scene just mentioned was described, and before night the sergeant was safely quartered in New York.

Middleton recovered the horse, cloak, and scabbard belonging to Champe, and returned to Tappan. Lee was grieved when he saw the supposed evidence that poor Champe was slain ; but equally great was his joy when he learned from Middleton that the sergeant had escaped safely on board one of the enemy's galleys. Four days afterward Lee received a letter from Champe, in a disguised hand, and without signature, informing him of the occurrence just narrated.

Champe was sent by Clinton, for interrogation, to his adjutant general. The faithfulness of the legion to which he had hitherto been attached was well known in the British army, and this desertion was regarded as an important sign of increasing defection among the Americans. This opinion Champe fostered by adroit answers to questions proposed. Sir Henry Clinton also questioned him closely ; and so sincere seemed to be the sergeant's desire to serve the king, that he won the entire confidence of the British general. Clinton

---

[1] The horses of Lee's legion were all shod by a farrier attached to the corps, and every shoe, alike in form, had a private mark put upon it. By this means the foot-prints of Champe's horse were recognized, and the course of the deserter made obvious to his pursuers.

[2] There is now a hamlet of that name there, situated on the high road from Hackensack to Hoboken.

gave Champe a couple of guineas, and recommended him to call upon General Arnold, who was engaged in raising an American legion, to be composed of Loyalists and deserters. This was exactly the course to which Champe had hoped events would tend. Arnold received him courteously, and assigned him quarters among his recruiting sergeants. The traitor asked him to join his legion, but Champe begged to be excused, on the plea that if caught by the rebels, he would surely be hanged; but promised Arnold that, if he changed his mind, he would certainly join his legion.

Champe found means to deliver the two letters before mentioned, and five days after his arrival in New York, he made arrangements with one of Washington's corre- October 25, spondents to assist him in abducting Arnold, and then communicated the facts to 1780. Major Lee.[1] He enlisted in the traitor's legion, so as to have free intercourse with him, and ascertain his night habits and pursuits. In the rear of Arnold's quarters was a garden, extending down to the water's edge.[2] Champe ascertained that it was Arnold's habit to return to his quarters at about midnight, and that previous to going to bed he always visited the garden. Adjoining the garden was a dark alley leading to the street. These circumstances were favorable to Champe's plans. He had arranged with two accomplices (one of whom was to have a boat in readiness) to seize and gag Arnold, on a certain night, in his garden, convey him to the alley, and from thence, through the most unfrequented streets, to the river. In case of detection while carrying the traitor, they were to represent him as a drunken soldier whom they were conveying to the guard-house. Once in the boat, they might pass in safety to Hoboken.

Champe carefully removed some of the palings between the garden and the alley, and replaced them so slightly that they might again be removed without noise. When all was arranged, he wrote to Lee, and appointed the third subsequent night for the de- November 5, livery of the traitor on the Jersey shore. On that evening, Lee and a small 1780. party left the camp, with three accoutered horses—one for Arnold, one for the sergeant, and one for his associate—and at midnight concealed themselves at an appointed place in the woods at Hoboken. Hour after hour passed, and the dawn came, but Champe and his prisoner did not arrive. Lee and his party returned to camp greatly disappointed. A few days afterward he received a letter from his sergeant, explaining the cause of his failure, and an assurance that present success was hopeless. On the very day when Champe was to execute his plan, Arnold changed his quarters, to superintend the embarkation of troops for an expedition southward, to be commanded by himself.[3] In this expedition the American le-

---

[1] In this first communication he assured Lee that his inquiries concerning the alleged defection of other American officers were satisfactory, and that no such defection existed.

[2] Arnold's quarters were at No. 3 Broadway, adjoining those of Sir Henry Clinton. The house is yet standing, and is represented, with Clinton's quarters, on page 592, of volume ii. The garden extended along the street to the northern boundary of the *Atlantic Hotel*, No. 5, where the dark alley, mentioned in the text, divided it from the premises No. 9, now known as the *Atlantic Garden*. The shore of the river was formerly a few yards west of Greenwich Street, West Street being all "made ground."

[3] Arnold received, as the price of his desertion from the Americans and attempted betrayal of the liberties of his country into the hands of the enemy, a commission as colonel, with a brevet rank of brigadier, in the British army, and the sum of nearly fifty thousand dollars. It may be mentioned, for the information of those unskilled in the technicalities of the military service, that the term *brevet* is used to a commission giving nominal rank higher than that for which pay is received. A brevet major serves and draws pay as a captain, and a brevet brigadier as colonel. Arnold was lower in office, both actual and nominal, among his new friends than he had been in the American army. But large bribes of gold was a salvo to that nice sense of honor for which he had so often wrangled. He was heartily despised by the British officers, and he was frequently insulted without possessing the power to show his resentment. Many anecdotes illustrative of this point have been related. It is said that, on one occasion, a British statesman, as he rose to make a speech in the House of Commons, saw Arnold in the gallery. "Mr. Speaker," he said, "I will not speak while that man (pointing toward Arnold) is in the house." George the Third introduced Arnold to Earl Balcarras, one of Burgoyne's officers at Bemis's Heights. "I know General Arnold and abominate traitors," was the quick reply of the earl, as he refused his hand and turned on his heel. When Talleyrand was about to come to America, he was informed that an American gentleman was in an adjoining room. He sought an interview, and asked for letters to his friends in America. "I was born in Amer-

gion was to be employed, and poor Champe, who had enlisted in it to carry out his plans, was in a sad dilemma. Instead of crossing the Hudson that night, with the traitor his prisoner, he found himself on board of a British transport, and that traitor his commander ! December 16, The expedition sailed, and Champe was landed on the shores of Virginia. He 1780. sought opportunities to escape, but found none, until after the junction with Cornwallis at Petersburg, where he deserted. He passed up toward the mountains, and into the friendly districts of North Carolina. Finally, he joined the legion of Major Lee, just after it had passed the Congaree in pursuit of Lord Rawdon. Great was the surprise of his old comrades when they saw him, and it was increased at the cordial reception which the deserter received at the hands of Lee. His story was soon told, and four-fold greater than before his desertion was the love and admiration of his corps for him. They felt proud of him, and his promotion would have been hailed by general acclamation. Knowing that he would immediately be hanged if caught by the enemy,. he was discharged from service. The commander-in-chief munificently rewarded him ; and seventeen years afterward, when President Adams appointed Washington to the chief command of the armies of the United States, then preparing to defend the country from the threatened hostility of the French, the chief sent to Colonel Lee for information concerning Champe, being determined to bring him forward in the capacity of a captain of infantry. But the gallant soldier had removed to Kentucky, and was asleep in the soil.[1]

A few months after my visit to Tappan, I made another tour to the vicinity. I passed two days in the romantic valley of the Ramapo, through which the New York and Erie rail-way courses. Every rocky nook, sparkling water-course, and shaded glen in that wild valley has a legendary charm. It is a ravine sixteen miles in extent, opening wide toward the fertile fields of Orange county. It was a region peculiarly distinguished by wild and daring adventure during the Revolution, and, at times, as important military ground. There the marauding Cow-boys made their rendezvous ; and from its dark coverts, Claudius Smith, the merciless freebooter, and his three sons, with their followers, sallied out and plundered the surrounding country.[2] Along the sinuous Ramapo Creek, before the war of the Revolution broke out, and while the ancient tribe of the Ramapaughs yet chased the deer on the

rugged hills which skirt the valley, iron-forges were established, and the hammer-peal of spreading civilization echoed from the neighboring crags. Not far distant from its waters the great chain which was stretched across the Hudson at West Point was wrought ;[3] and the remains of one of the Ramapo forges, built at the close of the war, now form a picturesque ruin on the margin of the rail-way.[4] A few miles below it, Ramapo village, with its extensive machinery, sends up a per-

ica, lived there till the prime of my life, but alas! I can call no man in America my friend," replied the stranger. That stranger w__ Arnold.

[1] See Lee's *Memoirs of the War in the Southern Department of the United States*, from page 270 to 284 The reader, by observing the dates of his correspondence with Washington, will perceive that Lee has con founded the effort of Ogden to save André by having Arnold given up, and the desertion of his sergeant, with the expedition of Sergeant Champe. In his account of Champe's maneuver, he makes the salvation of André a leading incentive to efforts to capture Arnold; but André was executed on the 2d of October, whereas Champe did not desert until the 20th of the same month.

[2] Claudius Smith was a large, fine-looking man, of strong mind, and a desperado of the darkest dye. Himself and gang were a terror to Orange county for a long time, and tempting rewards were offered for his apprehension. He was finally captured near Oyster Bay, on Long Island, and taken to Goshen, where he was chained to the jail floor, and a strong guard placed over him. He was hung in the village on the 22d of January, 1779, with Gordon and De la Mar—the former convicted of horse-stealing, and the latter of burglary. Smith's residence was in the lower part of the present village of Monroe, on the Erie rail way. Several murders were afterward committed by Smith's son Richard, in revenge for the hanging of his father ; and for a while the Whigs in that region suffered more from the desperate Cow-boys than be fore the death of their great leader. For a detailed account of transactions connected with Claudius Smith, see Eager's *History of Orange County*, p. 550–564.   [3] See page 700.

[4] This ruin is situated about half way between the Sloatsburgh station and Monroe works. The forge

petual hymn of industry from the wilderness. This village, now containing a population of three hundred,[1] is owned by the Piersons, the elder having established iron-works there fifty years ago. Jeremiah H. Pierson, the original proprietor, is yet living there at the age of eighty-four, and to the kind hospitality of himself and family I am indebted for much of the pleasures and profit of my visit to the Ramapo Valley. God has taken his eyesight from him, but mercifully vouchsafes good health, sound mind, sunny cheerfulness, and the surroundings of a happy family. I listened with interest to a narrative of his clear recollections of the past, and the traditions gathered from his scattered neighbors when he first sat down there in the almost wilderness. Not twenty years had elapsed since the war closed when he erected his forges, and the *sufferers* were living in small groups all around him. They have all passed away, and volumes of unwritten traditionary history are buried with them. October. 1850.

The American army under Washington was encamped in the vicinity of Ramapo for a few days in July, 1777. The head-quarters of Washington had been at Morristown during the previous winter and spring. Believing it prudent to act on the defensive, he had waited anxiously for Sir William Howe, who was quartered in New York city, to make some decided movement. Summer approached, and yet the British commander gave no intimations respecting his designs for a campaign. It was believed that he would either make a demonstration against the strong posts in the Highlands, or attempt a passage of the Delaware and a seizure of Philadelphia. Washington's position at Morristown was an eligible one for acting promptly and efficiently when Howe should move either way.

General Howe had a considerable force stationed at New Brunswick. This force was augmented early in May, and Washington received information that they had begun to build a portable bridge there, so constructed that it might be laid upon flat boats. Believing this to be a preparation for crossing the Delaware, Washington collected the new levies from Virginia and the Middle States, at Morristown, and ordered those from the eastward to assemble at Peekskill. Toward the close of May, the American army moved from Morristown, and encamped upon the heights of Middlebrook, in a very strong position, and commanding the country from New Brunswick to the Delaware. The maneuvers of detachments of the two armies in this vicinity in June[a] are noticed on page 331, vol. i. The British finally crossed over to Staten Island from Amboy[b] on the bridge which they had constructed at New Brunswick, and entirely evacuated the Jerseys. 1777. [a] 1777. [b] June 30.

The next day Washington received intelligence of the approach of Burgoyne from Canada, and at the same time spies and deserters from New York informed him that a fleet of large vessels and transports were preparing in the harbor of that city. The commander-in-chief was greatly perplexed. At first it appeared probable that Howe was preparing to sail with his army southward, go up the Delaware, and attack Philadelphia by land and by water ; but the intelligence that Washington continued to receive from the North made it appear more probable that a junction with Burgoyne, and the consequent possession of the Hudson River, by which the patriots of the Eastern and Middle States would be separated, and a free communication with Canada be established, would engage the efforts of Sir William Howe. The possession of the Hudson River had been a prominent object from the beginning of the war.

---

was built in 1783–4, by Solomon Townshend, of New York, to make bar-iron and anchors, and was named the Augusta Works. A sketch of the ruin forms a pretty frontispiece to *The Salamander* (or Hugo, as it is now called), a legend of the Ramapo Valley, by Mrs. Elizabeth Oakes Smith. The historic anecdote related in the introduction to this charming legend I also heard from the lips of the "venerable Mr. P . . . . .," through whose kindness I was enabled to visit the "Hopper House." The relics of the Revolution are pleasingly grouped in the introduction referred to.

[1] When the large cotton factory (the spindles of which are now idle) and the screw factory of Mr. Pierson were in operation here, the village contained about seven hundred inhabitants. The whole valley of the Ramapo has but three or four owners. Many thousand acres belong to the Townsends ; the Lorillard family own another immense tract ; Mr. M'Farland another ; the Sloats have considerable possessions, and the lower part belongs to the Piersons.

780   PICTORIAL FIELD-BOOK

March of the American Army toward the Highlands.   Howe's Destination determined.   The Clove.

Washington remained at Middlebrook with the main division of the army, anxiously awaiting the movements of the enemy, until toward the middle of July. He dispatched two regiments to Peekskill, on the Hudson, and had his whole army in readiness to march in that direction, if circumstances should require. When it was certainly known that the British army had actually embarked on board the fleet, Washington moved slowly toward the Highlands by way of Morristown, Ramapo,[1] and the Clove[2]. He encamped in the latter place on the 15th, eleven miles above the *Ramapo Pass* (of which I shall pres ently write), and immediately sent forward Lord Stirling, with a division, to Peeks-

July, 1777.

kill. He established his head-quarters at Ramapo on the 23d; but so much was that region infested with *Cow-boys* and other Tories, that it was with great difficulty that he could obtain correct information from a distance.[3] Northward from the present Ramapo village rises a range of lofty hills, upon the highest summit of which is upreared a huge mass of granite, shaped like a mighty dome, the top covered with trees. From this eminence, five hundred feet above the village, a small portion of New York Bay, Staten Island, and the ocean near Sandy Hook, may be distinctly seen on a clear day, the distance being about thirty-five miles. To this observatory, it is said, Washington was piloted, and with his glass saw a portion

TORN ROCK.[4]

of the fleet of the enemy near Sandy Hook. The Weehawken Hill obstructed a full view of New York Harbor, and the commander-in-chief was uncertain whether the whole fleet had dropped down to the Hook; but, on returning to his quarters at Ramapo, he received positive information that the British fleet had gone to sea. Convinced that Philadelphia was the destination of Howe, Washington recalled Stirling's division from Peekskill, broke up his encampment in the Clove, and the army pursued various routes toward the Delaware. The battle of Brandywine, and other events in the vicinity of Philadelphia, which occurred soon afterward, will be noticed in subsequent chapters.

On the return of Commodore Sir George Collier and General Matthews from a marauding expedition to Virginia, at the close of May, 1779, they sailed up the Hudson River to attack the forts in the Highlands. This expedition, as we have

June 1, 1779.

noticed on page 175, was under the command of Sir Henry Clinton. As soon as Washington was advised of this movement, he drew his troops from their cantonments in New Jersey, and, by rapid marches, reached the Clove on the 7th with five brigades and two Carolina regiments. He pressed forward to Smith's Clove, whence there were mountain passes to the forts in the Highlands, and there he encamped. Small detachments for observation and protection to couriers were stationed at different points from the encampment

[1] Ramapo, or Romopock, was a small settlement on the Ramapo River, about five miles south of the present Suffern's Station on the New York and Erie rail-way, and within the province of New Jersey. It was nearly seven miles below the present village of Ramapo, founded by Mr. Pierson.

[2] The Clove here mentioned was chiefly the Ramapo Valley extending to Smith's Clove, which continues northward from the former, in the vicinity of Turner's Station, on the New York and Erie rail-road, far in the rear of Haverstraw and Stony Point. Through this clove, by the way of Ramapo, was the best route for an army from New Windsor into the upper part of New Jersey. The main division of the Continental army was again encamped in the Clove in 1779, when General Wayne captured Stony Point.

[3] "I can not give you any certain account of General Howe's intended operations," wrote Washington to General Schuyler. "His conduct is puzzling and embarrassing beyond measure. So are the informations which I get. At one time the ships are standing up toward the North River; in a little while they are going up the Sound; and in an hour after they are going out of the Hook. I think in a day or two we must know something of his intentions."

[4] This view is from the verge of the dam above the Ramapo works, near the rail-way, looking northeast. The eminence is called Torn Rock, from its ragged appearance on its southeastern side. There is a deep fissure in a portion of the bare rock, from which comes up a sound like the ticking of a watch, caused by the water which percolates through the seams in the granite. A tradition was long current that Washington lost his watch in the fissure, and that. by some miraculous power, it continued to *tick !*

southward to old Ramapo, and strong intrenchments were thrown up at the *Pass*, a narrow gorge about half a mile below the present Ramapo village. The passage between the hills here is only wide enough for the stream, the rail-way, a wagon-road, and a narrow strip of meadow-land. The hills on each side rise abrupt and rocky. It was a place almost as easy to fortify and guard as the pass of old Thermopylæ. The ditch and bank from the wagon-road eastward are yet quite prominent. Large trees have overgrown them, and with care these mementoes of the past may be long preserved.

REMAINS OF INTRENCHMENTS AT THE RAMAPO PASS.[1]

While the army was encamped at Smith's Clove, the successful expedition of General Wayne against Stony Point was accomplished. This success, the subsequent evacuation of that post and of Verplanck's Point by the British, and the necessity for sending re-enforcements to General Lincoln at the South, caused the camp in the Clove to be broken up early in the autumn. The main portion of the army went into winter quarters at Morristown, where the commander-in-chief established himself, and strong detachments were stationed at different points among the Highlands.

1779

Once again, and for the last time, the Ramapo Valley became the temporary theater of military operations. It was in the summer of 1781, when the allied armies took up their line of march for Virginia to achieve the defeat of Cornwallis. They had conjoined upon the Hudson for the purpose of making an attack upon the head-quarters of the British army in the city of New York. The failure of Count De Grasse, commander of a French fleet then in the West Indies, to co-operate with the land forces, made Washington abandon this project, and turn his attention to the military operations at the South. To prevent obstacles being thrown in his way by Sir Henry Clinton, or re-enforcements being sent to Cornwallis, Washington kept up the appearance of a meditated attack upon New York.

The two armies, which had remained nearly six weeks in the vicinity of Dobbs's Ferry, crossed the Hudson at Verplanck's Point, and marched by different routes to Trenton, under the general command of Lincoln; some passing through the Ramapo Valley and the Pass to Morristown, and others taking the upper route above the Ringwood Iron-works. The French took the river route, by Tappan and the Hackensack Valley, to Newark and Perth Amboy. At the latter place they built ovens, constructed boats, collected forage, and made other movements indicative of preparations to commence an attack, first upon the British posts on Staten Island, and then upon New York. Previous to the passage of the Hudson, Washington had caused deceptive letters to be written and put in the way of being intercepted,[2] all of which deceived Sir Henry Clinton into the belief that an attack upon New

---

[1] This view is from the road, looking north toward the village of Ramapo. The remains of the intrenchments are seen along the right in the foreground. On the left, in the distance, is seen a glimpse of the hills on the other side of the narrow valley.

[2] One of the bearers of these letters was a young Baptist clergyman, named Montagnie, an ardent Whig, who was directed by Washington to carry a dispatch to Morristown. He directed the messenger to cross the river at King's Ferry, proceed by Haverstraw to the Ramapo Clove, and through the Pass to Morristown. Montagnie, knowing the Ramapo Pass to be in possession of the Cow-boys and other friends of the enemy, ventured to suggest to the commander-in-chief that the upper road would be the safest. "I shall be taken," he said, "if I go through the Clove." "Your duty, young man, is not to talk, but to obey!" replied Washington, sternly, enforcing his words by a vigorous stamp of his foot. Montagnie proceeded as directed, and, near the Ramapo Pass, was caught. A few days afterward he was sent to New York, where he was confined in the Sugar House, one of the famous provost prisons in the city. The day after his arrival, the contents of the dispatches taken from him were published in Rivington's Gazette with great parade, for they indicated a plan of an attack upon the city. The enemy was alarmed thereby, and active preparations were put in motion for receiving the besiegers. Montagnie now perceived why he was so positively instructed to go through the Ramapo Pass, where himself and dispatches were quite sure to be

York city was the grand object of the Americans. The allied armies had crossed the Delaware, and were far on their way toward the head of Elk, before the British commander was fully aware of their destination.

About four miles south of the Ramapo Pass, and three from Suffern's Station, on the road to Morristown, is the "Hopper House," where Washington made his head-quarters from the 2d until the 18th of September, 1780. The mansion was owned by —— Hopper, one of the most active Whigs of the day. He was often employed by Washington in the secret service, and frequently visited his friends in New York city while the enemy had possession of it. On such occasions, he obtained much valuable information respecting the strength of the enemy, without incurring suspicion, as he never committed a word to paper. The remains of the patriot rest beneath a small marble monument, in a family cemetery, upon a grassy knoll by the road side, not far from the mansion. This is the house wherein those letters of Washington, beginning with "Head-quarters, Bergen county," were written; it being in New Jersey, about two miles from the New

THE HOPPER HOUSE.[1]

York line. It was here that he received the news of the defeat of Gates at the disastrous battle near Camden, on the 16th of August, 1780; and from hence he set out on his journey to Hartford, on Monday, the 18th of September, to meet the French officers in council, the time when Arnold attempted to surrender West Point into the hands of the enemy. The venerable widow of Mr. Hopper resided there until her death in 1849, when she had reached the ninety-ninth year of her life. Her daughter, who was often dandled on the knee of Washington, is still living, but was absent on the day of my visit, and I was denied the gratification of viewing those relics of the Revolution which are preserved in the house with much care.[2]

Close by Suffern's Station is an old building coeval with the original Hopper house. It was the head-quarters of Lieutenant-colonel Aaron Burr, while stationed there in command of Malcolm's regiment in September, 1777. It has been sometimes erroneously called the head-quarters of Washington. While encamped here for the purpose of guarding the Ram-

---

seized. When they appeared in Rivington's Gazette, the allied armies were far on their way to the Delaware. Montagnie admired the wisdom of Washington, but disliked himself to be the victim. Mr. Pierson, from whom I obtained the narrative, received it from the lips of Montagnie himself.

Upon this incident Mrs. Elizabeth Oakes Smith (who also received the narrative from Mr. P.) founded her interesting prize tale called the *Ramapo Pass*. She also mentions it in her introduction to *The Salamander*.

[1] This view is from the road, looking northeast. The low part, on the left, is a portion of the old mansion of the Revolution, which contained the dining-hall. It was a long stone building. A part of it has been taken down, and the present more spacious edifice, of brick, was erected soon after the war.

[2] Mrs. Smith, in her introduction to *The Salamander*, makes mention of the centenarian, and of these relics. "The ancient matron," she says, "has none of the garrulity of old age; on the contrary, as she adverted to past scenes, a quiet stateliness grew upon her, in beautiful harmony with the subject. Rarely will another behold the sight, so pleasing to ourselves, of *five generations*, each and all in perfect health and intelligence, under the same roof-tree. She spoke of this with evident satisfaction, and of the length of time her ancestors had been upon the soil; in truth, we had never felt more sensibly the honorableness of gray hairs. . . . . We were shown the bed and furniture, remaining as when he [Washington] used them, for the room is kept carefully locked, and only shown as a particular gratification to those interested in all that concerns the man of men. Here were the dark chintz hangings beneath which he had slept; the quaint furniture; old walnut cabinets, dark, massive, and richly carved; a Dutch Bible, mounted with silver, with clasps and chain of same material, each bearing the stamp of antiquity, yet all in perfect preservation; large China bowls; antique mugs; paintings upon glass of cherished members of the Orange family. These and other objects of interest remain as at that day."

apo Pass, Colonel Burr performed an exploit which was long remembered in the neighborhood.   He received intelligence that the enemy were in considerable force at Hackensack, and advancing into the country.   Leaving a guard to protect the camp, Burr marched with the remainder of his effective men to Paramus, a distance of sixteen miles, in the direction of Hackensack.   They arrived there at sunset, and found the militia of the district gathered in great confusion. Having arranged them in order, Burr marched forward with thirty picked men, and at ten o'clock at night approached the pickets of the enemy.   When within three miles of Hackensack, Burr led his men

BURR'S HEAD-QUARTERS.

into the woods, ordered them to sleep until he should awaken them, and then went alone to reconnoiter.   A little before daylight he returned, aroused his men, and directed them to follow him, without speaking a word or firing a gun until ordered, on pain of death.   Leading them unobserved between the sentinels, until within a few yards of the picket-guard, he gave the word *Fire!*   His men rushed upon the enemy before they had time to take up their arms, and a greater portion of them were killed.   A few prisoners and some spoil was carried off by the Americans, without the loss of a man on their part.   Burr sent an order to Paramus by an express for all the troops to move, and to rally the country.   This success inspirited the militia, and they flocked in great numbers to the standard of Burr.   The enemy, thoroughly frightened, retreated in haste to Paulus's Hook (Jersey City), leaving behind them a greater portion of the plunder which they had collected.

We will now leave the Ramapo, and, saying farewell to the Hudson and its associations, wend our way toward the sunny South.

END OF VOLUME I.